The ColdFusion 5
Web Application Construction Kit

4th Edition

Ben Forta and Nate Weiss

with Leon Chalnick,

David E. Crawford,

John Cummings, and

David Golden

201 W. 103rd Street
Indianapolis, Indiana 46290

Contents at a Glance

The ColdFusion 5 Web Application Construction Kit, 4th Edition

International Standard Book Number: 0-7897-2584-3

Library of Congress Catalog Card Number: 2001116549

Printed in the United States of America

First Printing: July 2001

04 03 02 01 4 3 2 1

Associate Publisher
Dean Miller

Acquisitions Editor
Angela C. Kozlowski

Development Editor
Mark L. Kozlowski

Managing Editor
Thomas F. Hayes

Project Editor
Heather McNeill

Copy Editor
Megan Wade

Indexer
Becky Hornyak

Proofreader
Kaylene Riemen
Julie Cook

Technical Editors
Jason R. Wright
Jason Heaslet
Stephanie Juma
Robert Panico

Team Coordinator
Lynne Williams

Interior Designer
Ruth Harvey

Cover Designer
Dan Armstrong
Ruth Harvey

Page Layout
Gloria Schurick

Contents

III Building ColdFusion Applications

V Appendixes

About the Authors

Ben Forta is Macromedia Inc.'s product evangelist for the ColdFusion product line and is one of the best known and most trusted names within the ColdFusion community. He has almost 20 years of experience in the computer industry in product development, support, training, and product marketing. Ben has also authored *Advanced ColdFusion 4.0 Application Development* and *Certified ColdFusion Developer Study Guide* (both published by Que), as well as *JavaServer Pages Application Development*, *WAP Development with WML and WMLScript*, and *Sams Teach Yourself SQL in 10 Minutes* (all published by Sams). Ben coauthored the official Allaire ColdFusion training courses, writes regular columns on ColdFusion and Internet development, and is a much sought-after lecturer and speaker on ColdFusion and Internet technologies. Born in London, England, and educated in London, New York, and Los Angeles, Ben now lives in Oak Park, Michigan, with his wife Marcy and their six children. Ben welcomes your e-mail at `ben@forta.com` and invites you to visit his Web site at `http://www.forta.com/`.

Nate Weiss is currently the tech director and chief architect at OneCARE (`www.onecare.com`), a company committed to online product support and customer relations. Previously, he was the principal developer at ICES, Inc. (`www.icesventures.com`). He has been fortunate enough to speak at several ColdFusion developer conferences and user group meetings and was the original owner of the WDDX SDK (available from `www.Wddx.org`). Visit his Web site at `www.nateweiss.com`, which includes a number of ColdFusion custom tags and other goodies.

Leon Chalnick is the president of Advanta Solutions, Inc., a Macromedia Premier Consulting Partner in the Los Angeles area. He started and runs the Southern California ColdFusion User Group. Leon has worked on several versions of this book and spoken at all the national ColdFusion and Allaire conferences. A Northwestern M.B.A., Leon is also an avid guitarist who played professionally for more than seven years.

David E. Crawford has been developing with ColdFusion since version 1.0 and is a Macromedia Certified ColdFusion Developer. He is currently a senior programmer/analyst for Actek, Inc., a Macromedia ColdFusion Consulting Partner based in Birmingham, Alabama. He holds an A.A. in computer programming and a B.A. in computer information systems from Northwest Nazarene University.

John Cummings is a senior support engineer for Macromedia, Inc. He spends the majority of his time helping customers solve ColdFusion-related problems. John is also the author of several ColdFusion-related technical articles that can be found at various ColdFusion-centric Web sites. You can contact John by e-mailing him at `john@mauzy-broadway.com` or visiting his site at `http://www.mauzy-broadway.com`.

David Golden is a senior technical writer on the ColdFusion team at Macromedia. David can be contacted via e-mail at `d_golden73@hotmail.com`.

Dedication

To the ColdFusion development community, for half a decade of acceptance, trust, support, and encouragement.—Ben Forta

What is there to say or do, Jon? Naomi? Dolores? Stan Sr.?—Nate Weiss

I would like to dedicate my contributions to this book to the wonderful staff at Advanta Solutions!—Leon Chalnick

To my wife Laura, without whom none of my work would mean anything.—John Cummings

Acknowledgments

Thanks to my primary co-author, Nate Weiss, for taking a leadership role in this new and improved edition (and for creating Orange Whip Studios). Thanks also to authors Leon Chalnick, Dave Crawford, John Cummings, and David Golden for their outstanding contributions. Thanks to Joseph DeVore for the OWS graphics and images (and for redesigning my Web site). Thanks to everyone at Que for so many years of support and trust. Special thanks to Heather McNeill for keeping a watchful eye on all those little details so as to ensure the highest quality product. A very special thank you to my friend and acquisitions editor, Angela Kozlowski, without whom I'd probably never actually complete a book. And most of all, thanks to the hundreds and thousands of you who have encouraged me to keep writing and teaching. There can be nothing more gratifying than the knowledge that I have helped so many of you advance your careers and improve your lives, and I am both humbled and flattered by your constant support and encouragement. Thank you.—Ben Forta

Showers of thanks to my writing companions and sources of inspiration (specifically Stephanie Hawkins, Ben Forta, Jeanmarie and Stan Williams, Team Allaire, forums users everywhere, blue bell knoll-era Cocteau Twins, Sleater-Kinney, Tangerine Dream, Dr. Pepper, Patience, Fortitude, and the majestic Rose Reading Room at the Forty-Second Street Public Library in New York City, capital of the world). A *huge* shout out to Angela Kozlowski, Mark Kozlowski, and Heather McNeill at Que, and to the terrific tech editors who helped us deliver. Thanks also to my colleagues at OneCARE for their support (especially Ross and Fred for allowing me the time to work on this book, and Matt, John, and Stan for taking up almost all the slack in my pseudo-quasi-absence). Of course, thanks to everyone at Macromedia who helped contribute to the quality of this edition, either directly or indirectly (especially, but of course not limited to, Jeremy Allaire, Sim Simeonov, Damon Cooper, Tom Harwood, Alan Preston, Seth Horan, Xu Chen, Chris Kintzing, Karen Breault, and Amy Gauthier). Finally, thanks to Mom, Dad, Liz, Ken, Carrie, Gigi, Don, Judith, Robin, and Cousin Sarah, and yes, there will be a quiz.—Nate Weiss

I would like to acknowledge the patience and support my wife Nancy has provided me in the process of working on this book. I would also like to acknowledge help from Ralph Fiol, Ben Pate, Dan Chick, Joseph Flanigan, and Muliadi Jeo for their help with the chapter on development methodologies.—Leon Chalnick.

TELL US WHAT YOU THINK!

As the reader of this book, *you* are our most important critic and commentator. We value your opinion and want to know what we're doing right, what we could do better, what areas you'd like to see us publish in, and any other words of wisdom you're willing to pass our way.

As an associate publisher for Que, I welcome your comments. You can fax, e-mail, or write me directly to let me know what you did or didn't like about this book—as well as what we can do to make our books stronger.

Please note that I cannot help you with technical problems related to the topic of this book, and that due to the high volume of mail I receive, I might not be able to reply to every message.

When you write, please be sure to include this book's title and authors as well as your name and phone or fax number. I will carefully review your comments and share them with the authors and editors who worked on the book.

Fax: 317-581-4666

E-mail: angela.kozlowski@quepublishing.com

Mail: Angela Kozlowski
Que
201 West 103rd Street
Indianapolis, IN 46290 USA

INTRODUCTION

In this chapter

WHO SHOULD USE THIS BOOK

This book is written for anyone who wants to create cutting-edge Web-based applications.

If you are a Webmaster or Web page designer and want to create dynamic, data-driven Web pages, this book is for you. If you are an experienced database administrator who wants to take advantage of the Web to publish or collect data, this book is for you, too. If you are starting out creating your Web presence, but know you want to serve more than just static information, this book will help get you there. If you have used ColdFusion before and want to learn what's new in ColdFusion 5, this book is also for you. Even if you are an experienced ColdFusion user, this book provides you with invaluable tips and tricks and also serves as the definitive ColdFusion developer's reference.

This book teaches you how to create real-world applications that solve real-world problems. Along the way, you acquire all the skills you need to design, implement, test, and roll out world-class applications.

HOW TO USE THIS BOOK

This book is designed to serve two different, but complementary, purposes.

First, it is a complete tutorial of everything you need to know to harness ColdFusion's power. As such, the book is divided into four sections, and each section introduces new topics building on what has been discussed in prior sections. Ideally, you will work through these sections in order, starting with ColdFusion basics and then moving on to advanced topics.

Second, this book is an invaluable desktop reference tool. The appendixes and accompanying CD-ROM contain reference chapters that will be of use to you while developing ColdFusion applications. Those reference chapters are cross-referenced to the appropriate tutorial sections, so that step-by-step information is always readily available to you.

Note

Now in its fifth major release, ColdFusion has matured into a massive application, and a single volume could not do justice to all its features. As such, this book is being released in conjunction with a second book: *Advanced ColdFusion 5 Application Development* (Que, ISBN: 0-7897-2585-1). Some of the advanced chapters that appeared in prior editions of this book have been moved into that new book to facilitate better coverage of those topics.

PART I, "GETTING STARTED"

Part I of this book introduces ColdFusion and explains what exactly it is that ColdFusion enables you to accomplish. Internet fundamentals are also introduced; a thorough understanding of these is a prerequisite to ColdFusion application development. This part also includes coverage of databases, SQL, ColdFusion Studio, and everything else you need to know to get up and running quickly.

In Chapter 1, "Introducing ColdFusion," the core technologies ColdFusion is built on are introduced. The Internet and how it works are explained, as are DNS servers and URLs, Web servers and browsers, HTML, and Web server extensions. A good understanding of these technologies is a vital part of creating Web-based applications. This chapter also teaches you how ColdFusion works and explains the various components that comprise it.

Chapter 2, "Installing ColdFusion and ColdFusion Studio," goes over ColdFusion's hardware and operating-system prerequisites and walks you through the entire process of installing the ColdFusion Application Server and the ColdFusion Studio development environment. The sample applications used in this book are also installed here.

Chapter 3, "Building the Databases," provides a complete overview of databases and related terms. Databases are an integral part of almost every ColdFusion application, so database concepts and technologies must be well understood. Databases are mechanisms for storing and retrieving information, and almost every Web-based application you build will sit on top of a database of some kind. Key database concepts, such as tables, rows, columns, data types, keys, and indexes, are taught, as are the basics of the relational database model. You also learn the differences between client-server– and shared-file–based databases, as well as the pros and cons of each.

Chapter 4, "Accessing the ColdFusion Administrator," introduces the ColdFusion Administrator program. This Web-based program, written in ColdFusion itself, manages and maintains every aspect of your ColdFusion Application Server.

To whet your appetite, Chapter 5, "Previewing ColdFusion," walks you through creating several actual working applications (from very simple to quite complex) using ColdFusion Studio wizards. After that, you'll even get to try coding an application manually, too.

In Chapter 6, "Introduction to SQL," you learn the basics of the SQL language. SQL is a standard language for interacting with database applications, and all ColdFusion database manipulation is performed using SQL statements. The link between ColdFusion and your database itself is via ODBC, so this chapter introduces this technology and walks you through the process of creating ODBC data sources. This chapter also teaches you how to use the SQL `SELECT` statement.

Chapter 7, "SQL Data Manipulation," introduces three other important SQL statements: `INSERT`, `UPDATE`, and `DELETE`.

Chapter 8, "Introduction to ColdFusion Studio," introduces the ColdFusion development environment. ColdFusion Studio is a powerful HTML and CFML editor, and it is chock-full of features designed to make Web page design and application development a whole lot easier. You learn how to use the editor, the Tag Chooser, and the Expression Builder, as well as how to configure the environment to work the way you do. You also learn how to use Studio for remote development.

PART II, "USING COLDFUSION"

With the introductions taken care of, Part II quickly moves on to real development. Starting with language basics, and progressing to database-driven applications and more, the chapters here will make you productive using ColdFusion faster than you thought possible.

Chapter 9, "Using ColdFusion," introduces ColdFusion templates and explains how these are created and used. Variables are explained (including complex variable types, such as arrays and structures), as are CFML functions and the `<CFSET>` and `<CFOUTPUT>` tags.

Chapter 10, "CFML Basics," teaches all the major CFML program flow language elements. From if statements (using `<CFIF>`) to loops (using `<CFLOOP>`) to switch statements (using `<CFSWITCH>` and `<CFCASE>`) to template reuse (using `<CFINCLUDE>`), almost every tag used regularly by ColdFusion developers is explained here, and all with real, usable examples.

Chapter 11, "Creating Data-Driven Pages," is where you create your first data-driven ColdFusion application, albeit a very simple one. You also learn how to use `<CFQUERY>` to create queries that extract live data from your databases and how to display query results using `<CFOUTPUT>`. Various formatting techniques, including using tables and lists, are taught as well. One method of displaying data on the Web is data drill down (which has become very popular), and this approach to data interaction is also taught.

In Chapter 12, "ColdFusion Forms," you learn how to collect user-supplied data via HTML forms. This data can be used to build dynamic SQL statements that provide you with infinite flexibility in creating dynamic database queries. This chapter also teaches you how to create search screens that enable visitors to search on as many different fields as you allow.

Continuing with the topic of collecting data from users, Chapter 13, "Form Data Validation," explains the various techniques and options available for data validation. ColdFusion can generate JavaScript client-side validation code automatically, without you having to learn JavaScript. You learn how to use this feature and how to provide your own validation rules.

Chapter 14, "Using Forms to Add or Change Data," teaches you how to use forms to add, update, and delete data in database tables. The ColdFusion tags `<CFINSERT>` and `<CFUPDATE>` are introduced, and you learn how `<CFQUERY>` can be used to insert, update, and delete data.

Chapter 15, "Debugging and Troubleshooting," teaches you the types of things that can go wrong in ColdFusion application development and what you can do to rectify them. You learn how to use ColdFusion's debugging and logging features and the powerful integrated debugger; most importantly, you learn tips and techniques that can help you avoid problems in the first place.

In Chapter 16, "Using Macromedia Dreamweaver UltraDev with ColdFusion," you are introduced to another Macromedia product—UltraDev. UltraDev is a graphical-based application-generation tool, and it can be used to create complete ColdFusion applications with minimal coding.

Part III, "Building ColdFusion Applications"

Part II concentrated on ColdFusion coding. In Part III, all the ideas and concepts are brought together in the creation of complete applications.

Experienced developers know that it takes careful planning to write good code. Chapter 17, "Planning an Application," teaches important design and planning techniques you can leverage within your own development.

Chapter 18, "Working with Projects," teaches you how to use the integrated ColdFusion Studio project tool. This time-saving feature enables you to work with entire applications at once, and one-step deployment simplifies the publishing process.

In Chapter 19, "Introducing the Web Application Framework," you learn how to take advantage of the ColdFusion Web application framework to facilitate the use of persistent `CLIENT` variables, sophisticated parameter and variable manipulation, and customized error message handling. You also learn how to use the application template to establish applicationwide settings and options and how to use the `APPLICATION` scope (including locking).

Chapter 20, "Working with Sessions," teaches you all you need to know about `CLIENT` and `SESSION` variables, as well as HTTP cookies. These special data types play an important part in creating a complete application that can track a client's state.

Chapter 21, "Security with ColdFusion," introduces important security concepts and explains which you should worry about and why. You learn how to create login screens, access control, and more.

Code should always be written with reuse in mind; this is true of all development, and ColdFusion is no exception. The primary vehicle for code reuse in ColdFusion is the custom tag, and Chapter 22, "Building Reusable Components," introduces custom tags from the ground up.

Chapter 23, "Improving the User Experience," helps you create applications that really get used. You learn important user interface concepts, how to build sophisticated browse screens, and much more.

Developers are always looking for ways to tweak their code, squeezing a bit more performance wherever possible. Chapter 24, "Improving Performance," provides tips, tricks, and techniques you can use to create applications that will always be snappy and responsive.

In Chapter 25, "Enhancing Forms with Client-Side Java," you learn how to take advantage of the ColdFusion-supplied Java form controls. These controls include a Windows Explorer–style tree control, an editable grid control, a slider control, and a highly configurable text input control. You also learn how to embed your own Java applets using the `<CFAPPLET>` tag.

Macromedia Flash is fast becoming the tool of choice for the creation of rich, highly interactive, portable, and lightweight user interfaces. Chapter 26, "Integrating with Macromedia Flash," introduces Flash from a ColdFusion developer's perspective and explains how the two can be used together.

Chapter 27, "Graphing," introduces ColdFusion's new high-performance graphing engine. You learn how to use the `<CFGRAPH>` tag to create all sorts of business graphics (including bar charts, pie charts, and more) for use within your applications.

Chapter 28, "Interacting with E-mail," introduces ColdFusion's e-mail capabilities. ColdFusion enables you to create SMTP-based e-mail messages using its `<CFMAIL>` tag. You learn how to send e-mail messages containing user-submitted form fields, how to e-mail the results of a database query, and how to do mass mailings to addresses derived from database tables. Additionally, you learn how to retrieve mail from POP mail boxes using the `<CFPOP>` tag.

Chapter 29, "Online Commerce," teaches you how to perform real-time electronic commerce, including credit card authorization. You build an entire working shopping-cart application—one you can use as a stepping stone when writing your own shopping applications.

Part IV, "Advanced ColdFusion"

Part IV teaches you advanced ColdFusion capabilities and techniques. The chapters in this section have been written with the assumption that you are familiar with basic SQL syntax and are very comfortable creating ColdFusion templates.

Chapter 30, "ColdFusion Server Configuration," revisits the ColdFusion Administrator, this time explaining every option and feature, while providing tips, tricks, and hints you can use to tweak your ColdFusion server.

Chapter 31, "More About SQL and Queries," teaches you how to create powerful SQL statements using subqueries and joins and explains the advantages and disadvantages of each. You also learn how to calculate averages, totals, and counts and how to use the `EXISTS`, `NOT EXISTS`, and `DISTINCT` keywords.

Chapter 32, "Working with Stored Procedures," takes advanced SQL one step further by teaching you how to create stored procedures and how to integrate them into your ColdFusion applications.

Chapter 33, "Error Handling," teaches you how to create applications that can both report errors and handle error conditions gracefully. You learn how to use the `<CFTRY>` and `<CFCATCH>` tags and how these can be used as part of a complete error-handling strategy.

ColdFusion is primarily used to generate Web content, but that is not all it can do. In Chapter 34, "Generating Non-HTML Content," you learn how to use `<CFCONTENT>` to generate content for popular applications (such as Microsoft Word and Microsoft Excel), as well as cutting-edge technologies such as WAP.

Chapter 35, "Interacting with the Operating System," introduces the powerful and flexible ColdFusion `<CFFILE>` and `<CFDIRECTORY>` tags. You learn how to create, read, write, and append local files; manipulate directories; and even add file uploading features to your forms. You also learn how to spawn external applications when necessary.

Chapter 36, "Full-Text Searching with Verity," introduces the Verity search engine. Verity provides a mechanism that performs full-text searches against all types of data. The Verity engine is bundled with the ColdFusion Application Server, and the `<CFINDEX>` and `<CFSEARCH>` tags provide full access to Verity indexes from within your applications.

Chapter 37, "Event Scheduling," teaches you to create tasks that execute automatically and at timed intervals. You also learn how to dynamically generate static HTML pages using ColdFusion's scheduling technology.

In Chapter 38, "Managing Your Code," you learn about coding standards, documentation, version control, and more, as well as why these are all so important. You learn how to use ColdFusion's built-in version control system, as well as how to interface with existing version control systems of your own.

Continuing with the topic of coding standards, Chapter 39, "Development Methodologies," introduces several popular independent development methodologies designed specifically for ColdFusion development.

Part V, "Appendixes"

Appendix A, "ColdFusion Tag Reference," is an alphabetical listing of all CMFL tags and descriptions. It is designed to be used in conjunction with the complete searchable "ColdFusion Tag Reference" on the accompanying CD-ROM.

Appendix B, "ColdFusion Function Reference," is a complete listing of every CFML function organized by category. It is designed to be used in conjunction with the complete searchable "ColdFusion Function Reference" on the accompanying CD-ROM.

Appendix C, "Special ColdFusion Variables and Result Codes," lists every special variable, prefix, and tag result code available within your applications.

Appendix D, "Verity Search Language Reference," is a complete guide to the Verity search language. Using the information provided here, you will be able to perform incredibly complex searches with minimal effort.

Appendix E, "Sample Application Data Files," lists the format of the database tables used in the sample applications throughout this book.

The CD-ROM

At the request of many readers, the CFML Tag and Function references are being made available in electrontic format (to facilitate searching and printing as needed). The following two references are on the accompanying CD-ROM:

- "Coldfusion Tag Reference" (in PDF format) is the definitive reference for every ColdFusion tag, with descriptive explanations, syntax tables, and examples for each. Topics are cross referenced extensively to related topics and appropriate tutorial chapters in the book.
- "Coldfusion Function Reference" (in PDF format) is a complete reference of every CFML function organized by category. Thorough descriptions and examples are given for every function, and extensive cross-references are provided.

In addition, the accompanying CD-ROM contains everything you need to start writing ColdFusion applications, including

- Evaluation versions of ColdFusion 5 (for Windows, Windows NT, Windows 2000, Solaris, and Linux)
- Evaluation version of ColdFusion Studio 5
- Source code and databases for all the examples in this book
- Thirty add-on tags designed for use within your own applications
- Additional reference material and resources

Turn the page and start reading. In no time, you'll be creating powerful applications powered by ColdFusion.

PART I

Getting Started

CHAPTER 1

INTRODUCING COLDFUSION

In this chapter

THE BASICS

If you're embarking on learning ColdFusion then you undoubtedly have an interest in applications that are developer Web (shorthand for World Wide Web) based. ColdFusion is built on top of the Internet (and the Web), so before getting started, a good understanding of the Internet and related technologies is a must.

There is no need to introduce you to the Internet and the Web. The fact that you're reading this book is evidence enough that these are important to you (as they should be). The Web is everywhere—and Web site addresses appear on everything from toothpaste commercials to movie trailers to cereal boxes to car showrooms. In August 1981, 213 hosts (computers) were connected to the Internet. By the turn of the millennium that number had grown to about 100 million! And most of them are accessing the Web.

What has made the World Wide Web so popular? That, of course, depends on who you ask. But most will agree that these are the two primary reasons:

- **Ease of use**—Publishing information on the Web and browsing for information are relatively easy tasks.
- **Quantity of content**—With millions of Web pages from which to choose and thousands more being created each day, there are sites and pages to cater to almost every surfer's tastes.

A massive potential audience awaits your Web site and the services it offers. You could, and should, be offering much more than just static text and images. You need features such as the following:

- Dynamic, data-driven Web pages
- Database connectivity
- Intelligent, user-customized pages
- Sophisticated data collection and processing
- E-mail interaction

ColdFusion enables you to do all this—and more.

But you need to take a step back before starting ColdFusion development. As I mentioned, because ColdFusion takes advantage of existing Internet technologies, a prerequisite to ColdFusion development is a good understanding of the Internet, the World Wide Web, Web servers and browsers, and how all these pieces fit together.

THE INTERNET

Much ambiguity and confusion surround the Internet, so we'll start with a definition. Simply put, the Internet is the world's largest network.

The networks found in most offices today are *local area networks (LANs)*, comprised of a group of computers in relatively close proximity to each other and linked by special hardware and cabling (see Figure 1.1). Some computers are clients (more commonly known as *workstations*); others are servers (also known as *file servers*). All these computers can communicate with each other to share information.

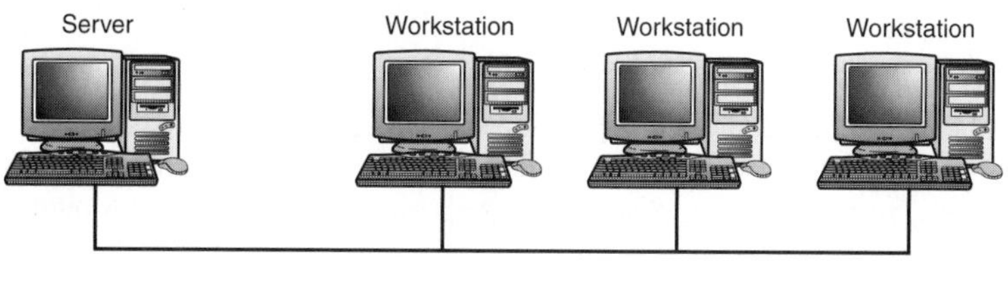

Figure 1.1
A LAN is a group of computers in close proximity linked by special cabling.

Now imagine a bigger network—one that spans multiple geographical locations. This type of network is typically used by larger companies with offices in multiple locations. Each location has its own LAN, which links the local computers together. All these LANs in turn are linked to each other via some communications medium. The linking can be anything from simple dial-up modems to high-speed T1 or T3 connections and fiber-optic links. The complete group of interconnected LANs, as shown in Figure 1.2, is called a *wide area network (WAN)*.

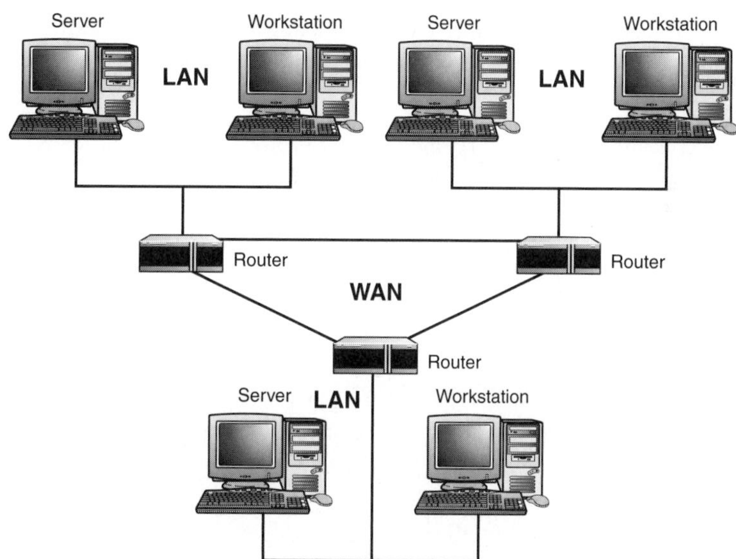

Figure 1.2
A WAN is made up of multiple, interconnected LANs.

WANs are used to link multiple locations within a single company. Suppose you need to create a massive network that links every computer everywhere. How would you do this?

You'd start by running high-speed *backbones*, connections capable of moving large amounts of data at once, between strategic locations—perhaps large cities or different countries.

These backbones would be similar to high-speed, multilane, interstate highways connecting various locations.

You'd build in fault tolerance to make these backbones fully redundant so that if any connection broke, at least one other way to reach a specific destination would be available.

You'd then create thousands of local links that would connect every city to the backbones over slower connections—like state highways or city streets. You'd allow corporate WANs, LANs, and even individual users with dial-up modems to connect to these local access points. Some would stay connected at all times, whereas others would connect as needed.

You'd create a common communications language so that every computer connected to this network could communicate with every other computer.

Finally, you'd devise a scheme to uniquely identify every computer connected to the network. This would ensure that information sent to a given computer actually reached the correct destination.

Congratulations, you've just created the Internet!

Even though this is an oversimplification, it is exactly how the Internet works.

The high-speed backbones do exist. Many are owned and operated by the large telecommunications companies.

The local access points, more commonly known as *points of presence (POPs)*, are run by phone companies, online services, cable companies, and local Internet service providers (also known as ISPs).

The common language is IP, the Internet protocol, except that the term *language* is a misnomer. A *protocol* is a set of rules governing behavior in certain situations. Foreign diplomats learn local protocol to ensure that they behave correctly in another country. The protocols ensure that no communication breakdowns or serious misunderstandings occur. Computers also need protocols to ensure that they can communicate with each other correctly and that data is exchanged correctly. IP is the protocol used to communicate across the Internet, so every computer connected to the Internet must be running a copy of IP.

The unique identifiers are IP *addresses*. Every computer, or host, connected to the Internet has a unique IP address. These addresses are made up of four sets of numbers separated by periods—`216.5.12.60`, for example. Some hosts have *fixed* (or *static*) IP addresses, whereas others have dynamically assigned addresses (assigned from a pool each time a connection is made). Regardless of how an IP address is obtained, no two hosts connected to the Internet can use the same IP address at any given time. That would be like two homes having the same phone number or street address. Information would end up in the wrong place all the time.

A Brief History of the Internet

The Internet has evolved over the past 30 years to become an incredibly important communications medium. What follows is a brief history of the Internet.

1969–The U.S. Department of Defense starts researching a new networking project–the first node in the network (ARPAnet) is established at UCLA and, soon after, nodes are set up at Stanford Research Institute, UCSB, and the University of Utah.

1971–The number of connected nodes reaches 15, as additional government and education institutions are brought online; the capability to send e-mail over the Internet is introduced.

1972–Telnet is introduced to permit remote host access over the Internet.

1973–The U.S. Defense Advanced Research Projects Agency begins work on the "Internetting Project," researching ways to link various kinds of packet networks; File Transfer Protocol (FTP) is introduced.

1977–E-mail specifications are formalized.

1983–Name server technology is developed at the University of Wisconsin.

1984–Domain Name Service (DNS) is introduced; the number of hosts connected to the Internet breaks 1,000.

1986–The U.S. National Science Foundation starts developing NFSNET, a major Internet backbone; Network News Transfer Protocol (NNTP) is introduced to enhance the performance of Usenet news.

1987–The number of hosts connected to the Internet tops 10,000.

1988–An Internet worm cripples the Internet, affecting more than 60,000 hosts; Internet Relay Chat (IRC) is introduced.

1989–The number of hosts connected to the Internet tops 100,000.

1990–Original ARPAnet is dismantled; the first commercial ISP comes online.

1991–Gopher is introduced; the World Wide Web is released by CERN, the European Laboratory for Particle Physics, located near Geneva, Switzerland.

1992–The number of hosts connected to the Internet tops 1,000,000; Veronica (a search tool) is introduced.

1993–The InterNIC is created to handle directory and domain registration services; Mosaic is developed; the number of known Web server tops 500; World Wide Web traffic accounts for about 1% of regular Internet traffic.

1994–The number of hosts connected to the Internet tops 3,000,000; the W3 standards organization is formed; the number of known Web servers tops 1,500 (200% growth in under a year).

1995–The World Wide Web becomes the service generating the most Internet traffic; InterNIC starts charging an annual fee for domain name registrations; ColdFusion (the first application server) is introduced; JavaScript is introduced.

1996–The Java development language promises to usher in a new era of portable application development; VRML (Virtual Reality Markup Language) debuts; 30 more countries register their own top-level domains; the number of hosts connected to the Internet tops 10,000,000; the number of regular Internet users worldwide tops 45,000,000 (close to 70% of them in the United States).

1997–The 2,000th RFC (Internet standards document) is published; human error at Network Solutions causes millions of hosts to be temporarily unreachable; 20 more countries register their own top-level domains; the number of hosts connected to the Internet reaches almost 20,000,000 (100% growth in a single year).

1998–Two millionth domain name is registered; the number of regular Internet users worldwide tops 100,000,000; XML picks up momentum as the ideal data exchange mechanism.

1999–Four millionth domain name is registered; the number of regular Internet users worldwide tops 150,000,000 (more than 50% of them in the United States); WAP (Wireless Application Protocol) is introduced.

2000–Ten millionth domain name is registered; the number of hosts connected to the Internet breaks 100,000,000.

INTERNET APPLICATIONS

The Internet itself is simply a massive communications network and offers very little to most users, which is why it took 20 years for the Internet to become the phenomenon is it today.

The Internet has been dubbed the Information Superhighway, and that analogy is quite accurate. Highways themselves are not nearly as exciting as the places you can get to by traveling them—and the same is true of the Internet. What makes the Internet so exciting are the applications that run over it and what you can accomplish with them.

The most popular application now is the World Wide Web. It is the Web that single-handedly transformed the Internet into a household word. In fact, many people mistakenly think that the World Wide Web is the Internet. This is definitely not the case, and Table 1.1 lists some of the more popular Internet-based applications.

TABLE 1.1 SOME INTERNET-BASED APPLICATIONS

Application	Description
E-mail	Simple Mail Transfer Protocol (SMTP) is the most popular e-mail delivery mechanism.
FTP	File Transfer Protocol is used to transfer files between hosts.
Gopher	This menu-driven document retrieval system was very popular before the creation of the World Wide Web.
IRC	Internet Relay Chat enables real-time, text-based conferencing over the Internet.
NFS	Network File System is used to share files among various hosts.
Newsgroups	Newsgroups are threaded discussion lists, of which thousands exist (accessed via NNTP).
Telnet	Telnet is used to log on to a host from a remote location.
WWW	The World Wide Web.

All these various applications—and many others—use IP to communicate across the Internet. The information transmitted by these applications is broken into *packets*, small blocks of data, which are sent to a destination IP address. The application at the receiving end processes the received information.

DNS

IP addresses are the only way to uniquely specify a host. When you want to communicate with a host—a Web server, for example—you must specify the IP address of the Web server you are trying to contact.

As you know from browsing the Web, you rarely specify IP addresses directly. You do, however, specify a hostname, such as `www.forta.com` (my Web site). If hosts are identified by IP addresses, how does your browser know which Web server to contact if you specify a hostname?

The answer is the Domain Name Service (DNS). DNS is a mechanism that maps hostnames to IP addresses. When you specify the destination address `www.forta.com`, your browser sends an address resolution request to a DNS server asking for the IP address of that host. The DNS server returns an actual IP address, in this case `216.5.12.60`. Your browser can then use this address to communicate with the host directly.

If you've ever mistyped a hostname, you've seen error messages similar to the one seen in Figure 1.3, which tell you the host could not be found, or that no DNS entry was found for the specified host. These error messages mean the DNS server was unable to resolve the specified hostname.

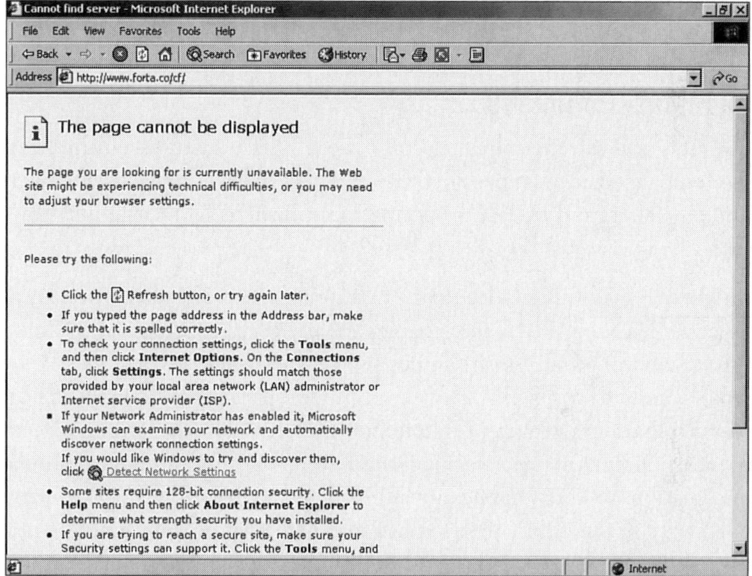

Figure 1.3
DNS errors often are caused by mistyping a URL.

DNS is never needed. Users can always specify the name of a destination host by its IP address to connect to the host. There are, however, some very good reasons not to:

- **IP addresses are hard to remember and easy to mistype**—Users are more likely to find `www.forta.com` than they are `216.5.12.60`.
- **IP addresses are subject to change**—For example, if you switch service providers, you might be forced to use a new set of IP addresses for your hosts. If users identified your site only by its IP address, they'd never be able to reach your host if the IP address changed. Your DNS name, however, stays the same even if your IP address switches. You need to change only the mapping so the hostname maps to the new, correct IP address (the new service provider usually handles that).

- **IP addresses must be unique, as already explained, but DNS names need not**—Multiple hosts, each with a unique IP address, can all share the same DNS name. This enables load balancing between servers, as well as the establishment of redundant servers (so that if a server goes down, another server will still process requests).
- **A single host, with a single IP address, can have multiple DNS names**—This enables you to create aliases if needed. For example, `ftp.forta.com`, `www.forta.com`, and even just plain `forta.com` might point to the same IP address, and thus the same server.

DNS servers are special software programs. Your ISP will often host your DNS entries, so you don't need to install and maintain your own DNS server software.

You can host your own DNS server and gain more control over the domain mappings, but in doing so, you inherit the responsibility of maintaining the server. If your DNS server is down, there won't be any way of resolving the hostname to an IP address, and no one will be able to find your site.

INTRANETS AND EXTRANETS

Intranets and extranets are currently two of the industry's favorite buzzwords. It was not too long ago that most people thought *intranet* was a typo; but in a very short period of time, intranets and extranets became recognized as legitimate and powerful new business tools.

An *intranet* is nothing more than a private Internet. In other words, it is a private network, usually a LAN or WAN, that enables the use of Internet-based applications in a secure and private environment. As on the public Internet, intranets can host Web servers, FTP servers, and any other IP-based services. Companies have been using private networks for years to share information. Traditionally, office networks have not been information friendly. Old private networks did not have consistent interfaces, standard ways to publish information, or client applications that were capable of accessing diverse data stores. The popularity in the public Internet has spawned a whole new generation of inexpensive and easy-to-use client applications. These applications are now making their way back into the private networks. The reason intranets are now getting so much attention is that they are a new solution to an old problem.

Extranets take this new communication mechanism one step further. *Extranets* are intranet-style networks that link multiple sites or organizations using intranet-related technologies. Many extranets actually use the public Internet as their backbones and employ encryption techniques to ensure the security of the data being moved over the network.

The two things that distinguish intranets and extranets from the Internet is who can access them and from where they can be accessed. Don't be confused by hype surrounding applications that claim to be intranet ready. If an application can be used over the public Internet, it will work on private intranets and extranets, too.

WEB SERVERS

As mentioned earlier, the most commonly used Internet-based application is now the World Wide Web. The recent growth of interest in the Internet is the result of growing interest in the World Wide Web.

The World Wide Web is built on a protocol called the Hypertext Transport Protocol (HTTP). HTTP is designed to be a small, fast protocol that is well suited for distributed, multimedia information systems and hypertext jumps between sites.

The Web consists of pages of information on hosts running Web-server software. The host is often referred to as the Web server, which is technically inaccurate. The Web server is software, not the computer itself. Versions of Web server software can run on almost all computers. There is nothing intrinsically special about a computer that hosts a Web server, and no rules dictate what hardware is appropriate for running a Web server.

The original World Wide Web development was all performed under various flavors of Unix. The majority of Web servers still run on Unix boxes, but this is changing. Now Web server versions are available for almost every major operating system. Web servers hosted on high-performance operating systems, such as Windows 2000 and Windows NT, are becoming more and more popular. This is because Unix is still more expensive to run than Windows 2000 and is also more difficult for the average user to use. Windows 2000 (built on top of Windows NT) has proven itself to be an efficient, reliable, and cost-effective platform for hosting Web servers. As a result, Windows' slice in the Web server operating system pie is growing.

What exactly is a Web server? A *Web server* is a program that serves Web pages upon request. Web servers typically don't know or care what they are serving. When a user at a specific IP address requests a specific file, the Web server tries to retrieve that file and send it back to the user. The requested file might be a Web page's HTML source code, a GIF image, a Flash file, a VRML world, or an AVI file. It is the Web browser that determines what should be requested, not the Web server. The server simply processes that request, as shown in Figure 1.4.

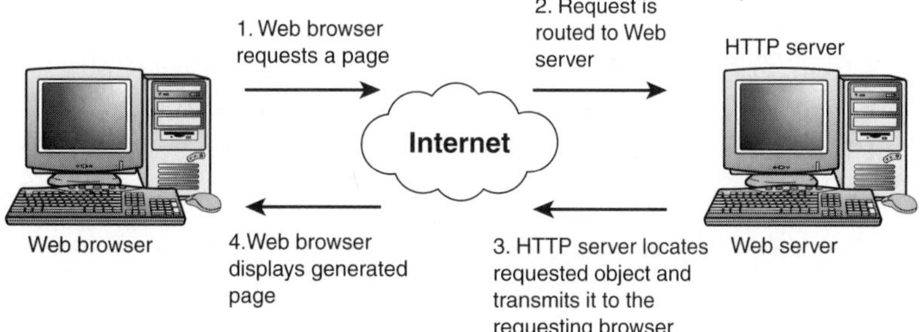
1. Web browser requests a page
2. Request is routed to Web server
HTTP server
Internet
Web browser
4.Web browser displays generated page
3. HTTP server locates requested object and transmits it to the requesting browser
Web server

Figure 1.4
Web servers process requests made by Web browsers.

It is important to note that Web servers typically do not care about the contents of these files. HTML code in a Web page, for example, is markup that the Web browser—not the Web server—will process. The Web server returns the requested page as is, regardless of what the page is and what it contains. If HTML syntax errors exist in the file, those errors will be returned along with the rest of the page.

Connections to Web servers are made on an as-needed basis. If you request a page from a Web server, an IP connection is made over the Internet between your host and the host running the Web server. The requested Web page is sent over that connection, and the connection is broken as soon as the page is received. If the received page contains references to additional information to be downloaded (for example, GIF or JPG images), each would be retrieved using a new connection. Therefore, it takes at least six requests, or *hits*, to retrieve all of a Web page with five pictures in it.

Note

This is why the number of hits is such a misleading measure of Web server activity. When you learn of Web servers that receive millions of hits in one day, it might not mean that there were millions of visitors. Hits do not equal the number of visitors or pages viewed. In fact, hits are a useful measure only of changes in server activity.

Web servers often are not the only IP-based applications running on a single host. In fact, aside from performance issues, there is no reason a single host cannot run multiple services. For example, a Web server, an FTP server, a DNS server, and an SMTP POP3 mail server can run at the same time. Each server is assigned a port address to ensure that each server application responds only to requests and communications from appropriate clients. If IP addresses are like street addresses, ports can be thought of as apartment or suite numbers. A total of 65,536 ports are available on every host—ports 0–1023 are the *Well Known Ports*, ports reserved for special applications and protocols (such as HTTP). Vendor-specific applications that communicate over the Internet (such as America Online's Instant Messenger, Microsoft SQL Server, and the Real Media player) typically use ports 1024–49151. No two applications can share a port.

Most servers use a standard set of port mappings, and some of the more common ports are listed in Table 1.2. Most Web servers use port 80, but you can change that. If desired, Web servers can be installed on nonstandard ports to "hide" Web servers, as well as host multiple Web servers on a single computer by mapping each one to a different port. Remember that if you do use a nonstandard port mapping, users will need to know the new port number.

TABLE 1.2 COMMON IP PORT NUMBERS

Port	Use
20	FTP
21	FTP
23	Telnet

Port	Use
25	SMTP
53	DNS
70	Gopher
80	HTTP
107	Remote Telnet service
109	POP2
110	POP3
119	NNTP
143	IMAP4, Interactive Mail Access Protocol version 4 (previously used by IMAP2)
194	IRC
220	IMAP3
389	LDAP, Lightweight Directory Access Protocol
443	HTTPS, HTTP running over secure sockets
540	UUCP, Unix to Unix Copy

Web Pages

Information on the World Wide Web is stored in *pages*. A page can contain any of the following:

- Text
- Headers
- Lists
- Menus
- Tables
- Forms
- Graphics
- Scripts
- Style sheets
- Multimedia

Web pages are constructed using a series of client-side technologies that are processed and displayed by Web browsers.

Web Browsers

Web browsers are client programs used to access Web sites and pages. The Web browser has the job of processing received Web pages and displaying them to the user. The browser attempts to display graphics, tables, forms, formatted text, or whatever the page contains.

The most popular Web browsers now in use are Netscape Navigator, shown in Figure 1.5, and Microsoft Internet Explorer, shown in Figure 1.6.

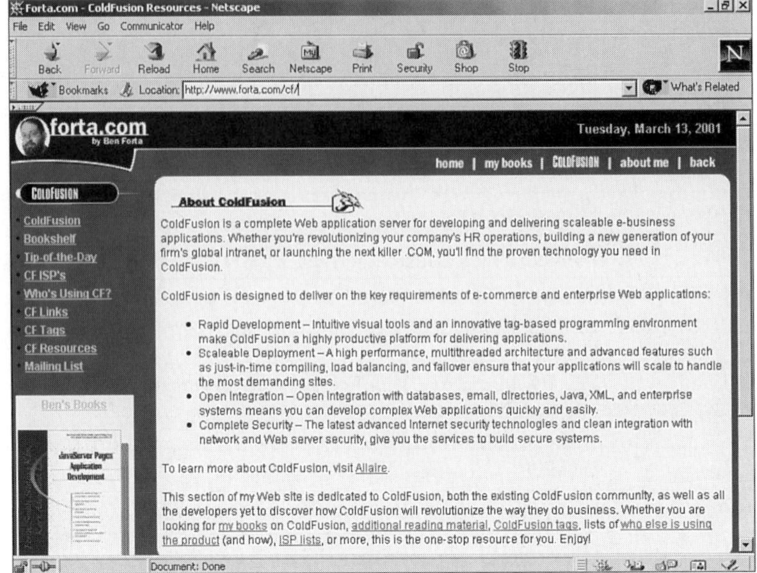

Figure 1.5 Netscape Navigator is the Web's most popular multiplatform browser.

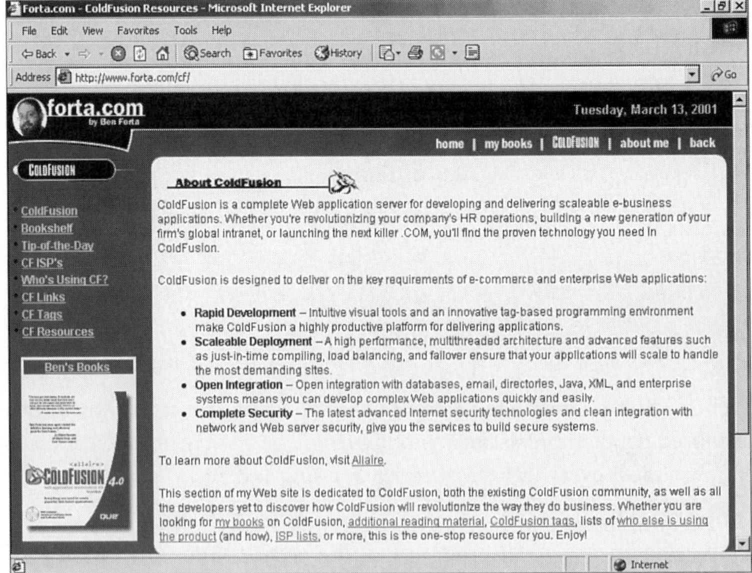

Figure 1.6 Microsoft Internet Explorer is the dominant browser on computers running Windows.

Web page designers have to pay close attention to the differences between browsers because different Web browsers support different HTML tags. Unfortunately, no one single browser supports every tag currently in use. Furthermore, the same Web page often looks different on two different browsers; every browser renders and displays Web page objects differently. Even the same browser running on different operating systems will often behave differently.

For this reason, most Web page designers use multiple Web browsers and test their pages in every one to ensure that the final output appears as intended. Without this testing, some Web site visitors will not see the pages you published correctly.

HTML

Web pages are plain text files constructed via Hypertext Markup Language (HTML). HTML is implemented as a series of easy-to-learn tags. Web page authors use these tags to mark up a page of text. Browsers then use these tags to render and display the information for viewing.

HTML is constantly being enhanced with new features and tags. To ensure backward compatibility, browsers must ignore tags they do not understand. For example, if you use the `<MARQUEE>` tag in an effort to create a scrolling text marquee, browsers that do not support this tag display the marquee text but do not scroll the text.

Web pages also can contain *hypertext jumps*, which are links to other pages or Web sites. Users can click links to jump to either other pages on the same site or any page on any site.

Pages on a Web server are stored in various directories. When requesting a Web page, a user might provide a full path (directory and filename) to specify a particular document.

You can specify a *default* Web page, a page that is sent back to the user when only a directory is specified, with a Web server. These default pages are often called `index.html` or `default.htm`. If no default Web page exists in a particular directory, you see either an error message or a list of all the available files, depending on how the server is set up.

JAVASCRIPT

HTML is a page markup language. It enables the creation and layout of pages and forms but not much else. Building intuitive and sophisticated user interfaces requires more than straight HTML—client-side scripting is necessary, too. Scripting enables you to write code (small programs) that runs within Web browsers.

The most popular client-side scripting language is JavaScript, which is supported (more or less) by almost every browser out there. Using JavaScript you can

- Perform form field validation
- Pop open windows
- Animate text and images
- Create drop-down menus or navigation controls
- Perform rudimentary text and numeric processing
- ...and much more

Note

The other major client-side scripting language is VBScript (modeled in Visual Basic). But VBScript is supported only in Microsoft Internet Explorer and is thus generally used less.

Scripting enables developers to trap and process *events*—things that occur within the browser. For example, a page being loaded, a form being submitted, and the mouse pointer moving over an image are all events, and scripts can be automatically executed by the Web browser when these occur. It is this that facilitates the types of features I just listed.

Script code is either embedded in the HTML file or stored in an external file and linked within the HTML code. Either way, the script is retrieved and processed by the Web browser.

Caution

Writing client-side scripts is more difficult than writing simple HTML. Not only are scripting languages harder to learn than HTML, there is an additional complexity in that various browsers support various levels of scripting. Writing portable scripts is possible, but it is not trivial.

OTHER CLIENT TECHNOLOGIES

Most new browsers also enable the use of add-on technologies that are supported either directly or via plug-in modules. Some of the most significant ones are

- **CSS (Cascading Style Sheets)**—Provide a means of separating presentation from content so that both can be more readily reused and managed.
- **DHTML (Dynamic HTML)**—A combination of HTML, scripting, and CSS that, when used together, provide extremely rich and powerful user-interface options.
- **Java applets**—Small programs that run within the Web browser (actually, they run within a Java Virtual Machine, but we'll not worry about that just yet). Applets were popular in the late '90s but are seldom used now because they are difficult to write; slow to download; and tend to be terribly incompatible with all the computers, operating systems, and browsers in use.
- **Macromedia Flash**—A technology that is now embedded in about 96% of all browsers in use. Flash provides a mechanism for creating rich and portable interactive user interfaces (complete with sound and animation), and Flash is being ported to all sorts of new platforms and devices.

URLs

So, now you know what Web servers, Web browsers, and Web pages are. The piece that links them all together is the URL.

Every Web page on the World Wide Web has an address. This is what you type into your browser to instruct it to load a particular Web page.

These addresses are called *Uniform Resource Locators (URLs)*. URLs are not just used to identify World Wide Web pages or objects. Files on an FTP server, for example, also have URL identifiers.

World Wide Web URLs consist of up to five parts (see Figure 1.7).

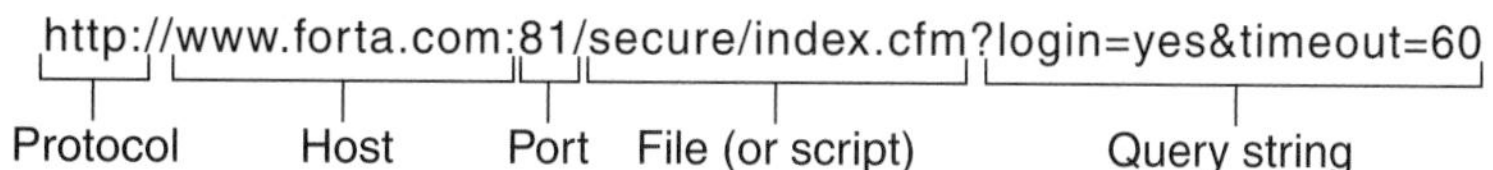

Figure 1.7 URLs consist of up to five parts.

- **The protocol to retrieve the object**—This is usually `http` for objects on the World Wide Web. If the protocol is specified then it must be followed by `://` (which separates the protocol from the hostname).
- **The Web server from which to retrieve the object**—This is specified as a DNS name or an IP address.
- **The host machine port on which the Web server is running**—If omitted, the specified protocol's default port is used; for Web servers, this is port 80. If specified, the port must be preceded by a colon (`:`).
- **The file to retrieve or the script to execute**—You learn more about the script later in this chapter.
- **Optional script parameters**—Also known as the *query string*. If a query string is specified, it must be preceded by a question mark (`?`).

Look at some sample URLs:

- `http://www.forta.com`—This URL points to a Web page on the host `www.forta.com`. Because no document or path was specified, the default document in the root directory is served.
- `http://www.forta.com/`—This URL is the same as the previous example and is actually the correct way to specify the default document in the root directory (although most Web browsers accept the previous example and insert the trailing slash automatically).
- `http://www.forta.com/books/`—This URL also points to a Web page on the host `www.forta.com`, but this time the directory `/books/` is specified. Because no page name was provided, the default page in the `/books/` directory is served.
- `http://216.5.12.60/books/`—This URL points to the same file as the previous example, but this time the IP address is used instead of the DNS name.
- `http://www.forta.com/books/topten.html`—Once again, this URL points to a Web page on the `www.forta.com` host. Both a directory and a filename are specified this time.

This retrieves the file `topten.html` from the `/books/` directory, instead of the default file.

- `http://www.forta.com:81/administration/index.html`—This is an example of a URL that points to a page on a Web server assigned to a nonstandard port. Because port `81` is not the standard port for Web servers, the port number must be provided.
- `http://www.forta.com/cf/tips/syndhowto.cfm`—This URL points to a specific page on a Web server, but not an HTML page. CFM files are ColdFusion templates, which are discussed later in this chapter.
- `http://www.forta.com/cf/tips/browse.cfm?search=tag`—This URL points to another ColdFusion file, but this time a parameter is passed to it. A `?` is always used to separate the URL itself (including the script to execute) from any parameter.
- `http://www.forta.com/cf/tips/browse.cfm?search=tag&s=1`—This URL is the same as the previous example, with one additional parameter. Multiple parameters are separated by ampersands (the `&` character).
- `http://www.forta.com/cgi/cfml.exe?template=//cf/tips/syndhowto.cfm`—This URL points to a script, rather than a Web page. `/cgi/` is the directory name (or directory map) to the location where the `cfml.exe` script is located. Anything after the `?` is parameters that are passed to the script. In this example, the Web server executes the script `cfml.exe` and passes the parameter `template=/cf/tips/syndhowto.cfm` to it.
- `ftp://ftp.forta.com/pub/catalog.zip`—This is an example of a URL that points to an object other than a Web page or script. The protocol `ftp` indicates that the object referred to is a file to be retrieved from an FTP server using the File Transfer Protocol. This file is `catalog.zip` in the `/pub/` directory.

Links in Web pages are references to other URLs. When a user clicks a link, the browser processes whatever URL it references.

UNDERSTANDING COLDFUSION

Now millions of Web sites exist that attract millions of visitors daily. Many Web sites are being used as electronic replacements for newspapers, magazines, brochures, and bulletin boards. The Web offers ways to enhance these publications using audio, images, animation, multimedia, and even virtual reality.

No one will dispute that these sites add value to the Net because information is knowledge, and knowledge is power. All this information is available at your fingertips—literally. Web sites, however, are capable of being much more than electronic versions of paper publications because of the underlying technology that makes the Web tick. Users can interact with you and your company, collect and process mission-critical information in real-time (allowing you to provide new levels of user support), and much more.

The Web is not merely the electronic equivalent of a newspaper or magazine—it is a communication medium that is limited only by the lack of innovation and creativity of Web site designers.

THE DYNAMIC PAGE ADVANTAGE

Dynamic pages (containing dynamic content) are what brings the Web to life. Linking your Web site to live data is a tremendous advantage, but the benefits of database interaction go beyond extending your site's capabilities.

Dynamic Web pages are becoming the norm for good reason. Consider the following:

- **Static Web pages**—Static Web pages are made up of text, images, and HTML formatting tags. These pages are manually created and maintained so that when information changes, so must the page. This usually involves loading the page into an editor, making the changes, reformatting text if needed, and then saving the file. Of course, not everyone in the organization can make these changes. The Webmaster or Web design team is responsible for maintaining the site and implementing all changes and enhancements. This often means that by the time information finally makes it onto the Web site, it's out of date.
- **Dynamic Web pages**—Dynamic Web pages contain very little text. Instead, they pull needed information from other applications. Dynamic Web pages communicate with databases to extract employee directory information, spreadsheets to display accounting figures, client-server database management systems to interact with order processing applications, and more. A database already exists. Why re-create it for Web page publication?

Creating dynamic pages enables you to create powerful applications that can include features such as these:

- Querying existing database applications for data
- Creating dynamic queries facilitating more flexible data retrieval
- Executing stored procedures (in databases that support them)
- Executing conditional code on-the-fly to customize responses for specific situations
- Enhancing the standard HTML form capabilities with data validation functions
- Dynamically populating form elements
- Customizing the display of dates, times, and currency values with formatting functions
- Easing the creation of data entry and data drill-down applications with wizards
- Generating e-mail automatically (perhaps in response to form submissions)
- Shopping carts and e-commerce sites
- Data syndication and affiliate programs
- ...and much more

Understanding Web Applications

As was explained earlier, Web servers do just that: They serve. Web browsers make requests, and Web servers fulfill those requests—they serve back the requested information to the browser. These are usually HTML files, as well as the other file types discussed previously.

And that's really all Web servers do. In the grand scheme of things, Web servers are actually pretty simple applications—they sit and wait for requests that they attempt to fulfill as soon as they arrive. Web servers do not let you interact with a database; they don't let you personalize Web pages; they don't let you process the results of a user's form submission; they do none of that. All they do is serve pages.

So how do you extend your Web server to do all the things just listed? That's where Web application servers come into play. A *Web application server* is a piece of software that extends the Web server, enabling it to do things it could not do by itself—kind of like teaching an old dog new tricks.

Here's how it all works. When a Web server receives a request from a Web browser, it looks at that request to determine whether it is a simple Web page or a page that needs processing by a Web application server. It does this by looking at the MIME type (or file extension). If the MIME type indicates that the file is a simple Web page (for example, it has an `HTM` extension) then the Web server fulfills the request and sends the file to the requesting browser as is. But if the MIME type indicates that the requested file is a page that needs processing by a Web application server (for example, it has a `CFM` extension) then the Web server passes it to the appropriate Web application server and returns the results that it gets back rather than the actual page itself. Figure 1.8 illustrates this concept (in contrast to simple HTTP processing seen previously in Figure 1.4).

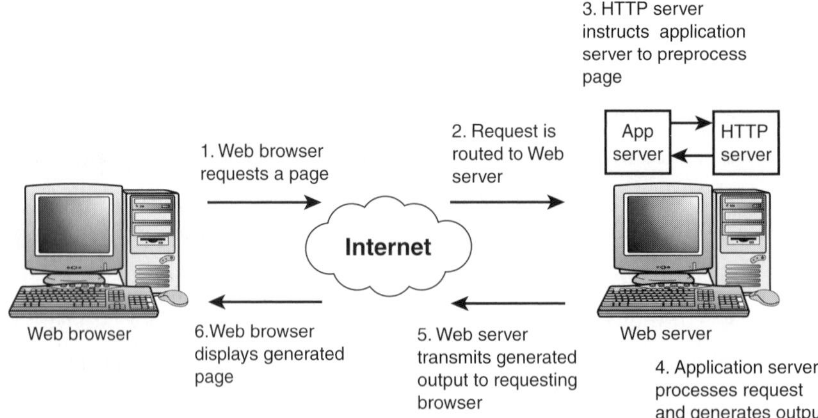

Figure 1.8 Web servers pass requests to Web application servers, which in turn pass results back to the Web server for transmission to the requesting browser.

In other words, Web application servers are page preprocessors. They process the requested page before it is sent back to the client (the browser), and in doing so they open the door to developers to do all sorts of interesting things on the server, things such as

- Creating guest books
- Conducting surveys
- Changing your pages on-the-fly based on date, time, first visit, and whatever else you can think of
- Personalizing pages for your visitors
- In fact, all the features listed previously

WHAT IS COLDFUSION?

Initially, developing highly interactive and data-rich sites was a difficult process. Writing custom Web-based applications was a job for experienced programmers only. A good working knowledge of Unix was a prerequisite, and experience with traditional development or scripting languages was a must.

But all that has changed. Macromedia's ColdFusion enables you to create sites every bit as powerful and capable as those listed earlier, without a long and painful learning curve. In fact, rather than being painful, the process is actually fun!

So, what exactly is ColdFusion? Simply put, ColdFusion is an application server—one of the very best out there (as well as the very first one out there; ColdFusion created the Application Server category).

ColdFusion does not require coding in traditional programming languages, although traditional programming constructs and techniques are fully supported. Instead, you create applications by extending your standard HTML files with high-level formatting functions, conditional operators, and database commands. These commands are instructions to the ColdFusion processor and form the building blocks on which to build industrial-strength applications.

This method of creating Web applications has significant advantages over conventional application development. Advantages include

- ColdFusion applications can be developed rapidly because no coding, other than use of simple HTML style tags, is required.
- ColdFusion applications are easy to test and roll out.
- The ColdFusion language contains all the processing and formatting functions you'll need (and the capability to create your own functions if you really run into a dead end).
- ColdFusion applications are easy to maintain because no compilation or linking step is required. The files you create are the files used by ColdFusion.
- ColdFusion provides all the tools you need to troubleshoot and debug applications, including a powerful remote interactive debugger.
- ColdFusion comes with all the hooks necessary to link to almost any database application.
- ColdFusion is fast, thanks to its scalable, multithreaded, service-based architecture.

COLDFUSION AND YOUR INTRANET OR EXTRANET

Although all the examples mentioned so far have been Internet sites, the benefits of ColdFusion apply to intranets and extranets, too.

Most companies have masses of information stored in various systems. Users often don't know what information is available or even how to access it.

ColdFusion bridges the gap between existing and legacy applications and your employees. It empowers employees with the tools to work more efficiently.

COLDFUSION EXPLAINED

You're now ready to take a look at ColdFusion so you can understand what it is and how it works its magic.

And if you're wondering why you went through all this discussion about the Internet and Web servers, here's where it will all fit together.

THE COLDFUSION APPLICATION SERVER

ColdFusion is an application server—a piece of software that (usually) resides on the same computer as your Web server, enabling the Web server to do things it would not normally know how to do.

ColdFusion is actually made up of several pieces of software (applications on Windows 95, 98, and Me; services on Windows NT and Windows 2000; and daemons on Linux, Solaris, and HP-UX). The ColdFusion Application Server is the program that actually parses (reads and interprets) and processes any supplied instructions.

Instructions are passed to ColdFusion using templates. A *template* looks much like any HTML file, with one big difference. Unlike HTML files, ColdFusion templates can contain special tags that instruct ColdFusion to perform specific operations. Listing 1.1 contains a sample ColdFusion template; it is one that you'll use later in this book.

LISTING 1.1 SAMPLE COLDFUSION TEMPLATE

```
<!--- Get movies sorted by release date --->
<CFQUERY DATASOURCE="ows" NAME="movies">
 SELECT MovieTitle, DateInTheaters
 FROM Films
 ORDER BY DateInTheaters
</CFQUERY>

<!--- Create HTML page --->
<HTML>
<HEAD>
```

```
<TITLE>Movies by Release Date</TITLE>
</HEAD>

<BODY>

<H1>Movies by Release Date</H1>

<!--- Display movies in list format --->
<UL>
<CFOUTPUT QUERY="movies">
 <LI><B>#Trim(MovieTitle)#</B> - #DateFormat(DateInTheaters)#</LI>
</CFOUTPUT>
</UL>

</BODY>

</HTML>
```

Earlier in this chapter, it was stated that Web servers typically return the contents of a Web page without paying any attention to the file contents.

That's exactly what ColdFusion does not do. When ColdFusion receives a request, it parses through the template looking for special ColdFusion tags (they all begin with `CF`) or ColdFusion variables and functions (always surrounded by pound signs). Any HTML or plain text is left alone and is output to the Web server untouched. Any ColdFusion instructions are processed, and any existing results are sent to the Web server (just like in Figure 1.8). The Web server can then send the entire output back to the requester's browser. As explained earlier, the request file type tells the Web server that a request is to be handled by an application server. ColdFusion files all have an extension of `.cfm` or `.cfml`, like this:

```
http://www.forta.com/books/index.cfm
```

When ColdFusion is installed, it configures your Web server so it knows that any file with an extension of `.cfm` (or `.cfml`) is a ColdFusion file. Then, whenever a ColdFusion file is requested, the Web server knows to pass the file to ColdFusion for processing rather than return it.

The ColdFusion Markup Language

Earlier it was stated that ColdFusion is an application server, which is true, but that is not all ColdFusion is. In fact, ColdFusion is two distinct technologies (that for now are coupled as one, but might not always remain that way):

- The ColdFusion Application Server
- The CFML language

And although the ColdFusion Application Server itself is important, ColdFusion's power comes from its capable and flexible language. ColdFusion Markup Language (CFML) is modeled after HTML, which makes it very easy to learn.

CFML extends HTML by adding tags with the following capabilities:

- Read data from, and update data to, databases and tables
- Create dynamic data-driven pages
- Perform conditional processing
- Populate forms with live data
- Process form submissions
- Generate and retrieve e-mail messages
- Interact with local files
- Perform HTTP and FTP operations
- Perform credit-card verification and authorization
- Read and write client-side cookies

And that's not even the complete list.

The majority of this book discusses ColdFusion pages (often called *templates*) and the use of CFML.

Linking to External Applications

One of ColdFusion's most powerful features is its capability to connect to data created and maintained in other applications. You can use ColdFusion to retrieve or update data in many applications, including the following:

- Corporate databases
- Client/server database systems (such as Microsoft SQL Server and Oracle)
- Spreadsheets
- Contact-management software
- ASCII-delimited files

ColdFusion accesses these applications via ODBC. ODBC, which is discussed in detail later in this book, is a standard interface that applications can use to interact with a diverse set of external data stores. In addition, ColdFusion also supports native database drivers for some databases.

Note

ODBC and the use of database drivers are explained in detail in Chapter 6, "Introduction to SQL."

EXTENDING COLDFUSION

As installed, ColdFusion will probably do most of what you need, interacting with most of the applications and technologies you'll be using. But in the event that you need something more, ColdFusion provides all the hooks and support necessary to communicate with just about any application or service in existence. Integration is made possible via

- C and C++
- Java
- COM
- CORBA

Note

These technologies and their uses are beyond the scope of this book and are covered in detail in the sequel *Advanced ColdFusion 5 Application Development* (Que, ISBN: 0-7897-2585-1).

BEYOND THE WEB

As was explained earlier, the Web and the Internet are not one and the same. The Web is an application that runs on top of the Internet, one of many applications. Others do exist, and you can use and take advantage of many of them.

One of the most exciting new technologies is Wireless Application Protocol (WAP), which can be used to power applications accessed via wireless devices (such as phones and PDAs).

As explained earlier, Web servers (and thus application servers) send content back to requesters without paying attention to what that content is. The requester (known as the *client* or *user agent*) is typically a Web browser, but it need not be. In fact, WAP browsers (the Internet browsers built into WAP devices) can also make requests to Web servers.

Note

WAP and generating WAP content using ColdFusion are discussed in Chapter 34, "Generating Non-HTML Content."

In other words, although ColdFusion is primarily used to generate Web content, it is not limited to doing so in any way, shape, or form. As seen in Figure 1.9, the same server can generate content for the Web, WAP, e-mail, and more.

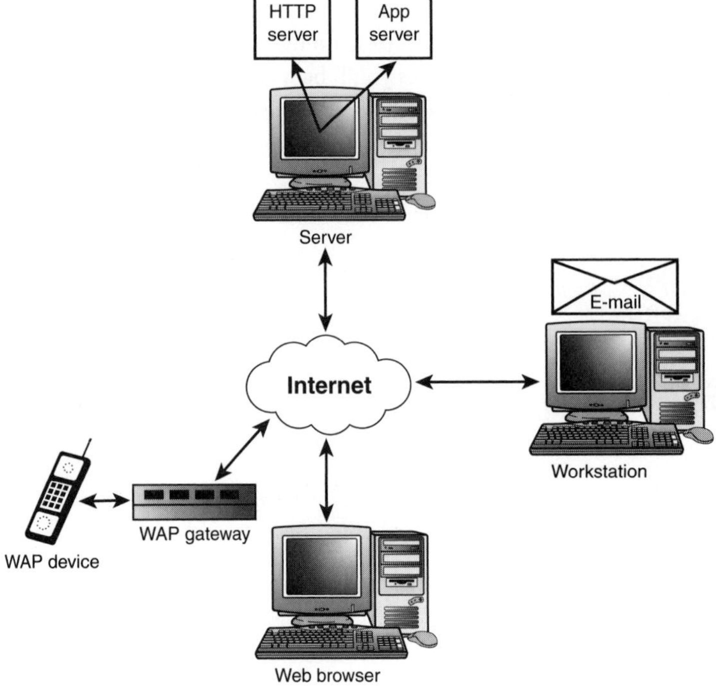

Figure 1.9
ColdFusion is client independent and can generate content for many types of clients, not just Web browsers.

POWERED BY COLDFUSION

You were probably planning to use ColdFusion to solve a particular problem or fill a specific need. Although this book helps you do just that, I hope that your mind is now racing and beginning to envision just what else ColdFusion can do for your Web site.

In its relatively short life, ColdFusion has proven itself to be a solid, reliable, and scalable development platform. ColdFusion 5 is the sixth major release of this product, and with each release it becomes an even better and more useful tool. It is easy to learn, fun to use, and powerful enough to create real-world, Web-based applications. With a minimal investment of your time, your Web site can be powered by ColdFusion.

CHAPTER 2

Installing ColdFusion and ColdFusion Studio

In this chapter

ColdFusion Server 5 represents the easiest-to-install version of ColdFusion to date. Before you begin the actual installation, read this section to make sure your system meets ColdFusion's requirements for hardware, software, and system configuration.

The first part of this chapter walks you through the preinstallation checklist to ensure that your system complies with ColdFusion Server's requirements. The second part of this chapter contains step-by-step instructions of installing ColdFusion Server on every supported platform. The third and final part of this chapter includes instructions for installing ColdFusion Studio.

The Two Flavors of ColdFusion: Professional and Enterprise

Like the previous version, ColdFusion 5 is sold in two versions: Professional and Enterprise. ColdFusion Enterprise contains powerful server management and scalability tools, security enhancements, and other sophisticated features. This book applies to both Professional and Enterprise editions of ColdFusion. Evaluation versions of ColdFusion Enterprise and ColdFusion Studio come bundled with this book's accompanying CD-ROM.

Preinstallation Checklist

To verify that ColdFusion will function at peak performance on your hardware platform, make sure you follow each of the three steps listed here:

- Check your hardware's specs. If your RAM or disk space is inadequate or your processor cannot handle the load, an upgrade will be necessary.
- Check your operating system's configuration. Just having a copy of Windows 2000 does not guarantee ColdFusion will function perfectly.
- Check your Web server. This is Web development. If you don't have the correct Web server installed or it does not function properly, you will not be able to test your ColdFusion applications.

Checking Your Hardware

At present, Allaire supports three hardware platforms for ColdFusion 5: Intel-based systems running Windows NT 4.0; Windows 2000; and several distributions of the Linux kernel, Sun SPARC systems running Solaris, and HP systems running HP-UX.

Intel-Based Systems

ColdFusion can be installed on Intel-based systems under Windows NT 4.0, Windows 2000, and several Linux distributions. The minimum recommended hardware is a Pentium-class machine running at 200MHz.

Windows NT and Windows 2000 systems should have no less than 128MB of RAM to run ColdFusion Professional and 200MB of free disk space. For ColdFusion Enterprise, 256MB of RAM and 400MB of free disk space are required.

All supported Linux distributions require the same system specifications as Windows.

Tip

For all platforms, keep in mind that installing additional RAM usually improves system performance to some extent. Also, the applications you create with ColdFusion will take up additional hard disk space.

Because this is Web development, ColdFusion works best when connected to a network via an Ethernet card. A modem can also be used.

Note

Broadband options continue to proliferate. Digital Subscriber Lines (DSLs) and cable modems are good alternatives when a T1 connection is not available.

Sun SPARC Systems

When installing ColdFusion on a Sun SPARC system, your system must have 256MB of RAM and 350MB of free disk space. ColdFusion supports Solaris 2.6, 7, and 8.

Again, your system should be connected to a network.

HP Systems

To use ColdFusion on HP systems, the system must be running HP-UX with a PA-RISC 1.1 or 2.0 processor. In addition, 128MB of RAM and 120MB of free disk space are required.

HP-UX systems should be connected to a network as well.

Choosing Your Hardware

You probably already know which hardware platform you will use for ColdFusion because it's likely the hardware you already own. If you have yet to decide, the following points should be kept in mind during your deliberations:

- Virtually all ColdFusion code will execute perfectly across all supported platforms. That means if you jump ship to another platform during or after development, your applications will require little, if any, porting.
- Intel-based systems are the most popular hardware platforms in the world, with the largest number of options and vendors. Also, Intel-based systems experts can be found more easily than those for any other platform.
- Depending on a variety of configuration options, Sun SPARC, and HP-UX systems might provide more scalability and performance than Windows.

Note

The CD-ROM contains evaluation versions of ColdFusion 5 Enterprise Edition and ColdFusion Studio for all platforms.

CHECKING YOUR OPERATING SYSTEM

The steps involved to ensure your operating system is properly configured to run ColdFusion depend on the operating system.

WINDOWS

Both ColdFusion 5 Professional and Enterprise run on Windows NT 4.0 Workstation and Server and Windows 2000 Professional and Server. If you use Windows 98, you should use ColdFusion 5 Professional.

The TCP/IP protocol must be installed for your Windows system to access other Web servers. If you can browse Web sites on the Internet or your intranet using a Web browser, TCP/IP is installed on your system.

If you receive error messages that the proper protocols have not been installed, do the following:

- For Windows 95, 98, and Me, right-click the Network Neighborhood icon on the desktop and select the Properties option to display the Network properties dialog box shown in Figure 2.1. The TCP/IP protocol should be shown in the Configuration tab. If it is not present, click the Add button to install it.

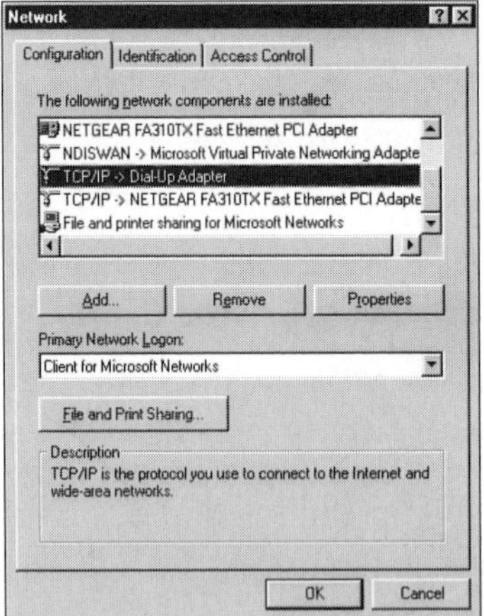

Figure 2.1
The Network dialog box in Windows 98 shows installed clients, protocols, and adapters.

- If you use Windows NT 4.0, right-click the Network Neighborhood icon and select Properties. The Network dialog box will appear listing all available protocols (see Figure 2.2). If TCP/IP does not appear, click the Add button to install it.

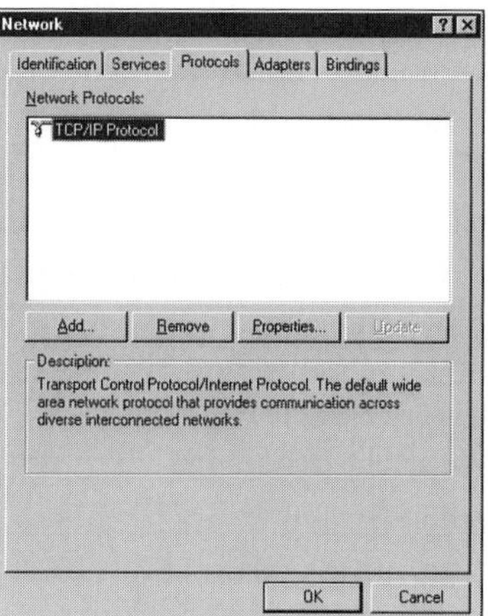

Figure 2.2
The Protocols tab in the Windows NT Network dialog box displays the installed protocols.

- If you use Windows 2000, right-click the My Network Places icon and select Properties. The Network and Dial-Up Connections dialog box will appear. In it, right-click the connection you want to configure (for example, Local Area Connection) to display the Properties dialog box shown in Figure 2.3. If TCP/IP has been installed, it will be listed. If TCP/IP does not appear, click the Install button to add it.

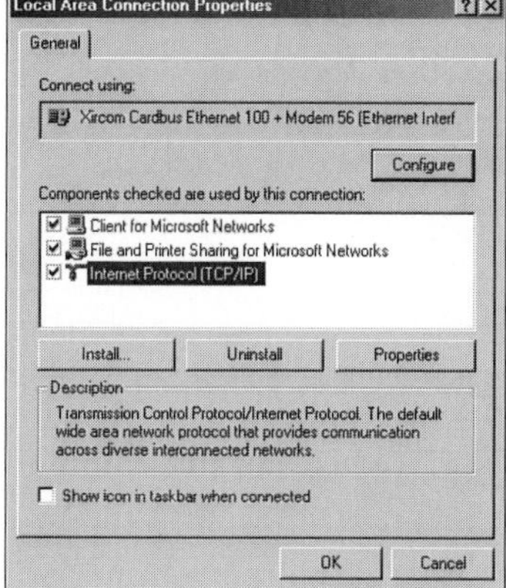

Figure 2.3
The Properties dialog box in Windows 2000's Network and Dial-Up Connections displays the installed protocols.

Note

To test whether your system's TCP/IP is working, open a command prompt and type `ping 127.0.0.1`. If the ping succeeds, TCP/IP is working.

LINUX

The rise in popularity of the Linux platform has taken the Web development community by storm. Today, ColdFusion 5 supports RedHat Linux 6.2 or greater, SuSE Linux 6.4 or greater, and Cobalt RAQ3/RAQ4 and XTR.

Because all Linux distributions are based on the same 2.x kernel, their installation procedures are similar. However, the procedures for manually configuring Web servers, especially Apache, depend on the distribution. Consult the ColdFusion documentation for more information.

SOLARIS

ColdFusion requires Solaris 2.6, 7, or 8. ColdFusion also needs the following patches and packages to be installed on each version of Solaris.

ColdFusion on Solaris 2.6:

- Solaris patch 105181-17 or higher (kernel patch)
- Solaris patch 105591-09 or higher (libc: Shared library patch for C++)
- Solaris patch 105210-25 or higher (libc: Shared library patch for C/C++)
- Solaris patch 105568-14 or higher (libthread: Shared library patch)

ColdFusion on Solaris 7:

- Solaris patch 106541-08 or higher (kernel patch)
- Solaris patch 106327-08 or higher (libc: Shared library patch for C++)
- Solaris patch 106980-07 or higher (libthread: Shared library patch)

ColdFusion on Solaris 8:

- None

ColdFusion on all Solaris versions requires the following packages:

- SUNWxcu4—XCU4 Utilities

> **Note**
>
> All patches and packages can be found at `http://access1.sun.com`.

HP-UX

ColdFusion 5 on HP-UX requires HP-UX 11 with the latest patches installed. HP-UX installation is more difficult than other platforms because the CD-ROM must be mounted prior to installation. Detailed instructions are included in the section "Installing ColdFusion on HP-UX."

CHOOSING YOUR OPERATING SYSTEM

You'll probably use the operating system with which you are the most familiar for your ColdFusion development. If you're still trying to decide, remember that your version of ColdFusion and your hardware platform dictate your choices of operating systems. Here are the options:

- **ColdFusion 5 Professional**—Requires Intel-based hardware running Windows 98; Windows NT 4.0; Windows 2000; RedHat Linux; SuSE Linux; Cobalt. It also supports HP hardware running HP-UX 11.
- **ColdFusion 5 Enterprise**—Runs on either Intel-based systems with Windows NT 4.0, Windows 2000, RedHat Linux, SuSE Linux, and Cobalt or Sun SPARC-based systems running Solaris.

Similar to hardware, you'll likely use the operating system you currently use for your ColdFusion development. If you're still undecided, here are some considerations:

- Essentially the same from a Web development perspective, Windows 98 serves as a very capable environment for developing and debugging ColdFusion applications. In addition, a multitude of applications are available for the three platforms.

Note

Windows 98 is intended for home use and should not be used in a deployment and production environment.

- Windows NT 4.0 (Workstation and Server) and 2000 (Professional, Server, and Advanced Server) feature stability and scalability enhancements that make them ideal for deployment and production environments.

Tip

The main difference between the Workstation/Professional versions of Windows NT 4.0/Windows 2000 is the number of concurrent sessions the operating system can accommodate. Workstation/Professional can handle 10 concurrent connections. However, Windows NT 4.0 Server and Windows 2000 Server do not have this limitation. Consult each version of Windows for detailed specifications.

- When compared to Windows, the Unix derivatives (the various Linux distributions, Solaris, and HP-UX) offer arguably more stability and scalability for deployment and production of Web applications. In particular, a very active Linux user community provides good, if unstructured, support for potential problems.
- Although Linux continues to make inroads into desktop applications and other computing arenas outside the server arena, Solaris and HP-UX's strengths remain solidly placed in the deployment and production of mission-critical Web applications.

Note

While HP-UX 11 is a 64-bit operating system, ColdFusion 5 supports only 32-bit operating systems at this time.

- You should use the operating system with which you are the most familiar. If you have used Windows almost exclusively, a switch to a different operating system can cause more problems than it solves.
- You must consider what the purpose of your ColdFusion application will be. If you're developing a Web application that must provide the highest level of scalability and reliability, a Unix-based operating system is probably your best choice.
- As the most popular operating system, Windows expertise and support are easier to come by than other operating systems. When tight deadlines loom, the last thing you want to be doing is searching discussion boards for a solution to an obscure bug.

CHECKING YOUR WEB SERVER

As explained in Chapter 1, "Introducing ColdFusion," Web servers are separate software programs that enable two-way communication between your system and other Web servers. A great number of Web servers are available for a great number of operating systems. You must choose the Web server that is compatible with your operating system and ColdFusion.

ColdFusion 5 supports most popular Web servers for the operating systems it supports. Table 2.1 lists which Web servers are supported on which ColdFusion platform.

TABLE 2.1 COLDFUSION-SUPPORTED WEB SERVERS

ColdFusion Version	IIS	Netscape/ iPlanet	Apache Web Server	Personal Web Server (Win 98, Me only)	Web Server API
ColdFusion Windows	4.0+	3.51+	1.3.6	Supported	Supported
ColdFusion Linux		4.1	1.3.6		
ColdFusion Solaris		3.6+	1.3.6		
ColdFusion HP-UX		3.6+	1.3.6		

Ask five Webmasters which Web server is best and you'll likely receive five different answers. Each Web server has advantages and disadvantages. Here are a few things to keep in mind when choosing which Web server is right for you:

- Windows 98 uses the Personal Web Server (PWS). PWS provides only basic Web server functionality and should not be used as a production Web server.
- Microsoft's Internet Information Server (IIS) is completely free and comes bundled with Windows NT 4 and Windows 2000. One of IIS's principal advantages is its capability to

use Windows' user lists and security options. This eliminates the complexity of maintaining multiple lists of passwords and security privileges. On the other hand, IIS users must have a network login to have a Web server login. At the time of this writing, the latest version of IIS for Windows NT is 4.0. Windows 2000 users should use IIS 5. Go to Microsoft's Web site to download the latest version (`http://www.microsoft.com`).

Tip

Windows NT 4.0 comes bundled with IIS 2.0. If you plan to use IIS, you should upgrade to IIS 4.0 for critical enhancements that make Web development on Windows much easier. Windows 2000 includes IIS 5.

- Netscape/iPlanet Web Server Enterprise Edition is one of the most popular commercial Web servers. It runs on Windows NT 4.0, Linux (with glibc-2.1.3-11 or later, gcc/egcs libstdc++ 2.9, and 2.2 kernel or later), HP-UX, and Sun Solaris. Enterprise Edition features Web-based administration and can be integrated with any LDAP-based directory server. At the time of this writing, the latest version of the Enterprise Edition is 4.1 SP5. Visit iPlanet's Web site to download an evaluation copy (`http://www.iplanet.com`).
- Apache is one of the oldest and still the most popular Web server on the Web. Completely free of charge, the Apache Web server is an open-source software project available for most operating systems, including Windows NT 4.0, Windows 2000, Linux, Solaris, and HP-UX. Apache has garnered a near-legendary reputation for reliability and scalability. With that stated, Apache is more difficult to install than IIS and Netscape/iPlanet Web Server. Also, support is provided through the Apache development community. At the time of this writing, the latest version of Apache is 1.3.19. Go to the Apache Web site to download the Web server (`http://www.apache.org`).

Because the applications you develop with ColdFusion are portable among all supported Web servers, your production Web server can differ from the Web server used for development with minimal changes in your ColdFusion code.

After you have installed a Web server, you must verify that it is working properly. To do this, start a Web browser and go to the URL `http://localhost/`. If everything is working, your Web server's default home page should appear.

Note

If the home page doesn't display, you must do a little troubleshooting. First, type **`ping 127.0.0.1`** at a command prompt. If the ping is successful, TCP/IP is working. More than likely, the problem lies with the Web server. For more information, consult the Web server's documentation.

FINAL INSTALLATION CHECKLIST

Ready to install ColdFusion? Almost. Before you begin the actual installation, quickly go through this final checklist to make sure your i's are dotted and your t's are crossed:

- Double-check your hardware's compliance with ColdFusion's system requirements.
- Make sure ColdFusion supports your operating system and that the required patches and packages have been properly installed. Don't forget the TCP/IP requirements of Windows.
- Verify that ColdFusion supports your Web server, as shown in Table 2.1. Also, validate that your Web server is working by entering **`http://localhost/`** in a Web browser. Remember to upgrade to IIS 4.0 in Windows NT 4.0.

That's it. Let's install ColdFusion 5!

INSTALLING COLDFUSION 5

ColdFusion is easier to install than ever. Nevertheless, with the variety of operating systems supported in ColdFusion 5, the installation procedures vary widely among operating systems. All ColdFusion installations contain two similarities:

1. Executing the ColdFusion installation file
2. Verifying the ColdFusion installation

The following sections describe the steps involved in installing ColdFusion 5 on Windows, Linux, Solaris, and HP-UX.

STARTING THE INSTALLATION ON WINDOWS

On the accompanying CD-ROM, you will find an evaluation copy of the Windows version of ColdFusion 5 Enterprise. Installation of ColdFusion 5 on Windows NT 4.0 and Windows 2000 are almost identical. The following Windows installation instructions apply to both versions of Windows.

> **Note**
>
> The installation instructions included in this section apply to both the evaluation versions of ColdFusion 5 and the full versions. If you are installing the full version of ColdFusion, simply enter the serial number that can be found in the software packaging.

WINDOWS STEP-BY-STEP INSTALLATION INSTRUCTIONS

To begin the installation, double-click the `coldfusion-50-win-us.exe` located in the Macromedia/ColdFusion/Server directory on the accompanying CD-ROM. If you are installing ColdFusion from a retail CD, double-click the `SETUP.EXE` file in the Windows directory. If you downloaded ColdFusion from the Web, execute the appropriate EXE file.

Tip

To install ColdFusion, make sure you log in to Windows NT or 2000 with LOCAL Administrator privileges.

As shown in Figure 2.4, ColdFusion's Install Wizard will begin, and a checklist screen will appear displaying the system information relevant to ColdFusion installation requirements. If your system requirements meet ColdFusion's requirements, a green check mark will show up next to the system component.

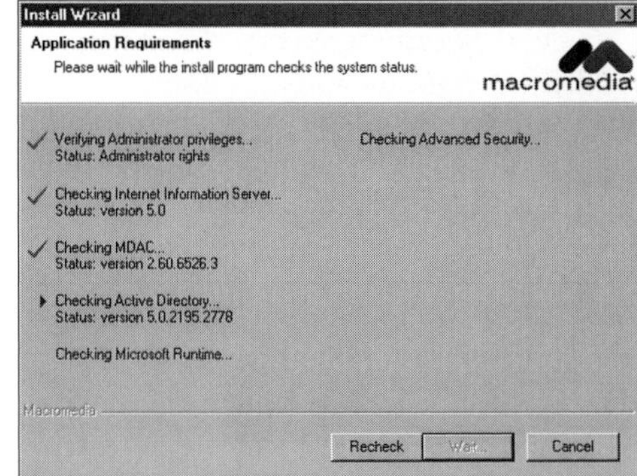

Figure 2.4
ColdFusion's Install Wizard checks your system for required components.

Note

If one or more of your system components does not meet ColdFusion's minimum requirements, a red X will appear next to the component. You should install the version required by ColdFusion as listed in the section "Checking Your Operating System," earlier in this chapter, and then click the Recheck button in ColdFusion's Install Wizard.

After your system meets the requirements and a green check mark appears beside each component, the Welcome dialog box appears next. When you are ready to proceed, click the Next button.

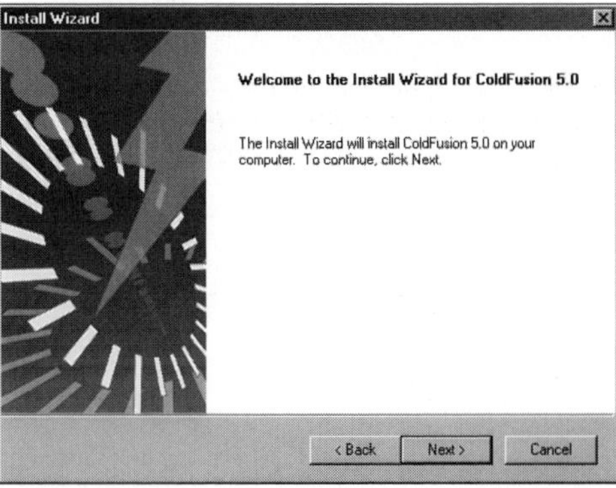

Figure 2.5
ColdFusion's Install Wizard guides you through the rest of the installation.

ColdFusion's license agreement will be displayed in the next dialog box (see Figure 2.6). If you agree, click the Yes button. If you do not agree, Click No and ColdFusion will not be installed.

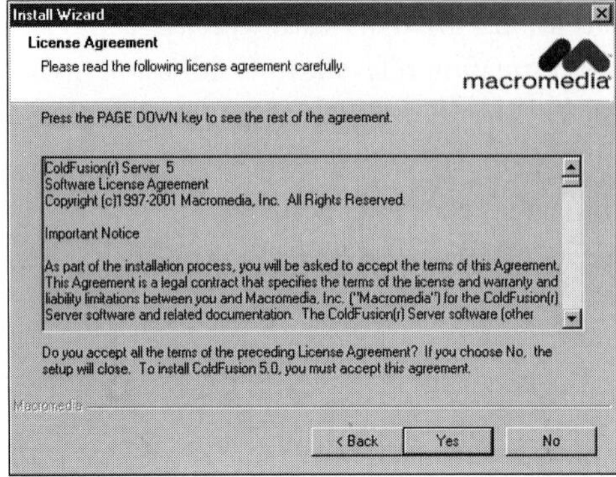

Figure 2.6
Read ColdFusion's license agreement and click the Yes or No button.

The following dialog box asks for your name, company, and serial number (see Figure 2.7). Enter the requested information and click Next.

Note

If you're installing the evaluation version of ColdFusion, leave the Serial Number text field blank.

Figure 2.7
Enter your name, company, and serial number in the Customer Information dialog box.

Install Wizard
Customer Information
Please enter your information.
macromedia
Please enter your name, the name of the company for whom you work and the product serial number.
User Name:
Julie Eisenstein
Company Name:
Orange Whip Studios
Serial Number:
Previous Serial Number:
Status
A blank serial number entitles you to a 30-day ColdFusion 5.0 Enterprise Evaluation. After 30-days, ColdFusion will revert to Single IP mode.
< Back
Next >
Cancel

In the next dialog box, the Install Wizard asks you to select the Web server to be used with ColdFusion (see Figure 2.8). The Install Wizard should automatically detect all Web servers installed on your system. Click the radio button beside your choice, and then click the Next button.

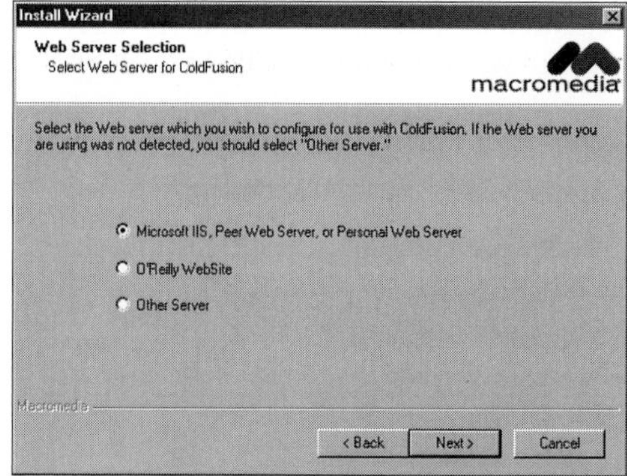

Figure 2.8
Choose the Web server that will be used with ColdFusion in the Web Server Selection dialog box.

Note

If you select Other Server, you must configure your Web server manually after the ColdFusion installation is complete. Refer to the ColdFusion documentation for instructions.

You now are prompted to choose the directory into which ColdFusion will be installed, as shown in Figure 2.9. If you want to install ColdFusion into the default `C:\CFusion` directory, click the Next button. If you want to install into a directory other than the default, click the Browse button to select an alternative.

In addition, you are prompted to select the Webroot directory into which the ColdFusion Administrator, documentation, and example application files will be installed. You also will save your CFML files in this directory. If you want to install into a directory other than the default, click the Browse button to select an alternative.

When you are finished, click the Next button.

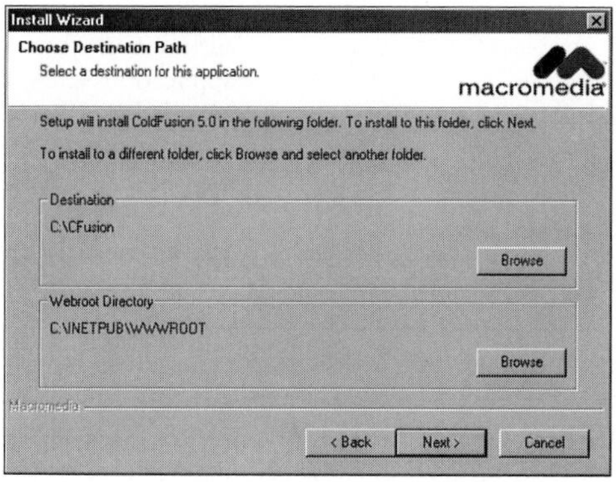

Figure 2.9
Select the installation and Webroot directories in the Choose Destination Path dialog box.

As shown in Figure 2.10, the Select Components dialog box displays next. In it, you choose which optional components of ColdFusion to install. Table 2.2 describes the available options.

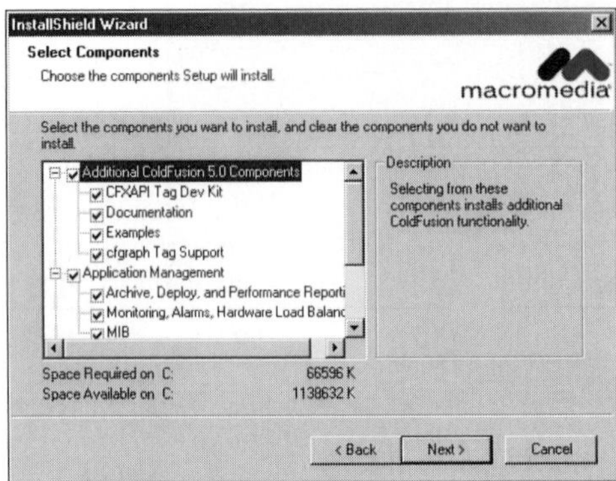

Figure 2.10
Select the optional ColdFusion components to install in the Select Components dialog box.

TABLE 2.2 SELECT COMPONENTS DIALOG BOX OPTIONS

Option	Description	Recommendations
CFXAPI Tag Dev Kit	Installs tools to develop custom tag	If you plan to develop your own custom tags using C++ and/or Java, this component is a necessity.
Documentation	Installs HTML versions of the official ColdFusion documentation	Although the documentation should not be installed in a production environment, the ColdFusion documentation provides a valuable reference when developing applications.
Examples	Installs sample ColdFusion applications	Although the sample applications should not be installed in a production environment, the sample applications represent a good way to get started building applications quickly.
cfgraph Tag Support	Installs graphing server	If you plan to use ColdFusion's built-in graphing functionality, you must install this component.
Archive, Deploy, and Performance Monitoring	Installs a server that allows you to archive and deploy applications and monitor their performance	If you want to use ColdFusion's archival, deployment, and performance monitoring features, select this component.

Option	Description	Recommendations
Monitoring, Alarms, and Hardware Load-Balancer	Installs support for tracking overall server performance and integrating with hardware load-balancers	If you want to monitor server performance, receive notifications when server thresholds are met, and integrate with hardware load-balancers, you should install this component.
MIB	Installs the Management Information Base (MIB) component	If you want to integrate ColdFusion with your network management system, install this component.
Load Balancing	Installs support for ClusterCATS	If you want to use ClusterCATS, ColdFusion's software-based load-balancing solution, select this component.
Web Server (IP) Failover	Configures your system to receive HTTP requests from other clustered servers	If you want to configure this system to receive HTTP requests from busy servers in the cluster.
Advanced Security	Installs the Advanced Security server	If you want to use ColdFusion's Advanced Security components, such as integrating with operating-system security policies and single sign-on, select this component.

Note

ClusterCATS and Application Management features are not supported on the Apache Web server, O'Reilly's WebSite Professional, and WebServer API. In addition, Windows NT Workstation and Windows 2000 Professional are not supported.

Note

If you install ClusterCATS, all monitoring, alarms, and load-balancing features are available in ClusterCATS Explorer. If you do not install ClusterCATS, you can access those features in the ColdFusion Administrator.

Note

If you want to use ColdFusion's MIB functionality, you first must install the Simple Network Management Protocol (SNMP) service for Windows, which can be found on your Windows NT 4.0 or Windows 2000 installation CD under Administration Tools.

The next dialog box prompts you to enter and confirm two passwords—one for the ColdFusion Administrator and one for ColdFusion Studio (Windows only) to access your ColdFusion server (see Figure 2.11).

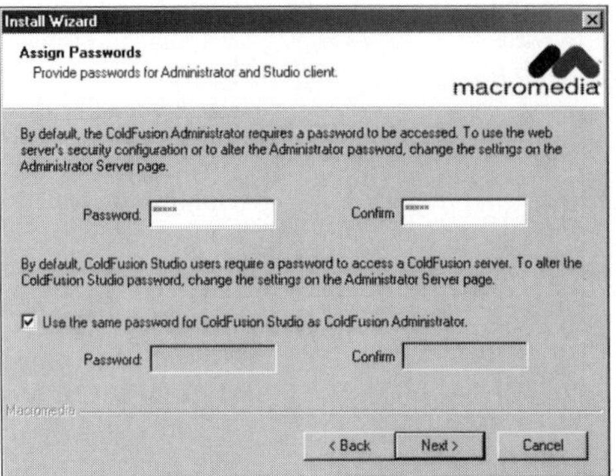

Figure 2.11
Enter and confirm passwords for ColdFusion Administrator and ColdFusion Studio in the Assign Passwords dialog box.

Tip

If you want, the passwords for ColdFusion Administrator and ColdFusion Studio can be the same.

The final dialog box before the actual installation lists your installation selections for review (see Figure 2.12). If everything checks out, click Next to begin transferring the program files.

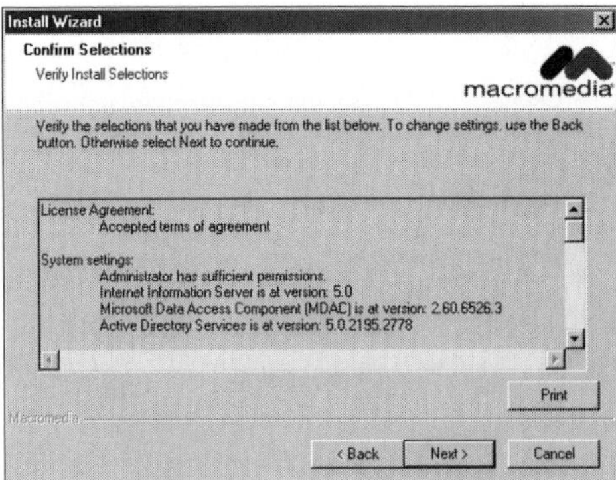

Figure 2.12
The Confirm Selections dialog box displays your installation selections.

Tip

Click the Print button in the Confirm Selections dialog box to get a hard copy of your installation selections.

The Install Wizard now configures your system and installs the ColdFusion files.

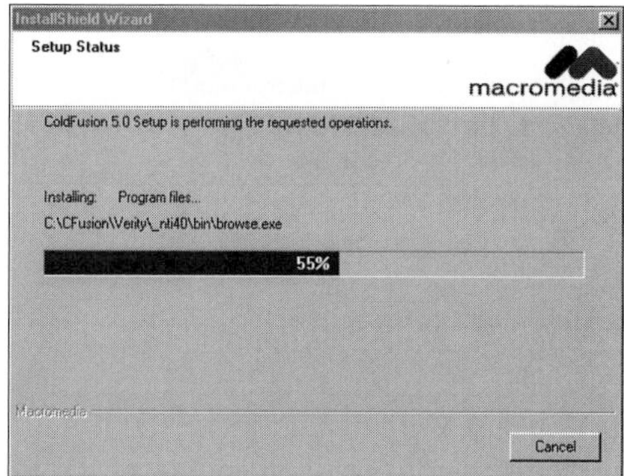

Figure 2.13
The Setup Status dialog box shows the installation progress and the files being installed.

After the installation completes, you are prompted to restart your computer (see Figure 2.14). Do so by clicking Finish.

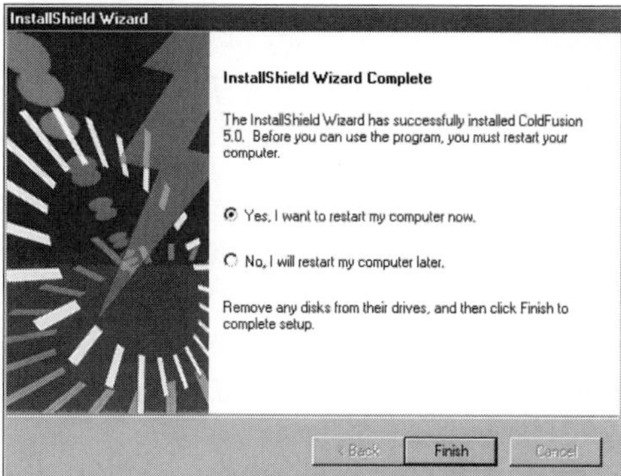

Figure 2.14
The InstallShield Complete dialog box prompts you to restart your computer.

MODIFYING, REPAIRING, OR UNINSTALLING COLDFUSION

Modifying, repairing, or uninstalling an installation is a snap in ColdFusion 5. Go to the Windows Control Panel and double-click the Add/Remove Programs icon. Next, click the ColdFusion 5 selection.

A Welcome dialog box appears in which you can choose to modify, repair, or remove the ColdFusion installation (see Figure 2.15). Modifying the installation enables you to add or subtract components from ColdFusion. When ColdFusion repairs the installation, it attempts to identify and reinstall a problematic component. Removing the installation uninstalls ColdFusion completely.

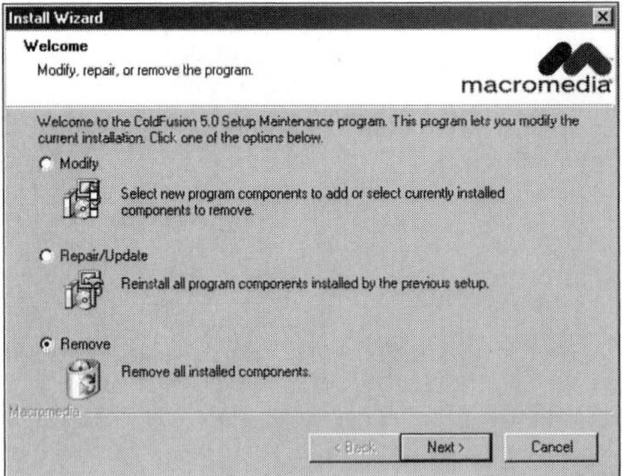

Figure 2.15
You can choose whether to modify, repair, or remove the ColdFusion installation in the Welcome dialog box.

INSTALLING COLDFUSION ON LINUX

On the accompanying CD-ROM, you will find an evaluation copy of the Linux version of ColdFusion Enterprise 5. Installation of ColdFusion 5 on Linux is almost as painless as a Windows installation. You should not experience any problems as long as your Linux distribution is officially supported by ColdFusion (see the section "Linux," earlier in this chapter, for supported distributions).

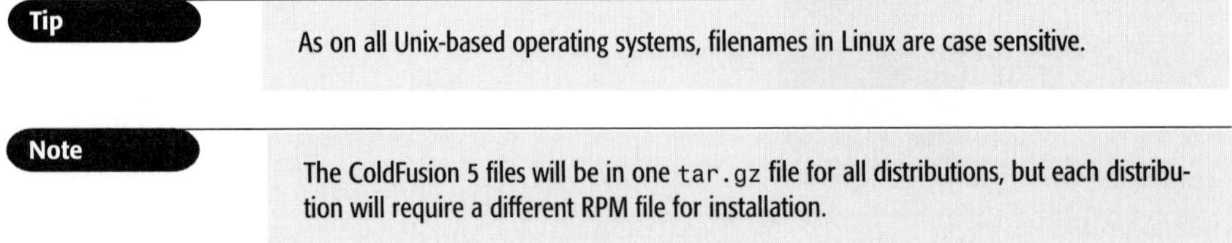

Tip

As on all Unix-based operating systems, filenames in Linux are case sensitive.

Note

The ColdFusion 5 files will be in one `tar.gz` file for all distributions, but each distribution will require a different RPM file for installation.

GENERAL LINUX STEP-BY-STEP INSTALLATION INSTRUCTIONS

The following are step-by-step instructions for installing ColdFusion for Linux:

1. Log in as root.
2. If you are installing from a CD-ROM, copy the gzipped tar file to a directory on your local disk. Using gunzip, uncompress the ColdFusion Server tar file by typing **`gunzip coldfusion-50-linux.tar.gz`**.
3. Untar the resulting tar file by typing **`tar -xvf coldfusion-50-linux.tar`**.
4. Go to the resulting directory by typing **`cd coldfusion-50-linux`**.
5. Run the ColdFusion Server installation script by entering the following command: **`./cfinstall`**.
6. After the installation begins, you are prompted to enter your ColdFusion license key. If you're installing the evaluation copy, just press Enter. If you're installing the full version of ColdFusion 5, enter the license key found in the package.

7. Type the name of the directory for the ColdFusion installation. If you select the default directory, it will be `/opt`. If you specify a directory other than the default `/opt`, the ColdFusion installation script will create a symbolic link between your directory and `/opt/coldfusion`.
8. Type the name of your Web server. If you are using Apache, press Enter. You are also prompted whether to configure Apache automatically for ColdFusion. Enter **`y`**. If you select Apache as your Web server and choose to configure it automatically for ColdFusion, you are prompted to enter the file path of your `httpd.conf` file.

Note

If you select Other Server, you must configure your Web server manually after the ColdFusion installation is complete. Refer to the ColdFusion documentation for instructions.

9. Type the path of your Web server's document root directory. If the default root directory works for your system (`home/httpd/html`), press Enter. The ColdFusion Administrator files and documentation will be installed in this directory.
10. You are now prompted whether to install the ColdFusion documentation. The documentation provides an invaluable reference and development guide. Type **`y`** or **`n`**. Next, choose whether to install the ColdFusion sample applications. The sample applications can get you started quickly but should not be installed in production environments as a security precaution. Enter **`y`** or **`n`**.
11. Type a password for ColdFusion Administrator, a Web-based interface to configure settings for ColdFusion. To verify your password, you are asked to enter your password again.
12. Type a password to connect to ColdFusion Server from ColdFusion Studio (Windows only). You are prompted again to verify your password.
13. Type a username to use with ColdFusion. The username must be an existing account. Pressing Enter assigns the default username (`nobody`).

Note

If you select Other Server, you must configure your Web server manually after the ColdFusion installation is complete. Refer to the ColdFusion documentation for instructions.

14. You are now prompted to choose whether or not you want to install any of ColdFusion's optional features. Table 2.3 describes the available options.

TABLE 2.3 OPTIONAL COLDFUSION COMPONENTS FOR LINUX

Option	Description	Recommendations
Reporting and Archive/Deploy	Installs a server that allows you to archive and deploy applications and monitor their performance	If you want to use ColdFusion's archival, deployment, and performance monitoring features, select this component.
Monitoring, Alarms, and Hardware Load-Balancer Integration	Installs support for tracking overall server performance and integrating with hardware load-balancers	If you want to monitor server performance, receive notifications when server thresholds are met, and integrate with hardware load-balancers, you should install this component.
ClusterCATS software load-balancing	Installs ClusterCATS	If you want to use ClusterCATS, ColdFusion's software-based load-balancing solution, select this component.
Web Server IP Failover	Configures your system to receive HTTP requests from other clustered servers	If you want to configure this system to receive HTTP requests from busy servers in the cluster.
MIB	Installs the Management Information Base (MIB) component	If you want to integrate ColdFusion with your network management system, install this component.

Note

ClusterCATS and Application Management features are not supported on SuSE and Cobalt. In addition, they do not support the Netscape/iPlanet Web server on any Linux distribution.

Note

If you install ClusterCATS, all monitoring, alarms, and load-balancing features are available in ClusterCATS Web Explorer. If you do not install ClusterCATS, you can access those features in the ColdFusion Administrator.

Note

If you want to use ColdFusion's MIB functionality, you must first install the Simple Network Management Protocol (SNMP) for Linux, UCD-SNMP 4.2. You can download UCD-SNMP at `http://www.sourceforge.org`.

15. Press Enter to enable the ColdFusion installation script to begin copying program files.

Note

When upgrading ColdFusion 5 on Linux from a previous version, refer to the ColdFusion documentation for instructions. Also, refer to the ColdFusion documentation for instructions on configuring your Web server to work with ColdFusion on Linux.

Note

For Linux, you must change the `/opt/coldfusion/bin/start` script to which database you will use. To do this, set the database-specific environment variable and edit the file path to the database in your `LD_LIBRARY_PATH` environment variable.

UNINSTALLING COLDFUSION ON LINUX

To uninstall ColdFusion on Linux, log in as root and enter **`/opt/coldfusion/uninstall/cfremove`**.

INSTALLING COLDFUSION ON SOLARIS

On the accompanying CD-ROM, you will find an evaluation copy of the Solaris version of ColdFusion Enterprise 5. Because Linux and Solaris are both based from Unix, their installation procedures are very similar. After you ensure that your version of Solaris matches ColdFusion's requirements (see the section "Solaris," earlier in this chapter), follow these step-by-step instructions to install ColdFusion on Solaris.

Tip

As on all Unix-based operating systems, filenames in Solaris are case sensitive.

SOLARIS STEP-BY-STEP INSTALLATION INSTRUCTIONS

1. Log in as root.
2. If you are installing from a CD-ROM, copy the gzipped tar file to a directory on your local disk. Using gunzip, uncompress the ColdFusion Server tar file by typing **`gunzip coldfusion-50-solaris.tar.gz`**.
3. Untar the resulting tar file by typing **`tar -xvf coldfusion-50-solaris.tar`**.
4. Go to the resulting directory by typing **`cd coldfusion-50-solaris`**.
5. Run the ColdFusion Server installation script by entering the following command: **`pkgadd -d coldfusion-50-solaris.pkg`**.
6. After the installation begins, you are prompted to enter your ColdFusion license key. If you're installing the evaluation copy, just press Enter. If you're installing the full version of ColdFusion 5, enter the license key found in the package.
7. Type the name of the directory for the ColdFusion installation. If you choose the default directory, it will be `/opt`.

8. Type the name of your Web server. If you are using Netscape/iPlanet Web Server Enterprise Edition, press Enter. If you want ColdFusion to configure your Web server automatically, enter **y** at the corresponding prompt. Also, enter your Web server's installation directory at the next prompt. Table 2.4 describes the optional ColdFusion components for Solaris.

> **Note**
>
> If you select Other Server, you must configure your Web server manually after the ColdFusion installation is complete. Refer to the ColdFusion documentation for instructions.

TABLE 2.4 OPTIONAL COLDFUSION COMPONENTS FOR SOLARIS

Option	Description	Recommendations
Reporting and Archive/Deploy	Installs a server that allows you to archive and deploy applications and monitor their performance	If you want to use ColdFusion's archival, deployment, and performance monitoring features, select this component.
Monitoring, Alarms, and Hardware Load-Balancer Integration	Installs support for tracking overall server performance and integrating with hardware load-balancers	If you want to monitor server performance, receive notifications when server thresholds are met, and integrate with hardware load-balancers, you should install this component.
ClusterCATS software load balancing	Installs ClusterCATS	If you want to use ClusterCATS, ColdFusion's software-based load-balancing solution, select this component.
Web Server IP Failover	Configures your system to receive HTTP requests from other clustered servers	If you want to configure this system to receive HTTP requests from busy servers in the cluster.
MIB	Installs the Management Information Base (MIB) component	If you want to integrate ColdFusion with your network management system, install this component.

Note

If you install ClusterCATS, all monitoring, alarms, and load-balancing features are available in ClusterCATS Web Explorer. If you do not install ClusterCATS, you can access those features in the ColdFusion Administrator.

Note

If you want to use ColdFusion's MIB functionality, you must first install Simple Network Management Protocol (SNMP) for Solaris. Consult the installation and configuration manual that accompanies ColdFusion for more information.

9. Type the path of your Web server's document root directory. The default root directory is determined by the Web server used.
10. Type `y` or `n` when prompted if you want to install Advanced Security. If you choose to install ColdFusion, you are prompted to enter a password for SiteMinder, ColdFusion's Advanced Security server. You are then prompted for the IP address and port of your security server. Additional prompts appear to ask for more information.

Note

Your security server must be running to install Advanced Security for ColdFusion.

11. You are now prompted about whether to install the ColdFusion documentation. The documentation provides an invaluable reference and development guide. Enter `y` or `n`. Next, choose whether to install the ColdFusion sample applications. The sample applications can get you started quickly but should not be installed in production environments as a security precaution. Enter `y` or `n`.
12. If you did not select Advanced Security, a dialog box appears asking for a password for ColdFusion Administrator, a Web-based interface to configure settings for ColdFusion. To verify your password, you are asked to enter your password again. Type a password to connect to ColdFusion Server from ColdFusion Studio. You are prompted again to verify your password.
13. Type a username to use with ColdFusion. The username must be an existing account. Pressing Enter assigns the default username (`nobody`).
14. Press Enter to enable the ColdFusion installation script to begin copying program files.

Note

When upgrading ColdFusion 5 on Solaris from a previous version, refer to the ColdFusion documentation for instructions.

Tip

For Solaris, you must change the `/opt/coldfusion/bin/start` script to which database you will use. To do this, set the database-specific environment variable and edit the file path to the database in your `LD_LIBRARY_PATH` environment variable.

Uninstalling ColdFusion on Solaris

To uninstall ColdFusion on Solaris, log in as root and enter **`pkgrm cfusion`**.

Installing ColdFusion on HP-UX

On the accompanying CD-ROM, you will find an evaluation copy of the HP-UX version of ColdFusion Enterprise 5. Installing ColdFusion 5 on HP-UX shares many similarities with Linux and Solaris. Be sure your version of HP-UX complies with ColdFusion's requirements (see the section "HP-UX," earlier in this chapter). The main difference is mounting the CD-ROM, which is explained next.

> **Tip**
>
> As on all Unix-based operating systems, filenames in HP-UX are case sensitive.

Mounting the ColdFusion CD-ROM on HP-UX

To support long filenames, ColdFusion 5 for HP-UX uses the Portable File System (PFS) commands and not the standard HP-UX `mount/unmount` commands. Therefore, you must mount the ColdFusion CD-ROM as follows:

1. Make a mount point for the CD-ROM, such as
   ```
   mkdir SD_CFCD
   ```
2. Make an entry in the PFS mount file, such as
   ```
   /code/dsk/CDROM   /DG_CFCD      pfs-rrip    xlat=unix  0
   ```
3. Start the PFS daemons by typing
   ```
   nohup /usr/sbin/pfs_mountd &
   nohup /usr/sbin/pfsd &
   ```
4. Next, mount the CD-ROM by typing
   ```
   /usr/sbin/pfs_mount /DG_CFCD.
   ```
5. You should now be able to see the CD-ROM by looking in the `/DG_CDROM` directory.

HP-UX Step-By-Step Installation Instructions

1. Log in as root.
2. Mount the CD-ROM as described previously.
3. Go to the `HPUX` directory on the CD-ROM.
4. Copy the `tar.gz` file to a temporary location on your hard disk.
5. Run gunzip on the `.gz` file, and untar the resulting tar file.
6. Change directory to the directory created by tar, and execute the `cfinstall` script.
7. After the installation begins, you are prompted to enter your ColdFusion license key. If you're installing the evaluation copy, just press Enter. If you're installing the full version of ColdFusion 5, enter the license key found in the package.

8. Type the name of the directory for the ColdFusion installation. If you choose the default directory, it will be `/opt`.
9. Type the name of your Web server.
10. Type the path of your Web server's document root directory. The default root directory is determined by the Web server used. ColdFusion's documentation will be installed in the Web server's root directory under `/cfdocs`.
11. Type a password for ColdFusion Administrator, a Web-based interface to configure settings for ColdFusion. To verify your password, you are asked to enter your password again.
12. Type a password to connect to ColdFusion Server from ColdFusion Studio. You are prompted again to verify your password.
13. Type a username to use with ColdFusion. The username must be an existing account. Pressing Enter assigns the default username (`nobody`).
14. Press Enter to enable the ColdFusion installation script to begin copying program files.

Tip

For HP-UX, you must change the `/opt/coldfusion/bin/start` script to which database you will use. To do this, set the database-specific environment variable and edit the file path to the database in your `SHLIB_PATH` environment variable.

UNINSTALLING COLDFUSION ON HP-UX

To uninstall ColdFusion on HP-UX, log in as root and enter `/opt/coldfusion/uninstall/cfremove`.

VERIFYING YOUR INSTALLATION

For all operating systems and platforms, you must test whether the ColdFusion installation was successful and whether the ColdFusion server is running. To verify your installation, follow these simple steps:

1. Type the following URL into a Web browser: **`http://127.0.0.1/CFIDE/administrator/docs/index.htm`.**
2. Click the link Validate That the Installation Was Successful.
3. In the next page, click the Test Installation button.

If your ODBC connections are working properly and ColdFusion is running, you will receive a greeting. If not, the error page should provide some information as to where the problem lies.

SUCCESS!

You just installed ColdFusion 5. Read the next section to learn more about installing ColdFusion Studio 4.5.2, which is also included on this book's CD-ROM.

INSTALLING COLDFUSION STUDIO

Targeted at ColdFusion developers, ColdFusion Studio 4.5 provides all the tools you need to develop ColdFusion applications. Although ColdFusion Studio is not required for ColdFusion development, it contains features that simplify and speed up your Web development projects.

Note

ColdFusion Studio 4.5.2 is the current version. ColdFusion Studio 5 should be available in the last half of 2001. Check the Macromedia Web site for availability.

ColdFusion Studio comes bundled with a single-user version of the ColdFusion, which enables you to test your Web applications on your local machine.

This book's accompanying CD-ROM contains a 30-day evaluation version of ColdFusion Studio. This is a complete version of Studio, and it comes complete with all documentation and Help. ColdFusion Studio resides in the `Macromedia/ColdFusion/Studio` directory on the CD-ROM as `ColdFusionStudio-452-win-eval-us.exe`.

Note

ColdFusion Studio is available only for Windows but works with ColdFusion Server on all platforms.

Tip

ColdFusion Studio should not be installed on the Web server itself. Studio can also be installed on a remote computer. It can communicate with a ColdFusion server over a TCP/IP connection.

CHECKING YOUR HARDWARE AND OPERATING SYSTEM

ColdFusion Studio requires a minimum of 32MB of RAM and 15MB of disk space. Windows 95, 98, Me, NT 4.0, or 2000 also is required to install ColdFusion Studio. Even though ColdFusion Studio is not available for Linux, Solaris, or HP-UX, you can use it with a ColdFusion server running on any operating system.

COLDFUSION STUDIO STEP-BY-STEP INSTALLATION INSTRUCTIONS

You will find that ColdFusion Studio 4.5 is even easier to install than ColdFusion itself.

Note

These installation instructions apply to the full version of ColdFusion Studio as well as the evaluation version. In the full version, you are prompted for a serial number that is included with the software.

Double-click `ColdFusionStudio-452-win-eval-us.exe`. If you have downloaded ColdFusion Studio, double-click that file instead. A welcome screen should appear, as shown in Figure 2.16. Click the Next button to proceed.

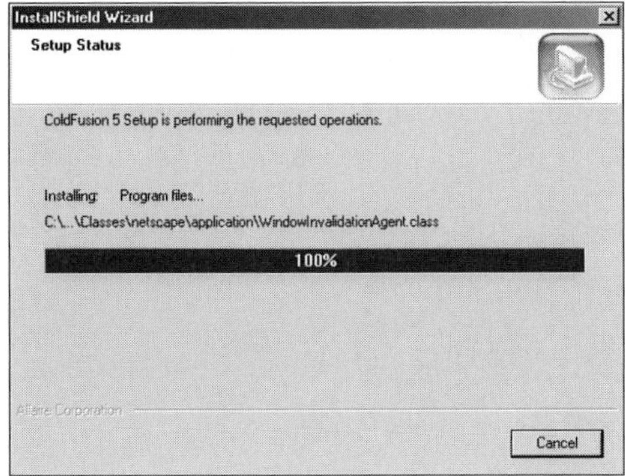

Figure 2.16
You first see the Welcome dialog box when installing ColdFusion Studio.

The Software License Agreement dialog box appears (see Figure 2.17). Click the Yes button to accept or the No button to decline. If you click No, ColdFusion Studio will not be installed.

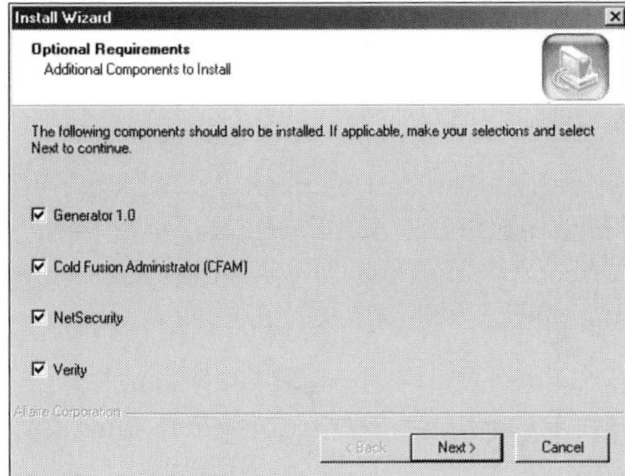

Figure 2.17
The Software License Agreement dialog box displays the terms of use for ColdFusion Studio.

Following the license agreement, the User Information dialog box appears (see Figure 2.18). Enter your name, company, and serial number (full version). Click the Next button.

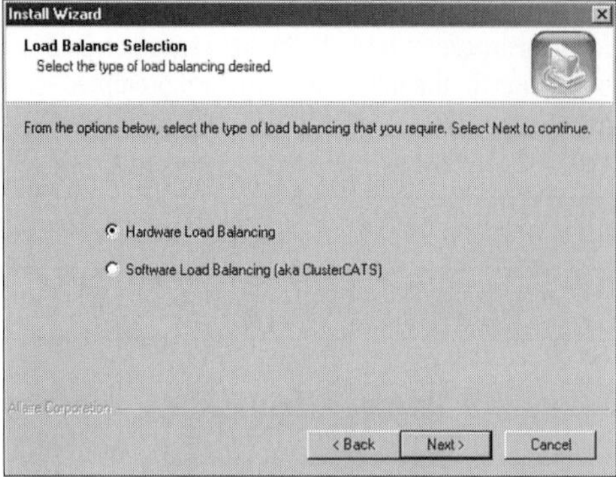

Figure 2.18
Enter your name, company, and serial number (full version only) in the User Information dialog box.

After you have provided this information, you are prompted to choose the file path into which ColdFusion Studio will be installed (see Figure 2.19). Click the Browse button to install into a directory other than the default. Click the Next button when finished.

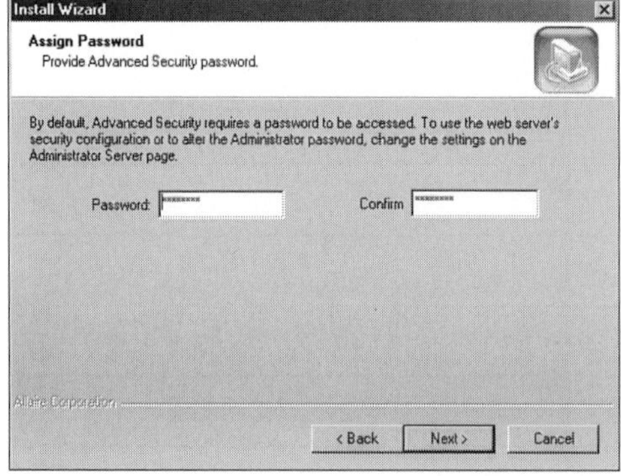

Figure 2.19
Specify the file path for the ColdFusion Studio installation in the Choose Destination Location dialog box.

The next dialog box prompts you to choose a file path into which TopStyle Lite will be installed (see Figure 2.20). TopStyle Lite is Bradbury Software's editing tool for Cascading Style Sheets. If you want a directory other than the default `\PROGRAM FILES\BRADBURY\TOPSTYLE2.0`, click the Browse button. When finished, click the Next button.

You are now asked to choose which components of ColdFusion Studio to install: ColdFusion Studio Program Files and Documentation (see Figure 2.21). If hard drive space permits, install both components. Click the Next button.

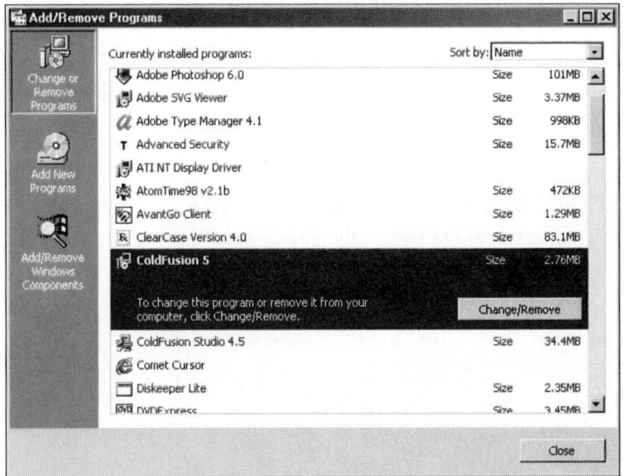

Figure 2.20
Select the file path for the TopStyle Lite installation in the Choose TopStyle Lite Destination Location dialog box.

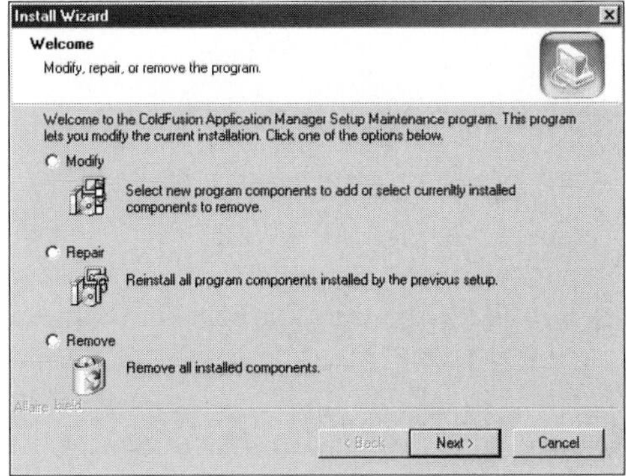

Figure 2.21
Select the ColdFusion Studio components to install in the Select Components dialog box.

In the following dialog box, shown in Figure 2.22, select the program group in which ColdFusion Studio icons will reside. Click the Next button.

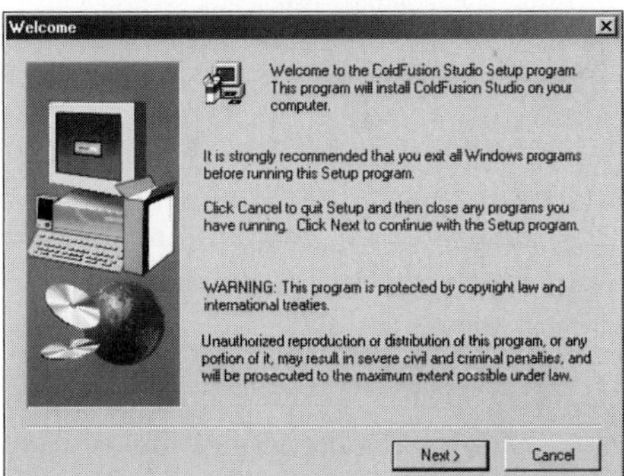

Figure 2.22
The Select Program Folder dialog box prompts you to select the program group for the ColdFusion Studio icons.

The last dialog box before the installation program starts copying files asks you to review your selections (see Figure 2.23). If you are satisfied with your choices, click the Next button. If you want to change anything, click the Back button to navigate to the appropriate dialog box.

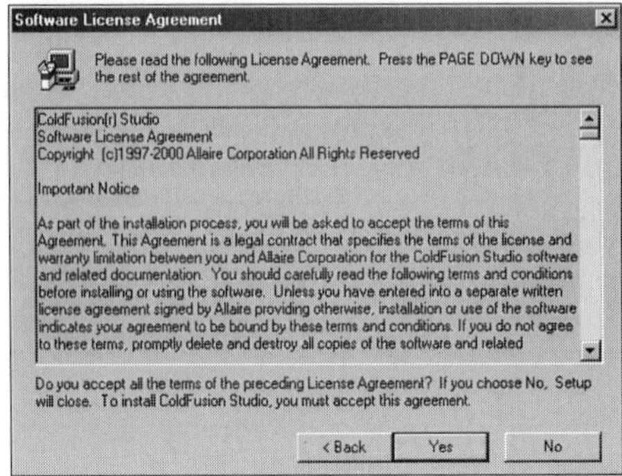

Figure 2.23
Review your installation selections in the Start Copying Files dialog box.

When the installation finishes, you might be prompted to restart your computer.

VERIFYING THE INSTALLATION

After you have restarted your computer, verifying the installation is a simple matter of running ColdFusion Studio by selecting it from the ColdFusion Studio 4.5 program group.

INSTALLING THIS BOOK'S SAMPLE APPLICATIONS

On the CD-ROM that accompanies this book, in the ows directory, you will find the sample application pages used in the following chapters. You should store all the sample applications in a folder named ows under the Web server root directory.

Note

If you use IIS in Windows, the Web server root is located at `C:\INETPUB\WWWROOT`. If you use Apache in Linux, the Web server root is usually located at `/USR/LOCAL/APACHE/HTDOCS`.

As you can see if you explore the ows directory, it contains numerous subdirectories, one for almost every chapter. You can either copy the ows directory to your Web server root or create the directories individually as you progress through the chapters.

The `images` folder (which contains the images for the sample applications) and `data` folder (which contains the Access database for the sample applications) must be copied to your Web server root.

Note

Copying the OWS database file to your system can cause your operating system to regard it as read-only. To read and write information to the database (a critical component of *database*-driven Web development), you must have read-write access to the database file.

Note

To update ColdFusion Studio with tag editors for ColdFusion 5, you must run the setup program `coldfusion_studio_tagupdate.exe` from the `Macromedia/ColdFusion/StudioTagUpdate` directory on the CD-ROM. It installs new tag editors and updated documentation.

ColdFusion Studio Update for ColdFusion 5

The ColdFusion Server 5 installation should update Studio with new tag editors and documentation automatically. However, if you install ColdFusion Studio after you install ColdFusion Server or you use a Unix-based operating system for ColdFusion Server, you must install the ColdFusion Studio update separately.

To install the ColdFusion Studio update:

1. On the CD-ROM accompanying this book, go the \CFServer50\ColdFusionServer5\StudioTagUpdate\ directory in Windows.
2. Run the coldfusion-studio-tagupdate.exe file. The resulting WinZip Self-Extractor dialog box displays (see Figure 2.24) lets you specify which directory the ColdFusion 5 Visual Tool Markup Language (VTML) files will be inserted. The default directory is C:\Program Files\Allaire\ColdFusion Studio 4.5 directory on your system. If ColdFusion Studio is installed in a different directory, enter it in the Unzip to Folder dialog box.

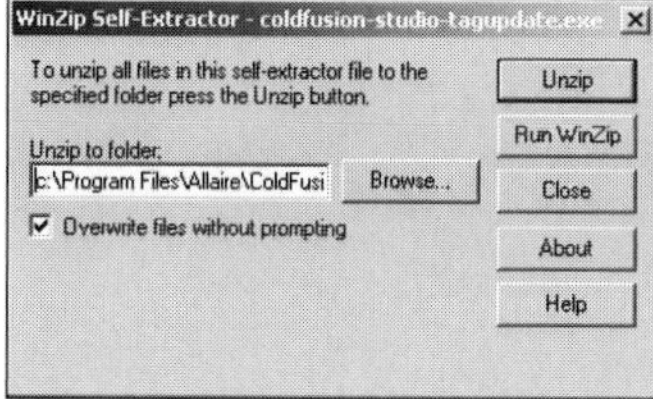

Figure 32.24 Select the ColdFusion Studio installation directory in the WinZip Self-Extractor dialog box.

3. Click the Unzip button. The updated files are installed.

And with that, you are ready to learn ColdFusion.

CHAPTER 3

Building the Databases

In this chapter

DATABASE FUNDAMENTALS

You have just been assigned a project. You must create and maintain a list of all the movies produced by your employer—Orange Whip Studios.

What do you use to maintain this list? Your first thought might be to use a word processor. You could create the list, one movie per line, and manually insert each movie's name so the list is alphabetical and usable. Your word processor provides you with sophisticated document-editing capabilities, so adding, removing, or updating movies is no more complicated than editing any other document.

Initially, you might think you have found the perfect solution—that is, until someone asks you to sort the list by release date and then alphabetically for each date. Now you must re-create the entire list, again sorting the movies manually and inserting them in the correct sequence. You end up with two lists to maintain. You must add new movies to both lists and possibly remove movies from both lists as well. You also discover that correcting mistakes or simply making changes to your list has become more complicated because you must make every change twice. Still, the list is manageable. You have only the two word-processed documents to be concerned with, and you can even open them both at the same time and make edits simultaneously.

Okay, the word processor is not the perfect solution, but it is still a manageable solution—that is, until someone else asks for the list sorted by director. As you fire up your word processor yet again, you review the entire list-management process in your mind. New movies must now be added to three lists. Likewise, any deletions must be made to all three lists. If a movie tag line changes, you must change just the multiple lists.

And then, just as you think you have the entire process worked out, your face pales and you freeze. What if someone else wants the list sorted by rating? And then, what if yet another department needs the list sorted in some other way? You panic, break out in a sweat, and tell yourself, "There must be a better way!"

This example is a bit extreme, but the truth is that a better way really does exist. You need to use a database.

DATABASES: A DEFINITION

Let's start with a definition. A *database* is simply a structured collection of similar data. The important words here are *structured* and *similar*, and the movie list is a perfect example of both.

Imagine the movie list as a two-dimensional grid or table, similar to that shown in Figure 3.1. Each horizontal row in the table contains information about a single movie. The rows are broken up by vertical columns. Each column contains a single part of the movie record. The `Movie Title` column contains movie titles, and so on.

Movies

Movie Title	Rating	Budget
Being Unbearably Light	5	300000
Charlie's Devils	1	750000
Closet Encounters of the Odd Kind	5	350000
Four Bar-Mitzvah's and a Circumcision	1	175000

Figure 3.1
Databases display data in an imaginary two-dimensional grid.

The movie list contains similar data for all movies. Every movie record, or row, contains the same type of information. Each has a title, tag line, budget amount, and so on. The data is also structured in that the data can be broken into logical columns, or fields, that contain a single part of the movie record.

Here's the rule of thumb: Any list of information that can be broken into similar records of structured fields should probably be maintained in a database. Product prices, phone directories, invoices, invoice line items, vacation schedules, and lists of actors and directors are all database candidates.

WHERE ARE DATABASES USED?

You probably use databases all the time, often without knowing it. If you use a software-based accounting program, you are using a database. All accounts payable, accounts receivable, vendor, and customer information is stored in databases. Scheduling programs use databases to store appointments and to-do lists. Even e-mail programs use databases for directory lists and folders.

These databases are designed to be hidden from you, the end user. You never add accounts receivable invoice records into a database yourself. Rather, you enter information into your accounting program, and it adds records to the database.

CLARIFICATION OF DATABASE-RELATED TERMS

Now that you understand what a database is, I must clarify some important database terms for you. In the SQL world (you learn about SQL in depth in Chapter 6, "Introduction to SQL"), this collection of data is called a *table*. The individual records in a table are called *rows*, and the fields that make up the rows are called *columns*. A collection of tables is called a *database*.

Picture a filing cabinet. The cabinet houses drawers, each of which contains groups of data. The cabinet is a means of keeping related but dissimilar information in one place. Each cabinet drawer contains a set of records. One drawer might contain employee records, whereas another drawer might contain sales records. The individual records within each drawer are different, but they all contain the same type of data, in fields.

The filing cabinet shown in Figure 3.2 is the database—a collection of drawers or tables containing related but dissimilar information. Each drawer contains one or more records, or rows, made up of different fields, or columns.

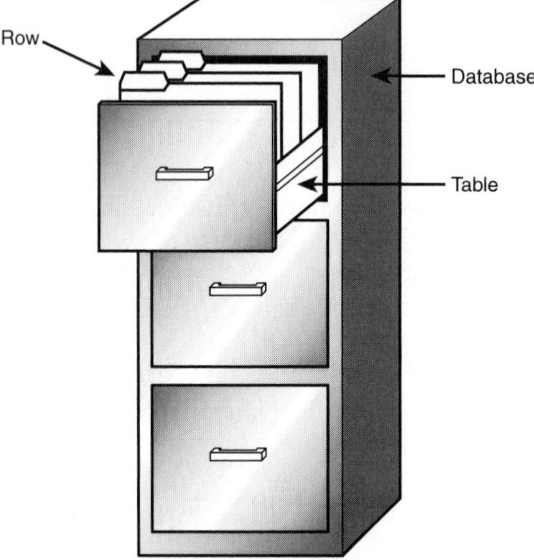

Figure 3.2
Databases store information in tables, columns, and rows, similarly to how records are filed in a filing cabinet.

DATA TYPES

Each row in a database table is made up of one or more columns. Each column contains a single piece of data, part of the complete record stored in the row. When a table is created, each of its columns needs to be defined. Defining columns involves specifying the column's name, size, and data type. The data type specifies what data can be stored in a column.

Data types specify the characteristics of a column and instruct the database as to what kind of data can be entered into it. Some data types allow the entry of free-form alphanumeric data. Others restrict data entry to specific data, such as numbers, dates, or true or false flags. A list of common data types is shown in Table 3.1.

TABLE 3.1 COMMON DATABASE DATA TYPES AND HOW THEY ARE USED

Data Type	Restrictions	Typical Use
Character	Upper- and lowercase text, numbers, symbols	Names, addresses, descriptions

Data Type	Restrictions	Typical Use
Numeric	Positive and negative numbers, decimal points	Quantities, numbers
Date	Dates, times	Dates, times
Money	Positive and negative numbers, decimal points	Prices, billing amounts, invoice line items
Boolean	`Yes` and `No` or `True` and `False`	On/off flags, switches
Binary	Non-text data	Pictures, sound, and video data

Most database applications provide a graphic interface to database creation, enabling you to select data types from a list. Microsoft Access uses a drop-down list box, as shown in Figure 3.3, and provides a description of each data type.

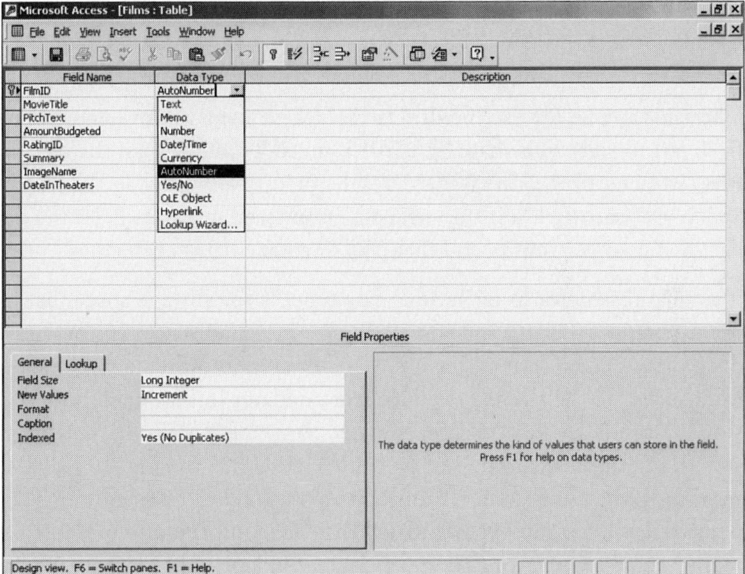

Figure 3.3
Microsoft Access uses a drop-down list box to enable you to select data types easily.

You use data types for several reasons, instead of just entering all data into simple text fields. One of the main reasons is to control or restrict the data a user can enter into that field. A field that has to contain a person's age, for example, could be specified as a numeric field. This way, the user cannot enter characters into it—only the digits 0–9 would be allowed. This restriction helps ensure that no invalid data is entered into your database.

Various data types are also used to control how data is sorted. Data entered in a text field is sorted one character at a time, as if it were left-justified. The digit 0 comes before 1, which comes before 9, which comes before *a*, and so on. Because each character is evaluated individually, a text field containing the number 10 is listed after 1 but before 2 because 10 is greater than 1 but less than 2, just as a 0 is greater than *a* but less than *b*. If the value being stored in this column is a person's age, correctly sorting the table by that column would be impossible. Data entered into a numeric field, however, is evaluated by looking at the complete value rather than a character at a time; 10 is considered greater than 2 instead of less than 2. Figure 3.4 shows how data is sorted if numbers are entered into a text field.

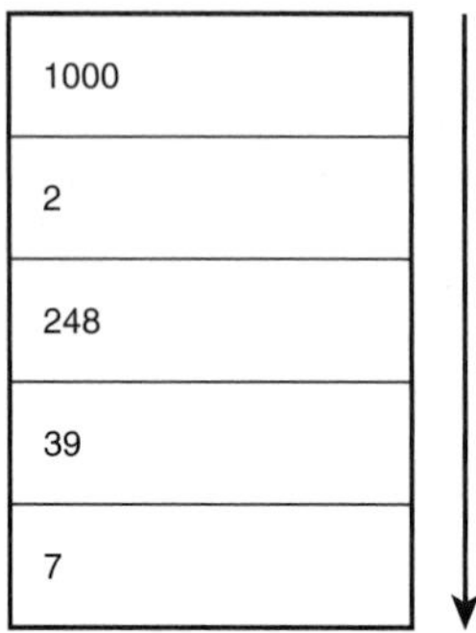

Figure 3.4
Unless you use the correct data type, data might not be sorted the way you want.

The same is true for date fields. Dates in these fields are evaluated one character at a time, from left to right. The date 02/05/01 is considered less than the date 10/12/99 because the first character of the date 02/05/01—the digit 0—is less than the first character of the date 10/12/99—the digit 1. If the same data is entered in a date field, the database evaluates the date as a complete entity and therefore sorts the dates correctly.

The final reason for using various data types is the storage space that plain-text fields take up. A text field that is large enough to accommodate up to 10 characters takes up 10 bytes of storage. Even if only 2 characters are entered into the field, 10 bytes are still stored. The extra space is reserved for possible future updates to that field. Some types of data can be stored more efficiently when not treated as text. For example, a 4-byte numeric field can store numeric values from 0 to over 4,000,000,000! Storing 4,000,000,000 in a text field requires 10 bytes of storage. Similarly, a 4-byte date/time field can store the date and time with accuracy to the minute. Storing that same information in a text field would take a minimum of 14 bytes or as many as 20 bytes, depending on how the data is formatted.

Note

Different database applications use different terms to describe the same data type. For example, Microsoft Access uses the term *text* to describe a data type that allows the entry of all alphanumeric data. Microsoft SQL Server calls this same data type `char` and uses text to describe variable-length text fields. After you determine the type of data you want a column to contain, refer to your database application's manuals to ensure that you use the correct term when making data type selections.

When you're designing a database, you should give careful consideration to data types. You usually cannot easily change the type of a field after the table is created. If you do have to change the type, you typically must create a new table and write routines to convert the data from one table to the new one.

Planning the size of fields is equally important. With most databases, you can't change the size of a field after the table is created. Getting the size right the first time and allowing some room for growth can save you much aggravation later.

Caution

When you're determining the size of data fields, always try to anticipate future growth. If you're defining a field for phone numbers, for example, realize that not all phone numbers follow the three-digit area code plus seven-digit phone number convention used in the United States. Paris, France, for example, has eight-digit phone numbers, and area codes in small towns in England can contain four or five digits.

USING A DATABASE

Back to the example. At this point, you have determined that a database will make your job easier and might even help preserve your sanity. You create a table with columns for movie title, tag line (or pitch text), release date, and the rest of the required data. You enter your movie list into the table, one row at a time, and are careful to put the correct data in each column.

Next, you instruct the database application to sort the list by movie title. The list is sorted in a second or less, and you print it out. Impressed, you try additional sorts—by rating and by budgeted amount. The results of these sorts are shown in Figures 3.5, 3.6, and 3.7.

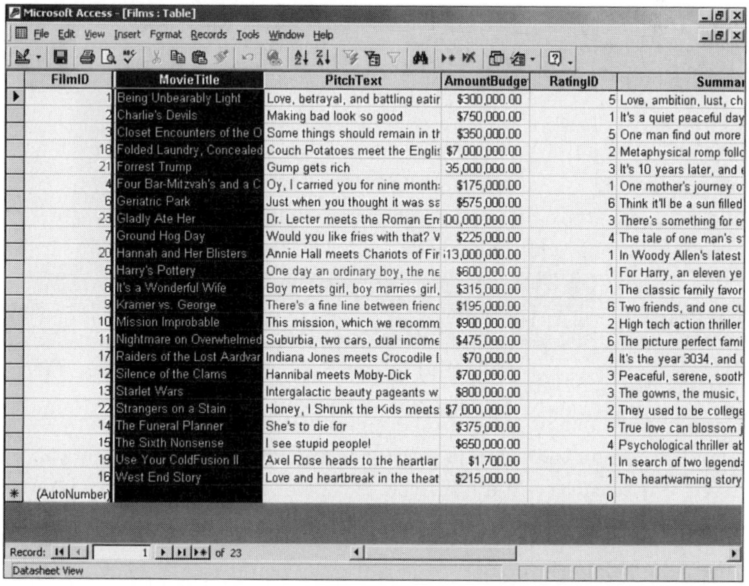

Figure 3.5
Data entered once in a Microsoft Access table can be sorted any way you want.

Microsoft Access - [Films : Table]

FilmID	MovieTitle	PitchText	AmountBudge	RatingID	Summai
1	Being Unbearably Light	Love, betrayal, and battling eatir	$300,000.00	5	Love, ambition, lust, ch
2	Charlie's Devils	Making bad look so good	$750,000.00	1	It's a quiet peaceful day
3	Closet Encounters of the O	Some things should remain in tl	$350,000.00	5	One man find out more
18	Folded Laundry, Concealed	Couch Potatoes meet the Englis	$7,000,000.00	2	Metaphysical romp follc
21	Forrest Trump	Gump gets rich	35,000,000.00	3	It's 10 years later, and
4	Four Bar-Mitzvah's and a C	Oy, I carried you for nine month:	$175,000.00	1	One mother's journey o
6	Geriatric Park	Just when you thought it was sa	$575,000.00	6	Think it'll be a sun filled
23	Gladly Ate Her	Dr. Lecter meets the Roman En	00,000,000.00	3	There's something for e
7	Ground Hog Day	Would you like fries with that? V	$225,000.00	4	The tale of one man's s
20	Hannah and Her Blisters	Annie Hall meets Chariots of Fir	13,000,000.00	1	In Woody Allen's latest
5	Harry's Pottery	One day an ordinary boy, the ne	$600,000.00	1	For Harry, an eleven ye
8	It's a Wonderful Wife	Boy meets girl, boy marries girl,	$315,000.00	1	The classic family favor
9	Kramer vs. George	There's a fine line between frienc	$195,000.00	6	Two friends, and one cu
10	Mission Improbable	This mission, which we recomm	$900,000.00	2	High tech action thriller
11	Nightmare on Overwhelmed	Suburbia, two cars, dual income	$475,000.00	6	The picture perfect fami
17	Raiders of the Lost Aardvar	Indiana Jones meets Crocodile I	$70,000.00	4	It's the year 3034, and
12	Silence of the Clams	Hannibal meets Moby-Dick	$700,000.00	3	Peaceful, serene, sootl
13	Starlet Wars	Intergalactic beauty pageants w	$800,000.00	3	The gowns, the music,
22	Strangers on a Stain	Honey, I Shrunk the Kids meets	$7,000,000.00	2	They used to be college
14	The Funeral Planner	She's to die for	$375,000.00	5	True love can blossom j
15	The Sixth Nonsense	I see stupid people!	$650,000.00	4	Psychological thriller ab
19	Use Your ColdFusion II	Axel Rose heads to the heartlar	$1,700.00	1	In search of two legend
16	West End Story	Love and heartbreak in the theat	$215,000.00	1	The heartwarming story
(AutoNumber)				0	

Record: 1 of 23

Datasheet View

Figure 3.6
Data sorted by rating.

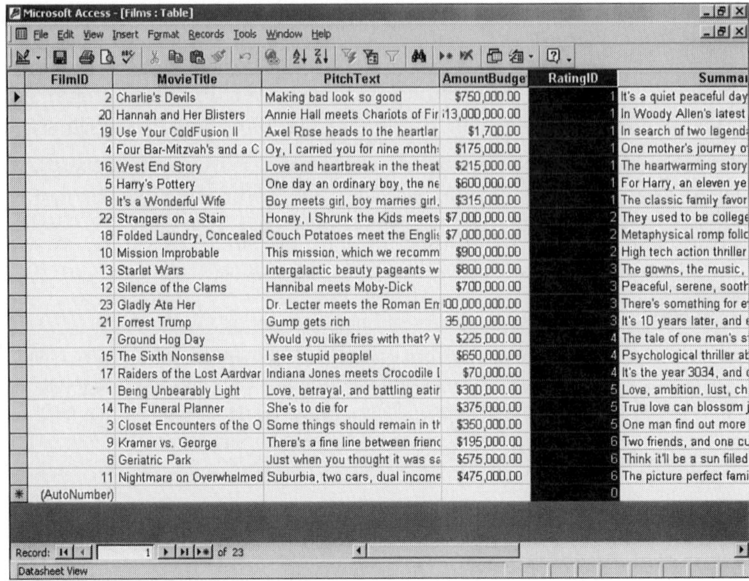
Microsoft Access - [Films : Table]

FilmID	MovieTitle	PitchText	AmountBudge	RatingID	Summar
2	Charlie's Devils	Making bad look so good	$750,000.00	1	It's a quiet peaceful day
20	Hannah and Her Blisters	Annie Hall meets Chariots of Fir	13,000,000.00	1	In Woody Allen's latest
19	Use Your ColdFusion II	Axel Rose heads to the heartlar	$1,700.00	1	In search of two legend
4	Four Bar-Mitzvah's and a C	Oy, I carried you for nine month	$175,000.00	1	One mother's journey o
16	West End Story	Love and heartbreak in the theat	$215,000.00	1	The heartwarming story
5	Harry's Pottery	One day an ordinary boy, the ne	$600,000.00	1	For Harry, an eleven ye
8	It's a Wonderful Wife	Boy meets girl, boy marries girl,	$315,000.00	1	The classic family favor
22	Strangers on a Stain	Honey, I Shrunk the Kids meets	$7,000,000.00	2	They used to be college
18	Folded Laundry, Concealed	Couch Potatoes meet the Englis	$7,000,000.00	2	Metaphysical romp follc
10	Mission Improbable	This mission, which we recomm	$900,000.00	2	High tech action thriller
13	Starlet Wars	Intergalactic beauty pageants w	$800,000.00	3	The gowns, the music,
12	Silence of the Clams	Hannibal meets Moby-Dick	$700,000.00	3	Peaceful, serene, sooth
23	Gladly Ate Her	Dr. Lecter meets the Roman Em	00,000,000.00	3	There's something for e
21	Forrest Trump	Gump gets rich	35,000,000.00	3	It's 10 years later, and
7	Ground Hog Day	Would you like fries with that? V	$225,000.00	4	The tale of one man's s
15	The Sixth Nonsense	I see stupid people!	$650,000.00	4	Psychological thriller at
17	Raiders of the Lost Aardvar	Indiana Jones meets Crocodile I	$70,000.00	4	It's the year 3034, and
1	Being Unbearably Light	Love, betrayal, and battling eatir	$300,000.00	5	Love, ambition, lust, ch
14	The Funeral Planner	She's to die for	$375,000.00	5	True love can blossom j
3	Closet Encounters of the O	Some things should remain in th	$350,000.00	5	One man find out more
9	Kramer vs. George	There's a fine line between frienc	$195,000.00	6	Two friends, and one cu
6	Geriatric Park	Just when you thought it was sa	$575,000.00	6	Think it'll be a sun filled
11	Nightmare on Overwhelmed	Suburbia, two cars, dual income	$475,000.00	6	The picture perfect fami
(AutoNumber)				0	

Record: 1 of 23
Datasheet View

Figure 3.7
Data sorted by budgeted amount.

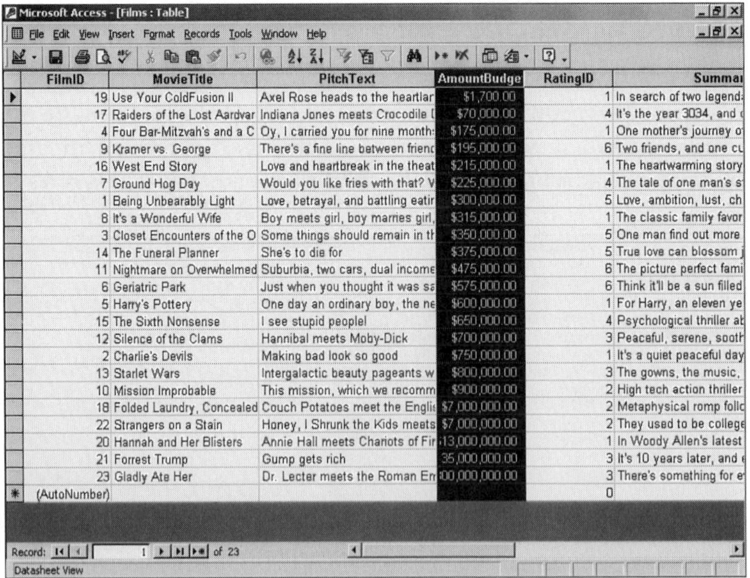
Microsoft Access - [Films : Table]

FilmID	MovieTitle	PitchText	AmountBudge	RatingID	Summar
19	Use Your ColdFusion II	Axel Rose heads to the heartlar	$1,700.00	1	In search of two legend
17	Raiders of the Lost Aardvar	Indiana Jones meets Crocodile I	$70,000.00	4	It's the year 3034, and
4	Four Bar-Mitzvah's and a C	Oy, I carried you for nine month	$175,000.00	1	One mother's journey o
9	Kramer vs. George	There's a fine line between frienc	$195,000.00	6	Two friends, and one cu
16	West End Story	Love and heartbreak in the theat	$215,000.00	1	The heartwarming story
7	Ground Hog Day	Would you like fries with that? V	$225,000.00	4	The tale of one man's s
1	Being Unbearably Light	Love, betrayal, and battling eatir	$300,000.00	5	Love, ambition, lust, ch
8	It's a Wonderful Wife	Boy meets girl, boy marries girl,	$315,000.00	1	The classic family favor
3	Closet Encounters of the O	Some things should remain in th	$350,000.00	5	One man find out more
14	The Funeral Planner	She's to die for	$375,000.00	5	True love can blossom j
11	Nightmare on Overwhelmed	Suburbia, two cars, dual income	$475,000.00	6	The picture perfect fami
6	Geriatric Park	Just when you thought it was sa	$575,000.00	6	Think it'll be a sun filled
5	Harry's Pottery	One day an ordinary boy, the ne	$600,000.00	1	For Harry, an eleven ye
15	The Sixth Nonsense	I see stupid people!	$650,000.00	4	Psychological thriller at
12	Silence of the Clams	Hannibal meets Moby-Dick	$700,000.00	3	Peaceful, serene, sooth
2	Charlie's Devils	Making bad look so good	$750,000.00	1	It's a quiet peaceful day
13	Starlet Wars	Intergalactic beauty pageants w	$800,000.00	3	The gowns, the music,
10	Mission Improbable	This mission, which we recomm	$900,000.00	2	High tech action thriller
18	Folded Laundry, Concealed	Couch Potatoes meet the Englis	$7,000,000.00	2	Metaphysical romp follc
22	Strangers on a Stain	Honey, I Shrunk the Kids meets	$7,000,000.00	2	They used to be college
20	Hannah and Her Blisters	Annie Hall meets Chariots of Fir	13,000,000.00	1	In Woody Allen's latest
21	Forrest Trump	Gump gets rich	35,000,000.00	3	It's 10 years later, and
23	Gladly Ate Her	Dr. Lecter meets the Roman Em	00,000,000.00	3	There's something for e
(AutoNumber)				0	

Record: 1 of 23
Datasheet View

You now have two or more lists, but you had to enter the information only once; because you were careful to break the records into multiple columns, you can sort or search the list in any way necessary. You just need to reprint the lists whenever your records are added, edited, or deleted. And the new or changed data is automatically sorted for you.

"Yes," you think to yourself, "this really is a better way."

A DATABASE PRIMER

You have just seen a practical use for a database. The movie list is a simple database that involves a single table and a small set of columns. Most well-designed database applications require many tables and ways to link them. You'll revisit the movie list when relational databases are introduced.

Your first table was a hit. You have been able to accommodate any list request, sorted any way anyone could need. But just as you are beginning to wonder what you're going to do with all your newfound spare time, your boss informs you that he'll need reports sorted by the director name.

"No problem," you say. You open your database application and modify your table. You add two new columns, one for the director's first name and one for the last name. Now, every movie record can contain the name of the director, and you even create a report of all movies including director information. Once again, you and your database have saved the day, and all is well.

Or so you think. Just when things are looking good, you receive a memo asking you to include movie expenses in your database so as to be able to run reports containing this information.

You think for a few moments and come up with two solutions to this new problem. The first solution is simply to add lots more columns to the table, three for each expenses item (date, description, and amount).

This, you realize, is not a long-term solution at all. How many expenses should you allow space for? Every movie can, and likely will, have a different set of expenses, and you have no way of knowing how many expenses you should accommodate for. Inevitably, whatever number you pick will not be enough at some point. In addition, adding all these extra columns, which will not be used by most records, is a tremendous waste of disk space. Furthermore, data manipulation becomes extremely complicated if data is stored in more than one column. If you need to search for specific expenses, you'd have to search multiple columns. This situation greatly increases the chance of incorrect results. It also makes sorting data impossible because databases sort data one column at a time, and you have data that must be sorted together spread over multiple columns.

Note

An important rule in database design is that if columns are seldom used by most rows, they probably don't belong in the table.

Your second solution is to create additional rows in the table, one for each expense for each movie. With this solution, you can add as many expenses as necessary without creating extra columns.

This solution, though, is not workable. Although it does indeed solve the problem of handling more than a predetermined number of expenses, doing so introduces a far greater problem. Adding additional rows requires repeating the basic movie information—things such as title and tag line—over and over, for each new row.

Not only does reentering this information waste storage space, it also greatly increases the likelihood of your being faced with conflicting data. If a movie title changes, for example, you must be sure to change every row that contains that movie's data. Failing to update all rows would result in queries and searches returning conflicting results. If you do a search for a movie and find two rows, both of which have different ratings, how would you know which is correct?

This problem is probably not overly serious if the conflicting data is the spelling of a name—but imagine that the data is customer billing information. If you reenter a customer's address with each order and then the customer moves, you could end up shipping orders to an incorrect address.

You should avoid maintaining multiple live copies of the same data whenever possible.

Note

Another important rule in database design is that data should never be repeated unnecessarily. As you multiply the number of copies you have of the same data, the chance of data-entry errors also multiplies.

Tip

One point worth mentioning here is that the "never duplicate data" rule does not apply to backups of your data. Backing up data is incredibly important, and you can never have too many backup plans. The rule of never duplicating data applies only to *live data*–data to be used in a production environment on an ongoing basis.

And while you are thinking about it, you realize that even your earlier solution for including director names is dangerous. After all, what will happen when a movie has two directors? You've allocated room for only one name.

UNDERSTANDING RELATIONAL DATABASES

The solution to your problem is to break the movie list into multiple tables. Let's start with the movie expenses.

The first table, the movie list, remains just that—a movie list. To link movies to other records, you add one new column to the list, a column containing a unique identifier for each movie. It might be an assigned movie number or a sequential value that is incremented as each new movie is added to the list. The important thing is that no two movies have the same ID.

Tip

Never reusing record-unique identifiers is generally a good idea. If the movie with ID number `105` is deleted, for example, that number should never be reassigned to a new movie. This policy guarantees that there is no chance of the new movie record getting linked to data that belonged to the old movie.

Next, you create a new table with several columns: movie ID, expense date, expense description, and expense amount. As long as a movie has no associated expenses, the second table—the expenses table—remains empty. When an expense is incurred, a row is added to the expenses table. The row contains the movie that uniquely identifies this specific movie and the expense information.

The point here is that no movie information is stored in the expenses table except for that movie ID, which is the same movie ID assigned in the movie list table. How do you know which movie the record is referring to when expenses are reported? The movie information is retrieved from the movie list table. When displaying rows from the expenses table, the database relates the row back to the movie list table and grabs the movie information from there. This relationship is shown later in this chapter, in Figure 3.8.

This database design is called a *relational database*. With it you can store data in various tables and then define *links*, or *relationships*, to find associated data stored in other tables in the database. In this example, a movie with two expenses would have two rows in the expenses table. Both of these rows contain the same movie ID, and therefore both refer to the same movie record in the movie table.

Note

The process of breaking up data into multiple tables to ensure that data is never duplicated is called *normalization*.

PRIMARY AND FOREIGN KEYS

Primary key is the database term for the column(s) that contains values which uniquely identify each row. A primary key is usually a single column, but doesn't have to be.

There are only two requirements for primary keys:

- **Every row must have a value in the primary key**—Empty fields, sometimes called *null fields*, are not allowed.
- **Primary key values can never be duplicated**—If two movies were to have the same ID, all relationships would fail. In fact, most database applications prevent you from entering duplicate values in primary key fields.

When you are asked for a list of all expenses sorted by movie, you can instruct the database to build the relationship and retrieve the required data. The movie table is scanned in alphabetical order, and as each movie is retrieved, the database application checks the expenses table for any rows that have a movie ID matching the current primary key. You can even instruct the database to ignore the movies that have no associated expenses and retrieve only those that have related rows in the expenses table.

Tip

Many database applications support a feature that can be used to auto-generate primary key values. Microsoft Access refers to this as an Auto Number field, SQL Server uses the term Identity, and other databases use other terms (for essentially the same thing). Using this feature, a correct and safe primary key is automatically generated every time a new row is added to the table.

Note

Not all data types can be used as primary keys. You cannot use columns with data types for storing binary data, such as sounds, images, variable-length records, or OLE links, as primary keys.

The movie ID column in the expenses table is not a primary key. The values in that column are not unique if any movie has more than one expense listed. All records of a specific movie's expenses contain the same movie ID. The movie ID is a primary key in a different table—the movie table. This is a *foreign key*. A foreign key is a nonunique key whose values are contained within a primary key in another table.

To see how the foreign key is used, assume that you have been asked to run a report to see which movies incurred expenses on a specific date. To do so, you instruct the database application to scan the expenses table for all rows with expenses listed on that date. The database application uses the value in the expenses table's movie ID foreign key field to find the name of the movie; it does so by using the movie table's primary key. This relationship is shown in Figure 3.8.

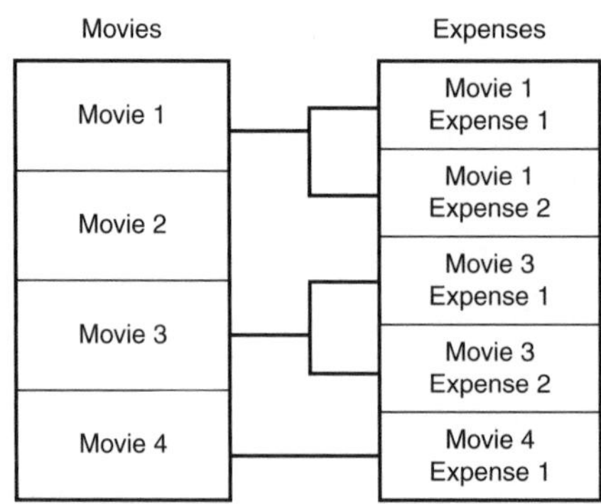

Figure 3.8
The foreign key values in one table are always primary key values in another table, allowing tables to be "related" to each other.

The relational database model helps overcome scalability problems. A database that can handle an ever-increasing amount of data without having to be redesigned is said to *scale well*. You should always take scalability into consideration when designing databases.

Now you've made a significant change to your original database, but what you've created is a manageable and scalable solution. Your boss is happy once again, and your database management skills save the day.

DIFFERENT KINDS OF RELATIONSHIPS

The type of relationship discussed up to this point is called a *one-to-many* relationship. This kind of relationship allows an association between a single row in one table and multiple rows in another table. In the example, a single row in the movie list table can be associated with many rows in the expenses table. The one-to-many relationship is the most common type of relationship in a relational database.

Two other types of relational database relationships exist: the *one-to-one* relationship and the *many-to-many* relationship.

The one-to-one relationship allows a single row in one table to be associated with no more than one row in another table. This type of relationship is used infrequently. In practice, if you run into a situation in which a one-to-one relationship is called for, you should probably revisit the design. Most tables that are linked with one-to-one relationships can simply be combined into one large table.

The many-to-many relationship is also used infrequently. The many-to-many relationship allows one or more rows in one table to be associated with one or more rows in another table. This type of relationship is usually the result of bad design. Most many-to-many relationships can be more efficiently managed with multiple one-to-many relationships.

MULTITABLE RELATIONSHIPS

Now that you understand relational databases, let's look at the directors problem again. You will recall that the initial solution was to add the directors directly into the movie table, but that was not a viable solution because it would not allow for multiple directors in a single movie.

Actually, an even bigger problem exists with the suggested solution. As I said earlier, relational database design dictates that data never be repeated. If the director's name was listed with the movie, any director who directed more than one movie would be listed more than once.

In other words, unlike the expenses—which are always associated with a single movie—directors can be associated with multiple movies, and movies can be associated with multiple directors. Two tables will not help here.

The solution to this type of relationship problem is to use three database tables:

- Movies are listed in their own table, and each movie has a unique ID.
- Directors are listed in their own table, and each director has a unique ID.
- A new third table is added, which relates the two previous tables.

For example, if movie number `105` was directed by director number `3`, a single row would be added to the third table. It would contain two foreign keys, the primary keys of each of the movie and director tables. To find out who directed movie number `105`, all you'd have to do is look at that third table for movie number `105` and you'd find that director `3` was the director. Then, you'd look at the directors table to find out who director `3` is.

That might sound overly complex for a simple mapping, but bear with me—this is all about to make a lot of sense.

If movie number `105` had a second director (perhaps director ID `5`), all you would need to do is add a second row to that third table. This new row would also contain `105` in the movie ID column, but it would contain a different director ID in the director column. Now you can associate two, three, or more directors with each movie. Each director is associated with a movie by simply adding one more record to that third table.

And if you wanted to find all movies directed by a specific director, you could do that too. First, you'd find the ID of the director in the directors table. Then, you'd search that third table for all movie IDs associated with the director. And then you'd scan the movies table for the names of those movies.

This type of multitable relationship frequently is necessary in larger applications, and you'll be using it later in this chapter. Figure 3.9 summarizes the relationships used.

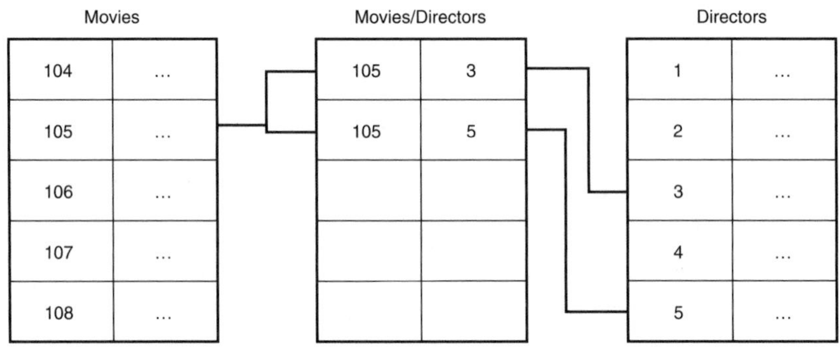

Figure 3.9
To relate multiple rows to multiple rows, a three-way relational table design should be used.

To summarize, two tables are used if the rows in one table might be related to multiple rows in a seconds table and when rows in the second table are only ever related to single rows in the first table. If, however, rows in both tables might be related to multiple rows, three tables must be used.

INDEXES

Database applications make extensive use of a table's primary key whenever relationships are used. It is therefore vital that accessing a specific row by primary key value be a fast operation. When data is added to a table, you have no guarantee that the rows are stored in any specific order. A row with a higher primary key value could be stored before a row with a lower value. You should make no assumptions about the actual physical location of any rows within your table.

Now take another look at the relationship between the movie list table and the expenses table. You have the database scan the expenses table to learn which movies have incurred expenses on specific dates; only rows containing that date are selected. This operation, however, returns only the movie IDs—the foreign key values. To determine to which movies these rows are referring, you have the database check the movie list table. Specific rows are selected—the rows that have this movie ID as their primary key values.

To find a specific row by primary key value, you could have the database application sequentially read through the entire table. If the first row stored is the one needed, the sequential read is terminated. If not, the next row is read, and then the next, until the desired primary key value is retrieved.

This process might work for small sets of data. Sequentially scanning hundreds, or even thousands, of rows is a relatively fast operation, particularly for a fast computer with plenty of available system memory. As the number of rows increases, however, so does the time it takes to find a specific row.

The problem of finding specific data quickly in an unsorted list is not limited to databases. Suppose you're reading a book on mammals and are looking for information on cats. You could start on the first page of the book and read everything, looking for the word *cat*. This approach might work if you have just a few pages to search through, but as the number of pages grows, so does the difficulty of locating specific words and the likelihood that you will make mistakes and miss references.

To solve this problem, books have indexes. An index allows rapid access to specific words or topics spread throughout the book. Although the words or topics referred to in the index are not in any sorted order, the index itself is. *Cat* is guaranteed to appear in the index somewhere after *bison*, but before *cow*. To find all references to *cat*, you would first search the index. Searching the index is a quick process because the list is sorted. You don't have to read as far as *dog* if the word you're looking for is *cat*. When you find *cat* in the index list, you also find the page numbers where cats are discussed.

Databases use indexes in much the same way. Database indexes serve the same purpose as book indexes—allowing rapid access to unsorted data. Just as book indexes list words or topics alphabetically to facilitate the rapid location of data, so do database table indexes list the values indexed in a sorted order. Just as book indexes list page numbers for each index listing, database table indexes list the physical location of the matching rows, as shown in Figure 3.10. After the database application knows the physical location of a specific row, it can retrieve that row without having to scan every row in the table.

However, two important differences exist between an index at the back of a book and an index to a database table. First, an index to a database table is *dynamic*. This means that every time a row is added to a table, the index is automatically modified to reflect this change. Likewise, if a row is updated or deleted, the index is updated to reflect this change. As a result, the index is always up-to-date and always useful. Second, unlike a book index, the table index is never explicitly browsed by the end user. Instead, when the database application is instructed to retrieve data, it uses the index to determine how to complete the request quickly and efficiently.

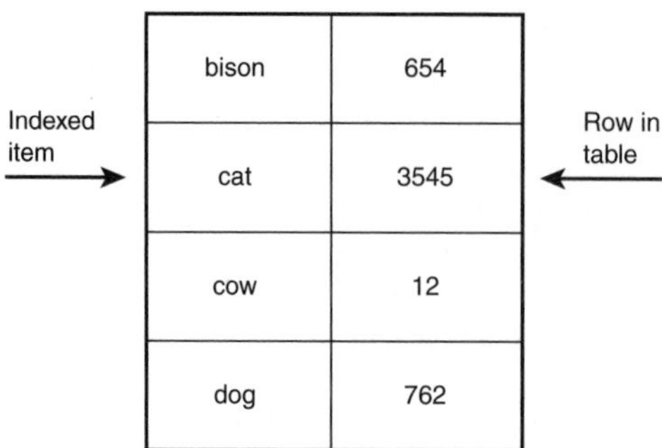

Figure 3.10
Database indexes are lists of rows and where they appear in a table.

The index is maintained by the database application and is used only by the database application. You never actually see the index in your database, and in fact, most modern database applications hide the actual physical storage location of the index altogether.

When you create a primary key for a table, it is automatically indexed. The database assumes the primary key will be used constantly for lookups and relationships and therefore does you the favor of creating that first index automatically.

When you run a report against the expenses table to find particular entries, the following process occurs. First, the database application scans the expenses table to find any rows that match the desired date. This process returns the IDs of any matching expenses. Next, the database application retrieves the matching movie for each expense row it has retrieved. It searches the primary key index to find the matching movie record in the movie list table. The index contains all movie IDs in order and, for each ID, lists the physical location of the required row. After the database application finds the correct index value, it obtains a row location from the index and then jumps directly to that location in the table. Although this process might look involved on paper, it actually happens very quickly and in less time than any sequential search would take.

Using Indexes

Now revisit your movies database. Movie production is up, and the number of movies in your movies table has grown, too. Lately, you've noticed that operations are taking longer than they used to. The alphabetical movie list report takes considerably longer to run, and the performance drops even further as more movies are added to the table. The database design was supposed to be a scalable solution, so why is the additional data bringing the system to its knees?

The solution here is the introduction of additional indexes. The database application automatically creates an index for the primary key. Any additional indexes have to be explicitly defined. To improve sorting and searching by rating, you just need an index on the rating column. With this index, the database application can instantly find the rows it is looking for without having to sequentially read through the entire table.

The maximum number of indexes a table can have varies from one database application to another. Some databases have no limit at all and allow every column to be indexed. That way, all searches or sorts can benefit from the faster response time.

Caution

Some database applications limit the number of indexes any table can have. Before you create dozens of indexes, check to see whether you should be aware of any limitations.

Before you run off and create indexes for every column in your table, you have to realize the tradeoff. As explained earlier, unlike an index at the end of a book, a database table index is dynamic. As data changes, so do the indexes, and updating indexes takes time. The more indexes a table has, the longer write operations take. Furthermore, each index takes up additional storage space, so unnecessary indexes waste valuable disk space.

When, then, should you create an index? The answer is entirely up to you. Adding indexes to a table makes read operations faster and write operations slower. You have to decide the number of indexes to create and which columns to index for each application. Applications that are used primarily for data entry have less need for indexes. Applications that are used heavily for searching and reporting can definitely benefit from additional indexes.

For example, you should probably index the movie list table by rating because you often will be sorting and searching by movie rating. You will seldom need to sort by movie summary, so you don't have any justification for indexing the summary column. You still can search or sort by summary if the need arises, but the search will take longer than a rating search. Likewise, the release date column might be a candidate for indexing. Whether you add indexes is up to you and your determination of how the application will be used.

Tip

With many database applications, you can create and drop indexes as needed. You might decide that you want to create additional temporary indexes before running a batch of infrequently used reports. They enable you to run your reports more quickly. You can drop the new indexes after you finish running the reports, which restores the table to its previous state. The only downside to doing so is that write operations are slower while the additional indexes are present. This slowdown might or might not be a problem; again, the decision is entirely up to you.

Indexing on More than One Column

Often, you might find yourself sorting data on more than one column; an example is indexing on last name plus first name. Your directors table might have more than one director with the same last name. To correctly display the names, you need to sort on last name plus first name. This way, Jack Smith always appears before Jane Smith, who always appears before John Smith.

Indexing on two columns—such as last name plus first name—is not the same as creating two separate indexes (one for last name and one for first name). You have not created an index for the first name column itself. The index is of use only when you're searching or sorting the last name column, or both the last name and first name.

As with all indexes, indexing more than one column often can be beneficial, but this benefit comes with a cost. Indexes that span multiple columns take longer to maintain and take up more disk space. Here, too, you should be careful to create only indexes that are necessary and justifiable.

UNDERSTANDING THE VARIOUS TYPES OF DATABASE APPLICATIONS

All the information described to this point applies equally to all databases. The basic fundamentals of databases, tables, keys, and indexes are supported by all database applications. At some point, however, databases start to differ. They can differ in price, performance, features, security, scalability, and more.

One decision you should make very early in the process is whether to use a *shared-file–based* database, such as Microsoft Access, or a *client/server* database application, such as Microsoft SQL Server and Oracle. Each has advantages and disadvantages, and the key to determining which will work best for you is understanding the difference between shared-file–based applications and client/server systems.

SHARED-FILE–BASED DATABASES

Databases such as Microsoft Access and Visual FoxPro and Borland dBASE are shared-file–based databases. They store their data in data files that are shared by multiple users. These data files usually are stored on network drives so they are easily accessible to all users who need them, as shown in Figure 3.11.

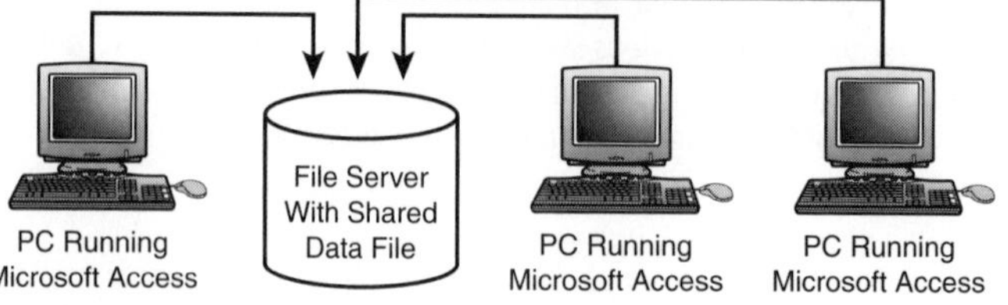

Figure 3.11
The data files in a shared-file–based database are accessed by all users directly.

When you access data from a Microsoft Access table, for example, that data file is opened on your computer. Any data you read is read by Microsoft Access running on your computer. Likewise, any data changes are made locally by the copy of Access running on your computer.

Considering this point is important when you're evaluating shared-file–based database applications. The fact that every running copy of Microsoft Access has the data files open locally has serious implications:

- **Shared data files are susceptible to data corruption**—Each user accessing the tables has the data files open locally. If the user fails to terminate the application correctly or the computer hangs, those files don't close gracefully. Abruptly closing data files like this can corrupt the file or cause garbage data to be written to it.
- **Shared data files create a great deal of unnecessary network traffic**—If you perform a search for specific expenses, the search takes place on your own computer. The database application running on your computer has to determine which rows it wants and which it does not. The application has to know of all the records—including those it will discard for this particular query—for this determination to occur. Those discarded records have to travel to your computer over a network connection. Because the data is discarded anyway, unnecessary network traffic is created.
- **Shared data files are insecure**—Because users have to open the actual data files with which they intend to work, they must have full access to those files. This also means that users can delete, either intentionally or accidentally, the entire data file with all its tables.

This is not to say that you should never use shared-file–based databases. The following are some reasons to use this type of database:

- Shared-file–based databases are inexpensive. The software itself costs far less than client/server database software. Furthermore, unlike client/server software, shared-file–based databases do not require dedicated hardware for database servers.
- Shared-file–based databases are easier to use and easier to learn than client/server–based databases.

CLIENT/SERVER–BASED DATABASES

Databases such as Microsoft SQL Server and Oracle are client/server–based databases. Client/server applications are split into two distinct parts. The *server* portion is a piece of software that is responsible for all data access and manipulation. This software runs on a computer called the *database server*. In the case of Microsoft SQL Server, it is a computer running Windows NT or 2000 and the SQL Server software.

Only the server software interacts with the data files. All requests for data, data additions and deletions, and data updates are funneled through the server software. These requests or changes come from computers running client software. The *client* is the piece of software with which the user interacts. If you request a list of movies sorted by rating, for example, the client software submits that request over the network to the server software. The server software processes the request; filters, discards, and sorts data as necessary; and sends the results back to your client software. This process is illustrated in Figure 3.12.

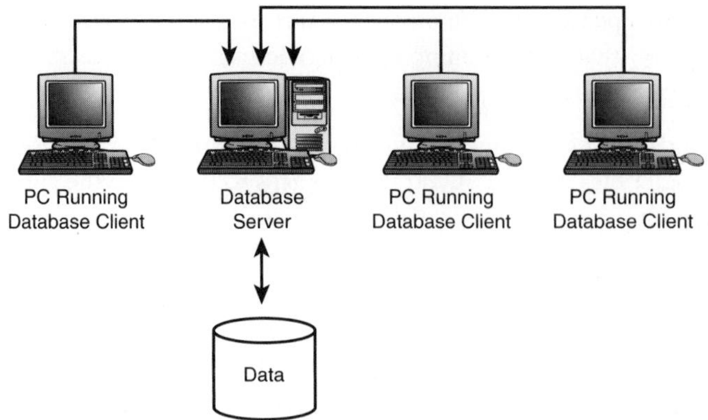

Figure 3.12
Client/server databases enable clients to perform database operations that are processed by the server software.

All this action occurs transparently to you, the user. The fact that data is stored elsewhere or that a database server is even performing all this processing for you is hidden. You never need to access the data files directly. In fact, most networks are set up so that users have no access to the data, or even the drives on which it is stored.

Client/server–based database servers overcome the limitations of shared-file–based database applications in the following ways:

- **Client/server–based data files are less susceptible to data corruption caused by incorrect application termination**—If a user fails to exit a program gracefully, or if her computer locks up, the data files do not get damaged. That is because the files are never actually open on that user's computer.
- **Client/server–based database servers use less network bandwidth**—Because all data filtering occurs on the server side, all unnecessary data is discarded before the results are sent back to the client software. Only the necessary data is transmitted over the network.
- **End users in a client/server database environment need never have access to the actual physical data files**—This lack of access helps ensure that the files are not deleted or tampered with.

As you can see, client/server databases are more secure and more robust than shared-file databases—but all this extra power and security comes with a price:

- **Running client/server databases is expensive**—The software itself is far more expensive than shared-file database applications. In addition, you need a database server to run a client/server database. It must be a high-powered computer that is often dedicated for just this purpose.
- **Client/server databases are more difficult to set up, configure, and administer**—Many companies hire full-time database administrators to do this job.

WHICH DATABASE PRODUCT TO USE

Now that you have learned the various types of database systems you can use, how do you determine which is right for your application?

Unfortunately, this question has no simple answer. You really need to review your application needs, the investment you are willing to make in the system, and which systems you already have in place.

To get started, try to answer as many of the following questions as possible:

Do you have an existing database system in place? If yes, is it current technology that is still supported by the vendor? Do you need to link to data in this system, or are you embarking on a new project that can stand on its own feet?

Do you have any database expertise or experience? If yes, with which database systems are you familiar?

Do you have database programmers or administrators in-house? If yes, with which systems are they familiar?

How many users do you anticipate will use the system concurrently?

How many records do you anticipate your tables will contain?

How important is database uptime? What is the cost associated with your database being down for any amount of time?

Do you have existing hardware that can be used for a database server?

These questions are not easy to answer, but the effort is well worth your time. The more planning you do up front, the better chance you have of making the right decision. Getting the job done right the first time will save you time, money, and aggravation later.

Of course, there is no way you can anticipate all future needs. At some point you might, in fact, need to switch databases. If you ever do have to migrate from one database to another, contact the database vendor to determine which migration tools are available. As long as you select known and established solutions from reputable vendors, you should be safe.

Tip

As a rule, shared-file–based databases should never be used on production servers.

Most developers opt to use client/server databases for production applications because of the added security and scalability. Shared file databases, however, often are used on development and testing machines because they are cheaper and easier to use.

This is a good compromise, and one that is highly recommended–client/server on production machines, shared-file on development machines (if necessary).

BUILDING THE OWS DATABASE TABLES

Now that you've reviewed the important database fundamentals, let's walk through the tables used in the Orange Whip Studios application (the database you'll be using throughout this book).

The database is made up of 11 tables, all of which are related. These relationships are graphically shown in Figure 3.13.

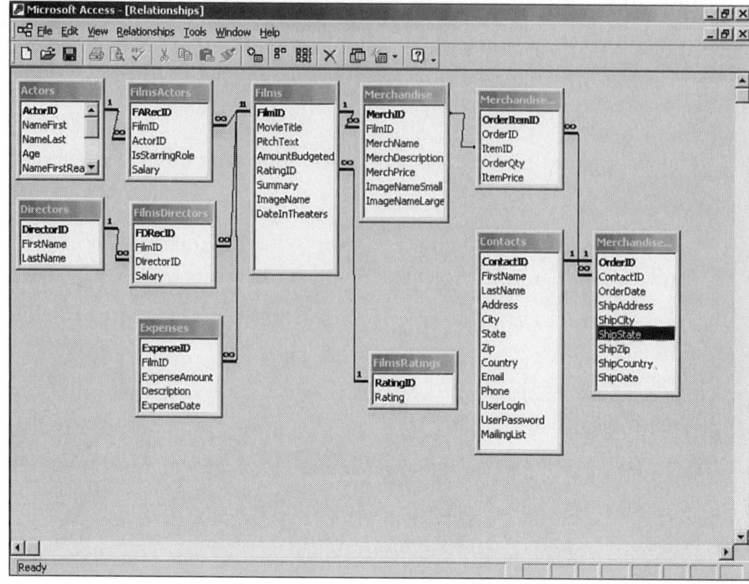

Figure 3.13
Many database applications allow relationships to be defined and viewed graphically.

> **Note**
>
> What follows is not a complete definition of the tables; it is a summary intended to provide a quick reference that will be of use to you when building the applications. You might want to bookmark this page for future reference.

> **Note**
>
> See Appendix E, "Sample Application Data Files," for a more thorough description of the tables used.

THE `Films` TABLE

The `Films` table contains the movies list.

TABLE 3.2 THE `Films` TABLE

Column	Data Type and Size	Description
`FilmID`	Numeric	Unique ID for each movie; can be populated manually when rows are inserted or automatically (if defined as an Auto Number field)
`MovieTitle`	Text	Movie title
`PitchText`	Text	Movie pitch text; the tag line

Column	Data Type and Size	Description
AmountBudgeted	Numeric, or currency	Amount budgeted for movie (may not be equal to the actual cost plus expenses)
RatingID	Numeric	ID of associated rating in the FilmRatings table
Summary	Memo or long text	Full movie summary stored in a variable-length text field (to enable longer summaries)
ImageName	Text	Filename of associated image (if there is one)
DateInTheaters	Date	Expected movie release date

The primary key for this table is the FilmID column.

This table contains a single foreign key:

- The RatingID column is related to the primary key of the FilmsRatings table.

The Expenses Table

The Expenses table contains the expenses associated with any movies listed in the Films table.

Table 3.3 The Expenses Table

Column	Data Type and Size	Description
ExpenseID	Numeric	Unique ID for each expense; can be populated manually when rows are inserted or automatically (if defined as an Auto Number field)
FilmID	Numeric	ID of associated movie
ExpenseAmount	Numeric, or currency	Expense amount
Description	Text	Expense description
ExpenseDate	Date	Expense date

The primary key for this table is the ExpenseID column.

This table contains a single foreign key:

- The FilmID column is related to the primary key of the Films table.

The Directors Table

The Directors table contains the directors list. This table is related to the Films table via the FilmsDirectors table.

TABLE 3.4 THE `Directors` TABLE

Column	Data Type and Size	Description
`DirectorID`	Numeric	Unique ID for each director; can be populated manually when rows are inserted or automatically (if defined as an Auto Number field)
`FirstName`	Text	Director's first name
`LastName`	Text	Director's last name

The primary key for this table is the `DirectorID` column.

This table contains no foreign keys.

THE `FilmsDirectors` TABLE

The `FilmsDirectors` table is used to relate the `Films` and `Directors` tables (so as to associate directors with their movies).

TABLE 3.5 THE `FilmsDirectors` TABLE

Column	Data Type and Size	Description
`FDRecID`	Numeric	Unique ID for each row; can be populated manually when rows are inserted or automatically (if defined as an Auto Number field)
`FilmID`	Numeric	ID of associated movie
`DirectorID`	Numeric	ID of associated director
`Salary`	Numeric, or currency	Actor's salary

The primary key for this table is the `FDRecID` column.

This table contains two foreign keys:

- The `FilmID` column is related to the primary key of the `Films` table.
- The `DirectorID` column is related to the primary key of the `Directors` table.

THE `Actors` TABLE

The `Actors` table contains the actors list. This table is related to the `Films` table via the `FilmsActors` table.

TABLE 3.6 THE `Actors` TABLE

Column	Data Type and Size	Description
`ActorID`	Numeric	Unique ID for each actor; can be populated manually when rows are inserted or automatically (if defined as an Auto Number field)
`NameFirst`	Text	Actor's first name
`NameLast`	Text	Actor's last name
`Age`	Numeric	Actor's age
`NameFirstReal`	Text	Actor's real first name
`NameLastReal`	Text	Actor's real last name
`AgeReal`	Numeric	Actor's real age (this one actually increases each year)
`IsEgomaniac`	Bit or Yes/No	Flag specifying whether actor is an egomaniac
`IsTotalBabe`	Bit or Yes/No	Flag specifying whether actor is a total babe
`Gender`	Text	Actor's gender (`M` or `F`)

The primary key for this table is the `ActorID` column.

This table contains no foreign keys.

THE `FilmsActors` TABLE

The `FilmsActors` table is used to relate the `Films` and `Actors` tables (so as to associate actors with their movies).

TABLE 3.7 THE `FilmsActors` TABLE

Column	Data Type and Size	Description
`FARecID`	Numeric	Unique ID for each row; can be populated manually when rows are inserted or automatically (if defined as an Auto Number field)
`FilmID`	Numeric	ID of associated movie
`ActorID`	Numeric	ID of associated actor
`IsStarringRole`	Bit or Yes/No	Flag specifying whether this is a starring role
`Salary`	Numeric or currency	Actor's salary

The primary key for this table is the `FARecID` column.

This table contains two foreign keys:

- The `FilmID` column is related to the primary key of the `Films` table.
- The `ActorID` column is related to the primary key of the `Actors` table.

THE FilmsRatings TABLE

The FilmsRatings table contains a list of film ratings used in the Films table (which is related to this table).

TABLE 3.8 THE FilmsRatings TABLE

Column	Data Type and Size	Description
RatingID	Numeric	Unique ID for each rating; can be populated manually when rows are inserted or automatically (if defined as an Auto Number field)
Rating	Text	Rating description

The primary key for this table is the RatingID column.

This table contains no foreign keys.

THE Contacts TABLE

The Contacts table contains a list of all contacts (including customers).

TABLE 3.9 THE Contacts TABLE

Column	Data Type and Size	Description
ContactID	Numeric	Unique ID for each contact; can be populated manually when rows are inserted or automatically (if defined as an Auto Number field)
FirstName	Text	Contact first name
LastName	Text	Contact last name
Address	Text	Contact address
City	Text	Contact city
State	Text	Contact state (or province)
Zip	Text	Contact ZIP code (or postal code)
Country	Text	Contact country
Email	Text	Contact e-mail address
Phone	Text	Contact phone number
UserLogin	Text	Contact login name
UserPassword	Text	Contact login password
MailingList	Bit or Yes/No	Flag specifying whether this contact is on the mailing list

The primary key for this table is the `ContactID` column.

This table contains no foreign keys.

THE `Merchandise` TABLE

The `Merchandise` table contains a list of merchandise for sale. Merchandise is associated with movies, so this table is related to the `Films` table.

TABLE 3.10 THE `Merchandise` TABLE

Column	Data Type and Size	Description
`MerchID`	Numeric	Unique ID for each item of merchandise; can be populated manually when rows are inserted or automatically (if defined as an Auto Number field)
`FilmID`	Numeric	ID of associated movie
`MerchName`	Text	Item name
`MerchDescription`	Text	Item description
`MerchPrice`	Numeric or currency	Item price
`ImageNameSmall`	Text	Filename of small image of item (if present)
`ImageNameLarge`	Text	Filename of large image of item (if present)

The primary key for this table is the `MerchID` column.

This table contains a single foreign key:

- The `FilmID` column is related to the primary key of the `Films` table.

THE `MerchandiseOrders` TABLE

The `MerchandiseOrders` table contains the orders for movie merchandise. Orders are associated with contacts (the buyer), so this table is related to the `Contacts` table.

TABLE 3.11 THE `MerchandiseOrders` TABLE

Column	Data Type and Size	Description
`OrderID`	Numeric	Unique ID of order (order number); can be populated manually when rows are inserted or automatically (if defined as an Auto Number field)
`ContactID`	Numeric	ID of associated contact
`OrderDate`	Date	Order date
`ShipAddress`	Text	Order ship to address
`ShipCity`	Text	Order ship to city

TABLE 3.11 CONTINUED

Column	Data Type and Size	Description
`ShipState`	Text	Order ship to state (or province)
`ShipZip`	Text	Order ship to ZIP code (or postal code)
`ShipCountry`	Text	Order ship to country
`ShipDate`	Date	Order ship date (when shipped)

The primary key for this table is the `OrderID` column.

This table contains a single foreign key:

- The `ContactID` column is related to the primary key of the `Contacts` table.

THE `MerchandiseOrdersItems` TABLE

The `MerchandiseOrdersItems` table contains the individual items within an order. Order items are associated with an order and the merchandise being ordered, so this table is related to both the `MerchandiseOrders` and `Merchandise` tables.

TABLE 3.12 THE `MerchandiseOrdersItems` TABLE

Column	Data Type and Size	Description
`OrderItemID`	Numeric	Unique ID of order items; can be populated manually when rows are inserted or automatically (if defined as an Auto Number field)
`OrderID`	Numeric	ID of associated order
`ItemID`	Numeric	ID of item ordered
`OrderQty`	Numeric	Item quantity
`ItemPrice`	Numeric or currency	Per-item price

The primary key for this table is the `OrderItemID` column.

This table contains two foreign keys:

- The `OrderID` column is related to the primary key of the `MerchandiseOrders` table.
- The `ItemID` column is related to the primary key of the `Merchandise` table.

Tip

Many database applications, including Microsoft Access and Microsoft SQL Server, provide interfaces to map relationships graphically. If your database application supports this feature, you might want to use it and then print the output for immediate reference.

CHAPTER 4

Accessing the ColdFusion Administrator

In this chapter

The ColdFusion server is a piece of software—an application. And as explained in Chapter 1, "Introducing ColdFusion," the software usually runs on a computer running Web server software. Production servers (servers that run finished and deployed applications) usually are connected to the Internet with a high-speed always-on connection. Development machines (used during the application development phase) often are standalone computers or workstations on a network and usually run locally installed Web server software and ColdFusion.

The ColdFusion Application Server software (I'll just call it ColdFusion for readability's sake) has all sorts of configuration and management options. Some must be configured before features will work (for example, connections to databases), whereas others are configured only if necessary (for example, the extensibility options). Yet others are purely management and monitoring related (for example, log file analysis).

All these configuration options are managed via a special program—the ColdFusion Administrator. The ColdFusion Administrator is a Web-based application; you access it using any Web browser, from any computer with an Internet connection. This is important because

- Local access to the computer running ColdFusion often is impossible (especially if hosting with an ISP or in an IT department).
- ColdFusion servers can be managed easily, without needing to install special client software.
- ColdFusion can be managed from any Web browser, even those running on platforms not directly supported by ColdFusion, and even on browsers not running on PCs.

Of course, such a powerful Web application needs to be secure (otherwise, anyone would be able to reconfigure your ColdFusion server!). At install time, you were prompted for a password with which to secure the ColdFusion Administrator—and without that password, you will not be able to access the program.

Note

If you are running ColdFusion Enterprise and installed the optional Advanced Security options, you'll be able to define multiple levels of security within the ColdFusion Administrator and grant access to specific features and options as necessary.

This feature is covered in detail in the sequel to this book, *Advanced ColdFusion 5 Application Development* (ISBN 0-7897-2585-1).

Note

Many ColdFusion developers abbreviate ColdFusion Administrator to CF Admin. So, if you hear people talking about "CF Admin," you'll know what they are referring to.

LOGGING IN TO (AND OUT OF) THE COLDFUSION ADMINISTRATOR

When ColdFusion is installed, a program group named ColdFusion Server 5 is created. Within that group is an option named ColdFusion Administrator that, if selected, launches the ColdFusion Administrator.

It is important to note that this menu option is just a shortcut, and you can access the ColdFusion Administrator by specifying the appropriate URL directly. This is especially important if ColdFusion is not installed locally, or if you simply want to bookmark the administrator directly.

Tip

As a rule, if you are serious about ColdFusion development, you should install a server locally. Although you can learn ColdFusion and write code against a remote server, not having access to the server will complicate both your learning and your ongoing development.

The URL for the ColdFusion Administrator is

```
http://localhost/CFIDE/Administrator/index.cfm
```

If, for some reason, `localhost` does not work, the IP address `127.0.0.1` can be used instead:

```
http://127.0.0.1/CFIDE/Administrator/index.cfm
```

Note

To access the ColdFusion Administrator on a remote server, use the same URL but replace `localhost` with the DNS name (or IP address) of that remote host.

So, using the Program Group option or any of the URLs listed previously, start your ColdFusion Administrator. You should see a login screen similar to the one shown in Figure 4.1.

Enter your password, and then click the Password button. Assuming your password is correct (you'll know if it is not), you'll see the Administrator Home Page, as shown in Figure 4.2.

The Home Page is divided into several regions:

- The upper-left section contains a Home button (use this to get back to the home page if you find yourself lost) and a Logout button.
- To the right of the Home and Logout buttons is a toolbar with links to Examples, Documentation, and other important information.

- The left side of the screen contains menus with all the administrative and configuration options. The Menus options change based on the menu choices directly above them.
- To the right of the menus is the main Administrator screen, which varies based on the menu options selected. When at the home page, this screen contains links to documentation, online support, training, product registration, the Security Zone, and much more.

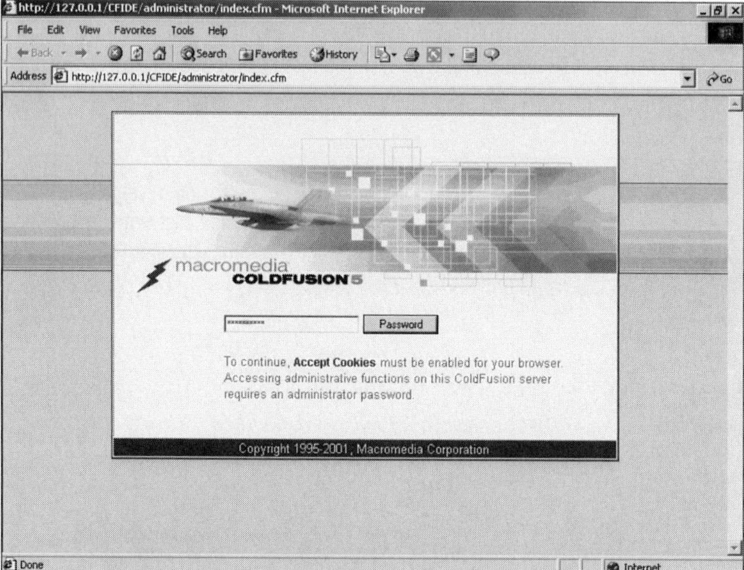

Figure 4.1
To prevent unauthorized use, access to the ColdFusion Administrator is password-protected.

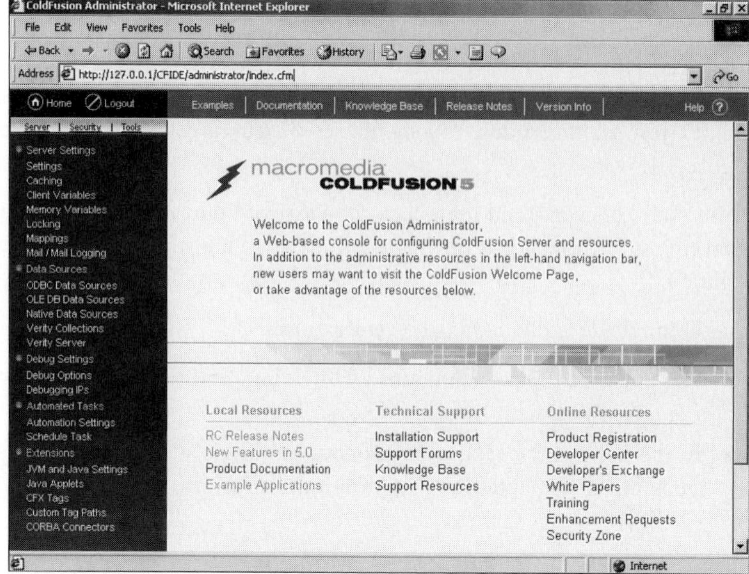

Figure 4.2
The ColdFusion Administrator Home Page provides instant access to help, documentation, and other important resources.

At the top right of the screen is a Help option. This link is always available, and additional help options are available as necessary.

Try logging out of the administrator (use the Logout button) and then log in again. You should get in the habit of always logging out of the administrator when you are finished using it.

Tip

If you are logged into the administrator, your login will timeout after a period of inactivity (forcing you to log in again). But don't rely on this. If you leave your desk or work in an environment in which others can access your computer, always explicitly log out of the ColdFusion Administrator when finished (or when you leave).

Using the ColdFusion Administrator

Let's take a brief look at the administrator and then configure the few options needed so that you can begin development. If you have logged out of the ColdFusion Administrator (or if you have yet to log in), log in now.

Note

This chapter does not provide full coverage of the ColdFusion Administrator. In fact, later in this book is an entire chapter (Chapter 30, "ColdFusion Server Configuration") that covers every Administrator option in detail.

Creating an ODBC Data Source

In Chapter 6, "Introduction to SQL," you learn about SQL, ODBC, and OLE-DB data sources, so don't worry if these terms are not familiar to you yet. For now, it is sufficient to know that for ColdFusion to interact with a database, a connection to that database must be defined. ColdFusion supports several forms of database connection, but the one you'll use (and indeed, the one that is most used) is ODBC (again, ODBC is explained in detail in Chapter 6).

ODBC is not a ColdFusion invention, and many programs other than ColdFusion use ODBC for data access. ODBC connections (called *data sources*) usually are defined at the operating-system level with special utilities (such as the ODBC Control Panel applet in Windows).

But, as explained earlier, ColdFusion developers often have no access to the server running ColdFusion, so configuring ODBC data sources the standard way is not always possible (and no standard Web interface exists for ODBC data source creation). To resolve this problem, the ColdFusion Administrator includes a set of screens that can be used to define ODBC data sources.

The Orange Whip Studios applications use a database that you will be using extensively, so let's create a data source for this database now.

> **Note**
>
> If you have not yet installed the sample file and databases, refer to the end of Chapter 2, "Installing ColdFusion and ColdFusion Studio."

Here are the steps to perform:

1. In the ColdFusion Administrator, select the ODBC Data Sources menu option (it's in the section labeled Data Sources); you'll see a screen similar to the one shown in Figure 4.3. Of course, the list of available data sources on your computer will likely differ from the figure.

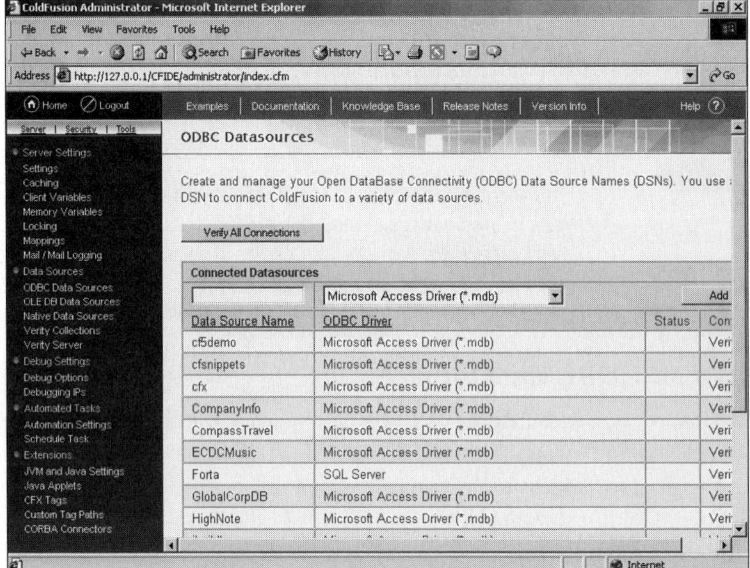

Figure 4.3
The ODBC Data Sources screen lists all defined ODBC data sources.

2. All defined ODBC data sources are listed in this screen, and data sources can be added and edited here as well. At the top of the screen enter **`ows`** as the name for the new data source and set the driver type to **`Microsoft Access Driver (*.mdb)`** (as shown in Figure 4.4); then click the Add button.
3. The Create ODBC Data Source screen, shown in Figure 4.5, prompts for any information necessary to define the data source. The only field necessary for a Microsoft Access data source is the Database File, so provide the full path to the `ows.mdb` file in this field (it usually is `\ows\data\ows.mdb` under the Web root). You also can click the Browser Server button to display a tree control (created using a Java applet) that can be used to browse the server's hard drive to locate the file interactively (as shown in Figure 4.6).

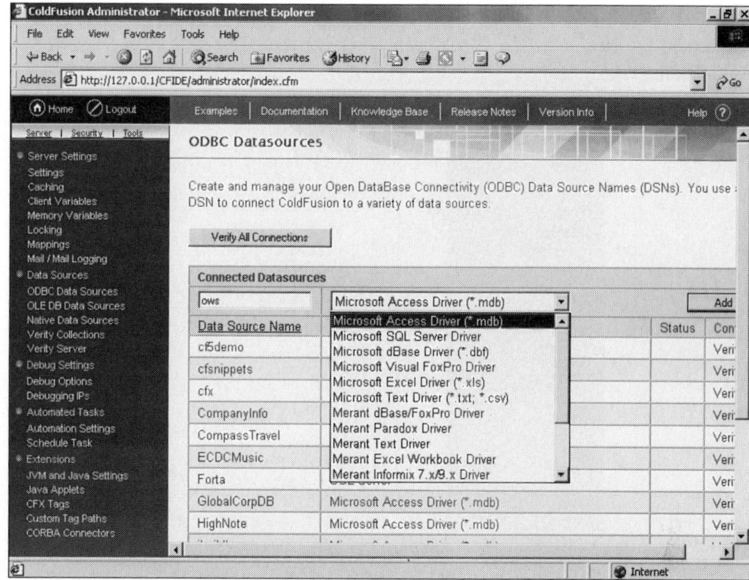

Figure 4.4
ODBC data sources can be defined (and edited) from within the ODBC Data Sources screen.

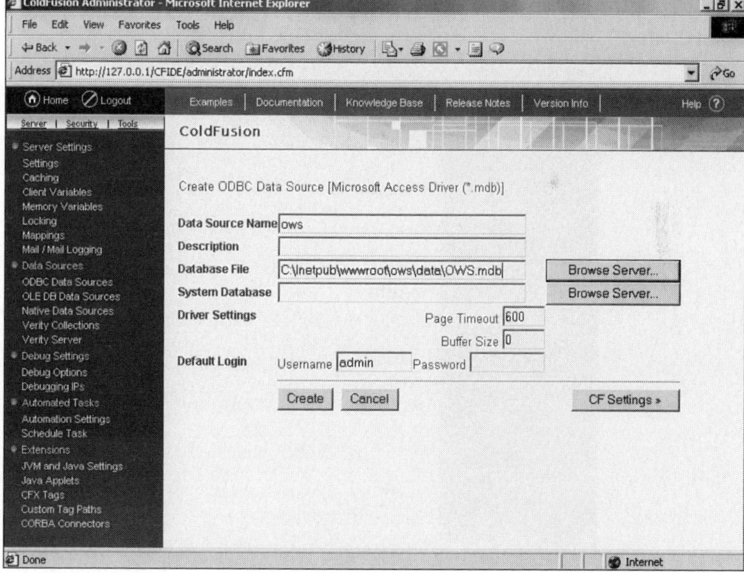

Figure 4.5
The Data Source screen varies based on the driver selected.

4. When you have filled in any required fields, click the Create button to create the new data source. The list of data sources will be redisplayed, and the new ows data source will be listed with a Status of OK (as shown in Figure 4.7). If the Status is Failed (as shown in Figure 4.8), click ows to make any necessary corrections.

You've now created an ODBC data source! You'll start using it in the next chapter.

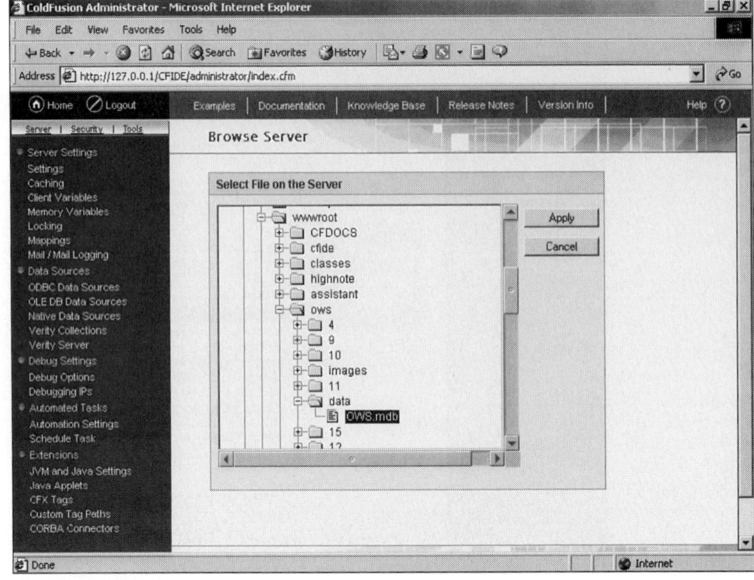

Figure 4.6
Files can be located interactively using the tree control driver browser.

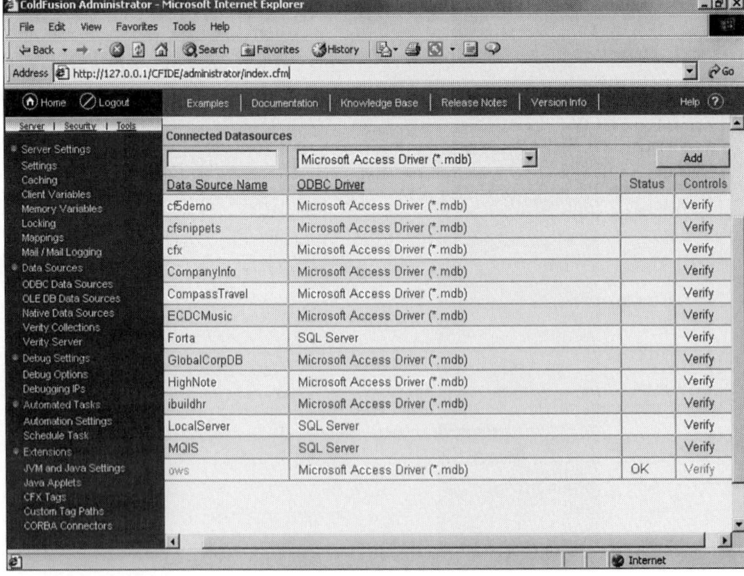

Figure 4.7
Newly created ODBC data sources are automatically verified, and the verification status is displayed.

Note

The options required in a data source definition vary based on the driver used. As such, the screen used to create and edit data sources varies based on the driver used.

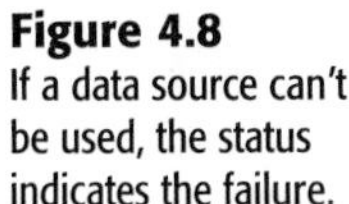

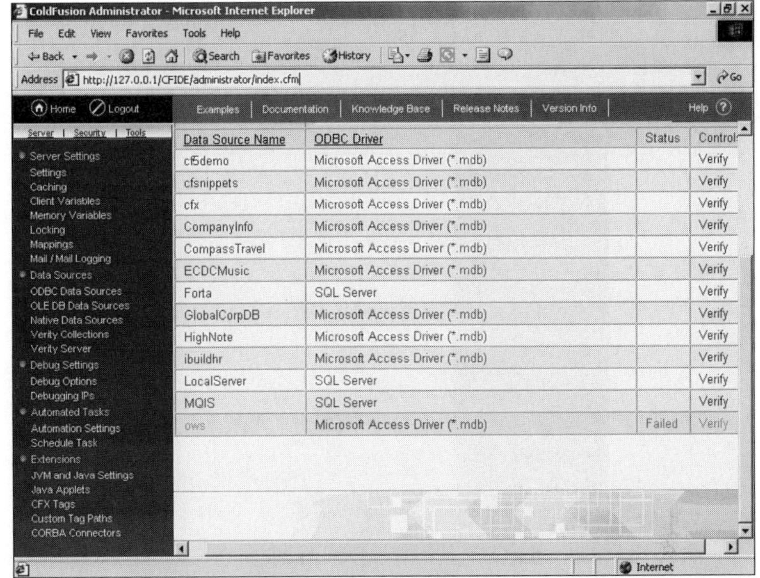

Figure 4.8
If a data source can't be used, the status indicates the failure.

Tip

ODBC data sources defined with the ColdFusion Administrator also can be used by any other application that supports ODBC. Similarly, data sources defined outside the ColdFusion Administrator can be used with ColdFusion.

Defining a Mail Server

Later in the book (in Chapter 28, "Interacting with E-mail"), you learn how to generate e-mail messages with ColdFusion. ColdFusion does not include a mail server; therefore, to generate e-mail the name of a mail server (an SMTP server) must be provided.

Note

If you do not have access to a mail server or do not know the mail server name, don't worry. You won't be using this feature for a while, and omitting this setting now will not preclude you from following along in the next lessons.

To set up your SMTP mail server, do the following:

1. In the ColdFusion Administrator, select the Mail/Mail Logging menu option (it's in the section labeled Server Settings); you'll see a screen similar to the one shown in Figure 4.9.
2. The first field (titled Mail Server) prompts for the mail server host (either the DNS name or IP address). Provide this information as requested.

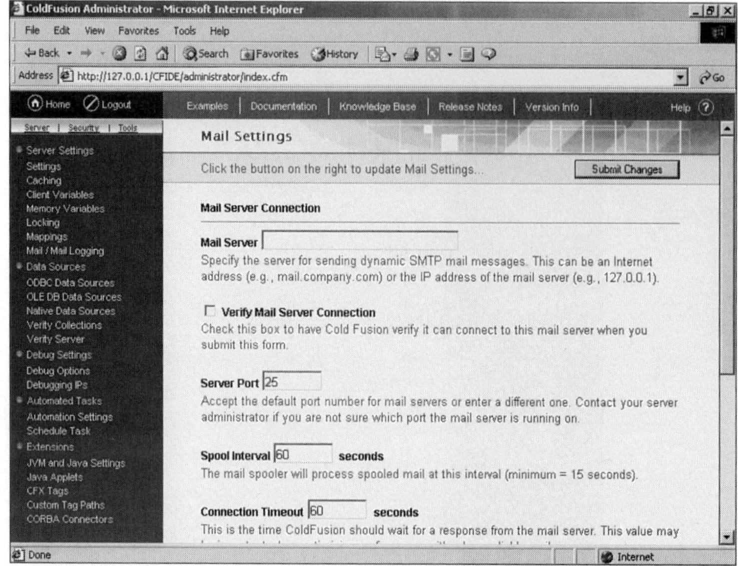

Figure 4.9
The Mail Settings screen is used to define the default SMTP mail server and other mail-related options.

3. Before you submit the form, you always should ensure that the specified mail server is valid (and accessible). To do this, check the Verify Mail Server Connection checkbox (below the Mail Server field).
4. Click the Submit Changes button (there is one at both the top and the bottom of the screen). Assuming the mail server was accessible, you'll see a screen similar to the one shown in Figure 4.10. (You'll see an error message if the specified server could not be accessed.)

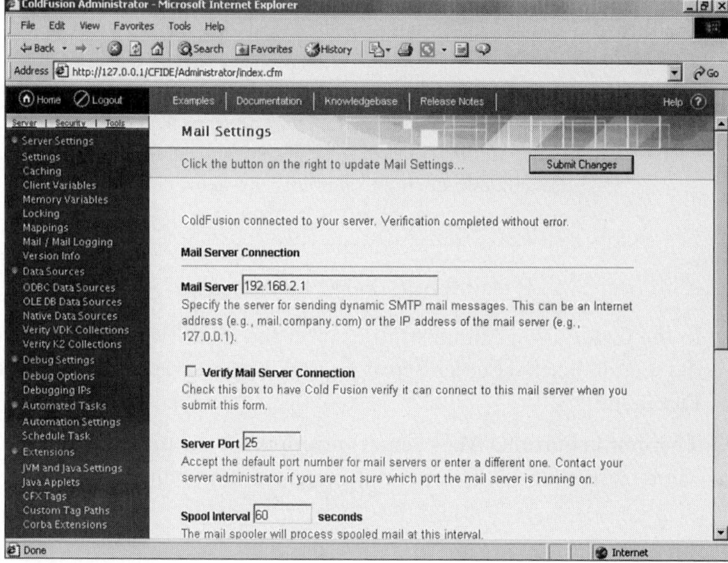

Figure 4.10
The Mail Settings screen optionally reports the mail server verification status.

You have now configured your mail server and can use ColdFusion to generate SMTP e-mail.

IDENTIFYING THE ADMINISTRATOR'S E-MAIL ADDRESS

If an error occurs within your ColdFusion applications, an error message (similar to the one shown in Figure 4.11) is displayed. Ideally, error messages should encourage users to report problems—after all, problems are much harder to find if you don't know they exist. ColdFusion can display an e-mail address in the standard error screens if one is provided.

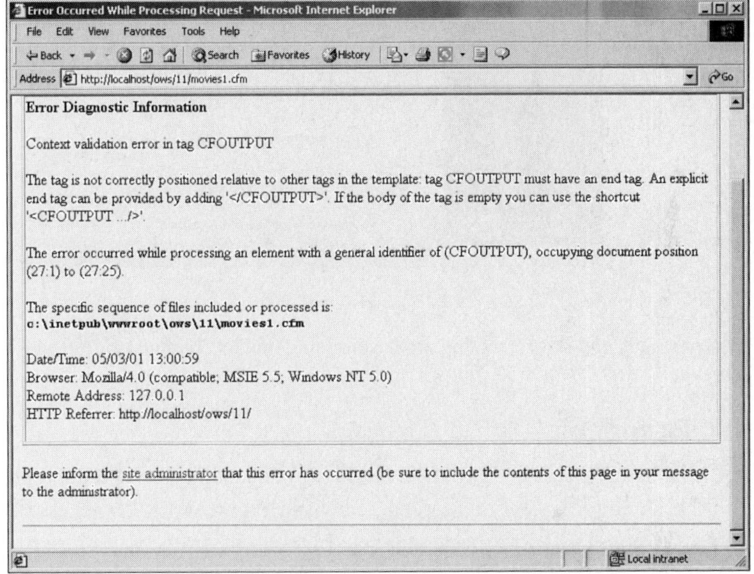

Figure 4.11
ColdFusion error messages can include an e-mail address if one is provided.

To provide an e-mail address to be used in error messages, do the following:

1. In the ColdFusion Administrator, select the Logging Settings menu option. (It's in the section labeled Logs and Statistics; you must click the Tools option at the top of the menu bar to switch to the Tools menu options.) You'll see a screen similar to the one shown in Figure 4.12.
2. The first field (titled Administrator E-Mail) prompts for the default e-mail to be used in error messages. Provide this information as requested.
3. Click the Submit Changes button to save your selection.

You have now configured the administrator e-mail address. We won't deliberately generate an error now (to test this setting). Believe me when I tell you that, like it or not, as you work through this book, you create enough error messages to be able to see this setting in action.

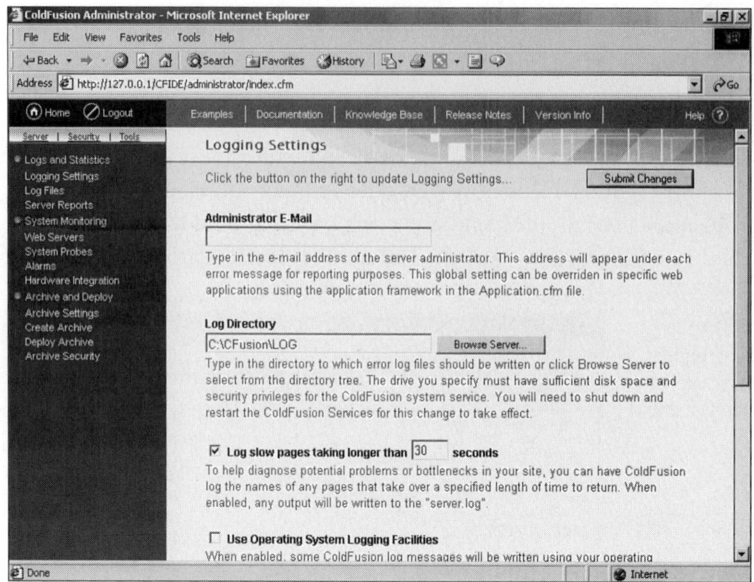

Figure 4.12
The Logging Settings page, primarily used to define log file settings, is also where the administrator e-mail address is specified.

➔ Error messages and error handling are covered in detail in Chapter 19, "Introducing the Web Application Framework," and Chapter 33, "Error Handling."

Enabling Debugging

The final screens you need to look at before proceeding are the debugging screens, starting with the Debugging Options screen, shown in Figure 4.13. To access this screen, select Debug Options (it's in the section labeled Debug Settings; you must switch back from the Tools menu to the Server menu).

I do not want you to turn on any of these options now, but I do want you to know where these options are (and how to get to them) so that you'll be ready to use them in Chapter 11, "Creating Data-Driven Pages."

Note

When you do turn on debugging, you should turn on all the options on this page except for the first. That one is used for performance monitoring and, in truth, is not a debug option at all.

Now go to the Debugging IP Address Restrictions screen (shown in Figure 4.14). To get to it, select the Debugging IPs option (it's also in the section labeled Debug Settings). This screen is used to define the IP addresses of clients who will receive debug output (this will make more sense in Chapter 11, I promise). Ensure that the address `127.0.0.1` is listed; if it is not, add it. If you don't have a locally installed ColdFusion (and are accessing a remote ColdFusion server), add your own IP address, too (type it and click the Add button).

Figure 4.13
The Debugging Options screen is used to enable and display debug output.

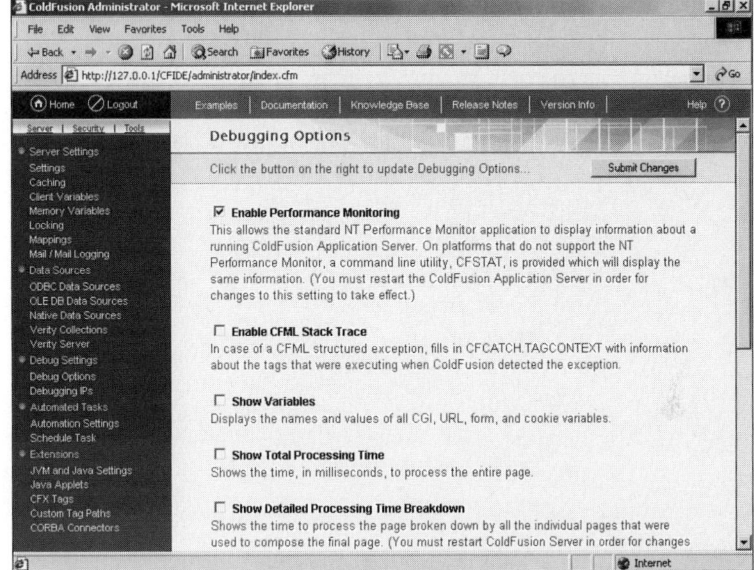

Figure 4.14
The Debugging IP Address Restrictions screen is used to define the IP address that will receive generated debug output.

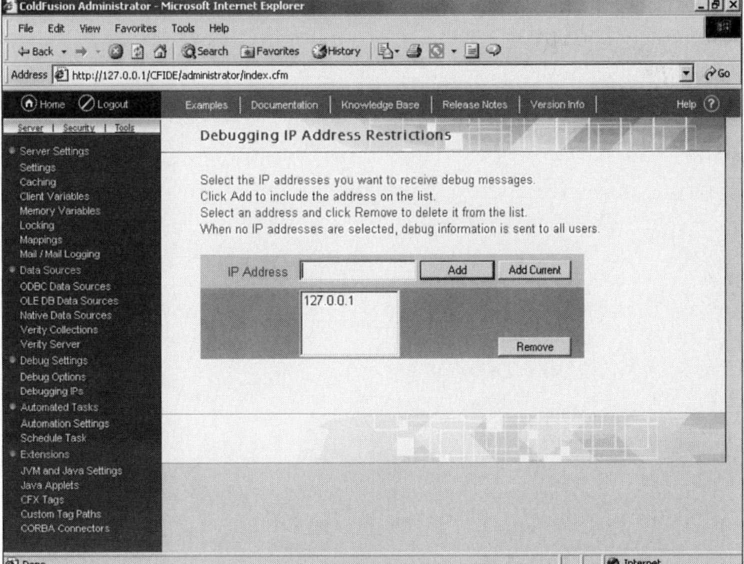

Debugging and the generated debug output are an important part of application development, as you'll see later in the book.

→ Chapter 15, "Debugging and Troubleshooting," covers the debugging options in detail.

For now, though, you are finished with the ColdFusion Administrator. So log out and proceed to the next chapter.

Note

Feel free to browse through the other administrator screens, but resist the urge to make changes to settings until you have studied Chapter 30.

CHAPTER 5

Previewing ColdFusion

In this chapter

PREPARING TO LEARN COLDFUSION

We're just about ready to go. But before we do, you need to know a little about the sample applications we'll be using and how they are used.

Orange Whip Studios is a low-budget movie studio waiting for its first big break. To help get there, a series of Web applications need to be created. These include

- A public Web site that will allow viewers to learn more about the movies
- Intranet screens for movie management (budgets, actors, directors, and more)
- A public e-commerce site allowing fans to buy movie goodies and memorabilia
- And more...

Your job, throughout this book, is to build these applications.

Tip

Most of the applications created in this book share common resources (images and data, for example) but are standalone—not requiring components created elsewhere. Although this is not typical of real-world application development, in this book this is deliberate and by design. By creating smaller, more focused applications, there is a far greater likelihood that you'll be able to reuse code and techniques in your own development. And this is both allowed and encouraged.

Here are a few things you must know about how the code and resources are managed:

- The Orange Whip Studios Web applications are created and stored in a folder named `ows` beneath the Web root.
- `ows` contains a folder named `images`, which—and this should come as no surprise—contains images used in many of the applications.
- The database used by the applications is stored in a folder named `data` beneath the `ows` folder.
- Web applications usually are organized into a directory structure that somehow maps to application features or sections. However, you won't do that here. To simplify the learning process, you'll be creating a folder beneath `ows` for each chapter in the book—`5` for Chapter 5, `6` for Chapter 6, and so on. The files created in each chapter should go in their appropriate folders.

Assuming you are running ColdFusion locally, and assuming you installed the files in the default locations, the URL to access the `ows` folder will be `http://localhost/ows` or `http://127.0.0.1/ows`. Folders beneath `ows`, such as the folder for Chapter 5 (this chapter) would be accessed as `http://localhost/ows/5` or `http://127.0.0.1/ows/5`.

Tip

Try to use `localhost` instead of `127.0.0.1` in your URLs. I only mentioned the IP address method so you know you can use it instead of `localhost` if needed, but from this point on we'll just use `localhost`.

Note

Chapter 2, "Installing ColdFusion and ColdFusion Studio," walked you through installing the sample application files. Chapter 4, "Accessing the ColdFusion Administrator," instructed you on how to set up the ODBC data source needed for these examples. If you did not perform these steps, please refer to those chapters and follow the instructions in each before proceeding. You will not be able to perform the lessons in this chapter (or any future chapter) until this has been done.

And now we're *really* ready to go.

USING THE APPLICATIONS WIZARDS

More often than not, you'll find yourself writing your own ColdFusion applications from scratch, which is why the majority of this book covers actual application design and coding. But, to help you get started and as a way to demonstrate basic ColdFusion coding concepts and design considerations, ColdFusion Studio comes with a set of wizards that will write basic applications for you.

Note

Because ColdFusion Studio 5 was not available at the time of this writing, the wizards used in this chapter are the ones in ColdFusion Studio 4.5.2. If you are using ColdFusion Studio 5 then your screens might look different. If this is the case, visit this book's Web site at `http://www.forta.com/books/0789725843/` for revised instructions.

And so, to get you started using ColdFusion and to ensure that everything is configured correctly, let's take a few minutes to experiment using some of these wizards.

Note

ColdFusion Studio comes with a whole set of wizards, and it even lets you write your own. Wizard creation is a very advanced topic and is not covered in this book. If you are interested in learning how to write your own wizards (and how to use the WIZML and VTML markup languages), see my book *Advanced ColdFusion 5 Application Development* (ISBN: 0-7897-2585-1).

The wizards are all accessed using Studio's File, New menu option. Chapter 8, "Introduction to ColdFusion Studio," takes a detailed look at ColdFusion Studio; for now, these are the steps needed to use the wizards:

1. Launch ColdFusion Studio.
2. The left pane in the Studio screen is the Resource tab. It has a set of tabs at the bottom, one of which is the Files tab (it has a picture of a computer on it); make sure this tab is selected.
3. The top half of the Resource pane shows an Explorer-style tree control used for drive and directory selection; find your application root directory (the one referred to previously) and make sure it is selected.
4. As explained previously, each chapter in this book has its own directory, so create a directory named `5` in the application root by right-clicking in the lower pane (where files are listed) and selecting Create Folder (specifying `5` as the folder name).
5. After it's created, the new folder will be displayed in the upper pane. Select the new folder to make it the current directory (so the files created by the wizards will be saved in it). Your screen should look similar to the one shown in Figure 5.1 (although your own directory list will likely differ slightly).

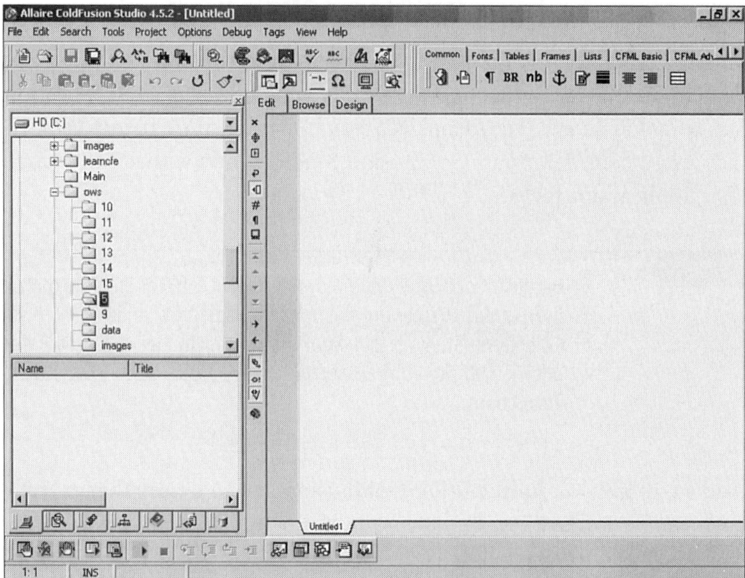

Figure 5.1
ColdFusion Studio's Resource pane contains a File tab that can be used to create and work with files and folders.

And with that, you're ready to begin.

Note

Make a note of how to create folders. You'll need to do this for each chapter in this book, and even though you'll be reminded to do so occasionally, I won't walk you through the exact steps each time.

THE RECORD VIEWER WIZARD

The first wizard you'll look at is the Record Viewer Wizard. This useful wizard creates an interactive database record viewer—enabling you to scroll through table records, viewing, editing, and deleting them as necessary. You use it to allow the viewing and editing of actors listed in the `Actors` table.

Here are the steps:

1. Make sure you've created the chapter folder (as described previously) and have selected it as the active folder.
2. Select New from the File menu to display the New Document dialog box, as seen in Figure 5.2.

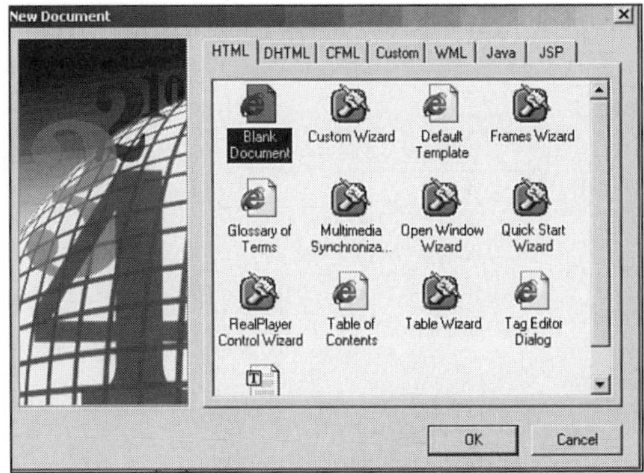

Figure 5.2
The Studio New Document dialog box is used to access templates and wizards.

3. The New Document dialog box contains tabs used to group and organize related wizards (and templates); select the CFML tab to display the ColdFusion wizards, as seen in Figure 5.3.
4. Double-click the Record Viewer Wizard icon to launch the wizard, seen in Figure 5.4.
5. You'll be prompted for an application title and a path into which generated files will be stored (see Figure 5.5). The latter should be correct (because you selected the correct folder before launching the wizard). Type **`OWS Actors`** as the title, and then click the Next button.
6. Next, the wizard will prompt you for the server and ODBC data source to use (see Figure 5.6). Select `localhost` as the server so the wizard will know which list of data sources to provide. Then select `ows` as the data source and click Next.
7. The wizard then prompts for the database table to use. Select `Actors` (see Figure 5.7) and click Next.

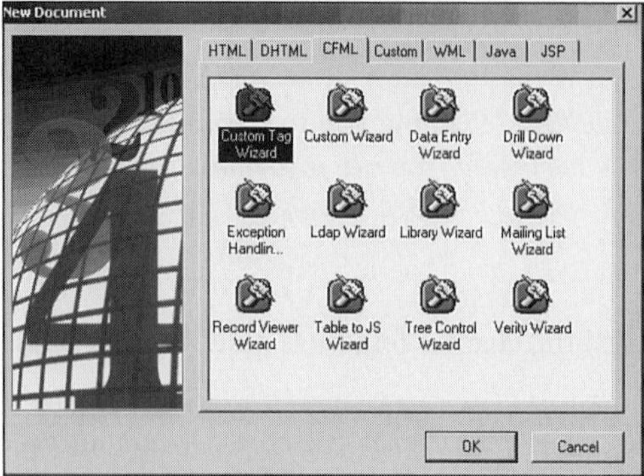

Figure 5.3
All ColdFusion-specific wizards are in the CFML tab.

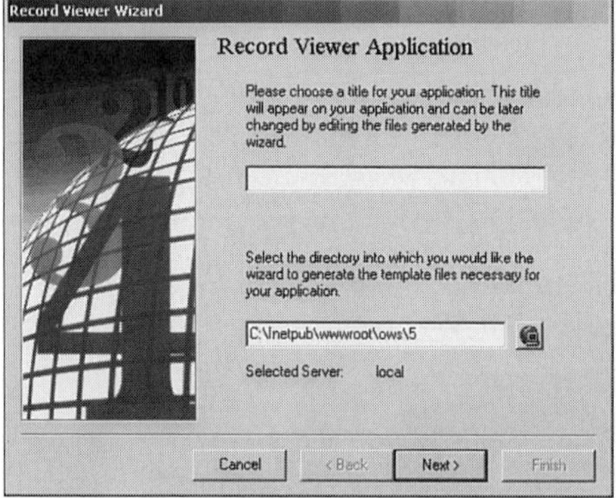

Figure 5.4
The Record Viewer Wizard creates a complete table browsing (and editing) utility.

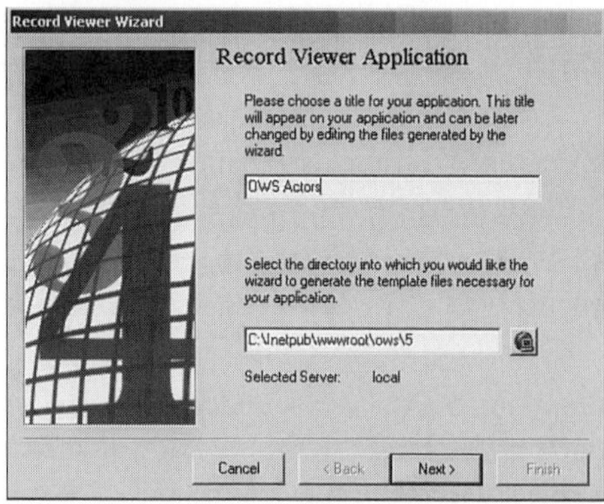

Figure 5.5
Every wizard-generated application is titled, and the title is used to construct the names of the generated files.

8. Now that the wizard knows which table you'll be using, it can retrieve a column list from that table and prompt you for the columns to be displayed (see Figure 5.8). To display all the columns, select the entire list (click the top column, and then Shift+click the last to select them all); then click Next.

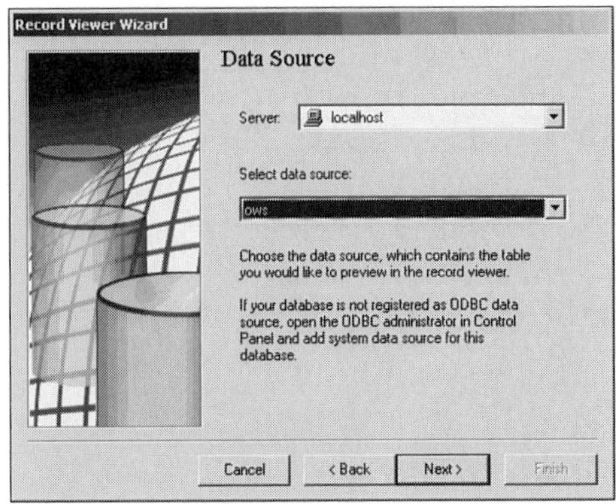

Figure 5.6
After a server is selected, the list of data sources automatically is populated with those available on the specified server.

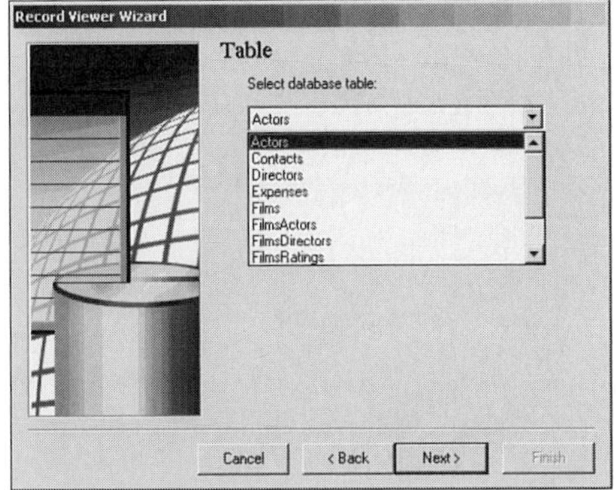

Figure 5.7
Table names are selected from lists retrieved automatically from the data source.

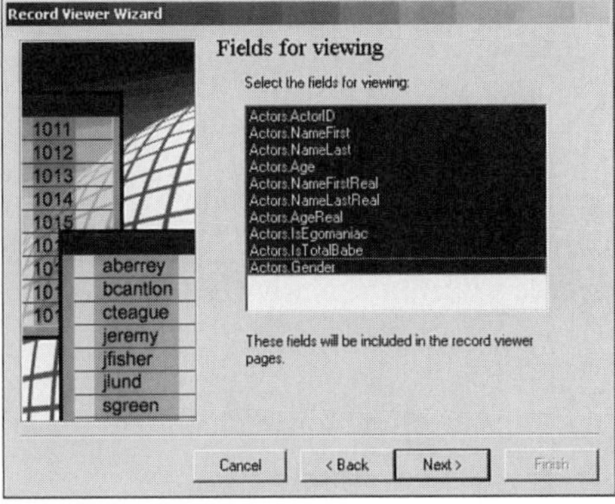

Figure 5.8
Multiple-column selection is performed using Shift+click or Ctrl+click.

9. The Record Viewer generated by this wizard is used for editing, too, so you'll be prompted for the columns that can be edited (see Figure 5.9). The `ActorID` column is a primary key that can't be edited, so select all the columns except `ActorID` and then click Next.

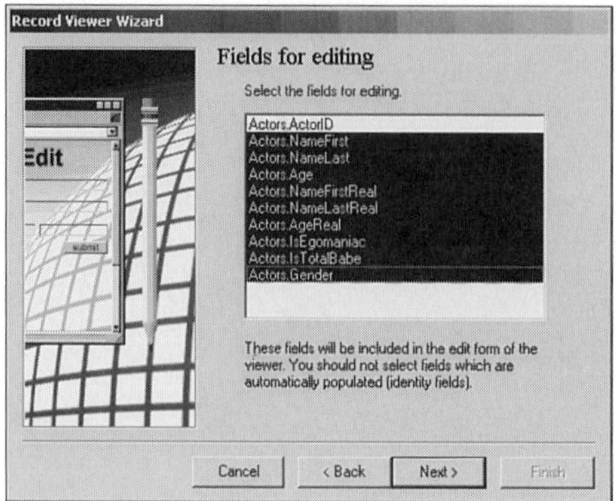

Figure 5.9
Not all columns are editable, so be careful to not select any columns that should not be edited.

10. The final piece of information needed by the wizard is the name of the table's primary key (so the code can correctly identify table rows). Select the `ActorID`, and then click Finish to generate the code (see Figure 5.10).

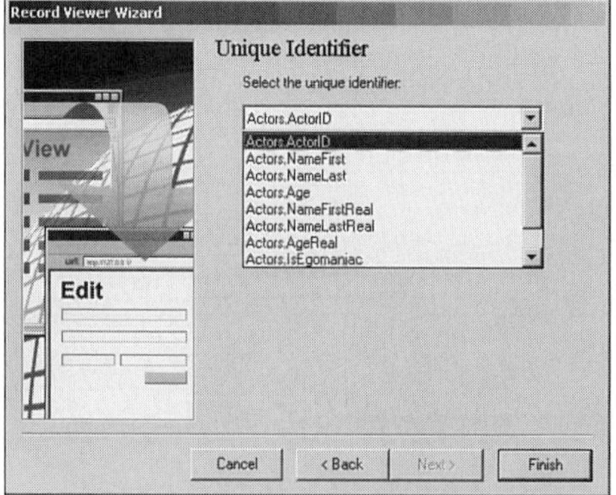

Figure 5.10
A table's primary key is needed to be able to uniquely identity rows within the table.

11. At this point the wizard generates the code. As seen in Figure 5.11, the wizard notifies you that it has completed the task of listing the files it created along with a description of each. Click Close to exit the wizard; the newly created CFM files will be opened in the Studio editor window.

Ready to try the application? Open your Web browser and go to the following URL:

```
http://localhost/ows/5/OWSActors_RecordView.cfm
```

You'll see the first actor record displayed (as seen in Figure 5.12), along with controls allowing you to scroll back and forth through the data. There are even Add, Edit, and Delete buttons that, well, add, edit, and delete (see Figure 5.13). Feel free to play with the application to see what it can do.

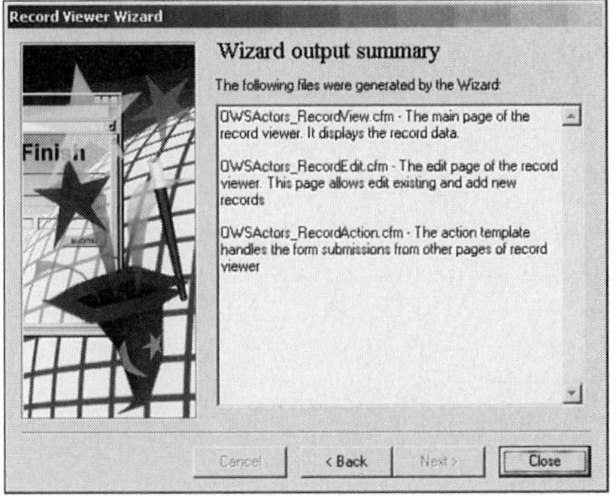

Figure 5.11
The Record Viewer table generates three CFM files.

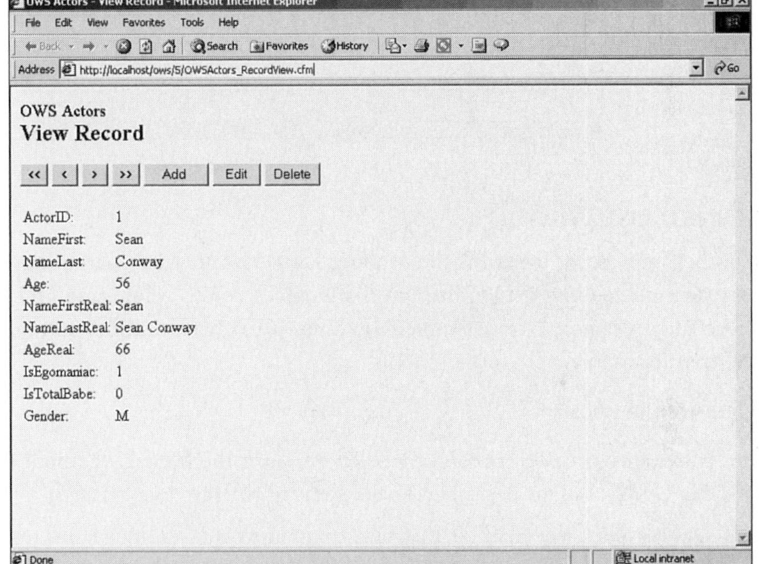

Figure 5.12
The Record Viewer application features a set of buttons that can be used to scroll through the data.

Caution

Feel free to experiment with the application, but realize that if you make changes to any data, your output might look different in applications created in future chapters. This is not a problem as long as you keep it in mind (so that you'll know why things look different later).

Now that was easy—a real working ColdFusion application, and you didn't even have to write a line of code.

Figure 5.13
The edit screen is used to edit data (as seen here), as well as to add new data.

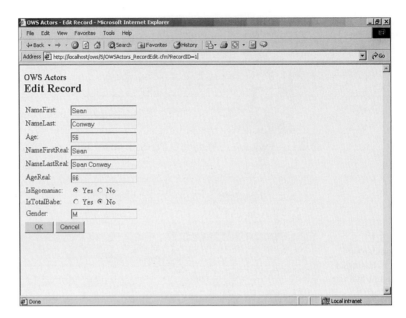

THE MAILING LIST WIZARD

Another interesting wizard is the Mailing List Wizard. As its name suggests, this wizard creates a simple mailing list application that enables you to send e-mail messages to one or more addresses in a database table. You'll use it to create a utility to e-mail the contacts in the `Contacts` table.

Here are the steps:

1. Make sure the correct folder is selected, open the New Document dialog box, and select the CFML tab (as described in the steps in the previous wizard).
2. Double-click the Mailing List Wizard icon to launch the wizard (as seen in Figure 5.14). Specify a title of **`OWS Contact Mailing`** and click Next (the path should be correct).

Figure 5.14
The Mailing List Wizard can greatly simplify database-driven e-mail operations.

3. You next are prompted for the server and data source to use (like in Figure 5.6 in the previous wizard). Select `localhost` as the server and `ows` as the data source, and click Next.
4. Next, you must specify the database table to be used (in a dialog box similar to the one seen in Figure 5.7). Select the `Contacts` table and click Next.
5. The code generated by this wizard will retrieve e-mail addresses from the `Contacts` table, so you need to specify the column in the table that contains the addresses. Select the `Email` column (as seen in Figure 5.15) and click Finish to generate the code.

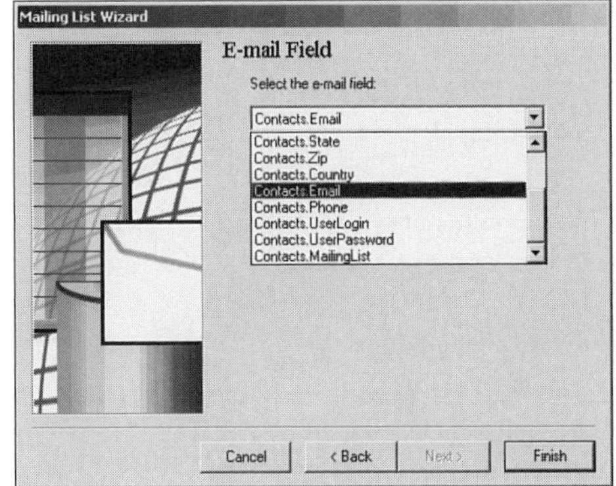

Figure 5.15
There is no way the wizard can automatically determine which column contains e-mail addresses, so you must select this yourself.

6. The wizard will create two files and then list them (with descriptions), as seen in Figure 5.16. Click Close to close the wizard.

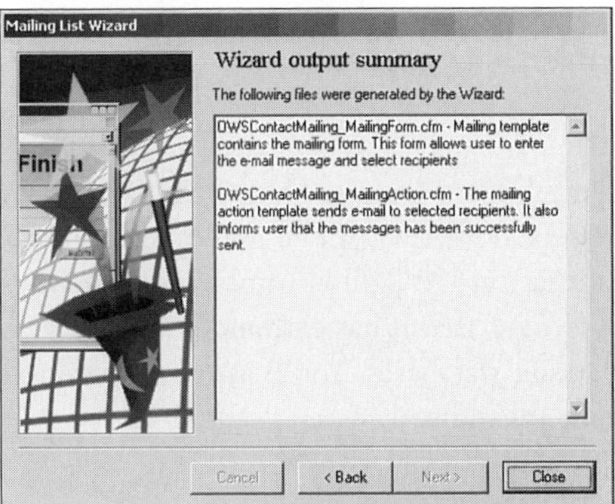

Figure 5.16
The Record Viewer table generates two CFM files.

To try the application, open a browser and go to this URL:

```
http://localhost/ows/5/OWSContactMailing_MailingForm.cfm
```

You'll see a screen (similar to the one shown in Figure 5.17) that enables you to select one or more e-mail addresses, specify the sender and subject, and enter the message to be sent.

It even allows you to select how the message should be sent—one message to all (where each recipient sees the names of all recipients) or one message to each recipient (recipients see no names other than their own).

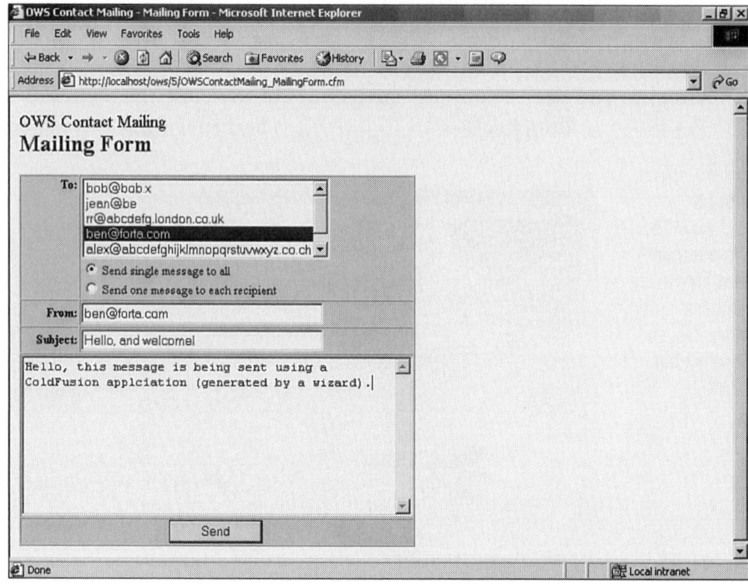

Figure 5.17
The Mailing List Wizard creates an application that lets you select one or more e-mail addresses, as well as other options.

Caution

The e-mail addresses in the `Contacts` table are not valid, so if you actually send messages using the application you just generated, they'll all bounce.

THE DATA DRILL-DOWN WIZARD

The last wizard deserves a special mention. The Data Drill-Down Wizard generates extremely powerful (and complex) code that can be used to create data drill-down interfaces (if you don't know what these are, it'll all become very clear when you try it out). What makes this wizard so special is that it has extremely sophisticated database handling that makes it usable with relational databases. You'll use the wizard to create an application enabling users to find movie merchandise.

Here are the steps:

1. Make sure the correct folder is selected, open the New Document dialog box, and select the CFML tab (as described in the steps in the first wizard).
2. Double-click the Drill-Down Wizard icon to launch the wizard (as seen in Figure 5.18). Specify a title of **`OWS Merchandise`** and click Next (the path should be correct).

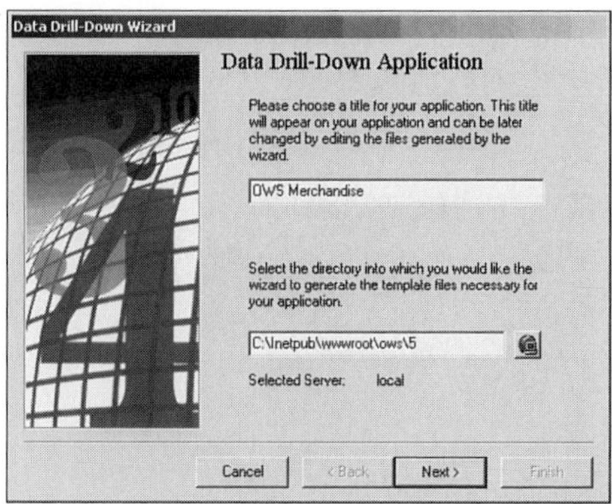

Figure 5.18
The Data Drill-Down Wizard is used to create highly interactive search interfaces.

3. Select `localhost` as the server and `ows` as the data source, and click Next.
4. Unlike the table selection screens seen in the previous two wizards, the screen shown in Figure 5.19 allows you to select multiple tables. Select the `Films` and `Merchandise` tables (Ctrl+click to select the second one), and click Next.

Figure 5.19
The Data Drill-Down Wizard enables the selection of multiple (related) tables.

5. The wizard needs to know how these tables are related so it can generate the appropriate SQL code. As seen in Figure 5.20, the wizard will try to determine the relationships automatically and will get them correct (as it did here) if the column names are consistent. You can change or modify the relationship information if necessary, but because the wizard got it right, click Next.
6. Data drill-down interfaces usually start with a search screen, so the wizard will prompt you for the columns that users will be able to search on (as seen in Figure 5.21). Select the `MovieTitle` column from the `Films` table and the `MerchName` and `MerchDescription` columns from the `Merchandise` table, and then click Next.

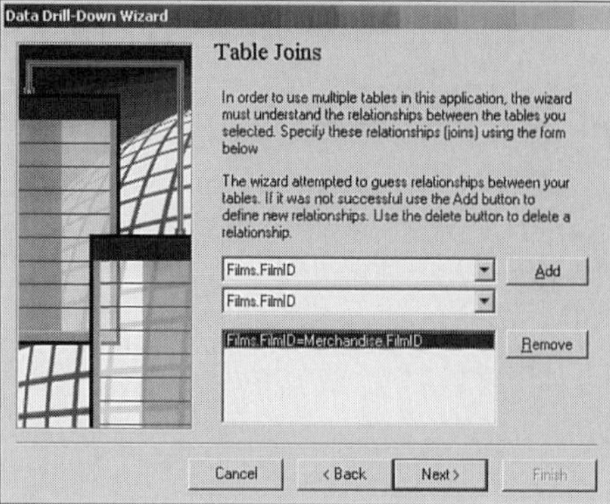

Figure 5.20
The wizard will try to determine table relationship automatically.

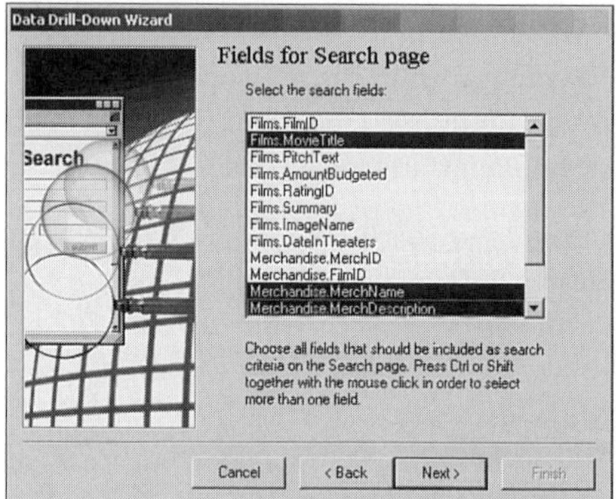

Figure 5.21
Select as many search fields as necessary; searches can be performed on one or more of them at once.

7. Next, the wizard will prompt for the columns to be displayed on the results page. Select the `MovieTitle` column from the `Films` table and the `MerchName`, `MerchDescription`, and `MerchPrice` columns from the `Merchandise` table (as seen in Figure 5.22); then click Next.

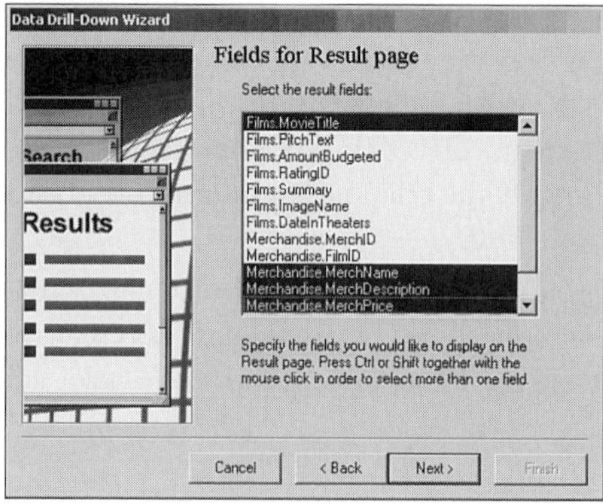

Figure 5.22
Search results are displayed in a tabular format containing the columns selected here.

8. The wizard will then prompt for the columns to be displayed in the details page (as seen in Figure 5.23). Select the `MovieTitle` and `PitchText` columns from the `Films` table and the `MerchName`, `MerchDescription`, and `MerchPrice` columns from the `Merchandise` table, and then click Next.

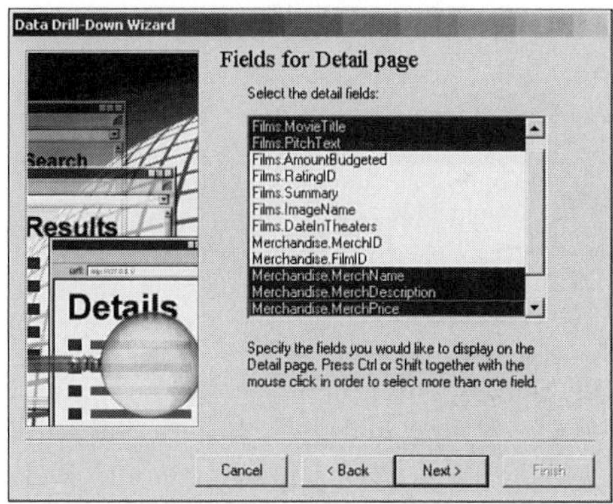

Figure 5.23
The details page displays a single record and thus has room for more information than the search results screen.

9. The last piece of information needed is the unique ID to be used for selecting items in the details page (as seen in Figure 5.24). Select the `MerchID` column in the `Merchandise` table, and click Finish.

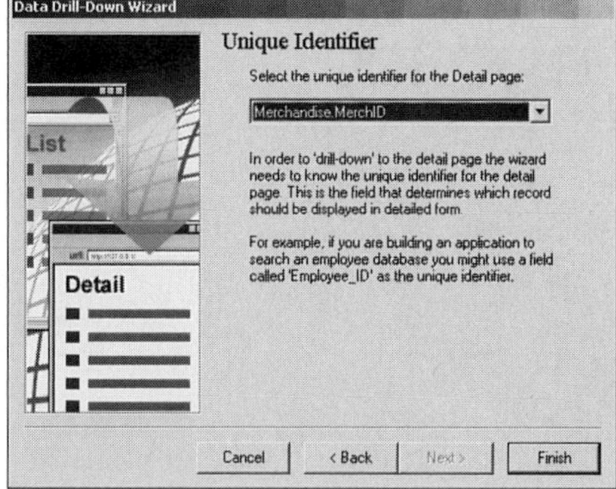

Figure 5.24
Because more than one table can be selected, the wizard requires that you specify which column (in which table) is to be used as the unique identifier.

10. The wizard will generate four complete CFM files and then list them and their descriptions (see Figure 5.25). Click Close to exit the wizard.

To try this application, open a browser and go to this URL:

```
http://localhost/ows/5/OWSMerchandise_Search.cfm
```

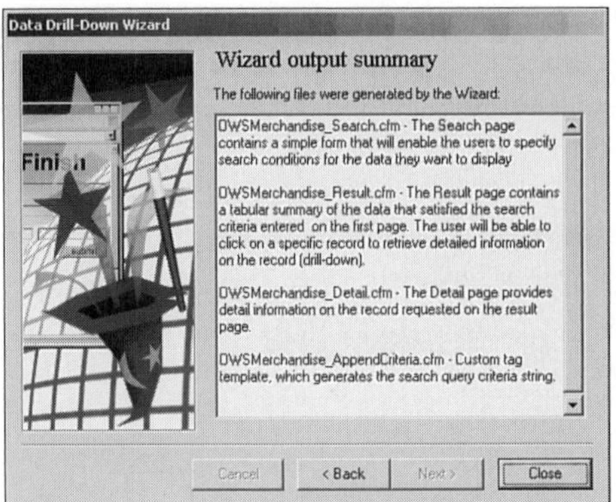

Figure 5.25
The Record Viewer table generates four CFM files.

You'll see a screen similar to the one shown in Figure 5.26. Enter search text in any of the search fields, select an optional search type, and then click the Submit Query button. You'll see a search results screen (as seen in Figure 5.27) allowing you to click the Detail link to see product details.

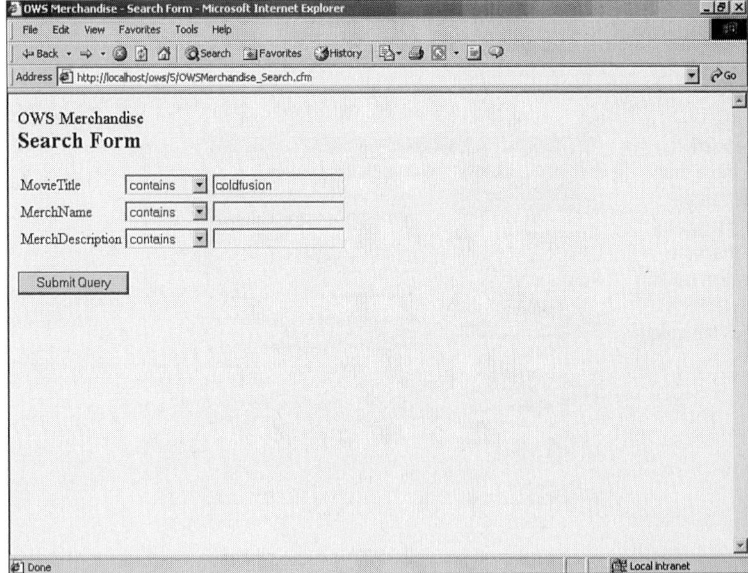

Figure 5.26
The search screen supports multiple columns and multiple search types.

As you can see, the wizards are both powerful and easy to use. Although the code they generate might not be exactly what you want, they often provide a good starting point (as well as usable code).

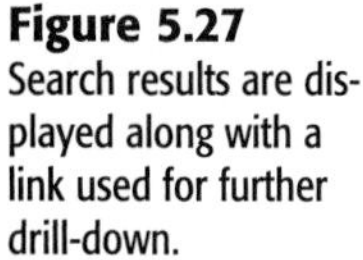

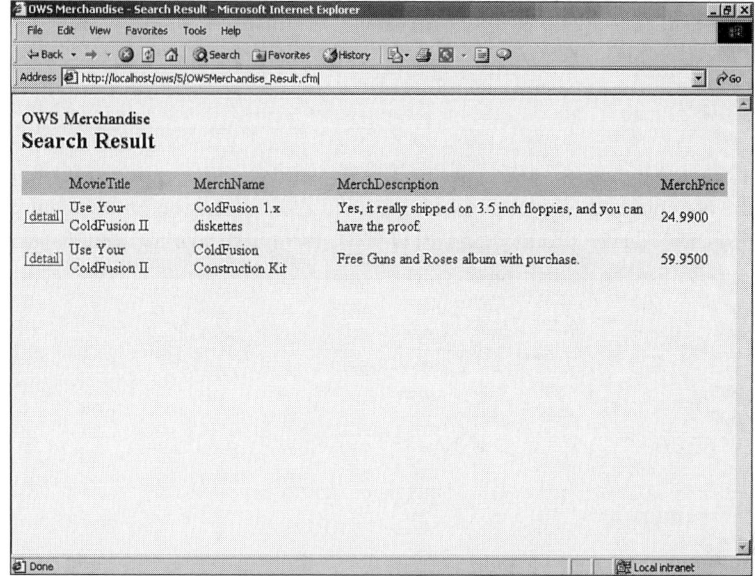

Figure 5.27
Search results are displayed along with a link used for further drill-down.

TRYING IT YOURSELF

As I already said, wizards are almost always not enough, which is why the majority of this book discusses coding. To give you a small test of what's to come, try this small (and very simple) application. We'll not go into the details of the code itself at this point; for now, concentrate on creating and executing CFM files so that they work (if these all work, you'll have a much easier time working through the book).

The `bday` application is really simple—it prompts for your name and date of birth and calculates your age (using simple date arithmetic). The application is made up of two files:

- `bday1.cfm` (shown in Listing 5.1) is the form that prompts for the name and date of birth.
- `bday2.cfm` (shown in Listing 5.2) processes the form and displays the results.

Create these two files (you can use ColdFusion Studio or any other editor) and enter the code exactly as it is shown in the listings. Save both files in the `5` directory.

LISTING 5.1 `bday1.cfm`

```
<HTML>
<BODY>
<FORM ACTION="bday2.cfm" METHOD="post">
Name: <INPUT TYPE="text" NAME="name">
<BR>
Date of birth: <INPUT TYPE="text" NAME="dob">
<BR>
<INPUT TYPE="submit">
```

LISTING 5.1 CONTINUED

```
</FORM>
</BODY>
</HTML>
```

The code in bday1.cfm is simple HTML—there is no ColdFusion code at all (and in fact, the file could have been named with an HTML extension and it would have still worked properly). bday1.cfm contains an HTML form with two form fields—name for the username and dob for the date of birth.

LISTING 5.2 bday2.cfm

```
<HTML>
<BODY>
<CFOUTPUT>
Hello #FORM.name#,
you are #DateDiff("YYYY", FORM.dob, Now())#.
</CFOUTPUT>
</BODY>
</HTML>
```

The code in bday2.cfm is a mixture of HTML and CFML. The name form field is used to display the Hello message, and the dob field is used to calculate the age.

To try the application, open a browser and go to the following URL:

```
http://localhost/ows/5/bday1.cfm
```

A form, similar to the one seen in Figure 5.28, will prompt you for your name and date of birth. Fill in the two fields, and then click the form submission button to display your age (see Figure 5.29).

Was that a little anticlimactic after the wizard-generated code? Perhaps. But you've now learned all you need to know about creating, saving, and executing ColdFusion applications. And now the fun starts.

Note

You might be wondering why I made you test your code in a browser instead of in Studio. The reason is that Studio requires a special configuration to be capable of executing CFM files. Remember (as was discussed in Chapter 1, "Introducing ColdFusion"), CFM files must be processed by a server before results can be displayed in a browser. Therefore, because you've yet to configure Studio, you can't browse CFM pages using the integrated browser yet. This is discussed in Chapter 8.

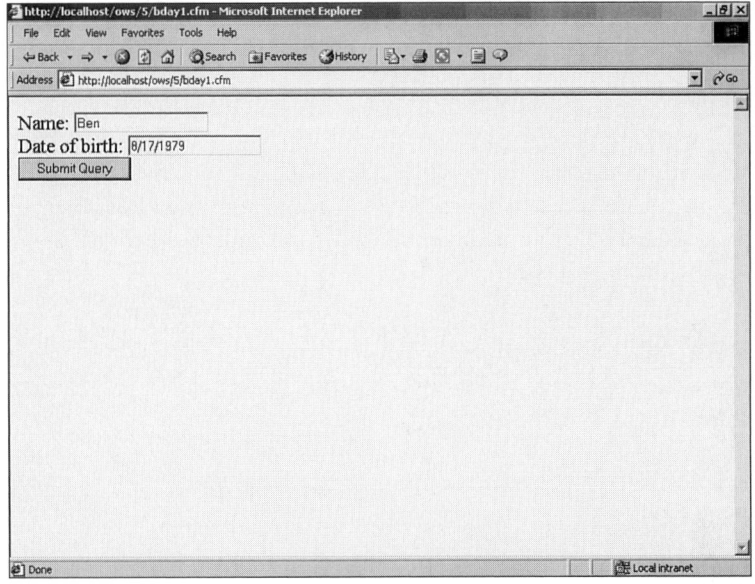

Figure 5.28
ColdFusion forms are created using standard HTML tags.

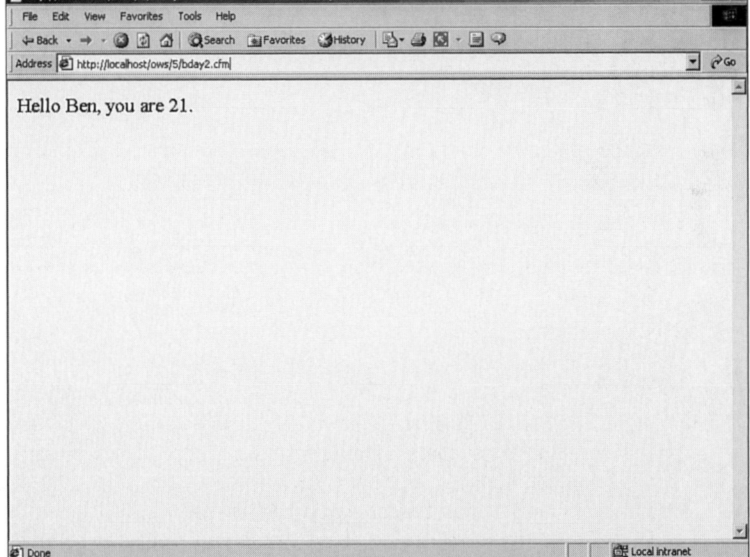

Figure 5.29
ColdFusion generates output displayed in a browser.

CHAPTER 6

Introduction to SQL

In this chapter

INTRODUCING SQL, THE STRUCTURED QUERY LANGUAGE

SQL, pronounced *sequel* or *S-Q-L*, is an acronym for Structured Query Language. SQL is a language you use to access and manipulate data in a relational database. It is designed to be both easy to learn and extremely powerful, and its mass acceptance by so many database vendors proves that it has succeeded in both.

In 1970, Dr. E. F. Codd, the man credited with being the father of the relational database, described a universal language for data access. In 1974, engineers at IBM's San Jose Research Center created the Structured English Query Language, or SEQUEL, built on Codd's ideas. This language was incorporated into System R, IBM's pioneering relational database system.

Toward the end of the 1980s, two of the most important standards bodies, the American National Standards Institute (ANSI) and the International Standards Organization (ISO), published SQL standards, opening the door to mass acceptance. With these standards in place, SQL was poised to become the de facto standard used by every major database vendor.

Although SQL has evolved a great deal since its early SEQUEL days, the basic language concepts and its founding premises have remained the same. The beauty of SQL is its simplicity. But don't let that simplicity deceive you. SQL is a powerful language, and it encourages you to be creative in your problem solving. You can almost always find more than one way to perform a complex query or to extract desired data. Each solution has pros and cons, and no solution is explicitly right or wrong.

Before you panic at the thought of learning a new language, let me reassure you that SQL really is easy to learn. In fact, you need to learn only four statements to be able to perform almost all the data manipulation you will need on a regular basis. Table 6.1 lists these statements.

TABLE 6.1 SQL-BASED DATA MANIPULATION STATEMENTS

Statement	Description
`SELECT`	Queries a table for specific data.
`INSERT`	Adds new data to a table.
`UPDATE`	Updates existing data in a table.
`DELETE`	Removes data from a table.

Each of these statements takes one or more keywords as parameters. By combining various statements and keywords, you can manipulate your data in as many ways as you can imagine.

ColdFusion provides you with all the tools you need to add Web-based interaction to your databases. ColdFusion itself, though, has no built-in database. Instead, it communicates with whatever database you select, passing updates and requests and returning query results.

Introducing ODBC

The communication between ColdFusion and the database usually takes place via a database interface called Open Database Connectivity, or ODBC. ODBC is a standard Application Programming Interface (API) for accessing information from different database systems and different storage formats.

Note

ColdFusion also supports database communication via other interfaces, but as they are infrequently used we'll just be discussing ODBC here. Any SQL taught in this chapter (and the next chapter) is applicable regardless of the interface used.

Working with Database System Differences

The purpose of ODBC is to enable you to access a diverse selection of databases and data formats without having to learn the features and peculiarities of each. ODBC provides a layer of abstraction, accomplished using database drivers, between your client application and the underlying database. The database drivers create a database-independent environment, as illustrated in Figure 6.1. This way, you can write one program and have it work with almost any major database system.

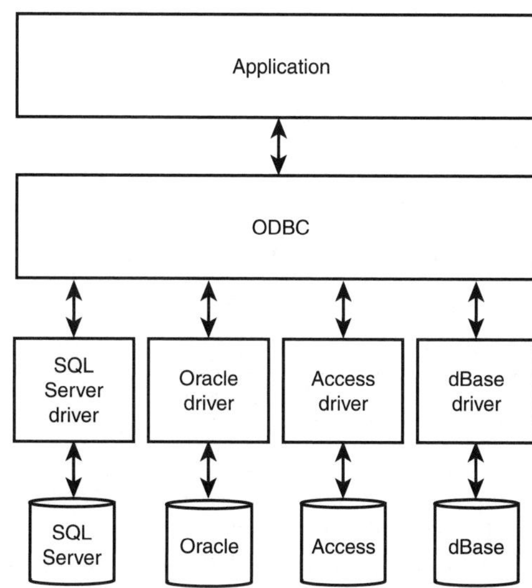

Figure 6.1
ODBC creates a database-independent development environment.

Of course, differences exist between database systems. Microsoft SQL Server and Oracle, for example, both require you to log in to the database server before you can manipulate any data. Based on your login, you are granted or denied access to specific tables or other objects. Microsoft Access, on the other hand, has no concept of login-based security. If you have access to the data file (the MDB file), you have full access to all data in it.

You will find other differences, too. To access Microsoft SQL Server, your client application must know the address of the server. It might be an IP address or an NT server name. To use Microsoft Access data files, however, you just need to know the drive and path to the data file.

Part of the job of ODBC is to hide these differences from your client application. To accomplish this feat, each ODBC driver has its own configuration options. When you select the SQL Server ODBC driver, you are asked for a server name, a server login name, and a password, as shown in Figure 6.2. When you select the Access ODBC driver, you are prompted for a file path, as shown in Figure 6.3.

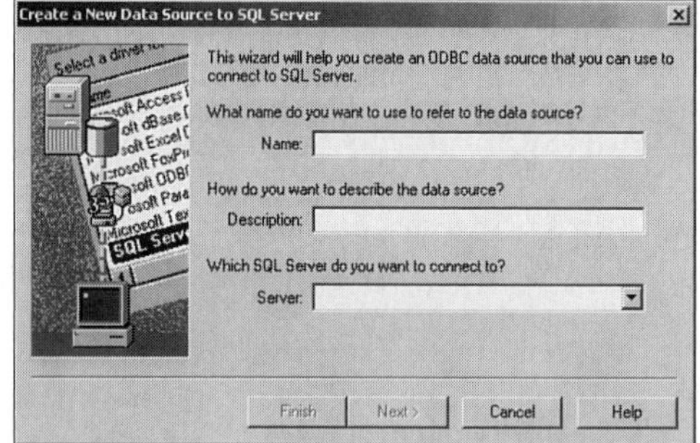

Figure 6.2
The Microsoft SQL Server ODBC driver prompts you for login information.

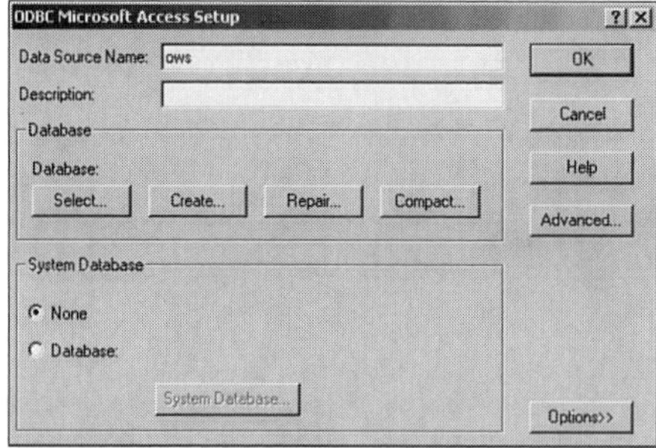

Figure 6.3
The Microsoft Access ODBC driver prompts you for the file path to the Access data file.

This way, your client software can load any ODBC driver and connect to a database. The ODBC driver you select will handle opening the database, whether it's opening a network file or logging in to a server. All your client software knows is that it must connect to a database; the details of how this process occurs are all hidden.

The ODBC Story

ODBC was created in an effort to allow Microsoft Excel, Microsoft's popular spreadsheet program, to access diverse data stores.

In April 1988, Microsoft's Kyle Geiger proposed a model that used database drivers to isolate the native data types of different database applications. This model, in conjunction with a standard application interface, would enable client software to communicate with any message store. To access a particular data store, all that would be required was a driver designed specifically for that data store.

While Geiger worked on his proposal, engineers at DEC, Lotus, and Sybase were working on much the same idea. The four companies joined forces, and between 1988 and 1992 they helped shape the specification.

The original name for this project was Microsoft Data Access API. In early 1989, the effort was renamed Open SQL, and then in the summer of 1989, it was renamed again to SQL Connectivity. Finally, in the winter of 1992, the name was changed one last time to Open Database Connectivity, or ODBC.

The beta version of ODBC 1.0 was released in March 1992, and in September 1992, version 1.0 finally was released. Shortly thereafter, in October 1992, the specification was reviewed and accepted by the ANSI SQL committee.

ODBC itself is not a language; the language used by ODBC is SQL. Part of the magic of the ODBC database driver is that it understands SQL and converts it to whatever is appropriate for any specific database. This way, you can use SQL commands to work with xBASE-based databases (such as Microsoft FoxPro and Borland dBASE) and ISAM databases (such as Btrieve), even though they have entirely different native languages.

And herein lies the power of ODBC. The combination of database independence and a common standard language grants ODBC clients a tremendous level of freedom—freedom to use any database they want, freedom to use different databases for different tasks seamlessly and simultaneously, and freedom to concentrate on application development without having to learn database-specific languages and APIs.

Applications that use ODBC do not interact with the underlying databases directly. Rather, they communicate with ODBC data sources. A data source is kind of a virtual database—it is a saved profile that includes the ODBC driver to be used as well as necessary configuration options and settings. Data sources typically are defined using operating system features (such as the Control Panel in Windows), but the ColdFusion Administrator (as seen in Chapter 4, "Accessing the ColdFusion Administrator") provides a Web-based interface to creating and managing data sources that is ideally suited for Web-based development.

Note

Don't confuse ODBC data sources and ODBC drivers. ODBC *drivers* are dynamic link libraries (DLLs) that communicate with a specific data store type. A *data source* is a complete database configuration that uses an ODBC driver to communicate with a specific database.

A data source communicates with only one database. To use an ODBC driver to communicate with two or more of the same type of databases, you must create multiple data sources that all use the same ODBC driver.

Tip

In Chapter 4, "Accessing the ColdFusion Administrator," I walked you through creating the ODBC data source that you'll use in this chapter. If you did not create the data source, please refer back to that chapter and do so now so you can follow along with the examples.

UNDERSTANDING ODBC AND COLDFUSION

ColdFusion is an ODBC client. ODBC enables you to use ColdFusion with whichever database you choose. If you're using Microsoft Access, ColdFusion uses the Access driver; if you're using Oracle, the Oracle ODBC driver is used instead. You can even use ODBC to read and write plain-text files. As long as you have the correct ODBC driver, ColdFusion will support that data store.

Because ColdFusion is an ODBC client, the database language used by ColdFusion is SQL. To truly exploit the power of ColdFusion, you must have a thorough understanding of SQL. Fortunately, by the end of this chapter, you will know enough basic SQL to start generating world-class ColdFusion applications.

Note

ColdFusion Enterprise also supports the use of native database drivers that can be used instead of ODBC. The discussion of the pros and cons of ODBC versus native drivers is beyond the scope of this chapter, but suffice it to say that a knowledge of SQL is necessary regardless of the interface used.

Tip

This chapter (and the next) is by no means a complete SQL tutorial, so a good book on SQL is a must for ColdFusion developers. If you want a crash course on all the major SQL language elements, you might want to pick a copy of my *Sams Teach Yourself SQL in 10 Minutes* (ISBN: 0-672-31664-1).

PREPARING TO WRITE SQL QUERIES

Now that you have a data source, all you need is a client application with which to access the data. Ultimately, the client you will use is ColdFusion; after all, that is why you're reading this book. But to start learning SQL, you are best off using a standalone query tool, such as Microsoft Query or George Poulose's Query Tool.

Tip

As you start developing ColdFusion applications, you will find that most data-retrieval problems are caused by incorrect SQL statements. Query tools, such as the ones described here, are useful debugging tools because they enable you to test SQL statements interactively–providing a powerful way to validate SQL queries and isolate data-retrieval problems.

MICROSOFT QUERY

Microsoft Query is a SQL query utility. It is a simple ODBC database frontend Microsoft supplies with many of its other applications, including Microsoft Office. With Microsoft Query, you can test ODBC connectivity, interactively build SQL statements, and view the results of SQL queries, all in an easy-to-use environment. Microsoft Query is therefore a useful development and prototyping tool, and one well worth learning.

Note

If you set up Microsoft Office using the minimum setup, you might not have Microsoft Query installed. If this is the case, run the Office setup program again and select Microsoft Query from the Database Tools option.

Tip

Can't find MS Query on your computer? It often is hidden with no icon displayed. Use the Windows Find function to search for `MSQ*.EXE`; you'll often find one or more copies scattered across your hard drive.

Now run Microsoft Query. When the program loads, you should see a screen similar to the one shown in Figure 6.4. Along the top of the screen is the toolbar that gives you quick access to commonly used functions.

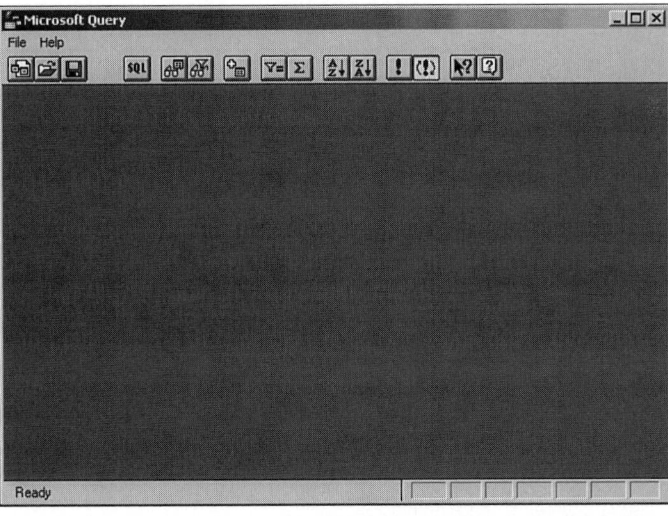

Figure 6.4 Microsoft Query is a multiple document interface (MDI) application. Using it, you can open multiple documents—or in this case, queries—at once.

Tip

The toolbar buttons in MS Query have ToolTips assigned to them. Just hold your mouse cursor over any button to display a pop-up title and a description in the status bar below.

To create a SQL query, select File, Execute SQL to open the Execute SQL dialog box, as shown in Figure 6.5. This dialog box enables you to type a SQL statement and then execute it (seeing the results if any are generated).

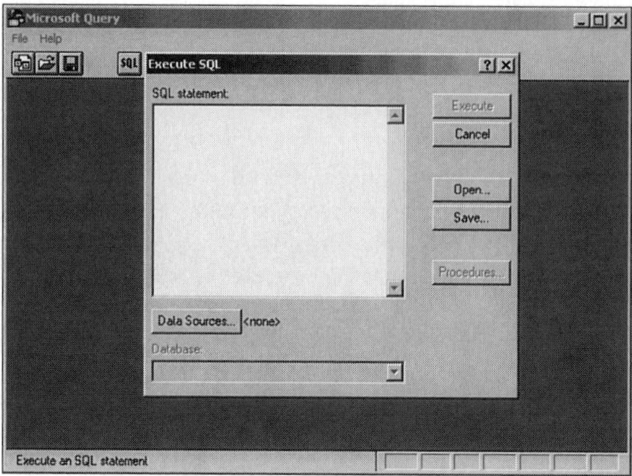

Figure 6.5
MS Query can be used to execute SQL statements typed directly into it.

The first thing you must do is tell MS Query which data source to use. Click the Data Sources button to display a dialog box similar to the one shown in Figure 6.6. Then select the desired data source (we'll be using the ows data source, so select that one), and click OK.

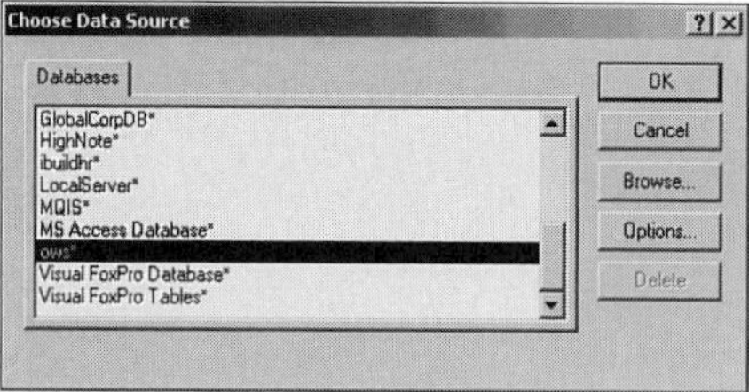

Figure 6.6
MS Query displays a list of all defined data sources, which can be selected and used.

After the data source is selected, you can type your SQL statement in the SQL Statement box and then click the Execute button to execute it. Results are displayed in a window that opens.

Tip

We'll use MS Query in this chapter to test manually entered SQL statements, but that is not all MS Query can do. If you select File, New and select a data source, you'll be able to use a wizard and query builder screens to build SQL statements interactively. But one warning, different versions of MS Query feature different screens and options, and not all features are available in all versions.

Query Tool

Query Tool is a wonderful little utility created by George Poulose. It provides interactive access to data sources and their contents, as well as SQL query execution and testing. If you can't find a copy of MS Query, you might want to take a look at this utility.

Tip

For your convenience, a copy of Query Tool is included on the accompanying CD. A copy also can be downloaded from this book's Web page: `http://www.forta.com/books/0789725843`.

When Query Tool is executed, the first thing it does is prompt you for the ODBC data source to be used (see Figure 6.7). Select the `ows` data source for the examples used in this chapter. (You might have to switch to the Machine Data Source pane to locate the data source.)

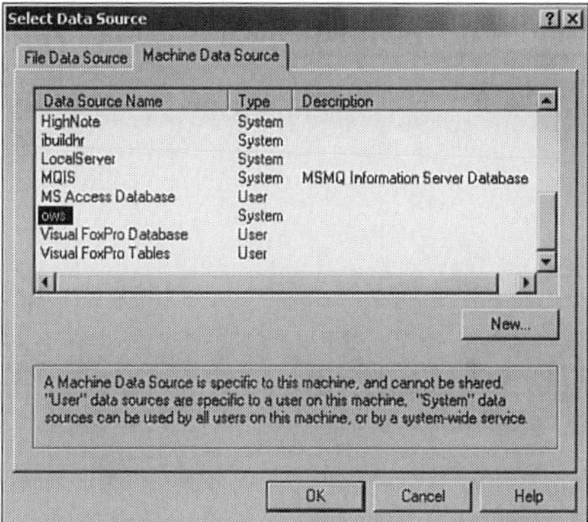

Figure 6.7 Query Tool automatically prompts you for the ODBC data source to use upon startup.

After a data source is selected, Query Tool displays a multipane screen (see Figure 6.8). The upper-left pane contains a tree control that can be used to browse the names of available tables and more. The upper-right pane is used to specify a SQL statement, and the bottom pane displays query results (if any exist) upon SQL statement execution. Execution occurs when the Execute Query button (the one with the blue arrow) is clicked or Query, Execute is selected.

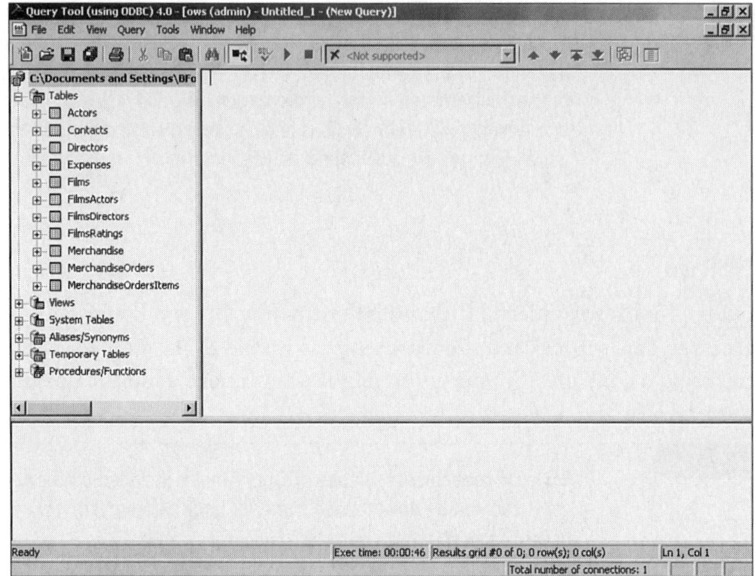

Figure 6.8
The Query Tool window is broken into multiple panes.

CREATING QUERIES

With all the preliminaries taken care of, you can roll up your sleeves and start writing SQL. The SQL statement you will use most is the SELECT statement. You use SELECT, as its name implies, to select data from a table.

Note

The following figures use MS Query, but the SQL and results will be the same regardless of the utility used.

Most SELECT statements require at least the following two parameters:

- What data you want to select, known as the *select list*. If you specify more than one item, you must separate each with a comma.
- The table (or tables) from which to select the data, specified with the FROM keyword.

The first SQL SELECT you will create is a query for a list of movies in the Films table. Type the code in Listing 6.1 as seen in Figure 6.9, and then execute the statement.

LISTING 6.1 SIMPLE SELECT STATEMENT

```
SELECT
MovieTitle
FROM Films
```

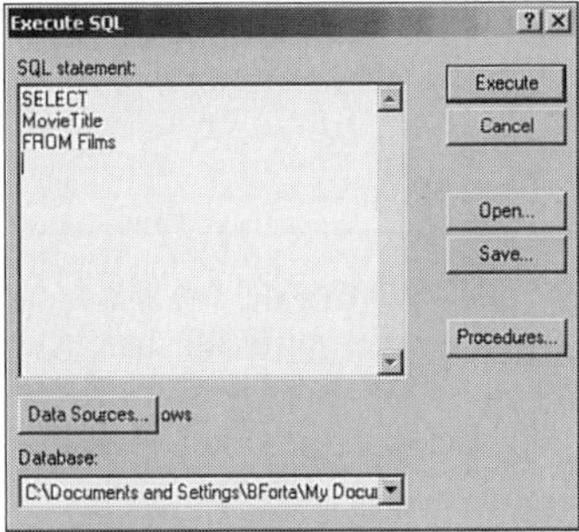

Figure 6.9
MS Query allows SQL statements to be entered manually and then executed.

That's it! You've written your first SQL statement. The results will be shown as seen in Figure 6.10 (assuming you are using MS Query).

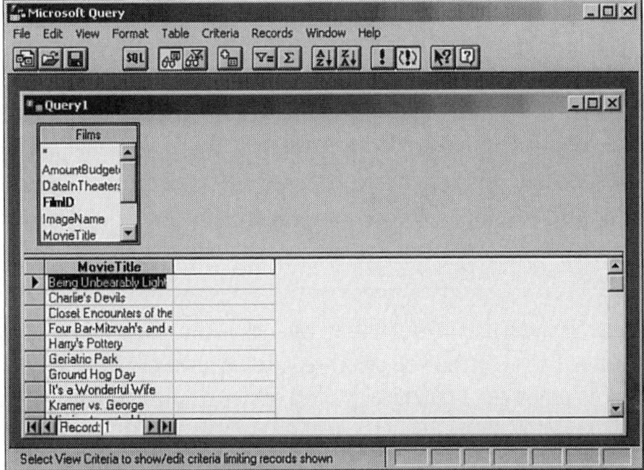

Figure 6.10
Microsoft Query displays query results in the data pane, the bottom part of the Query window.

Note

You can enter SQL statements on one long line or break them up over multiple lines. All whitespace characters (spaces, tabs, newline characters) are ignored when the command is processed. If you break a statement into multiple lines and indent parameters, you make the statement easier to read and debug.

Before you go any further, take a closer look at the SQL code you entered. The first parameter you pass to the `SELECT` statement is a list of the two columns you want to see. A column is specified by its name (for example, `MovieTitle`) or as *`table.column`* (such as `Films.MovieTitle`, where `Films` is the table name and `MovieTitle` is the column name).

Because you want to specify two columns, you must separate them with commas. No comma appears after the last column name, so if you have only one column in your select list, you don't need a comma.

Right after the select list, you specify the table on which you want to perform the query. You always precede the table name with the keyword FROM. The table is specified by name, in this case Films.

Note

SQL statements are not case sensitive; that is, you can specify the SELECT statement as SELECT, select, Select, or however you want. Common practice, however, is to enter all SQL keywords in uppercase and parameters in lowercase or mixed case. This way, you can read the SQL code and spot typos more easily.

Now modify the SELECT statement so it looks like the code in Listing 6.2; then execute it.

LISTING 6.2 SELECT ALL COLUMNS

```
SELECT
*
FROM Films
```

This time, instead of specifying explicit columns to select, you use an asterisk (*). The asterisk is a special select list option that represents all columns. The data pane now shows all the columns in the table in the order in which they appear in the table itself.

Caution

Generally, you should not use an asterisk in the select list unless you really need every column. Each column you select requires its own processing, and retrieving unnecessary columns can dramatically affect retrieval times as your tables get larger.

SORTING QUERY RESULTS

When you use the SELECT statement, the results are returned to you in the order in which they appear in the table. This is usually the order in which the rows were added to the table, typically not a sort order that is of much use to you. More often than not, when you retrieve data using a SELECT statement, you want to sort the query results. To sort rows, you need to add the ORDER BY clause. ORDER BY always comes after the table name; if you try to use it before, you generate a SQL error.

Now click the SQL button, enter the SQL code shown in Listing 6.3, and then click OK.

LISTING 6.3 SELECT WITH SORTED OUTPUT

```
SELECT MovieTitle, PitchText, Summary
FROM Films
ORDER BY MovieTitle
```

Your output is then sorted by the MovieTitle column, as shown in Figure 6.11.

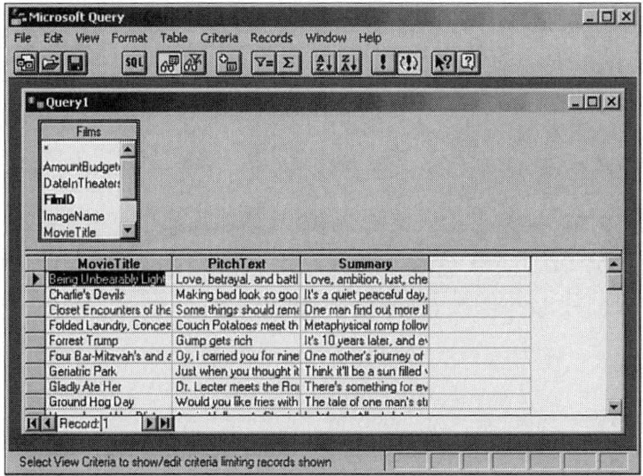

Figure 6.11
You use the `ORDER BY` clause to sort `SELECT` output.

What if you need to sort by more than one column? No problem. You can pass multiple columns to the `ORDER BY` clause. Once again, if you have multiple columns listed, you must separate them with commas. The SQL code in Listing 6.4 demonstrates how to sort on more than one column by sorting by `RatingID`, and then by `MovieTitle` within each `RatingID`. The sorted output is shown in Figure 6.12.

Listing 6.4 `SELECT` with Output Sorted on More Than One Column

```
SELECT RatingID, MovieTitle, Summary
FROM Films
ORDER BY RatingID, MovieTitle
```

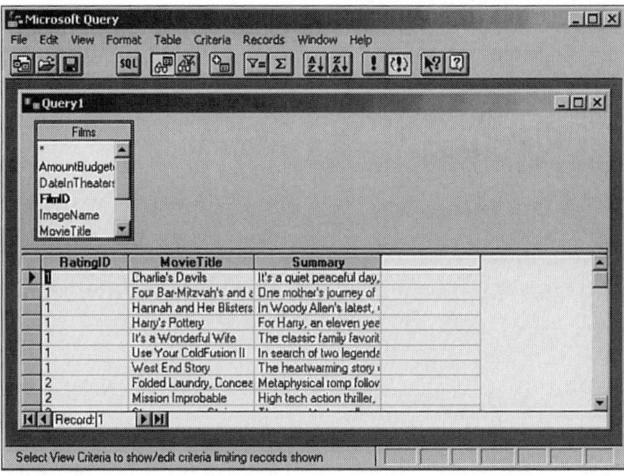

Figure 6.12
You can sort output by more than one column via the `ORDER BY` clause.

You also can use `ORDER BY` to sort data in descending order (Z–A). To sort a column in descending order, just use the `DESC` (short for descending) parameter. Listing 6.5 retrieves all the movies and sorts them by title in reverse order. Figure 6.13 shows the output that this SQL `SELECT` statement generates.

LISTING 6.5 SELECT WITH OUTPUT SORTED IN REVERSE ORDER

```
SELECT MovieTitle, PitchText, Summary
FROM Films
ORDER BY MovieTitle DESC
```

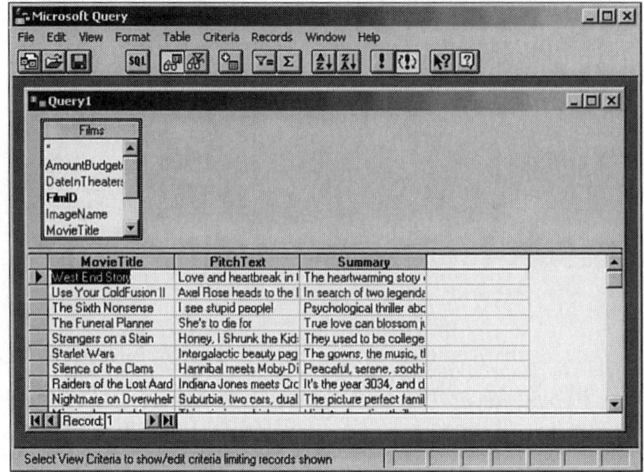

Figure 6.13
Using the ORDER BY clause, you can sort data in a descending sort sequence.

FILTERING DATA

So far, all your queries have retrieved all the rows in the table. You also can use the SELECT statement to retrieve only data that matches specific search criteria. To do so, you must use the WHERE clause and provide a restricting condition. If a WHERE clause is present, when the SQL SELECT statement is processed, every row is evaluated against the condition. Only rows that pass the restriction are selected.

If you use a WHERE clause, it must appear after the table name. If you use both the ORDER BY and WHERE clauses, the WHERE clause must appear after the table name but before the ORDER BY clause.

FILTERING ON A SINGLE COLUMN

To demonstrate filtering, modify the SELECT statement to retrieve only movies with a RatingID of 1. Listing 6.6 contains the SELECT statement, and the resulting output is shown in Figure 6.14.

LISTING 6.6 SELECT WITH WHERE CLAUSE

```
SELECT MovieTitle, PitchText, Summary
FROM Films
WHERE RatingID=1
ORDER BY MovieTitle DESC
```

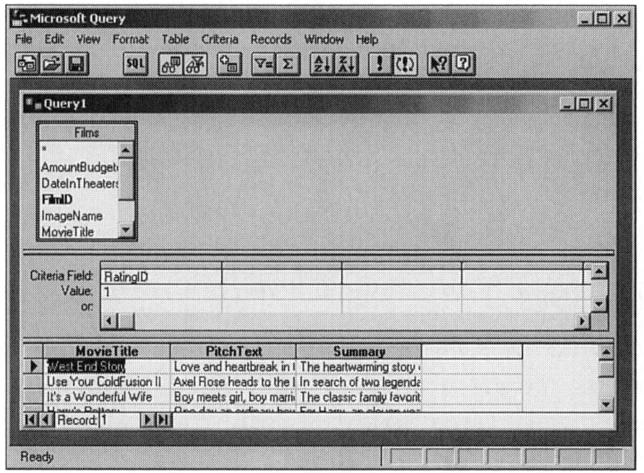

Figure 6.14
Using the WHERE clause, you can restrict the scope of a SELECT search.

FILTERING ON MULTIPLE COLUMNS

The `WHERE` clause also can take multiple conditions. To search for `Ben Forta`, you can specify a search condition in which the first name is `Ben` and the last name is `Forta`, as shown in Listing 6.7. As Figure 6.15 shows, only `Ben Forta` is retrieved.

LISTING 6.7 SELECT WITH MULTIPLE WHERE CLAUSES

```
SELECT FirstName, LastName, Email
FROM Contacts
WHERE FirstName='Ben' AND LastName='Forta'
```

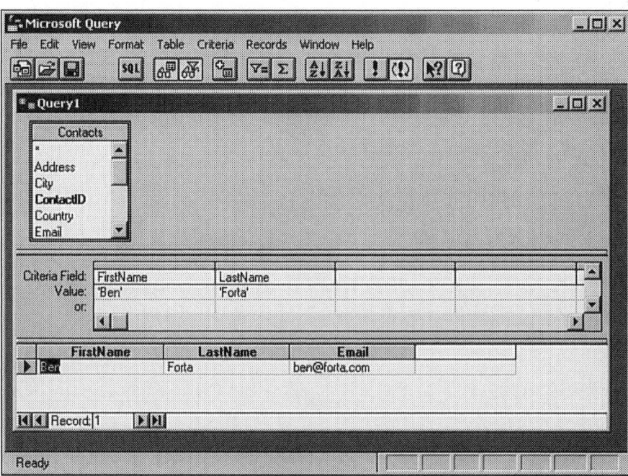

Figure 6.15
You can narrow your search with multiple WHERE clauses.

PART I CH 6

Note

Text passed to a SQL query must be enclosed within quotation marks. If you omit the quotation marks, the SQL parser thinks that the text you specified is the name of a column, and you receive an error because that column does not exist. Pure SQL allows strings to be enclosed within single quotation marks ('like this') or within double quotation marks ("like this").

But when passing text in a SQL statement to an ODBC driver, you *must* use single quotation marks. If you use double quotation marks, the ODBC parser treats the first double quotation mark as a statement terminator, ignoring all text after it.

THE AND AND OR OPERATORS

Multiple WHERE clauses can be evaluated as AND conditions or OR conditions. The example in Listing 6.7 is an AND condition. Only rows in which both the last name is Forta and the first name is Ben will be retrieved. If you change the clause to the following, contacts with a first name of Ben will be retrieved (regardless of last name) and contacts with a last name of Forta will be retrieved (regardless of first name):

```
WHERE FirstName='Ben' OR LastName='Forta'
```

You can combine the AND and OR operators to create any search condition you need. Listing 6.8 shows a WHERE clauses that can be used to retrieve only Ben Forta and Rick Richards.

LISTING 6.8 COMBINING WHERE CLAUSES WITH AND AND OR OPERATORS

```
SELECT NameFirst, NameLast, Email
FROM Contacts
WHERE FirstName='Ben' AND LastName='Forta'
 OR FirstName='Rick' AND LastName='Richards'
```

EVALUATION PRECEDENCE

When a WHERE clause is processed, the operators are evaluated in the following order of precedence:

- Parentheses have the highest precedence.
- The AND operator has the next level of precedence.
- The OR operator has the lowest level of precedence.

What does this mean? Well, look at the WHERE clause in Listing 6.8. The clause reads WHERE FirstName='Ben' AND LastName='Forta' OR FirstName='Rick' AND LastName='Richards'. AND is evaluated before OR so this statement looks for Ben Forta and Rick Richards, which is what we wanted.

But what would a WHERE clause of WHERE FirstName='Rick' OR FirstName='Ben' AND LastName='Forta' return? Does that statement mean *anyone whose first name is either Rick or Ben, and whose last name is Forta*, or does it mean *anyone whose first name is Rick, and also Ben Forta*? The difference is subtle, but if the former is true then only contacts with a last name of Forta will be retrieved, whereas if the latter is true then any Rick will be retrieved, regardless of last name.

So which is it? Because AND is evaluated first, the clause means *anyone whose first name is Rick, and also Ben Forta*, which might be what you want. And then again, it might not.

To prevent the ambiguity created by mixing AND and OR statements, parentheses are used to group related statements. Parentheses have a higher order of evaluation than both AND and OR, so they can be used to explicitly match related clauses. Consider the following WHERE clauses:

```
WHERE (FirstName='Rick' OR FirstName='Ben') AND (LastName='Forta')
```

This clause means *anyone whose first name is either Rick or Ben, and whose last name is Forta.*

```
WHERE (FirstName='Rick') OR (FirstName='Ben' AND LastName='Forta')
```

This clause means *anyone whose first name is Rick, and also Ben Forta.*

As you can see, the exact same set of WHERE clauses can mean very different things depending on where parentheses are used.

Tip

Always using parentheses whenever you have more than one WHERE clause is good practice. They make the SQL statement easier to read and easier to debug.

WHERE Conditions

For the examples to this point, you have used only the = (equal) operator. You filtered rows based on their being equal to a specific value. Many other operators and conditions can be used with the WHERE clause; they're listed in Table 6.2.

Table 6.2 WHERE Clause Search Conditions

Condition	Description
=	Equal to. Tests for equality
<>	Not equal to. Tests for inequality
<	Less than. Tests that the value on the left is less than the value on the right
<=	Less than or equal to. Tests that the value on the left is less than or equal to the value on the right
>	Greater than. Tests that the value on the left is greater than the value on the right
>=	Greater than or equal to. Tests that the value on the left is greater than or equal to the value on the right
BETWEEN	Tests that a value is in the range between two values; the range is inclusive

TABLE 6.2 CONTINUED

Condition	Description
EXISTS	Tests for the existence of rows returned by a subquery
IN	Tests to see whether a value is contained within a list of values
IS NULL	Tests to see whether a column contains a NULL value
IS NOT NULL	Tests to see whether a column contains a non-NULL value
LIKE	Tests to see whether a value matches a specified pattern
NOT	Negates any test

TESTING FOR EQUALITY: =

You use the = operator to test for value inequality. The following example retrieves only contacts whose last name is Smith:

```
WHERE LastName = 'Smith'
```

TESTING FOR INEQUALITY: <>

You use the <> operator to test for value inequality. The following example retrieves only contacts whose first name is not Kim:

```
WHERE FirstName <> 'Kim'
```

TESTING FOR LESS THAN: <

By using the < operator, you can test that the value on the left is less than the value on the right. The following example retrieves only contacts whose last name is less than C, meaning that their last name begins with an A or a B:

```
WHERE LastName < 'C'
```

TESTING FOR LESS THAN OR EQUAL TO: <=

By using the <= operator, you can test that the value on the left is less than or equal to the value on the right. The following example retrieves actors aged 21 or less:

```
WHERE Age <= 21
```

TESTING FOR GREATER THAN: >

You use the > operator to test that the value on the left is greater than the value on the right. The following example retrieves only movies with a rating of 3 or higher (greater than 2):

```
WHERE RatingID > 2
```

TESTING FOR GREATER THAN OR EQUAL TO: >=

You use the >= operator to test that the value on the right is greater than or equal to the value on the left. The following example retrieves only contacts whose first name begins with the letter J or higher:

```
WHERE FirstName >= 'J'
```

BETWEEN

Using the BETWEEN condition, you can test whether a value falls into the range between two other values. The following example retrieves only actors aged 20 to 30. Because the test is inclusive, ages 20 and 30 are also retrieved:

```
WHERE Age BETWEEN 20 AND 30
```

The BETWEEN condition is actually nothing more than a convenient way of combining the >= and <= conditions. You also could specify the preceding example as follows:

```
WHERE Age >= 20 AND Age <= 30
```

The advantage of using the BETWEEN condition is that it makes the statement easier to read.

EXISTS

Using the EXISTS condition, you can check whether a subquery returns any rows. Subqueries are explained in Chapter 31, "More About SQL and Queries."

IN

You can use the IN condition to test whether a value is part of a specific set. The set of values must be surrounded by parentheses and separated by commas. The following example retrieves contacts whose last name is Black, Jones, or Smith:

```
WHERE LastName IN ('Black', 'Jones', 'Smith')
```

The preceding example is actually the same as the following:

```
WHERE LastName = 'Black' OR LastName = 'Jones' OR LastName = 'Smith'
```

Using the IN condition does provide two advantages. First, it makes the statement easier to read. Second, and more importantly, you can use the IN condition to test whether a value is within the results of another SELECT statement.

IS NULL AND IS NOT NULL

A NULL value is the value of a column that is empty. The IS NULL condition tests for rows that have a NULL value; that is, the rows have no value at all in the specified column. IS NOT NULL tests for rows that have a value in a specified column.

The following example retrieves all contacts whose Email column is left empty:

```
WHERE Email IS NULL
```

To retrieve only the contacts who do have an e-mail address, use the following example:

```
WHERE Email IS NOT NULL
```

LIKE

Using the LIKE condition, you can test for string pattern matches using wildcards. Two wildcard types are supported. The % character means that anything from that position on is considered a match. You also can use [] to create a wildcard for a specific character.

The following example retrieves actors whose last name begins with the letter S. To match the pattern, a last name must have an S as the first character, and anything at all after it:

```
WHERE LastName LIKE 'S%'
```

To retrieve actors with an S anywhere in their last names, you can use the following:

```
WHERE LastName LIKE '%S%'
```

You also can retrieve just actors whose last name ends with S, as follows:

```
WHERE LastName LIKE '%S'
```

The LIKE condition can be negated with the NOT operator. The following example retrieves only actors whose last name does not begin with S:

```
WHERE LastName NOT LIKE 'S%'
```

Using the LIKE condition, you also can specify a wildcard on a single character. If you want to find all actors named Smith but are not sure whether the one you want spells his or her name Smyth, you can use the following:

```
WHERE LastName LIKE 'Sm[iy]th'
```

This example retrieves only names that start with *Sm*, then have an *i* or a *y*, and then a final *th*. With this example, as long as the first two characters are *Sm* and the last two are *th*, and as long as the middle character is *i* or *y*, the name is considered a match.

Tip

Using the powerful LIKE condition, you can retrieve data in many ways. But everything comes with a price, and the price here is performance. Generally, LIKE conditions take far longer to process than other search conditions, especially if you use wildcards at the beginning of the pattern. As a rule, use LIKE and wildcards only when absolutely necessary.

For even more powerful searching, LIKE may be combined with other clauses using AND and OR. And you may even include multiple LIKE clauses in a single WHERE clause.

CHAPTER 7

SQL Data Manipulation

In this chapter

ADDING DATA

Chapter 6, "Introduction to SQL," introduced ODBC, SQL, and data retrieval (using the `SELECT` statement). You'll probably find that you spend far more time retrieving data than you do inserting, updating, or deleting data (which is why we concentrated on `SELECT` first).

But you will need to insert data into tables at some point, so now let's take a look at data inserting using the `INSERT` statement.

Note

In this chapter, you will add, update, and delete rows from tables in the `ows` data source. The reason you delete any added rows is to ensure that any example code and screenshots later in the book actually look like you'd expect them to.

Feel free to add more rows if you'd like, but realize that if you do not clean up when you're finished, your screens will look different from the ones shown in the figures. This is not a problem, and you are welcome to do so; just keep it in mind so you know why things don't look the same.

USING THE `INSERT` STATEMENT

You use the `INSERT` statement to add data to a table. `INSERT` is usually made up of three parts:

- The table into which you want to insert data, specified with the `INTO` keyword.
- The column(s) into which you want to insert values. If you specify more than one item, each must be separated by a comma.
- The values to insert, which are specified with the `VALUES` keyword.

The `Directors` table contains the list of movie directors working with (or for) Orange Whip Studios. Directors cannot be assigned projects (associated with movies) if they are not listed in this table, so any new directors must be added immediately.

Note

As in the last chapter, Microsoft Query is used in this chapter for all screenshots. You can use it, too, or you can use any other SQL utility, including the ones mentioned in the previous chapter.

Run Microsoft Query and select File, Execute SQL to display the Execute SQL window. You'll notice that the Data Sources option is set to `<none>`, so you must select the `ows` data source (as you did in the previous chapter), as seen in Figure 7.1.

→ **See** Appendix E, "Sample Application Data Files," **p.XXX**, for an explanation of each of the data files and their contents.

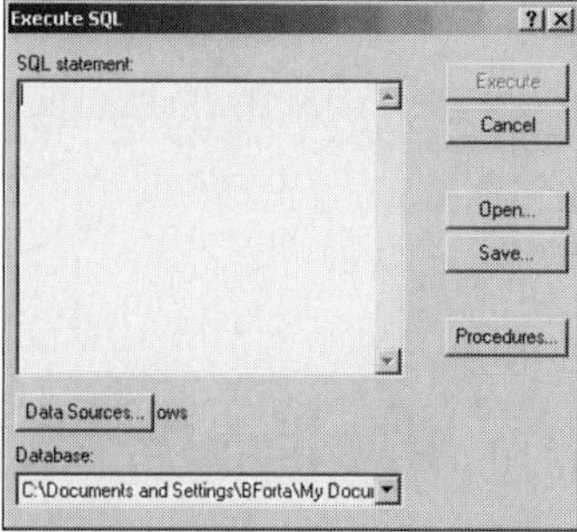

Figure 7.1
The Microsoft Query Execute SQL window is used to directly enter and execute any SQL statements.

Now you're ready to add the new director. The following code contains the SQL `INSERT` statement:

```
INSERT INTO Directors(FirstName, LastName)
VALUES('Benjamin', 'FORTA')
```

Enter this statement into the SQL Statement box (or whatever the equivalent is in your application), as seen in Figure 7.2. Feel free to replace my name with your own. When you're finished, click the Execute button to insert the new row. Assuming no problems occur, you should see a confirmation screen similar to the one shown in Figure 7.3.

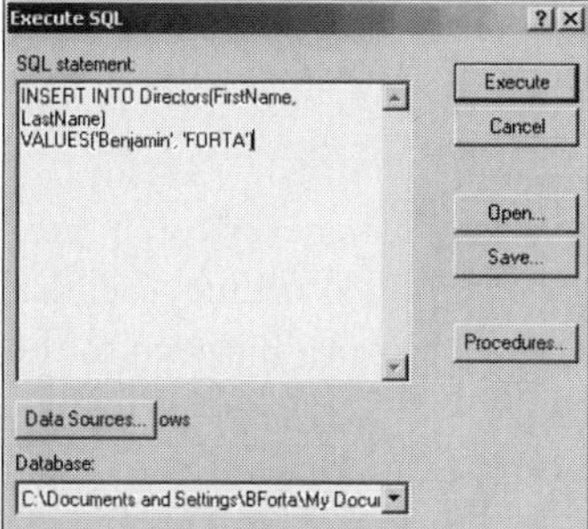

Figure 7.2
Type the statement into the SQL Statement box, and then click Execute.

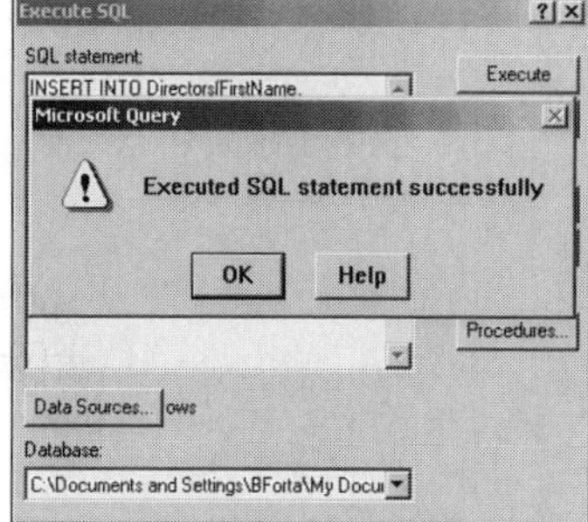

Figure 7.3
Microsoft Query notifies you regarding your SQL statements' successful execution.

UNDERSTANDING INSERT

Now that you've successfully inserted a row using the SQL INSERT statement, take a minute to look at the statement's syntax.

The first line of your statement reads as follows:

```
INSERT INTO Directors(FirstName, LastName)
```

The text immediately following the INTO keyword is the name of the table into which the new row is being inserted. In this case, it is the Directors table.

Next, the columns being added are specified. The columns are listed within parentheses, and if multiple columns are specified, each must be separated by a comma. A row in the Directors table requires both a FirstName and a LastName, so the INSERT statement specifies both columns.

Note

When you insert a row into a table, you can provide values for as many (or as few) columns as you prefer. The only restriction is that any columns defined as NOT NULL columns—meaning they can't be left empty—must have values specified. If you do not set a value for a NOT NULL column, the ODBC driver returns an error message and the row is not inserted.

The next line reads as follows:

```
VALUES('Benjamin', 'FORTA')
```

A value must be specified for every column listed whenever you insert a row. Values are passed to the VALUES keyword; all values are contained within parentheses, just like their column names. Two columns are specified, so two values are passed to the VALUES keyword.

Note

When inserting rows into a table, columns can be specified in any order. But be sure that the order of the values in the VALUES keyword exactly matches the order of the columns after the table name or you'll insert the wrong data into the columns.

To verify that the new director was added to the table, retrieve the complete list of directors using the following SQL statement:

```
SELECT * FROM Directors
```

As explained in Chapter 6, SELECT * means select all columns. As you can see in Figure 7.4, the new row was added to the table. Make a note of the DirectorID, which you'll need later to update or delete this row.

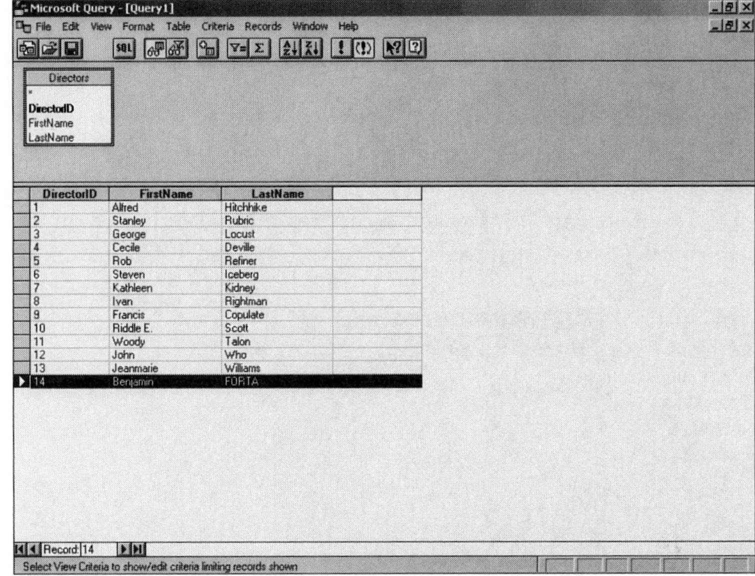

Figure 7.4
You can use Microsoft Query to execute SQL statements and verify the results of those statements.

Note

In the previous `INSERT` statement, no value was provided for the `DirectorID` column. So, where did that value come from? The `Directors` table was set up to automatically assign primary key values every time a new row is inserted. This is a feature supported by many databases–Access calls these AutoNumber columns, SQL Server uses the term Identity, and other databases have other names for the same feature. The end result is that you don't have to worry about creating unique values because the database does that for you.

Tip

`INSERT` can insert only one row at a time, unless the data being inserted is being retrieved from another table. In that case, a special form of the `INSERT` statement (called `INSERT SELECT`) can be used to insert all retrieved rows in a single operation.

Modifying Data

You use the SQL `UPDATE` statement to update one or more columns. This usually involves specifying the following:

- The table containing the data you want to update.
- The column or columns you want to update, preceded by the `SET` keyword. If you specify more than one item, each must be separated by a comma.
- An optional `WHERE` clause to specify which rows to update. If no `WHERE` clause is provided, all rows are updated.

Try updating a row. Open the Execute SQL window and enter the following SQL statement (ensuring that the ID number used in the `WHERE` clause is the `DirectorID` you noted earlier).

```
UPDATE Directors
SET FirstName='Ben'
WHERE DirectorID = 14
```

Your code should look similar to the example shown in Figure 7.5 (although the `DirectorID` might be different). Click Execute to perform the update. Microsoft Query displays a confirmation dialog box indicating that the operation completed successfully.

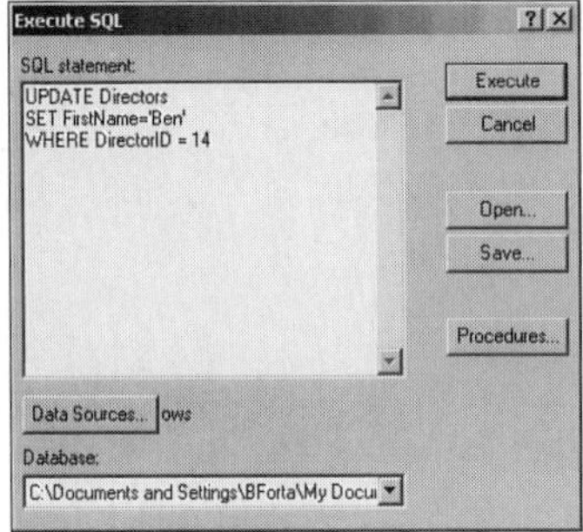

Figure 7.5
Update statements can be entered manually and entered on one line or broken over many lines.

If you now select the contents of the `Directors` table, you see that the new director's first name has been changed.

UNDERSTANDING UPDATE

Now, take a closer look at the SQL statement you just used. The first line issued the `UPDATE` statement and specified the name of the table to update. As with the `INSERT` and `DELETE` statements, the table name is required.

You next specified the column you wanted to change and its new value:

```
SET FirstName='Ben'
```

This is an instruction to update the `FirstName` column with the text `'Ben'`. The `SET` keyword is required for an `UPDATE` operation because updating rows without specifying what to update makes little sense.

The `SET` keyword can be used only once in an `UPDATE` statement. If you are updating multiple rows—for example, to change `Benjamin` to `Ben` and to set the `LastName` to `Forta` in one operation—the `SET` keyword would look like this:

```
SET FirstName='Ben', LastName='Forta'
```

When updating multiple columns, each column must be separated by a comma. The complete (revised) `UPDATE` statement would then look like this:

```
UPDATE Directors
SET FirstName='Ben', LastName='Forta'
WHERE DirectorID = 14
```

The last line of the code listing specifies a `WHERE` clause. The `WHERE` clause is optional in an `UPDATE` statement. Without it, all rows will be updated. The following code uses the primary key column to ensure that only a single row gets updated:

```
WHERE DirectorID = 14
```

To verify that the updates worked, try retrieving all the data from the `Directors` table. The results should be similar to those seen in Figure 7.6 (showing the updated final row).

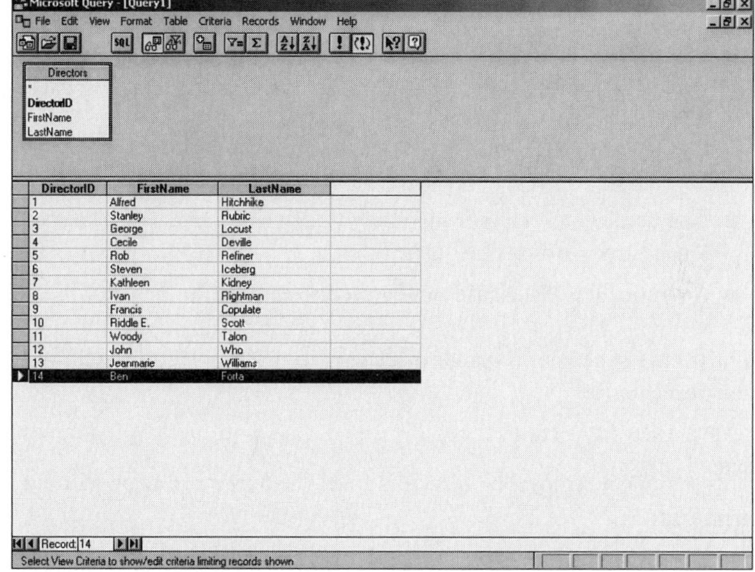

Figure 7.6
When experimenting with updates, it is a good idea to retrieve the table contents to check that the update worked properly.

> **Caution**
>
> Be sure to provide a `WHERE` clause when using the SQL `UPDATE` statement; otherwise, all rows will be updated.

MAKING GLOBAL UPDATES

You occasionally will want to update all rows in a table. To do this, you use `UPDATE`, too—you'd just omit the `WHERE` clause or specify a `WHERE` clause that matches multiple rows.

When updating multiple rows using a `WHERE` clause, always be sure to test that `WHERE` clause with a simple `SELECT` statement before executing the `UPDATE`. If the `SELECT` returns the correct data (the data you want updated), you'll know that it is safe to use with `UPDATE`. Failure to do this can result in you updating the wrong data!

> **Tip**
>
> Before executing `INSERT`, `UPDATE`, or `DELETE` operations that contain complex statements or `WHERE` conditions, you should test the statement or condition by using it in a

SELECT statement. If SELECT returns incorrect statement results or an incorrect subset of data filtered by the WHERE clause, you'll know that the statement or condition is incorrect.

The SELECT statement never changes any data, unlike INSERT, UPDATE, and DELETE. So, if an error exists in the statement or condition, you'll find out about it before any damage is done.

DELETING DATA

Deleting data from a table is even easier than adding or updating data—perhaps too easy.

You use the SQL DELETE statement to delete data. The statement takes only two parameters—one required and one optional:

- The name of the table from which to delete the data must be specified immediately following the words DELETE FROM.
- An optional WHERE clause can be used to restrict the scope of the deletion process.

The DELETE statement is dangerously easy to use. Look at the following line of code (but don't execute it):

```
DELETE FROM Directors
```

This statement removes all directors from the Directors table without any warnings or confirmation.

Tip

Some databases, client/server databases (such as Microsoft SQL Server and Oracle) in particular, offer safeguards against accidental (or malicious) deletions. There generally are two approaches to preventing mass deletion.

One is to create a *trigger* (a piece of code that runs on the server when specific operations occur) that verifies every DELETE statement and blocks any DELETE without a WHERE clause.

Another popular option is to restrict the use of DELETE without a WHERE clause based on login name. Only certain users, usually those with administrative rights, are granted permission to execute DELETE without a WHERE clause. Any other user attempting a mass DELETE will receive an error message, and the operation will abort.

Not all database systems support these techniques. Consult the database administrator's manuals to ascertain which safeguards are available to you.

The DELETE statement is most often used with a WHERE clause. For example, the following SQL statement deletes a single director from the Directors table (the one you just added):

```
DELETE FROM Directors
WHERE DirectorID=14
```

To verify that the row was deleted, retrieve all the `Directors` one last time (as seen in Figure 7.7).

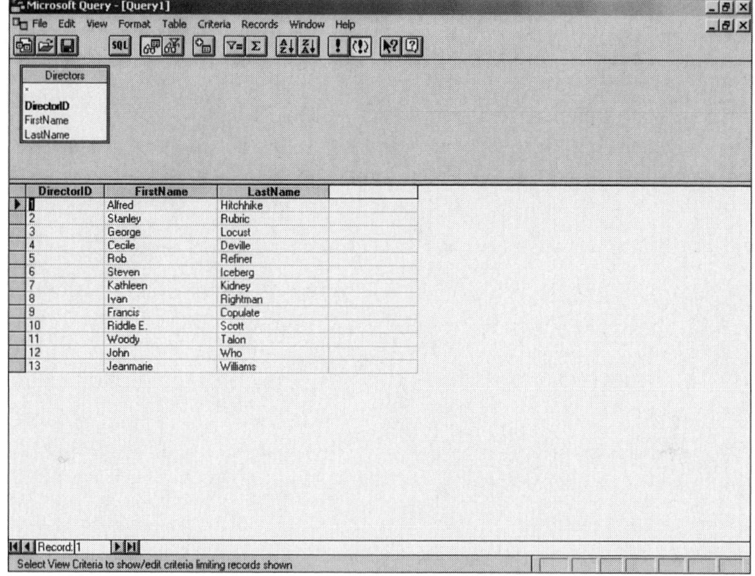

DirectorID	FirstName	LastName
1	Alfred	Hitchhike
2	Stanley	Rubric
3	George	Locust
4	Cecile	Deville
5	Rob	Refiner
6	Steven	Iceberg
7	Kathleen	Kidney
8	Ivan	Rightman
9	Francis	Copulate
10	Riddle E.	Scott
11	Woody	Talon
12	John	Who
13	Jeanmarie	Williams

Figure 7.7 Most databases delete rows immediately (as opposed to flagging them for deletion), and this will be reflected when listing the table contents.

As with all `WHERE` clauses, the `DELETE` statement's `WHERE` clause can be a `SELECT` statement that retrieves the list of rows to delete. If you do use a `SELECT` statement for a `WHERE` clause, be careful to test the `SELECT` statement first to ensure that it retrieves all the values you want, and only those values you want.

Tip

Feel free to `INSERT`, `UPDATE`, and `DELETE` rows as necessary, but when you're finished either clean up the changes or just copy overwrite the data file with the original (to restore it to its original state).

Note

Primary key values are never reused. If you `INSERT` rows after you have performed delete operations, the new rows will be assigned brand new IDs, and the old (deleted) IDs will not be reused. This behavior is a required part of how relational databases work as was explained in Chapter 3, "Building the Databases."

CHAPTER 8

Introduction to ColdFusion Studio

In this chapter

UNDERSTANDING COLDFUSION STUDIO

It is impossible to cover every aspect of Studio in one chapter, but I'll attempt to demonstrate some of the most important features to get you up and running. You are encouraged to experiment on your own. There is nothing in Studio that you can break by tinkering; the more you play with it, the more you'll discover, and the more useful a tool it will be.

To understand what ColdFusion Studio is and how it can simplify your application development, you first need to understand what it is not.

ColdFusion Studio (referred to as Studio from this point on) is not a WYSIWYG HTML generator. Nor is it an HTML authoring tool. It will not let you drag and drop page elements onto a page to generate the underlying HTML. In fact, it makes no effort to try to conceal HTML from you.

Quite the opposite. In fact, Studio tries very hard to expose all the underlying code, ensuring that you, the developer, have full control over it.

So what exactly is ColdFusion Studio?

ColdFusion Studio is an editor, much like Windows Notepad. With Studio you create and open files, write your code, and save files, just as you would in any other editor. But that's where the similarity ends. Unlike typical editors, Studio was designed from the ground up as a programmer's editor. It is based on HomeSite, the award-winning HTML editor used by more than a quarter of a million Web page designers and boasts a feature set that no other editor can match:

- Menus and toolbars provide shortcuts to the most common tags and functions.
- Multiple document interface.
- Automatic color coding of HTML, CFML, and other languages.
- Wizards and templates.
- Drag-and-drop editing and context-sensitive right–mouse-click options.
- Design mode to simplify the creation of some HTML elements (such as tables).
- Integrated image and thumbnail viewer.
- Edit dialog box for most HTML and CFML tags (and you can even create your own dialog box for your own tags).
- Pop-up help for all HTML and CFML tags.
- Automatic tag completion.
- Built-in expression builder.
- Built-in SQL query builder.
- Integrated project management.
- Built-in HTML validation.
- Open and save files over an Internet connection (using HTTP or FTP).
- Built-in support for version control systems.

The bottom line is that if you are serious about Web application development and serious about development with ColdFusion, ColdFusion Studio is a must.

Note

At the time that this book went to press, ColdFusion Studio 5 was not yet available. As such, the software described in this chapter is ColdFusion 4.5.2 with the add-on extensions for ColdFusion 5 support installed.

The information presented here will be of use in ColdFusion Studio 5 when it is available. If there are significant differences then, an electronic version of this chapter will be made available on the book's Web page `http://www.forta.com/books/0789725843/`.

RUNNING COLDFUSION STUDIO

If you haven't already done so, start Studio by selecting ColdFusion Studio from your Programs menu (which usually is in a group called ColdFusion Studio followed by a version number).

Note

If you have not yet installed ColdFusion Studio, now is a good time to do so. Refer to Chapter 2, "Installing ColdFusion and ColdFusion Studio," for installation instructions.

INTRODUCING COLDFUSION STUDIO

Start with a quick guided tour of the Studio environment shown in Figure 8.1.

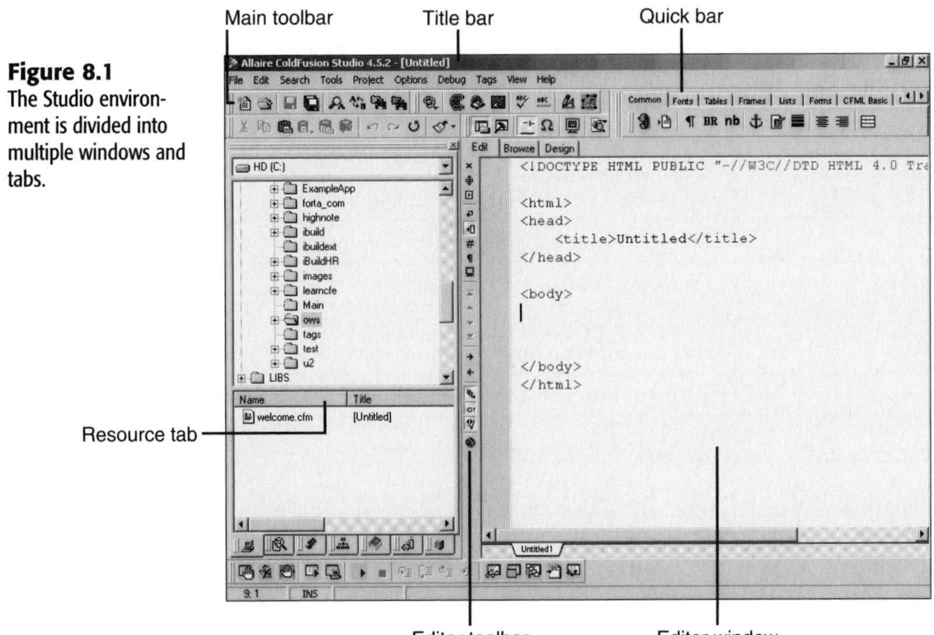

Figure 8.1
The Studio environment is divided into multiple windows and tabs.

The top of the screen has two toolbars. The main toolbar on the left contains buttons for opening and saving files; performing searches; cut, copy, and paste operations; undo and redo; search; and more. The Quick Bar toolbar on the right is actually a collection of tabbed toolbars containing dozens of tag shortcuts and wizards. Table 8.1 lists the tabs of the tag toolbar and what each one contains. The exact layout and placement of tabs is highly configurable. If your screen does not exactly match the one shown in Figure 8.1, it is because some tabs have been changed or relocated.

TABLE 8.1 COLDFUSION STUDIO TAG TOOLBARS

Tab	Description
ASP	Options useful to ASP developers
CFFORM	ColdFusion `<CFFORM>` tags, including the ColdFusion Java controls
CFML Advanced	Advanced ColdFusion tags, including `<CFCOOKIE>`, `<CFMAIL>`, `<CFPOP>`, `<CFLDAP>`, `<CFHTP>`, `<CFFTP>`, and the Verity interface tags
CFML Basic	Basic ColdFusion tags, including `<CFQUERY>`, `<CFOUTPUT>`, `<CFSET>`, and `<CFINCLUDE>`
CFML Flow	ColdFusion flow control tags, including `<CFIF>` and `<CFCASE>`
Common	Commonly used tags (paragraph and line breaks, bold, links, horizontal rules) and quick start options for creating header and body tags
Debug	Options to manage the debugger, including setting breakpoints, trace options, and setting debugger options
Edit	Copy, cut, paste, undo, redo, and related editing options
Fonts	Font face, color, and size control, and the heading tags
Forms	Forms and all form field types
Frames	Frame wizard and all the frame-related tags
JSP	Options useful to JSP developers
Linkbot	Options for use with the Linkbot utility
Lists	Menus, ordered lists, unordered lists, and list items
Script	JavaScript and other scripting-related options
Standard	File open, save, search, replace, and similar options
Tables	Table wizard, all the table tags, and a Quick Table button that creates a basic table for you based on the size you select
Tools	Color palette, link verification, spell checker, and other tools
View	Enable and disable tabs and views

You can select a button from any of these toolbars to automatically insert HTML or CFML tags into the document you are editing. Some buttons insert text, and others bring up dialog boxes, prompting you for additional information, inserting the text after you fill in the fields and click Apply.

To the left of the screen is the Resource Tab. This is a multipurpose tab that actually contains six tabs. Table 8.2 lists the tabs and what each is used for. You select the tab you want by clicking the tab selectors at the bottom of the Resource tab.

TABLE 8.2 COLDFUSION STUDIO RESOURCE TABS

Tab	Description
Files	Local files and directories in a Windows Explorer–style window, as well as access to remote files via RDS (explained later) and FTP.
Database	Access to ODBC (and other) data sources on either a local or remote server (which is discussed later).
Projects	Project management, create and work with entire projects rather than one file at a time.
Site View	Site-management features.
Snippets	Create your own code snippets that you can insert into any page.
Help	Help library.
Tag Inspector	Tag drill-down view of pages.

Tip

Hold your mouse over any button to display a pop-up description of what that button does.

The right side of the screen is the ColdFusion editor itself. This highly customizable editor is where you actually write your Web pages. If you click buttons on any of the tag toolbars, the code is inserted right where the flashing cursor is.

To the left of the Editor window is the editor toolbar, which contains 18 buttons you can use to control the editor itself. For example, clicking the top button closes the currently active file, and clicking the third option displays a pop-up list of all files currently open. Other buttons are used to turn on or off word wrap, text indentation, and pop-up help.

Tip

The Resource tab is a very important part of ColdFusion Studio, and you will probably want access to it at all times. However, it does take up a significant amount of screen space. To save space, you can hide and display the entire Resource tab by toggling the F9 key, thus displaying it only when necessary.

WORKING WITH FILES

Studio is an editor, and most of your time using Studio will be spent working with files. These will usually be plain HTML Web pages or ColdFusion application pages. Studio gives you several ways to create, open, and manipulate files:

- The File menu contains the standard file manipulation options, such as New, Open, Save, and Close.
- The main toolbar contains buttons for creating and opening files.
- Double-clicking any file in the Resource tab's local window opens that file for editing.

The Studio title bar shows the name of the file currently open and active in the editor. There is no limit to the number of files you can open at one time, but there's more on that when the multiple-document interface is discussed later in this chapter.

Note

If the active file has never been saved, it is named Untitled and that is the name displayed in Studio's title bar.

USING THE EDITOR

The heart of ColdFusion Studio is its editor. This is obviously where you do most of your work, and thus, this is where the Studio feature set shines.

This has been said before, but it bears repeating—Studio is not an HTML authoring tool, and it won't write HTML or CFML for you. Studio assumes that you, the developer, want to be in complete control of the application development effort. At the same time, Studio attempts to simplify the development process without getting in your way.

To demonstrate the Studio editor, open any HTML or CFML file. Use the File, Open menu option, click the Main Toolbar Open button, or just browse through the local files in the Resource tab and double-click any file to open it.

USING COLOR-CODING

The first thing you'll notice is that the text in the editor window is color-coded. Color-coding is used to highlight specific tags or text, and Studio performs all color-coding automatically. There are two primary reasons to use color-coding:

- Color-coded text makes it easy to quickly find specific tags or tag types. For example, all table-related tags are shown in one color, whereas all ColdFusion tags are shown in another.
- Color-coding makes finding mistakes in your code easier. If a tag or block of text does not display in the correct color, you'll know right away that you've made a typo there. If you do something as simple as omitting the > symbol from the end of the tag, you'll immediately see that the text after the tag is incorrectly color-coded.

Color-coding can be turned off by selecting Color Coding from the Setting dialog box in the Options menu, but there is seldom a reason to do so unless you are working with massive files (so large that Studio takes a significant amount of time to perform the color-coding). As a rule, you should always keep color-coding turned on.

Tip

> You can change the colors Studio uses for color-coding by selecting the Color Coding tab from the Options Settings dialog box (or by pressing F8).

Using Toolbars

As mentioned earlier, the tag toolbars provide shortcuts to commonly used HTML and CFML tags. Clicking any button on any tag toolbar either inserts tag text or displays a dialog box that prompts you for tag options. To try this out, follow these steps:

1. Close any files you have opened. (You can simply right-click the file in the Editor window and select Close.)
2. Type the text **`My first page written in Studio`** in the Editor window.
3. Highlight the text you just typed with your mouse.
4. Click the Bold button (the one with the big bold B on it) on the Fonts toolbar.

Studio automatically applies the HTML bold tags (`<B>` and `</B>`) to the highlighted text, as shown in Figure 8.2.

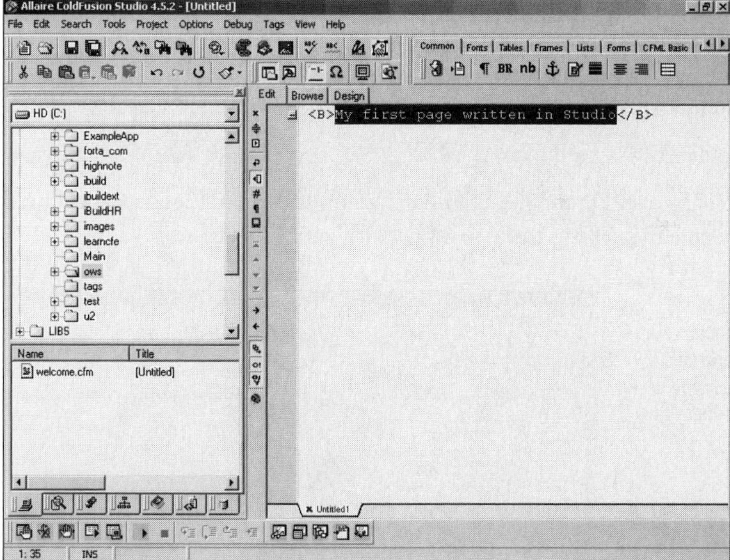

Figure 8.2 Studio enables you to highlight text and select a tag toolbar button to apply tags to that text.

Try another example. This time you create an HTML table:

1. Close any files you have opened. (You can simply right- click the file in the Editor window and select Close.)
2. Select the Tables Toolbar tag.
3. Click the Table Sizer button (the one on the right) to display a table selection box, as shown in Figure 8.3.

4. Move your mouse down and to the right to select the number of rows and columns you want in your HTML table.
5. When you have highlighted the number of desired rows and columns, click your mouse to make the selection.

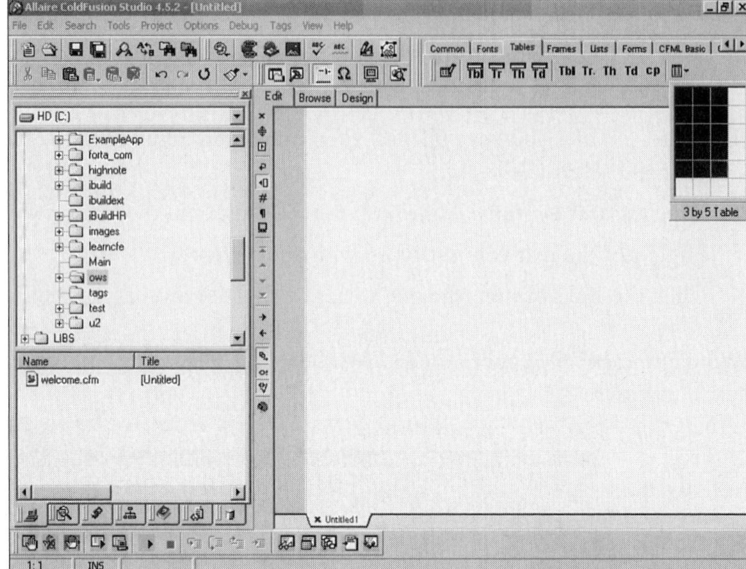

Figure 8.3
The Table Sizer button enables you to quickly generate code to create HTML tables.

As shown in Figure 8.4, Studio generates the HTML code for your table, and it even indents the cells to make working with your table easier.

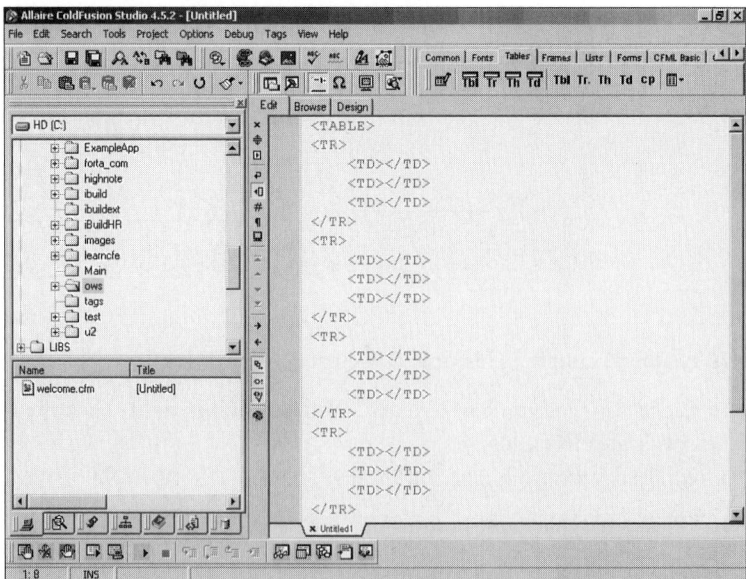

Figure 8.4
Studio automatically indents generated HTML table code to make working with tables easier.

As you can see, the tag toolbar buttons are both a tremendous timesaver and a way to help ensure that you don't mistype tags or tag attributes.

Caution

When clicking tag toolbar buttons, pay close attention to where you editor cursor is. Studio inserts the selected tag at the current cursor position. If the cursor is in the wrong place (in the middle of another tag, for example), that's where the text is inserted.

USING THE SPLIT-SCREEN EDITOR

Often you'll find yourself working with large files, needing to see and use different parts of the file at the same time. ColdFusion Studio enables you to split the editor screen in two so that two different parts of the same file can be displayed and edited at the same time.

To split the editor window, simply click the Split Current Document button in the Editor toolbar (the second one from the top), or you can select Split Editor from the Options menu. The screen will split, as seen in Figure 8.5, and you can even move the splitter bar up and down to change the window sizes as necessary.

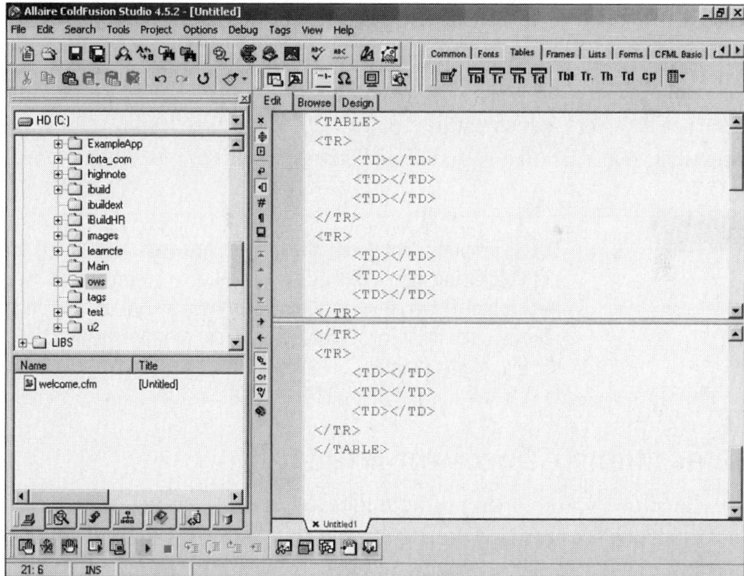

Figure 8.5
Split editor screen mode greatly simplifies working with long files.

BROWSING YOUR WEB PAGES

Because Studio is not a WYSIWYG authoring tool, what you see in the editor is code, not the generated output. To view the page your code creates, you must browse that page.

If you have Microsoft Internet Explorer installed on your computer, Studio can use it internally to display your page, as shown in Figure 8.6. To browse a page this way, just click the Browse tab above the Editor window. You can also use the F12 key to toggle between edit and browse modes.

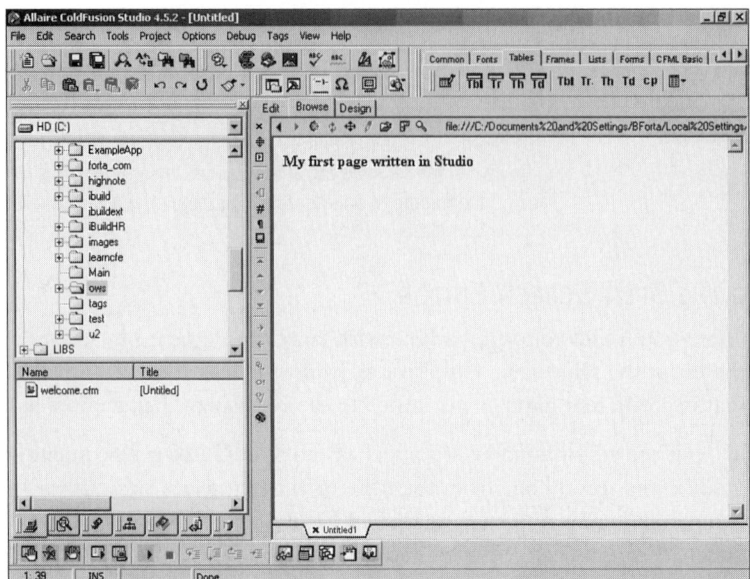

Figure 8.6
Studio can use Microsoft Internet Explorer as its internal browser if it is installed.

Web developers often need to view their pages in more than one browser. This is generally good practice because of browser incompatibilities and differences. Studio lets you configure external browsers, which can be spawned from within Studio as necessary. To set up external browsers, select Configure External Browsers from the Options menu.

Note

Unless properly configured, the internal browser can be used to view HTML files, but not ColdFusion files—ColdFusion files must be preprocessed by the ColdFusion Application Server. If you attempt to browse a CFM or CFML file, Studio will likely display an error message. Configuring Studio to properly display CFM files is explained at the end of this chapter.

USING THE MULTIPLE DOCUMENT INTERFACE

Studio allows you to open multiple files at once. When you open multiple files, each one has a tab at the bottom of the Editor window, as shown in Figure 8.7. You can click these tabs to switch between files. The tab belonging to the file that is actually open is shown brighter and in the foreground, so you'll always know which file you are looking at. In addition, the Studio title bar also shows the name of the currently active file.

The file tabs at the bottom of the Editor window have another important use. They indicate which files have been saved and which have not. The text in the tab changes to blue and an X is displayed to the left of the filename as soon as any changes are made to that file. After the file is saved, the text is displayed in black and the X is removed. This makes seeing which files have not been saved yet easy.

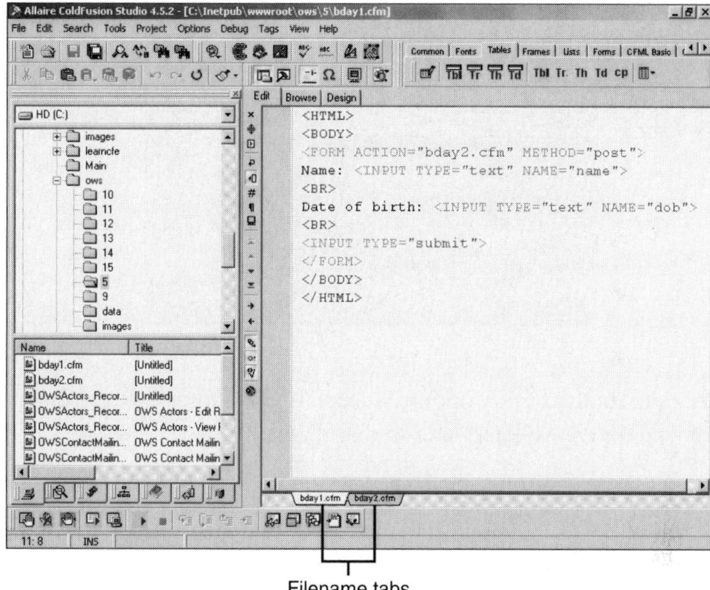

Figure 8.7
The ColdFusion Editor window displays a tab for each open document.

USING THE RIGHT MOUSE BUTTON

Right-clicking is probably the most important tip to remember when using Studio. Studio makes extensive use of the right mouse button, particularly in the Editor window. Studio's right mouse button support is *context sensitive*, which means the options displayed vary, based on where you right-click. Try right-clicking any tag. You'll see a pop-up menu similar to the one shown in Figure 8.8. You can select the Edit Tag option to display a context-sensitive tag dialog box, like the one shown in Figure 8.9.

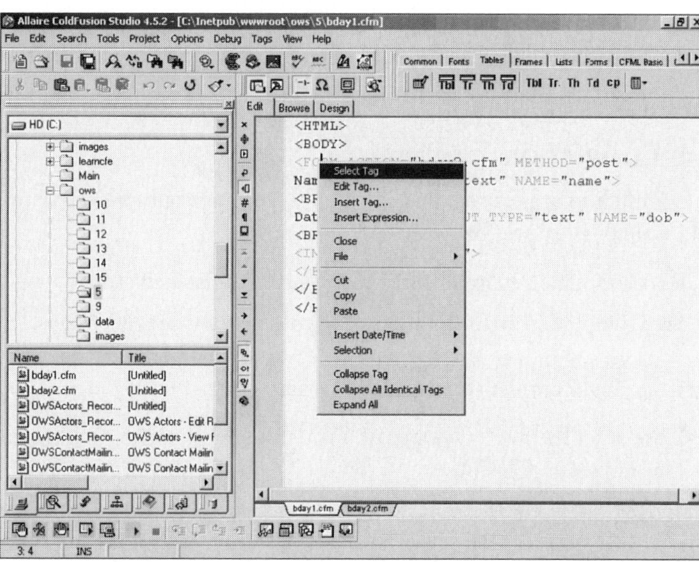

Figure 8.8
Clicking the right mouse button in Studio displays a pop-up, context-sensitive options menu.

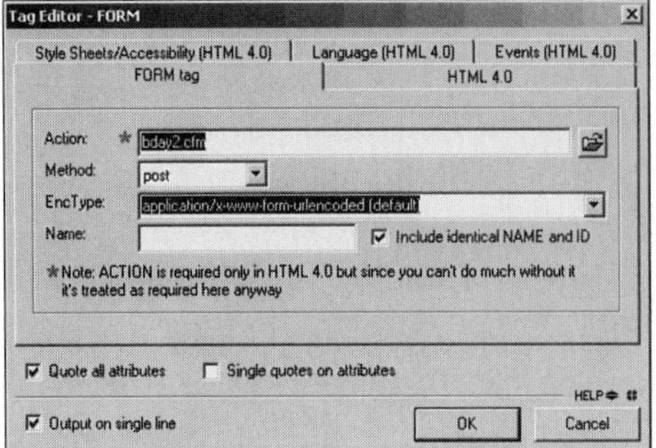

Figure 8.9
Selecting Edit Tag from the right mouse button menu displays a tag-specific editing dialog box.

Other right mouse button options include Insert Expression and Insert SQL Statement. These options are explored later in this chapter.

The right mouse button can also be used in the Resource tab. Right-click any file or directory to display a pop-up menu of relevant options.

Tip

Use the right mouse button extensively. Because it is context sensitive, you are always presented with a list of useful options.

GETTING HELP

ColdFusion developers have to remember the HTML language, CFML tags and functions, SQL interfaces, and communication with many other protocols and standards. That's a lot of information to remember, and most developers keep a selection of reference books and manuals close by at all times.

Studio greatly simplifies the process of finding the help you need. It boasts an extensive array of help-related features, all designed to give you immediate, useful, and relevant help. The following sections look at some of these features.

USING TAG COMPLETION

Tag Completion is a feature that lets Studio automatically finish writing tags for you. This is an invaluable feature for two reasons:

- Tag Completion helps ensure that you don't mistakenly miss a tag's required ending tag.
- Tag Completion writes end tags for you, helping prevent typos.

To try out Tag Completion, do the following:

1. Close any files you have opened. (You can simply right-click the file in the Editor window and select Close.)
2. In the Editor window, type `<UL>` (to create an unordered list).

As soon as you type the > at the end of `<UL>`, Studio automatically inserts the matching `</UL>` tag and places your cursor between them so you can continue typing.

Tip

Tag Completion can be disabled by clicking the Tag Completion button in the editor toolbar or in the Tag Help tab in the Options, Settings dialog box.

Tip

You can add tags to the list of tags to be completed in the Tag Help tab in the Options, Settings dialog box.

Using Tag Tips

Tag tips are inline, pop-up help dialog boxes shown right in your Editor window. Tag tips pop up if you press the F2 key while the typing cursor is on a tag. The Tag tips for the `<BODY>` tag are shown in Figure 8.10.

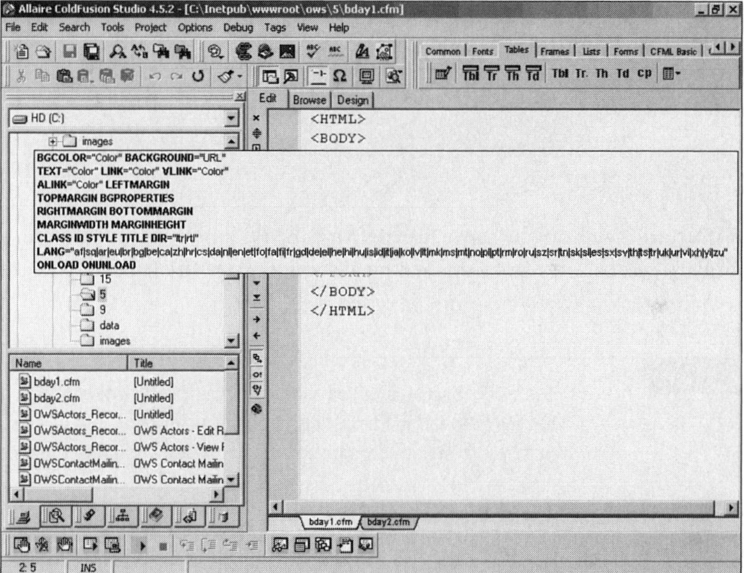

Figure 8.10
Tag tips appear right in the Editor window to provide tag-specific help.

Using Tag Insight and Function Insight

Tag Insight takes online help to the next level by providing pop-up, interactive, tag-specific, and function-specific help, as shown in Figure 8.11. To try this out, do the following:

1. Close any files you have opened. (You can simply right-click the file in the Editor window and select Close.)
2. In the Editor window, type **`<BODY`** and then wait a second or two.

3. Studio displays a pop-up selectable menu of all the attributes appropriate for the tag you are editing—the <BODY> tag in this case.
4. Select any attribute to insert it into your tag.

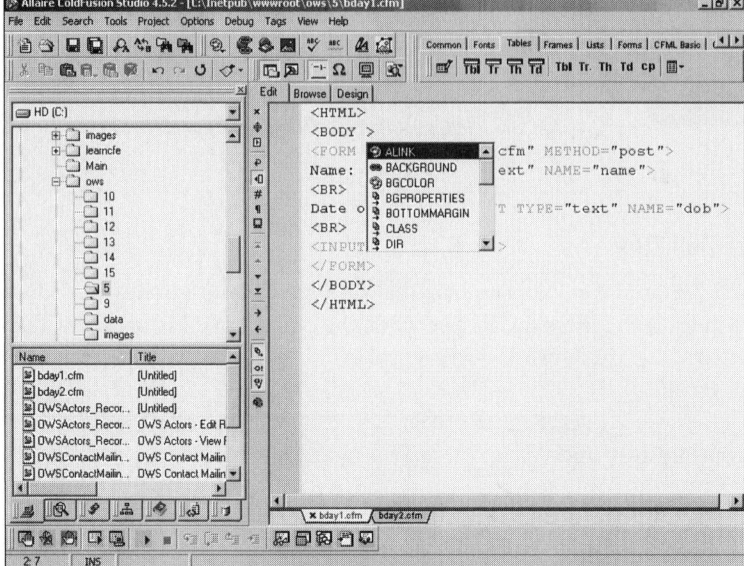

Figure 8.11
Tag Insight can be used to display interactive, tag-specific help.

Function Insight is the same feature for CFML functions and is used the same way. Function attributes are displayed for selection after the parentheses are opened (with the (character) or when a comma is typed.

Tip

Tag Insight can be disabled by clicking the Tag Insight button in the editor toolbar or in the Tag Help tab in the Options, Settings dialog box. You can also adjust the *delay* (the number of seconds Studio should wait before displaying the menu).

USING EDIT DIALOG BOX HELP

Studio can display tag-specific edit dialog boxes to help you create and edit tags. Any options you select or fill in are added as tag attributes to the tag when you click the Apply button.

Many of these edit dialog boxes, those for ColdFusion tags in particular, have optional syntax help built right into them. If help is available for a specific tag, two little buttons are displayed at the bottom right of the dialog box. These buttons toggle on and off the help display, in either the dialog box itself (as shown in Figure 8.12) or in a separate window.

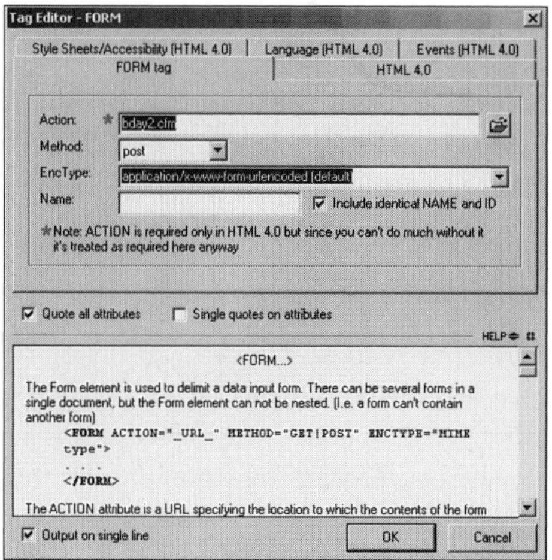

Figure 8.12
Many tag edit dialog boxes have built-in, embedded syntax help.

USING ONLINE HELP

In addition to all the help options just discussed, Studio also has a complete online searchable help library. To access the help, click the Help tab in the Resource tab (the one with a purple book with the yellow question mark). You'll see a list of Help References you can browse or search, as shown in Figure 8.13.

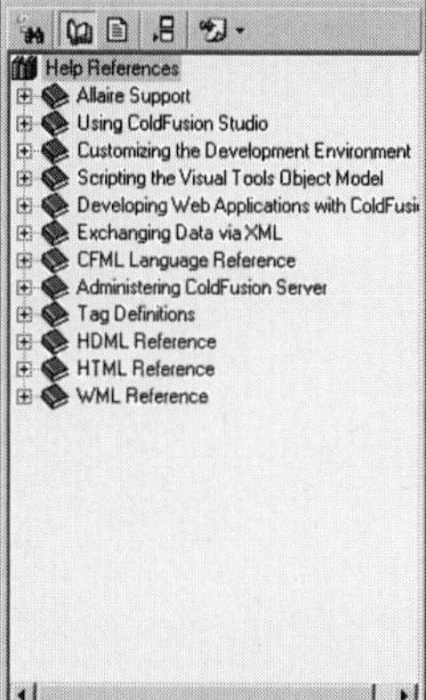

Figure 8.13
Studio comes with a complete, searchable reference library.

To search for a specific topic, click the Search button (the one with the binoculars on it). This displays a Help Search dialog box, where you can type in any search text.

Tip

Context-sensitive help for specific tags and functions also can be displayed as necessary by clicking the tag or function and pressing F1.

USING TAGS AND EXPRESSIONS

ColdFusion developers spend much of their time working with tags and expressions, so Studio provides interactive utilities to make both of these operations easier.

This section explores two of these interactive utilities: the Tag Chooser and the Expression Builder. Both of these tools, as well as other useful tools, are available as menu selections and as right-click options.

USING THE TAG CHOOSER

The Tag Chooser is a drill-down tree interface to HTML and CFML tags, as well as other tag types, such as HDML and VTML, and even to custom tags. It is accessible via the right-click menu in the Editor window or by selecting Tag Chooser from the Tools menu.

The Tag Chooser's primary purpose is to help you find the tag you are looking for by context or category. To try the Tag Chooser, do the following:

1. Close any files you have opened. (You can simply right-click the file in the Editor window and select Close.)
2. Right-click in the Editor window and select Insert Tag to display the Tag Chooser dialog box, as shown in Figure 8.14.
3. Expand the HTML tag list by double-clicking HTML tags or by clicking the + items symbol.
4. Select Tables to display the list of table-related tags.
5. Double-click the TABLE item to display the Table dialog box.
6. Click the Apply button to insert the tag into your document.

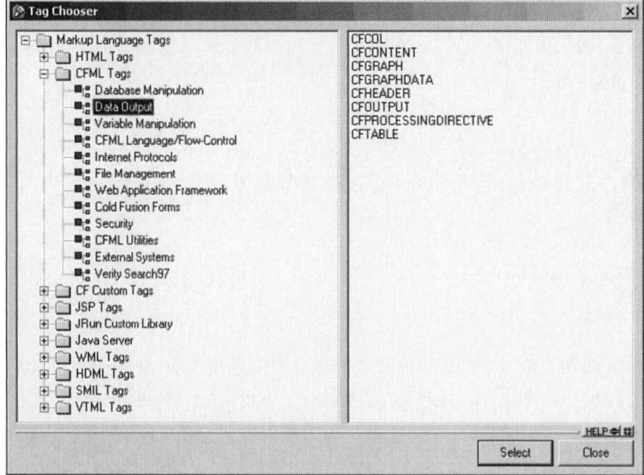

Figure 8.14
The Studio Tag Chooser lets you drill down through a list of tags to find what you are looking for.

Tip

The Tag Chooser dialog box can also display tag-specific help if you click either of the help buttons on the bottom right of the dialog box.

Using the Expression Builder

ColdFusion *expressions* are collections of references, ColdFusion functions, variables, and operators. Expressions are an important part of ColdFusion application development, so Studio provides an Expression Builder to help you construct and edit expressions. It is accessible via the right-click menu in the Editor window or by selecting Expression Builder from the Tools menu.

Note

Don't worry if you are unfamiliar with expressions; they are covered extensively throughout this book. For now, you are shown how to use the builder so you can take advantage of it later.

The Expression Builder, shown in Figure 8.15, works much like the Tag Chooser. You select the element type you want (function, constant, operator, or variable), and then drill down to find the specific expression element you are seeking. As you select elements, they are displayed at the top of the Expression Builder dialog box so you can see and edit the complete expression.

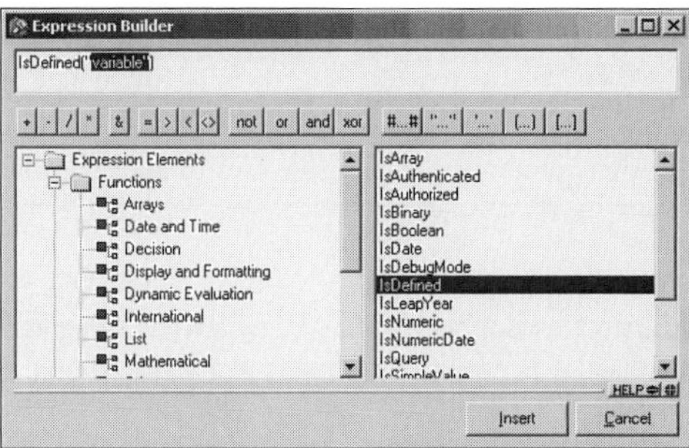

Figure 8.15 The Studio Expression Builder can be used to simplify creating and editing ColdFusion expressions.

After you have finished creating or editing an expression, clicking the Insert button places the expression into your document in the Editor window.

Tip

The Expression Builder dialog box can also display element-specific help if you click either of the help buttons on the bottom right of the dialog box.

ACCESSING COLDFUSION APPLICATION SERVER SERVICES

Unlike Web page development, ColdFusion application development usually involves a high level of integration with services on the ColdFusion Application Server machine. At a minimum, this integration involves ODBC data sources, as well as files and directories on the server.

Studio can be used to open and work with these services over any Internet connection. This enables developers to work from a computer located anywhere and still gain full access to the file system as well as to the ODBC data sources.

CONNECTING TO A COLDFUSION SERVER

To access these services, you first might tell Studio about your ColdFusion server and how to get to it. To do this, select the File tab on the Resource tab and select Allaire FTP & RDS.

Studio supports two forms of remote server connection, direct connection to ColdFusion servers, and FTP server connections. These are described in Table 8.3.

TABLE 8.3 SERVER TYPES SUPPORTED BY COLDFUSION STUDIO

Server	Description
RDS	Connecting to a ColdFusion server using RDS (Remote Development Services) gives you access to the server's filesystem and all system ODBC data sources. The connection is made via HTTP. Use this option to connect to a ColdFusion server.
FTP	Connecting to an FTP server gives you access to the filesystem on a remote host. Use this connection to transfer files to and from FTP servers.

Tip

Remote ColdFusion development should be performed using RDS. FTP should be used only when connecting to remote FTP servers and ideally should not be used for ColdFusion development at all.

To add a ColdFusion Server via RDS, follow these steps:

1. Select the File tab from the Resource tab.
2. Select Allaire FTP & RDS from the drop-down list box.
3. Right-click Allaire FTP & RDS and select Add RDS Server to display the server properties dialog box shown in Figure 8.16.
4. Enter any descriptive name in the Description field.
5. Specify the hostname or IP address of the server to connect to. Use `localhost` or `127.0.0.1` to connect to a local server.

6. Enter the Studio server password in the Password field, or leave it blank to be prompted for it each time you access the server. (If you do enter the password, you are not prompted for it again to gain server access; therefore, anyone who has access to Studio on your computer also has server access.)
7. Click OK to add the server.

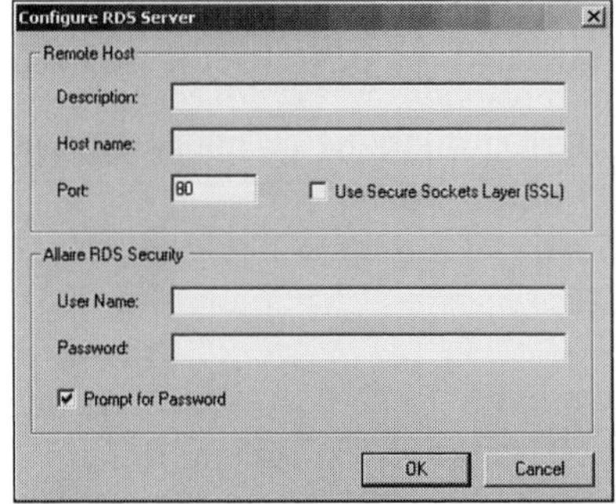

Figure 8.16
The Configure RDS Server dialog box is used to add a ColdFusion Server to the Studio remote server list.

You'll now see the server you added appear in the list of remote servers.

See Chapter 2 for more about setting up the Studio password ColdFusion installation.

ACCESSING SERVER FILES

To browse files on a remote server (either a ColdFusion or an FTP server), just expand the server name by clicking the + to its left. You are prompted for a password if you did not specify one when setting up the server; then Studio attempts to connect to the server. If the connection is successful, you see a tree control that lets you browse drives and directories available on the server, as shown in Figure 8.17. Click any directory to display its contents in the file pane.

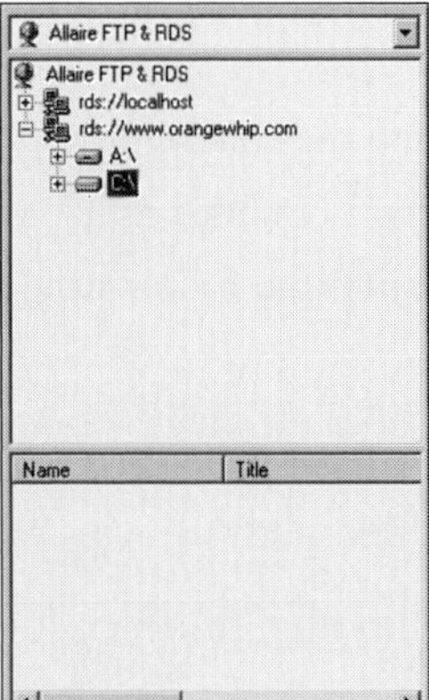

Figure 8.17
The Resource Tab file tab can be used to show files and directories on the ColdFusion server machine.

You can double-click any file to open it for editing, just as you would a local file. Studio automatically handles the retrieving of files from the server (using either HTTP or FTP) and saving the files back to the server.

ACCESSING SERVER DATA SOURCES

Accessing server data sources is similar to accessing files and directories. To access server data sources, you first must have configured a ColdFusion server for remote access within Studio. You cannot use FTP server connections for data source interaction.

To browse your server's data sources, select the Database tab in the Resource tab (the one with the yellow cylinder on it). You'll see the same ColdFusion servers that you set up in the Remote tab. Select a server from the drop-down list to display a list of data sources available on the server, as shown in Figure 8.18.

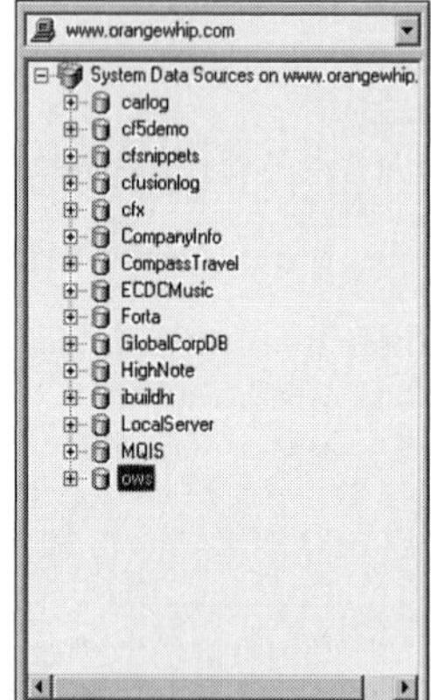

Figure 8.18
The Resource Tab gives you remote access to the ODBC data sources on the ColdFusion Server machine.

You can do several things with this list:

- Expand any data source to view the tables, views, and queries within it (as seen in Figure 8.19).
- Expand any table to see the list of columns and the column data types within it.
- Double-click a table or view to browse the data contained in it.
- Drag and drop any table, view, or field name into the Editor window.
- Access the SQL Query Builder.

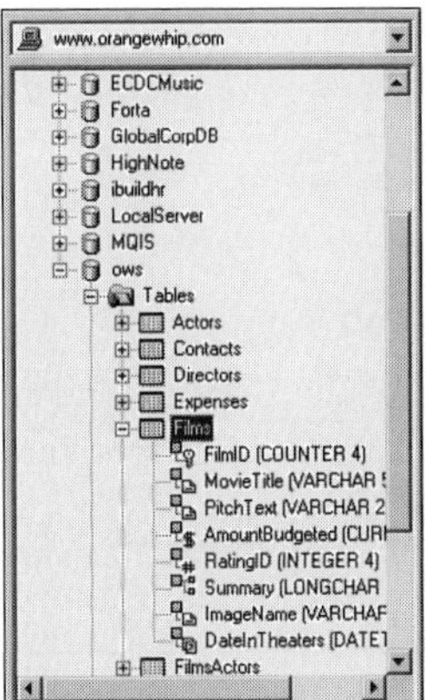

Figure 8.19
The Resource Tab enables you to drill down into remote data sources to see table and view names, as well as column data types and sizes.

CONFIGURING DEVELOPMENT MAPPINGS

As mentioned earlier, the integrated browser cannot process ColdFusion files unless configured to do so. Why? You will recall from Chapter 1, "Introducing ColdFusion," that CFML must be processed by the ColdFusion server—CFML is a server language, not a browser language.

HTML files usually are served by a Web server, but they can be opened locally, too. Using the File Open option in most browsers, pages can be opened and displayed without any server interaction. This is exactly what the Studio internal browser does when it displays HTML files—it opens them locally.

ColdFusion files can't be opened this way, though. If you use the browser File Open option to open the CFM file, ColdFusion will be incapable of processing the CFML, and some CFML code might even be displayed onscreen.

To be capable of browsing CFM files within Studio, Studio must actually submit the request to the server for processing, displaying the results (instead of the code itself). This round trip to the server and back happens automatically—after you configure it to do so. And the way you configure it is by defining development mappings.

Development mappings are defined in the Remote Development Settings screen, shown in Figure 8.20. To access this screen, either select the Development Mappings option from the Debug toolbar (it's the button with the picture of a computer in front of a page of code) or select Development Mappings from the Debug menu.

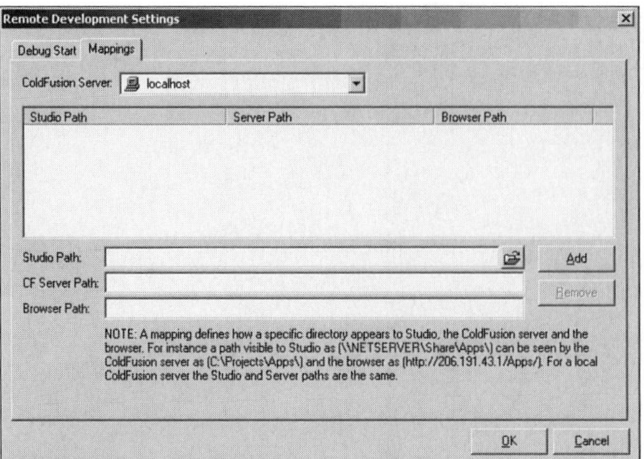

Figure 8.20
Use the Remote Development Settings dialog box to define mappings to ColdFusion servers to enable browsing (and debugging) ColdFusion applications.

Mappings are used to instruct ColdFusion Studio on how to access files when needed. For every file there are three paths that must be defined:

- **The Studio Path**—The path used by ColdFusion Studio to access a file. This can be specified using a drive and directory or using a UNC path.
- **The CF Server Path**—The path used by the ColdFusion server to access a file. This is the local path on the server itself and is always specified as a drive and directory.
- **The Browser Path**—The path that a Web browser on your computer would use to access this file, starting with `http://`.

Tip

When defining mappings for a local server, the Studio Path and the CF Server Path will be the same.

Here are the steps to define a local mapping that can be used for all ColdFusion pages under the Web root:

1. Development mappings are defined for each server individually (both the local server and all remote servers), and the server must be selected from the list of ColdFusion servers. Select the `localhost` server to define a mapping for your local ColdFusion server.
2. In the Studio Path field, specify the location of your Web root folder. If you are using Microsoft IIS, for example, this will likely be `c:\inetpub\wwwroot`.
3. In the CF Server Path field, specify the location of the Web root. Again, if you are using Microsoft IIS, this will likely be `c:\inetpub\wwwroot`.
4. In the Browser Path field, specify the URL to access the Web root. For local servers, this will usually be `http://127.0.0.1/`.
5. Your screen should look similar to the one shown in Figure 8.21. Click the Add button to add the mapping, and then click OK.

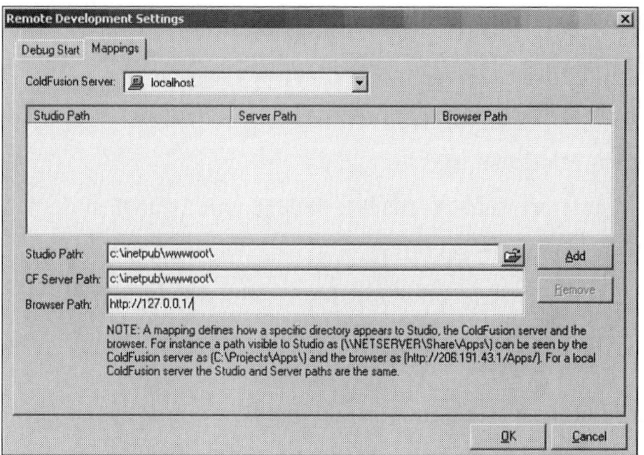

Figure 8.21
Mappings are defined for each individual server, and selecting a server displays the defined mappings.

You can now browse ColdFusion pages within Studio. To test this, open one of the files created in Chapter 5, "Previewing ColdFusion," and then click the Browse button. Studio will submit the page to ColdFusion for processing and then display the results as seen in Figure 8.22.

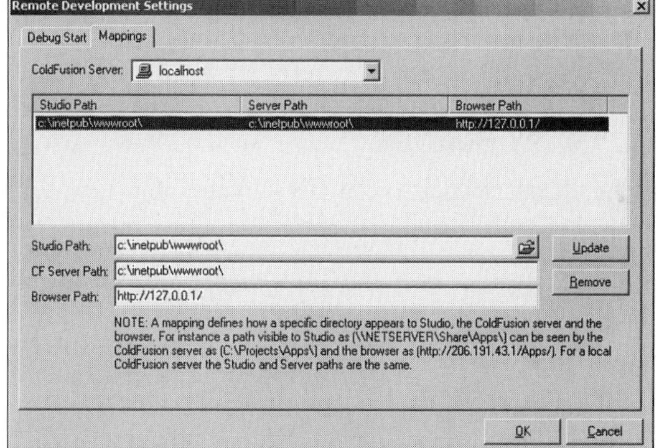

Figure 8.22
After development mappings are defined, ColdFusion pages can be browsed within ColdFusion Studio.

Using the SQL Query Builder

Almost every ColdFusion application uses some type of database integration. Although database integration is probably the most commonly used ColdFusion feature, learning SQL—the language used to interact with these databases—remains the single biggest hurdle facing ColdFusion developers.

For this reason, a graphical SQL generation tool has been added to ColdFusion Studio. This tool—the SQL Query Builder—helps ColdFusion developers construct powerful SQL statements without actually writing a single line of SQL code.

Some of the features built into the Query Builder include the following:

- Drag-and-drop interface simplifies field selection.
- Simple drop-down list boxes for filter and sort selection.
- Full support for relational queries and all JOIN types.
- Capability to generate SELECT, INSERT, DELETE, and UPDATE statements.
- Generated SQL shown in real time.
- SQL statements can be executed and any results displayed.
- Generates <CFQUERY> ready code.

Unlike other query builders built into database client applications, the ColdFusion Studio SQL Query Builder has been designed from scratch with the ColdFusion developer in mind. As such, learning to effectively use the Query Builder can dramatically improve the rate at which you roll out applications, and it can help you get the code right on the first try.

Note

As good as the SQL Query Builder is, it is no substitute for a good working knowledge of SQL. The Query Builder can help with your most common SQL statements, but at some point you will need to write SQL code directly. Whether it is to fine-tune the SQL code or to write statements not supported by the Query Builder, you must learn SQL if you are serious about ColdFusion development.

NAVIGATING THE SQL QUERY BUILDER

First, let's look at the Query Builder screen. To start the SQL Query Builder, do one of the following:

- Select Insert SQL Statement from the Tools menu. Select a server from the drop-down list box, select a table, and click New Query.
- Right-click in the Editor window and select Insert SQL Statement. Select a server from the drop-down list box, select a table, and click New Query.
- Within the <CFQUERY> Tag Editor dialog box, click the SQL Query Builder button (to the right of the SQL Statement field). Select a server from the drop-down list box, select a table, and click New Query.
- Right-click any table in the Database tab in the Resource windows and select New Query.

This opens the Query Builder, as seen in Figure 8.23.

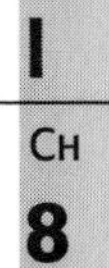

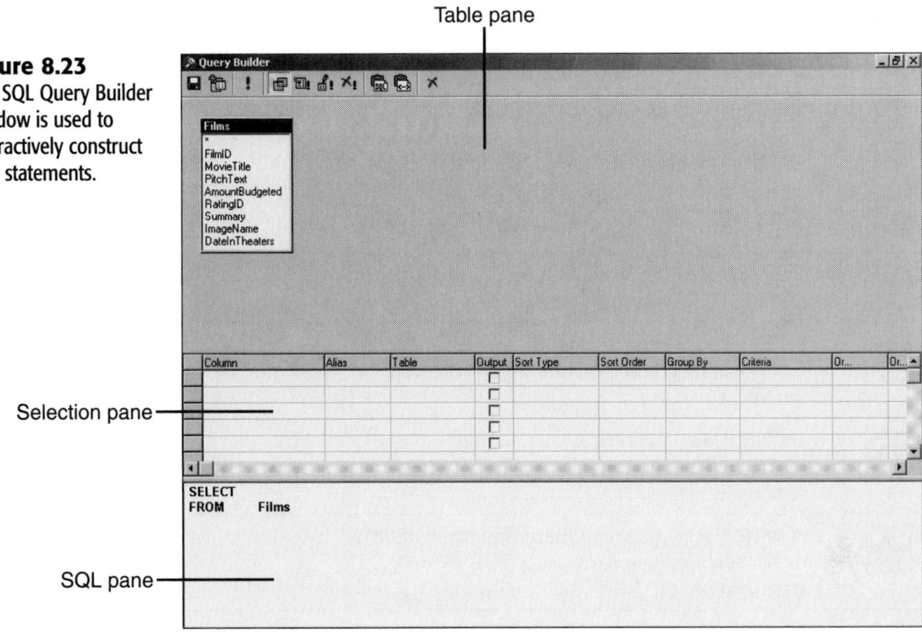

Figure 8.23
The SQL Query Builder window is used to interactively construct SQL statements.

Note

The SQL Query Builder is password-protected to prevent unauthorized access to the databases. If you are not already logged in to the ColdFusion Remote Development Server, you are prompted for a password at this point. Enter the ColdFusion Studio password as specified during system installation (or in the ColdFusion Administrator).

As seen in Figure 8.23, the Query Builder window is divided into three sections, with a standard Windows toolbars at the top.

The top portion of the window is the Table pane. This is where you are presented with a graphical representation of the tables in your SQL query. You can add and remove tables, define relationships between tables, and select the columns you want included in the query.

The middle portion of the window is the Selection pane. This is where the list of currently selected columns is displayed. You can add and remove columns, attach criteria to perform data filtering, specify search orders and grouping, and pass subqueries.

The bottom portion of the window is the SQL pane. This is where the Query Builder shows you the SQL code being constructed. As you make changes in the two upper panes, the SQL code in the SQL pane changes in real time. The final code, as it appears in this pane, is what gets pasted into your application.

Using the Toolbar

The SQL Query Builder window has no menus. All selections are made using the items in the two panes and the toolbar. The toolbar buttons are described in Table 8.4.

TABLE 8.4 SQL QUERY BUILDER TOOLBAR BUTTONS

Button	Effect
	Save Query enables you to save the query for reuse. Queries are saved on the ColdFusion server, enabling queries to be shared by multiple users.
	Add Tables is used to add tables to a query.
	Run Query executes the SQL code appearing in the SQL pane. Results are displayed in a pop-up window.
	`SELECT` Query puts the Query Builder in `SELECT` mode, enabling you to create a SQL `SELECT` statement.
	`INSERT` Query puts the Query Builder in `INSERT` mode, enabling you to create a SQL `INSERT` statement.
	`UPDATE` Query puts the Query Builder in `UPDATE` mode, enabling you to create a SQL `UPDATE` statement.
	`DELETE` Query puts the Query Builder in `DELETE` mode, enabling you to create a SQL `DELETE` statement.
	Copy SQL to Clipboard copies the SQL code from the SQL pane to the Windows Clipboard so you can paste into other applications.
	Copy `CFQUERY` to Clipboard copies the SQL code formatted as a complete `<CFQUERY>` tag from the SQL pane to the Windows Clipboard.
	Close Query Builder quits the Query Builder.

The majority of SQL statements you write will be SQL `SELECT` statements, so the Query Builder window opens in the default `SELECT` mode. To generate SQL code for `INSERT`, `UPDATE`, or `DELETE` operations, you must switch the mode using the toolbar buttons shown in Table 8.4.

GENERATING SQL SELECT STATEMENTS

Before you can start creating your SQL statement, you must select at least one database table. If you open the Query Builder while a database table is selected in the Database tab, that table will be preselected in the Table pane. If no database table is highlighted, the Query Builder will prompt you for the initial table to use.

To try this, follow these steps:

1. Select the Database tab in the Resource Tab.
2. Select the `localhost` server.

3. Expand the ows datasource.
4. Select the `Films` table, and then right-click and select New Query to launch the SQL Query Builder.

The Query Builder begins constructing right away; this is shown in the SQL pane in Figure 8.24.

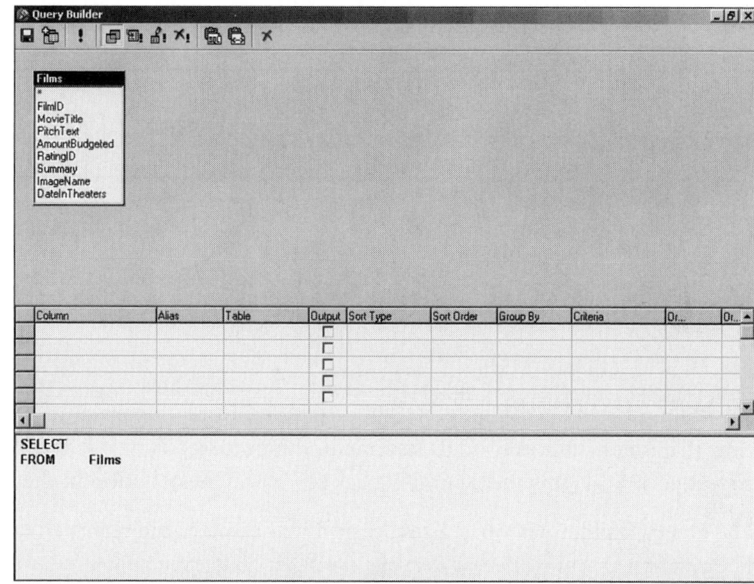

Figure 8.24
The SQL Query Builder constructs SQL statements as options are selected.

Note

For more information on the SQL `SELECT` statement, see Chapter 6, "Introduction to SQL."

SELECTING TABLE COLUMNS

The SQL in the SQL pane is not yet a valid SQL statement. The next thing you need to do is select the columns to be retrieved. The following are several ways to add columns to your statement:

- Double-click any column in any of the tables in the Table pane to add that column to the Selection pane.
- Drag a column from the Table pane and drop it into the Columns area, which is in the Selection pane grid.
- Click any line in the Columns area to display a drop-down list box of all the columns that can be added to the selection; click any one to select it.

Select the `MovieTitle` and `Summary` columns from the `Films` table. Notice how, as you select each column, the SQL statement in the SQL pane reflects that change. Your screen should now look similar to the one in Figure 8.25.

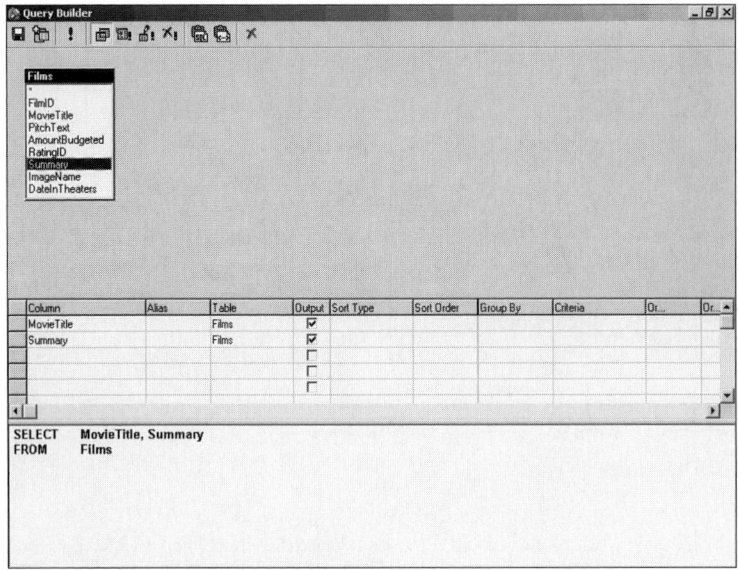

Figure 8.25
The SQL Query Builder enables you to add columns to your table in three ways.

TESTING SQL STATEMENTS

Now that you have a valid SQL statement, the next step is to test that it works as intended. To test your SQL statement, simply click the Run Query button in the toolbar.

The Query Builder will open a results grid that displays the retrieved data for browsing. The results window's title bar displays the SQL code executed, similar to the example shown in Figure 8.26.

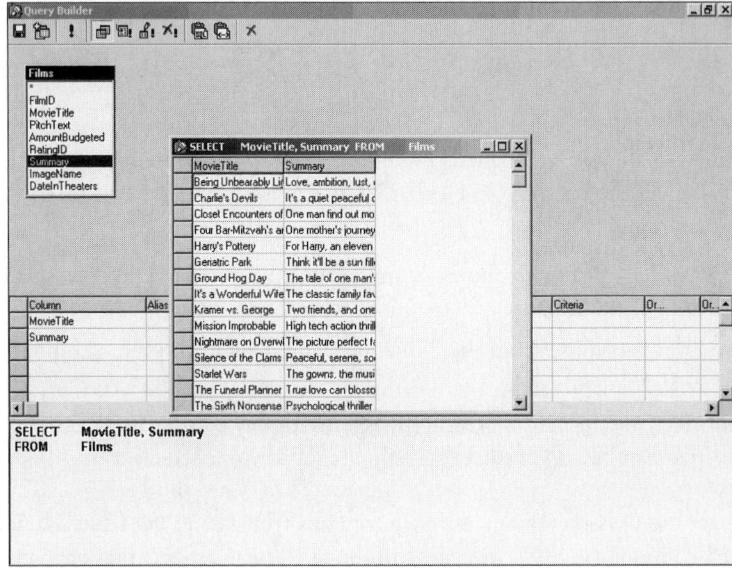

Figure 8.26
SQL statements can be tested directly in the Query Builder, and results are displayed in a results grid.

To close the results window, just click the Close Window button (on the right with an X).

Caution

The Query Builder lets you execute any valid SQL statement. When you execute a SQL statement, the Query Builder submits the statement over the TCP/IP connection to the ColdFusion server for processing; the returned data is then displayed. Be careful not to execute a statement that could return very large resultsets because this could take a very long time to return, giving you the impression that Studio has hung.

JOINING TABLES

As explained in Chapter 3, "Building the Databases," relational database applications store data in multiple related tables. When related tables are used in a single statement (so as to retrieve data from them), they are *joined*. Additionally, the SQL Query Builder fully supports table joins. To join the `FilmsRatings` table to the query you just created, do the following:

1. Click the Add Tables button (the one with the yellow plus sign and the tables) to display a list of available tables.
2. Select the `FilmsRatings` table and click Add to add it to the query.
3. Click Done to close the Add Tables dialog box.
4. Click the `RatingsID` column in the `Films` table and drag it to the `RatingsID` column in the `FilmsRatings` table to join the two tables.

The SQL Query Builder will display a link identifying the join, and the SQL code will be updated with the join condition (the `WHERE` clause), as seen in Figure 8.27.

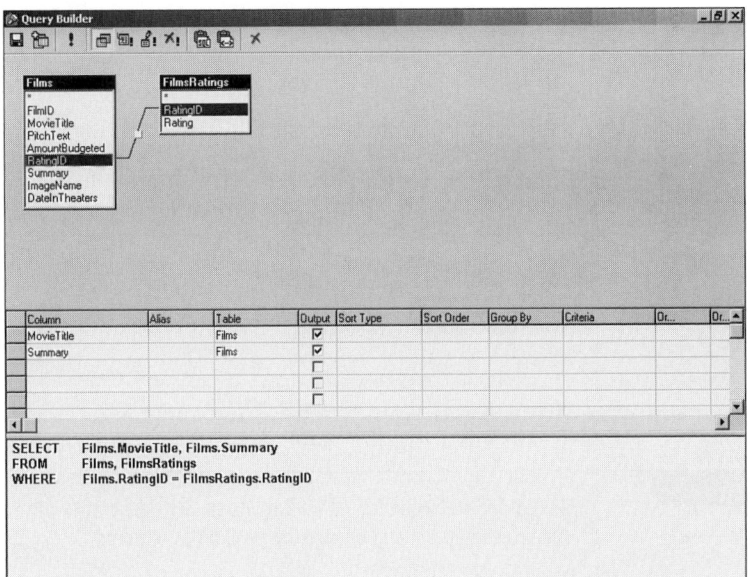

Figure 8.27
The SQL Query Builder enables you to interactively join database tables.

Now add the `Rating` column (in table `FilmsRatings`) to the query, and then test the query using the Run Query button (as described previously).

Tip

To change the join type, or to remove a join, right-click the square in the link line between the two tables.

SORTING RESULTS

Now sort the returned data. SQL results are sorted by columns in the retrieved columns list. Multiple columns can be selected, in which case the data is sorted by the first column and then by the second.

You will sort the data by `Rating` and then by `MovieTitle`. Here's how to do that:

1. In the Selection Pane grid, click the Sort Type column on the `Rating` row. Select Ascending from the drop-down list.
2. Click the Sort Type column on the `MovieTitle` row and set it to Ascending as well.

The SQL pane now shows an `ORDER BY` clause, which sorts the retrieved data, as seen in Figure 8.28. Data is now sorted by `Rating`; within each `Rating` it's sorted by `MovieTitle`. To verify that this worked, try running the query using the Run Query button.

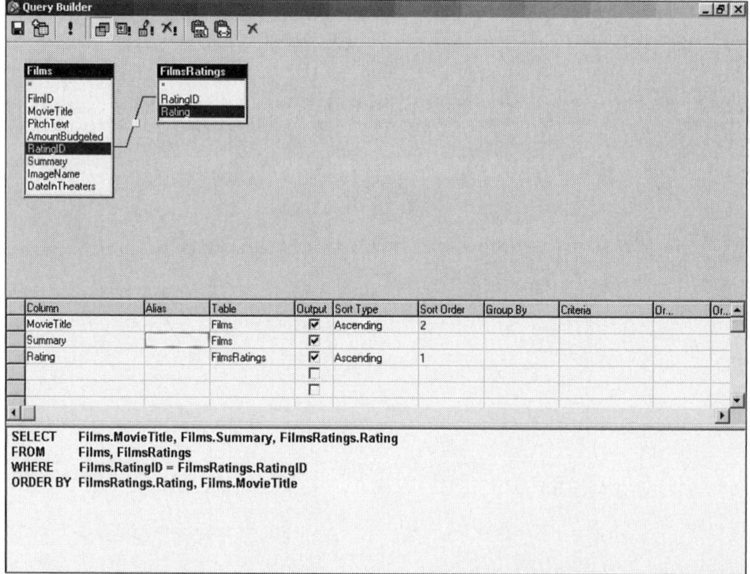

Figure 8.28 Retrieved data can be sorted as necessary by specifying the Sort Type.

Tip

To reorder the sequence within the `ORDER BY` clause, click the Sort Order column in the Selection pane and change the position as required.

FILTERING DATA

So far, you have retrieved all the data in the tables. Next, you add SQL `WHERE` clauses using the Query Builder filtering tools.

To apply filtering within Query Builder, all you do is specify a search criteria in the `Criteria` column for the required row. For example, to find all movies with a rating of `General`, type the following into the `Rating` row's Criteria box:

```
='General'
```

As soon as you click anywhere outside that Criteria box, the SQL code in the SQL pane is updated to include your `WHERE` clause. You can test this query to verify that it returns the required data.

When you typed that criteria, you might have noticed that the Criteria box has a built-in drop-down list box with a selection of common criteria types, as shown in Figure 8.29. You can select any of these to help you construct your SQL `WHERE` clauses.

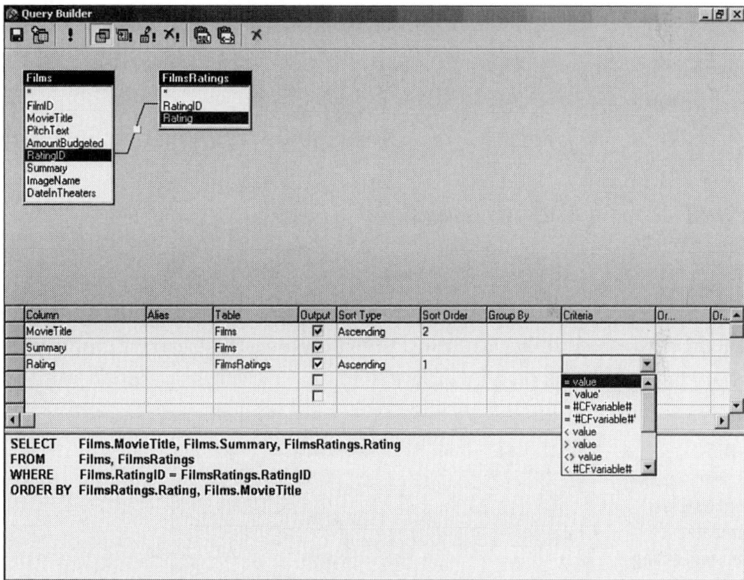

Figure 8.29
The Criteria drop-down list box contains common `WHERE` clause conditions for selection.

Many of the selections in the drop-down list box contain the text `value` or `#CFvariable#`. These are designed to be placeholders. You replace the word `value` with an actual value (as you did with the word `General`), and the word `#CFvariable#` with the name of a ColdFusion variable to be used within your `WHERE` clause.

Note

There are two versions of each `value` and `#CFvariable#` in the Criteria drop-down list box. One is enclosed within single quotation marks, and the other is not. Because SQL is not typeless, it is your responsibility to enclose values and variables within single quotation marks when constructing `WHERE` clauses. Selecting the correct option from this list can help ensure that you do not inadvertently omit this.

`<CFQUERY>` SQL `SELECT` statements often contain ColdFusion variables within their `WHERE` clauses. For example, you might be retrieving all employees whose last name is whatever value was specified in a form field. This type of `WHERE` clause can't easily be tested outside the ColdFusion environment because the variables used do not exist until the submitted form is processed by ColdFusion.

Fortunately, the SQL Query Builder has a very elegant solution to this problem. To demonstrate it, perform the following steps:

1. Click in the Criteria box for the `Rating` field.
2. Select ='#CFvariable#' from the drop-down list box.
3. Replace the text `CFvariable` with the text **`FORM.Rating`**. (Be sure to leave the single quotation marks and pound signs intact.)
4. Click any box other than the Criteria box you are editing, so that the SQL pane sees the changes.
5. Click the Run Query button.

The SQL code you are trying to run is invalid. The SQL was not processed under ColdFusion control, and therefore the variables it refers to do not exist yet. To compensate for this, and to simulate ColdFusion processing, the Query Builder prompts you to enter the query parameters as seen in Figure 8.30.

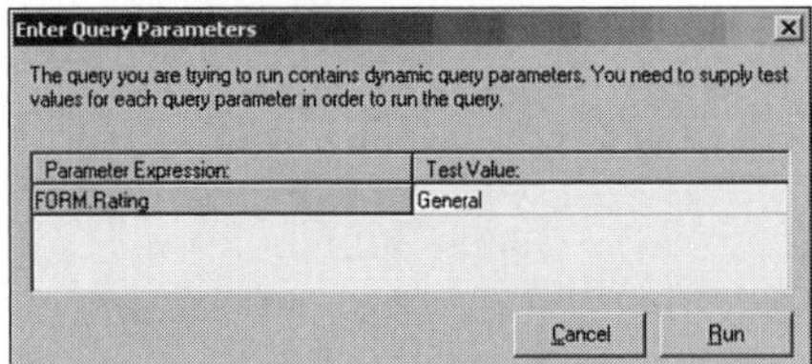

Figure 8.30
Manually setting query parameters enables you to simulate ColdFusion processing dynamic SQL statements.

You can provide a value here for each field in your query (there is one in the example), and the Query Builder will then process the SQL as if ColdFusion itself were processing it. For more information on the SQL `WHERE` clause, see Chapter 6.

ADVANCED DATA FILTERING

The filter you just created is a simple SQL `WHERE` clause, with a single criterion. The Query Builder can also be used to build more complex `WHERE` clauses, including `AND` and `OR` clauses and any combination thereof.

AND clauses are created by making multiple selections of the fields to be filtered on, once for each condition. To create an AND clause, simply add a condition in another row's Criteria field.

To create an OR clause condition, simply add an additional condition in any of the Or columns to the right of the Criteria field. Each additional OR condition must go in its own Or field.

Note

There is no limit to the number of AND clauses that can be included in a WHERE clause, and up to four OR conditions per column can be used in the WHERE clause.

Tip

Depending on the SQL code needed and the filter criteria used, often you can use a single criterion with an IN operator instead of creating multiple OR clauses.

USING QUERY BUILDER SQL STATEMENTS

After you have created and tested your SQL statements in the SQL Query Builder, you have several options. You can execute it as is, copy and paste the SQL code, or save the code for reuse. Use the Copy SQL to Clipboard toolbar button to copy and paste the SQL code from the SQL pane.

POPULATING <CFQUERY> TAGS

The <CFQUERY> tag is introduced in Chapter 11, "Creating Data-Driven Pages." <CFQUERY> is used to execute SQL queries within your ColdFusion code.

If you launched the Query Builder from within the <CFOUTPUT> Tag Editor dialog box, you have the option of pasting the SQL code back into that dialog box. To do this, follow these steps:

1. Click the Close Query Builder button.
2. You are prompted to save the query. Select Yes if you plan to use this query again; otherwise, select No.
3. You are then prompted to reinsert the query into your code; select Yes.
4. The <CFQUERY> Tag Editor displays the final SQL code and automatically sets the data source correctly, as seen in Figure 8.31.

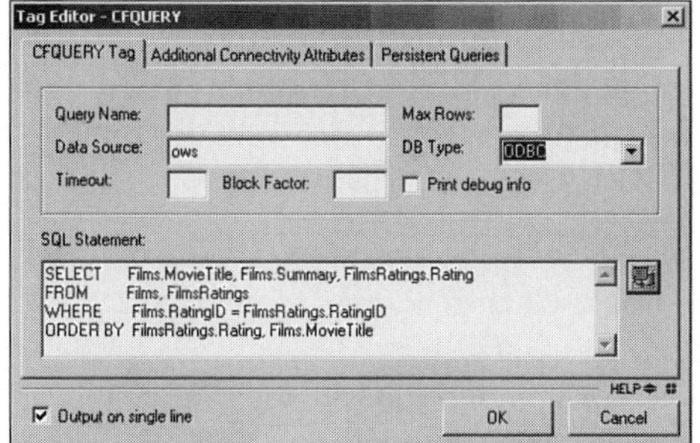

Figure 8.31 The Query Builder can insert generated SQL directly into the *<CFQUERY>* Tag Editor.

REUSING QUERIES

As mentioned earlier, SQL statements created with the Query Builder can be saved for future use. ColdFusion Studio saves generated queries on the ColdFusion server. This enables anyone connected to that ColdFusion server to reuse existing queries.

Perform the following steps to reuse a saved query:

1. Open the Database tab in the ColdFusion Studio Resource tab.
2. Connect to the desired ColdFusion server (providing the password if required).
3. Expand the desired data source to display a Queries selection.
4. Expand the Queries option to display the list of saved queries.
5. Drag the desired query from the list to the Editor window. As shown in Figure 8.32, ColdFusion Studio creates a complete `<CFQUERY>` tag at the location that the query was dropped.

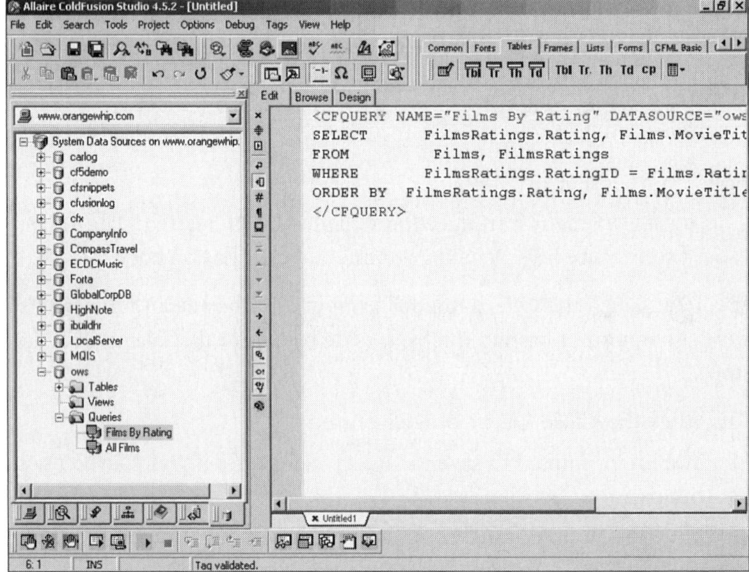

Figure 8.32 Drag and drop an existing database query to create a fully populated `<CFQUERY>` tag containing the query's SQL statement.

GENERATING OTHER SQL STATEMENTS

More often than not, you'll find yourself using the Query Builder to construct SQL `SELECT` statements—but that is not all the Query Builder can do. To assist you in writing SQL `INSERT`, `UPDATE`, and `DELETE` statements, these are also supported by the Query Builder.

GENERATING SQL `INSERT` STATEMENTS

The SQL Query Builder can't be used to generate simple SQL `INSERT` statements like this:

```
INSERT INTO Directors(FirstName, LastName)
VALUES('Ben', 'Forta')
```

The Query Builder can be used to build only SQL INSERT SELECT statements, which are used to insert the results of a SELECT statement into another table.

To generate a SQL INSERT statement, you must switch SQL Query Builder to Insert mode by clicking the INSERT Query button in the toolbar. The Query Builder then prompts you for the name of the table into which you will be inserting data.

To create an INSERT statement, follow these steps:

1. Select the table into which data is to be inserted.
2. Right-click the table and select Remove Table. This removes it from the Table pane but retains the table as the destination for the inserted data in the SQL pane.
3. Click the Add Tables (or right-click in the Table pane and select Add Table) to select the tables from which data is to be selected for insertion.
4. Select the columns to be inserted using any of the selection methods described in the "Selecting Table Columns" section.
5. Click the Append To column for the first row in the columns grid, and select the field into which the data is to be inserted from the drop-down list box.
6. Repeat step 5 for every column listed in Columns.
7. If they are not already chosen, select the columns to be used for the SELECT WHERE clause.
8. Specify the criteria for the SELECT WHERE clause as explained in the sections "Filtering Data" and "Advanced Data Filtering."

Caution

Be sure you always specify a WHERE clause criteria. Otherwise, you will insert every selected row into the destination table.

For more information on the SQL INSERT statement, see Chapter 7, "SQL Data Manipulation."

GENERATING SQL UPDATE STATEMENTS

To generate a SQL UPDATE statement, you must switch the SQL Query Builder to Update mode by clicking the UPDATE Query button in the toolbar. The Query Builder then prompts you for the name of the table whose data you will be updating.

To create an UPDATE statement, follow these steps:

1. Select the table to be updated.
2. Select the columns to be updated using any of the selection methods described in the "Selecting Table Columns" section.
3. Specify the new value for each field in that field's New Value box. You can specify either a literal value or a ColdFusion variable.

4. If they are not already chosen, select the columns to be used for the WHERE clause.
5. Specify the criteria for the UPDATE WHERE clause as explained in the sections "Filtering Data" and "Advanced Data Filtering."

Caution

Be sure you always specify a WHERE clause criteria. Otherwise, you will update every row in the table with the new values.

Note

Putting single quotation marks around values or variables in the New Value column if they are needed is your responsibility.

For more information on the SQL UPDATE statement, see Chapter 7.

GENERATING SQL DELETE STATEMENTS

To generate a SQL DELETE statement, you must switch the SQL Query Builder to Delete mode by clicking the DELETE Query button in the toolbar. The Query Builder then prompts you for the name of the table whose data you will be deleting.

To create a DELETE statement, follow these steps:

1. Select the table from which to delete data.
2. Select the columns to be used for the WHERE clause using any of the selection methods described in the "Selecting Table Columns" section.
3. Specify the criteria for the DELETE WHERE clause as explained in the sections "Filtering Data" and "Advanced Data Filtering."

Caution

Be sure you always specify a WHERE clause criteria. Otherwise, you will delete every row in the table with the new values.

For more information on the SQL DELETE statement, see Chapter 7.

JUST USE IT

As you can see, ColdFusion Studio is a powerful and flexible editor designed with ColdFusion developers in mind. As such, it does much more than edit files. The integrated Tag Chooser, Expression Builder, and SQL Query Builder all serve to simplify the application development process. With extensive built-in help options and support for remote development, Studio is an invaluable tool. Start using it and you'll wonder how you managed without it.

PART II

Using ColdFusion

CHAPTER 9

USING COLDFUSION

In this chapter

WORKING WITH TEMPLATES

Back in Chapter 5, "Previewing ColdFusion," you created several applications (both using wizards and writing code manually). ColdFusion applications are made up of one or more files—files with a `.CFM` extension. These files often are referred to as *templates*; you'll see the terms *templates*, *files*, and even *pages* used somewhat interchangeably—just so you know, they all refer to the same thing. (I'll explain why the term *templates* is used in a moment.)

CREATING TEMPLATES

As already explained, ColdFusion templates are plain text files. These files can be created with several types of programs:

- ColdFusion Studio (introduced in Chapter 8, "Introduction to ColdFusion Studio")
- Macromedia HomeSite (the most popular code-based HTML and Web editor)
- Macromedia UltraDev (introduced in Chapter 16, "Using Macromedia Dreamweaver UltraDev with ColdFusion")
- Windows Notepad

Obviously, the best choice for ColdFusion developers, as already seen, is ColdFusion Studio. So that's what you'll use here (and throughout the rest of this book).

To create a new ColdFusion file (or template; as I said, the terms are used interchangeably), simply open ColdFusion Studio. The editor will be ready for you to start typing code, and what you save is the ColdFusion file (as long as you save it with a `.CFM` extension, that is).

The code shown in Listing 9.1 is the contents of a simple ColdFusion file named `hello1.cfm`. Actually, at this point no ColdFusion code exists in the listing—it is all straight HTML and text, but we'll get to that soon. Launch ColdFusion Studio (if it is not already open), and type the code as shown in Listing 9.1.

LISTING 9.1 `hello1.cfm`

```
<HTML>
<HEAD>
   <TITLE>Hello 1</TITLE>
</HEAD>

<BODY>

Hello, and welcome to ColdFusion!

</BODY>
</HTML>
```

Note

Tag case is not important, so `<BODY>` or `<body>` or `<Body>` can be used—it's your choice.

SAVING TEMPLATES

Before ColdFusion can process pages, they must be saved onto the ColdFusion server. If you are developing against a local server (ColdFusion running on your own computer) then you can save the files locally; if you are developing against a remote server then you must save your code on that server.

Where you save your code is extremely important—the URL used to access the page is based on where files are saved (and how directories and paths are configured on the server).

All the files you create throughout this book will go in directories beneath the `ows` directory under the Web root (as discussed in Chapter 5). To save the code you just typed (Listing 9.1), create a new directory under `ows` and then save the code as `hello1.cfm`. To save the file, either select Save from the File menu or click the Save button in the Studio toolbar.

Tip

Forgotten how to create directories in ColdFusion Studio? Here's a reminder: Select the directory in which the new directory is to be created, right-click in the file pane below, and select Create Folder.

Of course, you can also create directories using Windows Explorer (or any other application), but if you do so while Studio is open, you'll need to refresh the list in Studio so it sees the new directory.

EXECUTING TEMPLATES

Now, let's test the code. Open your Web browser and go to this URL:

```
http://localhost/ows/9/hello1.cfm
```

You should see a page similar to the one shown in Figure 9.1. Okay, so I admit that this is somewhat anticlimactic, but wait; it'll get better soon enough.

There's another way to browse the code you write. Assuming it is a page that can be executed directly (meaning it is not one that needs to be processed after another page—for example, a page that expects to be processed after a form is submitted), you can browse it directly in Studio by selecting the Browse tab above the editor window (see Figure 9.2).

Tip

For the Browse tab to work, ColdFusion Studio must have Development Mappings defined. If you run into problems using the Browse tab, the first thing to check is that these mappings exist (Alt+M usually displays the Remote Development Mappings dialog box). Mappings, and how to define them, is explained in Chapter 8; refer to that chapter if necessary.

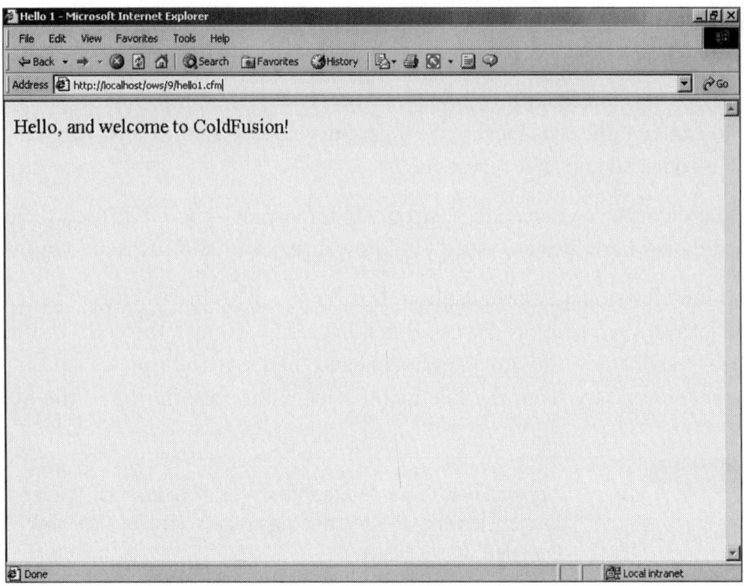

Figure 9.1
ColdFusion-generated output usually is viewed in any Web browser.

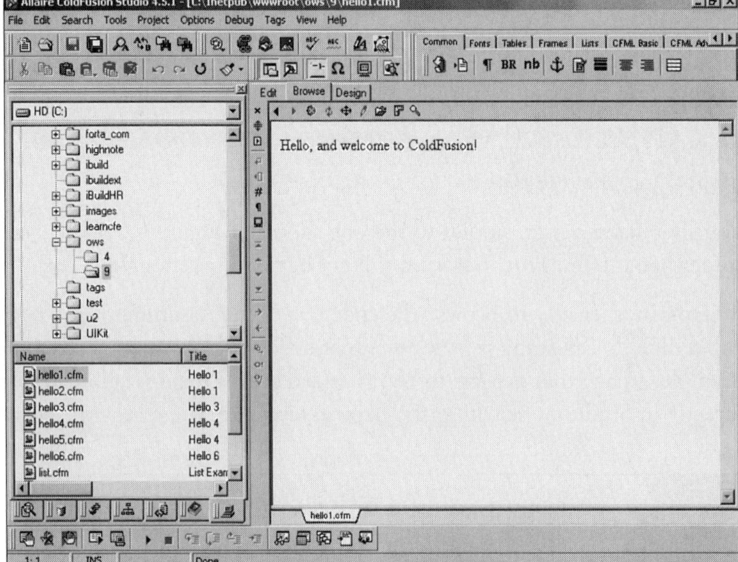

Figure 9.2
If configured correctly, you'll be able to browse much of your ColdFusion code within Studio itself.

TEMPLATES EXPLAINED

I promised to explain why ColdFusion files are often referred to as templates. Chapter 1, "Introducing ColdFusion," explains that ColdFusion pages are processed differently from Web pages—when requested, Web pages are sent to the client (the browser) as is, whereas ColdFusion files are processed and the generated results are returned to the client instead.

In other words, ColdFusion files are never sent to the client, but what they create is. And depending on what a ColdFusion file contains, it likely will generate multiple different outputs all from that same single `.CFM` file. And thus the term *template*.

USING FUNCTIONS

And this is where it starts to get interesting. CFML (the ColdFusion Markup Language) is made up of two primary language elements:

- **Tags**—Perform operations, such as accessing a database, evaluating a condition, and flagging text for processing.
- **Functions**—Return (and possibly process) data and do things such as getting the current date and time, converting text to uppercase, and rounding a number to its nearest integer.

Writing ColdFusion code requires the use of both tags and functions. The best way to understand this is to see it in action. Listing 9.2 contains a revised hello page. Type the code in a new page, and save it as `hello2.cfm` in the `ows/9` directory.

LISTING 9.2 `hello2.cfm`

```
<HTML>
<HEAD>
   <TITLE>Hello 2</TITLE>
</HEAD>

<BODY>

Hello, and welcome to ColdFusion!
<BR>
<CFOUTPUT>
It is now #Now()#
</CFOUTPUT>

</BODY>
</HTML>
```

After you have saved the page, try it by browsing it (either in a Web browser or right within Studio). The URL will be `http://localhost/ows/9/hello2.cfm`. The output should look similar to Figure 9.3 (of course, your date and time will probably be different).

Now, before we go any further, let's take a look at the code in Listing 9.3. You will recall that when ColdFusion processes a `.CFM` file, it looks for CFML code to be processed and returns any other code to the client as is. So, the first line of code is

```
<HTML>
```

Figure 9.3
ColdFusion code can contain functions, including one that returns the current date and time.

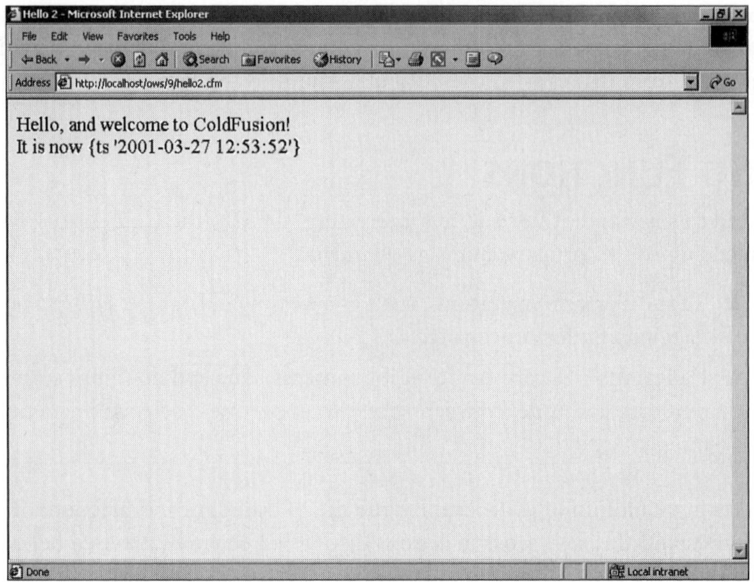

That is not CFML code—it's plain HTML. Therefore, ColdFusion ignores it and sends it on its way (to the client browser). The next few lines are also HTML code:

```
   <TITLE>Hello 2</TITLE>
</HEAD>

<BODY>

Hello, and welcome to ColdFusion!
<BR>
```

No ColdFusion language elements exist there, so ColdFusion ignores the code and sends it to the client as is.

But the next three lines of code are not HTML:

```
<CFOUTPUT>
It is now #Now()#
</CFOUTPUT>
```

`<CFOUTPUT>` is a ColdFusion tag (all ColdFusion tags begin with `CF`). `<CFOUTPUT>` is used to mark a block of code to be processed by ColdFusion. All text between the `<CFOUTPUT>` and `</CFOUTPUT>` tags is scanned, character by character, and any special instructions within that block are processed.

In the example, the following line was between the `<CFOUTPUT>` and `</CFOUTPUT>` tags:

```
It is now #Now()#
```

The text `It is now` is not an instruction, so it is sent to the client as is. But the text `#Now()#` *is* a ColdFusion instruction—within strings of text instructions are delimited by pound signs (the `#` character). `#Now()#` is an instruction telling ColdFusion to execute a function named `Now()`—a function that returns the current date and time. Thus the output in Figure 9.3 is generated.

The entire block of text from `<CFOUTPUT>` until `</CFOUTPUT>` is referred to as a *<CFOUTPUT> block*. Not all the text in a `<CFOUTPUT>` block need be CFML functions. In the previous example, literal text was used, too, and that text was sent to the client untouched. As such, you also could have entered the code like this:


```
It is now <CFOUTPUT>#Now()#</CFOUTPUT>
```

Only the `#Now()#` expression needs ColdFusion processing, so only it really needs to be within the `<CFOUTPUT>` block. But what if you had not placed the expression within a `<CFOUTPUT>` block? Try it—remove the `<CFOUTPUT>` tags, save the page, and execute it. You'll see output similar to that in Figure 9.4—obviously not what you want. Because any content not within a `<CFOUTPUT>` block is sent to the client as is, using `Now()` outside a `<CFOUTPUT>` block causes the text `Now()` to be sent to the client instead of the data returned by `Now()`. Why? Because if it's outside a `<CFOUTPUT>` block, ColdFusion will never process it.

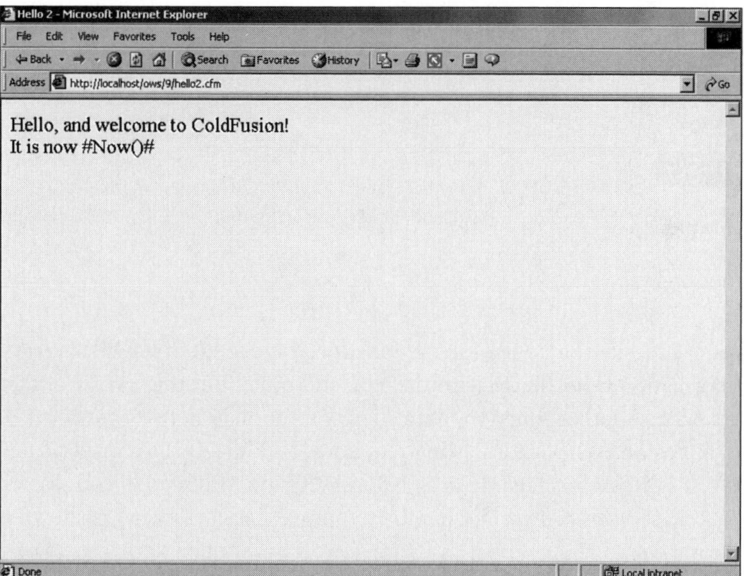

Figure 9.4
If expressions are sent to the browser, it usually means you have omitted the `<CFOUTPUT>` tags.

Omitting the pound signs has a similar effect. Put the `<CFOUTPUT>` tags back where they belong, but change `#Now()#` to `Now()` (removing the pound signs from before and after it). Then save the page, and execute it. The output will look similar to Figure 9.5. Why? Because all `<CFOUTPUT>` does is flag a block of text as needing processing by ColdFusion.

However, ColdFusion does not process *all* text between the tags—instead, it looks for expressions delimited by pound signs, and any text *not* within pound signs is assumed to be literal text that is to be sent to the client as is.

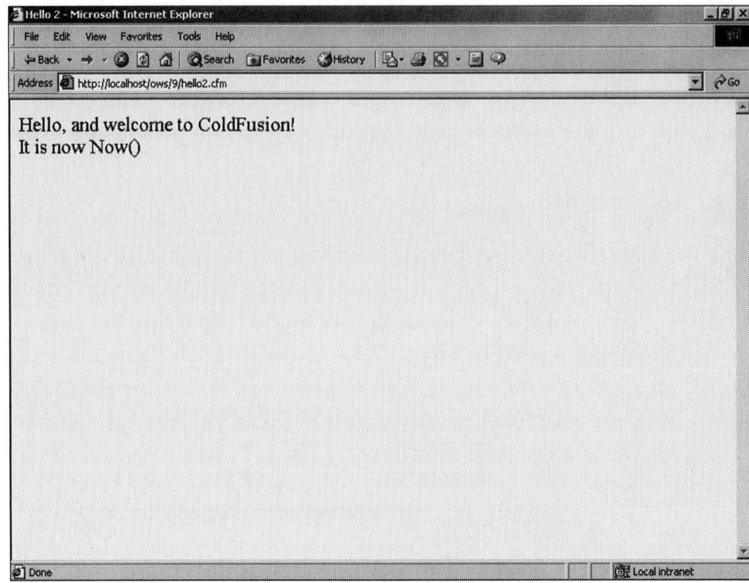

Figure 9.5
signs are needed around all expressions; otherwise, the expression is sent to the client instead of being processed.

> **Note**
> <CFOUTPUT> has another important use when working with database-driven content. More information about that can be found in Chapter 11, "Creating Data-Driven Pages."

`Now()` is a function, one of many functions supported in CFML. `Now()` is used to retrieve information from the system (the date and time), but the format of that date is not entirely readable. Another function, `DateFormat()`, can help here. `DateFormat()` is one of ColdFusion's output formatting functions, and its job is to format dates so they are readable (in all types of formats). Listing 9.3 is a revision of the code you just used; save it as `hello3.cfm` and browse the file to see output similar to what is shown in Figure 9.6.

LISTING 9.3 `hello3.cfm`

```
<HTML>
<HEAD>
   <TITLE>Hello 3</TITLE>
</HEAD>

<BODY>
```

```
Hello, and welcome to ColdFusion!
<BR>
<CFOUTPUT>
It is now #DateFormat(Now())#
</CFOUTPUT>

</BODY>
</HTML>
```


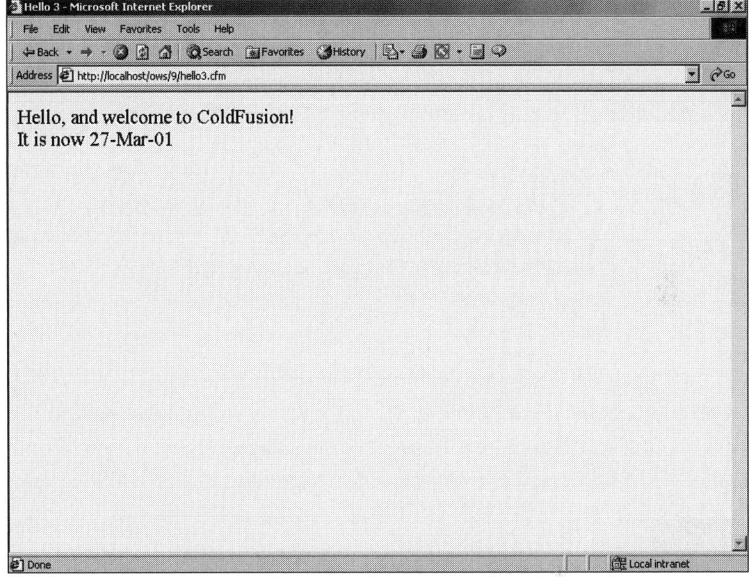

Figure 9.6 ColdFusion features a selection of output formatting functions that can be used to better control generated output.

`DateFormat()` is an example of a function that accepts (and requires) that data must be passed to it—after all, it needs to know which date you want to format for display. `DateFormat()` can accept dates as hard-coded strings (as in `#DateFormat("12/13/01")#`), as well as dates returned by other expressions, such as the `Now()` function. `#DateFormat(Now())#` tells ColdFusion to format the date returned by the `Now()` function.

Note

Passing a function as a parameter to another function is referred to as *nesting*. In this chapter's example, the `Now()` function is said to be *nested* in the `DateFormat()` function.

`DateFormat()` takes a second optional attribute, too: a format mask used to describe the output format. Try replacing the `#DateFormat(Now())#` in your code with any of the following (and try each to see what they do):

- `#DateFormat(Now(), "MMMM-DD-YYYY")#`
- `#DateFormat(Now(), "MM/DD/YY")#`
- `#DateFormat(Now(), "DDD, MMMM DD, YYYY")#`

Parameters passed to a function are always separated by commas. Commas are not used if a single parameter is passed, but when two or more parameters exist, every parameter must be separated by a comma.

You've now seen a function that takes no parameters, a function that takes a required parameter, and a function that takes both required and optional parameters. All ColdFusion functions, and you'll be using many of them, work the same way—some take parameters, and some do not. But all functions, regardless of parameters, return a value.

> **Note**
>
> It is important to remember that # is not part of the function–the functions you used here were `DateFormat()` and `Now()`. The pound signs were used to delimit (mark) the expressions, but they are not part of the expression itself.

I know I have already said this, but it is worth repeating—CFML code is processed on the server, not on the client. The CFML code you write is *never* sent to the Web browser. What is sent to the browser? Most browsers feature a View Source option that displays code as received. If you view the source of for page `hello3.cfm` you'll see something like this:

```
<HTML>
<HEAD>
   <TITLE>Hello 3</TITLE>
</HEAD>

<BODY>

Hello, and welcome to ColdFusion!
<BR>

It is now 27-Mar-01


</BODY>
</HTML>
```

As you can see, there is no CFML code here at all. The `<CFOUTPUT>` tags, the functions, the pound signs—all have been stripped out by the ColdFusion Server, and what was sent to the client is the output that they generated.

> **Tip**
>
> Viewing the generated source is an invaluable debugging trick. If you ever find that output is not being generated as expected, viewing the source can help you understand exactly what was generated and why.

USING VARIABLES

Now that you've had the chance to use some basic functions, it's time to introduce variables. Variables are an important part of just about every programming language, and CFML is no exception. A *variable* is a container that stores information in memory on the server. Variables are named, and the contents of the container are accessed via that name. Let's look at a simple example, seen in Listing 9.4. Type the code, save it as `hello4.cfm`, and browse it. You should see a display similar to the one shown in Figure 9.7.

LISTING 9.4 `hello4.cfm`

```
<HTML>
<HEAD>
   <TITLE>Hello 4</TITLE>
</HEAD>

<BODY>

<CFSET FirstName="Ben">
<CFOUTPUT>
Hello #FirstName#, and welcome to ColdFusion!
</CFOUTPUT>

</BODY>
</HTML>
```

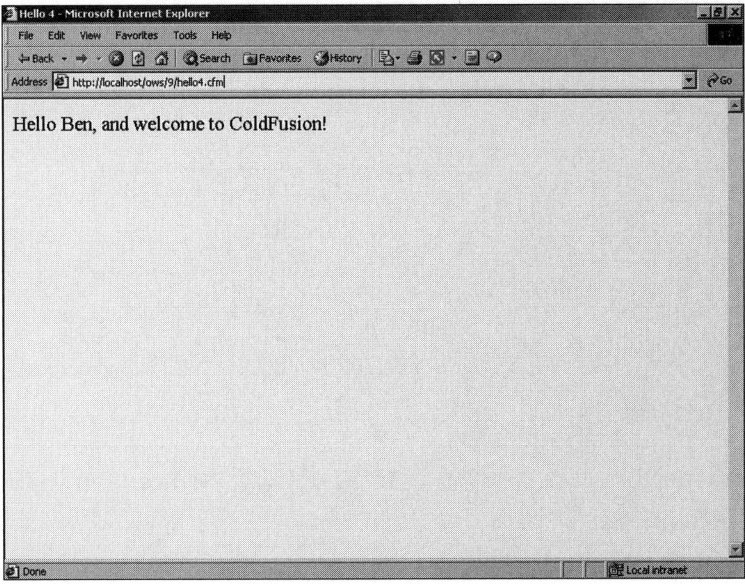

Figure 9.7 Variables are replaced by their contents when content is generated.

The code in Listing 9.4 is similar to the previous code listings. It starts with plain HTML that is sent to the client as is. Then a new tag is used, `<CFSET>`:

```
<CFSET FirstName="Ben">
```

<CFSET> is used to set variables. Here, a variable named `FirstName` is created, and a value of `"Ben"` is stored in it. After it's created, that variable will exist until the page has finished processing and can be used as seen in the next line of code:

```
Hello #FirstName#, and welcome to ColdFusion!
```

This line of code was placed in a <CFOUTPUT> block so ColdFusion would know to replace `#FirstName#` with the contents of `FirstName`. The generated output is then

```
Hello Ben, and welcome to ColdFusion!
```

Variables can be used as many times as necessary, as long as they exist. Try moving the <CFSET> statement after the <CFOUTPUT> block, or delete it altogether. Executing the page now will generate an error, similar to the one seen in Figure 9.8. This error message is telling you that you referred to (tried to access) a variable that does not exist. The error message tells you the name of the variable that caused the problem, as well as the line and column in your code (to help you find and fix the problem easily). More often than not, this error is caused by typos.

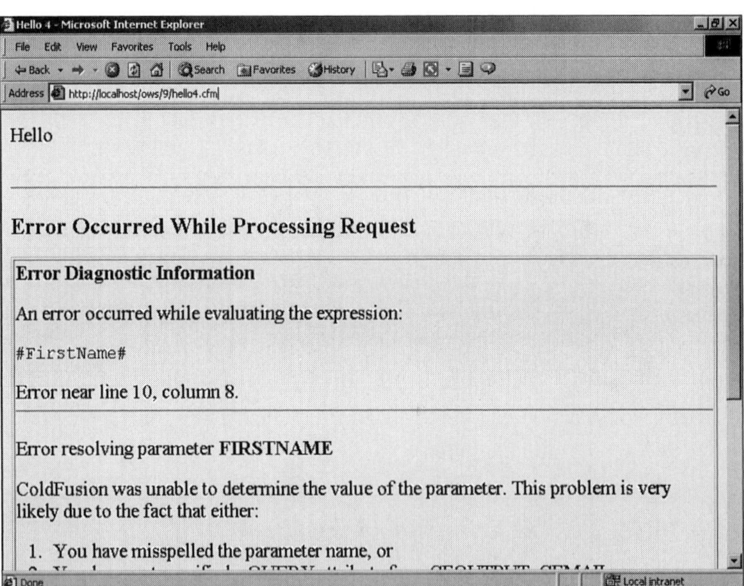

Figure 9.8
ColdFusion produces an error if a referenced variable does not exist.

Note

Regular variables exist only in the page that creates them. If you define a variable named `FirstName` in one page, you can't use it in another page unless you explicitly pass it to that page (see Chapter 11).

An exception to this rule does exist. In Chapter 20, "Working with Sessions," you learn how to create and use variables that persist across requests (each page access is known as a *request*).

Listing 9.5 contains a new version of the code, this time using the variable `FirstName` five times. Try this listing for yourself (feel free to replace my name with your own). The output is shown in Figure 9.9.

LISTING 9.5 `hello5.cfm`

```
<HTML>
<HEAD>
   <TITLE>Hello 5</TITLE>
</HEAD>

<BODY>

<CFSET FirstName="Ben">
<CFOUTPUT>
Hello #FirstName#, and welcome to ColdFusion!<P>
Your name in uppercase: #UCase(FirstName)#<BR>
Your name in lowercase: #LCase(FirstName)#<BR>
Your name in reverse: #Reverse(FirstName)#<BR>
Characters in your name: #Len(FirstName)#<BR>
</CFOUTPUT>

</BODY>
</HTML>
```


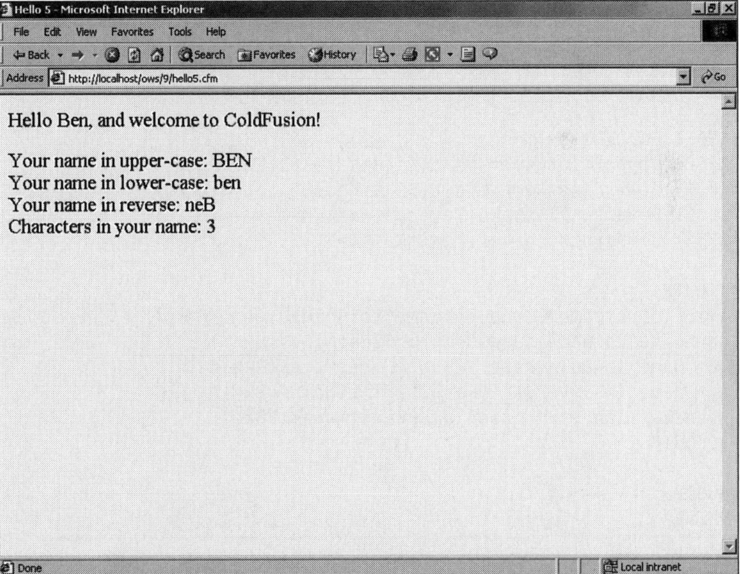

Figure 9.9 There is no limit to the number of functions that can be used in one page, which enables you to render content as you see fit.

Let's take a look at the code in Listing 9.5. A `<CFSET>` is used to create a variable named `FirstName`. That variable is used once by itself (the Hello message), and then four times with functions. `UCase()` converts a string to uppercase, `LCase()` converts a string to lowercase, `Reverse()` reverses the string, and `Len()` returns the length of a string (the number of characters in it).

But functions such as `UCase()` don't truly convert strings; instead, they return converted strings. The difference is subtle but important. Look at the following line of code:

```
Your name in uppercase: #UCase(FirstName)#
```

`UCase()` returns `FirstName` converted to uppercase, but the contents of `FirstName` itself are intact. `FirstName` was not modified; a copy was made and modified instead, and that copy was returned. To save the uppercase `FirstName` to a variable, you must do something like this:

```
<CFSET UpperFirstName=UCase(FirstName)>
```

Here a new variable, `UpperFirstName`, is created. `UpperFirstName` is assigned the value that is returned by `UCase(FirstName)`, the uppercase `FirstName`. And this new variable can be used like any other variable, and as often as necessary. Listing 9.6 contains a modified version of the previous listing. Try it for yourself—the output will be exactly the same as in Figure 9.9.

LISTING 9.6 `hello6.cfm`

```
<HTML>
<HEAD>
   <TITLE>Hello 6</TITLE>
</HEAD>

<BODY>

<CFSET FirstName="Ben">
<CFSET UpperFirstName=UCase(FirstName)>
<CFSET LowerFirstName=LCase(FirstName)>
<CFSET ReverseFirstName=Reverse(FirstName)>
<CFSET LenFirstName=Len(FirstName)>

<CFOUTPUT>
Hello #FirstName#, and welcome to ColdFusion!<P>
Your name in uppercase: #UpperFirstName#<BR>
Your name in lowercase: #LowerFirstName#<BR>
Your name in reverse: #ReverseFirstName#<BR>
Characters in your name: #LenFirstName#<BR>
</CFOUTPUT>

</BODY>
</HTML>
```

This code deserves a look. Five `<CFSET>` tags now exist, and five variables are created. The first creates the `FirstName` variable, just like in the previous examples. The next creates a new variable named `UpperFirstName`, which contains the uppercase version of `FirstName`. And then `LowerFirstName`, `ReverseFirstName`, and `LenFirstName` are each created with additional `<CFSET>` statements.

The <CFOUTPUT> block here contains no functions at all. Rather, it just displays the contents of the variables that were just created. In this particular listing there is actually little value in doing this, aside from the fact that the code is a little more organized this way. The real benefit in saving function output to variables is realized when a function is used many times in a single page. Then, instead of using the same function over and over, you can use it once, save the output to a variable, and just use that variable instead.

One important point to note here is that variables can be overwritten. Look at the following code snippet:

```
<CFSET FirstName="Ben">
<CFSET FirstName="Nate">
```


Here, `FirstName` is set to `Ben` and then set again to `Nate`. Variables can be overwritten as often as necessary, and whatever the current value is when accessed (displayed, or passed to other functions), that's the value that will be used.

Knowing that, what do you think the following line of code does?

```
<CFSET FirstName=UCase(FirstName)>
```

This is an example of variable overwriting, but here the variable being overwritten is the variable itself. I mentioned earlier that functions such as `UCase()` do not convert text; they return a converted copy. So how could you really convert text? By using code such as the line just shown. `<CFSET FirstName=UCase(FirstName)>` sets `FirstName` to the uppercase version of `FirstName`, effectively overwriting itself with the converted value.

VARIABLE NAMING

This would be a good place to discuss variable naming. When you create a variable you get to name it, and the choice of names is up to you. However, you need to know a few rules about variable naming:

- Variable names can contain alphanumeric characters but can't begin with a number (so `result12` is okay, but `4thresult` is not).
- Variable names can't contain spaces. If you need to separate words, use underscores (for example, `monthly_sales_figures` instead of `monthly sales figures`).
- Aside from the underscore, nonalphanumeric characters can't be used in variable names (so `Sales!`, `SSN#`, and `first-name` are all invalid).
- Variable names are case insensitive (`FirstName` is the same as `FIRSTNAME` which is the same as `firstname`).

Other than that, you can be as creative as necessary with your names. Pick any variable name you want; just be careful not to overwrite existing variables by mistake.

Tip

Avoid the use of abbreviated variable names, such as `fn` or `c`. Although these are valid names, what they stand for is not apparent just by looking at them. Yes, `fn` is less

keystrokes than `FirstName`, but the first time you (or someone else) has to stare at the code trying to figure out what a variable is for, you'll regret saving that little bit of time. As a rule, make variable names descriptive.

USING PREFIXES

ColdFusion supports many variable types, and you'll become very familiar with them as you work through this book. For example, local variables (the type you just created) are a variable type. Submitted form fields are a variable type, as are many others.

ColdFusion variables can be referenced in two ways:

- The variable name itself
- The variable name with the type as a prefix

For example, the variable `FirstName` that you used a little earlier is a local variable (type `VARIABLES`). So, that variable can be referred to as `FirstName` (as you did previously) and as `VARIABLES.FirstName`. Both are valid, and both will work (you can try editing file `hello6.cfm` to use the `VARIABLES` prefix to try this).

So, should you use prefixes? Well, there are pros and cons. Here are the pros:

- Using prefixes improves performance. ColdFusion will have less work to do finding the variable you are referring to if you explicitly provide the full name (including the prefix).
- If multiple variables exist with the same name but are of different types, the only way to be 100% sure that you'll get the variable you want is to use the prefix.

As for the cons, there is just one:

- If you omit the prefix then multiple variable types will be accessible (perhaps form fields and URL parameters, which are discussed in the following chapters). If you provide the type prefix, you restrict access to the specified type, and although this does prevent ambiguity (as just explained), it does make your code a little less reusable.

The choice is yours, and there is no real right or wrong. You can use prefixes if you see fit, and not use them if not. If you don't specify the prefix, ColdFusion will find the variable for you. And if multiple variables of the same name do exist (with differing types) then a predefined order of precedence is used (don't worry if these types are not familiar yet, they will become familiar soon enough, and you can refer to this list when necessary):

- Query results
- Local variables (`VARIABLES`)
- `CGI` variables
- `FILE` variables

- URL parameters
- FORM fields
- COOKIE values
- CLIENT variables

In other words, if you refer to #FirstName# (without specifying a prefix) and that variable exists both as a local variable (VARIABLES.FirstName) and as a FORM field (FORM.FirstName), VARIABLES.FirstName will be used automatically.

Note

An exception to this does exist. Some ColdFusion variable types must *always* be accessed with an explicit prefix; these are covered in later chapters.

WORKING WITH EXPRESSIONS

I've used the term *expressions* a few times in this chapter. What is an expression? The official ColdFusion documentation explains that expressions are "language constructs that allow you to create sophisticated applications." A better way to understand it is that expressions are strings of text made up of one or more of the following:

- Literal text (strings), numbers, dates, times, and other values
- Variables
- Operators (+ for addition, & for concatenation, and so on)
- Functions

So, UCase(FirstName) is an expression, as is "Hello, my name is Ben", 12+4, and DateFormat(Now()). And even though many people find it hard to articulate exactly what an expression is, realize that expressions are an important part of the ColdFusion language.

BUILDING EXPRESSIONS

Expressions are typed where necessary. Expressions can be passed to a <CFSET> statement as part of an assignment, used when displaying text, and passed to almost every single CFML tag (except for the few that take no attributes).

Simple expressions can be used, such as those discussed previously (variables, functions, and combinations thereof). But more complex expressions can be used, too, and expressions can include arithmetic, string, and decision operators (you'll use these in the next few chapters).

When using expressions, pound signs are used to delimit ColdFusion functions and variables within a block of text. So, how would you display the # itself? Look at the following code snippet:

```
<CFOUTPUT>
#1: #FirstName#
</CFOUTOUT>
```

You can try this yourself if you so feel inclined; you'll see that ColdFusion generates an error when it processes the code (see Figure 9.10).

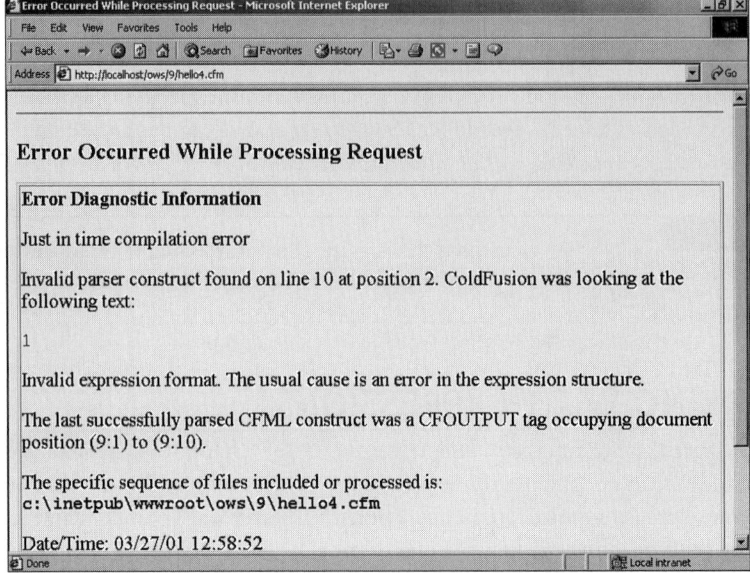

Figure 9.10
Pound signs in text must be escaped; otherwise, ColdFusion produces an error.

What causes this error? Well, when ColdFusion encounters the # at the start of the line, it assumes you are delimiting a variable or a function and tries to find the matching # (which of course does not exist). The solution is to *escape* the pound sign (flag it as being a real pound sign), as follows:

```
<CFOUTPUT>
##1: #FirstName#
</CFOUTOUT>
```

When ColdFusion encounters ##, it knows that # is not delimiting a variable or function. Instead, it correctly displays a single #.

When To Use #, and When Not To

Before we go any further, let's clarify exactly when pound signs are needed and when they're not.

Simply put, pound signs are needed to flag functions and variables within a string of text.

So, in this first example, the pound signs are obviously needed:

```
Hello #VARIABLES.FirstName#
```

But what about when a variable is used within a tag, like this?

```
<CFSET UpperFirstName=UCase(FirstName)>
```

Here pound signs are not necessary because ColdFusion assumes that anything passed to a tag is a function or variable unless explicitly defined as a string. So, the following is incorrect:

```
<CFSET #UpperFirstName#=#UCase(FirstName)#>
```

This code will actually work (ColdFusion is very forgiving), but it is still incorrect and should not be used.

This next example declares a variable and assigns a value that is a string, so no pound signs are needed here:

```
<CFSET FirstName="Ben">
```


But if the string contains variables, pound signs would be necessary. Look at this next example: `FullName` is assigned a string, but the string contains two variables (`FirstName` and `LastName`) and those variables must be enclosed within pound signs (otherwise ColdFusion will assign the text, not the variable values):

```
<CFSET FullName="#FirstName# #LastName#">
```

Incidentally, the previous line of code is functionally equivalent to the following:

```
<CFSET FullName=FirstName & " " & LastName>
```

Here pound signs are not necessary because the variables are not being referred to within a string.

Again, the rule is this—only use pound signs when referring to variables and functions within a block of text. Simple as that.

USING COLDFUSION DATA TYPES

The variables you have used thus far are simple variables, are defined, and contain a value. ColdFusion supports three advanced data types that I'll briefly introduce now.

Note

This is just an introduction to lists, arrays, and structures. All three are used repeatedly throughout the rest of this book, so don't worry if you do not fully understand them by the time you are done reading this chapter. Right now, the intent is to ensure that you know these exist and what they are. You'll have lots of opportunities to use them soon enough.

LISTS

Lists are used to group together related information. Lists are actually strings (plain text)—what makes them lists is that a delimiter is used to separate items within the string. For example, the following is a comma-delimited list of five U.S. states:

```
California,Florida,Michigan,Massachusetts,New York
```

The next example is also a list. Even though it might not look like a list, a sentence is a list delimited by spaces:

```
This is a ColdFusion list
```

Lists are created just like any other variables. For example, this next line of code uses the `<CFSET>` tag to create a variable named `fruit` that contains a list of six fruits:

```
<CFSET fruit="apple,banana,cherry,grape,mango,orange">
```

Listing 9.7 demonstrates the use of lists. Type the code and save it as `list.cfm` in the `9` directory; then execute it. You should see an output similar to the one shown in Figure 9.11.

LISTING 9.7 `list.cfm`

```
<HTML>
<HEAD>
   <TITLE>List Example</TITLE>
</HEAD>

<BODY>

<CFSET fruit="apple,banana,cherry,grape,mango,orange">
<CFOUTPUT>
Complete list: #fruit#<BR>
Number of fruit in list: #ListLen(fruit)#<BR>
First fruit: #ListFirst(fruit)#<BR>
Last fruit: #ListLast(fruit)#<BR>
<CFSET fruit=ListAppend(fruit, "pineapple")>
Complete list: #fruit#<BR>
Number of fruit in list: #ListLen(fruit)#<BR>
First fruit: #ListFirst(fruit)#<BR>
Last fruit: #ListLast(fruit)#<BR>
</CFOUTPUT>

</BODY>
</HTML>
```

Let's walk through the code. A `<CFSET>` is used to create a list, which is simply a string. Therefore, a simple variable assignment can be used.

Next comes the `<CFOUTPUT>` block, starting with displaying `#fruit#` (the complete list). The next line of code uses the `ListLen()` function to return the number of items in the list (there are `6` of them). Individual list members can be retrieved using `ListFirst()` (used here to get the first list element), `ListLast()` (used here to get the last list element), and `ListGetAt()` (used to retrieve any list element, but not used in this example).

Then another `<CFSET>` tag is used, as follows:

```
<CFSET fruit=ListAppend(fruit, "pineapple")>
```

This code uses the `ListAppend()` function to add an element to the list. You will recall that functions return copies of modified variables, not modified variables themselves. So the `<CFSET>` tag assigns the value returned by `ListAppend()` to `fruit`, effectively overwriting the list with the new revised list.

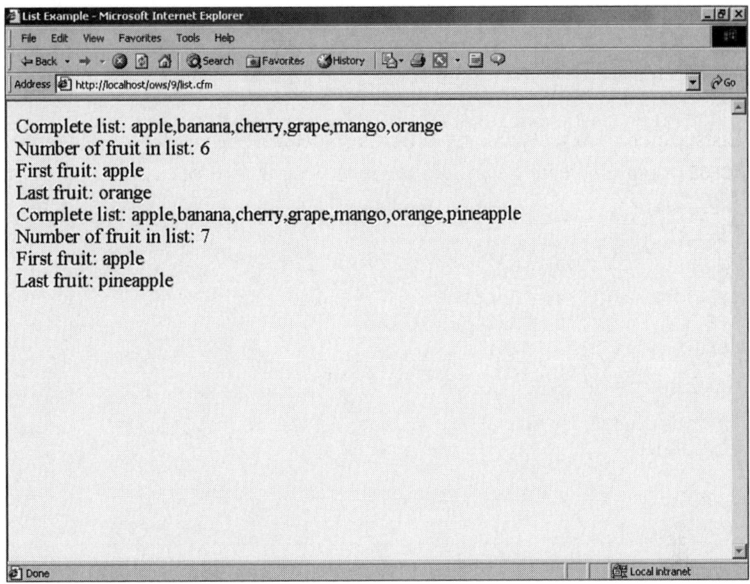

Figure 9.11
Lists are useful for grouping related data into simple sets.

Then the number of items, as well as the first and last items, are displayed again. This time `7` items are in the list, and the last item has changed to `pineapple`.

As you can see, lists are very easy to use and provide a simple mechanism for grouping related data.

Note

I mentioned earlier that a sentence is a list delimited by spaces. The default list delimiter is indeed a comma. Actually, though, *any* character can be used as a list delimiter, and every list function takes an optional delimiter attribute if necessary.

ARRAYS

Arrays, like lists, store multiple values in a single variable. But unlike lists, arrays can contain far more complex data (including lists and even other arrays).

Unlike lists, arrays support multiple dimensions. A single dimensional array is actually quite similar to a list: It's a linear collection. A two-dimensional array is more like a grid (imagine a spreadsheet), and data is stored in rows and columns. ColdFusion also supports three-dimensional arrays, which can be envisioned as cubes of data.

If this all sounds somewhat complex, well, it is. Arrays are not as easy to use as lists are, but they are far more powerful (and far quicker). Listing 9.8 contains a simple block of code that creates an array and displays part of it; the output is shown in Figure 9.12. To try it out, type the code and save it as `array.cfm`.

LISTING 9.8 `array.cfm`

```
<HTML>
<HEAD>
   <TITLE>Array Example</TITLE>
</HEAD>

<BODY>

<CFSET names=ArrayNew(2)>
<CFSET names[1][1]="Ben">
<CFSET names[1][2]="Forta">
<CFSET names[2][1]="Nate">
<CFSET names[2][2]="Weiss">

<CFOUTPUT>
The first name in the array #names[1][1]# #names[1][2]#
</CFOUTPUT>

</BODY>
</HTML>
```

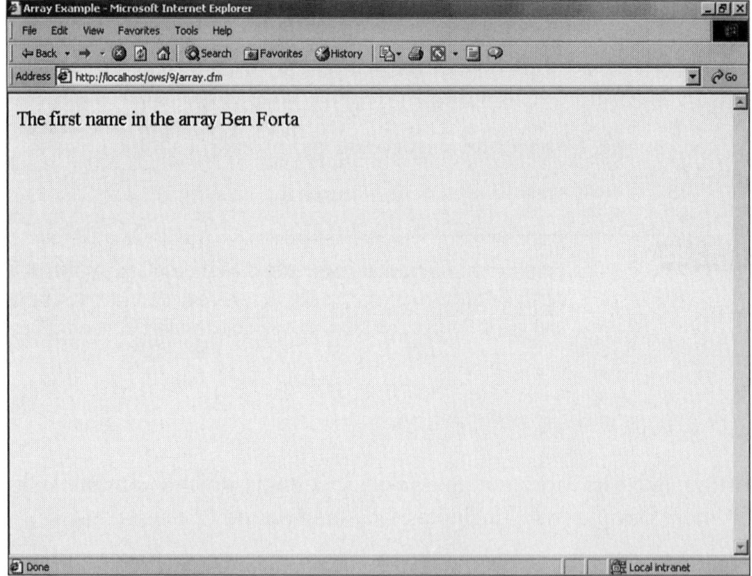

Figure 9.12
Arrays treat data as if it were in a one-, two-, or three-dimensional grid.

Arrays are created using the `ArrayNew()` function. `ArrayNew()` requires that the desired dimension be passed as a parameter, so the following code creates a two-dimensional array named `names`:

```
<CFSET names=ArrayNew(2)>
```

Array elements are set using `<CFSET>`, just like any other variables. But unlike other variables, when array elements are set the element number must be specified using an index (a relative position starting at 1). So, in a single dimensional array, names[1] would refer to the first element and names[6] would refer to the sixth. In two-dimensional arrays, both dimensions must be specified, as seen in these next four lines (taken from Listing 9.8):

```
<CFSET names[1][1]="Ben">
<CFSET names[1][2]="Forta">
<CFSET names[2][1]="Nate">
<CFSET names[2][2]="Weiss">
```


names[1][1] refers to the first element in the first dimension—think of it as the first column of the first row in a grid. names[1][2] refers to the second column in that first row, and so on.

When accessed, even for display, the indexes must be used. Therefore, the following line of code

```
The first name in the array #names[1][1]# #names[1][2]#
```

generates this output:

```
The first name in the array Ben Forta
```

As you can see, although they're not as easy to use as lists, arrays are a very flexible and powerful language feature.

STRUCTURES

Structures are the most powerful and flexible data type within ColdFusion, so powerful in fact that many internal variables (including ones listed in Appendix C, "Special ColdFusion Variables and Result Codes") are structures internally.

Simply put, structures provide a way to store data within data. Unlike arrays, structures have no special dimensions and are not like grids. Rather, they can be thought of as top-level folders that can store data, or other folders, which in turn can store data, or other folders, and so on. Structures can contain lists, arrays, and even other structures.

To give you a sneak peek at what structures look like, see Listing 9.9. Give it a try yourself; save the file as structure.cfm, and you should see output as shown in Figure 9.13.

LISTING 9.9 structure.cfm

```
<HTML>
<HEAD>
   <TITLE>Structure Example</TITLE>
</HEAD>

<BODY>

<CFSET contact=StructNew()>
<CFSET contact.FirstName="Ben">
<CFSET contact.LastName="Forta">
<CFSET contact.EMail="ben@forta.com">
```

LISTING 9.9 CONTINUED

```
<CFOUTPUT>
E-Mail:
<A HREF="mailto:#contact.EMail#">#contact.FirstName# #contact.LastName#</A>
</CFOUTPUT>

</BODY>
</HTML>
```

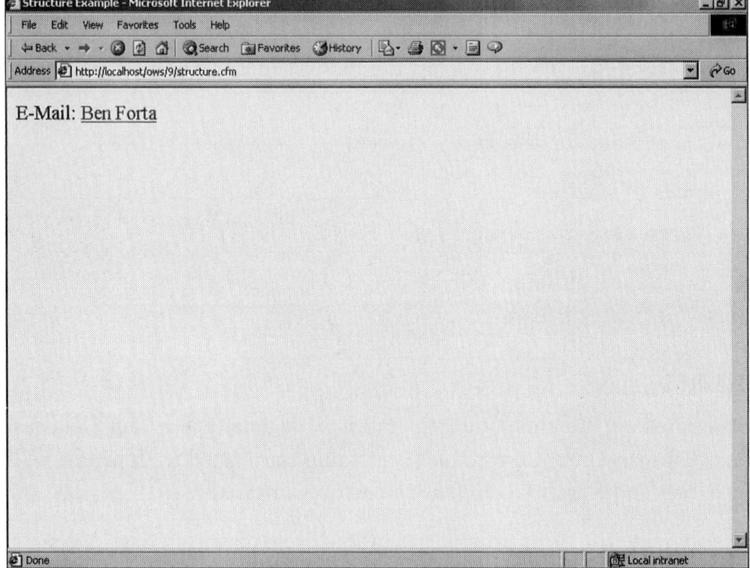

Figure 9.13 Structures are the most powerful data type in ColdFusion and are used internally extensively.

Structures are created using `StructNew()`, which—unlike `ArrayNew()`—takes no parameters. After a structure is created, variables can be set inside it. The following three lines of code all set variables with the `contact` structure:

```
<CFSET contact.FirstName="Ben">
<CFSET contact.LastName="Forta">
<CFSET contact.EMail="ben@forta.com">
```

To access structure members, simply refer to them by name. `#contact.FirstName#` accesses the `FirstName` member of the `contact` structure. Therefore, the code

```
<A HREF="mailto:#contact.EMail#">#contact.FirstName# #contact.LastName#</A>
```

generates this output:

```
<A HREF="mailto:ben@forta.com">Ben Forta</A>
```

And that's just scratching the surface. Structures are incredibly powerful, and you'll use them extensively as you work through this book.

Note

For simplicity's sake, I have described only the absolute basic form of structure use. ColdFusion features an entire set of structure manipulation functions that can be used to better take advantage of structures–you use some of them in the next chapter, "CFML Basics."

COMMENTING YOUR CODE

The last introductory topic I want to mention is commenting your code. Many books leave this to the very end, but I believe it is so important that I am introducing the concept right here—before you start real coding.

The code you have worked with thus far has been short, simple, and rather self-explanatory. But as you start building bigger and more complex applications, your code will become more involved and more complex. And then comments become vital. The reasons to comment your code include

- If you make code as self-descriptive as possible, when you revisit it at a later date you'll remember what you did, and why.
- This is even truer if others have to work on your code. The more detailed and accurate comments are, the easier (and safer) it will be to make changes or corrections when necessary.
- Commented code is much easier to debug than uncommented code.
- Commented code tends to be better organized, too.

And that's just the start of it.

Listing 9.10 is a revised version of `hello6.cfm`; all that has changed is the inclusion of comments. And as you can see from Figure 9.14, this has no impact on generated output whatsoever.

LISTING 9.10 `hello7.cfm`

```
<!---
Name:        hello7.cfm
Author:      Ben Forta (ben@forta.com)
Description: Demonstrate use of comments
Created:     3/27/01
--->

<HTML>
<HEAD>
   <TITLE>Hello 7</TITLE>
</HEAD>

<BODY>
```

LISTING 9.10 CONTINUED

```
<!--- Save name --->
<CFSET FirstName="Ben">

<!--- Save converted versions of name --->
<CFSET UpperFirstName=UCase(FirstName)>
<CFSET LowerFirstName=LCase(FirstName)>
<CFSET ReverseFirstName=Reverse(FirstName)>

<!--- Save name length --->
<CFSET LenFirstName=Len(FirstName)>

<!--- Display output --->
<CFOUTPUT>
Hello #FirstName#, and welcome to ColdFusion!<P>
Your name in uppercase: #UpperFirstName#<BR>
Your name in lowercase: #LowerFirstName#<BR>
Your name in reverse: #ReverseFirstName#<BR>
Characters in your name: #LenFirstName#<BR>
</CFOUTPUT>

</BODY>
</HTML>
```

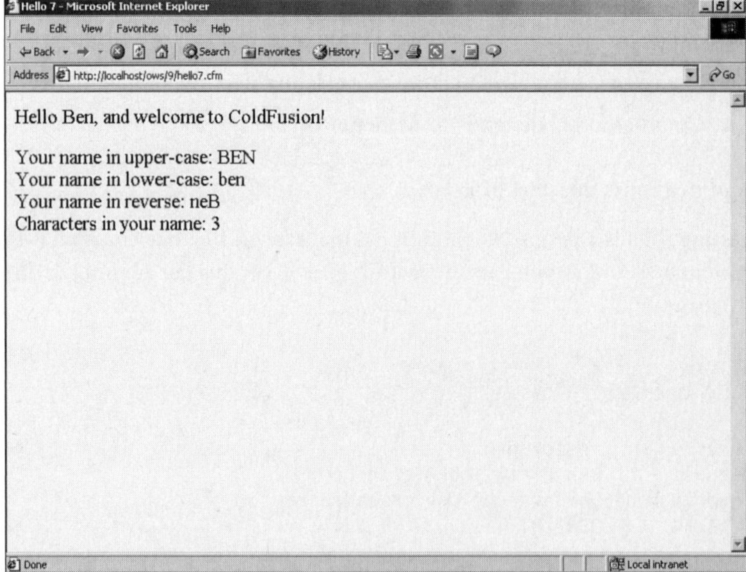

Figure 9.14 ColdFusion comments in your code are never sent to the client browser.

Comments are typed between `<!---` and `--->` tags. Comments should never be nested and should never be mismatched (such as having a starting tag without an end tag, or vice versa).

Note

ColdFusion uses `<!---` and `--->` to delimit comments. HTML uses `<!--` and `-->` (two hyphens instead of three). Within ColdFusion code, always use ColdFusion comments and not HTML comments. The latter will be sent to the client (they won't be displayed, but they will still be sent), whereas the former won't.

Tip

Commenting code is a useful debugging technique. When you are testing code and need to eliminate specific lines, you can *comment them out* temporarily by wrapping them within `<!---` and `--->` tags.

CHAPTER 10

CFML Basics

In this chapter

WORKING WITH CONDITIONAL PROCESSING

Chapter 9, "Using ColdFusion," introduced two ColdFusion tags (`<CFOUTPUT>` and `<CFSET>`), functions, and variables. This chapter takes CFML one step further, adding conditional and programmatic processing—the stuff that starts to add real power to your code.

The code you wrote in the last chapter was linear—ColdFusion started at the top of the page and processed every line in order. And although that works for simple applications, more often than not you'll need to write code that does various things based on conditions, such as the following:

- Displaying different messages based on the time of day or day of week
- Personalizing content based on user login
- Informing users of the status of searches or other operations
- Displaying (or hiding) options based on security level

All these require intelligence within your code to facilitate decision making. Conditional processing is the mechanism by which this is done, and ColdFusion supports two forms of conditional processing:

- If statements, created using `<CFIF>` and related tags
- Switch statements, created using `<CFSWITCH>` and `<CFCASE>`

Let's start by taking a look at these in detail.

IF STATEMENTS

If statements are a fundamental part of most development languages, and even though the syntax varies from one language to the next, the basic concepts and options are the same. If statements are used to create conditions that are evaluated, enabling you to perform actions based on the result.

The conditions passed to if statements always evaluate to `TRUE` or `FALSE`, and any condition that can be expressed as a `TRUE` / `FALSE` (or `YES` / `NO`) question is valid. Here are some examples of valid conditions:

- Is today Monday?
- Does variable `FirstName` exist?
- Were any rows retrieved from a database?
- Does variable one equal variable two?
- Is a specific word in a sentence?

More complex conditions (multiple conditions) are allowed, too:

- Is today Sunday or Saturday?
- Was a credit card number provided, and if yes, has it been validated?

- Does the currently logged-in user have a first name of `Ben` and a last name of `Forta`, or a first name of `Nate` and a last name of `Weiss`?

The common denominator here is that all these conditions can be answered with `TRUE` or `FALSE`, so they are all valid conditions.

Note

In ColdFusion the words `TRUE` and `FALSE` can be used when evaluating conditions. In addition, `YES` can be used in lieu of `TRUE`, and `NO` can be used in lieu of `FALSE`.

It is also worth noting that *all* numbers are either `TRUE` or `FALSE`: `0` is `FALSE`, and any other number (positive or negative) is `TRUE`.

BASIC IF STATEMENTS

ColdFusion if statements are created using the `<CFIF>` tag. `<CFIF>` takes no attributes; instead, it takes a condition. For example, the following `<CFIF>` statement checks to see whether a variable named `FirstName` contains the value `Ben`:

```
<CFIF FirstName IS "Ben">
```

The keyword `IS` is an operator used to test for equality. Other operators are supported, too, as listed in Table 10.1.

TABLE 10.1 CFML EVALUATION OPERATORS

Operator	Shortcut	Description
EQUAL	IS, EQ	Tests for equality
NOT EQUAL	IS NOT, NEQ	Tests for nonequality
GREATER THAN	GT	Tests for greater than
GREATER THAN OR EQUAL TO	GTE	Tests for greater than or equal to
LESS THAN	LT	Tests for less than
LESS THAN OR EQUAL TO	LTE	Tests for less than or equal to
CONTAINS		Tests whether a value is contained within a second value
DOES NOT CONTAIN		Tests whether a value is not contained within a second value

Most CFML operators have shortcuts you can use. The `IS` operator used in the previous code example is actually a shortcut for `EQUAL`, and that condition is actually

```
<CFIF FirstName EQUAL "Ben">
```

To test whether `FirstName` is not `Ben`, you could use the following code:

```
<CFIF FirstName IS NOT "Ben">
```

or

```
<CFIF FirstName NEQ "Ben">
```

or

```
<CFIF FirstName NOT EQUAL "Ben">
```

or even

```
<CFIF NOT FirstName IS "Ben">
```

In this last snippet, the `NOT` operator is used to negate a condition.

Ready to try `<CFIF>` yourself? Listing 10.1 contains a simple application that checks to see whether it is the weekend (see Figure 10.1). Save the file as `if1.cfm`, and to execute it go to this URL:

```
http://localhost/ows/10/if1.cfm
```

Tip

Don't forget to create the `10` directory under `ows`; all the code created in this chapter should go in that directory.

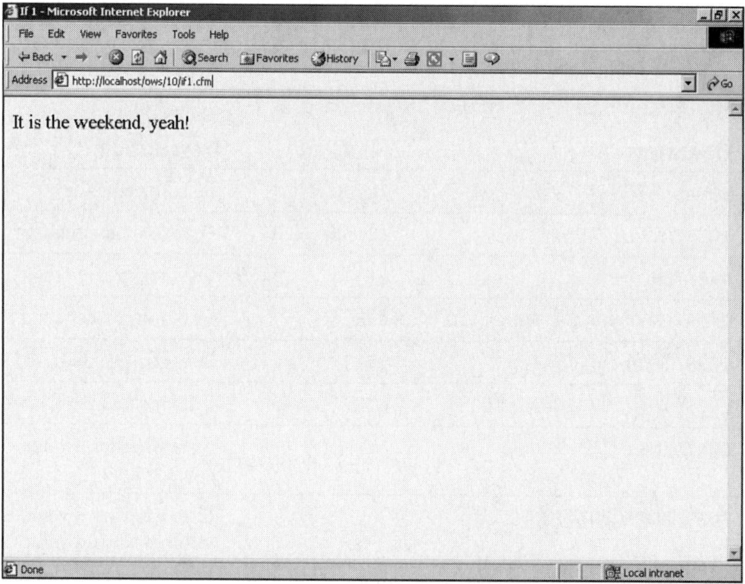

Figure 10.1
`<CFIF>` statements can be used to display output conditionally.

LISTING 10.1 `if1.cfm`

```
<!---
Name:        if1.cfm
Author:      Ben Forta (ben@forta.com)
Description: Demonstrate use of <CFIF>
```

```
Created:     3/27/01
--->

<HTML>
<HEAD>
   <TITLE>If 1</TITLE>
</HEAD>

<BODY>

<!--- Is it the weekend? --->
<CFIF DayOfWeek(Now()) IS 1>
   <!--- Yes it is, great! --->
   It is the weekend, yeah!
</CFIF>

</BODY>
</HTML>
```


The code in Listing 10.1 should be pretty self-explanatory. A comment header describes the code, and then the standard HTML `<HEAD>` and `<BODY>` tags are used to create the page. Then comes the `<CFIF>` statement:

```
<CFIF DayOfWeek(Now()) IS 1>
```

As you already have seen, `Now()` is a function that returns the current system date and time. `DayOfWeek()` is a function that returns the day of the week for a specified date (a variable, a literal, or another function). `DayOfWeek(Now())` returns the current day of the week: `1` for Sunday, `2` for Monday, `3` for Tuesday, and so on. The condition `DayOfWeek(Now()) IS 1` is then simply checks to see whether it is Sunday—if it is Sunday then the condition evaluates to `TRUE`, and if not, it evaluates to `FALSE`.

If it's `TRUE`, the text between the `<CFIF>` and `</CFIF>` tags is displayed. It's as simple as that.

MULTICONDITION IF STATEMENTS

A couple of problems exist with Listing 10.1, the most important of which is that weekends are made up of both Sundays and Saturdays. Therefore, the code to check whether it is the weekend needs to check for both days.

Listing 10.2 contains a revised version of the code; save this file as `if2.cfm`, and then execute it.

Tip

So as not to have to retype all the code as you make changes, use Studio's File, Save As menu option to save the file with the new name, and then edit the newly saved file.

LISTING 10.2 `if2.cfm`

```
<!---
Name:        if2.cfm
```

LISTING 10.2 CONTINUED

```
Author:       Ben Forta (ben@forta.com)
Description: Demonstrate use of multiple conditions
Created:      3/27/01
--->

<HTML>
<HEAD>
   <TITLE>If 2</TITLE>
</HEAD>

<BODY>

<!--- Is it the weekend? --->
<CFIF (DayOfWeek(Now()) IS 1) OR (DayOfWeek(Now()) IS 7)>
   <!--- Yes it is, great! --->
   It is the weekend, yeah!
</CFIF>

</BODY>
</HTML>
```

The code is the same as Listing 10.1, except for the `<CFIF>` statement itself:

```
<CFIF (DayOfWeek(Now()) IS 1) OR (DayOfWeek(Now()) IS 7)>
```

This statement contains two conditions, one that checks whether the day of the week is `1` (Sunday), and one that checks whether it is `7` (Saturday). If it is Sunday or Saturday, the message is displayed correctly—problem solved.

To tell ColdFusion to test for either condition, the `OR` operator is used. By using `OR` if either of the specified conditions is `TRUE`, the condition returns `TRUE`. `FALSE` is returned only if *neither* condition is `TRUE`. This is in contrast to the `AND` operator, which requires that both conditions are `TRUE` and returns `FALSE` if only one or no conditions are `TRUE`. Look at the following code snippet:

```
<CFIF (FirstName IS "Ben") AND (LastName IS "Forta")>
```

For this condition to be `TRUE`, the `FirstName` must be `Ben` and the `LastName` must be `Forta`. `Ben` with any other `LastName` or `Forta` with any other `FirstName` fails the test.

`AND` and `OR` are logical operators (sometimes called *Boolean* operators). These two are the most frequently used logical operators, but others are supported, too, as listed in Table 10.2.

TABLE 10.2 CFML LOGICAL OPERATORS

Operator	Description
AND	Returns TRUE only if both conditions are TRUE
OR	Returns TRUE if at least one condition is TRUE
XOR	Returns TRUE if either condition is TRUE, but not if both or neither are TRUE

Operator	Description
EQV	Tests for equivalence and returns TRUE if both conditions are the same (either both TRUE or both FALSE, but not if one is TRUE and one is FALSE)
IMP	Tests for implication; returns FALSE only when the first condition is TRUE and the second is FALSE
NOT	Negates any other logical operator

Note

You probably noticed that when multiple conditions (either AND or OR) were used, each condition was enclosed within parentheses. This is not required but is generally good practice. Not only does it make the code cleaner and easier to read, but it also prevents bugs from being introduced by expressions being evaluated in ways other than you expected. For example, if both AND and OR are used in a condition, AND is always evaluated before OR, which might or might not be what you want. Parentheses are evaluated before AND, so by using parentheses you can explicitly manage the order of evaluation.

IF AND ELSE

The code in Listing 10.2 is logically correct: If it is Sunday or Saturday then it is indeed the weekend, and the weekend message is displayed. But what if it is not Sunday or Saturday? Right now, nothing is displayed at all—that must be fixed.

Listing 10.3 contains the revised code, capable of displaying a non-weekend message if necessary (see Figure 10.2). Save this code as `if3.cfm`, and then execute it.

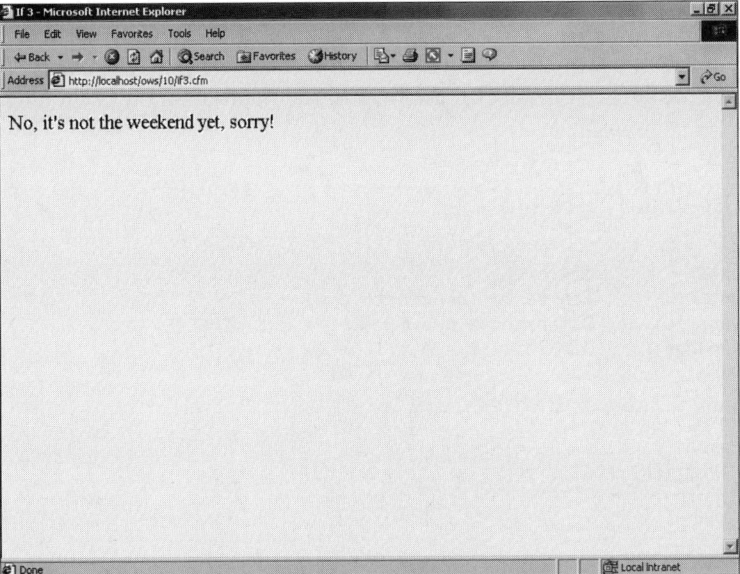

Figure 10.2
<CFELSE> enables the creation of code to be executed when a <CFIF> test fails.

LISTING 10.3 `if3.cfm`

```
<!---
Name:        if3.cfm
Author:      Ben Forta (ben@forta.com)
Description: Demonstrate use of <CFIF> and <CFELSE>
Created:     3/27/01
--->

<HTML>
<HEAD>
   <TITLE>If 3</TITLE>
</HEAD>

<BODY>

<!--- Is it the weekend? --->
<CFIF (DayOfWeek(Now()) IS 1) OR (DayOfWeek(Now()) IS 7)>
   <!--- Yes it is, great! --->
   It is the weekend, yeah!
<CFELSE>
   <!--- No it is not :-( --->
   No, it's not the weekend yet, sorry!
</CFIF>

</BODY>
</HTML>
```

The only real difference between Listings 10.2 and 10.3 is the introduction of a new tag—`<CFELSE>`. `<CFIF>` is used to define code to be executed when a condition is `TRUE`, and `<CFELSE>` defines code to be executed when a condition is `FALSE`. `<CFELSE>` takes no attributes and can be used only between `<CFIF>` and `</CFIF>` tags. The new code will now display `It is the weekend, yeah!` if it is Sunday or Saturday and `No, it's not the weekend yet, sorry!` if not. Much better.

But before you move on, Listing 10.4 contains one more refinement—a cleaner `<CFIF>` statement. Save Listing 10.4 as `if4.cfm`, and then execute it (it should do exactly what Listing 10.3 did).

LISTING 10.4 `if4.cfm`

```
<!---
Name:        if4.cfm
Author:      Ben Forta (ben@forta.com)
Description: Demonstrate use of <CFIF> and <CFELSE>
Created:     3/27/01
--->

<HTML>
<HEAD>
   <TITLE>If 4</TITLE>
</HEAD>

<BODY>
```

```
<!--- Is it the weekend? --->
<CFSET weekend=(DayOfWeek(Now()) IS 1) OR (DayOfWeek(Now()) IS 7)>

<!--- Let the user know --->
<CFIF weekend>
   <!--- Yes it is, great! --->
   It is the weekend, yeah!
<CFELSE>
   <!--- No it is not :-( --->
   No, it's not the weekend yet, sorry!
</CFIF>

</BODY>
</HTML>
```

The more complex conditions become, the harder they are to read. So, many developers prefer to save the results of executed conditions to variables for later use. Look at this line of code (from Listing 10.4):

```
<CFSET weekend=(DayOfWeek(Now()) IS 1) OR (DayOfWeek(Now()) IS 7)>
```


Here, `<CFSET>` is used to create a variable named `weekend`. The value stored in this variable is whatever the condition returns. So, if it is a weekend (Sunday or Saturday), `weekend` will be `TRUE`, and if it is not a weekend then `weekend` will be `FALSE`.

Note

See Chapter 9, "Using ColdFusion," for detailed coverage of the `<CFSET>` tag.

After `weekend` is set, it can be used in the `<CFIF>` statement:

```
<CFIF weekend>
```

If `weekend` is `TRUE` then the first block of text is displayed; otherwise, the `<CFELSE>` text is displayed.

But what is `weekend` being compared to? In every condition thus far, you have used an operator (such as `IS`) to test a condition. Here, however, no operator is used; so what is `weekend` being tested against?

Actually, `weekend` is indeed being tested; it is being compared to `TRUE`. Within a `<CFIF>` the comparison is optional, and if it's omitted, a comparison to `TRUE` is assumed. So, `<CFIF weekend>` is functionally the same as

```
<CFIF weekend IS TRUE>
```

The `weekend` variable contains either `TRUE` or `FALSE`. If it's `TRUE`, the condition is effectively

```
<CFIF TRUE IS TRUE>
```

which obviously evaluates to `TRUE`. But if `weekend` is `FALSE`, the condition is

```
<CFIF FALSE IS TRUE>
```

which obviously is `FALSE`.

Note

I said that `weekend` contained either `TRUE` or `FALSE`, but feel free to test that for yourself. If you add the following line to your code, you'll be able to display the contents of `weekend`:

```
<CFOUTPUT>#weekend#</CFOUTPUT>
```

As you can see, you have a lot of flexibility when it comes to writing `<CFIF>` statements.

Multiple If Statements

There's one more feature of `<CFIF>` that you need to look at—support for multiple independent conditions (as opposed to one condition made up of multiple conditions).

The best way to explain this is with an example. In the previous listings you displayed a message on weekends. But what if you wanted to display different messages on Sunday and Saturday? You could create multiple `<CFIF> </CFIF>` blocks, but there is a better way.

Listing 10.5 contains yet another version of the code; this time the filename should be `if5.cfm`.

Listing 10.5 `if5.cfm`

```
<!---
Name:        if5.cfm
Author:      Ben Forta (ben@forta.com)
Description: Demonstrate use of <CFIF>
Created:     3/27/01
--->

<HTML>
<HEAD>
   <TITLE>If 5</TITLE>
</HEAD>

<BODY>

<!--- Get day of week --->
<CFSET dow=DayOfWeek(Now())>

<!--- Let the user know --->
<CFIF dow IS 1>
   <!--- It's Sunday --->
   It is the weekend! But make the most of it, tomorrow it's back to work.
<CFELSEIF dow IS 7>
   <!--- It's Saturday --->
   It is the weekend! And even better, tomorrow is the weekend too!
<CFELSE>
   <!--- No it is not :-( --->
   No, it's not the weekend yet, sorry!
</CFIF>

</BODY>
</HTML>
```

Let's take a look at the previous code. A `<CFSET>` is used to create a variable named `dow`, which contains the day of the week (the value returned by `DayOfWeek(Now())`, a number from `1` to `7`).

The `<CFIF>` statement checks to see whether `dow is 1`, and if `TRUE`, displays the Sunday message (see Figure 10.3). Then a `<CFELSEIF>` is used to provide an alternative `<CFIF>` statement:

```
<CFELSEIF dow IS 7>
```

The `<CFELSEIF>` checks to see whether `dow is 7`, and if `TRUE`, displays the Saturday message (see Figure 10.4). And then finally, `<CFELSE>` is used to display text if neither the `<CFIF>` nor the `<CFELSEIF>` are `TRUE`.

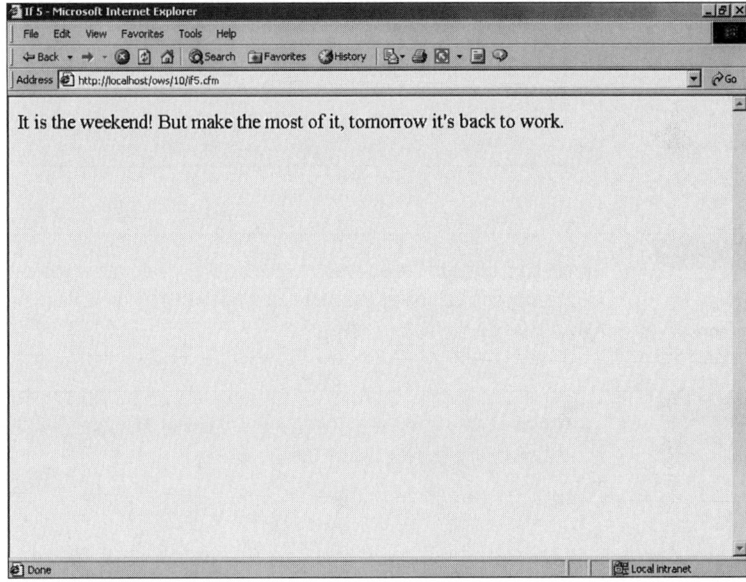

Figure 10.3
If `dow` is `1`, the Sunday message is displayed.

> **Note**
>
> `<CFELSEIF>` is essentially a combined `<CFELSE>` and `<CFIF>`, and thus its name.

Aside from being more readable, there is another benefit in saving conditions' results to variables (as you did here with the `dow` variable and previously with `weekend`). As a rule, you should avoid repeating code—with the exact same expressions (getting the day of the week) used in multiple places, you run the risk that one day you'll update the code and not make all the changes in all the required locations. If just a single expression must be changed, that potential problem is avoided.

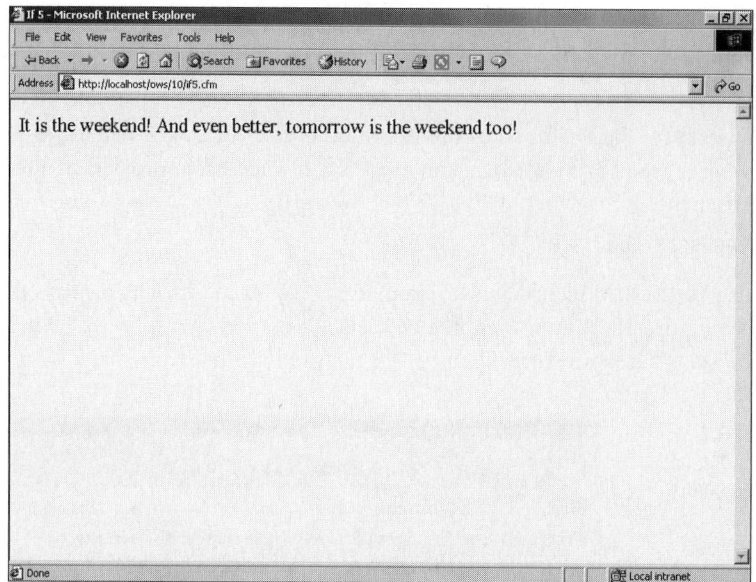

Figure 10.4
If dow is 7, the Saturday message is displayed.

Tip

No limit exists to the number of `<CFELSEIF>` statements you use within a `<CFIF>` tag, but you can never use more than one `<CFIF>` or `<CFELSE>`.

Note

Use of `<CFELSEIF>` and `<CFELSE>` is optional. However, if `<CFELSE>` is use, it must always be the last tag before the `</CFIF>`.

PUTTING IT ALL TOGETHER

`<CFIF>` is one of the most frequently used tags in CFML. So before we move on to the next subject, let's walk through one more example—a slightly more complex one.

Guess the Number is a simple game, similar to *I'm thinking of a number between 1 and 10, guess what number I am thinking of.* ColdFusion picks a random number, you guess a number, and ColdFusion will tell you whether you guessed the correct number.

Listing 10.6 contains the code for `guess1.cfm`. Save it in the `10` directory, but do not execute it in the integrated browser (using the Browse tab). Instead, use this URL to execute it:

`http://localhost/ows/10/guess1.cfm?guess=`*n*

Replace *n* with a number from 1 to 10. For example, if you guess 5, use this URL:

`http://localhost/ows/10/guess1.cfm?guess=5`

You'll see an output similar to the ones shown in Figures 10.5 and 10.6 (actually, if you reload the page often enough, you'll see both figures).

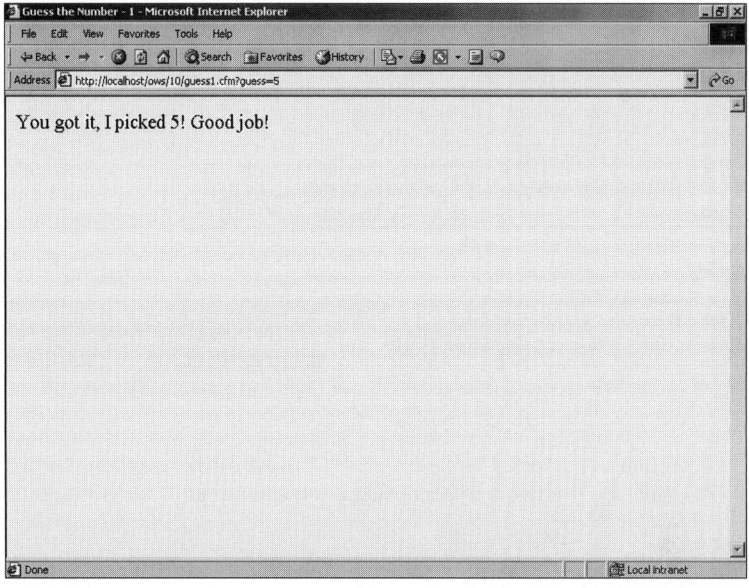

Figure 10.5
`URL.guess` matched the number ColdFusion picked.

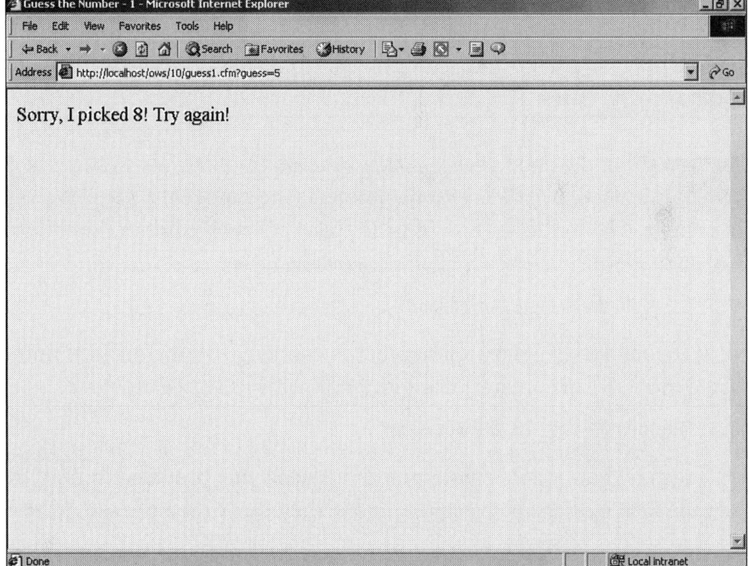

Figure 10.6
`URL.guess` did not match the number ColdFusion picked.

Listing 10.6 guess1.cfm

```
<!---
Name:        guess1.cfm
Author:      Ben Forta (ben@forta.com)
Description: Demonstrate use of multiple if statements
```

LISTING 10.6 CONTINUED

```
Created:     3/27/01
--->

<HTML>
<HEAD>
   <TITLE>Guess the Number - 1</TITLE>
</HEAD>

<BODY>

<!--- Pick a random number --->
<CFSET RandomNumber=RandRange(1, 10)>

<!--- Check if matched --->
<CFIF RandomNumber IS URL.guess>
   <!--- It matched --->
   <CFOUTPUT>
   You got it, I picked #RandomNumber#! Good job!
   </CFOUTPUT>
<CFELSE>
   <!--- No match --->
   <CFOUTPUT>
   Sorry, I picked #RandomNumber#! Try again!
   </CFOUTPUT>
</CFIF>

</BODY>
</HTML>
```

The first thing the code does is pick a random number. To do this, the `RandRange()` function is used—`RandRange()` takes two parameters (the range) and returns a random number within that range. The following line of code thus returns a random number from 1 to 10 (inclusive) and saves it in a variable named `RandomNumber`:

```
<CFSET RandomNumber=RandRange(1, 10)>
```

Next, the randomly generated number is compared to the guessed number (which was passed as a URL parameter) using the following `<CFIF>` statement:

```
<CFIF RandomNumber IS URL.guess>
```

`URL.guess` is the variable containing the `guess` value provided in the URL. If the two match then the first message is displayed, and if they don't then the second message is displayed.

Note

`URL` variables, and how they are used, are covered in detail in Chapter 11, "Creating Data-Driven Pages." For now, though, it is sufficient to know that variables passed as parameters to a URL are accessible via the `URL` scope.

But what if no guess parameter was specified? You will recall from Chapter 9 that referring to a variable that does not exist generates an error. Therefore, you should modify the code to check that URL.guess exists before using it. Listing 10.7 contains the modified version of the code; save this file as guess2.cfm.

LISTING 10.7 guess2.cfm

```
<!---
Name:        guess2.cfm
Author:      Ben Forta (ben@forta.com)
Description: Demonstrate use of multiple if statements
Created:     3/27/01
--->

<HTML>
<HEAD>
   <TITLE>Guess the Number - 2</TITLE>
</HEAD>

<BODY>

<!--- Pick a random number --->
<CFSET RandomNumber=RandRange(1, 10)>

<!--- Check if number was passed --->
<CFIF IsDefined("URL.guess")>

   <!--- Yes it was, did it match? --->
   <CFIF RandomNumber IS URL.guess>
      <!--- It matched --->
      <CFOUTPUT>
      You got it, I picked #RandomNumber#! Good job!
      </CFOUTPUT>
   <CFELSE>
      <!--- No match --->
       <CFOUTPUT>
       Sorry, I picked #RandomNumber#! Try again!
       </CFOUTPUT>
   </CFIF>

<CFELSE>

   <!--- No guess specified, give instructions --->
   You did not guess a number.<BR>
   To guess a number, reload this page adding
   <B>?guess=n</B> (where n is the guess, for
   example, ?guess=5). Number should be between
   1 and 10.

</CFIF>

</BODY>
</HTML>
```

Listing 10.7 introduces a new concept in `<CFIF>` statements—nested `<CFIF>` tags. Let's take a look at the code. The first `<CFIF>` statement is

```
<CFIF IsDefined("URL.guess")>
```

`IsDefined()` is a CFML function that checks whether a variable exists. `IsDefined("URL.guess")` returns `TRUE` if `guess` was passed on the URL and `FALSE` if not. Using this function, you can process the guess only if it actually exists. So, the entire code block (complete with `<CFIF>` and `<CFELSE>` tags) is within the `TRUE` block of the outer `<CFIF>` and the original `<CFIF>` block is now nested—it is a `<CFIF>` within a `<CFIF>`.

This then also enables you to add another `<CFELSE>` block—on the outer `<CFIF>`. Remember, the outer `<CFIF>` checks whether `URL.guess` exists, so `<CFELSE>` can be used to display a message if it does not. Therefore, not only will the code no longer generate an error if `guess` was not specified, it will also provide help and instruct the user appropriately (see Figure 10.7).

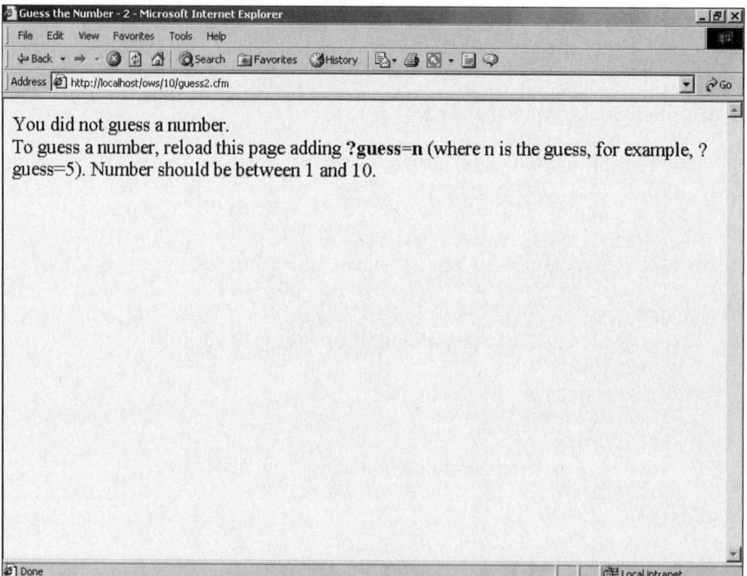

Figure 10.7
By checking for the existence of expected variables, your applications are capable of providing assistance and instructions if necessary.

Tip

The code in Listing 10.7 clearly demonstrates the value of indenting your code. The code within each `<CFIF>` block is indented, and the deeper the nesting, the further the indentation. This type of formatting is extremely popular among professional developers because it makes finding matching code blocks (or mismatched code blocks) much easier.

As a rule, nesting should be avoided unless absolutely necessary. Nesting really isn't necessary in this game. Listing 10.8 takes the game code one step further, this time using `<CFELSEIF>` and multiple clause conditions to create tighter (and better performing) code. Save Listing 10.8 as `guess3.cfm`.

LISTING 10.8 guess3.cfm

```
<!---
Name:        guess3.cfm
Author:      Ben Forta (ben@forta.com)
Description: Demonstrate use of multiple if statements
Created:     3/27/01
--->

<HTML>
<HEAD>
   <TITLE>Guess the Number - 3</TITLE>
</HEAD>

<BODY>

<!--- Pick a random number --->
<CFSET RandomNumber=RandRange(1, 10)>

<!--- Check if number was passed --->
<CFIF IsDefined("URL.guess") AND (RandomNumber IS URL.guess)>
   <!--- It matched --->
   <CFOUTPUT>
   You got it, I picked #RandomNumber#! Good job!
   </CFOUTPUT>
<CFELSEIF IsDefined("URL.guess") AND (RandomNumber IS NOT URL.guess)>
   <!--- Did not match --->
   <CFOUTPUT>
    Sorry, I picked #RandomNumber#! Try again!
   </CFOUTPUT>
<CFELSE>
   <!--- No guess specified, give instructions --->
   You did not guess a number.<BR>
   To guess a number, reload this page adding
   <B>?guess=n</B> (where n is the guess, for
   example, ?guess=5). Number should be between
   1 and 10.
</CFIF>

</BODY>
</HTML>
```

Again, the code starts with the random number generation. Then this `<CFIF>` statement is used:

```
<CFIF IsDefined("URL.guess") AND (RandomNumber IS URL.guess)>
```

As explained earlier, `AND` requires that both conditions be `TRUE`. Therefore, the first message is displayed only if `URL.guess` exists and if the numbers match. The second condition is in a `<CFELSEIF>` statement:

```
<CFELSEIF IsDefined("URL.guess") AND (RandomNumber IS NOT URL.guess)>
```

Here, too, `IsDefined()` is used to check that `URL.guess` exists. The second condition is `TRUE` only when the numbers do not match, in which case the second message is displayed.

The `<CFELSE>` here is evaluated only if `<CFIF>` and `<CFELSEIF>` are both not evaluated, in which case it would be clear that `URL.guess` was not defined.

The same result occurs, but this time without nesting.

Caution

As a rule, don't nest unless you really have to. Although nesting is legal within your code, nested code tends to be easier to make mistakes in, harder to debug, and slower to execute.

Note

Take a look at this line of code again:

```
<CFIF IsDefined("URL.guess") AND (RandomNumber IS URL.guess)>
```

You might be wondering why an error would not be generated if `URL.guess` did not exist. After all, if the `IsDefined()` returns `FALSE`, should the next condition cause an error because `URL.guess` is being referred to?

The truth is, prior to ColdFusion 4 this is exactly what would have happened: An error would have been generated because both conditions were always evaluated. As of ColdFusion 4, *short-circuit evaluation* is supported. What this means is that conditions that do not affect a result are never evaluated. In an `AND` condition, if the first condition returns `FALSE` then the result will always be `FALSE`, regardless of whether the second condition returns `TRUE` or `FALSE`. Similarly, in an `OR` condition, if the first condition is `TRUE` then the result will always be `TRUE`, regardless of whether the second condition is `TRUE` or `FALSE`. With short-circuit evaluation, conditions that do not affect the final result are not executed (to save processing time). So, in the previous example, if `IsDefined("URL.guess")` returns `FALSE`, `RandomNumber IS URL.guess` is never evaluated.

Let's finish this game application with one last revision. Listing 10.9 should be saved as file `guess4.cfm`.

LISTING 10.9 `guess4.cfm`

```
<!---
Name:        guess4.cfm
Author:      Ben Forta (ben@forta.com)
Description: Demonstrate use of multiple if statements
Created:     3/27/01
--->

<HTML>
<HEAD>
```

```
   <TITLE>Guess the Number - 4</TITLE>
</HEAD>

<BODY>

<!--- Set range --->
<CFSET GuessLow=1>
<CFSET GuessHigh=10>

<!--- Pick a random number --->
<CFSET RandomNumber=RandRange(GuessLow, GuessHigh)>

<!--- Was a guess specified? --->
<CFSET HaveGuess=IsDefined("URL.guess")>

<!--- If specified, did it match? --->
<CFSET Match=(HaveGuess) AND (RandomNumber IS URL.guess)>

<!--- Feedback --->
<CFOUTPUT>
<CFIF Match>
   <!--- It matched --->
   You got it, I picked #RandomNumber#! Good job!
<CFELSEIF HaveGuess>
   <!--- Did not match --->
   Sorry, I picked #RandomNumber#! Try again!
<CFELSE>
   <!--- No guess specified, give instructions --->
   You did not guess a number.<BR>
   To guess a number, reload this page adding
   <B>?guess=n</B> (where n is the guess, for
   example, ?guess=5). Number should be between
   #GuessLow# and #GuessHigh#.
</CFIF>
</CFOUTPUT>

</BODY>
</HTML>
```


Quite a few changes were made in Listing 10.9. First, the range high and low values are now variables, defined as follows:

```
<!--- Set range --->
<CFSET GuessLow=1>
<CFSET GuessHigh=10>
```

By saving these to variables, changing the range (perhaps to allow numbers 1–20) will be easier. These variables are passed to the `RandRange()` function and are used in the final output (when instructions are given if no `guess` was specified), so the allowed range is included in the instructions.

Next, the simple assignment `<CFSET HaveGuess=IsDefined("URL.guess")>` sets variable `HaveGuess` to either `TRUE` (if `guess` was specified) or `FALSE`. The next assignment sets a variable named `Match` to `TRUE` if the numbers match (and `guess` was specified) or to `FALSE`. In other words, two simple <CFSET> statements contain all the necessary intelligence and decision making, and because the results are saved to variables, using this information is very easy indeed.

This makes the display code much cleaner. <CFIF Match> displays the first message if the correct guess was provided. <CFELSEIF HaveGuess> is executed only if the <CFIF> failed, which must mean the guess was wrong. In addition, the <CFELSE> displays the instructions (with the correct range included automatically).

It does not get much cleaner than that.

SWITCH STATEMENTS

All the conditional processing used thus far has involved <CFIF> statements. But, as I stated at the beginning of this chapter, ColdFusion also supports another form of conditional processing–switch statements.

The best way to understand switch statements is to see them used. Listing 10.10 should be saved as file switch.cfm.

LISTING 10.10 switch.cfm

```
<!---
Name:        switch.cfm
Author:      Ben Forta (ben@forta.com)
Description: Demonstrate use of <CFSWITCH> and <CFCASE>
Created:     3/27/01
--->

<HTML>
<HEAD>
   <TITLE>Switch</TITLE>
</HEAD>

<BODY>

<!--- Get day of week --->
<CFSET dow=DayOfWeek(Now())>

<!--- Let the user know --->
<CFSWITCH EXPRESSION="#dow#">

   <!--- Is it Sunday? --->
   <CFCASE VALUE="1">
   It is the weekend! But make the most of it, tomorrow it's back to work.
   </CFCASE>

   <!--- Is it Saturday? --->
   <CFCASE VALUE="7">
   It is the weekend! And even better, tomorrow is the weekend too!
   </CFCASE>
```

```
    <!--- If code reaches here it's not the weekend --->
    <CFDEFAULTCASE>
    No, it's not the weekend yet, sorry!
    </CFDEFAULTCASE>
</CFSWITCH>

</BODY>
</HTML>
```

If you have executed Listing 10.10 (you should have), you'd have noticed that it does exactly what Listing 10.5 (file `if5.cfm`) does. But the code here is very different.

First the day of the week is saved to variable `dow` (as you did earlier), but then that variable is passed to a `<CFSWITCH>` statement:

```
<CFSWITCH EXPRESSION="#dow#">
```


`<CFSWITCH>` takes an `EXPRESSION` to evaluate; here, the value in `dow` is used. The `EXPRESSION` is a string, so pound signs are needed around `dow` (otherwise, the text `dow` will be evaluated instead of the value of that variable).

`<CFSWITCH>` statements include `<CFCASE>` statements, which each match a specific value that `EXPRESSION` could return. The first `<CFCASE>` is executed if `EXPRESSION` is `1` (Sunday) because `1` is specified as the `VALUE` in `<CFCASE VALUE="1">`. Similarly, the second `<CFCASE>` is executed if `EXPRESSION` is `7` (Saturday). Whichever `<CFCASE>` matches the `EXPRESSION` is the one that is processed, and in this example, the text between the `<CFCASE>` and `</CFCASE>` tags is displayed.

If no `<CFCASE>` matches the `EXPRESSION`, the optional `<CFDEFAULTCASE>` block is executed—`<CFDEFAULTCASE>` is similar to `<CFELSE>` in a `<CFIF>` statement.

As already stated, the end result is exactly the same as in the example using `<CFIF>`. So, why would you use `<CFSWITCH>` over `<CFIF>`? There are two reasons:

- `<CFSWITCH>` usually executes more quickly than `<CFIF>`.
- `<CFSWITCH>` code tends to be neater and more manageable.

But you can't always use `<CFSWITCH>`. Unlike `<CFIF>`, `<CFSWITCH>` can be used only if all conditions are checking against the same `EXPRESSION`—the conditions are all the same, just the values being compared against differ. If you need to check a set of entirely different conditions, `<CFSWITCH>` would not be an option (which is why you could not use it in the game example).

Note

Although the example here uses `<CFSWITCH>` to display text, that is not all this tag can do. In fact, just about any code you can imagine can be placed between `<CFCASE>` and `</CFCASE>`.

Tip

<CFCASE> tags are evaluated in order, so placing the values that you expect to match more frequently before those that will match much less frequently makes sense. Doing so can improve application performance slightly because ColdFusion will not have to evaluate values unnecessarily.

This is also true of sets of <CFIF> and <CFELSEIF> statements: Conditions that are expected to match more frequently should be moved higher up the list.

Using Looping

Loops are another fundamental language element supported by most development platforms. *Loops* do just that—they loop. Loops provide a mechanism with which to repeat tasks, and ColdFusion supports several types of loops, all via the <CFLOOP> tag:

- Index loops, used to repeat a set number of times
- Conditional loops, used to repeat until a specified condition becomes FALSE
- Query loops, used to iterate through database query results
- List loops, used to iterate through a specified list
- Collection loops, used to loop through structures

You won't use all these loop types here, but to acquaint you with <CFLOOP>, let's look at a few examples.

The Index Loop

One of the most frequently used loops is the index loop, used to loop a set number of times (from a specified value to another specified value). To learn about this loop, you'll generate a simple list (see Figure 10.8). Type the code in Listing 10.11, and save it in 10 as loop1.cfm.

Listing 10.11 loop1.cfm

```
<!---
Name:        loop1.cfm
Author:      Ben Forta (ben@forta.com)
Description: Demonstrate use of <CFLOOP FROM TO>
Created:     3/27/01
--->

<HTML>
<HEAD>
   <TITLE>Loop 1</TITLE>
</HEAD>

<BODY>

<!--- Create list --->
<UL>
```

```
<!--- Loop from 1 to 10 --->
<CFLOOP FROM="1" TO="10" INDEX="i">
   <!--- Write item --->
   <CFOUTPUT><LI>Item #i#</LI></CFOUTPUT>
</CFLOOP>

<!--- End list --->
</UL>

</BODY>
</HTML>
```

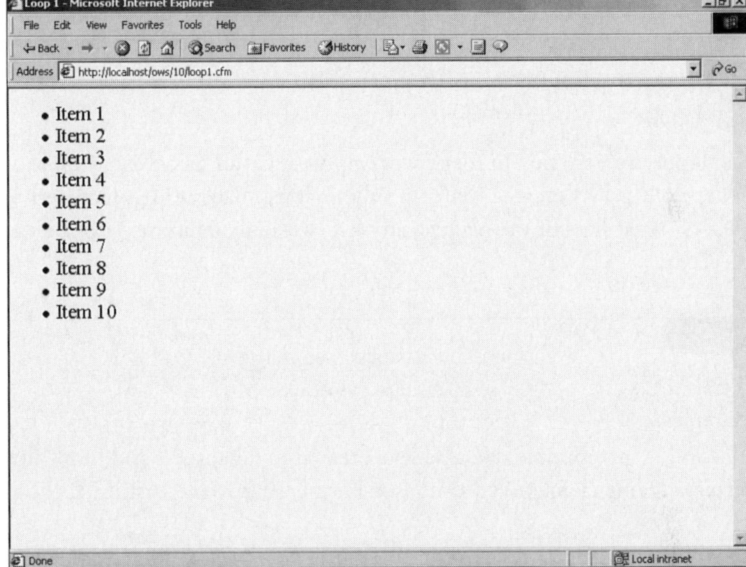

Figure 10.8
Loops can build lists and other display elements automatically.

<CFLOOP> is used to create a block of code to be executed over and over. The code in Listing 10.11 creates a simple loop that displays a list of numbers (in an HTML unordered list) from 1 to 10. The HTML unordered list is started before the <CFLOOP> (you wouldn't want to start it in the loop, because you'd be starting a new list on each iteration) and ends after the </CFLOOP>. The loop itself is created using the following code:

```
<CFLOOP FROM="1" TO="10" INDEX="i">
```

In an index loop the `FROM` and `TO` values must be specified and the code between <CFLOOP> and </CFLOOP> is repeated that many times. Here, `FROM="1"` and `TO="10"`, so the loop repeats 10 times. Within the loop itself, a variable named in the `INDEX` attribute contains the current increment, so `i` will be `1` the first time around, `2` the second time, and so on.

Within the loop, the value of `i` is displayed in a list item using the following code:

```
<CFOUTPUT><LI>Item #i#</LI></CFOUTPUT>
```

The first time around, when `i` is `1`, the generated output will be

```
<LI>Item 1</LI>
```

and on the second loop it will be

```
<LI>Item 2</LI>
```

and so on.

Tip

Want to loop backward? You can. Use the `STEP` attribute to specify how to count from the `FROM` value to the `TO` value. `STEP="-1"` makes the count go backward, one number at a time.

The List Loop

List loops are designed to make working with ColdFusion lists simple and error-free. Whether it is lists created by form submissions, manual lists, lists derived from database queries (regardless of the origin), any list (with any delimiter) can be iterated over using `<CFLOOP>`.

Note

For information about lists, see Chapter 9.

The following example uses the lists created in Chapter 9 and loops through the list displaying one element at a time (see Figure 10.9). Save Listing 10.12 as `loop2.cfm`.

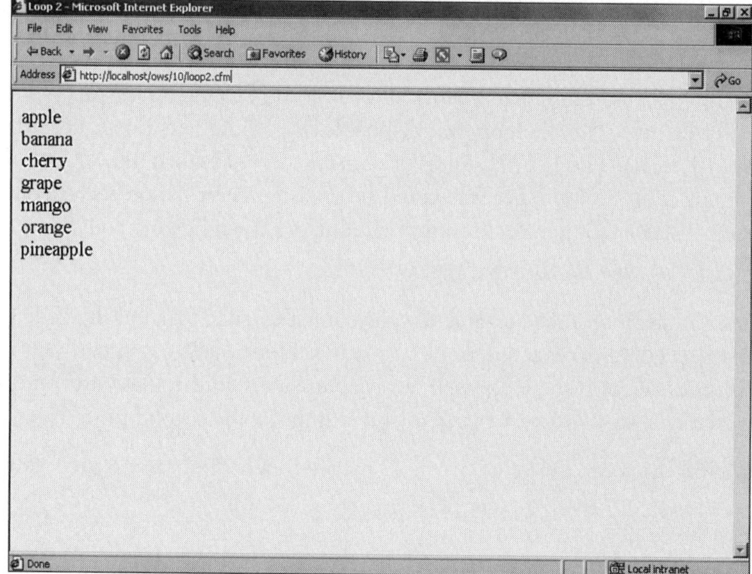

Figure 10.9 Any lists, with any delimiter, can be iterated using `<CFLOOP>`.

LISTING 10.12 `loop2.cfm`

```
<!---
Name:        loop2.cfm
Author:      Ben Forta (ben@forta.com)
Description: Demonstrate use of <CFLOOP LIST>
Created:     3/27/01
--->

<HTML>
<HEAD>
   <TITLE>Loop 2</TITLE>
</HEAD>

<BODY>

<!--- Create list --->
<CFSET fruit="apple,banana,cherry,grape,mango,orange,pineapple">

<!--- Loop through list --->
<CFLOOP LIST="#fruit#" INDEX="i">
   <!--- Write item --->
   <CFOUTPUT>#i#<BR></CFOUTPUT>
</CFLOOP>

</BODY>
</HTML>
```

`<CFSET>` is used to create the list (a comma-delimited list of fruit). `<CFLOOP>` takes the list to be processed in the `LIST` attribute, and because `LIST` accepts a string, pound signs must be used around the variable name `fruit`.

`<CFLOOP>` repeats the loop once for every element in the list. In addition, within the loop, it makes the current element available in the variable specified in the `INDEX` attribute—in this example, `i`. So, `i` is `apple` on the first iteration, `banana` on the second iteration, and so on.

Note

Lists also can be looped over using index loops. `FROM="1" TO="#ListLen(fruit)#"` sets the `TO` and `FROM` properly. Within the loop, `ListGetAt()` can be used to obtain the element.

NESTED LOOPS

Similar to the `<CFIF>` and `<CFSWITCH>` statements, loops can be nested. Nesting loops enables the creation of extremely powerful code, as long as you are very careful in constructing the loops. Listing 10.13 contains a practical example of nested loops, using three loops to display a table of Web browser-safe colors (seen in Figure 10.10). Save the code as `loop3.cfm`.

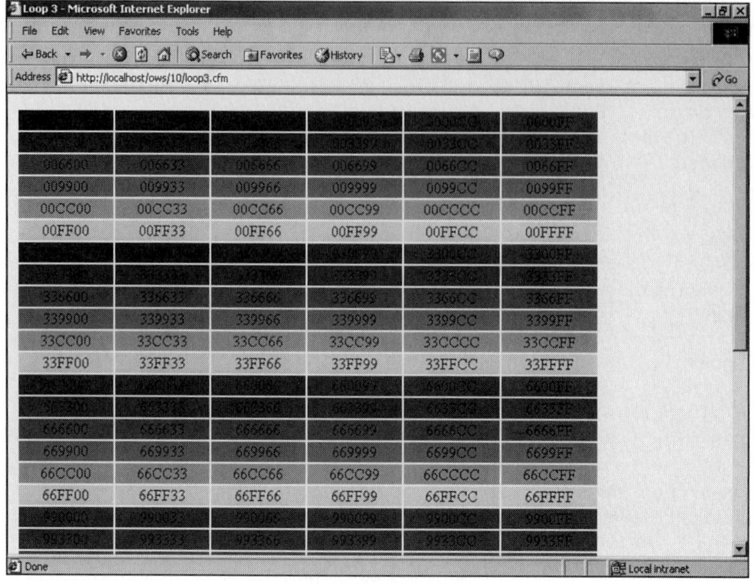

Figure 10.10 Displaying the Web browser-safe color palette requires the use of three nested loops.

LISTING 10.13 loop3.cfm

```
<!---
Name:        loop3.cfm
Author:      Ben Forta (ben@forta.com)
Description: Demonstrate use of nested loops
Created:     3/27/01
--->

<HTML>
<HEAD>
   <TITLE>Loop 3</TITLE>
</HEAD>

<BODY>

<!--- Hex value list --->
<CFSET hex="00,33,66,99,CC,FF">

<!--- Create table --->
<TABLE>

<!--- Start RR loop --->
<CFLOOP INDEX="red" LIST="#hex#">
   <!--- Start GG loop --->
   <CFLOOP INDEX="green" LIST="#hex#">
      <TR>
      <!--- Start BB loop --->
      <CFLOOP INDEX="blue" LIST="#hex#">
         <!--- Build RGB value --->
         <CFSET rgb=red&green&blue>
         <!--- And display it --->
         <CFOUTPUT>
```

```
            <TD BGCOLOR="#rgb#" WIDTH="100" ALIGN="center">#rgb#</TD>
            </CFOUTPUT>
         </CFLOOP>
         </TR>
      </CFLOOP>
</CFLOOP>

</TABLE>

</BODY>
</HTML>
```

Listing 10.13 warrants explanation. Colors in Web pages are expressed as RGB values (as in red, green, blue). The idea is that by adjusting the amount of red, green, and blue within a color, every possible color can be created. RGB values are specified using hexadecimal notation, and don't panic if you have forgotten base-n arithmetic—it's quite simple, actually. The amount of color is specified as a number, from `0` (none) to `255` (all). But instead of 0–255, the hexadecimal equivalents (00–FF) are used. So, pure red is all red and no green or blue, or FF0000; yellow is all red and green and no blue, or FFFF00.

Still confused? Execute the code and you'll see a complete list of colors and the RGB value for each.

To list all the colors, the code must loop through all possible combinations—list all shades of red, and within each shade of red list each shade of green, and within each shade of green list each shade of blue. In the innermost loop, a variable named `rgb` is created as follows:

```
<CFSET rgb=red&green&blue>
```

On the very first iteration red, green, and blue are all `00`, so `rgb` is `000000`. On the next iteration red and green are still `00`, but blue is `33`, so `rgb` is `000033`. By the time all the loops have been processed, a total of 1,296 colors has been generated (6 to the power of 3, for you mathematicians out there, because each color has six possible shades as defined in variable `hex`).

And although the exact mechanics of RGB value generation are not that important here, the key is that loops can be nested quite easily and within each loop the counters and variables created at an outer loop are visible and usable.

REUSING CODE

All developers write code (or should write code) with reuse in mind. The many reasons this is a good idea include

- **Saving time**—If it is written once, don't write it again.
- **Easier maintenance**—Make a change in one place and any code that uses it gets that change automatically.
- **Easier debugging**—Fewer copies exist out there that will need to be fixed.
- **Group development**—Developers can share code more easily.

Most of the code reuse in this book involves ColdFusion code, but to demonstrate basic reuse, let's look at a simple example.

Orange Whip Studios is building a Web site, slowly. Figure 10.11 shows a home page (still being worked on), and Figure 10.12 shows a contact us page (also being worked on). Both pages have a lot in common—both have the same header, the same logo, and the same copyright notice. If you were writing plain HTML, you'd have no choice but to copy all the code that creates those page components into every page you were creating.

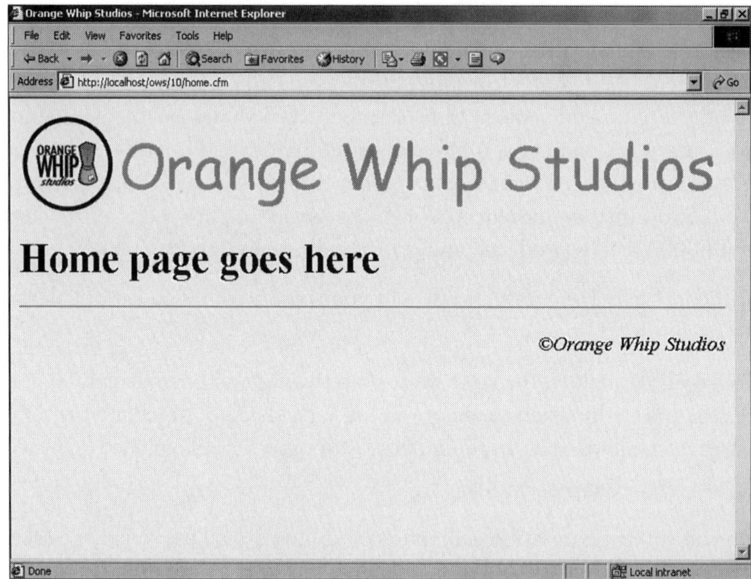

Figure 10.11
The home page contains basic logos and branding.

But you're using ColdFusion, and ColdFusion makes code reuse incredibly simple. The CFML `<CFINCLUDE>` tag is used to include one page in another. `<CFINCLUDE>` specifies the name of a file to include, and at runtime, when ColdFusion encounters a `<CFINCLUDE>` tag, it reads the contents of the specified file and processes it as if it were part of the same file.

To demonstrate this, look at Listings 10.14 and 10.15. The former is `ows_header.cfm`, and the latter is `ows_footer.cfm`. Between the two files, all the formatting for the Orange Whip Studios pages is present.

LISTING 10.14 `ows_header.cfm`

```
<HTML>
<HEAD>
   <TITLE>Orange Whip Studios</TITLE>
</HEAD>

<BODY>
```

```
<!--- Header --->
<TABLE WIDTH="100%">
<TR>
<TD>
   <IMG SRC="../images/logo_c.gif" WIDTH="101" HEIGHT="101" ALT="" BORDER="0">
</TD>
<TD>
   <FONT FACE="Comic Sans MS" SIZE="7" COLOR="#FF8000">Orange Whip Studios</FONT>
</TD>
</TR>
</TABLE>
<P>
```

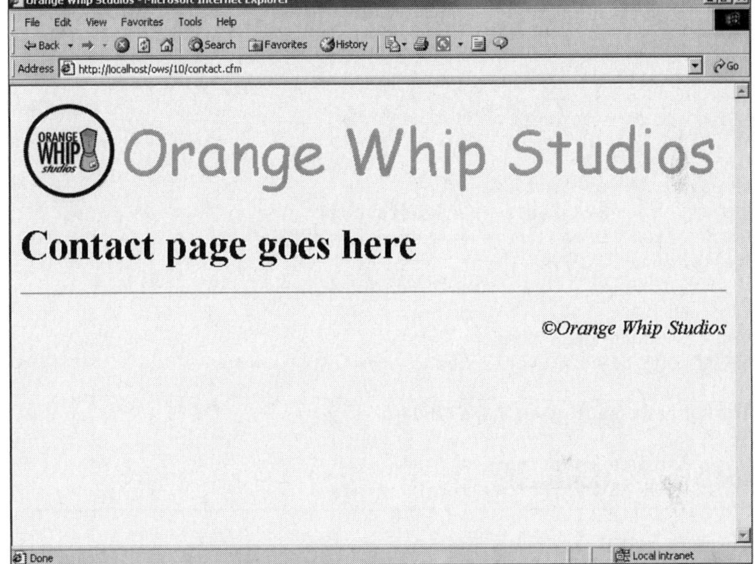

Figure 10.12 The Contact page contains the same elements as the home page.

LISTING 10.15 `ows_footer.cfm`

```
<P>
<HR>
<P ALIGN="right">
<I>&copy;Orange Whip Studios</I>
</P>

</BODY>
</HTML>
```

Now that the page header and footer have been created, `<CFINCLUDE>` can be used to include them in the pages. Listing 10.16 is `home.cfm`, and Listing 10.17 is `contact.cfm`.

Listing 10.16 home.cfm

```
<!---
Name:        home.cfm
Author:      Ben Forta (ben@forta.com)
Description: Demonstrate use of <CFINCLUDE>
Created:     3/27/01
--->

<!--- Include page header --->
<CFINCLUDE TEMPLATE="ows_header.cfm">

<H1>Home page goes here</H1>

<!--- Include page footer --->
<CFINCLUDE TEMPLATE="ows_footer.cfm">
```

Listing 10.17 contact.cfm

```
<!---
Name:        contact.cfm
Author:      Ben Forta (ben@forta.com)
Description: Demonstrate use of <CFINCLUDE>
Created:     3/27/01
--->

<!--- Include page header --->
<CFINCLUDE TEMPLATE="ows_header.cfm">

<H1>Contact page goes here</H1>

<!--- Include page footer --->
<CFINCLUDE TEMPLATE="ows_footer.cfm">
```

As you can see, very little code exists in Listings 10.16 and 10.17. Each listing contains two `<CFINCLUDE>` statements: The first includes file `ows_header.cfm` (Listing 10.14), and the second includes file `ows_footer.cfm` (Listing 10.15). ColdFusion includes those two files and generates the output seen previously in Figures 10.11 and 10.12. The content that is unique to each page can be placed between the two `<CFINCLUDE>` tags.

To see the real value here, modify `ows_header.cfm` (change colors, text, or anything else) and then reload `home.cfm` and `contact.cfm` to see your changes automatically applied to both.

Note

ColdFusion supports another form of code reuse—custom tags. This subject is covered in detail in Chapter 22, "Building Reusable Components."

Revisiting Variables

The last tag this chapter discusses is `<CFPARAM>`. You won't use this tag here, but in preparation for the next chapters, I'll explain what this tag is and how it is used.

Earlier in this chapter, you used a function named `IsDefined()`, which is used to check whether a variable exists. You used `IsDefined()` to simply check for a variable's existence, but what if you wanted to create a variable with a default value if it did not exist? You could do something similar to this:

```
<CFIF NOT IsDefined("FirstName")>
   <CFSET FirstName="Ben">
</CFIF>
```

Why would you want to do this? Well, as a rule, you should not include data validation code in the middle of your core code. This is bad practice for several reasons, the most important of which are that it helps create unreliable code, makes debugging difficult, and makes code reuse very difficult. So, best practices dictate that all variable validation occur before your core code. If required variables are missing, throw an error, redirect the user to another page, or do something else. If optional variables are missing, define them and assign default values. Either way, by the time you get to your core code, you should have no need for variable checking of any kind—that should all have been done already.

And thus the type of code I just showed you.

`<CFPARAM>` has several uses, but the most common use is simply a way to shortcut the previous code. Look at the following:

```
<CFPARAM NAME="FirstName" DEFAULT="Ben">
```

When ColdFusion processes this line, it checks to see whether a variable named `FirstName` exists. If it does then the tag is ignored and processing continues. If, however, the variable does not exist, it will be created right then and there and assigned the value specified in `DEFAULT`. So, by using `<CFPARAM>` you can ensure that after that tag has been processed, one way or another the variable referred to exists. And that makes writing clean code that much easier.

Tip

`<CFPARAM>` can be used to check for (and create) variables in specific scopes, including `URL` and `FORM`. This can greatly simplify the processing of passed values, as you will see in the coming chapters.

CHAPTER 11

Creating Data-Driven Pages

In this chapter

Accessing Databases

In the past few chapters, you created and executed ColdFusion templates. You worked with different variable types, conditional processing, code reuse, and more.

But this chapter is where it starts to get really interesting—now it's time to learn how to connect to databases to create complete dynamic and data-driven pages.

Note

The examples in this chapter, and indeed all the chapters that follow, use the data in the `ows` data sources and database. These must be present before continuing.

And I'll remind you just this once, all the files created in this chapter need to go in a directory named `11` under the application root (the `ows` directory under the Web root).

For your first application, you will create a page that lists all movies in the `Films` table.

Static Web Pages

Before you create your first data-driven ColdFusion template, let's take a look at how *not* to create this page.

Listing 11.1 contains the HTML code for the movie list Web page. The HTML code is relatively simple; it contains header information and then a list of movies, one per line, separated by line breaks (the HTML `<BR>` tag).

Listing 11.1 `movies.htm`—**HTML Code for Movie List**

```
<!DOCTYPE HTML PUBLIC "-//W3C//DTD HTML 4.0 Transitional//EN">
<HTML>
<HEAD>
    <TITLE>Orange Whip Studios - Movie List</TITLE>
</HEAD>

<BODY>

<H1>Movie List</H1>

Being Unbearably Light<BR>
Charlie's Devils<BR>
Closet Encounters of the Odd Kind<BR>
Folded Laundry, Concealed Ticket<BR>
Forrest Trump<BR>
Four Bar-Mitzvah's and a Circumcision<BR>
Geriatric Park<BR>
Gladly Ate Her<BR>
Ground Hog Day<BR>
Hannah and Her Blisters<BR>
Harry's Pottery<BR>
It's a Wonderful Wife<BR>
Kramer vs. George<BR>
```

```
Mission Improbable<BR>
Nightmare on Overwhelmed Street<BR>
Raiders of the Lost Aardvark<BR>
Silence of the Clams<BR>
Starlet Wars<BR>
Strangers on a Stain<BR>
The Funeral Planner<BR>
The Sixth Nonsense<BR>
Use Your ColdFusion II<BR>
West End Story<BR>

</BODY>
</HTML>
```

Figure 11.1 shows the output this code listing generates.

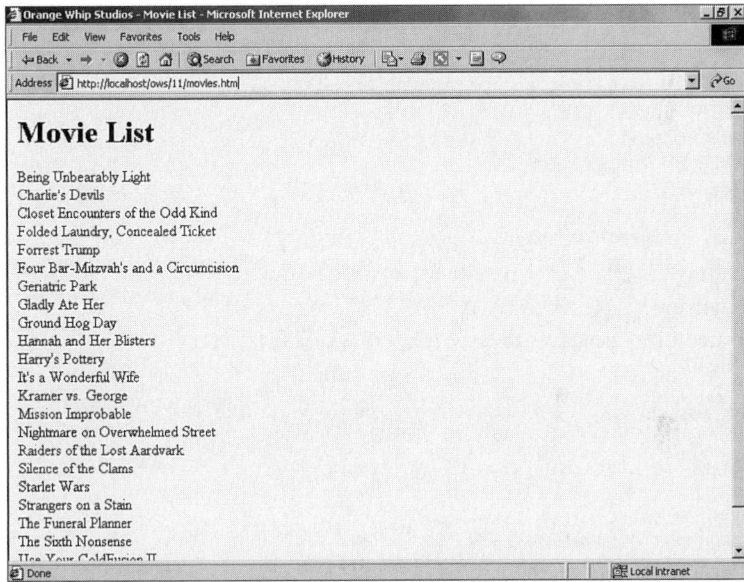

Figure 11.1
You can create the movie list page as a static HTML file.

DYNAMIC WEB PAGES

Why is a static HTML file not the way to create the Web page? What would you have to do when a new movie is created, or when a movie is dropped? What would you do if a movie title or tag line changed?

You could directly modify the HTML code to reflect these changes, but you already have all this information in a database. Why would you want to have to enter it all again? You'd run the risk of making mistakes—information being misspelled, entries out of order, and possibly missing movies altogether. As the number of movies in the list grows, so will the potential for errors occurring. In addition, visitors will be looking at inaccurate information during the period between updating the table and updating the Web page.

A much easier and more reliable solution is to have the Web page display the contents of your `Films` table; this way any table changes are immediately available to all viewers. The Web page would be dynamically built based on the contents of the `Films` table.

To create your first data-driven ColdFusion template, enter the code as it appears in Listing 11.2 and save it in the `11` directory as `movies1.cfm`. (Don't worry if the ColdFusion code does not make much sense yet; I explain it in detail in just a moment.)

LISTING 11.2 `movies1.cfm`—THE BASIC MOVIE LIST

```
<!---
Name:        movies1.cfm
Author:      Ben Forta (ben@forta.com)
Description: First data-driven Web page
Created:     4/1/01
--->

<!--- Get movie list from database --->
<CFQUERY NAME="movies" DATASOURCE="ows">
SELECT MovieTitle
FROM Films
ORDER BY MovieTitle
</CFQUERY>

<!--- Create HTML page --->
<!DOCTYPE HTML PUBLIC "-//W3C//DTD HTML 4.0 Transitional//EN">
<HTML>
<HEAD>
    <TITLE>Orange Whip Studios - Movie List</TITLE>
</HEAD>

<BODY>

<H1>Movie List</H1>

<!--- Display movie list --->
<CFOUTPUT QUERY="movies">
#MovieTitle#<BR>
</CFOUTPUT>

</BODY>
</HTML>
```

Now, execute this page in your browser as

```
http://localhost/ows/11/movies1.cfm
```

The results are shown in Figure 11.2.

UNDERSTANDING DATA-DRIVEN TEMPLATES

Now compare Figure 11.1 to Figure 11.2. Can you see the difference between them? Look carefully.

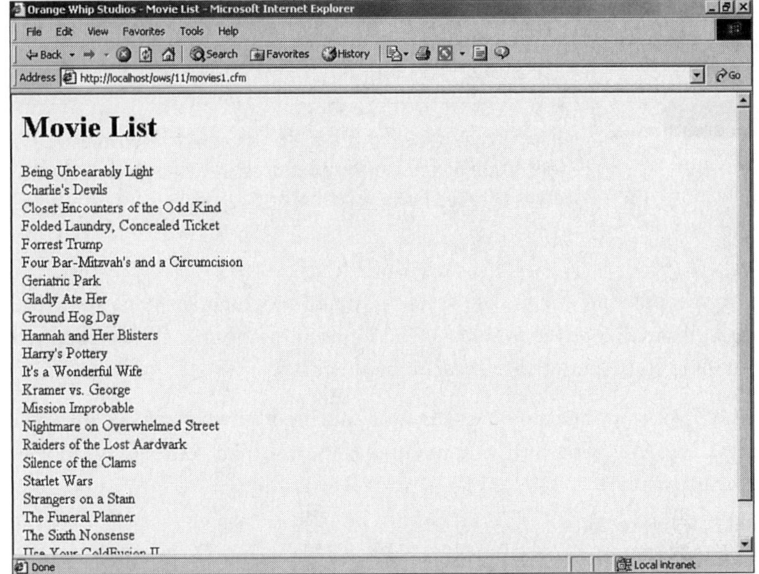

Figure 11.2
Ideally, the movie list page should be generated dynamically, based on live data.

Give up? The truth is that there is no difference at all. The screen shots are identical, and if you looked at the HTML source that generated Figure 11.2, you'd see that aside from a lot of extra whitespace, the dynamically generated code is exactly the same as the static code you entered in Listing 11.1 and nothing like the (much shorter) dynamic code you entered in Listing 11.2.

How did the code in Listing 11.2 become the HTML source code that generated Figure 11.1? Let's review the code listing carefully.

The <CFQUERY> Tag

Listing 11.2 starts off with a comment block (as should all the code you write). Then comes a ColdFusion tag called `<CFQUERY>`, which submits any SQL statement to an ODBC data source. The SQL statement is usually a SQL `SELECT` statement, but it could also be an `INSERT`, an `UPDATE`, a `DELETE`, a stored procedure call, or any other SQL statement.

Note

See Chapter 4, "Accessing the ColdFusion Administrator," for information on how to create ODBC data sources.

See Chapter 6, "Introduction to SQL," for an overview of ODBC and SQL statements.

The `<CFQUERY>` tag has several attributes, or parameters, that are passed to it when used. The `<CFQUERY>` in Listing 11.2 uses only two attributes:

- `NAME`—This attribute is used to name the query and any returned data.
- `DATASOURCE`—This attribute contains the name of the ODBC data source to be used.

The query NAME you specified is Movies. This name will be used later when you process the results generated by the query.

Note

Query names passed to <CFQUERY> need not be unique to each query within your page. If you do reuse query names, subsequent <CFQUERY> calls will overwrite the results retrieved by the earlier query.

You specified ows for the DATASOURCE attribute, which is the name of the data source you created in Chapter 4. DATASOURCE is required; without it ColdFusion would not know which database to execute the SQL statement against.

The SQL statement to be executed is specified between the <CFQUERY> and </CFQUERY> tags. The following SQL statement was used, which retrieves all movie titles sorted alphabetically:

```
SELECT MovieTitle
FROM Films
ORDER BY MovieTitle
```

Tip

The SQL statement in Listing 11.2 is broken up over many lines to make the code more readable. Although it is perfectly legal to write a long SQL statement that is wider than the width of your browser, these generally should be broken up over as many lines as needed.

ColdFusion pays no attention to the actual text between the <CFQUERY> and </CFQUERY> tags (unless you include CFML tags or functions, which we'll get to later in this chapter). Whatever is between those tags gets sent to the data source for processing.

When ColdFusion encounters a <CFQUERY> tag, it creates an ODBC request and submits it to the specified data source. The results, if any, are stored in a temporary buffer and are identified by the name specified in the NAME attribute. All this happens before ColdFusion processes the next line in the template.

Note

You will recall that ColdFusion tags (including the <CFQUERY> tag) are never sent to the Web server for transmission to the browser. Unlike HTML tags, which are browser instructions, CFML tags are ColdFusion instructions.

Note

ColdFusion does not validate the SQL code you specify. If syntax errors exist in the SQL code, ColdFusion will not let you know because that's not its job. The data source will return error messages if appropriate, and ColdFusion will display those to you. But it is the data source (and the database or database driver) that returns those error messages, not ColdFusion.

It is important to note that, at this point, no data has been displayed. <CFQUERY> retrieves data from a database table, but it does not display that data. Actually, it does nothing at all with the data—that's your job. All it does is execute a specified SQL statement when the </CFQUERY> tag is reached. <CFQUERY> has no impact on generated content at all, and retrieved data is never sent to the client (unless you send it).

The next lines in the template are standard HTML tags, headers, title, and headings. Because these are not ColdFusion tags, they are sent to the Web server and then on to the client browser.

Using <CFOUTPUT> to Display <CFQUERY> Data

Next, the query results are displayed, one row per line. To loop through the query results, the <CFOUTPUT> tag is used.

<CFOUTPUT> is the same ColdFusion output tag you used earlier (in Chapter 9, "Using ColdFusion"). This time, however, you use it to create a code block that is used to output the results of a <CFQUERY>. For ColdFusion to know which query results to output, the query name is passed to <CFOUTPUT> in the QUERY attribute. The name provided is the same that was assigned to the <CFQUERY> tag's NAME attribute. In this case, the NAME is Movies.

Caution

The query NAME passed to <CFQUERY> must be a valid (existing) query; otherwise, ColdFusion will generate an error.

The code between <CFOUTPUT QUERY="Movies"> and </CFOUTPUT> is the output code block. ColdFusion uses this code once for every row retrieved. Because 23 rows are currently in the Films table, the <CFOUTPUT> code is looped through 23 times. And any HTML or CFML tags within that block are repeated as well—once for each row.

Note

So what is the minimum number of times a <CFOUTPUT> code block will be processed? Well, that depends on whether you are using the QUERY attribute. Without a QUERY, the code block is processed once. However, with a QUERY block, it is processed once if a single row exists in the query, and not at all if the query returned no results.

Tip

You'll notice that I put the SQL query at the very top of the page instead of right where it was needed (in the middle of the output). This is the recommended way to write your code–queries should be organized at the top of the page, all together. This will help you write cleaner code and will also simplify any testing and debugging if (or rather, when) the need arises.

Using Table Columns

As explained in Chapter 9, ColdFusion uses `#` to delimit expressions and variables. ColdFusion expressions also can be columns retrieved by a `<CFQUERY>`. Whatever column name is specified is used; ColdFusion replaces the column name with the column's actual value. When ColdFusion processed the output block, it replaced `#MovieTitle#` with the contents of the `MovieTitle` column that was retrieved in the `Movies` query. Each time the output code block is used, that row's `MovieTitle` value is inserted into the HTML code.

ColdFusion-generated content can be treated as any other content in an HTML document; any of the HTML formatting tags can be applied to them. In this example, the query results must be separated by a line break (the `<BR>` tag).

Look at the following line of code:

```
#MovieTitle#<BR>
```

That code becomes the following for the movie `Being Unbearably Light`:

```
Being Unbearably Light<BR>
```

Figure 11.2 shows the browser display this template creates. It is exactly the same result as Figure 11.1, but without any actual data in the code. The output of Listing 11.2 is dynamically generated—each time the page is refreshed, the database query is executed and the output is generated.

Note

Want to prove this for yourself? Open the database and make a change to any of the movie titles and then refresh the Web page–you'll see that the output will reflect the changes as soon as they are made.

Tip

If you are thinking that constantly rereading the database tables seems unnecessary and likely to impact performance, you're right. Chapter 24, "Improving Performance," teaches tips and techniques to optimize the performance of data-driven sites.

The Dynamic Advantage

To see the real power of data-driven pages, take a look at Listing 11.3. This is the same code as in Listing 11.2, but a column has been added to the SQL statement (retrieving

PitchText as well now) and the output has been modified so that it displays both the MovieTitle and PitchText columns. Save this file as movies2.cfm (you can edit movies1.cfm and use Studio's Save As option to save it as movies2.cfm, if you find that easier). Now, execute this page in your browser as follows:

```
http://localhost/ows/11/movies2.cfm
```

Figure 11.3 shows the output generated by the revised code.

LISTING 11.3 movies2.cfm—THE EXTENDED MOVIE LIST

```
<!---
Name:        movies2.cfm
Author:      Ben Forta (ben@forta.com)
Description: Retrieving multiple database columns
Created:     4/1/01
--->

<!--- Get movie list from database --->
<CFQUERY NAME="movies" DATASOURCE="ows">
SELECT MovieTitle, PitchText
FROM Films
ORDER BY MovieTitle
</CFQUERY>

<!--- Create HTML page --->
<!DOCTYPE HTML PUBLIC "-//W3C//DTD HTML 4.0 Transitional//EN">
<HTML>
<HEAD>
    <TITLE>Orange Whip Studios - Movie List</TITLE>
</HEAD>

<BODY>

<H1>Movie List</H1>

<!--- Display movie list --->
<CFOUTPUT QUERY="movies">
<B>#MovieTitle#</B><BR>
#PitchText#<P>
</CFOUTPUT>

</BODY>
</HTML>
```

So what changed in Listing 11.3? Two things. First, the SQL statement passed to <CFQUERY> now retrieves two columns:

```
SELECT MovieTitle, PitchText
FROM Films
ORDER BY MovieTitle
```

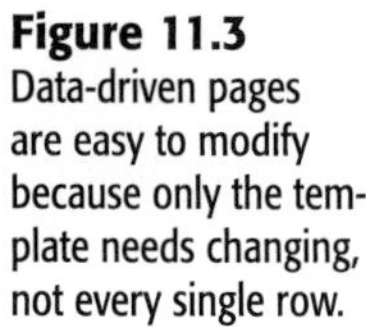

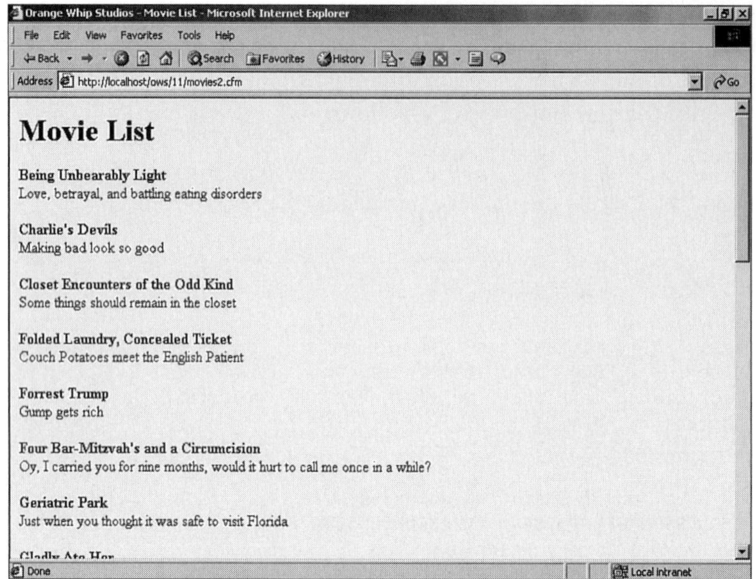

Figure 11.3 Data-driven pages are easy to modify because only the template needs changing, not every single row.

And second, the code within the `<CFOUTPUT>` block now reads

```
<CFOUTPUT QUERY="movies">
<B>#MovieTitle#</B><BR>
#PitchText#<P>
</CFOUTPUT>
```

As you can see, two table columns are now used, each delimited by pound signs. The `MovieTitle` is displayed in bold (using `<B>` and `</B>` tags) and is followed by a line break; on the next line `PitchText` is displayed followed by a paragraph break. So, for the first row displayed, the previous code becomes

```
<B>Being Unbearably Light</B><BR>
Love, betrayal, and battling eating disorders<P>
```

Compare that to what you'd have had to change in `movies.htm` to update a static page to look like Figure 11.3, and you'll start to appreciate the dynamic page advantage.

Excited? You should be. Welcome to ColdFusion and the wonderful world of dynamic data-driven Web pages!

Displaying Database Query Results

Listings 11.2 and 11.3 displayed data in simple line-by-line outputs. But that is not all you can do with ColdFusion—in fact, there is no type of output that *can't* be generated with ColdFusion. ColdFusion has absolutely nothing to do with formatting and generating output; as long as you can write what you want (in HTML, JavaScript, DHTML, or any other client technology), ColdFusion generates the output dynamically.

To better understand this, let's take a look at some alternative output options.

Displaying Data Using Lists

HTML features support for two list types—ordered lists (in which each list item is automatically numbered) and unordered lists (in which list items are preceded by bullets). Creating HTML lists is very simple:

1. Start the list with `<UL>` (for an unordered list) or `<OL>` (for an ordered list).
2. End the list with a matching `</UL>` or `</OL>`.
3. Between the list's start and end tags, specify the list members (called *list items*) between `<LI>` and `</LI>` tags.

For example, the following is a simple bulleted (unordered) list containing two names:

```
<UL>
    <LI>Ben Forta</LI>
    <LI>Nate Weiss</LI>
</UL>
```

So, how would you display the movie list in an unordered list? Listing 11.4 contains the code, which you should save as `movies3.cfm`. Execute the code in your browser; the output should look similar to Figure 11.4.

Listing 11.4 movies3.cfm—The Movie List in an Unordered List

```
<!---
Name:        movies3.cfm
Author:      Ben Forta (ben@forta.com)
Description: Data-driven HTML list
Created:     4/1/01
--->

<!--- Get movie list from database --->
<CFQUERY NAME="movies" DATASOURCE="ows">
SELECT MovieTitle, PitchText
FROM Films
ORDER BY MovieTitle
</CFQUERY>

<!--- Create HTML page --->
<!DOCTYPE HTML PUBLIC "-//W3C//DTD HTML 4.0 Transitional//EN">
<HTML>
<HEAD>
    <TITLE>Orange Whip Studios - Movie List</TITLE>
</HEAD>

<BODY>

<H1>Movie List</H1>

<!--- Display movie list --->
<UL>
<CFOUTPUT QUERY="movies">
<LI><B>#MovieTitle#</B> - #PitchText#</LI>
```

LISTING 11.4 CONTINUED

```
</CFOUTPUT>
</UL>

</BODY>
</HTML>
```

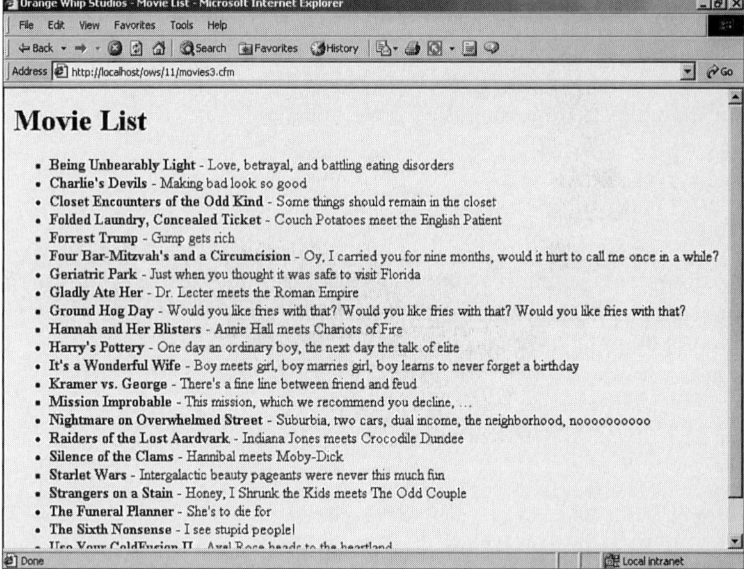

Figure 11.4
HTML unordered lists are a simple way to display data-driven output.

Let's review Listing 11.4 together. It should look familiar because it is essentially the same code as Listing 11.3 (`movies2.cfm`), only the actual data output has changed. The new output code looks similar to this:

```
<UL>
<CFOUTPUT QUERY="movies">
<LI><B>#MovieTitle#</B> - #PitchText#</LI>
</CFOUTPUT>
</UL>
```

As you can see, the list is started before the `<CFOUTPUT>` tag, and it is ended after the `</CFOUTPUT>` tag. This is important—everything within the output block is repeated once for every row retrieved. Therefore, if the list was started *inside* the output block, 23 lists would be generated, with each containing a single movie—instead of a single list containing 23 movies. Only the data to be repeated should be placed inside the output block.

The output code itself is simple. For the first row, the code

```
<LI><B>#MovieTitle#</B> - #PitchText#</LI>
```

becomes

```
<LI><B>Being Unbearably Light</B> - Love, betrayal, and battling eating
➥disorders</LI>
```

A valid list item with the movie title in bold (using <B> and </B>) is followed by the tag line.

Tip

As you can see, changing output formatting affects (or should affect) only an isolated portion of your code. As such, many developers first test whether their code works using simple output (line breaks or lists) before they write complex user interfaces. This can make development much easier (debugging core code and the user interface at the same time is not fun).

Caution

Be careful when placing code within an output block. Only code that is to be repeated for each row should be placed between <CFOUTPUT> and </CFOUTPUT>. Any other code should go outside the tags.

DISPLAYING DATA USING TABLES

Probably the layout feature most frequently used (and most useful) is tables. HTML tables enable you to create grids that can contain text, graphics, and more. Tables are used to facilitate a more controlled page layout, including placing content side by side, in columns, and wrapped around images.

Creating tables involves three sets of tags:

- <TABLE> and </TABLE>—Used to create the table
- <TR> and </TR>—Used to create rows in the table
- <TD> and </TD>—Used to insert cells within a table row (<TH> and </TH> also can be used for header cells—essentially data cells formatted a little differently)

So, a simple table with a header row, two columns, and two rows of data (as seen in Figure 11.5) might look like this:

```
<TABLE>
    <TR>
        <TH>First Name</TH>
        <TH>Last Name</TH>
    </TR>
    <TR>
        <TD>Ben</TD>
        <TD>Forta</TD>
    </TR>
    <TR>
        <TD>Nate</TD>
        <TD>Weiss</TD>
    </TR>
</TABLE>
```

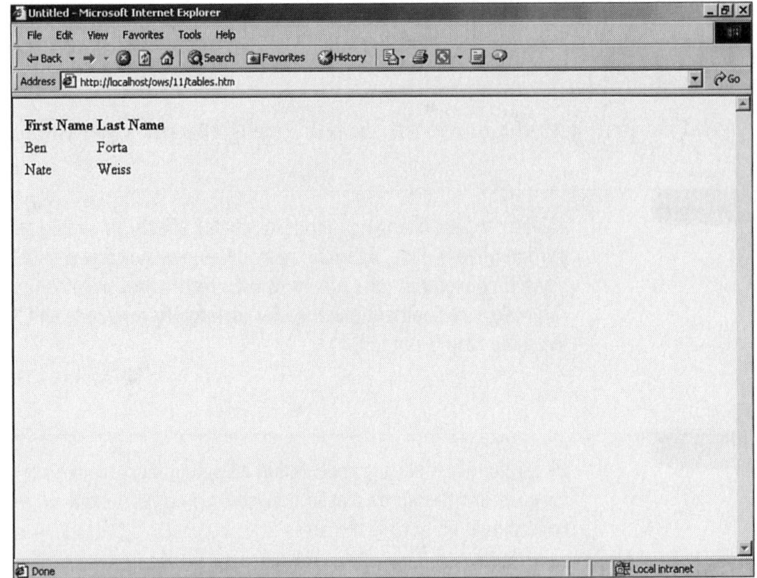

Figure 11.5 HTML tables are constructed using tags to create the table, rows, and individual cells.

Note

There is a lot more to HTML tables than I just explained. For detailed coverage of tables, consult a copy of *Sams Teach Yourself Web Publishing with HTML and XHTML in 21 Days* (ISBN: 0-672-32077-0).

Tip

The ColdFusion Studio Table toolbar contains a table creation wizard as well as buttons and shortcuts to simplify table creation and manipulation.

So, with that, let's modify the movie listing to display the list in an HTML table. Listing 11.5 contains a modified version of the code (again, you can use Save As to create a copy of the previous version for editing). Save the file as `movies4.cfm`, and then execute it to display an output similar to that shown in Figure 11.6.

LISTING 11.5 `movies4.cfm`—**THE MOVIE LIST IN AN HTML TABLE**

```
<!---
Name:        movies4.cfm
Author:      Ben Forta (ben@forta.com)
Description: Data-driven HTML table
Created:     4/1/01
--->

<!--- Get movie list from database --->
<CFQUERY NAME="movies" DATASOURCE="ows">
SELECT MovieTitle, PitchText
```

```
FROM Films
ORDER BY MovieTitle
</CFQUERY>

<!--- Create HTML page --->
<!DOCTYPE HTML PUBLIC "-//W3C//DTD HTML 4.0 Transitional//EN">
<HTML>
<HEAD>
    <TITLE>Orange Whip Studios - Movie List</TITLE>
</HEAD>

<BODY>

<H1>Movie List</H1>

<!--- Display movie list --->
<TABLE BORDER="1">
<CFOUTPUT QUERY="movies">
<TR>
 <TD>#MovieTitle#</TD>
 <TD>#PitchText#</TD>
</TR>
</CFOUTPUT>
</TABLE>

</BODY>
</HTML>
```


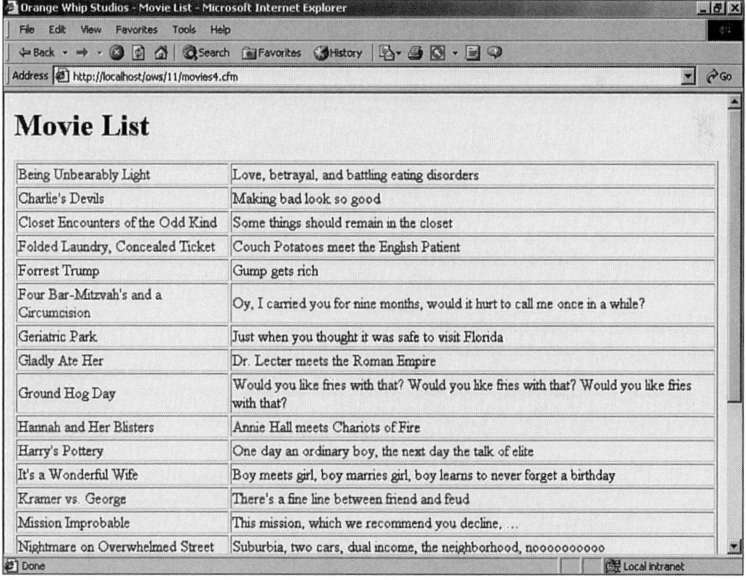

Figure 11.6 Tables provide a convenient mechanism to display data in a grid-like format.

Once again, the code in Listing 11.5 is similar to the previous examples, and once again, it is only the output block that has changed.

The table is created using the code `<TABLE BORDER="1">`—a table with a border. The `<TABLE>` and `</TABLE>` tags are placed *outside* the output block (you want a single table, not a table for each row).

The table needs a new table row for each row in the query. So, the `<TR>` and `</TR>` tags are within the output loop, and within them are two cells (containing `MovieTitle` and `PitchText`).

As you can see in Figure 11.6, this code creates a single table with as many rows as there are query rows (23 in this example).

Tip

Viewing the source code generated by ColdFusion is useful when debugging template problems. When you view the source, you are looking at the complete output as it was sent to your browser. If you ever need to ascertain why a Web page does not look the way you intended it to look, a good place to start is comparing your template with the source code it generated.

You'll probably find yourself using tables extensively, so, to ensure that dynamic HTML table creation is properly understood, another example is in order.

This time the table will contain two rows for each query row. The first will contain two cells—one for the title and tag line and one for the release date. The second row will contain the movie summary (and because the summary can be lengthy, its cell spans both columns). The output generated can be seen in Figure 11.7.

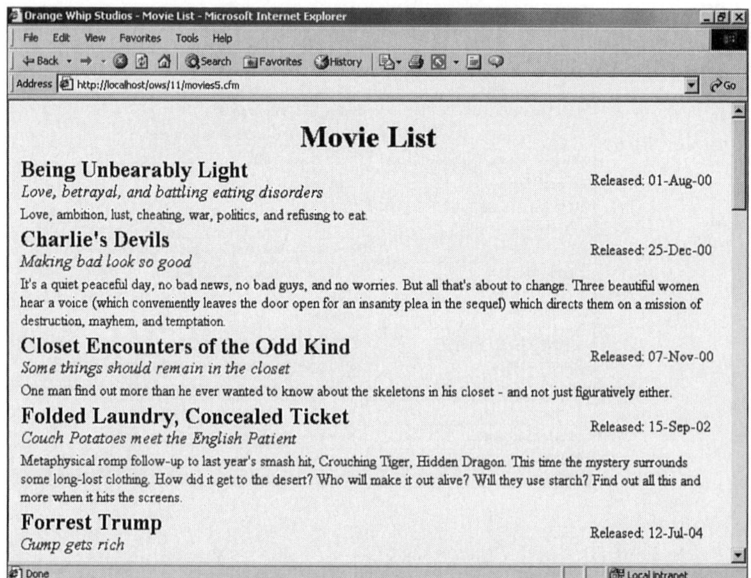

Figure 11.7
For greater control, HTML tables can contain cells that span two or more columns (and rows).

Listing 11.6 contains the revised code; this time save the file as `movies5.cfm` and execute it in your browser.

Listing 11.6 movies5.cfm—The Movie List in an HTML Table

```
<!---
Name:        movies5.cfm
Author:      Ben Forta (ben@forta.com)
Description: Data-driven HTML table
Created:     4/1/01
--->

<!--- Get movie list from database --->
<CFQUERY NAME="movies" DATASOURCE="ows">
SELECT MovieTitle, PitchText, Summary, DateInTheaters
FROM Films
ORDER BY MovieTitle
</CFQUERY>

<!--- Create HTML page --->
<!DOCTYPE HTML PUBLIC "-//W3C//DTD HTML 4.0 Transitional//EN">
<HTML>
<HEAD>
    <TITLE>Orange Whip Studios - Movie List</TITLE>
</HEAD>

<BODY>

<!--- Display movie list --->
<TABLE>
<TR>
 <TH COLSPAN="2"><FONT SIZE="+3">Movie List</FONT></TH>
</TR>
<CFOUTPUT QUERY="movies">
<TR>
 <TD>
  <FONT SIZE="+2"><B>#MovieTitle#</B></FONT><BR>
  <FONT SIZE="+1"><I>#PitchText#</I></FONT>
 </TD>
 <TD>Released: #DateFormat(DateInTheaters)#</TD>
</TR>
<TR>
 <TD COLSPAN="2">#Summary#</TD>
</TR>
</CFOUTPUT>
</TABLE>

</BODY>
</HTML>
```

A few changes have been made in Listing 11.6. First, the `<CFQUERY> SELECT` statement has been modified to retrieve two additional columns—`Summary` contains the movie summary, and `DateInTheaters` contains the movie's public release date.

In addition, a new row has been added *before* the <CFOUTPUT> tag containing the following line of code:

```
<TH COLSPAN="2"><FONT SIZE="+3">Movie List</FONT></TH>
```

This creates a header cell (header contents usually are centered and displayed in bold) containing the text `Movie List` as a table title. Because the table is two columns wide, the title must span both columns, so the optional attribute `COLSPAN="2"` is specified.

The output block itself creates two rows (two sets of <TR> and </TR> tags). The first contains two cells—one with the `MovieTitle` and `PitchText` (with a line break between them) and the other with the release date formatted for display using the `DateFormat()` function. The second row contains a single cell spanning both columns and displaying `Summary`.

Note

The `DateFormat()` function was introduced in Chapter 9.

Tip

Pay close attention to which code you place within and without the <CFOUTPUT> block. Misplacing a <TR> or </TD> tag could result in a badly formatted HTML table, and some browsers might opt to not even display that table.

As you can see, as long as you know the basic HTML syntax and know what needs to be repeated for each database row and what doesn't, creating dynamic data-driven output is quick and painless.

Tip

ColdFusion features a tag named <CFTABLE> that can be used to automate the entire process of creating data-driven HTML tables. Although this tag works, I recommend against using it. HTML tables are not difficult to learn and create, and doing so is well worth the effort because you'll find that you have far more control over the exact format and output.

Caution

I know I have said it several times already, but because this is one of the most common beginners' mistakes (and a very aggravating one to debug at that), I'll say it one last time.

When creating dynamic output, pay special attention to what needs to be repeated and what does not. Anything that needs to be displayed once per row (either before or after the row) must go in the output block; anything else must not.

Note

HTML tables are a useful way to format data, but a cost is associated with using tables. For a browser to correctly display a table, it cannot display any part of that table until it has received the entire table from the Web server. This is because any row, even one near the end of the table, can affect the width of columns and how the table will be formatted. Therefore, if you display data in a table, the user will see no data at all until all the data is present. If you were to use another type of display–a list, for example–the data would be displayed as it was received. The reality of it is that the page likely will take as long to fully load with or without tables. The disadvantage of using tables is that it takes longer for any data to appear. Actual ColdFusion processing time is identical regardless of whether tables are used, but the user perception could be one of a slower application if you create large HTML tables.

Using Query Variables

So far, you have displayed data retrieved using database queries. But sometimes you'll need access to data about queries (and not just data within queries). For example, if you wanted to display the number of movies retrieved, where would you get that count from?

To simplify this type of operation, ColdFusion includes special variables in every query. Table 11.1 lists these variables, and as you can see, `RecordCount` can provide the number of rows retrieved.

Table 11.1 Query Variables

Variable	Description
`ColumnList`	Names of columns in query results (comma-delimited list)
`ExecutionTime`	Query execution time (in milliseconds)
`RecordCount`	Number of rows in a query

To demonstrate using these special variables, create the file `movies6.cfm`, as shown in Listing 11.7. This code, which is based on `movies5.cfm`, generates the output seen in Figure 11.8. Save the code, and execute it in your browser.

Listing 11.7 `movies6.cfm`—Using Query Variables

```
<!---
Name:        movies6.cfm
Author:      Ben Forta (ben@forta.com)
Description: Using query variables
Created:     4/1/01
--->

<!--- Get movie list from database --->
<CFQUERY NAME="movies" DATASOURCE="ows">
```

LISTING 11.7 CONTINUED

```
SELECT MovieTitle, PitchText, Summary, DateInTheaters
FROM Films
ORDER BY MovieTitle
</CFQUERY>

<!--- Create HTML page --->
<!DOCTYPE HTML PUBLIC "-//W3C//DTD HTML 4.0 Transitional//EN">
<HTML>
<HEAD>
    <TITLE>Orange Whip Studios - Movie List</TITLE>
</HEAD>

<BODY>

<!--- Display movie list --->
<TABLE>
<TR>
 <CFOUTPUT>
 <TH COLSPAN="2">
  <FONT SIZE="+3">Movie List (#Movies.RecordCount# movies)</FONT>
 </TH>
 </CFOUTPUT>
</TR>
<CFOUTPUT QUERY="movies">
<TR>
 <TD>
  <FONT SIZE="+2"><B>#CurrentRow#: #MovieTitle#</B></FONT><BR>
  <FONT SIZE="+1"><I>#PitchText#</I></FONT>
 </TD>
 <TD>Released: #DateFormat(DateInTheaters)#</TD>
</TR>
<TR>
 <TD COLSPAN="2">#Summary#</TD>
</TR>
</CFOUTPUT>
</TABLE>

</BODY>
</HTML>
```

So, what changed here? Only two modifications were made to this code. The title (above the output block) now reads as follows:

```
Movie List (#Movies.RecordCount# movies)
```

`#Movies.RecordCount#` returns the number of rows retrieved—in this case, `23`. Like any other expression, the text `Movies.RecordCount` must be enclosed within pound signs and must be between `<CFOUTPUT>` and `</CFOUTPUT>` tags. But unlike many other expressions, here the prefix `Movies` is required. Why? Because this code is not within a query-driven `<CFOUTPUT>` (there is no `QUERY` attribute). Therefore, for ColdFusion to know which query's count you want, you must specify it.

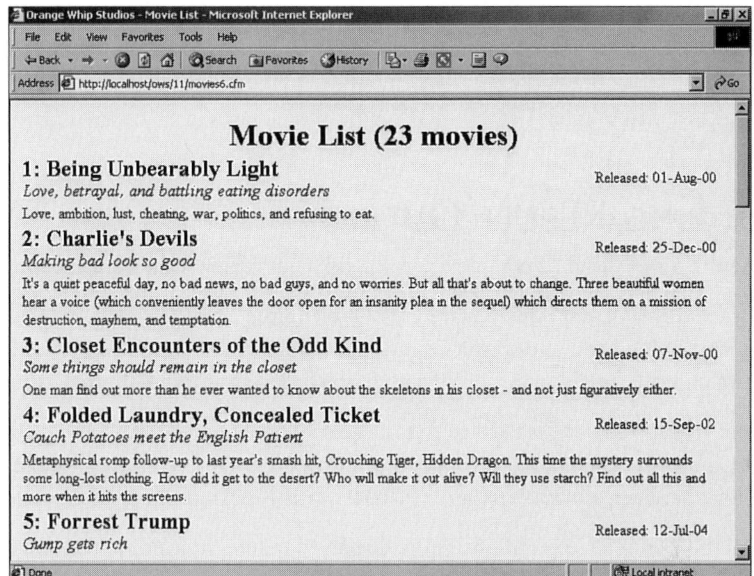

Figure 11.8 `RecordCount` can be accessed to obtain the number of rows in a query.

Tip

Here the query name prefix is required because the query was not specified in the `<CFOUTPUT>` loop. Within an output loop, the query name is not required, but it can be used to prevent ambiguity (for example, if there were variables with the same names as table columns).

Here you use `RecordCount` purely for display purposes. But as you will see later in this chapter, it can be used in other ways, too (for example, checking to see whether a query returned any data at all).

Incidentally, why is `Movies.RecordCount` not in a `<CFOUTPUT QUERY="Movies">` block? I'll not answer that one because the last time I explained it, I said it would be the last time I'd do so. (That was your hint.)

The other line of code that changed is the movie title display, which now has `#CurrentRow#:` in front of it. `CurrentRow` is another special variable, but this time it's in `<CFOUTPUT>` instead of `<CFQUERY>`. Within an output loop, `CurrentRow` keeps a tally of the iterations—it contains `1` when the first row is processed, `2` when the second row is processed, and so on. In this example, it's used to number the movies (as seen in Figure 11.8). You also could use it to perform fancy formatting (for example, alternating the background color for every other row).

Note

The value in CurrentRow is not the row's unique ID (primary key). In fact, the number has nothing to do with the table data at all. It is merely a loop counter and should never be relied on as anything else.

Grouping Result Output

Before a new level of complexity is introduced, review how ColdFusion processes queries.

In ColdFusion, data queries are created using the <CFQUERY> tag. <CFQUERY> performs a SQL operation and retrieves results if any exist. Results are stored temporarily by ColdFusion and remain only for the duration of the processing of the template that contained the query.

The <CFOUTPUT> tag is used to output query results. <CFOUTPUT> takes a query name as an attribute and then loops through all the rows that were retrieved by the query. The code block between <CFOUTPUT> and </CFOUTPUT> is repeated once for every row retrieved.

All the examples created until now displayed results in a single list or single table.

What would you do if you wanted to process the results in subsets? For example, suppose you wanted to list movies by rating. You could change the SQL statement in the <CFQUERY> to set the sort order to be RatingID and then by MovieTitle.

This would retrieve the data in the correct order, but how would you display it? If you used <CFOUTPUT> as you have until now, every row created by the <CFOUTPUT> block would have to be the same. If one had the rating displayed, all would have to because every row that is processed is processed with the same block of code.

Look at Figure 11.9. As you can see, the screen contains nested lists. The top-level list contains the rating IDs, and within each rating ID is a second list containing all the movies with that rating. How would you create an output like this?

Listing 11.8 ratings1.cfm—**Grouping Query Output**

```
<!---
Name:        ratings1.cfm
Author:      Ben Forta (ben@forta.com)
Description: Query output grouping
Created:     4/1/01
--->

<!--- Get movie list from database --->
<CFQUERY NAME="movies" DATASOURCE="ows">
SELECT MovieTitle, RatingID
FROM Films
ORDER BY RatingID, MovieTitle
</CFQUERY>

<!--- Create HTML page --->
<!DOCTYPE HTML PUBLIC "-//W3C//DTD HTML 4.0 Transitional//EN">
<HTML>
```

```
<HEAD>
    <TITLE>Orange Whip Studios - Movies by Rating</TITLE>
</HEAD>

<BODY>

<!--- Display movie list --->
<UL>
<!--- Loop through ratings --->
<CFOUTPUT QUERY="movies" GROUP="RatingID">
<LI>#RatingID#</LI>
 <UL>
 <!--- For each rating, list movies --->
 <CFOUTPUT>
  <LI>#MovieTitle#</LI>
 </CFOUTPUT>
 </UL>
</CFOUTPUT>
</UL>

</BODY>
</HTML>
```

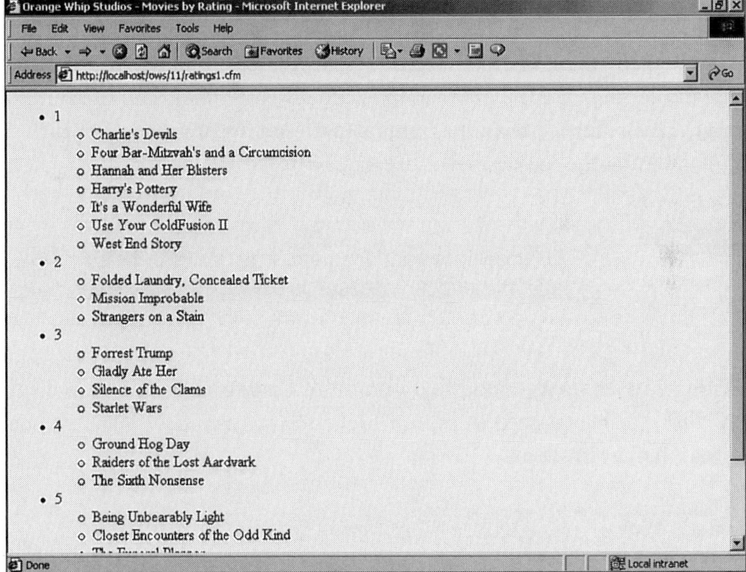

Figure 11.9 Grouped data can be displayed properly using the `<CFOUTPUT>` `GROUP` attribute.

Listing 11.8 contains the code for a new page; save this as `ratings1.cfm` and execute it in your browser.

Listing 11.8 starts with the comment block, followed by a `<CFQUERY>` that retrieves all the movies (title and rating only) sorted by `RatingID` and `MovieTitle` (by `RatingID` and within each `RatingID` by `MovieTitle`).

The display section of the code starts by creating an unordered list—this is the outer list, which contains the ratings.

Then, `<CFOUTPUT>` is used again to create an output block, but this time the `GROUP` attribute has been added. `GROUP="RatingID"` tells the output block to loop through the outer loop only when `RatingID` changes. In other words, the outer loop is processed once per group value. So, in this example, it's processed once per `RatingID` value—regardless of the number of movies with that `RatingID`.

Then, the `RatingID` is displayed, and a second unordered list is started—this is for the inner list within each `RatingID`.

Next, comes a second `<CFOUTPUT>` block that displays the `MovieTitle`. No `QUERY` is specified here; ColdFusion does not need one. Why? Because `GROUP` is being used, ColdFusion knows which query is being used and loops through the inner `<CFOUTPUT>` only as long as `RatingID` does not change.

As soon as `RatingID` changes, the inner `<CFOUTPUT>` loop stops and the inner list is terminated with a `</UL>`.

This repeats until all rows have been processed, at which time the outer `<CFOUTPUT>` terminates and the final `</UL>` is generated.

So, how many times is each `<CFOUTPUT>` processed? The movie list contains 23 rows with a total of 6 ratings. So the outer loop is processed 6 times, and the inner loop is processed 23 times. This outer list contains 6 items (each `RatingID` value), and each item contains a sublist containing the movies with that `RatingID`.

Note

For grouping to work, groups must be created in the exact same order as the sort order (the `ORDER BY` clause) in the SQL statement itself.

Listing 11.9 contains a modified version of Listing 11.8, this time displaying the results in an HTML table (as seen in Figure 11.10). Save Listing 11.9 as `ratings2.cfm`, and then execute it in your browser.

Listing 11.9 ratings2.cfm—Grouping Query Output

```
<!---
Name:        ratings2.cfm
Author:      Ben Forta (ben@forta.com)
Description: Query output grouping
Created:     4/1/01
--->

<!--- Get movie list from database --->
<CFQUERY NAME="movies" DATASOURCE="ows">
SELECT MovieTitle, RatingID
FROM Films
ORDER BY RatingID, MovieTitle
```

```
</CFQUERY>

<!--- Create HTML page --->
<!DOCTYPE HTML PUBLIC "-//W3C//DTD HTML 4.0 Transitional//EN">
<HTML>
<HEAD>
    <TITLE>Orange Whip Studios - Movies by Rating</TITLE>
</HEAD>

<BODY>

<!--- Display movie list --->
<TABLE>
<!--- Loop through ratings --->
<CFOUTPUT QUERY="movies" GROUP="RatingID">
<TR VALIGN="top">
<TH>
 #RatingID#
</TH>
<TD>
 <!--- For each rating, list movies --->
 <CFOUTPUT>
 #MovieTitle#<BR>
 </CFOUTPUT>
</TD>
</TR>
</CFOUTPUT>
</TABLE>

</BODY>
</HTML>
```


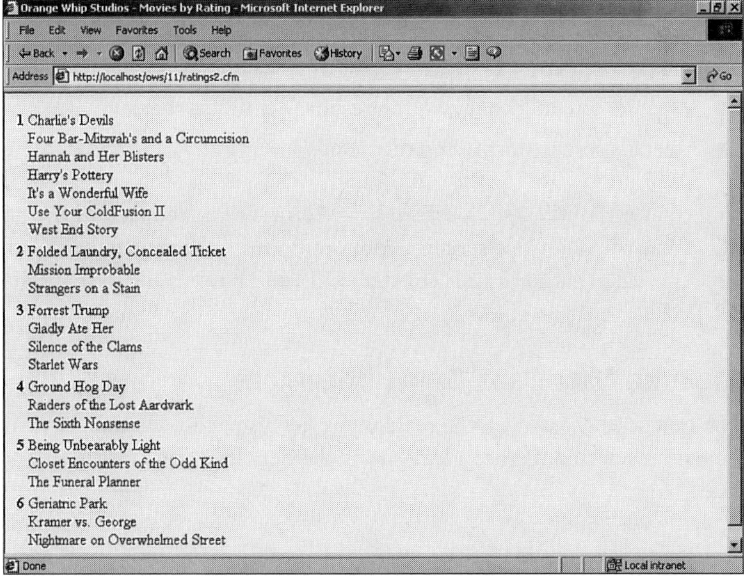

Figure 11.10
Grouped data can be used in lists, tables, and any other form of data presentation.

The only thing that has changed in Listing 11.10 is the output code. Again, the `<CFOUTPUT>` tags are nested—the outer loops through `RatingID` and the inner loops through the movies.

The HTML table is created before any looping occurs (you want only one table). Then, for each `RatingID` a new table row is created containing two cells. The left cell contains the `RatingID`, and the right cell contains the movies.

To do this, the inner `<CFOUTPUT>` loop is used in that right cell (between the `<TD>` and `</TD>` tags) so that, for each `RatingID` listed on the left, all the appropriate movies are listed on the right.

Tip

A single level of grouping is used here, but there is no limit to the number of levels in which data can be grouped. To group multiple levels (groups within groups), you simply need an additional `<CFOUTPUT>` per group (and of course, the SQL statement must sort the data appropriately).

Using Data Drill-Down

Now that you've learned almost everything you need to know about the `<CFOUTPUT>` tag, let's put it all together in a complete application.

You saw an example of a data drill-down application in Chapter 5, "Previewing ColdFusion." As was explained there, data drill-down is a popular form of user interface within Web applications because it enables the progressive and gradual selection of desired data.

Data drill-down applications usually are made up of three levels of interface:

- A search screen
- A results screen (displaying the results of any searches)
- A details screen (displaying the details for any row selected in the results screen)

You won't create the search screen here (forms are introduced in the next chapter), but you will create the latter two screens. Your application will display a list of movies (similar to the screens created earlier in this chapter) and will allow visitors to click any movie to see detailed information about it.

Implementing Data Drill-Down Interfaces

The first screen you need to create is the details page—the one that will be displayed when a movie is selected. Figure 11.11 shows the details for one movie.

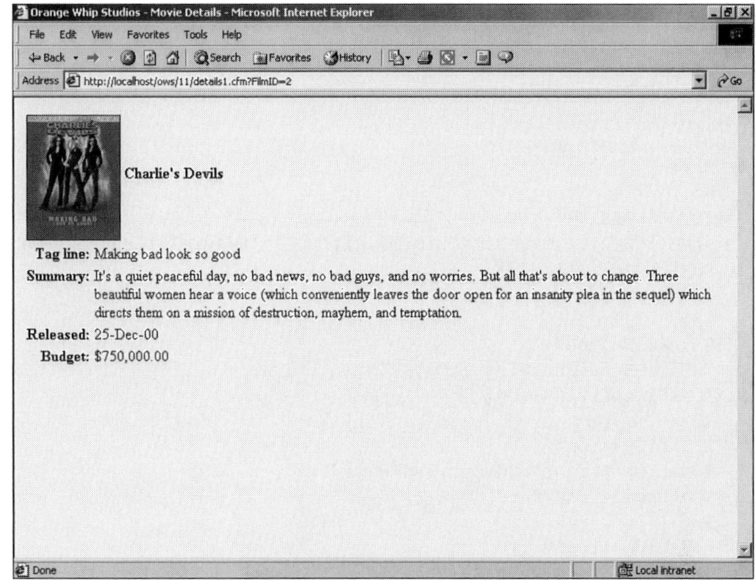

Figure 11.11 In data drill-down applications, the details page displays all the details for a specific record.

Listing 11.10 contains the code for the file `details1.cfm`. Save the code, and then execute it in your browser with this URL:

```
http://localhost/ows/11/details1.cfm?FilmID=2
```

You should see a screen similar to the one shown in Figure 11.11.

LISTING 11.10 details1.cfm—DATA DRILL-DOWN DETAILS

```
<!---
Name:        details1.cfm
Author:      Ben Forta (ben@forta.com)
Description: Data drill-down details
Created:     4/1/01
--->

<!--- Get a movie from database --->
<CFQUERY NAME="movie" DATASOURCE="ows">
SELECT FilmID, MovieTitle, PitchText,
       Summary, DateInTheaters, AmountBudgeted
FROM Films
WHERE FilmID=#URL.FilmID#
</CFQUERY>

<!--- Create HTML page --->
<!DOCTYPE HTML PUBLIC "-//W3C//DTD HTML 4.0 Transitional//EN">
<HTML>
<HEAD>
    <TITLE>Orange Whip Studios - Movie Details</TITLE>
</HEAD>
```

Listing 11.10 Continued

```
<BODY>

<!--- Display movie details --->
<CFOUTPUT QUERY="movie">
 <TABLE>
  <TR>
   <TD COLSPAN="2">
    <IMG SRC="../images/f#FilmID#.gif" ALT="#MovieTitle#" ALIGN="MIDDLE">
    <B>#MovieTitle#</B>
   </TD>
  </TR>
  <TR VALIGN="top">
   <TH ALIGN="right">Tag line:</TH>
   <TD>#PitchText#</TD>
  </TR>
  <TR VALIGN="top">
   <TH ALIGN="right">Summary:</TH>
   <TD>#Summary#</TD>
  </TR>
  <TR VALIGN="top">
   <TH ALIGN="right">Released:</TH>
   <TD>#DateFormat(DateInTheaters)#</TD>
  </TR>
  <TR VALIGN="top">
   <TH ALIGN="right">Budget:</TH>
   <TD>#DollarFormat(AmountBudgeted)#</TD>
  </TR>
 </TABLE>
</CFOUTPUT>

</BODY>
</HTML>
```

There are several important things to point out in Listing 11.10. Let's start with the SQL statement:

```
SELECT FilmID, MovieTitle, PitchText,
       Summary, DateInTheaters, AmountBudgeted
FROM Films
WHERE FilmID=#URL.FilmID#
```

The `WHERE` clause here is used to select a specific movie by its primary key (`FilmID`). But instead of comparing it to a real number, a ColdFusion variable is used—`#URL.FilmID#`.

> **Note**
>
> See Chapter 6 for a detailed explanation of the `SELECT` statement and its `WHERE` clause.

Earlier I said that ColdFusion paid no attention to the text between `<CFQUERY>` and `</CFQUERY>`, but that is not entirely true. When ColdFusion prepares the `SELECT` statement to be sent to the database driver, it checks for any CFML (tags, functions, or expressions).

When it encounters #URL.FilmID#, it replaces that expression with whatever the value of the URL parameter FilmID is. So, if the URL parameter FilmID had a value of 2, the generated SQL would look like this:

```
SELECT FilmID, MovieTitle, PitchText,
       Summary, DateInTheaters, AmountBudgeted
FROM Films
WHERE FilmID=2
```

This is why I had you append ?FilmID=2 to the URL when you executed this page. Without a FilmID parameter, this code would have failed, but we'll get to that in a moment.

The beauty of this technique is that it allows the same details page to be used for an unlimited number of database records—each FilmID specified generates a different page. If FilmID were 10, the SQL statement would have a WHERE clause of FilmID=10, and so on.

Note

URL variables were briefly introduced in Chapter 10, "CFML Basics."

The rest of the code in Listing 11.10 is rather self-explanatory. The details are displayed in an HTML table with the title spanning two columns. Dates are formatted using the DateFormat() function, and monetary amounts are formatted using the DollarFormat() function (which, as its name suggests, formats numbers as dollar amounts).

Note

Support for other currencies also are available via the locale functions.

One interesting line of code, though, is the <IMG> tag (used to display the movie poster image):

```
<IMG SRC="../images/f#FilmID#.gif" ALT="#MovieTitle#" ALIGN="MIDDLE">
```

Binary data, like images, cannot be stored in databases and accessed easily. So, how can images be associated with database rows? One solution, the one used here, is to store the images in a directory and name them using the primary key values. Therefore, in this example, the image for FilmID 2 is f2.gif, and that image is stored in the images directory under the application root. By using #FilmID# in the filename, images can be referred to dynamically. In this example, for FilmID 2 the <IMG> tag becomes

```
<IMG SRC="../images/f2.gif" ALT="Charlie's Devils" ALIGN="MIDDLE">
```

Try executing Listing 11.10 again, but this time do not pass the FilmID parameter. What happens when you execute the code? You probably received an error message similar to the one in Figure 11.12 telling you that you were referring to a variable that does not exist. You can't use URL.FilmID in your SQL statement if no URL parameter named FilmID exists.

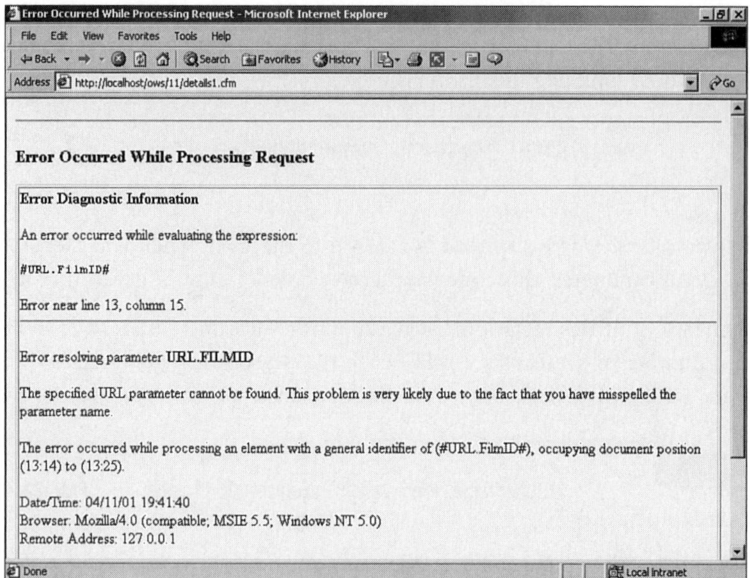

Figure 11.12 You can't refer to a variable that does not exist because an error message will be generated.

The solution (which you looked at briefly in Chapter 10) is to check that the variable exists before using it. Listing 11.11 contains an updated version of the code; save it as `details2.cfm` and execute it. What happens now if no `FilmID` is specified?

LISTING 11.11 details2.cfm—DATA DRILL-DOWN DETAILS

```
<!---
Name:        details2.cfm
Author:      Ben Forta (ben@forta.com)
Description: Data drill-down details with basic validation
Created:     4/1/01
--->

<!--- Make sure FilmID was passed --->
<CFIF NOT IsDefined("URL.FilmID")>
 <!--- It wasn't, send to movie list --->
 <CFLOCATION URL="movies6.cfm">
</CFIF>

<!--- Get a movie from database --->
<CFQUERY NAME="movie" DATASOURCE="ows">
SELECT FilmID, MovieTitle, PitchText,
       Summary, DateInTheaters, AmountBudgeted
FROM Films
WHERE FilmID=#URL.FilmID#
</CFQUERY>

<!--- Create HTML page --->
<!DOCTYPE HTML PUBLIC "-//W3C//DTD HTML 4.0 Transitional//EN">
```

```
<HTML>
<HEAD>
    <TITLE>Orange Whip Studios - Movie Details</TITLE>
</HEAD>

<BODY>

<!--- Display movie details --->
<CFOUTPUT QUERY="movie">
 <TABLE>
  <TR>
   <TD COLSPAN="2">
    <IMG SRC="../images/f#FilmID#.gif" ALT="#MovieTitle#" ALIGN="MIDDLE">
    <B>#MovieTitle#</B>
   </TD>
  </TR>
  <TR VALIGN="top">
   <TH ALIGN="right">Tag line:</TH>
   <TD>#PitchText#</TD>
  </TR>
  <TR VALIGN="top">
   <TH ALIGN="right">Summary:</TH>
   <TD>#Summary#</TD>
  </TR>
  <TR VALIGN="top">
   <TH ALIGN="right">Released:</TH>
   <TD>#DateFormat(DateInTheaters)#</TD>
  </TR>
  <TR VALIGN="top">
   <TH ALIGN="right">Budget:</TH>
   <TD>#DollarFormat(AmountBudgeted)#</TD>
  </TR>
 </TABLE>
</CFOUTPUT>

</BODY>
</HTML>
```


The only thing that has changed in Listing 11.11 is the inclusion of the following code *before* the `<CFQUERY>` tag:

```
<!--- Make sure FilmID was passed --->
<CFIF NOT IsDefined("URL.FilmID")>
 <!--- It wasn't, send to movie list --->
 <CFLOCATION URL="movies6.cfm">
</CFIF>
```

If `FilmID` was not passed then the user should never have gotten to this page, so why not send her where she belongs? `<CFLOCATION>` is a ColdFusion tag that redirects users to other pages (or even other sites). So, the `<CFIF>` statement checks to see whether `URL.FilmID` exists (using the `IsDefined()` function). If it does not, the user is sent to the `movies6.cfm` page automatically. Now the SQL code can't execute without a `FilmID`. Therefore, if no `FilmID` exists, the `<CFQUERY>` tag is never even reached.

Note

The `IsDefined()` function was introduced in Chapter 10.

So far so good, but you're not there yet. Two other possible trouble spots still exist. Try executing the following URL:

```
http://localhost/ows/11/details2.cfm?FilmID=1
```

`1` is a valid `FilmID`, so the movie details are displayed. But `FilmID 1` does not have a movie image, which means the `<IMG>` tag is pointing to a nonexistent image, causing a browser error (as seen in Figure 11.13).

In addition, try this URL:

```
http://localhost/ows/11/details2.cfm?FilmID=1000
```

No movie with a `FilmID` of `1000` exists, so no movie is displayed, but no error message is displayed either.

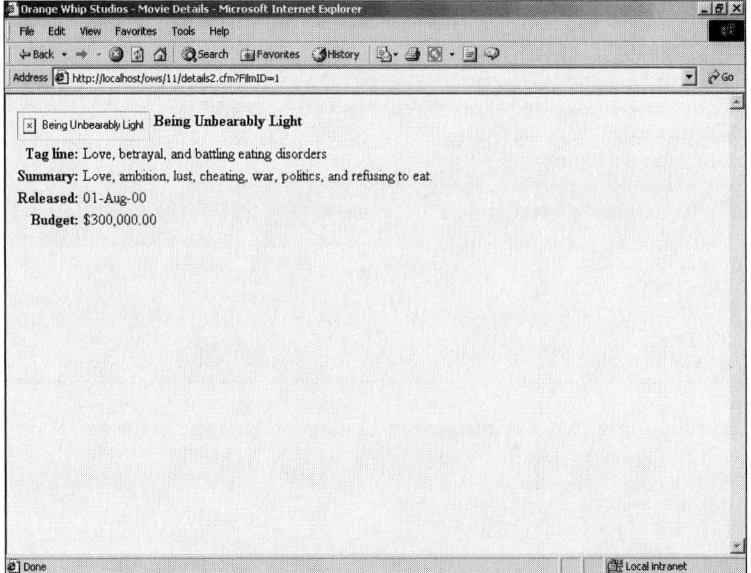

Figure 11.13 When referring to images dynamically, care must be taken to ensure that the image actually exists.

Neither of these problems is critical, but they should be addressed anyway. Listing 11.12 contains a final version of the details page; save this file as `details3.cfm`.

LISTING 11.12 `details3.cfm`—**DATA DRILL-DOWN DETAILS**

```
<!---
Name:        details3.cfm
Author:      Ben Forta (ben@forta.com)
Description: Data drill-down details with complete validation
```

```
Created:     4/1/01
--->

<!--- Movie list page --->
<CFSET list_page="movies7.cfm">

<!--- Make sure FilmID was passed --->
<CFIF NOT IsDefined("URL.FilmID")>
 <!--- It wasn't, send to movie list --->
 <CFLOCATION URL="#list_page#">
</CFIF>

<!--- Get a movie from database --->
<CFQUERY NAME="movie" DATASOURCE="ows">
SELECT FilmID, MovieTitle, PitchText,
       Summary, DateInTheaters, AmountBudgeted
FROM Films
WHERE FilmID=#URL.FilmID#
</CFQUERY>

<!--- Make sure valid FilmID was passed --->
<CFIF movie.RecordCount IS 0>
 <!--- It wasn't, send to movie list --->
 <CFLOCATION URL="#list_page#">
</CFIF>

<!--- Build image paths --->
<CFSET image_src="../images/f#movie.FilmID#.gif">
<CFSET image_path=ExpandPath(image_src)>

<!--- Create HTML page --->
<!DOCTYPE HTML PUBLIC "-//W3C//DTD HTML 4.0 Transitional//EN">
<HTML>
<HEAD>
    <TITLE>Orange Whip Studios - Movie Details</TITLE>
</HEAD>

<BODY>

<!--- Display movie details --->
<CFOUTPUT QUERY="movie">
 <TABLE>
  <TR>
   <TD COLSPAN="2">
    <!--- Check of image file exists --->
    <CFIF FileExists(image_path)>
     <!--- If it does, display it --->
     <IMG SRC="#image_src#" ALT="#MovieTitle#" ALIGN="MIDDLE">
    </CFIF>
     <B>#MovieTitle#</B>
   </TD>
  </TR>
  <TR VALIGN="top">
   <TH ALIGN="right">Tag line:</TH>
   <TD>#PitchText#</TD>
  </TR>
  <TR VALIGN="top">
```

LISTING 11.12 CONTINUED

```
    <TH ALIGN="right">Summary:</TH>
    <TD>#Summary#</TD>
   </TR>
   <TR VALIGN="top">
    <TH ALIGN="right">Released:</TH>
    <TD>#DateFormat(DateInTheaters)#</TD>
   </TR>
   <TR VALIGN="top">
    <TH ALIGN="right">Budget:</TH>
    <TD>#DollarFormat(AmountBudgeted)#</TD>
   </TR>
  </TABLE>
</CFOUTPUT>

<P>

<!--- Link back to movie list --->
<CFOUTPUT><A HREF="#list_page#">[Movie list]</A></CFOUTPUT>

</BODY>
</HTML>
```

A lot has changed here, so let's walk through the code together.

The first line of code is a `<CFSET>` statement that sets a variable named `list_page` to `movies7.cfm`. You'll see why this was done in a moment.

Next comes the check for the `URL` parameter `FilmID`. If it is not present, `<CFLOCATION>` is used to redirect the user to the page referred to in variable `list_page` (the movie list, same as before).

Then comes the query itself—same as before; no changes there.

After the query comes a new `<CFIF>` statement that checks to see whether `Movie.RecordCount IS 0`. You will recall that `RecordCount` lets you know how many rows were retrieved by a query, so if `RecordCount IS 0`, you know that no rows were retrieved. The only way this could happen is if an invalid `FilmID` were specified, in which case `<CFLOCATION>` would be used to send the user back to the movie list page—one problem solved. (Earlier I said that I'd show you an alternative use for `RecordCount`; well, I just did.)

Next comes a set of two `<CFSET>` statements:

```
<!--- Build image paths --->
<CFSET image_src="../images/f#movie.FilmID#.gif">
<CFSET image_path=ExpandPath(image_src)>
```

The goal here is to check that the movie image exists before the `<IMG>` tag is used to insert it. ColdFusion provides a function named `FileExists()` that can be used to check for the existence of files, but there is a catch.

Images always have at least two paths by which they are referred—the actual path on disk and the URL (usually a relative URL). So, in this example, the image for `FilmID 2` would have a path on disk that might look similar to `c:\inetpub\wwwroot\ows\images\f2.gif` and a URL that might look similar to `..\images\f2.gif`. Usually, you care about only the URL—the actual physical location of a file is not important within the browser. But to check for a file's existence, you do need the actual path (that is what you must pass to `FileExists()`). And the code you used to build the path (using `#FilmID#` in the `SRC`) was a relative path.

Enter the two `<CFSET>` statements. The first simply creates a variable named `image_src` that contains the dynamically generated relative filename (in the case of `FilmID 2`, it would be `..\images\f2.gif`), the same technique used in the `<IMG>` tag in the previous versions of this code. The second uses a ColdFusion function named `ExpandPath()` that converts relative paths to complete physical paths (here saving that path to `image_path`).

At this point, no determination has been made as to whether to display the image. All you have done is created two variables, each containing a path—one physical, suitable for using with `FileExists()`, and one relative, suitable for use in an `<IMG>` tag.

Next comes the details display, which is the same as it was before, except now the `<IMG>` tag is enclosed within a `<CFIF>` statement that checks whether `FileExists(image_path)`. If the image exists, `FileExists()` returns `TRUE` and the `<IMG>` tag is inserted using `image_src` as the `SRC`. If `FileExists()` returns `FALSE` (meaning the movie had no image), the `<IMG>` tag is not generated—problem two solved.

Note

Of course, the two variables `image_path` and `image_src` are not actually necessary, and the code would have worked if the processing was all done inline. But, the approach used here is cleaner, more intuitive, easier to read and will help you write better code.

At the very bottom of the page is a new link that enables users to get back to the movie list page. This link also uses the `list_page` variable. And by now, I hope the reason that a variable for the movie link URL is used is blatantly obvious. The code now has three locations that refer to the movie list file. Had they all been hard-coded, making changes would involve more work and would be more error-prone (the likelihood of you missing one occurrence grows with the number of occurrences). By using a variable, all that needs to change is the variable assignment at the top of the page—the rest all works as is.

The last thing to do is to update the movie listing page so it contains links to the new `details3.cfm` page. Listing 11.13 contains the revised movie listing code (based on `movies6.cfm`). Save it as `movies7.cfm`, and then execute it to see a page similar to the one shown in Figure 11.14.

Listing 11.13 `movies7.cfm`—**Data Drill-Down Results Page**

```
<!---
Name:        movies7.cfm
Author:      Ben Forta (ben@forta.com)
Description: Data drill-down
```

LISTING 11.13 CONTINUED

```
Created:     4/1/01
--->

<!--- Get movie list from database --->
<CFQUERY NAME="movies" DATASOURCE="ows">
SELECT FilmID, MovieTitle, PitchText, Summary, DateInTheaters
FROM Films
ORDER BY MovieTitle
</CFQUERY>

<!--- Create HTML page --->
<!DOCTYPE HTML PUBLIC "-//W3C//DTD HTML 4.0 Transitional//EN">
<HTML>
<HEAD>
    <TITLE>Orange Whip Studios - Movie List</TITLE>
</HEAD>

<BODY>

<!--- Display movie list --->
<TABLE>
<TR>
 <CFOUTPUT>
   <TH COLSPAN="2">
     ➥<FONT SIZE="+3">Movie List (#Movies.RecordCount# movies)</FONT>
   ➥</TH>
 </CFOUTPUT>
</TR>
<CFOUTPUT QUERY="movies">
<TR>
 <TD>
  <FONT SIZE="+2">
  <B>#CurrentRow#: <A HREF="details3.cfm?FilmID=#URLEncodedFormat
➥(Trim(FilmID))#">#MovieTitle#</A></B>
  </FONT>
  <BR>
  <FONT SIZE="+1">
  <I>#PitchText#</I>
  </FONT>
 </TD>
 <TD>Released: #DateFormat(DateInTheaters)#</TD>
</TR>
<TR>
 <TD COLSPAN="2">#Summary#</TD>
</TR>
</CFOUTPUT>
</TABLE>

</BODY>
</HTML>
```

Just two changes have been made in Listing 11.13. The `SELECT` statement in the `<CFQUERY>` now also retrieves the `FilmID` column—you need that to pass to the details page. (You will recall that the details page needs the `FilmID` passed as a URL parameter.)

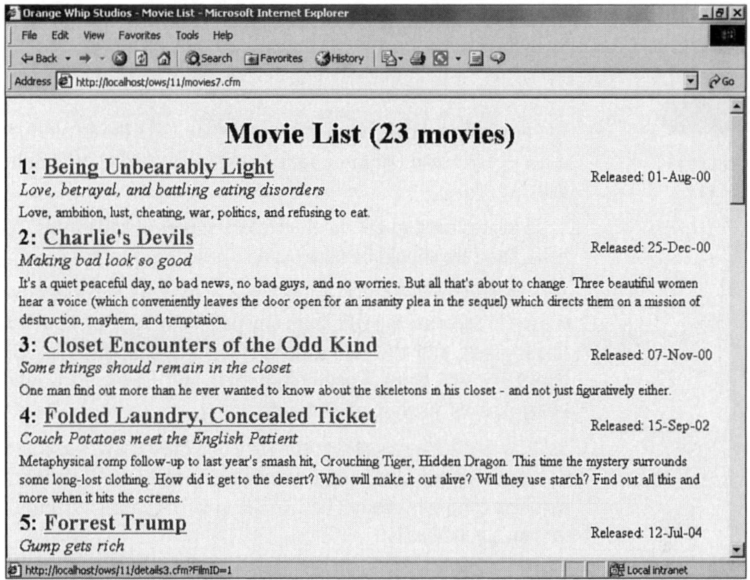

Figure 11.14 Dynamically generated URLs make creating data drill-down interfaces easy.

The display of `MovieTitle` has been changed to read

```
<A HREF="details3.cfm?FilmID=#URLEncodedFormat(Trim(FilmID))#">#MovieTitle#</A>
```

The HTML `<A HREF="">` tag is used to create links to other pages. The text between the `<A>` and `</A>` tags is clickable, and when it's clicked, the user is taken to the URL specified in the `HREF` attribute. So, the tag `<A HREF="details3.cfm">Click here</A>` displays the text `Click here`, which, if clicked, takes the user to page `details3.cfm`.

But you need `FilmID` to be passed to the details page, so for `FilmID 1` the `HREF` needed would read

```
<A HREF="details3.cfm?FilmID=1>Being Unbearably Light</A>
```

And for `FilmID 2` it would have to be

```
<A HREF="details3.cfm?FilmID=2>Charlie's Devils</A>
```

The links are created using the `FilmID` column so that the URL parameter `FilmID` is correctly populated with the appropriate value for each movie. As ColdFusion loops through the movies, it creates a link for each one of them. The links all point to the same page—`details3.cfm`. The only thing that differs is the value passed to the `FilmID` parameter, and this value is then used in `details3.cfm` to display the correct movie. So, for the movie with `FilmID` of `1`, the URL correctly becomes

```
<A HREF="details3.cfm?FilmID=1>Being Unbearably Light</A>
```

Try it out; you should be able to click any movie to see the details and then click the link at the bottom of the details page to get back.

Pretty impressive for just two files containing less than 150 lines of ColdFusion code (including all HTML and comments).

Note

You probably noticed that when constructing URLs for an `HREF`, two functions were used, `Trim()` and `URLEncodedFormat()`, instead of just referring to the column directly.

`Trim()` was used to get rid of any extra spaces (if any existed). URLs have size limitations, and care should be taken to not waste URL space.

The `URLEncodedFormat()` function is even more important. As you already know, `?` is used to separate the URL from any parameters passed to it, `=` is used to assign parameter values, and `&` is used to separate parameters. Of course, this means that these characters can't be used within URL parameter values; many others can't be used, either (spaces, periods, and so on).

So, how are these values passed? They're passed using a special format in which characters are replaced by a set of numbers that represent them. On the receiving end, the numbers can be converted back to the original characters (and ColdFusion does this for you automatically).

The `URLEncodedFormat()` function takes a string and returns a version of it that is URL safe.

When you populate a URL from a variable (any variable, including a database column), you run the risk that the values used might contain these illegal characters—characters that need to be converted. Therefore, you always should use `URLEncodedFormat()` (as was done in the previous example) so that if any invalid characters exist, they will be converted automatically and transparently. (Even in this chapter's example, in which you know `FilmID` contains only numbers that are safe, it still pays to encode the values in case someone changes something someday.)

Displaying Data Using Frames

Another form of data drill-down, albeit a less popular one, involves the use of HTML *frames*. Frames enable you to split your browser window in two or more windows and control what gets displayed within each. ColdFusion templates are very well suited for use within frames.

Creating frames involves creating multiple templates (or HTML pages). Each window in a frame typically displays a different template; you need two templates if you have two windows. In addition, one more page is always used to lay out and create the frames.

When the frames are created, each window is titled with a unique name. In a nonframed window, the new page is opened in the same window every time you select a hyperlink, replacing whatever contents were there previously. In a framed window, you can use the window name to control the destination for any output.

Figure 11.15 shows a frames-based version of the movie listing application. As you can see, movies are listed on the left, and when a movie is selected its details are displayed on the right.

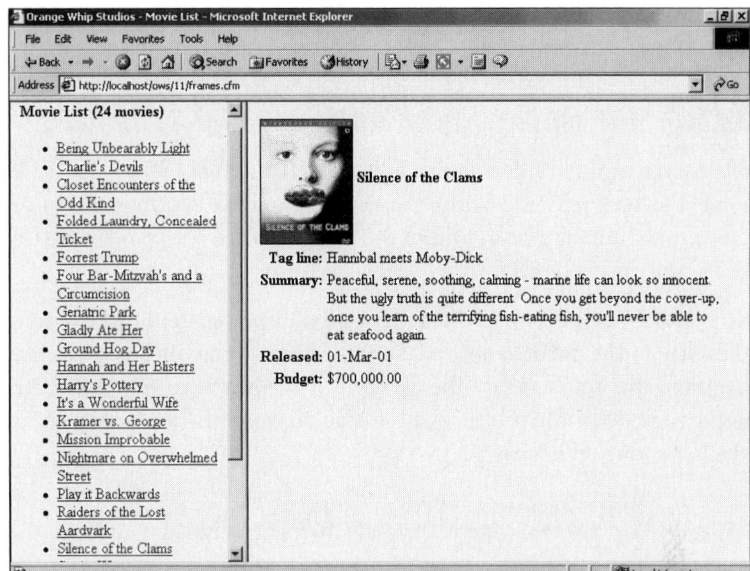

Figure 11.15 Frames-based interfaces are effective for data drill-down applications.

Now that you know how frames work, the first thing you need to do is create the template to define and create the frames. The code for template `frames.cfm` is shown in Listing 11.14.

LISTING 11.14 `frames.cfm`—COLDFUSION-POWERED FRAMES

```
<!---
Name:        frames.cfm
Author:      Ben Forta (ben@forta.com)
Description: Frames for frames-based data drill-down
Created:     4/1/01
--->

<!DOCTYPE HTML PUBLIC "-//W3C//DTD HTML 4.0 Transitional//EN">
<HTML>
<HEAD>
    <TITLE>Orange Whip Studios - Movie List</TITLE>
</HEAD>

<!-- frames -->
<FRAMESET COLS="250,*">
    <FRAME NAME="left" SRC="movies.cfm">
    <FRAME NAME="right" SRC="blank.cfm">
</FRAMESET>
```

This template first defines the frames. `<FRAMESET COLS="250,*">` creates two columns (or windows)—one 250 pixels wide and the other as wide as the remaining space allows.

Tip

Sizes also can be specified as percentages, so `<FRAMESET COLS="50%,50%">` would create two windows, each `50%` of the width of the browser.

The two columns are then defined: `<FRAME NAME="left" SRC="movies.cfm">` creates the left frame; the `NAME` attribute names the window; and the `SRC` attribute specifies the name of the template to initially display within the window when the frame is first displayed. Listing 11.15 contains the code for the file `movies.cfm`.

No movie is selected when the frame is first displayed, and therefore no information exists to display in the details window (the right frame). You obviously can't display movie information in that frame before the user selects the movie to view, so instead you display an empty page. `SRC="blank.cfm"` loads a blank page in the frame named `right`, the source for which is shown in Listing 11.16.

LISTING 11.15 movies.cfm—MOVIE LIST FOR LEFT FRAME

```
<!---
Name:        movies.cfm
Author:      Ben Forta (ben@forta.com)
Description: Left frame for data drill-down
Created:     4/1/01
--->

<!--- Get movie list from database --->
<CFQUERY NAME="movies" DATASOURCE="ows">
SELECT FilmID, MovieTitle
FROM Films
ORDER BY MovieTitle
</CFQUERY>

<BODY>

<CFOUTPUT>
<B>Movie List (#Movies.RecordCount# movies)</B>
</CFOUTPUT>

<!--- Movie list --->
<UL>
 <CFOUTPUT QUERY="movies">
  <LI><A HREF="details.cfm?FilmID=#URLEncodedFormat(Trim(FilmID))#
➥" TARGET="right">#MovieTitle#</A>
 </CFOUTPUT>
</UL>

</BODY>
```

LISTING 11.16 blank.cfm—INITIAL BLANK RIGHT FRAME

```
<!---
Name:        blank.cfm
```

```
Author:      Ben Forta (ben@forta.com)
Description: Blank initial frame content
Created:     4/1/01
--->

<BODY>
</BODY>
```

Listing 11.15 (`movies.cfm`) contains code similar to the code used in previous listings in this chapter. The only difference is the link itself. The `<A>` tag now contains a new attribute: `TARGET="right"`. `TARGET` specifies the name of the target window in which to open the URL. Because you named the right window `right` (you named the left window `left`), when a link is clicked in the left window, the appropriate URL is opened in the right window.

Tip

Frames can be named with any names you want, but be careful not to reuse frame names unless you want to reuse the same frame.

Tip

To open links in a new window (effectively creating a frame as needed), use the target of _new.

The link itself is a file named `details.cfm` (a modified version of the details files created earlier). Listing 11.17 contains the source for this file.

Listing 11.17 details.cfm—Movie Details for Right Frame

```
<!---
Name:        details.cfm
Author:      Ben Forta (ben@forta.com)
Description: Detail for frames-based data drill-down
Created:     4/1/01
--->

<!--- Make sure FilmID was passed --->
<CFIF NOT IsDefined("URL.FilmID")>
 <!--- This should never happen --->
 <CFLOCATION URL="blank.cfm">
</CFIF>

<!--- Get a movie from database --->
<CFQUERY NAME="movie" DATASOURCE="ows">
SELECT FilmID, MovieTitle, PitchText,
       Summary, DateInTheaters, AmountBudgeted
FROM Films
WHERE FilmID=#URL.FilmID#
</CFQUERY>

<!--- Make sure valid FilmID was passed --->
<CFIF movie.RecordCount IS 0>
```

Listing 11.17 Continued

```
 <!--- This should never happen --->
 <CFLOCATION URL="blank.cfm">
</CFIF>

<!--- Build image paths --->
<CFSET image_src="../images/f#movie.FilmID#.gif">
<CFSET image_path=ExpandPath(image_src)>

<!--- Create HTML page --->
<BODY>

<!--- Display movie details --->
<CFOUTPUT QUERY="movie">
 <TABLE>
  <TR>
   <TD COLSPAN="2">
    <!--- Check if image file exists --->
    <CFIF FileExists(image_path)>
     <!--- If it does, display it --->
     <IMG SRC="#image_src#" ALT="#MovieTitle#" ALIGN="MIDDLE">
    </CFIF>
    <B>#MovieTitle#</B>
   </TD>
  </TR>
  <TR VALIGN="top">
   <TH ALIGN="right">Tag line:</TH>
   <TD>#PitchText#</TD>
  </TR>
  <TR VALIGN="top">
   <TH ALIGN="right">Summary:</TH>
   <TD>#Summary#</TD>
  </TR>
  <TR VALIGN="top">
   <TH ALIGN="right">Released:</TH>
   <TD>#DateFormat(DateInTheaters)#</TD>
  </TR>
  <TR VALIGN="top">
   <TH ALIGN="right">Budget:</TH>
   <TD>#DollarFormat(AmountBudgeted)#</TD>
  </TR>
 </TABLE>
</CFOUTPUT>

<P>

</BODY>
```

Listing 11.17 should be self-explanatory by this point. The only real change here is that if no `FilmID` is passed, or if `FilmID` is invalid (neither condition should ever actually occur, but it pays to be safe), file `blank.cfm` is loaded. You could change this to display an appropriate error message if you want.

After you have created all four files (`frame.cfm`, `blank.cfm`, `movies.cfm`, and `details.cfm`), execute the application in your browser by going to the following URL:

```
http://localhost/ows/11/frames.cfm
```

You should see a screen similar to the one shown previously in Figure 11.15. Try clicking any link on the left; the appropriate movie will be displayed on the right.

And there you have it—two simple tags, `<CFQUERY>` and `<CFOUTPUT>`, generating any output you can imagine.

Debugging Dynamic Database Queries

Before we finish this chapter, there is something you should be aware of. Look at the following code:

```
<!--- Get a movie from database --->
<CFQUERY NAME="movie" DATASOURCE="ows">
SELECT FilmID, MovieTitle, PitchText,
       Summary, DateInTheaters, AmountBudgeted
FROM Films
WHERE FilmID=#URL.FilmID#
</CFQUERY>
```


As you now know, this code builds a dynamic SQL statement—the expression `#URL.FilmID#` is replaced by the contents of that variable to construct a complete SQL `SELECT` statement at runtime.

This particular example is a simple one, a single expression is used in a simple `WHERE` clause. But as the complexity of the expressions (or the number of them) increases, so does the chance that you'll introduce problems in your SQL. And to find these problems, you'll need to know exactly what SQL was generated by ColdFusion—taking into account all dynamic processing.

Fortunately, ColdFusion enables you to do this. In Chapter 4, "Accessing the ColdFusion Administrator," I mentioned the debugging screens (and told you that we'd use them in this chapter). The debugging screens can be used to append debug output to the bottom of generated pages, as seen in Figure 11.16.

As you can see, the appended output contains database query information (including the SQL, number of rows retrieved, and execution time), page execution time, passed parameters, CGI variables, and much more.

To try this for yourself, see Chapter 4 for instructions on turning on debug output. Once enabled, execute any page in your browser and the debug output will be appended automatically.

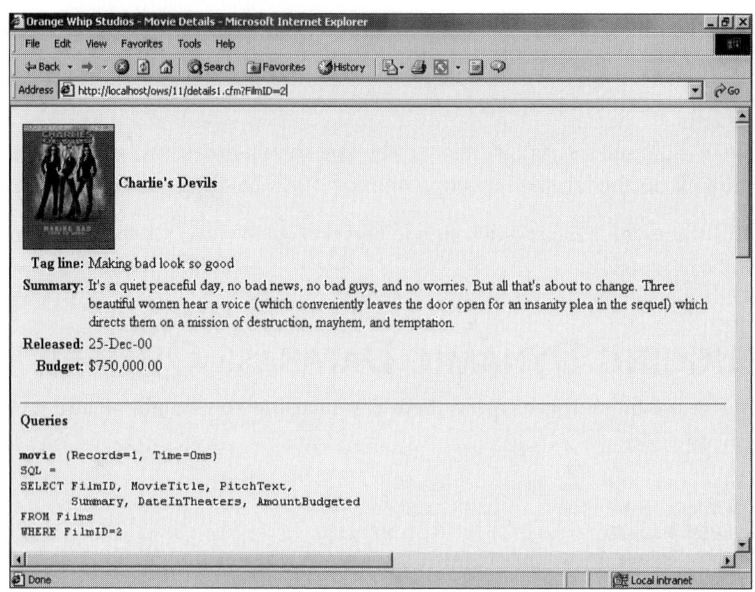

Figure 11.16
Debug output can be used to discover the dynamic SQL generated by ColdFusion.

CHAPTER 12

ColdFusion Forms

In this chapter

USING FORMS

In Chapter 11, "Creating Data-Driven Pages," you learned how to create ColdFusion templates that dynamically display data retrieved from databases. The `Films` table has just 23 rows, so the data fit easily within a Web browser window and required only minimal scrolling.

What do you do if you have hundreds or thousands of rows? Displaying all that data in one long list is impractical. Scrolling through lists of movies to find the one you want just doesn't work well. The solution is to enable users to search for what they want by specifying what they are looking for. You can allow them to enter a title, actors, or part of the tag-line, and then you can display only the movies that meet the search criteria.

To accomplish this solution, you need to do two things. First, you must create your search form using the HTML `<FORM>` tags. Second, you must create a template that builds SQL `SELECT` statements dynamically based on the data collected and submitted by the form.

Note

See Chapter 6, "Introduction to SQL," for an explanation of the `SELECT` statement.

CREATING FORMS

Before you can create a search form, you need to learn how ColdFusion interacts with HTML forms. Listing 12.1 contains the code for a sample form that prompts for a first and last name. Create this template, and then save it in a new folder named `12` (under the Web root directory) as `forms1.cfm`.

LISTING 12.1 `forms1.cfm`—HTML FORMS CAN BE USED TO COLLECT AND SUBMIT DATA TO COLDFUSION FOR PROCESSING

```
<!---
Name:        forms1.cfm
Author:      Ben Forta (ben@forta.com)
Description: Detail for frame based data drill-down
Created:     4/15/01
--->

<!DOCTYPE HTML PUBLIC "-//W3C//DTD HTML 4.0 Transitional//EN">

<HTML>
<HEAD>
    <TITLE>Learning ColdFusion Forms 1</TITLE>
</HEAD>

<BODY>

<!--- Movie search form --->
<FORM ACTION="forms2.cfm" METHOD="POST">
```

```
Please enter the movie name and then click
<B>Process</B>.
<P>
Movie:
<INPUT TYPE="text" NAME="MovieTitle">
<BR>
<INPUT TYPE="submit" VALUE="Process">

</FORM>

</BODY>
</HTML>
```

Execute this code to display the form, as shown in Figure 12.1.

This form is simple, with a single data entry field and a submit button, but it helps clearly demonstrate how forms are used to submit data to ColdFusion.

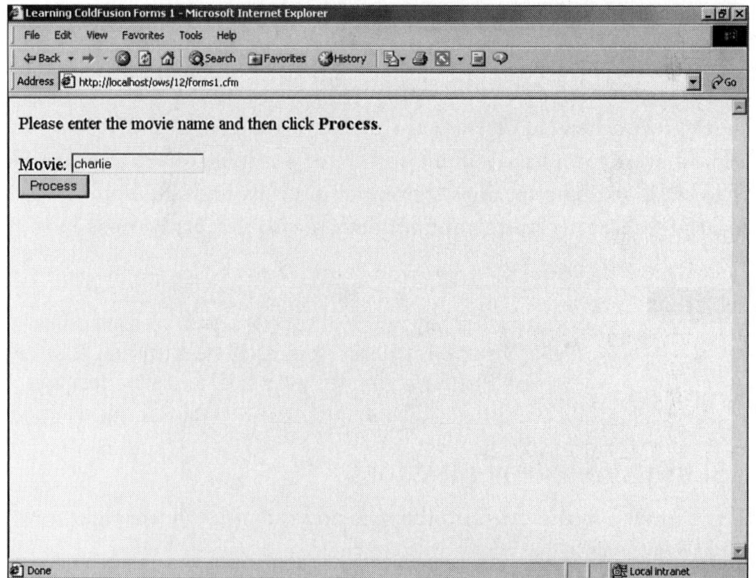

Figure 12.1
You can use HTML forms to collect data to be submitted to ColdFusion.

Using HTML Form Tags

You create HTML forms by using the `<FORM>` tag. `<FORM>` usually takes two parameters passed as tag attributes. The `ACTION` attribute specifies the name of the script or program the Web server should execute in response to the form's submission. To submit a form to ColdFusion, you specify the name of the ColdFusion template that will process the form. The following example specifies that the template `forms2.cfm` should process the submitted form:

```
ACTION="forms2.cfm"
```

The METHOD attribute specifies how data is sent back to the Web server. All ColdFusion forms must be submitted as type POST.

Caution

> The default submission type is not POST; it is usually GET. If you omit the METHOD="POST" attribute from your form tag, you run the risk of losing form data—particularly in long forms or forms with TEXTAREA controls.

Your form has only a single data entry field: <INPUT TYPE="text" NAME="MovieTitle">. This is a simple text field. The NAME attribute in the <INPUT> tag specifies the name of the field, and ColdFusion uses this name to refer to the field when it is processed.

Each field in a form usually is given a unique name. If two fields have the same name, both sets of values are returned to be processed and are separated by a comma. You usually want to be able to validate and manipulate each field individually, so each field should have its own name. The notable exceptions are the check box and radio button input types, which will be described shortly.

The last item in the form is an <INPUT> of type submit. The submit <INPUT> type creates a button that, when clicked, submits the form contents to the Web server for processing. Almost every form has a submit button (or a graphic image that acts like a submit button). The VALUE attribute specifies the text to display within the button, so <INPUT TYPE="submit" VALUE="Process"> creates a submit button with the text Process in it.

Tip

> When you're using an INPUT type of submit, you always should specify button text by using the VALUE attribute. If you don't, the default text Submit Query (or something similar) is displayed, and this text is likely to confuse your users.

Form Submission Error Messages

If you enter a movie title into the field and submit the form right now, you will receive a ColdFusion error message similar to the one shown in Figure 12.2. This error says that template forms2.cfm cannot be found.

This error message, of course, is perfectly valid. You submitted a form to be passed to ColdFusion and processed it with a template, but you have not created that template yet. Your next task, then, is to create a template to process the form submission.

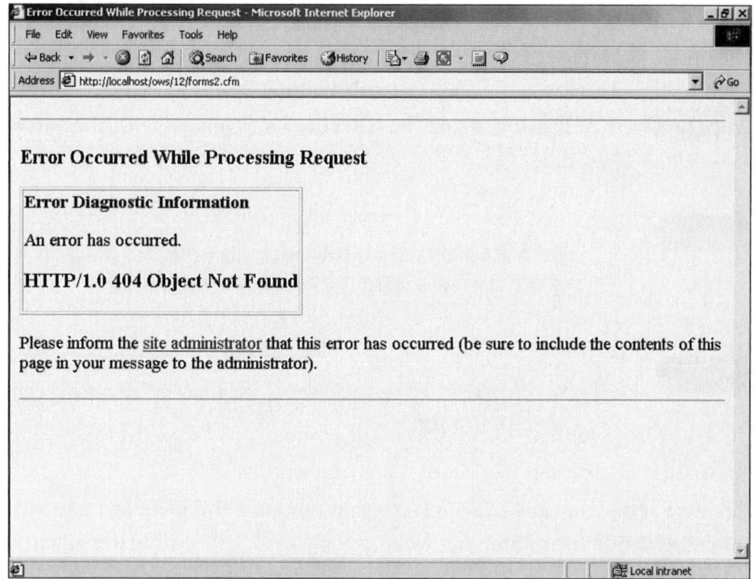

Figure 12.2 ColdFusion returns an error message when it cannot process your request.

Processing Form Submissions

To demonstrate how to process returned forms, you must create a simple template that echoes the movie title you entered. The template is shown in Listing 12.2.

Listing 12.2 `forms2.cfm`—Processing Form Fields

```
<!---
Name:        forms2.cfm
Author:      Ben Forta (ben@forta.com)
Description: Introduction to forms
Created:     4/15/01
--->

<!DOCTYPE HTML PUBLIC "-//W3C//DTD HTML 4.0 Transitional//EN">

<HTML>
<HEAD>
    <TITLE>Learning ColdFusion Forms 2</TITLE>
</HEAD>

<BODY>

<!--- Display search text --->
<CFOUTPUT>
<B>Movie title:</B> #FORM.MovieTitle#
</CFOUTPUT>

</BODY>
</HTML>
```

PROCESSING TEXT SUBMISSIONS

By now the `CFOUTPUT` tag should be familiar to you; you use it to mark a block of code that ColdFusion should parse and process. The line `<B>Movie title:</B> #FORM.MovieTitle#` is processed by ColdFusion. `#FORM.MovieTitle#` is replaced with the value you entered in the `MovieTitle` form field.

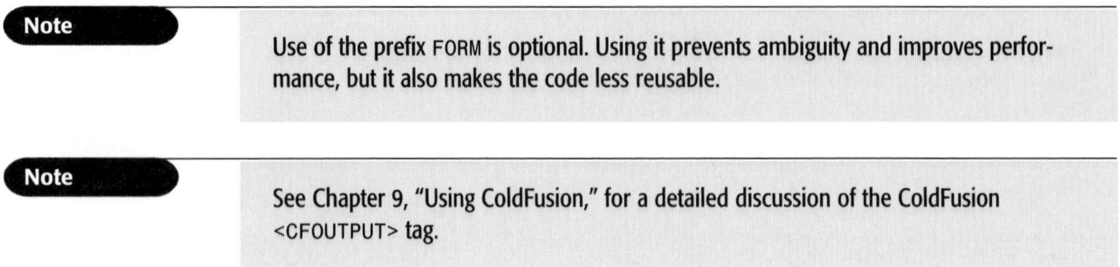

Note Use of the prefix `FORM` is optional. Using it prevents ambiguity and improves performance, but it also makes the code less reusable.

Note See Chapter 9, "Using ColdFusion," for a detailed discussion of the ColdFusion `<CFOUTPUT>` tag.

Create a template called `forms2.cfm` that contains the code in Listing 12.2 and save it. Then resubmit your name by clicking the form's submit button again. This time you should see a browser display similar to the one shown in Figure 12.3. Whatever name you enter in the Movie field in Form 1 is displayed.

As you can see, `FORM` fields are used in ColdFusion like any other variable type.

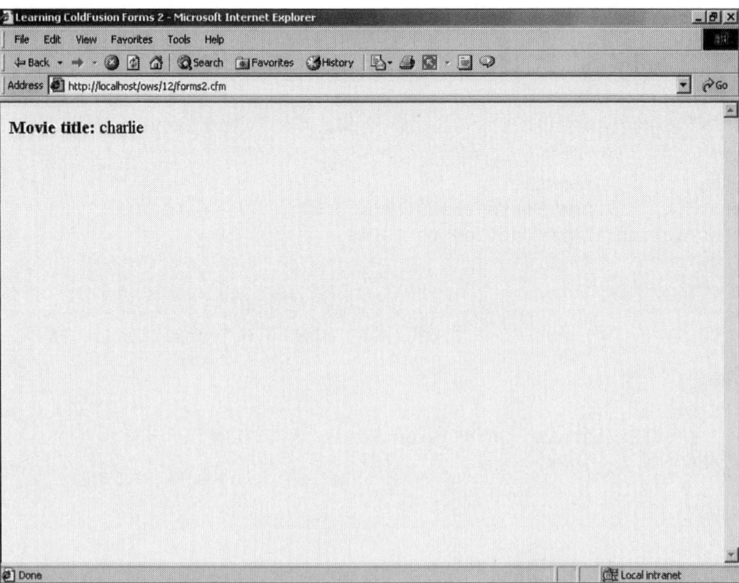

Figure 12.3 Submitted form fields can be displayed simply by referring to the field name.

PROCESSING CHECK BOXES AND RADIO BUTTONS

Other input types you will frequently use are check boxes and radio buttons. *Check boxes* are used to select options that have one of two states: on or off, yes or no, and true or false. To ask a visitor whether he wants to be added to a mailing list, for example, you would create a check box field. If the user selects the box, his name is added to the mailing list; if the user does not select the box, his name is not added.

Radio buttons are used to select one of at least two mutually exclusive options. You can implement a field prompting for payment type with options such as Cash, Check, Credit card, or P.O.

The code example in Listing 12.3 creates a form that uses both option buttons and check box fields.

LISTING 12.3 forms3.cfm—USING OPTION BUTTONS AND CHECK BOXES

```
<!---
Name:        forms3.cfm
Author:      Ben Forta (ben@forta.com)
Description: Introduction to forms
Created:     4/15/01
--->

<!DOCTYPE HTML PUBLIC "-//W3C//DTD HTML 4.0 Transitional//EN">

<HTML>

<HEAD>
    <TITLE>Learning ColdFusion Forms 3</TITLE>
</HEAD>

<BODY>

<!--- Payment and mailing list form --->
<FORM ACTION="forms4.cfm" METHOD="POST">

Please fill in this form and then click <B>Process</B>.
<P>
<!--- Payment type radio buttons --->
Payment type:<BR>
<INPUT TYPE="radio" NAME="PaymentType" VALUE="Cash">Cash<BR>
<INPUT TYPE="radio" NAME="PaymentType" VALUE="Check">Check<BR>
<INPUT TYPE="radio" NAME="PaymentType" VALUE="Credit card">Credit card<BR>
<INPUT TYPE="radio" NAME="PaymentType" VALUE="P.O.">P.O.
<P>
<!--- Mailing list checkbox --->
Would you like to be added to our mailing list?
<INPUT TYPE="checkbox" NAME="MailingList" VALUE="Yes">
<P>
<INPUT TYPE="submit" VALUE="Process">

</FORM>

</BODY>

</HTML>
```

Figure 12.4 shows how this form appears in your browser.

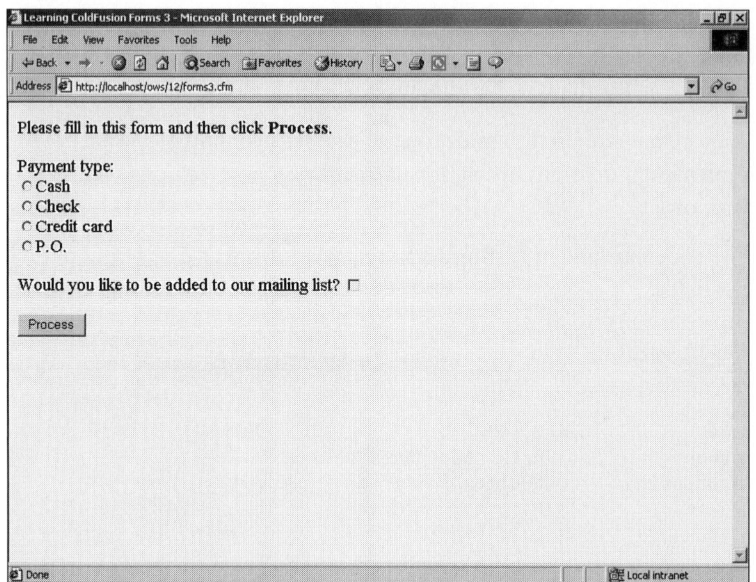

Figure 12.4
You can use input types of option buttons and check boxes to facilitate the selection of options.

Before you create `forms4.cfm` to process this form, you should note a couple of important points. First, look at the four lines of code that make up the Payment Type radio button selection:

```
<INPUT TYPE="radio" NAME="PaymentType" VALUE="Cash">Cash<BR>
<INPUT TYPE="radio" NAME="PaymentType" VALUE="Check">Check<BR>
<INPUT TYPE="radio" NAME="PaymentType" VALUE="Credit card">Credit card<BR>
<INPUT TYPE="radio" NAME="PaymentType" VALUE="P.O.">P.O.
```

Each one contains the exact same `NAME` attribute—`NAME="PaymentType"`. The four `<INPUT>` fields have the same name so your browser knows they are part of the same set. If each radio button had a separate name, the browser would not know that these buttons are mutually exclusive and thus would allow the selection of more than one button.

Another important point is that, unlike `<INPUT>` type text, radio buttons do not prompt the user for any textual input. Therefore, you must use the `VALUE` attribute for the browser to associate a particular value with each radio button. The code `VALUE="Cash"` instructs the browser to return the value `Cash` in the `PaymentType` field if that radio button is selected.

Now that you understand radio button and check box fields, you're ready to create a template to process them. Create a template called `forms4.cfm` using the template code in Listing 12.4.

LISTING 12.4 forms4.cfm—PROCESSING OPTION BUTTONS AND CHECK BOXES

```
<!---
Name:        forms4.cfm
Author:      Ben Forta (ben@forta.com)
```

```
Description: Introduction to forms
Created:     4/15/01
--->

<!DOCTYPE HTML PUBLIC "-//W3C//DTD HTML 4.0 Transitional//EN">

<HTML>

<HEAD>
    <TITLE>Learning ColdFusion Forms 4</TITLE>
</HEAD>

<BODY>

<!--- Display feedback to user --->
<CFOUTPUT>

<!--- Payment type --->
Hello,<BR>
You selected <B>#FORM.PaymentType#</B> as your payment type.<BR>

<!--- Mailing list --->
<CFIF MailingList IS "Yes">
 You will be added to our mailing list.
<CFELSE>
 You will not be added to our mailing list.
</CFIF>

</CFOUTPUT>

</BODY>

</HTML>
```


The form processing code in Listing 12.4 displays the payment type the user selects. The field `PaymentType` is fully qualified with the `FORM` field type to prevent name collisions.

When the check box is selected, the value specified in the `VALUE` attribute is returned; in this case, the value is `Yes`. If the `VALUE` attribute is omitted, the default value of `on` is returned.

Note

See Chapter 10, "CFML Basics," for details on using the `<CFIF>` tag.

Now, execute `forms3.cfm` in your browser, select a payment option, and then select the check box. Click the Process button. Your browser display should look similar to the one shown in Figure 12.5.

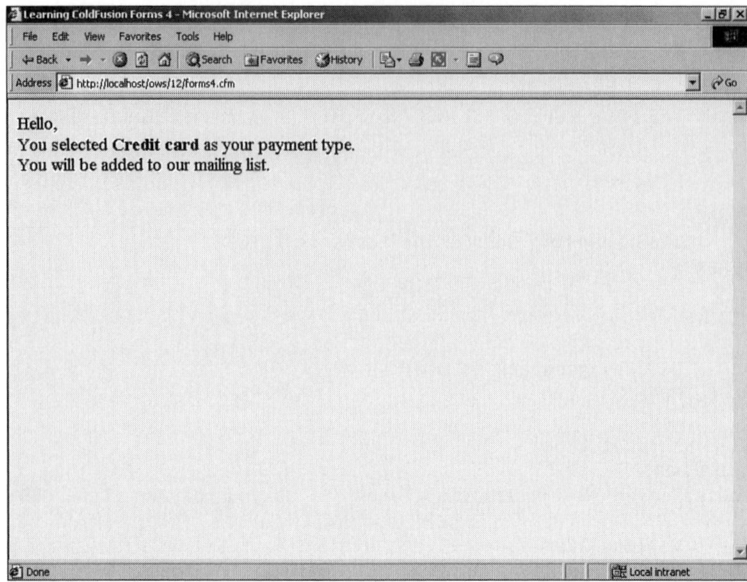

Figure 12.5
You can use ColdFusion templates to process user-selected options.

That worked exactly as intended, so now get ready to complicate things a little. Reload template `forms3.cfm` and submit it without selecting a payment type or with the `MailingList` check box not selected. ColdFusion generates an error message, as shown in Figure 12.6. As you can see, the field you do not select generates an `Error resolving parameter` error.

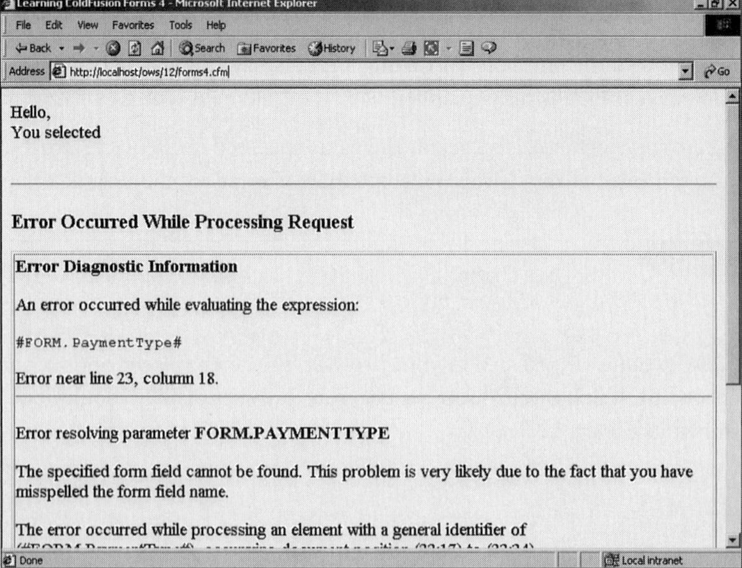

Figure 12.6
Option buttons or check boxes that are submitted with no value generate a ColdFusion error.

Check the code in Listing 12.3 to verify that the form fields do in fact exist. Why does ColdFusion report that the form field does not exist? That is one of the quirks of HTML forms. If you select a check box, the `on` value is submitted; however, *nothing* is submitted if you do not select the check box—not even an empty field. The same is true of radio buttons: If you make no selection, the field is not submitted at all. (This behavior is the exact opposite of the text `<INPUT>` type, which returns empty fields as opposed to no field.)

How do you work around this limitation? You can choose from a couple of solutions.

The first: Modify your form processing script to check which fields exist by using the `#IsDefined()#` function and, if the field exists, process it.

The second: The simpler solution is to prevent the browser from omitting fields that are not selected. You can modify the radio button field so that one radio button is preselected. This way, users will have to make a selection or use the preselected option. To preselect a radio button, just add the attribute `CHECKED` to it.

Check boxes are trickier because by their nature they must be able to be turned off. Check boxes are used for on/off states, and, when the check box is off, there is no value to submit. The solution here is to set a default value in the `ACTION` template. As you have already learned, this can be done easily using the `<CFPARAM>` tag. Look at this code:

```
<CFPARAM NAME="FORM.MailingList" DEFAULT="No">
```

When ColdFusion encounters this line, it checks to see whether a variable named `FORM.MailingList` exists. If it does, processing continues. If it does not exist, though, ColdFusion creates the variable and sets the value to whatever is specified in the `DEFAULT` attribute. The key here is that either way—whether the variable exists or not—the variable does exist after the `<CFPARAM>` tag is processed. It is therefore safe to refer to that variable further down the template code.

The updated form is shown in Listing 12.5. The first option button in the `PaymentType` field is modified to read `<INPUT TYPE="radio" NAME="PaymentType" VALUE="Cash" CHECKED>`. The `CHECKED` attribute ensures that a button is checked. The `MailingList` check box has a `VALUE` of `Yes` when it is checked, and the `<CFPARAM>` in the action page ensures that if `MailingList` is not checked, the value automatically is set to `No`.

Listing 12.5 forms5.cfm—Pre-Selecting Form Field Values

```
<!---
Name:        forms5.cfm
Author:      Ben Forta (ben@forta.com)
Description: Introduction to forms
Created:     4/15/01
--->

<!DOCTYPE HTML PUBLIC "-//W3C//DTD HTML 4.0 Transitional//EN">

<HTML>

<HEAD>
```

LISTING 12.5 CONTINUED

```
   <TITLE>Learning ColdFusion Forms 5</TITLE>
</HEAD>

<BODY>

<!--- Payment and mailing list form --->
<FORM ACTION="forms4.cfm" METHOD="POST">

Please fill in this form and then click <B>Process</B>.
<P>
<!--- Payment type radio buttons --->
Payment type:<BR>
<INPUT TYPE="radio" NAME="PaymentType" VALUE="Cash" CHECKED>Cash<BR>
<INPUT TYPE="radio" NAME="PaymentType" VALUE="Check">Check<BR>
<INPUT TYPE="radio" NAME="PaymentType" VALUE="Credit card">Credit card<BR>
<INPUT TYPE="radio" NAME="PaymentType" VALUE="P.O.">P.O.
<P>
<!--- Mailing list checkbox --->
Would you like to be added to our mailing list?
<INPUT TYPE="checkbox" NAME="MailingList" VALUE="Yes">
<P>
<INPUT TYPE="submit" VALUE="Process">

</FORM>

</BODY>

</HTML>
```

Create and save this template as `forms5.cfm`, and then add the following code to the top of `forms4.cfm`:

```
<!--- Initialize variables --->
<CFPARAM NAME="MailingList" DEFAULT="No">
```

Try using it and experiment with the two fields. You'll find that this form is reliable and robust, and it does not generate ColdFusion error messages, no matter which options are selected (or not).

PROCESSING LIST BOXES

Another field type you will frequently use is the list box. Using list boxes is an efficient way to enable users to select one or more options. If a list box is created to accept only a single selection, you can be guaranteed that a value is always returned. If you don't set one of the options to be preselected, the first one in the list is selected. An option always has to be selected.

List boxes that allow multiple selections also allow no selections at all. If you use a multiple-selection list box, you once again have to find a way to ensure that ColdFusion does not generate `Error resolving parameter` errors.

Listing 12.6 contains the same data-entry form you just created, but it replaces the option buttons with a list box. Save this template as `forms6.cfm`, and then test it with your browser.

Listing 12.6 forms6.cfm—Using a <SELECT> List Box for Options

```
<!---
Name:        forms6.cfm
Author:      Ben Forta (ben@forta.com)
Description: Introduction to forms
Created:     4/15/01
--->

<!DOCTYPE HTML PUBLIC "-//W3C//DTD HTML 4.0 Transitional//EN">

<HTML>

<HEAD>
    <TITLE>Learning ColdFusion Forms 6</TITLE>
</HEAD>

<BODY>

<!--- Payment and mailing list form --->
<FORM ACTION="forms4.cfm" METHOD="POST">

Please fill in this form and then click <B>Process</B>.
<P>
<!--- Payment type select list --->
Payment type:<BR>
<SELECT NAME="PaymentType">
    <OPTION VALUE="Cash">Cash</OPTION>
    <OPTION VALUE="Check">Check</OPTION>
    <OPTION VALUE="Credit card">Credit card</OPTION>
    <OPTION VALUE="P.O.">P.O.</OPTION>
</SELECT>
<P>
<!--- Mailing list checkbox --->
Would you like to be added to our mailing list?
<INPUT TYPE="checkbox" NAME="MailingList" VALUE="Yes">
<P>
<INPUT TYPE="submit" VALUE="Process">

</FORM>

</BODY>

</HTML>
```

For this particular form, the browser display shown in Figure 12.7 is probably a better user interface. The choice of whether to use radio buttons or list boxes is yours, and no hard and fast rules exist as to when to use one versus the other. The following guidelines, however, might help you determine which to use:

- If you need to allow the selection of multiple items or of no items at all, use a list box.

- List boxes take up less screen space. With a list box, 100 options take up no more precious real estate than a single option.
- Radio buttons present all the options to the users without requiring mouse clicks (and statistically, users more often than not select options that are readily visible).

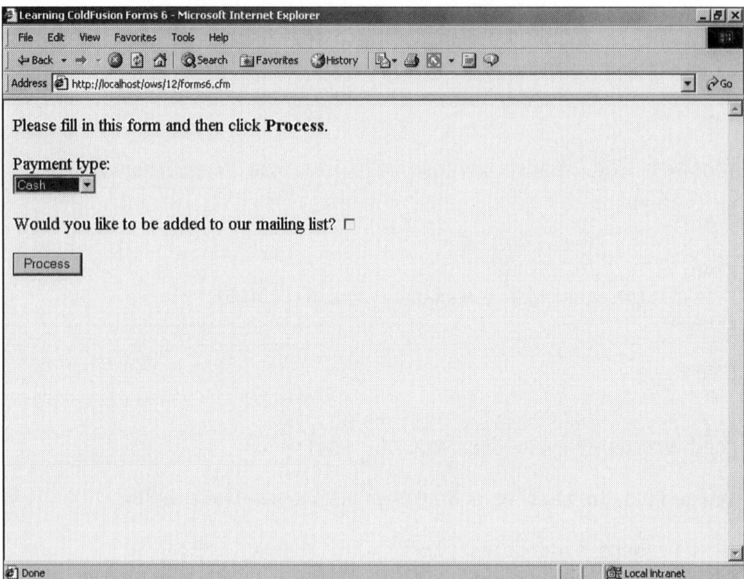

Figure 12.7
You can use HTML list boxes to select one or more options.

PROCESSING TEXT AREAS

Text area fields are boxes in which the users can enter free-form text. When you create a text area field, you specify the number of rows and columns of screen space it should occupy. This area, however, does not restrict the amount of text users can enter. The field scrolls both horizontally and vertically to enable the users to enter more text.

Listing 12.7 creates an HTML form with a text area field for user comments. The field's width is specified as a number of characters that can be typed on a single line; the height is the number of lines that are displayed without scrolling.

Tip

The `<TEXTAREA>` `COLS` attribute is specified as a number of characters that can fit on a single line. This setting is dependent on the font in which the text is displayed, and the font is browser specific. Be sure you test any `<TEXTAREA>` fields in more than one browser because a field that fits nicely in one might not fit at all in another.

LISTING 12.7 forms7.cfm—USING A TEXT AREA FIELD

```
<!---
Name:        forms7.cfm
Author:      Ben Forta (ben@forta.com)
Description: Introduction to forms
Created:     4/15/01
--->

<!DOCTYPE HTML PUBLIC "-//W3C//DTD HTML 4.0 Transitional//EN">

<HTML>

<HEAD>
    <TITLE>Learning ColdFusion Forms 7</TITLE>
</HEAD>

<BODY>

<!--- Comments form --->
<FORM ACTION="forms8.cfm" METHOD="POST">

Please enter your comments in the box provided, and then click <B>Send</B>.
<P>
<TEXTAREA NAME="Comments" ROWS="6" COLS="40"></TEXTAREA>
<P>
<INPUT TYPE="submit" VALUE="Send">

</FORM>

</BODY>

</HTML>
```


Listing 12.8 contains ColdFusion code that displays the contents of a <TEXTAREA> field.

LISTING 12.8 forms8.cfm—PROCESSING FREE-FORM TEXT AREA FIELDS

```
<!---
Name:        forms8.cfm
Author:      Ben Forta (ben@forta.com)
Description: Introduction to forms
Created:     4/15/01
--->

<!DOCTYPE HTML PUBLIC "-//W3C//DTD HTML 4.0 Transitional//EN">

<HTML>

<HEAD>
    <TITLE>Learning ColdFusion Forms 8</TITLE>
</HEAD>

<BODY>

<!--- Display feedback to user --->
```

LISTING 12.8 CONTINUED

```
<CFOUTPUT>

Thank you for your comments. You entered:
<P>
<B>#FORM.comments#</B>

</CFOUTPUT>

</BODY>

</HTML>
```

Figure 12.8 shows the <TEXTAREA> field you created, and Figure 12.9 shows how ColdFusion displays the field.

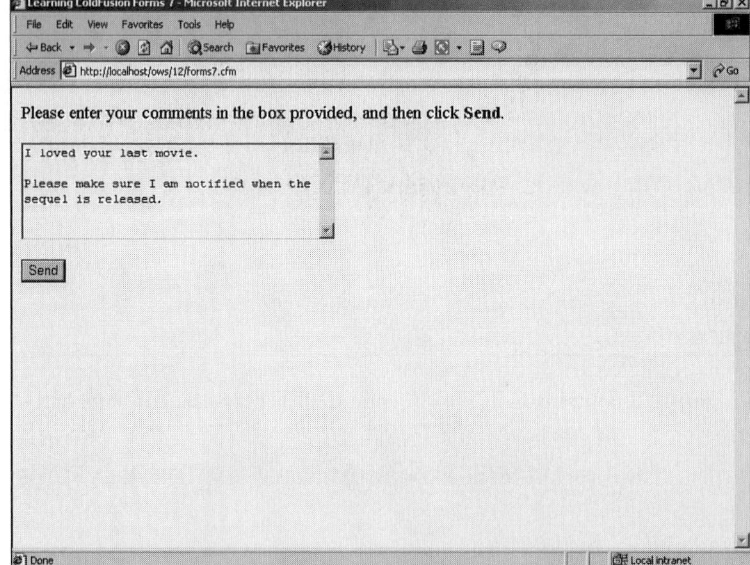

Figure 12.8
The HTML <TEXTAREA> field is a means by which you can accept free-form text input from users.

Try entering line breaks (by pressing the Enter key) in the text field and then submit it. What happens to the line breaks? Line break characters are considered whitespace characters (just like spaces) by your browser, and all whitespace is ignored by browsers. "WHITE-SPACE IS IGNORED" is displayed no differently than "WHITESPACE   IS IGNORED."

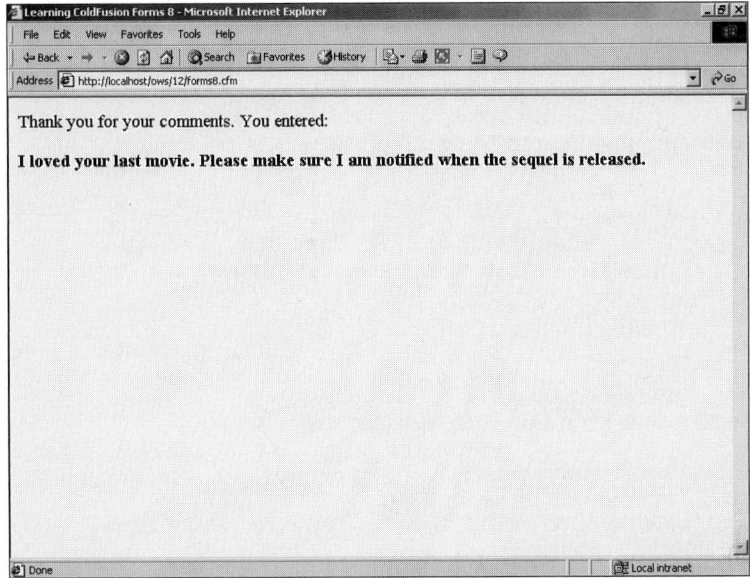

Figure 12.9 Without ColdFusion output functions, <TEXTAREA> fields are not displayed with line breaks preserved.

The only way to display line breaks is to replace the line break with an HTML paragraph tag: <P>. You therefore have to parse through the entire field text and insert <P> tags wherever necessary. Fortunately, ColdFusion makes this task a simple one. The ColdFusion `#ParagraphFormat()#` function automatically replaces every double line break with a <P> tag. (Single line breaks are not replaced because ColdFusion has no way of knowing whether the next line is a new paragraph or part of the previous one.)

Tip

The ColdFusion `Replace()` and `ReplaceList()` functions can be used instead of `ParagraphFormat()` to have greater control over the paragraph formatting. These functions are explained in Appendix B, "ColdFusion Function Reference."

The code in Listing 12.9 contains the same comments form as the one in Listing 12.7, with two differences. First, default field text is provided. Unlike other <INPUT> types, <TEXTAREA> default text is specified between <TEXTAREA> and </TEXTAREA> tags—not in a `VALUE` attribute.

Second, you use the `WRAP` attribute to wrap text entered into the field automatically. `WRAP="VIRTUAL"` instructs the browser to wrap to the next line automatically, just as most word processors and editors do.

Listing 12.9 `forms9.cfm`—The HTML <TEXTAREA> Field with Wrapping Enabled

```
<!---
Name:        forms9.cfm
Author:      Ben Forta (ben@forta.com)
Description: Introduction to forms
```

LISTING 12.9 CONTINUED

```
Created:     4/15/01
--->

<!DOCTYPE HTML PUBLIC "-//W3C//DTD HTML 4.0 Transitional//EN">

<HTML>

<HEAD>
    <TITLE>Learning ColdFusion Forms 9</TITLE>
</HEAD>

<BODY>

<!--- Comments form --->
<FORM ACTION="forms10.cfm" METHOD="POST">

Please enter your comments in the box provided, and then click <B>Send</B>.
<P>
<TEXTAREA NAME="Comments" ROWS="6" COLS="40" WRAP="virtual">
Enter your comments here ...
</TEXTAREA>
<P>
<INPUT TYPE="submit" VALUE="Send">

</FORM>

</BODY>

</HTML>
```

Note

Some older browsers do not support the `<TEXTAREA>` `WRAP` attribute. These browsers ignore the attribute and require the users to enter line breaks manually. Because the attribute is ignored when not supported, you can safely use this option when necessary; your forms do not become incompatible with older browsers.

Listing 12.10 shows the template to display the user-supplied comments. The Comments field code is changed to `#ParagraphFormat(FORM.Comments)#`, ensuring that multiple line breaks are maintained and displayed correctly, as shown in Figure 12.10.

LISTING 12.10 `forms10.cfm`—USING THE `ParagraphFormat()` FUNCTION TO PRESERVE LINE BREAKS

```
<!---
Name:        forms10.cfm
Author:      Ben Forta (ben@forta.com)
Description: Introduction to forms
Created:     4/15/01
--->
```

```
<!DOCTYPE HTML PUBLIC "-//W3C//DTD HTML 4.0 Transitional//EN">

<HTML>

<HEAD>
    <TITLE>Learning ColdFusion Forms 10</TITLE>
</HEAD>

<BODY>

<!--- Display feedback to user --->
<CFOUTPUT>

Thank you for your comments. You entered:
<P>
<B>#ParagraphFormat(FORM.comments)#</B>

</CFOUTPUT>

</BODY>

</HTML>
```

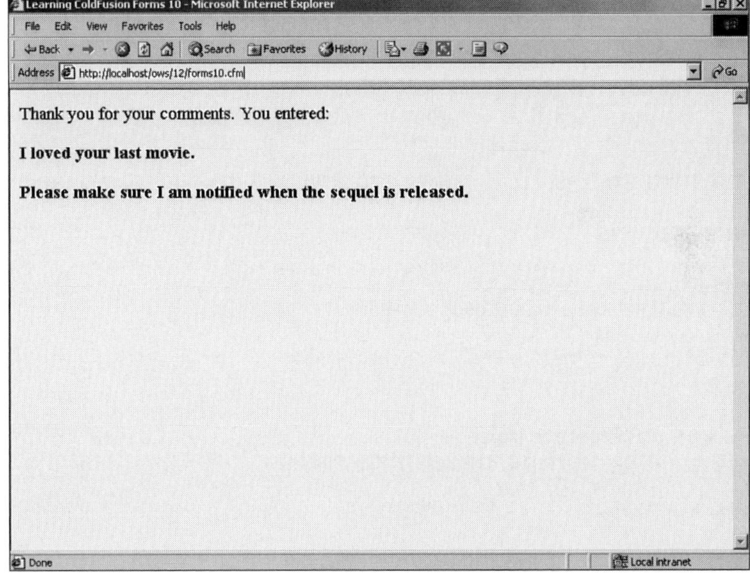

Figure 12.10 You should use the ColdFusion `ParagraphFormat()` function to display `<TEXTAREA>` fields with their line breaks preserved.

Processing Buttons

The HTML forms specification supports only two types of buttons. Almost all forms, including all the forms you create in this chapter, have a submit button. Submit, as its name implies, instructs the browser to submit the form fields to a Web server.

Tip

Most newer browsers actually require no submit button at all and force a submit if the Enter key is pressed.

The second supported button type is reset. *Reset* clears all form entries and restores default values if any existed. Any text entered into `<INPUT TYPE="text">` or `<TEXTAREA>` fields is cleared, as are any check box, list box, and option button selections. Many forms have reset buttons, but you never need more than one.

On the other hand, you might want more than one submit button. For example, if you're using a form to modify a record, you could have two submit buttons: one for Update and one for Delete. (Of course, you also could use two forms to accomplish this task.) If you create multiple submit buttons, you must name the button with the `NAME` attribute and be sure to assign a different `VALUE` attribute for each. The code in Listing 12.11 contains a reset button and two submit buttons.

LISTING 12.11 `forms11.cfm`**—TEMPLATE WITH A RESET BUTTON AND MULTIPLE SUBMIT BUTTONS**

```
<!---
Name:        forms11.cfm
Author:      Ben Forta (ben@forta.com)
Description: Introduction to forms
Created:     4/15/01
--->

<!DOCTYPE HTML PUBLIC "-//W3C//DTD HTML 4.0 Transitional//EN">

<HTML>

<HEAD>
    <TITLE>Learning ColdFusion Forms 11</TITLE>
</HEAD>

<BODY>

<!--- Update/delete form --->
<FORM ACTION="forms12.cfm" METHOD="POST">

<P>

Movie:
<INPUT TYPE="text" NAME="MovieTitle">

<P>
<!--- Submit buttons --->
<INPUT TYPE="submit" NAME="Operation" VALUE="Update">
<INPUT TYPE="submit" NAME="Operation" VALUE="Delete">
<!--- Reset button --->
<INPUT TYPE="reset" VALUE="Clear">
```

```
</FORM>

</BODY>

</HTML>
```

The result of this code is shown in Figure 12.11.

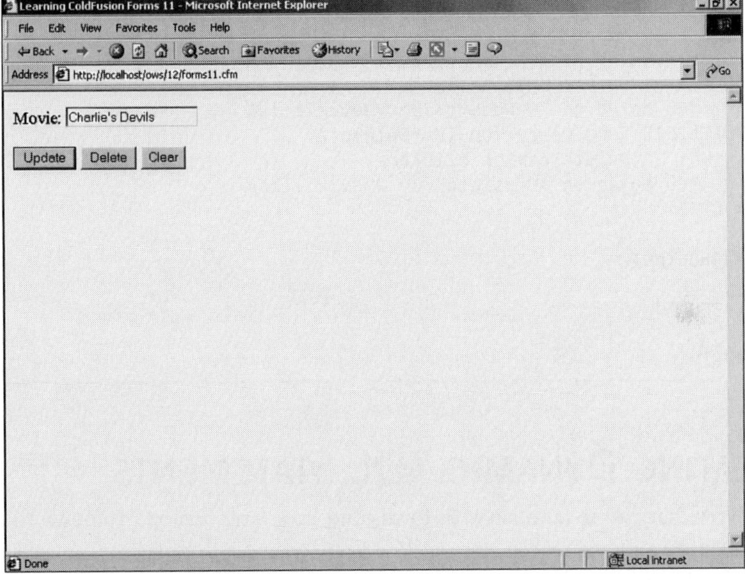

Figure 12.11 When you're using multiple submit buttons, you must assign a different value to each button.

When you name submit buttons, you treat them as any other form field. Listing 12.12 demonstrates how to determine which submit button was clicked. The code `<CFIF FORM.Operation IS "Update">` checks whether the Update button was clicked, and `<CFELSEIF FORM.Operation IS "Delete">` checks whether Delete was clicked, but only if Update was not clicked.

Listing 12.12 forms12.cfm—ColdFusion Example of Multiple Submit Button Processing

```
<!---
Name:        forms12.cfm
Author:      Ben Forta (ben@forta.com)
Description: Introduction to forms
Created:     4/15/01
--->

<!DOCTYPE HTML PUBLIC "-//W3C//DTD HTML 4.0 Transitional//EN">

<HTML>
```

LISTING 12.12 CONTINUED

```
<HEAD>
    <TITLE>Learning ColdFusion Forms 12</TITLE>
</HEAD>

<BODY>

<!--- User feedback --->
<CFOUTPUT>

<CFIF FORM.Operation IS "Update">
    <!--- Update button clicked --->
    You opted to <B>update</B> #MovieTitle#
<CFELSEIF FORM.Operation IS "Delete">
    <!--- Delete button clicked --->
    You opted to <B>delete</B> #MovieTitle#
</CFIF>

</CFOUTPUT>

</BODY>

</HTML>
```

CREATING DYNAMIC SQL STATEMENTS

Now that you're familiar with forms and how ColdFusion processes them, you can return to creating a movie search screen. The first screen enables visitors to search for a movie by title. Because this requires text input, you will need an `<INPUT>` field of type text. The field name can be anything you want, but using the same name as the table column to which you're comparing the value is generally a good idea.

Tip

When you're creating search screens, you can name your form fields with any descriptive name you want. When you're creating insert and update forms, however, the field name must match the table column names so ColdFusion knows which field to save with each column. For this reason, you should get into the habit of always naming form fields with the appropriate table column name.

The code in Listing 12.13 contains a simple HTML form, not unlike the test forms you created earlier in this chapter. The form contains a single text field called `MovieTitle` and a submit button.

Listing 12.13 search1.cfm—Code Listing for Movie Search Screen

```
<!---
Name:        search1.cfm
Author:      Ben Forta (ben@forta.com)
Description: Creating search screens
Created:     4/15/01
--->

<!DOCTYPE HTML PUBLIC "-//W3C//DTD HTML 4.0 Transitional//EN">

<HTML>

<HEAD>
    <TITLE>Orange Whip Studios - Movies</TITLE>
</HEAD>

<BODY>

<!--- Page header --->
<CFINCLUDE TEMPLATE="header.cfm">

<!--- Search form --->
<FORM ACTION="results1.cfm" METHOD="POST">

<TABLE ALIGN="center" BORDER="1">
    <TR>
        <TD>
            Movie:
        </TD>
        <TD>
            <INPUT TYPE="text" NAME="MovieTitle">
        </TD>
    </TR>
    <TR>
        <TD COLSPAN="2" ALIGN="center">
            <INPUT TYPE="submit" VALUE="Search">
        </TD>
   </TR>
</TABLE>

</FORM>

</BODY>

</HTML>
```

Save this form as search1.cfm, and then execute it to display a screen similar to the one shown in Figure 12.12.

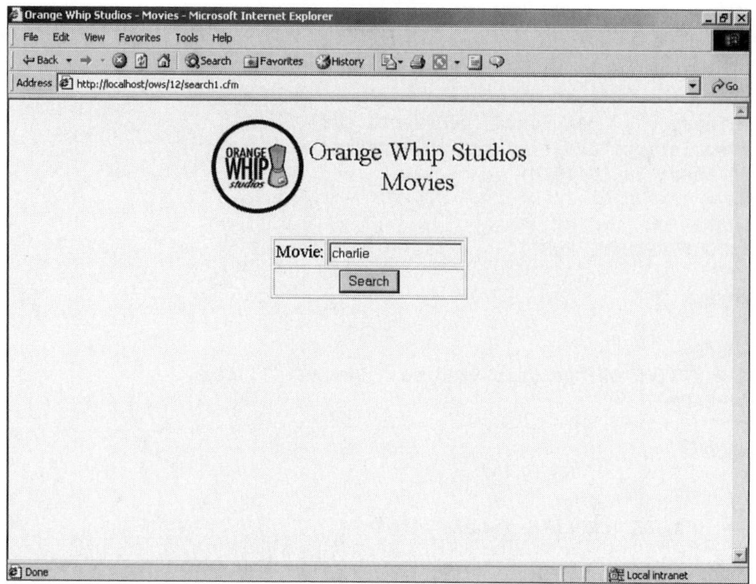

Figure 12.12 The movie search screen enables users to search by movie title.

Listing 12.13 starts off with a comment block, followed by the standard HTML headers and `<BODY>` tag. Then a `<CFINCLUDE>` tag is used to include a common header, file `header.cfm` (which puts the logo and title at the top of the page).

Note

See Chapter 10 for information on using the `<CFINCLUDE>` tag.

The form itself is placed inside an HTML table—this is a very popular technique that can be used to better control form field placement. The form contains a single field, `MovieTitle`, and a submit button.

The `<FORM> ACTION` attribute specifies which ColdFusion template should be used to process this search. The code `ACTION="results1.cfm"` instructs ColdFusion to use the template `results1.cfm`, which is shown in Listing 12.14. Create this template and save it as `results1.cfm`.

LISTING 12.14 results1.cfm—USING A PASSED FORM FIELD IN A SQL WHERE CLAUSE

```
<!---
Name:        results1.cfm
Author:      Ben Forta (ben@forta.com)
Description: Creating search screens
Created:     4/15/01
--->

<!--- Get movie list from database --->
<CFQUERY NAME="movies" DATASOURCE="ows">
```

```
SELECT MovieTitle, PitchText, Summary, DateInTheaters
FROM Films
WHERE MovieTitle LIKE '%#FORM.MovieTitle#%'
ORDER BY MovieTitle
</CFQUERY>

<!--- Create HTML page --->
<!DOCTYPE HTML PUBLIC "-//W3C//DTD HTML 4.0 Transitional//EN">
<HTML>
<HEAD>
    <TITLE>Orange Whip Studios - Movies</TITLE>
</HEAD>

<BODY>

<!--- Page header --->
<CFINCLUDE TEMPLATE="header.cfm">

<!--- Display movie list --->
<TABLE>
<TR>
 <CFOUTPUT>
 <TH COLSPAN="2">
  <FONT SIZE="+3">Movie List (#Movies.RecordCount# movies)</FONT>
 </TH>
 </CFOUTPUT>
</TR>
<CFOUTPUT QUERY="movies">
<TR>
 <TD>
  <FONT SIZE="+2"><B>#CurrentRow#: #MovieTitle#</B></FONT><BR>
  <FONT SIZE="+1"><I>#PitchText#</I></FONT>
 </TD>
 <TD>Released: #DateFormat(DateInTheaters)#</TD>
</TR>
<TR>
 <TD COLSPAN="2">#Summary#</TD>
</TR>
</CFOUTPUT>
</TABLE>

</BODY>
</HTML>
```

The code in Listing 12.14 is based on the movie lists created in the last chapter, so most of the code should be very familiar. The only big change here is in the `<CFQUERY>` tag.

The `WHERE` clause in Listing 12.14 contains a ColdFusion field rather than a static value. You will recall that when ColdFusion parses templates, it replaces field names with the values contained within the field. So, look at the following `WHERE` clause:

```
WHERE MovieTitle LIKE '%#FORM.MovieTitle#%'
```

`#FORM.MovieTitle#` is replaced with whatever was entered in the `MovieTitle` form field. If the word `her` was entered then the `WHERE` clause becomes

```
WHERE MovieTitle LIKE '%her%'
```

which will find all movies with the text `her` anywhere in the `MovieTitle`. If you search for all movies beginning with `C`, the code `WHERE MovieTitle LIKE '%#FORM.MovieTitle#%'` would become `WHERE MovieTitle LIKE '%C%'`. And so on. You can do this with any clauses, not just the `LIKE` operator.

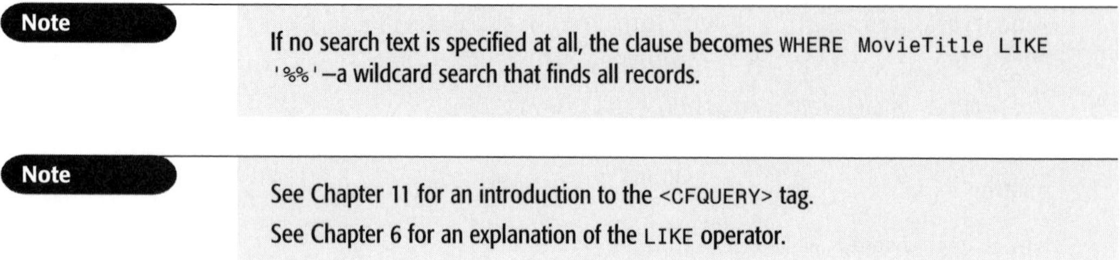

Note

If no search text is specified at all, the clause becomes `WHERE MovieTitle LIKE '%%'`—a wildcard search that finds all records.

Note

See Chapter 11 for an introduction to the `<CFQUERY>` tag.

See Chapter 6 for an explanation of the `LIKE` operator.

You use a `LIKE` clause to enable users to enter partial text. The clause `WHERE MovieTitle = 'her'` finds only movies with a title of `her`; movies with `her` in the name along with other text are not retrieved. Using a wildcard, as in `WHERE MovieTitle LIKE '%her%'`, enables users to also search on partial names.

Try experimenting with different search strings. The sample output should look similar to the output shown in Figure 12.13. Of course, depending on the search criteria you specify, you'll see different search results.

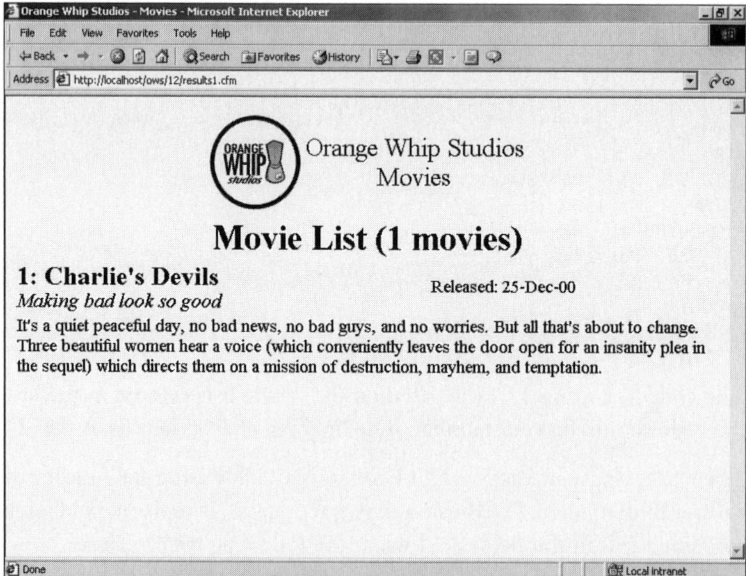

Figure 12.13 By building `WHERE` clauses dynamically, you can create different search conditions on-the-fly.

To complete the application, try copying the movie detail page (created in Chapter 11) and modify `results1.cfm` so that it enables the drill-down of the displayed search results. You'll then have a complete drill-down application.

BUILDING TRULY DYNAMIC STATEMENTS

When you roll out your movie search screen, you are immediately inundated with requests. "Searching by title is great, but what about by tag-line or rating?" your users ask. Now that you have introduced the ability to search for data, your users want to be able to search on several fields.

Adding fields to your search screen is simple enough. Add two fields: one for tag-line and one for rating. The code for the updated search screen is shown in Listing 12.15.

LISTING 12.15 search2.cfm—MOVIE SEARCH SCREEN

```
<!---
Name:        search2.cfm
Author:      Ben Forta (ben@forta.com)
Description: Creating search screens
Created:     4/15/01
--->

<!DOCTYPE HTML PUBLIC "-//W3C//DTD HTML 4.0 Transitional//EN">

<HTML>

<HEAD>
    <TITLE>Orange Whip Studios - Movies</TITLE>
</HEAD>

<BODY>

<!--- Page header --->
<CFINCLUDE TEMPLATE="header.cfm">

<!--- Search form --->
<FORM ACTION="results2.cfm" METHOD="POST">

<TABLE ALIGN="center" BORDER="1">
    <TR>
        <TD>
            Movie:
        </TD>
        <TD>
            <INPUT TYPE="text" NAME="MovieTitle">
        </TD>
    </TR>
    <TR>
        <TD>
            Tag line:
        </TD>
        <TD>
            <INPUT TYPE="text" NAME="PitchText">
        </TD>
    </TR>
    <TR>
        <TD>
            Rating:
```

LISTING 12.15 CONTINUED

```
        </TD>
        <TD>
            <INPUT TYPE="text" NAME="RatingID"> (1-6)
        </TD>
    </TR>
    <TR>
        <TD COLSPAN="2" ALIGN="center">
            <INPUT TYPE="submit" VALUE="Search">
        </TD>
    </TR>
</TABLE>

</FORM>

</BODY>

</HTML>
```

This form enables the users to specify text in one of three fields, as shown in Figure 12.14.

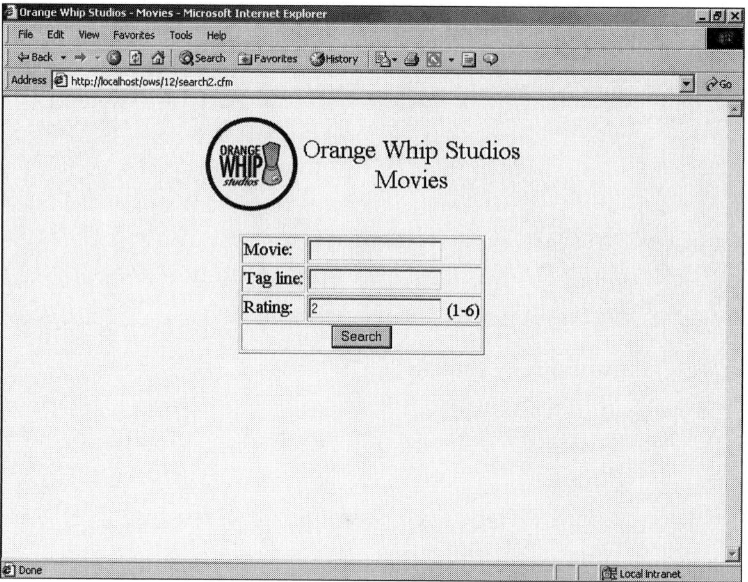

Figure 12.14 The movie search screen now allows searching by three fields.

You must create a search template before you can actually perform a search. The complete search code is shown in Listing 12.16; save this file as `results2.cfm`.

LISTING 12.16 `results2.cfm`—BUILDING SQL STATEMENTS DYNAMICALLY

```
<!---
Name:       results2.cfm
Author:     Ben Forta (ben@forta.com)
```

```
Description: Creating search screens
Created:     4/15/01
--->

<!--- Get movie list from database --->
<CFQUERY NAME="movies" DATASOURCE="ows">
SELECT MovieTitle, PitchText, Summary, DateInTheaters
FROM Films
<!--- Search by movie title --->
<CFIF FORM.MovieTitle IS NOT "">
    WHERE MovieTitle LIKE '%#FORM.MovieTitle#%'
</CFIF>
<!--- Search by tag line --->
<CFIF FORM.PitchText IS NOT "">
    WHERE PitchText LIKE '%#FORM.PitchText#%'
</CFIF>
<!--- Search by rating --->
<CFIF FORM.RatingID IS NOT "">
    WHERE RatingID = #FORM.RatingID#
</CFIF>
ORDER BY MovieTitle
</CFQUERY>

<!--- Create HTML page --->
<!DOCTYPE HTML PUBLIC "-//W3C//DTD HTML 4.0 Transitional//EN">
<HTML>
<HEAD>
    <TITLE>Orange Whip Studios - Movies</TITLE>
</HEAD>

<BODY>

<!--- Page header --->
<CFINCLUDE TEMPLATE="header.cfm">

<!--- Display movie list --->
<TABLE>
<TR>
 <CFOUTPUT>
 <TH COLSPAN="2">
  <FONT SIZE="+3">Movie List (#Movies.RecordCount# movies)</FONT>
 </TH>
 </CFOUTPUT>
</TR>
<CFOUTPUT QUERY="movies">
<TR>
 <TD>
  <FONT SIZE="+2"><B>#CurrentRow#: #MovieTitle#</B></FONT><BR>
  <FONT SIZE="+1"><I>#PitchText#</I></FONT>
 </TD>
 <TD>Released: #DateFormat(DateInTheaters)#</TD>
</TR>
<TR>
 <TD COLSPAN="2">#Summary#</TD>
</TR>
</CFOUTPUT>
</TABLE>
```

LISTING 12.16 CONTINUED

```
</BODY>
</HTML>
```

UNDERSTANDING DYNAMIC SQL

Before you actually perform a search, take a closer look at the template in Listing 12.16. The `<CFQUERY>` tag is similar to the one you used in the previous search template, but in this one the SQL `SELECT` statement in the SQL attribute is incomplete. It does not specify a `WHERE` clause with which to perform a search, nor does it specify a search order. No `WHERE` clause is specified because the search screen has to support not one, but four search types, as follows:

- If none of the three search fields is specified, no `WHERE` clause should be used so that all movies can be retrieved.
- If a movie title is specified, the `WHERE` clause must filter data to find only movies containing the specified title text. For example, if `the` is specified as the search text, the `WHERE` clause has to be `WHERE MovieTitle LIKE '%the%'`.
- If tag-line text is specified, the `WHERE` clause needs to filter data to find only movies containing the specified text. For example, if `bad` is specified as the search text, the `WHERE` clause must be `WHERE PitchText LIKE '%bad%'`.
- If you're searching by rating and specify `2` as the search text, a `WHERE` clause of `WHERE RatingID = 2` is necessary.

How can a single search template handle all these search conditions? The answer is dynamic SQL.

When you're creating dynamic SQL statements, you break the statement into separate common SQL and specific SQL. The common SQL is the part of the SQL statement you always want. The sample SQL statement has two common parts:

```
SELECT MovieTitle, PitchText, Summary, DateInTheaters
FROM Films
```

and

```
ORDER BY MovieTitle
```

The common text is all the SQL statement you need if no search criteria is provided. If, however, search text is specified, the number of possible `WHERE` clauses is endless.

Take another look at Listing 12.16 to understand the process of creating dynamic SQL statements. The code `<CFIF FORM.MovieTitle IS NOT "">` checks to see that the `MovieTitle` form field is not empty. This condition fails if no text is entered into the `MovieTitle` field in the search form, in which case any code until the `</CFIF>` is ignored.

Note

See Chapter 10 for details on using <CFIF>.

If a value does appear in the MovieTitle field, the code WHERE MovieTitle LIKE '#FORM.MovieTitle#%' is processed and appended to the SQL statement. #FORM.MovieTitle# is a field and is replaced with whatever text is entered in the MovieTitle field. If the is specified as the text for which to search, this statement translates to WHERE MovieTitle LIKE '%the%'. This text is appended to the previous SQL statement, which now becomes the following:

```
SELECT MovieTitle, PitchText, Summary, DateInTheaters
FROM Films
WHERE MovieTitle LIKE '%the%'
```

All you need now is the ORDER BY clause. Even though ORDER BY is fixed and does not change with different searches, it must be built dynamically because the ORDER BY clause must come after the WHERE clause, if one exists. After ColdFusion processes the code ORDER BY MovieTitle, the finished SQL statement reads as follows:

```
SELECT MovieTitle, PitchText, Summary, DateInTheaters
FROM Films
WHERE MovieTitle LIKE '%the%'
ORDER BY MovieTitle
```

Note

You can't use double quotation marks in a SQL statement. When ColdFusion encounters a double quotation mark, it thinks it has reached the end of the SQL statement. It then generates an error message because extra text appears where ColdFusion thinks there should be none. To include text strings with the SQL statement, use only single quotation marks.

Similarly, if a RatingID is specified (for example, the value 2) as the search text, the complete SQL statement reads as follows:

```
SELECT MovieTitle, PitchText, Summary, DateInTheaters
FROM Films
WHERE RatingID = 2
ORDER BY MovieTitle
```

The code <CFIF FORM.MovieTitle IS NOT ""> evaluates to FALSE because FORM.MovieTitle is actually empty; ColdFusion therefore checks the next condition, which is also FALSE, and so on. Because RatingID was specified, the third <CFIF> condition is TRUE and the previous SELECT statement is generated.

Note

You might have noticed that there are single quotation marks around FORM.MovieTitle and FORM.PitchText but not FORM.RatingID. Why? Because MovieTitle and PitchText have text data types in the database table, whereas RatingID is numeric. SQL is not typeless, and it will require that you specify quotes where needed to create strings if that is what is expected.

So, one template is capable of generating four different sets of SQL SELECT statements, of which the values can be dynamic. Try performing various searches, but for now, use only one form field at a time.

CONCATENATING SQL CLAUSES

Now try entering text in two search fields, or all three of them. What happens? You probably generated an error similar to the one shown in Figure 12.15.

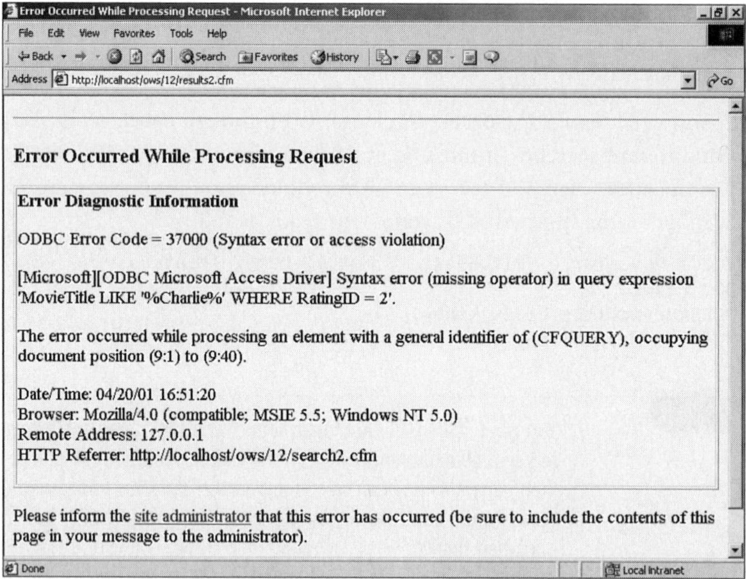

Figure 12.15
Dynamic SQL must be generated carefully to avoid building invalid SQL.

Why did this happen? Well, what if the was specified as the MovieTitle and 2 as the RatingID. Walk through the <CFIF> statements to work out what the generated SQL would look like. The first condition will be TRUE, the second will be FALSE, and the third will be TRUE. The SELECT statement would therefore look like this:

```
SELECT MovieTitle, PitchText, Summary, DateInTheaters
FROM Films
WHERE MovieTitle LIKE '%the%'
WHERE RatingID = 2
ORDER BY MovieTitle
```

Obviously, this is not a valid SELECT statement—only one WHERE clause is allowed. The correct syntax for this statement is

```
SELECT MovieTitle, PitchText, Summary, DateInTheaters
FROM Films
WHERE MovieTitle LIKE '%the%'
 AND RatingID = 2
ORDER BY MovieTitle
```

So, how would you generate this code? You could not hard-code any condition with a WHERE or an AND because you wouldn't know whether it was the first clause. Yes, the MovieTitle clause, if used, will always be the first, but it might not always be used.

One obvious solution (which I suggest you avoid at all costs) is to use embedded <CFIF> statements to intelligently include WHERE or AND as necessary. However, this type of code is very complex and error-prone.

A better solution would be to never need WHERE at all—only use AND. How can you do this? Look at the following SQL statement:

```
SELECT MovieTitle, PitchText, Summary, DateInTheaters
FROM Films
WHERE 0=0
 AND MovieTitle LIKE '%the%'
 AND RatingID = 2
ORDER BY MovieTitle
```

WHERE 0=0 is a dummy clause. Obviously 0 is equal to 0, so WHERE 0=0 retrieves every row in the table. For each row the database checks to see whether 0 is 0, which it of course is. This is a legal WHERE clause, but it does nothing because it is always TRUE.

So why use it? Simple. Now that there is a WHERE clause, you can safely use AND for every dynamic condition. If no other condition exists then only the WHERE 0=0 will be evaluated; however, if additional conditions do exist, no matter how many, they can all be appended using AND.

Note

There is nothing magical about WHERE 0=0; you can use any condition that will always be TRUE: WHERE 'A'='A', WHERE primary key = primary key (using the table's primary key), and just about anything else you want.

Listing 12.17 contains a revised search page (this time using a drop-down list box for the rating); save it as search3.cfm. Figure 12.16 shows the new and improved search screen.

Listing 12.18 contains the revised results page; save it as results3.cfm.

Listing 12.17 search3.cfm—Revised Movie Search Screen

```
<!---
Name:        search3.cfm
Author:      Ben Forta (ben@forta.com)
Description: Creating search screens
Created:     4/15/01
--->

<!DOCTYPE HTML PUBLIC "-//W3C//DTD HTML 4.0 Transitional//EN">

<HTML>

<HEAD>
    <TITLE>Orange Whip Studios - Movies</TITLE>
```

LISTING 12.17 CONTINUED

```
</HEAD>

<BODY>

<!--- Page header --->
<CFINCLUDE TEMPLATE="header.cfm">

<!--- Search form --->
<FORM ACTION="results3.cfm" METHOD="POST">

<TABLE ALIGN="center" BORDER="1">
    <TR>
        <TD>
            Movie:
        </TD>
        <TD>
            <INPUT TYPE="text" NAME="MovieTitle">
        </TD>
    </TR>
    <TR>
        <TD>
            Tag line:
        </TD>
        <TD>
            <INPUT TYPE="text" NAME="PitchText">
        </TD>
    </TR>
    <TR>
        <TD>
            Rating:
        </TD>
        <TD>
            <SELECT NAME="RatingID">
                <OPTION VALUE=""></OPTION>
                <OPTION VALUE="1">General</OPTION>
                <OPTION VALUE="2">Kids</OPTION>
                <OPTION VALUE="3">Accompanied Minors</OPTION>
                <OPTION VALUE="4">Teens</OPTION>
                <OPTION VALUE="5">Adults</OPTION>
                <OPTION VALUE="6">Mature Audiences</OPTION>
            </SELECT>
        </TD>
    </TR>
    <TR>
        <TD COLSPAN="2" ALIGN="center">
            <INPUT TYPE="submit" VALUE="Search">
        </TD>
   </TR>
</TABLE>

</FORM>

</BODY>

</HTML>
```

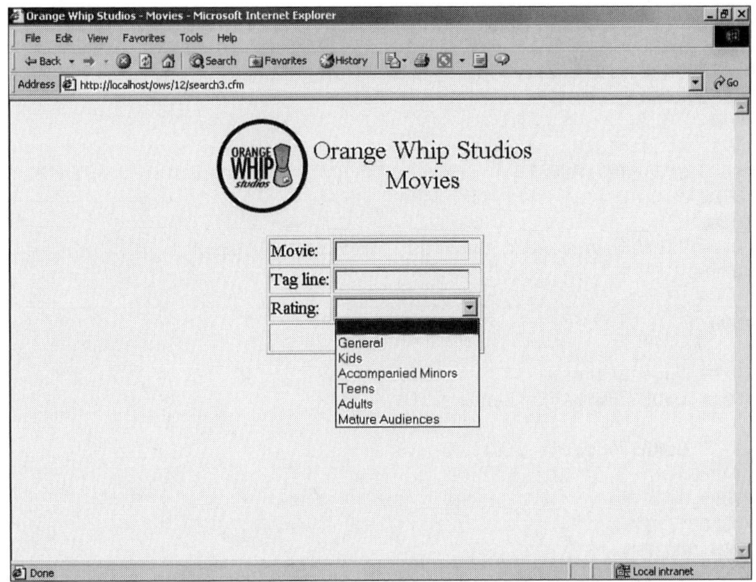

Figure 12.16 Drop-down list boxes are well suited for selections of one of a set of finite options.

The only change in Listing 12.17 is the drop-down list box for the `RatingID`. Manually entering `1` to `6` is not intuitive and is highly error-prone. For finite lists such as this drop-down list, boxes are a better option. This does not change the form field processing, though—either way, `RatingID` is sent to the `ACTION` page, shown in Listing 12.18.

LISTING 12.18 `results3.cfm`—**CONCATENATING SQL CLAUSES**

```
<!---
Name:        results3.cfm
Author:      Ben Forta (ben@forta.com)
Description: Creating search screens
Created:     4/15/01
--->

<!--- Get movie list from database --->
<CFQUERY NAME="movies" DATASOURCE="ows">
SELECT MovieTitle, PitchText, Summary, DateInTheaters
FROM Films
WHERE 0=0
<!--- Search by movie title --->
<CFIF FORM.MovieTitle IS NOT "">
    AND MovieTitle LIKE '%#FORM.MovieTitle#%'
</CFIF>
<!--- Search by tag line --->
<CFIF FORM.PitchText IS NOT "">
    AND PitchText LIKE '%#FORM.PitchText#%'
</CFIF>
<!--- Search by rating --->
<CFIF FORM.RatingID IS NOT "">
    AND RatingID = #FORM.RatingID#
</CFIF>
```

LISTING 12.18 CONTINUED

```
ORDER BY MovieTitle
</CFQUERY>

<!--- Create HTML page --->
<!DOCTYPE HTML PUBLIC "-//W3C//DTD HTML 4.0 Transitional//EN">
<HTML>
<HEAD>
    <TITLE>Orange Whip Studios - Movies</TITLE>
</HEAD>

<BODY>

<!--- Page header --->
<CFINCLUDE TEMPLATE="header.cfm">

<!--- Display movie list --->
<TABLE>
<TR>
 <CFOUTPUT>
 <TH COLSPAN="2">
  <FONT SIZE="+3">Movie List (#Movies.RecordCount# movies)</FONT>
 </TH>
 </CFOUTPUT>
</TR>
<CFOUTPUT QUERY="movies">
<TR>
 <TD>
  <FONT SIZE="+2"><B>#CurrentRow#: #MovieTitle#</B></FONT><BR>
  <FONT SIZE="+1"><I>#PitchText#</I></FONT>
 </TD>
 <TD>Released: #DateFormat(DateInTheaters)#</TD>
</TR>
<TR>
 <TD COLSPAN="2">#Summary#</TD>
</TR>
</CFOUTPUT>
</TABLE>

</BODY>
</HTML>
```

The `<CFQUERY>` in Listing 12.18 now contains a dummy clause and then three optional `AND` clauses, each within a `<CFIF>` statement. So, what will this do?

- If no form fields are filled in then only the dummy `WHERE` clause will be used.
- If any single form field is filled in then the `WHERE` clause will contain the dummy and a single real clause appended using `AND`.
- If any two form fields are filled in then the `WHERE` clause will have three clauses, one dummy and two real.
- If all three clauses are filled in then the `WHERE` clause will contain four clauses, one dummy and three real.

In other words, a single template can now generate eight different combinations of `WHERE` clauses, and each can have an unlimited number of values. All that in less than 20 lines of code—it doesn't get much more powerful than that.

After you create the template, use your browser to perform various combinations of searches. You'll find that this new search template is both powerful and flexible. Indeed, this technique for creating truly dynamic SQL `SELECT` statements will likely be the basis for some sophisticated database interaction in real-world applications.

Creating Dynamic Search Screens

There is one final improvement to be made to your application. The list of ratings used in the search form have been hard-coded (refer to Listing 12.17). Remember that you're creating data-driven applications. Everything in your application should be data-driven. You don't want to have to manually enter data, not even in list boxes. Rather, you want the list box to be driven by the data in the `FilmsRatings` table. This way, you can acquire changes automatically when ratings are added or when a rating name changes.

Listing 12.19 is identical to Listing 12.17, with the exception of the addition of a new `<CFQUERY>` and a `<CFOUTPUT>` block to process its contents.

Listing 12.19 `search4.cfm`—**Data-Driven Forms**

```
<!---
Name:        search3.cfm
Author:      Ben Forta (ben@forta.com)
Description: Creating search screens
Created:     4/15/01
--->

<!--- Get ratings --->
<CFQUERY DATASOURCE="ows" NAME="ratings">
SELECT RatingID, Rating
FROM FilmsRatings
ORDER BY RatingID
</CFQUERY>

<!DOCTYPE HTML PUBLIC "-//W3C//DTD HTML 4.0 Transitional//EN">

<HTML>

<HEAD>
    <TITLE>Orange Whip Studios - Movies</TITLE>
</HEAD>

<BODY>

<!--- Page header --->
<CFINCLUDE TEMPLATE="header.cfm">

<!--- Search form --->
<FORM ACTION="results3.cfm" METHOD="POST">
```

LISTING 12.19 CONTINUED

```
<TABLE ALIGN="center" BORDER="1">
    <TR>
        <TD>
            Movie:
        </TD>
        <TD>
            <INPUT TYPE="text" NAME="MovieTitle">
        </TD>
    </TR>
    <TR>
        <TD>
            Tag line:
        </TD>
        <TD>
            <INPUT TYPE="text" NAME="PitchText">
        </TD>
    </TR>
    <TR>
        <TD>
            Rating:
        </TD>
        <TD>
            <SELECT NAME="RatingID">
                <OPTION VALUE=""></OPTION>
                <CFOUTPUT QUERY="ratings">
                    <OPTION VALUE="#RatingID#">#Rating#</OPTION>
             </CFOUTPUT>
         </SELECT>
        </TD>
    </TR>
    <TR>
        <TD COLSPAN="2" ALIGN="center">
            <INPUT TYPE="submit" VALUE="Search">
        </TD>
   </TR>
</TABLE>

</FORM>

</BODY>

</HTML>
```

The code in Listing 12.19 demonstrates a data-driven form. The <CFQUERY> at the top of the template should be familiar to you by now. It creates a result set called ratings, which contains the ID and name of each rating in the database.

The drop-down list box also has been changed. The <SELECT> tag creates the list box, and it is terminated with the </SELECT> tag, as before. The individual entries in the list box are specified with the <OPTION> tag, but here that tag is within a <CFOUTPUT> block. This block is executed once for each row retrieved by the <CFQUERY>, creating an <OPTION> entry for each one.

As it loops through the `ratings` resultset, the `<CFQUERY>` block creates the individual options, using the `RatingID` field as the `VALUE` and `Rating` as the description. So, when ColdFusion processes `RatingID 1` (`General`), the code generated is

```
<OPTION VALUE="1">General</OPTION>
```

The end result is exactly the same as the screen shown previously in Figure 12.16, but this time it is populated by a database query (instead of being hard-coded).

Also notice that a blank `<OPTION>` line is included in the list box. Remember that list boxes always must have a selection, so if you want to allow your users to not select any option, you need to give them a *no option* option (the blank option).

And there you have it—dynamic data-driven forms used to perform dynamic data-driven searches using dynamic data-driven SQL.

CHAPTER 13

Form Data Validation

In this chapter

UNDERSTANDING FORM VALIDATION

HTML forms are used to collect data from users by using several field types. Forms are used for data entry, as front-end search engines, for filling out orders, for signing guest books, providing user names and passwords to secure applications, and much more. Although forms have become one of the most important features in HTML, these forms provide almost no data validation tools.

This becomes a real problem when developing Web-based applications. As a developer, you need to be able to control what data users can enter into what fields. Without that, your programs will constantly be breaking due to mismatched or unanticipated data. And thus far, you have used forms only as search front ends—when forms are used to insert or update database tables (as you'll see in Chapter 14, "Using Forms to Add or Change Data"), this becomes even more critical.

Thankfully, ColdFusion provides a complete and robust set of tools with which to implement form data validation, both client-side and server-side.

Since its inception, HTML has always provided Web page developers with a variety of ways to format and display data. With each revision to the HTML specification, additional data display mechanisms have been made available. As a result, HTML is a powerful data-publishing tool.

Although its data presentation options continue to improve, HTML's data collection capabilities leave much to be desired. In fact, they have barely changed at all since the language's very early days.

HTML data collection is performed using forms. HTML forms support the following field types:

- Free-form text fields
- Select box (or drop-down list boxes)
- Radio buttons
- Check boxes
- Multiline text boxes
- Password (hidden input) boxes

Note

See Chapter 12, "ColdFusion Forms," for more information about HTML forms and using them with ColdFusion.

So what's wrong with this list? Actually, nothing at all. These field types are all the standard fields you would expect to be available to you in any development language. What is wrong, however, is that these fields have extremely limited capabilities. There are two primary limitations:

- Incapability to mark fields as required
- Incapability to define data types or filters—only accepting digits, a ZIP code, or a phone number, for instance

What this means is that there is no simple way to tell HTML to disallow form submission if certain fields are left empty. Similarly, HTML cannot be instructed to accept only certain values or types of data in specific fields.

HTML itself has exactly one validation option, the `MAXLENGTH` attribute, which can be used to specify the maximum number of characters that can be entered in a text field. But that's it. No other validation options are available.

To work around these limitations, HTML developers have typically adopted two forms of validation options:

- Server-side validation
- Client-side validation

COMPARING SERVER-SIDE AND CLIENT-SIDE VALIDATION

Server-side validation involves checking for required fields or invalid values after a form has been submitted. The script on the server first validates the form and then continues processing only if all validation requirements are met. Typically, an error message is sent back to the user's browser if validation fails; the user then makes the corrections and resubmits the form. Of course, the form submission must be validated again upon resubmission, and the process must be repeated if the validation fails again.

Client-side scripting enables the developer to embed instructions to the browser within the HTML code. Because HTML itself provides no mechanism for doing this, developers have resorted to using scripting languages, such as JavaScript (supported by both Netscape Navigator and Microsoft Internet Explorer) or VBScript (supported by Microsoft Internet Explorer only). These interpreted languages support basic data manipulation and user feedback and are thus well suited for form validation. To validate a form, the page author would create a function to be executed as soon as a Submit button is clicked. This function would perform any necessary validation and allow the submission to proceed only if the validation check was successful. The advantage of this approach is that the user does not have to submit a form to find out an error occurred in it. Notification of any errors occurs prior to form submission.

UNDERSTANDING THE PROS AND CONS OF EACH OPTION

Neither of these options is perfect, and they are thus often used together, complementing each other. Table 13.1 lists the pros and cons of each option.

TABLE 13.1 THE PROS AND CONS OF CLIENT AND SERVER FORM VALIDATION

Validation Type	Pros	Cons
Server-side	Most flexible form of validation. Validation is browser independent and even supports non-HTML browsers.	User must submit data before validation occurs; any errors require correction and resubmission.
Client-side	Validation occurs prior to form submission, allowing for a more intuitive and less aggravating user interface.	Not all browsers support scripting languages. Languages have high learning curves.

From a user's perspective, client-side validation is preferable. Obviously, users want to know what is wrong with the data they entered *before* they submit the form for processing. From a developer's perspective, however, server-side validation is simpler to code, guaranteed to always work regardless of the browser used, and less likely to fall victim to browser incompatibilities.

Tip

Form field validation should never be considered optional, and you should get in the habit of always using some type of validation in each and every form you create. Failure to do so will inevitably cause errors and broken applications later.

USING SERVER-SIDE VALIDATION

As mentioned earlier, server-side validation involves adding code to your application that performs form field validation after the form is submitted. In ColdFusion this usually is achieved with a series of `<CFIF>` statements that check each field's value and data types. If any validation steps fail, processing can be terminated with the `<CFABORT>` function, or the user can be redirected to another page (maybe the form itself) using `<CFLOCATION>`.

Two ways to perform server-side validation are available in ColdFusion. Let's look at basic server-side validation first, and then you'll use embedded validation codes to automate the validation where possible.

USING BASIC SERVER-SIDE VALIDATION

The code shown in Listing 13.1 is a simple login prompt used to gain access to an intranet site. The file, which should be saved as `login1.cfm` (in a new directory named `13`), prompts for a user ID and password. HTML's only validation rule, `MAXLENGTH`, is used in both form fields to restrict the number of characters that can be entered. The form itself is shown in Figure 13.1.

LISTING 13.1 `login1.cfm`—**LOGIN SCREEN SHOWN IN FIGURE 13.1**

```
<!---
Name:        login1.cfm
Author:      Ben Forta (ben@forta.com)
Description: Form field validation demo
Created:     4/15/01
--->

<!DOCTYPE HTML PUBLIC "-//W3C//DTD HTML 4.0 Transitional//EN">

<HTML>

<HEAD>
    <TITLE>Orange Whip Studios - Intranet</TITLE>
</HEAD>

<BODY>

<!--- Page header --->
<CFINCLUDE TEMPLATE="header.cfm">

<!--- Login form --->
<FORM ACTION="process.cfm" METHOD="POST">

<TABLE ALIGN="center" BGCOLOR="orange">
    <TR>
        <TD ALIGN="right">
            ID:
        </TD>
        <TD>
            <INPUT TYPE="text" NAME="LoginID" MAXLENGTH="5">
        </TD>
    </TR>
    <TR>
        <TD ALIGN="right">
            Password:
        </TD>
        <TD>
            <INPUT TYPE="password" NAME="LoginPassword" MAXLENGTH="20">
        </TD>
    </TR>
    <TR>
        <TD COLSPAN="2" ALIGN="center">
            <INPUT TYPE="submit" VALUE="Login">
        </TD>
   </TR>
</TABLE>

</FORM>

</BODY>

</HTML>
```

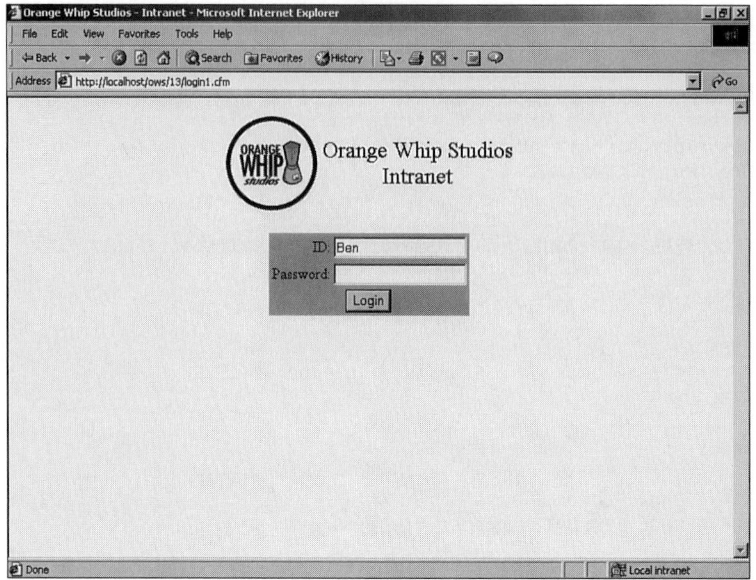

Figure 13.1
HTML forms support basic field types, such as text and password boxes.

This particular form gets submitted to a template named `process.cfm` (specified in the `ACTION` attribute). That template is responsible for validating the user input and processing the login only if all the validation rules passed. The validation rules necessary here are

- Login ID is required.
- Login ID must be numeric.
- Login password is required.

To perform this validation, three `<CFIF>` statements are used, as shown in Listing 13.2.

LISTING 13.2 `process.cfm`**—BASIC SERVER-SIDE VALIDATION CODE**

```
<!---
Name:        process.cfm
Author:      Ben Forta (ben@forta.com)
Description: Form field validation demo
Created:     4/15/01
--->

<!DOCTYPE HTML PUBLIC "-//W3C//DTD HTML 4.0 Transitional//EN">

<HTML>

<HEAD>
    <TITLE>Orange Whip Studios - Intranet</TITLE>
</HEAD>

<BODY>
```

```
<!--- Page header --->
<CFINCLUDE TEMPLATE="header.cfm">

<!--- Make sure LoginID is not empty --->
<CFIF Len(Trim(LoginID)) IS 0>
 <H1>ERROR! ID cannot be left blank!</H1>
 <CFABORT>
</CFIF>

<!--- Make sure LoginID is a number --->
<CFIF IsNumeric(LoginID) IS "No">
 <H1>ERROR! Invalid ID specified!</H1>
 <CFABORT>
</CFIF>

<!--- Make sure LoginPassword is not empty --->
<CFIF Len(Trim(LoginPassword)) IS 0>
 <H1>ERROR! Password cannot be left blank!</H1>
 <CFABORT>
</CFIF>

<CENTER>
<H1>Intranet</H1>
</CENTER>

</BODY>

</HTML>
```

The first `<CFIF>` checks the length of `LoginID` after trimming it with the `Trim()` function. The `Trim()` function is necessary to trap space characters that are technically valid characters in a text field but are not valid here. If the `Len()` function returns `0`, an error message is displayed, and the `<CFABORT>` statements halts further processing.

Tip

Checking the length of the trimmed string (to determine whether it is empty) is functionally the same as doing a comparison against an empty string, like this:

```
<CFIF Trim(LoginID) IS "">
```

The reason I used `Len()` to get the string length (instead of comparing it to `""`) is that numeric comparisons are processed more quickly than string comparisons. For even greater performance, I could have eliminated the comparison value and used the following:

```
<CFIF NOT Len(Trim(LoginID))>
```


The second `<CFIF>` statement checks the data type. The `IsNumeric()` function returns `TRUE` if the passed value was numeric (contained only digits, for example) or `FALSE` if not. Once again, if the `<CFIF>` check fails, an error is displayed and `<CFABORT>` halts further processing, as shown in Figure 13.2. The third `<CFIF>` checks that a password was specified (and that that the field was not left blank).

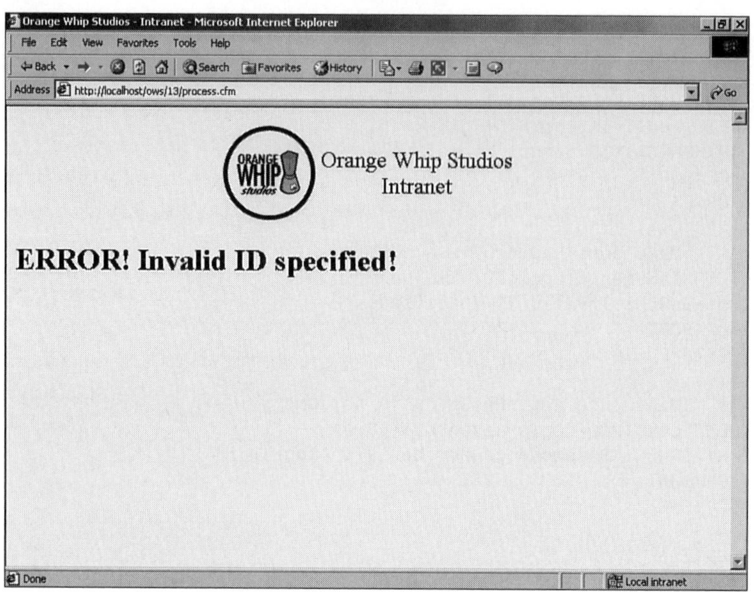

Figure 13.2 <CFIF> statements can be used to perform validation checks and then display error messages if the checks fail.

This form of validation is the most powerful and flexible of all the validation options available to you. There is no limit to the number of `<CFIF>` statements you can use, and there is no limit to the number of functions or tags you can use within them. You can even perform database operations (perhaps to check that a password matches) and use the results in comparisons.

Note

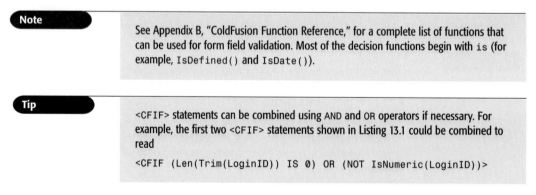

See Appendix B, "ColdFusion Function Reference," for a complete list of functions that can be used for form field validation. Most of the decision functions begin with `is` (for example, `IsDefined()` and `IsDate()`).

Tip

`<CFIF>` statements can be combined using AND and OR operators if necessary. For example, the first two `<CFIF>` statements shown in Listing 13.1 could be combined to read

```
<CFIF (Len(Trim(LoginID)) IS 0) OR (NOT IsNumeric(LoginID))>
```

The big downside here, however, is that this type of validation code is neither clean nor manageable. If you were to add or rename a field, for example, you'd have to remember to update the destination form (the form to which the fields get submitted, as specified in the `<FORM> ACTION` attribute), as well as the form itself. As your forms grow in complexity, so does the likelihood of your forms and their validation rules getting out of sync.

USING COLDFUSION EMBEDDED FORM VALIDATION

To work around this problem, ColdFusion enables developers to embed basic form validation instructions within an HTML form. These instructions are embedded as hidden form fields. They get sent to the user's browser along with the rest of the form fields, but they are not displayed to the user. Nonetheless, when the user submits the form back to the Web server, those hidden fields are submitted too. ColdFusion can then use them to perform automatic field validation.

To add a validation rule, you must add a hidden field to the form—you will need to add one hidden field for each validation rule necessary. The field name must be the name of the field to validate, followed by the validation rule—for example, `_required` (an underscore followed by the word `required`) to flag a field as required. The field's `VALUE` attribute can be used to specify the error message to be displayed if the validation fails. This next line of code tells ColdFusion that the `LoginID` field is required and that the error message `ID is required!` should be displayed if it's not present:

```
<INPUT TYPE="hidden" NAME="LoginID_required" VALUE="ID is required!">
```

ColdFusion supports seven basic validation rules, as listed in Table 13.2. It is important to remember that even though the validation rules are being sent to the browser as hidden form fields, the actual validation still occurs on the server after the form has been submitted.

TABLE 13.2 FORM FIELD VALIDATION RULE SUFFIXES

Suffix	Description
`_date`	Date in most common date formats, such as MM/DD/YY and MM/DD/YYYY (year is optional, and will default to the current year if omitted)
`_eurodate`	Same as `_date`, but with day before month (European format)
`_float`	Numeric data, decimal point allowed
`_integer`	Numeric data, decimal point not allowed
`_range`	Range of values; the minimum and maximum values (or just one of them) must be specified in the `VALUE` attribute as `MIN=` and `MAX=`—for example, `"MIN=5 MAX=10"`
`_required`	Field is required and can't be left blank
`_time`	Time in most common time formats

Note

There is no limit to the number of validation rules you can embed in a form. The only restriction is that every validation rule must be embedded as a separate hidden field. So, to flag a field as required and numeric, you'd need two embedded rules, as shown in Listing 13.3.

To demonstrate using these validation rules, update the login prompt screen created earlier. Listing 13.3 shows the updated form to which three lines of code have been added. Save this file as `login2.cfm`.

Listing 13.3 `login2.cfm`— **Login Prompt Screen with Embedded Field Validation Rules**

```
<!---
Name:        login2.cfm
Author:      Ben Forta (ben@forta.com)
Description: Form field validation demo
Created:     4/15/01
--->

<!DOCTYPE HTML PUBLIC "-//W3C//DTD HTML 4.0 Transitional//EN">

<HTML>

<HEAD>
    <TITLE>Orange Whip Studios - Intranet</TITLE>
</HEAD>

<BODY>

<!--- Page header --->
<CFINCLUDE TEMPLATE="header.cfm">

<!--- Login form --->
<FORM ACTION="process.cfm" METHOD="POST">

<TABLE ALIGN="center" BGCOLOR="orange">
    <TR>
        <TD ALIGN="right">
            ID:
        </TD>
        <TD>
            <INPUT TYPE="text" NAME="LoginID" MAXLENGTH="5">
            <INPUT TYPE="hidden"
                   NAME="LoginID_required"
                   VALUE="ID is required!">
            <INPUT TYPE="hidden"
                   NAME="LoginID_integer"
                   VALUE="Invalid ID specified!">
        </TD>
    </TR>
    <TR>
        <TD ALIGN="right">
            Password:
        </TD>
        <TD>
            <INPUT TYPE="password" NAME="LoginPassword" MAXLENGTH="20">
            <INPUT TYPE="hidden"
                   NAME="LoginPassword_required"
                   VALUE="Password is required!">
        </TD>
    </TR>
    <TR>
        <TD COLSPAN="2" ALIGN="center">
            <INPUT TYPE="submit" VALUE="Login">
        </TD>
   </TR>
```

```
</TABLE>

</FORM>

</BODY>

</HTML>
```

The first rule specifies that the `LoginID` field is a required field. The second rule further specifies that only numeric data can be entered into the `LoginID` field. And finally, the third rule flags the `LoginPassword` field as required, too.

So, what happens if the validation rules fail? The screen shown in Figure 13.3 is what gets displayed if non-numeric data was entered into the login field and the password field was left blank.

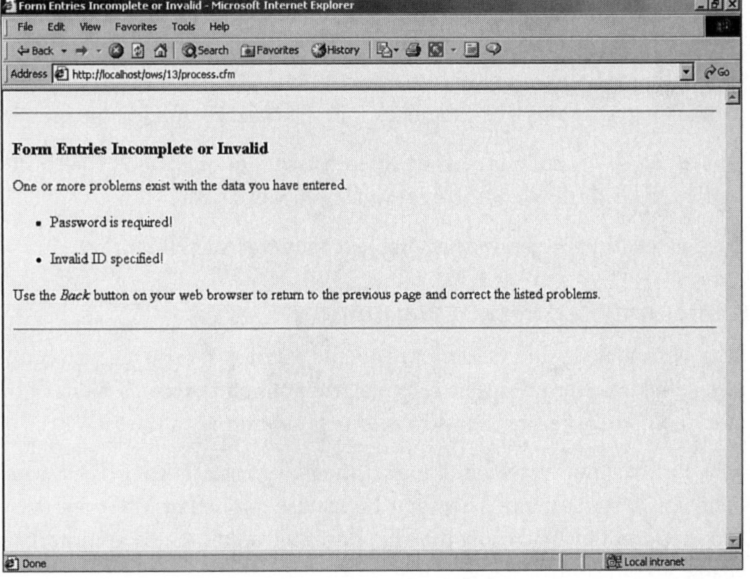

Figure 13.3 When using embedded form field validation, ColdFusion automatically displays an error message listing which checks failed.

Note

The screen shown in Figure 13.3 is the default validation error screen. This screen can be changed using the `<CFERROR>` tag.

Note

See Chapter 19, "Introducing the Web Application Framework," for information about using `<CFERROR>`.

As you can see, the ColdFusion validation rules are both simple and effective. And best of all, because the validation rules are embedded into the form itself, your forms and their rules are less likely to get out of sync.

Tip

Validation rules can be embedded anywhere in your form, either before or after the field being validated. To make maintaining your code easier, you should establish guidelines governing rule placement. Two popular standards are grouping all the rules together at the very top of the form, and listing validation rules right after the field they validate (as you did in Listing 13.3).

Of course, when validation errors occur the user will still have to go back to the form to make any corrections. The benefits of embedded validation rules are really only developer benefits—embedded validation does nothing to improve the user experience. For that you need client-side validation.

USING CLIENT-SIDE VALIDATION

The biggest drawback in using server-side validation is that the validation occurs after form submission. This means that if any validation rules fail, the user must go back to the form, make the corrections, and resubmit it to the server. To make matters worse, many browsers lose the data in the form fields when the Back button is clicked, forcing the user to reenter all the data.

Obviously, this is not a user-friendly interface. Too many good Web sites have lost visitors because their forms were too aggravating to work with.

Fortunately, an alternative is available: client-side validation.

UNDERSTANDING CLIENT-SIDE VALIDATION

To perform client-side validation, you add a series of browser instructions to your Web page. The browser interprets these instructions and executes them right on the client (the user's computer) before the form ever gets submitted to the server.

These instructions are written in scripting languages, such as JavaScript (supported by both Netscape Navigator and Microsoft Internet Explorer) or VBScript (based on Visual Basic and supported by Microsoft Internet Explorer only). These are interpreted languages that enable you to control browser behavior.

Note

Don't confuse JavaScript with Java. Java is a true compiled object-oriented application development language, one that can be used to write entire programs. JavaScript (including JScript, which is a variant of JavaScript) is an interpreted language designed to control Web browsers. Unlike Java, JavaScript cannot access anything on your computer other than your Web browser.

To validate a form, you write a script that will trap the form submission and allow it to proceed only if a series of validation checks have passed. If any checks fail, you would display an error message and prevent the form from being submitted.

Of course, to do this, you'd have to learn JavaScript or VBScript.

USING <CFFORM>

To simplify the process of embedding client-side validation scripting code into your forms, ColdFusion includes a tag called `<CFFORM>`. `<CFFORM>` is an extremely powerful tag that actually has several distinct functions. The function you are most interested in here is its support for client-side JavaScript.

Note

See Chapter 25, "Enhancing Forms with Client-Side Java," for more information about `<CFFORM>` and how to use its Java applets to extend your forms.

So, what can `<CFFORM>` do for you here? Simply put, `<CFFORM>` can *automatically* generate JavaScript code to handle most forms of data validation. And the best part of it is that you don't even have to know or learn JavaScript.

To see `<CFFORM>` in action, once again modify your login screen.

The code in Listing 13.4 is essentially the same code as your original form (refer to Listing 13.1). The only thing you've changed is replacing `<FORM>` with `<CFFORM>` and `</FORM>` with `</CFFORM>`. Make these changes and save the file as `login3.cfm`.

LISTING 13.4 `login3.cfm`—CODE FOR <CFFORM>-DRIVEN LOGIN FORM

```
<!---
Name:        login3.cfm
Author:      Ben Forta (ben@forta.com)
Description: Form field validation demo
Created:     4/15/01
--->

<!DOCTYPE HTML PUBLIC "-//W3C//DTD HTML 4.0 Transitional//EN">

<HTML>

<HEAD>
    <TITLE>Orange Whip Studios - Intranet</TITLE>
</HEAD>

<BODY>

<!--- Page header --->
<CFINCLUDE TEMPLATE="header.cfm">

<!--- Login form --->
<CFFORM ACTION="process.cfm">

<TABLE ALIGN="center" BGCOLOR="orange">
    <TR>
        <TD ALIGN="right">
            ID:
        </TD>
        <TD>
            <INPUT TYPE="text" NAME="LoginID" MAXLENGTH="5">
```

LISTING 13.4 CONTINUED

```
        </TD>
    </TR>
    <TR>
        <TD ALIGN="right">
            Password:
        </TD>
        <TD>
            <INPUT TYPE="password" NAME="LoginPassword" MAXLENGTH="20">
        </TD>
    </TR>
    <TR>
        <TD COLSPAN="2" ALIGN="center">
            <INPUT TYPE="submit" VALUE="Login">
        </TD>
   </TR>
</TABLE>

</CFFORM>

</BODY>

</HTML>
```

So, what happens when ColdFusion processes this form? The best way to understand it is to look at the code this template generates. You can do this by selecting the View Source option in your browser. The code you see should look similar to this:

```
<!DOCTYPE HTML PUBLIC "-//W3C//DTD HTML 4.0 Transitional//EN">

<HTML>

<HEAD>
    <TITLE>Orange Whip Studios - Intranet</TITLE>

<script LANGUAGE=JAVASCRIPT TYPE="text/javascript" >

<!--

function  _CF_checkCFForm_1(_CF_this)

    {

    return true;

    }

//-->

</script>

</HEAD>

<BODY>

<TABLE ALIGN="center">
```

```
 <TR>
  <TD><IMG SRC="../images/logo_c.gif" ALT="Orange Whip Studios"></TD>
  <TD ALIGN="center"><FONT SIZE="+2">Orange Whip Studios<BR>Intranet</FONT></TD>
 </TR>
</TABLE>

<FORM NAME="CFForm_1" ACTION="process.cfm"
➥METHOD=POST onSubmit="return _CF_checkCFForm_1(this)">

<TABLE ALIGN="center" BGCOLOR="orange">
    <TR>
        <TD ALIGN="right">
            ID:
        </TD>
        <TD>
            <INPUT TYPE="text" NAME="LoginID" MAXLENGTH="5">
        </TD>
    </TR>
    <TR>
        <TD ALIGN="right">
            Password:
        </TD>
        <TD>
            <INPUT TYPE="password" NAME="LoginPassword" MAXLENGTH="20">
        </TD>
    </TR>
    <TR>
        <TD COLSPAN="2" ALIGN="center">
            <INPUT TYPE="submit" VALUE="Login">
        </TD>
   </TR>
</TABLE>

</FORM>

</BODY>

</HTML>
```

The first thing you'll notice is that a JavaScript function has been added to the top of the page. The function currently always returns `true` because no validation rules have been set up yet. As you add validation rules to `<CFFORM>`, this function will automatically be expanded.

Note

Unlike CFML, JavaScript is case sensitive, so `true` and `false` can't be replaced with `TRUE` and `FALSE`.

The `<CFFORM>` and `</CFFORM>` tags in your code (refer to Listing 13.4) have been replaced with standard HTML `<FORM>` and `</FORM>` tags.

The `<FORM>` tag itself now has a `NAME` attribute with a unique value that was assigned by ColdFusion.

Caution

<CFFORM> enables you to provide a name yourself, in which case ColdFusion would use your own name instead of generating one for you. If you do specify your own name, be sure that each form on your page is uniquely named.

And finally, an `onSubmit` attribute was added. This is the JavaScript instruction to your browser that tells it to execute the JavaScript function specified prior to submitting the form to the server. If the specified function returns `true`, the form submission will continue. If the function returns `false`, the submission will be canceled.

Note

Actually, I lied. There was one other change in Listing 13.4. If you look carefully, you'll notice that I omitted the `METHOD` from the form—something I said you should never do. Why did I do this? Take a look at the generated code again; you'll see that ColdFusion automatically put the `METHOD="POST"` in there for me. That's another useful <CFFORM> feature.

USING <CFINPUT>

<CFFORM> creates the foundation on which to build JavaScript validation. To specify the validation rules themselves, you have to use the <CFINPUT> tag. <CFINPUT> does the same thing as the standard HTML <INPUT> tag and takes the same attributes as parameters. But it also takes additional optional attributes, attributes you can use to specify validation rules.

Look at this code sample:

```
<CFINPUT TYPE="text" NAME="LoginID" SIZE="5" MAXLENGTH="5" REQUIRED="Yes">
```

It looks just like a standard <INPUT> tag. The only differences are <CFINPUT> instead of <INPUT> and the extra `REQUIRED` attribute, which has a value of `Yes`.

And yet this code does so much more than <INPUT>. This <CFINPUT> tag instructs ColdFusion to generate the JavaScript code required to flag this field as required.

So, update your login screen once again.

Listing 13.5 is yet another updated version of your login screen (this is file `login4.cfm`). This time the `LoginID` field's <INPUT> tag has been replaced with a <CFINPUT> tag.

LISTING 13.5 login4.cfm—LOGIN PROMPT SCREEN WITH <CFINPUT> USED TO FLAG REQUIRED FIELD

```
<!---
Name:        login4.cfm
Author:      Ben Forta (ben@forta.com)
Description: Form field validation demo
Created:     4/15/01
--->

<!DOCTYPE HTML PUBLIC "-//W3C//DTD HTML 4.0 Transitional//EN">
```

```
<HTML>

<HEAD>
    <TITLE>Orange Whip Studios - Intranet</TITLE>
</HEAD>

<BODY>

<!--- Page header --->
<CFINCLUDE TEMPLATE="header.cfm">

<!--- Login form --->
<CFFORM ACTION="process.cfm">

<TABLE ALIGN="center" BGCOLOR="orange">
    <TR>
        <TD ALIGN="right">
            ID:
        </TD>
        <TD>
            <CFINPUT TYPE="text" NAME="LoginID"
                     MAXLENGTH="5" REQUIRED="Yes">
        </TD>
    </TR>
    <TR>
        <TD ALIGN="right">
            Password:
        </TD>
        <TD>
            <INPUT TYPE="password" NAME="LoginPassword" MAXLENGTH="20">
        </TD>
    </TR>
    <TR>
        <TD COLSPAN="2" ALIGN="center">
            <INPUT TYPE="submit" VALUE="Login">
        </TD>
   </TR>
</TABLE>

</CFFORM>

</BODY>

</HTML>
```


When ColdFusion processes this new form, it generates no fewer than 70 lines of JavaScript code (as shown here), and all automatically:

```
<!DOCTYPE HTML PUBLIC "-//W3C//DTD HTML 4.0 Transitional//EN">

<HTML>

<HEAD>
    <TITLE>Orange Whip Studios - Intranet</TITLE>

<script LANGUAGE=JAVASCRIPT TYPE="text/javascript" >
```

```
<!--

function _CF_onError(form_object, input_object, object_value, error_message)
    {
    alert(error_message);
           return false;
    }

function _CF_hasValue(obj, obj_type)
    {
    if (obj_type == "TEXT" || obj_type == "PASSWORD")
    {
        if (obj.value.length == 0)
              return false;
        else
              return true;
        }
    else if (obj_type == "SELECT")
    {
        for (i=0; i < obj.length; i++)
            {
        if (obj.options[i].selected)
            return true;
        }

           return false;
    }
    else if (obj_type == "SINGLE_VALUE_RADIO"
             || obj_type == "SINGLE_VALUE_CHECKBOX")
    {

        if (obj.checked)
            return true;
        else
               return false;
    }
    else if (obj_type == "RADIO" || obj_type == "CHECKBOX")
    {

        for (i=0; i < obj.length; i++)
            {
        if (obj[i].checked)
            return true;
        }

           return false;
    }
    }

function  _CF_checkCFForm_1(_CF_this)

    {

    if  (!_CF_hasValue(_CF_this.LoginID, "TEXT" ))

        {
```

```
        if  (!_CF_onError(_CF_this, _CF_this.LoginID,
                           CF_this.LoginID.value,
                           "Error in LoginID text."))

            {

            return false;

            }

        }

    return true;

    }

//-->

</script>

</HEAD>

<BODY>

<TABLE ALIGN="center">
 <TR>
  <TD><IMG SRC="../images/logo_c.gif" ALT="Orange Whip Studios"></TD>
  <TD ALIGN="center"><FONT SIZE="+2">Orange Whip Studios<BR>Intranet</FONT></TD>
 </TR>
</TABLE>

<FORM NAME="CFForm_1" ACTION="process.cfm"
                      METHOD=POST onSubmit="return
                      CF_checkCFForm_1(this)">

<TABLE ALIGN="center" BGCOLOR="orange">
    <TR>
        <TD ALIGN="right">
            ID:
        </TD>
        <TD>
            <INPUT TYPE="text" NAME="LoginID" MAXLENGTH="5">
        </TD>
    </TR>
    <TR>
        <TD ALIGN="right">
            Password:
        </TD>
        <TD>
            <INPUT TYPE="password" NAME="LoginPassword" MAXLENGTH="20">
        </TD>
    </TR>
    <TR>
        <TD COLSPAN="2" ALIGN="center">
            <INPUT TYPE="submit" VALUE="Login">
        </TD>
```

```
    </TR>
</TABLE>

</FORM>

</BODY>

</HTML>
```

As you can see, the `<CFINPUT>` tag has been replaced by a standard HTML `<INPUT>` tag. In fact, the generated tag looks exactly the same as the `<INPUT>` tag looked before you added the `<CFINPUT>` `REQUIRED` attribute. That attribute was used by ColdFusion to generate the JavaScript code, which ensures that a blank `LoginID` field cannot be submitted. If the user tries to submit the form, the JavaScript will pop up an error message box, as shown in Figure 13.4.

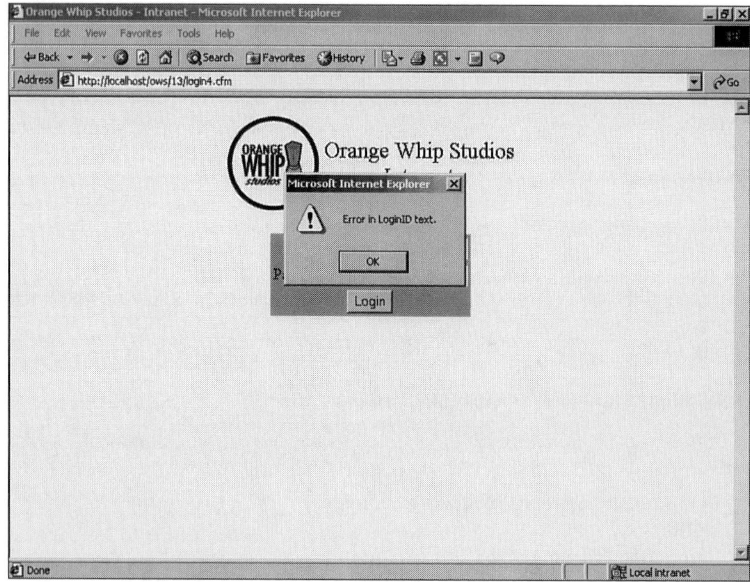

Figure 13.4
Unless otherwise specified, a default error message is used when JavaScript validation rules fail.

> **Note**
>
> The pop-up error box is a standard browser dialog box that varies from browser to browser, and there is no way to change what it looks like. The only thing you can change is the actual error message itself.

USING <CFINPUT> VALIDATION OPTIONS

So far, you have used `<CFINPUT>` to flag fields as required. And if you were impressed with that, wait, there's more. `<CFINPUT>` also lets you specify data type validation rules, as well as customized error messages.

To provide these capabilities, `<CFINPUT>` supports all the attributes supported by HTML `<INPUT>`, as well as some additional ones. These are listed in Table 13.3.

TABLE 13.3 <CFINPUT> ATTRIBUTES

Attribute	Description
MESSAGE	Error message text to pop up if this field's validation fails.
ONERROR	The name of a JavaScript function to execute if a validation rule fails, overriding the default error function.
ONVALIDATE	To override the default JavaScript validation code, and to use your own JavaScript, specify the JavaScript function name here.
RANGE	Range of valid values (for numeric data only) specified as `minimum,maximum`.
REQUIRED	Set to `Yes` to flag field as required, default is `No`.
VALIDATE	One of the nine supported data validation types, as listed in Table 13.4.

The `<CFINPUT>` `VALIDATE` attribute takes a data type as a value. The supported data types are listed in Table 13.4.

TABLE 13.4 <CFINPUT> DATA VALIDATION TYPES

Type	Description
creditcard	Blanks and dashes are stripped, and the number is verified using the mod10 algorithm.
date	Verifies U.S. date entry in the form mm/dd/yyyy.
eurodate	Verifies valid European date entry in the form dd/mm/yyyy.
float	Verifies a floating-point entry.
integer	Verifies an integer entry.
social_security_number	Social Security number in the form ###-##-#### (the hyphen separator can be replaced with a blank).
telephone	Verifies a telephone entry; telephone data must be entered as ###-###-#### (the hyphen separator can be replaced with a blank); the area code and exchange must begin with a digit between `1` and `9`.
time	Verifies a time entry in the form hh:mm:ss.
zipcode	(U.S. formats only) Number can be a 5-digit or 9-digit ZIP in the form #####-#### (the hyphen separator can be replaced with a blank).

Note

There is no way to add your own validation types to `<CFINPUT>`. Any additional validation rules must be written manually (using a client-side scripting language).

Now that you've seen what `<CFINPUT>` can do, update your login screen one final time. The code shown in Listing 13.6 uses `<CFINPUT>` tags for both input fields and flags both of them as required fields. In addition, the LoginID field has a validation type of integer, which prevents the user from entering non-numeric data in it. And finally, both fields have custom error messages specified using the MESSAGE attribute. If validation fails, the specified error message is displayed, as shown in Figure 13.5.

LISTING 13.6 login5.cfm—THE COMPLETED PROMPT FORM, WITH JAVASCRIPT VALIDATION

```
<!---
Name:        login5.cfm
Author:      Ben Forta (ben@forta.com)
Description: Form field validation demo
Created:     4/15/01
--->

<!DOCTYPE HTML PUBLIC "-//W3C//DTD HTML 4.0 Transitional//EN">

<HTML>

<HEAD>
    <TITLE>Orange Whip Studios - Intranet</TITLE>
</HEAD>

<BODY>

<!--- Page header --->
<CFINCLUDE TEMPLATE="header.cfm">

<!--- Login form --->
<CFFORM ACTION="process.cfm">

<TABLE ALIGN="center" BGCOLOR="orange">
    <TR>
        <TD ALIGN="right">
            ID:
        </TD>
        <TD>
            <CFINPUT TYPE="text"
                     NAME="LoginID"
                     MESSAGE="Valid numeric ID is required!"
                     VALIDATE="integer"
                     REQUIRED="Yes"
                     MAXLENGTH="5">
        </TD>
    </TR>
    <TR>
        <TD ALIGN="right">
            Password:
        </TD>
        <TD>
            <CFINPUT TYPE="password"
                     NAME="LoginPassword"
                     MESSAGE="Password is required!"
                     REQUIRED="Yes"
                     MAXLENGTH="20">
        </TD>
    </TR>
```

```
    <TR>
        <TD COLSPAN="2" ALIGN="center">
            <INPUT TYPE="submit" VALUE="Login">
        </TD>
    </TR>
</TABLE>

</CFFORM>

</BODY>

</HTML>
```

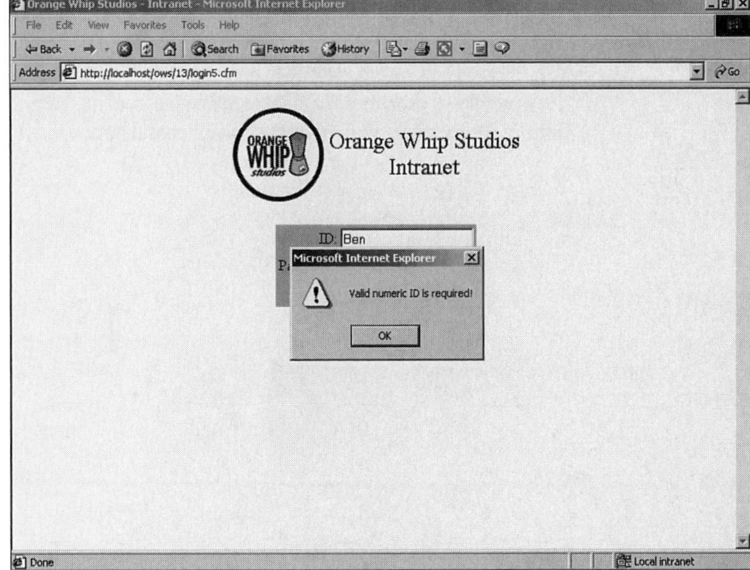

Figure 13.5
The <CFINPUT> MESSAGE attribute can be used to customize the displayed error message.

As you can see, with <CFINPUT>, implementing client-side validation is a clean and simple process—ColdFusion does it for you.

PUTTING IT ALL TOGETHER

Before you run off and plug <CFFORM> and <CFINPUT> into all your templates, there are some other details that you should know:

- **Not all browsers support JavaScript**—Also, those that don't will generally ignore it, enabling your forms to be submitted without being validated.
- **You should combine the use of JavaScript validation with server-side validation using embedded fields**—These will never fail validation if the browser does support JavaScript, and if the browser does not, at least you have some form of validation.

- **Older browsers (including some versions of Netscape 3) might have trouble with some of the generated JavaScript**—So, be sure you test your forms in as many different browsers as possible.
- **The JavaScript code can be quite lengthy**—This will increase the size of your Web page and thus the time it takes to download it from your Web server.

Note

One form of form processing that is gaining popularity is server-side validation with a twist. Instead of aborting processing and displaying validation errors, you can redisplay the original form (containing all the information entered by the user), flagging the fields that need correction with an indicator and a message.

To create this type of interface, you must create your form with the capability to display existing values (as explained in the last chapter), as well as with all the conditional logic necessary to display messages where and when needed.

This is not trivial code to write, but keep the idea in mind. When you are ready to tackle it, it's definitely an interface worthy of consideration for your applications.

CHAPTER 14

Using Forms to Add or Change Data

In this chapter

ADDING DATA WITH COLDFUSION

Now that you have learned all about forms and form data validation (in the previous two chapters), it's time to combine the two so as to be able to add and update table data.

Note

See Chapter 12, "ColdFusion Forms," to learn about HTML forms and how to use them within your ColdFusion applications.

See Chapter 13, "Form Data Validation," for coverage of form field validation techniques and options.

When you created the movie search forms in Chapter 12, you had to create two templates for each search. One created the user search screen that contains the search form, and the other performs the actual search using the ColdFusion `<CFQUERY>` tag. ColdFusion developers usually refer to these as the `<FORM>` and `ACTION` pages (because one contains the form and the other is the file specified as the `<FORM> ACTION`).

Breaking an operation into more than one template is typical of ColdFusion, as well as all Web-based data interaction. As explained in Chapter 1, "Introduction to ColdFusion," a browser's connection to a Web server is made and broken as necessary. An HTTP connection is made to a Web server whenever a Web page is retrieved. That connection is broken as soon as that page is retrieved. Any subsequent pages are retrieved with a new connection that is used just to retrieve that page.

There is no real way to keep a connection alive for the duration of a complete process—when searching for data, for example. Therefore, the process must be broken up into steps, and as shown in Chapter 12, each step is a separate template.

Adding data via your Web browser is no different. You generally need at least two templates to perform the insertion. One displays the form you use to collect the data, and the other processes the data and inserts the record.

Adding data to a table involves the following steps:

1. Display a form to collect the data. The names of any input fields should match the names of the columns in the destination table.
2. Submit the form to ColdFusion for processing. ColdFusion adds the row via the ODBC driver using a SQL statement.

CREATING AN ADD RECORD FORM

Forms used to add data are no different from the forms you created to search for data. The form is created using the standard HTML `<FORM>` and `<INPUT>` tags, as shown in Listing 14.1. Save this file as `insert1.cfm` (in the `14` directory under `ows`). You'll be able to execute the page to display the form, but don't submit it yet (you've yet to create the `ACTION` page).

LISTING 14.1 insert1.cfm—NEW MOVIE FORM

```
<!---
Name:        insert1.cfm
Author:      Ben Forta (ben@forta.com)
Description: Table row insertion demo
Created:     4/20/01
--->

<!--- Get ratings --->
<CFQUERY DATASOURCE="ows" NAME="ratings">
SELECT RatingID, Rating
FROM FilmsRatings
ORDER BY RatingID
</CFQUERY>

<!--- Page header --->
<CFINCLUDE TEMPLATE="header.cfm">

<!--- New movie form --->
<CFFORM ACTION="insert2.cfm">

<TABLE ALIGN="center" BGCOLOR="orange">
    <TR>
        <TH COLSPAN="2">
            <FONT SIZE="+1">Add a Movie</FONT>
        </TH>
    </TR>
    <TR>
        <TD>
            Movie:
        </TD>
        <TD>
            <CFINPUT TYPE="Text"
                     NAME="MovieTitle"
                     MESSAGE="MOVIE TITLE is required!"
                     REQUIRED="Yes"
                     SIZE="50"
                     MAXLENGTH="100">
        </TD>
    </TR>
    <TR>
        <TD>
            Tag line:
        </TD>
        <TD>
            <CFINPUT TYPE="Text"
                     NAME="PitchText"
                     MESSAGE="TAG LINE is required!"
                     REQUIRED="Yes"
                     SIZE="50"
                     MAXLENGTH="100">
        </TD>
    </TR>
    <TR>
        <TD>
            Rating:
        </TD>
```

LISTING 14.1 CONTINUED

```
        <TD>
            <!--- Ratings list --->
            <SELECT NAME="RatingID">
                <CFOUTPUT QUERY="ratings">
                    <OPTION VALUE="#RatingID#">#Rating#</OPTION>
                </CFOUTPUT>
            </SELECT>
        </TD>
    </TR>
    <TR>
        <TD>
            Summary:
        </TD>
        <TD>
            <TEXTAREA NAME="summary"
                      COLS="40"
                      ROWS="5"
                      WRAP="virtual"></TEXTAREA>
        </TD>
    </TR>
    <TR>
        <TD>
            Budget:
        </TD>
        <TD>
            <CFINPUT TYPE="Text"
                     NAME="AmountBudgeted"
                     MESSAGE="BUDGET must be a valid numeric amount!"
                     VALIDATE="integer"
                     REQUIRED="NO"
                     SIZE="10"
                     MAXLENGTH="10">
        </TD>
    </TR>
    <TR>
        <TD>
            Release Date:
        </TD>
        <TD>
            <CFINPUT TYPE="Text"
                     NAME="DateInTheaters"
                     MESSAGE="RELEASE DATE must be a valid date!"
                     VALIDATE="date"
                     REQUIRED="NO"
                     SIZE="10"
                     MAXLENGTH="10">
        </TD>
    </TR>
    <TR>
        <TD>
            Image File:
        </TD>
        <TD>
            <CFINPUT TYPE="Text"
                     NAME="ImageName"
                     REQUIRED="NO"
```

```
                    SIZE="20"
                    MAXLENGTH="50">
        </TD>
    </TR>
    <TR>
        <TD COLSPAN="2" ALIGN="center">
            <INPUT TYPE="submit" VALUE="Insert">
        </TD>
    </TR>
</TABLE>

</CFFORM>

<!--- Page footer --->
<CFINCLUDE TEMPLATE="footer.cfm">
```

Note

Listing 14.1 contains a form, not unlike all the forms created in Chapters 12 and 13. This form uses form techniques and validation options described in both of those chapters; refer to them if necessary.

The file `insert1.cfm` (and indeed all the files in this chapter) includes common header and footer files (`header.cfm` and `footer.cfm`, respectively). These files contain the HTML page layout code, including any logos. They are included in each file (using `<CFINCLUDE>` tags) to facilitate code reuse (and to keep codee listings shorter and more manageable). Listings 14.2 and 14.3 contain the code for these two files.

Note

`<CFINCLUDE>` and code reuse are introduced in Chapter 10, "CFML Basics."

LISTING 14.2 `header.cfm`—**MOVIE FORM PAGE HEADER**

```
<!---
Name:        header.cfm
Author:      Ben Forta (ben@forta.com)
Description: Header for Intranet screens
Created:     4/20/01
--->

<!DOCTYPE HTML PUBLIC "-//W3C//DTD HTML 4.0 Transitional//EN">

<HTML>

<HEAD>
    <TITLE>Orange Whip Studios - Intranet</TITLE>
</HEAD>

<BODY>

<TABLE ALIGN="center">
 <TR>
  <TD><IMG SRC="../images/logo_c.gif" ALT="Orange Whip Studios"></TD>
```

LISTING 14.2 CONTINUED

```
  <TD ALIGN="center">
   <FONT SIZE="+2">Orange Whip Studios<BR>Movie Maintenance</FONT>
  </TD>
 </TR>
</TABLE>
```

LISTING 14.3 footer.cfm—MOVIE FORM PAGE FOOTER

```
<!---
Name:        footer.cfm
Author:      Ben Forta (ben@forta.com)
Description: Footer for Intranet screens
Created:     4/20/01
--->

</BODY>

</HTML>
```

The <FORM> ACTION attribute specifies the name of the template to be used to process the insertion; in this case it's insert2.cfm.

Each <INPUT> or <CFINPUT> field has a field name specified in the NAME attribute. These names correspond to the names of the appropriate columns in the Films table.

Tip

Studio users can take advantage of the built-in drag-and-drop features when using table and column names within your code. Simply open the Resource tab's Database tab, select the server you are using, open the data source, and expand the tables item to display the list of tables within the data source. You can then drag the table name into your source code. Similarly, expanding the table name displays a list of the fields within that table, and those too can be dragged into your source code.

You also specified the SIZE and MAXLENGTH attributes in each of the text fields. SIZE is used to specify the size of the text box within the browser window. Without the SIZE attribute, the browser uses its default size, which varies from one browser to the next.

The SIZE attribute does not restrict the number of characters that can entered into the field. SIZE="50" creates a text field that occupies the space of 50 characters, but the text scrolls within the field if you enter more than 50 characters. To restrict the number of characters that can be entered, you must use the MAXLENGTH attribute. MAXLENGTH="100" instructs the browser to allow no more than 100 characters in the field.

The SIZE attribute primarily is used for aesthetics and the control of screen appearance. MAXLENGTH is used to ensure that only data that can be handled is entered into a field. Without MAXLENGTH, users could enter more data than would fit in a field, and that data would be truncated upon database insertion (or might even generate database errors).

Tip

You should always use both the `SIZE` and `MAXLENGTH` attributes for maximum control over form appearance and data entry. Without them, the browser will use its defaults—and there are no rules governing what these defaults should be.

Each of the text fields uses client-side validation, and the `RatingID` field is a drop-down list box populated with a `<CFQUERY>` (just as you did in the last chapter).

The Add a Movie form is shown in Figure 14.1.

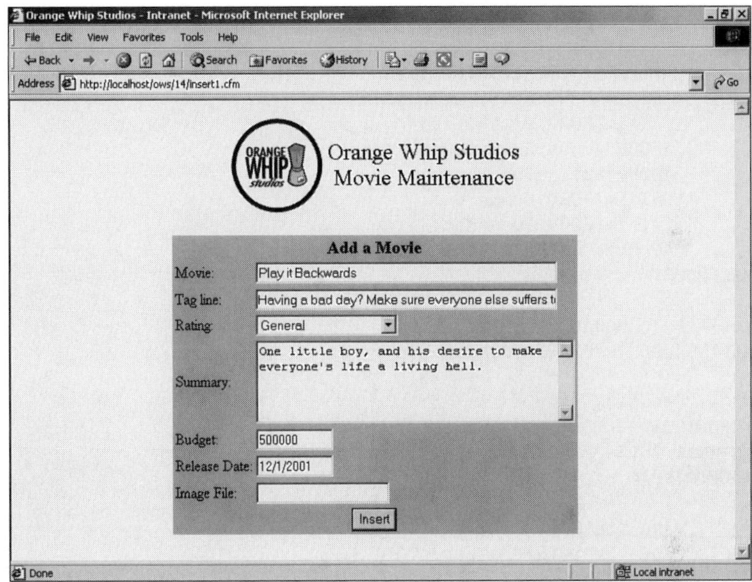

Figure 14.1 HTML forms can be used as a front end for data insertion.

PROCESSING ADDITIONS

The next thing you need is a template to process the actual data insertion—the `ACTION` page mentioned earlier. In this page use the SQL `INSERT` statement to add the new row to the `Films` table.

Note

See Chapter 7, "SQL Data Manipulation," for an explanation of the `INSERT` statement.

As shown in Listing 14.4, the `<CFQUERY>` tag can be used to pass any SQL statement—not just `SELECT` statements. The SQL statement here is `INSERT`, which adds a row to the `Films` table and sets the values in seven columns to the form values passed by the browser.

LISTING 14.4 `insert2.cfm`—ADDING DATA WITH THE SQL `INSERT` STATEMENT

```
<!---
Name:        insert2.cfm
```

LISTING 14.4 CONTINUED

```
Author:      Ben Forta (ben@forta.com)
Description: Table row insertion demo
Created:     4/20/01
--->

<!--- Insert movie --->
<CFQUERY DATASOURCE="ows">
INSERT INTO Films(MovieTitle,
                  PitchText,
                  AmountBudgeted,
                  RatingID,
                  Summary,
                  ImageName,
                  DateInTheaters)
VALUES('#Trim(FORM.MovieTitle)#',
       '#Trim(FORM.PitchText)#',
       #FORM.AmountBudgeted#,
       #FORM.RatingID#,
       '#Trim(FORM.Summary)#',
       '#Trim(FORM.ImageName)#',
       #CreateODBCDate(FORM.DateInTheaters)#)
</CFQUERY>

<!--- Page header --->
<CFINCLUDE TEMPLATE="header.cfm">

<!--- Feedback --->
<CFOUTPUT>
<H1>New movie #FORM.MovieTitle# added</H1>
</CFOUTPUT>

<!--- Page footer --->
<CFINCLUDE TEMPLATE="footer.cfm">
```

Listing 14.4 is pretty self-explanatory. The `<CFQUERY>` tag performs the actual `INSERT` operation. The list of columns into which values are to be assigned is specified, as is the matching `VALUES` list (these two lists must match exactly, both the columns and their order).

Each of the values used is from a `FORM` field, but some differences do exist in how the fields are used:

- All string fields have their values enclosed within single quotation marks.
- The two numeric fields (`AmountBudgeted` and `RatingID`) have no single quotation marks around them.
- The date field (`DateInTheaters`) is formatted as a date using the `CreateODBCDate()` function.

It is important to remember that SQL is not typeless, so it is your job to use quotation marks where necessary to explicitly type variables.

Tip

Any time you pass dates to an ODBC data source, use the `CreateODBCDate()` function (or the `CreateODBCTime()` and `CreateODBCDateTime()` functions). These functions all take in a variety of formats and covert them into a format that is guaranteed to work with all ODBC database drivers. If you do not use these functions, you run the risk of generating errors if the dates are not in the exact format expected by the database.

Note

Notice that the `<CFQUERY>` in Listing 14.4 has no `NAME` attribute. `NAME` is an optional attribute and is necessary only if you need to manipulate the data returned by `<CFQUERY>`. Because the operation here is an `INSERT`, no data is returned; the `NAME` attribute is therefore unnecessary.

Save Listing 14.4 as `insert2.cfm`, and then try submitting a new movie using the form in `insert1.cfm`. You should see a screen similar to the one shown in Figure 14.2.

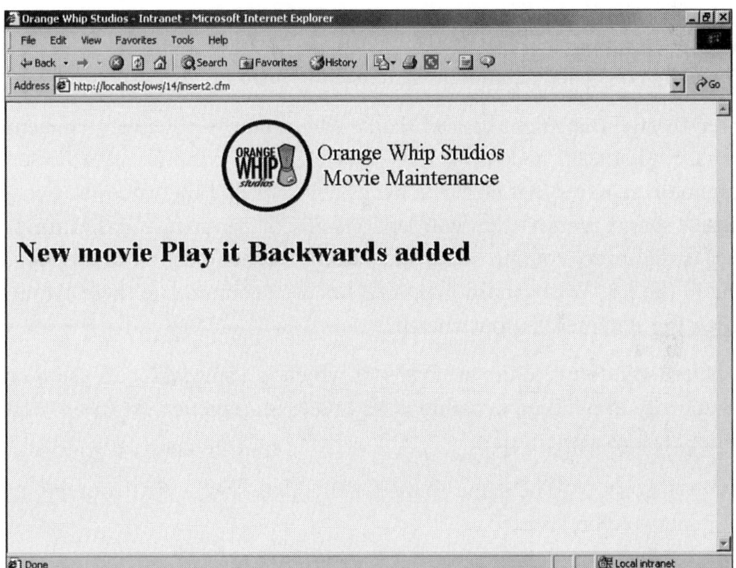

Figure 14.2 Data can be added via ColdFusion using the SQL `INSERT` statement.

Note

You can verify that the movie was added by browsing the table using any of the search templates you created in Chapter 12.

INTRODUCING <CFINSERT>

The example in Listing 14.4 demonstrates how to add data to a table using the standard SQL `INSERT` command. This works very well if you have to provide data for only a few columns, and if those columns are always provided. If the number of columns can vary, using SQL `INSERT` gets rather complicated.

For example, assume you have two or more data-entry forms for similar data. One might collect a minimal number of fields, whereas another collects a more complete record. How would you create a SQL INSERT statement to handle both sets of data?

You could create two separate templates, with a different SQL INSERT statement in each, but that's a situation you should always try to avoid. As a rule, you should try to avoid having more than one template perform a given operation. That way you don't run the risk of future changes and revisions being applied incorrectly. If a table name or column name changes, for example, you won't have to worry about forgetting one of the templates that references the changed column.

Tip

As a rule, you should never create more than one template to perform a specific operation. This helps prevent introducing errors into your templates when updates or revisions are made. You are almost always better off creating one template with conditional code than creating two separate templates.

Another solution is to use dynamic SQL. You could write a basic INSERT statement and then gradually construct a complete statement by using a series of <CFIF> statements.

Even though this might be a workable solution, it is not a very efficient one. The conditional SQL INSERT code is far more complex than conditional SQL SELECT. The INSERT statement requires that both the list of columns and the values be dynamic. In addition, the INSERT syntax requires that you separate all column names and values by commas. This means that every column name and value must be followed by a comma—except the last one in the list. Your conditional SQL has to accommodate these syntactical requirements when the statement is constructed.

A better solution is to use <CFINSERT>, which is a special ColdFusion tag that hides the complexity of building dynamic SQL INSERT statements. <CFINSERT> takes the following parameters as attributes:

- DATASOURCE—The name of the ODBC data source that contains the table to which the data is to be inserted.
- TABLENAME—The name of the destination table.
- FORMFIELDS—An optional comma-separated list of fields to be inserted. If this attribute is not provided, all the fields in the submitted form are used.

Look at the following ColdFusion tag:

```
<CFINSERT DATASOURCE="ows" TABLENAME="Films">
```

This code does exactly the same thing as the <CFQUERY> tag in Listing 14.4. When ColdFusion processes a <CFINSERT> tag, it builds a dynamic SQL INSERT statement under the hood. If a FORMFIELDS attribute is provided, the specified field names are used. No FORMFIELDS attribute was specified in this example, so ColdFusion automatically uses the form fields that were submitted, building the list of columns and the values dynamically.

<CFINSERT> even automatically handles the inclusion of single quotation marks where necessary.

Listing 14.5 contains a revised version of insert2.cfm; save this file as insert3.cfm.

LISTING 14.5 insert3.cfm—ADDING DATA WITH THE <CFINSERT> TAG

```
<!---
Name:        insert3.cfm
Author:      Ben Forta (ben@forta.com)
Description: Table row insertion demo
Created:     4/20/01
--->

<!--- Insert movie --->
<CFINSERT DATASOURCE="ows" TABLENAME="Films">

<!--- Page header --->
<CFINCLUDE TEMPLATE="header.cfm">

<!--- Feedback --->
<CFOUTPUT>
<H1>New movie #FORM.MovieTitle# added</H1>
</CFOUTPUT>

<!--- Page footer --->
<CFINCLUDE TEMPLATE="footer.cfm">
```

Try modifying the form in template insert1.cfm so that it submits the form to template insert3.cfm instead of insert2.cfm; then add a record. You'll see that the code in Listing 14.5 does exactly the same thing as the code in Listing 14.4, but with a much simpler syntax and interface.

Change file insert1.cfm so that it uses insert3.cfm as its ACTION page (instead of insert2.cfm). Then try adding a movie; your browser display should look no different from it did before.

CONTROLLING <CFINSERT> FORM FIELDS

<CFINSERT> instructs ColdFusion to build SQL INSERT statements dynamically. ColdFusion automatically uses all submitted form fields when building this statement.

Sometimes you might want ColdFusion to not include certain fields. For example, you might have hidden fields in your form that are not table columns, such as the hidden field shown in Listing 14.6. That field might be there as part of a security system you have implemented; it is not a column in the table. If you try to pass this field to <CFINSERT>, ColdFusion passes the hidden Login field as a column to the database. Obviously, this generates an ODBC error, as seen in Figure 14.3, because no Login column exists in the Films table.

LISTING 14.6 insert4.cfm—TEMPLATE THAT ADDS A MOVIE

```
<!---
Name:        insert4.cfm
```

Listing 14.6 Continued

```
Author:      Ben Forta (ben@forta.com)
Description: Table row insertion demo
Created:     4/20/01
--->

<!--- Get ratings --->
<CFQUERY DATASOURCE="ows" NAME="ratings">
SELECT RatingID, Rating
FROM FilmsRatings
ORDER BY RatingID
</CFQUERY>

<!--- Page header --->
<CFINCLUDE TEMPLATE="header.cfm">

<!--- New movie form --->
<CFFORM ACTION="insert5.cfm">

<!--- Login field --->
<INPUT TYPE="hidden" NAME="Login" VALUE="Ben">

<TABLE ALIGN="center" BGCOLOR="orange">
    <TR>
        <TH COLSPAN="2">
            <FONT SIZE="+1">Add a Movie</FONT>
        </TH>
    </TR>
    <TR>
        <TD>
            Movie:
        </TD>
        <TD>
            <CFINPUT TYPE="Text"
                     NAME="MovieTitle"
                     MESSAGE="MOVIE TITLE is required!"
                     REQUIRED="Yes"
                     SIZE="50"
                     MAXLENGTH="100">
        </TD>
    </TR>
    <TR>
        <TD>
            Tag line:
        </TD>
        <TD>
            <CFINPUT TYPE="Text"
                     NAME="PitchText"
                     MESSAGE="TAG LINE is required!"
                     REQUIRED="Yes"
                     SIZE="50"
                     MAXLENGTH="100">
        </TD>
    </TR>
    <TR>
        <TD>
            Rating:
```

```
        </TD>
        <TD>
            <!--- Ratings list --->
            <SELECT NAME="RatingID">
                <CFOUTPUT QUERY="ratings">
                    <OPTION VALUE="#RatingID#">#Rating#</OPTION>
                </CFOUTPUT>
            </SELECT>
        </TD>
    </TR>
    <TR>
        <TD>
            Summary:
        </TD>
        <TD>
            <TEXTAREA NAME="summary"
                      COLS="40"
                      ROWS="5"
                      WRAP="virtual"></TEXTAREA>
        </TD>
    </TR>
    <TR>
        <TD>
            Budget:
        </TD>
        <TD>
            <CFINPUT TYPE="Text"
                     NAME="AmountBudgeted"
                     MESSAGE="BUDGET must be a valid numeric amount!"
                     VALIDATE="integer"
                     REQUIRED="NO"
                     SIZE="10"
                     MAXLENGTH="10">
        </TD>
    </TR>
    <TR>
        <TD>
            Release Date:
        </TD>
        <TD>
            <CFINPUT TYPE="Text"
                     NAME="DateInTheaters"
                     MESSAGE="RELEASE DATE must be a valid date!"
                     VALIDATE="date"
                     REQUIRED="NO"
                     SIZE="10"
                     MAXLENGTH="10">
        </TD>
    </TR>
    <TR>
        <TD>
            Image File:
        </TD>
        <TD>
            <CFINPUT TYPE="Text"
                     NAME="ImageName"
                     REQUIRED="NO"
                     SIZE="20"
```

Listing 14.6 Continued

```
                        MAXLENGTH="50">
        </TD>
    </TR>
    <TR>
        <TD COLSPAN="2" ALIGN="center">
            <INPUT TYPE="submit" VALUE="Insert">
        </TD>
    </TR>
</TABLE>

</CFFORM>

<!--- Page footer --->
<CFINCLUDE TEMPLATE="footer.cfm">
```

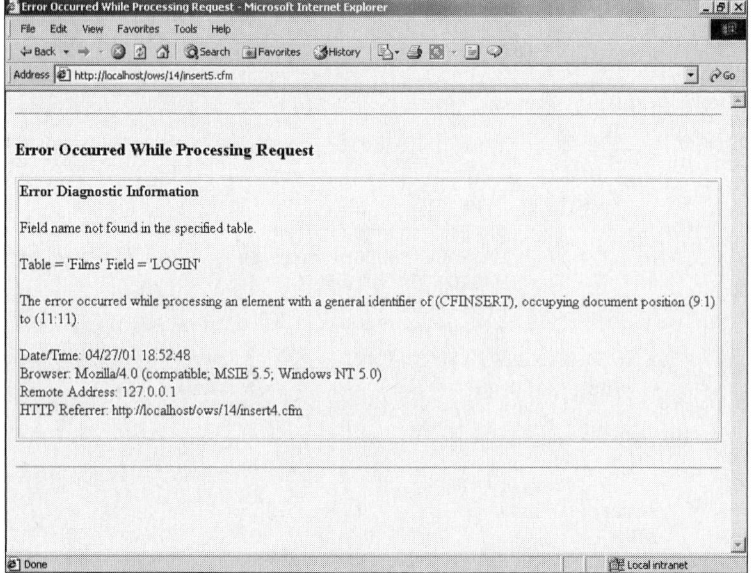

Figure 14.3 A ODBC error message is generated if ColdFusion tries to insert fields that are not table columns.

To solve this problem, you must use the `FORMFIELDS` attribute. `FORMFIELDS` instructs ColdFusion to process only form fields that are in the list. Any other fields are ignored.

It is important to note that `FORMFIELDS` is not used to specify which fields ColdFusion should process. Rather, it specifies which fields should *not* be processed. The difference is subtle. Not all fields listed in the `FORMFIELDS` value need be present. They are processed *if* they are present; if they are not present, they are not processed (so no error will be generated). Any fields not listed in the `FORMFIELDS` list are completely ignored.

Listing 14.7 contains an updated data insertion template. The `<CFINSERT>` tag now has a `FORMFIELDS` attribute, so now ColdFusion knows to ignore the hidden `Login` field in `insetr4.cfm`.

LISTING 14.7 insert5.cfm—USING THE <CFINSERT> FORMFIELDS ATTRIBUTE TO SPECIFY WHICH FIELDS TO AVOID PROCESSING

```
<!---
Name:        insert5.cfm
Author:      Ben Forta (ben@forta.com)
Description: Table row insertion demo
Created:     4/20/01
--->

<!--- Insert movie --->
<CFINSERT DATASOURCE="ows"
          TABLENAME="Films"
          FORMFIELDS="MovieTitle,PitchText,AmountBudgeted,
➥RatingID,Summary,ImageName,DateInTheaters">

<!--- Page header --->
<CFINCLUDE TEMPLATE="header.cfm">

<!--- Feedback --->
<CFOUTPUT>
<H1>New movie #FORM.MovieTitle# added</H1>
</CFOUTPUT>

<!--- Page footer --->
<CFINCLUDE TEMPLATE="footer.cfm">
```

COLLECTING DATA FOR MORE THAN ONE INSERT

Another situation in which <CFINSERT> FORMFIELDS can be used is when a form collects data that needs to be added to more than one table. You can create a template that has two or more <CFINSERT> statements by using FORMFIELDS.

As long as each <CFINSERT> statement has a FORMFIELDS attribute that specifies which fields are to be used with each INSERT, ColdFusion correctly executes each <CFINSERT> with its appropriate fields.

<CFINSERT> VERSUS SQL INSERT

Adding data to tables using the ColdFusion <CFINSERT> tag is simpler and helps prevent the creation of multiple similar templates.

Why would you ever avoid using <CFINSERT>? Is there ever a reason to use SQL INSERT instead of <CFINSERT>?

The truth is that both are needed. <CFINSERT> can be used only for simple data insertion to a single table. If you want to insert the results of a SELECT statement, you could not use <CFINSERT>. Similarly, if you want to insert values other than FORM fields—perhaps variables or URL parameters—you'd be unable to use <CFINSERT>.

Here are some guidelines to help you decide when to use each method:

- Whenever possible, use `<CFINSERT>` to add data to ODBC tables.
- If you find that you need to add specific form fields—and not all that were submitted—use the `<CFINSERT>` tag with the `FORMFIELDS` attribute.
- If `<CFINSERT>` cannot be used because you need a complex `INSERT` statement or are using fields that are not form fields, use SQL `INSERT`.

UPDATING DATA WITH COLDFUSION

Updating data with ColdFusion is similar to inserting data. You generally need two templates to update a row—a data-entry form template and a data update template. The big difference between a form used for data addition and one used for data modification is that the latter needs to be populated with existing values, similar to the screen shown in Figure 14.4.

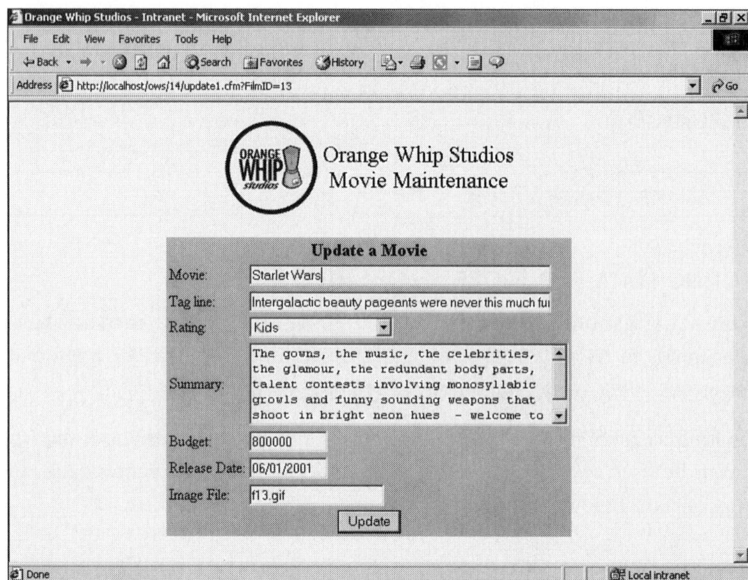

Figure 14.4
When using forms to update data, the form fields usually need to populated with existing values.

BUILDING A DATA UPDATE FORM

Populating an HTML form is a simple process. First, you must retrieve the row to be updated from the table. You do this with a standard `<CFQUERY>`; the retrieved values are then passed as attributes to the HTML form.

Listing 14.8 contains the code for `update1.cfm`, a template that updates a movie. Save it as `update1.cfm`, and then execute it. Be sure to append the `FilmID`—for example, `?FilmID=13`—as a `URL` parameter. Your screen should look similar to the one shown in Figure 14.4.

Listing 14.8 update1.cfm—Movie Update Form

```
<!---
Name:        update1.cfm
Author:      Ben Forta (ben@forta.com)
Description: Table row update demo
Created:     4/20/01
--->

<!--- Check that FilmID was provided --->
<CFIF NOT IsDefined("URL.FilmID")>
 <H1>You did not specify the FilmID</H1>
 <CFABORT>
</CFIF>

<!--- Get the film record --->
<CFQUERY DATASOURCE="ows" NAME="film">
SELECT FilmID, MovieTitle, PitchText,
       AmountBudgeted, RatingID,
       Summary, ImageName, DateInTheaters
FROM Films
WHERE FilmID=#URL.FilmID#
</CFQUERY>

<!--- Get ratings --->
<CFQUERY DATASOURCE="ows" NAME="ratings">
SELECT RatingID, Rating
FROM FilmsRatings
ORDER BY RatingID
</CFQUERY>

<!--- Page header --->
<CFINCLUDE TEMPLATE="header.cfm">

<!--- Update movie form --->
<CFFORM ACTION="update2.cfm">

<!--- Embed primary key as a hidden field --->
<CFOUTPUT>
<INPUT TYPE="hidden" NAME="FilmID" VALUE="#Film.FilmID#">
</CFOUTPUT>

<TABLE ALIGN="center" BGCOLOR="orange">
    <TR>
        <TH COLSPAN="2">
            <FONT SIZE="+1">Update a Movie</FONT>
        </TH>
    </TR>
    <TR>
        <TD>
            Movie:
        </TD>
        <TD>
            <CFINPUT TYPE="Text"
                     NAME="MovieTitle"
                     VALUE="#Trim(film.MovieTitle)#"
                     MESSAGE="MOVIE TITLE is required!"
                     REQUIRED="Yes"
```

Listing 14.8 Continued

```
                    SIZE="50"
                    MAXLENGTH="100">
        </TD>
    </TR>
    <TR>
        <TD>
            Tag line:
        </TD>
        <TD>
            <CFINPUT TYPE="Text"
                    NAME="PitchText"
                    VALUE="#Trim(film.PitchText)#"
                    MESSAGE="TAG LINE is required!"
                    REQUIRED="Yes"
                    SIZE="50"
                    MAXLENGTH="100">
        </TD>
    </TR>
    <TR>
        <TD>
            Rating:
        </TD>
        <TD>
            <!--- Ratings list --->
            <SELECT NAME="RatingID">
                <CFOUTPUT QUERY="ratings">
                    <OPTION VALUE="#RatingID#"
➥<CFIF ratings.RatingID IS film.RatingID>SELECTED</CFIF>>#Rating#</OPTION>
                </CFOUTPUT>
            </SELECT>
        </TD>
    </TR>
    <TR>
        <TD>
            Summary:
        </TD>
        <TD>
            <CFOUTPUT>
            <TEXTAREA NAME="summary"
                     COLS="40"
                     ROWS="5"
                     WRAP="virtual">#Trim(Film.Summary)#</TEXTAREA>
            </CFOUTPUT>
        </TD>
    </TR>
    <TR>
        <TD>
            Budget:
        </TD>
        <TD>
            <CFINPUT TYPE="Text"
                    NAME="AmountBudgeted"
                    VALUE="#Int(film.AmountBudgeted)#"
                    MESSAGE="BUDGET must be a valid numeric amount!"
                    VALIDATE="integer"
                    REQUIRED="NO"
```

```
                        SIZE="10"
                        MAXLENGTH="10">
            </TD>
        </TR>
        <TR>
            <TD>
                Release Date:
            </TD>
            <TD>
                <CFINPUT TYPE="Text"
                        NAME="DateInTheaters"
                        VALUE="#DateFormat(film.DateInTheaters, "MM/DD/YYYY")#"
                        MESSAGE="RELEASE DATE must be a valid date!"
                        VALIDATE="date"
                        REQUIRED="NO"
                        SIZE="10"
                        MAXLENGTH="10">
            </TD>
        </TR>
        <TR>
            <TD>
                Image File:
            </TD>
            <TD>
                <CFINPUT TYPE="Text"
                        NAME="ImageName"
                        VALUE="#Trim(film.ImageName)#"
                        REQUIRED="NO"
                        SIZE="20"
                        MAXLENGTH="50">
            </TD>
        </TR>
        <TR>
            <TD COLSPAN="2" ALIGN="center">
                <INPUT TYPE="submit" VALUE="Update">
            </TD>
        </TR>
</TABLE>

</CFFORM>

<!--- Page footer --->
<CFINCLUDE TEMPLATE="footer.cfm">
```

There is a lot to look at in Listing 14.8. And don't submit the form yet; you have yet to create the `ACTION` page.

To populate a form with data to be updated, you must first retrieve that row from the table. Therefore, you must specify a `FilmID` to use this template. Without it, ColdFusion would not know which row to retrieve. To ensure that the `FilmID` is passed, the first thing you do is check for the existence of the `FilmID` parameter. The following code returns `TRUE` only if `FilmID` was not passed, in which case an error message is sent back to the user and template processing is halted with the `<CFABORT>` tag:

```
<CFIF NOT IsDefined("URL.FilmID")>
```

Without the `<CFABORT>` tag, ColdFusion continues processing the template. An error message is generated when the `<CFQUERY>` statement is processed because the `WHERE` clause `WHERE FilmID = #URL.FilmID#` references a nonexistent field.

The first `<CFQUERY>` tag retrieves the row to be edited, and the passed URL is used in the `WHERE` clause to retrieve the appropriate row. The second `<CFQUERY>` retrieves the list of ratings for the `<SELECT>` control. To populate the data-entry fields, the current field value is passed to the `<INPUT>` (or `<CFINPUT>`) `VALUE` attribute. Whatever is passed to `VALUE` is displayed in the field, so `VALUE="#Film.MovieTitle#"` displays the `MovieTitle` table column.

Note

The query name is necessary here as a prefix because it is not being used within a `<CFOUTPUT>` associated with a query.

Note

`<CFINPUT>` is a ColdFusion tag, so you can pass variables and columns to it without needing to use `<CFOUTPUT>`. If you were using `<INPUT>` instead of `<CFINPUT>` then the `<INPUT>` tags would need to be within a `<CFOUTPUT>` block.

This is actually another benefit of using `<CFINPUT>` instead of `<INPUT>`—`<CFINPUT>` makes populating form fields with dynamic data much easier.

To ensure that no blank spaces exist after the retrieved value, the fields are trimmed with the ColdFusion `Trim()` function before they are displayed. Why would you do this? Some databases, such as Microsoft SQL Server, pad text fields with spaces so they take up the full column width in the table. The `MovieTitle` field is a 255-character–wide column, so a movie title could have a lot of spaces after it. The extra space can be very annoying when you try to edit the field. To append text to a field, you'd first have to backspace or delete all those extra characters.

Tip

When populating forms with table column values, you always should trim the field first. Unlike standard browser output, spaces in form fields are not ignored. Removing them allows easier editing. The ColdFusion `Trim()` function removes spaces at the beginning and end of the value. If you want to trim only trailing spaces, you could use the `RTrim()` function instead. See Appendix B, "ColdFusion Function Reference," for a complete explanation of the ColdFusion `Trim()` functions.

Dates and numbers are also being formatted specially. By default, dates are displayed in a rather unusable format (and a format that will not be accepted upon form submission). Therefore, `DateFormat()` is used to format the date in a usable format.

The `AmountBudgeted` column allows numbers with decimal points; to display the number within the trailing decimal point and zeros, the `Int()` function can be used to round the number to an integer. You also could have used `NumberFormat()` for more precise number formatting.

One hidden field exists in the FORM. The following code creates a hidden field called FilmID, which contains the ID of the movie being updated:

```
<INPUT TYPE="hidden" NAME="FilmID" VALUE="#Film.FilmID#">
```

This hidden field must be present. Without it, ColdFusion has no idea which row you were updating when the form was actually submitted. Also, because it is an <INPUT> field (not <CFINPUT>), it must be enclosed within <CFOUTPUT> tags.

Remember that HTTP sessions are created and broken as necessary, and every session stands on its own two feet. ColdFusion might retrieve a specific row of data for you in one session, but it does not know that in the next session. Therefore, when you update a row, you must specify the primary key so ColdFusion knows which row to update. Hidden fields are one way of doing this because they are sent to the browser as part of the form, but they are never displayed and thus cannot be edited. However, they are still form fields, and they are submitted along with all other form fields intact upon form submission.

PROCESSING UPDATES

Just as with adding data, there are two ways to update rows in a table. The code in Listing 14.9 demonstrates a row update using the SQL UPDATE statement.

Note See Chapter 7 for an explanation of the UPDATE statement.

LISTING 14.9 update2.cfm—UPDATING A TABLE WITH THE SQL UPDATE STATEMENT

```
<!---
Name:        update2.cfm
Author:      Ben Forta (ben@forta.com)
Description: Table row update demo
Created:     4/20/01
--->

<!--- Update movie --->
<CFQUERY DATASOURCE="ows">
UPDATE Films
SET MovieTitle='#Trim(FORM.MovieTitle)#',
    PitchText='#Trim(FORM.PitchText)#',
    AmountBudgeted=#FORM.AmountBudgeted#,
    RatingID=#FORM.RatingID#,
    Summary='#Trim(FORM.Summary)#',
    ImageName='#Trim(FORM.ImageName)#',
    DateInTheaters=#CreateODBCDate(FORM.DateInTheaters)#
WHERE FilmID=#FORM.FilmID#
</CFQUERY>

<!--- Page header --->
<CFINCLUDE TEMPLATE="header.cfm">

<!--- Feedback --->
<CFOUTPUT>
<H1>Movie #FORM.MovieTitle# updated</H1>
```

Listing 14.9 Continued

```
</CFOUTPUT>

<!--- Page footer --->
<CFINCLUDE TEMPLATE="footer.cfm">
```

This SQL statement updates the seven specified rows for the movie whose ID is the passed `FORM.FilmID`.

To test this update template, try executing template `update1.cfm` with different `FilmID` values (passed as URL parameters), and then submit your changes.

Introducing <CFUPDATE>

Just as you saw earlier in regards to inserting data, hard-coded SQL statements are neither flexible nor easy to maintain. ColdFusion provides a simpler way to update rows in database tables.

The `<CFUPDATE>` tag is similar to the `<CFINSERT>` tag discussed earlier in this chapter. `<CFUPDATE>` requires just two attributes: the ODBC data source and the name of the table to update.

Just like `<CFINSERT>`, the following attributes are available to you:

- `DATASOURCE`—The name of the ODBC data source that contains the table to which the data is to be updated.
- `TABLENAME`—The name of the destination table.
- `FORMFIELDS`—An optional comma-separated list of fields to be updated. If this attribute is not provided, all the fields in the submitted form are used.

When using `<CFUPDATE>`, ColdFusion automatically locates the row you want to update by looking at the table to ascertain its primary key. All you have to do is ensure that the primary key value is passed, as you did in Listing 14.8 using a hidden field.

The code in Listing 14.10 performs the same update as that in Listing 14.9, but it uses the `<CFUPDATE>` tag rather than the SQL `UPDATE` tag. Obviously, this code is more readable, reusable, and accommodating of form-field changes you might make in the future.

Listing 14.10 `update3.cfm`—Updating Data with the `CFUPDATE` Tag

```
<!---
Name:        update3.cfm
Author:      Ben Forta (ben@forta.com)
Description: Table row update demo
Created:     4/20/01
--->

<!--- Update movie --->
<CFUPDATE DATASOURCE="ows" TABLENAME="Films">
```

```
<!--- Page header --->
<CFINCLUDE TEMPLATE="header.cfm">

<!--- Feedback --->
<CFOUTPUT>
<H1>Movie #FORM.MovieTitle# updated</H1>
</CFOUTPUT>

<!--- Page footer --->
<CFINCLUDE TEMPLATE="footer.cfm">
```

To use this code, you must change the <FORM> ACTION attribute in update1.cfm so that it points to update3.cfm. Make this change, and try updating several movies.

<CFUPDATE> Versus SQL UPDATE

Just as with adding data, the choice to use <CFUPDATE> or SQL UPDATE is yours. The guidelines as to when to use each option are similar as well.

The following are some guidelines that help you decide when to use each method:

- Whenever possible, use <CFUPDATE> to update data to ODBC tables.
- If you find that you need to update specific form fields—not all that were submitted—use the <CFUPDATE> tag with the FORMFIELDS attribute.
- If <CFUPDATE> can't be used because you need a complex UPDATE statement or you are using fields that are not form fields, use SQL UPDATE.
- If you ever need to update all rows in a table, you must use SQL UPDATE.

Deleting Data with ColdFusion

Unlike adding and updating data, ColdFusion provides no efficient way to delete data. DELETE is always a dangerous operation, and the ColdFusion developers didn't want to make it too easy to get rid of the wrong data.

To delete data in a ColdFusion template, you must use the SQL DELETE statement, as shown in Listing 14.11. The code first checks to ensure that a FilmID was passed; it terminates if the URL.FilmID field is not present. If a FilmID is passed, a <CFQUERY> is used to pass a SQL DELETE statement to the ODBC data source.

Note

See Chapter 7 for an explanation of the DELETE statement.

Listing 14.11 delete1—Deleting Table Data with the SQL DELETE Statement

```
<!---
Name:        delete1.cfm
Author:      Ben Forta (ben@forta.com)
```

LISTING 14.11 CONTINUED

```
Description: Table row delete demo
Created:     4/20/01
--->

<!--- Check that FilmID was provided --->
<CFIF NOT IsDefined("FilmID")>
 <H1>You did not specify the FilmID</H1>
 <CFABORT>
</CFIF>

<!--- Delete a movie --->
<CFQUERY DATASOURCE="ows">
DELETE FROM Films
WHERE FilmID=#FilmID#
</CFQUERY>

<!--- Page header --->
<CFINCLUDE TEMPLATE="header.cfm">

<!--- Feedback --->
<H1>Movie deleted</H1>

<!--- Page footer --->
<CFINCLUDE TEMPLATE="footer.cfm">
```

No `<CFDELETE>` tag exists in ColdFusion. The only way to delete rows is using a SQL `DELETE`.

REUSING FORMS

You can now add to as well as update and delete from your `Films` table. But what if you need to change the form? What if you needed to add a field, or change validation, or update colors? Any changed needed to be made to the Add form also must be made to the Update form.

With all the effort you have gone to in the past few chapters to prevent any duplication of effort, this seems counterproductive.

Indeed it is.

The big difference between an Add and an Update form is whether the fields are prefilled to show current values. Using ColdFusion conditional expressions, you can create a single form that can be used for both adding and updating data.

To do this, all you need is a way to conditionally include the `VALUE` attribute in `<INPUT>`. After all, look at the following two `<INPUT>` statements:

```
<INPUT TYPE="text" NAME="MovieTitle">
<INPUT TYPE="text" NAME="MovieTitle" VALUE="#MovieTitle#">
```

The first `<INPUT>` is used for new data; there is no prefilled `VALUE`. The second is for editing, and thus the field is populated with an initial `VALUE`.

It would therefore not be difficult to create <INPUT> fields with <CFIF> statements embedded in them, conditionally including the VALUE. Look at the following code:

```
<INPUT TYPE="text" NAME="MovieTitle"
    <CFIF IsDefined("URL.FilmID")>
        VALUE="#MovieTitle#"
    </CFIF>
>
```

This <INPUT> field includes the VALUE attribute only if the FilmID was passed (meaning that this is an edit operation as opposed to an add operation). Using this technique, a single form field can be used for both adds and edits.

This is perfectly valid code, and this technique is quite popular. The only problem with it is that the code can get very difficult to read. All those embedded <CFIF> statements, one for every row, make the code quite complex. There is a better solution.

VALUE can be empty: The attribute VALUE="" is perfectly legal and valid. So why not *always* use VALUE, but conditionally populate it? The best way to demonstrate this is to try it, so Listing 14.12 contains the code for edit1.cfm—a new dual purpose form.

Listing 14.12 edit1.cfm—Combination Insert and Update Form

```
<!---
Name:        edit1.cfm
Author:      Ben Forta (ben@forta.com)
Description: Dual purpose form demo
Created:     4/20/01
--->

<!--- Check that FilmID was provided --->
<!--- If yes, edit, else add --->
<CFSET EditMode=IsDefined("URL.FilmID")>

<!--- If edit mode then get row to edit --->
<CFIF EditMode>

    <!--- Get the film record --->
    <CFQUERY DATASOURCE="ows" NAME="film">
    SELECT FilmID, MovieTitle, PitchText,
           AmountBudgeted, RatingID,
           Summary, ImageName, DateInTheaters
    FROM Films
    WHERE FilmID=#URL.FilmID#
    </CFQUERY>

    <!--- Save to variables --->
    <CFSET MovieTitle=Trim(film.MovieTitle)>
    <CFSET PitchText=Trim(film.PitchText)>
    <CFSET AmountBudgeted=Int(film.AmountBudgeted)>
    <CFSET RatingID=film.RatingID>
    <CFSET Summary=Trim(film.Summary)>
    <CFSET ImageName=Trim(film.ImageName)>
    <CFSET DateInTheaters=DateFormat(film.DateInTheaters, "MM/DD/YYYY")>

    <!--- Form text --->
```

LISTING 14.12 CONTINUED

```
    <CFSET FormTitle="Update a Movie">
    <CFSET ButtonText="Update">

<CFELSE>

    <!--- Save to variables --->
    <CFSET MovieTitle="">
    <CFSET PitchText="">
    <CFSET AmountBudgeted="">
    <CFSET RatingID="">
    <CFSET Summary="">
    <CFSET ImageName="">
    <CFSET DateInTheaters="">

    <!--- Form text --->
    <CFSET FormTitle="Add a Movie">
    <CFSET ButtonText="Insert">

</CFIF>

<!--- Get ratings --->
<CFQUERY DATASOURCE="ows" NAME="ratings">
SELECT RatingID, Rating
FROM FilmsRatings
ORDER BY RatingID
</CFQUERY>

<!--- Page header --->
<CFINCLUDE TEMPLATE="header.cfm">

<!--- Add/update movie form --->
<CFFORM ACTION="edit2.cfm">

<CFIF EditMode>
    <!--- Embed primary key as a hidden field --->
    <CFOUTPUT>
    <INPUT TYPE="hidden" NAME="FilmID" VALUE="#Film.FilmID#">
    </CFOUTPUT>
</CFIF>

<TABLE ALIGN="center" BGCOLOR="orange">
    <TR>
        <TH COLSPAN="2">
            <CFOUTPUT>
            <FONT SIZE="+1">#FormTitle#</FONT>
            </CFOUTPUT>
        </TH>
    </TR>
    <TR>
        <TD>
            Movie:
        </TD>
        <TD>
            <CFINPUT TYPE="Text"
                     NAME="MovieTitle"
                     VALUE="#MovieTitle#"
```

```
                        MESSAGE="MOVIE TITLE is required!"
                        REQUIRED="Yes"
                        SIZE="50"
                        MAXLENGTH="100">
            </TD>
        </TR>
        <TR>
            <TD>
                Tag line:
            </TD>
            <TD>
                <CFINPUT TYPE="Text"
                        NAME="PitchText"
                        VALUE="#PitchText#"
                        MESSAGE="TAG LINE is required!"
                        REQUIRED="Yes"
                        SIZE="50"
                        MAXLENGTH="100">
            </TD>
        </TR>
        <TR>
            <TD>
                Rating:
            </TD>
            <TD>
                <!--- Ratings list --->
                <SELECT NAME="RatingID">
                    <CFOUTPUT QUERY="ratings">
                        <OPTION VALUE="#RatingID#" <CFIF ratings.RatingID
➥IS VARIABLES.RatingID>SELECTED</CFIF>>#Rating#</OPTION>
                    </CFOUTPUT>
                </SELECT>
            </TD>
        </TR>
        <TR>
            <TD>
                Summary:
            </TD>
            <TD>
                <CFOUTPUT>
                <TEXTAREA NAME="summary"
                         COLS="40"
                         ROWS="5"
                         WRAP="virtual">#Summary#</TEXTAREA>
                </CFOUTPUT>
            </TD>
        </TR>
        <TR>
            <TD>
                Budget:
            </TD>
            <TD>
                <CFINPUT TYPE="Text"
                        NAME="AmountBudgeted"
                        VALUE="#AmountBudgeted#"
                        MESSAGE="BUDGET must be a valid numeric amount!"
                        VALIDATE="integer"
                        REQUIRED="NO"
```

LISTING 14.12 CONTINUED

```
                      SIZE="10"
                      MAXLENGTH="10">
      </TD>
   </TR>
   <TR>
      <TD>
         Release Date:
      </TD>
      <TD>
         <CFINPUT TYPE="Text"
                      NAME="DateInTheaters"
                      VALUE="#DateInTheaters#"
                      MESSAGE="RELEASE DATE must be a valid date!"
                      VALIDATE="date"
                      REQUIRED="NO"
                      SIZE="10"
                      MAXLENGTH="10">
      </TD>
   </TR>
   <TR>
      <TD>
         Image File:
      </TD>
      <TD>
         <CFINPUT TYPE="Text"
                      NAME="ImageName"
                      VALUE="#ImageName#"
                      REQUIRED="NO"
                      SIZE="20"
                      MAXLENGTH="50">
      </TD>
   </TR>
   <TR>
      <TD COLSPAN="2" ALIGN="center">
         <CFOUTPUT>
         <INPUT TYPE="submit" VALUE="#ButtonText#">
         </CFOUTPUT>
      </TD>
  </TR>
</TABLE>

</CFFORM>

<!--- Page footer --->
<CFINCLUDE TEMPLATE="footer.cfm">
```

The code first determines whether the form will be used for an Add or an Update. How can it know this? The difference between how the two are called is in the URL—whether `FilmID` is passed. The code `<CFSET EditMode=IsDefined("URL.FilmID")>` created a variable named `EditMode`, which will be `TRUE` if `URL.FilmID` exists and `FALSE` if not. This variable can now be used as necessary throughout the page.

Next comes a `<CFIF>` statement. If editing (`EditMode` is `TRUE`) then a `<CFQUERY>` is used to retrieve the current values. The fields retrieved by that `<CFQUERY>` are saved in local variables using multiple <CFSET> tags. No <CFQUERY> is used if it is an insert operation, but <CFSET> is used to create empty variables.

By the time the </CFIF> has been reached, a set of variables have been created. They'll either contain values (from the Films table) or be empty. But either way, they are usable as VALUE attributes in <INPUT> and <CFINPUT> tags.

Look at the <CFINPUT> fields themselves. You'll notice that no conditional code exists within them as did before. Instead, every <INPUT> tag has a VALUE attribute regardless of whether this is an insert or an update. The value in the VALUE attribute is a ColdFusion variable—a variable that is set at the top of the template, not a database field.

The rest of the code in the template uses these variables, without needing any conditional processing. Even the page title and Submit button text can be initialized in variables this way, so <CFIF> tags are not necessary for them, either.

The primary key, embedded as a hidden field, is necessary only if a movie is being edited, so the code to embed that field is enclosed within a <CFIF> statement:

```
<CFIF EditMode>
    <!--- Embed primary key as a hidden field --->
    <CFOUTPUT>
    <INPUT TYPE="hidden" NAME="FilmID" VALUE="#Film.FilmID#">
    </CFOUTPUT>
</CFIF>
```

Even the form header (at the top of the page) and the text of the Submit button are populated using variables. This way the <FORM> is completely reusable:

```
<INPUT TYPE="submit" VALUE="#ButtonText#">
```

This form is submitted to the same ACTION page regardless of whether data is being added or updated. Therefore, the ACTION page also must support both additions and updates. Listing 14.13 contains the new ACTION template, edit2.cfm.

Listing 14.13 edit2.cfm—Combination Insert and Update Page

```
<!---
Name:        edit2.cfm
Author:      Ben Forta (ben@forta.com)
Description: Dual purpose form demo
Created:     4/20/01
--->

<CFSET EditMode=IsDefined("FORM.FilmID")>

<CFIF EditMode>
    <!--- Update movie --->
    <CFUPDATE DATASOURCE="ows" TABLENAME="Films">
    <CFSET action="updated">
<CFELSE>
    <!--- Add movie --->
    <CFINSERT DATASOURCE="ows" TABLENAME="Films">
    <CFSET action="added">
</CFIF>
```

Listing 14.13 Continued

```
<!--- Page header --->
<CFINCLUDE TEMPLATE="header.cfm">

<!--- Feedback --->
<CFOUTPUT>
<H1>Movie #FORM.MovieTitle# #action#</H1>
</CFOUTPUT>

<!--- Page footer --->
<CFINCLUDE TEMPLATE="footer.cfm">
```

This code also first determines the `EditMode`—this time by checking for a `FORM` field named `FilmID` (the hidden form field). If `EditMode` is `TRUE`, a `<CFUPDATE>` is used to update the row; otherwise, a `<CFINSERT>` is used to insert it. The same `<CFIF>` statements also is used to set a variable that is used later in the page when providing user feedback.

It's clean, simple, and reusable.

Creating a Complete Application

Now that you've created add, modify, and delete templates, let's put it all together and create a finished application.

The following templates are a combination of all you have learned in this and previous chapters.

The template shown in Listing 14.14 is the main movie maintenance page. It displays all the movies in the `Films` table and provides links to edit and delete them (using the data drill-down techniques discussed in previous chapters); it also has a link to add a new movie. The administration page is shown in Figure 14.5.

Listing 14.14 `movies.cfm`—Movie List Maintenance Page

```
<!---
Name:        movies.cfm
Author:      Ben Forta (ben@forta.com)
Description: Movie maintenance application
Created:     4/20/01
--->

<!--- Get all movies --->
<CFQUERY DATASOURCE="ows" NAME="movies">
SELECT FilmID, MovieTitle
FROM Films
ORDER BY MovieTitle
</CFQUERY>

<!--- Page header --->
<CFINCLUDE TEMPLATE="header.cfm">

<TABLE ALIGN="center" BGCOLOR="orange">
```

```
    <!--- Loop through movies --->
    <CFOUTPUT QUERY="movies">
        <TR>
            <!--- Movie name --->
            <TD><B>#MovieTitle#</B></TD>
            <!--- Edit link --->
            <TD><A HREF="edit3.cfm?FilmID=#FilmID#">[Edit]</A></TD>
            <!--- Delete link --->
            <TD><A HREF="delete2.cfm?FilmID=#FilmID#"">[Delete]</A></TD>
        </TR>
    </CFOUTPUT>

    <TR>
        <TD></TD>
        <!--- Add movie link --->
        <TD COLSPAN="2" ALIGN="center"><A HREF="edit3.cfm">[Add]</A></TD>
    </TR>

</TABLE>

<!--- Page footer --->
<CFINCLUDE TEMPLATE="footer.cfm">
```

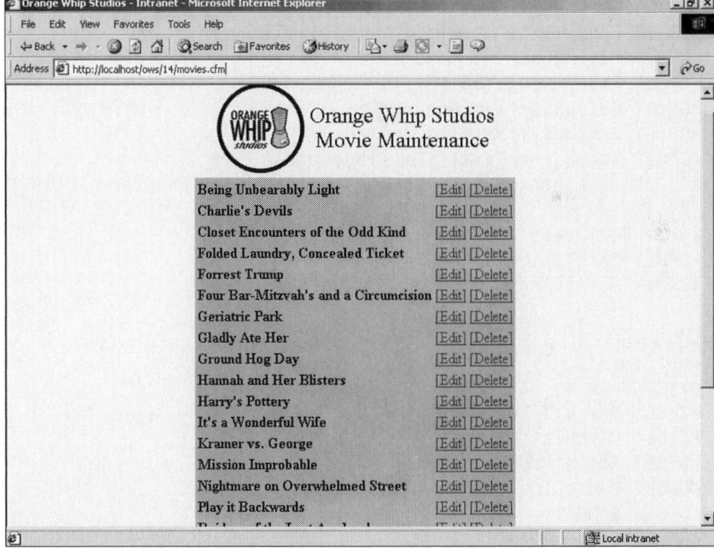

Figure 14.5
The movie administration page is used to add, edit, and delete movies.

Listing 14.14 has two links for each movie, an edit link (that links to `edit3.cfm` passing the `FilmID`) and a delete link (`delete2.cfm`, also passing the `FilmID`). The add link at the bottom of the page also points to `edit3.cfm` but does not pass a `FilmID` (so the form will be used as an add form).

Listing 14.15 is essentially the same reusable add and update form you created earlier.

Listing 14.15 `edit3.cfm`—**Movie Add and Update Form**

```
<!---
Name:        edit3.cfm
Author:      Ben Forta (ben@forta.com)
Description: Dual purpose movie edit form
Created:     4/20/01
--->

<!--- Check that FilmID was provided --->
<!--- If yes, edit, else add --->
<CFSET EditMode=IsDefined("URL.FilmID")>

<!--- If edit mode then get row to edit --->
<CFIF EditMode>

    <!--- Get the film record --->
    <CFQUERY DATASOURCE="ows" NAME="film">
    SELECT FilmID, MovieTitle, PitchText,
           AmountBudgeted, RatingID,
           Summary, ImageName, DateInTheaters
    FROM Films
    WHERE FilmID=#URL.FilmID#
    </CFQUERY>

    <!--- Save to variables --->
    <CFSET MovieTitle=Trim(film.MovieTitle)>
    <CFSET PitchText=Trim(film.PitchText)>
    <CFSET AmountBudgeted=Int(film.AmountBudgeted)>
    <CFSET RatingID=film.RatingID>
    <CFSET Summary=Trim(film.Summary)>
    <CFSET ImageName=Trim(film.ImageName)>
    <CFSET DateInTheaters=DateFormat(film.DateInTheaters, "MM/DD/YYYY")>

    <!--- Form text --->
    <CFSET FormTitle="Update a Movie">
    <CFSET ButtonText="Update">

<CFELSE>

    <!--- Save to variables --->
    <CFSET MovieTitle="">
    <CFSET PitchText="">
    <CFSET AmountBudgeted="">
    <CFSET RatingID="">
    <CFSET Summary="">
    <CFSET ImageName="">
    <CFSET DateInTheaters="">

    <!--- Form text --->
    <CFSET FormTitle="Add a Movie">
    <CFSET ButtonText="Insert">

</CFIF>

<!--- Get ratings --->
<CFQUERY DATASOURCE="ows" NAME="ratings">
SELECT RatingID, Rating
```

```
FROM FilmsRatings
ORDER BY RatingID
</CFQUERY>

<!--- Page header --->
<CFINCLUDE TEMPLATE="header.cfm">

<!--- Add/update movie form --->
<CFFORM ACTION="edit4.cfm">

<CFIF EditMode>
    <!--- Embed primary key as a hidden field --->
    <CFOUTPUT>
    <INPUT TYPE="hidden" NAME="FilmID" VALUE="#Film.FilmID#">
    </CFOUTPUT>
</CFIF>

<TABLE ALIGN="center" BGCOLOR="orange">
    <TR>
        <TH COLSPAN="2">
            <CFOUTPUT>
            <FONT SIZE="+1">#FormTitle#</FONT>
            </CFOUTPUT>
        </TH>
    </TR>
    <TR>
        <TD>
            Movie:
        </TD>
        <TD>
            <CFINPUT TYPE="Text"
                     NAME="MovieTitle"
                     VALUE="#MovieTitle#"
                     MESSAGE="MOVIE TITLE is required!"
                     REQUIRED="Yes"
                     SIZE="50"
                     MAXLENGTH="100">
        </TD>
    </TR>
    <TR>
        <TD>
            Tag line:
        </TD>
        <TD>
            <CFINPUT TYPE="Text"
                     NAME="PitchText"
                     VALUE="#PitchText#"
                     MESSAGE="TAG LINE is required!"
                     REQUIRED="Yes"
                     SIZE="50"
                     MAXLENGTH="100">
        </TD>
    </TR>
    <TR>
        <TD>
            Rating:
        </TD>
        <TD>
```

LISTING 14.15 CONTINUED

```
            <!--- Ratings list --->
            <CFSELECT NAME="RatingID"
                      QUERY="ratings"
                      VALUE="RatingID"
                      DISPLAY="Rating"
                      SELECTED="#VARIABLES.RatingID#">
            </CFSELECT>
        </TD>
    </TR>
    <TR>
        <TD>
            Summary:
        </TD>
        <TD>
            <CFOUTPUT>
            <TEXTAREA NAME="summary"
                      COLS="40"
                      ROWS="5"
                      WRAP="virtual">#Summary#</TEXTAREA>
            </CFOUTPUT>
        </TD>
    </TR>
    <TR>
        <TD>
            Budget:
        </TD>
        <TD>
            <CFINPUT TYPE="Text"
                     NAME="AmountBudgeted"
                     VALUE="#AmountBudgeted#"
                     MESSAGE="BUDGET must be a valid numeric amount!"
                     VALIDATE="integer"
                     REQUIRED="NO"
                     SIZE="10"
                     MAXLENGTH="10">
        </TD>
    </TR>
    <TR>
        <TD>
            Release Date:
        </TD>
        <TD>
            <CFINPUT TYPE="Text"
                     NAME="DateInTheaters"
                     VALUE="#DateInTheaters#"
                     MESSAGE="RELEASE DATE must be a valid date!"
                     VALIDATE="date"
                     REQUIRED="NO"
                     SIZE="10"
                     MAXLENGTH="10">
        </TD>
    </TR>
    <TR>
        <TD>
            Image File:
        </TD>
```

```
        <TD>
            <CFINPUT TYPE="Text"
                     NAME="ImageName"
                     VALUE="#ImageName#"
                     REQUIRED="NO"
                     SIZE="20"
                     MAXLENGTH="50">
        </TD>
    </TR>
    <TR>
        <TD COLSPAN="2" ALIGN="center">
            <CFOUTPUT>
            <INPUT TYPE="submit" VALUE="#ButtonText#">
            </CFOUTPUT>
        </TD>
   </TR>
</TABLE>

</CFFORM>

<!--- Page footer --->
<CFINCLUDE TEMPLATE="footer.cfm">
```

There are only two changes in `edit3.cfm`. The `ACTION` has been changed to point to a new file—`edit4.cfm`. In addition, look at the `RatingID` field. It uses a new tag named `<CFSELECT>`. This tag, which can be used only within `<CFFORM>` and `</CFFORM>` tags, simplifies the creation of dynamic data-driven `<SELECT>` controls. The code

```
<CFSELECT NAME="RatingID"
          QUERY="ratings"
          VALUE="RatingID"
          DISPLAY="Rating"
          SELECTED="#VARIABLES.RatingID#">
</CFSELECT>
```

is functionally the same as

```
<SELECT NAME="RatingID">
    <CFOUTPUT QUERY="ratings">
        <OPTION VALUE="#RatingID#" <CFIF ratings.RatingID
➥IS VARIABLES.RatingID>SELECTED</CFIF>>#Rating#</OPTION>
    </CFOUTPUT>
</SELECT>
```

Obviously, the `<CFSELECT>` is much cleaner and simpler. It creates a `<SELECT>` control named `RatingID` that is populated with the `ratings` query, using the `RatingID` column as the value and displaying the `Rating` column. Whatever value is in the variable `RatingID` will be used to preselect the selected option in the control.

Listings 14.16 and 14.17 perform the actual data insertions, updates, and deletions. The big change in these templates is that they themselves provide no user feedback at all. Instead, they return to the administration screen using the `<CFLOCATION>` tag as soon as they finish processing the database changes. `<CFLOCATION>` is used to switch from the current template being processed to any other URL, including another ColdFusion template. The following sample code instructs ColdFusion to switch to the `movies.cfm` template:

```
<CFLOCATION URL="movies.cfm">
```

This way, the updated movie list is displayed, ready for further processing, as soon as any change is completed.

LISTING 14.16 edit4.cfm—MOVIE INSERT AND UPDATE PROCESSING

```
<!---
Name:        edit4.cfm
Author:      Ben Forta (ben@forta.com)
Description: Dual purpose edit page
Created:     4/20/01
--->

<!--- Edit or update? --->
<CFIF IsDefined("FORM.FilmID")>
    <!--- Update movie --->
    <CFUPDATE DATASOURCE="ows" TABLENAME="Films">
<CFELSE>
    <!--- Add movie --->
    <CFINSERT DATASOURCE="ows" TABLENAME="Films">
</CFIF>

<!--- When done go back to movie list --->
<CFLOCATION URL="movies.cfm">
```

LISTING 14.17 delete2.cfm—MOVIE DELETE PROCESSING

```
<!---
Name:        delete2.cfm
Author:      Ben Forta (ben@forta.com)
Description: Delete a movie
Created:     4/20/01
--->

<!--- Check that FilmID was provided --->
<CFIF NOT IsDefined("FilmID")>
 <H1>You did not specify the FilmID</H1>
 <CFABORT>
</CFIF>

<!--- Delete a movie --->
<CFQUERY DATASOURCE="ows">
DELETE FROM Films
WHERE FilmID=#FilmID#
</CFQUERY>

<!--- When done go back to movie list --->
<CFLOCATION URL="movies.cfm">
```

And there you have it—a complete application featuring data display, edit and delete using data-drill down, and reusable data-driven add and edit forms. Extremely powerful, and not complicated at all.

CHAPTER 15

DEBUGGING AND TROUBLESHOOTING

In this chapter

DEBUGGING COLDFUSION APPLICATIONS

As with any development tool, sooner or later you're going to find yourself debugging or troubleshooting a ColdFusion problem. Many applications and interfaces have to work seamlessly for a ColdFusion application to function correctly. The key to quickly isolating and correcting problems is a thorough understanding of ColdFusion, ODBC data sources, SQL syntax, URL syntax, and your Web server—and more importantly, how they all work with each other.

If the prospect of debugging an application sounds daunting, don't panic. Thankfully, ColdFusion has powerful built-in debugging and error-reporting features. These capabilities, coupled with logical and systematic evaluation of trouble spots, enable you to diagnose and correct all sorts of problems.

This chapter teaches you how to use the ColdFusion debugging tools and introduces techniques that help you quickly locate the source of a problem. More importantly, because an ounce of prevention is worth a pound of cure, guidelines and techniques that will help prevent common errors from occurring in the first place are introduced.

UNDERSTANDING WHAT CAN GO WRONG

As an application developer, sooner or later you are going to have to diagnose, or *debug*, a ColdFusion application problem. Because ColdFusion relies on so many other software components to work its magic, there are a lot of places where things can go wrong.

As you are reading this chapter, the following assumptions are made:

- You are familiar with basic ColdFusion concepts.
- You understand how ColdFusion uses ODBC for all database interaction.
- You are familiar with basic SQL syntax and use.

If you are not familiar with any of these topics, it is strongly recommended that you read the chapters about them before proceeding.

Note

See Chapter 1, "Introducing ColdFusion," for more information on how ColdFusion works and how all the pieces fit together to create a complete application.

See Chapter 3, "Building the Databases," for a detailed explanation of databases, tables, rows, columns, keys, and other database-related terms.

See Chapter 6, "Introduction to SQL," for more information about ODBC drivers and data sources and how ColdFusion uses them for all database interaction.

See Chapter 8, "Introduction to ColdFusion Studio," for an overview of ColdFusion Studio and its debugging capabilities.

Almost all ColdFusion problems fall into one of the following categories:

- Web server configuration problems
- ODBC driver errors
- SQL statement syntax or logic errors
- ColdFusion syntax errors
- URL and path problems
- Logic problems within your code

Let's look at each of these potential problem areas to learn what can go wrong in each.

DEBUGGING WEB SERVER CONFIGURATION PROBLEMS

You should almost never encounter problems caused by Web server misconfiguration during routine, day-to-day operations. These types of problems almost always occur either during the initial ColdFusion setup or while testing ColdFusion for the first time. After ColdFusion in installed and configured correctly, it will stay that way.

The only exception to this is the possibility of you receiving a `ColdFusion Application Server not currently running` error when attempting to execute a ColdFusion script. This error, shown in Figure 15.1, is generated when the Web server ColdFusion extensions cannot communicate with the ColdFusion Application Server. (Figure 15.1 is the Windows NT and Windows 2000 error message; other operating systems display similar messages.)

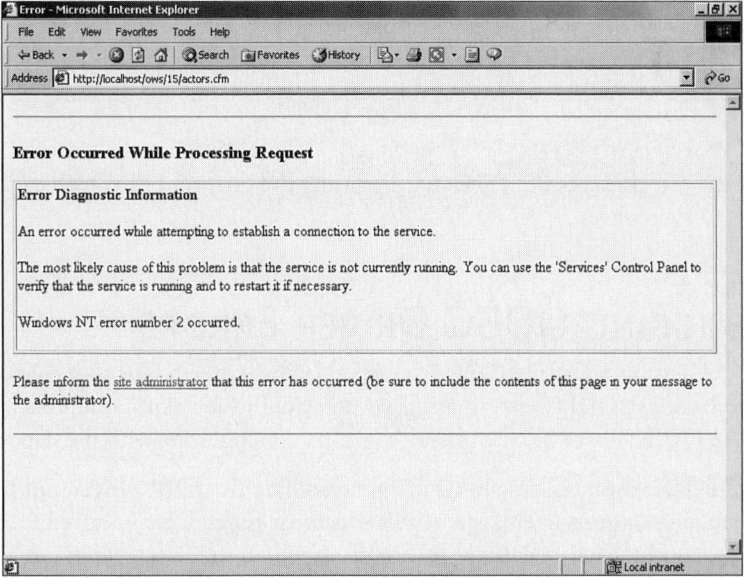

Figure 15.1
The ColdFusion Application Server must be running; otherwise, all ColdFusion requests will generate an error message.

The Application Server must be running for ColdFusion to process templates. Steps to verifying that the server is running, and starting it if it is not, differ based on your operating system:

- If you are running ColdFusion on a Windows NT or Windows 2000 machine, you should run the Service applet in the Windows Control Panel. It will display whether the service is running and will enable you to start it if is not.
- If you are running Windows 95, Windows 98, or Windows Me, you'll see the ColdFusion icon on the taskbar (near the clock) when the Application Server is running. If it is not running, select ColdFusion from the ColdFusion program groups under your Start button menu.
- If you are running ColdFusion on Unix, use the `ps` command to list running processes to see whether ColdFusion is running.

Tip

Windows NT and Windows 2000 services can be started automatically every time the server is restarted. The service Startup option must be set to Automatic for a service to start automatically. Windows 95, Windows 98, and Windows 2000 users can automatically start ColdFusion by ensuring that the ColdFusion Application Server is in the Programs, Startup group. This setting is turned on by the ColdFusion installation procedure and typically should be left on at all times. However, if the service does not automatically start, check these options.

Tip

If your operating system features a mechanism by which to automatically restart services or daemons upon shutdown, use it.

One other situation worth noting is when you are prompted to save a file every time you request a ColdFusion page. If this is the case then one of two things is happening:

- ColdFusion is not installed on the server correctly.
- You are accessing URLs locally (using the browser File, Open option) instead of via the Web server.

Debugging ODBC Driver Errors

ColdFusion relies on ODBC (or native database drivers) for all its database interaction. You will receive ODBC error messages when ColdFusion can't communicate with the appropriate ODBC driver or when the driver can't communicate with the database.

ODBC error messages always are generated by an ODBC driver, not by ColdFusion. ColdFusion merely displays whatever error message it has received from the ODBC driver, and unfortunately ODBC error messages tend to often be cryptic or even misleading. However, ColdFusion often adds its own suggestions to the error screen to help you diagnose the problem, as shown in Figure 15.2.

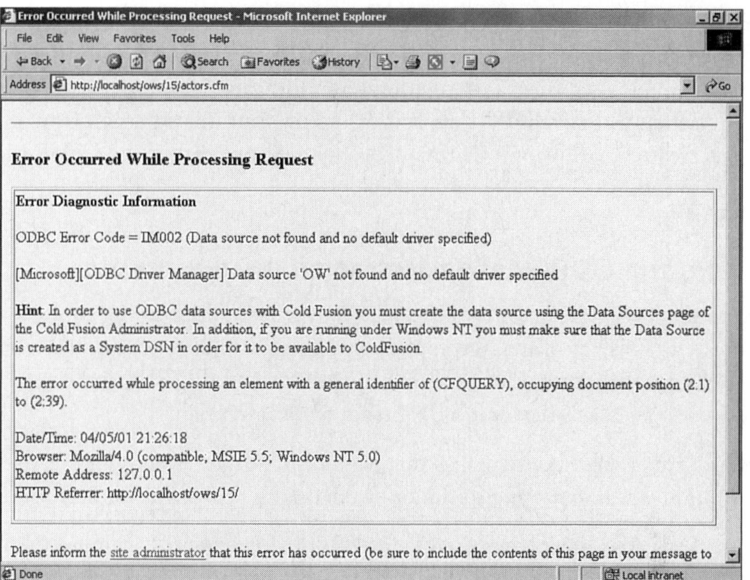

Figure 15.2
ColdFusion attempts to display useful information along with ODBC error messages.

ODBC error messages always contain an error number, which in and of itself is pretty useless. A text message that describes the problem follows the error number, however. The text of these messages varies from driver to driver, so it would be pointless to list all the possible error messages here. Instead, the more common symptoms and how to fix the problems that cause them are listed.

Tip

You can use the ColdFusion Administrator to verify that an ODBC data source is correctly set up and attached to the appropriate data file. To do this, run the ColdFusion Administrator and select the ODBC Data Sources menu option. Each listed data source has a Verify link next to it, which you can click to verify that ODBC can connect to the database properly.

Receiving the ODBC Error Message `Data Source Not Found`

ColdFusion communicates with databases via ODBC drivers. These drivers access data sources—external data files. If the ODBC driver reports that the data source could not be found, check the following:

- Make sure you have created the ODBC data source.
- Verify that the data source name is spelled correctly. ODBC data source names are not case sensitive, so don't worry about that.

- Under Windows NT and Windows 2000, ODBC data sources are *user login specific*. This means if you create a data source from within the ODBC Control Panel applet while logged in as a user without administrator privileges, only that user will have access to that ODBC data source. To prevent this situation from occurring, always create ColdFusion's ODBC data sources from within the ColdFusion Administrator program.

RECEIVING THE ODBC ERROR MESSAGE `File Not Found`

You might get the error message `File not found` when trying to use a data source you have created. This error message applies only to data sources that access data files directly (such as Microsoft Access, Microsoft Excel, and Borland dBASE), and not to client/server database systems (such as Microsoft SQL Server and Oracle).

`File not found` simply means that the ODBC driver could not locate the data file in the location it was expecting to find it. To diagnose this problem, perform the following steps:

1. Data files must be created before ODBC data sources can use them. If you have not yet created the data file, you must do so before proceeding.
2. Check the ODBC data source settings, verify that the file name is spelled correctly, and ensure that the file exists.
3. If you have moved the location of a data file, you must manually update any ODBC data sources that reference it.

RECEIVING LOGIN OR PERMISSION ERRORS WHEN TRYING TO ACCESS A DATA STORE

Some database systems, such as Microsoft SQL Server, Sybase, and Oracle, require that you log on to a database before you can access it. When setting up an ODBC data source to this type of database, you must specify the login name and password the driver should use to gain access.

The following steps help you locate the source of this problem:

1. Verify that the login name and password are spelled correctly. (You will not be able to see the password—only asterisks are displayed in the password field.)
2. On some database systems, passwords are case sensitive. Ensure that you have not left the Caps Lock key on by mistake.
3. Verify that the name and password you are using does indeed have access to the database to which you are trying to connect. You can do this using a client application that came with your database system.
4. Verify that the login being used actually has rights to the specific tables and views you are using and to the specific statements (`SELECT`, `INSERT`, and so on). Many better DBMSs enable administrators to grant or deny rights to specific objects and specific operations on specific objects.

Tip

When you are testing security- and rights-related problems, be sure you test using the same login and password as the ones used in the data source definition.

Receiving the ODBC Error Message `Unknown Table`

After verifying that the data source name and table names are correct, you might still get `unknown table` errors. A very common problem, especially with client/server databases such as Microsoft SQL Server, is forgetting to provide a fully qualified table name. You can do this in two ways:

- **Explicitly provide the fully qualified table name whenever it is passed to a SQL statement**—Fully qualified table names are usually made up of three parts, separated by periods. The first is the name of the database containing the table; the second is the owner name (usually specified as `dbo`); the third is the actual table name itself.
- **Some ODBC drivers, such as the Microsoft SQL Server driver, enable you to specify a default database to be used if none is explicitly provided**—If this option is set, its value is used whenever a fully qualified name is not provided.

Tip

If your ODBC driver allows you to specify a default database name, use that feature. This enables you to write fewer and simpler hard-coded SQL statements.

Debugging SQL Statement or Logic Errors

Debugging SQL statements is one of the two types of troubleshooting you'll spend most of your debugging time doing (the other is debugging ColdFusion syntax errors, which we'll get to next). You will find yourself debugging SQL statements if you run into either of these situations:

- ColdFusion reports SQL syntax errors. Figure 15.3, for example, is an error caused by misspelling a table name in a SQL statement.
- No syntax errors are reported, but the specified SQL statement did not achieve the expected results.

Obviously, a prerequisite to debugging SQL statements is a good working knowledge of the SQL language. I'm assuming you are already familiar with the basic SQL statements and are comfortable using them.

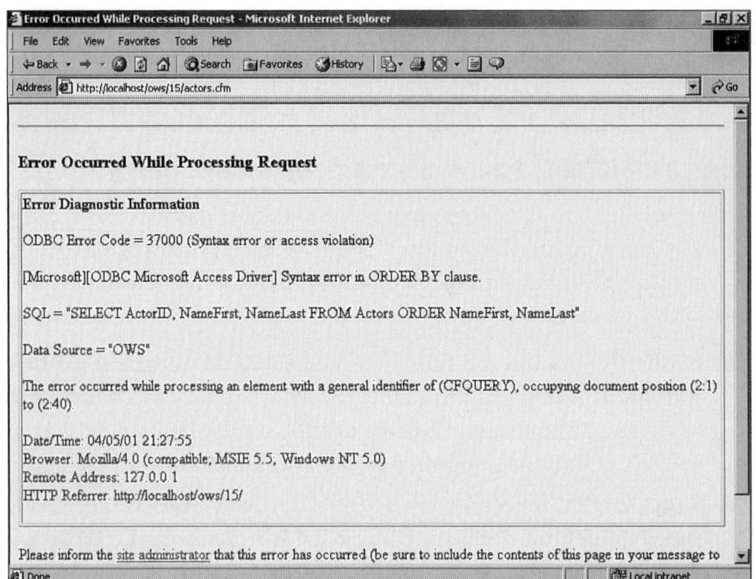
Error Occurred While Processing Request - Microsoft Internet Explorer

Error Occurred While Processing Request

Error Diagnostic Information

ODBC Error Code = 37000 (Syntax error or access violation)

[Microsoft][ODBC Microsoft Access Driver] Syntax error in ORDER BY clause.

SQL = "SELECT ActorID, NameFirst, NameLast FROM Actors ORDER NameFirst, NameLast"

Data Source = "OWS"

The error occurred while processing an element with a general identifier of (CFQUERY), occupying document position (2:1) to (2:40).

Date/Time: 04/05/01 21:27:55
Browser: Mozilla/4.0 (compatible; MSIE 5.5; Windows NT 5.0)
Remote Address: 127.0.0.1
HTTP Referrer: http://localhost/ows/15/

Please inform the site administrator that this error has occurred (be sure to include the contents of this page in your message to

Figure 15.3 ColdFusion displays the SQL error reported by ODBC and often attempts to provide hints of its own.

Note

See Chapter 7, "SQL Data Manipulation," for information about basic SQL statements and examples of their uses.

Tip

The Debug Options screen in the ColdFusion Administrator contains a checkbox labeled Show SQL and Data Source Name. During development, turn on this option so that the full SQL statement and data source name is displayed in any database-related error messages.

The keys to successfully debugging SQL statements are as follows:

1. Isolate the problem. Debugging SQL statements inside ColdFusion templates can be tricky, especially when creating dynamic SQL statements. Try executing the same statement from within another ODBC client, such as Microsoft Query or ColdFusion Studio, and then replacing dynamic parameters with fixed values if appropriate.
2. The big difference between ColdFusion SQL statements and statements entered into any other ODBC client is the use of ColdFusion fields. If you are using ColdFusion fields within your statement, verify that you are enclosing them within quotation marks when necessary. If the value is a string, it must be enclosed in single quotation marks. If it is a number, it must not be enclosed in quotation marks. (And be sure double quotation marks are never used within SQL statements because this will terminate the statement prematurely.)

3. Look at the bigger picture. Dynamic SQL statements are one of ColdFusion's most powerful features, but this power comes with a price. When you create a dynamic SQL statement, you are effectively relinquishing direct control over the statement itself and are allowing it to be changed based on other conditions. This means that the code for a single ColdFusion query can be used to generate an infinite number of queries. Because some of these queries might work—and others might not—debugging dynamic SQL requires that you be able to determine exactly what the dynamically created SQL statement looks like. Thankfully, ColdFusion makes this an easy task, as you will see later in the section "Using the ColdFusion Debugging Options."
4. Break complex SQL statements into smaller, simpler statements. If you are debugging a query that contains subqueries, verify that the subqueries properly work independently of the outer query.

Caution

Be careful to not omit pound signs from around variable names in your SQL code. Consider the following SQL statement:

```
DELETE Actors
WHERE ActorID=ActorID
```

What the code is supposed to do is delete a specific actor, the one whose ID is specified in `ActorID`. But because pound signs were omitted, instead of passing the actor ID, the name of the actor ID column is passed. The result? Every row in the `Actors` table is deleted instead of just the one–all because of missing pound signs. The correct statement should have looked like this:

```
DELETE Actors
WHERE ActorID=#ActorID#
```

Incidentally, this is why you should always test `WHERE` clauses in a `SELECT` before using them in a `DELETE` or `UPDATE`.

Whenever a SQL syntax error occurs, ColdFusion displays the SQL statement it submitted. The fully constructed statement is displayed if your SQL statement was constructed dynamically.

The field names are displayed as submitted if the error occurred during an `INSERT` or `UPDATE` operation, but the values are replaced with question marks (except for `NULL` values, which are displayed as `NULL`).

Note

If you ever encounter strange ODBC error messages about mismatched data types or incorrect numbers of parameters, the first thing you should check is that you have not mistyped any table or column names and that you have single quotation marks where necessary. More often than not, that is what causes that error.

Tip

If you are using ColdFusion Studio (and you should be), you can completely avoid typos in table and column names by using the Studio database drag-and-drop support. To do this, open the Database tab in the Resource tab, select the desired data source, and expand the tables to find the table and column you need. You can then click the table or column name and just drag it to the Editor window, where it will be inserted when you release the mouse key.

DEBUGGING COLDFUSION SYNTAX ERRORS

Debugging ColdFusion syntax errors is the other type of troubleshooting you'll find yourself doing. Thankfully, and largely as a result of the superb ColdFusion error-reporting and debugging capabilities, these are usually the easiest bugs to find.

ColdFusion syntax errors are usually one of the following:

- Mismatched pound signs or quotation marks
- Mismatched begin and end tags; a `<CFIF>` without a matching `</CFIF>`, for example
- Incorrectly nested tags
- A tag with a missing or an incorrectly spelled attribute
- Missing quotation marks around tag attributes
- Using double quotation marks instead of single to delimit strings when building SQL statements
- Illegal use of tags

If any of these errors occur, ColdFusion generates a descriptive error message, as shown in Figure 15.4. The error message lists the problematic code (and a few lines before and after it) and identifies exactly what the problem is.

Caution

If your template contains HTML forms, frames, or tables, you might have trouble viewing generated error messages. If an error occurs in the middle of a table, for example, that table will never be terminated, and there is no way to know how the browser will attempt to render the partial table. If the table is not rendered and displayed properly, you will not see the error message.

Tip

If you think an error has occurred but no error message is displayed, you can view the source in the browser. The generated source will contain any error messages that were included in the Web page but not displayed.

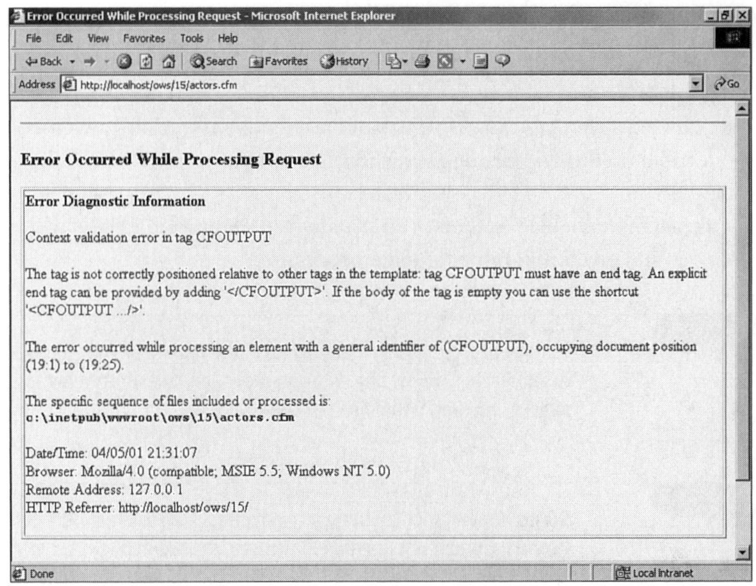

Figure 15.4
ColdFusion generates descriptive error messages when syntax errors occur.

One of the most common ColdFusion errors is missing or mismatched tags. Indenting your code, as shown in the following, is a good way to ensure that all tags are correctly matched:

```
<CFIF some condition here>
   <CFOUTPUT>
      Output code here
      <CFIF another condition>
         Some other output code here
      </CFIF>
   </CFOUTPUT>
<CFELSE>
   Some action here
</CFIF>
```

ColdFusion Studio users should take advantage of Studio's Tag Insight, Tag Tips, and Tag Completion features to avoid common mismatching problems. The right-click menu's Edit Tag option is also useful in helping prevent typos in tags and their attributes.

Note

See Chapter 8 for more information about ColdFusion Studio and its tag options.

INSPECTING VARIABLE CONTENTS

Sometimes problems throw no errors at all—this occurs when your code is syntactically valid but a logic problem exists somewhere. Aside from using the interactive debugger (which is discussed shortly), the primary means to locating this type of bug is to inspect variable contents during processing. Two ways to do this are available:

- Embed variable display code as necessary in your page, dumping the contents of variables to the screen (or to HTML comments you can view using View Source in your browser).
- The `<CFDUMP>` tag can display the contents of any variable, even complex variables, and can be used to aid debugging when necessary.

By displaying variable contents, you usually can determine what various code blocks are doing at any given point during page processing.

Tip

You can use `<CFABORT>` anywhere in the middle of your template to force ColdFusion to halt further processing. You can move the `<CFABORT>` tag farther down the template as you verify that lines of code work.

Tip

During development, when you find yourself alternating between needing debugging information and not needing it, you can enclose debug code in `<CFIF IsDebugMode()>` and `</CFIF>`. This way your debug output will be processed only if debugging is enabled.

USING THE DOCUMENT VALIDATOR

To help you catch syntax errors before your site goes live, ColdFusion Studio has an integrated validator. The validator can be used to check for mismatched tags, unknown variables, missing pound signs, and other common errors.

To use the validator, open the file to be checked in Studio and then select Validate Document from the Tools menu. ColdFusion Studio validates your code and lists any errors in a results window at the bottom of the screen, as seen in Figure 15.5.

To quickly jump to the problematic code, just double-click the error message in the results window. As seen in Figure 15.6, the Studio Validator displays the same error message as ColdFusion itself does at runtime and even highlights the trouble spot in the Edit window. This enables you to fix errors before you roll out your application.

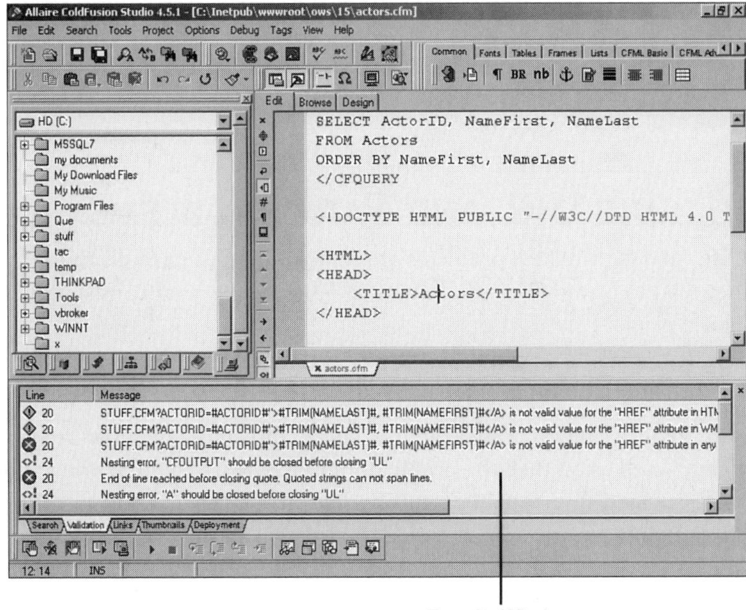

Figure 15.5 The ColdFusion Studio Validator lists any errors in a results window.

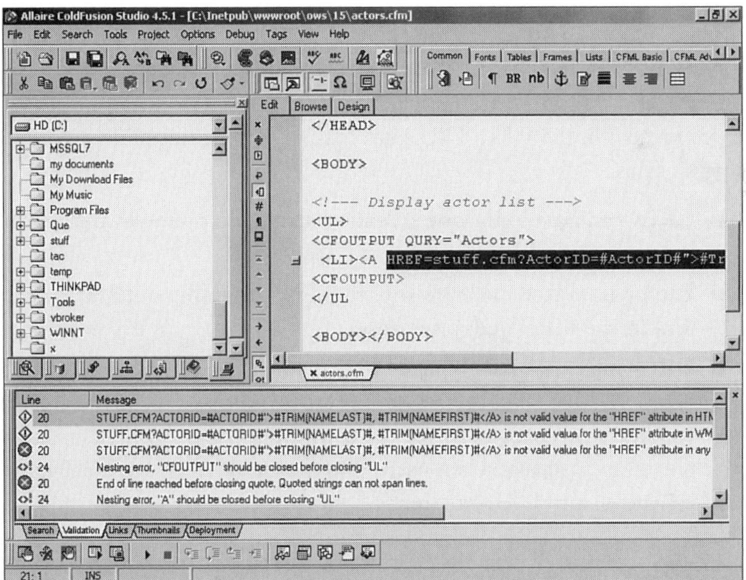

Figure 15.6 The ColdFusion Studio Validator can flag problem code for you.

Tip

To quickly validate the current document while you are editing it, press Shift+F6.

Note

You can customize the behavior of the validator, including specifying what gets validated and which tags to validate. To do this, select Settings from the Options menu, and then select the Validation tab.

DEBUGGING URL AND PATH PROBLEMS

URL- and path-related problems are some of the easiest to diagnose and resolve because they tend to be rather binary in nature—they either work consistently or they fail consistently.

IMAGES ARE NOT DISPLAYED

If image files (and other files) are not always displayed when you reference them from within ColdFusion then the problem might be path related. If you are using relative paths (and you generally should be), ensure that the path as it is sent to the browser is valid. Having too many or too few periods and slashes in the path is a common culprit.

Tip

Most browsers let you check image paths (constructing full URLs from relative paths in your code) by right-clicking the image and viewing the properties.

PASSING PARAMETERS THAT ARE NOT PROCESSED

Parameters you pass to a URL can't be processed by ColdFusion, even though you see them present in the URL. URLs are finicky little beasts, and you have to abide by the following rules:

- **URLs can have only one question mark character in them**—The question mark separates the URL itself from the query.
- **Each parameter must be separated by an ampersand (&) to pass multiple parameters in the URL query section.**
- **URLs must not have spaces in them**—If you are generating URLs dynamically based on table column data, you must be sure to trim any spaces from those values. If you must use spaces, replace them with plus signs. ColdFusion correctly converts the plus signs to spaces when used. Use the ColdFusion `URLEncodedFormat()` function to convert text to URL-safe text.

Tip

ColdFusion debug output, discussed in the following section, lists all passed URL parameters. This is an invaluable debugging tool.

DEBUGGING FORM PROBLEMS

If a form is submitted without data, it can cause an error. Web browsers submit data to Web servers in two ways. These ways are called `GET` and `POST`, and the submission method for use is specified in the `FORM METHOD` attribute.

As a rule, forms being submitted to ColdFusion always should be submitted using the `POST` method. The default method is `GET`, so if you omit or misspell `METHOD="POST"`, ColdFusion will be incapable of processing your forms correctly.

You occasionally might get an `Unknown variable` error message when referring to form fields in the action template. Radio buttons, check boxes, and list boxes are not submitted if no option was selected. It is important to remember this when referring to form fields in an action template. If you refer to a check box without first checking for its existence (and then selecting it), you'll generate an error message.

The solution is to always check for the existence of any fields or variables before using them. Alternatively, you can use the `<CFPARAM>` tag to assign default values to fields, thereby ensuring that they always exist.

Note

See Chapter 12, "ColdFusion Forms," for more information about working with form fields and working with specific form controls.

How can you check which form fields were actually submitted and what their values are? Enable ColdFusion debugging—any time you submit a form, its action page contains a debugging section that describes the submitted form. This is shown in Figure 15.7. A field named `FORM.FORMFIELDS` contains a comma-delimited list of all the submitted fields, as well as a list of the submitted fields and their values.

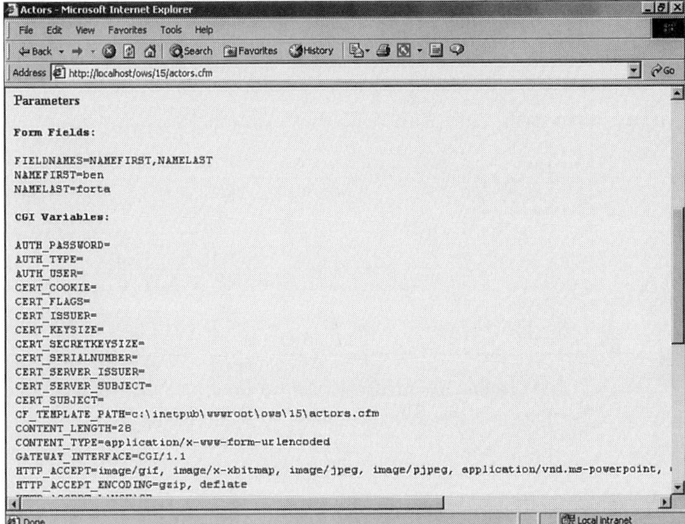

Figure 15.7
ColdFusion displays form-specific debugging information if debugging is enabled.

Here are some other things to look for:

- Ensure all form fields have names.
- Ensure related check boxes or radio buttons have the same name.
- Ensure form field names are specified within double quotation marks.
- Ensure form field names have no spaces or other special characters in them.
- Ensure that all quotation marks around attribute values match.

All these are HTML related, not ColdFusion related. But every one of them can complicate working with forms, and HTML itself will not generate errors upon form generation.

USING THE COLDFUSION DEBUGGING OPTIONS

The ColdFusion debugging options are enabled or disabled via the ColdFusion Administrator, as explained in Chapter 4, "Accessing the ColdFusion Administrator."

The ColdFusion debugging options work by appending debugging information to the end of any generated Web pages, as shown in Figure 15.8. The exact information displayed varies, based on the options you selected and the contents of your template.

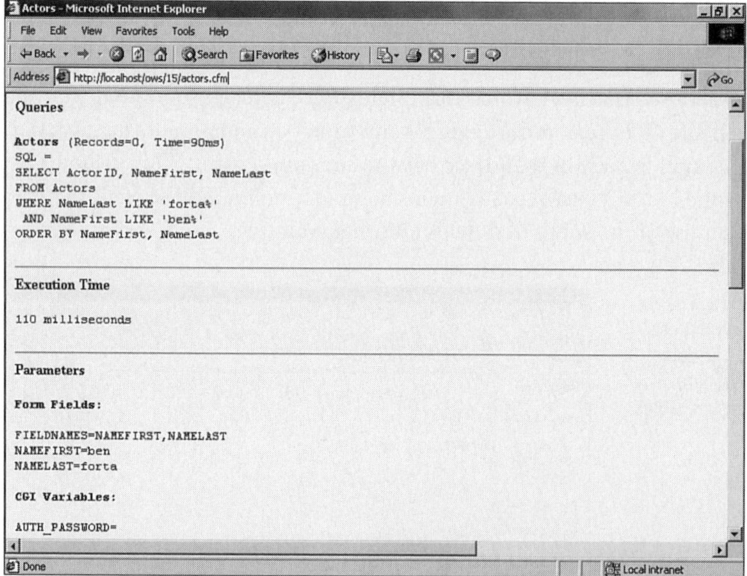

Figure 15.8
ColdFusion can append debugging information to any generated Web page.

Note

See Chapter 30, "ColdFusion Server Configuration," for a detailed explanation of each of the available debug output options and settings.

Tip

You can restrict the display of debugging information to specific IP addresses. If you enable debugging, you should use this feature to prevent debugging screens from being displayed to your site's visitors.

Caution

At a minimum, the local host IP address (`127.0.0.1`) should be specified. If no IP address is in the list, debugging information will be sent to anyone who browses any ColdFusion page.

You often will find yourself needing temporary access to debug information for specific IP addresses. You'll find a CFX tag, `<CFX_Debug>`, on the CD-ROM that enables you to simply turn on and off debug information without having to access the ColdFusion Administrator.

USING THE STUDIO REMOTE DEBUGGER

ColdFusion Studio features a complete integrated remote debugger. Key features of the debugger include the following:

- Debug applications running on any server—local or across any IP connection
- Create breakpoints to examine code where necessary
- Examine variables and expressions mid-execution
- Analyze query results in real-time
- Browse the tag stack dynamically
- Monitor output generation

Full coverage of all the features of this powerful tool are beyond the scope of this chapter. What follows, however, should be enough information to get you up and running using the debugger.

Note

The debugger can be used to debug code only on a server configured as a remote RDS server within ColdFusion Studio. To debug local files, you must have a local RDS server configured. For more information on configuring RDS servers, see Chapter 8.

THE DEBUGGER TOOLBAR

The ColdFusion Debugger is controlled using the Debugger toolbar. This is usually at the bottom of the Studio window, as seen in Figure 15.9.

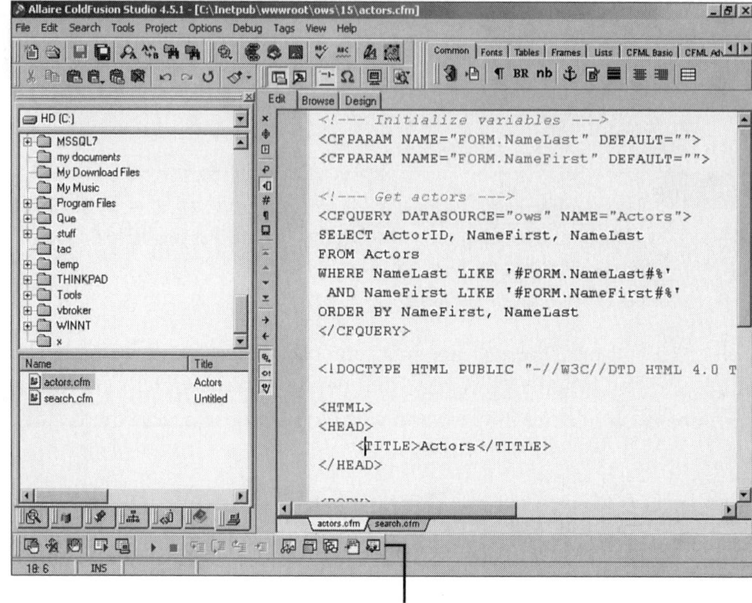

Figure 15.9
The ColdFusion Studio Debugger is controlled using the Debugger toolbar.

The Debugger toolbar contains the following buttons:

- Displays list of breakpoints
- Clears all breakpoints
- Toggles the current breakpoint
- Debugger settings
- Debugger mappings
- Starts debugger
- Stops debugger
- Steps into code
- Steps over code
- Steps out of current code block

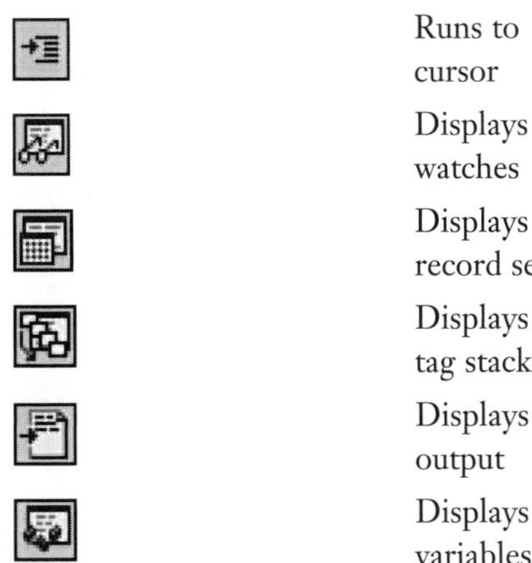

	Runs to cursor
	Displays watches
	Displays record sets
	Displays tag stack
	Displays output
	Displays variables

Using the Debugger

To use the debugger, open the page to be debugged in the Editor window. You can set *breakpoints* (points in your code where the debugger should stop and wait for your input) by clicking the line number in the gray bar to the left of the Editor window. You can place breakpoints only on CFML code. Figure 15.10 shows a breakpoint on a `<CFOUTPUT>` tag. When a breakpoint is set, the line of code is displayed with a red background.

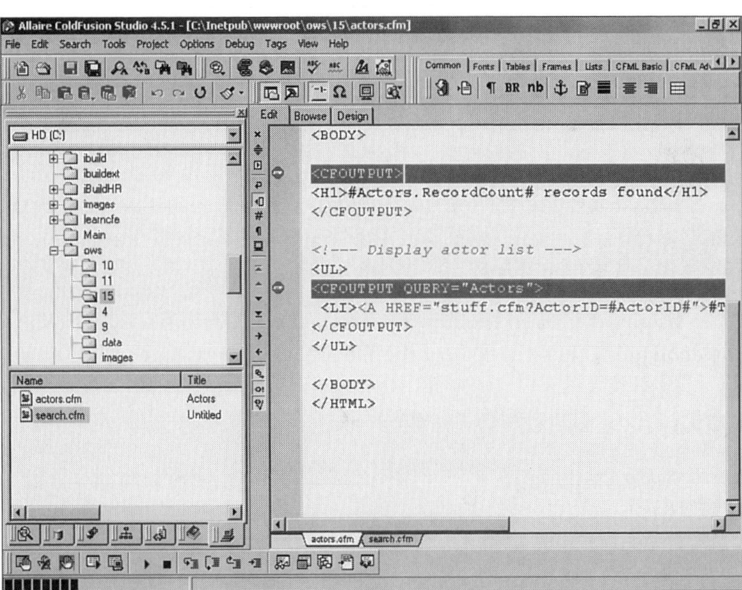

Figure 15.10 The ColdFusion Studio Debugger highlights breakpoints in your code and positions the cursor at the active breakpoint.

Tip

To remove a single breakpoint, click the line number twice. To remove all breakpoints, click the Clear All Breakpoints button in the Debugger toolbar.

To use the debugger, either click the Start Debugging button in the Debugger toolbar or select Start from the Debug menu. You will be prompted with a Remote Development Settings dialog box, as shown in Figure 15.11.

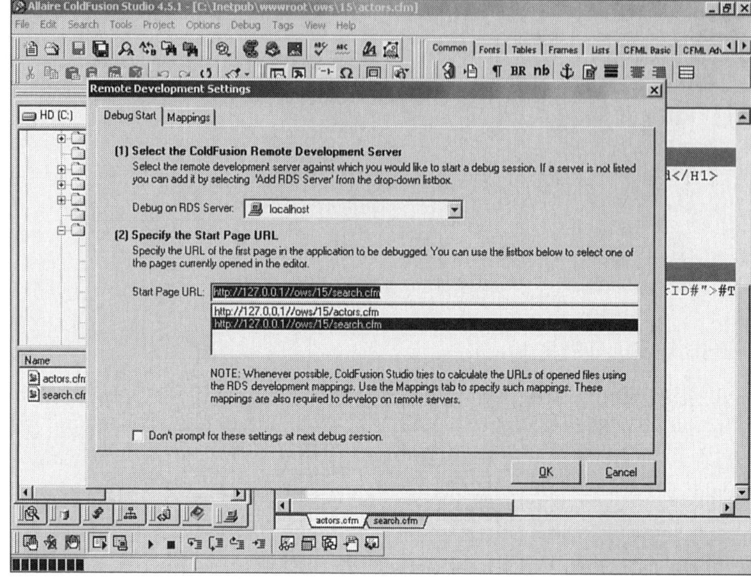

Figure 15.11
Debugger settings, including the initial file to load, are specified in the Remote Development Settings dialog box.

In the Debug on RDS Server field, specify the server to debug against. The default value here should be correct.

In the Start Page URL box, specify the URL in which to start the debugger. By default, Studio constructs a URL for the currently selected file. If you are debugging a page that must be called from another page (for example, a form action page), you must specify that initial page URL in this field.

After you have entered the information into these two fields, click the OK button to start the debugger. This will display the Debug window, as shown in Figure 15.12.

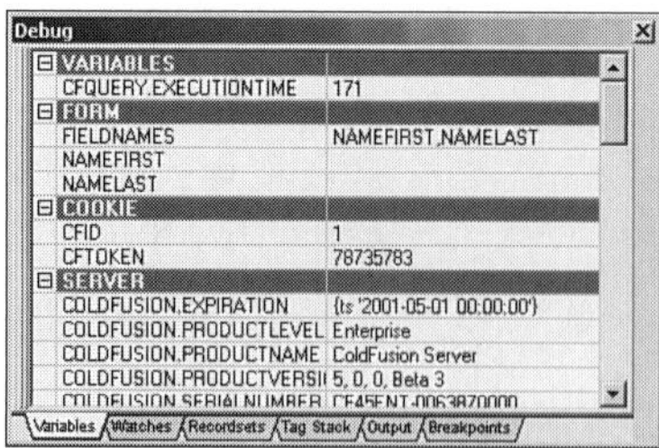

Figure 15.12
The Debug window hovers over the Studio window, enabling you to browse your files and access debug options at the same time.

After the debugger has started, you should execute the program until the first breakpoint has been reached. To do this, use the program in the Studio Browse window. You might have to move the Debug window out of the way to get to the page.

THE BREAKPOINTS PANE

As soon as a breakpoint is reached, the debugger stops execution and highlights the breakpoint with a blue background. In Figure 15.13, the Debug window displays the breakpoint that was reached.

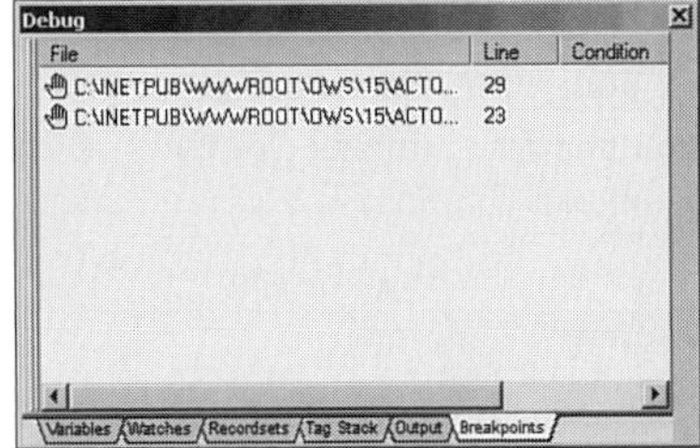

Figure 15.13 The Breakpoints pane in the Debug window shows all breakpoints and enables the adding, editing, and deleting of breakpoints.

THE VARIABLES PANE

After code execution has stopped, you can use any of the debugging options by selecting the tabs in the Debug window. To display a list of all variables and their values, click the Variables tab. The variables are categorized by type, as shown in Figure 15.14, and each type can be expanded or closed as necessary.

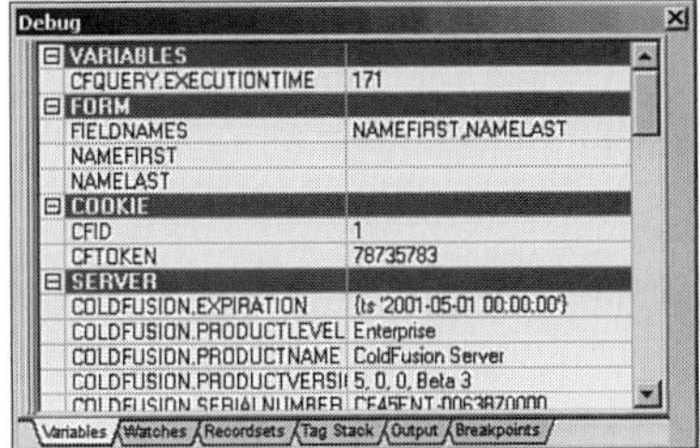

Figure 15.14 The Variables pane shows the current values of all variables, categorized by type.

THE WATCHES PANE

The Watches pane lets you enter variables or expressions you can monitor, as shown in Figure 15.15. As they change, their values are updated in this window. To evaluate an expression once, type it in the expression field and click the Evaluate button. To watch (*monitor*) an expression, type it in the expression field and click the Watch button.

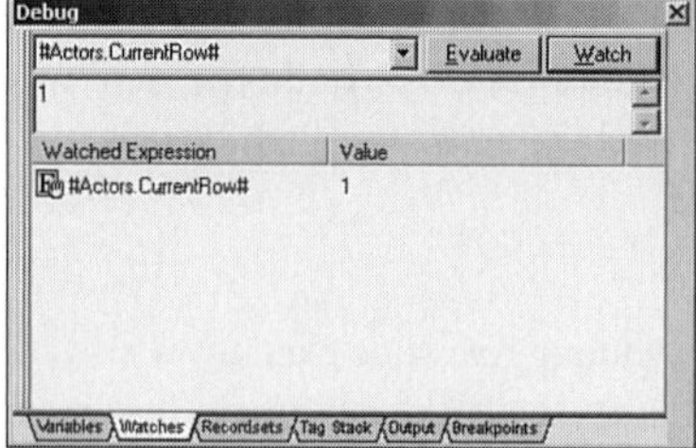

Figure 15.15
The Watches pane shows all the expressions being watched and enables the real-type evaluation of expressions.

THE RECORDSETS PANE

The Recordsets tab displays a list of all queries that have been executed up to the breakpoint. As shown in Figure 15.16, the query name, number of rows retrieved, and the SQL statement are listed in this tab.

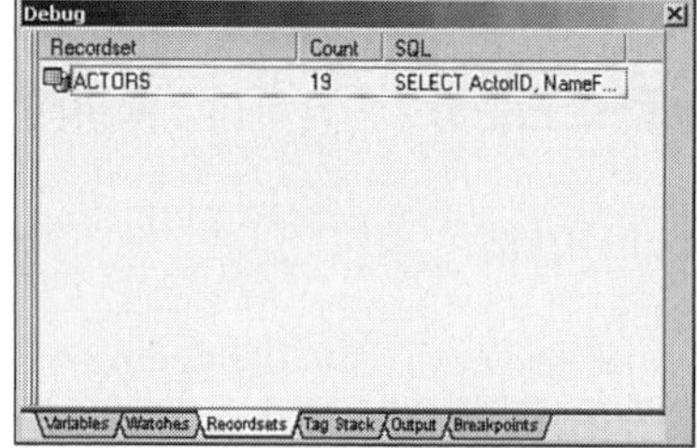

Figure 15.16
The Recordsets pane shows all executed queries and their details.

THE TAG STACK PANE

The Tag Stack pane shown in Figure 15.17 shows the current page being executed and the calling tag stack, if one exists. If you are debugging a page that has been called or included from any other page, those pages are listed in descending order.

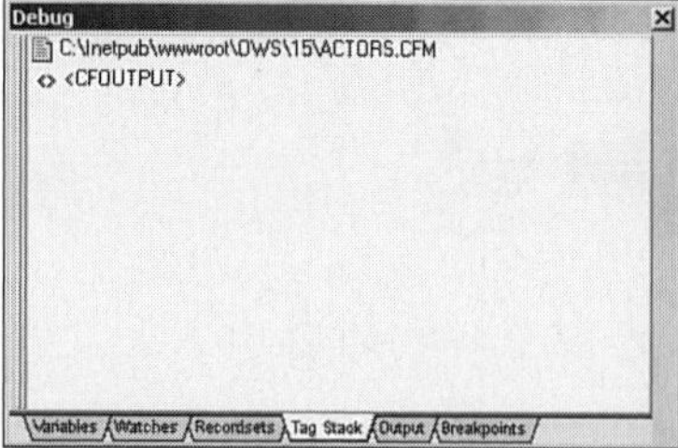

Figure 15.17
The Tag Stack pane displays the order of tag execution so as to be able to determine how a line of code was reached.

THE OUTPUT PANE

The Output pane, shown in Figure 15.18, displays the HTML output as it is being generated. The data shown here is post-processing data—the same data that will be sent back to the client browser.

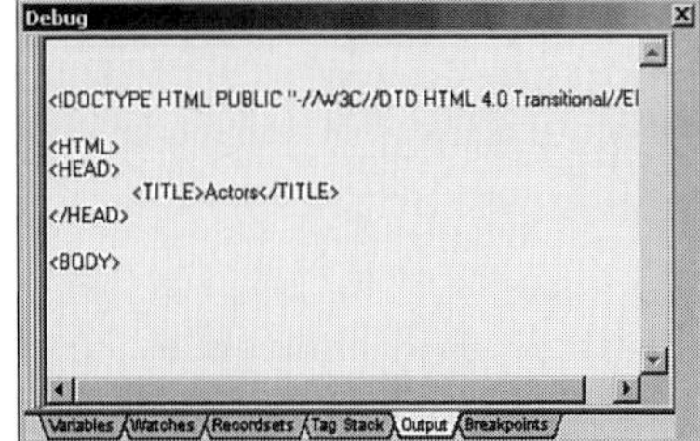

Figure 15.18
The Output pane shows generated client output as it is being generated.

Customizing the Debugger

The Debug pane can be opened, closed, moved, and broken out into multiple panes. Each of the panes can be undocked and repositioned as necessary, as shown in Figure 15.19. To move a pane, select and drag it by clicking the double vertical lines to the left of the pane.

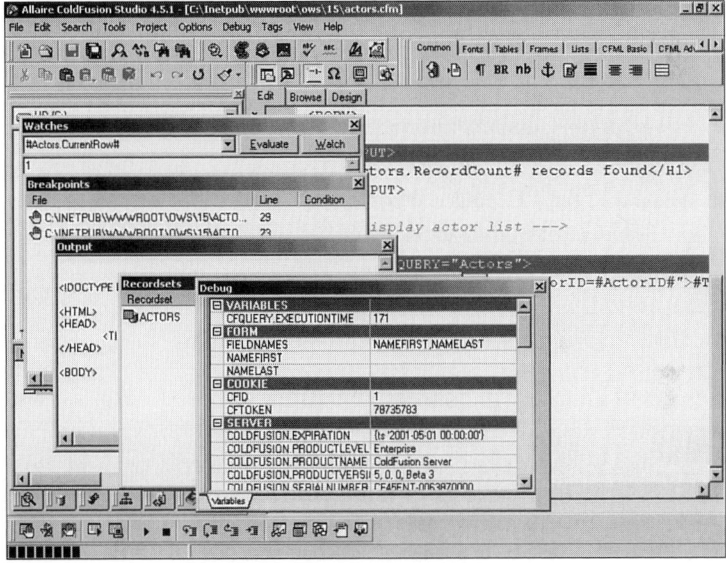

Figure 15.19
The individual debugger panes can be undocked and moved as necessary.

As you can see, the remote debugger provides industrial-strength tools to aid you in pinpointing code trouble spots—the type of tool not yet seen in the Internet application development space.

Using the ColdFusion Log Files

ColdFusion logs all warnings and errors to log files, which aids you and Allaire Technical Support in troubleshooting problems. ColdFusion log files are created when the ColdFusion service starts. You can delete these log files if they get too large or move them to another directory for processing. If you do move or delete the log files, ColdFusion creates new ones automatically.

Tip

If you are having trouble locating the ColdFusion log files, check the Debugging screen in the ColdFusion Administrator program. That is where the location of the log files is specified.

All the ColdFusion log files are plain-text, comma-delimited files. You can import these files into a database or spreadsheet application of your choice for analysis. The ColdFusion Administrator includes a sophisticated log file viewer that enables you to browse, search, and analyze log file data as necessary.

Note

See Chapter 30 for more information on the ColdFusion Administrator's log file viewing options.

ColdFusion creates several log files. Some of the important ones are

- `application.log`—Contains generated CFML errors, `404` errors, and other runtime error conditions and messages
- `server.log`—Contains information about the ColdFusion Application Server itself, including server stop and start times
- `webserver.log`—Contains errors pertaining to files and paths, in particular missing files and "object not found" error messages
- `schedule.log`—Logs scheduled event execution

In addition to the standard log files, specific operations (such as restoring an archive) can create their own log files, too.

Tip

Some errors are browser related. If you are having a hard time reproducing reported error messages, try to determine which version of which browser the user was running and on which platform. You might find that you have run into browser bugs (yes, some versions of popular browsers are very buggy). To help you find these problems, the log files list any identification information provided by a browser, along with the error message.

PREVENTING PROBLEMS

As mentioned earlier, the best approach to troubleshooting ColdFusion problems (and indeed any development problems) is to prevent them from ever occurring in the first place.

Bugs are inevitable. As the size of an application grows, so does the likelihood of a bug being introduced. As an application developer, you need to have two goals in mind:

1. Develop 100% bug-free code.
2. In the event that your code is not 100% bug-free, make sure that it is easy to debug.

As an application developer myself, I know that these are lofty goals. The reality of it is that application development almost always takes longer than planned, and sacrifices have to be made if release dates are to be met. Code quality is usually the first thing that gets sacrificed.

Of course, sooner or later these sacrifices come back to haunt you. Then come the long debugging sessions, rapid code fixes, software upgrades, and possibly even data conversion. Then, because the rapidly patched code often introduces bugs of its own, the whole cycle starts again.

Although there is no sure-fire way of preventing all bugs, some guidelines and coding practices can both help prevent many of them and make finding them easier when they do occur. Here are my 10 Commandments of ColdFusion development:

I. Plan Before You Code

We've all done it, and probably more than once. ColdFusion makes it so easy to start coding that you're often tempted to start projects by firing up ColdFusion Studio and creating CFM files. That's a bad thing indeed. Nothing is more harmful to your development efforts than failing to plan properly, and you should be spending more time planning that coding, not less. And I don't mean planning your IPO. Planning involves thinking through every aspect of your application, from database design to UI considerations, from resource management to schedules and deliverables, and from feature lists with implementation details to language and presentation. You'd never build a house without detailed blueprints (well, you might try, but you'd never get the necessary permission to begin work), and building an application is no different. I am constantly amazed by the number of applications I am asked to look at that have no supporting documentation. And these aren't just from small development shops—I am talking about some of the largest and most respected corporations, too. Scalability problems? I would not doubt it. I'd actually be amazed if such an application ever *did* scale. You can't expect an application that grew in spite of its developers to scale. Nor can you expect it to be bug-free, manageable, or delivered on time. Yes, I know that detailed planning takes time, time none of us have. But in the long run you'll come out ahead.

II. Organize Your Application

An extension of planning your application is organizing it (along with any other applications). Applications are made up of lots of little bits and pieces, and keeping them organized is imperative. This includes directory structures and determining where common files should go, moving images to their own directory (or server), breaking long files into smaller, more manageable (and more reusable) ones, and even ensuring consistent organization among different applications. And going back to the prior commandment, Plan Before You Code, all organization should be documented in detail as part of that plan.

III. Set Coding Standards

This is an interesting one, and one I get asked about often. Allaire has not published formal recommendations on coding standards, nor in my opinion should they. Allaire's job is to create killer tools and products for developers, and our job is to use them however works best for us. I don't believe that a single set of coding standards would work for all developers, but at the same time, I don't believe any developer should be writing code that does not adhere to a standard—*any* standard. Coding standards include everything from filenaming and directory-naming conventions, to variable-naming conventions, to code organization and ordering within your source, to error-handling, to componentization, and much more. For example, if all variables that contain dates begin with `dt`, for example, then references to a variable named `dtOrderDate` become self-explanatory. The purpose of coding standards is to ensure some level of consistency in your code. Whether it is to allow other developers to understand and work with your code or simply so that you'll know what the heck you did (and why) six months down the line, coding standards provide a mechanism to create code that describes and explains itself. There is no right or wrong coding standard, as long as it is used. The only thing wrong about coding standards is not using one.

IV. Comment Your Code

This is an obvious one, but apparently few of us have the time to pay attention to the obvious. So, I'll say it once again: All code must be commented. (For the record, I'd fire an employee on the spot for turning in code that is not commented; that's how serious an offense I believe this one to be.) Every source code file needs a descriptive header listing a description, the author information, the creation date, a chronological list of changes, any dependencies and assumptions, and any other relevant information. In addition, every conditional statement, every loop, every set of variable assignments, and every include or component reference must be commented with a simple statement explaining what is being done and why. It's a pain, I know. But the next time you (or anyone else) has to work with the code, you'll appreciate the effort immeasurably. And you might even be able to safely make code changes without breaking things in the process.

V. Never Make Changes on a Live Server

This is another obvious one, but one worth stating anyway. All development and testing *must* occur on servers established for just that purpose. Yes, this means you'll need additional hardware, but the cost of a new box is nothing compared to the cost of bringing down your application because that little change was not as little as you expected. Write your code, test it, debug it as necessary, deploy it to a testing server, test it some more, and test it some more, and then finally deploy it to your live production server. And don't repeat this process too often. Instead of uploading slightly changed versions of your application every day, collect the changes, test them some more, and deploy them monthly, or weekly, or whenever works best for you. The key here is that your production server is sacred; don't touch it at all unless you have to—and the less frequently, the better. And never, ever, make changes on live servers, even minor ones. Nothing is ever as minor and as isolated as it seems, and there is no change that is worth crashing a server over.

VI. Functionality First, Then Features

This is yet another obvious one, and a common beginner's mistake. Yes, writing fancy DHTML menu-generation code is far more fun that writing data-entry validation routines, but the latter is far more important to the success of your application. Concentrate on creating a complete working application; then pretty it up as necessary. Do so and increase the chance that you'll finish on schedule for a change. The final result might not be as cool as you'd like, but there is something to be said for an application that actually works, even an uncool one. Furthermore, (as explained in the next commandment) debugging logic problems is difficult when the code is cluttered with fancy formatting and features.

VII. Build and Test Incrementally

Testing and debugging complete applications is difficult. The bigger an application is, the more components that are used, and the more developers working on a project, all make debugging and testing anything but trivial. When you develop core components of your application, test them. Write little test routines, hard-code, or smoke-and-mirror as necessary, but however you do it, do it. Obviously, you'll have to test your complete application when you're finished and some problems won't come to light until then, but the more you can test code blocks in isolation, the better.

VIII. Never Reinvent the Wheel, and Plan Not To

This is one I have written about extensively. Write code with reuse in mind, and reuse code whenever possible. When designing your code, put the extra time in up front to ensure it is not hard-coded or highly task specific unless it absolutely has to be. The benefits? Being able to reuse existing code shortens your development time. You also stand a far greater chance of creating bug-free code when you use components that have already been used and tested. Plus, if you do make subsequent fixes and corrections, all code that uses the improved components benefit. This has a lot of benefits and no downside whatsoever.

IX. Use All the Tools at Your Disposal, Not Just ColdFusion

ColdFusion applications are usually not standalone entities. They rely on database servers, mail servers, and much more. In addition, ColdFusion can leverage COM, CORBA, C/C++ code, and all sorts of Java-based bits and pieces. Use these tools, as many as necessary, and always attempt to select the best one for a specific job. The best ColdFusion applications are not the ones written purely in ColdFusion; they are the ones that leverage the best technologies for the job, all held together by ColdFusion.

X. Implement Version Control and Source Code Tracking

Source code changes, and changes are dangerous. As your applications grow, so does the need for tracking changes and source code control. Select a version control package that works for you, and use it. Key features to look for are the ability to lock files (so no one else edits a file while you edit it—if that does happen, someone's changes will be lost), the ability to view change history (what changed, by whom, and when), the ability to roll back complete applications (so that when the latest upgrade bombs you can easily roll back an entire application to a prior known state), the ability to create and check file dependencies (so you'll know what other code is affected by changes you make), and reporting. In addition, if you can integrate the product with ColdFusion Studio, that's even better. The bottom line: I don't care which product you use, just use one.

Note

Chapter 22, "Building Reusable Components," teaches the basics of code reuse and creating your own components.

Chapter 39, "Development Methodologies," introduces several independent coding methodologies and standards, including the most popular one—Fusebox.

Note

Java, COM, CORBA, and C and their use with ColdFusion are covered in detail in the sequel to this book, *Advanced ColdFusion 5 Application Development* (ISBN: 0-7897-2585-1).

CHAPTER 16

USING MACROMEDIA DREAMWEAVER ULTRADEV WITH COLDFUSION

In this chapter

OVERVIEW

ColdFusion Studio no longer holds the monopoly on ColdFusion integrated development environments (IDEs). With the introduction of Dreamweaver UltraDev, Web professionals now have two choices for a ColdFusion IDE. However, UltraDev and ColdFusion Studio approach ColdFusion development in very different ways. Whereas ColdFusion Studio offers a code-centric editing environment, UltraDev leverages Dreamweaver's renowned Web page design interface to produce an elegant yet powerful visual development environment.

Many veteran ColdFusion developers are completely satisfied with ColdFusion Studio and see little need for a visual. On the other hand, other developers will be very interested in finding out what UltraDev has to offer the ColdFusion development community. For those developers who are curious, the following list contains a few points that make UltraDev potentially attractive for ColdFusion development:

- Visual Web page design and ColdFusion development in one package
- Extensibility with an active enthusiast community constantly building Dreamweaver and Dreamweaver UltraDev Extensions
- Development flexibility by having the option to develop in ASP and JSP as well as ColdFusion
- Tight integration with other Macromedia Web development tools, such as Flash, Fireworks, and so on

Choosing between UltraDev and ColdFusion Studio likely will come down to personal choice. Working directly with the code in a capable text-editing environment such as ColdFusion Studio will remain attractive to many ColdFusion developers. However, as UltraDev evolves and its ColdFusion capabilities refine and increase, it promises to become a more popular choice for ColdFusion development.

Tip

Many developers find that Studio is better suited for low-level coding and that UltraDev is better suited for live prototyping. Both clients have legitimate uses; you just need to determine which works best for you in which scenarios.

Note

Future versions of ColdFusion Studio and UltraDev likely will evolve to the point that you won't need to use two applications at all. Everything discussed in this chapter pertains to the current shipping product (UltraDev 4).

THE ULTRADEV ENVIRONMENT

After installing UltraDev but before configuring it for ColdFusion development, you should familiarize yourself with the UltraDev development environment.

THE DOCUMENT WINDOW

In UltraDev, you will build your ColdFusion application in the document window, as shown in Figure 16.1. The document window can display four types of views for developing ColdFusion applications:

- **Code**—Shows the actual code in your page
- **Design**—Provides a WYSIWYG environment in which you can visually develop ColdFusion applications
- **Code and Design**—Divides and displays both the code and the visual environment
- **Live Data**—Displays what the page will look like as rendered by your ColdFusion server

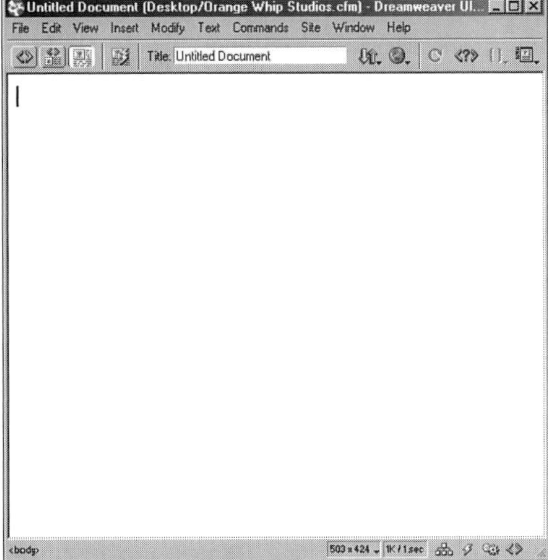

Figure 16.1
UltraDev's document window displays a number of views to develop ColdFusion applications.

THE DATA BINDINGS AND SERVER BEHAVIORS PANELS

In addition to the document window, UltraDev uses floating panels, windows, and toolbars to organize its development tools. Almost all your development tasks in UltraDev will be accomplished using one panel or another, or a combination of multiple panels. For ColdFusion-specific development tasks, you will principally use the Data Bindings and Server Behaviors panels.

THE SITE WINDOW

The Site window lets you manage all files associated with your Web application (see Figure 16.2). To display the Site window, select the Windows menu in a document window and select either Site Files or Site Map.

The Site window displays files using a Windows Explorer–like interface with hierarchical file trees. With the buttons in the upper-left corner of the Site window, you can browse files by site (the Site Files button), application server (the Application Server button), or site map (the Site Map button).

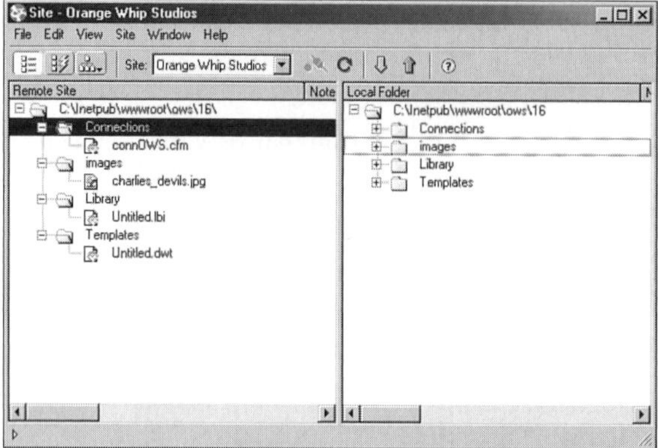

Figure 16.2
The Site window enables you to organize and manage the files for your Web application.

Note

Before you can use the Site window, you must set up your Web application in UltraDev. See the section "Configuring UltraDev for ColdFusion," later in this chapter, for more information.

Tip

You can configure the Site window by opening the Edit menu and selecting Preferences. In the Preferences dialog box, click Site to display the configuration options.

THE DATA BINDINGS PANEL

UltraDev's Data Bindings panel functions as the window to your database (see Figure 16.3). To display the Data Bindings window, open the Windows menu in a document window and select Data Bindings.

In the Data Bindings panel, you can define and call recordsets and stored procedures without writing a single line of SQL. You can also create and use a variety of variables, such as CGI, URL, form, and session variables. See the section "Building Form, Results, and Details Pages," later in this chapter, for more information.

THE SERVER BEHAVIORS PANEL

The Server Behaviors panel shares the same window as the Data Bindings panel (see Figure 16.4). To display the Server Behaviors panel, open the Windows menu in a document window and select Server Behaviors.

Figure 16.3
The Data Bindings panel enables you to create recordsets and variables.

In the Server Behaviors panel, you can add predefined ColdFusion logic, such as inserting or editing a record, or create your own ColdFusion logic. See the section "Building Form, Results, and Details Pages," later in this chapter, for more information.

Figure 16.4
The Server Behaviors panel gives you the ability to insert predefined ColdFusion logic and create your own.

THE CODE INSPECTOR

The Code Inspector displays the actual code for your pages (see Figure 16.5). To start the Code Inspector, open the Windows menu and select Code Inspector.

The Code Inspector provides basic text editing features, including basic syntax coloring, word wrap, line numbers, highlighting invalid HTML, and automatic indent.

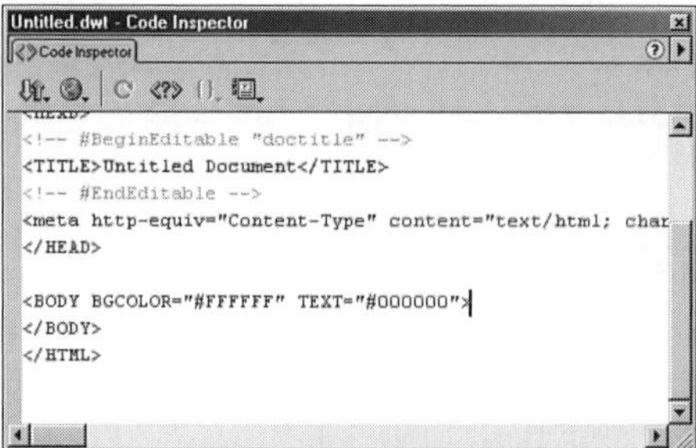

Figure 16.5
The Code Inspector enables you view edit the actual code.

Tip

If you want to use a text-editing environment, UltraDev includes an OEM version of HomeSite 4.5. It can be installed from the UltraDev CD-ROM. You can also use ColdFusion Studio. To integrate an external text editor with UltraDev, such as HomeSite or ColdFusion Studio, follow these steps:

1. Open the Edit menu and select Preferences.
2. Click the File Types/Editors option.
3. In the External Code Editor text box, enter the file path for the EXE file of your text editor.

CONFIGURING ULTRADEV FOR COLDFUSION

Before you can develop any ColdFusion applications, you first must set up UltraDev for ColdFusion development. Creating a site in UltraDev and defining its characteristics accomplishes this.

For the purposes of this chapter, let's assume that you're setting up UltraDev for the Orange Whip Studios sample application that accompanies this book.

CREATING YOUR SITE

A *site* is UltraDev terminology for a Web development project. All your ColdFusion development will take place inside the context of the site you create.

To create a site, follow these steps:

1. If it is not already running, start UltraDev.
2. In the document window, select Windows from the menu bar and click Site Files (or press F8). The Site window appears.
3. In the Site window's menu bar, select Site and click New Site. The Site Definitions dialog box appears.

   In the Site Definitions box, you will notice a vertical bar on the left. It contains the following choices:

- Local Info
- Remote Info
- Application Server
- Design Notes
- Site Map Layout
- File View Columns

In each of these sections, you can set all the definitions for your site.

4. In the Local Info screen of the Site Definitions dialog box, type **`Orange Whip Studios`** in the Site Name text box (see Figure 16.6). In the Local Root Folder text box, enter **`C:\Inetpub\wwwroot\ows\16\`**. Click the file icon to the right of the text box to spawn a file chooser dialog box.
5. Click Remote Info in the left window. If your ColdFusion server is located on your local machine or network, select Local/Network in the Access drop-down menu (see Figure 16.7). Enter the file path for the directory in which you will be storing your ColdFusion files (for example, **`C:\Inetpub\wwwroot\ows\16\`** for a local directory) in the Remote Folder text box.

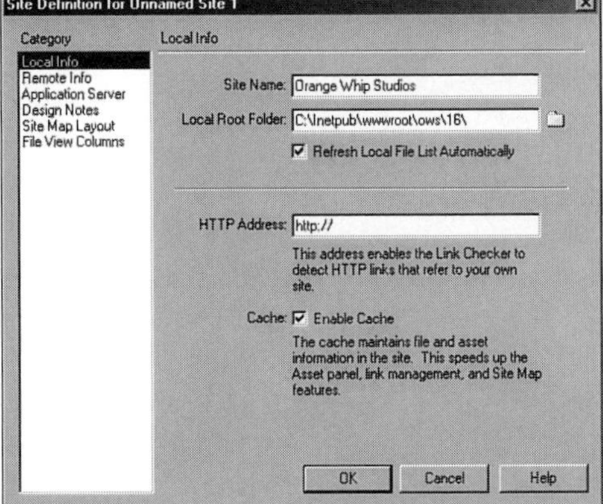

Figure 16.6
Name your site and supply the root folder in the Local Info screen of the Site Definitions dialog box.

Tip

In the Remote Info screen, you can also configure UltraDev to use a remote server over FTP. In addition, you can use a source control system, such as SourceSafe or WebDAV.

Don't click OK just yet. You will use the same Site Definitions dialog box to establish your other site definitions.

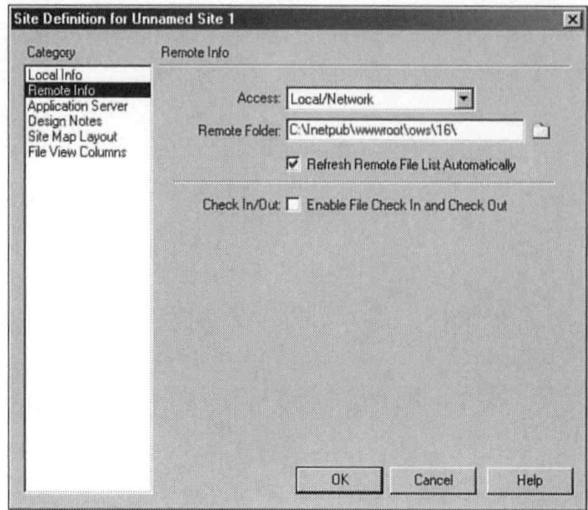

Figure 16.7
Select your access method and specify the directory where your application files will reside in the Remote Info screen of the Site Definitions dialog box.

SETTING COLDFUSION AS YOUR APPLICATION SERVER

To configure the Orange Whip Studio site for ColdFusion, complete the following steps:

1. In the Site Definitions dialog box, click Application Server.
2. Select ColdFusion 4.0 from the Server Model drop-down menu (see Figure 16.8).
3. Select Local/Network from the Access drop-down menu.

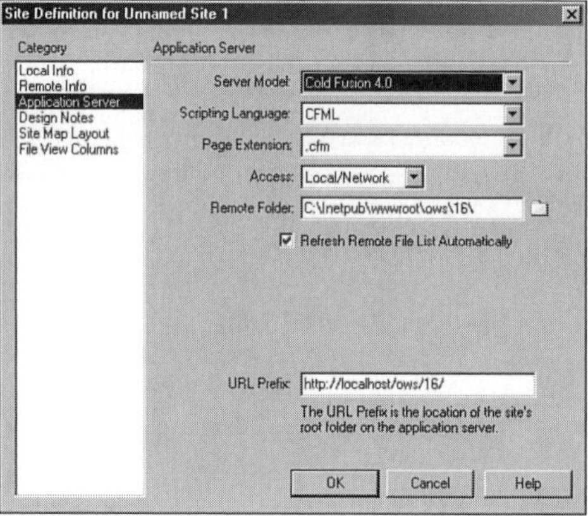

Figure 16.8
In the Application Server screen of the Site Definitions dialog box, select ColdFusion 4.0.

Note

Even though UltraDev 4 is designed for ColdFusion 4.04, UltraDev's prepackaged CFML tools work seamlessly on ColdFusion 5.

Click the OK button, and you're finished. Next, let's set up the data source connections for UltraDev.

ESTABLISHING DATA SOURCES

UltraDev requires a DSN connection to communicate with your database. To establish a connection with your database, follow these steps:

1. In UltraDev's document window, select Modify from the menu bar and click Connections. The Connections dialog box appears.
2. Click the New button. When you click the New button, a submenu appears; select Data Source Name in the submenu. The Data Source Name dialog box appears (see Figure 16.9).
3. Enter **connOWS** in the Connection Name text box. In the Data Source Name (DSN) drop-down menu, select OWS. Click the Login button, enter your ColdFusion Administrator username and password, and click OK.

Note

An ODBC data source must be established in Windows for UltraDev to reference.

4. Enter your ColdFusion Administrator username in the User Name text box and your ColdFusion Administrator password in the Password text box.
5. Click the Test button to verify that the DSN connection works.

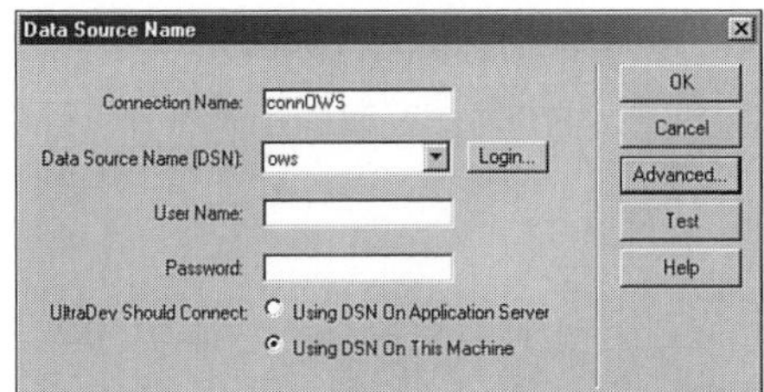

Figure 16.9 Establish your UltraDev DSN connection in the Data Source Name dialog box.

Congratulations, UltraDev is now ready to develop ColdFusion applications.

BUILDING FORM, RESULTS, AND DETAILS PAGES

As a demonstration of ColdFusion development with UltraDev, you will build a simple expense reporting application for the Accounting Department of Orange Whip Studios. Using this application, accounting personnel can select a film and view the total expenses associated with it. In addition, they can click the total expense figure and see a breakdown of individual expenses.

For this application, you need three pages:

- A form page in which the user selects the film
- A results page in which the user views the total expenses
- A details page in which the user views the details of each expense

Let's start with the form page.

BUILDING THE FORM PAGE

Ensure that Orange Whip Studios is selected in the Site window. The form page consists of an HTML table, one menu, and a submit button. Do the following:

1. In the File menu of the Site window, select New File. Rename the file `form.cfm`. Repeat this step to create two more files named `results.cfm` and `detail.cfm`. Open `form.cfm`.
2. To create the table, select the Windows menu in the `form.cfm Document window and` click Object (see Figure 16.10). In the Objects toolbar, click the Insert Table button, and create a table with two columns and three rows.

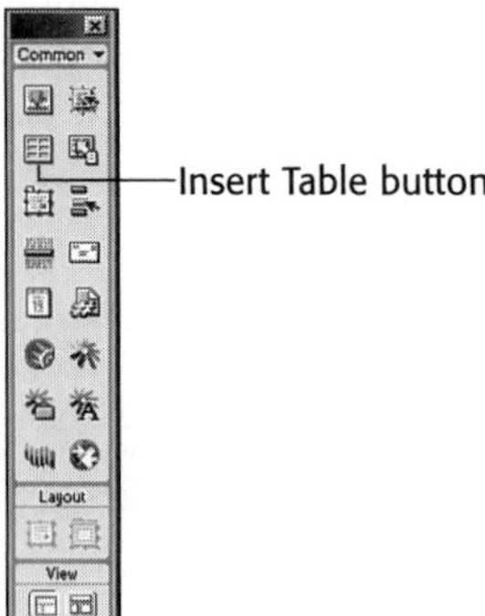

Figure 16.10
To create a table, click the Table button in the Objects toolbar.

3. Highlight the top row and right-click. In the submenu that appears, select Table and Merge Cells. Repeat this for the bottom row.
4. Type **`Current Expenses by Film`** in the top row and make the text bold. In the next row, type **`Select Film:`** in the left cell and leave the right cell blank for now. Also, leave the bottom row empty.
5. Next, you create the menu. Place your cursor in the right cell of the second row. At the top of the Objects toolbar, click the small down arrow labeled Common. In the submenu that appears, select Forms. Next, click the Insert List/Menu button. A dialog box appears that asks whether you want to insert a `FORM` tag. Click No. A menu appears in the cell.

   You could enter each film title, or you could leverage ColdFusion to make the menu dynamic. To do this, you must first create a recordset. Go to the Data Bindings panel and click the + button. In the submenu that appears, click RecordSet (Query). In the RecordSet dialog box, enter **`GetFilmTitles`** in the Name text field and select connOWS in the Connection drop-down menu. You want to populate the menu with film titles, so select Films in the Table drop-down menu. Now, click the Selected radio button. You obviously need the `MovieTitle` column. However, because this is a form page, you also need to pass a value to the results page. Let's use `FilmID`. So, while holding down the Ctrl key, click FilmID. Click OK. The recordset `GetFilmTitles` now displays in the Data Bindings panel (see Figure 16.11).

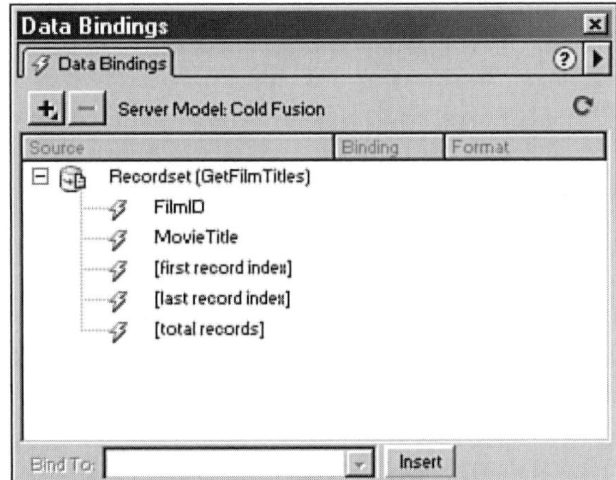

Figure 16.11 The `GetFilmTitles` recordset now displays in the Data Bindings panel.

6. Make sure the menu is selected. If it is not already open, open the Windows menu in the document window and select Properties. The Properties panel lets you modify attributes for most elements in the document window (see Figure 16.12).

Figure 16.12 The Properties panel lets you define and change attributes for page elements.

7. In the Properties panel, enter **`FilmSelection`**. This identifies the form variable you will reference in the results page. Now, click the List Values button, which spawns the List Values dialog box (see Figure 16.13). Click the + button. In the Item Label column, notice the lightning bolt button. Click it and the Dynamic Data dialog box appears, which is almost an exact replica of the Data Bindings panel.

Because you want the list to contain movie titles, select MovieTitles. Notice the code in the Code text box. You can edit the code if you want. Click OK. Back in the List Values dialog box, the Item Label and Item Value columns contain an entry for the MovieTitles column.

Click OK.

Wait a minute. Although you want the movie titles for the item labels, you want `FilmID` to be assigned to the item values. Fortunately, you don't need to go back into the List Values dialog box to change this. In the Data Bindings panel, Item Selection is assigned to the Value column. Select FilmID, and click the down arrow next to the Value column. In the submenu that appears, select Item Value. That's it.

8. With your mouse, select the form field (the red box surrounding the menu). The Properties panel changes to show the `<FORM>` tag attributes. To specify where to send the form variable, enter the file path to the `results.cfm` file in the Action text box, and ensure that Post is selected in the Method drop-down menu.
9. Place your cursor in the bottom row and click the Insert button on the Object toolbar. By default, UltraDev inserts a Submit button. Click No when UltraDev asks you to insert a form.
10. Place the cursor outside the table, and click the Insert Form button in the Objects pane. A red broken-line box appears below the table. Select the whole table and press Ctrl+X on your keyboard to cut the table. Be sure the cursor is sitting inside the form box and press Ctrl+V on your keyboard to paste the table. Your table should now look similar to the one in Figure 16.13.
11. Save `form.cfm`.

That's it. Now let's move on to `results.cfm`.

Figure 16.13
Here is the table with the form controls added. The red boxes indicate the presence of forms.

BUILDING THE RESULTS PAGE

When the user selects a film and clicks the Submit button, you want the results page to display the movie title, the total expenses for the movie, and the amount of the budget for the movie. In addition, you want the user to be able to click the total expenses and see a breakdown of the individual expenses.

Therefore, you need a table that displays the movie title, total expenses, and budget. Let's start by creating the recordset:

1. In the Site window, open `results.cfm`.
2. In the Data Bindings panel, click the + button and select RecordSet (Query). In the RecordSet dialog box, enter **`GetTotalExpenses`** in the Name text box and select connOWS in the Connection drop-down menu. In the Table drop-down menu, select Expenses and click the Selected radio button. Select FilmID and ExpenseAmount.

   Because you want to display the total expenses for only the movie the user selects, you must use the form variable passed by the form page. The easiest way to do that is to revert to the previous dialog box by clicking the Simple button. In the Filter drop-down menu, select FilmID. In the drop-down menu to the right, select =. Below the Filter drop-down menu, select Form variable. Finally, enter **`FilmSelection`** in the text box to the right of Form variable (see Figure 16.14).

   Now you have a problem. You need the *total* expenses for each movie. Because the current dialog box provides no obvious facility for using aggregate SQL functions, you must edit the SQL directly. To do so, click the Advanced button. The RecordSet dialog box changes to display a more detailed interface to the database (see Figure 16.14). The `SELECT` and `FROM` statements already appear in the SQL text box, as does a `WHERE` clause for the form variable.

   In the SQL text box, replace FilmID and ExpenseAmount with the following statement directly after `SELECT`: **`SUM(ExpenseAmount) AS TotalExpense`**.

   This adds the values of all the columns in the `ExpenseAmount` column and designates the sum as `TotalExpense`. Click OK. The `GetTotalExpenses` recordset now displays in the Data Bindings panel.
3. Create another recordset that simply selects `MovieTitle`, `BudgetAmount`, and `FilmID` from the `Movies` table. Just like step 1, make the `FilmID` equal to the variable `Form.FilmSelection`.
4. Create a table with four rows and two columns. Merge the cells in the bottom and top rows. In the left cell of the second row, type **`Total Current Expenses`**. In the left cell of the third row, type **`Budget`**. In the bottom row, type **`To see individual expenses, click total expenses value.`**

Figure 16.14
The Advanced RecordSet dialog box enables you to edit SQL statements directly, as well as other functions.

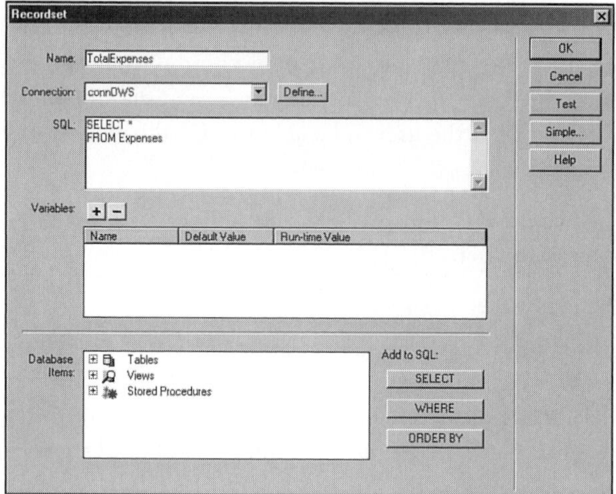

5. In the top row, you want to show the title of the movie. To do this, go to the Server Behaviors panel. Ensure that your cursor is sitting in the top row, and click the + button. In the submenu that appears, click Dynamic Elements and select Dynamic Text.

   The Dynamic Text dialog box displays the `GetExpenses` and `GetMovieTitle` recordsets. You want the movie title, so select MovieTitle. Click OK. The variable `GetMovieTitle.MovieTitle` now appears in light blue surrounded by brackets.

6. Next, insert the total expenses variable. Ensure that your cursor is sitting in the right cell of the second row, and click the + button. Select Dynamic Elements and then Dynamic Text. In the Dynamic Text dialog box, select TotalExpense. Because this is a dollar figure, you must format the variable output. In the Format drop-down menu, select Currency–Dollar Format (see Figure 16.15). Click OK.

7. To insert the budget variable, use the Data Binding panel. Again, you could drag and drop BudgetAmount from the Data Binding panel to the right cell of the third row. Instead, though, use the Insert button at the bottom of the Data Bindings panel. Ensure that your cursor is sitting in the target cell, and select BudgetAmount so that it is highlighted. Next, click the Insert button. The `GetMovieTitle.BudgetAmount` variable appears in the cell. Because this is another dollar amount, scroll the Data Bindings panel to the right. You will see a small down-arrow button in the Format column. Click it, and a submenu appears. In the Format submenu, select Currency and then Dollar Format. The table should now appear as shown in Figure 16.16.

8. Let's see what the table looks like so far in a Web browser. Click the Live Data View button in the Document window toolbar. This activates ColdFusion Server to process the page and return the output (see Figure 16.17). Click the button again to return to the normal view.

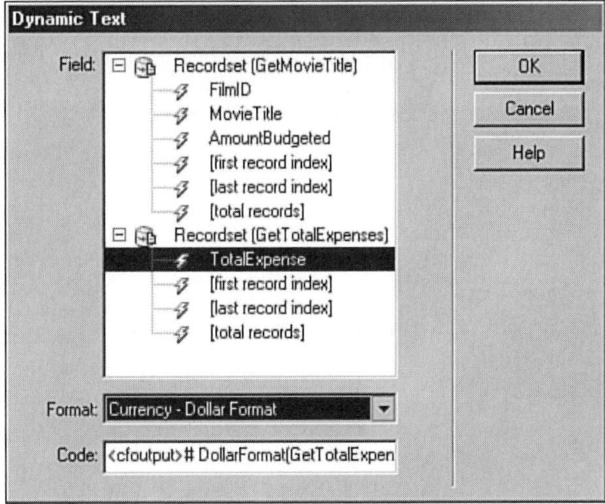

Figure 16.15
The Dynamic Text dialog box lets you insert variables easily and format the output in one click.

Figure 16.16
The table contains text and dynamic text.

9. Finally, you need to make the total expenses value clickable so users can see the individual expense. Start by highlighting the `GetTotalExpenses.TotalExpense` variable. In the Server Behaviors panel, click the + button and select Go to Detail Page. The Go to Detail Page dialog box appears (see Figure 16.18).

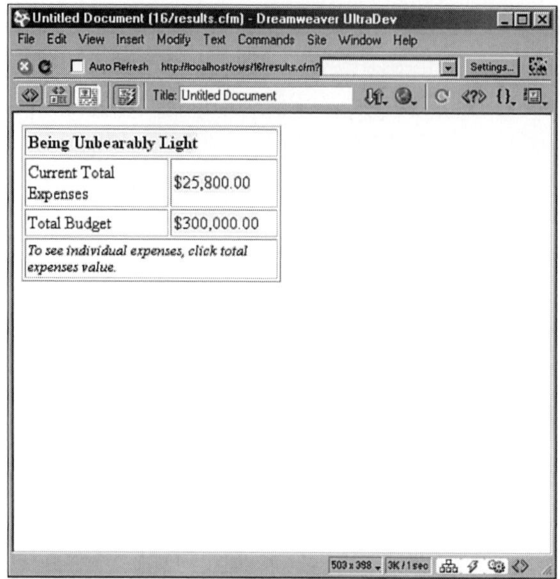

Figure 16.17 The Live Data View displays an approximation of what the results page would look like in a Web browser.

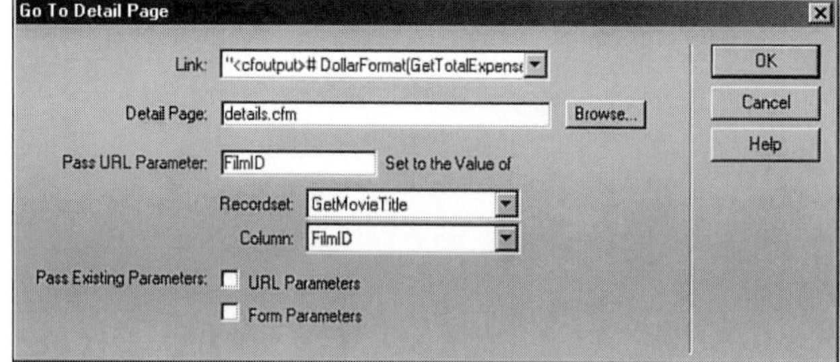

Figure 16.18 The Go to Detail Page dialog box enables you to designate the detail page to pass variables and which variables to pass.

In this dialog box, the `TotalExpense` variable should already be selected in the Link drop-down menu. In the Detail Page text box, enter the file path to `detail.cfm`. You want to display the details of all expenses related to a file, so in the Pass URL Parameter box, enter **`FilmID`**. In the RecordSet drop-down menu, you must choose which recordset value the URL parameter will pass: `GetTotalExpenses` or `GetMovieTitle`. Because you want to display the individual expenses on the details page of a specific movie, select GetTotalExpenses. In the Column drop-down menu, select FilmID. Click OK. The `TotalExpense` variable now appears as a hyperlink.

Note

In the Pass Existing Parameters section of the Go to Detail Page dialog box, you can also assign the variable passed by the form page to pass on to the details page. Click either URL or Form to enable this feature.

BUILDING THE DETAILS PAGE

You're nearing the finish. For the last page, you need two separate tables—one table to display general information about the movie and one table to display individual expense dates, descriptions, and amounts. Also, you need three recordsets—one to get the individual expenses, one to get the movie title and related information, and one to add up the total expenses. Let's get to it:

1. In the Site window, open `details.cfm`.
2. Create three recordsets named `GetExpenseDetails`, `GetMovieInfo`, and `GetTotalExpenses`. In the `GetExpenseDetails` recordset, select the Expenses table and the `FilmID`, `ExpenseAmount`, `Description`, and `ExpenseDate` columns. Filter the recordset by selecting the FilmID equal to the URL parameter `FilmID`. (Remember, the results page is passing this variable.) In the `GetMovieInfo` recordset, select the Films table and the `FilmID`, `MovieTitle`, `AmountBudgeted`, and `DateInTheaters` columns. Similar to the `ExpenseDetails` recordset, filter the recordset by selecting the FilmID equal to the URL parameter `FilmID`. In the `GetTotalExpenses` recordset, select the Expenses table and set the FilmID equal to the URL parameter `FilmID`. Click the Advanced button, and enter the same aggregate SQL function as you used in the results page. Your Data Bindings Panel should look similar to the one in Figure 16.19.
3. At the top of the page, type **`Expense Report for`** and insert the `GetMovieInfo.MovieTitle` variable by dragging and dropping it after `for`. Highlight the line, and increase its font size to `4` in the Properties panel.
4. Create a table with three rows and two columns. In the left column, enter **`Premiere Date`** in the first row, **`Budget`** in the second row, and **`Total Expenses to Date`** in the third row. In the right column, insert the `GetMovieInfo.DateInTheaters` variable in the first row, the `GetMovieInfo.AmountBudgeted` variable in the second row, and the `GetTotalExpenses.TotalExpense` in the third row. The first variable should be formatted as a date, and the second and third variables should be formatted as dollar amounts. The table should look similar to the one in Figure 16.20.

   Here is the same table in the Live Data view (see Figure 16.21).

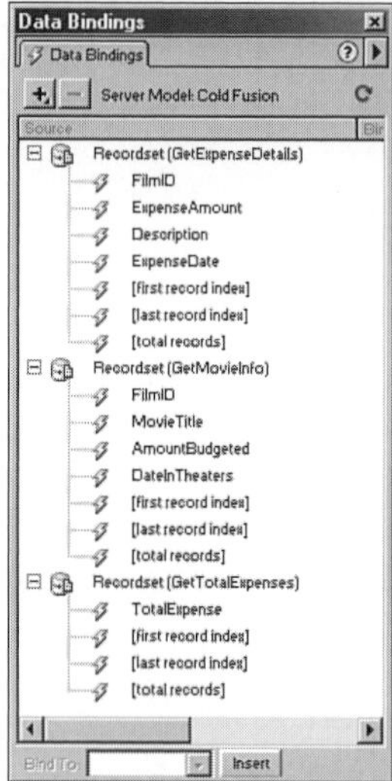

Figure 16.19
The Data Bindings panel for `details.cfm` is crowded with recordsets.

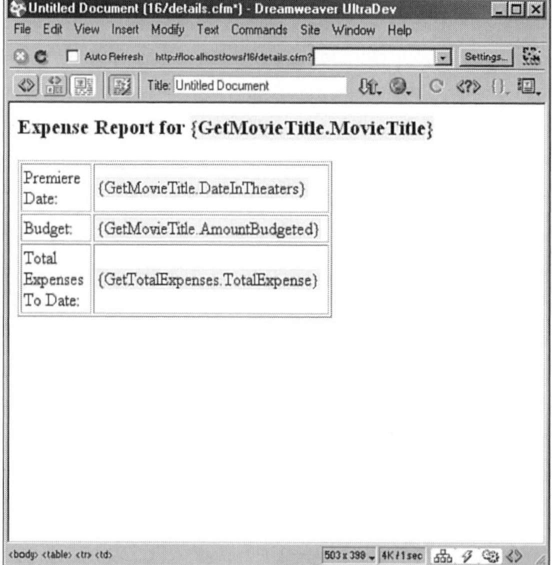

Figure 16.20
The first table in `details.cfm` contains general information about the movie selected by the user, including dynamic text fields for the premiere date, budget, and total expenses.

5. In the Document window below the table created in step 4, press Enter on your keyboard and create another table with two rows and three columns. On the top row, type **`Date`** in the first column, **`Description`** in the second column, and **`Amount`** in the third column. Make all these words bold.

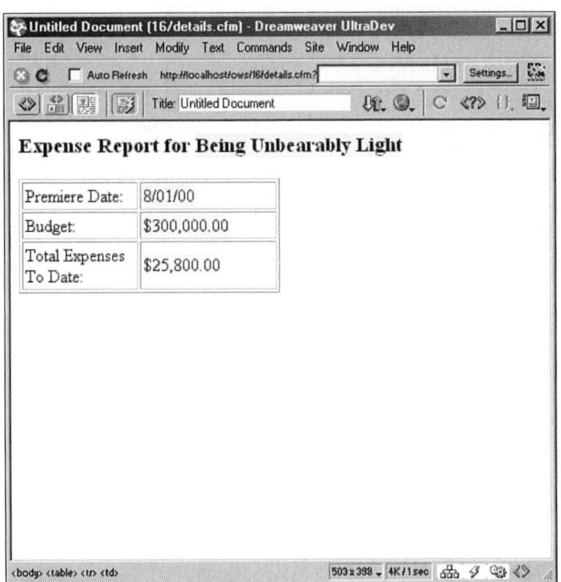

Figure 16.21
The Live Data view of the first table in `details.cfm` shows the values returned by ColdFusion for the variables.

6. The individual expenses returned by ColdFusion for each movie likely will be more than one. Therefore, you must configure the second row to repeat for every record returned. To do this, highlight the second row with your cursor. In the Server Behaviors panel, click the + button and select Repeat Region. The Repeat Region dialog box appears (see Figure 16.22). Select GetExpenseDetails in the RecordSet drop-down menu, and click the All Records radio button in the Show section. Click OK. A thin gray line labeled Repeat appears around the second row.

Note

Ensure that you always configure a page element, such as a row or a column, to repeat before inserting any dynamic text or form controls. Otherwise, UltraDev creates nested `<CFOUTPUT>` tags.

7. In the second row, finish by inserting `GetExpenseDetails.ExpenseDate` in the first column and giving it a date format. Then insert `GetExpenseDetails.Description` in the second column, and insert `GetExpenseDetails.ExpenseAmount` in the third column and give it a dollar currency format. The results are shown in Figure 16.23.

Figure 16.24 shows the completed page in the Live Data view.

Congratulations, you've built a ColdFusion application with Dreamweaver UltraDev.

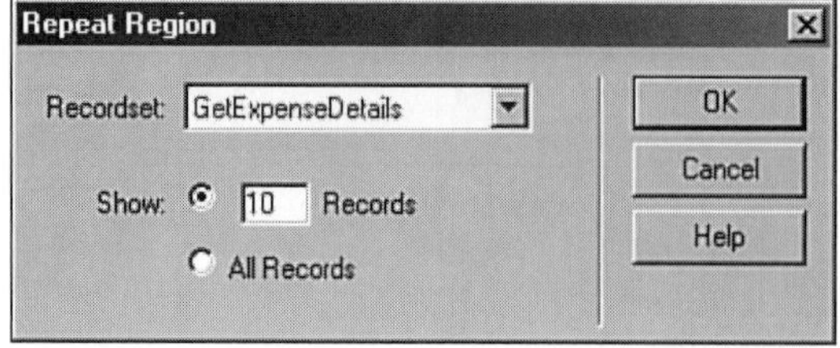

Figure 16.22
In the Repeat Record dialog box, configure the second row to repeat for each record returned by ColdFusion.

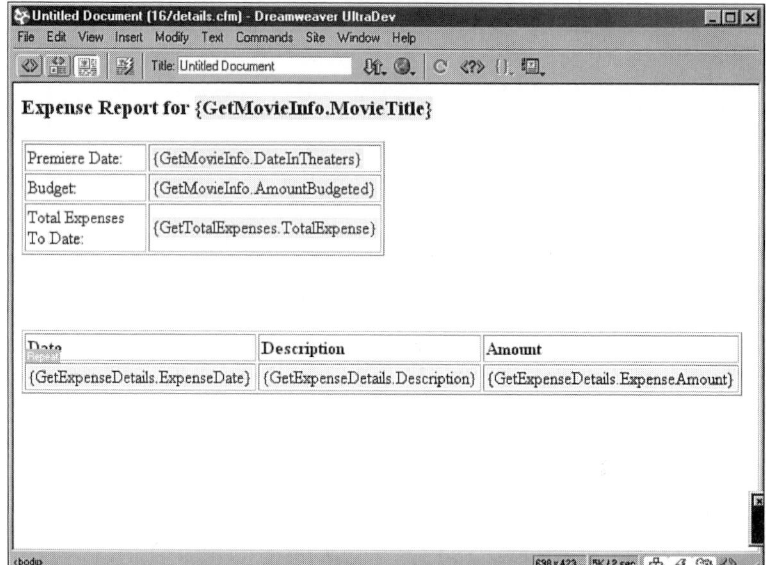

Figure 16.23
The second row in `details.cfm` contains the individual expenses of the movie, including dynamic text fields for the expense date, expense description, and amount.

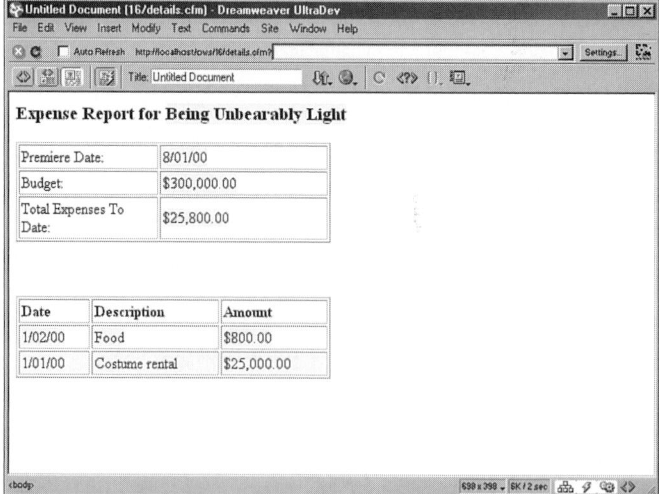

Figure 16.24
Shown in the Live Data view, you can see the completed page. The text highlighted in yellow is dynamic.

A Note on the ColdFusion Code Generated by UltraDev

You just created a ColdFusion application without typing a single line of code. UltraDev generated the CFML code for you, enabling you to concentrate on the user experience. For example, Listing 16.1 shows the `<CFQUERY>` code from `results.cfm`.

Listing 16.1 results.cfm—<CFQUERY>

```
<!---
Name:        results.cfm
Author:      David Golden (d_golden73@hotmail.com)
Description: results page
Created:     5/01/01
--->
<cfinclude template="Connections/connOWS.cfm">
<cfparam name="FORM.FilmSelection" default="1">
<cfparam name="GetMovieTitle__MMColParam" default="#FORM.FilmSelection#">
<cfquery name="GetMovieTitle" datasource=#MM_connOWS_DSN#
➥ username=#MM_connOWS_USERNAME# password=#MM_connOWS_PASSWORD#>
SELECT FilmID, MovieTitle, AmountBudgeted FROM Films WHERE FilmID
➥ = #GetMovieTitle__MMColParam#
</cfquery>
<cfparam name="GetTotalExpenses__MMColParam" default="#FORM.FilmSelection#">
<cfquery name="GetTotalExpenses" datasource=#MM_connOWS_DSN#
➥ username=#MM_connOWS_USERNAME# password=#MM_connOWS_PASSWORD#>
SELECT SUM(ExpenseAmount) AS TotalExpense FROM Expenses WHERE FilmID
➥ = #GetTotalExpenses__MMColParam#
</cfquery>
<cfscript> MM_paramName = "";
</cfscript>
<cfscript>
// *** Go To Record and Move To Record: create strings for maintaining
➥ URL and Form parameters

// create the list of parameters which should not be maintained
MM_removeList = "&index=";
If (MM_paramName NEQ "") MM_removeList = MM_removeList
➥ & "&" & MM_paramName & "=";
MM_keepURL=""; MM_keepForm=""; MM_keepBoth=""; MM_keepNone="";

// add the existing URL parameters to the MM_keepURL string
MM_params=ListToArray(CGI.QUERY_STRING,"&");
For (i=1; i LTE ArrayLen(MM_params); i=i+1) {
  If (FindNoCase("&" & GetToken(MM_params[i],1,"=") & "=",MM_removeList) Is 0)
    MM_keepURL = MM_keepURL & "&" & MM_params[i];
}
```

LISTING 16.1 CONTINUED

```
// add the existing Form variables to the MM_keepForm string
If (IsDefined("FORM.FieldNames")) {
  MM_params=ListToArray(FORM.FieldNames,",");
  For (i=1; i LTE ArrayLen(MM_params); i=i+1) {
    If (FindNoCase("&" & MM_params[i] & "=",MM_removeList) Is 0)
      MM_keepForm = MM_keepForm & "&" & LCase(MM_params[i])
➥ & "=" & URLEncodedFormat(Evaluate("FORM." & MM_params[i]));
  }
}

// create the Form + URL string and remove the initial '&' from
➥ each of the strings
MM_keepBoth = MM_keepURL & MM_keepForm;
If (MM_keepURL NEQ "") MM_keepURL = RemoveChars(MM_keepURL,1,1);
If (MM_keepForm NEQ "") MM_keepForm = RemoveChars(MM_keepForm,1,1);
If (MM_keepBoth NEQ "") MM_keepBoth = RemoveChars(MM_keepBoth,1,1);
</cfscript>
```

As you can see, UltraDev uses `<CFSCRIPT>` extensively to perform functions that usually are performed using CFML tag attributes. Although this does increase the average size of CFML files produced by UltraDev when compared to ColdFusion Studio, the code should run perfectly on any ColdFusion release after 4.0.

Note

Future versions of UltraDev probably will generate plain CFML, relying less on `<CFSCRIPT>`.

Note

For an introduction to the UltraDev development in general, look for *Sams Teach Yourself Dreamweaver UltraDev 4 in 21 Days* (ISBN: 0-672-31901-2).

Building ColdFusion Applications

CHAPTER 17

Planning an Application

In this chapter

GETTING STARTED ON YOUR APPLICATION

When many developers get a new project to work on, their first instinct is usually to start coding right away. It's easy to understand why. Those first few hours or days of coding can be a lot of fun. The "inner geek" in each of us gets a special thrill from sinking its teeth into a new project, watching an application take shape, and carving something unique and useful out of thin air. Plus, there's often a deadline looming, so it often seems like the best idea just to start writing code as soon as humanly possible.

The problem is that even the simplest applications have a way of becoming much more complicated than they seemed at first. Nine times out of ten, if you take the time to plan your application and development process right from the start, you really will do a better job in less time. Of course, people say that about almost everything in life. But in Web application development, it really is true.

Admit it! Your inner geek is already telling you to skip this chapter and get on with the coding. Resist the geek, if you can. The advice in this chapter will mean a bit more work for you upfront. You might find that you even need to write a few documents. But you probably will end up doing more cool stuff and less tedious work if you know exactly where your application is headed at all times. Really. Seriously. Honest. Your inner geek might even buy you a drink when you're done.

DEFINING THE PROJECT

The first thing to do is to ensure that the project is as completely defined as possible. You need to know exactly what type of application to build, and that usually means doing some research and asking lots of questions.

In a perfect world, you would already have a written description of the application that defines its every aspect. You would know exactly what the expectations are for the project, and who will be testing it, using it, and benefiting from it. You would have complete understandings of every aspect of the project, from what technologies should be used, to how the database should look.

In reality, you might have only a short description, such as "we want to personalize our online store," or "we need an accounting section in the company intranet." Sounds great, but you can't exactly start working yet.

THE IMPORTANCE OF BEING INSPIRED

If you can, try to have a "vision" about the project early on. Make it ambitious. Figure out how people are thinking about the project, and try to come up with some twist or feature that takes it to a whole new level—something you would be happy to see as an end user and that you would be proud to have implemented as a developer.

Why? Because it's important for you to be as interested in the project as you can. If you're having fun during the development process, the application will most likely turn out better. So, if at first the application sounds like something you've done or seen a million times before, try to think of something to add to make it unique. Even if the project already sounds difficult or daunting, think of some way to make it even more of a challenge.

Then, after you have gotten yourself excited about the project, try to get everyone else excited about it, too. Come up with a trademark-sounding name or code name for the project (perhaps from a favorite movie or a play on words based on the name of your competition). Talk about the project as if it were the cure for all diseases, as if it were going to save the world. Sell the thing. Even if it's filled with irony, your enthusiasm will bubble over onto the next desk or into the next room. At the very least, the project will be a little bit more fun. And how can that not be a good thing?

UNDERSTANDING THE PROJECT

Now that you're enthused about the project, you need to get yourself educated as well. Before you go any further, be sure you know the answers to the following:

- **Internet, Intranet, or Extranet?** Most projects will fall into one of these three categories. Be sure you know which one yours falls into, and why. It is usually obvious when a project is an Internet project because it targets end users. Sometimes the difference between intranets and extranets can be more subtle, especially if the application is meant to be used by your company's business partners as well as in house. Even though it's just a word, be sure you and your client or boss *agree* on the word.
- **Totally new or "Version 2.0"?** You should know whether you are replacing an existing Web application. If so, why? What exactly is wrong with the current one? To what extent should you be using the existing application as a guide? Is the original just showing its age, or was it a total disaster from its very conception?
- **New process or existing process?** You should know whether your application is creating something totally new ("we have never had anything in place to do this"), or a modification of a current process ("we have always done this, but it was partly on paper and partly in a spreadsheet").
- **Integrating with existing site?** You should know whether your application is going to sit within the context of a larger Web site. If so, how will people get to your part of the site? How will they get back? Do you need to keep the navigation consistent?
- **Integrating with other systems?** Does any back-end or legacy integration need to be done? Perhaps your application needs to receive periodic updates from some type of batch process that occurs within the organization. If so, learn as much about the existing systems as you can.
- **Existing database schemas?** Frequently, there is some type of existing database that at least part of your application will need to be aware of. Perhaps a table of customers and their IDs already exists somewhere within the organization. Find out whether your application can add tables and columns to this database or whether it should have its own database. Remember that ColdFusion generally has no problem dealing with information from multiple databases.

CONDUCTING A FEW INTERVIEWS

We recommend that you conduct a few informal interviews amongst the people who might actually be using your application when it's completed. Depending on the project, that might mean people within the company or just a few potential end users you find out on the street. Ask these people what they would like to see in the application. How could it be even more useful to them?

Tip

> A fun question to ask is, "If there were only a single button to click in this new application, what should it be?" At first, you might get sarcastic answers, such as, "It should find me a better husband," or "It should do my job for me," but after you start getting serious answers, they can be quite telling.

These potential users will likely tell you more about how your application will actually be used than your normal contacts within the company can. They often are more likely to be able to describe what they need in ordinary terms. You might find that you think about the project differently after a couple of these short interviews, and you might end up reevaluating the importance of various features.

Tip

> If your application is meant to replace or improve some process these people perform manually or with some earlier application, you might want to observe them doing their jobs for a short amount of time. You might find that they end up spending most of their time doing task "X," whereas you were thinking of the application as assisting mainly with task "Y."

This interview process serves another, more subtle purpose as well. It associates a real person—a face, or several faces—with the project for you. When you reach a stumbling block later, or when you design a form, you can have these people in mind (hmmm, what would that cute accountant like to see here?). Perhaps without totally realizing it, you will actually be creating the application *for* these people. When it's finished, you are likely to have improved their day-to-day work experiences or somehow made things more fun or easier for people using your application at home. You'll find it more rewarding, and your application will have much more perceived value.

SETTING EXPECTATIONS

This is perhaps the most important thing to nail down as early as possible. Even the most savvy people have a way of expecting things from an application that they never told you about.

Try to sit down and discuss the following with your boss or client. Keep in mind that many of these items are matters of give and take. You might want to keep framing the discussion by using words such as "the upside of doing this would be X, but the downside would be Y." Consider the following:

- **How fast for modem users?** If you're lucky, you are building an intranet that will never be used outside the local network. If not, you probably have to consider the poor folks connecting at 56K. Try to come up with an expected level of service for modem users (perhaps the first page must come up in 15 seconds or less and all other pages in 10 seconds or less). Depending on to whom you are talking, talking in terms of image size (no more than 50KB of images per page) might be easier than talking in terms of download time. It's often best to talk in terms of file size with graphic artists and in terms of download time with everyone else.
- **What screen resolution and color depth?** Most developers and graphic artists have great computer monitors that display lots of pixels at a time. But many people have only 640×480 screens. If those people are important to you, and the application is starting to have a luxurious, cinematic layout that uses a lot of horizontal space, it's often helpful to point out that some people are going to have to scroll to see the important elements on the page.
- **How much does security matter?** You should know to what extent your application needs to be secure. Many applications need some level of security (based on a password of some kind, as discussed in Chapter 21, "Security with ColdFusion"), but do they need more? Should the pages be further secured using HTTPS and SSL, or restricted according to IP address? Or should it be secured even further, using client certificates? Where will the application sit in terms of the company's firewall, assuming the company has one?
- **Number of concurrent users?** You should determine what the expectations for the application are in terms of performance. If your client is thinking about the application getting a million hits per minute, but you only have an old 486 computer to host the thing on, that could be a problem. Of course, ColdFusion is inherently scalable, and you could always use a cluster of better servers later, but it can't hurt to ensure that you and your boss or client are in some kind of agreement in terms of load expectations.
- **Browser compatibility?** Does the application need to be capable of looking great with every browser ever made, from the first beta of Netscape Navigator to the latest service pack for Internet Explorer? Probably not. But you do need to determine exactly what the expectations are. Point out that if you are using client-side features, such as JavaScript or Dynamic HTML, the more browsers you need to support, the more testing you might need to do.
- **Platforms (Win, Mac, and so on)?** Unfortunately, today's Web browsers often display the same page differently on a Mac versus a Windows machine, and so on. If you need to support only one platform (if you are building an intranet for a strictly Linux shop), your job might be a lot easier. Again, just be sure you and your client agree on what the expectations are.

KNOWING THE PLAYERS

Unless you are producing every aspect of the application on your own—including artwork, testing, and deployment—you need to know who is going to be working on the various aspects of the project. Depending on the circumstances, you might need to assemble a team on your own.

Commonly, a team consists of the following basic positions. Even if one person is performing more than one function, be sure you know who is who:

- **ColdFusion Coders**—How many people will be programming the application? Just you, or a team of 20? Are the coders all under your control, or do they have their own chains of command or other responsibilities?
- **Graphic Artists**—Who will be coming up with any needed graphics, banners, and buttons? Who will be designing the overall look and feel of the application? Who will come up with the site's navigation and structure?
- **Database People**—Who will be in charge of developing the database structure or making changes to any existing tables? Does that person see herself as a developer (designing tables for applications and so on), or more of a database administrator (tuning the database, adjusting indexes, scheduling maintenance, and the like)?
- **Project Managers**—Who will be in charge of ensuring that the various elements of the project are being completed on time and meeting all the requirements? Who will keep an eye on everyone's schedules? Who will that person report to within the company? Who will report to that person within your team?

FACT FINDING

Next, it's time to do a bit of research. This might sound like a lot of work, but the truth is you can often do the research suggested here in a couple of hours. It is almost always time well spent.

LOOKING AT SIMILAR SITES

Spend some time searching the Internet for sites that are similar to your project. Even if you can't find a Web site that does the exact same thing as the application you're building, at least try to find a few sites that are in the same conceptual space or that have pages that present the same type of information that your application will be.

For example, let's say one of your pages is going to be an "Advanced Search" type of page, and another will be a page with data presented in rows and columns. Find the best examples of those types of pages that you can. What about them do you like? What don't you like? How does the use of color or spacing affect your opinion of the existing pages? When do the best sites use a button instead of a link, and why? When do graphics help, and when do they just get in the way?

Deciding Which Technologies to Use

You also should research and decide which technologies you will use. Most likely, ColdFusion will give you most of the functionality you need, but you still need to answer a few questions:

- **What database system?** You need to decide which type of relational database system (RDBMS) you will use. Many smaller Web applications are built using Access (.mdb) tables as their information stores, and there is nothing wrong with this for smaller applications. Most people will advise you to consider a server-based database product (such as Oracle, MySQL, or SQLServer) for larger-scale applications.
- **Any scripting or Dynamic HTML?** ColdFusion makes all its decisions on the server side, just before a page is delivered to the browser. Sometimes, your application will benefit from some type of client-side scripting using JavaScript or perhaps Dynamic HTML. If so, decide where you will use scripting, and to what end.
- **Any Flash, video, or other multimedia?** Depending on the project, you might need to include dynamic, interactive content, such as Macromedia Flash movies, Shockwave presentations, or 3D worlds in your pages. You also might want to present video to your users via the RealVideo player, Windows Media Player, QuickTime, or some other client-side technology. In general, such content requires that a plug-in be installed on each user's browser, but many plug-ins (Flash in particular) are commonly installed by default when the user installs a browser. Plug-ins generally can be installed automatically for Internet Explorer users (especially under Windows) but usually must be downloaded and installed manually for other browsers and platforms. Keep these issues in mind as you discuss the project. Can you actually require the Flash Player (or whatever other plug-in) for your application, or is it just used to add to the user's experience when available?
- **What to put in custom tags?** You should decide whether you will build any reusable custom tags while you are constructing your application. If you will, you might want to sketch out what each custom tag will do and what each tag's attributes might be. (CFML custom tags are discussed in Chapter 22, "Building Reusable Components.")
- **Any custom-built extensions?** Depending on the situation, you might want (or need) to code certain parts of your application using a different programming language, such as C++, Java, or Visual Basic. You might, for instance, compile a CFX tag to use within your ColdFusion templates. Or, you might create a COM object, servlet, or Java class, which you can also invoke within your ColdFusion template code. These subjects are not discussed in this book, but they are discussed in great detail in our companion book, *Advanced ColdFusion 5 Application Development* (Que, ISBN: 0-7897-2585-1).

Investigating Existing Custom Tags

The ColdFusion Developer's Exchange site is a great place to look for any existing custom tags that might help you build your application more quickly. Using these prebuilt extensions to ColdFusion often enables you to get your application finished more easily. Why reinvent the wheel if someone else has already done the work and is willing to share it with you for free (or for a nominal charge)?

The Developer's Exchange is located at `http://www.allaire.com/developer/gallery`.

SEARCHING THE COLDFUSION FORUMS

Another good place to go during the planning phase is the Online Support Forums for ColdFusion, which is a place where other users discuss problems and answer questions for each other. Support engineers from Allaire/Macromedia also participate in the forum discussions.

Try running searches for the type of application you are building or for specific features you might not have fully formed in your mind yet. You likely will find message threads that discuss various approaches of displaying the type of information you need to present, as well as any pitfalls or gotchas to keep in mind. You also probably will find code snippets and examples you can adapt.

The ColdFusion Support Forums are located at `http://forums.allaire.com`.

INVESTIGATING STANDARD OR THIRD-PARTY EXTENSIONS

As mentioned earlier, ColdFusion can invoke and communicate with Java classes and COM objects. You don't have to write any Java, C++, or Visual Basic code to use them; instead, you use them via CFML's `CreateObject()` function or via the `<CFOBJECT>` tag. Although using them might not be quite as seamless and ideal as using custom tags, the basic idea is the same: Why reinvent the wheel when someone has already done the work for you?

Therefore, it is worth a quick look on the Internet to see whether either of the following can help with some part of the functionality your application is meant to provide:

- **Third-party COM or ActiveX Objects**—With only a few exceptions, any nonvisual COM or ActiveX component can be used with ColdFusion. A good way to look for these items is to consult the Components sections of the various Active Server Pages sites out there—just about any COM/ActiveX object marketed toward ASP developers can be used in your ColdFusion templates. Of course, these components can be used only if you are using ColdFusion under Windows. For more on this topic, check out `http://www.cfcomet.com`.
- **Java Classes**—It is also worth checking for any Java classes that could provide specific chunks of functionality you need. For instance, if you need a platform-agnostic way to deal with reading the public keys associated with a server's SSL certificate, for instance, you could take a look at the classes provided by the `java.security.cert` package in the standard Java Development Kit (JDK) from http://`www.javasoft.com`. Of course, you could look beyond the JDK as well; a great number of third-party products can be invoked via Java, which generally means you can invoke them via ColdFusion.

A real discussion of how to use these objects in your ColdFusion templates is beyond the scope of this book. See *Advanced ColdFusion 5.0 Development* for complete explanations and examples. Also, see Appendix A, “ColdFusion Tag Reference,” to learn more about the `<CFOBJECT>` tag, and see Appendix B, “ColdFusion Function Reference,” to learn about the `CreateObject()` function.

PLANNING THE PROCESS

By now, you probably have met with your client or boss a few times and have done your initial research. You have a pretty good idea about what your application is going to be about. You probably also are beginning to have a strong sense about how it will be laid out. In other words, you should be starting to see the application in your mind. Time to get that down on paper. Then you can start doing the real work!

DESIGN DOCUMENTS

Even the most accomplished developers sometimes jump in without writing anything down on paper first. Those same developers will tell you that in most instances, working this way turns out to be a mistake. Sooner or later, you realize you forgot some feature your boss or client was expecting. Without documents, whether you really forgot the feature—or whether your client simply didn’t mention it—can’t be proven. In short, it simply can’t hurt to put things down on paper.

SPECIFICATION DOCUMENT

At the very least, you should have some type of project specifications document that describes the application in plain English and lists all the critical elements or features. This document should also include approximations of how long you think each item will take to complete.

The document should have a big picture or executive summary portion that, if read by an outsider, will provide an understanding about what the project is about. It should also have a detailed portion that is as specific as possible about individual features.

You also might want the document to prioritize the various elements or features; it could be that a shopping cart and an events calendar are both required elements, but that the events calendar is to be your primary focus. Most importantly, the specifications document should include the expectations that you have agreed upon for the project (see the section “Setting Expectations,” earlier in this chapter).

FLOWCHARTS AND STORYBOARDS

Depending on the project and your client, you might want to put together some visual aids, such as flowcharts or storyboards, that visually explain the various pages that will make up your application and what elements will be visible on each.

If you own a copy of the software product called Visio, you could use it to lay out flowcharts or storyboards. You could also use just about any other drawing program (such as PowerPoint) or just plain old paper or whiteboards. These flowcharts might be *logical* (mapping out the flow of decisions a template will make or the flow of choices your users might make) or *physical* (representing the pages in your application and the sequence or links from one to the other).

You might even end up with sketches of each page, which certainly can't hurt. In any case, be sure the important elements and features from your specification document are represented.

MILESTONES DOCUMENT

Just as most analysts stress the importance of setting boundaries in your personal life, most developers recommend establishing *milestones* during the development of an application. Milestones are like checkpoints along the way to an application's completion. You might try to set five milestones, say, each representing approximately 20% of the application's features or pages. After each milestone, your client or boss should take a look, give you any preliminary feedback, and generally let you know that you are on the right track.

Milestones are good for everyone involved. For your boss or client, she gets a positive feeling of progress whenever a milestone is reached. You also get a positive feeling of accomplishment, but more importantly, you are ensuring that your boss or client is reasonably satisfied with the development at a number of junctures. This involvement protects you a bit—if your boss or client has reviewed your progress as you reach these milestones, you know there's little chance of her disliking the whole project at the end because of some misunderstanding.

PLANNING THE TESTING PHASE

You should now have a good roadmap for the development of your project, in the form of your specifications and milestones documents (see the previous section). Next, you should also put together a similar type of roadmap regarding testing. No matter how great a coder you are, at least one bug is bound to be in your application the first time around. It's important that you and your client or boss expect and leave time for some type of beta or testing phase.

WHO CAN HELP WITH Q/A?

Somebody should be assigned the job of overseeing quality assurance for your application. In other words, it should be somebody's job to go through the application and ensure that everything actually works as intended. Do all the links work? What if certain form fields are left out? What if a user submits a form more than once?

The Q/A folks also can be the ones ensuring that your application meets all the expectations agreed upon earlier (see the section "Setting Expectations," earlier in this chapter). If you agreed on a maximum download time for modem users, trying some of the pages using a modem can be part of the Q/A process. If you agreed on IE and Netscape compatibility, someone should view the application using each relevant browser.

You also might want a list to be made of all the items in your application that should be tested whenever you update the code. That way, your Q/A team (which might simply be you) has a simple checklist of links, mouse clicks, form submissions, and so on that must be able to be completed successfully before an iteration of the application can be said to really work.

Beta Testing

In addition to internal Q/A work, it's often a good idea to have some kind of semipublic beta test, in which real users (rather than those you have been interacting with during the development) get to put the application through its paces. Everyday users have a way of finding even the most obscure problems. Navigation elements that seem intuitive to you might be completely baffling to average folks. Or, they might consistently miss the most important button on the page.

Depending on the application, the appropriate beta testers can be selected people within the company (perhaps the same folks you interviewed while you were defining the project, as discussed earlier in this chapter). They might be a select group of the company's customers, or you might decide to open up the beta site to the general public.

Tracking Bug Reports

You might want to set up a way for people to report bugs in the application, so a central place exists where you can see a list of open issues to be fixed. This will also keep your client or boss off your back as you complete the project. Let's face it: People like to see progress. Anyone who can report bugs through some type of official channel—and see that the bug has been fixed a few days later—will be impressed with your professionalism.

You can approach bug tracking in many ways. Various commercial project-management applications are available that include bug-tracking functionality. You also can use ColdFusion to put together a simple bug-tracker Web application that your Q/A people and beta users can use whenever they find a bug. Just be sure the bug tracker doesn't have any bugs of its own!

Tip

If you do create a Web-based bug tracker, you could include a link to it whenever a ColdFusion error message gets displayed for whatever reason. See "Customizing Error Messages" in Chapter 19, "Introducing the Web Application Framework," for details.

Separate Development Environment

This isn't always possible, but you should plan to have a separate development environment (server or set of servers) that will be used only by you (and the rest of your development team, if there is one). While your Q/A people are checking out the application and finding bugs, you can be working on those bugs without worrying whether the Q/A people can still work while you're making changes. Many people get to this place by installing a Web server, the ColdFusion server, and a database server all on their own workstations. Performance might not be optimal, but it is usually fine for development.

Staging/Production

Again, depending on budget and resources, this isn't always possible, but most developers will recommend having separate staging and production environments. The *staging* environment is a server or set of servers your boss or client visits to review your progress. It's also the server your Q/A or beta users visit. The *production* server is where the final code goes after everyone is satisfied with it, and it is the server your actual end users visit. Any updates to the code are made first to staging tested there, and then moved to production.

Ideally, the staging and production environments should be as identical as possible (same hardware, same software versions, and so on), so no surprise incompatibilities or other issues occur.

While You Are Working

The last thing to plan out before you start coding is how you will continue to document the project as you go along. After all, if you've gone through the work to create all those great flowcharts and other design documents, it would be kind of silly not to keep them up to date while you work.

Charting Page Flow

One of the most valuable things to have at any time is an up-to-date list of important pages and the links between them. ColdFusion Studio's Projects feature can help you with this by letting you organize your application files and enabling you to perform global searches through all the templates in your project (see Chapter 18, "Working with Projects"). But sometimes there's just no replacement for a proper paper document (perhaps a Visio drawing) that you can keep pegged to your wall for reference.

Plus, if you keep your page-flow document up to date throughout, you'll have that much more to refer to if you need to make adjustments to the application a year from now.

And let's not forget that clients and bosses always like to see documents with recent dates on them, no matter what's actually *in* the documents.

Include Files and Custom Tags

Another handy document to keep current while you work is a list of include files and custom tags. You learned about include files in Chapter 10, "CFML Basics," and you will learn about custom tags in Chapter 22. Although both types of files are handy because they enable you to isolate and reuse your code, it can sometimes be easy to forget which files rely on which other files. Therefore, a simple spreadsheet or document that keeps track of these interdependencies can really help.

Commenting Style

Throughout this book, we try to encourage you to comment your code as much as possible. Any code, ColdFusion or otherwise, is a hundred times more valuable if it is thoroughly commented. And it becomes a *thousand* times more valuable if all the code for an application is commented in a consistent style.

You should decide ahead of time how you will comment your code, and stick to it while you work. For instance, you might make resolutions similar to the following:

- A header comment should be at the top of each .cfm file that explains the purpose of the file, when it was first written, and the original author's name.
- When anyone makes a significant change to the file, the header comment should be amended, explaining which portions were added or changed. Over time, you'll be left with a simple revision history for each file.
- The header comment also might list the variables used within the template and what they are for. If the file is a custom tag, perhaps each attribute should be listed and explained.
- Perhaps each significant change or addition to a file should be noted in place with an explanation, date, and the developer's initials.
- You could demand that there be at least one line of comment before each CFML tag, perhaps with a few exceptions, such as `<CFOUTPUT>`.

Naming Conventions

Some developers are strict about naming conventions, and often for very good reasons. We're not going to suggest any specific sets of naming conventions here because different people have different ideas about what makes sense. It's probably something that you and your team should decide on your own.

That said, here are a few ideas:

- Because short variable names can result in cryptic-looking code, you might require that every variable name consist of at least two words, with the first letter of each word in uppercase. So instead of variable names such as `tot` and `fn`, you would have names such as `CurrentTotal` and `FirstName`.
- Many coders like to use the first letter of each variable's name to suggest the type of information the variable will hold. For instance, you could use `sFirstName` and `sShipAddress` instead of `FirstName` and `ShipAddress`. This enables you to instantly see that the actual values will be strings. Similarly, you might use something such as `dFirstVisit` for dates and `nCurrentPrice` or `iProductsOrdered` for numbers. You also could use similar naming conventions for the columns in your database tables.

- Similarly, some people find that having the names of their database tables start with a `t` or `tbl`, such as `tCustomers` or `tblCustomers`, is useful. Sometimes people also choose to come up with a convention to indicate the relationship between related tables, such as calling a table `tCustomers_Orders` or `rCustomers2Orders` if the table relates rows from the `tCustomers` and `tOrders` tables.
- Some developers like to put all forms into a separate include file and start the filename with `frm`, as in `frmNewUser.cfm` or perhaps `frm_NewUser.cfm`. Other people do something similar with each `<CFQUERY>` tag, ending up with files with names such as `qryGetDirectors` and so on. See Chapter 39, "Development Methodologies," for more information.

KEEPING THE DIRECTORY STRUCTURE IN MIND

There are no hard and fast rules about how to organize your ColdFusion templates and other files into folders, but you should put some real thought into it and come up with a scheme that makes sense to you.

Here are some things to keep in mind:

- **Make every effort to keep the directory structure of your application as organized as possible**—For instance, it often makes sense to have a folder that corresponds to each high-level section of the site (the sections that appear on your main navigation bar, or the sections accessible from the application's home page).
- **Folders are like friends: Unless they are too full of themselves, the more you have, the better**—It is almost always better to have lots of directories with relatively few files in them, rather than only a few directories with hundreds of files in each.
- **Decide where your images and other media files will be kept**—For instance, this book calls for keeping them all in a single folder named `images`. You might decide to maintain a number of subfolders within `images`. Of course, you could also decide to use an entirely different strategy, perhaps keeping your image files in the same folders as the templates that use them. Just choose a method and stick with it.
- **In general, it is most convenient to use long, descriptive filenames**—However, if you will be displaying a link to a particular template many, many times on a page (for each record in a database, say), a long filename might add to the size of the final HTML code your template generates. Try to use somewhat shorter filenames for templates that will be linked to extremely often. The same goes for images that will be included in pages frequently.

Tip

The Yahoo! site is a good place to look for an example of a site that exposes a very sensible, hierarchical URL structure, but where each portion of the URL is kept very short (often just a letter or two).

Moving Targets and Feature Creep

Unless you are particularly blessed by the gods of application development, you will deal with the twin evils of *moving targets* and *feature creep*. These scorned, ugly creatures are sometimes so filthy and wretched as to be barely distinguishable from one another. Moving targets, of course, are those aspects of an application that your client or boss keeps changing her mind about from one day to the next. Feature creep is what happens if little extra features keep getting piled onto the application while you work. Either one will keep you from getting your project done on time.

On the other hand, it's only natural that the best suggestions and most exciting eureka moments will come while the application is being built. Development is a creative process, and you or others might stumble upon a really brilliant idea that just *has* to be in there. Therefore, you should probably plan on making a few concessions or adjustments during the development process. Have some type of agreement in place about how to deal with incoming ideas.

CHAPTER 18

Working with Projects

In this chapter

One of the most useful features of the ColdFusion Studio environment is its excellent take on the notion of Web projects. Of course, most Web development environments include some way of grouping files together into some kind of container called a project, or perhaps a Web or site. ColdFusion Studio's notion of projects is a particularly useful spin on this idea.

In keeping with Studio's general design philosophy of giving you what you need without getting in the way, you'll find that Studio's Project features can help you stay organized and maintain consistency while you work on an application. They can even help you keep your sanity when things get hectic. In this chapter, you'll see exactly how.

Support for Projects has been an important part of Studio for quite some time, but the feature set got an almost complete overhaul when version 4.5 of Studio was released. If you haven't taken a look at Projects lately, you're especially encouraged to take a close look at this chapter.

About ColdFusion Studio Projects

In ColdFusion Studio, a *project* is simply any collection of files that you want to be able to work with conveniently. First, you tell Studio which files belong in the project. Then you get to look at and work with them collectively, which makes a lot of things easier.

Generally, you should create a project for each application that you create with ColdFusion. At its simplest, that just means identifying the root folder your .cfm files sit in on your Web server. Sometimes, you also might want to include files that sit in other places as well. Studio lets you collect any number of files into a single project, and the files don't have to be in the same location on your computer. The files might be on different drives, or even on different machines.

In any case, after you've established which files the project includes, all of the following become easier:

- **Seeing all your files at a glance**—Studio lets you easily drill across all files in a project. For instance, you can get a single list of all the image files used in your application, even if they are located in several different folders. You can even open all the files in a project at once.
- **Searching and Replacing**—After you've set up a project in Studio, you can use its great Extended Search and Replace feature against all files in the project at once. Of course, you can use Extended Search and Replace across directories on your drive, without using projects at all. But it is often handy to be able to search all files in a project, no matter how many directories the files might be located in. See the "Project-Wide Search & Replace" section in this chapter for details.
- **Deploying your application**—Most developers do their coding against a development Web server of some kind, which might just be their local machines. When the code is finished, you can deploy the application to some other server, perhaps at an ISP or in your company's IT department. Studio lets you deploy all your project files in one swoop.

- **Doing due diligence**—Studio can encode all files in a project so your source code is not easily read by someone you might not want to see it (such as a client or your boss). It can also check all the HTML links in the project, so you can see whether links become broken after you change a filename.

When to Create a Project

How projects are defined, and which files are placed in them, is entirely up to you. You can create projects that contain entire applications, small subsets of an application, or any combination thereof.

As you'll see, Studio projects are structured in a flexible fashion that lets you treat even a very complicated application as a single project. So, you'll most likely create a Studio project for each ColdFusion Web application you work on. That said, if an application is particularly complicated, or has several sections that you think of as being separate from one another, you might decide to create several projects.

Tip

Having several projects for a large application can be especially handy if you think you'll often want to deploy various sections to the live Web server independently from one another.

Using Projects

This section explains how to create a project and how to use it as an alternative way to get to and edit your files (instead of using the normal Files tab). A project's main job is to provide a customized view of your computer's filesystem, tailored to show you exactly what you need to work on in your application. Think of the project as a home base for your application within the ColdFusion Studio environment.

Introducing Studio's Projects Tab

The Projects tab is part of the Resource tab, as shown in Figure 18.1. To activate it, just click the Projects icon (the small globe with a yellow plus sign) at the bottom of the Resource tab.

Tip

If the Projects icon is not showing, another way to get to the Projects tab is to select View, Resource Windows, Projects from Studio's main menu bar.

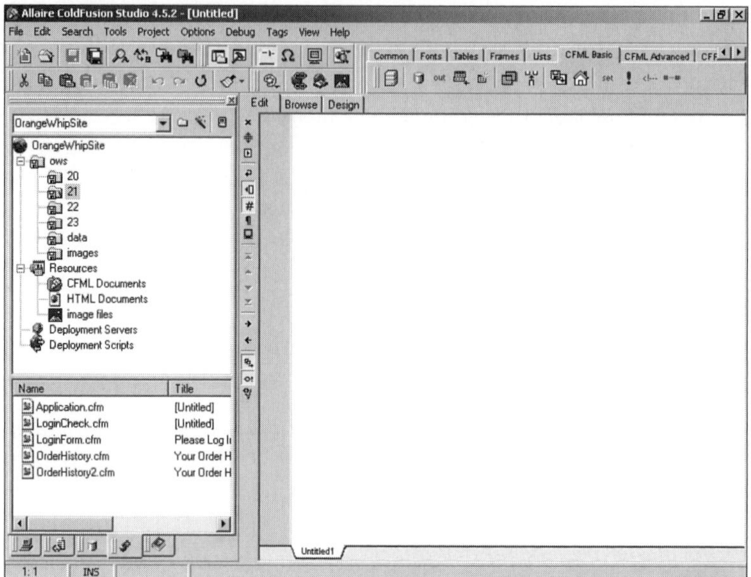

Figure 18.1
The Projects tab has two panes, with Folders on top and Files beneath.

As you can see, the Projects tab is split into two panes, which at first glance look similar to the two panes in the Files tab, with which you are already familiar. After you create a project, the top pane shows the various folders in the project, and the bottom pane shows the individual files. A drop-down list also appears at the very top of the Projects tab, which is for choosing among the projects that have been set up.

Tip

Remember, you can always show or hide the entire Resource tab by pressing the F9 key on your keyboard or by clicking the Resource Tab button on the View toolbar.

CREATING STUDIO PROJECTS

Creating a new project is simple. Simply click the New Project button (the little magic wand icon) at the top of the Projects tab. Or, if you prefer, select Project, New Project from Studio's main menu bar. In either case, the New Project dialog box will appear, as shown in Figure 18.2.

Tip

You can also bring up the New Project dialog box by right-clicking the top pane (under the drop-down list) and selecting New Project from the pop-up menu.

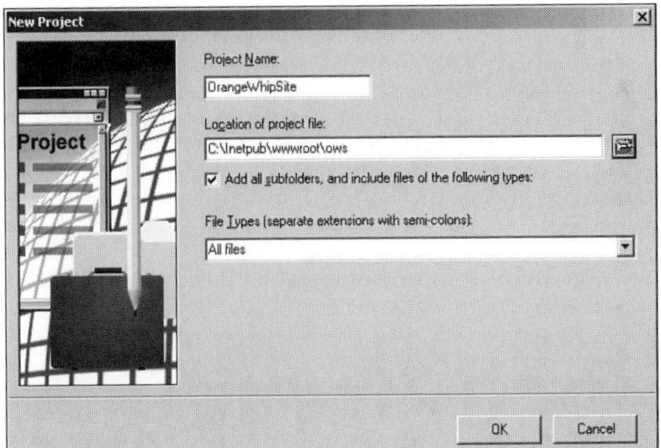

Figure 18.2
The New Project dialog box is used to create new Studio Projects.

After you have the New Project dialog box onscreen, just follow these steps to create your project:

1. Specify a name for the project in the Project Name field. The name should be as descriptive as possible and should be unique to the project you're creating. Feel free to use spaces and other punctuation in the name.
2. In the Location of Project File field, specify the root directory that contains the files to be included in the project. If your application's files aren't all together in a single root folder, just pick one of the folders for now (whichever one you would most consider the main folder). You'll be able to add other files and folders later.
3. By default, all files within the specified directory are included in the project. All subfolders (and files in the subfolders) are included as well. To adjust what gets included, you can uncheck the check box marked Add All Subfolders, and Include Files of the Following Types. You can also provide the specific files you want to include in the project by filling in the File Types field. For instance, if you want only your ColdFusion code files to be included in the project, you would enter **`cfm`** here. If you want to include ColdFusion files plus image files, you might enter **`cfm;jpeg;gif`** here.

When you click OK, the new project is created and opened for you. Your screen will now look similar to Figure 18.1. Notice that the name of the new project is now displayed in the drop-down list and is also visible at the top of the tree structure in the top pane of the Projects tab.

EDITING FILES IN A PROJECT

After you have the project you want to work with open in the Projects tab, doing your everyday editing is similar to how you'd work normally (that is, using the Files tab). You open, edit, and save files in the same basic way.

For the moment, ignore the special items marked Resources, Deployment Servers, and Deployment Scripts (refer to Figure 18.1). They are discussed later in this chapter, in the sections "Filtering Your Files with Project Resources" and "Deploying Projects." That leaves the main root folder, which you specified while you were creating the project. It shows up as a folder icon in the top pane of the Projects tab.

Clicking the folder icon for your application's root folder causes the bottom pane to show the files in the folder. If you accepted the default File Types options when you created the project, this list is the same as if you were looking at the folder in the normal Files tab. If you provided specific file types, you'll notice that only the files with the extensions you listed are shown because they are the only files being considered part of the project.

Here are a few things to try as you explore the Projects tab:

- If folders exist within your application's root folder, you can drill down into the subfolders just as you'd expect to be able to in the Windows Explorer or the Files tab.
- If you double-click one of the files in the bottom pane, it is opened in the editor window, just as if you had opened it normally. You can also right-click the file and select Edit, Insert As Link, or any of the other options that would normally appear for the file.
- Just as with the normal File tab, you can drag an image file from the bottom pane into the editor window, which automatically creates the appropriate `<IMG>` tag. Dragging other types of files into the editor creates `<A>` tags (hyperlinks).
- If you right-click a file in the bottom pane, you can select Remove from Project from the pop-up menu. The file will no longer be associated with the project, but it will not be actually deleted from disk.

Note

The Remove from Project selection mentioned previously is not available if the folder has been modified to be an auto include folder. You'll find out about auto include folders in the section, "Setting Up Auto Include Folders."

OPENING EXISTING PROJECTS

To reopen your new project later, you can simply select it from the drop-down list at the top of the Projects tab (refer to Figure 18.1). Or, if you prefer, you can choose it by selecting Reopen Project from the Projects menu in Studio's main menu bar.

Tip

You also can reopen a project by opening the .apf file that was created in the folder location you specified when creating the project (refer to Figure 18.2). Or, double-click the .apf file from the Windows Explorer; Studio will open with the project open and ready for you. (The .apf file is where the information about folder locations and so on is kept. You should have no need to edit it manually.)

GETTING THE MOST OUT OF PROJECT FOLDERS

Because most of the value of Studio's Project features come from being able to collect files together in a way that makes sense to you, it's important to understand the various ways you can specify which files are considered part of your project. Depending on your needs, you will either use physical folders or virtual folders to hold the files in your project. Let's take a look at the differences.

PHYSICAL FOLDERS

The normal type of project folder is called a *physical folder*. It's called a physical folder because it corresponds directly to an actual directory on your machine's drive. Think of these project folders as aliases for the actual directories they are based on.

If you've been following along with this chapter, you already have a project with a physical folder in it. When you used the New Project dialog box to create a new project (refer to Figure 18.2), a physical folder was added to your project with the same name as the root folder you provided in the Location field (refer to Figure 18.1).

If you right-click that folder and select Properties, you'll see that it has been set up as a physical folder (see Figure 18.3). The Directory Path field indicates the underlying Windows-style folder on which the project folder is based.

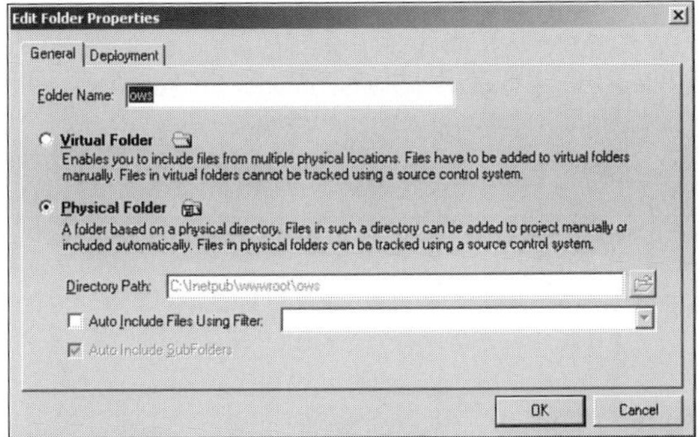

Figure 18.3
The Edit Folder Properties dialog box shows whether a folder is physical or virtual.

Tip

If you want, you can change the name of the folder as it appears in the Projects tab, simply by editing the Folder Name field in this dialog box. The name of the underlying directory (as shown in the Directory Path field) will not be changed. This enables you to have descriptive aliases for your folders, without actually changing anything on disk.

Note

Don't change the folder name if you plan to use the Project Deployment feature, unless you want the name of the folder to be different in the deployed version of your application. See the "Deploying Projects" section, later in this chapter.

HOW PROJECT FOLDERS WORK BY DEFAULT

By default, the project folder that is automatically included when creating a new project is set up as shown in Figure 18.3. As the dialog box explains, the folder is a physical folder, meaning it represents a physical directory on your hard drive (or network). As you can see, the auto include options are not enabled by default.

With this type of folder, when you want a new file to be considered part of your project, you must add it to the folder on your own. This is great if you want to be especially selective about which files are included in your project. Unlike the normal Windows-style directory on which it is based, this type of project folder will not become cluttered with every file that might have to sit in the directory for whatever reason. It contains only what you want it to contain. It's like living in some kind of pleasant fantasy, where you don't have to see everyone else's files, just the ones that are relevant to you.

ADDING ADDITIONAL FILES TO A FOLDER

Say you just wrote a new CFML file in the same root folder you specified when you created the project. Of course, now you want it to be considered part of your project. Simply right-click the appropriate project folder and select the Add Files to Folder option. Now select the new file and click OK. The file is now a part of the project folder and will remain there unless you specifically remove it.

Tip

Of course, you can add more than one file at a time. Just hold down the Shift or Ctrl key while selecting the files you want to add. The keys behave the same way as they do in the Windows Explorer and elsewhere.

Tip

You also can set things up so that new subdirectories will automatically become part of your project. See "Setting Up Auto Include Folders," later in this chapter.

Because this is a physical folder and thus has a correlation to the underlying directory, you will find that you can't add a file that sits in some other directory without copying or moving the file first. As a courtesy, Studio can do that moving or copying for you. Try adding a file from some folder other than the one your project folder is based on. You will get a special prompt, as shown in Figure 18.4. You can then click Copy or Move, depending on whether you want the file to be copied or moved into the underlying directory.

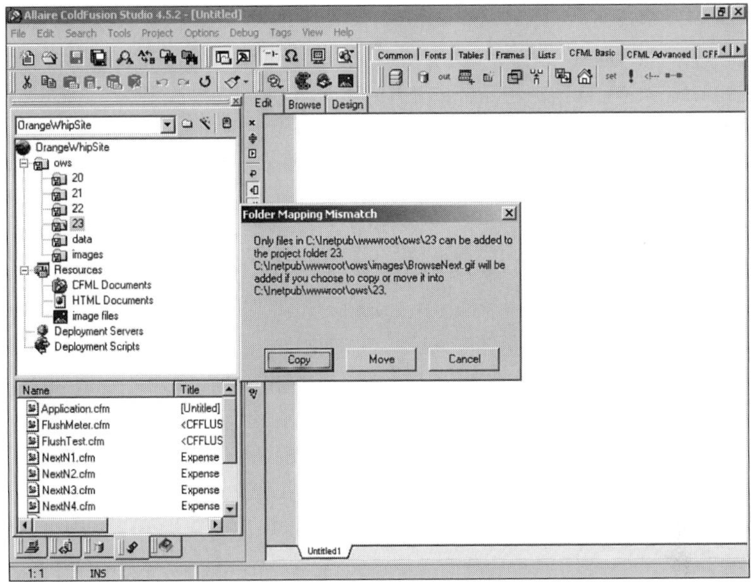

Figure 18.4
Studio prompts you if you try to add a file from another directory to a physical folder.

ADDING ANOTHER FOLDER

Okay, so you know how to add a new file to a project folder. What about a new directory? Let's say you just added a new subdirectory to your application's directory structure. It's not going to appear as a subfolder to your existing project folder until you specifically add it to your project.

To add the new subdirectory to your project, follow these steps:

1. Right-click the project folder that represents the new directory's parent, and select Add Folder from the pop-up menu. The Add a Project Folder dialog box appears, which looks the same as the one shown in Figure 18.3.
2. Leave the Physical Folder option selected (as opposed to Virtual Folder).
3. Type a name for the new project folder in the Folder Name field.
4. Provide the location of your new directory in the Directory Path field.

Tip

> You also can set things up so that new subdirectories will automatically become part of your project. See "Setting Up Auto Include Folders," later in this chapter.

It's important to note something here. As you just learned, you can easily add a project folder to another project folder, for when you add a new subdirectory to the original directory. But when you are filling out the Directory Path field for the new project folder, you are allowed to choose any directory at all, even a directory on a different drive or computer. This means you can create a structure of nested project folders that represent directories in entirely disparate locations. The way the folders are nested doesn't need to have anything to do with how the actual directories are organized on disk.

In short, you can organize the project folders in any way that makes sense for the work you're doing. It's a good way to deal with a large Web application, which might have evolved into a complex directory structure that might not make as much sense as it should. Rather than reorganizing the directories (which might mean having to correct many links and other references), you can just come up with a project folder structure that makes sense to you and access the files that way.

REMOVING FILES AND PROJECT FOLDERS

Of course, sometimes you must remove a file or folder from a project. Presumably, this is because you no longer feel that it's relevant to the work you are doing.

To remove a file from a project, simply right-click the file (in the lower pane of the Projects tab), and select Remove from Project from the pop-up menu. Studio will prompt you for confirmation. When you click OK, the file is removed from your project.

To remove a project folder from a project, right-click the folder (in the top pane of the Projects tab), and select Remove Folder from the pop-up menu. Again, Studio will prompt you for confirmation. When you click Yes, the folder is removed from your project.

Note

Removing a file or project folder from a project doesn't affect the actual file or folder on disk at all. All you are doing is removing the alias from your project; you are not deleting the actual file or folder from your hard drive.

SETTING UP AUTO INCLUDE FOLDERS

So far, you have been learning about project folders that require you to add any new files manually. You've also seen that any new subdirectories also have to be added to the project folder manually. Often, that's exactly what you want, so your structure of project folders doesn't become unnecessarily crowded with files you don't need to focus on as a developer. But this kind of extra step can also be tedious, especially when you are first building your application and creating many new files and folders.

Studio enables you to set up a project folder as an auto include folder. After you do this, any new files you add to the underlying directory become part of the project. You can also have Studio automatically add any new subdirectories to your project for you. In other words, the project folder will behave more like a normal Windows directory.

To add an auto include folder to your project, you follow the same steps as you would normally (see "Adding Another Folder," earlier in this chapter). The only difference is that you will check the two Auto Include check boxes, as shown in Figure 18.5.

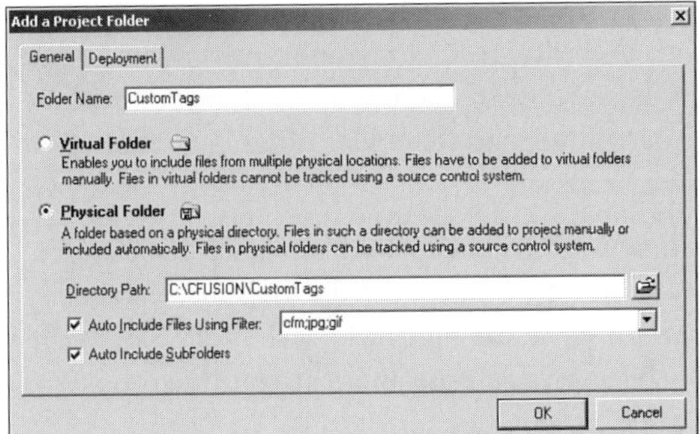

Figure 18.5 Enabling the auto include options eliminates the need to add new files or folders manually.

Checking the Auto Include Files Using Filter check box causes new files to be automatically included in your project. By default, the Filter field is set to All Files. If you want, you can restrict the files that get automatically added by providing whatever file extensions are appropriate. Separate multiple extensions with semicolons. For instance, to include only CFML templates and images in the folder, type **`cfm;jpg;gif`**, as shown in Figure 18.5.

Checking the Auto Include Subfolders check box causes new directories to automatically show up as new project folders in your project, nested within the folder you're adding. If that's not what you want, you can leave this check box empty.

Note

You also have access to these same options for existing project folders. Just right-click the folder and select Properties from the pop-up menu.

Tip

If you find that you usually want your project folders to be set up as auto include folders, you can change Studio's defaults easily. See "Adjusting the Default Settings for Projects," later in this chapter.

VIRTUAL FOLDERS

By now, you are familiar with the type of project folder called a physical folder, and you've seen how it lets you create a filtered, customized view of the directories involved in an application. You've also seen how such a project folder can be turned into an auto include folder that changes as the underlying directory structure changes.

Studio provides another type of project folder, called a *virtual folder*. Virtual folders are designed for situations in which you want a number of individual files to be included in your project but don't want to include folders for all the directories that the files sit in. In other words, it's a way to collect any random set of files together and have them be included in your project for organizational purposes. Unlike a physical folder, this type of folder doesn't map in any way to a directory on your hard drive. It's just a convenient visual container, known only to Studio and yourself.

For example, your company might have a global Cascading Style Sheet (.css) file that is shared across your entire Web site. It might be in some directory somewhere called `CSS`. Elsewhere, there might be a couple of commonly used images, such as company logos, in a directory called `Pics`. You will refer to these files often in your application, so you want them to be a part of your project.

This would be a great time to add a virtual folder to your project. You could call the folder `Corporate Look and Feel` and tell Studio that the CSS file and the logos belong there. Now you don't have to go searching for the logos whenever you want to drag them onto a page you're working on. They'll always be right there at your fingertips.

To add a virtual folder to your project, follow the same steps as you would for a physical folder (see "Adding Another Folder," earlier in this chapter). The only thing you do differently is to select the Virtual Folder option in the Add a Project Folder dialog box (Figure 18.5).

Your new virtual folder will be empty at first. To add files to it, follow the steps described in the "Adding Additional Files to a Folder" section earlier in this chapter. To remove files, follow the instructions in the "Removing Files and Project Folders" section, also earlier in this chapter.

WORKING WITH REMOTE FILES

One of the great things about Studio is the way it lets you treat files on a remote server in nearly the same way as you treat files on your local network. In fact, whenever you add a new physical folder to your project, you can choose a directory on any server that has been registered with Studio (that is, any server that appears under Allaire FTP & RDS).

Follow these steps to add a project folder that refers to a directory on a remote machine:

1. Be sure the remote machine has been added as an Allaire RDS or FTP server in Studio (see Chapter 8, "Introduction to ColdFusion Studio," for instructions).
2. Bring up the Add a Project Folder dialog box as you would normally, by right-clicking (see "Adding Another Folder," earlier in this chapter).
3. Click the little folder icon next to the Directory Path field. The Select Directory dialog box appears.
4. Expand the Allaire FTP & RDS item (within the My Computer part of the tree); then drill down to the desired server and folder, as shown in Figure 18.6. Depending on how the server is configured, you might have to enter a password to do so.

You'll notice that a slightly different icon is used to represent a project folder that refers to a remote server, but otherwise they can be used in the same way. Clicking the folder will show you the files in it, and you can open any of those files and work with them normally. Whenever you save changes to such a file, the changes are saved on the remote server for you.

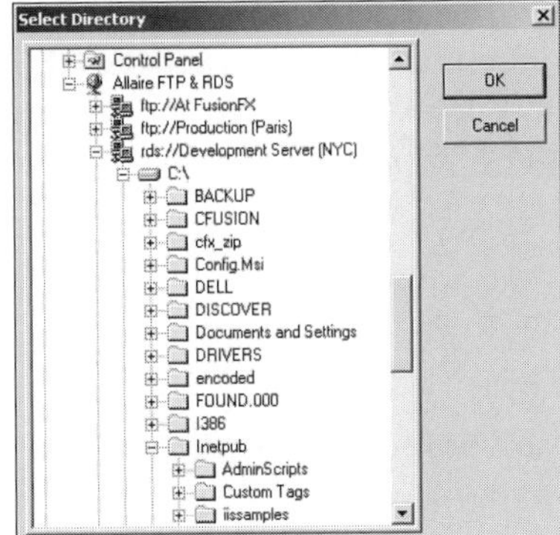

Figure 18.6
Your project can include files and folders on remote servers.

In addition, all the other project-wide goodies Studio provides will transparently interact with the remote servers as necessary. For instance, when using the Extended Search and Replace feature on the entire project (see "Project-Wide Search & Replace," later in this chapter), you automatically search through any files that sit on remote machines.

Note

You can also add individual files from remote servers to your project. For instance, whenever you add an individual file to a virtual folder, you can drill down through the Allaire FTP & RDS section of the directory tree (see "Adding Additional Files to a Folder," earlier in this chapter).

Filtering Your Files with Project Resources

You've seen the various ways you can include files in your project and how you can organize them into whatever kind of meta-hierarchy of folders you want. You might end up with a lot of project folders in your project. That's often all you need to be able to work with your files conveniently.

However, sometimes you might want a way to drill *across* the files in your project, rather than drilling *down*. For instance, your application might contain several JavaScript (.js) files, located in various folders. You might want a quick way to access them all at once. Or, you might want to quickly scan through all the images in your project. Studio provides a feature called *project resources* that addresses this need quite nicely.

The Default Resource Filters

Whenever you have a project open in the Projects tab, you'll see a Resources item as a part of the project (refer to Figure 18.1). If you expand this item, you'll see that three Resources are defined there by default: one for CFML documents, one for HTML documents, and one for images.

Clicking any of the resources causes all the corresponding files in the project to be displayed in the lower pane of the Projects tab. For instance, if you click the CFML Documents resource, you'll see all the .cfm files in your project; if you click the Images resource, you'll see all the GIF, JPEG, and PNG files in your project. You can then work with the files as you would normally.

It's a simple feature, but a very handy one.

ADDING YOUR OWN RESOURCE FILTERS

You can also add your own resources to a project. For instance, you might want to add a resource called Script Files that shows you all your JavaScript and VBScript files. You also might want another resource called Style Sheets so you can easily see all your CSS files.

Follow these steps to add a new resource to your project:

1. Right-click the resources item for your project (in the upper pane of the Projects tab) and select Add Resource from the pop-up menu. The Add Resource Folder dialog box appears, as shown in Figure 18.7.
2. Provide a descriptive name in the Resource Name field.
3. Provide a Resource Filter that includes the appropriate file extension(s). Separate multiple file extensions with semicolons.
4. When you click OK, the new resource is added and is ready for use.

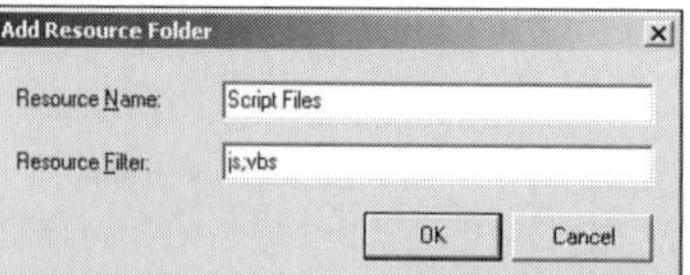

Figure 18.7
Customized resource filters are yet another convenient way to access your files.

If you want to adjust the filter or name of the resource later, just right-click the resource and select Properties from the pop-up menu. To delete a resource, right-click the resource and select Remove Resource.

ADJUSTING THE DEFAULT SETTINGS FOR PROJECTS

If you find that you always like to add a few extra resource filters to your project or wish that Studio would automatically set up the root folder as an auto include folder when you create a new project, you should definitely pay a visit to the Projects section of Studio's Settings dialog box (shown in Figure 18.8).

For instance, I've adjusted my copy of Studio so that a script files resource filter is always included whenever I create a new project. Also, I find that the HTML Documents resource is not particularly helpful to me (because all my HTML code is in ColdFusion templates), so I've unchecked it to ensure it doesn't get included in new projects. Finally, I've adjusted the Default Project Folder Type so that a new project's root folder is set up to auto include its subfolders and files.

Tip

Remember, you can get to the Settings dialog box anytime by pressing your F8 key.

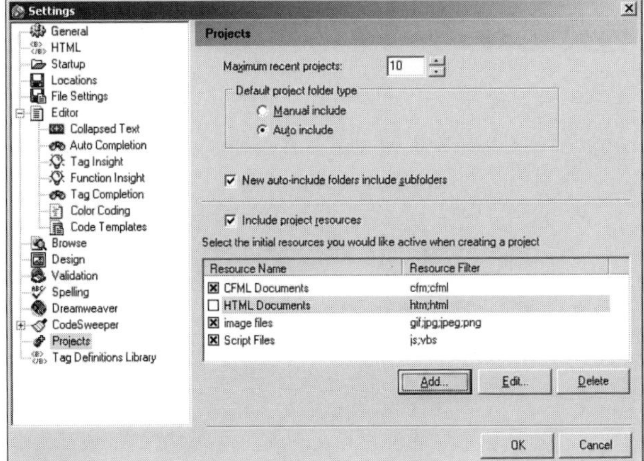

Figure 18.8
You can easily change the defaults for new projects in Studio's Settings dialog box.

USING PROJECTS TO EASE CODE MAINTENANCE

In Studio, projects are about more than just keeping your application's files handy and organized. Studio also has great features that help you maintain your code, and even get it deployed from your development server to your live servers (assuming that you're fortunate enough to have a separate development environment).

Let's take a look at two code-maintenance features Studio provides for projects: Search & Replace and Link Verification.

PROJECTWIDE SEARCH & REPLACE

Both the Extended Find and Extended Replace dialog boxes allow you to select an entire project when doing a search. All files in your project will be searched, regardless of which actual directories or servers your application's files are sitting in.

To perform a projectwide Find or Replace, follow these steps:

1. Bring up the Extended Find or Extended Replace dialog box as you would normally, either using the buttons on the Standard toolbar or using the Edit menu.
2. Fill out the Find What and Replace With fields as you would normally, and select whatever options (such as Match Case) are appropriate.
3. Select the In Project option, and then select the project you want to search from the drop-down list (see Figure 18.9). If the project isn't in the drop-down list, click the button to the right of the list and locate your project's .apf file, which is most likely in the root folder you specified while creating the project.

Tip

You can get to the Extended Find dialog box quickly by pressing Shift+Ctrl+F on your keyboard. For Extended Replace, press Shift+Ctrl+R.

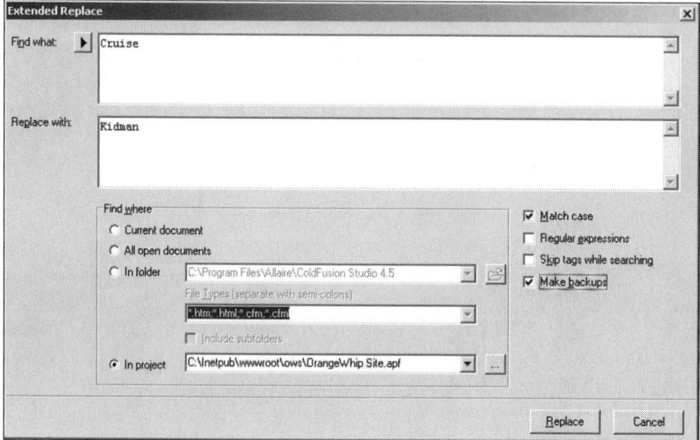

Figure 18.9
Being able to perform Search and Replace operations over an entire project can be a real timesaver.

VERIFYING ALL LINKS IN A PROJECT

The Verify Links feature can also be used to ensure that all links in your project are still valid. You might want to use it from time to time, especially after you have renamed some files or folders, or if you have recently copied and pasted some code from some other application. Or, perhaps you were on vacation and suspect that your boss might have messed something up while you were gone.

To verify all the links in your project, follow these steps:

1. Right-click your project (the small globe in the upper pane of the Projects tab) and select Verify Links from the pop-up menu. The Verify Links in Project dialog box appears, as shown in Figure 18.10.
2. If you want, select a Root URL option. Normally, you can accept the default option (Set Each File's Root URL to Itself), which means that any relative links are assumed to be relative to the location of the file itself. However, if your project contains files that are included (via the `<CFINCLUDE>` tag) in other files, relative links might need to be considered relative to some fixed URL. Generally, you would enter the URL of your application's root folder here.
3. If you want, adjust the Timeout value. The default value is 15 seconds, which means that if Studio doesn't get a response from the Web server while checking for the existence of a particular file or image, it marks that link as bad and moves on to the next one. You could decrease this value if you wanted to ensure that each link was at a very responsive Web server or increase it if you know and accept that some of the links will take longer to get to (perhaps you have some links to sites in other countries).

4. If your workstation is sitting behind a proxy server, click the Proxy button and provide the appropriate proxy name and port. You should supply the same values with which your Web browser is configured (you can probably find them under Internet Settings in the Control Panel, using the LAN Settings button on the Connections tab).
5. Click OK to begin the link verification process. The Results pane will appear and begin to list which links are still valid and which are not.

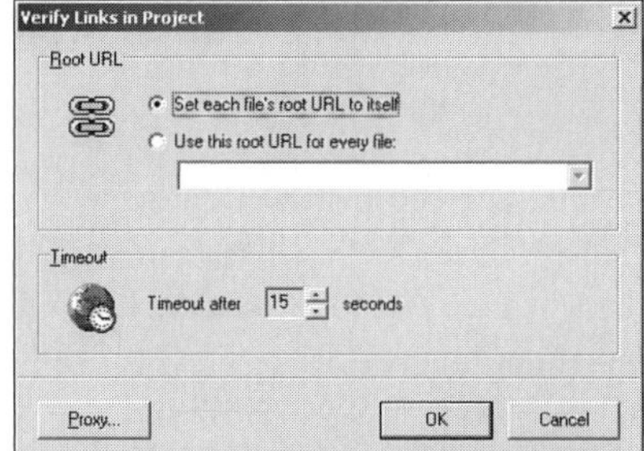

Figure 18.10
You can use Studio's Verify Links feature against all files in your project.

DEPLOYING PROJECTS

Sooner or later, it's got to happen. You've tweaked the code as much as you can. Your company's executives have all seen the great new features you've been working on, and they want to see it on the company's production Web server yesterday. It's time to deploy your application.

Traditionally, the process of deploying an application has generally meant copying the files from your development environment and then copying the code to your production servers. If your production servers are elsewhere, perhaps in some type of hosted or co-located facility, that often means opening an FTP client or a program such as pcAnywhere and copying the files that way. It might even mean copying the files via the command line or putting together some kind of DOS-style batch file to do the updating.

In short, it's a far cry from an integrated solution. If your application's files don't all sit within the same root folder, you must be careful to copy all the files to the correct locations. If you are operating multiple ColdFusion servers in a cluster or round-robin configuration, everything gets that much more complicated and that much more error prone.

Studio's Project Deployment functionality provides a way to get your deployment tasks done much more quickly and easily. It provides the following features:

- All files in your project will be deployed (copied) to the correct locations, even if they have to end up in a number of folders on the target server.
- The files can be deployed via your local network, FTP, or ColdFusion's own Remote Directory Service (RDS).
- To save time, you can specify that only the files that have changed since the last update should be deployed.

- You can deploy to multiple machines, updating all your servers at once.
- Studio can encode the files as they are deployed, so your valuable source code never gets posted to the live servers in such a way that it can be readily opened and read.
- The process can be customized via common scripting languages.

TELLING STUDIO WHERE TO DEPLOY THE FILES

For Studio to deploy your project, it needs to know two things: to which server(s) to deploy and where to place the files on each server. Generally, you must specify this information only once—the first time you deploy your project.

Before you begin, you should decide whether you plan to deploy your files via your local network or over the Internet via Allaire FTP & RDS. If you can see the target server in your Windows Network Neighborhood or via a mapped network drive, you can deploy via the local network. Otherwise, you must deploy via Allaire FTP & RDS. See Chapter 8 for information about how to set up Allaire FTP & RDS in Studio.

SPECIFYING A DEPLOYMENT PATH

The first thing to do is to tell Studio where the files should be placed on the server(s) to which you want to deploy your application. For instance, if your application is currently contained within a folder called `MyApp` within your development Web server's document root, you probably want the files to be placed in a folder that is also called `MyApp` within the document root of the Web servers to which you are deploying. In such a case, the location of the target Web server's document root is called the *deployment path*.

To specify the deployment path for your project, follow these steps:

1. Right-click your project (the small blue globe in the upper pane of the Projects tab) and select Properties from the pop-up menu. The Edit Project Properties dialog box appears.
2. Click the folder icon to the right of the Deployment Path field. The Select Directory dialog box appears, looking similar to Figure 18.6, seen earlier in this chapter.
3. Navigate through the tree of directory structures until you find the correct location to deploy to. If the target Web server is on your local network, you can drill down through the Network Neighborhood to find the appropriate folder. If the target Web server is elsewhere and you want to deploy the files over the Internet, you can drill down through the Allaire FTP & RDS section of the tree.
4. When you click OK in the Select Directory dialog box, the Deployment Path is filled in for you, as shown in Figure 18.11. If you selected a path on an Allaire FTP or RDS server, the server-specific parts of the path are automatically left off. This is to facilitate deploying your files to multiple servers.

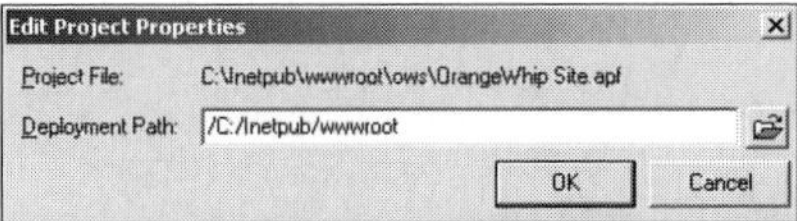

Figure 18.11 Specifying the deployment path is the first step toward deploying your project.

> **Note**
>
> Remember, in most cases, the Deployment Path for the project will simply be the target Web server's document root. The files in your various project folders will be deployed relative to the deployment path.

ALTERNATIVE LOCATIONS FOR SPECIFIC FOLDERS

You might have certain files that should be deployed to a location different from the rest of the files. For instance, your application might rely on some CFML custom tags, which would need to be placed in the target server's special CustomTags folder for your application to work correctly. Or, you might need to update some type of companywide style sheet, which must be placed in a folder called Global, instead of the folder where the rest of your files are going.

To allow for this kind of situation, Studio enables you to override the default deployment path (which you specified in the previous section) on a folder-by-folder basis. If you needed to, you could actually specify a different deployment location for each folder in your project.

To specify a deployment location for a project folder, follow these steps:

1. Right-click the project folder and select Properties from the pop-up menu. The Edit Folder Properties dialog box appears.
2. Click the Deployment tab.
3. Select the Specific Deployment Location option, as shown in Figure 18.12.
4. Provide the desired location by using the folder icon next to the Deployment Path box. The Select Directory dialog box will appear, just as it did when you were specifying the deployment path for the project as a whole.

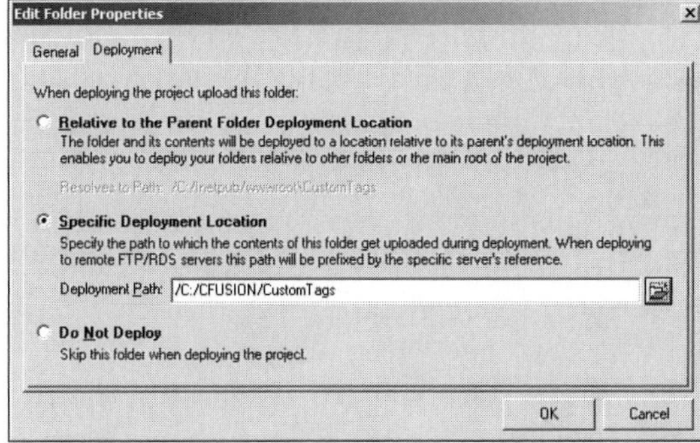

Figure 18.12 You can specify deployment locations for individual folders in your project.

THE DEPLOYMENT WIZARD

Now that you've given Studio the deployment path information it needs to successfully deploy your project, you can perform the actual deployment quite easily. A Deployment Wizard is provided to guide you through the process of deploying your application. Let's take a look at the wizard, step by step.

Start the Deployment Wizard by clicking the small blue computer icon (which looks alarmingly similar to a Mac Classic) at the upper-right corner of the Projects tab. You can also start the wizard by selecting Project and then selecting Deployment Wizard from Studio's main menu bar.

SELECTING THE DEPLOYMENT TYPE

The first step of the wizard asks you to choose between Direct Deployment and Scriptable Deployment. We'll discuss the second option later in this chapter; for the moment, just leave Direct Deployment selected, as shown in Figure 18.13. Click the Next button.

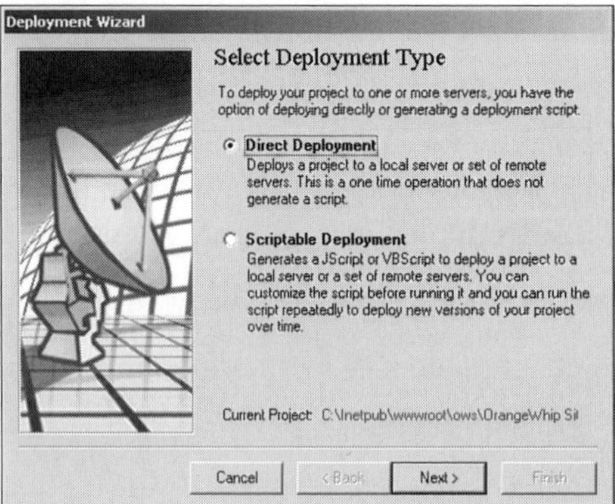

Figure 18.13 The Deployment Wizard guides you through the process of deploying your application.

SELECTING THE DEPLOYMENT DESTINATION AND OTHER OPTIONS

The second step of the wizard, shown in Figure 18.14, asks you to select the deployment destination and some other options. Fill this page out as follows:

- **Local/Network Deployment or Remote RDS/FTP Deployment**—Select Local/Network Deployment if you can see the destination for your files in your Windows Network Neighborhood or via a mapped network drive. Otherwise, select Remote RDS/FTP Deployment, which will send your files over the Internet.
- **Create Any Missing Folders/Directories**—In general, you should leave this check box checked. Only uncheck it if you know for sure that the directory structure already exists on the target server(s). This will save Studio the step of having to check all the folders beforehand, which can save some time.
- **Upload Only Newer Files**—In general, you should leave this check box checked. It causes Studio not to bother copying a file if a file with the same date already exists on

the target server. This can save a considerable amount of time, especially if you have large files or if your connection to the target server is slow. If, for some reason, you think the files might have gotten out of sync, you can uncheck this option, causing all files to be sent to the server, even if they are unchanged from the last update.

- **Encrypt CFML Files**—Leave this option unchecked for now. This option is discussed in the section "Encoding Your Source Code for Safety," later in this chapter.
- **Force Lower Case Filenames**—If you need to check this box because of some type of special Web server requirement, you can do so. Checking this option causes all files to be created with lowercase filenames on the target server(s).
- **Disable Logging**—By default, Studio maintains a log of each deployment process. Unless you provide a different filename in this dialog box, the log will be written to a text file called `Deployment.log` in Studio's program directory. If you want, you can tell Studio not to create this log file by checking this box.

When you are finished filling out this second step of the wizard, click Next.

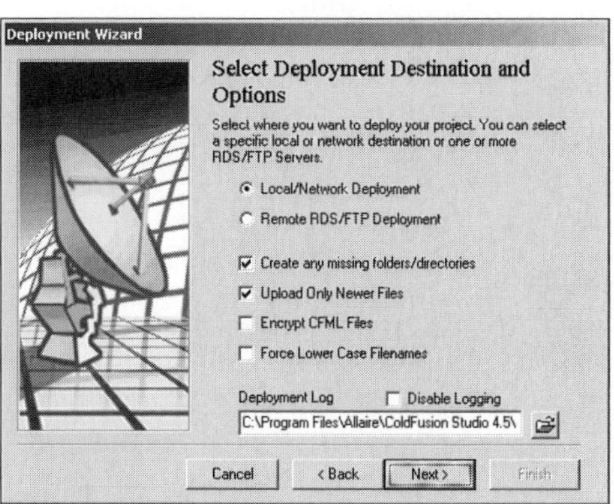

Figure 18.14 The second step of the Deployment Wizard enables you to set a number of options to control the deployment process.

Selecting the Deployment Servers

If you selected Remote RDS/FTP Deployment in the second step, you now are presented with a third step, titled Select Remote Deployment Servers, as shown in Figure 18.15. Many developers need to deploy their applications to only a single server; others, however, need to deploy their applications to many servers in a server farm or to several mirror servers located in various cities around the world.

Simply check off the servers to which you want your application to be deployed. All servers that have been previously registered with the Allaire FTP & RDS feature will be displayed as possible choices. Please see Chapter 8 for instructions on how to add a server to Allaire FTP & RDS.

When you are finished selecting the servers to deploy, click Next.

Tip

As the text in Figure 18.15 notes, you can specify default deployment servers for the project so you don't have to spend time checking off the correct ones each time you go through the wizard to deploy. See "Specifying Default Deployment Servers," later in this chapter.

Note

Because you are not able to specify a separate deployment location for each remote server, the files are placed in the same location on all servers that you select in this step. If this is a problem—for instance, if the Web server document root is not in the same location or drive on each machine—you must run through the wizard separately for each server that is set up differently.

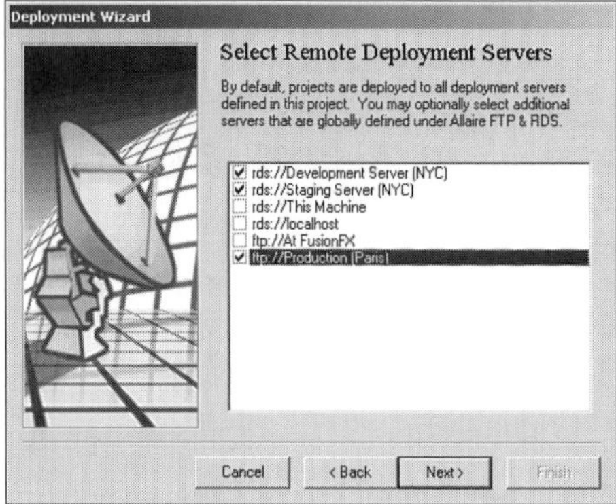

Figure 18.15
The third step of the wizard asks you to specify to which servers to deploy. This step is skipped if you are deploying over your local network.

STARTING THE DEPLOYMENT PROCESS

The wizard should now be ready to start deploying your application, as shown in Figure 18.16. Click the Finish button to begin the deployment process. Studio should immediately begin sending your files to the server (or servers) you specified.

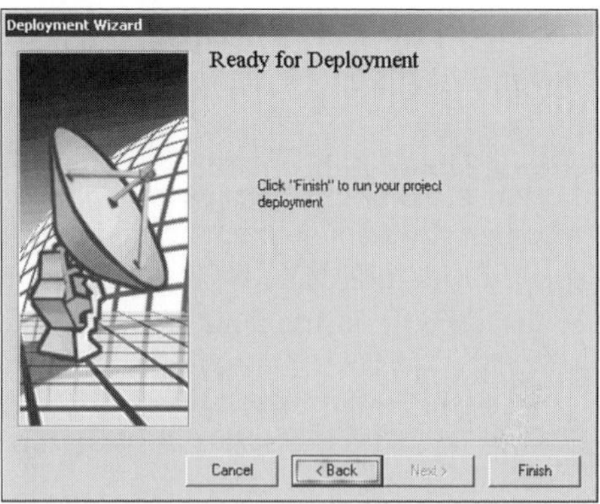

Figure 18.16
After you have answered the wizard's questions, a single click begins the deployment process.

The actual deployment process might take some time or occur almost instantly, depending on the size of your application and image files, the number of target servers, and the speed of your connection. Studio will keep you updated on its progress by showing you the status of each file-copy operation in the Results pane, as shown in Figure 18.17.

Tip

If you want, you can toggle the Results button in the View toolbar to hide or show the deployment status. You can also select Results from the View menu to do the same thing.

Tip

The information being shown to you in the Results pane is the same information being placed in the deployment log (refer to Figure 18.14).

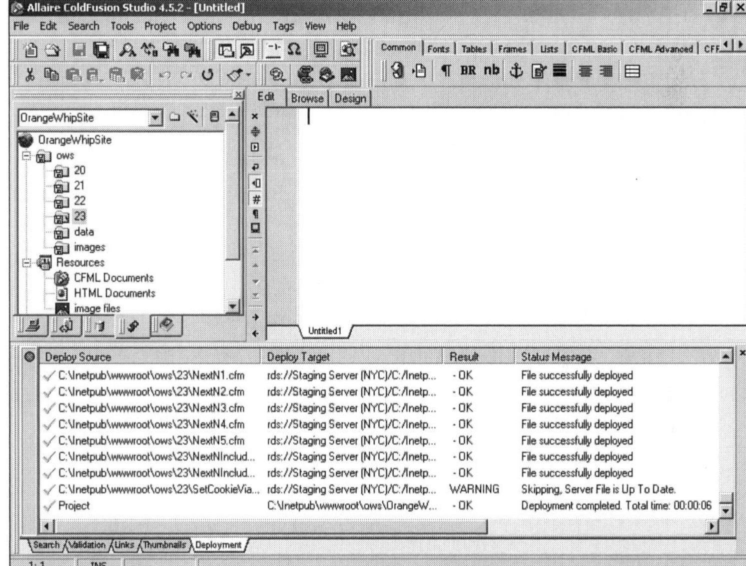

Figure 18.17
As Studio deploys your application, you can monitor its progress in the Results pane.

Tip

If you want to print out the results of your deployment, right-click in the Results pane and select Browse from the pop-up menu. This converts the results into a simple Web page and opens it in your browser. From there, you can use your browser's print function to get a hard copy.

Specifying Default Deployment Servers

If you selected Remote RDS/FTP Deployment, the third step of the Deployment Wizard asks you to choose to which servers to deploy. If you want, you can specify that certain servers be set as default servers for your project. From then on, those servers will be already checked for you when you get to the third step of the wizard, so you can just click the Next button to start the deployment.

To specify a default server for your project, follow these steps:

1. Right-click the Deployment Servers item for your project (the globe on a stand icon in the upper pane of the Resource tab, as shown in Figure 18.1) and select Add FTP Server or Add RDS Server from the pop-up menu.
2. The Configure RDS Server or Configure FTP Server dialog box appears, as appropriate. Fill in the fields in the dialog box and click OK. See Chapter 8 for instructions on how to set up an RDS or FTP server.

KEEPING SPECIFIC FOLDERS FROM BEING DEPLOYED

In some situations, you might have a project folder in your project that doesn't need to be deployed. Perhaps the folder contains some notes of your own or source artwork files (such as Photoshop .psd files or Flash .fla files) that don't need to be sent to your Web servers. But you might not want to remove these items from the project because you find that having everything together while you're working is convenient.

Studio enables you to specify that any given project folder should be skipped during the deployment process. To do so, follow these steps:

1. Right-click the project folder and select Properties from the pop-up menu. The Edit Folder Properties dialog box appears.
2. Click the Deployment tab (refer to Figure 18.12).
3. Select the Do Not Upload option.

ENCODING YOUR SOURCE CODE FOR SAFETY

As you have already learned, people using your application have no way to view your actual ColdFusion templates. The ColdFusion server interprets the CFML code in your templates and sends the resulting Web pages back to the Web browser. Even if users use the View Source option in their browsers, all they see is the final HTML code your templates generate.

However, people who have direct access to your .cfm files can of course open them in ColdFusion Studio (or any other text editor) and look at your code. This might not be desirable, especially if you are writing code you (or your company) are planning to sell.

To address this issue, ColdFusion servers can process CFML templates that have been encoded in a special way. After it's encoded, a template just looks like garbage if you try to view it in a text editor. It's no longer readable by people, but any ColdFusion server can read and interpret it just as well as the original.

Two ways to encode your templates are available: automatically as part of a Studio deployment process and manually, using the Windows command line.

Caution

Encoding is a one-way process; you can encrypt a template, but no tools are supplied by Macromedia to get your code back if you lose the original version of the file.

WHAT ENCODING IS (AND WHAT IT IS NOT)

It's important not to mistake ColdFusion's template-encoding feature for more than it actually is. It is not a bulletproof security measure. There is no means for managing any kind of public or private signing key; therefore, if you somehow figured out the decoding algorithm, you would be able to decode any encoded template, not just your own. It's just a simple mechanism to keep people from being able to casually look through your code. There are even rumors of decoding programs possibly being available through the hacker community.

The feature still has plenty of value. Presumably, if you are selling your code to another party, you have already copyrighted your code and have probably notified the party that the code is your property and that they may not alter or attempt to reverse-engineer your templates. Encoding your templates means people would have to make a real effort to get at your code. No one could say they didn't understand that they weren't supposed to look at your code. They also couldn't say they just stumbled upon it while looking through a Web server's document root or were just taking a look out of curiosity. At the very least, it's a good way to help keep the honest people honest.

ENCODING WHILE DEPLOYING FROM STUDIO

Studio enables you to easily encode your templates while you deploy them. Simply check the Encrypt CFML Files check box during the Select Deployment Destination and Options step of the Deployment Wizard (refer to Figure 18.14). All your project files will be encoded before being placed on the servers to which you're deploying. This means the original version of the files need never sit on your production servers.

After deploying, if you were to try to open one of the encoded files, it would look something similar to the garbage text shown in Figure 18.18. As you can see, there's no way you could possibly know what's going on in the code from looking at it.

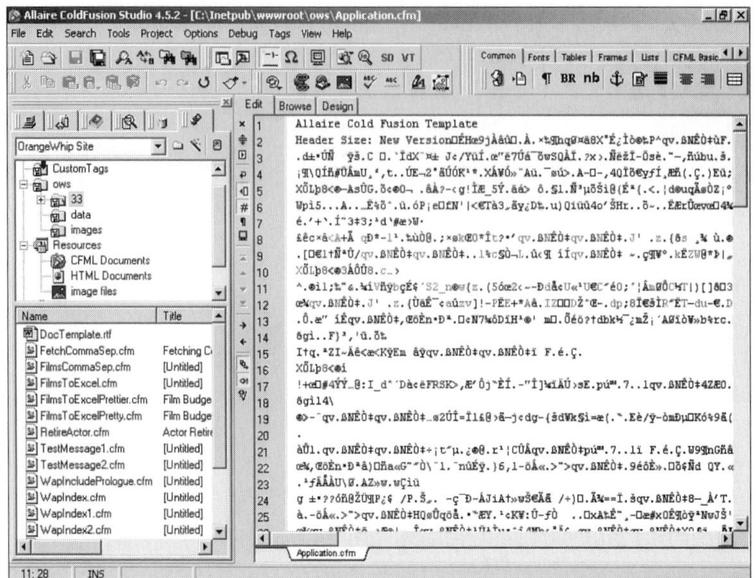

Figure 18.18 Encoded templates look like garbage when opened in Studio or any other text editor.

ENCODING ON THE COMMAND LINE

You can also encrypt templates using the `cfencode.exe` command-line utility that ships with ColdFusion. You might find this method to be more convenient if you just need to encode a few of your templates.

You will find the `cfcrypt.exe` file in the BIN folder within ColdFusion's program folder, which is located at `C:\CFUSION\BIN` in a typical installation. The syntax for using the command-line utility is as follows:

```
cfcrypt infile outfile [/r /q] [/h "message"] /v "2"
```

Table 18.1 explains what each of the parameters means.

TABLE 18.1 PARAMETERS FOR THE `cfcrypt.exe` COMMAND-LINE UTILITY

Parameter	Description
`infile`	The file(s) you want to encode. This can be the path to a single file, or you can use the normal DOS-style wildcards (? and *) to specify multiple files at once.
`outfile`	Path and filename of the output file. You can skip this parameter if you want. If you do, the input file(s) will be encoded in place, meaning that the original version of the files will be lost. Be sure you have a normal copy of the file because you will have no way to get your code back from the encoded version. To ensure you're not overwriting your files accidentally, you will get a warning message if you omit this parameter.
`/r`	If you include this switch and use wildcards for `infile`, any matching files in any subdirectories will also be encoded.
`/q`	Suppresses the warning message that gets displayed if you omit the `outfile` parameter.

TABLE 18.1 CONTINUED	
`/h`	This enables you to include a short header message at the beginning of your encoded files. Later, if someone opens the file in a text editor, he will see this message on the first line of the file (before the encrypted garbage).
`/v`	Required parameter that allows encoding using a specified version number. You always should use a value of `2` here, unless you want your templates to be capable of running on a version of ColdFusion Server prior to 4.0, in which case you should use `1`.

As an example, the following command encodes all .cfm files within the MyApp folder and all its subdirectories. The original version of the file is not changed at all. The encoded version is placed into the `c:\Encoded` folder, keeping the structure of subdirectories intact. You could then distribute the encoded version without worrying about people being able to easily read your code:

```
c:\CFUSION\BIN\cfencode C:\Inetpub\wwwroot\MyApp\*.cfm
➥C:\Encoded /r /h "Visit www.mycompany.com for updates and support." /v "2"
```

The command-line encoder is handy for encoding CFML custom tags you want to distribute or sell. See Chapter 22, "Building Reusable Components," for information about creating custom tags. The following command encodes the `MyCustomTag.cfm` file in ColdFusion's special CustomTags folder. The encoded version would be placed in the `c:\Encoded` folder:

```
c:\CFUSION\BIN\cfencode C:\CFUSION\CustomTags\MyCustomTag.cfm
➥ C:\Encoded\MyCustomTag.cfm /h "Copyright 2001 by My Company, Inc.
➥All rights reserved." /v "2"
```


Note

Because switches usually are optional with command-line utilities, a common mistake is to think that the `/v` switch can be left off. It is, however, required. Also note the quotation marks around the `/v` value, which is somewhat unusual for a command-line utility.

CREATING DEPLOYMENT SCRIPTS

So far this section has been dealing with deployment tasks in which you want the deployment to start right away. Studio also lets you do your deploying another way, via *deployment scripts*. Deployment scripts are special script files that carry out a particular deployment task, just like the normal deployments you have already learned about. After you have a deployment script that does what you need, you can just run the script to perform the actual deployment, rather than interacting with the wizard again.

WHEN TO CREATE A DEPLOYMENT SCRIPT

Many developers find that the wizard-based deployment works just fine for them and have no reason to create deployment scripts. Others find them incredibly handy—it all depends on the situation at hand.

Two main situations exist in which you might want to create a deployment script:

- You find you are deploying often, and always in the same way (using the same options in each step of the Deployment Wizard). If you created a script, you would then have a way to begin the deployment with one click.
- You want to customize the deployment process in some way. Perhaps you want to automatically archive the files currently on the target servers before the deployment begins. Maybe you need the list of deployment servers to come from an external file or database table, or you need to ensure that certain changes in a database structure get migrated over to the target servers as part of the deployment process. You would use the Deployment Wizard once to create a basic deployment script, then edit the script to suit your needs.

The first situation is easy to deal with and explain. The second situation is a bit more complicated. To be able to fully understand and customize a deployment script, you must be at least somewhat familiar with VBScript or JScript. You also must learn about the `DeploymentManager` object provided by Studio's Visual Tools Object Model (VTOM), which provides you with the programmatic hooks you need to customize the deployment process.

Unfortunately, a discussion of how to customize a deployment script is beyond the scope of this book. It is discussed in full in *Advanced ColdFusion 5 Application Development 2nd Edition* (0-7897-2585-1), the companion volume to this book.

CREATING A DEPLOYMENT SCRIPT

To create a deployment script, follow these steps:

1. Start the Deployment Wizard as you would normally.
2. During the first step of the wizard, select the Scriptable Deployment option (refer to Figure 18.13). When you click Next, a new step titled Define Script Properties appears, as shown in Figure 18.19.
3. Provide a descriptive name for your script in the Deployment Task Name field. This name will appear as a part of your project in the Projects tab.
4. If you want, you can change the Script Language option from JScript to VBScript. This option is relevant only if you plan to read and customize the script. If so, you should choose the language you are more familiar with. If you don't know either but are familiar at all with JavaScript, Java, C++, or similar languages, the JScript option will probably produce code that is more familiar to you.
5. You also can provide a specific location or filename for your script in the Save Script to File field. Otherwise, just accept the default filename the wizard suggests, which is based on the task name.

When you click Next, the Select Script Type step of the wizard appears, as shown in Figure 18.20. If you are not planning to customize your script, the Project-wide Upload Script is recommended because it is the simplest of the three. If you are planning to customize the script, you should select Project Element Iterator Script, unless you just want the script to contain a hard-coded reference to each file that exists in your project right now. If so, select File-by-File Deployment Script.

Complete the rest of the wizard as you would normally.

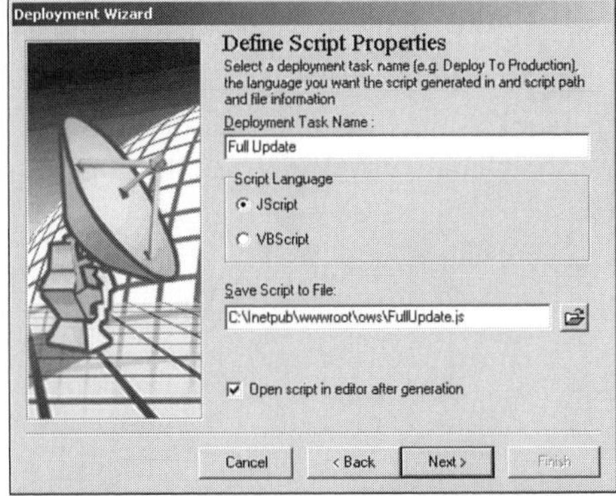

Figure 18.19
You have your choice of scripting languages when creating a deployment script.

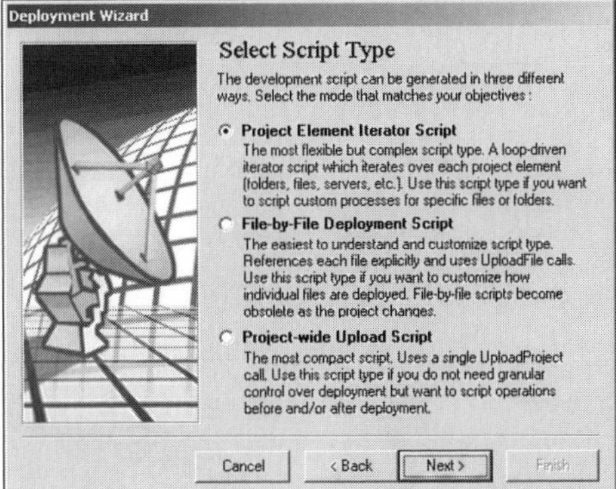

Figure 18.20
You have three types of deployment scripts from which to choose.

Tip

After you've created a deployment script, you could easily create a toolbar button to run it. Just right-click a toolbar and select Customize. In the Customize dialog box, select Add Custom Button; then select the Execute an ActiveScript File option and specify your deployment script in the Script File field. See Chapter 8, "Introduction to ColdFusion Studio," for more information.

Running a Deployment Script

After you run through the Deployment Wizard with the Scriptable Deployment option, your new script appears as a part of your project, nested within the Deployment Scripts item (refer to Figure 18.1). To run the script, simply right-click it and select Run Script from the pop-up menu. The script begins immediately, and the Results tab appears to show you the progress of the deployment process (refer to Figure 18.17).

CUSTOMIZING YOUR SCRIPTS

Again, a discussion of how to customize a deployment script is unfortunately beyond the scope of this book. If you want to learn how to customize a deployment script, several good sources of information are available:

- If you have the *Advanced ColdFusion 5 Application Development* book, see the "Scripting ColdFusion Studio" chapter.
- In Studio's Help tab, take a look at the Scripting the Visual Tools Object Model section. Pay particular attention to the DeploymentManager Object page, which explains the scripting methods and properties specific to deployment.
- Create a new script by using the Deployment Wizard; then open it in Studio. The code the wizard produces is fairly well commented. Depending on your situation, you might be able to figure out what you need to change just by examining the file and referring to the Help pages mentioned previously.

Note

To edit an existing script, right-click it and select Open Script from the pop-up menu. To change the name of the script as it appears in the Projects tab, right-click it and select Properties. To remove the script from your project, right-click it and select Remove.

CHAPTER 19

Introducing the Web Application Framework

In this chapter

ColdFusion provides a small but very important set of features for building sophisticated Web applications. The features all have to do with making all your ColdFusion templates for a particular site or project behave as if they were related to one another—that is, to make them behave as a single application. These features are referred to collectively as the *Web application framework*.

The Web application framework is designed to help you with the following:

- **Consistent Look and Feel**—The application framework enables you to easily include a consistent header or footer at the top and bottom of every page in your application. It also lets you apply the same look and feel to any error messages that might need to be displayed to the user.
- **Sharing Variables Between Pages**—So far, the variables you have worked with in this book all "die" when each page request has been processed. The Web application framework changes this, giving you a variety of ways to maintain the values of variables between page requests. The variables can be maintained on a per-user, per-session, or application-wide basis.
- **Before and After Processing**—The application framework gives you an easy way to execute custom code you want just *before* each page request. A common use for this capability is to provide password security for your application. You can also execute custom code just *after* the request.

Considered together, it's the Web application framework that really lets you present a Web experience to your users. Without these features, your individual templates would always stand on their own, acting as little miniprograms. The framework is the force that binds all your templates together.

USING APPLICATION.CFM

To get started with the Web application framework, you first must create a special file called `Application.cfm`. In most respects, this file is just an ordinary ColdFusion template. Even though you can put any CFML code in the template that you want, you should generally not do so. `Application.cfm` has special uses, as you will see.

Only two things make `Application.cfm` special:

- The code in your `Application.cfm` file will be automatically included just before any of your application pages. The behavior is just as if you included the file using an ordinary `<CFINCLUDE>` tag at the very top of each of your regular .cfm files.
- You can't visit an `Application.cfm` page directly. If you attempt to visit an `Application.cfm` page with a browser, you will receive an error message from ColdFusion.

The `Application.cfm` file is sometimes referred to as the *application template*. It might not sound all that special so far, but you will find that these two special properties actually go a long way toward making your applications more cohesive and easier to develop.

Note

On Unix/Linux systems, filenames are case sensitive. The `Application.cfm` file must be spelled exactly as shown here, using a capital A. Even if you are doing your development with Windows systems in mind, pay attention to the case so ColdFusion will be capable of finding the file if you decide to move your application to a Linux or Unix server later.

PLACEMENT OF `Application.cfm`

As stated previously, the code in your `Application.cfm` file is automatically executed just before each of the pages that make up your application. You might be wondering how exactly ColdFusion does this. How will it know which files make up your application and which ones do not?

The answer is quite simple: Whenever a user visits a .cfm page, ColdFusion looks to see whether a file named `Application.cfm` exists in the same directory as the requested page. If so, ColdFusion automatically includes it, just as if you had put a `<CFINCLUDE>` tag at the top of the requested template.

If no `Application.cfm` exists in the same folder as the requested page, ColdFusion looks in that folder's parent folder. If no `Application.cfm` file exists there, it looks in *that* parent's folder, and so on, until there are no more parent folders to look in.

All this means is that you should do something you were probably already going to do anyway. Namely, you should put all the ColdFusion templates for a particular application within a single folder, somewhere within your Web server's document root. Let's call that directory your *application folder*. Within the application folder, you can organize your ColdFusion templates using any structure of subfolders you want. Now, if you put an `Application.cfm` file in the application folder, all of its code will automatically be included in all your application's templates. It's that simple.

For instance, consider the folder structure shown in Figure 19.1. Here, the application folder is the folder named `OrangeWhip`, which is sitting within the Web server's document root. Some basic Web pages are located in there, such as the company's home page (`Index.cfm`), a How To Contact Us page (`ContactUs.cfm`), and a Company Info page (`Company.cfm`).

Because a file called `Application.cfm` also exists in this folder, it automatically is included every time a user visits `Index.cfm` or `ContactUs.cfm`. It also is included whenever a user visits any of the ColdFusion templates stored in the Intranet or Store folders, or any of the subfolders of the Intranet folder. No matter how deep the subfolder structure gets, the `Application.cfm` file in the OrangeWhip folder will be automatically included.

A BASIC `Application.cfm` TEMPLATE

Take a look at Listing 19.1, which is a simple `Application.cfm` file. Because the two `<CFSET>` tags are executed before each page request, the `DataSource` and `CompanyName` variables can be referred to within any of the application's ColdFusion templates. For instance, the value of the `DataSource` variable will always be `ows`.

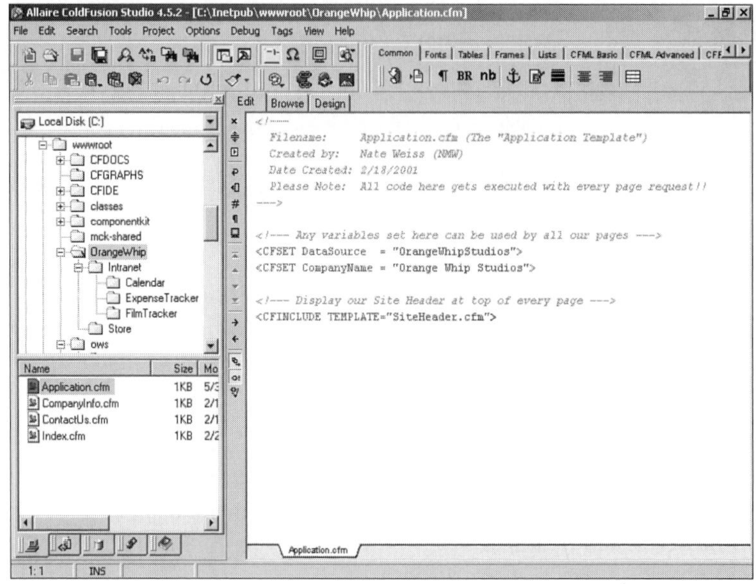

Figure 19.1
The `Application.cfm` file gets included before any of your application's templates.

To try this listing out, be sure to save it as `Application.cfm`, not `Application1.cfm`.

Listing 19.1 `Application1.cfm`—**A Simple Application Template**

```
<!---
  Filename:     Application.cfm (The "Application Template")
  Created by:   Nate Weiss (NMW)
  Date Created: 2/18/2001
  Please Note:  All code here gets executed with every page request!!
--->

<!--- Any variables set here can be used by all our pages --->
<CFSET DataSource  = "ows">
<CFSET CompanyName = "Orange Whip Studios">

<!--- Display our Site Header at top of every page --->
<CFINCLUDE TEMPLATE="SiteHeader.cfm">
```

Tip

Later, you can refer to this variable as the `DATASOURCE` attribute for all the `<CFQUERY>` tags in the application. That way, if the data source name changes later, for whatever reason, you will need to update your code in only one place, rather than in each individual `<CFQUERY>` tag.

In addition, the `<CFINCLUDE>` tag in Listing 19.1 ensures that the company's standard page header will be shown at the top of each page. Listing 19.2 shows the `SiteHeader.cfm` template itself. Note that it can use the `CompanyName` variable that gets set by `Application.cfm`.

If this were your application, you would no longer have to put that <CFINCLUDE> tag at the top of the Index.cfm or CompanyInfo.cfm pages (see Figure 19.1), and you wouldn't have to remember to include it in any new templates. ColdFusion would now be taking care of that for you.

LISTING 19.2 SiteHeader.cfm—SIMPLE HEADER THAT IS INCLUDED ON EACH PAGE BY Application.cfm

```
<!---
  Filename:     SiteHeader.cfm
  Created by:   Nate Weiss (NMW)
  Date Created: 2/18/2001
  Please Note:  Included in every page by Application.cfm
--->

<HTML>
<HEAD>
  <TITLE><CFOUTPUT>#CompanyName#</CFOUTPUT></TITLE>
</HEAD>

<BODY>
<FONT FACE="sans-serif" SIZE="2">
```

USING ONREQUESTEND.CFM

The Web application framework also reserves the special OnRequestEnd.cfm filename, which automatically is included at the very end of every page request, rather than at the beginning. Similar to the Application.cfm file, this file cannot be visited directly using a Web browser.

ColdFusion looks for OnRequestEnd.cfm in the same folder in which it finds Application.cfm. So, for OnRequestEnd.cfm to be executed, just place it in the same location in which your Application.cfm file is sitting (your application folder).

Listing 19.3 demonstrates one common use for OnRequestEnd.cfm. It has just one line of code, which is a simple <CFINCLUDE> tag to include the SiteFooter.cfm template at the bottom of every page. Listing 19.4 shows the SiteFooter.cfm file itself, which displays a copyright notice. The net effect is that the copyright notice is displayed at the bottom of every page in the application, as shown in Figure 19.2.

Of course, there are other ways to get this effect. You could forget about this OnRequestEnd.cfm business and just put the <CFINCLUDE> tag at the bottom of every page in your application. But that might be tedious, and you might forget to do it sometimes. Or, you could just put the copyright notice in the OnRequestEnd.cfm file and get rid of the SiteFooter.cfm file altogether. That would be fine, but leaving them in separate files can keep things more manageable if the footer becomes more complicated in the future.

LISTING 19.3 `OnRequestEnd.cfm`**—INCLUDING A SITE FOOTER AT THE BOTTOM OF EVERY PAGE**

```
<!---
  Filename:     OnRequestEnd.cfm
  Created by:   Nate Weiss (NMW)
  Date Created: 2/18/2001
  Please Note:  All code here gets executed with every page request!!
--->

<!--- Display our Site Footer at bottom of every page --->
<CFINCLUDE TEMPLATE="SiteFooter.cfm">
```

Note

On Unix/Linux systems, filenames are case sensitive. The `OnRequestEnd.cfm` file must be spelled exactly as shown here. Even if you are doing your development with Windows systems in mind, pay attention to the case so ColdFusion will be capable of finding the file if you decide to move your application to a Linux or Unix server later.

LISTING 19.4 `SiteFooter.cfm`**—SIMPLE FOOTER THAT GETS INCLUDED BY** `OnRequestEnd.cfm`

```
<!---
  Filename:     SiteFooter.cfm
  Created by:   Nate Weiss (NMW)
  Date Created: 2/18/2001
  Please Note:  Included in every page by OnRequestEnd.cfm
--->

<!--- Display copyright notice at bottom of every page --->
<CFOUTPUT>
  <FONT SIZE="1" FACE="sans-serif" COLOR="Silver">
  <P>(c) #Year(Now())# #CompanyName#. All rights reserved.<BR>
</CFOUTPUT>

</BODY>
</HTML>
```

Tip

The expression `#Year(Now())#` is a simple way to display the current year. You also could use `#DateFormat(Now(), "yyyy")#` to get the same effect. You can find out more about the `DateFormat`, `Year`, and `Now` functions in Appendix B, "ColdFusion Function Reference."

Listing 19.5 provides preliminary code for Orange Whip Studio's home page. As you can see, it is just a simple message that welcomes the user to the site. Of course, in practice, this is where you would provide links to all the interesting parts of the application. The point of this template is to demonstrate that the site header and footer are now going to be automatically included at the top and bottom of all ordinary ColdFusion templates in this folder (or its subfolders), as shown in Figure 19.2. Note that this template is also able to use the `CompanyName` variable that was set in the `Application.cfm` file.

LISTING 19.5 `Index1.cfm`—A BASIC HOME PAGE FOR ORANGE WHIP STUDIOS

```
<!---
  Filename:     Index.cfm
  Created by:   Nate Weiss (NMW)
  Date Created: 2/18/2001
  Please Note:  Header and Footer are automatically provided
--->

<CFOUTPUT>
  <BLOCKQUOTE>
  <P>Hello, and welcome to the home of
  #CompanyName# on the web!  We certainly
  hope you enjoy your visit.  We take pride in
  producing movies that are almost as good
  as the ones they are copied from.  We've
  been doing it for years.  On this site, you'll
  be able to find out about all our classic films
  from the golden age of Orange Whip Studios,
  as well as our latest and greatest new releases.
  Have fun!<BR>
  </BLOCKQUOTE>
</CFOUTPUT>
```

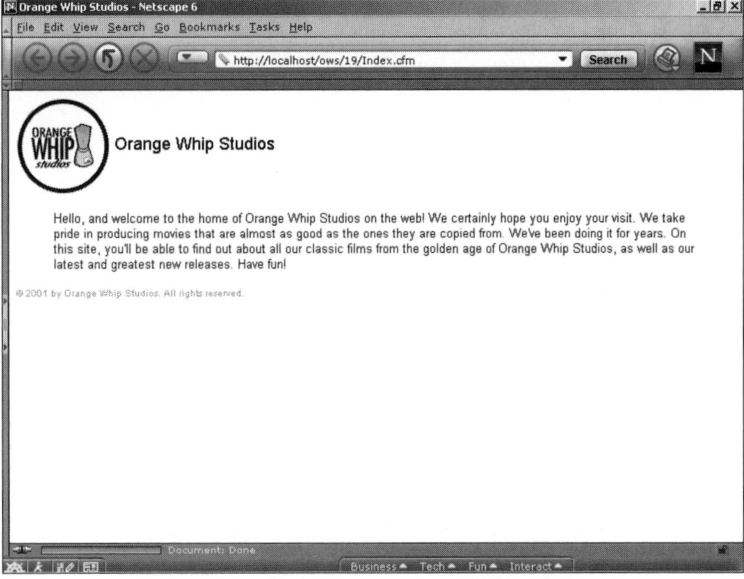

Figure 19.2 The application framework makes keeping things consistent throughout your site easy.

CUSTOMIZING THE LOOK OF ERROR MESSAGES

The Web application framework provides a simple way to customize the look of error messages that can occur while users are accessing your pages. As you know, error messages might appear because of syntax problems in your code, because of database connection problems, or just because the user has left out one or more required fields while he is filling out a form.

The application framework enables you to customize any of these error messages. You can even hide them from the user's view entirely if you want. This enables you to maintain a consistent look and feel throughout your application, even when those dreaded error messages occur.

INTRODUCING THE <CFERROR> TAG

You use the `<CFERROR>` tag to specify how error messages should be displayed. Customizing the error messages that appear throughout your application is generally a two-step process:

1. First, you create an *error display template*, which displays the error message along with whatever graphics or other formatting you consider appropriate.
2. Next, you include a `<CFERROR>` tag that tells ColdFusion to display errors using the error display template you just created. In general, you place the `<CFERROR>` tag in your `Application.cfm` file.

Table 19.1 shows the attributes supported by the `<CFERROR>` tag.

TABLE 19.1 <CFERROR> TAG ATTRIBUTES

Attribute	Description
`TYPE`	The type of error you want to catch and display using your customized error display template. The allowable values are `Request`, `Validation`, `Monitor`, and `Exception`. The first two types are covered in this chapter; the latter two are discussed in Chapter 33, "Error Handling." If you don't supply this attribute, it is assumed to be `Request`, but it is best to always supply it.
`TEMPLATE`	Required. The relative path and filename of your customized error display template. You specify the filename in the same way as you would specify an include file with the `<CFINCLUDE>` tag.
`MAILTO`	Optional. An e-mail address for a site administrator that the user could use to send some type of notification that the error occurred. The only purpose of this attribute is to pass an appropriate e-mail address to your error display template. It does not actually send any e-mail messages on its own.
`EXCEPTION`	Optional. The specific exception that you want to catch and display using your customized error display template. The default value is `Any`, which is appropriate for most circumstances. See Chapter 33 for a discussion of the other values you can supply here.

The next two sections discuss how to customize the error messages displayed for *exception errors* (syntax errors, database errors, and so on) and *validation errors* (when the user fails to fill out a form correctly).

REQUEST VERSUS EXCEPTION ERROR TEMPLATES

If you want to customize the way error messages are displayed, you first must create an error display template. This template is displayed to the user whenever a page request cannot be completed because of some type of uncaught error condition.

ColdFusion actually allows you to create two types of error display templates:

- **Request Error Display Templates**—The simplest way to show a customized error message. You can include whatever images or formatting you want so that the error matches your site's look and feel. However, CFML tags, such as `<CFOUTPUT>`, `<CFSET>`, or `<CFINCLUDE>`, are not allowed. CFML functions and variables also are not allowed.
- **Exception Error Display Templates**—These are more flexible. You can use whatever CFML tags you want. For instance, you might want to have ColdFusion automatically send an e-mail to the Webmaster when certain types of errors occur. The main caveat is that ColdFusion cannot display such a template for certain serious errors.

In general, the best practice is to create one template of each type. The exception template is displayed most of the time, unless the error is so serious that ColdFusion cannot safely continue interpreting CFML tags, in which case the request template is displayed. The request template also kicks in if the exception template *itself* causes an error or cannot be found.

Tip

If you don't care about being able to use CFML tags in these error display templates, you can just create the request template and skip creating the exception one.

Note

For those history buffs out there, the request type of error display template is somewhat of a holdover from earlier versions of ColdFusion. At one time, you could never respond intelligently to any type of error. Thankfully, those days are over.

CREATING A CUSTOMIZED REQUEST ERROR PAGE

To create the request display template, do the following:

1. Create a new ColdFusion template called `ErrorRequest.cfm`, located in the same directory as your `Application.cfm` file. Include whatever images or formatting you want, using whatever `<IMG>` or other tags you would normally. Remember to *not* put any CFML tags in this template.

2. Include the special `ERROR.Diagnostics` variable wherever you want the actual error message to appear, if you want it to appear at all. Contrary to what you are used to, the variable should *not* be between `<CFOUTPUT>` tags.
3. If you want, you can include the special `ERROR.MailTo` variable to display the e-mail address of your site's Webmaster or some other appropriate person. You also can use any of the other variables shown in Table 19.2.
4. Include a `<CFERROR>` tag in your `Application.cfm` file, with the `TYPE` attribute set to `Request` and the `TEMPLATE` attribute set to `ErrorRequest.cfm`. This is what associates your error display template with your application.

Listing 19.6 is a good example of a request error display template. Note that no `<CFOUTPUT>` or other CFML tags are present. Also note that the only variables used are the special `ERROR` variables mentioned previously.

LISTING 19.6 ErrorRequest.cfm—CUSTOMIZING THE DISPLAY OF ERROR MESSAGES

```
<!---
  Filename:     ErrorRequest.cfm
  Created by:   Nate Weiss (NMW)
  Date Created: 2/18/2001
  Please Note:  Included via <CFERROR> in Application.cfm
--->

<HTML>
<HEAD><TITLE>Error</TITLE></HEAD>
<BODY>

<!--- Display sarcastic message to poor user --->
<h2>Who Knew?</h2>
<P>We are very sorry, but a technical problem prevents us from
showing you what you are looking for.  Unfortunately, these things
happen from time to time, even though we have only the most
top-notch people on our technical staff.  Perhaps all of
our programmers need a raise, or more vacation time. As always,
there is also the very real possibility that SPACE ALIENS
(or our rivals at Mirimax Studios) have sabotaged our Web site.<BR>
<P>That said, we will naturally try to correct this problem
as soon as we possibly can.  Please try again shortly.

<!--- Provide "mailto" link so user can send e-mail --->
<P>If you want, you can
<A HREF="mailto:#ERROR.MailTo#">send the Webmaster an e-mail</A>.
<P>Thank you.<BR>

<!--- Display the actual error message --->
<BLOCKQUOTE>
  <HR><FONT SIZE="-1" COLOR="Gray">#ERROR.Diagnostics#</FONT>
</BLOCKQUOTE>

</BODY>
</HTML>
```

Note

ColdFusion also provides the `<CFTRY>` and `<CFCATCH>` tags, which enable you to trap specific errors and respond to or recover from them as appropriate. See Chapter 33, "Error Handling," for details.

Listing 19.7 shows how to use the `<CFERROR>` tag in your `Application.cfm` file. Note that the e-mail address `webmaster@orangewhipstudios.com` is being provided as the tag's `MAILTO` attribute, which means that the Webmaster's e-mail address will be inserted in place of the `ERROR.MailTo` reference in Listing 19.8. Figure 19.3 shows how an error message would now be shown if you were to make a coding error in one of your templates.

To test this listing, save it as `Application.cfm`, not `Application2.cfm`.

Listing 19.7 `Application2.cfm`—**Use of the** `<CFERROR>` **Tag in** `Application.cfm`

```
<!---
  Filename:     Application.cfm (The "Application Template")
  Created by:   Nate Weiss (NMW)
  Date Created: 2/18/2001
  Please Note:  All code here gets executed with every page request!!
--->

<!--- Any variables set here can be used by all our pages --->
<CFSET DataSource  = "ows">
<CFSET CompanyName = "Orange Whip Studios">
<CFSET ErrorEmail  = "webmaster@orangewhipstudios.com">

<!--- Display Custom Message for "Request" Errors --->
<CFERROR
  TYPE="Request"
  TEMPLATE="ErrorRequest.cfm"
  MAILTO="#ErrorE-mail#">

<!--- Display our Site Header at top of every page --->
<CFINCLUDE TEMPLATE="SiteHeader.cfm">
```


Additional Error Variables

In Listing 19.6, you saw how the `ERROR.Diagnostics` variable can be used to show the user which specific error actually occurred. A number of additional variables can be used in the same way. You will see a several of these used in Listing 19.8 in the next section.

Note

Note that the `ERROR.GeneratedContent` variable is not available in request error display templates.

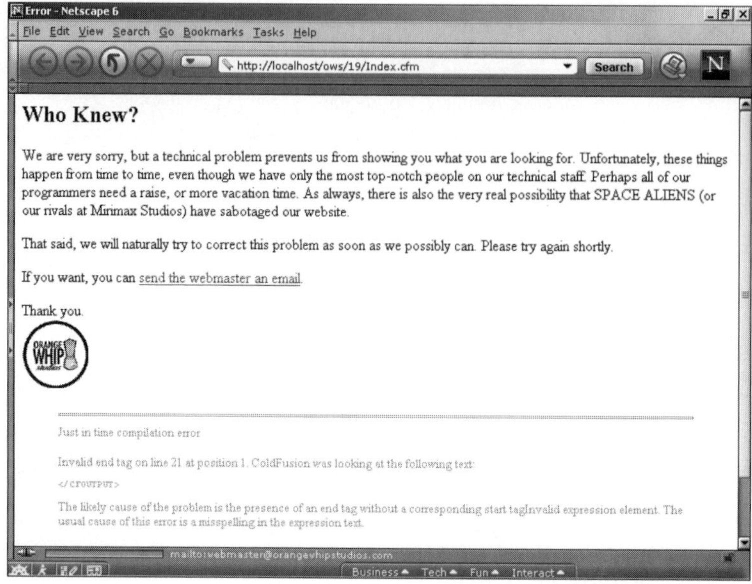

Figure 19.3 Customized error pages help maintain your application's look and feel.

TABLE 19.2 SPECIAL ERROR VARIABLES AVAILABLE IN AN ERROR DISPLAY TEMPLATE

Attribute	Description
`ERROR.Browser`	The browser that was used when the error occurred, as reported by the browser itself. This is the same value that is normally available to you as the `#CGI.HTTP_USER_AGENT#` variable, which generally includes the browser version number and operating system.
`ERROR.DateTime`	The date and time that the error occurred, in the form MM/DD/YY HH:MM:SS. You can use the `DateFormat()` function to format the date differently in an exception template, but not in a request template.
`ERROR.Diagnostics`	The actual error message. In general, this is the most important thing to include (or to decide not to include) in an error display template. Please note that the exact text of this message can be affected by the settings currently enabled in the Debugging page of the ColdFusion Administrator. For instance, if the Display the Template Path in Error Messages check box is checked, this message will reveal the complete path of the ColdFusion template that caused the error. See Chapter 15, "Debugging and Troubleshooting," for details.
`ERROR.GeneratedContent`	The actual HTML that had been generated by the requested ColdFusion template (and any included templates and so on) up until the moment that the error occurred. You could use this to display the part of the page that had been successfully generated. This variable is not available in the request type of error display template.

Attribute	Description
`ERROR.HTTPReferer`	The page the user was coming from when the error occurred, assuming that the user got to the problem page via a link or form submission. This value is reported by the browser and can sometimes be blank (especially if the user visited the page directly by typing its URL). Note the incorrect spelling of the word *referrer*.
`ERROR.MailTo`	An e-mail address, presumably for a site administrator or Webmaster, as provided to the `<CFERROR>` tag. See the following examples to see how this actually should be used.
`ERROR.QueryString`	The query string provided to the template in which the error occurred. In other words, everything after the `?` sign in the page's URL. This is the same value that is normally available to you as the `#CGI.QUERY_STRING#` variable.
`ERROR.RemoteAddress`	The IP address of the user's machine.
`ERROR.Template`	Filename of the ColdFusion template (.cfm file) in which the error occurred.

Note

These are the only variables you can use in *request* error display templates. You can use all types of ColdFusion variables in exception error display templates, discussed next.

CREATING A CUSTOMIZED EXCEPTION ERROR PAGE

You already have seen how to create a request error display template, in which you are prevented from using any CFML tags or functions. Now you can create an exception error template, in which you *are* able to use whatever CFML tags and functions you want.

For instance, Listing 19.8 is similar to Listing 19.6, but it does not display the `ERROR.Diagnostics` message to the user. This means that the user will not know which type of error actually occurred. After all, your users might not care about the specifics, and you might not want them to see the actual error message in the first place. In addition, instead of allowing the user to send an e-mail message to the Webmaster, this template has ColdFusion send an e-mail message to the Webmaster automatically, via the `<CFMAIL>` tag.

LISTING 19.8 `ErrorException.cfm`—**SENDING AN E-MAIL WHEN AN ERROR OCCURS**

```
<!---
  Filename:      ErrorException.cfm
  Created by:    Nate Weiss (NMW)
  Date Created: 2/18/2001
  Please Note:   Included via <CFERROR> in Application.cfm
--->
```

LISTING 19.8 CONTINUED

```
<HTML>
<HEAD><TITLE>Error</TITLE></HEAD>
<BODY>

<!--- Display sarcastic message to poor user --->
<h2>Who Knew?</h2>
<P>We are very sorry, but a technical problem prevents us from
showing you what you are looking for.  Unfortunately, these things
happen from time to time, even though we have only the most
top-notch people on our technical staff.  Perhaps all of
our programmers need a raise, or more vacation time. As always,
there is also the very real possibility that SPACE ALIENS
(or our rivals at Mirimax Studios) have sabotaged our website.<BR>
<P>That said, we will naturally try to correct this problem
as soon as we possibly can.  Please try again shortly.
Thank you.<BR>

<!--- Maybe the company logo will make them feel better --->
<IMG SRC="../images/logo_b.gif" WIDTH="73" HEIGHT="73" ALT="" BORDER="0">

<!--- Send an email message to site administrator --->
<!--- (or whatever address provided to <CFERROR>) --->
<CFIF ERROR.MailTo NEQ "">
  <CFMAIL
    TO="#ERROR.MailTo#"
    FROM="errorsender@orangewhipstudios.com"
    SUBJECT="Error on Page #ERROR.Template#">
    Error Date/Time: #ERROR.DateTime#
    User's Browser:  #ERROR.Browser#
    URL Parameters:  #ERROR.QueryString#
    Previous Page:   #ERROR.HTTPReferer#
    ------------------------------------
    #ERROR.Diagnostics#
  </CFMAIL>
</CFIF>
```

Now all you have to do is add a second `<CFERROR>` tag to your `Application.cfm` file, this time specifying `TYPE="Exception"`. You should put this `<CFERROR>` tag right after the first one, so the first one can execute if some problem occurs with your exception error display template. Listing 19.9 (in the next section) shows how this would look in your `Application.cfm` file.

Note

Because sending automated error e-mails is a great way to show how exception templates can be used, the `<CFMAIL>` tag has been introduced a bit ahead of time. Its use in Listing 19.8 should be fairly self-explanatory: The ColdFusion server sends a simple e-mail message to the Webmaster. The e-mail will contain the error message, date, browser version, and so on because of the `ERROR` variables referred to between the opening and closing `<CFMAIL>` tags. See Chapter 28, "Interacting with E-mail," for details.

Tip

The Webmaster could also look in ColdFusion's logs to see any errors that might be occurring throughout the application. See Chapter 15, "Debugging and Troubleshooting," for details.

Creating a Customized Validation Error Page

Now, your application responds in a friendly and consistent manner, even when problems occur in your code. The Web application framework also enables you to customize the page that appears if a user's form input doesn't comply with the validation rules you have set up using the hidden form fields technique (as described in Chapter 13, "Form Data Validation").

To create your own validation error display template, follow the same steps you performed to create your request template (see the section "Creating a Customized Request Error Page," earlier in this chapter). The only differences are that you use the special `ERROR` variables listed in Table 19.3 instead of those in Table 19.2, and that you should specify `TYPE="Validation"` in the `<CFERROR>` tag you include in your `Application.cfm` file.

Table 19.3 Special ERROR Variables Available in an Validation Display Template

Attribute	Description
`ERROR.InvalidFields`	The actual problems with the way the user has filled out the form. The text is preformatted as a bulleted list (the text includes `<UL>` and `<LI>` tags). In general, you would always want to include this in your error display template; otherwise, the user wouldn't have any indication of what she did wrong.
`ERROR.ValidationHeader`	The default text that normally appears above the bulleted list of problems when you are not using a customized error message. The message reads, "Form Entries Incomplete or Invalid.... One or more problems exist with the data you have entered." You can include this variable in your template if you want this wording to appear. Otherwise, you can just provide your own text.
`ERROR.ValidationFooter`	The default text that normally appears above the bulleted list of problems when you are not using a customized error message. The message reads, "Use the Back button on your Web browser to return to the previous page and correct the listed problems."

Listing 19.9 shows a completed validation error display template. Figure 19.4 shows how it would look to the end user, if he were to submit a form without filling it out correctly.

Listing 19.10 shows how your `Application.cfm` file would look at this point. Note that it now contains three `<CFERROR>` tags: one for each type of error display template you've learned to create in this chapter.

Listing 19.9 `ErrorValidation.cfm`—**Customizing the Display of Form Validation Messages**

```
<!---
  Filename:      ErrorValidation.cfm
  Created by:    Nate Weiss (NMW)
  Date Created: 2/18/2001
  Please Note:   Included via <CFERROR> in Application.cfm
--->

<HTML>
<HEAD><TITLE>Form Fields Missing or Incomplete</TITLE></HEAD>
<BODY>

<!--- Introductory Message --->
<IMG SRC="../images/logo_b.gif" WIDTH="73" HEIGHT="73" ALT="" ALIGN="absmiddle"
➥BORDER="0">
<FONT SIZE="4">Please take a moment...</FONT><BR CLEAR="all">
Maybe it's because we are in the entertainment business and thus have lost
touch with the kinds of problems that ordinary people have, but we can't
quite figure out how to deal with the information you just provided.
Here are the "problems" that we need you to correct:

<!--- Display actual form-field problems --->
#ERROR.InvalidFields#

<!--- Link back to previous page --->
<P>Please
<A HREF="javascript:history.back()">return to the form</A>
and correct these minor problems.<BR>
Or, just use your browser's Back button.<BR>
</BODY>
</HTML>
```

Listing 19.10 `Application3.cfm`—**Using Request, Exception, and Validation Templates Together**

```
<!---
  Filename:      Application.cfm (The "Application Template")
  Created by:    Nate Weiss (NMW)
  Date Created: 2/18/2001
  Please Note:   All code here gets executed with every page request!!
--->

<!--- Any variables set here can be used by all our pages --->
<CFSET DataSource  = "ows">
<CFSET CompanyName = "Orange Whip Studios">
<CFSET ErrorEmail  = "webmaster@orangewhipstudios.com">

<!--- Display Custom Message for "Request" Errors --->
<CFERROR
  TYPE="Request"
  TEMPLATE="ErrorRequest.cfm"
  MAILTO="#ErrorEmail#">
```

```
<!--- Display Custom Message for "Exception" Errors --->
<CFERROR
  TYPE="Exception"
  EXCEPTION="Any"
  TEMPLATE="ErrorException.cfm"
  MAILTO="#ErrorEmail#">

<!--- Display Custom Message for "Validation" Errors --->
<CFERROR
  TYPE="Validation"
  TEMPLATE="ErrorValidation.cfm">

<!--- Display our Site Header at top of every page --->
<CFINCLUDE TEMPLATE="SiteHeader.cfm">
```

Note

ColdFusion also provides the `<CFTRY>` and `<CFCATCH>` tags, which allow you to trap specific errors and respond to or recover from them as appropriate. See Chapter 33 for details.

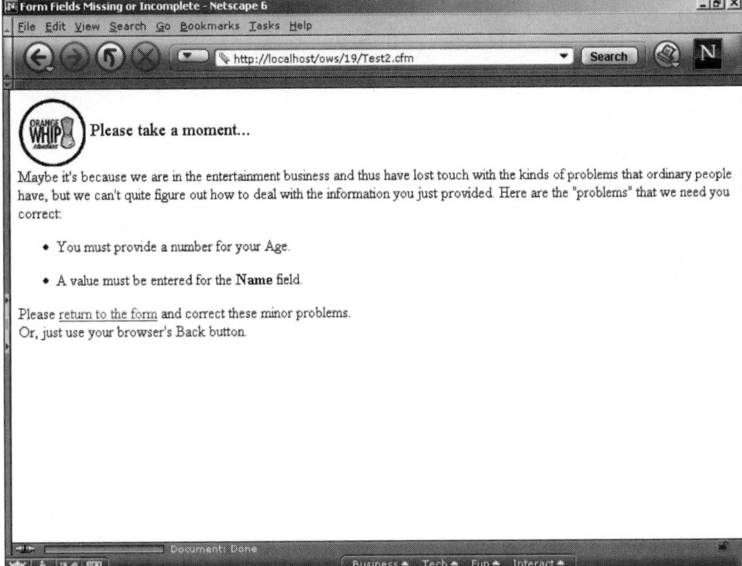

Figure 19.4
A customized display template makes it less jarring for users that fail to fill out a form correctly.

PART III CH 19

USING APPLICATION VARIABLES

So far in this chapter, you have seen how ColdFusion's Web application framework features help you maintain a consistent look and feel throughout your application. You also have seen how easy setting up before and after processing with the special application templates (`Application.cfm` and `OnRequestEnd.cfm`) is. In other words, your pages are starting to look and behave cohesively.

Next, you learn how your application's templates can start sharing variables between page requests. Basically, this is the part where your application gets a piece of the server's memory in which to store values. This is where it gets a brain.

WHAT ARE APPLICATION VARIABLES?

Pretend it's Oscar season. Orange Whip Studios wants to put a featured movie in a little box on its home page, and it's your job to get that done. The studio wants the featured movie to be different each time the home page is viewed, shamelessly rotating through all its movies.

Hmmm. You could retrieve all the movies from the database for each page request and somehow pick one at random, but that wouldn't guarantee that the same movie didn't get picked three or four times in a row. What you want is some way to remember your current spot in the list of movies, so they all get shown evenly, in order. You consider making a table to remember which movies have been shown and then deleting all rows from the table when it's time to rotate through them again, but that seems like overkill. You wish there was some kind of variable that would persist between page requests, instead of dying at the bottom of each page like the ColdFusion variables you're used to.

That's exactly what application variables are for. Instead of setting a variable called `LastMovieID`, you could call it `APPLICATION.LastMovieID`. After you set this variable value to `5`, say, it remains set at `5` until you change it again (or until the server is restarted). In essence, application variables enable you to set aside a little piece of ColdFusion's memory, which your application can use for its own purposes.

WHEN TO USE APPLICATION VARIABLES

Generally, you can use application variables whenever you need a variable to be shared among all pages and all visitors to your application. The variable is kept in ColdFusion's memory, and any page in your application can access or change its value. If some code on one of your pages changes the value of an application variable, the next hit to any of your application's pages will reflect the new value.

This means you should not use application variables if you want a separate copy of the variable to exist for each visitor to your site. In other words, application variables should not be used for anything personalized because they do not attempt to distinguish between your site's visitors. Chapter 20, "Working with Sessions," explains how to create variables that are maintained separately for each visitor.

So, consider application variables for things such as the following:

- Rotating banner ads evenly, so that all ads get shown the same number of times
- Rotating other types of content, such as the featured movie problem mentioned previously, or products that might be on sale
- Keeping counters of various types of events, such as the number of people currently online or the number of hits since the server was started

- Maintaining some type of information that changes only occasionally or perhaps doesn't change at all, but can take a bit of time to compute or retrieve

Do not use application variables for per-user tasks, such as these:

- Maintaining a shopping cart
- Remembering a user's e-mail address or username from visit to visit
- Keeping a list of the pages a user has visited while he has been on your site

INTRODUCING THE <CFAPPLICATION> TAG

As a part of the Web application framework, ColdFusion provides a tag called `<CFAPPLICATION>`, which is used primarily for enabling various types of persistent variables. Application variables are one type of persistent variable; you learn about two other types—client and session variables—in Chapter 20.

Application variables can be used only after a `<CFAPPLICATION>` tag has been encountered, which tells ColdFusion where to store the variables in its memory. Because you generally want to share the variables throughout your application, it is almost always best to put the `<CFAPPLICATION>` tag in your `Application.cfm` file.

The tag takes a number of attributes, most of which are relevant only for session and client variables, discussed in the next chapter. For now, only two attributes are important, as shown in Table 19.4.

TABLE 19.4 <CFAPPLICATION> TAG ATTRIBUTES RELEVANT TO APPLICATION VARIABLES

Attribute	Description
NAME	A name for your application. The name can be anything you want, up to 64 characters long. ColdFusion uses this name internally to store and look up your application variables for you. It should be unique per application. This attribute is required to enable the use of application variables.
APPLICATIONTIMEOUT	Optional. How long you want your application variables to live in the server's memory. If you don't provide this value, it defaults to whatever is set up in the Variables page of the ColdFusion Administrator. See the section "Application Variable Timeouts," later in this chapter.

ENABLING APPLICATION VARIABLES

Listing 19.11 shows how your `Application.cfm` page is continuing to evolve. The `<CFAPPLICATION>` tag is now present, in addition to the `<CFERROR>` and other tags you learned about earlier in this chapter. Therefore, you can start using application variables in any ColdFusion templates in the same folder (or subfolders) as `Application.cfm`.

Listing 19.11 Application4.cfm—Using <CFAPPLICATION> to Enable Application Variables

```
<!---
  Filename:     Application.cfm (The "Application Template")
  Created by:   Nate Weiss (NMW)
  Date Created: 2/18/2001
  Please Note:  All code here gets executed with every page request!!
--->

<!--- Name our application, and enable Application variables --->
<CFAPPLICATION
  NAME="OrangeWhipSite">

<!--- Any variables set here can be used by all our pages --->
<CFSET DataSource  = "ows">
<CFSET CompanyName = "Orange Whip Studios">
<CFSET ErrorEmail  = "webmaster@orangewhipstudios.com">

<!--- Display Custom Message for "Request" Errors --->
<CFERROR
  TYPE="Request"
  TEMPLATE="ErrorRequest.cfm"
  MAILTO="#ErrorEmail#">

<!--- Display Custom Message for "Exception" Errors --->
<CFERROR
  TYPE="Exception"
  EXCEPTION="Any"
  TEMPLATE="ErrorException.cfm"
  MAILTO="#ErrorEmail#">

<!--- Display Custom Message for "Validation" Errors --->
<CFERROR
  TYPE="Validation"
  TEMPLATE="ErrorValidation.cfm">

<!--- Display our Site Header at top of every page --->
<CFINCLUDE TEMPLATE="SiteHeader.cfm">
```

Note

ColdFusion maintains your application variables based on the <CFAPPLICATION> tag's NAME attribute. Therefore, it is important that no other applications on the same ColdFusion server use the same NAME. If they do, ColdFusion will consider them to be the same application and will share the variables amongst all the combined pages. Changing a variable in one also changes it in the other, and so on.

Using Application Variables

Now that application variables have been enabled, using them is quite simple. Basically, you create or set an application variable the same way you would set a normal variable, generally using the <CFSET> tag. The only difference is the presence of the word APPLICATION, followed by a dot. For instance, the following line would set the APPLICATION.OurHitCount variable to 0. The variable would then be available to all pages in the application and would hold the value of 0 until it was changed:

```
<CFSET APPLICATION.OurHitCount = 0>
```

You can use application variables in any of the same places you would use ordinary ones. For instance, the following lines add one to an application variable and then output the new value, rounded to the nearest thousandth:

```
<CFSET APPLICATION.OurHitCount = APPLICATION.OurHitCount + 1>
<CFOUTPUT>#Round(APPLICATION.OurHitCount / 1000)># thousand</CFOUTPUT>
```

You also can use application variables with ColdFusion tags, such as <CFIF>, <CFPARAM>, and <CFOUTPUT>. See Chapter 9, "Using ColdFusion," and Chapter 10, "CFML Basics," if you want to review the use of variables in general.

PUTTING APPLICATION VARIABLES TO WORK

Application variables can make getting the little featured movie widget up and running relatively easy. Again, the idea is for a callout-style box, which cycles through each of Orange Whip Studio's films, to display on the site's home page. The box should change each time the page is accessed, rotating through all the movies evenly.

Listing 19.12 shows one simple way to get this done, using application variables. You'll note that the template is broken into two separate parts. The first half is the interesting part, in which an application variable called MovieList is used to rotate the featured movie correctly. The second half simply outputs the name and description to the page, as shown in Figure 19.5.

Note

Ignore the <CFLOCK> tags shown in Listing 19.12 for the moment. They are extremely important and are discussed in the next section, but for now just focus on the use of application variables.

LISTING 19.12 FeaturedMovie.cfm—USING APPLICATION VARIABLES TO TRACK CONTENT ROTATION

```
<!--- Need to lock when accessing shared data --->
<CFLOCK TIMEOUT="10">

  <!--- List of movies to show (list starts out empty) --->
  <CFPARAM NAME="Application.MovieList" TYPE="string" DEFAULT="">

  <!--- If this is the first time we're running this,  --->
  <!--- Or we have run out of movies to rotate through --->
  <CFIF ListLen(Application.MovieList) EQ 0>
    <!--- Get all current FilmIDs from the database --->
    <CFQUERY NAME="GetFilmIDs" DATASOURCE="#DataSource#">
      SELECT FilmID FROM Films
```

LISTING 19.12 CONTINUED

```
      ORDER BY MovieTitle
    </CFQUERY>

    <!--- Turn FilmIDs into a simple comma-separated list --->
    <CFSET Application.MovieList = ValueList(GetFilmIDs.FilmID)>
  </CFIF>

  <!--- Pick the first movie in the list to show right now --->
  <CFSET ThisMovieID = ListGetAt(Application.MovieList, 1)>
  <!--- Re-save the list, as all movies *except* the first --->
  <CFSET Application.MovieList = ListDeleteAt(Application.MovieList, 1)>
</CFLOCK>



<!--- Now that we have chosen the film to "Feature", --->
<!--- Get all important info about it from database. --->
<CFQUERY NAME="GetFilm" DATASOURCE="#DataSource#">
  SELECT
    MovieTitle, Summary, Rating,
    AmountBudgeted, DateInTheaters
  FROM Films f, FilmsRatings r
  WHERE FilmID = #ThisMovieID#
  AND f.RatingID = r.RatingID
</CFQUERY>

<!--- Now Display Our Featured Movie --->
<CFOUTPUT>
  <!--- Define formatting for our "feature" display --->
  <STYLE TYPE="text/css">
    TH.fm {background:RoyalBlue;color:white;text-align:left;
           font-family:sans-serif;font-size:10px}
    TD.fm {background:LightSteelBlue;
           font-family:sans-serif;font-size:12px}
  </STYLE>

  <!--- Show info about featured movie in HTML Table --->
  <TABLE WIDTH="150" ALIGN="right" BORDER="0" CELLSPACING="0">
    <TR><TH CLASS="fm">
      Featured Film
    </TH></TR>
    <!--- Movie Title, Summary, Rating --->
    <TR><TD CLASS="fm">
      <B>#GetFilm.MovieTitle#</B><BR>
      #GetFilm.Summary#<BR>
      <P ALIGN="right">Rated: #GetFilm.Rating#</P>
    </TD></TR>
    <!--- Cost (rounded to millions), release date --->
    <TR><TH CLASS="fm">
      Production Cost $#Round(GetFilm.AmountBudgeted / 1000000)# Million<BR>
      In Theaters #DateFormat(GetFilm.DateInTheaters, "mmmm d")#<BR>
    </TH></TR>
  </TABLE>
  <BR CLEAR="all">
</CFOUTPUT>
```

As you can see, the top half of the template is pretty simple. The idea is to use an application variable called `MovieList` to hold a list of available movies. If 20 movies are in the database, the list holds 20 movie IDs at first. The first time the home page is visited, the first movie is featured and then removed from the list, leaving 19 movies in the list. The next time, the second movie is featured (leaving 18), and so on until all the movies have been featured. Then the process starts over again.

Looking at the code line by line, you can see how this actually happens:

1. First, the `<CFPARAM>` tag is used to set the `APPLICATION.MovieList` variable to an empty string if it doesn't exist already. Because the variable will essentially live forever once set, this line has an effect only the first time this template runs (until the server is restarted).
2. Next, the `<CFIF>` tag is used to test whether the `MovieList` variable is currently empty. It is empty if this is the first time the template has run or if all the available movies have been featured in rotation already. If the list is empty, it is filled with the list of current movie IDs. Getting the current list is a simple two-step process of querying the database and then using the `ValueList` function to create the list from the query results.
3. Now, the `ListGetAt()` function is used to get the first movie's ID from the list. The value is placed in the `ThisMovieID` variable. This is the movie to feature on the page.
4. Finally, the `ListDeleteAt()` function is used to chop off the first movie ID from the `APPLICATION.MovieList` variable. The variable now holds one fewer movie. Eventually, its length will dwindle to zero, in which case step 2 will occur again, repeating the cycle.

Tip

Because you are interested in the first element in the list, you could use `ListFirst()` in place of the `ListGetAt()` function shown in Listing 19.11, if that reads more clearly for you. You also could use `ListRest()` instead of the `ListDeleteAt()` function. See Appendix B for details.

Now that the movie to feature has been picked (it's in the `ThisMovieID` variable), actually displaying the movie's name and other information is straightforward. The `<CFQUERY>` in the second half of Listing 19.12 selects the necessary information from the database, and then a simple HTML table is used to display the movie in a nicely formatted box.

At this point, Listing 19.12 can be visited on its own, but it really was meant to show the featured movie on Orange Whip's home page. Simply include the template using the `<CFINCLUDE>` tag, as shown in Listing 19.13.

Figure 19.5 shows the results.

Listing 19.13 `Index2.cfm`—**Including the Featured Movie in the Company's Home Page**

```
<!---
  Filename:     Index.cfm
  Created by:   Nate Weiss (NMW)
  Date Created: 2/18/2001
  Please Note:  Header and Footer are automatically provided
--->

<CFOUTPUT>
  <P>Hello, and welcome to the home of
  #CompanyName# on the web!  We certainly
  hope you enjoy your visit.  We take pride in
  producing movies that are almost as good
  as the ones they are copied from.  We've
  been doing it for years.  On this site, you'll
  be able to find out about all our classic films
  from the golden age of Orange Whip Studios,
  as well as our latest and greatest new releases.
  Have fun!<BR>
</CFOUTPUT>

<!--- Show a "Featured Movie" --->
<CFINCLUDE TEMPLATE="FeaturedMovie.cfm">
```

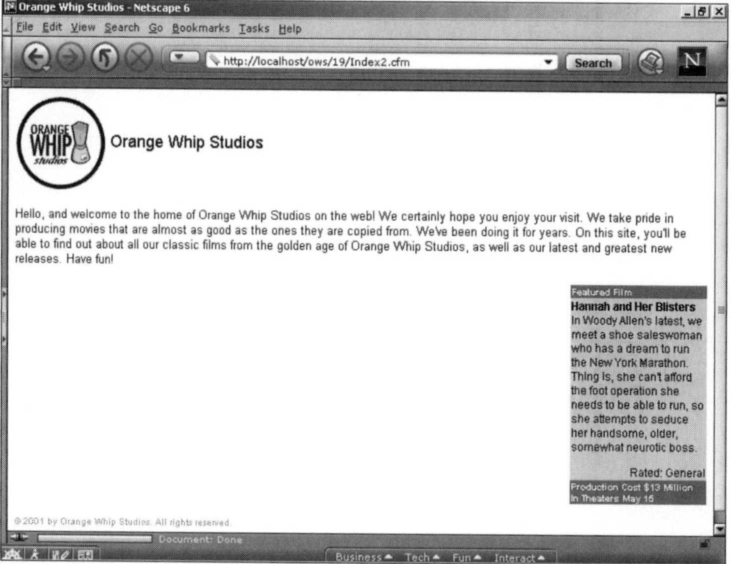

Figure 19.5 Application variables enable the featured movie to be rotated evenly amongst all page requests.

Preventing Memory Corruption with Locking

Earlier, in Listing 19.12, you probably noticed the `<CFLOCK>` tags surrounding the portion of the code having to do with the `APPLICATION.MovieList` variable. Those `<CFLOCK>` tags are extremely important.

ColdFusion is a *multithreaded* application. This means the server can process more than one page request at a time. Generally speaking, this is a wonderful feature. Because the server can in effect do more than one thing at a time, it can tend to two or three (or fifty) visitors to your application, all at the same moment.

Multithreading does bring one serious drawback to the table. Unless you take steps to prevent it, two page requests can set the same application variable at the same time. In addition, one visitor's request can read the value of a variable at the same moment that another page is changing its value. If this occurs, ColdFusion's memory can become corrupted, and the server could become unstable. You might start to see strange error messages, and the server will likely need to be restarted eventually.

Of course, solutions do exist. Any of the following will address the issue:

- You can use the `<CFLOCK>` tag to mark the areas of your code that set, change, access, or display application variables. The `<CFLOCK>` tag ensures that those potentially problematic parts of your code don't execute at the same time as other potentially problematic parts. In other words, you keep your code tread-safe yourself. That's what this section is all about.
- In the Locking page of the ColdFusion Administrator, you can enable the Automatic Read Locking setting for the Application Scope. Then, you will need to use `<CFLOCK>` only around code that sets or changes the values of application variables. You can access or display the values of the variables without locking them. This is more convenient than the first option if you use application variables frequently in your code but only change their values in a few places. There is a small performance hit for enabling this option.
- In the Server Settings page of the ColdFusion Administrator, you can set the Limit Simultaneous Requests To value to `1`. This guarantees that your whole application will be thread-safe, which means you can use application variables freely without having to worry about locking them. If your server is not hit very hard, or if all your pages are processed quickly (no long-running queries or other time-intensive processing in any of them), this can be a great solution for you. Otherwise, performance might suffer if you do this. See Chapter 30 for details.

Tip

Make it a habit to use `<CFLOCK>` tags whenever you use application variables, even if you are just outputting their values.

<CFLOCK> TAG SYNTAX

You already have seen the `<CFLOCK>` tag in action in Listing 19.12, and you might have already figured out what some of the attributes do. Generally, you just place opening and closing `<CFLOCK>` tags around any part of your code that deals with application variables (or session variables, which are discussed in the next chapter). Table 19.5 takes a closer look at the tag's syntax.

Table 19.5 <CFLOCK> Tag Syntax

Attribute	Description
SCOPE	The type of persistent variables you are using between the <CFLOCK> tags. Allowable values are Application, Session, and Server. You would use a <CFLOCK> with SCOPE="Application" around any code that uses application variables. You would set this value to Session around code that uses session variables, which are discussed in the next chapter. The use of server variables is not discussed in this book and is generally discouraged.
TYPE	Optional. The type, or strength, of the lock. Allowable values are Exclusive and ReadOnly. The next code example discusses the difference between the two. If you don't provide a TYPE, the default of Exclusive is assumed.
TIMEOUT	Required. The length of time, in seconds, that ColdFusion will wait to obtain the lock. If another visitor's request has a similar <CFLOCK> on it, ColdFusion will wait for this many seconds for the locked part of the other request to finish before proceeding. Generally, 10 is a sensible value to use here.
THROWONTIMEOUT	Optional. The default is Yes, which means an error message will be displayed if ColdFusion cannot obtain the lock within the TIMEOUT period you specified. (You can catch this error using <CFCATCH> to deal with the situation differently. See Chapter 33, "Error Handling," for details.)
NAME	Optional. You can provide a NAME attribute instead of SCOPE. NAME is for using <CFLOCK> in a different way from what is being discussed here. It is mainly for locking access to files, directories, or external programs. This use of <CFLOCK> is discussed in the companion book, *Advanced ColdFusion 5.0 Development*.

When ColdFusion encounters an opening <CFLOCK> tag in your code, it requests a lock from the server. It keeps the lock until it encounters the closing </CFLOCK> tag in your code, at which point it releases the lock. While your template has the lock, all other templates that want that same type of lock must wait in line. ColdFusion pauses the other templates (right at their opening <CFLOCK> tags) until your template releases the lock.

Tip

If it helps, think of locks as being similar to hall passes back in grade school. If you wanted to go to the bathroom, you needed to get a pass from the teacher. Nobody else would be able to go to the bathroom until you came back and returned the pass. This was to protect the students (and the bathroom) from becoming, um, corrupted, right?

Application Variable Timeouts

By default, application variables are kept on the server almost indefinitely. They die only if two whole days pass without any visits to any of the application's pages. After two days of inactivity, ColdFusion considers the APPLICATION scope to have expired, and all associated application variables are flushed from its memory.

If one of your applications uses a large number of application variables but is used only very rarely, you could consider decreasing the amount of time that the APPLICATION scope takes to expire. This would enable ColdFusion to reuse the memory taken up by the application variables. In actual practice, there might not be that many situations in which this flexibility is useful, but you should still know what your options are if you want to think about ways to tweak the way your applications behave.

Two ways are available to adjust the application timeout period from its two-day default value. You can use the ColdFusion Administrator or the APPLICATIONTIMEOUT attribute of the <CFAPPLICATION> tag.

Adjusting Timeouts Using APPLICATIONTIMEOUT

As shown in Table 19.4, the <CFAPPLICATION> tag takes an optional APPLICATIONTIMEOUT attribute. You can use this to explicitly specify how long an unused APPLICATION scope will remain in memory before it expires.

The APPLICATIONTIMEOUT attribute expects a ColdFusion *time span* value, which is a special type of numeric information used to describe a period of time in terms of days, hours, minutes, and seconds. All this means is that you must specify the application timeout using the CreateTimeSpan() function, which takes four numeric arguments to represent the desired number of days, hours, minutes, and seconds, respectively. For more information about the CreateTimeSpan() function, see Appendix B.

For instance, to specify that an application should time out after two hours of inactivity, you would use code such as the following:

```
<CFAPPLICATION
  NAME="OrangeWhipSite"
  APPLICATIONTIMEOUT="#CreateTimeSpan(0,2,0,0)#">
```


Note

If you do not specify an APPLICATIONTIMEOUT attribute, the Default Timeout value in the Variables page of the ColdFusion Administrator is used. See the next section, "Adjusting Timeouts Using the ColdFusion Administrator," for details.

Note

If you specify an APPLICATIONTIMEOUT that exceeds the Maximum Timeout value in the Variables page of the ColdFusion Administrator, the Maximum Timeout in the Administrator is used instead. See the next section, "Adjusting Timeouts Using the ColdFusion Administrator," for details.

Adjusting Timeouts Using the ColdFusion Administrator

To adjust the amount of time that each application's APPLICATION scope should live before it expires, follow these steps:

1. Navigate to the Variables page of the ColdFusion Administrator.
2. Under Default Timeout, fill in the days, hours, minutes, and seconds fields for application variables, as shown in Figure 19.6.
3. If you want, you also can adjust the Maximum Timeout for application variables here. If any developers attempt to use a longer timeout with the `APPLICATIONTIMEOUT` attribute of the `<CFAPPLICATION>` tag, this value will be used instead (no error message is displayed).
4. Click Apply.

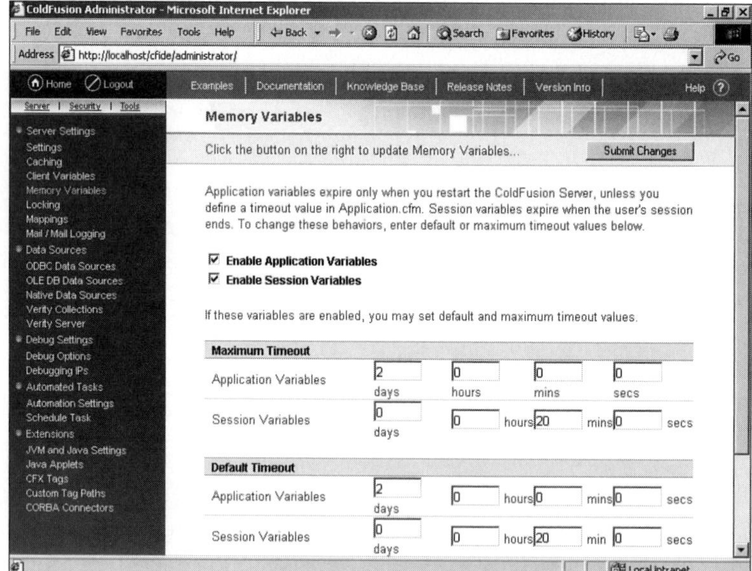

Figure 19.6
You can adjust when an application expires using the Variables page of the ColdFusion Administrator.

CHAPTER 20

Working with Sessions

In this chapter

In the last chapter, "Introducing the Web Application Framework," you learned about *application variables*, which live in your ColdFusion server's memory between page requests. You also learned that application variables are shared between all pages in your application. There are plenty of uses for application variables, but because they are not maintained separately for each user, they don't go far in helping you create a personalized site experience.

This chapter continues the discussion of the Web application framework, focusing on the features that let you track variables on a per-user basis. This opens up all kinds of opportunities for keeping track of what each user needs, wants, has seen, or is interacting with. And in true ColdFusion style, it's all very easy to learn and use.

ADDRESSING THE WEB'S STATELESSNESS

The basic building blocks of the Web—that is, TCP/IP, HTTP, and HTML—don't directly address any notion of a session on the Web. Users don't log in to the Web. Nor do they ever log out. So, without some additional work, each page visit stands alone, in its own context. Content is requested by the browser, the server responds, and that's the end of it. No connection is maintained, and the server is not notified when the user leaves the site altogether.

Out of the box, HTTP and HTML don't even provide a way to know who the user is or where he is. As a user moves from page to page in your site—perhaps interacting with things along the way—there's no way to track his progress or choices along the way. As far as each page request is concerned, there's only the current moment, with no future and no past. The Web is thus said to be *stateless* because it doesn't provide any built-in infrastructure to track the *state* (or status or condition) of what a user is doing.

What does the Web's statelessness mean to you, as a Web developer? It means that without some type of server-side mechanism to simulate the notion of a session, you would have no way to remember that a user has put something into a shopping cart, say, or to remember the fact that the user has logged in to your site. So, essentially, the problem is that the Web itself provides no short-term memory for remembering the contents of shopping carts and other types of choices users make during a visit. You need something to provide that short-term memory for you. That's exactly what you learn about in this chapter.

THE PROBLEM OF MAINTAINING STATE

The fact that HTTP and HTML are stateless is certainly no accident. A main reason the Web is so wildly popular is the fact that it is so simple. The Web probably wouldn't have gotten to be so big so fast if a whole infrastructure had needed to be in place for logging in and logging out of each web server, or if it assumed that one needed to maintain a constant connection to a server to keep one's current session open.

The simplicity of the sessionless approach also enables the tremendous scalability that Web applications—and the Web as a whole—benefit from. It's what makes Web applications so thin and lightweight and what enables Web servers to serve so many people simultaneously. So, the Web's statelessness is by design, and most people should be glad that it is.

Except for us Web developers. Our lives would probably be a lot easier if some kind of universal user ID existed, issued by, um, the United Nations or something. That couldn't be faked. And that could identify who the user was, no matter what computer he was sitting at. Until that happens, we need another way to track a user's movements as he moves through our own little pieces of the Web.

SOLUTIONS PROVIDED BY COLDFUSION

Expanding on the Web application framework—which already sets part of the server's brain aside to deal with each application—ColdFusion provides three types of variables that help you maintain the state of a user's visit from page to page and between visits.

Similar to application variables (which you learned about in the last chapter), all three of these are *persistent* variables because they stay alive between page requests. However, they are different from application variables because they are maintained separately for each browser that visits your site. It's almost as if ColdFusion had a tiny little part of its memory set aside for each visitor.

COOKIES

Cookies are a simple mechanism for asking a browser to remember something, such as a user's favorite color or perhaps some type of ID number. The information is stored in the client machine's memory (or on one of its drives). You can store only a small amount of information using cookies, and users generally have a way to turn off cookies in their browsers' settings. Unfortunately, cookies have gotten a lot of bad press in the past few years, so many users do choose to turn them off at the browser level.

CLIENT VARIABLES

Client variables are similar to cookies, except that the information is stored on the server, rather than on the client machine. The values are physically stored in the server's registry or in a database. Client variables are designed to hold semipermanent data, such as preferences that should live for weeks or months between a user's visits.

SESSION VARIABLES

Similar to client variables, *session variables* are stored on the server. However, instead of being stored physically, they are simply maintained in the server's RAM. Session variables are designed to hold temporary data, such as items in a shopping cart or steps in some type of wizard-style data entry mechanism that takes the user several pages to complete.

CHOOSING WHICH TYPE OF VARIABLES TO USE

With three types of per-visitor variables from which to choose, developers sometimes have a hard time figuring out which is the best type to use for a particular task. We certainly recommend that you look through this whole chapter before you start using any of them in your own application. However, in the future, you might want to refresh your memory about which type to use. Table 20.1 lists the pros and cons of cookies, client variables, and session variables. In addition, Figure 20.1 is a simple decision tree that should help guide you through the process of choosing which type of variable to use.

TABLE 20.1 PROS AND CONS OF COOKIES VERSUS CLIENT VARIABLES VERSUS SESSION VARIABLES

Variable	Pros	ConsType
COOKIE	Not ColdFusion specific, so are familiar to most developers. Can persist for same visit only, or until a specific date/time.	Very limited storage capacity. User can turn them off. Simple values only (no arrays, structures, and so on). Have a bad reputation.
CLIENT	Much larger storage capacity. Values never leave server. Persist between server restarts. Cookies not needed to retain values during single visit. Can persist for months. Stored in server's registry or in any database.	Cookies required to remember values between visits. Simple values only (no arrays, structures, and so on), but see <CFWDDX> note in this chapter.
SESSION	High performance—stored in ColdFusion's RAM only. Complex values okay (arrays, structures, and so on). Can be used without cookies.	Values do not persist between server restarts. RAM-resident, so must be locked with <CFLOCK>.

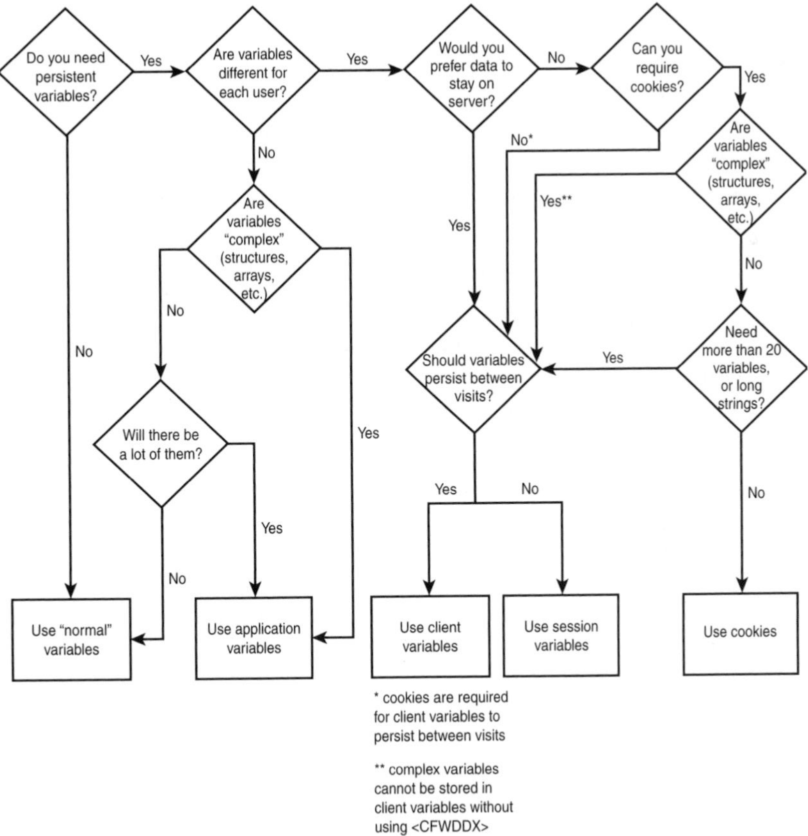

Figure 20.1
Choosing whether to use application variables, cookies, client variables, or session variables.

USING COOKIES TO REMEMBER PREFERENCES

Cookies are simple variables that can be stored on a client machine. Basically, the server asks the browser to remember a variable with such-and-such a name and such-and-such a value. The browser returns the variable to the server as it requests successive pages from that same server. In other words, after the server sets the value on the browser, the browser continues to remind the server about it as the user moves from page to page. The net effect is that each site essentially has a small portion of the browser's memory in which to store little bits of information.

Note

Cookies first appeared in early versions of Netscape Navigator and have since been adopted by nearly all browser software. As of this writing, the original specification document for cookies is still available at `http://www.netscape.com/newsref/std/cookie_spec.html`. It is somewhat of an interesting read, if only because it underscores how important Netscape's early innovations have become to today's Web. No substantive changes have been made to the cookie specification since.

Introducing the COOKIE Scope

Cookies are not something specific to ColdFusion. Any server-side scripting programming environment can set them (they can even be set by client-side languages such as JavaScript). Depending on the language, the actual code necessary to set or retrieve a cookie varies quite a bit. The best implementations keep coders from having to understand the details of the actual communication between the browser and server. It's best if the coder can just concentrate on the task at hand.

In ColdFusion, the notion of cookies is exposed to you via the simple, elegant `COOKIE` scope. Similar to the `APPLICATION` scope you learned about in the previous chapter, the `COOKIE` scope is automatically maintained by ColdFusion. Setting a variable within the `COOKIE` scope instructs the browser to remember the cookie. Referring to a variable within the `COOKIE` scope reads the value of the cookie on the browser's machine.

For instance, the following line asks the user's browser to remember a cookie variable called `MyMessage`. The value of the cookie is `"Hello, World!"`:

```
<CFSET COOKIE.MyMessage = "Hello, World!">
```

From that point on, you could output the value of `#COOKIE.MyMessage#` in your CFML code, between `<CFOUTPUT>` tags. The `"Hello, World"` message would be output in place of the variable.

Simple Exercise

Here is a simple exercise that will help illustrate what's going on when you use cookies. First, temporarily change your browser's preferences to notify you whenever a cookie is being set.

To be notified when a cookie is set on your browser, follow these guidelines:

- If you are using a Netscape 4 browser, select Preferences from the Edit menu; then check the Warn Me Before Accepting a Cookie box on the Advanced page of the Preferences dialog box.
- If you are using Internet Explorer 5, select Internet Options from the Tools menu, and then select the Security tab. Make sure the appropriate zone is selected; then select Custom Level and check the Prompt options for both Allow Cookies That Are Stored on Your Computer and Allow Per-Session Cookies.
- If you are using some other browser or version, the steps you take might be slightly different, but you should have some way to turn on some type of notification when cookies are set.

Now, use your browser to visit the `CookieSet.cfm` template shown in Listing 20.1. You should see a prompt similar to the one shown in Figure 20.2. The prompt might look different depending on browser and version, but it generally will show you the name and value of the cookie being set. Note that you can even refuse to allow the cookie to be set. Go ahead and let the browser keep the cookie by clicking OK.

If you now visit the `CookieShow.cfm` template shown in Listing 20.2, you will see the message `you started your visit at`, followed by the exact time you visited Listing 20.1. Click your browser's Reload button a few times, so you can see that the value does not change. The value persists between page requests. If you go back to Listing 20.1, the cookie will be reset to a new value.

Close your browser, reopen it, and visit the `CookieShow.cfm` template again. You will see an error message from ColdFusion, telling you that the `COOKIE.TimeVisitStart` variable does not exist. By default, cookies expire when the browser is closed. Therefore, the variable is no longer passed to the server with each page request and is unknown to ColdFusion.

LISTING 20.1 `CookieSet.cfm`—**SETTING A COOKIE**

```
<HTML>
<HEAD><TITLE>Cookie Demonstration</TITLE></HEAD>
<BODY>

<!--- Set a cookie to remember the time right now --->
<CFSET COOKIE.TimeVisitStart = TimeFormat(Now(), "h:mm:ss tt")>

The cookie has been set.

</BODY>
</HTML>
```

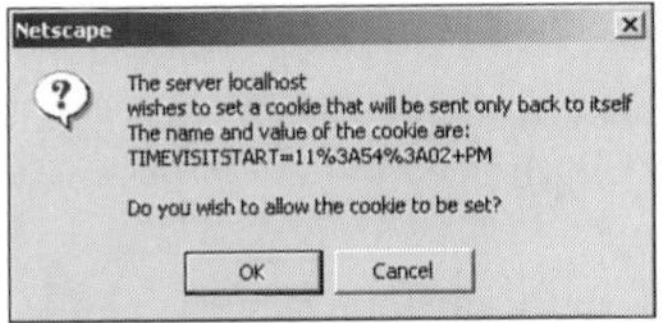

Figure 20.2 `CookieShow.cfm`—Users can configure their browsers to notify them when cookies are being set.

LISTING 20.2 `CookieShow.cfm`—**DISPLAYING A COOKIE'S VALUE**

```
<HTML>
<HEAD><TITLE>Cookie Demonstration</TITLE></HEAD>
<BODY>

<CFOUTPUT>
  You started your visit at:
  #COOKIE.TimeVisitStart#<BR>
</CFOUTPUT>

</BODY>
</HTML>
```


USING COOKIES

You easily can build on the last example to make it a more useful real-world example. For instance, you wouldn't want the Time Started value to keep being reset every time the user visited the first page. So, it would probably make sense to first test for the cookie's existence and only set the cookie if it doesn't already exist. Also, it would probably be sensible to remember the full date/time value of the user's first visit, rather than just the time.

So, instead of

```
<CFSET COOKIE.TimeVisitStart = TimeFormat(Now(), "h:mm:ss tt")>
```

you could use

```
<CFIF IsDefined("COOKIE.VisitStart") EQ "No">
  <CFSET COOKIE.VisitStart = Now()>
</CFIF>
```

In fact, the `IsDefined` test and the `<CFSET>` tag can be replaced with a single `<CFPARAM>` tag:

```
<CFPARAM NAME="COOKIE.VisitStart" TYPE="date" DEFAULT="#Now()#">
```

This `<CFPARAM>` tag can be placed in your `Application.cfm` file so it is encountered before each page request is processed. You can now be assured that ColdFusion will set the cookie the first time the user hits your application, no matter what page she starts on, and that you will never get a `parameter doesn't exist` error message because the cookie is guaranteed to always be defined. As discussed previously, the cookie will be reset if the user closes and reopens her browser.

Note

If you need a quick reminder on the difference between `<CFSET>` and `<CFPARAM>`, see Chapter 9, "Using ColdFusion," and Chapter 10, "CFML Basics."

You could then output the time elapsed in your application by outputting the difference between the cookie's value and the current time. You could put this code wherever you wanted in your application, perhaps as part of some type of header or footer message. For instance, the following code would display the number of minutes that the user has been using the application:

```
<CFOUTPUT>
  Minutes Elapsed: #DateDiff("n", COOKIE.VisitStart, Now())#
</CFOUTPUT>
```

The next two listings bring these lines together. Listing 20.3 is an `Application.cfm` file that includes the `<CFPARAM>` tag shown previously. Listing 20.4 is a file called `ShowTimeElapsed.cfm`, which can be used to display the elapsed time in any of the current application's pages by using `<CFINCLUDE>`. You also can visit Listing 20.4 on its own—Figure 20.3 shows what the results would look like.

Be sure to save Listing 20.3 as `Application.cfm`, not `Application1.cfm`.

Listing 20.3 `Application1.cfm`—**Defining a Cookie Variable in** `Application.cfm`

```
<!---
  Filename:     Application.cfm
  Created by:   Nate Weiss (NMW)
  Date Created: 2/18/2001
  Please Note:  Executes for each page request
--->
```

```
<!--- If no "VisitStart" cookie exists, create it --->
<!--- Its value will be the current date and time --->
<CFPARAM NAME="COOKIE.VisitStart" TYPE="date" DEFAULT="#Now()#">
```

LISTING 20.4 `ShowTimeElapsed.cfm`—**PERFORMING CALCULATIONS BASED ON COOKIES**

```
<!---
  Filename:      ShowTimeElapsed.cfm
  Created by:    Nate Weiss (NMW)
  Date Created: 2/18/2001
  Please Note:   Can be <CFINCLUDED> in any page in your application
--->

<!--- Find number of seconds passed since visit started  --->
<!--- (difference between cookie value and current time) --->
<CFSET SecsSinceStart = DateDiff("s", COOKIE.VisitStart, Now())>

<!--- Break it down into numbers of minutes and seconds --->
<CFSET MinutesElapsed = Int(SecsSinceStart / 60)>
<CFSET SecondsElapsed = SecsSinceStart MOD 60>

<!--- Display the minutes/seconds elapsed --->
<CFOUTPUT>
  Minutes Elapsed:
  #MinutesElapsed#:#NumberFormat(SecondsElapsed, "00")#
</CFOUTPUT>
```

Because `COOKIE.VisitStart` always is a ColdFusion date/time value, getting the raw number of seconds since the visit started is easy—you use the `DateDiff` function. If the difference in seconds between the cookie value and the present moment (the value returned by the `Now` function) is 206, you know that 206 seconds have passed since the cookie was set.

Because most people would be more comfortable seeing time expressed in minutes and seconds, Listing 20.4 does some simple math on the raw number of seconds elapsed. First, it calculates the number of whole minutes that have elapsed, by dividing `SecsSinceStart` by 60 and rounding down to the nearest integer. Next, it calculates the number of seconds to display after the number of minutes by finding the modulus (which is the remainder left when `SecsSinceStart` is divided by 60).

Tip

See Appendix B, "ColdFusion Function Reference," for explanations of the `DateDiff`, `Int`, and `Now` functions.

GAINING MORE CONTROL WITH <CFCOOKIE>

You already have learned how to set cookies using the `<CFSET>` tag and the special `COOKIE` scope (Listings 19.1–19.3). Using that technique, setting cookies is as simple as setting normal variables. However, sometimes you will want to have more control over how cookies get set.

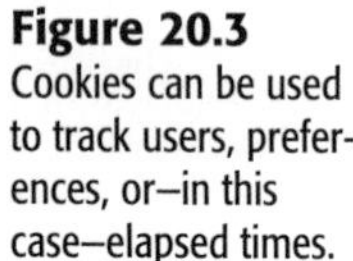

Figure 20.3
Cookies can be used to track users, preferences, or—in this case—elapsed times.

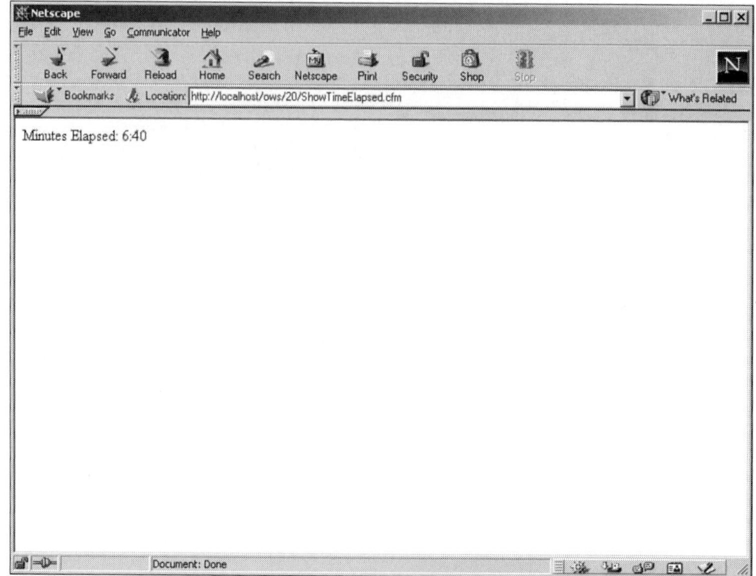

INTRODUCING THE <CFCOOKIE> TAG

To provide you with additional control, ColdFusion provides the `<CFCOOKIE>` tag, which is an alternative syntax for setting cookie variables. Once set, you can access or display the cookies as you have learned so far, by referring to them in the special `COOKIE` scope.

Table 20.2 introduces the attributes available when using `<CFCOOKIE>`.

TABLE 20.2 <CFCOOKIE> TAG SYNTAX

Attribute	Purpose
`NAME`	Required. The name of the cookie variable. If you use `NAME="VisitStart"`, the cookie will thereafter become known as `COOKIE.VisitStart`.
`VALUE`	Required. The value of the cookie. To set the cookie's value to the current date and time, use `VALUE="#Now()#"`.
`EXPIRES`	Optional. When the cookie should expire. You can provide any of the following: ■ A specific expiration date (such as `3/18/2002`) or a date/time value. ■ The number of days you want the cookie to exist before expiring, such as `10` or `90`. ■ The word `NEVER`, which is a shortcut for setting the expiration date way into the future, such that it will effectively never expire. ■ The word `NOW`, which is a shortcut for setting the expiration date in the recent past, such that it is already considered expired. This is how you delete a cookie.

Attribute	Purpose
	If you do not specify an EXPIRES attribute, the cookie will do what it does normally, which is to expire when the user closes her browser. See the section "Controlling Cookie Expiration," later in this chapter.
DOMAIN	Optional. You can use this attribute to share the cookie with other servers within your own Internet domain. By default, the cookie is visible only to the server that set it. See the section "Controlling How Cookies Are Shared," later in this chapter.
PATH	Optional. You can use this attribute to specify which pages on your server should be able to use this cookie. By default, the cookie can be accessed by all pages on the server once set. See the section "Controlling How Cookies Are Shared," later in this chapter.
SECURE	Optional. Whether the cookie should be sent back to the server only if a secure connection is being used. The default is No. See the section "Controlling How Cookies Are Shared," later in this chapter.

Controlling Cookie Expiration

The most common reason for using <CFCOOKIE> instead of a simple <CFSET> is to control how long the cookie will live before it expires. For instance, looking back at the Application.cfm file shown in Listing 20.3, what if you didn't want the Elapsed Time counter to start over each time the user closed her browser?

Say you wanted the elapsed time to keep counting for up to a week. You would replace the <CFPARAM> line in Listing 20.3 with the following:

```
<!--- If no "VisitStart" cookie exists, create it --->
<CFIF IsDefined("COOKIE.VisitStart") EQ "No">
  <CFCOOKIE
    NAME="VisitStart"
    VALUE="#Now()#"
    EXPIRES="7">
</CFIF>
```

Controlling How Cookies Are Shared

Netscape's original cookie specification defines three additional concepts that have not been discussed yet. All three of them have to do with giving you more granular control over which pages your cookies are visible to:

- **A domain can be specified as each cookie is set**—The basic idea is that a cookie should only ever be visible to the server that set the cookie originally. This is to protect the user's privacy. However, if a company is running several Web servers, it is considered fair that a cookie set on one should be visible to the others. Specifying a domain for a cookie makes it visible to all servers within that domain.
- **In addition, a path can be specified as each cookie is set**—This enables you to control whether the cookie should be visible to the entire Web server (or Web servers) or just a part of it. For instance, if a cookie will be used only by the pages within the ows

folder in the Web server's root, it might make sense for the browser to not return the cookie to any other pages, even on the same server. The path could be set to /ows, which would ensure that the cookie is visible only to the pages within the ows folder. This way, two applications on the same server can each set cookies with the same name without them overwriting one another, as long as the applications use different paths when setting the cookies.

- **A cookie can be marked as secure only**—This means that it should be returned to the server only when a secure connection is being used (that is, if the page's URL starts with https:// instead of http://). If the browser is asked to visit an ordinary (not secure) page on the server, the cookie is not sent and thus is not visible to the server.

As a ColdFusion developer, you have access to these three concepts by way of the DOMAIN, PATH, and SECURE attributes of the <CFCOOKIE> tag. As Table 20.2 showed, all three attributes are optional.

Let's say you have three servers, named one.orangewhip.com, two.orangewhip.com, and three.orangewhip.com. To set a cookie that would be shared among the three servers, you take the portion of the domain names they share, including the first dot. The following code would set a cookie visible to all three servers (and any other servers whose hostnames end in .orangewhip.com):

```
<!--- Share cookie over our whole domain --->
<CFCOOKIE
  NAME="VisitStart"
  VALUE="#Now()#"
  DOMAIN=".orangewhip.com">
```

The next example uses the PATH attribute to share the cookie among all pages that have a /ows at the beginning of the path portion of their URLs (the part after the hostname). For instance, the following would set a cookie that would be visible to a page with a path of /ows/Home.cfm and /ows/store/checkout.cfm, but not /owintra/login.cfm:

```
<!--- Only share cookie within ows folder --->
<CFCOOKIE
  NAME="VisitStart"
  VALUE="#Now()#"
  PATH="/ows">
```

And finally, this example uses the SECURE attribute to tell the browser to make the cookie visible only to pages that are at secure (https://) URLs. In addition, the cookie will expire in 30 days and be shared among the servers in the orangewhip.com domain, but only within the /ows portion of each server:

```
<!--- This cookie is shared but confidential --->
<CFCOOKIE
  NAME="VisitStart"
  VALUE="#Now()#"
  EXPIRES="30"
  DOMAIN=".orangewhip.com"
  PATH="/ows"
  SECURE="Yes">
```

Tip

You can specify that you want to share cookies only within a particular subdomain. For instance, `DOMAIN=".intranet.orangewhip.com"` shares the cookie within all servers that have `.intranet.orangewhip.com` at the end of their hostnames. However, there must always be a leading dot at the beginning of the `DOMAIN` attribute.

Note

You cannot share cookies based on IP addresses. To share cookies between servers, the servers must have Internet domain names.

Note

The `DOMAIN` attribute is commonly misunderstood. Sometimes, people assume that you can use it to specify other domains with which to share the cookies. `DOMAIN`, however, can be used only to specify whether to share the cookies with other servers in the same domain.

Sharing Cookies with Other Applications

Because cookies are not a ColdFusion-specific feature, cookies set with, say, Active Server Pages are visible in ColdFusion's `COOKIE` scope, and cookies set with `<CFCOOKIE>` are visible to other applications, such as PHP, Perl, or Java Server Pages. The browser doesn't know which language is powering which pages. All it cares about is whether the domain, path, secure, and expires requirements have been met. If so, it makes the cookie available to the language.

Tip

If you find that cookies set in another language don't seem to be visible to ColdFusion, the problem might be the path part of the cookie. For instance, whereas ColdFusion sets the path to `/` by default so that the cookie is visible to all pages on the server, JavaScript sets the path to match the path of the current page by default. Try setting the path part of the cookie to `/` to make it behave more like one set with ColdFusion. The syntax to do this varies from language to language.

Cookie Limitations

There are some pretty serious restrictions on what you can store in cookies:

- **Only simple strings can be stored**—Because dates and numbers can be expressed as strings, you can store them as cookies. But no ColdFusion-specific data types, such as arrays and structures, can be specified as the value for a cookie.
- **The cookie specification establishes that a maximum of 20 cookies can be set within any one domain**—This prevents cookies from eventually taking up a lot of room on the user's hard drive. Browsers might or might not choose to enforce this limit.

- **Each cookie can be only four kilobytes in length or less**—Also, the name of the cookie is considered toward the four-kilobyte limit.
- **According to the original specification, the browser is not obligated to store more than 300 cookies (total, considering all cookies set by all the world's servers together)**—The browser can delete the least recently used cookie when the 300-cookie limit has been reached. That said, many modern browsers choose not to enforce this limit.

USING CLIENT VARIABLES

Client variables are similar to cookies, except that they are stored on the server, rather than on the client (browser) machine. In many situations, you can use the two almost interchangeably. So, because you're already familiar with cookies, learning how to use client variables will be a snap. Instead of using the `COOKIE` prefix before a variable name, you simply use the `CLIENT` prefix instead.

Okay, there's a little bit more to it than that. But not much.

Note

Before you can use the `CLIENT` prefix, you must enable ColdFusion's Client Management feature. See the section "Enabling Client Variables," later in this chapter.

Note

This might be a bit confusing at this point, but it's worth noting that client variables can also be configured so that they are stored on the browser machine, if you take special steps in the ColdFusion Administrator. They then become essentially equivalent to cookies. See the section "Adjusting How Client Variables Are Stored," later in this chapter.

HOW DO CLIENT VARIABLES WORK?

Client variables work like this:

1. The first time a particular user visits your site, ColdFusion generates a unique ID number to identify the user's browser.
2. ColdFusion sets this ID number as a cookie called `CFID` on the user's browser. From that point on, the browser identifies itself to ColdFusion by presenting this ID.
3. When you set a client variable in your code, ColdFusion stores the value for you on the server side, without sending anything to the browser machine. It stores the `CFID` number along with the variable, to keep them associated internally.
4. Later, when you access or output the variable, ColdFusion simply retrieves the value based on the variable name and the `CFID` number.

For the most part, this process is hidden to you as a developer. You simply use the CLIENT scope prefix in your code—ColdFusion takes care of the rest.

Enabling Client Variables

Before you can use client variables in your code, you must enable them using the <CFAPPLICATION> tag. In the last chapter, you learned how to use this tag to enable application variables. <CFAPPLICATION> takes several additional attributes that are relevant to client variables, as shown in Table 20.3.

Table 20.3 Additional <CFAPPLICATION> Attributes Relevant to Client Variables

Attribute	Description
NAME	An optional name for your application. For more information about the NAME attribute, see the section "Enabling Application Variables" in Chapter 19, "Introducing the Web Application Framework."
CLIENTMANAGEMENT	Yes or No. Setting this value to Yes enables client variables for the rest of the page request. Assuming that the <CFAPPLICATION> tag is placed in your Application.cfm file, client variables will be enabled for all pages in your application.
CLIENTSTORAGE	Optional. You can set this attribute to the word Registry, which means the actual client variables will be stored in your server's Registry. You can also provide a data source name here, which will cause the variables to be stored in a database. If you omit this attribute, it defaults to Registry unless you have changed the default in the ColdFusion Administrator. For details, see "Adjusting How Client Variables Are Stored," later in this chapter.
SETCLIENTCOOKIES	Optional. The default is Yes, which allows ColdFusion to automatically set the CFID cookie on each browser, which it uses to track client variables properly for each browser. You can set this value to No if you don't want the cookies to be set. But if you do so, you will need to do a bit of extra work. For details, see "Adjusting How Client Variables Are Stored," later in this chapter.
SETDOMAINCOOKIES	Optional. The default is No, which tells ColdFusion to set the CFID cookie so that it is visible to the current server only. If you have several ColdFusion servers operating in a cluster together, you can set this to Yes to share client variables between all your ColdFusion servers. For details, see "Adjusting How Client Variables Are Stored," later in this chapter.

For now, just concentrate on the CLIENTMANAGEMENT attribute (the others are discussed later). Listing 20.5 shows how easy it is to enable client variables for your application. After you save this code in the Application.cfm file for your application, you can start using client variables. (Be sure to save Listing 20.5 as Application.cfm, not Application2.cfm.)

Note

If you attempt to use client variables without enabling them first, an error message will be displayed.

LISTING 20.5 `Application2.cfm`—**ENABLING CLIENT VARIABLES IN** `Application.cfm`

```
<!---
  Filename:     Application.cfm
  Created by:   Nate Weiss (NMW)
  Date Created: 2/18/2001
  Please Note:  Executes for each page request
--->

<!--- Any variables set here can be used by all our pages --->
<CFSET DataSource  = "ows">
<CFSET CompanyName = "Orange Whip Studios">

<!--- Name our application, and enable Client and Application variables --->
<CFAPPLICATION
  NAME="OrangeWhipSite"
  CLIENTMANAGEMENT="Yes"
  CLIENTSTORAGE="Registry">
```

USING CLIENT VARIABLES

Client variables are ideal for storing things such as user preferences, recent form entries, and other types of values that you don't want to force your users to provide over and over again.

REMEMBERING VALUES FOR NEXT TIME

For instance, consider a typical search form, in which the user types what he is looking for and then submits the form to see the search results. It might be nice if the form could remember what the user's last search was.

The code in Listing 20.6 does just that. The basic idea is that the form's search criteria field will already be filled in for the user, using the value of a variable called `SearchPreFill`. The value of this variable is set at the top of the page and will set to the last search the user ran, if available. If no last search information exists (if this is the first time the user has used this page), it will be blank.

LISTING 20.6 `SearchForm1.cfm`—**USING CLIENT VARIABLES TO REMEMBER THE USER'S LAST SEARCH**

```
<!---
  Filename:     SearchForm.cfm
  Created by:   Nate Weiss (NMW)
  Date Created: 2/18/2001
  Please Note:  Maintains "last" search via Client variables
--->

<!--- Determine value for "Search Pre-Fill" feature --->
<!--- When user submits form, save search criteria in client variable --->
<CFIF IsDefined("Form.SearchCriteria")>
  <CFSET CLIENT.LastSearch = Form.SearchCriteria>
  <CFSET SearchPreFill     = Form.SearchCriteria>
```

```
<!--- If not submitting yet, get prior search word (if possible) --->
<CFELSEIF IsDefined("CLIENT.LastSearch")>
  <CFSET SearchPreFill = CLIENT.LastSearch>

<!--- If no prior search criteria exists, just show empty string --->
<CFELSE>
  <CFSET SearchPreFill = "">
</CFIF>


<HTML>
<HEAD><TITLE>Search Orange Whip</TITLE></HEAD>
<BODY>
  <H2>Search Orange Whip</H2>

  <!--- Simple search form, which submits back to this page --->
  <CFFORM ACTION="#CGI.SCRIPT_NAME#" METHOD="Post">

    <!--- "Search Criteria" field --->
    Search For:
    <CFINPUT NAME="SearchCriteria" VALUE="#SearchPreFill#"
      REQUIRED="Yes"
      MESSAGE="You must type something to search for!">

    <!--- "Submit" button --->
    <INPUT TYPE="Submit" VALUE="Search"><BR>

  </CFFORM>

</BODY>
</HTML>
```

The first part of this template (the `<CFIF>` part) does most of the work because it's in charge of setting the `SearchPreFill` variable that creates the illusion of memory for the user. There are three different conditions to deal with. If the user currently is submitting the form to run his search, his search criteria should be saved in a client variable called `CLIENT.LastSearch`. If the user is not currently submitting the form but has run a search in the past, his last search criteria should be retrieved from the `LastSearch` client variable. If no last search is available, the `IsDefined("CLIENT.LastSearch")` test will fail, and `SearchPreFill` should just be set to an empty string.

The rest of the code is an ordinary form. The only thing to note is the fact that the value of the `SearchPreFill` variable is passed to the `<CFINPUT>` tag that presents the user with the search field.

If you visit this page in your browser, the search field will be blank the first time you visit it. To test the use of client variables, type a word or two to search for and submit the form. Of course, no actual search takes place because no database code exists in the example yet, but the form should correctly remember the search criteria you typed. You can close the browser and reopen it, and the value should still be there.

Note

In fact, assuming that you haven't changed anything in the ColdFusion Administrator to the contrary, the value of `CLIENT.LastSearch` will continue to be remembered until the user leaves the site for 90 days or more.

Using Several Client Variables Together

There is no set limit on the number of client variables you can use. Listing 20.7 builds on the search form from Listing 20.6, this time allowing the user to specify how many records should be returned by the search. A second client variable called `LastMaxRows` is used to remember the value, using the same simple `<CFIF>` logic that was used in the previous listing.

Listing 20.7 `SearchForm2.cfm`—Using Several Client Variables to Remember Search Preferences

```
<!---
  Filename:     SearchForm.cfm
  Created by:   Nate Weiss (NMW)
  Date Created: 2/18/2001
  Please Note:  Maintains "last" search via Client variables
--->

<!--- When user submits form, save search criteria in Client variable --->
<CFIF IsDefined("Form.SearchCriteria")>
  <CFSET CLIENT.LastSearch  = Form.SearchCriteria>
  <CFSET CLIENT.LastMaxRows = Form.SearchMaxRows>
<!--- If not submitting yet, get prior search word (if possible) --->
<CFELSEIF IsDefined("CLIENT.LastSearch") AND IsDefined("CLIENT.LastMaxRows")>
  <CFSET SearchCriteria = CLIENT.LastSearch>
  <CFSET SearchMaxRows  = CLIENT.LastMaxRows>
<!--- If no prior search criteria exists, just show empty string --->
<CFELSE>
  <CFSET SearchCriteria = "">
  <CFSET SearchMaxRows  = 10>
</CFIF>



<HTML>
<HEAD><TITLE>Search Orange Whip</TITLE></HEAD>
<BODY>
  <H2>Search Orange Whip</H2>

  <!--- Simple search form, which submits back to this page --->
  <CFFORM ACTION="#CGI.SCRIPT_NAME#" METHOD="Post">

    <!--- "Search Criteria" field --->
    Search For:
    <CFINPUT NAME="SearchCriteria" VALUE="#SearchCriteria#"
      REQUIRED="Yes"
      MESSAGE="You must type something to search for!">
```

```
    <!--- "Submit" button --->
    <INPUT TYPE="Submit" VALUE="Search"><BR>

    <!--- "Max Matches" field --->
    <I>show up to
    <CFINPUT NAME="SearchMaxRows" VALUE="#SearchMaxRows#" SIZE="2"
      REQUIRED="Yes" VALIDATE="integer" RANGE="1,500"
      MESSAGE="Provide a number from 1-500 for search maximum.">
    matches</I><BR>
  </CFFORM>

  <!--- If we have something to search for, do it now --->
  <CFIF SearchCriteria NEQ "">
    <!--- Get matching film entries from database --->
    <CFQUERY NAME="GetMatches" DATASOURCE="#DataSource#">
      SELECT FilmID, MovieTitle, Summary
      FROM Films
      WHERE MovieTitle LIKE '%#SearchCriteria#%'
         OR Summary    LIKE '%#SearchCriteria#%'
      ORDER BY MovieTitle
    </CFQUERY>

    <!--- Show number of matches --->
    <CFOUTPUT>
      <HR><I>#GetMatches.RecordCount# records found for
      "#SearchCriteria#"</I><BR>
    </CFOUTPUT>

    <!--- Show matches, up to maximum number of rows --->
    <CFOUTPUT QUERY="GetMatches" MAXROWS="#SearchMaxRows#">
      <P><B>#MovieTitle#</B><BR>
      #Summary#<BR>
    </CFOUTPUT>
  </CFIF>
</BODY>
</HTML>
```

Next, the actual search is performed, using simple LIKE code in a <CFQUERY> tag. When the results are output, the user's maximum records preference is provided to the <CFOUTPUT> tag's MAXROWS attribute. Any rows beyond the preferred maximum are not shown. (If you want to brush up on the <CFQUERY> and <CFOUTPUT> code used here, see Chapter 11, "Creating Data-Driven Pages.")

Not only does this version of the template remember the user's last search criteria, but it actually reruns the user's last query before the user even submits the form. This means the user's last search results will be redisplayed each time the page is visited, making the search results appear to be persistent. The results are shown in Figure 20.4.

You easily could change this behavior by changing the second <CFIF> test to IsDefined("Form.SearchCriteria"). The last search would still appear prefilled in the search form, but the search itself wouldn't be rerun until the user clicked the Search button. Use client variables in whatever way makes sense for your application.

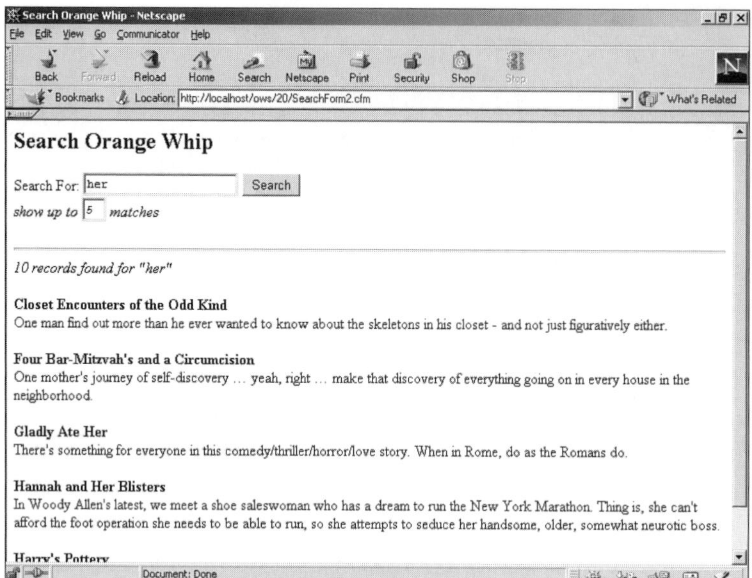

Figure 20.4 Client variables make maintaining the state of a user's recent activity easy.

Tip

To improve performance, you could add a `CACHEDWITHIN` or `CACHEDAFTER` attribute to the `<CFQUERY>` tag, which enables ColdFusion to deliver any repeat searches directly from the server's RAM memory. For details, see Chapter 24, "Improving Performance."

Note

Say 15 matching records exist in the database, but the user has typed `10` in the Show Up To field. This template will show only the first 10 matches, but the records found message will reflect the full 15. Therefore, the user will know that more records exist to be seen. You could consider adding a `MAXROWS` attribute to the `<CFQUERY>` tag as well, which would cause only 10 records to be retrieved from the database in the first place. The records found message would then show 10 instead of 15.

Deleting Client Variables

Once set, client variables become stored semipermanently. Client variables are deleted only if a user's browser doesn't return to your site for longer than 90 days. In the next section, you learn how to adjust the number of days that the variables are kept, but sometimes you still will need to delete a client variable programmatically.

Note

It is important to understand that each client variable does not have its own expiration date. Client variables do not expire individually; the whole client record is what expires. So, it's not that a client variable is deleted 90 days after it was set. Rather, the client

> variable (and all other client variables assigned to the user's machine) is deleted after the user lets 90 days pass before revisiting any pages in the application. For more information about tweaking the expiration system, see "Adjusting How Long Client Variables Are Kept," in the next section.

ColdFusion provides a `DeleteClientVariable()` function that enables you to delete individual client variables by name. The function takes one argument, which is the name of the client variable you want to delete (the name is not case sensitive). Another handy housekeeping function is the `GetClientVariablesList()` function, which returns a comma-separated list of the client variable names that have been set for the current browser.

Listing 20.8 shows how these two functions can be used together to delete all client variables that have been set for a user's browser. You could use code such as this on some "Start Over" type of page, or if the user has chosen to log out of some type of special area.

Listing 20.8 `DeleteClientVars.cfm`—**Deleting All Client Variables That Have Been Set for the Current Browser**

```
<!---
  Filename:     DeleteClientVars.cfm
  Created by:   Nate Weiss (NMW)
  Date Created: 2/18/2001
--->
<HTML>
<HEAD><TITLE>Clearing Your Preferences</TITLE></HEAD>
<BODY>

<H2>Clearing Your Preferences</H2>

<!--- For each client variable set for this browser... --->
<CFLOOP LIST="#GetClientVariablesList()#" INDEX="ThisVarName">
  <!--- Go ahead and delete the client variable! --->
  <CFSET DeleteClientVariable(ThisVarName)>

  <CFOUTPUT>#ThisVarName# deleted.<BR></CFOUTPUT>
</CFLOOP>

<P>Your preferences have been cleared.

</BODY>
</HTML>
```


Adjusting How Client Variables Are Stored

Out of the box, ColdFusion stores client variables in the server's Registry and will delete all client variables for any visitors who haven't returned to your site for 90 days or more. You can, of course, tweak these behaviors to suit your needs. This section discusses the client-variable storage options available to you.

ADJUSTING HOW LONG CLIENT VARIABLES ARE KEPT

Normally, client variables are maintained on what amounts to a permanent basis for users who visit your site at least once every 90 days. If a user actually lets 90 days pass without visiting your site (shame on her!), all her client variables automatically are purged by ColdFusion. This helps keep the client variable store from becoming ridiculously large.

To adjust this value from the default of 90 days, do the following:

1. Open the ColdFusion Administrator.
2. Navigate to the Client Variables page.
3. Click the Registry link, under Storage Name.
4. Change the Purge Data for Clients that Remain Unvisited For value to the number of days you want; then click Submit Changes.

> **Note**
>
> It's important to understand that there isn't a separate timeout for each individual client variable. The only time client variables are automatically purged is if the client browser hasn't visited the server at all for 90 days (or whatever the purge data setting has been set to, using the previous procedure).

STORING CLIENT VARIABLES IN A DATABASE

You can have ColdFusion store your client variables in a database, instead of in the Registry. This will appeal to people who just don't like the idea of the Registry being used in this way, or who find that they must make the Registry very large to accommodate the number of client variables they need to maintain.

This feature is particularly important if you are running several servers in a cluster. You can have all the servers in the cluster keep your application's client variables in the same database, thereby giving you a way to persist variables between pages without worrying about what will happen if the user ends up at a different server in the cluster on her next visit. See the section "Sharing Client Variables Between Servers," later in this chapter.

> **Note**
>
> When using the term *Registry*, we are referring to the Windows Registry, assuming that ColdFusion Server is installed on a Windows machine. On other platforms, ColdFusion ships with a Registry replacement, which is used for Registry-resident client variables and which you can read and write to using the `<CFREGISTRY>` tag. So, Linux and Unix users don't have to change or remove code that would otherwise be accessing the Windows Registry, and can still use the default client storage mechanism of the Registry. See Appendix A, "ColdFusion Tag Reference," for details about `<CFREGISTRY>`.

To store your client variables in a database, follow these steps:

1. Create a new database to hold the client variables. You don't need to create any tables in the database; ColdFusion will do that on its own. If you want, you can use an existing database, but we recommend that you use a fresh, dedicated database for storing client variables.
2. Use the ColdFusion Administrator to create a new data source for your new database. See Chapter 6, "Introduction to SQL," for details.
3. Navigate to the Client Variables page of the ColdFusion Administrator.
4. Select your new data source from the drop-down list, and then click the Add Client Variable Store button. The Add/Edit Client Store page appears, as shown in Figure 20.5.
5. Adjust the Purge Data for Clients that Remain Unvisited For value as desired. This value is described previously in the section "Adjusting How Long Client Variables Are Kept." As the page in the Administrator notes, if you are using the client variable database in a cluster situation, this option should be enabled for only one server in the cluster. If you are not using a cluster, you should keep this option enabled.
6. Check the Disable Global Client Variable Updates check box unless you are particularly interested in the accuracy of the `HITCOUNT` and `LASTVISIT` properties (see Appendix C, "Special ColdFusion Variables and Result Codes"). In general, we recommend that you check this option because it can greatly lessen the strain on the database. The only side effect is that client variables will be purged based on the last time a client variable was set or changed, rather than the last time the user visited your site.
7. Leave the Create Client Database Tables option checked, unless you have already gone through this process for this same database in the past.
8. Click the Submit Changes button.

You now can supply the new data source name to the `CLIENTSTORAGE` attribute of the `<CFAPPLICATION>` tag (refer to Table 20.3). All your application's client variables now will be stored in the database instead of in the Registry.

Tip

If you go back to the Client Variables page of the ColdFusion Administrator and change the Client Variable Storage Mechanism value to the data source you just created, it will be used for all applications that don't specify a `CLIENTSTORAGE` attribute at all (refer to Table 20.3).

Sharing Client Variables Between Servers

As explained at the beginning of this section, ColdFusion tracks each browser by automatically setting its own client-tracking cookie called `CFID`. Normally, it sets this cookie such that it is sent back only to the same server that set it. If you have three ColdFusion servers, each visitor will be given a different `CFID` number for each server, which in turn means that client variables will be maintained separately for each server.

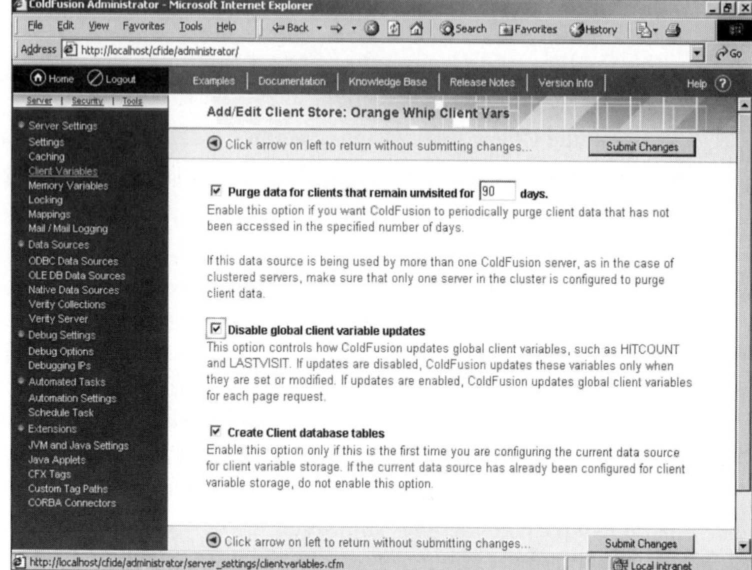

Figure 20.5
You can have ColdFusion store your application's client variables in a database, rather than the Registry.

In many situations, especially if you are operating several servers in a cluster, you will want client variables to be shared between the servers, so that a `CLIENT.LastSearch` variable set by one server will be visible to the others.

To share client variables between servers, do the following:

1. Have ColdFusion store your application's client variables in a database, rather than in the Registry. Be sure to do this on all servers in question. For instructions, see the section "Storing Client Variables in a Database," earlier in this chapter.
2. Add a `SETDOMAINCOOKIES="Yes"` attribute to your application's `<CFAPPLICATION>` tag. This causes ColdFusion to set the `CFID` cookie in such a way that it will be shared among all servers in the same Internet domain. This is the rough equivalent of using the `DOMAIN` attribute in a `<CFCOOKIE>` tag.

Now, you can use client variables in your code as you would normally. No matter which server a user visits, ColdFusion will store all client variables in the common database you set up.

Note

For cookies to be shared between servers, they all must be members of the same top-level Internet domain (for instance, `orangewhip.com`).

Note

For more information about using client variables in a clustered environment, see the "Managing Session State in Clusters" chapter in the companion volume, *Advanced ColdFusion 5 Application Development* (ISBN: 0-7897-2585-1).

Backing Up Your Server's Client Variables

If you are keeping client variables in a database, you can back up all client variables by simply backing up the database itself. If it's an Access or some other type of file-based database, that entails making a backup copy of the database (.mdb) file itself. Otherwise, you must use whatever backup facility is provided with your database software.

If you are keeping client variables in the Registry, you can make a copy of the appropriate portion of the Registry. To do so on a Windows machine, follow these steps:

1. Open the Registry Editor by selecting Run from the Windows Start menu and then typing **`regedit`** in the Run dialog box.
2. Navigate to the following Registry branch (folder):
   `HKEY_LOCAL_MACHINE\SOFTWARE\Allaire\ColdFusion\CurrentVersion\Clients`
3. Select Export Registry File from the Registry menu; then save the file wherever you want. Be sure to leave the Selected Branch option selected.

To back up the Registry on a Unix/Linux machine, back up this file:

```
<installdir>/coldfusion/.windu.hostname/windu_reg.dat
```

Storing Client Variables As a Cookie

You can, somewhat paradoxically, tell ColdFusion to store your application's client variables in cookies on the user's machine, rather than storing them on the server side. You do this by setting the `CLIENTSTORAGE` attribute of the `<CFAPPLICATION>` tag to `Cookie`. This basically enables you to continue using the `CLIENT` prefix even if you want the variables to essentially be stored as cookies.

This might be useful, for instance, in situations in which you are selling your code as a third-party application and want your licensees to have the option of not using a server-side data store. Unfortunately, the various size limitations for cookies will apply (see the section "Cookie Limitations," earlier in this chapter). Because this is a somewhat esoteric subject, it isn't discussed in full here. Please consult the ColdFusion documentation for more information about this feature.

Note

The cookie storage mechanism for client variables can be useful in a clustered environment or a site that gets an extremely large number of discrete visitors. For more information about using client variables in a clustered environment, see the "Managing Session State in Clusters" chapter in the companion volume, *Advanced ColdFusion 5 Application Development* (ISBN: 0-7897-2585-1).

USING CLIENT VARIABLES WITHOUT REQUIRING COOKIES

Earlier in this chapter, you learned that ColdFusion maintains the association between a browser and its client variables by storing a CFID cookie on the browser machine. That would seem to imply that client variables will not work if a user's browser doesn't support cookies or if the user has disabled cookies in his browser's preferences. Don't worry. All is not completely lost.

Actually, ColdFusion normally sets two cookies with which to track client variables: the CFID value already mentioned and a randomly generated CFTOKEN value. Think of CFID and CFTOKEN as being similar to a username and password, respectively. Only if the CFID and CFTOKEN are both valid will ColdFusion be capable of successfully looking up the appropriate client variables. If the browser does not provide the values for whatever reason (perhaps because the user has configured the browser not to use cookies or because a firewall between the user and your server is stripping them out of each page request), ColdFusion will not be capable of looking up the browser's client variables. In fact, ColdFusion will be forced to consider the browser to be a new, first-time visitor, and it will generate a new CFID and CFTOKEN for the browser—which, of course, means that all client variables that might have been set during previous pages or visits will be lost.

You can still use client variables without requiring cookies, but you must do a bit more work. Basically, you need to make the CFID and CFTOKEN available to ColdFusion yourself, by passing the values manually in the URL to every single page in your application.

So, if you want your client variables to work for browsers that don't (or won't) support cookies, you must include the CFID and CFTOKEN as URL parameters. So, a link such as

```
<A HREF="MyPage.cfm">Click Here</A>
```

would need to be changed to the following, which would need to be between <CFOUTPUT> tags:

```
<A HREF="MyPage.cfm?CFID=#CLIENT.CFID#&CFTOKEN=#CLIENT.CFTOKEN#">Click Here</A>
```

ColdFusion provides a shortcut property you can use to make this task a bit less tedious. Instead of providing the CFID and CFTOKEN in the URL, you can just pass the special CLIENT.URLTOKEN property, which always holds the current CFID and CFTOKEN name/value pairs together in one string, including the & and = signs. This means the previous line of code can be shortened to the following, which would still need to be between <CFOUTPUT> tags:

```
<A HREF="MyPage.cfm?#CLIENT.URLTOKEN#">Click Here</A>
```

You must be sure to pass CLIENT.URLTOKEN in every URL, not just in links. For instance, if you are using a <FORM> (or <CFFORM>) tag, you must pass the token value in the form's ACTION, such as this:

```
<FORM ACTION="MyPage.cfm?#CLIENT.URLTOKEN#" METHOD="Post">
```

If you are using frames, you must pass the token value in the SRC attribute, such as this:

```
<FRAME SRC="MyPage.cfm?#CLIENT.URLTOKEN#">
```

And so on. Basically, you must look through your code and ensure that whenever you see one of your .cfm templates in a URL of any type, that you correctly pass the token value.

Tip

Remember that the token value must always be between `<CFOUTPUT>` tags, unless the URL is being passed as an attribute to a CFML tag (any tag that starts with `CF`, such as `<CFFORM>`).

Note

If users bookmark one of your pages, the `CFID` and `CFTOKEN` information should be part of the bookmarked URL, so their client variables should not be lost even if their browsers don't support cookies. However, if they just type your site's URL into their browsers directly, it's unlikely that they will include the `CFID` and `CFTOKEN`. Therefore, ColdFusion will be forced to consider them as new visitors, which in turn means that the prior visit's client variables will be lost. ColdFusion will eventually purge the lost session (see the section "Adjusting How Long Client Variables Are Kept," earlier in this chapter).

Note

In addition to the `CFID`, `CFTOKEN`, and `URLTOKEN` properties mentioned here, several other automatically maintained properties of the `CLIENT` scope are available, including `HITCOUNT`, `LASTVISIT`, and `TIMECREATED`. See Appendix C, "Special ColdFusion Variables and Result Codes."

STORING COMPLEX DATA TYPES IN CLIENT VARIABLES

As mentioned earlier, you can store only simple values (strings, numbers, dates, and Boolean values) in the `CLIENT` scope. If you attempt to store one of ColdFusion's complex data types (structures, arrays, queries, and object references) as a client variable, you get an error message.

You can, however, use the `<CFWDDX>` tag to transform a complex value into an XML-based string. In this serialized form, the value can be stored as a client variable. Later, when you want to use the variable, you can use `<CFWDDX>` again to transform it from the string format back into its complex form.

There isn't space to fully discuss the `<CFWDDX>` tag here, but the following code snippets will be enough to get you started. For more information about `<CFWDDX>`, see Appendix A. For more information about the WDDX technology in general and how it can be used to do much more than just this, consult our companion volume, *Advanced ColdFusion 5.0 Development* or visit `http://www.openwddx.org`.

Assuming, for instance, that `MyStruct` is a structure, the following would store it in the `CLIENT` scope:

```
<CFWDDX
  ACTION="CFML2WDDX"
  INPUT="#MyStruct#"
  OUTPUT="Client.MyStructAsWddx">
```

Later, to retrieve the value, the following could be used:

```
<CFWDDX
  ACTION="WDDX2CFML"
  INPUT="#Client.MyStructAsWddx#"
  OUTPUT="MyStruct">
```

You then could refer to the values in `MyStruct` normally in your code. If you made any changes to the structure, you would need to re-store it using the first snippet.

Tip

You can use the `IsSimpleValue()` function to test whether a value can be stored in the `CLIENT` scope without using this WDDX technique. See Appendix B for details.

You can use the `IsWDDX()` function to test whether a client variable actually contains a valid WDDX value. See Appendix B for details.

USING SESSION VARIABLES

This chapter already has covered a lot of ground. You have learned about cookies and client variables and how they can be used to make an application aware of its individual users and what they are doing. ColdFusion's Web application framework provides one more type of persistent variable to discuss: session variables.

WHAT ARE SESSION VARIABLES?

Session variables are similar to client variables in that they are stored on the server, rather than in the browser's memory. Unlike client variables, however, session variables persist only for a user's current session. You'll learn exactly how a session is defined later, but for now, think of it as being a synonym for a user's visit to your site. Session variables, then, should be thought of as per-visit variables, whereas client variables are per-user variables intended to persist between each user's visits.

Session variables are not stored physically in the server's Registry or in a database. Instead, they are stored in the server's RAM. This makes sense, considering the fact that they are intended to persist for only a short time. Also, because ColdFusion doesn't need to physically store and retrieve the variables, you can expect session variables to work a bit more quickly than client variables.

ENABLING SESSION VARIABLES

Similar to client variables, you must enable session variables using the `<CFAPPLICATION>` tag before you can use them in your code. Table 20.4 lists the additional attributes relevant to session variables. In general, all you need to do is specify a `NAME` and then set `SESSIONMANAGEMENT="Yes"`.

TABLE 20.4 <CFAPPLICATION> ATTRIBUTES RELEVANT TO SESSION VARIABLES

Attribute	Purpose
NAME	A name for your application; this attribute is required for session variables. For more information about the NAME attribute, see the section "Enabling Application Variables" in Chapter 19.
SESSIONMANAGEMENT	Yes or No. Set to Yes to enable the use of session variables. If you attempt to use session variables in your code without setting this attribute to Yes, an error message will be displayed when the code is executed.
SESSIONTIMEOUT	Optional. How long you want your session variables to live in the server's memory. If you don't provide this value, it defaults to whatever is set up in the Variables page of the ColdFusion Administrator. See the section "When Does a Session End?" later in this chapter.

For example, to enable session management, you might use something such as this in your Application.cfm file:

```
<!--- Name our application, and enable Session and Application variables --->
<CFAPPLICATION
  NAME="OrangeWhipSite"
  SESSIONMANAGMENT="Yes">
```

Note

Session variables can be disabled globally (for the entire server) in the ColdFusion Administrator. If the Enable Session Variables option on the Memory Variables page of the Administrator has been unchecked, you will not be able to use session variables, regardless of what you set the SESSIONMANAGEMENT attribute to.

USING SESSION VARIABLES

After you have enabled session variables using <CFAPPLICATION>, you can start using them in your code. ColdFusion provides a special SESSION variable scope, which works similarly to the CLIENT and COOKIE scopes you are already familiar with. You can set and use session variables by simply using the SESSION prefix in front of a variable's name.

For instance, instead of the CLIENT.LastSearch used in the SearchForm.cfm examples earlier in this chapter, you could call the variable SESSION.LastSearch. The examples would still work in essentially the same way. The only difference in behavior would be that the memory of each user's last search would last only a short time (until the end of the session), rather than a long time (90 days, by default).

And, for something such as search results, the shorter memory provided by the use of session variables might feel more intuitive for the user. That is, a user might expect the search page to remember her last search phrase during the same visit, but she might be surprised or irritated if it remembered search criteria from weeks or months in the past.

Often, you will find it best to use session and client variables together in the same application. Things that should be remembered for only the current visit belong in session variables, whereas things that should be remembered between visits should be kept in client variables.

USING SESSION VARIABLES FOR MULTIPLE-PAGE DATA ENTRY

Session variables can be especially handy for data-entry processes that require the user to fill out a number of pages. For instance, say you have been asked to put together a data-entry interface for Orange Whip Studio's intranet. The idea is for your users to be able to add new films to the studio's database. A number of pieces of information will need to be supplied by the user (title, director, actors, and so on).

The most obvious solution would be to just create one long, complex form. However, you have been specifically asked not to do this because it might confuse the interns the company hires to do its data-entry tasks.

Carefully considering your options, you decide to present the data-entry screens in a familiar wizard format, with Next and Back buttons the users can use to navigate between the steps. However, it is important that nothing actually gets entered into the database until the user has finished all the steps. This means the wizard must remember everything the user has entered, even though she will be able to freely move back and forth between the steps.

Hmm. You could pass everything from step to step as hidden form fields, but that sounds like a lot of work, and it feels wrong to put the burden of remembering all that data on the client. You'd like to keep the information on the server side. You could create some type of temporary tables in your database and keep updating the temporary values until the user is finished, but that also sounds like a lot of work. Plus, how would you keep the values separate for each user? And what if the user abandons the wizard partway through?

The answer, of course, is to use session variables. They are perfect for this type of situation. You need to track the information for only a short time, so session variables are appropriate in that respect. Also, session variables aren't kept permanently on the server, so you won't be storing any excess data if the user doesn't finish the wizard.

MAINTAINING STRUCTURES IN THE SESSION SCOPE

For instance, the following code snippet creates a new structure called `SESSION.MovWiz`. The structure contains several pieces of information, most of which start out blank (set to an empty string). Because the variable is in the `SESSION` scope, a separate version of the structure is kept for each user, but only for the user's current visit. The `StepNum` value is in charge of tracking which step of the data-entry wizard each user is currently on:

```
<CFIF NOT IsDefined("SESSION.MovWiz")>
  <!--- If structure undefined, create/initialize it --->
  <CFSET SESSION.MovWiz = StructNew()>
  <!--- Represents current wizard step; start at one --->
  <CFSET SESSION.MovWiz.StepNum = 1>
  <!--- We will collect these from user; start blank --->
  <CFSET SESSION.MovWiz.MovieTitle  = "">
  <CFSET SESSION.MovWiz.PitchText   = "">
  <CFSET SESSION.MovWiz.DirectorID  = "">
```

```
  <CFSET SESSION.MovWiz.ActorIDs     = "">
  <CFSET SESSION.MovWiz.StarActorID = "">
</CFIF>
```

Updating the values in the SESSION.MovWiz structure is simple enough. Assume for the moment that the wizard contains Back and Next buttons named GoBack and GoNext, respectively. The following snippet would increment the StepNum part of the structure by one when the user clicks the Next button and decrement it by one if the user clicks Back:

```
<!--- If user clicked "Back" button, go back a step --->
<CFIF IsDefined("Form.GoBack")>
  <CFSET SESSION.MovWiz.StepNum = SESSION.MovWiz.StepNum - 1>
<!--- If user clicked "Next" button, go forward one --->
<CFELSEIF IsDefined("Form.GoNext")>
  <CFSET SESSION.MovWiz.StepNum = SESSION.MovWiz.StepNum + 1>
</CFIF>
```

The other values in the MovWiz structure can be accessed and updated in a similar way. For instance, to present the user with a text-entry field for the new movie's title, you could use something such as this:

```
<CFINPUT
  NAME="MovieTitle"
  VALUE="#SESSION.MovWiz.MovieTitle#">
```

The input field will be prefilled with the current value of the MovieTitle part of the MovWiz structure. If the previous snippet was in a form and submitted to the server, the value the user typed could be saved back into the MovWiz structure using the following line:

```
<CFSET SESSION.MovWiz.MovieTitle = Form.MovieTitle>
```

Putting It All Together

The code in Listing 20.9 combines all the previous snippets into a simple, intuitive wizard interface that users will find familiar and easy to use. The listing is a bit longer than usual, but each part is easy to understand.

The idea here is to create a self-submitting form page that changes depending on which step of the wizard the user is on. The first time the user comes to the page, he sees Step 1 of the wizard. He submits the form, which calls the template again, and sees Step 2, and so on.

This data-entry wizard will collect information from the user in five steps, as follows:

1. The film's title and one-line description, which eventually will be placed in the Films table
2. The film's director (the user can choose only one director), which is inserted in the FilmsDirectors table
3. The actors that will be in the movie (the user can choose any number of actors), which will be inserted in the FilmsActors table
4. Which of the film's actors will get top billing, which sets the IsStarringRole column of the FilmsActors table to true
5. A final confirmation screen, with a Finish button

Caution

The following examples use variables in the SESSION scope without locking the accesses with the <CFLOCK> tag. This is an acceptable practice if the Single Threaded Sessions option is checked in the Locking page of the ColdFusion Administrator. Otherwise, you must add <CFLOCK> tags around all accesses to the SESSION scope. See the section "Locking Revisited," later in this chapter.

LISTING 20.9 NewMovieWizard.cfm—USING SESSION VARIABLES TO BRING A USER THROUGH A MULTISTEP PROCESS

```
<!---
  Filename:     NewMovieWizard.cfm
  Created by:   Nate Weiss (NMW)
  Date Created: 3/2/2001
  Please Note:  Session variables must be enabled
--->

<!--- Total Number of Steps in the Wizard --->
<CFSET NumberOfSteps = 5>

<!--- The SESSION.MovWiz struct holds user's entries --->
<!--- as he moves through wizard. Make sure it exists! --->
<CFIF NOT IsDefined("SESSION.MovWiz")>
  <!--- If structure undefined, create/initialize it --->
  <CFSET SESSION.MovWiz = StructNew()>
  <!--- Represents current wizard step; start at one --->
  <CFSET SESSION.MovWiz.StepNum = 1>
  <!--- We will collect these from user; start blank --->
  <CFSET SESSION.MovWiz.MovieTitle  = "">
  <CFSET SESSION.MovWiz.PitchText   = "">
  <CFSET SESSION.MovWiz.DirectorID  = "">
  <CFSET SESSION.MovWiz.ActorIDs    = "">
  <CFSET SESSION.MovWiz.StarActorID = "">
</CFIF>


<!--- If user just submitted MovieTitle, remember it --->
<!--- Do same for the DirectorID, Actors, and so on. --->
<CFIF IsDefined("Form.MovieTitle")>
  <CFSET SESSION.MovWiz.MovieTitle = Form.MovieTitle>
  <CFSET SESSION.MovWiz.PitchText  = Form.PitchText>
<CFELSEIF IsDefined("Form.DirectorID")>
  <CFSET SESSION.MovWiz.DirectorID = Form.DirectorID>
<CFELSEIF IsDefined("Form.ActorID")>
  <CFSET SESSION.MovWiz.ActorIDs = Form.ActorID>
<CFELSEIF IsDefined("Form.StarActorID")>
  <CFSET SESSION.MovWiz.StarActorID = Form.StarActorID>
</CFIF>


<!--- If user clicked "Back" button, go back a step --->
<CFIF IsDefined("Form.GoBack")>
  <CFSET SESSION.MovWiz.StepNum = URL.StepNum - 1>
<!--- If user clicked "Next" button, go forward one --->
```

```
<CFELSEIF IsDefined("Form.GoNext")>
  <CFSET SESSION.MovWiz.StepNum = URL.StepNum + 1>
<!--- If user clicked "Finished" button, we're done --->
<CFELSEIF IsDefined("Form.GoDone")>
  <CFLOCATION URL="NewMovieCommit.cfm">
</CFIF>


<HTML>
<HEAD><TITLE>New Movie Wizard</TITLE></HEAD>
<BODY>

<!--- Show title and current step --->
<CFOUTPUT>
  <B>New Movie Wizard</B><BR>
  Step #SESSION.MovWiz.StepNum# of #NumberOfSteps#<BR>
</CFOUTPUT>


<!--- Data Entry Form, which submits back to itself --->
<CFFORM
  ACTION="NewMovieWizard.cfm?StepNum=#SESSION.MovWiz.StepNum#"
  METHOD="POST">

  <!--- Display the appropriate wizard step --->
  <CFSWITCH EXPRESSION="#SESSION.MovWiz.StepNum#">
    <!--- Step One: Movie Title --->
    <CFCASE VALUE="1">
      <!--- Show text entry field for title --->
      What is the title of the movie?<BR>
      <CFINPUT
        NAME="MovieTitle"
        SIZE="50"
        VALUE="#SESSION.MovWiz.MovieTitle#">

      <!--- Show text entry field for short description --->
      <P>What is the "pitch" or "one-liner" for the movie?<BR>
      <CFINPUT
        NAME="PitchText"
        SIZE="50"
        VALUE="#SESSION.MovWiz.PitchText#">
    </CFCASE>

    <!--- Step Two: Pick Director --->
    <CFCASE VALUE="2">
      <!--- Get list of directors from database --->
      <CFQUERY NAME="GetDirectors" DATASOURCE="#DataSource#">
        SELECT DirectorID, FirstName+' '+LastName As FullName
        FROM Directors
        ORDER BY LastName
      </CFQUERY>

      <!--- Show all Directors in SELECT list --->
      <!--- Pre-select if user has chosen one --->
      Who will be directing the movie?<BR>
      <CFSELECT
        SIZE="#GetDirectors.RecordCount#"
```

LISTING 20.9 CONTINUED

```
      QUERY="GetDirectors"
      NAME="DirectorID"
      DISPLAY="FullName"
      VALUE="DirectorID"
      SELECTED="#SESSION.MovWiz.DirectorID#"/>
  </CFCASE>


  <!--- Step Three: Pick Actors --->
  <CFCASE VALUE="3">
    <!--- Get list of actors from database --->
    <CFQUERY NAME="GetActors" DATASOURCE="#DataSource#">
      SELECT * FROM Actors
      ORDER BY NameLast
    </CFQUERY>

    What actors will be in the movie?<BR>
    <!--- For each actor, display check box --->
    <CFLOOP QUERY="GetActors">
      <!--- Should check box be pre-checked? --->
      <CFSET IsChecked = ListFind(SESSION.MovWiz.ActorIDs, ActorID)>
      <!--- Check box itself --->
      <CFINPUT
        TYPE="Checkbox"
        NAME="ActorID"
        VALUE="#ActorID#"
        CHECKED="#IsChecked#">
      <!--- Actor name --->
      <CFOUTPUT>#NameFirst# #NameLast#</CFOUTPUT><BR>
    </CFLOOP>
  </CFCASE>

  <!--- Step Four: Who is the star? --->
  <CFCASE VALUE="4">
    <CFIF SESSION.MovWiz.ActorIDs EQ "">
      Please go back to the last step and choose at least one
      actor or actress to be in the movie.
    <CFELSE>
      <!--- Get actors who are in the film --->
      <CFQUERY NAME="GetActors" DATASOURCE="#DataSource#">
        SELECT * FROM Actors
        WHERE ActorID IN (#SESSION.MovWiz.ActorIDs#)
        ORDER BY NameLast
      </CFQUERY>

      Which one of the actors will get top billing?<BR>
      <!--- For each actor, display radio button --->
      <CFLOOP QUERY="GetActors">
        <!--- Should radio be pre-checked? --->
        <CFSET IsChecked = SESSION.MovWiz.StarActorID EQ ActorID>
        <!--- Radio button itself --->
        <CFINPUT
          TYPE="Radio"
          NAME="StarActorID"
          VALUE="#ActorID#"
```

```
          CHECKED="#IsChecked#">
        <!--- Actor name --->
        <CFOUTPUT>#NameFirst# #NameLast#</CFOUTPUT><BR>
      </CFLOOP>
    </CFIF>
  </CFCASE>

  <!--- Step Five: Final Confirmation --->
  <CFCASE VALUE="5">
    You have successfully finished the New Movie Wizard.<BR>
    Click the Finish button to add the movie to the database.<BR>
    Click Back if you need to change anything.<BR>
  </CFCASE>
</CFSWITCH>


<P>
<!--- Show Back button, unless at first step --->
<CFIF SESSION.MovWiz.StepNum GT 1>
  <INPUT TYPE="Submit" NAME="GoBack" VALUE="&lt;&lt; Back">
</CFIF>
<!--- Show Next button, unless at last step --->
<!--- If at last step, show Finish button --->
<CFIF SESSION.MovWiz.StepNum LT NumberOfSteps>
  <INPUT TYPE="Submit" NAME="GoNext" VALUE="Next &gt;&gt;">
<CFELSE>
  <INPUT TYPE="Submit" NAME="GoDone" VALUE="Finish">
</CFIF>
</CFFORM>

</BODY>
</HTML>
```

Note

To help keep this code as clear as possible, Listing 20.9 does not prevent the user from leaving the various form fields blank. See Listing 20.11 for a version that validates the user's entries, using the techniques introduced in Chapter 13, "Form Data Validation."

First, a variable called `NumberOfSteps` is defined, set to `5`. This keeps the `5` from needing to be hardcoded throughout the rest of the template. Next, the `SESSION.MovWiz` structure is defined, using the syntax shown in the first code snippet, which appeared before this listing. The structure contains a default value for each piece of information that will be collected from the user.

Next, a `<CFIF>` / `<CFELSEIF>` block is used to determine whether the step the user just completed contains a form element named `MovieTitle`. If so, the corresponding value in the `SESSION.MovWiz` structure is updated with the form's value, thus remembering the user's entry for later. The other possible form fields are also tested for within this block of code in the same manner.

Next, the code checks to see whether a form field named GoBack was submitted to the form. If so, it means the user clicked the Back button in the wizard interface (see Figure 20.6). Therefore, the StepNum value in the MovWiz structure should be decremented by one, effectively moving the user back a step. An equivalent test is performed for fields named GoNext and GoFinish. If the user clicks GoFinish, he is redirected to another template called NewMovieCommit.cfm, which actually takes care of inserting the records in the database.

The rest of the code's job is to display the correct form to the user, depending on which step he is on. If he is on step one, the first CFCASE tag kicks in, causing form fields for the movie's title and short description to be displayed. Each of the form fields is prefilled with the current value of the corresponding value from SESSION.MovWiz. That means the fields will be blank when the user begins, but if he later clicks the Back button to get back to the first step, he will see the value that he previously entered. That is, a session variable is being used to maintain the state of the various steps of the wizard.

The other <CFCASE> sections are all similar to the first. Each presents form fields to the user (check boxes, radio buttons, and so on), always prefilled or preselected with the current values from SESSION.MovWiz. As the user clicks Next or Back to submit the values for a particular step, his entries are stored in the SESSION.MovWiz structure by the code near the top of the template.

The last bit of code simply decides whether to show Next, Back, and Finish buttons for each step of the wizard. As the user would expect, the Finish button is shown only on the last step, the Next button is shown for all steps except the last, and the Back button is shown on all steps except the first.

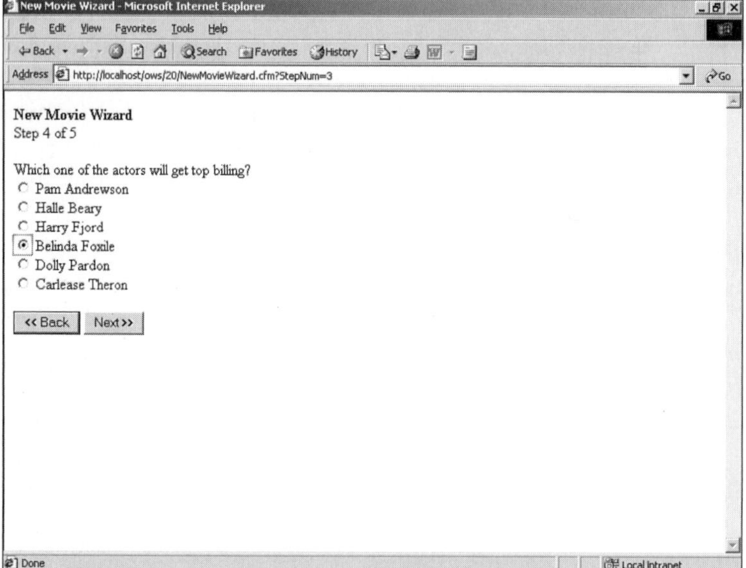

Figure 20.6
Session variables are perfect for creating wizard-style interfaces.

Deleting Session Variables

Unlike the CLIENT scope, the SESSION variable scope is actually just a ColdFusion structure. So, rather than using some type of specific function to delete a session variable (perhaps called DeleteSessionVariable()), you use the same StructDelete() function you use to remove a value from any other structure.

For instance, to delete the SESSION.MovWiz variable, you could use the following line:

```
<CFSET StructDelete(SESSION, "MovWiz")>
```

Note

> Do not use the StructClear() function on the SESSION scope itself, as in StructClear(SESSION). This will erase the session itself, rather than all session variables, which can lead to undesirable results. For more information, see Article 14143, "ColdFusion 4.5 and the StructClear(Session) Function" in the Macromedia/Allaire Knowledge Base.

Tip

> If you need to delete all variables from the SESSION scope at once, see the section "Expiring a Session Programmatically," later in this chapter.

Listing 20.10 is the NewMovieCommit.cfm template that is called when the user clicks the Finish button on the last step of the New Movie Wizard (refer to Listing 20.9). Most of this listing is made up of ordinary <CFQUERY> code, simply inserting the values from the SESSION.MovWiz structure into the correct tables in the database.

After all the records are inserted, the MovWiz variable is removed from the SESSION structure, using the syntax shown previously. At that point, the user can be directed back to the NewMovieWizard.cfm template, where he can enter another movie. The wizard code will see that the MovWiz structure no longer exists for the user and therefore will create a new structure, with blank initial values for the movie title and other information.

Listing 20.10 NewMovieCommit.cfm—Session Variables Can Be Deleted When No Longer Necessary

```
<!---
  Filename:     NewMovieCommit.cfm
  Created by:   Nate Weiss (NMW)
  Date Created: 2/18/2001
--->


<!--- Insert Film Record --->
<CFQUERY DATASOURCE="#DataSource#">
  INSERT INTO Films(MovieTitle, PitchText)
  VALUES ('#SESSION.MovWiz.MovieTitle#', '#SESSION.MovWiz.PitchText#')
</CFQUERY>
```

```
<!--- Get ID number of just-inserted film --->
<CFQUERY DATASOURCE="#DataSource#" NAME="GetNew">
  SELECT Max(FilmID) As NewID FROM Films
</CFQUERY>
<!--- Insert Director Record --->
<CFQUERY DATASOURCE="#DataSource#">
  INSERT INTO FilmsDirectors(FilmID, DirectorID, Salary)
  VALUES (#GetNew.NewID#, #SESSION.MovWiz.DirectorID#, 0)
</CFQUERY>
<!--- Insert Actor Records --->
<CFLOOP LIST="#SESSION.MovWiz.ActorIDs#" INDEX="ThisActor">
  <CFSET IsStar = IIF(ThisActor EQ SESSION.MovWiz.StarActorID, 1, 0)>
  <CFQUERY DATASOURCE="#DataSource#">
    INSERT INTO FilmsActors(FilmID, ActorID, Salary, IsStarringRole)
    VALUES (#GetNew.NewID#, #ThisActor#, 0, #IsStar#)
  </CFQUERY>
</CFLOOP>


<!--- Remove MovWiz variable from SESSION Structure --->
<!--- User will be started over on return to Wizard --->
<CFSET StructDelete(SESSION, "MovWiz")>


<!--- Display message to user --->
<HTML>
<HEAD><TITLE>Movie Added</TITLE></HEAD>
<BODY>
 <H2>Movie Added</H2>
 <P>The movie has been added to the database.

 <!--- Link to go through the Wizard again --->
 <P><A HREF="NewMovieWizard.cfm">Enter Another Movie</A>
</BODY>
</HTML>
```

One interesting thing about the wizard metaphor is that people expect wizards to adapt themselves based on the choices users make along the way. For instance, the last step of this wizard (in which the user indicates which of the movie's stars will get top billing) looks different depending on the previous step (in which the user selects which stars are in the movie at all). You also could decide to skip certain steps based on the film's budget, add more steps if the director and actors have worked together before, and so on. This would be relatively hard to do if you were collecting all the information on one long form.

As you can see in Listing 20.10, this version of the wizard doesn't collect information about salaries to be inserted into the `FilmsActors` and `FilmsDirectors` tables. It also doesn't perform any data validation. For instance, the user can leave the movie title blank without getting any kind of error message. If you want, take a look at the `NewMovieWizard2.cfm` and `NewMovieCommit2.cfm` templates (Listings 20.11 and 20.12). This slightly expanded version of the wizard adds some data validation for the form elements and adds another step in which the user enters financial information.

Caution

The following examples use variables in the SESSION scope without locking the accesses with the <CFLOCK> tag. This is an acceptable practice if the Single Threaded Sessions option is checked in the Locking page of the ColdFusion Administrator. Otherwise, you must add <CFLOCK> tags around all accesses to the SESSION scope. See the section "Locking Revisited," later in this chapter.

LISTING 20.11 NewMovieWizard2.cfm—**EXPANDED VERSION OF NEW MOVIE WIZARD, WITH BUDGETING STEP AND FORM VALIDATION**

```
<!---
  Filename:     NewMovieWizard2.cfm
  Created by:   Nate Weiss (NMW)
  Date Created: 3/2/2001
  Please Note:  Session variables must be enabled
--->

<!--- Total Number of Steps in the Wizard --->
<CFSET NumberOfSteps = 6>

<!--- The SESSION.MovWiz struct holds user's entries --->
<!--- as they move thru wizard. Make sure it exists! --->
<CFIF (NOT IsDefined("SESSION.MovWiz")) OR (NOT IsDefined("URL.StepNum"))>
  <!--- If structure undefined, create/initialize it --->
  <CFSET SESSION.MovWiz = StructNew()>
  <!--- Represents current wizard step; start at one --->
  <CFSET SESSION.MovWiz.StepNum = 1>
  <!--- We will collect these from user; start blank --->
  <CFSET SESSION.MovWiz.MovieTitle  = "">
  <CFSET SESSION.MovWiz.PitchText   = "">
  <CFSET SESSION.MovWiz.DirectorID  = "">
  <CFSET SESSION.MovWiz.DirectorSal = "">
  <CFSET SESSION.MovWiz.ActorIDs    = "">
  <CFSET SESSION.MovWiz.StarActorID = "">
  <CFSET SESSION.MovWiz.MiscExpense = "">
  <CFSET SESSION.MovWiz.ActorSals   = StructNew()>
</CFIF>


<!--- If user just submitted MovieTitle, remember it --->
<!--- Do same for the DirectorID, Actors, and so on. --->
<CFIF IsDefined("Form.MovieTitle")>
  <CFSET SESSION.MovWiz.MovieTitle = Form.MovieTitle>
  <CFSET SESSION.MovWiz.PitchText  = Form.PitchText>
<CFELSEIF IsDefined("Form.DirectorID")>
  <CFSET SESSION.MovWiz.DirectorID = Form.DirectorID>
<CFELSEIF IsDefined("Form.ActorID")>
  <CFSET SESSION.MovWiz.ActorIDs = Form.ActorID>
<CFELSEIF IsDefined("Form.StarActorID")>
  <CFSET SESSION.MovWiz.StarActorID = Form.StarActorID>
<CFELSEIF IsDefined("Form.DirectorSal")>
  <CFSET SESSION.MovWiz.DirectorSal = Form.DirectorSal>
  <CFSET SESSION.MovWiz.MiscExpense = Form.MiscExpense>
  <!--- For each actor now in the movie, save their salary --->
```

LISTING 20.11 CONTINUED

```
  <CFLOOP LIST="#SESSION.MovWiz.ActorIDs#" INDEX="ThisActor">
    <CFSET SESSION.MovWiz.ActorSals[ThisActor] = Form["ActorSal#ThisActor#"]>
  </CFLOOP>
</CFIF>


<!--- If user clicked "Back" button, go back a step --->
<CFIF IsDefined("Form.GoBack")>
  <CFSET SESSION.MovWiz.StepNum = URL.StepNum - 1>
<!--- If user clicked "Next" button, go forward one --->
<CFELSEIF IsDefined("Form.GoNext")>
  <CFSET SESSION.MovWiz.StepNum = URL.StepNum + 1>
<!--- If user clicked "Finished" button, we're done --->
<CFELSEIF IsDefined("Form.GoDone")>
  <CFLOCATION URL="NewMovieCommit2.cfm">
</CFIF>


<HTML>
<HEAD><TITLE>New Movie Wizard</TITLE></HEAD>
<BODY>

<!--- Show title and current step --->
<CFOUTPUT>
  <B>New Movie Wizard</B><BR>
  Step #SESSION.MovWiz.StepNum# of #NumberOfSteps#<BR>
</CFOUTPUT>


<!--- Data Entry Form, which submits back to itself --->
<CFFORM
  ACTION="NewMovieWizard2.cfm?StepNum=#SESSION.MovWiz.StepNum#"
  METHOD="POST">

  <!--- Display the appropriate wizard step --->
  <CFSWITCH EXPRESSION="#SESSION.MovWiz.StepNum#">
    <!--- Step One: Movie Title --->
    <CFCASE VALUE="1">
      <!--- Show text entry field for title --->
      What is the title of the movie?<BR>
      <CFINPUT
        NAME="MovieTitle"
        SIZE="50"
        REQUIRED="Yes"
        MESSAGE="Please don't leave the movie title blank."
        VALUE="#SESSION.MovWiz.MovieTitle#">

      <!--- Show text entry field for title --->
      <P>What is the "pitch" or "one-liner" for the movie?<BR>
      <CFINPUT
        NAME="PitchText"
        SIZE="50"
        REQUIRED="Yes"
        MESSAGE="Please provide the pitch text first."
        VALUE="#SESSION.MovWiz.PitchText#">
    </CFCASE>
```

```
<!--- Step Two: Pick Director --->
<CFCASE VALUE="2">
  <!--- Get list of directors from database --->
  <CFQUERY NAME="GetDirectors" DATASOURCE="#DataSource#">
    SELECT DirectorID, FirstName+' '+LastName As FullName
    FROM Directors
    ORDER BY LastName
  </CFQUERY>

  <!--- Show all Directors in SELECT list --->
  <!--- Pre-select if user has chosen one --->
  Who will be directing the movie?<BR>
  <CFSELECT
    SIZE="#GetDirectors.RecordCount#"
    QUERY="GetDirectors"
    NAME="DirectorID"
    DISPLAY="FullName"
    VALUE="DirectorID"
    REQUIRED="Yes"
    MESSAGE="You must choose a director first."
    SELECTED="#SESSION.MovWiz.DirectorID#"/>
</CFCASE>

<!--- Step Three: Pick Actors --->
<CFCASE VALUE="3">
  <!--- Get list of actors from database --->
  <CFQUERY NAME="GetActors" DATASOURCE="#DataSource#">
    SELECT * FROM Actors
    ORDER BY NameLast
  </CFQUERY>

  What actors will be in the movie?<BR>
  <!--- For each actor, display checkbox --->
  <CFLOOP QUERY="GetActors">
    <!--- Should checkbox be pre-checked? --->
    <CFSET IsChecked = ListFind(SESSION.MovWiz.ActorIDs, ActorID)>
    <!--- Checkbox itself --->
    <CFINPUT
      TYPE="Checkbox"
      NAME="ActorID"
      VALUE="#ActorID#"
      REQUIRED="Yes"
      MESSAGE="You must choose at least one actor first."
      CHECKED="#IsChecked#">
    <!--- Actor name --->
    <CFOUTPUT>#NameFirst# #NameLast#</CFOUTPUT><BR>
  </CFLOOP>
</CFCASE>


<!--- Step Four: Who is the star? --->
<CFCASE VALUE="4">
  <CFIF SESSION.MovWiz.ActorIDs EQ "">
    Please go back to the last step and choose at least one
    actor or actress to be in the movie.
  <CFELSE>
    <!--- Get actors who are in the film --->
```

Listing 20.11 Continued

```
      <CFQUERY NAME="GetActors" DATASOURCE="#DataSource#">
        SELECT * FROM Actors
        WHERE ActorID IN (#SESSION.MovWiz.ActorIDs#)
        ORDER BY NameLast
      </CFQUERY>

      Which one of the actors will get top billing?<BR>
      <!--- For each actor, display radio button --->
      <CFLOOP QUERY="GetActors">
        <!--- Should radio be pre-checked? --->
        <CFSET IsChecked = SESSION.MovWiz.StarActorID EQ ActorID>
        <!--- Radio button itself --->
        <CFINPUT
          TYPE="Radio"
          NAME="StarActorID"
          VALUE="#ActorID#"
          REQUIRED="Yes"
          MESSAGE="Please select the starring actor first."
          CHECKED="#IsChecked#">
        <!--- Actor name --->
        <CFOUTPUT>#NameFirst# #NameLast#</CFOUTPUT><BR>
      </CFLOOP>
    </CFIF>
  </CFCASE>


  <!--- Step Five: Expenses and Salaries --->
  <CFCASE VALUE="5">
    <!--- Get actors who are in the film --->
    <CFQUERY NAME="GetActors" DATASOURCE="#DataSource#">
      SELECT * FROM Actors
      WHERE ActorID IN (#SESSION.MovWiz.ActorIDs#)
      ORDER BY NameLast
    </CFQUERY>

    <!--- Director's Salary --->
    <P>How much will we pay the Director?<BR>
    <CFINPUT
      TYPE="Text"
      SIZE="10"
      NAME="DirectorSal"
      REQUIRED="Yes"
      VALIDATE="float"
      MESSAGE="Please provide a number for the director's salary."
      VALUE="#SESSION.MovWiz.DirectorSal#">

    <!--- Salary for each actor --->
    <P>How much will we pay the Actors?<BR>
    <CFLOOP QUERY="GetActors">
      <!--- Grab actors's salary from ActorSals structure --->
      <!--- Initialize to "" if no salary for actor yet --->
      <CFIF NOT StructKeyExists(SESSION.MovWiz.ActorSals, ActorID)>
        <CFSET SESSION.MovWiz.ActorSals[ActorID] = "">
      </CFIF>
      <!--- Text field for actor's salary --->
```

```
        <CFINPUT
          TYPE="Text"
          SIZE="10"
          NAME="ActorSal#ActorID#"
          REQUIRED="Yes"
          VALIDATE="float"
          MESSAGE="Please provide a number for each actor's salary."
          VALUE="#SESSION.MovWiz.ActorSals[ActorID]#">
        <!--- Actor's name --->
        <CFOUTPUT>for #NameFirst# #NameLast#<BR></CFOUTPUT>
      </CFLOOP>

      <!--- Additional Expenses --->
      <P>How much other money will be needed for the budget?<BR>
      <CFINPUT
        TYPE="Text"
        NAME="MiscExpense"
        REQUIRED="Yes"
        VALIDATE="float"
        MESSAGE="Please provide a number for additional expenses."
        SIZE="10"
        VALUE="#SESSION.MovWiz.MiscExpense#">
    </CFCASE>


    <!--- Step Six: Final Confirmation --->
    <CFCASE VALUE="6">
      You have successfully finished the New Movie Wizard.<BR>
      Click the Finish button to add the movie to the database.<BR>
      Click Back if you need to change anything.<BR>
    </CFCASE>
  </CFSWITCH>


  <P>
  <!--- Show Back button, unless at first step --->
  <CFIF SESSION.MovWiz.StepNum GT 1>
    <INPUT TYPE="Submit" NAME="GoBack" VALUE="&lt;&lt; Back">
  </CFIF>
  <!--- Show Next button, unless at last step --->
  <!--- If at last step, show "Finish" button --->
  <CFIF SESSION.MovWiz.StepNum LT NumberOfSteps>
    <INPUT TYPE="Submit" NAME="GoNext" VALUE="Next &gt;&gt;">
  <CFELSE>
    <INPUT TYPE="Submit" NAME="GoDone" VALUE="Finish">
  </CFIF>
</CFFORM>

</BODY>
</HTML>
```

PART III CH 20

LISTING 20.12 NEWMOVIECOMMIT2.CFM—EXPANDED VERSION OF WIZARD COMMIT CODE

```
<!---
  Filename:     NewMovieCommit2.cfm
  Created by:   Nate Weiss (NMW)
```

LISTING 20.12 CONTINUED

```
  Date Created: 2/18/2001
--->

<!--- Compute Total Budget --->
<!--- First, add the Director's salary and miscellaneous expenses --->
<CFSET TotalBudget = SESSION.MovWiz.MiscExpense + SESSION.MovWiz.DirectorSal>
<!--- Now add the salary for each actor in the movie --->
<CFLOOP LIST="#SESSION.MovWiz.ActorIDs#" INDEX="ThisActor">
  <CFSET ThisSal = SESSION.MovWiz.ActorSals[ThisActor]>
  <CFSET TotalBudget = TotalBudget + ThisSal>
</CFLOOP>

<!--- Insert Film Record --->
<CFQUERY DATASOURCE="#DataSource#">
  INSERT INTO Films(MovieTitle, PitchText, AmountBudgeted)
  VALUES ('#SESSION.MovWiz.MovieTitle#',
➥ '#SESSION.MovWiz.PitchText#', #TotalBudget#)
</CFQUERY>
<!--- Get ID number of just-inserted film --->
<CFQUERY DATASOURCE="#DataSource#" NAME="GetNew">
  SELECT Max(FilmID) As NewID FROM Films
</CFQUERY>
<!--- Insert Director Record --->
<CFQUERY DATASOURCE="#DataSource#">
  INSERT INTO FilmsDirectors(FilmID, DirectorID, Salary)
  VALUES (#GetNew.NewID#,
➥ #SESSION.MovWiz.DirectorID#, #SESSION.MovWiz.DirectorSal#)
</CFQUERY>
<!--- Insert Actor Records --->
<CFLOOP LIST="#SESSION.MovWiz.ActorIDs#" INDEX="ThisActor">
  <CFSET IsStar  = IIF(ThisActor EQ SESSION.MovWiz.StarActorID, 1, 0)>
  <CFQUERY DATASOURCE="#DataSource#">
    INSERT INTO FilmsActors(FilmID, ActorID, Salary, IsStarringRole)
    VALUES (#GetNew.NewID#,
➥ #ThisActor#, #SESSION.MovWiz.ActorSals[ThisActor]#, #IsStar#)
  </CFQUERY>
</CFLOOP>

<!--- Remove MovWiz variable from SESSION Structure --->
<!--- User will be started over on return to Wizard --->
<CFSET StructDelete(SESSION, "MovWiz")>


<!--- Display message to user --->
<HTML>
<HEAD><TITLE>Movie Added</TITLE></HEAD>
<BODY>
 <H2>Movie Added</H2>
 <P>The movie has been added to the database.

 <!--- Link to go through the Wizard again --->
 <P><A HREF="NewMovieWizard2.cfm">Enter Another Movie</A>
</BODY>
</HTML>
```

One item of note in these slightly expanded versions is that the new `ActorSals` part of the `SESSION.MovWiz` structure is itself a structure. The fact that you can use complex data types, such as structures and arrays, is one important advantage that session variables have over client variables and cookies.

OTHER SESSION VARIABLE EXAMPLES

A number of other examples in this book use session variables. You might want to skim through the code listings outlined here to see what other types of things session variables can be used for:

- Session variables are used to track the logged-in status of users in Chapter 21, "Security with ColdFusion."
- Session variables are used to help users check their e-mail messages from a ColdFusion template in Chapter 28, "Interacting with E-mail."
- The Ad Server examples in Chapter 34, "Generating Non-HTML Content," use session variables to track which ads have been shown on which pages on a per-visit basis.

USING SESSION VARIABLES WITHOUT REQUIRING COOKIES

ColdFusion tracks sessions using the same `CFID` and `CFTOKEN` cookie mechanism that it uses to track client variables. Therefore, you must take special steps if you need session variables to work even if a user's browser doesn't support cookies. See "Using Client Variables Without Requiring Cookies," earlier in this chapter, for specific instructions.

LOCKING REVISITED

Caution

This section discusses a way to get around having to lock all accesses to session variables with `<CFLOCK>`. If you do not have control over the ColdFusion Administrator, you must use `<CFLOCK>` around every read or write to the `SESSION` scope.

Note

We are assuming that you have read the "Preventing Memory Corruption with Locking" section in Chapter 19. If you haven't yet, please take a look at that section before you continue here.

PART III

CH 20

Similar to application variables, session variables are kept in the server's RAM. This means that the same types of memory-corruption problems can occur if session variables are being read and accessed by two different page requests at the same time. (See the section "Preventing Memory Corruption with Locking" in Chapter 19.)

However, *unlike* application variables, it is somewhat unlikely that your application will ever really need two page requests to be able to access the same `SESSION` structure at the same time. Users are usually moving from page to page in your site, visiting just one ColdFusion template at a time. In general, the only times when a single session would need to request more than one page at the same moment would be when a user first opens a frames-based page or if the user clicks the Reload button on her browser repeatedly.

For this reason, ColdFusion has a Single-Threaded Sessions option you can enable in the ColdFusion Administrator. After it's enabled, ColdFusion processes only one page request per session at a time. If the user's browser happens to request more than one page at the same time (which would most likely happen when the user is opening a frames-based page), the user's page requests are queued and processed one at a time. Of course, page requests from other sessions are processed normally.

What all this means is that you don't have to use `<CFLOCK>` to lock each access to the `SESSION` scope as long as you enable this option in the ColdFusion Administrator. ColdFusion essentially does this for you, almost as if you had put a `<CFLOCK>` of `TYPE="Exclusive"` and `SCOPE="Session"` at the top and bottom of every one of your pages. As long as you don't have a lot of frames-based pages that are accessed extremely frequently and that wouldn't need `<CFLOCK>` tags ordinarily, there is really no reason not to enable this feature. In fact, it's a bit of a puzzle why this feature isn't enabled by default when ColdFusion is installed.

To enable the Single Threaded Session option, follow these steps:

1. Navigate to the Locking page of the ColdFusion Administrator.
2. Check the Single Threaded Sessions option.
3. Select the No Automatic Checking or Locking option for the Session scope, unless you are using one of the other options for debugging purposes.
4. Click Submit Changes.

Note

A small performance penalty exists for enabling this feature but not an appreciable one. And there's no guarantee that the `<CFLOCK>` tags you would have to put in yourself otherwise wouldn't carry approximately the same performance penalty at the end of the day.

Caution

If you do not enable this option, you must lock your accesses to the `Session` scope with the `<CFLOCK>` tag, with the `SCOPE` attribute set to `Session`. If you are setting session variables, you will use a `TYPE` attribute of `Exclusive`; if you are only accessing or outputting session variables, you can use `TYPE="ReadOnly"`. For details, see the section "Preventing Memory Corruption with Locking" in Chapter 19.

WHEN DOES A SESSION END?

Developers often wonder when exactly a session ends. The simple answer is that ColdFusion's Session Management feature is based on time. By default, the behavior is that a particular session is considered to be expired if more than 20 minutes pass without another request from the same client. At that point, the SESSION scope associated with that browser is freed from the server's memory.

Of course, you can adjust this timeout period to whatever you feel is appropriate, as discussed in the next section.

Default Behavior

As far as ColdFusion is concerned, a session does not automatically end when the user closes her browser. You can see this yourself by visiting one of the session examples discussed in this book, such as the New Movie Wizard (refer to Listing 20.9). Fill out the wizard partway, and then close your browser. Now reopen it. Nothing has happened to your session's copy of the SESSION scope, so you still are on the same step of the wizard that you were before you closed your browser. As far as ColdFusion is concerned, you just reloaded the page.

Adjusting the Session Timeout Period

You can adjust the session timeout period for your session variables following the same basic steps you take to adjust the timeout period for application variables. That is, you can adjust the default timeout of 20 minutes using the ColdFusion Administrator, or you can use the SESSIONTIMEOUT attribute of the <CFAPPLICATION> tag to set a specific session timeout for your application.

For specific instructions, see the section "Application Variable Timeouts" in Chapter 19.

Expiring a Session Programmatically

If you want to expire a session in your code, you can do so by using a <CFAPPLICATION> tag such as the one in your Application.cfm file, except with a SESSIONTIMEOUT length of 0 seconds. For instance, if you wanted to give your users some type of log-out link, you could have a SessionLogout.cfm template that contains something such as the following:

```
<!--- Expire the session --->
<CFAPPLICATION
  NAME="OrangeWhipSite"
  SESSIONMANAGEMENT="Yes"
  SESSIONTIMEOUT="#CreateTimeSpan(0,0,0,0)#">
```


Ending the Session when the Browser Closes

One option is to set the SETCLIENTCOOKIES attribute of the <CFAPPLICATION> to No, which means that the CFID and CFTOKEN cookies ColdFusion normally uses to track each browser's session (and client) variables will not be maintained as persistent cookies on each client machine. If you are not using client variables, or don't need your client variables to persist after the user closes his browser, this can be a viable option.

If you do decide to set SETCLIENTCOOKIE="No", you must manually pass the CFID and CFTOKEN in the URL for every page request, as if the user's browser did not support cookies at all.

See the section "Using Client Variables Without Requiring Cookies," earlier in this chapter, for specific instructions.

If you want to use `SETCLIENTCOOKIE="No"` but don't want to pass the `CFID` and `CFTOKEN` in every URL, you could set the `CFID` and `CFTOKEN` as cookies on your own, as nonpersistent cookies. This means the values would be stored as cookies on the user's browser, but the cookies would expire when users close their browsers. The most straightforward way to get this effect is to use two `<CFSET>` tags in your `Application.cfm` file, just after your `<CFAPPLICATION>` tag, as follows:

```
<!--- Name our application, and enable Session and Application variables --->
<CFAPPLICATION
  NAME="OrangeWhipSite"
  SESSIONMANAGEMENT="Yes"
  SETCLIENTCOOKIES="No">

<!--- Preserve Session/Client variables only until browser closes --->
<CFSET Cookie.CFID    = SESSION.CFID>
<CFSET Cookie.CFTOKEN = SESSION.CFTOKEN>
```

This technique essentially causes ColdFusion to lose all memory of the client machine when the user closes the browser. When the user returns next time, it will not present any `CFID` to the server, and ColdFusion will be forced to issue a new `CFID` value, effectively abandoning any session or client variables that were associated with the browser in the past.

A completely different technique is to set your own nonpersistent cookie, perhaps called `Cookie.BrowserOpen`. If a user closes the browser, the cookie no longer exists. Therefore, you can use the cookie's nonexistence as a cue to expire the session programmatically, as discussed in the previous section. You could use code such as the following in your `Application.cfm` file:

```
<!--- If our BrowserOpen cookie is not sent --->
<CFIF NOT IsDefined("Cookie.BrowserOpen")>
  <!--- Expire the session, if any --->
  <CFAPPLICATION
    NAME="OrangeWhipSite"
    SESSIONMANAGEMENT="Yes"
    SESSIONTIMEOUT="#CreateTimeSpan(0,0,0,0)#">

  <!--- Set cookie, to expire when browser closes --->
  <CFSET Cookie.BrowserOpen = "Yes">
</CFIF>

<!--- Name our application, and enable Session and Application variables --->
<CFAPPLICATION
  NAME="OrangeWhipSite"
  SESSIONMANAGEMENT="Yes">
```

Unfortunately, there is also a downside to this technique. If the user's browser doesn't support cookies, or if the user has cookies turned off in the browser's preferences, the session will be expired with every page request. However, as long as you know that cookies will be supported (for instance, in an intranet application), it will serve you well.

CHAPTER 21

Security with ColdFusion

In this chapter

At this point, you have learned how to create interactive, data-driven pages for your users and have started to see how your applications can really come alive using the various persistent scopes provided by ColdFusion's Web application framework. Now is a good time to learn how to lock down your application pages so they require a username and password and show only the right information to the right people.

OPTIONS FOR SECURING YOUR APPLICATION

This section briefly outlines four approaches you can take if you need to secure access to your ColdFusion templates:

- SSL encryption
- Basic authentication
- Application-based security
- ColdFusion advanced security

You can use more than one of these options at the same time if you want. The third item, which we call *application-based security*, is what this chapter focuses on.

SSL ENCRYPTION

Most of today's Web servers enable you to make a connection between the browser and the server more secure by using encryption. After encryption has been enabled, your ColdFusion templates and related files become available at URLs that begin with `https://` instead of `http://`. The HTML code your templates generate is scrambled on its way out of the Web server. Provided that everything has been set up correctly, browsers can unscramble the HTML and use it normally. The framework that makes this all possible is called the Secure Sockets Layer (SSL).

Browsers generally indicate that a page is encrypted by showing a small key or lock icon in the browser's status bar. You probably have encountered many such sites on the Internet yourself, especially on pages where you were asked to provide a credit card number.

This topic is not discussed in detail here because encryption is enabled at the Web-server level and doesn't affect the ColdFusion Application Server directly. You don't need to do anything special in your ColdFusion templates for it to work properly. The encryption and decryption are taken care of by your Web server and each user's browser.

You might want to look into turning on your Web server's encryption options for sections of your applications that need to display or collect valuable pieces of information. For instance, most users hesitate to enter a credit card number if the page is not secure, so you should think about using encryption during any type of checkout process in your applications.

Tip

If you are working on a company intranet project, you might consider enabling SSL for your entire application, especially if employees will access it from outside your local network.

The steps you take to enable encryption differ depending on which Web server software you are using (Apache, Netscape/iPlanet, Microsoft IIS, and so on). You will need to consult your Web server's documentation for details. Along the way, you will learn a bit about public keys and private keys, and you probably will need to purchase a SSL certificate on an annual basis from a company such as VeriSign. VeriSign's Web site is also a good place to look if you want to find out more about SSL and HTTPS technology in general. Visit them on the Web at `http://www.verisign.com`.

Note

If you want your code to be capable of detecting whether a page is being accessed with an `https://` URL, you can use one of the variables in the `CGI` scope to make this determination. The variables might have slightly different names from Web server to Web server, but they generally start with `HTTPS`. For instance, on a Microsoft IIS server, the value of `CGI.HTTPS` is `on` or `off`, depending on whether the page is being accessed in an encrypted context. We recommend that you turn on the Show Variables debugging option in the ColdFusion Administrator to see which HTTPS-related variables are made available by your Web server software.

BASIC AUTHENTICATION

Nearly all Web servers provide support for something called HTTP basic authentication. *Basic authentication* is a method for password-protecting your Web documents and images and usually is used to protect static files, such as straight HTML files. However, you can certainly use basic authentication to password-protect your ColdFusion templates. Users will be prompted for their usernames and passwords via a dialog box presented by the browser, as shown in Figure 21.1. You will not have control over the look or wording of the dialog box, which varies from browser to browser.

Basic authentication is not the focus of this chapter. However, it is a quick, easy way to put a password on a particular folder, individual files, or an entire Web site. It is usually best for situations in which you want to give the same type of access to everyone who gets a password. With basic authentication, you don't need to write any ColdFusion code to control which users are allowed to see what. Depending on the Web server software you are using, the usernames and passwords for each user might be kept in a text file, an LDAP server, an ODBC database, or some type of proprietary format.

To find out how to enable basic authentication, see your Web server's documentation.

Tip

When basic authentication is used, you should be able to find out which username the user provided by examining either the `#CGI.AUTH_USER#` variable or the `#CGI.REMOTE_USER#` variable. The exact variable name depends on the Web server software you are using.

Note

Microsoft's Web servers and browsers extend the idea of basic authentication by providing a proprietary option called Integrated Windows Authentication (also referred to as *NTLM* or *Challenge/Response Authentication*), which enables people to access a Web server using their Windows usernames and passwords. For purposes of this section of this book, consider Windows Authentication to be in the same general category as basic authentication. That is, it is not covered specifically in this book and is enabled at the Web-server level.

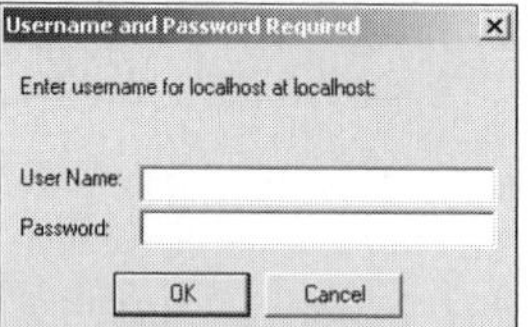

Figure 21.1
Basic authentication prompts the user to log in using a standard dialog box.

APPLICATION-BASED SECURITY

The term *application-based security* is used here to cover any situation in which you give your users an ordinary Web-based form to log in with. Most often, this means using the same HTML form techniques you already know to present this form to the user and then using a database query to verify that the username and password he typed was valid.

This method of security gives you the most control over the user experience, such as what the login page looks like, when it is presented, how long users remain logged in, and what they have access to. In other words, by creating a home-grown security or login process, you get to make it work however you need it to. The downside, of course, is that you must do a bit of extra work to figure out exactly what you need and how to get it done. That's what this chapter is all about.

COLDFUSION ADVANCED SECURITY

ColdFusion also provides several specialized tags and functions for creating login and authentication schemes. These tags and functions tie in with ColdFusion's advanced security features, which enable you to use the ColdFusion Administrator to set up *security contexts*. Security contexts define which users can look at which items. You can define users and groups in a database, or you can have ColdFusion look up users from an LDAP directory or a Windows domain.

These features are not included with a default ColdFusion installation and are not covered in this book. They are covered in the "Implementing Advanced Security" chapter in our companion volume, *Advanced ColdFusion 5.0 Application Development*. If you are curious about what these features can do for you and how you can access them in your code, see the `<CFAUTHENTICATE>` and `<CFIMPERSONATE>` tags in Appendix A, "ColdFusion Tag Reference." See also `IsAuthorized()`, `AuthenticatedUser()`, `IsAuthenticated()`, and `AuthenticatedContext()` in Appendix B, "ColdFusion Function Reference."

Using ColdFusion to Control Access

The remainder of this chapter discusses how to build your own form-based security mechanism. In general, putting something similar to this in place requires three large steps:

- Deciding which pages or information should be password-protected
- Creating a login page and verifying the user's username and password
- Restricting access to pages or information based on who the user is

Deciding What to Protect

Your first step is to decide exactly what it is you are trying to protect with your security measures. Of course, this step doesn't involve writing any code, but we strongly recommend that you think this through as thoroughly as possible. You should spend some time just thinking about what type of security measures your applications need and how users will gain access.

Be sure you have answers to these questions:

- **Does the whole application need to be secured or just a portion of it?** For company intranets, you usually want to secure the whole application. For Internet sites available to the general public, you usually want to secure only certain sections ("Members Only" or "Registered Users" areas, for instance).
- **What granularity of access do you need?** Some applications need to lock only certain people out of certain folders or pages. Others need to lock people out at a more granular, data-aware level. For instance, if you are creating some type of Manage Your Account page, you aren't trying to keep a registered user out of the page. Instead, you need to ensure that the users can see and change only their own account information.
- **When should the user be asked for her username and password?** When she first enters your application, or only when she tries to get something that requires it? The former might make the security seem more cohesive to the user, whereas the latter might be more user friendly.

We also recommend that you put some thought into the following questions. These have to do with how passwords will be maintained, rather than what they will protect:

- **Should usernames and passwords become invalid after a period of time?** For instance, if a user has purchased some type of 30-day membership to your site, what happens on the 31st day?
- **Does the user need a way to change her password? What about her username?**
- **Should certain users be able to log in only from certain IP addresses?** Or should they be able to log in during certain times of the day, or days of the week?

- **How will usernames and passwords be managed?** Do you need to implement some notion of user groups, such as users in an operating system? Do you need to be able to grant rights to view certain items on a group level? What about on an individual user level?

The answers to these questions will help you create whatever database tables or other validation mechanics will be necessary to implement the security policies you have envisioned. You will learn where and when to refer to any such custom tables as you work through the code examples in this chapter.

USING SESSION VARIABLES FOR AUTHENTICATION

An effective and straightforward method for handling the mechanics of user logins is outlined in the following section. Basically, the strategy is to turn on ColdFusion's session management features, as you learned about in Chapter 20, "Working with Sessions," and use session variables to track whether each user has logged in. There are many ways to go about this, but it can be as simple as setting a single variable in the `SESSION` scope after a user logs in.

Note

Before you can use the `SESSION` scope in your applications, you need to enable it using the `<CFAPPLICATION>` tag. See Chapter 20 for details.

CHECKING AND MAINTAINING LOGIN STATUS

For instance, assume for the moment that the user has just filled out a username/password form (more on that later), and you have verified that the username and password are correct. You could then use a line such as the following to remember that the user is logged in:

```
<CFSET SESSION.IsLoggedIn = "Yes">
```

As you learned in the last chapter, the `IsLoggedIn` variable is tracked for the rest of the user's visit (until his session times out). From this point forward, if you wanted to ensure that the user was logged in before showing him something, all you would need to do would be to check for the presence of the variable:

```
<CFIF NOT IsDefined("SESSION.IsLoggedIn")>
  Sorry, you don't have permission to look at that.
  <CFABORT>
</CFIF>
```

And, with that, you have modest security. Clearly, this isn't final code yet, but that really is the basic idea. A user will not be able to get past the second snippet unless his session has already encountered the first. The rest of the examples in this chapter are just expanded variations on these two code snippets.

So, all you have to do is put these two lines in the correct places. The first line must be wrapped within whatever code validates a user's password (probably by checking in some type of database table), and the second line must be put on whatever pages you need to protect.

Restricting Access to Your Application

Assume for the moment that you want to require your users to log in as soon as they enter your application. You could put a login form on your application's front page or home page, but what if a user doesn't go through your front page for whatever reason? For instance, if he uses a bookmark or types the URL for some other page, he would bypass your login screen. So, you need to figure out a way to ensure that the user gets prompted for a password on the first page request for each session, regardless of which page he actually is asking for.

A great solution is to use the special `Application.cfm` file set aside by ColdFusion's Web application framework, which you learned about in Chapter 19, "Introducing the Web Application Framework." You will recall that if you create a template called `Application.cfm`, it automatically is included before each page request. This means you could put some code in `Application.cfm` to see whether the `SESSION` scope is holding an `IsLoggedIn` value, as discussed previously. If it's not holding a value, the user must be presented with a login form. If it is holding a value, the user has already logged in previously during the current session.

With that in mind, take a look at the `Application.cfm` file shown in Listing 21.1.

Listing 21.1 `Application.cfm`—**Sending a User to a Login Page if Not Logged In**

```
<!---
  Filename:     Application.cfm
  Created by:   Nate Weiss (NMW)
  Date Created: 3/5/2001
--->

<!--- Any variables set here can be used by all our pages --->
<CFSET DataSource  = "ows">
<CFSET CompanyName = "Orange Whip Studios">

<!--- Name our application and enable session variables --->
<CFAPPLICATION
  NAME="OrangeWhipSite"
  SESSIONMANAGEMENT="Yes">

<!--- If user is not logged in, force him to now --->
<CFIF NOT IsDefined("SESSION.Auth.IsLoggedIn")>
  <CFINCLUDE TEMPLATE="LoginForm.cfm">
  <CFABORT>
</CFIF>
```

Caution

This template uses variables in the SESSION scope without locking the accesses with the <CFLOCK> tag. This is an acceptable practice if the Single Threaded Sessions option is checked in the Locking page of the ColdFusion Administrator. Otherwise, you must add <CFLOCK> tags around all accesses to the SESSION scope. See the section "Locking Revisited" in Chapter 20.

First, session variables are enabled using the <CFAPPLICATION> tag. Then, an IsDefined() test is used to check whether the IsLoggedIn value is present. If it's not, a <CFINCLUDE> tag is used to include the template called LoginForm.cfm, which presents a login screen to the user. Note that a <CFABORT> tag is placed directly after the <CFINCLUDE> so that nothing further is presented to the user.

The net effect is that all pages in your application have now been locked down and will never appear until you create code that sets the SESSION.Auth.IsLoggedIn value.

Note

Soon, you will see how the Auth structure can be used to hold other values relevant to the user's login status. If you do not need to track any additional information along with the login status, you could use a variable named SESSION.IsLoggedIn instead of SESSION.Auth.IsLoggedIn. However, it's not much extra work to add the Auth structure, and it gives you some extra flexibility.

CREATING A LOGIN PAGE

The next step is to create a login page, where the user can enter her username and password. The code in Listing 21.1 is a simple example. Of course, this code doesn't actually do anything when submitted yet, but it's helpful to see that most login pages are built with ordinary <FORM> or <CFFORM> code. Nearly all login pages are some variation of this skeleton.

Figure 21.2 shows what the form will look like to your users.

Tip

Use TYPE="Password" wherever you ask your users to type a password, as shown in Listing 21.1. That way, as the user types, her password will be masked so that someone looking over her shoulder can't see her password.

LISTING 21.2 LoginForm.cfm—A BASIC LOGIN PAGE

```
<!---
  Filename:     LoginForm.cfm
  Created by:   Nate Weiss (NMW)
  Date Created: 3/7/2001
--->
```

```
<!--- If the user is now submitting "Login" form, --->
<!--- Include "Login Check" code to validate user --->
<CFIF IsDefined("Form.UserLogin")>
  <CFINCLUDE TEMPLATE="LoginCheck.cfm">
</CFIF>



<HTML>
<HEAD>
  <TITLE>Please Log In</TITLE>
</HEAD>

<!--- Place cursor in "User Name" field when page loads--->
<BODY onLoad="document.LoginForm.UserLogin.focus();">

<!--- Start our Login Form --->
<CFFORM ACTION="#CGI.SCRIPT_NAME#" NAME="LoginForm" METHOD="POST">
  <!--- Make the UserLogin and UserPassword fields required --->
  <INPUT TYPE="Hidden" NAME="UserLogin_required">
  <INPUT TYPE="Hidden" NAME="UserPassword_required">

  <!--- Use an HTML table for simple formatting --->
  <TABLE BORDER="0">
    <TR><TH COLSPAN="2" BGCOLOR="Silver">Please Log In</TH></TR>
    <TR>
      <TH>Username:</TH>
      <TD>

      <!--- Text field for "User Name" --->
      <CFINPUT
        TYPE="Text"
        NAME="UserLogin"
        SIZE="20"
        VALUE=""
        MAXLENGTH="100"
        REQUIRED="Yes"
        MESSAGE="Please type your Username first.">

      </TD>
    </TR><TR>
      <TH>Password:</TH>
      <TD>

      <!--- Text field for Password --->
      <CFINPUT
        TYPE="Password"
        NAME="UserPassword"
        SIZE="12"
        VALUE=""
        MAXLENGTH="100"
        REQUIRED="Yes"
        MESSAGE="Please type your Password first.">

      <!--- Submit Button that reads "Enter" --->
      <INPUT TYPE="Submit" VALUE="Enter">
```

LISTING 21.2 CONTINUED

```
        </TD>
      </TR>
    </TABLE>

</CFFORM>

</BODY>
</HTML>
```

Note

In general, users will not be visiting `LoginForm.cfm` directly; instead, the code in Listing 21.2 gets included by the `<CFIF>` test performed in the `Application.cfm` page (Listing 21.1) the first time the user accesses some other page in the application (such as the `OrderHistory.cfm` template shown in Listing 21.4).

Please note that this form's `ACTION` attribute is set to `#CGI.SCRIPT_NAME#`. The special `CGI.SCRIPT_NAME` variable always holds the relative URL to the currently executing ColdFusion template. So, for example, if the user is being presented with the login form after requesting a template called `HomePage.cfm`, this form will re-request that same page when submitted. In other words, this form always submits back to the URL of the page on which it is appearing.

Tip

The `CGI.SCRIPT_NAME` can come in handy in any situation in which your code needs to be capable of reloading or resubmitting the currently executing template. See Appendix C, "Special ColdFusion Variables and Result Codes," for details.

When the form is actually submitted, the `Form.UserLogin`value will exist, indicating that the user has typed a username and password that should be checked for accuracy. As a result, the `<CFINCLUDE>` tag fires, which includes the password-validation code in the `LoginCheck.cfm` template (see Listing 21.3).

The Text and Password fields on this form use the `REQUIRED` and `MESSAGE` client-side validation attributes provided by `<CFINPUT>` and `<CFFORM>`. The two `Hidden` fields add server-side validation. See Chapter 13, "Form Data Validation," if you need to review these form field validation techniques.

Tip

This template's `<BODY>` tag has JavaScript code in its `onLoad` attribute, which causes the cursor to be placed in the `UserLogin` field when the page loads. You must consult a different reference for a full discussion of JavaScript, but you can use this same basic technique to cause any form element to have focus when a page first loads.

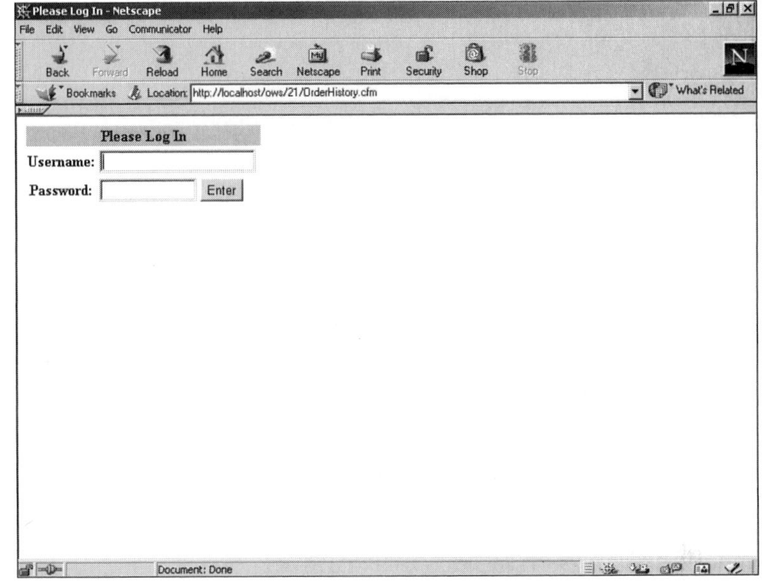

Figure 21.2
Users are forced to log in before they can access sensitive information in this application.

Note

JavaScript is case sensitive, so the `onLoad` code must be capitalized correctly; otherwise, scripting error messages will pop up in the browser. Of course, you can just leave out the `onLoad` code altogether if you want.

Verifying the Login Name and Password

Listing 21.3 provides simple code for your `LoginCheck.cfm` template. This is the template that will be included when the user attempts to gain access by submitting the login form from Listing 21.2.

The most important line in this template is the `<CFSET>` line that sets the `SESSION.Auth.IsLoggedIn` variable to `Yes`. After this value is set for the session, the `IsDefined()` test in the `Application.cfm` file (refer to Listing 21.1) will succeed and the user will be able to view pages normally.

Listing 21.3 `LoginCheck.cfm`—**Granting Access when the Username and Password Are Correct**

```
<!---
  Filename:     LoginCheck.cfm
  Created by:   Nate Weiss (NMW)
  Date Created: 2/18/2001
  Please Note:  Included by LoginForm.cfm
--->
```

LISTING 21.3 CONTINUED

```
<!--- Make sure we have Login name and Password --->
<CFPARAM NAME="Form.UserLogin" TYPE="string">
<CFPARAM NAME="Form.UserPassword" TYPE="string">

<!--- Find record with this Username/Password --->
<!--- If no rows returned, password not valid --->
<CFQUERY NAME="GetUser" DATASOURCE="#DataSource#">
  SELECT ContactID, FirstName
  FROM Contacts
  WHERE UserLogin    = '#Form.UserLogin#'
    AND UserPassword = '#Form.UserPassword#'
</CFQUERY>

<!--- If the username and password are correct --->
<CFIF GetUser.RecordCount EQ 1>
  <!--- Remember user's logged-in status, plus --->
  <!--- ContactID and First Name, in structure --->
  <CFSET SESSION.Auth = StructNew()>
  <CFSET SESSION.Auth.IsLoggedIn = "Yes">
  <CFSET SESSION.Auth.ContactID  = GetUser.ContactID>
  <CFSET SESSION.Auth.FirstName  = GetUser.FirstName>

  <!--- Now that user is logged in, send them --->
  <!--- to whatever page makes sense to start --->
  <CFLOCATION URL="#CGI.SCRIPT_NAME#">
</CFIF>
```

Caution

This template uses variables in the `SESSION` scope without using the `<CFLOCK>` tag. This is acceptable only if the Single Threaded Sessions option is enabled. See the section "Locking Revisited" in Chapter 20.

Tip

The query in this template can be adapted or replaced with any type of database or lookup procedure you need. For instance, rather than looking in a database table, you could query an LDAP server to get the user's first name. For more information about LDAP, see the `<CFLDAP>` tag in Appendix A, or consult our companion volume, *Advanced ColdFusion 5.0 Development*.

First, the two `<CFPARAM>` tags ensure that the login name and password are indeed available as form fields, which they should be unless a user has somehow been directed to this page in error. Next, a simple `<CFQUERY>` tag attempts to retrieve a record from the `Contacts` table where the `UserLogin` and `UserPassword` columns match up to the username and password the user entered in the login form. If this query returns a record, the user has, by definition, entered a valid username and password and thus should be considered logged in.

Assume for the moment that the username and password are correct. The value of GetUser.RecordCount is therefore 1, so the code inside the <CFIF> block executes. A new structure called Auth is created in the SESSION scope, and three values are placed within the new structure. The most important of the three is the IsLoggedIn value, which is used here in the same basic way that was outlined in the original code snippets near the beginning of this chapter.

The user's unique ID number (his ContactID) is also placed in the SESSION.Auth structure, as well as his first name. The idea here is to populate the SESSION.Auth structure with whatever information is pertinent to the fact that the user has indeed been authenticated. Therefore, any little bits of information that might be helpful to have later in the user's session can be saved in the Auth structure now.

Tip

By keeping the SESSION.Auth.FirstName value, for instance, you will be able to display the user's first name on any page, which will give your application a friendly, personalized feel. And, by keeping the SESSION.Auth.ContactID value, you will be able to run queries against the database based on the user's authenticated ID number.

Finally, the <CFLOCATION> tag is used to redirect the user to the current value of CGI.SCRIPT_NAME. Because CGI.SCRIPT_NAME also was used for the ACTION of the login form, this value will still reflect the page for which the user was originally looking, before the login form appeared. The browser will respond by re-requesting the original page. This time, the SESSION.Auth.IsLoggedIn test in Application.cfm (refer to Listing 21.1) will not <CFINCLUDE> the login form, and the user will thus be allowed to see the content he originally was looking for.

Note

The underlying assumption here is that no two users can have the same UserLogin and UserPassword. You must ensure that this rule is enforced in your application. For instance, when a user first chooses (or is assigned) his username and password, there needs to be a check in place to ensure that nobody else already has them.

PERSONALIZING BASED ON LOGIN

After Listings 21.1–21.3 are in place, the SESSION.Auth structure is guaranteed to exist for all your application's pages. What's more, the user's unique ID and first name will be available as SESSION.Auth.ContactID and SESSION.Auth.FirstName, respectively. This makes providing users with personalized pages, such as Manage My Account or My Order History, easy.

Listing 21.4 shows a template called OrderHistory.cfm, which enables a user to review the merchandise orders she has placed in the past. Because the authenticated ContactID is readily available, getting this done in a reasonably secure fashion is easy. In most respects, this is just a data display template, the likes of which you learned about in Chapter 11, "Creating Data-Driven Pages." The only new concept here is the notion of using authenticated identification information from the `SESSION` scope (in this case, the `ContactID`).

LISTING 21.4 `OrderHistory.cfm`—PERSONALIZING CONTENT BASED ON LOGIN

```
<!---
  Filename:     OrderHistory.cfm
  Created by:   Nate Weiss (NMW)
  Date Created: 3/5/2001
--->

<!--- Retrieve user's orders, based on ContactID --->
<CFQUERY NAME="GetOrders" DATASOURCE="#DataSource#">
  SELECT OrderID, OrderDate,
    (SELECT Count(*)
     FROM MerchandiseOrdersItems oi
     WHERE oi.OrderID = o.OrderID) AS ItemCount
  FROM MerchandiseOrders o
  WHERE ContactID = #SESSION.Auth.ContactID#
  ORDER BY OrderDate DESC
</CFQUERY>

<HTML>
<HEAD>
  <TITLE>Your Order History</TITLE>
</HEAD>
<BODY>

<!--- Personalized message at top of page--->
<CFOUTPUT>
  <h2>Your Order History</h2>
  <P><B>Welcome back, #SESSION.Auth.FirstName#</B>!<BR>
  You have placed <B>#GetOrders.RecordCount#</B>
  orders with us to date.</P>
</CFOUTPUT>


<!--- Display orders in a simple HTML table --->
<TABLE BORDER="1" WIDTH="300" CELLPADDING="5" CELLSPACING="2">
  <!--- Column headers --->
  <TR>
    <TH>Date Ordered</TH>
    <TH>Items</TH>
  </TR>

  <!--- Display each order as a table row --->
  <CFOUTPUT QUERY="GetOrders">
    <TR>
      <TD>
        <A HREF="OrderHistory.cfm?OrderID=#OrderID#">
          #DateFormat(OrderDate, "mmmm d, yyyy")#
        </A>
      </TD>
      <TD>
```

```
        <B>#ItemCount#</B>
      </TD>
    </TR>
  </CFOUTPUT>
</TABLE>

</BODY>
</HTML>
```

Caution

This template uses variables in the SESSION scope without using the <CFLOCK> tag. This is acceptable only if the Single Threaded Sessions option is enabled. See the section "Locking Revisited" in Chapter 20.

First, a fairly ordinary <CFQUERY> tag is used to retrieve information about the orders the user has placed. Because the user's authenticated ContactID is being used in the WHERE clause, you can be certain that you will be retrieving the order information appropriate only for this user.

Next, a personalized message is displayed to the user, including her first name. Then the order records are displayed using an ordinary <CFOUTPUT QUERY> block. The order records are displayed in a simple tabular format using simple HTML table formatting. Figure 21.3 shows what the results will look like for the end user.

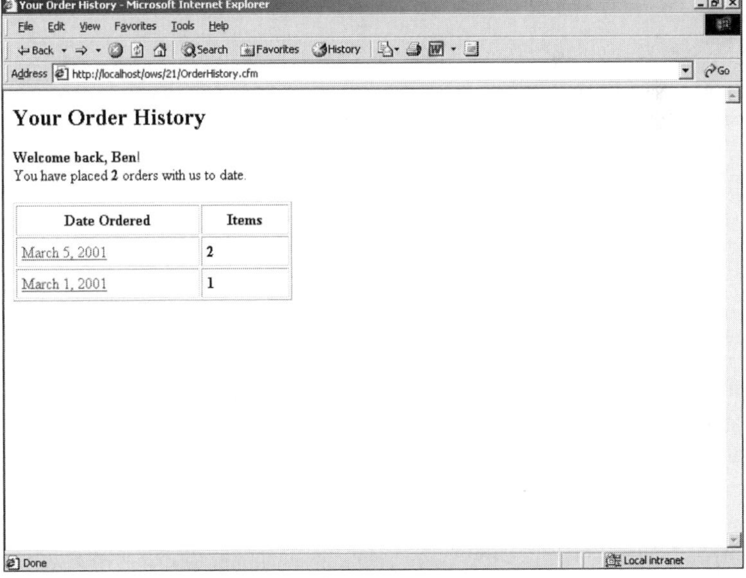

Figure 21.3
After a user is authenticated, providing a personalized experience is easy.

BEING CAREFUL WITH PASSED PARAMETERS

When you are dealing with sensitive information, such as account or purchase histories, you need to be more careful when passing parameters from page to page. It's easy to let yourself feel that your work is done after you force your users to log in. Of course, forcing them to log in is an important step, but your code still needs to check things internally before it exposes sensitive data.

RECOGNIZING THE PROBLEM

Here's a scenario that illustrates a potential vulnerability. After putting together the `OrderHistory.cfm` template shown in Listing 21.4, you realize that people will need to be able to see the details of each order, such as the individual items purchased. You decide to enable the user to click in each order's Order Date column to see the details of that order. You decide, sensibly, to turn each order's date into a link that passes the desired order's ID number as a URL parameter.

So, you decide to change this:

```
#DateFormat(OrderDate, "mmmm d, yyyy")#
```

to this:

```
<A HREF="OrderHistory.cfm?OrderID=#OrderID#">
  #DateFormat(OrderDate, "mmmm d, yyyy")#
</A>
```

This is fine. When the user clicks the link, the same template is executed—this time with the desired order number available as `URL.OrderID`. You just need to add an `IsDefined()` check to see whether the URL parameter exists, and if so, run a second query to obtain the detail records (item name, price, and quantity) for the desired order. After a bit of thought, you come up with the following:

```
<CFIF IsDefined("URL.OrderID")>
  <CFQUERY NAME="GetDetail" DATASOURCE="#DataSource#">
    SELECT m.MerchName, oi.ItemPrice, oi.OrderQty
    FROM Merchandise m, MerchandiseOrdersItems oi
    WHERE m.MerchID = oi.ItemID
    AND oi.OrderID  = #URL.OrderID#
  </CFQUERY>
</CFIF>
```

The problem with this code is that it doesn't ensure that the order number passed in the URL indeed belongs to the user. After the user notices that the order number is being passed in the URL, he might try to play around with the passed parameters just to, ahem, see what happens. And, indeed, if the user changes the `?OrderID=5` part of the URL to, say, `?OrderID=10`, he will be able to see the details of some other person's order. Depending on what type of application you are building, this kind of vulnerability could be a huge problem.

CHECKING PASSED PARAMETERS

The problem is relatively easy to address. You just need to ensure that, whenever you retrieve sensitive information based on a URL or FORM parameter, you somehow verify that the parameter is one the user has the right to request. In this case, you must ensure that the URL.OrderID value is associated with the user's ID number, SESSION.Auth.ContactID.

In this application, the easiest policy to enforce is probably ensuring that each query involves the SESSION.Auth.ContactID value somewhere in its WHERE clause. Therefore, to turn the unsafe query shown previously into a safe one, you would add another subquery or inner join to the query, so the Orders table is directly involved. After the Orders table is involved, the query can include a check against its ContactID column.

A safe version of the snippet shown previously would be the following, which adds a subquery at the end to ensure the OrderID is a legitimate one for the current user:

```
<CFIF IsDefined("URL.OrderID")>
  <CFQUERY NAME="GetDetail" DATASOURCE="#DataSource#">
    SELECT m.MerchName, oi.ItemPrice, oi.OrderQty
    FROM Merchandise m, MerchandiseOrdersItems oi
    WHERE m.MerchID = oi.ItemID
    AND oi.OrderID  = #URL.OrderID#
    AND oi.OrderID IN
      (SELECT o.OrderID FROM MerchandiseOrders o
       WHERE o.ContactID = #SESSION.Auth.ContactID#)
  </CFQUERY>
</CFIF>
```

Another way to phrase the query, using an additional join, would be

```
<CFIF IsDefined("URL.OrderID")>
  <CFQUERY NAME="GetDetail" DATASOURCE="#DataSource#">
    SELECT
      m.MerchName, m.MerchPrice,
      oi.ItemPrice, oi.OrderQty
    FROM
    (Merchandise m INNER JOIN
    MerchandiseOrdersItems oi
      ON m.MerchID = oi.ItemID) INNER JOIN
    MerchandiseOrders o
      ON o.OrderID = oi.OrderID
    WHERE o.ContactID = #SESSION.Auth.ContactID#
      AND oi.OrderID  = #URL.OrderID#
  </CFQUERY>
</CFIF>
```

With either of these snippets, if the user alters the OrderID in the URL, it doesn't matter. Because the ContactID is now part of the query's WHERE criteria, it will return zero records if the requested OrderID is not consistent with the session's authenticated ContactID. Thus, the user will only ever be able to view his own orders.

PUTTING IT TOGETHER AND GETTING INTERACTIVE

The `OrderHistory2.cfm` template shown in Listing 21.5 builds on the previous version (refer to Listing 21.4) by adding the ability for the user to view details about each order. The code is a bit longer than before, but there really aren't any big surprises here. The main additions are to display the detail information. Some formatting has also been applied to make the template look nicer when displayed to the user.

LISTING 21.5 `OrderHistory2.cfm`—SAFELY PROVIDING DETAILS ABOUT A USER'S ORDERS

```
<!---
  Filename:     OrderHistory2.cfm
  Created by:   Nate Weiss (NMW)
  Date Created: 3/5/2001
--->

<!--- Retrieve user's orders, based on ContactID --->
<CFQUERY NAME="GetOrders" DATASOURCE="#DataSource#">
  SELECT OrderID, OrderDate,
    (SELECT Count(*)
     FROM MerchandiseOrdersItems oi
     WHERE oi.OrderID = o.OrderID) AS ItemCount
  FROM MerchandiseOrders o
  WHERE ContactID = #SESSION.Auth.ContactID#
  ORDER BY OrderDate DESC
</CFQUERY>

<!--- Determine if a numeric OrderID was passed in URL --->
<CFSET ShowDetail = IsDefined("URL.OrderID") AND IsNumeric(URL.OrderID)>

<!--- If an OrderID was passed, get details for order --->
<!--- Query must check against ContactID for security --->
<CFIF ShowDetail>
  <CFQUERY NAME="GetDetail" DATASOURCE="#DataSource#">
    SELECT m.MerchName, oi.ItemPrice, oi.OrderQty
    FROM Merchandise m, MerchandiseOrdersItems oi
    WHERE m.MerchID = oi.ItemID
    AND oi.OrderID  = #URL.OrderID#
    AND oi.OrderID IN
      (SELECT o.OrderID FROM MerchandiseOrders o
       WHERE o.ContactID = #SESSION.Auth.ContactID#)
  </CFQUERY>

  <!--- If no Detail records, don't show detail --->
  <!--- User may be trying to "hack" URL params --->
  <CFIF GetDetail.RecordCount EQ 0>
    <CFSET ShowDetail = False>
  </CFIF>
</CFIF>


<HTML>
<HEAD>
  <TITLE>Your Order History</TITLE>
```

an easy way to set up various access levels, where `1` might be for normal employees, `2` for supervisors, `3` for managers, `4` for executives, and `100` for developers. So, if only security level `3` and above should be able to view a page, you could do something similar to this:

```
<CFIF SESSION.Auth.UserLevel LT 3>
  Access denied!
  <CFABORT>
</CFIF>
```

Access Rights, Users, and Groups

Depending on the application, you might need something more sophisticated than what is suggested in the previous code snippets. If so, you might want to consider creating database tables to represent some notion of access rights, users, and groups. A typical implementation would establish a many-to-many relationship between users and groups, so that a user can be in more than one group and each group can have any number of users. In addition, a one-to-many relationship generally would exist between groups and access rights. Tables with names such as `GroupsUsers` and `GroupsRights` would maintain the relationships.

After the tables were in place, you could adapt the code examples in this chapter to enforce the rules established by the tables. For instance, assuming that you had a table called `Rights`, which had columns named `RightID` and `RightName`, you might put a query similar to the following after the `GetUser` query in `LoginCheck.cfm` (refer to Listing 21.3):

```
<!--- Find what rights user has from group membership --->
<CFQUERY NAME="GetRights" DATASOURCE="#DataSource#">
  SELECT r.RightName
  FROM Rights r, GroupsContacts gu, GroupsRights gr
  WHERE r.RightID    = gr.RightID
    AND gu.GroupID   = gr.GroupID
    AND gu.ContactID = #SESSION.Auth.ContactID#
</CFQUERY>

<!--- Save comma-separated list of rights in SESSION --->
<CFSET SESSION.Auth.RightsList = ValueList(GetRights.RightName)>
```

Now, `SESSION.Auth.RightsList` would be a list of string values that represented the rights the user should be granted. The user is being granted these rights because the rights have been granted to the groups she is in.

After the previous code is in place, code such as the following could be used to find out whether a particular user is allowed to do something, based on the rights she has actually been granted:

```
<CFIF ListFind(SESSION.Auth.RightsList, "SalesAdmin">
  <A HREF="SalesData.cfm">Sacred Sales Data</A>
</CFIF>
```

or

```
<CFIF NOT ListFind(SESSION.Auth.RightsList, "SellCompany">
  Access denied.
  <CFABORT>
</CFIF>
```

CHAPTER 22

Building Reusable Components

In this chapter

INTRODUCING CFML CUSTOM TAGS

One of the most wonderful things about ColdFusion is its extensibility. A number of methods are available to extend ColdFusion to do things that it doesn't do out of the box. There are a number of fairly traditional, compiled ways you can extend it, such as via Java, C++, servlets, XML, and more. These techniques are covered in detail in our companion volume, *Advanced ColdFusion 5 Application Development* (ISBN: 0-7897-2585-1).

But the coolest, easiest, and perhaps most powerful way to extend ColdFusion is by creating CFML *custom tags*. Custom tags enable you to add your own tags to the CFML language, for whatever purpose you want. Best of all, custom tags are written using ColdFusion's own native language, CFML. This means you already know most of what you need to know and can get started right away.

THE BASIC IDEA

The idea behind custom tags is simple: to enable ColdFusion developers such as yourself to take chunks of ordinary CFML code and package them into reusable modules. From that point on, you can refer to the modules by name, using the familiar tag-based syntax you already expect from ColdFusion. You get to define attributes for your tags, just like regular CFML tags. Your tags can run queries, generate HTML, and perform calculations. There are almost no special requirements or limitations.

Generally, custom tags are written so they are self contained and goal oriented. They take care of whatever processing is necessary to get a particular task, or a set of related tasks, done. Thought of this way, custom tags can be considered a rough equivalent to what many other programming languages would call a *class*, but custom tags aren't as formally defined as that and are not necessarily object oriented. Truth is, custom tags can be many different things, depending on your needs.

WHY MODULARITY IS A GOOD THING

As you soon will see, custom tags are easy to write. However, as easy as they are, you generally need to put a some additional thought into how exactly you want them to work. A process that might take you a half-hour to code as a normal ColdFusion template might take an extra 10 or 15 minutes to implement as a custom tag, because you will need to put some extra thought into how your code should be modularized.

So, if it takes extra time, why bother with all this modularity business? The answer, of course, is that breaking your code into independent, manageable chunks has a number of significant advantages.

MODULARITY MEANS MORE FUN

Let's face it. The idea of creating your own tags—your very own extensions to the CFML language itself—is, well, it's just cool! And the fact that you get to write them using the ordinary ColdFusion syntax you already know and love makes it really easy to get excited about writing them. When you're excited as a programmer, you naturally are more creative, more ambitious, and more productive. There's nothing like a burst of enthusiasm to boost your productivity. It's as close to an adrenaline rush as many of us coders are going to get, at least at our day jobs.

Modularity Means Being Self-Contained

Because custom tags are modular, they usually end up being entirely self contained. For instance, you might create a custom tag called `<CF_PlaceOrder>` that takes care of all aspects of placing an order, whatever that means in practice for your application. Because this custom tag is self contained, other developers can place the tag in their templates wherever they need to, without worrying about what your custom tag actually does internally.

Modules Are Easy to Maintain

In addition, when a custom tag is used, any changes can be made in just one place. Again, consider a hypothetical custom tag called `<CF_PlaceOrder>`. If some new step needs to be added to the actual processing of each order, the custom tag can be updated without anyone needing to touch each template that uses the tag. Additionally, because custom tags generally represent self-contained, well-defined chunks of code that do just one thing and do it well, they usually are easier to maintain by various members of a team. Their single-mindedness and sense of purpose tend to make them more self-documenting and easier to understand than ordinary templates.

Modularity Encourages Code Reuse

Why reinvent the wheel? If someone else already has written code that gets a particular task done, it almost always is easier and more efficient to simply reuse that code, freeing you up to get on to the next item in your schedule. And, conversely, if you write some code that solves a problem, why not package it in such a way that you can easily use it again later?

Modules Can Be Traded or Sold

You don't even have to know how to write a custom tag to take advantage of them. Hundreds of custom tags are available—most of them free—which you can download and use in your own applications. What's more, most publicly available custom tags are unencrypted, so you can adapt them to suit your needs if they do almost what you need them to do but not quite. Of course, you can share your custom tags with others if they help solve a common problem. And, if one of your custom tags is particularly great, others will likely be glad to buy it from you.

How to Use Custom Tags

It is sometimes said that lazy people make the best programmers because they tend to solve problems by taking advantage of proven, working solutions that are already in place. Often, it really is a great idea to reuse work that others have done. So, before you get started on a project or before you tackle a piece of code, you should see whether someone has already written a custom tag that does what you need. If so, you can just use it in your code and move on to your next task. It's almost as if you are getting the entire ColdFusion developer community to help you write the code for your application.

FINDING TAGS ON THE DEVELOPERS EXCHANGE

A number of places are available where you can look for custom tags online. By far, the largest and most popular is the Developers Exchange portion of Allaire's own Web site. Thousands of custom tags are there for the taking. In many situations, a simple search will reveal that someone else has already solved your problem for you.

The Developers Exchange is located at `http://www.allaire.com/developer/gallery`. You can run keyword searches to find tags or browse through tags by category, popularity, or the date they were posted (see Figure 22.1).

Note

Other items are available besides custom tags at the Developers Exchange, so when you run a search, be sure to specify that you want to find custom tags only.

Tip

Another good place to look for custom tags is the CFXtras site, at `http://www.cfxtras.com`.

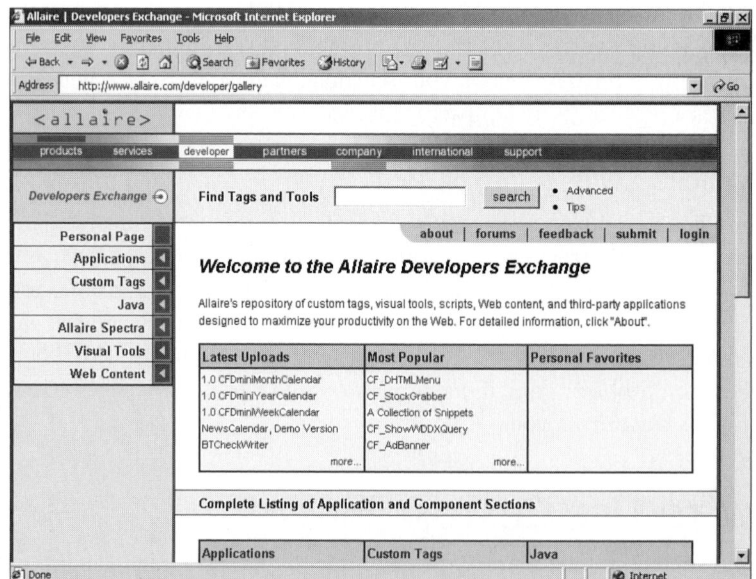

Figure 22.1
The Developers Exchange on the Allaire Web site is a great place to look for publicly available custom tags.

How to Install a Custom Tag

Each custom tag is represented by a single ColdFusion template (.cfm) file. Generally, the .cfm file and some type of documentation are placed together in a .zip file for easy downloading.

There really isn't any special installation step. All you have to do is place the custom tag template into the special `CustomTags` folder on your ColdFusion server's drive.

To install a custom tag, follow these steps:

1. Find the custom tag you want and download the .zip file that contains the tag. If you have been given the .cfm file directly, rather than in a .zip file, go to step 3.
2. Open the .zip file, using a utility such as WinZip from `http://www.winzip.com`, and find the custom tag template (.cfm) file itself. The template's filename will be the name of the custom tag, without the `CF_` prefix. So, if you have downloaded a custom tag called `<CF_PlaceOrder>`, you should look for a file called `PlaceOrder.cfm`.
3. Place the custom tag template file into the `CustomTags` folder, which is located within the `CFUSION` folder on your ColdFusion server's drive. In a default Windows installation, this is the `c:\CFUSION\CustomTags` folder.

That's it. The custom tag is now installed, and you can start using it in your code.

Tip

If you want to organize the custom tag templates you download (or write yourself) into subfolders within the `CustomTags` folder, go ahead. As long as they are somewhere within the `CustomTags` folder, ColdFusion will find them and let you use them in your applications.

Note

If you don't have access to the special `CustomTags` folder, or if you plan to use the custom tag in just one or two of your own templates, you can just place the custom tag template into the folder where you plan to use it. See "Placing Custom Tags in the Current Directory," later in this chapter.

Note

Some custom tags might require other tags or files to be present as well. The documentation that comes with the tag should point out what you need to know.

Note

If, after you download a tag, you find that no ColdFusion template exists with the appropriate filename, you might have downloaded a *CFX tag*, which is different from a CFML custom tag. CFX tags are compiled with a language such as Java or C++ and must be registered in the ColdFusion Administrator before they can be used. Instead of a template (.cfm) file, they are represented by one or more Dynamic Link Library (.dll) or Java Class (.class) files. See Chapter 30, "ColdFusion Server Configuration," for details.

USING CUSTOM TAGS

After you install a custom tag by placing its template in the special `CustomTags` folder, you are ready to use it in your code. For your convenience, two custom tags have been included on this book's CD-ROM for you, in the folder for this chapter. The custom tags are included as .zip files, just as if you had downloaded them from the Developers Exchange (shown previously in Figure 22.1) or some other source. Table 22.1 provides information about the tags.

Before you try the following code listings, install these tags according to the directions in the last section. That is, extract the `CoolImage.cfm` and `TwoSelectsRelated.cfm` templates from the Zip files included on the CD-ROM, and place them in the special `CustomTags` folder on your ColdFusion server.

TABLE 22.1 THIRD-PARTY CUSTOM TAGS INCLUDED ON THE CD-ROM FOR THIS CHAPTER

Custom Tag	Custom Tag Template	What It Does
`<CF_CoolImage>`	`CoolImage.cfm` (in `CoolImage.zip`)	Creates a rollover image on the current page. When a user hovers the mouse over the image, the image changes to something else (usually a glowing or highlighted version of the first image).
`<CF_TwoSelectsRelated>`	`TwoSelectsRelated.cfm` (in `TwoSelectsRelated.zip`)	Places two correlated `<SELECT>`lists or drop-down lists on the current page. When the user selects an item in the first list, the choices in the second list change.

USING `<CF_CoolImage>`

Users and graphic designers seem to love rollover images, in which an image changes when you move your mouse over it, usually to suggest that the image is live and can (should! must!) be clicked. Normally, you must write or borrow some JavaScript to get this done.

Listing 22.1 shows how you can use the `<CF_CoolImage>` custom tag to easily place a rollover image on one of your pages. If you visit this listing in your Web browser, you will see that the image does indeed roll over properly when you move your mouse over it.

Listing 22.1 UseCoolImage.cfm—**Using the <CF_CoolImage> Custom Tag to Create a Rollover Effect**

```
<HTML>
<HEAD><TITLE>Using a Custom Tag</TITLE></HEAD>
<BODY>
<H2>Using a Custom Tag</H2>
Hover your mouse over the logo, baby, yeah!<P>

  <!--- Display a "Mouse Rollover" Image via groovy --->
  <!--- <CF_CoolImage> Custom Tag by Jeremy Allaire --->
  <!--- The tag will include all needed code for us --->
  <CF_CoolImage
    ImgName="MyImage"
    Src="Logo.gif"
    OverSrc="LogoOver.gif"
    Width="300"
    Height="51"
    Border="0"
    HREF="http://www.macromedia.com/"
    Alt="Click for Macromedia Home Page">

</BODY>
</HTML>
```

The attributes for `<CF_CoolImage>` are fairly self-explanatory and are not detailed here (you can look them up on the Developers Exchange if you want). The purpose of this listing is to show you how to use a custom tag in your code and give you a sense of the types of things you can do with custom tags.

Note

If memory serves, this was one of the very first custom tags ever posted for public download. It was written by none other than Jeremy Allaire, one of the fathers of ColdFusion. This author remembers very fondly when he first saw it, only then realizing what custom tags were really all about. The tag has since been improved on a bit by others, but it remains a classic and is quite interesting as a bit of history!

Thinking About Custom Tags As Abstractions

If you visit `UseCoolImage.cfm` and then view its HTML code using your browser's View Source option, you will see that all the appropriate JavaScript and HTML code has been generated for you, based on the attributes you provided to the tag in Listing 22.1. There isn't space to go into a line-by-line explanation of the generated code here, but because the custom tag takes care of writing it correctly for you, you don't really *need* to understand it.

In fact, that's the great thing about the tag. It enables you to focus on the task at hand—inserting a rollover image—without worrying about the actual code you normally would need to write. It enables you to think about the rollover at a higher, or more abstract, level. Developers often refer to this type of phenomenon as *abstraction*.

The more a tag wraps up several concepts or coding steps into one task-based or goal-oriented chunk, the more the tag can be said to be a helpful abstraction of the underlying concepts. In more formal languages, the process of abstraction often becomes locked up in rules about object-orientation or classes. ColdFusion doesn't impose any such rules; you are free to make your custom tags do whatever you want them to and have them represent whatever level of abstraction you feel is appropriate.

Tip

Of course, if you want to know more about the JavaScript code generated by `<CF_CoolImage>`, you can easily decipher it with the help of a JavaScript reference text or online JavaScript tutorial.

USING `<CF_TwoSelectsRelated>`

So you can begin to get a sense of the variety of effects and behaviors you can get from custom tags, here is another example, this time using the `<CF_TwoSelectsRelated>` custom tag, which is also included on this book's CD-ROM. This custom tag enables you to quickly add two `<SELECT>` lists to your page, which become actively correlated via JavaScript. Again, the goal of the tag is to present developers with an abstraction of the basic idea of related inputs, without each developer needing to concentrate on getting the tedious JavaScript code exactly right.

Listing 22.2 shows how the tag can be used in your own applications. Here, it is used to display a list of ratings. When the user clicks a rating in the first list, the corresponding list of films is displayed in the second list, as shown in Figure 22.2.

LISTING 22.2 `UsingTwoSelectsRelated.cfm`—USING THE `<CF_TwoSelectsRelated>` TAG TO DISPLAY CORRELATED INFORMATION

```
<!--- Get ratings and associated films from database --->
<CFQUERY DATASOURCE="ows" NAME="GetRatedFilms">
  SELECT
    r.RatingID, r.Rating,
    f.FilmID, f.MovieTitle
  FROM FilmsRatings r INNER JOIN Films f
  ON r.RatingID = f.RatingID
  ORDER BY r.RatingID, f.MovieTitle
</CFQUERY>


<HTML>
<HEAD><TITLE>Using a Custom Tag</TITLE></HEAD>
<BODY>
<H2>Using a Custom Tag</H2>

  <!--- This custom tag will only work in a form --->
  <FORM>

    <!--- Show ratings and films in correlated SELECT lists --->
    <!--- via custom tag, which generates all needed script --->
```

```
    <CF_TwoSelectsRelated
      QUERY="GetRatedFilms"
      NAME1="RatingID"
      NAME2="FilmID"
      DISPLAY1="Rating"
      DISPLAY2="MovieTitle"
      SIZE1="5"
      SIZE2="5"
      FORCEWIDTH1="30"
      FORCEWIDTH2="50">

  </FORM>

</BODY>
</HTML>
```

This code queries the Orange Whip Studios database to get a list of ratings and related films. The query variable is then provided to the `QUERY` attribute of the `<CF_TwoSelectsRelated>` custom tag. When the tag executes, it outputs two ordinary `<SELECT>` tags—the first with a `NAME` attribute as provided to the `NAME1` attribute of the custom tag and the other with a `NAME` attribute as provided to `NAME2`. The appropriate number of `<OPTION>` tags is also generated for each `<SELECT>` list, with each `<OPTION>`'s display text and `VALUE` attribute coming from the results of the `GetRatedFilms` query, as specified by the `VALUE1`, `VALUE2`, `DISPLAY1`, and `DISPLAY2` attributes provided to the custom tag. In addition, the appropriate JavaScript code is generated to give the lists an actively related effect. If you visit Listing 22.2 in your browser, you can test the behavior. And if you view the page's source code using your browser's View Source option, you will see that about 75 lines of HTML and JavaScript code were generated for you, depending on the actual records in the database.

Again, the purpose of this listing is not to teach you the syntax for this custom tag in particular (you can learn more about that in the tag's documentation, which is included in the .zip on the CD-ROM), as much as it is to give you an idea about how to use custom tags and the types of things they can do for you.

Changing the Custom Tag Search Path

As you have already learned, when you use a custom tag in one of your ColdFusion templates, the ColdFusion Application Server looks in the special `CustomTags` folder for the corresponding custom tag template. So, when you use the `<CF_TwoSelectsRelated>` custom tag in your own code, ColdFusion looks for the `TwoSelectsRelated.cfm` file in the `c:\CFUSION\CustomTags` folder (assuming you are running ColdFusion on a Windows machine and accepted the default installation options).

If you want, you can change the location of the special `CustomTags` folder or specify additional folders for ColdFusion to look in. For instance, say you want to place the custom tags for the Orange Whip Studios project in a folder called `C:\OrangeWhipCustomTags`, instead of `C:\CFUSION\CustomTags`. ColdFusion lets you add this new folder to the *custom tag search path*. The custom tag search path is simply a list of folders ColdFusion looks through whenever you call a custom tag in one of your application templates. When ColdFusion is first installed, only one folder is in the search path (the `CustomTags` folder within `CFUSION`).

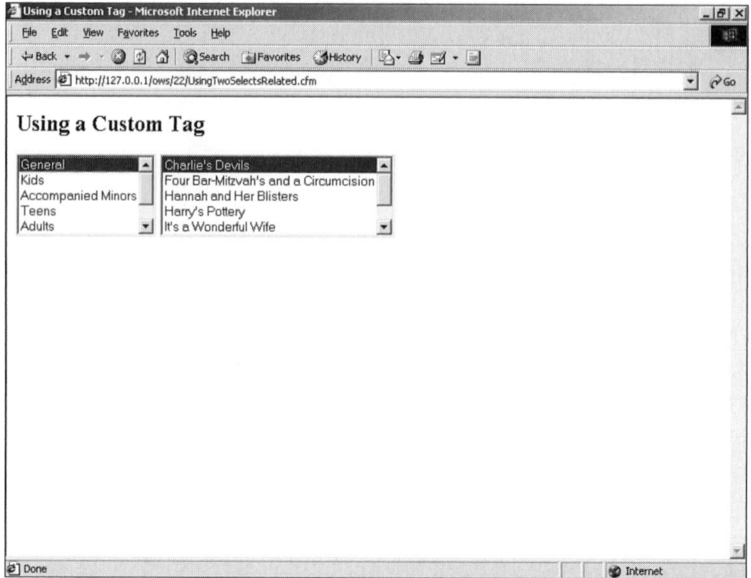

Figure 22.2
Some custom tags create user-interface widgets, such as these related select lists.

After a new folder is added to the search path, you are free to place some custom tags in the new folder and others in the original `CustomTags` folder. Now, when you first refer to a custom tag in your own templates, the ColdFusion server first looks in the special `CustomTags` folder (and its subfolders) and then in your newly specified folder (and any of its subfolders).

Note

If all this path searching sounds like a lot of overhead for ColdFusion to incur, don't worry. After ColdFusion successfully finds a custom tag template in the search paths you have configured, it remembers the template's location for all subsequent requests (until the server is restarted or until the server's template cache is exhausted). In other words, the custom tag search path is searched only once per custom tag per server restart, so there isn't much of a penalty for adding folders to the search path.

Tip

If you are familiar with Java, you will recognize that the custom tag search path is comparable to the class path for the Java interpreter.

To add a folder to the custom tag search path, follow these steps:

1. Navigate to the Custom Tag Paths page of the ColdFusion Administrator.
2. Specify the path and name of the folder you want to add to the custom tag search path, as shown in Figure 22.3. You can use the Browse Server button to avoid having to type the folder's path manually.
3. Click the Add Path button. The new folder appears in the list of custom tag paths.
4. Now you can place your custom tag templates in the folder you just added or in the original.

You also can remove folders from the custom tag search path, using the Delete button shown in Figure 22.3. After you remove a folder from the search path, ColdFusion will no longer find custom tag templates in that folder.

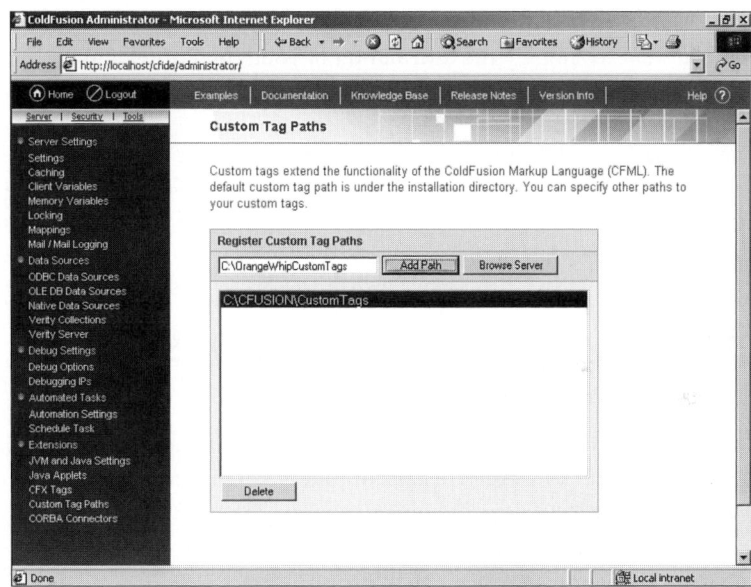

Figure 22.3
You can add folders to the custom tag search path with the ColdFusion Administrator.

> **Note**
>
> Throughout this chapter, you will find instructions to save files in the special `CustomTags` folder. Whenever the `CustomTags` folder is mentioned, you could also use any folders that you might have added to the custom tag search path.

Placing Custom Tags in the Current Directory

Sometimes placing custom tag templates in the special `CustomTags` folder is not possible or convenient (see the section "How to Install a Custom Tag," earlier in this chapter). For instance, if your ColdFusion application is being hosted by an Internet service provider (ISP), you might not have access to the `CustomTags` folder.

In such a situation, you can place the custom tag template (`CoolImage.cfm`, for example) in the same folder as the template you want to actually use the custom tag in. When ColdFusion encounters the custom tag in your code, it first will look for the appropriate file in the current folder. (It will not automatically look in the parent folder or subfolders of the current folder.) If ColdFusion can't find the .cfm file for the custom tag in the current folder, it then will look in the special `CustomTags` folder (and its subfolders).

Placing the custom tag template in the current folder is a good solution when

- You don't have access to the special `CustomTags` folder, as mentioned previously.
- You are still developing and testing the custom tag.
- You know you won't use the custom tag extensively, so you don't mind it being available only to code templates in the current folder.
- You want to simplify the distribution of your application and would therefore rather not require that the custom tag template be dealt with separately.

These situations aside, it is generally recommended that you use the special `CustomTags` folder as described earlier in this chapter. You will be able to find all your custom tags in one place, and you won't have to maintain multiple copies of the same custom tag template (one for each folder in which you want to use the tag).

CONTROLLING TEMPLATE LOCATIONS WITH <CFMODULE>

ColdFusion provides an alternative way to use custom tags in your templates, which is helpful in a number of situations. Instead of calling your custom tags using the usual `<CF_` prefix, you use the `<CFMODULE>` tag. You don't need to change anything in the custom tag template itself. Any custom tag can be used with either method.

INTRODUCING THE <CFMODULE> TAG

The `<CFMODULE>` tag is used to execute a ColdFusion template as a *module*, which is just another name for a CFML custom tag. Basically, you specify which custom tag you want to use by using the `NAME` or `TEMPLATE` attribute. Then, you add whatever additional attributes you need to pass to the tag, just as you would if you were calling the module using the normal `<CF_`-style custom tag syntax.

Table 22.2 explains the attributes you can supply to the `<CFMODULE>` tag.

Note

You provide either the `NAME` attribute *or* the `TEMPLATE` attribute when using `<CFMODULE>`. You do not provide both.

TABLE 22.2 <CFMODULE> TAG SYNTAX

Attribute	Purpose
NAME	The name of the custom tag you want to use, not including the <CF_ prefix. ColdFusion will look for the tag in the current folder and then the special CustomTags folder, just as it would if you were calling the custom tag normally. So, instead of using <CF_FilmRecord> in your code, you would use <CFMODULE> with NAME="FilmRecord".
TEMPLATE	The filename of the custom tag template, including the .cfm extension. You can provide a relative path to the template, just like the TEMPLATE attribute of the <CFINCLUDE> tag. ColdFusion will not automatically look for the tag in the special CustomTags folder because you are specifying the location explicitly. So, instead of using <CF_FilmRecord> in your code, you might use <CFMODULE> with TEMPLATE="FilmRecord.cfm".
ATTRIBUTECOLLECTION	Optional, and for special cases only. A structure that contains name/value pairs to be considered as attributes. See the section "Passing Attributes with ATTRIBUTECOLLECTION," later in this chapter.

CALLING MODULES BY NAME

As mentioned previously, you can use <CFMODULE> to call modules either by name with the NAME attribute or by template location with the TEMPLATE attribute. In this section, you learn about calling modules by name.

UNDERSTANDING THE NAME ATTRIBUTE

At its simplest, you can use <CFMODULE> to call custom tags by simply providing the name of the tag, without the customary <CF_ prefix. ColdFusion will use the same logic as it does normally to find the corresponding template file (first looking in the current directory and then looking in the special CustomTags folder). Provide <CFMODULE> with whatever additional attributes you normally would supply to the custom tag.

For instance, you might have a custom tag called <CF_FilmRecord>, which is normally called with two attributes called Action and FilmID, like this:

```
<!--- Delete movie --->
<CF_FilmRecord
  Action="Delete"
  FilmID="5">
```

To call the tag with <CFMODULE>, you would use the following:

```
<!--- Delete movie --->
<CFMODULE
  NAME="FilmRecord"
  Action="Delete"
  FilmID="5">
```

No huge advantage exists to using <CFMODULE> in this way, over the traditional <CF_ method. As shown previously, it is simply an alternative syntax you can use if you prefer.

Note

One advantage, which can be helpful in certain situations, is that the NAME attribute can be determined dynamically. For example, you could create a string variable called CallThisModule, which would hold the name of the module you wanted to call—based on whatever logic you needed. You could then call <CFMODULE> with TEMPLATE="#CallThisModule#" to execute the module. There would be no way to accomplish this using the traditional <CF_ syntax.

USING DOT NOTATION TO AVOID CONFLICTS

As you learned earlier, you can place custom tag templates anywhere within the special CustomTags folder. You can place them in the CustomTags folder itself, or you can create any number of folders and subfolders with the CustomTags folder. (see the section "Using Custom Tags," earlier in this chapter).

In general, this is a great feature. The only problem is that more than one custom tag with the same filename could exist. For instance, what if two of your Web applications are running on the same ColdFusion server, and both use <CF_PlaceOrder> custom tags that do different things internally? You could place one in a subfolder of CustomTags called OrangeWhip and the other in a subfolder called PetStore, but you would have no way to tell ColdFusion which one of these to actually use at any given time. ColdFusion would simply use the first one it found for all requests, regardless of which folder the calling template was in.

To address this type of situation, ColdFusion allows you to use dot notation in <CFMODULE>'s NAME attribute, where the dots indicate subfolders within the special CustomTags folder.

For instance, to specify that you want to use the version of the PlaceOrder module located within the OrangeWhip subfolder of the CustomTags folder, you would use the following:

```
<!--- Place order via custom tag --->
<CFMODULE
  NAME="OrangeWhip.PlaceOrder">
```

Or, to specify that you want to use the custom tag template FilmRecord.cfm that is located in a folder called TagObjects within a folder called OrangeWhip within the special CustomTags folder, you would use the following:

```
<!--- Delete movie --->
<CFMODULE
  NAME="OrangeWhip.TagObjects.FilmRecord"
  Action="Delete"
  FilmID="5">
```

As you can see, the ability to use this special dot notation enables you to set up hierarchies of custom tag modules, simply by establishing subfolders nested within the special CustomTags folder. This can be important if your application will be installed on a server along with other ColdFusion applications.

CALLING MODULES BY TEMPLATE LOCATION

You also can use <CFMODULE> with its TEMPLATE attribute, instead of the NAME attribute, to explicitly specify the location of your custom tag template. Use this method in situations in which you don't want ColdFusion to attempt to find your tag's template automatically (in the current folder or the CustomTags folder or anywhere else).

Note

The TEMPLATE attribute effectively takes away the magic effect of your custom tags appearing to become part of ColdFusion. As such, using the word *module* instead of *custom tag* starts to make more sense.

The TEMPLATE attribute works just like the TEMPLATE attribute of the <CFINCLUDE> tag. You can provide a relative path to the template, using slashes to indicate subdirectories. You can also use the usual URL-style ../ notation to indicate the parent folder.

For instance, just as all images for the Orange Whip Studios project are being stored in the images subfolder within the ows folder, you could keep all your modules within a subfolder called modules. Then, assuming you want to call a template from a different subfolder of ows (such as a subfolder called 22 for this chapter of this book), you could refer to the custom tag template using a relative path that starts with ../modules/, as shown in the following code.

So, instead of this:

```
<!--- Delete movie --->
<CF_FilmRecord
  Action="Delete"
  FilmID="5">
```

or this

```
<!--- Delete movie --->
<CFMODULE
  NAME="FilmRecord"
  Action="Delete"
  FilmID="5">
```

you might use something such as this:

```
<!--- Delete movie --->
<CFMODULE
  TEMPLATE="../modules/FilmRecord.cfm"
  Action="Delete"
  FilmID="5">
```

Note

You can't provide an absolute filesystem-style path to the TEMPLATE attribute, so drive letters or UNC paths are not allowed.

WRITING CUSTOM TAGS THAT DISPLAY INFORMATION

Now that you understand how to use existing custom tags, it's time to learn how to write your own. This section introduces you to the basic concepts involved when creating a custom tag. As you will soon see, it's an easy and productive way to write your code. And it's fun, too!

WRITING YOUR FIRST CUSTOM TAG

It's traditional to illustrate a new language or technique with a "Hello, World" example. Listing 22.3 shows a custom tag that outputs a `"Hello, World"` message in the current Web page, formatted with ordinary HTML table syntax.

Be sure to save this listing as `HelloWorld.cfm`. Remember, you can save it in either the special `CustomTags` folder or the same folder you are using as you follow along in this chapter.

LISTING 22.3 `HelloWorld.cfm`—**A SIMPLE CUSTOM TAG TEMPLATE**

```
<TABLE BORDER="5" CELLPADDING="5">
  <TR><TH BGCOLOR="Yellow">
    <B>Hello, World, from Orange Whip Studios.</B><BR>
  </TH></TR>
  <TR><TD BGCOLOR="Orange">
    Orange whip... two orange whips... three orange whips!<BR>
  </TD></TR>
</TABLE>
```

Now, you can use the custom tag just by adding a `CF_` prefix to the tag's filename (without the `.cfm` part). This means that you have just created a custom tag called `<CF_HelloWorld>`, which can be used in code as shown in Listing 22.4.

LISTING 22.4 `UsingHelloWorld.cfm`—**TESTING THE** `<CF_HelloWorld>` **CUSTOM TAG**

```
<HTML>
<HEAD><TITLE>Testing &lt;CF_HelloWorld&gt;</TITLE></HEAD>
<BODY>

  <!--- Display Hello World Message, via Custom Tag --->
  <CF_HelloWorld>

</BODY>
</HTML>
```

It's a start, but this custom tag is not terribly exciting. Of course, it will always output the same exact thing. In fact, at this point, you could just replace the reference to the custom tag in Listing 22.4 with an ordinary `<CFINCLUDE>` tag and the results would be the same:

```
<!--- Display Hello World Message, via Custom Tag --->
<CFINCLUDE TEMPLATE="HelloWorld.cfm">
```

Things get a lot more interesting after you start making custom tags that accept attributes, just like ColdFusion's built-in tags.

Introducing the ATTRIBUTES Scope

In order to make your own custom tags really useful, you will want the tags to accept tag attributes, just as normal CFML and HTML tags do. ColdFusion makes this very easy by defining a special ATTRIBUTES scope for use within your custom tag templates.

The ATTRIBUTES scope is a ColdFusion structure that is automatically populated with any attributes provided to the custom tag when it is actually used in code. For instance, if an attribute called Message is provided to a tag, as in

```
<CF_HelloWorld Message="Country and Western">
```

then the special ATTRIBUTES scope will contain a Message value, set to Country and Western. You could output this value onto the page by referring to #ATTRIBUTES.Message# between <CFOUTPUT> tags within the custom tag template.

Outputting Attribute Values

Listing 22.5 shows another custom tag called <CF_HelloWorldMessage>, which is almost the same as <CF_HelloWorld> from Listing 22.3. The difference is the fact that this tag accepts an attribute called Message, which gets displayed as part of the "Hello, World" message, as shown in Figure 22.4.

Listing 22.5 HelloWorldMessage.cfm—Defining Attributes for Your Custom Tags

```
<!--- Tag Attributes --->
<CFPARAM NAME="ATTRIBUTES.Message" TYPE="string">

<!--- Output message in HTML table format --->
<TABLE BORDER="5" CELLPADDING="5">
  <TR><TH BGCOLOR="Yellow">
    <B>Hello, World, from Orange Whip Studios.</B><BR>
  </TH></TR>
  <TR><TD BGCOLOR="Orange">
    <CFOUTPUT>#ATTRIBUTES.Message#</CFOUTPUT><BR>
  </TD></TR>
</TABLE>
```

The <CFPARAM> tag at the top of Listing 22.5 makes it clear that a Message parameter is expected to be provided to the tag and that it is expected to be a string value. The <CFOUTPUT> block near the end outputs the value of the Message parameter provided to the tag, as shown in Figure 22.4. Listing 22.6 shows how to supply the Message parameter the tag now expects.

Note

For this listing to work, you must save the previous listing (Listing 22.5) as HelloWorldMessage.cfm, either in the same folder as Listing 22.6 or in the special CustomTags folder.

LISTING 22.6 `UsingHelloWorldMessage.cfm`**—SUPPLYING ATTRIBUTES TO YOUR CUSTOM TAGS**

```
<HTML>
<HEAD><TITLE>Testing &lt;CF_HelloWorldMessage&gt;</TITLE></HEAD>
<BODY>

  <!--- Display Hello World Message, via Custom Tag --->
  <CF_HelloWorldMessage
    Message="We're getting the band back together!">

</BODY>
</HTML>
```

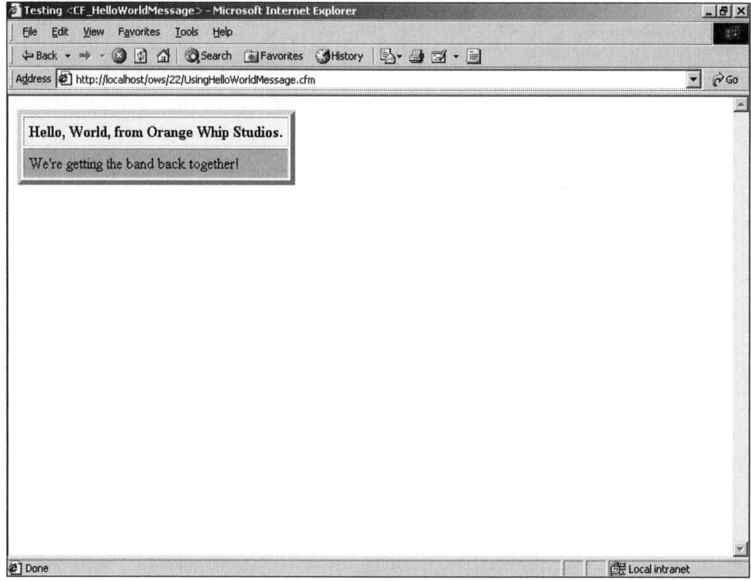

Figure 22.4
The `<CF_HelloWorldMessage>` custom tag displays any message in a consistent manner.

Note

Attribute names are not case sensitive. There is no way to determine whether a parameter was passed to a tag with code such as `Message="Hello"` or `MESSAGE="Hello"`. Of course, the case of each attribute's value is preserved, so there is a difference between `Message="Hello"` and `Message="HELLO"`.

USING `<CFPARAM>` TO DECLARE ATTRIBUTES

You actually don't *have* to include the `<CFPARAM>` tag in Listing 22.5. As long as the `Message` attribute is actually provided when the tag is used, and as long as the parameter is a string value, the `<CFPARAM>` tag doesn't do anything. It only has any effect if the attribute is omitted (or provided with a value that can't be converted to a string), in which case it displays an error message.

However, we strongly suggest that you declare each of a custom tag's attributes with a <CFPARAM> tag at the top of the tag's template, for the following reasons:

- Always having your custom tag's attributes formally listed as <CFPARAM> tags at the top of your templates makes your custom tag code clearer and more self-documenting.
- Specifying the expected data type with <CFPARAM>'s TYPE attribute acts as a convenient sanity check in case someone tries to use your tag in an unexpected way.
- If you declare all your tag's attributes using <CFPARAM> tags at the top of a tag's template, you know that the rest of the template will never run if the attributes are not provided properly when the tag is actually used. This prevents problems or data inconsistencies that could arise from partially executed code.
- As discussed in the next section, you easily can make any of your tag's attributes optional by simply adding a DEFAULT attribute for the corresponding <CFPARAM> tag.

See Chapter 10, "CFML Basics," for more information about the <CFPARAM> tag.

Note

You can use the <CFTRY> and <CFCATCH> tags to provide friendly error messages when the attributes passed to a custom tag do not comply with the rules imposed by the custom tag's <CFPARAM> tags. See the version of the <CF_PlaceOrder> custom tag presented in Chapter 33, "Error Handling," for an example.

MAKING ATTRIBUTES OPTIONAL OR REQUIRED

When you are first working on a new custom tag, one of the most important things to consider is which attributes your new tag will take. You want to ensure that the attribute names are as clear, intuitive, and self-describing as possible.

Often, you will want to make certain attributes *optional*, so they can be omitted when the tag is actually used. That way, you can provide lots of attributes (and thus a lot of flexibility and customizability) for your tags, without over-burdening users of your tags with a lot of unnecessary typing if they just want a tag's normal behavior.

USING <CFPARAM> TO ESTABLISH DEFAULT VALUES

The most straightforward way to declare an optional attribute for a custom tag is to provide a DEFAULT attribute to the corresponding <CFPARAM> tag at the top of the tag's template.

For instance, take a look at the version of the <CF_HelloWorldMessage> tag shown in Listing 22.7. This version is the same as the previous one (shown previously in Listing 22.5), except that it defines five new attributes: TopMessage, TopColor, BottomColor, TableBorder, and TablePadding. The values are given sensible default values using the DEFAULT attribute.

LISTING 22.7 `HelloWorldMessage2.cfm`**—MAKING CERTAIN ATTRIBUTES OPTIONAL**

```
<!--- Tag Attributes --->
<CFPARAM NAME="ATTRIBUTES.Message" TYPE="string">
<CFPARAM NAME="ATTRIBUTES.TopMessage" TYPE="string"
  DEFAULT="Hello, World, from Orange Whip Studios.">
<CFPARAM NAME="ATTRIBUTES.TopColor" TYPE="string" DEFAULT="Yellow">
<CFPARAM NAME="ATTRIBUTES.BottomColor" TYPE="string" DEFAULT="Orange">
<CFPARAM NAME="ATTRIBUTES.TableBorder" TYPE="numeric" DEFAULT="5">
<CFPARAM NAME="ATTRIBUTES.TablePadding" TYPE="numeric" DEFAULT="5">

<!--- Output message in HTML table format --->
<CFOUTPUT>
  <TABLE BORDER="#ATTRIBUTES.TableBorder#"
➥CELLPADDING="#ATTRIBUTES.TablePadding#">
    <TR><TH BGCOLOR="#ATTRIBUTES.TopColor#">
      <B>#ATTRIBUTES.TopMessage#</B><BR>
    </TH></TR>
    <TR><TD BGCOLOR="#ATTRIBUTES.BottomColor#">
      #ATTRIBUTES.Message#<BR>
    </TD></TR>
  </TABLE>
</CFOUTPUT>
```

So, if the tag is explicitly provided with a `TopColor` value when it is used, that value will be available as `ATTRIBUTES.TopColor`. If not, the `DEFAULT` attribute of the `<CFPARAM>` tag kicks in and provides the default value of `Yellow`. The same goes for the other new attributes: If values are supplied at runtime, the supplied values are used; if not, the default values kick in.

Tip

There's generally no harm in defining more attributes than you think people will usually need, as long as you supply default values for them. As a rule of thumb, you can try to provide attributes for just about every string or number used by your tag, rather than hard-coding them. This is what Listing 22.7 does.

Assuming you save Listing 22.7 as a custom tag template called `HelloWorldMessage.cfm`, you would now be able to use any of the following in your application templates:

```
<CF_HelloWorldMessage
  Message="We're getting the band back together!">

<CF_HelloWorldMessage
  TopMessage="Message of the Day"
  Message="We're getting the band back together!">

<CF_HelloWorldMessage
  Message="We're getting the band back together!"
  TopColor="Beige"
  BottomColor="##FFFFFF"
  TableBorder="0">
```

USING FUNCTIONS TO TEST FOR ATTRIBUTES

Instead of using the <CFPARAM> tag, you can use the IsDefined() function to test for the existence of tag attributes. This is largely a matter of personal preference. For instance, instead of this:

```
<CFPARAM NAME="ATTRIBUTES.Message" TYPE="string">
```

you could do this:

```
<CFIF IsDefined("ATTRIBUTES.Message") EQ "No">
  <CFABORT SHOWERROR="You must provide a Message attribute">
</CFIF>
```

Or, instead of this:

```
<CFPARAM NAME="ATTRIBUTES.TopColor" TYPE="string" DEFAULT="Yellow">
```

you could do this:

```
<CFIF NOT IsDefined("ATTRIBUTES.TopColor")>
  <CFSET ATTRIBUTES.TopColor="Yellow">
</CFIF>
```

Note

Because the ATTRIBUTES scope is implemented as a ColdFusion structure, you also can use CFML's various structure functions to test for the existence of tag attributes. For instance, instead of IsDefined("Attributes.TopColor")—shown in the previous code snippet—you could use StructKeyExists(ATTRIBUTES, "TopColor") to get the same effect.

Tip

Because the special ATTRIBUTES scope exists only when a template is being called as a custom tag, you can use IsDefined("ATTRIBUTES") if you want to be able to detect whether the template is being visited on its own or included via a regular <CFINCLUDE> tag.

DECIDING WHO YOU ARE DEVELOPING FOR

Before you get started on a new custom tag, it's often helpful to think about who the audience for your new tag will be. You can keep the audience in mind as you think about the tag's functionality and what its attributes and default behavior should be.

Custom tags generally fall into one of these two groups:

- **Application-Specific Tags**—Display something or perform some type of action that makes sense only within your application (or within your company). These tags generally either have something to do with your application's specific database schema or are in charge of maintaining or participating in some kind of business rules or processes specific to your company. This type of tag extends the CFML language to the exclusive benefit of your application, perhaps creating a kind of tool set for your code's internal use.

- **General-Purpose Tags**—Don't have anything specific to do with your application; instead they provide some type of functionality you might need in a variety of scenarios. Rather than being of interest mainly to yourself or your programming team, these tags are of interest to the ColdFusion developer community at large. This type of tag extends the CFML language for all ColdFusion programmers who download or purchase the tag.

The type of code you use to write the two types of tags is not categorically different. But it is still helpful to keep the tag's audience (which might just be yourself, or could be ColdFusion developers all over the world) in mind as you work. If you are creating an application-specific tag, think about the various people on your team or people who might need to look at the code in the future. If you are creating a general-purpose tag, think about or imagine a few fellow developers, using your tag in various types of contexts.

Now, thinking about these people, ask yourself these questions:

- **How can you name the tag so that its purpose is self-explanatory?** In general, the longer the tag name, the better. Also, the tag name should hint at not only what the tag *does*, but what it *does it to*. So, something such as `<CF_DisplayMovie>` or `<CF_ShowMovieCallout>` is better than just `<CF_Movie>` or `<CF_Display>`, even if the shorter names are easier to type or seem obvious to you.
- **How can you name the attributes so that they are also self-explanatory?** Again, there is usually little harm in using long attribute names. Often, longer attribute names make code that uses the tags more self-documenting.
- **Which attributes will the audience need, and which should be optional versus required?** A good rule of thumb is that the tag's optional attributes should have sensible enough default values so that the tag works in a useful way with only the required attributes. The optional attributes should be gravy.

Tip

> If you want, try to make your tag's name and attribute names come together in such a way that the tag's use in code almost reads like a sentence. It's really great when a tag's purpose can be understood simply from looking at its usage in actual code templates.

QUERYING AND DISPLAYING OUTPUT

Now that you know how to create a custom tag that accepts a few attributes to control its behavior, it's time to try creating a custom tag that really gets something useful done. This section demonstrates how easy creating tags that look up and display information is. You can then reuse these tags throughout your application.

RUNNING QUERIES IN CUSTOM TAGS

You can use any tag in the CFML language within a custom tag template, including `<CFQUERY>`, `<CFOUTPUT>`, and `<CFSET>`. Listing 22.8 takes the movie-display code from the `FeaturedMovie.cfm` template in Chapter 19, "Introducing the Web Application Framework," and turns it into a custom tag called `<CF_ShowMovieCallout>`.

The first half of the `FeaturedMovie.cfm` example randomly determines which of the available movies to show, and the second half queries the database for the selected movie and displays its title, description, and other information. This custom tag does the work of the second half of that example (that is, it just shows a movie's information, without the randomizing aspect). It takes just one required attribute, a numeric attribute called `FilmID`. Within the custom tag, the `ATTRIBUTES.FilmID` value can be used in the criteria for a `<CFQUERY>` to retrieve the appropriate film information.

At its simplest, this tag can be used like the following, which is a neat, tidy, and helpful abstraction of the CFML, HTML, and CSS code the tag generates:

```
<!--- Show movie number five, formatted nicely --->
<CF_ShowMovieCallout
  FilmID=5">
```

LISTING 22.8 `ShowMovieCallout.cfm`—**QUERYING AND DISPLAYING INFORMATION ABOUT A PARTICULAR FILM RECORD**

```
<!---
  <CF_ShowMovieCallout> Custom Tag
  Retrieves and displays the given film

  Example of Use:
  <CF_ShowMovieCallout
    FilmID="5">
--->

<!--- Tag Attributes --->
<!--- FilmID Attribute is Required --->
<CFPARAM NAME="ATTRIBUTES.FilmID" TYPE="numeric">
<!--- Whether to reveal cost/release dates (optional) --->
<CFPARAM NAME="ATTRIBUTES.ShowCost" TYPE="boolean" DEFAULT="Yes">
<CFPARAM NAME="ATTRIBUTES.ShowReleaseDate" TYPE="boolean" DEFAULT="Yes">
<!--- Optional formatting and placement options --->
<CFPARAM NAME="ATTRIBUTES.TableAlign" TYPE="string" DEFAULT="right">
<CFPARAM NAME="ATTRIBUTES.TableWidth" TYPE="string" DEFAULT="150">
<CFPARAM NAME="ATTRIBUTES.Caption" TYPE="string" DEFAULT="Featured Film">
<!--- Use "ows" datasource by default --->
<CFPARAM NAME="ATTRIBUTES.DataSource" TYPE="string" DEFAULT="ows">

<!--- Get important info about film from database --->
<CFQUERY NAME="GetFilm" DATASOURCE="#ATTRIBUTES.DataSource#">
  SELECT
    MovieTitle, Summary,
    AmountBudgeted, DateInTheaters
  FROM Films
```

LISTING 22.8 CONTINUED

```
  WHERE FilmID = #ATTRIBUTES.FilmID#
</CFQUERY>

<!--- Display error message if record not fetched --->
<CFIF GetFilm.RecordCount NEQ 1>
  <CFTHROW
    MESSAGE="Invalid FilmID Attribute"
    DETAIL="Film #ATTRIBUTES.FilmID# does not exist!">
</CFIF>


<!--- Format a few queried values in local variables --->
<CFSET ProductCost = Ceiling(Val(GetFilm.AmountBudgeted) / 1000000)>
<CFSET ReleaseDate = DateFormat(GetFilm.DateInTheaters, "mmmm d")>

<!--- Now Display The Specified Movie --->
<CFOUTPUT>
  <!--- Define formatting for film display --->
  <STYLE TYPE="text/css">
    TH.fm {background:RoyalBlue;color:white;text-align:left;
           font-family:sans-serif;font-size:10px}
    TD.fm {background:LightSteelBlue;
           font-family:sans-serif;font-size:12px}
  </STYLE>

  <!--- Show information about featured movie in HTML table --->
  <TABLE
    WIDTH="#ATTRIBUTES.TableWidth#"
    ALIGN="#ATTRIBUTES.TableAlign#"
    BORDER="0"
    CELLSPACING="0">

    <TR><TH CLASS="fm">
      #ATTRIBUTES.Caption#
    </TH></TR>
    <!--- Movie Title, Summary, Rating --->
    <TR><TD CLASS="fm">
      <B>#GetFilm.MovieTitle#</B><BR>
      #GetFilm.Summary#<BR>
    </TD></TR>
    <!--- Cost (rounded to millions), release date --->
    <CFIF ATTRIBUTES.ShowCost OR ATTRIBUTES.ShowReleaseDate>
      <TR><TH CLASS="fm">
        <!--- Show Cost, if called for --->
        <CFIF ATTRIBUTES.ShowCost>
          Production Cost $#ProductCost# Million<BR>
        </CFIF>
        <!--- Show release date, if called for --->
        <CFIF ATTRIBUTES.ShowReleaseDate>
          In Theaters #ReleaseDate#<BR>
        </CFIF>
      </TH></TR>
    </CFIF>
  </TABLE>
  <BR CLEAR="all">
</CFOUTPUT>
```

Tip

It is often helpful to put an Example of Use comment at the top of your custom tag as shown here, even if you provide better documentation elsewhere. If nothing else, the hint will serve as a quick reminder to you if you need to revise the tag later.

At the top of this listing, a number of `<CFPARAM>` tags are used to make clear what the tag's required and optional parameters will be. Only the `FilmID` attribute is required; because its `<CFPARAM>` tag doesn't have a `DEFAULT` attribute, ColdFusion will throw an error message if a `FilmID` is not provided at runtime. The `ShowCost` and `ShowReleaseDate` attributes are Boolean values, meaning that either `Yes` or `No` (or an expression that evaluates to `True` or `False`) can be supplied when the tag is actually used; the `DEFAULT` for each is defined to be `Yes`. The `TableAlign`, `TableWidth`, `Caption`, and `DataSource` attributes are also given sensible default values so they can be omitted when the tag is used.

Next, the `<CFQUERY>` named `GetFilm` retrieves information about the appropriate film, using the value of `ATTRIBUTES.FilmID` in the `WHERE` clause. Then, two local variables called `ProductionCost` and `ReleaseDate` are set to formatted versions of the `AmountBudgeted` and `DateInTheaters` columns returned by the query.

Note

These two variables are referred to as *local* because they exist only in the context of this custom tag template itself, not in the calling template where the tag is used. The `GetFilm` query is also a local variable. See the section "Local Variables in Custom Tags," later in this chapter, for more information.

Custom tags should be capable of dealing reasonably gracefully with unexpected situations. For that reason, a `<CFIF>` block is used right after the `<CFQUERY>` to ensure that the query retrieved one record as expected. If not, a `<CFTHROW>` tag is used to halt all processing with a customized, diagnostic error message. For more information about `<CFTHROW>`, see Chapter 33, "Error Handling."

Note

The error message generated by the `<CFTHROW>` tag will be displayed using the appropriate look and feel template if the `<CFERROR>` tag is used in `Application.cfm`, as discussed in Chapter 19.

The rest of the template is essentially unchanged from the `FeaturedMovie.cfm` template as it originally appeared in Chapter 19. The film's title, summary, and other information are shown in an attractive table format. The `<CFIF>` logic at the end of the template enables the display of the `Production Cost` and `Release Date` to be turned off by setting the `ShowCost` or `ShowReleaseDate` attributes of the tag to `No`.

After Listing 22.8 is saved as a custom tag template called `ShowMovieCallout.cfm` (in the special `CustomTags` folder or in the same folder as the templates in which you want to use the tag), it is ready for use. Listing 22.9 shows how easily the tag can be used in your application's templates. The results are shown in Figure 22.5.

LISTING 22.9 UsingShowMovieCallout.cfm—USING THE <CF_ShowMovieCallout> CUSTOM TAG

```
<HTML>
<HEAD><TITLE>Movie Display</TITLE></HEAD>
<BODY>
  <!--- Page Title and Text Message --->
  <h2>Movie Display Demonstration</h2>
  <P>Any movie can be displayed at any time by using
  the <B>&lt;CF_ShowMovieCallout&gt;</B> tag.  All you
  need to do is to pass the appropriate FilmID to the tag.
  If the formatting needs to be changed in the future, only
  the custom tag's template will need to be edited.<BR>

  <!--- Display Film information as a "callout", via custom tag --->
  <CF_ShowMovieCallout
    FilmID="20">

</BODY>
</HTML>
```

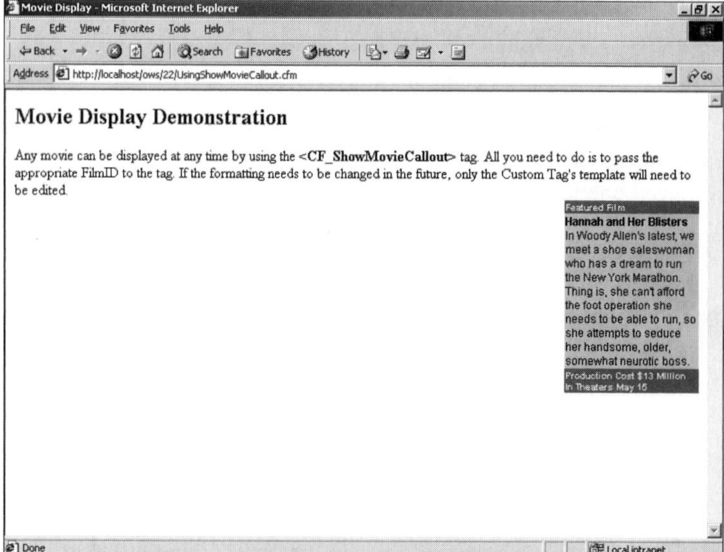

Figure 22.5
Using the <CF_ShowMovieCallout> tag, any film can be displayed with just one line of code.

LOCAL VARIABLES IN CUSTOM TAGS

In the previous section, it was pointed out that the `GetFilm`, `ProductCost`, and `ReleaseDate` variables are local variables, meaning the variables exist only within the scope of the custom tag template itself.

This is an important aspect of ColdFusion's custom tag functionality. Whenever a custom tag is executed, it gets a private area in the server's memory to store its own variables. Unless you use a scope prefix (such as `ATTRIBUTES`, `APPLICATION`, or `SESSION`), all references to variables in the custom tag template refer only to this private area. The result is what some other programming languages call a *namespace*—an interim memory space for the tag to do its work, without needing to worry about how it will affect the template in which it is being used.

For instance, if you attempt to display the value of the `ProductCost` variable in Listing 22.9, after the `<CF_ShowMovieCallout>` tag, you would get an error message saying that the variable doesn't exist. The variable exists only within the custom tag's template itself. After the tag finishes its work, all its variables are discarded and are no longer available.

This is what enables custom tags to be so modular and independent. Because they don't affect the variables in the templates in which they run, they are free to create variables and run queries in any way they need to. All kinds of problems would arise if this were not the case.

For instance, what if Listing 22.9 needs to run its own query named `GetFilms` before it uses the `<CF_ShowMovieCallout>` tag? If it weren't for the fact that custom tags have their own local variables, the `<CFQUERY>` inside the custom tag template would overwrite any variable called `GetFilms` that was set before the tag was called. This could lead to all sorts of strange and unexpected behavior (especially if you were using a custom tag that you did not write because you would need to know all the variable names the custom tag uses internally and avoid using them in your templates).

In short, remember these important points:

- Variables in custom tags are always local, unless you specify a special scope name (discussed shortly).
- Variables set before the tag is used are not available within the custom tag itself.
- Similarly, variables set in the custom tag's template are not available as normal variables in code that uses the tag.
- The `ATTRIBUTES` scope enables you to pass specific values into the tag.
- The special `CALLER` scope, which you will learn about shortly, enables you to access or set specific variables in the calling template.

CUSTOM TAGS VERSUS <CFINCLUDE>

Earlier in this book, you learned about the `<CFINCLUDE>` tag, which enables you to put ordinary CFML code in a separate template and include it elsewhere, wherever you need to use it. You might be thinking that including a template with the `<CFINCLUDE>` tag is pretty similar to calling a custom tag. That's true, but custom tags are more sophisticated because they have their own variable namespaces, as explained above.

So, yes, you often can get the same results using <CFINCLUDE> instead of creating a custom tag, but your code usually will be harder to maintain and debug because variables set in the calling template might interfere with the way the included template behaves, and vice versa.

CUSTOM TAGS THAT PROCESS DATA

So far, this chapter has concentrated on creating custom tags that display information, such as the <CF_ShowMovieCallout> custom tag. Many of the custom tags you will write are likely to be similar to <CF_ShowMovieCallout>, in that they will be in charge of wrapping up several display-related concepts (querying the database, including formatting, outputting the information, and so on).

However, you also can create custom tags that have different purposes in life: to process or gather information. This type of custom tag generally doesn't generate any HTML to be displayed on the current page. Instead, these tags just perform some type of processing, often returning a calculated result of some kind to the calling template.

Tip

You might call these tags nonvisual, or perhaps number crunchers, just to set them apart from tags that generate something visual, such as the <CF_ ShowMovieCallout> and <CF_HelloWorldMessage> examples you have already seen.

INTRODUCING THE CALLER SCOPE

ColdFusion defines two special variable scopes that come into play only when creating custom tags:

- ATTRIBUTES scope—You have already learned about this scope, which is used to pass specific information to a custom tag each time it is used.
- CALLER scope—Gives a custom tag a way to set and use variables in the template in which the tag is being used (the *calling template*).

The special CALLER scope is easy to understand and use. Within a custom tag template, you just prefix any variable name with CALLER (using dot notation) to access the corresponding variable in the calling template. Through the CALLER scope, you have full read/write access to all variables known to the calling template, meaning you can set variables as well as access their current values. For instance, you can set variables in the calling template using an ordinary <CFSET> tag.

RETURNING VARIABLES TO THE CALLING TEMPLATE

Let's say you are writing a custom tag called <CF_PickFeaturedMovie>, which will choose a movie from the list of available films. In the calling template, you plan on using the tag like so:

```
<CF_PickFeaturedMovie>
```

Inside the custom tag template (PickFeaturedMovie.cfm), you could set a variable using the special CALLER prefix, such as this:

```
<CFSET Caller.FeaturedFilmID = 5>
```

Using this prefix, FeaturedFilmID would then be available in the calling template as a normal variable. For instance, this code snippet would call the custom tag and then output the value of the variable it returns:

```
<CF_PickFeaturedMovie>
<CFOUTPUT>
  The featured Film ID is:
  #FeaturedFilmID#
</CFOUTPUT>
```

Of course, using these snippets, the value of FeaturedFilmID will always be 5, so the custom tag wouldn't be all that useful. Listing 22.10 shows how to expand the previous snippets into a useful version of the <CF_PickFeaturedMovie> custom tag. This tag borrows the featured movie selection code from the FeaturedMovie.cfm template that originally appeared in Chapter 19 and was adapted further in Chapter 20, "Working with Sessions." The purpose of the code is to select a single film's ID number in such a way that all films are rotated evenly on a per-session basis.

Listing 22.10 PickFeaturedMovie1.cfm—Setting a Variable in the Calling Template

```
<!--- Tag Attributes --->
<!--- Use "ows" datasource by default --->
<CFPARAM NAME="ATTRIBUTES.DataSource" TYPE="string" DEFAULT="ows">

<!--- Need to lock when accessing shared data --->
<CFLOCK SCOPE="Session" TIMEOUT="10">

  <!--- List of movies to show (list starts out empty) --->
  <CFPARAM NAME="SESSION.MovieList" TYPE="string" DEFAULT="">

  <!--- If this is the first time we're running this,  --->
  <!--- Or we have run out of movies to rotate through --->
  <CFIF SESSION.MovieList EQ "">
    <!--- Get all current FilmIDs from the database --->
    <CFQUERY NAME="GetFilmIDs" DATASOURCE="#ATTRIBUTES.DataSource#">
      SELECT FilmID FROM Films
      ORDER BY MovieTitle
    </CFQUERY>

    <!--- Turn FilmIDs into a simple comma-separated list --->
    <CFSET SESSION.MovieList = ValueList(GetFilmIDs.FilmID)>
  </CFIF>

  <!--- Pick the first movie in the list to show right now --->
  <CFSET ThisMovieID = ListFirst(SESSION.MovieList)>
  <!--- -save the listas all movies *except* the first --->
  <CFSET SESSION.MovieList = ListRest(SESSION.MovieList)>

  <!--- Return chosen movie to calling template --->
  <CFSET CALLER.FeaturedFilmID = ThisMovieID>
</CFLOCK>
```

The <CFPARAM> tag at the top of this custom tag template establishes a single optional attribute for the tag called DataSource, which will default to ows if not provided explicitly. Except for the final <CFSET> line, the remainder of the code is copied literally from the version presented in Chapter 20. Because the final <CFSET> uses the special CALLER scope, the featured movie the tag has chosen is available for the calling template to use normally.

Listing 22.11 shows how this version of the <CF_PickFeaturedMovie> custom tag can be put to use in actual code. This code assumes you have saved Listing 22.10 as PickFeaturedMovie.cfm (not PickFeaturedMovie1.cfm) in the current directory or in the special CustomTags folder.

LISTING 22.11 UsingPickFeaturedMovie1.cfm—**USING A VARIABLE SET BY A CUSTOM TAG**

```
<HTML>
<HEAD><TITLE>Movie Display</TITLE></HEAD>
<BODY>
  <!--- Page Title and Text Message --->
  <h2>Movie Display Demonstration</h2>
  <P>The appropriate "Featured Movie" can be obtained by
  using the <B>&lt;CF_PickFeaturedMovie&gt;</B> tag.
  The featured movie can then be displayed using the
  <B>&lt;CF_ShowMovieCallout&gt;</B> tag.<BR>

  <!--- Pick rotating Featured Movie to show via custom tag --->
  <CF_PickFeaturedMovie>

  <!--- Display film information as callout via custom tag --->
  <CF_ShowMovieCallout
    FilmID="#FeaturedFilmID#">

</BODY>
</HTML>
```

Note

The CALLER scope is for use only within custom tag templates. Don't use it in your ordinary ColdFusion templates. Doing so won't generate an error message, but it could lead to unexpected results.

Note

If you are calling a custom tag from within another custom tag, the CALLER scope of the innermost tag will refer to the local variables in the first custom tag template, not the variables in the top-level page template. To access the variables of the top-level template from the innermost tag, you must use CALLER.CALLER.VariableName instead of CALLER.VariableName. In some cases, this can be a pain; the REQUEST scope provides an effective solution, as explained in the section "The REQUEST Scope," later in this chapter.

First, the <CF_PickFeaturedMovie> custom tag from Listing 22.10 is called. As the custom tag executes, it selects the film ID it feels is appropriate and saves the value in the FeaturedFilmID variable in the calling template (which, in this case, is Listing 22.11). Next, the featured movie is actually displayed to the user, using the <CF_ShowMovieCallout> custom tag presented earlier in this chapter.

Tip

These two custom tags (<CF_PickFeaturedMovie> and <CF_ShowMovieCallout>) each do something useful on their own and can be used together, as shown here. As you design custom tags for your applications, this type of synergy between tags is a nice goal to try to shoot for.

Of course, for Listing 22.11 to work, session management needs to be enabled by including a <CFAPPLICATION> tag in the application's Application.cfm file (see Chapter 20 for details):

```
<!--- Name our application and enable application variables --->
<CFAPPLICATION
  NAME="OrangeWhipSite"
  SESSIONMANAGEMENT="Yes">
```

Note

The more a custom tag relies on variables in the calling template, the less modular it becomes. So, although the CALLER scope gives you read/write access to variables in the calling template, you should use it mainly for setting new variables, rather than accessing the values of existing ones. If you find that you are accessing the values of many existing variables in the calling template, it might be that you should just be writing a normal <CFINCLUDE> style template rather than a custom tag, or that the values should be passed in to the tag explicitly as attributes.

Variable Names As Tag Attributes

In the version of the <CF_PickFeaturedMovie> custom tag shown in Listing 21.10, the selected film ID is always returned to the calling template as a variable named FeaturedFilmID. Often, allowing a custom tag to accept an additional attribute is helpful to determine the name of the return variable in which the custom tag will place information.

For instance, for the <CF_PickFeaturedMovie> custom tag, you might add an attribute called ReturnVariable, which determines the calling template to specify the variable in which to place the featured film's ID number.

So, to use the tag, you would change this line from Listing 22.10:

```
<!--- Pick rotating featured movie to show via custom tag --->
<CF_PickFeaturedMovie>
```

to this:

```
<!--- Pick rotating featured movie to show via custom tag --->
<CF_PickFeaturedMovie
  ReturnVariable="FeaturedFilmID">
```

This makes the custom tag less intrusive because it doesn't demand that any particular variable names be set aside for its use. If, for whatever reason, the developer coding the calling template wants the selected film to be known as `MyFeaturedFilmID` or `ShowThisMovieID`, she can simply specify that name for the `ReturnVariable` attribute. The calling template is always in control.

Note

Also, code that uses the `<CF_PickFeaturedMovie>` tag will be a bit more self-documenting and easier to understand because it is now evident from where exactly the `FeaturedFilmID` variable is coming.

Note

If you think about it, a number of ColdFusion's own CFML tags use this same technique. The most obvious example is the `NAME` attribute of the `<CFQUERY>` tag, which is indeed an attribute that tells the tag in which variable to store its results. The `NAME` attributes of the `<CFDIRECTORY>` and `<CFSEARCH>` tags are similar, as are the `OUTPUT` attribute for `<CFWDDX>` and the `VARIABLE` attributes for `<CFFILE>` and `<CFSAVEOUTPUT>`. See Appendix A, "ColdFusion Tag Reference," for details.

USING <CFPARAM> WITH TYPE="VariableName"

You already have seen the `<CFPARAM>` tag used throughout this chapter to make it clear which attributes a custom tag expects and to ensure that the data type of each attribute is correct. When you want the calling template to accept a variable name as one of its attributes, you can set the `TYPE` of the `<CFPARAM>` tag to `variableName`.

Therefore, the next version of the `<CF_PickFeaturedMovie>` custom tag will include the following lines:

```
<!--- Variable name to return selected FilmID as --->
<CFPARAM NAME="ATTRIBUTES.ReturnVariable" TYPE="variableName">
```

When the `<CFPARAM>` tag is encountered, ColdFusion ensures that the actual value of the attribute is a legal variable name. If it's not, it displays an error message stating the variable name is illegal. This makes for a very simple sanity check. It ensures the tag isn't being provided with something such as `ReturnValue="My Name"`, which likely would result in a much uglier error message later because spaces are not allowed in ColdFusion variable names.

Note

In ColdFusion, variable names must start with a letter, and all the other characters can be only letters, numbers, and underscores. Any string that does not conform to these rules will not get past a `<CFPARAM>` of `TYPE="variableName"`.

The Problem with Setting a Variable Dynamically

After the <CFPARAM> tag shown previously is added to the <CF_PickFeaturedMovie> custom tag template, the template can refer to Attributes.ReturnVariable to get the desired variable name. Now the final <CFSET> variable in Listing 22.10 just needs to be changed so that it uses the dynamic variable name instead of the hard-coded variable name of FeaturedFilmID. Developers sometimes get confused about how exactly to do this.

Here's the line as it stands now, from Listing 22.10:

```
<!--- Return chosen movie to calling template --->
<CFSET CALLER.FeaturedFilmID = ThisMovieID>
```

People often try to use syntax similar to the following to somehow indicate that the value of Attributes.ReturnVariable should be used to determine the name of the variable in the CALLER scope:

```
<!--- Return chosen movie to calling template --->
<CFSET CALLER.#Attributes.ReturnVariable# = ThisMovieID>
```

Or

```
<!--- Return chosen movie to calling template --->
<CFSET #CALLER.##Attributes.ReturnVariable### = ThisMovieID>
```

These are not legal because ColdFusion does not understand that you want the value of Attributes.ReturnVariable to be evaluated before the <CFSET> is actually performed. ColdFusion will just get exasperated with you and display an error message.

Using Quoted <CFSET> Syntax

ColdFusion provides a somewhat odd-looking solution to this problem. You simply surround the left side of the <CFSET> expression (the part before the = sign) with quotation marks. This forces ColdFusion to first evaluate the variable name as a string, before attempting to actually perform the variable-setting. The resulting code looks a bit strange, but it actually works very nicely and is relatively easy to read.

So, this line from Listing 22.10:

```
<!--- Return chosen movie to calling template --->
<CFSET CALLER.FeaturedFilmID = ThisMovieID>
```

can be replaced with this:

```
<!--- Return chosen movie to calling template --->
<CFSET "CALLER.#ATTRIBUTES.ReturnVariable#" = ThisMovieID>
```

Listing 22.12 shows the completed version of the <CF_PickFeaturedMovie> custom tag. This listing is identical to Listing 22.10, except for the first and last lines, which are the <CFPARAM> line and the updated <CFSET> line shown previously.

LISTING 22.12 `PickFeaturedMovie2.cfm`—**REVISED VERSION OF** `<CF_PickFeaturedMovie>` **CUSTOM TAG**

```
<!--- Tag Attributes --->
<!--- Variable name to return selected FilmID as --->
<CFPARAM NAME="ATTRIBUTES.ReturnVariable" TYPE="variableName">
<!--- Use "ows" datasource by default --->
<CFPARAM NAME="ATTRIBUTES.DataSource" TYPE="string" DEFAULT="ows">

<!--- Need to lock when accessing shared data --->
<CFLOCK SCOPE="Session" TIMEOUT="10">

  <!--- List of movies to show (list starts out empty) --->
  <CFPARAM NAME="SESSION.MovieList" TYPE="string" DEFAULT="">

  <!--- If this is the first time we're running this,  --->
  <!--- Or we have run out of movies to rotate through --->
  <CFIF SESSION.MovieList EQ "">
    <!--- Get all current FilmIDs from the database --->
    <CFQUERY NAME="GetFilmIDs" DATASOURCE="#ATTRIBUTES.DataSource#">
      SELECT FilmID FROM Films
      ORDER BY MovieTitle
    </CFQUERY>

    <!--- Turn FilmIDs into a simple comma-separated list --->
    <CFSET SESSION.MovieList = ValueList(GetFilmIDs.FilmID)>
  </CFIF>

  <!--- Pick the first movie in the list to show right now --->
  <CFSET ThisMovieID = ListFirst(SESSION.MovieList)>
  <!--- Resave the list as all movies *except* the first --->
  <CFSET SESSION.MovieList = ListRest(SESSION.MovieList)>

  <!--- Return chosen movie to calling template --->
  <CFSET "CALLER.#ATTRIBUTES.ReturnVariable#" = ThisMovieID>
</CFLOCK>
```

Listing 22.13 shows how to use this new version of the custom tag. This listing is nearly identical to Listing 22.11, except for the addition of the `ReturnVariable` attribute. Note how much clearer the cause and effect now are. In Listing 22.11, the `FeaturedFilmID` variable seemed to appear out of nowhere. Here, it is very clear where the `ShowThisMovieID` variable is coming from.

Note

This listing assumes that you have saved the code shown in Listing 22.12 as a template called `PickFeaturedMovie.cfm` (not `PickFeaturedMovie2.cfm`). Of course, you would need to save it in the special `CustomTags` folder or in the same folder as this listing.

LISTING 22.13 `UsingPickFeaturedMovie2.cfm`—**USING THE** `ReturnVariable` **ATTRIBUTE**

```
<HTML>
<HEAD><TITLE>Movie Display</TITLE></HEAD>
<BODY>
  <!--- Page Title and Text Message --->
  <h2>Movie Display Demonstration</h2>
  <P>The appropriate featured movie can be obtained by
  using the <B>&lt;CF_PickFeaturedMovie&gt;</B> tag.
  The featured movie can then be displayed using the
  <B>&lt;CF_ShowMovieCallout&gt;</B> tag.<BR>

  <!--- Pick rotating featured movie to show via custom tag --->
  <CF_PickFeaturedMovie
    ReturnVariable="ShowThisMovieID">

  <!--- Display film information as callout via custom tag --->
  <CF_ShowMovieCallout
    FilmID="#ShowThisMovieID#">

</BODY>
</HTML>
```

USING THE `SetVariable()` FUNCTION

Another way to solve this type of problem is with the `SetVariable()` function. This function accepts two parameters. The first parameter is a string specifying the name of a variable, and the second parameter is the value you want to store in the specified variable. (The function also returns the new value as its result, which is not generally helpful in this situation.)

So, this line from Listing 22.12:

```
<!--- Return chosen movie to calling template --->
<CFSET "CALLER.#ATTRIBUTES.ReturnVariable#" = ThisMovieID>
```

could be replaced with this:

```
<!--- Return chosen movie to calling template --->
<CFSET Temp = SetVariable("CALLER.#Attributes.ReturnVariable#", ThisMovieID)>
```

And, because the result of the function is unnecessary here, this line can be simplified to just this:

```
<!--- Return chosen movie to calling template --->
<CFSET SetVariable("CALLER.#Attributes.ReturnVariable#", ThisMovieID)>
```

Either method (the quoted `<CFSET>` syntax mentioned previously or the `SetVariable()` method shown here) produces the same results. Use whichever method you prefer.

CUSTOM TAGS THAT ENCAPSULATE BUSINESS RULES

Often, it is helpful to create custom tags to represent the business rules or logic your application needs to enforce or adhere to. After these custom tags are written correctly, you can rest assured that your application will not violate the corresponding business rules.

For instance, looking at the tables in the ows example database, it is easy to see that several tables will be involved when someone wants to place an order from Orange Whip Studio's online store. For each order, a record will be added to the MerchandiseOrders table, and several records can be added to the MerchandiseOrdersItems table (one record for each item the user has in his shopping cart). In addition, you will need to verify the user's credit card number and perhaps send a confirmation e-mail as an acknowledgement of the user's order. In a real-world application, you also might need to decrease the current number of items on hand after the order has been placed, and so on.

All those steps could be placed in a single custom tag. It could be called something such as <CF_PlaceMerchandiseOrder> and take a few simple and easily understood parameters that represent everything necessary to successfully complete an order. The tag might look similar to this when used in code:

```
<!--- Place order for selected items and get new Order ID --->
<CF_PlaceMerchandiseOrder
  ContactID="4"
  MerchIDList="2,6,9"
  ShipToCurrentAddress="Yes"
  SendReceiptViaEmail="Yes"
  ReturnVariable="NewOrderID">
```

In fact, a version of the <CF_PlaceMerchandiseOrder> tag is developed in Chapter 29, "Online Commerce."

CUSTOM TAGS THAT REPRESENT OBJECTS

Depending on the application you are working on, you might want to consider creating a custom tag that loosely represents a type of object and the things that can be done with the object. There are many ways to conceive of and approach such an undertaking. This section suggests one particularly simple approach. Some others are described in Chapter 39, "Development Methodologies."

ColdFusion provides several native CFML tags that encapsulate all the built-in functionality for a particular target item. For instance, the <CFFILE> tag takes an ACTION attribute that can be set to Copy, Move, Delete, Write, and so on. That is, the <CFFILE> tag can be said to represent a type of object (a file object), and the various ACTION values are the things that can be done to the object. Similarly, the ACTION attribute for the <CFCOLLECTION> tag can be used to do all the various things available for a Verity collection (such as Create, Repair, Delete, and Optimize). Thus, the <CFCOLLECTION> tag can be loosely thought of as an object (or if you prefer, an object class) that represents a Verity collection, or perhaps the Verity engine.

Note

If you are familiar with object-oriented programming (OOP), you might find it a bit of a stretch to call <CFFILE> or <CFCOLLECTION> an object or objectclass. Clearly, the object metaphor isn't perfect and certainly isn't meant to suggest that CFML is truly object-oriented or that custom tags represent some type of true object-oriented framework. This discussion is just about thinking of certain CFML tags as being somewhat similar to the real objects that object-oriented programmers are familiar with.

Creating a custom tag to encapsulate several related actions that all center on the same idea or type of object can be useful. For instance, the Orange Whip Studios project has an important database table called `Films`. It might make sense to think of each film as a sort of object that various actions can be performed upon. All these actions could be encapsulated within a custom tag called, say, `<CF_Film>` or `<CF_FilmRecord>`. Similar to `<CFFILE>` or `<CFCOLLECTION>`, this tag could have an `ACTION` attribute that can be set to values such as `Create`, `Update`, and `Delete`. If `Action="Create"`, the tag would insert a new record in the `Films` table. If `Action="Delete"`, the tag would delete a record from the `Films` table.

Defining the Actions

Listing 22.14 shows how the template for such a custom tag, called `<CF_FilmRecord>`, might be structured. As you can see, no actual processing is being done yet. All this code does is establish one required parameter for the custom tag, called `Action`. In addition, it has an optional parameter that can be used to set the datasource name.

Listing 22.14 `FilmRecord1.cfm`—**Code Skeleton for the** `<CF_FilmRecord>` **Custom Tag**

```
<!--- Tag Attributes --->
<CFPARAM NAME="ATTRIBUTES.Action" TYPE="string">
<CFPARAM NAME="ATTRIBUTES.DataSource" TYPE="string" DEFAULT="ows">

<!--- ** Different processing for the various Actions --->
<CFSWITCH EXPRESSION="#ATTRIBUTES.Action#">

  <!--- ** Action="Create" --->
  <CFCASE VALUE="Create">
  </CFCASE>

  <!--- ** Action="Update" --->
  <CFCASE VALUE="Update">
  </CFCASE>

  <!--- ** Action="Delete" --->
  <CFCASE VALUE="Delete">
  </CFCASE>

  <!--- ** Action="GetData" --->
  <CFCASE VALUE="GetData">
  </CFCASE>
```

Listing 22.14 Continued

```
  <!--- ** Action="ShowInCallout" --->
  <CFCASE VALUE="ShowInCallout">
  </CFCASE>

  <!--- Show error if an unknown Action attribute is provided --->
  <CFDEFAULTCASE>
    <CFTHROW
      DETAIL="Unknown Action parameter."
      MESSAGE="Allowable values are Create, Update, Delete, GetData, and
ShowInCallout.">
  </CFDEFAULTCASE>
</CFSWITCH>
```

As you can see, this listing simply sets up a `<CFSWITCH>` block to handle the various possible values of the `Action` attribute. If `Action="Create"`, the code between the first set of `<CFCASE>` tags executes. If `Action="Delete"`, the second `<CFCASE>` executes, and so on. The `<CFDEFAULTCASE>` tag at the end executes and displays an error message if the provided `Action` doesn't get processed by any of the `<CFCASE>` tags.

Just as with `<CFFILE>` and `<CFCOLLECTION>`, this tag needs to take different attributes depending on which `Action` is being performed. If `Action="Delete"`, the only additional piece of information necessary is a `FilmID` attribute, indicating the film to delete. If `Action="Create"`, however, the tag requires different attributes to work with, such as the `MovieTitle` and `AmountBudgeted` attributes that represent the title and budget for the new film, respectively.

Adding Action-Specific Tag Attributes

Listing 22.15 builds on Listing 22.14, this time using `<CFPARAM>` tags to define the additional attributes that are appropriate for each `Action`.

Listing 22.15 `FilmRecord2.cfm`**—Adding Action-Specific Parameters for the** `<CF_FilmRecord>` **Custom Tag**

```
<!--- Tag Attributes --->
<CFPARAM NAME="ATTRIBUTES.Action" TYPE="string">
<CFPARAM NAME="ATTRIBUTES.DataSource" TYPE="string" DEFAULT="ows">

<!--- ** Different processing for the various Actions --->
<CFSWITCH EXPRESSION="#ATTRIBUTES.Action#">

  <!--- ** Action="InsertNew" --->
  <CFCASE VALUE="Create">
    <!--- Additional Parameters for this Action --->
    <CFPARAM NAME="ATTRIBUTES.MovieTitle" TYPE="string">
    <CFPARAM NAME="ATTRIBUTES.PitchText" TYPE="string">
    <CFPARAM NAME="ATTRIBUTES.AmountBudgeted" TYPE="numeric">
    <CFPARAM NAME="ATTRIBUTES.ReturnVariable" TYPE="variableName">

  </CFCASE>
```

```
  <!--- ** Action="Update" --->
  <CFCASE VALUE="Update">
    <!--- Additional Parameter for this Action --->
    <CFPARAM NAME="ATTRIBUTES.FilmID" TYPE="numeric">
  </CFCASE>


  <!--- ** Action="Delete" --->
  <CFCASE VALUE="Delete">
    <!--- Additional Parameter for this Action --->
    <CFPARAM NAME="ATTRIBUTES.FilmID" TYPE="numeric">
  </CFCASE>


  <!--- ** Action="GetData" --->
  <CFCASE VALUE="GetData">
    <!--- Additional Parameter for this Action --->
    <CFPARAM NAME="ATTRIBUTES.FilmID" TYPE="numeric">
    <CFPARAM NAME="ATTRIBUTES.ReturnVariable" TYPE="variableName">
  </CFCASE>


  <!--- ** Action="ShowInCallout" --->
  <CFCASE VALUE="ShowInCallout">
    <!--- Additional Parameter for this Action --->
    <CFPARAM NAME="ATTRIBUTES.FilmID" TYPE="numeric">
  </CFCASE>


  <!--- Show error if an unknown Action attribute is provided --->
  <CFDEFAULTCASE>
    <CFTHROW
      DETAIL="Unknown Action parameter."
      MESSAGE="Allowable values are Create, Update, Delete, GetData, and
ShowInCallout.">
  </CFDEFAULTCASE>

</CFSWITCH>
```

As you can see, Listing 22.15 specifies that if `Action="Create"` then the tag must be provided with four additional attributes. A new record will be inserted into the `Films` table, with the title, description, and budget provided by the `MovieTitle`, `PitchText`, and `AmountBudgeted` attributes, respectively. Then, the `FilmID` for the newly-inserted film will be returned to the calling template as specified by the `ReturnVariable` attribute (see the section "Returning Variables to the Calling Template," earlier in this chapter).

The other `Action` values (`Update`, `Delete`, `GetData`, and `ShowInCallout`) are provided with attributes in the same basic way.

Processing Each Action

Now that the tag's additional attributes have been defined for each possible value of the `Action` attribute, you easily can flesh out the custom tag so it can actually perform each of the actions. Listing 22.16 shows the completed `<CF_FilmRecord>` custom tag. This listing appears to be somewhat long at first, but the code within each `<CFCASE>` block is quite simple.

Remember to save this listing as a custom tag template named `FilmRecord.cfm`, rather than `FilmRecord3.cfm`.

LISTING 22.16 `FilmRecord3.cfm`—**THE COMPLETE** `<CF_FilmRecord>` **CUSTOM TAG**

```
<!--- Tag Attributes --->
<CFPARAM NAME="ATTRIBUTES.Action" TYPE="string">
<CFPARAM NAME="ATTRIBUTES.DataSource" TYPE="string" DEFAULT="ows">

<!--- Examples of use:
  <!--- Create a new record in Films table --->
  <CF_FilmRecord
    Action="Create"
    MovieTitle="movie_title"
    PitchText="pitch_text"
    AmountBudgeted="number"
    ReturnVariable="variable_name">

  <!--- Update an existing record in Films table --->
  <CF_FilmRecord
    Action="Update"
    FilmID="film_id_number"
    MovieTitle="movie_title"
    PitchText="pitch_text"
    AmountBudgeted="number">

  <!--- Delete an existing record from Films table --->
  <CF_FilmRecord
    Action="Delete"
    FilmID="film_id_number">

  <!--- Retrieve an existing record from Films table --->
  <CF_FilmRecord
    Action="GetData"
    FilmID="film_id_number"
    ReturnVariable="variable_name">

  <!--- Display film record as a callout on page --->
  <CF_FilmRecord
    Action="ShowInCallout"
    FilmID="film_id_number">
--->

<!--- ** Different processing for the various Actions --->
<CFSWITCH EXPRESSION="#ATTRIBUTES.Action#">

  <!--- ** Action="Create" --->
  <CFCASE VALUE="Create">
    <!--- Additional Parameters for this Action --->
    <CFPARAM NAME="ATTRIBUTES.MovieTitle" TYPE="string">
    <CFPARAM NAME="ATTRIBUTES.PitchText" TYPE="string">
    <CFPARAM NAME="ATTRIBUTES.AmountBudgeted" TYPE="numeric">
```

```
  <CFPARAM NAME="ATTRIBUTES.ReturnVariable" TYPE="variableName">

  <!--- Insert Film Record --->
  <CFQUERY DATASOURCE="#ATTRIBUTES.DataSource#">
    INSERT INTO Films(
      MovieTitle,
      PitchText,
      AmountBudgeted)
    VALUES (
      '#ATTRIBUTES.MovieTitle#',
      '#ATTRIBUTES.PitchText#',
      #ATTRIBUTES.AmountBudgeted#)
  </CFQUERY>
  <!--- Get ID number of just-inserted film --->
  <CFQUERY DATASOURCE="#ATTRIBUTES.DataSource#" NAME="GetNew">
    SELECT Max(FilmID) As NewID FROM Films
  </CFQUERY>
  <!--- Return new FilmID to calling template --->
  <CFSET "Caller.#ATTRIBUTES.ReturnVariable#" = GetNew.NewID>
</CFCASE>


<!--- ** Action="Update" --->
<CFCASE VALUE="Update">
  <!--- Additional Parameter for this Action --->
  <CFPARAM NAME="ATTRIBUTES.FilmID" TYPE="numeric">

  <!--- Were MovieTitle/PitchText/AmountBudgeted given? --->
  <CFSET HasTitle  = IsDefined("ATTRIBUTES.MovieTitle")>
  <CFSET HasPitch  = IsDefined("ATTRIBUTES.PitchText")>
  <CFSET HasBudget = IsDefined("ATTRIBUTES.AmountBudgeted")>

  <!--- Assuming at least one of the three was given --->
  <CFIF HasTitle OR HasPitch OR HasBudget>
    <!--- Update Record in database --->
    <CFQUERY DATASOURCE="#ATTRIBUTES.DataSource#">
      UPDATE Films SET
      <CFIF HasTitle>
        MovieTitle = '#ATTRIBUTES.MovieTitle#'
        <CFIF HasPitch OR HasBudget>,</CFIF>
      </CFIF>
      <CFIF HasPitch>
        PitchText  = '#ATTRIBUTES.PitchText#'
        <CFIF HasBudget>,</CFIF>
      </CFIF>
      <CFIF HasBudget>
        AmountBudgeted = #ATTRIBUTES.AmountBudgeted#
      </CFIF>
      WHERE FilmID = #ATTRIBUTES.FilmID#
    </CFQUERY>
  </CFIF>
</CFCASE>


<!--- ** Action="Delete" --->
<CFCASE VALUE="Delete">
  <!--- Additional Parameter for this Action --->
```

Listing 22.16 Continued

```
  <CFPARAM NAME="ATTRIBUTES.FilmID" TYPE="numeric">

  <!--- Delete Record from database --->
  <CFQUERY DATASOURCE="#ATTRIBUTES.DataSource#">
    DELETE FROM Films
    WHERE FilmID = #ATTRIBUTES.FilmID#
  </CFQUERY>
</CFCASE>


<!--- ** Action="GetData" --->
<CFCASE VALUE="GetData">
  <!--- Additional Parameter for this Action --->
  <CFPARAM NAME="ATTRIBUTES.FilmID" TYPE="numeric">
  <CFPARAM NAME="ATTRIBUTES.ReturnVariable" TYPE="variableName">

  <!--- Get Film Record --->
  <CFQUERY DATASOURCE="#ATTRIBUTES.DataSource#" NAME="GetFilm">
    SELECT * FROM Films
    WHERE FilmID = #ATTRIBUTES.FilmID#
  </CFQUERY>

  <!--- Get Associated Actor Records --->
  <CFQUERY DATASOURCE="#ATTRIBUTES.DataSource#" NAME="GetActors">
    SELECT * FROM Actors
    WHERE ActorID IN
      (SELECT ActorID FROM FilmsActors
       WHERE FilmID = #ATTRIBUTES.FilmID#)
  </CFQUERY>

  <!--- Get Associated Merchandise Records --->
  <CFQUERY DATASOURCE="#ATTRIBUTES.DataSource#" NAME="GetMerch">
    SELECT * FROM Merchandise
    WHERE FilmID = #ATTRIBUTES.FilmID#
  </CFQUERY>

  <!--- Create a Structure and place query results in it --->
  <CFSET s = StructNew()>
  <CFSET s.Film   = GetFilm>
  <CFSET s.Actors = GetActors>
  <CFSET s.Merch  = GetMerch>

  <!--- Return Structure to calling template --->
  <CFSET "Caller.#ATTRIBUTES.ReturnVariable#" = s>
</CFCASE>


<!--- ** Action="ShowInCallout" --->
<CFCASE VALUE="ShowInCallout">
  <!--- Additional Parameter for this Action --->
  <CFPARAM NAME="ATTRIBUTES.FilmID" TYPE="numeric">

  <!--- Display Film info as "callout", via Custom Tag --->
  <CF_ShowMovieCallout
    FilmID="#ATTRIBUTES.FilmID#"
```

```
      DataSource="#Attributes.DataSource#">
  </CFCASE>


  <!--- Show error if an unknown Action attribute is provided --->
  <CFDEFAULTCASE>
    <CFTHROW
      DETAIL="Unknown Action parameter."
      MESSAGE="Allowable values are Create, Update, Delete, GetData,
➥ and ShowInCallout.">
  </CFDEFAULTCASE>

</CFSWITCH>
```

The first <CFCASE> tag is for when the custom tag is called with an `Action` attribute of `Create`. The job for the tag in this case is to insert a new record into the `Films` table. This is done with a simple `INSERT` query that inserts the values passed to the tag via the `MovieTitle`, `PitchText`, and `AmountBudgeted` attributes. A follow-up query uses SQL's `Max` function to grab the `FilmID` of the just-inserted film record. Finally, the new ID number is returned to the calling template using the quoted <CFSET> syntax discussed earlier (see the section "Returning Variables to the Calling Template," earlier in this chapter).

The next <CFCASE> tag fires if the custom tag is called with `Action="Update"`. Here, the job of the tag is to update an existing record in the `Films` table. This code requires a `FilmID` attribute via the usual <CFPARAM> tag but doesn't use <CFPARAM> tags to declare the `MovieTitle`, `PitchText`, and `AmountBudgeted` attributes. Instead, the `IsDefined()` function is used to set variables called `HasTitle`, `HasPitch`, and `HasBudget`. The `HasTitle` variable is `True` if a `Title` attribute was passed to the tag and is `False` if it's not. The three `Has` variables are then used to dynamically construct a query that updates the record in the `Films` table. If all three attributes were provided to the tag, all three columns are updated in the table. If only a new `MovieTitle` is provided, only `HasTitle` is `True` and only the `MovieTitle` column is updated, leaving the other columns alone.

The next <CFCASE> fires if `Action="Delete"`. Here the tag's job is very simple: delete the record from the `Films` table. A single <CFQUERY> gets this done.

The <CFCASE> for `Action="GetData"` is somewhat interesting. So far, you have seen only custom tags that return simple values to the calling template. This code illustrates how easy returning a structure to the calling template, which could contain just about any amount of information, is. Here, three separate <CFQUERY> tags are used to get the appropriate records from the `Films`, `Actors`, and `Merchandise` tables. Because of the way Orange Whip Studio's database tables are designed, the `GetFilms` query should always return one record, whereas the `GetActors` and `GetMerch` queries can return many records each. Then a new structure called `s` is created, and the three queries are placed into the structure as name/value pairs called `Film`, `Actors`, and `Merch`. Finally, the structure is returned to the calling template using the `ReturnVariable` technique. If the calling template provided a `ReturnVariable` of `FilmInfo`, it would later be capable of outputting `FilmInfo.Film.MovieTitle` to display the film's title or examining `FilmInfo.Actors.RecordCount` to determine how many actors starred in the film.

The last <CFCASE> is for Action="ShowInCallout", which uses the <CF_ShowMovieCallout> tag that was presented earlier in this chapter. This illustrates how easy using custom tags inside other custom tags is. Now a developer could use <CF_ShowMovieCallout> or <CF_FilmRecord> with ACTION="ShowInCallout" interchangeably. In this case, that doesn't present much of an advantage, but it is still interesting to think of the <CF_FilmRecord> tag as being capable of doing so many things, all having to do with the common concept (or object) of a film record.

USING THE CUSTOM TAG "OBJECT"

Listing 22.17 shows how the completed <CF_FilmRecord> tag can be used to create a new film record in a database, update an existing film record, display the record, and delete the record. Again, the <CF_FilmRecord> tag can be thought of as representing a FilmRecord object, and the various actions can be thought of as the various methods available for that type of object.

LISTING 22.17 UsingFilmRecord.cfm—USING THE VARIOUS ACTIONS PROVIDED BY <CF_FilmRecord>

```
<HTML>
<HEAD><TITLE>Using &lt;CF_UsingFilmRecord&gt;</TITLE></HEAD>
<BODY>
  <H2>Using &lt;CF_UsingFilmRecord&gt;</H2>

  <!--- Create a film record --->
  <CF_FilmRecord
    Action="Create"
    MovieTitle="The Bruise Brothers"
    PitchText="Identical twins fight to the finish."
    AmountBudgeted="5000"
    ReturnVariable="NewFilmID">

  <!--- Display new Film ID --->
  <P>Inserted film record.  New FilmID is:
  <CFOUTPUT>#NewFilmID#</CFOUTPUT>

  <!--- Update a film record --->
  <CF_FilmRecord
    Action="Update"
    FilmID="#NewFilmID#"
    AmountBudgeted="5000000">

  <!--- Update a film record --->
  <CF_FilmRecord
    Action="Update"
    FilmID="#NewFilmID#"
    PitchText="Identical twins fight in a futuristic boxing match!">

  <!--- Show film in callout --->
  <CF_FilmRecord
    Action="ShowInCallout"
    FilmID="#NewFilmID#">
```

```
  <!--- Get information about the film --->
  <CF_FilmRecord
    Action="GetData"
    FilmID="#NewFilmID#"
    ReturnVariable="FilmData">

  <!--- Display title of movie --->
  <P>Retrieved film information.  The title is:
  <CFOUTPUT>#FilmData.Film.MovieTitle#</CFOUTPUT>

  <!--- Delete a film --->
  <CF_FilmRecord
    Action="Delete"
    FilmID="#NewFilmID#">

  <P>Film has been deleted.

</BODY>
</HTML>
```


Learning More About Object-Based Custom Tags

As you can see, a single custom tag now provides a library of actions or processes related to a common theme (the concept of a film record). Many developers are attracted to thinking about custom tags in this way.

Several groups have put together formalized ways of thinking about ColdFusion templates (and custom tags in particular) as objects. See Chapter 39 for more information on this topic.

Custom Tags for General-Purpose Use

So far in this chapter, you have learned how to make custom tags that are mainly for internal use within your application or company. That is, although the `<CF_FilmRecord>` and `<CF_ShowMovieCallout>` custom tags can be enormously helpful while building projects for Orange Whip Studios, they probably are not all that helpful to the average ColdFusion programmer.

In contrast, sometimes you will find yourself writing a custom tag you know will be helpful not only to yourself but to other developers as well. If so, you can package it and make it available to others via the Developers Exchange on the Allaire Web site, either for free or for a charge.

For instance, perhaps you have a need to convert sentences to title case, meaning that the first letter of each word should be capitalized. You could write a custom tag, perhaps called `<CF_TextToTitleCase>`, to get the job done. After the tag is complete, you could share it with other developers you know or even post it for free download for the entire ColdFusion developer community to use.

Listing 22.18 shows code that creates the `<CF_TextToTitleCase>` custom tag. The tag has two attributes—`Input` and `Output`. The tag looks at the text passed to it via the `Input` attribute, capitalizes the first letter of each word, and returns the capitalized version of the string back to the calling template by storing it in the variable specified by the `Output` attribute.

Note

The `Output` attribute here works just like the `ReturnVariable` attribute in some of the other examples in this chapter. Depending on the situation, simplified attribute names, such as `Input` and `Output`, can be easier for other developers to use. In other cases, more verbose attribute names, such as `TextToConvert` and `ReturnVariable`, might make more sense. Geeky as this might sound, coming up with the names is part of the fun.

LISTING 22.18 `TextToTitleCase.cfm`—**SOURCE CODE FOR THE** `<CF_TextToTitleCase>` **CUSTOM TAG**

```
<!--- Tag Parameters --->
<CFPARAM NAME="Attributes.Input" TYPE="string">
<CFPARAM NAME="Attributes.Output" TYPE="variableName">

<!--- Local Variable --->
<CFSET Result = "">

<!--- For each word in the input --->
<CFLOOP LIST="#Attributes.Input#" INDEX="ThisWord" DELIMITERS=" ">
  <!--- Grab the first letter and convert it to uppercase --->
  <CFSET FirstLetter = UCase( Mid(ThisWord, 1, 1) )>
  <!--- Grab remaining letters and convert them to lowercase --->
  <CFSET RestOfWord = LCase( Mid(ThisWord, 2, Len(ThisWord)-1) )>

  <!--- Append the completed, capitalized word to the result --->
  <CFSET Result = ListAppend(Result, FirstLetter & RestOfWord, " ")>
</CFLOOP>

<!--- Return the result to the calling template --->
<CFSET "Caller.#Attributes.Output#" = Result>
```

Listing 22.18 relies on the idea that a set of words (similar to a sentence) can be thought of as a list, just like an ordinary, comma-separated list of values. The only difference is that the list is delimited by spaces instead of commas. Therefore, by supplying a space as the delimiter to ColdFusion's list functions, such as `ListAppend()`, you easily can treat each word individually or loop through the list of words in a sentence.

Tip

For more information about lists, see the various list functions (such as `ListFind()`, `ListGetAt()`, and `ListDeleteAt()`) in Appendix B, "ColdFusion Function Reference." See also the discussion about CFML data types in Chapter 9, "Using ColdFusion."

First, two `<CFPARAM>` tags declare the tag's `Input` and `Output` attributes, and a variable called `Result` is set to an empty string. Then, a `<CFLOOP>` tag is used to loop over the words supplied by the `Input` attribute. For each word, the first letter is capitalized and stored in the `FirstLetter` variable. The remaining letters, if any, are stored in the `RestOfWord` variable. So, when the `FirstLetter` and `RestOfWord` variables are concatenated together using the `&` operator, they form the capitalized form of the current word. The `ListAppend()` function is then used to append the word to the list of capitalized words in `Result`, again using the space character as the delimiter. When the `<CFLOOP>` is finished, all the words in `Input` have been capitalized and the tag's work is done. It then passes the completed `Result` back to the calling template using the usual quoted `<CFSET>` syntax.

Note

Because of the way ColdFusion's list functionality behaves, consecutive space characters from the original string are not preserved in the tag's output. ColdFusion treats multiple delimiters as a single delimiter. So, if the `Input` contained three words with five spaces between each word, the resulting `Output` would still contain three words (in title case), but with only one space between each word. This is the defined, documented behavior and is not a bug. Depending on the situation, the multiple-delimiter behavior can work for you or against you. Just keep it in mind.

Listing 22.19 shows how this custom tag can be used—either by you or by other developers—in actual code. Figure 22.6 shows what the results look like in a browser.

LISTING 22.19 `UsingTextToTitleCase.cfm`—**USING THE** `<CF_TextToTitleCase>` **CUSTOM TAG**

```
<HTML>
<HEAD><TITLE>Using &lt;CF_TextToTitleCase&gt;</TITLE></HEAD>
<BODY>
  <H2>Using &lt;CF_TextToTitleCase&gt;</H2>

  <!--- Text to convert to title case --->
  <CFSET OriginalText = "The rest of the band's around back.">

  <!--- Convert text to title case via custom tag --->
  <CF_TextToTitleCase
    Input="#OriginalText#"
    Output="FixedCase">

  <!--- Output the text, now in title case --->
  <CFOUTPUT>
    <P><B>Original Text:</B><BR>
    #OriginalText#<BR>

    <P><B>Processed Text:</B><BR>
    #FixedCase#<BR>
  </CFOUTPUT>

</BODY>
</HTML>
```

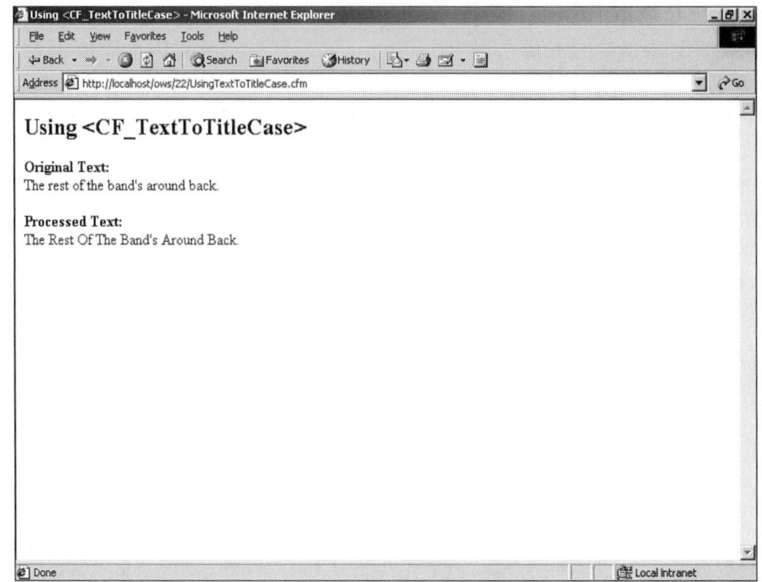

Figure 22.6
The `<CF_TextToTitleCase>` custom tag capitalizes the first letter of each word in a string.

Tip

If you want a more sophisticated custom tag for doing a variety of capitalization tasks, including special handling of acronyms and names, see the `<CF_Capitalize>` custom tag by Tim Hoffman, in the Developers Exchange on the Allaire Web site.

You could use this custom tag to ensure that the titles of all new movies entered in the `Films` table were capitalized in title case. This becomes especially easy if the only way records are added to the `Films` table is by using the `<CF_FilmRecord>` custom tag with `Action="Create"`. You would just need to place the `<CF_TextToTitleCase>` tag in the appropriate spot within `FilmRecord.cfm` (refer to Listing 22.16).

Instead of this line, adapted from Listing 22.16:

```
<!--- Insert Film Record --->
<CFQUERY DATASOURCE="#ATTRIBUTES.DataSource#">
  INSERT INTO Films(MovieTitle, PitchText, AmountBudgeted)
  VALUES ('#ATTRIBUTES.MovieTitle#','#ATTRIBUTES.PitchText#',
➥#ATTRIBUTES.AmountBudgeted#)
</CFQUERY>
```

You could use

```
<!--- Convert film's title to title case via custom tag --->
<CF_TextToTitleCase
  Input="#ATTRIBUTES.MovieTitle#"
  Output="TitleCase">

<!--- Insert film record --->
<CFQUERY DATASOURCE="#ATTRIBUTES.DataSource#">
```

```
  INSERT INTO Films(MovieTitle, PitchText, AmountBudgeted)
  VALUES ('#TitleCase#', '#ATTRIBUTES.PitchText#', #ATTRIBUTES.AmountBudgeted#)
</CFQUERY>
```

If appropriate, you could also add similar code to the `Action="Update"` portion of the template. Listing 22.20 (FilmRecord4.cfm, on the CD-ROM for this book) shows an updated version of the `<CF_FilmRecord>` tag that uses `<CF_TextToTitleCase>` in both places.

Sharing Your Custom Tags

As explained in the section "Finding Tags on the Developers Exchange," earlier in this chapter, the Developers Exchange on the Allaire Web site is the first place most ColdFusion developers go when they are looking for custom tags to purchase or download. If you want to share one of your custom tags with others, consider posting it to the Developers Exchange.

Tip

Many developers also make personal custom tag pages of their own. For instance, you can find many custom tags and other ColdFusion goodies by the authors of this book at `www.forta.com` and `www.nateweiss.com`.

Note

This book was printed shortly before Allaire merged with Macromedia. By the time you read this, the Developers Exchange might have been moved to a new location within the Macromedia Web site, `www.macromedia.com`, perhaps under a different name.

Providing Documentation

If you are going to make one of your custom tags available to other developers, you should write some type of short documentation for the tag. No formal guidelines exist for doing this, but it is customary to write the documentation in a simple HTML (.htm) file and include it in a .zip file along with the custom tag template itself. So, for the `<CF_TextToTitleCase>` custom tag, you might create a documentation file called `CF_TextToTitleCase.htm`.

Tip

ColdFusion Studio's Design tab can be handy when writing a short documentation file. Just create a new HTML file, select the Design tab, and write your custom tag documentation right there in Studio.

At the very least, your documentation should describe what the tag is meant to do and provide a list of its attributes. In general, the more verbose, the better. If your documentation is not clear, you might start getting questions via e-mail from developers who are using the tag. Rest assured, they *will* find you!

Tip

You will find that many developers don't know how to install a custom tag and often start fooling around in the ColdFusion Administrator or the Registry instead of just placing your template in the special `CustomTags` folder. It is therefore recommended that you quickly mention in your documentation how to install the tag.

In addition, it is recommended that you include a sample ColdFusion template (.cfm file) showing how the custom tag should actually be used in code. For instance, for the `<CF_TextToTitleCase>` custom tag, you could simply include the `UsingTextToTitleCase.cfm` template from Listing 22.19.

Posting to the Developers Exchange

Posting your custom tag to the Developers Exchange on the Allaire Web site is simple. If you are going to allow people to download your tag for free, all you need to do is create a .zip file that contains your custom tag template, plus any documentation or examples, as discussed previously. Then go to the Developers Exchange and follow the submit links to post your tag to the exchange.

Visit the Developers Exchange at `http://www.allaire.com/developer/gallery/`.

Selling Your Custom Tags

As of this writing, the Developers Exchange on Allaire's Web site does not accept payment for commercial tags. Therefore, if you want to sell your custom tags, you must either set up a secured payment processing and download area of your own (see Chapter 29) or use a specialized third-party site to handle this for you.

Tip

The CFXtras Web site at `http://www.cfextras.com` is a good example of such a site. Signing up as a tag author and beginning selling your custom tags right away is easy. The site retains a portion of each payment made to you as a service fee.

Studio Dialog Boxes for Your Custom Tags

You can create customized Tag Editor dialog boxes for your custom tags for use in ColdFusion Studio or HomeSite. People then could right-click one of your custom tags in the editor and select Edit Tag to get to your customized dialog box. You also can customize Studio's Tag Inspector, Tag Chooser, and toolbars so they are aware of your custom tags and their attributes.

These capabilities are especially attractive for those interested in distributing their custom tags to other ColdFusion developers, whether for fun or profit. For more information, see our companion volume, *Advanced ColdFusion 5 Application Development* (ISBN: 0-7897-2585-1).

ADDITIONAL CUSTOM TAG TOPICS

In this chapter, you have learned quite a bit about how to use and write custom tags and the various types of roles they can play in your applications. There are still a number of advanced custom tag concepts that just can't be covered completely in this book.

The following topics are covered, however, in our companion volume, *Advanced ColdFusion 5 Application Development*.

PAIRED CUSTOM TAGS

You can create paired custom tags that expect opening and closing tags to be placed in the calling template, just as CFML's own `<CFOUTPUT>` tag expects a matching `</CFOUTPUT>` tag to be present. ColdFusion provides a special structure called `ThisTag`, which can be used to create such tags.

For more information, see our companion volume, *Advanced ColdFusion 5 Application Development*. You can also search for `ThisTag` in ColdFusion Studio's online documentation.

ASSOCIATING NESTED CUSTOM TAGS

You also can create families of custom tags that can be used together and that access each other's attributes and other information when they are used. The tags usually are nested within each other—often to gather multiple sets of attributes. Many of ColdFusion's native tags have special subtags that are used to gather additional information from you, the coder. For instance, consider the `<CFMAILPARAM>` tag, which is used only between opening and closing `<CFMAIL>` tags (see Chapter 28, "Interacting with E-mail"), or the `<CFCATCH>` and `<CFRETHROW>` tags, which are used only between `<CFTRY>` tags (see Chapter 33).

You generally create such tag families using the `<CFASSOCIATE>` tag, which is explained in our companion volume, *Advanced ColdFusion 5 Application Development*.

Note

A great example of this type of custom tag is the extremely popular `<CF_DHTMLMenu>` custom tag by Ben Forta. It is included on the CD-ROM for this chapter for your perusal.

PASSING ATTRIBUTES WITH ATTRIBUTECOLLECTION

In addition to the special `NAME` and `TEMPLATE` attribute names (discussed in the section "Controlling Template Locations with `<CFMODULE>`," earlier in this chapter), a third attribute name exists that you should avoid defining for your custom tags: `ATTRIBUTECOLLECTION`. The `ATTRIBUTECOLLECTION` attribute name is reserved by ColdFusion for a special use: If a structure variable is passed to a custom tag as an attribute called `ATTRIBUTECOLLECTION`, the values in the structure become part of the `ATTRIBUTES` scope inside the custom tag template.

That is, instead of doing this:

```
<!--- Delete movie --->
<CFMODULE
  NAME="FilmRecord"
  Action="Delete"
  FilmID="5">
```

you could do this:

```
<!--- Delete movie --->
<CFSET Attribs = StructNew()>
<CFSET Attribs.Action = "Delete">
<CFSET Attribs.FilmID = 5>
<CFMODULE
  NAME="FilmRecord"
  ATTRIBUTECOLLECTION="#Attribs#">
```

This is really only useful in certain specialized situations, perhaps if you are calling a custom tag *recursively* (using the custom tag within the custom tag's own template, so that the tag calls itself repeatedly when used). You would be able to call a tag a second time within itself, passing the second tag the same attributes that were passed to the first, by specifying `ATTRIBUTESCOLLECTION="#Attributes#"`.

THE REQUEST SCOPE

In addition to the `CALLER` and `ATTRIBUTES` scopes, ColdFusion defines a third special variable scope called `REQUEST`, which is relevant to a discussion of custom tags. Although it is not specifically part of ColdFusion's custom tag framework, it comes into play only in situations in which you have custom tags that might in turn use other custom tags.

MAKING VARIABLES AVAILABLE TO ALL CUSTOM TAGS

Consider the code for the `<CF_FilmRecord>` tag shown previously in Listing 22.16. It defines an optional `DataSource` attribute, which defaults to `ows`. That value is then passed to the `<CF_ShowMovieCallout>` tag from Listing 22.8. Wouldn't it be more convenient to be able to use the `DataSource` variable defined in the `Application.cfm` file, similar to earlier templates? That way, if your application needed to use a different data source name, you could just make the change in one place, in `Application.cfm`.

But how could you refer to that `DataSource` variable? Normally, you would refer to it directly in the `DATASOURCE` attribute for each `<CFQUERY>` tag, as in the `DATASOURCE="#DataSource#"` attribute that has appeared in previous chapters. Of course, in a custom tag template, that variable wouldn't exist because the tag has its own local variable scope. You could access the value using the `CALLER` scope, as in `DATASOURCE="#CALLER.DataSource#"`, but there is a problem with that, too. When `<CF_FilmRecord>` calls `<CF_ShowMovieCallout>`, the code template for `<CF_ShowMovieCallout>` won't be capable of referring to `CALLER.DataSource` because there is no local variable named `DataSource` in the calling template. In this situation, `<CF_ShowMovieCallout>` could refer to `CALLER.CALLER.DataSource` and that would work, but your code will just continue to get messier and messier if you begin to nest tags several levels deep.

The answer is the REQUEST scope, which is a special scope shared among all ColdFusion templates participating in the page request—whether they are included via <CFINCLUDE>, called as a custom tag, or called via <CFMODULE>.

This means you can change these lines in the Application.cfm file:

```
<!--- Any variables set here can be used by all our pages --->
<CFSET DataSource  = "ows">
<CFSET CompanyName = "Orange Whip Studios">
```

to this:

```
<!--- Any variables set here can be used by all our pages --->
<CFSET REQUEST.DataSource  = "ows">
<CFSET REQUEST.CompanyName = "Orange Whip Studios">
```

Then you will be able to provide the REQUEST.DataSource variable to the DATASOURCE attribute of every <CFQUERY> tag in your application, regardless of whether the query is in a custom tag.

Maintaining Per-Request Flags and Counters

The REQUEST scope can also be used to create custom tags that are aware of how many times they have been included on a page. For instance, if you look at the code for the <CF_FilmRecord> tag in Listing 22.16, you will see it includes a <STYLE> block that defines how the callout box will appear. If this custom tag was included several times on the same page, that <STYLE> block will be included several times in the page's source, which will cause the final page to have a longer download time than it should.

You could use the REQUEST scope to ensure the <STYLE> block gets included in the page's source code only once by surrounding the block with a <CFIF> test that checks to see whether a variable called REQUEST.CalloutStyleIncluded has been set. If not, the <STYLE> block should be included in the page. If it has been set, the tag knows the block has already been included on the page, presumably because the tag has already been used earlier on the same page.

So, the <STYLE> block in ShowMovieCallout.cfm would be adjusted to look similar to the following:

```
<!--- If the <STYLE> is not included in this page yet --->
<CFIF IsDefined("REQUEST.CalloutStyleIncluded") EQ "No">
  <!--- Define formatting for film display --->
  <STYLE TYPE="text/css">
    TH.fm {background:RoyalBlue;color:white;text-align:left;
           font-family:sans-serif;font-size:10px}
    TD.fm {background:LightSteelBlue;
           font-family:sans-serif;font-size:12px}
  </STYLE>
```

```
  <!--- Remember that the <STYLE> has been included --->
  <CFSET REQUEST.CalloutStyleIncluded = "Yes">
</CFIF>
```

Listing 22.21 provides the complete code for the revised `ShowMovieCallout.cfm` template.

LISTING 22.21 `ShowMovieCallout2.cfm`—**TRACKING VARIABLES BETWEEN TAG INVOCATIONS**

```
<!---
  <CF_ShowMovieCallout> Custom Tag
  Retrieves and displays the given film

  Example of Use:
  <CF_ShowMovieCallout
    FilmID="5">
--->

<!--- Tag Attributes --->
<!--- FilmID Attribute is Required --->
<CFPARAM NAME="ATTRIBUTES.FilmID" TYPE="numeric">
<!--- Whether to reveal cost/release dates (optional) --->
<CFPARAM NAME="ATTRIBUTES.ShowCost" TYPE="boolean" DEFAULT="Yes">
<CFPARAM NAME="ATTRIBUTES.ShowReleaseDate" TYPE="boolean" DEFAULT="Yes">
<!--- Optional formatting and placement options --->
<CFPARAM NAME="ATTRIBUTES.TableAlign" TYPE="string" DEFAULT="right">
<CFPARAM NAME="ATTRIBUTES.TableWidth" TYPE="string" DEFAULT="150">
<CFPARAM NAME="ATTRIBUTES.Caption" TYPE="string" DEFAULT="Featured Film">
<!--- Use "ows" datasource by default --->
<CFPARAM NAME="ATTRIBUTES.DataSource" TYPE="string" DEFAULT="ows">

<!--- Get important info about film from database --->
<CFQUERY NAME="GetFilm" DATASOURCE="#ATTRIBUTES.DataSource#">
  SELECT
    MovieTitle, Summary,
    AmountBudgeted, DateInTheaters
  FROM Films
  WHERE FilmID = #ATTRIBUTES.FilmID#
</CFQUERY>

<!--- Display error message if record not fetched --->
<CFIF GetFilm.RecordCount NEQ 1>
  <CFTHROW
    MESSAGE="Invalid FilmID Attribute"
    DETAIL="Film #ATTRIBUTES.FilmID# does not exist!">
</CFIF>


<!--- Format a few queried values in local variables --->
<CFSET ProductCost = Ceiling(Val(GetFilm.AmountBudgeted) / 1000000)>
<CFSET ReleaseDate = DateFormat(GetFilm.DateInTheaters, "mmmm d")>

<!--- Now Display The Specified Movie --->
<CFOUTPUT>
  <!--- If the <STYLE> not included in this page yet --->
  <CFIF IsDefined("REQUEST.CalloutStyleIncluded") EQ "No">
```

```
   <!--- Define formatting for film display --->
   <STYLE TYPE="text/css">
     TH.fm {background:RoyalBlue;color:white;text-align:left;
            font-family:sans-serif;font-size:10px}
     TD.fm {background:LightSteelBlue;
            font-family:sans-serif;font-size:12px}
   </STYLE>

   <!--- Remember that the <STYLE> has been included --->
   <CFSET REQUEST.CalloutStyleIncluded = "Yes">
 </CFIF>

 <!--- Show info about featured movie in HTML Table --->
 <TABLE
   WIDTH="#ATTRIBUTES.TableWidth#"
   ALIGN="#ATTRIBUTES.TableAlign#"
   BORDER="0"
   CELLSPACING="0">

   <TR><TH CLASS="fm">
     #ATTRIBUTES.Caption#
   </TH></TR>
   <!--- Movie Title, Summary, Rating --->
   <TR><TD CLASS="fm">
     <B>#GetFilm.MovieTitle#</B><BR>
     #GetFilm.Summary#<BR>
   </TD></TR>
   <!--- Cost (rounded to millions), release date --->
   <CFIF ATTRIBUTES.ShowCost OR ATTRIBUTES.ShowReleaseDate>
     <TR><TH CLASS="fm">
       <!--- Show Cost, if called for --->
       <CFIF ATTRIBUTES.ShowCost>
         Production Cost $#ProductCost# Million<BR>
       </CFIF>
       <!--- Show release date, if called for --->
       <CFIF ATTRIBUTES.ShowReleaseDate>
         In Theaters #ReleaseDate#<BR>
       </CFIF>
     </TH></TR>
   </CFIF>
  </TABLE>
  <BR CLEAR="all">
</CFOUTPUT>
```

Note

Because the REQUEST scope is not shared between page requests, you do not need to use the <CFLOCK> tag when setting or accessing REQUEST variables.

CHAPTER 23

Improving the User Experience

In this chapter

USABILITY CONSIDERATIONS

This chapter concentrates on issues regarding the overall user experience and various ways it can be improved. The phrase *user experience* is purposefully a bit vague and is hard to measure quantitatively. Different people will define it differently. For the purposes of this discussion, think of the quality of the user experience as being affected mainly by the combination of application performance, usability, and friendliness.

In other words, do users have a pleasant experience when they use your application?

PUTTING YOURSELF IN THE USER'S SHOES

One of the best ways to ensure that your application is pleasant for your users to use is to simply keep them in mind as you do your development work. When you are deep into a development project, perhaps rushing to meet a deadline, it's easy to just produce code that works well enough for you to move on to the next task, without asking yourself whether it's really good enough for the user.

So, even if you are not responsible for the design or navigation, you still should keep the user in mind as you put together each data-entry screen or code each query. If users are happy, your application will probably be successful. If they spend too much time waiting or get confused, your application will probably not be successful. In most situations, especially applications aimed at the general public, it's as simple as that.

THINKING ABOUT NAVIGATION

Entire books have been written on great ways to set up navigation elements for Web sites. Navigation elements should not only look good, but also be clear and easy to use. There shouldn't be too many choices, especially on the first page of your application. At the same time, you will notice that most Web sites try to ensure that the most important content is no more than three levels (clicks) deep into the navigation structure. Most usability scholars agree that the most important or most commonly used items should appear before the less important items, even at the cost of the order being somewhat less predictable.

Studying the navigation elements used by your favorite Web sites—the ones you use often—can be helpful. What do these sites have in common? What is the theory behind the navigation on each page? For instance, does it adapt itself to context, or does it remain exactly consistent from page to page? Why are some things on the home page but other things on a second-level page? Try to come up with rules that explain which items appear on which pages, and where. For instance, some sites tend to put verbs in a toolbar at the top of each page and nouns in the left margin. Other sites might do the reverse. Try to come up with similar rules for what goes where within your own application.

Tip

Good discussions on navigation and other design elements can be found on a number of developer-related Web sites. One good place to start is the Dimitry's Design Lab section at the WebReference Web site (`http://www.webreference.com/dlab`).

WHY IT'S GOOD TO BE PREDICTABLE

When describing a friend or a spouse, the word *predictable* doesn't sound like much of a compliment. But when describing a Web application, predictability is almost always something that should be actively pursued and cherished. As users move from page to page, they will feel most comfortable if they can predict, even intuit, what is going to appear next.

ANTICIPATING THE USER'S NEXT MOVE

As you are putting together a page, don't just think about what the user is going to do on that page. Try to figure out what the user is likely to do *next*. If the user is filling out a registration form, he might want to know what your company's privacy policy is. Or, if the user is reading a press release, he might appreciate links to the company's corporate information and information about its management team.

In general, on any page, try to put yourself in the user's shoes and ask yourself whether it's clear how to get to the next step or the next piece of information.

SCRIPTING, ROLLOVERS, AND WIDGETS

JavaScript and Dynamic HTML can go a long way toward making your applications feel more exciting to your users. They also can cause problems of their own. For instance, image rollovers are great when used judiciously but can really slow a page down if too many rollovers are used.

In particular, Dynamic HTML functionality is notorious for behaving differently from browser to browser, version to version, and platform to platform. If you are going to use Dynamic HTML, try to find cross-browser scripts you can adapt until you come to understand what all the specific limitations are. As a start, `www.webreference.com`, `www.builder.com`, and `www.dhtmlzone.com` are good places to look for scripts that work reasonably well in various browsers.

DEALING WITH PROBLEMS GRACEFULLY

Hopefully, your application will never encounter any serious problems or error conditions. Unfortunately, as great as ColdFusion is, your application is bound to run into some type of problem at some point. Try to ensure that any error messages still seem friendly and encouraging to the user and don't cause her to lose her trust in your Web site.

For instance, consider customizing all error messages so that they match the look and feel of your site. For instructions, see the section "Customizing the Look of Error Messages" in Chapter 19, "Introducing the Web Application Framework." See also Chapter 33, "Error Handling."

EASING THE BROWSER'S BURDEN

If an application isn't running as fast as you want it to, you usually should try to look for a source of trouble on the server side, such a `<CFQUERY>` tag that is taking longer to execute than it should. However, you also should spend some time thinking about how much work the browser machine is doing to display your pages.

DEALING WITH IMAGE SIZE

No matter how ardently you work to make your application generate sensible HTML, and no matter how hard you work to ensure all your queries and other server-side code runs quickly, it is all too easy to slow down your pages with a lot of large images. Not only can large images take a long time to download, they also take up room in the browser machine's memory, which can have an effect on the user's computer (depending on how much RAM and virtual memory the user has available).

Here are some suggestions to keep image size in check:

- **Create or resave your images using a program that knows how to compress or optimize images for use on the Web**—In general, you give up a bit of image quality for a smaller file size; the trade-off is generally worth it. For instance, recent versions of Adobe Photoshop include the terrific Save for Web option on the File menu, which enables you to preview how your images will look after they are optimized. Macromedia's Fireworks product also does a great job at compressing image files and generally optimizing them for display on the Web. Other tools, some of them free or shareware, can provide similar results. One place to look for such programs is `www.shareware.com`.
- **Create or resave any JPEG images using a progressive JPEG option, so the images can be displayed in greater and greater detail as they are downloaded**—This is more pleasant for the user because she doesn't have to wait for the whole image to download before she can get a sense of the image. In Photoshop, this is also available in the Save for Web dialog box (see the previous bullet).
- **The `WIDTH` and `HEIGHT` attributes you supply to an `<IMG>` tag don't have to reflect the actual width and height of the image file**—You could, for instance, create an image file that is 50×50 pixels, yet provide `WIDTH` and `HEIGHT` attributes of `100` each. The image's file size would be much smaller, but it would take up the same amount of space on the page. Of course, it would appear pixilated, but depending on the nature of the artwork, that might be fine.
- **If you don't know an image's `WIDTH` and `HEIGHT`, you can determine the width and height by reading the dimensions dynamically using a custom tag or CFX tag**—This occurs in situations such as when you are dealing with images that have been uploaded from users (see Chapter 35, "Interacting with the Operating System"). A number of such tags are available from the ColdFusion Developers Exchange Web site. See Chapter 22, "Building Reusable Components," for details about the Developers Exchange.

- **Always try to provide a sensible ALT attribute for each <IMG> tag to describe what the image is about**—Most browsers display any text you provide in an ALT tag while the image is loading or as a tooltip when the user hovers her mouse over the image. This enables the user to anticipate what each image is going to be before it is actually displayed.
- **Consider using the LOWSRC attribute for your larger <IMG> tags**—The LOWSRC attribute enables a smaller version of the image to be displayed while the full-size image is being downloaded. At the time of this writing, no versions of Internet Explorer support LOWSRC, but it will still be of benefit to Netscape users. Consult the HTML Reference section of ColdFusion Studio's online help for details.

And, of course, you must think about whether your larger images are really necessary. Can they be eliminated, or at least be made a bit smaller? Look at some of your favorite Web sites—the ones you actually use on a daily basis. How many images do you see? Most likely, not that many. Most popular Web sites use other techniques to give visual impact to parts of a page (especially type size and background colors) and use images quite sparingly.

Tip

In any case, always provide WIDTH and HEIGHT attributes for each <IMG> tag. This enables the browser to display the rest of the page correctly before the images have been loaded. Without WIDTH and HEIGHT, the browser might have to wait until all the images have loaded to display anything, or it might have to reflow the document several times as each image is loaded. (The exact behavior in the absence of WIDTH and HEIGHT varies from browser to browser.)

USING TABLES WISELY

HTML tables are a great way to display information in any type of rows-and-columns format, such as the Next N examples shown later in this chapter. Here are a few tips to help you make the most of them, without placing an undue burden on the browser:

- **Whenever possible, provide WIDTH attributes for each <TH> or <TD> cell in the table**—This usually speeds up the display of the table. The exact behavior, however, varies somewhat from browser to browser.
- **You can specify the WIDTH attribute for an entire table as a percentage**—For instance, WIDTH="100%" tells the browser to make the table take up the entire available width of the page. You can also use percentages for the widths of each <TH> and <TD> cell. For instance, if three <TD> cells were in a table row, you could use WIDTH="50%" for the first one and WIDTH="25%" for the second two. This is helpful when you want content to spread itself evenly across the page, regardless of screen resolution. If the user resizes the page, the table automatically resizes itself as well.
- **You should try not to control an entire page's layout using tables**—This is because tables usually cannot be displayed incrementally, which means the table often will not be displayed until the closing </TABLE> tag is encountered. So, if your whole page is laid out using a single, large table, the page might not be displayed at all until the

whole page has been received (regardless of what you do with the <CFFLUSH> tag discussed later in this chapter). Sometimes, however, a table can be displayed incrementally. The exact behavior varies from browser to browser. See the COLS attribute for the <TABLE> tag in an HTML reference for details.

USING FRAMES WISELY

Frames are a nice way to separate sections of a page. A frames-based page usually takes a bit longer to appear at first because each frame must be fetched by the browser by submitting a separate page request to the server. However, after the frameset is loaded, subsequent page requests can be pretty quick (assuming that only one frame needs to be replaced, rather than the whole page).

However, some users find frames confusing—especially if a lot of them are used on a page, each with its own scrollbar. If you choose to use frames in your application, you should try to ensure that the layout is such that the content of each frame does not need to scroll.

Note

If you are using session variables, the introduction of frames makes locking all accesses to the SESSION scope especially important to prevent memory corruption. This can be done for you automatically using the ColdFusion Administrator. See Chapter 20, "Working with Sessions," for details.

USING EXTERNAL SCRIPT AND STYLE FILES

The use of JavaScript and Cascading Style Sheets (CSS) is not discussed specifically in this book, but they often become important parts of ColdFusion applications. CSS and JavaScript code usually are included as part of the HTML document itself, generally in the <HEAD> section. If you will use the same JavaScript functions or CSS classes over and over again, on a number of pages, you should consider moving the script or CSS code into separate files.

This way, the browser must download the file only once, at the beginning of each session (depending on how the browser's caching preferences have been set up by the user), rather than as a part of each page. This can make your pages display more quickly, especially for modem users—and especially if your script or CSS code is rather long.

To move frequently used JavaScript functions into a separate file, just save the JavaScript code to a file with a .js extension. The file should not include opening and closing <SCRIPT> tags; it should contain only the JavaScript code itself. Next, in place of the original <SCRIPT> block, include a reference to the .js file using the SRC attribute of the <SCRIPT> tag, like this (the closing <SCRIPT> tag is required):

```
<SCRIPT LANGUAGE="JavaScript" SRC="MyScripts.js"></SCRIPT>
```

Similarly, to move frequently used CSS code into a separate file, save the CSS code to a file with a .css extension. The file should not include any <STYLE> tags—just the CSS code itself. Now, in place of the original <STYLE> block, include a reference to the .css file using the <LINK> tag:

```
<LINK REL="stylesheet" TYPE="text/css" HREF="MyStyles.css">
```

Browser Compatibility Issues

Not all browsers support all HTML tags. For instance, Internet Explorer does not support the <LAYER> and <SPACER> tags that are supported by Netscape Communicator, and Netscape browsers don't support the <MARQUEE> tag provided by IE. Support for various tags also differs from browser version to browser version—for instance, the <IFRAME> tag was not supported in Netscape browsers until version 6.0. Support for more advanced technologies, such as JavaScript and Dynamic HTML, differ even more widely from browser to browser.

You can use the automatic CGI.HTTP_USER_AGENT variable to determine which browser is being used to access the currently executing template. The HTTP_USER_AGENT value is a string provided by the browser for identification purposes. You can look at the string using ColdFusion's string functions to determine the browser and version number. For instance, the following line of code can be placed in Application.cfm to determine whether the user is using a Microsoft Internet Explorer browser:

```
<CFSET REQUEST.IsIE = HTTP_USER_AGENT contains "MSIE">
```

You then could use the REQUEST.IsIE variable in any of your application's pages (including custom tags or modules) to display Internet Explorer–specific content when appropriate:

```
<CFIF REQUEST.IsIE>
  <!--- Internet Explorer content goes here --->
<CFELSE>
  <!--- Non-IE content goes here --->
</CFIF>
```

Note

If you find that you need to perform more sophisticated tests about the user's environment, you might consider using a tool such as BrowserHawk from cyScape. BrowserHawk gives you a clean, managed way to determine what the user's browser is (version number, platform) and what its capabilities are (frames, DHTML, scripting, installed plug-ins, screen resolution, and so on). For your convenience, an evaluation version of BrowserHawk has been included on this book's CD-ROM.

Remembering Settings

One way to make your application more usable and helpful for your users is to remember certain settings or actions as they interact with it. For instance, in Chapter 20, ColdFusion's Client Management feature was used to remember the words the user last searched for. When a user returns to the search page later, he finds that his last search phrase is already filled in for him. This can improve the user experience both by saving the user time and by making him feel at home.

Remembering Usernames and Passwords

If your application requires users to log in by providing a username and password, you might consider adding some type of "remember me" option on the login form. This would cause the username to be prefilled for the user when he next needs to log in. You can use the same basic technique used in the `SearchForm1.cfm` and `SearchForm2.cfm` templates from Chapter 20. Instead of using the `CLIENT` scope to remember the last search phrase, use it to remember and prefill the username.

Note

Of course, this makes your application less secure because anyone with physical access to the user's machine could see the user's username.

Other Helpful Settings to Remember

Many other things can be remembered between user visits to save the user time and make him feel more at home:

- If the user has indicated which country he lives in, you could show him content relevant to his country each time he returns to your site, perhaps even translated into the appropriate language.
- If the user has a favorite color, you could store the color in the `CLIENT` scope and use it to set the `BGCOLOR` for the `<BODY>` tags at the top of each page.

Avoiding the Big Brother Effect

After you start thinking about remembering settings for the user, it becomes clear that you probably could retain just about everything each user does, on which pages, and when. However, if your application begins to flaunt its knowledge of the user's actions in a way that is perceived as excessive, you might start to lose the trust of your users. People like it when sites are personalized for them, but no one likes to feel as if their every move is being watched and recorded. Also, be sure you aren't violating any type of privacy statement your company or client has made publicly available.

Creating Next N Records Interfaces

Sooner or later, you probably will run into a situation in which you need to build what we call a *Next N interface*. A Next N interface is any Web page that enables the user to view a large number of records—say, 10 or 20 at a time. You probably have seen such interfaces yourself on a number of Web sites. They are very common on search engine Web sites, which might have 1,000 records to look through. Instead of showing you all 1,000 records at once, buttons or links labeled Next and Back move you through the records in more reasonable chunks.

ADVANTAGES OF NEXT N INTERFACES

This type of interface has a number of advantages:

- **Familiarity**—Because Next N interfaces are so common, many users expect them whenever they are presented with a large number of records. If they see a ton of records without such an interface, your application might seem unfinished.
- **Performance**—As discussed earlier, good performance is part of providing a good user experience. Because Next N interfaces put an upper boundary on the size of the generated HTML, pages that use them usually are easier on both the browser machine and the ColdFusion server.
- **Readability**—Most importantly, Next N interfaces usually enable the user to more easily find the information she is looking for, simply because reading a small page is faster than reading a large one.

WHEN TO CREATE A NEXT N INTERFACE

It will usually be obvious when you need to add a Next N interface to a particular display page. Other times, though, it is not so obvious and only becomes evident over time, as the number of records in the database grows. A year after an application is deployed, what seemed to be a nice, compact data-display page when you wrote it could get to the point where it is slow and unmanageable. So, you should consider creating some variation on the Next N interface presented in this chapter whenever you think the user might sometime need to look at a large number of records.

Tip

You might come up with an internal user interface policy stipulating that whenever a user will be presented with more than 50 records, a Next N interface should be implemented. You might pick a larger cutoff point if your users have fast connection speeds, or choose a smaller cutoff if many users will connect via slow modems.

CREATING THE BASIC INTERFACE

Say you have been asked to create a simple expense report area for Orange Whip Studio's intranet. The only instruction you have been given is to create a page in which employees can review all expenses. After talking with a few of the employees in the accounting department, you learn that they are usually most interested in viewing the most recent expenses. You decide to display the expense records in reverse order (the most recent expense first), with a Next 10 interface. This way, users can see the new expenses right away and page through the older records 10 at a time.

This section presents four versions of a typical Next N interface, with each version getting a bit more sophisticated.

Limiting the Number of Records Shown

A number of approaches can be taken to create a Next N interface. Listing 23.1 demonstrates a simple, effective technique that easily can be adapted to suit your needs.

The code relies on a URL parameter named `StartRow`, which tells the template which records to display. The first time the page is displayed, `StartRow` defaults to `1`, which causes rows 1–10 to be displayed. When the user clicks the Next button, `StartRow` is passed as `11`, so rows 11–20 are displayed. The user can continue to click Next (or Back) to move through all the records.

Note

Before this listing will work, the `REQUEST.DataSource` variable needs to be set in your `Application.cfm` file, as shown in Listing 23.2.

Note

Listing 23.3, later in this chapter, also must be in place before this listing will work.

Listing 23.1 `NextN1.cfm`—**A Simple Next N Interface**

```
<!--- Retrieve expense records from database --->
<CFQUERY NAME="GetExp" DATASOURCE="#REQUEST.DataSource#">
  SELECT
    f.FilmID, f.MovieTitle,
    e.Description, e.ExpenseAmount, e.ExpenseDate
  FROM
    Expenses e INNER JOIN Films f
    ON e.FilmID = f.FilmID
  ORDER BY
    e.ExpenseDate DESC
</CFQUERY>


<!--- Number of rows to display per Next/Back page  --->
<CFSET RowsPerPage = 10>
<!--- What row to start at? Assume first by default --->
<CFPARAM NAME="URL.StartRow" DEFAULT="1" TYPE="numeric">

<!--- We know the total number of rows from query   --->
<CFSET TotalRows = GetExp.RecordCount>
<!--- Last row is 10 rows past the starting row, or --->
<!--- total number of query rows, whichever is less --->
<CFSET EndRow = Min(URL.StartRow + RowsPerPage - 1, TotalRows)>
<!--- Next button goes to 1 past current end row  --->
<CFSET StartRowNext = EndRow + 1>
<!---"Back button goes back N rows from start row --->
<CFSET StartRowBack = URL.StartRow - RowsPerPage>


<!--- Page Title --->
<HTML>
<HEAD><TITLE>Expense Browser</TITLE></HEAD>
```

```
<BODY>
<CFOUTPUT><H2>#REQUEST.CompanyName# Expense Report</H2></CFOUTPUT>


<TABLE WIDTH="600" BORDER="0" CELLSPACING="0" CELLPADDING="1" COLS="3">
  <!--- Row at top of table, above column headers --->
  <TR>
    <TD COLSPAN="2">
      <!--- Message about which rows are being displayed --->
      <CFOUTPUT>
        Displaying <B>#URL.StartRow#</B> to <B>#EndRow#</B>
        of <B>#TotalRows#</B> Records<BR>
      </CFOUTPUT>
    </TD>
    <TD></TD>
    <TD ALIGN="right">
      <!--- Provide Next/Back links --->
      <CFINCLUDE TEMPLATE="NextNIncludeBackNext.cfm">
    </TD>
  </TR>

  <!--- Row for column headers --->
  <TR>
    <TH WIDTH="100">Date</TH>
    <TH WIDTH="250">Film</TH>
    <TH WIDTH="150">Expense</TH>
    <TH WIDTH="100">Amount</TH>
  </TR>

  <!--- For each query row that should be shown now --->
  <CFLOOP QUERY="GetExp" StartRow="#URL.StartRow#" ENDROW="#EndRow#">
    <CFOUTPUT>
      <TR VALIGN="baseline">
        <TD WIDTH="100">#LSDateFormat(ExpenseDate)#</TD>
        <TD WIDTH="250">#MovieTitle#</TD>
        <TD WIDTH="150"><EM>#Description#</EM></TD>
        <TD WIDTH="100">#LSCurrencyFormat(ExpenseAmount)#</TD>
      </TR>
    </CFOUTPUT>
  </CFLOOP>

  <!--- Row at bottom of table, after rows of data --->
  <TR>
    <TD WIDTH="100"></TD>
    <TD WIDTH="250"></TD>
    <TD WIDTH="150"></TD>
    <TD WIDTH="100" ALIGN="right">
      <!--- Provide Next/Back links --->
      <CFINCLUDE TEMPLATE="NextNIncludeBackNext.cfm">
    </TD>
  </TR>
</TABLE>


</BODY>
</HTML>
```

Note

This listing relies on the STARTROW and ENDROW attributes for the <CFLOOP> tag. See Chapter 10, "CFML Basics," and Appendix A, "ColdFusion Tag Reference," for detailed information about <CFLOOP>.

First, a query named GetExp is run, which retrieves all expense records from the Expenses table, along with the associated MovieTitle for each expense. The records are returned in reverse date order (most recent expenses first). Next, a variable called RowsPerPage is set to the number of rows that should be displayed to the user at one time. Of course, this value can be adjusted to 20, 50, or whatever you feel is appropriate.

Tip

You could set the RowsPerPage variable in Application.cfm if you wanted to use the same value in a number of different Next N interfaces throughout your application.

The URL.StartRow parameter is established via the <CFPARAM> tag and given a default value of 1 if it is not actually supplied in the URL. Then, a TotalRows variable is set to the number of rows returned by the GetExp query.

Tip

Sometimes it's worth setting a variable just to keep your code clear. In this template, you could skip the <CFSET> for the TotalRows variable and just use GetExp.RecordCount in its place throughout the rest of the code. But the name of the TotalRows variable helps make the role of the value easier to understand, and virtually no performance penalty will exist for the extra line of code.

Next, a variable called EndRow is calculated, which determines which row should be the last one to appear on a given page. In general, the EndRow is simply RowsPerPage past the StartRow. However, the EndRow should never go past the total number of rows in the query, so the Min function is used to ensure that the value is never greater than TotalRows. This becomes important when the user reaches the last page of search results. The URL.StartRow and EndRow values are passed to the STARTROW and ENDROW attributes of the <CFLOOP> that displays the expense records, effectively throttling the display so it shows only the appropriate records for the current page.

StartRowNext and StartRowBack represent what the new StartRow value should be if the user clicks the Next or Back link. If the user clicks Next, the page is reloaded at one row past the current EndRow. If the user clicks Back, the display moves back by the value stored in RowsPerPage (which is 10 in this example).

After this small set of variables has been calculated, the rest of the template is really quite simple. An HTML table is used to display the expense results. The first row of the table displays a message about which rows are currently being shown. It also displays Next and Back links, as appropriate, by including the NextNIncludeBackNext.cfm template (see Listing 23.3). The next row of the table displays some simple column headings. Then, the

<CFLOOP> tag is used to output a table row for each record returned by the GetExp query, but only for the rows from URL.StartRow through EndRow. Finally, the last row of the HTML table repeats the Next and Back links under the expense records, using a second <CFINCLUDE> tag.

Note

For now, don't worry about the fact that the query must be rerun each time the user clicks the Next or Back link. ColdFusion's query-caching feature can be used to ensure that your database is not queried unnecessarily. See Chapter 24, "Improving Performance," for details.

The Application.cfm file shown in Listing 23.2 establishes the REQUEST.DataSource and REQUEST.CompanyName variables used in Listing 23.1. Because they are set in the special REQUEST scope, these variables are available for use within any of this folder's templates, including any custom tags.

This is an excellent way to establish global settings for an application, such as data source names, and is used in most of the Application.cfm templates in the second half of this book. For more information about this use of the special REQUEST scope, see the section "The REQUEST Scope" in Chapter 22, "Building Reusable Components."

Listing 23.2 Application.cfm—**Providing Application Settings for This Chapter's Examples**

```
<!---
  Filename:     Application.cfm
  Created by:   Nate Weiss (NMW)
  Date Created: 2/18/2001
  Please Note:  Executes for each page request
--->

<!--- Any variables set here can be used by all our pages --->
<CFSET REQUEST.DataSource = "ows">
<CFSET REQUEST.CompanyName = "Orange Whip Studios">
```

Adding Next and Back Buttons

Listing 23.3 provides the code that includes the Back and Next links above and below the expense records. The idea here is simple: to show Back and Next links when appropriate. The Back link should be shown whenever the StartRowBack value is greater than 0, which should always be the case unless the user is looking at the first page of records. The Next link should be shown as long as the StartRowNext value is not after the last row of the query, which would be the case only when the user is at the last page of records.

Listing 23.3 NextNIncludeBackNext.cfm—**Including Back and Next Buttons**

```
<!--- Provide Next/Back links --->
<CFOUTPUT>
  <!--- Show link for Back, if appropriate --->
```

LISTING 23.3 CONTINUED

```
  <CFIF StartRowBack GT 0>
    <A HREF="#CGI.SCRIPT_NAME#?StartRow=#StartRowBack#">
      <IMG SRC="../images/BrowseBack.gif" WIDTH="40" HEIGHT="16"
        ALT="Back #RowsPerPage# Records" BORDER="0"></A>
  </CFIF>
  <!--- Show link for Next, if appropriate --->
  <CFIF StartRowNext LT TotalRows>
    <A HREF="#CGI.SCRIPT_NAME#?StartRow=#StartRowNext#">
      <IMG SRC="../images/BrowseNext.gif" WIDTH="40" HEIGHT="16"
        ALT="Next #RowsPerPage# Records" BORDER="0"></A>
  </CFIF>
</CFOUTPUT>
```

As you can see, the Next and Back links always reload the current page, passing the appropriate `StartRow` parameter in the URL. Now the user can navigate through the all the query's records in digestible groups of 10. Figure 23.1 shows what the results look like in a browser.

Note

Because the `CGI.SCRIPT_NAME` variable is used for the Back and Next links, this code continues to provide the correct links even if you change the filename for Listing 23.1. If you find this confusing, you could replace the `CGI.SCRIPT_NAME` with the name of the template the user will be accessing (in this case, `NextN1.cfm`). See Appendix C, "Special ColdFusion Variables and Result Codes," for more information about this handy CGI variable.

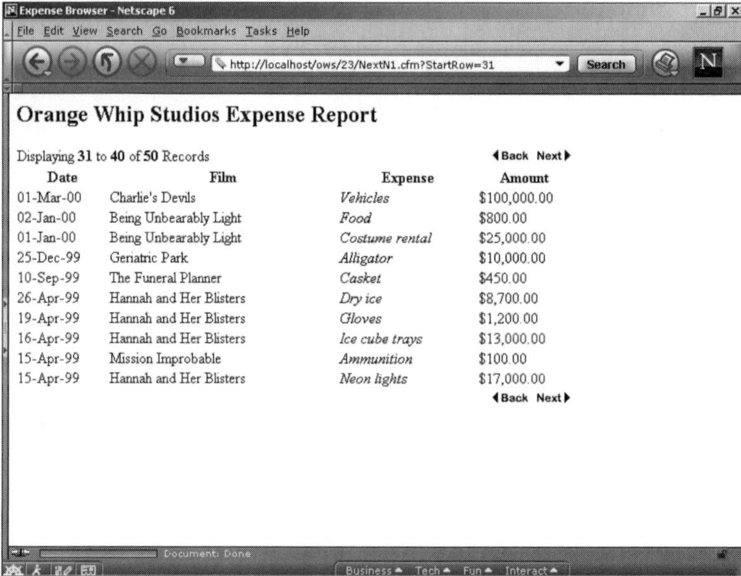

Figure 23.1
Creating a simple Next 10 type of interface for your users is easy.

ALTERNATING ROW COLORS FOR READABILITY

Listing 23.4 is a revised version of Listing 23.1. This version just adds some basic formatting via CSS syntax and presents the rows of data with alternating colors, as shown in Figure 23.2.

LISTING 23.4 `NextN2.cfm`—**ADDING CSS-BASED FORMATTING TO THE NEXT N INTERFACE**

```
<!--- Retrieve expense records from database --->
<CFQUERY NAME="GetExp" DATASOURCE="#REQUEST.DataSource#">
  SELECT
    f.FilmID, f.MovieTitle,
    e.Description, e.ExpenseAmount, e.ExpenseDate
  FROM
    Expenses e INNER JOIN Films f
    ON e.FilmID = f.FilmID
  ORDER BY
    e.ExpenseDate DESC
</CFQUERY>


<!--- Number of rows to display per Next/Back page  --->
<CFSET RowsPerPage = 10>
<!--- What row to start at? Assume first by default --->
<CFPARAM NAME="URL.StartRow" DEFAULT="1" TYPE="numeric">

<!--- We know the total number of rows from query   --->
<CFSET TotalRows    = GetExp.RecordCount>
<!--- Last row is 10 rows past the starting row, or --->
<!--- total number of query rows, whichever is less --->
<CFSET EndRow       = Min(URL.StartRow + RowsPerPage - 1, TotalRows)>
<!--- Next button goes to 1 past current end row  --->
<CFSET StartRowNext = EndRow + 1>
<!--- Back button goes back N rows from start row --->
<CFSET StartRowBack = URL.StartRow - RowsPerPage>


<!--- Page Title --->
<HTML>
<HEAD><TITLE>Expense Browser</TITLE></HEAD>
<BODY>
<CFOUTPUT><H2>#REQUEST.CompanyName# Expense Report</H2></CFOUTPUT>

<!--- Simple style sheet for formatting --->
<STYLE>
  TH       {font-family:sans-serif;font-size:smaller;
            background:navy;color:white}
  TD       {font-family:sans-serif;font-size:smaller}
  TD.DataA {background:silver;color:black}
  TD.DataB {background:lightgrey;color:black}
</STYLE>

<TABLE WIDTH="600" BORDER="0" CELLSPACING="0" CELLPADDING="1">
  <!--- Row at top of table, above column headers --->
  <TR>
    <TD WIDTH="500" COLSPAN="3">
```

LISTING 23.4 CONTINUED

```
      <!--- Message about which rows are being displayed --->
      <CFOUTPUT>
        Displaying <B>#URL.StartRow#</B> to <B>#EndRow#</B>
        of <B>#TotalRows#</B> Records<BR>
      </CFOUTPUT>
    </TD>
    <TD ALIGN="right">
      <!--- Provide Next/Back links --->
      <CFINCLUDE TEMPLATE="NextNIncludeBackNext.cfm">
    </TD>
  </TR>

  <!--- Row for column headers --->
  <TR>
    <TH WIDTH="100">Date</TH>
    <TH WIDTH="250">Film</TH>
    <TH WIDTH="150">Expense</TH>
    <TH WIDTH="100">Amount</TH>
  </TR>

  <!--- For each query row that should be shown now --->
  <CFLOOP QUERY="GetExp" StartRow="#URL.StartRow#" ENDROW="#EndRow#">
    <!--- Use class "DataA" or "DataB" for alternate rows --->
    <CFSET Class = IIF(GetExp.CurrentRow MOD 2 EQ 0, "'DataA'", "'DataB'")>

    <CFOUTPUT>
      <TR VALIGN="baseline">
        <TD CLASS="#Class#" WIDTH="100">#LSDateFormat(ExpenseDate)#</TD>
        <TD CLASS="#Class#" WIDTH="250">#MovieTitle#</TD>
        <TD CLASS="#Class#" WIDTH="150"><I>#Description#</I></TD>
        <TD CLASS="#Class#" WIDTH="100">#LSCurrencyFormat(ExpenseAmount)#</TD>
      </TR>
    </CFOUTPUT>
  </CFLOOP>

  <!--- Row at bottom of table, after rows of data --->
  <TR>
    <TD WIDTH="100"></TD>
    <TD WIDTH="250"></TD>
    <TD WIDTH="150"></TD>
    <TD WIDTH="100" ALIGN="right">
      <!--- Provide Next/Back links --->
      <CFINCLUDE TEMPLATE="NextNIncludeBackNext.cfm">
    </TD>
  </TR>
</TABLE>


</BODY>
</HTML>
```

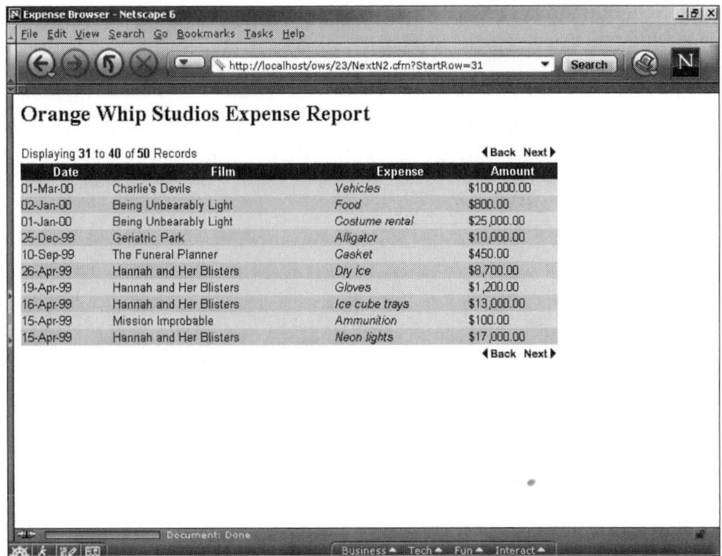

Figure 23.2
The background colors of table cells can be alternated to make the display easier to read.

Defining Styles

The `<STYLE>` block in Listing 23.4 specifies that all `<TH>` cells should be displayed with white lettering on a navy background. Also, two style classes for `<TD>` cells are defined, called `DataA` and `DataB`. By displaying alternate rows with these two classes, the expenses are displayed with alternating background colors, as shown in Figure 23.2.

Inside the `<CFLOOP>` tag, the code alternates between the `DataA` and `DataB` style classes by using ColdFusion's `MOD` operator. The `MOD` operator simply returns the *modulus* of two numbers, which is the remainder left over when the first number is divided by the second. When the `CurrentRow` is an even number, dividing it by `2` results in a remainder of `0`, so the `Class` variable is set to `DataA`. Otherwise, `Class` is set to `DataB`. The `Class` variable is then used as the `CLASS` attribute for the `<TD>` cells that display each row of expenses. The result is the pleasant-looking rendition of the Next N interface shown in Figure 23.2.

Tip

The `DataA` and `DataB` style classes could vary in more than just background color. They could use different typefaces, font colors, bolding, and so on. See a CSS reference for details.

Note

If you don't want to use CSS-based formatting, you could use the `IIF()` test in Listing 23.4 to switch between two color names instead of class names. Then, you would feed the result to the `BGCOLOR` attribute of the `<TD>` tags, instead of the `CLASS` attribute. This would ensure that the rows displayed with alternating colors, even for browsers that don't support CSS (CSS support appeared in Version 4.0 of Internet Explorer and Netscape Communicator). Of course, you could also choose to alternate both the `CLASS` and `BGCOLOR` values.

A NOTE ON THE USE OF IIF()

The line that sets the Class attribute uses the IIF() function, which enables you to choose between two expressions depending on a condition. The IIF() function is comparable to the ? and : operators used in JavaScript and some other languages. The first parameter is the condition, the second parameter determines what the result should be when the condition is True, and the third is what the result should be when condition is False.

When IIF() is used to switch between two strings, as shown previously in Listing 23.4, the second and third parameters must have two sets of quotes because they each will be evaluated as expressions. If the second parameter were written as "DataA" instead of "'DataA'", an error would result because ColdFusion would try to return the value of a variable called DataA, which does not exist. The inner set of single quotation marks tells ColdFusion that the literal string DataA should be returned. For details, see IIF() in Appendix B, "ColdFusion Function Reference."

The IIF() function is used here because it often improves code readability in cases such as this, due to its brevity. If, however, you find it confusing, you could achieve the same result by replacing the single <CFSET> line with this:

```
<CFIF GetExp.CurrentRow MOD 2 EQ 0>
  <CFSET Class = "DataA">
<CFELSE>
  <CFSET Class = "DataB">
</CFIF>
```

LETTING THE USER BROWSE PAGE-BY-PAGE

Many Next N interfaces you see on the Web provide numbered page-by-page links in addition to the customary Back and Next links. If there are 50 records to display, and 10 records are shown per page, the user can use links labeled 1–5 to jump to a particular set of 10 records. This not only gives the user a way to move through the records quickly, but the collection of clickable page numbers also serves as a visual cue or meter that provides a sense of how many records there are to look through.

For clarity, the page-by-page links are implemented in a separate file called NextNIncludePageLinks.cfm. Listing 23.5 shows the code for this new file.

LISTING 23.5 NextNIncludePageLinks.cfm—CREATING PAGE-BY-PAGE LINKS FOR BROWSING RECORDS

```
<!--- Simple "Page" counter, starting at first "Page" --->
<CFSET ThisPage = 1>

<!--- Loop thru row numbers, in increments of RowsPerPage --->
<CFLOOP FROM="1" TO="#TotalRows#" STEP="#RowsPerPage#" INDEX="PageRow">
  <!--- Detect whether this "Page" currently being viewed --->
  <CFSET IsCurrentPage = (PageRow GTE URL.StartRow) AND (PageRow LTE EndRow)>

  <!--- If this "Page" is current page, show without link --->
  <CFIF IsCurrentPage>
    <CFOUTPUT><B>#ThisPage#</B></CFOUTPUT>
```

```
  <!--- Otherwise, show with link so user can go to page  --->
  <CFELSE>
    <CFOUTPUT>
      <A HREF="#CGI.SCRIPT_NAME#?StartRow=#PageRow#">#ThisPage#</A>
    </CFOUTPUT>
  </CFIF>

  <!--- Increment ThisPage variable --->
  <CFSET ThisPage = ThisPage + 1>
</CFLOOP>
```


Similar to the Back and Next code shown in Listing 23.3, this template's job is to generate a number of links that reload the current template, passing the appropriate `StartRow` parameter in the URL.

First, a variable named `ThisPage` is set to `1`. This variable is incremented as each page-by-page link is displayed. Next, a `<CFLOOP>` tag is used to create each page-by-page link. Because the `STEP` attribute is set to the value of `RowsPerPage`, the `PageRow` variable increments by `10` for each iteration of the loop, until it exceeds `TotalRows`. So, the first time through the loop, `ThisPage` and `PageRow` are both `1`. The second time through the loop, `ThisPage` is `2` and `PageRow` is `11`, and so on.

The next `<CFSET>` determines whether the user is already looking at the page of results currently being considered by the loop. If the current value of `PageRow` is between the `StartRow` and `EndRow` values (refer to Listing 23.4), `IsCurrentPage` is `True`. Now the page number can be displayed by outputting the value of `ThisPage`. If `ThisPage` is the page currently being viewed, it is shown in boldface. If not, the page number is presented as a link to the appropriate page by passing the value of `PageRow` in the URL as the `StartRow` parameter. Now the user can see where she is in the records by looking for the boldface number, and she can jump to other pages by clicking the other numbers, as shown in Figure 23.3.

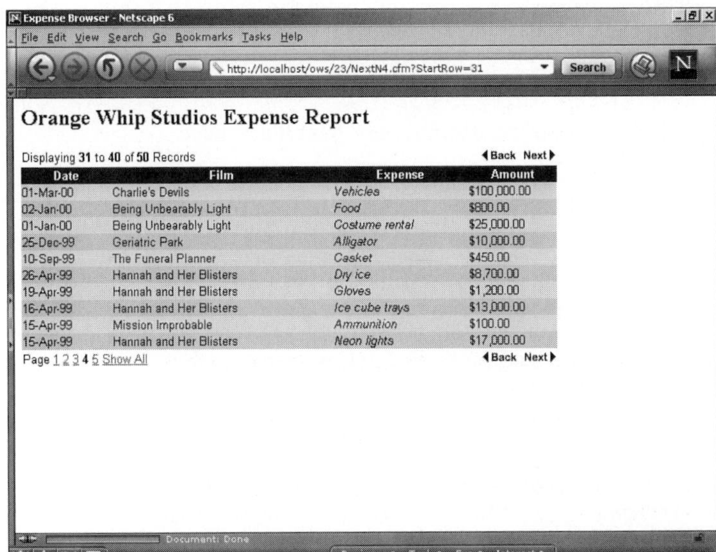

Figure 23.3
The completed interface includes Back, Next, Page-by-Page, and Show All links for easy navigation.

Now that the code has been written, it can be included in the Next N interface with a simple `<CFINCLUDE>` tag, like so:

```
<!--- Shortcut links for "Pages" of search results --->
Page <CFINCLUDE TEMPLATE="NextNIncludePageLinks.cfm">
```

Listing 23.6 (on this book's CD-ROM) builds on the previous version (refer to Listing 23.4) by adding the `<CFINCLUDE>` tag shown previously. The code is otherwise unchanged.

You can also see this `<CFINCLUDE>` tag in the next version of this template (see Listing 23.7).

Adding a Show All Option

Although Next N interfaces are great for keeping your pages from getting too large to navigate properly, your users sometimes might need a way to see all the records at once (for instance, when they need to print a hard copy). Therefore, it's worth considering the addition of a Show All link, which essentially serves to override the Next N interface if the user so desires.

Listing 23.7 is the final version of the Next N interface, which now includes a Show All option, as well as the page-by-page navigation included in the previous version. As you can see, only a few lines of new code were necessary to put the Show All option into place.

Listing 23.7 NextN4.cfm—Adding a Way to View All Records at Once

```
<!--- Retrieve expense records from database --->
<CFQUERY NAME="GetExp" DATASOURCE="#REQUEST.DataSource#">
  SELECT
    f.FilmID, f.MovieTitle,
    e.Description, e.ExpenseAmount, e.ExpenseDate
  FROM
    Expenses e INNER JOIN Films f
    ON e.FilmID = f.FilmID
  ORDER BY
    e.ExpenseDate DESC
</CFQUERY>


<!--- Number of rows to display per Next/Back page  --->
<CFSET RowsPerPage = 10>
<!--- What row to start at? Assume first by default --->
<CFPARAM NAME="URL.StartRow" DEFAULT="1" TYPE="numeric">
<!--- Allow for Show All parameter in the URL --->
<CFPARAM NAME="URL.ShowAll" TYPE="boolean" DEFAULT="No">

<!--- We know the total number of rows from query   --->
<CFSET TotalRows     = GetExp.RecordCount>
<!--- Show all on page if ShowAll is passed in URL   --->
<CFIF URL.ShowAll>
  <CFSET RowsPerPage = TotalRows>
</CFIF>
<!--- Last row is 10 rows past the starting row, or --->
<!--- total number of query rows, whichever is less --->
<CFSET EndRow       = Min(URL.StartRow + RowsPerPage - 1, TotalRows)>
<!--- Next button goes to 1 past current end row  --->
```

```
<CFSET StartRowNext = EndRow + 1>
<!--- Back button goes back N rows from start row --->
<CFSET StartRowBack = URL.StartRow - RowsPerPage>


<!--- Page Title --->
<HTML>
<HEAD><TITLE>Expense Browser</TITLE></HEAD>
<BODY>
<CFOUTPUT><H2>#REQUEST.CompanyName# Expense Report</H2></CFOUTPUT>

<!--- Simple style sheet for formatting --->
<STYLE>
  TH       {font-family:sans-serif;font-size:smaller;
            background:navy;color:white}
  TD       {font-family:sans-serif;font-size:smaller}
  TD.DataA {background:silver;color:black}
  TD.DataB {background:lightgrey;color:black}
</STYLE>

<TABLE WIDTH="600" BORDER="0" CELLSPACING="0" CELLPADDING="1">
  <!--- Row at top of table, above column headers --->
  <TR>
    <TD WIDTH="500" COLSPAN="3">
      <!--- Message about which rows are being displayed --->
      <CFOUTPUT>
        Displaying <B>#URL.StartRow#</B> to <B>#EndRow#</B>
        of <B>#TotalRows#</B> Records<BR>
      </CFOUTPUT>
    </TD>
    <TD WIDTH="100" ALIGN="right">
      <CFIF NOT URL.ShowAll>
        <!--- Provide Next/Back links --->
        <CFINCLUDE TEMPLATE="NextNIncludeBackNext.cfm">
      </CFIF>
    </TD>
  </TR>

  <!--- Row for column headers --->
  <TR>
    <TH WIDTH="100">Date</TH>
    <TH WIDTH="250">Film</TH>
    <TH WIDTH="150">Expense</TH>
    <TH WIDTH="100">Amount</TH>
  </TR>

  <!--- For each query row that should be shown now --->
  <CFLOOP QUERY="GetExp" StartRow="#URL.StartRow#" ENDROW="#EndRow#">
    <!--- Use class "DataA" or "DataB" for alternate rows --->
    <CFSET Class = IIF(GetExp.CurrentRow MOD 2 EQ 0, "'DataA'", "'DataB'")>

    <CFOUTPUT>
      <TR VALIGN="baseline">
        <TD CLASS="#Class#" WIDTH="100">#LSDateFormat(ExpenseDate)#</TD>
        <TD CLASS="#Class#" WIDTH="250">#MovieTitle#</TD>
        <TD CLASS="#Class#" WIDTH="150"><I>#Description#</I></TD>
        <TD CLASS="#Class#" WIDTH="100">#LSCurrencyFormat(ExpenseAmount)#</TD>
      </TR>
```

LISTING 23.7 CONTINUED

```
    </CFOUTPUT>
  </CFLOOP>

  <!--- Row at bottom of table, after rows of data --->
  <TR>
    <TD WIDTH="500" COLSPAN="3">
      <CFIF NOT URL.ShowAll>
        <!--- Shortcut links for "Pages of search results --->
        Page <CFINCLUDE TEMPLATE="NextNIncludePageLinks.cfm">
        <!--- Show All link --->
        <CFOUTPUT>
          <A HREF="#CGI.SCRIPT_NAME#?ShowAll=Yes">Show All</A>
        </CFOUTPUT>
      </CFIF>
    </TD>
    <TD WIDTH="100" ALIGN="right">
      <CFIF NOT URL.ShowAll>
        <!--- Provide Next/Back links --->
        <CFINCLUDE TEMPLATE="NextNIncludeBackNext.cfm">
      </CFIF>
    </TD>
  </TR>
</TABLE>


</BODY>
</HTML>
```

Near the top of the template, a new URL parameter called `ShowAll` is introduced and given a default value of `No`. Two lines later, a simple `<CFIF>` test is used to set the `RowsPerPage` variable to the value of `TotalRows` if `URL.ShowAll` is `True`. Therefore, if the page is accessed with `ShowAll=Yes` in the URL, the page displays all the records in one large group.

The rest of the template is mostly unchanged from the last version. The only difference is the addition of a few `<CFIF>` tests throughout, so the Back, Next, and page-by-page links are not shown when in show all mode. The final results are shown in Figure 23.3.

Note

Again, for now, don't worry about the fact that the query must be rerun each time the user clicks Next, Back, Show All, or one of the numbered page links. ColdFusion's query-caching feature can be used to ensure that your database is not hit too hard. See Chapter 24, "Improving Performance," for details.

RETURNING PAGE OUTPUT RIGHT AWAY WITH CFFLUSH

By default, the output of all ColdFusion templates is automatically *buffered* by the server, which means the HTML for the entire page is sent to the browser at once, after all processing has been completed. In general, this isn't a problem. In fact, it enables

ColdFusion to pull off a number of cool tricks internally (see the section "When You Can't Flush the Buffer," later in this chapter).

That said, in some instances you will want ColdFusion to return the HTML it generates right away, as the template is executing. The browser will be capable of receiving and displaying the HTML as it is generated. Meanwhile, ColdFusion can be finishing the remainder of the template. The act of telling ColdFusion to send back the generated output right away is called *clearing the page buffer*.

WHEN TO CLEAR THE BUFFER

The two basic situations in which you might want to clear the page buffer are as follows:

- **Large Pages**—If the template you are working on will output a lot of information, such as a long article all on one page, or some type of report that will have many records, you might want to flush the page buffer after every 1,000 characters of HTML have been generated. This causes the page to appear to display more quickly because the user can start reading the page before it has been completely received. It can also be easier on the ColdFusion server because the entire page will never have to be in its RAM at the same time.
- **Long-Running Pages**—Sometimes one of your templates might need to perform some type of operation that is inherently slow, but that doesn't necessarily output a large amount of HTML. For instance, if the user is placing an order, verifying his credit card number might take 10 or 15 seconds (see Chapter 29, "Online Commerce"). By clearing the page buffer several times during the order process, you can display a series of "please wait" messages so the user can see that something is actually happening.

In both of the previous situations, clearing the page buffer judiciously can make your applications appear to be more responsive because they give more feedback to the user sooner. That can mean a better user experience.

Caution

In our opinion, you should not just start clearing the page buffer regularly in all your ColdFusion templates. In particular, it is *not* recommended that you place a `<CFFLUSH>` tag in your `Application.cfm` file. See the section "When You Can't Flush the Buffer," later in this chapter.

THE EXCEPTION, NOT THE RULE

Most ColdFusion pages don't fall into either of the categories discussed previously. That is, most of your application's templates will not generate tons and tons of HTML code, and most of them will complete their executions normally in well under a second.

So, clearing the page buffer usually doesn't have much impact on the average ColdFusion template. And after the page buffer has been cleared, a number of features can no longer be used and will generate error messages (see the section "When You Can't Flush the Buffer," later in this chapter).

In short, the capability to flush the page buffer is helpful for dealing with certain special situations, as outlined previously. Unless the template you are working on will produce a large amount of output or will take a long time to process, just let ColdFusion buffer the page normally.

INTRODUCING THE <CFFLUSH> TAG

ColdFusion 5 provides a new tag called `<CFFLUSH>` that lets you clear the server's page buffer programmatically. As soon as ColdFusion encounters a `<CFFLUSH>` tag, it sends anything the template has generated so far to the browser. If the browser can, it displays that content to the user while ColdFusion continues working on the template.

The `<CFFLUSH>` tag takes just one attribute—`INTERVAL`—which is optional. You can use `<CFFLUSH>` without `INTERVAL`; that simply causes the page buffer to be flushed at the moment the tag is encountered. If you provide a number to `INTERVAL`, ColdFusion continues to flush the page cache whenever that many bytes have been generated by your template. So, `INTERVAL="1000"` causes the page buffer to be cleared after every 1,000 bytes, which would mean after every 1,000th character or so.

Tip

If you're not familiar with what a *byte* is, don't worry about it. Just think of the `INTERVAL` attribute as specifying a number of characters, rather than a number of bytes. Basically, each character in the normal English character set takes up a byte in a computer's memory.

FLUSHING THE OUTPUT BUFFER FOR LARGE PAGES

Consider the Show All option shown in Listing 23.7, earlier in this chapter. Over time, hundreds or thousands of records could exist in the `Expenses` table, causing the Show All display to become extremely large. Therefore, it becomes a good candidate for `<CFFLUSH>` tag.

For instance, near the top of Listing 23.7, you could change this code:

```
<!--- Show all on page if ShowAll is passed in URL   --->
<CFIF URL.ShowAll>
  <CFSET RowsPerPage = TotalRows>
</CFIF>
```

to this:

```
<!--- Show all on page if ShowAll is passed in URL   --->
<CFIF URL.ShowAll>
  <CFSET RowsPerPage = TotalRows>

  <!--- Flush the page buffer every 5,000 characters --->
  <CFFLUSH INTERVAL="5000">
</CFIF>
```

Now, the page should begin to be sent to the user's browser in 5,000-character chunks, instead of all at once. The result is that the page should display more quickly when the Show All option is used. Note, however, that the difference might not be particularly noticeable until the Expenses table starts to get quite large. Even then, the difference will likely be more noticeable for modem users.

FLUSHING THE OUTPUT BUFFER FOR LONG-RUNNING PROCESSES

You already have seen how <CFFLUSH> can help with templates that return large pages to the browser. You also can use <CFFLUSH> to help deal with situations in which a lengthy process needs to take place (such as verifying and charging a user's credit card or executing a particularly complex record-updating process).

SIMULATING A LONG-RUNNING PROCESS

To keep the examples in this chapter simple, the following code snippet is used to simulate some type of time-consuming process. Because this code should never be used in an actual, real-world application, it is not explained in detail here. The basic idea is to create a <CFLOOP> that keeps looping over and over again until a specified number of seconds have passed.

For instance, this will force ColdFusion to spin its wheels for five seconds:

```
<CFSET InitialTime = Now()>
<CFLOOP CONDITION="DateDiff('s', InitialTime, Now()) LT 5"></CFLOOP>
```

See Appendix B for more information about the Now() and DateDiff() functions.

Caution

The previous code snippet is a very inefficient way to cause ColdFusion to pause for a specified amount of time and should not be used in your own production code. It will cause ColdFusion to hog the CPU during the time period specified. It is used in this chapter only as a placeholder for whatever time-consuming process you might need to execute in your own templates.

Tip

The <CF_WaitFor> custom tag, available from http://www.nateweiss.com, can be used to safely cause ColdFusion to wait for a specified number of seconds on Windows systems. It will not, however, work on ColdFusion servers running on other platforms.

DISPLAYING A PLEASE-WAIT TYPE OF MESSAGE

The FlushTest.cfm template shown in Listing 23.8 demonstrates how you can use the <CFFLUSH> tag to output page content before and after a lengthy process. Here, the user is asked to wait while an order is processed.

LISTING 23.8 FlushTest.cfm—DISPLAYING MESSAGES BEFORE AND AFTER A LENGTHY PROCESS

```
<HTML>
<HEAD><TITLE>&lt;CFFLUSH&gt; Example</TITLE></HEAD>
<BODY>
```

LISTING 23.8 CONTINUED

```
  <!--- Initial message --->
  <P><STRONG>Please Wait</STRONG><BR>
  We are processing your order.<BR>
  This process may take up to several minutes.<BR>
  Please do not reload or leave this page until the process is complete.<BR>

  <!--- Flush the page output buffer --->
  <!--- The above code is sent to the browser right now --->
  <CFFLUSH>

  <!--- Time-consuming process goes here --->
  <!--- Here, ColdFusion is forced to wait for 5 seconds --->
  <!--- Do not use this CFLOOP technique in actual code! --->
  <CFSET InitialTime = Now()>
  <CFLOOP CONDITION="DateDiff('s', InitialTime, Now()) LT 5"></CFLOOP>

  <!--- Display "Success" message --->
  <P><STRONG>Thank You.</STRONG><BR>
  Your order has been processed.<BR>

</BODY>
</HTML>
```

As you can see, the code is very simple. First, a "please wait" message is displayed, using ordinary HTML tags. Then, the `<CFFLUSH>` tag is used to flush the page buffer, enabling the user to see the message immediately. Next, the time-consuming process is performed (you would replace the `<CFLOOP>` snippet with whatever is appropriate for your situation). The rest of the page can then be completed normally.

If you visit this template with your browser, you should see the please wait message alone on the page at first. After about five seconds, the thank you message will appear. This gives your application a more responsive feel for your users.

DISPLAYING A GRAPHICAL PROGRESS METER

With the help of some simple JavaScript code, you can create a graphical progress meter while a particularly long process executes. The code shown in Listing 23.9 is similar to the previous listing, except that it assumes the time-consuming process the template needs to accomplish has several steps. When the page first appears, it shows an image of a progress indicator that reads `0%`. As each step of the lengthy process is completed, the image is updated so the indicator reads `25%`, `50%`, `75%`, and finally `100%`.

LISTING 23.9 `FlushMeter.cfm`—DISPLAYING A PROGRESS METER BY SWAPPING IMAGES VIA JAVASCRIPT

```
<HTML>
<HEAD><TITLE>&lt;CFFLUSH&gt; Example</TITLE></HEAD>
<BODY>
```

```
  <!--- Initial Message --->
  <P><STRONG>Please Wait</STRONG><BR>
  We are processing your order.<BR>

  <!--- Create the "Meter" image object --->
  <!--- Initially, it displays a blank GIF --->
  <IMG NAME="Meter" SRC="../images/PercentBlank.gif"
    WIDTH="200" HEIGHT="16" ALT="" BORDER="0">

  <!--- Flush the page buffer --->
  <CFFLUSH>

  <!--- Loop from 0 to 25 to 50 to 75 to 100 --->
  <CFLOOP FROM="0" TO="100" STEP="25" INDEX="i">
    <!--- Time-consuming process goes here --->
    <!--- Here, ColdFusion waits for 5 seconds as an example --->
    <!--- Do not use this technique in actual code! --->
    <CFSET InitialTime = Now()>
    <CFLOOP CONDITION="DateDiff('s', InitialTime, Now()) LT 2"></CFLOOP>

    <!--- Change the SRC attribute of the Meter image --->
    <CFOUTPUT>
      <SCRIPT LANGUAGE="JavaScript">
        document.images["Meter"].src = '../images/Percent#i#.gif';
      </SCRIPT>
    </CFOUTPUT>
    <CFFLUSH>
  </CFLOOP>

  <!--- Display "Success" message --->
  <P><STRONG>Thank You.</STRONG><BR>
  Your order has been processed.<BR>
</BODY>
</HTML>
```


First, an ordinary `<IMG>` tag is used to put the progress indicator on the page. The image's `SRC` attribute is set to the `PercentBlank.gif` image, which is just an empty, transparent (*spacer*) image that won't show up (except as empty space) on the page. The `<CFFLUSH>` tag is used to ensure that the browser receives the `<IMG>` tag code and displays the placeholder image right away.

Next, the `<CFLOOP>` tag is used to simulate some type of time-consuming, five-step process. Because of the `STEP` attribute, the value of `i` is `0` the first time through the loop, then `25`, then `50`, then `75`, and then `100`. Each time through the loop, a `<SCRIPT>` tag is output that contains JavaScript code to change the `src` property of the meter `<IMG>`, which causes the meter effect. The buffer is flushed with `<CFFLUSH>` after each `<SCRIPT>` tag, so the browser can receive and execute the script right away. The first time through the loop, the `<IMG>` is set to display the `Percent0.gif` file, then `Percent25.gif`, and so on. The end result is a simple progress meter that can help your users feel like they are still connected during whatever time-consuming processes they initiate. Figure 23.4 shows what the meter looks like in a browser.

Note

> Full coverage of the use of an image's `src` property to swap the images it displays can't be included here. For more information, consult a JavaScript reference book, or the scripting reference section under HTML Reference in ColdFusion Studio's online help.

If the user's browser doesn't support JavaScript, the `<IMG>` tag will simply continue to display the `PercentBlank.gif` image, which the user won't even notice because it is invisible.

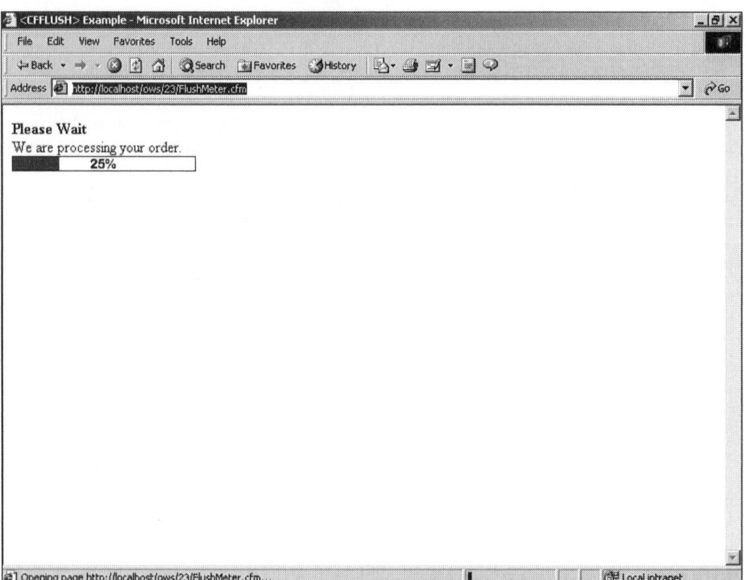

Figure 23.4
The `<CFFLUSH>` tag enables you to display progress indicators during lengthy processes.

FLUSHING THE OUTPUT BUFFER BETWEEN TABLE ROWS

In Listing 23.7, a Show All link was added to the Next N interface for browsing Orange Whip Studio's expenses. Depending on the number of rows in the `Expenses` table, that page could produce quite a bit of output. You might want to consider flushing the page output buffer after every few rows of data, so the user will start to see the rows while the page is being generated.

Listing 23.10 shows how you can add a `<CFFLUSH>` in the middle of an output loop, so groups of rows get sent back to the browser right away. In this example, the rows are sent back in groups of five; in practice, you might want to choose a higher number, such as 20 or 30 rows.

LISTING 23.10 `NextN5.cfm`—SENDING CONTENT TO THE BROWSER AFTER EVERY FIFTH ROW OF DATA

```
<!--- Retrieve expense records from database --->
<CFQUERY NAME="GetExp" DATASOURCE="#REQUEST.DataSource#">
  SELECT
    f.FilmID, f.MovieTitle,
```

```
    e.Description, e.ExpenseAmount, e.ExpenseDate
  FROM
    Expenses e INNER JOIN Films f
    ON e.FilmID = f.FilmID
  ORDER BY
    e.ExpenseDate DESC
</CFQUERY>


<!--- Number of rows to display per Next/Back page  --->
<CFSET RowsPerPage = 10>
<!--- What row to start at? Assume first by default --->
<CFPARAM NAME="URL.StartRow" DEFAULT="1" TYPE="numeric">
<!--- Allow for Show All parameter in the URL --->
<CFPARAM NAME="URL.ShowAll" TYPE="boolean" DEFAULT="No">

<!--- We know the total number of rows from query   --->
<CFSET TotalRows = GetExp.RecordCount>
<!--- Show all on page if ShowAll passed in URL   --->
<CFIF URL.ShowAll>
  <CFSET RowsPerPage = TotalRows>
</CFIF>
<!--- Last row is 10 rows past the starting row, or --->
<!--- total number of query rows, whichever is less --->
<CFSET EndRow = Min(URL.StartRow + RowsPerPage - 1, TotalRows)>
<!--- Next button goes to 1 past current end row  --->
<CFSET StartRowNext = EndRow + 1>
<!--- Back button goes back N rows from start row --->
<CFSET StartRowBack = URL.StartRow - RowsPerPage>


<!--- Page Title --->
<HTML>
<HEAD><TITLE>Expense Browser</TITLE></HEAD>
<BODY>
<CFOUTPUT><H2>#REQUEST.CompanyName# Expense Report</H2></CFOUTPUT>

<!--- simple style sheet for formatting --->
<STYLE>
  TH       {font-family:sans-serif;font-size:smaller;
            background:navy;color:white}
  TD       {font-family:sans-serif;font-size:smaller}
  TD.DataA {background:silver;color:black}
  TD.DataB {background:lightgrey;color:black}
</STYLE>

<TABLE WIDTH="600" BORDER="0" CELLSPACING="0" CELLPADDING="1">
  <!--- Row at top of table, above column headers --->
  <TR>
    <TD WIDTH="500" COLSPAN="3">
      <!--- Message about which rows are being displayed --->
      <CFOUTPUT>
        Displaying <B>#URL.StartRow#</B> to <B>#EndRow#</B>
        of <B>#TotalRows#</B> Records<BR>
      </CFOUTPUT>
    </TD>
    <TD WIDTH="100" ALIGN="right">
      <CFIF NOT URL.ShowAll>
```

PART III CH 23

LISTING 23.10 CONTINUED

```
      <!--- Provide Next/Back links --->
      <CFINCLUDE TEMPLATE="NextNIncludeBackNext.cfm">
    </CFIF>
  </TD>
</TR>

<!--- Row for column headers --->
<TR>
  <TH WIDTH="100">Date</TH>
  <TH WIDTH="250">Film</TH>
  <TH WIDTH="150">Expense</TH>
  <TH WIDTH="100">Amount</TH>
</TR>

<!--- For each query row that should be shown now --->
<CFLOOP QUERY="GetExp" StartRow="#URL.StartRow#" ENDROW="#EndRow#">
  <!--- Use class "DataA" or "DataB" for alternate rows --->
  <CFSET Class = IIF(GetExp.CurrentRow MOD 2 EQ 0, "'DataA'", "'DataB'")>

  <!--- Actual data display --->
  <CFOUTPUT>
    <TR VALIGN="baseline">
      <TD CLASS="#Class#" WIDTH="100">#LSDateFormat(ExpenseDate)#</TD>
      <TD CLASS="#Class#" WIDTH="250">#MovieTitle#</TD>
      <TD CLASS="#Class#" WIDTH="150"><I>#Description#</I></TD>
      <TD CLASS="#Class#" WIDTH="100">#LSCurrencyFormat(ExpenseAmount)#</TD>
    </TR>
  </CFOUTPUT>

  <!--- If showing all records, flush the page buffer after every 5th row --->
  <CFIF URL.ShowAll>
    <CFIF GetExp.CurrentRow MOD 5 EQ 0>
      <!--- End the current table --->
      </TABLE>
      <!--- Flush the page buffer --->
      <CFFLUSH>
      <!--- Start a new table --->
      <TABLE WIDTH="600" BORDER="0" CELLSPACING="0" CELLPADDING="1">
      <!--- Simulate a time-intensive process --->
      <CFSET InitialTime = Now()>
      <CFLOOP CONDITION="DateDiff('s', InitialTime, Now()) LT 1"></CFLOOP>
    </CFIF>
  </CFIF>

</CFLOOP>

<!--- Row at bottom of table, after rows of data --->
<TR>
  <TD WIDTH="500" COLSPAN="3">
    <CFIF NOT URL.ShowAll>
      <!--- Shortcut links for "Pages" of search results --->
      Page <CFINCLUDE TEMPLATE="NextNIncludePageLinks.cfm">
      <!--- Show All Link --->
      <CFOUTPUT>
        <A HREF="#CGI.SCRIPT_NAME#?ShowAll=Yes">Show All</A>
      </CFOUTPUT>
```

```
      </CFIF>
    </TD>
    <TD WIDTH="100" ALIGN="right">
      <CFIF NOT URL.ShowAll>
        <!--- Provide Next/Back links --->
        <CFINCLUDE TEMPLATE="NextNIncludeBackNext.cfm">
      </CFIF>
    </TD>
  </TR>
</TABLE>


</BODY>
</HTML>
```


This code listing is mostly unchanged from the previous version (refer to Listing 23.7). The only significant change is the addition of the <CFIF> block at the end of the <CFLOOP> block. The code in this block executes only if the user has clicked the Show All link, and only if the current row number is evenly divisible by 5 (that is, only for every fifth row).

If both of these conditions are true, the current <TABLE> tag (the one opened near the top of the listing) is closed with a closing </TABLE> tag. The page buffer is then flushed using <CFFLUSH>, and a new table is started with an opening <TABLE> tag that matches the one from the top of the listing. In other words, the expense records are shown as a series of five-row tables that are each sent to the browser individually, rather than as one long table that gets sent to the browser at once. Because each of these minitables is complete, with beginning and ending <TABLE> tags, the browser can display them as it receives them (most browsers can't properly render a table until the closing </TABLE> tag has been encountered).

After the page buffer is cleared, this template waits for one second, using the same time-delay technique that was used in the progress meter example (refer to Listing 23.9). Again, you should never use this technique in your actual code templates. It is used here as a simple way of causing ColdFusion to pause for a moment, so you can see the effect of the page flushes.

If you visit Listing 23.10 with your Web browser and click the Show All link, you will see that the rows of data are presented to you in small groups, with a one-second pause between each group. This proves that the buffer is being cleared, and that a user accessing a very long page over a slow connection would at least be able to begin viewing the records before the entire page had been received.

Of course, in practice, you wouldn't have the time-delay loop at all. It is only included here to make the effect easier to see while developing.

When You Can't Flush the Buffer

This section has introduced the <CFFLUSH> tag and pointed out several situations in which it can be helpful. However, because it causes the content your templates generate to be sent to the browser in pieces—rather than the whole page at once—certain ColdFusion tags and features that depend on being capable of manipulating the page as a whole cannot be used after a <CFFLUSH> tag.

Restrictions on Cookie Use

After the <CFFLUSH> tag has been used on a page, telling ColdFusion to set a cookie in the browser is no longer possible. This is because cookies are set by sending special HTTP headers to the browser, and all HTTP headers must be sent to the browser before any actual HTML content. So, after a <CFFLUSH> tag has been used, sending any additional headers to the browser is no longer possible, which in turn means that it's too late for ColdFusion to set any cookies.

If you really need to set a cookie after a <CFFLUSH>, you can use JavaScript to set the cookie. For your convenience, a custom tag called <CF_SetCookieViaJS> has been included on the CD-ROM for this book. The custom tag supports three attributes—COOKIENAME, COOKIEVALUE, and EXPIRES—which correspond to the NAME, VALUE, and EXPIRES attributes for the regular <CFCOOKIE> tag. The EXPIRES attribute is optional.

So, instead of

```
<CFCOOKIE
  NAME="MyCookie"
  VALUE="My Value">
```

You would use

```
<CF_SetCookieViaJS
  CookieName="MyCookie"
  CookieValue="My Value">
```

Please note that the cookie will be set only if the user's browser supports JavaScript and if JavaScript has not been disabled.

Caution

This custom tag is not supported and is merely presented as a workaround for situations in which you must set a cookie after a <CFFLUSH> tag. Whenever possible, it is recommended that you set cookies using the usual <CFCOOKIE> and <CFSET> methods explained in Chapter 20.

Tip

If you are somewhat familiar with JavaScript, you could study the SetCookieViaJS.cfm custom tag template (on the CD-ROM) as an example of how custom tags can be used to generate JavaScript code.

Note

The PATH, SECURE, and DOMAIN attributes from <CFCOOKIE> are not supported by this custom tag, but they could easily be added by editing the custom tag template. See Chapter 22 for information about building custom tags.

Restrictions on <CFLOCATION>

After a <CFFLUSH> tag has been encountered, you can no longer use the <CFLOCATION> tag to redirect the user to another page. This is because <CFLOCATION> works by sending a redirect header back to the browser. After the first <CFFLUSH> tag has been encountered on a page, the page's headers have already been sent to the browser; thus, it is too late to redirect the browser to another page using the usual methods provided by HTTP alone.

There are a few workarounds to this problem. Both rely on the browser to interpret your document in a certain way, and they are not part of the standard HTTP protocol. That said, these methods should work fine with most browsers.

The first workaround is to include a <META> tag in the document, with an HTTP-EQUIV attribute set to Refresh. Then, provide the URL for the next page in the CONTENT attribute, as shown in the following. Most browsers interpret this as an instruction to go to the specified page as soon as the tag is encountered.

So, instead of this:

```
<CFLOCATION URL="MyNextPage.cfm">
```

you would use this:

```
<META HTTP-EQUIV="Refresh" CONTENT="0; URL=MyNextPage.cfm">
```

Note

If you want the redirect to occur after five seconds rather than right away, you could change the 0 in the previous snippet to 5. See the topic titled Client Pull in ColdFusion Studio's online help for more information about this use of the <META> tag.

Another workaround is to use JavaScript. The following snippet could also be used in place of the <CFLOCATION> shown previously. However, if JavaScript is disabled or not supported by the client, nothing will happen. See the scripting reference in ColdFusion Studio for more information about this use of the document.location object:

```
<SCRIPT LANGUAGE="JavaScript">
<!--
  document.location.href ="MyNextPage.cfm";
//-->
</SCRIPT>
```

OTHER RESTRICTIONS

Several other tags cannot be used after a <CFFLUSH> tag has been encountered, for the same basic reasons the <CFCOOKIE> and <CFLOCATION> tags cannot be used (they all need to write header information).

These tags cannot be used after a <CFFLUSH>:

- <CFCONTENT>
- <CFCOOKIE>
- <CFFORM>
- <CFHEADER>
- <CFHTMLHEAD>
- <CFLOCATION>

CHAPTER 24

Improving Performance

In this chapter

OPTIONS IN THE COLDFUSION ADMINISTRATOR

This chapter discusses a number of ways to improve the performance of your ColdFusion templates, some of which are a bit involved. Before getting into the specific solutions discussed in the rest of this chapter, you should be aware of a number of server-wide options provided by the ColdFusion Administrator that can affect the overall performance of your applications.

The Administrator options most likely to have a direct effect on performance are

- **Limit Simultaneous Requests**—This option on the Settings page of the Administrator should be set to a fairly low number (but higher than 1) for best performance.
- **Suppress Whitespace by Default**—This option on the Settings page should be enabled for best performance.
- **Enforce Strict Attribute Validation**—This option on the Settings page should be enabled for best performance.
- **Template Cache Size**—This option on the Caching page should be set to a number greater than the total file sizes of all your ColdFusion templates for best performance.
- **Trusted Cache**—This option on the Caching page should be enabled for best performance, but only after you have completely finished writing your code.
- **Maintain Database Connections**—This option for each of your data sources should be enabled for best performance.

You are encouraged to consult Chapter 30, "ColdFusion Server Configuration," for details on each of these options.

IMPROVING QUERY PERFORMANCE WITH CACHING

Nearly all ColdFusion applications have a database at their heart, and most ColdFusion templates contain at least one `<CFQUERY>` or other database interaction. In fact, depending on the type of application you are building, your ColdFusion templates might be solely about getting information in and out of a database. In such a situation, ColdFusion is basically behaving as *database middleware*, sitting between your database and your Web server.

Because database access is such an integral part of ColdFusion development, the server provides a number of features to help you improve the performance of your database queries. This section helps you understand which options are available to you and how to make the most of them.

In particular, this section discusses the following:

- Query caching, which cuts down on the amount of interaction between your database and ColdFusion. This can improve performance dramatically.
- Helping ColdFusion deal with larger query results, via the `BLOCKFACTOR` attribute.

Note

It used to be easier to think of ColdFusion as simply being a database middleware application. In fact, very early versions of ColdFusion were so database centric that what we now call CFML was known as DBML, and tags such as `<CFOUTPUT>` and `<CFIF>` were known as `<DBOUTPUT>` and `<DBIF>`. With the addition of more services such as e-mail, HTTP, LDAP, graphing, file manipulation, Java integration, and content streaming, ColdFusion has since expanded and matured into something much more interesting: a Web application server.

UNDERSTANDING QUERY CACHING

To help improve performance, ColdFusion provides a wonderful feature called *query caching*. Basically, the idea is to allow ColdFusion to keep frequently used query results in its internal memory, rather than retrieving the results from the database over and over again.

You tell ColdFusion to cache a query by adding a `CACHEDWITHIN` or `CACHEDAFTER` attribute to the `<CFQUERY>` tag. If one of your templates is visited often, and contains a query that will not return different results each time it is run, you usually can give the page an instant performance boost by simply using one of these two special attributes. Table 24.1 explains what each of the attributes does.

TABLE 24.1 `<CFQUERY>` ATTRIBUTES RELEVANT FOR QUERY CACHING

Attribute	Purpose
`CACHEDWITHIN`	Optional. Tells ColdFusion to cache the query results for a period of time, which you can specify in days, hours, minutes, or seconds. You specify the time period using the `CreateTimeSpan()` function.
`CACHEDAFTER`	Optional. Tells ColdFusion to cache the query results based on a particular date and time. This attribute is generally less useful in real-world applications than `CACHEDWITHIN`. If you know that your database will be updated at a certain moment in time, perhaps after some type of external batch process, you can specify that date and time (as a ColdFusion date value) here.

Query caching is really easy to use. Say you use the following query in one of your ColdFusion templates:

```
<CFQUERY NAME="GetFilms" DATASOURCE="ows">
  SELECT * FROM Films
</CFQUERY>
```

Assuming that the data in the `Films` table doesn't change very often, it would probably be sufficient to only query the database occasionally, rather than with every page request. For instance, you might decide that the database really only needs to be checked for new or changed data every 15 minutes. Within each 15-minute period, the data from a previous query can just be reused. To get this effect, simply add a `CACHEDWITHIN` attribute that uses `CreateTimeSpan()` to specify a 15-minute interval, like this:

```
<CFQUERY NAME="GetFilms" DATASOURCE="ows"
  CACHEDWITHIN="#CreateTimeSpan(0,0,15,0)#">
```

```
  SELECT * FROM Films
</CFQUERY>
```

> **Note**
>
> See Appendix B, "ColdFusion Function Reference," for information about the `CreateTimeSpan()` function.

That's all you have to do. The first time the query is run, ColdFusion will interact with the database normally and retrieve the film records. But instead of discarding the records when the page request is finished—as it would normally—ColdFusion stores the query results in the server's RAM. The next time the template is visited, ColdFusion uses the records in its memory, instead of contacting the database again. It continues to do so for 15 minutes after the first query was run (or until the ColdFusion server is restarted). After the 15 minutes, the records are flushed from the server's RAM. Then, the next time the template is visited, the records are retrieved afresh from the database.

There's more. Queries aren't cached on a per-page basis. They are cached on a server-wide basis. If two `<CFQUERY>` tags on two different pages specify the exact same SQL code, `DATASOURCE`, and `NAME`, they will share the same cache. That is, the first time either page is accessed, the database is contacted and the records are retrieved. Then, for the next 15 minutes (or whatever interval you specify), a visit to either page will use the cached copy of the query results.

> **Note**
>
> If the two `<CFQUERY>` tags specify `USERNAME`, `PASSWORD`, `DBTYPE`, `DBSERVER`, or `DBNAME` attributes, all these attributes must be the same as well. If not, the two `<CFQUERY>` tags will be cached independently of one another (each will operate on its own 15-minute cycle).

> **Note**
>
> The SQL statements in the two `<CFQUERY>` tags must be exactly the same, even considering whitespace such as tabs, indenting, and spaces. If they're not the same, the two queries will be cached independently.

Clearly, if a query is at all time-consuming, the performance benefits can be tremendous. Every template that uses the cached query will be sped up. Plus, if the database and ColdFusion are on different machines, using query caching will likely cut down dramatically on network traffic. This tends to improve performance as well, depending on how your local network is configured.

> **Note**
>
> Of course, a possible disadvantage to caching a query is that changes to the data in the database will not be reflected right away. Any new records (or updates or deletes) will "show up" only after the cache interval has expired. See the section "Refreshing a Cached Query Programmatically," later in this chapter.

USING CACHED QUERIES

One obvious situation in which ColdFusion's query caching feature can be of great benefit is when building a Next N type of record-browsing interface, such as the one presented in Chapter 23, "Improving the User Experience."

Listing 24.1 takes the `NextN4.cfm` template from Listing 23.7 of Chapter 23 and adds a `CACHEDWITHIN` attribute to the `<CFQUERY>` at the top of the template. Now ColdFusion does not need to keep rerunning the query as the user browses through the pages of records.

LISTING 24.1 `NextNCached.cfm`—ADDING THE `CACHEDWITHIN` ATTRIBUTE TO SPEED UP RECORD BROWSING

```
<!--- Retrieve expense records from database --->
<!--- Query will be cached for 15 minutes at a time --->
<CFQUERY NAME="GetExp" DATASOURCE="#REQUEST.DataSource#"
  CACHEDWITHIN="#CreateTimeSpan(0,0,15,0)#">
  SELECT
    f.FilmID, f.MovieTitle,
    e.Description, e.ExpenseAmount, e.ExpenseDate
  FROM
    Expenses e INNER JOIN Films f
    ON e.FilmID = f.FilmID
  ORDER BY
    e.ExpenseDate DESC
</CFQUERY>


<!--- Number of rows to display per Next/Back page  --->
<CFSET RowsPerPage = 10>
<!--- What row to start at? Assume first by default --->
<CFPARAM NAME="URL.StartRow" DEFAULT="1" TYPE="numeric">
<!--- Allow for Show All parameter in the URL --->
<CFPARAM NAME="URL.ShowAll" TYPE="boolean" DEFAULT="No">

<!--- We know the total number of rows from query   --->
<CFSET TotalRows = GetExp.RecordCount>
<!--- Show all on page if ShowAll passed in URL   --->
<CFIF URL.ShowAll>
  <CFSET RowsPerPage = TotalRows>
</CFIF>
<!--- Last row is 10 rows past the starting row, or --->
<!--- total number of query rows, whichever is less --->
<CFSET EndRow = Min(URL.StartRow + RowsPerPage - 1, TotalRows)>
<!--- Next button goes to 1 past current end row  --->
<CFSET StartRowNext = EndRow + 1>
<!--- Back button goes back N rows from start row --->
<CFSET StartRowBack = URL.StartRow - RowsPerPage>


<!--- Page Title --->
<HTML>
<HEAD><TITLE>Expense Browser</TITLE></HEAD>
<BODY>
<CFOUTPUT><H2>#REQUEST.CompanyName# Expense Report</H2></CFOUTPUT>
```

Listing 24.1 Continued

```
<!--- Simple style sheet for formatting --->
<STYLE>
  TH       {font-family:sans-serif;font-size:smaller;
            background:navy;color:white}
  TD       {font-family:sans-serif;font-size:smaller}
  TD.DataA {background:silver;color:black}
  TD.DataB {background:lightgrey;color:black}
</STYLE>

<TABLE WIDTH="600" BORDER="0" CELLSPACING="0" CELLPADDING="1">
  <!--- Row at top of table, above column headers --->
  <TR>
    <TD WIDTH="500" COLSPAN="3">
      <!--- Message about which rows are being displayed --->
      <CFOUTPUT>
        Displaying <B>#URL.StartRow#</B> to <B>#EndRow#</B>
        of <B>#TotalRows#</B> Records<BR>
      </CFOUTPUT>
    </TD>
    <TD WIDTH="100" ALIGN="right">
      <CFIF NOT URL.ShowAll>
        <!--- Provide Next/Back links --->
        <CFINCLUDE TEMPLATE="NextNIncludeBackNext.cfm">
      </CFIF>
    </TD>
  </TR>

  <!--- Row for column headers --->
  <TR>
    <TH WIDTH="100">Date</TH>
    <TH WIDTH="250">Film</TH>
    <TH WIDTH="150">Expense</TH>
    <TH WIDTH="100">Amount</TH>
  </TR>

  <!--- For each query row that should be shown now --->
  <CFLOOP QUERY="GetExp" StartRow="#URL.StartRow#" ENDROW="#EndRow#">
    <!--- Use class "DataA" or "DataB" for alternate rows --->
    <CFSET Class = IIF(GetExp.CurrentRow MOD 2 EQ 0, "'DataA'", "'DataB'")>

    <CFOUTPUT>
      <TR VALIGN="baseline">
        <TD CLASS="#Class#" WIDTH="100">#LSDateFormat(ExpenseDate)#</TD>
        <TD CLASS="#Class#" WIDTH="250">#MovieTitle#</TD>
        <TD CLASS="#Class#" WIDTH="150"><I>#Description#</I></TD>
        <TD CLASS="#Class#" WIDTH="100">#LSCurrencyFormat(ExpenseAmount)#</TD>
      </TR>
    </CFOUTPUT>
  </CFLOOP>

  <!--- Row at bottom of table, after rows of data --->
  <TR>
    <TD WIDTH="500" COLSPAN="3">
      <CFIF NOT URL.ShowAll>
        <!--- Shortcut links for "Pages" of search results --->
        Page <CFINCLUDE TEMPLATE="NextNIncludePageLinks.cfm">
```

```
        <!--- Show All link --->
        <CFOUTPUT>
          <A HREF="#CGI.SCRIPT_NAME#?ShowAll=Yes">Show All</A>
        </CFOUTPUT>
      </CFIF>
    </TD>
    <TD WIDTH="100" ALIGN="right">
      <CFIF NOT URL.ShowAll>
        <!--- Provide Next/Back links --->
        <CFINCLUDE TEMPLATE="NextNIncludeBackNext.cfm">
      </CFIF>
    </TD>
  </TR>
</TABLE>

</BODY>
</HTML>
```


If you want, you can watch which queries are actually being cached by turning on the Show Query Information option on the Debug Options page of the ColdFusion Administrator. Whenever a query is being returned from the cache, the words `Cached Query` will show up where the execution time would ordinarily be displayed, as shown in Figure 24.1. When the cache timeout expires, you will see the execution time reappear in milliseconds, as it does normally.

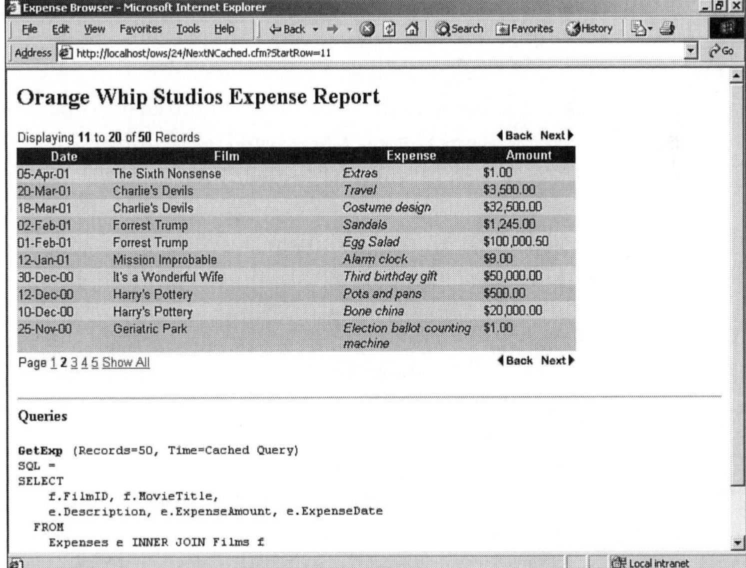

Figure 24.1 Cached queries are fetched directly from ColdFusion's internal memory, which can greatly improve performance.

Refreshing a Cached Query Programmatically

Query caching is used most often for queries that do not change often over time, or in situations where it is acceptable for your application to show information that might be slightly out of date. However, you might run into situations in which you want a query to be cached for several hours at a time (because the underlying data hardly ever changes), but where it is very important for changes to the database to be reflected right away.

ColdFusion doesn't provide a specific attribute for flushing a cache query, but you can achieve the same effect by including a `<CFQUERY>` tag with a negative `CACHEDWITHIN` value right after a relevant change is made to the database. This will force ColdFusion to contact the database and fetch the updated records. From that point on, the updated version of the query results will be what is shared with other pages that use the same query.

> **Note**
>
> This technique is not effective if the database is being updated not via ColdFusion, but via some other application.

For instance, say you are using the following cached query in your code:

```
<CFQUERY NAME="GetFilms" DATASOURCE="ows"
  CACHEDWITHIN="#CreateTimeSpan(0,3,0,0)#">
  SELECT * FROM Films
</CFQUERY>
```

Left to its own devices, this query's cache will be refreshed only every three hours. Now say that some other page updates one of the film records, perhaps using a `<CFUPDATE>` tag, like so:

```
<CFUPDATE DATASOURCE="ows" TABLENAME="Films">
```

Again, left to its own devices, the `SELECT` query will continue to show the cached records until the three-hour timeout expires. Only then will the changes made by the `<CFUPDATE>` be fetched from the database. However, you could force the updated records into the cache by placing the following query right after the `<CFUPDATE>`:

```
<CFQUERY NAME="GetFilms" DATASOURCE="ows"
➥CACHEDWITHIN="#CreateTimeSpan(0,0,0,-1)#">
  SELECT * FROM Films
</CFQUERY>
```

Now, when the first `SELECT` query is next executed, it will read the updated records from the cache. Your application will be always be showing the most current version of the records, even though it is usually reading the records from the query cache.

> **Caution**
>
> The SQL statements in the two `<CFQUERY>` tags (the one that uses the `CACHEDWITHIN` of three hours and the one that uses the negative `CACHEDWITHIN` value) must be exactly the same, even considering indenting and other whitespace. The `NAME` and `DATASOURCE` attributes must also be identical, as well as any `USERNAME`, `PASSWORD`, `DBTYPE`, `DBSERVER`, or `DBNAME` attributes you might be providing. If not, the queries will be considered separate for caching purposes, which means that the second query will not have the desired effect of refreshing the first.

Limiting the Number of Cached Queries

To ensure your cached queries don't take up crippling amounts of the server's RAM, ColdFusion imposes a server-wide limit on the number of queries that can be cached at any given time. By default, the limit is set to 100 cached queries. If a new `<CFQUERY>` tag that uses `CACHEDWITHIN` or `CACHEDAFTER` is encountered after 100 queries are already in the cache, the oldest query is dropped from the cache and is replaced with the new query.

You can increase this limit by editing the Limit the Maximum Number of Cached Queries on the Server field on the Caching page of the ColdFusion Administrator. Keep in mind that it's the final SQL code that determines how a query is cached. So, if you use a ColdFusion variable in the SQL portion of a `<CFQUERY>` tag, and the query is run with 10 different variable values during a given period, that will count as 10 queries toward the limit of 100. See Chapter 30 for details.

Caution

Unfortunately, there is currently no way to limit the number of cached queries based on the amount of memory they actually take up. The only way to limit them is by number, which means that a very small query might push a very large query out of the cache after the limit has been reached. Perhaps a future release of ColdFusion will allow cached queries to be limited by total memory consumption, rather than only by number.

Controlling How Many Records Are Fetched at Once

Normally, ColdFusion retrieves each record from your database individually. This doesn't necessarily take a long time because the ODBC and other database drivers supported by ColdFusion are generally quite efficient.

That said, if you know a query will return more than a few records, you can speed up ColdFusion a bit by giving it a hint about how many records are likely to be returned. You provide this hint by providing a `BLOCKFACTOR` attribute in your `<CFQUERY>` tags. The `BLOCKFACTOR` should be a reasonable guess as to how many records might be returned by the query.

However, you should not provide a `BLOCKFACTOR` that is less than the number of records returned by the query. If you do, your database driver will tell ColdFusion that the specified `BLOCKFACTOR` is invalid, and ColdFusion will try again—this time subtracting one from the value you supplied and so on until the `BLOCKFACTOR` does not exceed the total number of records. This could slow down your query. Unfortunately, ColdFusion can't determine the appropriate `BLOCKFACTOR` automatically.

For instance, if you know that there will be 25 records or more in the `Films` table for the foreseeable future, you should provide a `BLOCKFACTOR` of `25`, like this:

```
<CFQUERY NAME="GetFilms" DATASOURCE="ows" BLOCKFACTOR="25">
  SELECT * FROM Films
</CFQUERY>
```

The larger the number of records involved, the more effect the BLOCKFACTOR is likely to have on overall query performance. Don't obsess about getting the BLOCKFACTOR exactly right. Just think of it as a way to let ColdFusion know whether to expect a large number of records or just one or two. At the very least, consider providing a BLOCKFACTOR="100" attribute for all queries that will be returning hundreds or thousands of records.

Tip

If you are using stored procedures, it's worth noting that the <CFSTOREDPROC> tag also supports the BLOCKFACTOR attribute. See Chapter 32, "Working with Stored Procedures," for details.

Note

Currently, the maximum value allowed by BLOCKFACTOR is 100. If a query might return hundreds or thousands of records, you should still go ahead and set BLOCKFACTOR=100. Because ColdFusion will be retrieving the records in 100-record chunks, performance often can be improved rather dramatically.

Note

The BLOCKFACTOR attribute is currently supported only for ODBC drivers and the ORACLE native database driver. Also, some ODBC drivers ignore or reduce the actual block factor behind the scenes.

CACHING PAGE OUTPUT

You already have learned that ColdFusion allows you to cache query results. It also provides a *page caching* feature, which enables you to cache the complete page HTML generated by each of your templates. Similar to query caching, ColdFusion's page caching feature is designed to improve the overall performance of your Web pages.

The idea is simple. If you have certain ColdFusion templates that can be somewhat time-consuming or that can get hit fairly often, you can have ColdFusion cache them for a specified period of time. This can have a huge effect on overall application performance. The caching can take place on the browser machine, on the server machine, or on both.

INTRODUCING THE <CFCACHE> TAG

If you want ColdFusion to cache a page, just place the <CFCACHE> tag at the top of the template, before any other CFML or HTML tags. The most important attribute for the <CFCACHE> tag is the ACTION attribute, which tells ColdFusion whether you want the page to be cached on the client machine, on the ColdFusion server machine, or on both.

CLIENT-SIDE PAGE CACHING

The <CFCACHE> tag can provide two types of caching: *client-side* page caching and *server-side* page caching. Both are of great benefit. First, you will learn about client-side page caching, which is of particular relevance when putting together personalized pages that might take a bit of time to display. Then, you will learn about server-side page caching, which is most useful when putting together nonpersonalized pages that get hit very often.

Background

All modern Web browsers provide some type of internal page-caching mechanism. As you use your Web browser to visit sites, it makes local copies of the HTML for each page, along with local copies of any images or other media files the pages contain. If you go back to that same page later, the browser can show you the local copies of the files, rather than refetching them from the Web server. Your browser also provides a few settings you can use to control where the cached files are kept and how large the collection of all cached files can get. If it weren't for your browser's cache, most casual Web browsing would be much slower than it is.

Normally, the browser just relies on these settings to determine whether to display a page from its local cache or to recontact the Web server. If you haven't adjusted any of these settings yourself, your own browser is probably set to use the cached copy of a page until you close the browser. When you re-open the browser and visit that same page, the browser recontacts the Web server and fetches the page afresh.

Note

To view the current cache settings for a Netscape browser, select Edit, Preferences, Advanced, Cache. For Internet Explorer, select Internet Options from the Tools menu, and then click the Settings button under Temporary Internet Files.

Gaining More Control

The `<CFCACHE>` tag gives you programmatic control over when the browser should use its local, cached copy to display a page to the user. You use the `TIMEOUT` attribute to tell ColdFusion how old the browser's cached version of the page can be before it should be refetched from the server. If the browser fetched its local copy of the page *after* the date you specify, it uses the local copy to show the page to the user. If not, it visits the template normally. The attributes relevant for this use of the `<CFCACHE>` tag are summarized in Table 24.2.

Table 24.2 `<CFCACHE>` Tag Attributes Relevant for Client-Side Caching

Attribute	Purpose
`ACTION`	Must be set to `CLIENTCACHE` to use client-side caching only. You can also set this attribute to several other values to enable server-side caching, which is described in the next section. It can also be set to `OPTIMAL`, which uses both client-side and server-side mechanisms (see the section "ColdFusion-Optimized Caching," later in this chapter).
`TIMEOUT`	Optional. A date and time that indicate how long you want a cached version of a page to be used. Generally, you specify this attribute using the `DateAdd()` function, as shown in the following examples.

For instance, if you wanted the browser to feel free to use its local copy of a page for six hours at a time, you would include the following at the top of your ColdFusion template:

```
<!--- Let browser use a cached version of --->
<!--- this page, from up to six hours ago --->
<CFCACHE
  ACTION="CLIENTCACHE"
  TIMEOUT="#DateAdd("h", -6, Now())#">
```

Tip

If you wanted all pages in an application to be cached, you could simply place the `<CFCACHE>` tag at the top of your `Application.cfm` file.

The first time a user visits the page, ColdFusion will process the template normally and send the generated page back to the browser. The browser then will store the page in its local cache. The next time the user visits the same page, the browser will quickly contact the server, providing the server with the exact date and time that the page was visited the first time (that is, the date and time the local copy was saved). If the browser tells the server that its local copy is *not older* than the date specified in `TIMEOUT`, the server then tells the browser to just show the local copy to the user and immediately stop processing the rest of your template. Otherwise, ColdFusion tells the browser that the local copy is now out of date; processes the rest of your code normally; and returns the newly generated version to the browser, where it can be cached locally for the *next* six hours (or whatever interval you specify).

WHAT IT MEANS

In other words, using `<CFCACHE>`, you can keep the amount of interaction between the browser and server to a minimum. Yes, the browser will contact the Web server, and ColdFusion will begin executing your template code. But as soon as ColdFusion encounters the `<CFCACHE>` tag, which should be at the top of your CFML code, ColdFusion will often be able to tell the browser to just use its local copy of the page. This is a fast operation because only the initial handshake between browser and server is necessary to determine whether the local copy can be used.

This improves performance in three important ways:

- **First, the browser can display the template more quickly**—This is because it can just use its local copy instead of waiting for it to be regenerated by your template code and refetched over the Net. The longer the page or more time-consuming your CFML code is, the greater the benefit.
- **Second, the amount of work ColdFusion needs to do is lessened**—As long as the browser's local copy is still valid, ColdFusion can stop processing your template as soon as the `<CFCACHE>` tag is encountered. This frees up ColdFusion to complete its next task more quickly, which is of benefit to all your users. The more often your pages are viewed repeatedly by the same users, the greater the benefit.

- **Third, by reducing the number of times complete pages need to be sent back to browsers, traffic on your local network is kept to a minimum**—This makes better use of your network bandwidth. Again, the more often your pages are viewed repeatedly by the same users, the greater the benefit.

Tip

With Netscape browsers, you can override the client-side cache for a particular page request by doing what Netscape calls a *super reload* (which means holding down the Shift key while clicking the browser's Reload button). This can be useful while testing on your pages. You can do the same with most versions of Internet Explorer by holding down the Ctrl key (or equivalent) while clicking the browser's Refresh button.

Server-Side Page Caching

You also can use the `<CFCACHE>` tag to enable ColdFusion's *server-side* page caching mechanism. Similar to client-side caching, the idea is to take advantage of a previously generated version of your template code. However, with server-side caching, we're not talking about the cached copy of the page that might be on the browser machine. Instead, it's a cached copy of the page that ColdFusion stores on the server's drive.

Enabling the Server-Side Cache

To enable server-side caching for one of your templates, place a `<CFCACHE>` tag at the top of the template, before your other CFML and HTML tags. As you can see in Table 24.3, a number of attributes are relevant for using `<CFCACHE>` for server-side caching. However, they are all optional, and most of them are relevant only if your template is secured via SSL encryption or a username and password. Most of the time, you can just specify `ACTION="CACHE"` and whatever `TIMEOUT` you desire.

Table 24.3 <CFCACHE> Tag Attributes Relevant for Server-Side Caching

Attribute	Purpose
`ACTION`	Set this attribute to `CACHE` to enable server-side caching for your template. It can also be set to `OPTIMAL`, which uses both client-side and server-side mechanisms (see the section "ColdFusion-Optimized Caching," later in this chapter). If this attribute is omitted, it defaults to `CACHE`.
`TIMEOUT`	Optional. As with client-side caching, this is a date and time that indicate how long you want a cached version of a page to be used. Generally, you specify this attribute using the `DateAdd()` function, as shown in the following examples. If omitted, ColdFusion will continue to use the cached version forever, even after the server is restarted.
`CACHEDIRECTORY`	Optional. The directory in which you want ColdFusion to store cached versions of the page. If omitted, ColdFusion stores the cached versions in the same directory as the template itself.

TABLE 24.3 CONTINUED

Attribute	Purpose
USERNAME	Optional. If the template you want to cache normally requires the user to enter a username and password, you must provide the appropriate username here. Depending on the Web server software you are using, remember that the username might be case sensitive.
PASSWORD	Optional. If the template you want to cache normally requires the user to enter a username and password, you must provide the appropriate password here. Again, depending on your Web server, the password might be case sensitive.
PROTOCOL	Optional. Specify either `http://` (the default) or `https://`, depending on whether the template you want to cache is being served using SSL encryption. Normally, you can just omit this attribute.
PORT	Optional. If the Web server is serving documents at a nonstandard HTTP port, specify that port number here. Otherwise, you can omit this attribute, in which case it defaults to `80`—the port number usually used for the Web.

For instance, the following snippet could be placed at the top of any of your ColdFusion templates. This tells ColdFusion that your template code only needs to actually be executed once every 30 minutes (at most):

```
<!--- Let browser use a cached version of --->
<!--- this page, from up to six hours ago --->
<CFCACHE
  ACTION="CACHE"
  TIMEOUT="#DateAdd("m", -30, Now())#">
```

The first time the template is accessed, ColdFusion processes your code as it would normally. Before it sends the generated page back to the browser, though, it also saves it as a separate, static file on the server's drive. The next time the page is accessed, ColdFusion simply sends back the static version of the file, without executing any of your code that appears after the `<CFCACHE>` tag. It will continue to send this same static version back to all visitors until 30 minutes have passed. After the 30 minutes have elapsed, the next page request reexecutes your template normally.

For most situations, that's all you have to do. Your visitors will immediately begin to see greater performance. The more often your pages are hit and the longer your template code takes to execute, the larger the benefit.

Listing 24.2 is a simple example that demonstrates the effect. The template uses the `TimeFormat()` function to output the current time. At the top of the template, the `<CFCACHE>` tag is used to allow the page to be cached for 30 seconds at a time. Try visiting this page repeatedly with your browser.

Listing 24.2 ServerSideCache.cfm—Testing the Server-Side Cache Mechanism

```
<!--- Cache this template for 30 seconds at a time --->
<CFCACHE
  ACTION="CACHE"
  TIMEOUT="#DateAdd('s', -30, Now())#">

<HTML>
<HEAD><TITLE>Caching Demonstration</TITLE></HEAD>
<BODY>

  <!--- Display the current time --->
  <P>This page was generated at:
  <CFOUTPUT>#TimeFormat(Now(), "h:mm:ss tt")#</CFOUTPUT>

</BODY>
</HTML>
```


The first time you visit this template, it displays the current time. For the next 30 seconds, subsequent page accesses will continue to show that same time, which proves your template code is not being reexecuted. Regardless of whether you access the page using another browser or from another machine, you click the browser's Reload or Refresh button, or you close and reopen the browser, you will continue to see the original time message until the 30 seconds have elapsed. Then, the next page request will once again reflect the current time, which will then be used for the *next* 30 seconds.

Caution

Remember, if you are using <CFCACHE> for server-side caching (that is, with an ACTION of CACHE or OPTIMAL), the page will not be regenerated for each user. In particular, ensure that the page does not depend on any variables being kept in the CLIENT, COOKIE, or SESSION scopes because the generated page will be shared with other users, without checking that the other users' CLIENT, COOKIE, or SESSION variables are the same. So, in general, personalized pages should not be cached with server-side caching. For personalized pages, enable client-side caching with ACTION="CLIENTCACHE" instead.

Caching Pages That Use URL Parameters

ColdFusion maintains a separate cached version of your page for each combination of URL parameters with which it gets accessed. Each version expires on its own schedule, based on the TIMEOUT parameter you provide. In other words, you don't need to do anything special to use server-side caching with pages that use URL parameters to pass ID numbers or any other information.

ColdFusion does not cache the result of a form submission, regardless of whether the target page contains a <CFCACHE> tag. So, <CFCACHE> is disabled whenever the CGI.REQUEST_METHOD variable is set to POST.

Note

Remember, if you are using <CFCACHE> for server-side caching, the page will not be regenerated for each user. See the important caution in the previous section.

SPECIFYING THE CACHE DIRECTORY

By default, ColdFusion stores the cached versions of your templates in the same directory as the template itself. If, after visiting Listing 24.2, you take a look in the directory in which you saved the listing, you will notice that ColdFusion has placed a file there called `cfcache.map`, which ColdFusion uses to track which pages have been cached and when. In addition, you will also find a `tmp` file there, which is the actual cached copy of Listing 24.2. A new `tmp` file will appear in the folder whenever you visit a different template that uses server-side caching. In addition, a different `tmp` file will appear for each set of URL parameters supplied to the templates when they are visited.

If you use server-side caching for many of your templates, or if they accept several different URL parameters, your directories can become somewhat crowded with all the `tmp` files. There's no harm in it, but it can become annoying. If you want, you can use the `CACHEDIRECTORY` attribute to tell ColdFusion where to store the `cfcache.map` and `tmp` files. You must provide a fully qualified filesystem path to a folder on your server's drive (or local network, although this is not recommended).

For instance, the following would tell ColdFusion to store its cache files in a folder called `cachefiles`.

```
<!--- Cache this template for 20 minutes at a time --->
<CFCACHE
  ACTION="CACHE"
  TIMEOUT="#DateAdd('m', -20, Now())#"
  CACHEDIRECTORY="c:\cachefiles">
```

Note

You would, of course, need to create the `cachefiles` directory on the server machine before this will work.

Tip

The `CACHEDIRECTORY` does not have to be within your application's root folder or within the Web server's document root. Just ensure that it's not read-only.

The following uses the `GetTempDirectory()` function to tell ColdFusion to store its cache files in whichever directory the operating system sets aside for temporary files (commonly `c:\WINNT\temp` in a typical Windows installation). See Appendix B for more information about `GetTempDirectory()`:

```
<!--- Cache this template for 20 minutes at a time --->
<CFCACHE
  ACTION="CACHE"
  TIMEOUT="#DateAdd('m', -20, Now())#"
  CACHEDIRECTORY="#GetTempDirectory()#">
```

Tip

You can use the same CACHEDIRECTORY for all your application's templates. To make this easier, you could set a variable in your Application.cfm file and supply that variable to the CACHEDIRECTORY attribute for each <CFCACHE> tag. This is the same technique used for <CFQUERY>'s DATASOURCE attribute in many of the code examples in this book. For more information, see Chapter 19, "Introducing the Web Application Framework."

Note

If the directory you specify in the CACHEDIRECTORY attribute does not exist, it is ignored. They will be cached in the template's directory.

COLDFUSION-OPTIMIZED CACHING

As noted earlier in Tables 24.2 and 24.3, you can also provide a value of OPTIMAL to the ACTION attribute of the <CFCACHE> tag. This causes client-side caching *and* server-side caching to be used. For each page request, ColdFusion will first determine whether the browser has an appropriate version of the page in its local cache. If not, ColdFusion determines whether it has an appropriate version of the page in its own server-side cache. Only if there isn't an appropriate version in either cache will your template code be reexecuted.

The result is greatly enhanced performance in most situations.

FLUSHING THE PAGE CACHE

Earlier in this chapter, you learned about query caching and how a cached query can be refreshed when the data in the underlying database tables change. You have the same type of option available for server-side page caching, via the FLUSH action provided by the <CFCACHE> tag. You also can delete ColdFusion's cache files manually.

USING ACTION="FLUSH"

To flush a page from the cache before it would time out on its own, simply use the <CFCACHE> tag with ACTION="FLUSH". Table 24.4 shows the attributes relevant for flushing the server-side page cache.

TABLE 24.4 <CFCACHE> TAG ATTRIBUTES RELEVANT FOR SERVER-SIDE CACHE FLUSHING

Attribute	Purpose
ACTION	Must be set to FLUSH to flush pages from the server-side cache.
DIRECTORY	Optional. The directory that contains the cached versions of your pages. In other words, provide the same value here as you provide to the CACHEDIRECTORY attribute elsewhere.
EXPIREURL	Optional. A URL reference that represents which cache files should be deleted. If you don't provide this attribute, the cache will be flushed for all files in the specified directory. You can use an * character in this attribute as a simple wildcard.

So, if one of your templates makes some type of change that should be reflected immediately in your application, even in pages that would otherwise still be cached, you could use the following line to delete all cached pages in the current directory. You would place this code in the change template, right after the <CFQUERY> or whatever else is making the actual changes:

```
<!--- Flush the server-side page cache --->
<CFCACHE
  ACTION="FLUSH">
```

If you don't need to expire all cached pages from the directory, you can provide an EXPIREURL attribute. For instance, suppose you are using server-side caching to cache a template called ShowMovie.cfm, and that movie accepts a URL parameter called FilmID. After some kind of update to the Films table, you might want to flush the ShowMovie.cfm template from the cache, but only for the appropriate FilmID. To do so, you might use code such as the following:

```
<!--- Flush the server-side page cache --->
<CFCACHE
  ACTION="FLUSH"
  EXPIREURL="ShowMovie.cfm?FilmID=#FORM.FilmID#">
```

Or, to flush the cache for all versions of the ShowMovie.cfm template (regardless of URL parameters), but to leave all other cached pages in the directory alone, you would use something such as this:

```
<!--- Flush the server-side page cache --->
<CFCACHE
  ACTION="FLUSH"
  EXPIREURL="ShowMovie.cfm?*">
```

The previous snippets assume that the change template is in the same folder as the display pages that need to be flushed from the cache. If it's not, you can specify the appropriate directory using the DIRECTORY attribute.

DELETING THE CACHE FILES YOURSELF

You can also flush the cache files yourself, by simply deleting the appropriate tmp or cfcache.map files (see the section "Specifying the Cache Directory," earlier in this chapter). You can do this manually, via some type of batch file, or programmatically in your ColdFusion code via the <CFFILE> tag (see Chapter 35, "Interacting with the Operating System").

Note

In the ColdFusion documentation, Macromedia recommends against deleting the cache files manually. Presumably, this is because the internals of the server-side caching mechanism might change in a future version.

`DeleteCacheFiles.cfm` is a custom tag called `<CF_DeleteCacheFiles>`, which has been created and included on the CD-ROM for this chapter for your convenience. The custom tag will delete all server-side cached pages in a directory. It takes one optional parameter, `CacheDirectory`, which corresponds to the `CACHEDIRECTORY` attribute of the `<CFCACHE>` tag.

Note

> The tag does not make any attempt to flush the pages based on any kind of timeout. If you want, you could add such functionality yourself as a learning exercise. You would use the `DateLastModified` column returned by the `<CFDIRECTORY>` tag used in Listing 24.3. See Chapter 35, "Interacting with the Operating System," for details about `<CFDIRECTORY>`.

CONTROLLING WHITESPACE

One of the side effects of CFML's tag-based nature is the fact that whitespace characters (such as tabs, spaces, and return characters) that you use to indent your CFML code usually are passed on to the browser as part of the final generated page. In certain cases, this whitespace can considerably inflate the size of the generated HTML content, which in turn can have a negative effect on performance. ColdFusion provides several options for dealing with these extraneous whitespace characters.

UNDERSTANDING THE PROBLEM

In a ColdFusion template, you use CFML and HTML tags together. The processing instructions for the server are intermingled with what you actually want to generate. That is, there is no formal separation between the code parts of your template and the content parts. Most other Web scripting environments separate code from content, generally forcing you to put the HTML code you want to generate into some type of `Write()` function or special block delimited by characters such as `<%` and `%>` (depending on the language).

The fact that you get to use CFML tags right in the body of your document is a big part of what makes ColdFusion development so powerful. There is a disadvantage, however. Often ColdFusion can't easily determine which of the whitespace characters in a template are just to indent the code for clarity and which ones are actually intended to be sent to the browser as part of the final, generated page. When ColdFusion can't make the distinction, it errs on the side of caution and includes the whitespace in the final content.

AUTOMATIC WHITESPACE CONTROL

The good news is that ColdFusion already does a lot to eliminate excess whitespace from your generated pages. ColdFusion includes an automatic whitespace elimination feature, which is enabled by default. As long as you haven't disabled it, much whitespace is already being pulled out of your documents for you, before the generated page is sent to the browser.

Enabling Whitespace Suppression

On the Settings page of the ColdFusion Administrator, there is an option called Suppress Whitespace by Default. When enabled, portions of your template that contain only CFML tags will have the whitespace removed from them before the page is returned to the browser. Conceptually, it's as if ColdFusion looks at the template, finds the areas that contain only CFML tags, removes any whitespace (extra spaces, tabs, indenting, new lines, or hard returns) from those areas, and then processes the template.

Note

Whenever you enable or disable this setting in the Administrator, you must manually restart the ColdFusion Application Server before the change will take effect.

It's easy to see this in action. To do so, follow these steps:

1. Visit the `NextNCached.cfm` template (refer to Listing 24.1) with your Web browser.
2. Use the browser's View Source option to see the final HTML code the template generated. Leave the source code window open.
3. On the Settings page of the ColdFusion Administrator, uncheck the Suppress Whitespace by Default option, and submit the changes.
4. Restart the ColdFusion Application Server so that the change can go into effect.
5. Visit the `NextNCached.cfm` template again, and view source.

If you compare the two versions of the page source, you will see that the second version has a lot more blank lines and other whitespace in it. In particular, it has a lot more whitespace at the very top, which is all the whitespace that surrounds the comments and various `<CFQUERY>`, `<CFPARAM>`, and `<CFSET>` tags at the top of Listing 24.1. The first version of the page source has eliminated that whitespace from the top of the document.

There are very few situations in which this automatic suppression of whitespace would be undesirable. In general, then, it is recommended that you leave the Suppress Whitespace by Default option enabled in the ColdFusion Administrator.

Controlling Whitespace Suppression Programmatically

You can turn off ColdFusion's automatic whitespace suppression feature for specific parts of your document. Such situations are generally few and far between because whitespace is usually ignored in HTML, so there is usually no need to preserve it.

However, there are a few situations in which you wouldn't want ColdFusion to remove whitespace for you. For instance, a few rarely used HTML tags do consider whitespace to be significant. The `<PRE>` tag is one, and the `<XMP>` tag is another. If you are using either of these tags in a Web page document, ColdFusion's whitespace suppression might eliminate the very whitespace you are trying to display between the `<PRE>` or `<XMP>` tags. You might run into the same problem when composing an e-mail message programmatically using the `<CFMAIL>` tag (see Chapter 28, "Interacting with E-mail").

In such a situation, you can use the SUPPRESSWHITESPACE="No" attribute of the <CFPROCESSINGDIRECTIVE> tag to disable the automatic suppression of whitespace. Place the tag around the block of code that is sensitive to whitespace characters, like so:

```
<CFPROCESSINGDIRECTIVE SUPPRESSWHITESPACE="No">
  <PRE>
    ...whitespace-sensitive code here...
  </PRE>
</CFPROCESSINGDIRECTIVE>
```

For details, see the <CFPROCESSINGDIRECTIVE> tag in Appendix A, "ColdFusion Tag Reference."

SUPPRESSING WHITESPACE OUTPUT WITH <CFSILENT>

Unfortunately, ColdFusion cannot always correctly identify which parts of your code are made up of only CFML tags and thus should have whitespace automatically removed from them. This is most often the case with code loops created by <CFLOOP> and <CFOUTPUT>.

For instance, try adding the following code snippet to Listing 24.1, right after the <CFQUERY> tag:

```
<!--- Total up all expenses over 1,000 --->
<CFSET bigExpenses = 0>
<CFLOOP QUERY="GetExp">
  <CFIF GetExp.ExpenseAmount GT 1000>
    <CFSET BigExpenses = BigExpenses + GetExp.ExpenseAmount>
  </CFIF>
</CFLOOP>
```

Now visit the page with your browser and view source. You will see that a large number of lines have been added to the page. If you move through these lines with the left and right arrow keys on your keyboard, you will see that these lines hold the various spaces or tabs that were used to indent the code.

To solve the problem, use the <CFSILENT> tag, which causes *all* output (even actual text and HTML tags) to be suppressed. The <CFSILENT> tag takes no attributes. Simply wrap it around any code blocks that might generate extraneous whitespace when executed, such as <CFLOOP> or <CFOUTPUT> loops that perform calculations but that don't generate any output the browser needs to receive.

For instance, the previous snippet would become the following, which would not add any wasteful lines of spaces and other whitespace to the final page source that gets sent to the browser:

```
<CFSILENT>
  <!--- Total up all expenses over 1,000 --->
  <CFSET bigExpenses = 0>
  <CFLOOP QUERY="GetExp">
    <CFIF GetExp.ExpenseAmount GT 1000>
      <CFSET BigExpenses = BigExpenses + GetExp.ExpenseAmount>
    </CFIF>
  </CFLOOP>
</CFSILENT>
```

Note

The <CFSILENT> tag doesn't just suppress whitespace output. It suppresses all output, even output you would generally want to be sent to the browser (such as HTML code and text).

SUPPRESSING SPECIFIC WHITESPACE WITH <CFSETTING>

For situations in which ColdFusion's automatic suppression isn't suppressing all the whitespace in your generated pages (for instance, the first <CFLOOP> snippet in the previous section), but where <CFSILENT> is too drastic, you can use the <CFSETTING> tag to suppress output in a more selective manner.

For instance, if you view the page source for Listing 24.1 again, you will notice that some excess whitespace exists between each of the page-by-page links generated by the NextNIncludePageLinks.cfm template (which was covered in Chapter 23). However, wrapping the <CFSILENT> tag around the code won't solve the problem because that would suppress the desired output (the page-by-page links) as well as the undesired output (the whitespace).

The <CFSETTING> tag takes a few optional attributes, but the only one relevant to this discussion is the ENABLECFOUTPUTONLY attribute. When this attribute is set to Yes, all output is suppressed (similar to the <CFSILENT> tag), *except* for <CFOUTPUT> blocks. Any HTML code or text that should be sent to the browser must be between <CFOUTPUT> tags, even if the code doesn't include any ColdFusion variables or expressions.

Listing 24.3 is a revised version of the NextNIncludePageLinks.cfm template from Listing 23.5 in Chapter 23. This version is nearly the same as the original, except that <CFSETTING> tags have been placed at the top and bottom of the template (the first turns the ENABLECFOUTPUTONLY attribute on, and the second one turns it back off). In addition, spaces have been added before each of the closing </CFOUTPUT> tags.

LISTING 24.3 NextNIncludePageLinks2.cfm—SUPPRESSING ALL OUTPUT NOT BETWEEN <CFOUTPUT> TAGS

```
<!--- Control Whitespace Output --->
<CFSETTING ENABLECFOUTPUTONLY="Yes">

<!--- Simple Page counter, starting at first "Page" --->
<CFSET ThisPage = 1>

<!--- Loop thru row numbers, in increments of RowsPerPage --->
<CFLOOP FROM="1" TO="#TotalRows#" STEP="#RowsPerPage#" INDEX="PageRow">
  <!--- Detect whether this "Page" currently being viewed --->
  <CFSET IsCurrentPage = (PageRow GTE URL.StartRow) AND (PageRow LTE EndRow)>

  <!--- If this "Page" is current page, show without link --->
  <CFIF IsCurrentPage>
    <CFOUTPUT><B>#ThisPage#</B> </CFOUTPUT>
  <!--- Otherwise, show with link so user can go to page  --->
  <CFELSE>
```

```
    <CFSET LinkURL = "#CGI.SCRIPT_NAME#?StartRow=#PageRow#">
    <CFOUTPUT><A HREF="#LinkURL#">#ThisPage#</A> </CFOUTPUT>
  </CFIF>

  <!--- Increment ThisPage variable --->
  <CFSET ThisPage = ThisPage + 1>
</CFLOOP>

<!--- Control Whitespace Output --->
<CFSETTING ENABLECFOUTPUTONLY="No">
```

If you save Listing 24.3 as `NextNIncludePageLinks.cfm`, visit Listing 24.1 again, and then view source, you will see that the page-by-page links are no longer surrounded by a large number of extra lines and whitespace characters. In fact, all the page-by-page links are on a single line of code, separated only by a single space (the space that was added before the closing `</CFOUTPUT>` tags, as noted previously). The result can mean faster performance on the browser machine, especially for modem users.

See Appendix A for more information about the `<CFSETTING>` tag.

CUSTOM TAG SOLUTIONS

Between the `<CFSILENT>`, `<CFSETTING>`, and `<CFPROCESSINGDIRECTIVE>` techniques you have learned about in this section, you now will be able to deal with the generation of excessive whitespace in your ColdFusion pages. One more alternative is to use the `<CF_StripWhitespace>` custom tag, which is available for download from the ColdFusion Developer Exchange (`http://www.allaire.com/developer/gallery`) or from `http://www.nateweiss.com`. This custom tag can intelligently remove whitespace from the HTML code your templates generate. There is a small performance penalty for using this custom tag, which grows as the size of the generated source code grows. However, the end-user performance gained from the shortened page source can often overcome the small amount of time the ColdFusion server takes to execute the custom tag.

CHAPTER 25

Enhancing Forms with Client-Side Java

In this chapter

About ColdFusion's Java-Based Form Controls

In Chapter 12, "ColdFusion Forms"; Chapter 13, "Form Data Validation"; and Chapter 14, "Using Forms to Add or Change Data," you learned a great deal about creating forms for your Web applications. Not only did you learn about using standard HTML forms using `<FORM>`, `<INPUT>`, and `<SELECT>` tags, you also learned how to take advantage of ColdFusion's beefed-up, JavaScript-enriched encapsulations of those tags (`<CFFORM>`, `<CFINPUT>`, and `<CFSELECT>`).

ColdFusion also provides a collection of useful Java-based form controls, which you can use to create forms that present or collect information in ways that aren't possible with the standard HTML form controls. The controls are

- **Tree Control**—Similar to the tree-based file-navigation pane in the Windows Explorer, the `<CFTREE>` form control provides a professional-looking, compact, and intuitive way to present hierarchical information to your users.
- **Grid Control**—Somewhat similar to a spreadsheet application, the `<CFGRID>` form control provides an easy way for your users to view or edit rows and columns of data. New features for ColdFusion 5 are the capabilities to add check boxes, drop-down lists, and color-coding to the grid.
- **Slider Control**—The `<CFSLIDER>` control is ideal for situations in which you want to collect a rating, ranking, or some other numeric value that falls within a definite range.
- **Text Input Control**—ColdFusion also provides a Java-based text input applet, which—like the `<CFINPUT>` tags you learned about in Chapters 13 and 14—can be used to get validated text input from the user. In most cases, `<CFINPUT>` is better.

About the Java Controls and the Java Plug-In

The Java-based form controls included with ColdFusion have been completely rewritten and updated for version 5 of the application server. They are compatible with nearly all versions of the major browsers (even Netscape 6). You don't need to know anything about Java to use these controls; the deployment of the applets is taken care of by the ColdFusion server.

Before the controls will work on a user's browser, the Java Plug-in must be installed on the user's machine. The Java Plug-in enables Java applets (such as `<CFTREE>`, `<CFGRID>`, and `<CFSLIDER>`) to run using a Java runtime environment provided by the plug-in, rather than the Java virtual machine provided by the browser, if any.

If the Java Plug-in has never been installed, it is installed automatically if the user is using Internet Explorer (IE downloads and installs the plug-in from your ColdFusion server). If the user is using Netscape or some other browser, she might have to download and install the plug-in before the controls will work. For more information about the Java Plug-in, visit `http://www.javasoft.com/products/plugin`.

Note

In either case, you need to be aware that the initial Java Plug-in software is an approximately 5MB download. The download should need to be performed only once per machine, but you might want to consider *not* using these controls in applications geared toward people who might be accessing your pages via a slow connection.

Note

Previous versions of ColdFusion supported an ENABLECAB attribute for <CFFORM>, which caused the <CFFORM> Java applets to be available for Internet Explorer users more quickly than for Netscape users because all the Java classes needed by the applets were delivered in a single Windows Cabinet (.cab) file. In ColdFusion 5, the classes are now delivered in a single Java Archive (.jar) file for both IE and Netscape users, which results in good performance for all supported browsers. The ENABLECAB attribute is thus no longer necessary, has been deprecated from the CFML language, and is nonfunctional in ColdFusion 5. You don't have to remove it from your existing templates, but you should leave it out of any new ones.

USING <CFTREE>

The <CFTREE> tag creates one of the most powerful and useful controls in ColdFusion—a branched tree control for the display of data. To add a tree control to a form, use opening and closing <CFTREE> tags, which control the tree's width, height, and other basic attributes.

Then, within the <CFTREE> tag pair, add one or more <CFTREEITEM> tags for each item you want to be displayed in the tree. Of course, as you would expect from ColdFusion, the <CFTREEITEM> tags easily can be generated from the results of a query.

Table 25.1 shows the attributes supported by the <CFTREE> tag, which creates the shell for the tree control itself. Table 25.2 explains the attributes for the <CFTREEITEM> tag, which populates the tree with actual information to show to the user.

Don't worry too much about how many attributes exist for these tags. As you will soon see, these tags are actually very easy to use.

TABLE 25.1 <CFTREE> TAG ATTRIBUTES

Name	Status	Description
NAME	Required	A name for the tree control, similar to the NAME attribute for other form elements, such as <INPUT> and <CFSELECT>.
BORDER	Optional	Places a border around the tree. Default is Yes.
HSCROLL	Optional	Yes or No. Determines whether to show a horizontal scrollbar. Default is Yes.
VSCROLL	Optional	Yes or No. Determines whether to show a vertical scrollbar. Default is Yes.

TABLE 25.1 CONTINUED

Name	Status	Description
REQUIRED	Optional	Yes or No. User must select an item in the tree control. Default is No.
MESSAGE	Optional	Message text to appear if REQUIRED="Yes" and the user attempts to submit the form without selecting an item in the tree first.
DELIMITER	Optional	The character used to separate elements in the *treename.path* form variable that is provided when a form that contains a tree is submitted. The default is \. See the section "Getting the Chosen Tree Item When the Form Is Submitted," later in this chapter.
COMPLETEPATH	Optional	Yes passes the root level of the tree in the *treename.path* form variable that is provided when a form that contains a tree is submitted. If omitted or No, the root level is not included. It is recommended that you set this value to Yes when using trees for data entry. See the section, "Getting the Chosen Tree Item When the Form Is Submitted," later in this chapter.
HIGHLIGHTHREF	Optional	Relevant only if the tree contains <CFTREEITEM> tags that specify an HREF attribute (see Table 25.2). Yes shows such items as underlined so they look like ordinary Web page hyperlinks; No gets rid of the underlining. Default is Yes.
APPENDKEY	Optional	Relevant only if the tree contains <CFTREEITEM> tags that specify an HREF attribute. Yes passes a URL variable called CFTREEITEMKEY when a user clicks such a tree item. The value of CFTREEITEMKEY indicates the VALUE of the selected <CFTREEITEM>. The default is Yes. In general, it is more straightforward to simply pass whatever URL parameters you want by adding them to the HREF attribute yourself, as shown in Listing 25.2, later in this chapter.

Note

In addition, the <CFTREE> tag supports the look and feel attributes (such as LOOKANDFEEL and FONTSIZE) listed in Table 25.3. See the section "Controlling the Look and Feel," later in this chapter.

TABLE 25.2 <CFTREEITEM> TAG ATTRIBUTES

Name	Status	Description
DISPLAY	Optional	Optional. The label to display to the user for the tree item. If you don't provide a value for DISPLAY, the VALUE attribute (see the following) is used as the default.

Name	Status	Description
VALUE	Required	The underlying value (such as an ID number) that corresponds with the tree item. When the form is submitted, the value of the user-selected item will be available to the receiving template as the FORM variable specified by the NAME parameter of the <CFTREE> tag.
PARENT	Optional	The value of the tree item's parent, if any. Use this parameter to control which tree items are nested within other items. If you provide a value for PARENT, and the value corresponds with the VALUE of some other item in the tree, the new item will appear nested within the parent item, in a nested folder-like manner. If you don't provide a value for PARENT (or if the specified parent item doesn't exist in the tree), the new item becomes a root item in the tree (that is, not nested within any other items at all).
EXPAND	Optional	Yes or No. If Yes (the default), the tree item is expanded when the page first appears, revealing its children (if any). If No, the tree item is tree is closed when the page first appears; its children don't appear until the user expands the tree item by clicking it.
IMG	Optional	Image name or filename for the tree item. A number of images are supplied and can be specified using only the image name (no file extension): folder floppy fixed cd document element The default image that appears when you don't specify an IMG value of your own varies depending on the LOOKANDFEEL attribute of the <CFTREE> tag. To specify your own custom image, specify the path and file extension:IMG="../images/filmicon.gif"
IMGOPEN	Optional	The image to display when the tree item is expanded. You can use the same values or paths previously described for the IMG attribute.
HREF	Optional	URL to associate with the tree item or a query column for a tree that is populated from a query. If HREF is a query column, the HREF value is the value populated by the query. If HREF is not recognized as a query column, it is assumed that the HREF text is an actual HREF.
TARGET	Optional	Relevant only if the HREF attribute is specified. Target frame to activate if the user clicks the item. You can supply any of the values that you would normally supply to the TARGET attribute of an <A> or <FORM> tag (_parent, _self, _top, _blank, or a frame name you have defined yourself).

TABLE 25.2 CONTINUED

Name	Status	Description
QUERY	Optional	Query name used to generate data for the tree item. If you provide a query name here, a tree item is generated for each row of the query. If you provide a QUERY attribute, the values you supply to the VALUE, DISPLAY, HREF, TARGET, and IMG attributes should be column names. In practice, using this QUERY attribute can get confusing rather quickly and often doesn't provide the flexibility required to create the trees you need for your application. It is generally recommended that you use a <CFLOOP> tag to iterate over the query, instead of using this attribute.
QUERYASROOT	Optional	Relevant only if you are providing a QUERY attribute. If Yes, the query itself appears as a item in the tree, using the query's name as the DISPLAY attribute. The default is No.

Listing 25.1 shows how to use <CFTREE> and <CFTREEITEM> to put together a basic tree. As you can see in Figure 25.1, this tree contains five items, which correspond to the five <CFTREEITEM> tags in Listing 25.1. The first item, labeled Orange Whip Studios, has no PARENT attribute and so appears at the root level of the tree. Because the Films and Cast Members items specify a PARENT attribute that corresponds to the VALUE of the first item (its value is root), they appear nested within the Orange Whip Studios item. Similarly, because the Actresses and Actors specify Cast as their PARENT, and because Cast is the VALUE of the Cast Members item, they appear nested within Cast Members when the form is displayed.

LISTING 25.1 TreeControl1.cfm—BUILDING A SIMPLE TREE CONTROL WITH <CFTREE>

```
<HTML>
<HEAD><TITLE>Seeing The Forest For The Trees</TITLE></HEAD>
<BODY>


<!--- Tree controls must appear between <CFFORM> tags --->
<CFFORM ACTION="#CGI.SCRIPT_NAME#" METHOD="POST">

  <!--- Tree control --->
  <CFTREE
    NAME="NavTree"
    WIDTH="300"
    HEIGHT="400"
    BORDER="Yes"
    APPENDKEY="No">

    <!--- Root tree item --->
    <CFTREEITEM VALUE="root" DISPLAY="Orange Whip Studios" EXPAND="Yes">
    <!--- Tree item for films --->
    <CFTREEITEM PARENT="root" VALUE="Films" DISPLAY="Films" EXPAND="No">
    <!--- Tree item for actors --->
    <CFTREEITEM PARENT="root" VALUE="Cast" DISPLAY="Cast Members" EXPAND="Yes">
    <!--- Tree item for actors --->
    <CFTREEITEM PARENT="Cast" VALUE="CastFemale" DISPLAY="Actresses" EXPAND="No">
```

```
    <!--- Tree item for actors --->
    <CFTREEITEM PARENT="Cast" VALUE="CastMale" DISPLAY="Actors" EXPAND="No">

  </CFTREE>
</CFFORM>

</BODY>
</HTML>
```

As you can see in Figure 25.1, no really helpful information is being presented to the user yet. This example is here mainly to help you see how the PARENT and VALUE attributes work together to define the relationships between the items in a tree. The next listing adds more tree items that correspond to information in the database, which will make the tree a bit more interesting.

Note

Previous versions of ColdFusion supported an ENABLECAB attribute for <CFFORM>. The ENABLECAB attribute is thus no longer needed, has been deprecated from the CFML language, and is nonfunctional in ColdFusion 5.

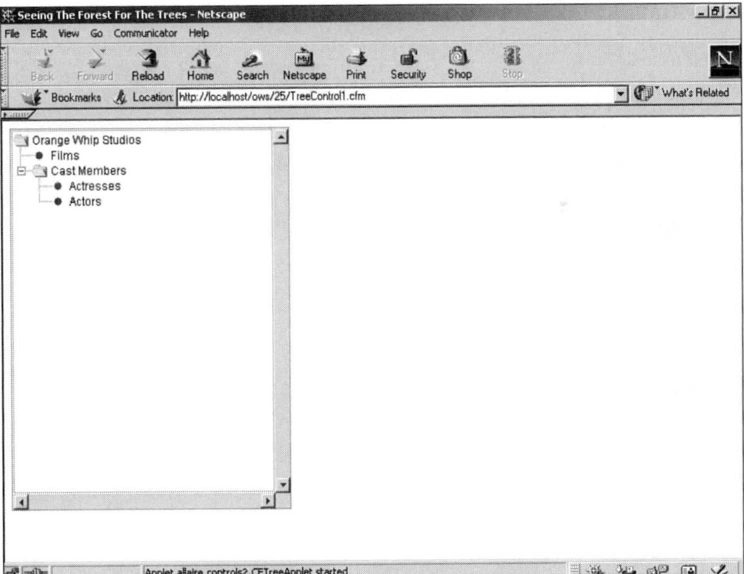

Figure 25.1
A simple <CFTREE> example.

USING QUERIES TO GENERATE TREE ITEMS

Frequently, you will want to create trees that contain information from a database. For instance, you might use <CFQUERY> to run a query named GetFilms and then add a tree item for each film to a tree you're building.

There are two ways to add items to a tree based on the results of a query. The easiest, most flexible method is to use an ordinary `<CFLOOP>` tag that loops over the rows of your query. Within the `<CFLOOP>`, place a `<CFTREEITEM>` tag to include a tree item for each row returned by the query. Of course, you can refer to the query's columns in the `VALUE`, `DISPLAY`, and other attributes of the `<CFTREEITEM>` tag.

The second method is to use the `QUERY` attribute of the `<CFTREEITEM>` tag. This method is a bit more concise because it allows you to skip the `<CFLOOP>`, but it is generally more tedious to use in practice because any formatting, filtering, and so on must be done at the query level. The `<CFLOOP>` method gives you more flexibility and makes your code easier to understand; it is the one that is shown in the examples in this chapter.

Listing 25.2 expands on the tree created in Listing 25.1. This version includes the same static tree elements as the first version. It then adds tree items for each of Orange Whip Studio's quality films and actors. The films are organized by rating.

LISTING 25.2 `TreeControl2.cfm`—**ADDING QUERIED INFORMATION TO A** `<CFTREE>`

```
<HTML>
<HEAD><TITLE>Seeing The Forest For The Trees</TITLE></HEAD>
<BODY>

<!--- Get list of ratings from database --->
<CFQUERY NAME="GetRatings" DATASOURCE="ows">
  SELECT RatingID, Rating
  FROM FilmsRatings
  ORDER BY Rating
</CFQUERY>

<!--- Get information about films from database --->
<CFQUERY NAME="GetFilms" DATASOURCE="ows">
  SELECT FilmID, MovieTitle, RatingID
  FROM Films
  ORDER BY MovieTitle
</CFQUERY>

<!--- Fetch a listing of current actors from the database --->
<CFQUERY NAME="GetActors" DATASOURCE="ows">
  SELECT ActorID, NameFirst, NameLast, Gender
  FROM Actors
  ORDER BY NameLast, NameFirst
</CFQUERY>


<!--- Tree controls must appear between <CFFORM> tags --->
<CFFORM ACTION="#CGI.SCRIPT_NAME#" METHOD="POST">

  <!--- Tree control --->
  <CFTREE
    NAME="NavTree"
    WIDTH="300"
    HEIGHT="400"
    BORDER="Yes"
    APPENDKEY="No">
```

```
<!--- Root tree item --->
<CFTREEITEM VALUE="root" DISPLAY="Orange Whip Studios" EXPAND="Yes">
<!--- Tree item for films --->
<CFTREEITEM PARENT="root" VALUE="Films" DISPLAY="Films" EXPAND="No">
<!--- Tree item for actors --->
<CFTREEITEM PARENT="root" VALUE="Cast" DISPLAY="Cast Members" EXPAND="Yes">
<!--- Tree item for actors --->
<CFTREEITEM PARENT="Cast" VALUE="CastFemale" DISPLAY="Actresses" EXPAND="No">
<!--- Tree item for actors --->
<CFTREEITEM PARENT="Cast" VALUE="CastMale" DISPLAY="Actors" EXPAND="No">

<!--- For each rating, generate a tree item --->
<!--- Specify Films as its parent, so it appears within films visually --->
<CFLOOP QUERY="GetRatings">
  <CFTREEITEM
    PARENT="Films"
    VALUE="Rating #RatingID#"
    DISPLAY="#Rating#">
</CFLOOP>


<!--- For each film, generate a tree item --->
<CFLOOP QUERY="GetFilms">
  <!--- Film should appear in tree according to its rating --->
  <CFSET ParentItem = "Rating #GetFilms.RatingID#">

  <!--- Generate actual tree item --->
  <CFTREEITEM
    PARENT="#ParentItem#"
    VALUE="#FilmID#"
    DISPLAY="#MovieTitle#"
    HREF="ShowFilm.cfm?FilmID=#FilmID#">
</CFLOOP>


<!--- Tree item for each actor --->
<CFLOOP QUERY="GetActors">
  <!--- Place under Actors or Actresses as appropriate --->
  <CFIF GetActors.Gender EQ "F">
    <CFSET ParentItem = "CastFemale">
  <CFELSE>
    <CFSET ParentItem = "CastMale">
  </CFIF>

  <!--- Generate actual tree item --->
  <CFTREEITEM
    PARENT="#ParentItem#"
    VALUE="#ActorID#"
    DISPLAY="#NameFirst# #NameLast#"
    EXPAND="No"
    HREF="ShowActor.cfm?ActorID=#ActorID#">
</CFLOOP>

  </CFTREE>
</CFFORM>

</BODY>
</HTML>
```

Within each of the <CFLOOP> tags, a variable called ParentItem is set to determine which tree item the film or actor should appear within. For films, the ParentItem is determined by the film's rating; for actors, the ParentItem is determined by the actor's gender. The ParentItem variable is then fed to the PARENT attribute of <CFTREEITEM>, which causes the hierarchical relationship between the items to be expressed visually to the user.

Figure 25.2 shows how Listing 25.2 looks when viewed in a browser. As you can see, tree controls are a great way to present a lot of information to the user in a familiar, organized manner. Because each of the generated <CFTREEITEM> tags for films and actors has HREF attributes, the user will be able to click the film or actor name to be taken to some type of detail page for that film or actor.

Note

Please note that the ShowActor.cfm and ShowFilm.cfm templates referred to in Listing 25.2 are not provided as examples for this chapter, so you will get Not Found errors if you actually try to click the underlined items in the tree (as shown in Figure 25.2). If you want, you could quickly put ShowActor.cfm and ShowFilm.cfm templates together that query the database based on the ActorID or FilmID parameters the <CFTREEITEM> tags pass in the URL.

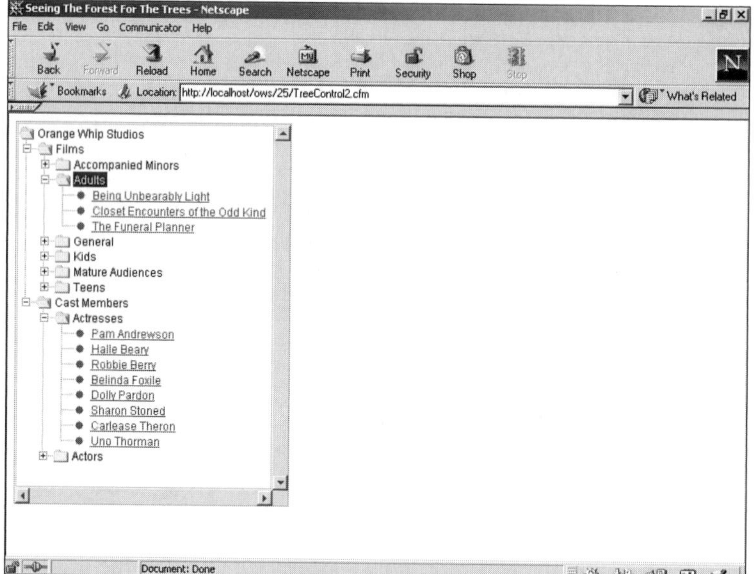

Figure 25.2
This version of the <CFTREE> includes queried information about films and actors.

Using Trees for Data Entry

So far, the trees you have seen have all used the <CFTREEITEM> tag's HREF attribute to create links for the user to click. In other words, so far the tree control essentially has been used as a navigational construct—a structured container for URLs. As you already have seen in Listings 25.1 and 25.2, this can be a useful way to use the <CFTREE> tag.

You also can use the <CFTREE> tag to create a tree about data entry, rather than navigation. For instance, you might create a data-entry form for adding new expenses into the Expenses table, and you might want the user to identify a category for the new expense. If these categories are organized in a category/subcategory fashion, a natural and efficient way to display the categories is with a <CFTREE> control (look ahead at Figure 25.3 to see what we're talking about).

WORKING WITH CATEGORIES AND SUBCATEGORIES

A number of ways are available to provide a category/subcategory structure for things such as expenses, company departments, parts explosions, and so on. This section explains one of the most common and flexible approaches.

The basic idea is simple. You create a database table with columns called CatID, ParentCatID, and Description (or similar names). After the table has been created, fill it with categories and subcategories. For a top-level category, leave the ParentCatID column blank. For a subcategory, set the ParentCatID column to the parent category's CatID. This simple technique enables you to easily represent a hierarchical category structure in your database. You can have as many categories and subcategories as you need, and they can be nested within each other as deeply as you want. To move a category within some other category, you need only change its ParentCatID value.

There is no such table in the Orange Whip Studios sample database, so let's will use a text file to hold the category and subcategory entries. The text file is shown in Listing 25.3.

Note

Normally, you would just create a ExpenseCats table in your database, rather than keeping the category information in a separate file. In fact, you might want to create such a table and adapt the following example to use that table instead. Just create the table with columns named CatID, ParentCatID, and Description and fill it with the rows of data shown in Listing 25.3.

LISTING 25.3 ExpenseCats.txt—SAMPLE CATEGORIES AND SUBCATEGORIES FOR EXPENSES

```
CatID,ParentCatID,Description
1,,One-Time Expenses
2,1,Props and Sets
3,2,Special Effects
4,,Recurring Expenses
5,4,Food and Catering
6,4,Travel
7,1,Miscellaneous
8,3,Make-Up
9,3,Explosives
10,1,Properties
```

This simple text file establishes two top-level categories, named One-Time Expenses and Recurring Expenses (they are top-level categories because their ParentCatID values have been left blank). Within the One-Time Expenses category are three subcategories—called Props and Sets, Miscellaneous, and Properties (they are subcategories of One-Time Expenses because their ParentCatID values match the CatID value for One-Time Expenses). Within Props and Sets is a subcategory named Special Effects; Special Effects has two subcategories named Explosives and Make-Up, and so on.

Note

The ExpenseCats.txt text file is queried using the Merant Text driver that ships with ColdFusion, using an ODBC connection string to connect to the file. See Chapter 31, "More About SQL and Queries," and Chapter 33, "Error Handling," for information and other examples of using <CFQUERY> with the DBTYPE="query" and CONNECTSTRING attributes.

DISPLAYING CATEGORIES AND SUBCATEGORIES IN A TREE

Listing 25.4 shows how the category and subcategory information from Listing 25.3 can be displayed in a <CFTREE>. The <CFTREE> control is part of a data-entry form that requires the user to select an expense category from the tree, select a film from a drop-down list, and provide a description and expense amount. The form is shown in Figure 25.3.

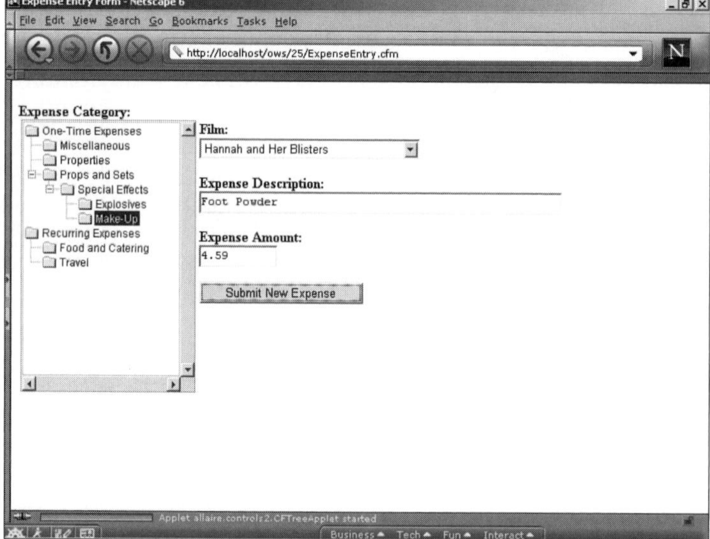

Figure 25.3 The <CFTREE> tag can be used as a data-entry control in your application's forms.

LISTING 25.4 ExpenseEntry.cfm—DISPLAYING CATEGORIES AND SUBCATEGORIES IN A DATA-ENTRY FORM

```
<!--- If the form is being submitted --->
<CFIF IsDefined("FORM.Description")>
  <!--- Database insertion code would go here. The chosen expense --->
  <!--- category from tree would be available as #FORM.ExpenseCat.node# --->
</CFIF>
```

```
<!--- Construct connection string so we can query ExpCats.txt file --->
<CFSET Driver = "{MERANT 3.70 ColdFusion OEM 32-BIT TextFile (*.*)}">
<CFSET DBDir  = GetDirectoryFromPath(GetCurrentTemplatePath())>
<CFSET ConStr = "DRIVER=#Driver#;DB=#DBDir#;FLN=1;tT=COMMA;UT=GUESS">

<!--- Query ExpCats.txt file for list of expense categories --->
<CFQUERY DBTYPE="dynamic" CONNECTSTRING="#ConStr#" NAME="GetCats">
  SELECT * FROM ExpenseCats.txt> tag>
  ORDER BY ParentCatID, Description
</CFQUERY>

<!--- Query Films.txt file for list of films --->
<CFQUERY NAME="GetFilms" DATASOURCE="ows">
  SELECT * FROM Films
  ORDER BY MovieTitle
</CFQUERY>

<HTML>
<HEAD><TITLE>Expense Entry Form</TITLE></HEAD>
<BODY>

<!--- Tree controls must appear between <CFFORM> tags --->
<CFFORM ACTION="#CGI.SCRIPT_NAME#" METHOD="POST">

  <!--- Tree control --->
  <B>Expense Category:</B><BR>
  <CFTREE
    NAME="ExpenseCat"
    WIDTH="200"
    HEIGHT="300"
    BORDER="Yes"
    COMPLETEPATH="Yes"
    REQUIRED="Yes"
    MESSAGE="Please pick a category from the tree." > tag>
    ALIGN="LEFT">

    <!--- For each category, generate a tree item --->
    <CFLOOP QUERY="GetCats">
      <CFTREEITEM
        PARENT="#GetCats.ParentCatID#"
        VALUE="#GetCats.CatID#"
        DISPLAY="#GetCats.Description#"
        IMG="folder">
    </CFLOOP>
  </CFTREE>

  <!--- Drop-down list of films --->
  <B>Film:</B><BR>
  <CFSELECT
    NAME="FilmID"
    QUERY="GetFilms"
    VALUE="FilmID"
    DISPLAY="MovieTitle"
    MESSAGE="Please choose a Film first."/><BR>

  <!--- Text entry field for expense description --->> tag>
  <P><B>Expense Description:</B><BR>
  <CFINPUT NAME="Description" SIZE="50" MAXLENGTH="200"
```

LISTING 25.4 CONTINUED

```
    REQUIRED="Yes" MESSAGE="Please don't leave the Description blank."><BR>

  <!--- Text entry field for expense amount --->
  <P><B>Expense Amount:</B><BR>
  <CFINPUT NAME="ExpenseAmount" SIZE="10" MAXLENGTH="200"
    REQUIRED="Yes" VALIDATE="float"
    MESSAGE="You must fill in an amount first."><BR>

  <!--- Submit button for form --->
  <P><INPUT TYPE="Submit" VALUE="Submit New Expense">
</CFFORM>

</BODY>
</HTML>
```

Note

The `ALIGN="LEFT"` attribute used in the `<CFTREE>` tag in this listing is explained in the section "Controlling the Look and Feel," later in this chapter.

First, a query named `GetCats` is run, which gets the category information from the `ExpenseCats.txt` file. If the category information was in a table in your database, you would just use an ordinary `<CFQUERY>` instead of the `TYPE="dynamic"` query being used here. A normal query named `GetFilms` also is used to get a list of current films from the database.

Next, the data entry form is created using the `<CFFORM>` tag. The form's `ACTION` is set to `#CGI.SCRIPT_NAME#`, which means the `ExpenseEntry.cfm` file will be called again when the user submits the form. See Appendix C, "Special ColdFusion Variables and Result Codes," for more information about this `CGI` variable.

The most important control within the form is the `<CFTREE>` tag, which allows the user to pick the appropriate expense category from the tree. The `REQUIRED` attribute is used to ensure that the user has indeed selected a category in the tree before he can submit the form; if not, he sees the message supplied to the `MESSAGE` attribute. Note that `REQUIRED` and `MESSAGE` work just like the equivalent attributes for the `<CFINPUT>` tag; see Chapter 13 for more information about this type of data validation.

Within the `<CFTREE>` tag pair, a `<CFLOOP>` is used to add a tree item for each row in the `GetCats` query. Because the `PARENT` and `VALUE` attributes are supplied with the category's `CatID` and `ParentCatID` values, the tree will visually reflect the category/subcategory structure implied by the data in the `ExpenseCats.txt` file (refer to Listing 25.3).

The rest of the form is straightforward and will be familiar to you if you have read Chapters 13 and 14. If you have not, you might want to take a glance at those chapters now if the use of `<CFINPUT>` and `<CFSELECT>` is unfamiliar to you.

Getting the Chosen Tree Item When the Form Is Submitted

After a form with a <CFTREE> on it is submitted, ColdFusion makes the user's choice available to you in the FORM scope, similar to other types of form fields. However, instead of providing you with just a single value, ColdFusion provides you with two values for each tree in the form. The first value is called Node and indicates the VALUE of the <CFTREEITEM> that the user selected before submitting the form. The second value is called Path and indicates the parent tree items of the selected item, if any.

Both values are named after the NAME of the <CFTREE> tag, using dot notation. For instance, after the form in Listing 25.4 is submitted, there will be a variable called FORM.ExpenseCat.Node, which would hold a value of 9 if the user has selected the Explosives item in the tree. There will also be a variable called FORM.ExpenseCat.Path, which will be set to 1\2\3\9 to indicate that the selected category was 9, which was nested within category 3 (Special Effects), which was in category 2 (Props and Sets), which was in category 1 (One-Time Expenses).

Listing 25.4 doesn't actually insert a record into the Expenses table when the form is submitted because the Expenses table doesn't currently have a column to hold the expense category number. If you were to add such a column (called ExpenseCatID, for instance), you could populate the column when the form was submitted by using a query similar to the following. You would place this between the <CFIF> tags at the top of the template:


```
<CFQUERY DATASOURCE="ows">
  INSERT INTO Expenses(FilmID, ExpenseCatID, ExpenseAmount, Description)
  VALUES (#FORM.FilmID#, #FORM.ExpenseCat.Node#,
          #FORM.ExpenseAmount#, '#FORM.Description#')
</CFQUERY>
```

Note that the FORM.ExpenseCat.Node variable is used to supply the value for the fictitious ExpenseCatID column.

Controlling the Look and Feel

ColdFusion enables you to control the look and feel of the <CFTREE> and other Java-based controls discussed in this chapter (<CFGRID>, <CFSLIDER>, and <CFTEXTINPUT>). Table 25.3 lists the additional attributes you can add to these tags to tweak the way they appear in your application's pages. If you want, you can experiment a bit with these attributes by adding them to the <CFTREE> tag in Listing 25.4.

Table 25.3 Common Attributes for Controlling the Look of the Java-Based <CFFORM> Controls

Name	Status	Description
LOOKANDFEEL	Optional	Setting that describes the general look and feel of the control, such as the way its borders are drawn and the general three-dimensional effect it has. Valid values for this attribute are Windows, Metal, and Motif. The default is the Windows look and feel. This attribute is new for ColdFusion 5.

Table 25.3 Continued

Name	Status	Description
FONT	Optional	Font name for text.
FONTSIZE	Optional	Font size for text.
BOLD	Optional	Enter Yes for boldface text and No for regular text. This has the same effect as <B></B> in HTML. The default is No.
ITALIC	Optional	Enter Yes for italicized text and No for normal text. This has the same effect as <I></I> in HTML. Default is No.
ALIGN	Optional	Alignment value for the CFFORM element. Valid entries are top, middle, left, right, bottom, baseline, texttop, absbottom, and absmiddle. Similar to the ALIGN attribute of the HTML <IMG> tag.
BORDER	Optional	Whether to show a border around the control. Yes or No.
VSPACE	Optional	Amount of vertical space to reserve as an invisible margin (gutter) above and below the control. You can use VSPACE and HSPACE together to ensure the control doesn't appear to be too close to other elements on the page. Similar to the VSPACE attribute of the HTML <IMG> tag.
HSPACE	Optional	Amount of horizontal space to reserve as an invisible margin (gutter) to the left and right of the control. You can use VSPACE and HSPACE together to ensure the control doesn't appear to be too close to other elements on the page. Similar to the HSPACE attribute of the HTML <IMG> tag.
WIDTH	Optional	The control's width, in pixels.
HEIGHT	Optional	The control's height, in pixels.

If the Control Does Not Load

Normally, you should be able to just go ahead and start using the <CFTREE>, <CFGRID>, and <CFSLIDER> controls discussed in this chapter. However, if your ColdFusion templates are being served on a virtual Web server (that is, a single machine that hosts a number of Web sites, each with its own document root), or if certain directories have been deleted, you might need to take a few extra steps before the controls will work.

Basically, the user's Web browser must be capable of accessing a file called CFJava2.jar, at the URL /CFIDE/classes/CFJava2.jar. After a typical ColdFusion installation, this should already be the case (there will be a folder within your Web server's document root called CFIDE, which will contain a folder called classes, which will contain the CFJava2.jar file). However, after ColdFusion is installed, some administrators tend to delete this directory.

In any case, if the Java-based controls do not appear to load properly—especially if a class-not-found error is displayed in the browser's status line—try to visit the following

URL in your browser (substituting `www.yourcompany.com` with the hostname for your ColdFusion server):

```
http://www.yourcompany.com/CFIDE/classes/CFJava2.jar
```

If you get a `Not Found`, `Forbidden`, `404`, or some similar error message, that the browser is incapable of accessing the `CFJava2.jar` file for one reason or another. There are generally two ways to solve this problem:

- **Create a folder called `CFIDE` within your document root, and copy the `classes` folder (including the `CFJava2.jar` file) into it**—You would copy the file from the Web server's default document root, if you have access to it, or from some other ColdFusion server (perhaps your local machine). If the folder already exists, ensure that the `CFJava2.jar` file is still there and doesn't have some kind of password (or other type of access control) protecting it.
- **Or, using your Web server software's configuration tools, create a virtual folder or virtual directory called `CFIDE` that points to the `CFIDE` folder in the Web server's default document root**—This assumes that the folder hasn't been deleted. The steps you take to accomplish this will vary depending on the Web server software you are using.

USING CFGRID

In early versions of ColdFusion, the <CFGRID> was simply a method of presenting spreadsheet-style grids of information to your users. Over the years, the <CFGRID> tag has become a capable data-entry tool as well (meaning that users can edit the information in the grid and submit it to the server for processing). The current version enables the adding of new data rows, deleting of rows, sorting of columns, and instant updating of all data in the grid. It even allows you to show check boxes and drop-down lists within the grid and provides a simple way to color-code individual cells on-the-fly. In short, the tag provides a nice, clean way of exposing spreadsheet-type data on a Web page.

As with the other <CFFORM> tags, you really have to build some sample applications to see what this tag looks like and what it does. <CFGRID> has more than 30 attributes you can use to customize its appearance and behavior. Any attributes set in the <CFGRID> tag affect the entire grid. You can also specify options for specific rows or columns by passing attributes to <CFGRIDCOLUMN> and <CFGRIDROW>. Options passed to <CFGRIDCOLUMN> and <CFGRIDROW> override any options set at the <CFGRID> level.

Table 25.4 is an abbreviated list of the attributes supported by <CFGRID>. We've shortened the list here to make it easier for you to concentrate on the most important attributes. The complete list is provided in Appendix A, "ColdFusion Tag Reference."

TABLE 25.4 AN ABBREVIATED LIST OF <CFGRID> TAG ATTRIBUTES

Name	Status	Description
NAME	Optional	A name for the grid, which should be unique for the form.
QUERY	Optional	The name of the query to be displayed in the grid. Required unless you use the <CFGRIDROW> tag (see Table 25.6, later in this chapter).
MAXROWS	Optional	Maximum number of query rows to display; same as the MAXROWS attribute for the <CFOUTPUT> tag.
COLHEADERS	Optional	Yes to display column headers at the top of the grid; No to hide column headers. Default is Yes. You have further control over the column headers via COLHEADERALIGN, COLHEADERFONT, COLHEADERFONTSIZE, COLHEADERTEXTCOLOR, COLHEADERITALIC, and COLHEADERBOLD (see Appendix A for details).
ROWHEADERS	Optional	Yes to display row headers at the left edge of the grid; No to hide row headers. Default is Yes. You have further control over the look of the row headers via ROWHEADERALIGN, ROWHEADERFONT, ROWHEADERFONTSIZE, ROWHEADERITALIC, ROWHEADERBOLD, ROWHEADERWIDTH, ROWHEIGHT, and ROWHEADERTEXTCOLOR.
SELECTMODE	Optional	Controls how users can select cells, if at all, and enables editing. Valid entries are BROWSE (no selecting or editing), EDIT (user can edit the data in the grid), SINGLE (user can select a single cell, but can't edit it), ROW (user can select only whole rows at a time), and COLUMN (user can select only whole columns at a time). The default is BROWSE.
INSERT	Optional	Relevant only if SELECTMODE="EDIT". If set to Yes, the user is provided with a button to add new records to the grid. The label shown on the button can be controlled with INSERTBUTTON (see Appendix A). Default is No.
DELETE	Optional	Relevant only if SELECTMODE="EDIT". If set to Yes, the user is provided with a button to delete records from the grid. The label shown on the button can be controlled with DELETEBUTTON (see Appendix A). Default is No.

Note

The <CFGRID> tag also supports most of the look and feel attributes listed in Table 25.3, earlier in this chapter.

The <CFGRID> tag can be used alone or in conjunction with <CFGRIDCOLUMN> and <CFGRIDROW> tags. When used alone, the grid simply displays all the data returned by the query specified in its QUERY attribute. All columns are displayed, and you don't have much control over the individual columns (in terms of width, header, and so on). But it's ridiculously easy. Listing 25.5 shows how to use <CFGRID> in this way, and Figure 25.4 shows the results.

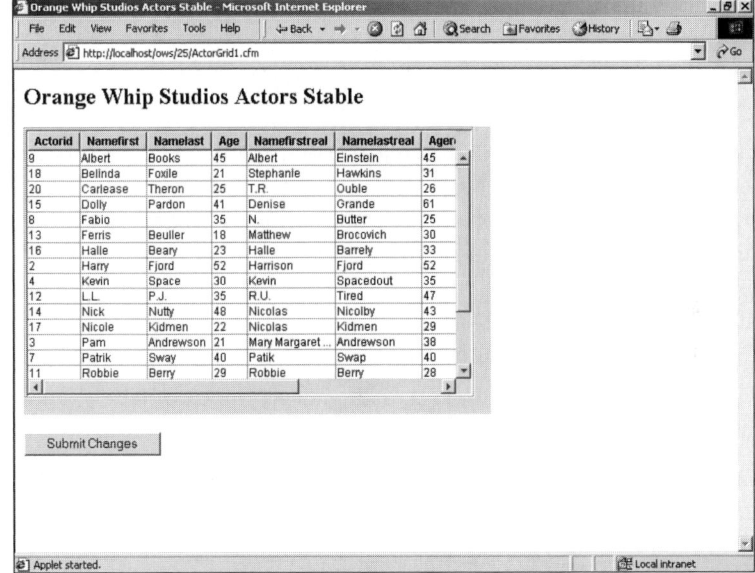

Figure 25.4 When used without <CFGRIDCOLUMN>, the <CFGRID> tag produces a default grid based on the column names in the query.

LISTING 25.5 ActorGrid1.cfm—A SIMPLE <CFGRID> EXAMPLE

```
<!--- Get list of Actors from database --->
<CFQUERY NAME="GetActors" DATASOURCE="ows">
  SELECT * FROM Actors
  ORDER BY NameFirst, NameLast
</CFQUERY>


<HTML>
<HEAD><TITLE>Orange Whip Studios Actors Stable</TITLE></HEAD>
<BODY>
<H2>Orange Whip Studios Actors Stable</H2>


<!--- Data entry form --->
<CFFORM ACTION="#CGI.SCRIPT_NAME#" METHOD="Post">

  <!--- Grid control for expenses --->
  <CFGRID
    NAME="ActorGrid"
    QUERY="GetActors"
    WIDTH="500"
    HEIGHT="300"
```

LISTING 25.5 ActorGrid1.cfm—A SIMPLE <CFGRID> EXAMPLE

```
    ROWHEADERS="No"
    COLHEADERBOLD="Yes"
    COLHEADERALIGN="CENTER">
  </CFGRID>

  <P><INPUT TYPE="Submit" VALUE="Submit Changes">
</CFFORM>

</BODY>
</HTML>
```

This example uses the minimum code necessary for a grid. No <CFGRIDCOLUMN> tag is needed because the database fields were used as the default column names. In general, the resulting grid will be too clunky to present to end users, but it will probably be good enough for putting together quick administrative pages for you (or your team's) own use.

ADDING <CFGRIDCOLUMN> TAGS

To produce more sophisticated grids, you must add <CFGRIDCOLUMN> tags between your opening and closing <CFGRID> tags. This enables you to set display options for each individual column, such as header labels, column widths, alignments, and so on.

Table 25.5 is an abbreviated list of the attributes supported by <CFGRIDCOLUMN>. We've shortened the list here to make it easier for you to concentrate on the most important attributes. The complete list is provided in Appendix A.

TABLE 25.5 AN ABBREVIATED LIST OF <CFGRIDCOLUMN> ATTRIBUTES

Name	Status	Description
NAME	Required	A name for the column; this should be the name of the query column you want to display in this column of the grid.
HEADER	Optional	Text to display in the column's header; the NAME attribute's text is used if this is omitted.
WIDTH	Optional	The width of the column, in pixels.
DISPLAY	Optional	Yes or No. If set to No, the column is hidden from view but is still submitted to the server when the form is submitted. In general, you use DISPLAY="No" for a table's ID number column. Similar conceptually to an <INPUT> form field of TYPE="Hidden". Default is Yes.
TYPE	Optional	Controls how the column can be sorted by the user by clicking the column header. If numeric, the user can sort the column numerically. If text or textnocase, the column is sorted alphabetically (text_nocase is generally more user friendly).

Name	Status	Description
		You can also set TYPE="boolean" to make check boxes appear in the column instead of text values. This is a new feature in ColdFusion 5 and is a great way to enable users to turn a database table's Yes/No or Bit type columns on and off. You also can set TYPE="Image" to display images in the grid; see Appendix A or the ColdFusion documentation for details.
DATAALIGN	Optional	The alignment for the data shown in the column. Valid entries are Left, Right, and Center. Defaults to Left.
NUMBERFORMAT	Optional	A formatting mask for displaying numbers. You can use the same mask characters supported by the NumberFormat() function (see Appendix B).
TEXTCOLOR	Optional	The color of the text in the column's cells, as a named color or hexadecimal RBG value. The color can change conditionally in real time, based on a formula you provide; see the section "Conditional Color Coding" for more information.
BGCOLOR	Optional	The background color for the column's cells, as a named color or hexadecimal RBG value. The color can change conditionally in real time, based on a formula you provide; see the section "Conditional Color Coding" for more information.
VALUES	Optional	If you provide a VALUES attribute and the column is editable (see SELECTMODE attribute in Table 25.4), the column becomes a drop-down list. The VALUES attribute is assumed to be a ColdFusion list, in which each list value creates a new choice in the drop-down list. Similar conceptually to the VALUE attribute of the <CFSELECT> tag (see Chapter 14).
VALUESDISPLAY	Optional	Relevant only if you provide a VALUES attribute. A list of values to show in the drop-down list. The VALUESDISPLAY attribute should also be a ColdFusion list, in which each list value is the user-friendly version of the corresponding list value in VALUES. Similar conceptually to the DISPLAY attribute of the <CFSELECT> tag.
VALUESDELIMITER	Optional	Relevant only if you provide a VALUES attribute. The delimiter character to use for the lists supplied to the VALUES and VALUESDISPLAY attributes. If the individual VALUESDISPLAY values might contain commas, you should change this to a delimiter that will not show up in your data, such as a semicolon or pipe character. See Chapter 9, "Using ColdFusion," for more information about ColdFusion lists and delimiters.

Listing 25.6 builds on the code from Listing 25.5, this time using `<CFGRIDCOLUMN>` tags to set individual attributes for each column that should be displayed in the grid. As you can see in Figure 25.5, the `ActorID` column is hidden from view, and the widths and alignments and number masks of the other columns have been tweaked to make the grid more visually pleasing.

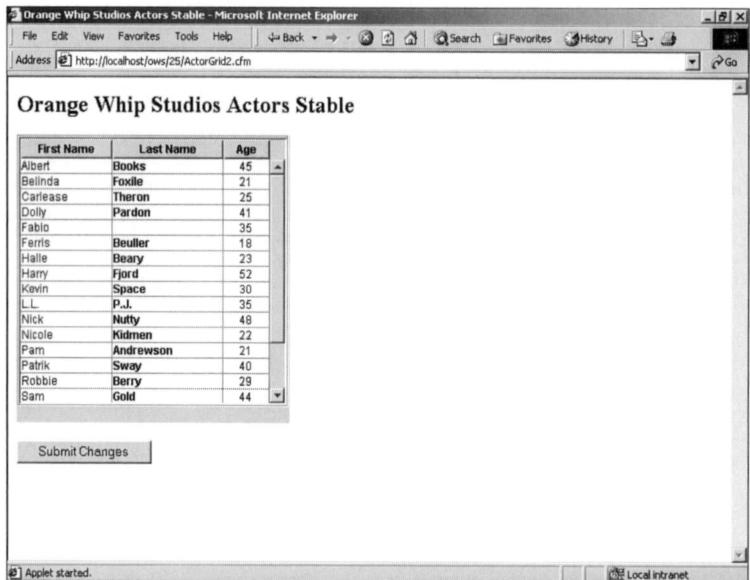

Figure 25.5
The `<CFGRIDCOLUMN>` tag gives you additional control over the display of your grids.

Listing 25.6 ActorGrid2.cfm—Using <CFGRIDCOLUMN> to Control the Display of Individual Columns

```
<!--- Get list of Actors from database --->
<CFQUERY NAME="GetActors" DATASOURCE="ows">
  SELECT * FROM Actors
  ORDER BY NameFirst, NameLast
</CFQUERY>


<HTML>
<HEAD><TITLE>Orange Whip Studios Actors Stable</TITLE></HEAD>
<BODY>
<H2>Orange Whip Studios Actors Stable</H2>


<!--- Data entry form --->
<CFFORM ACTION="#CGI.SCRIPT_NAME#" METHOD="Post">

  <!--- Grid control for expenses --->
  <CFGRID
    NAME="ActorGrid"
    QUERY="GetActors"
    WIDTH="295"
```

```
    HEIGHT="300"
    ROWHEADERS="No"
    COLHEADERBOLD="Yes"
    COLHEADERALIGN="CENTER"
    SELECTMODE="ROW">
    <!--- Hidden column for ActorID - does not actually get displayed --->
    <CFGRIDCOLUMN
      NAME="ActorID"
      DISPLAY="No">
    <!--- Column for actor's first name --->
    <CFGRIDCOLUMN
      NAME="NameFirst"
      HEADER="First Name"
      WIDTH="100">
    <!--- Column for actor's last name --->
    <CFGRIDCOLUMN
      NAME="NameLast"
      HEADER="Last Name"
      WIDTH="120"
      BOLD="Yes">
    <!--- Column for actor's age--->
    <CFGRIDCOLUMN
      NAME="Age"
      HEADER="Age"
      DATAALIGN="Center"
      WIDTH="50"
      NUMBERFORMAT="999.">
  </CFGRID>

  <P><INPUT TYPE="Submit" VALUE="Submit Changes">
</CFFORM>

</BODY>
</HTML>
```

MAKING EDITABLE GRIDS

To make a grid editable, set the SELECTMODE of the <CFGRID> column to EDIT. The user will then be able to edit the data in the grid, almost as if she were using a spreadsheet program such as Microsoft Excel. If you enable the INSERT and DELETE options for the <CFGRID> (see Table 25.5), she will even be able to insert new records and delete existing ones from the grid.

Tip

If you want the user to be able to edit only certain columns, set the SELECT attribute of the <CFGRIDCOLUMN> tag (see Table 25.5).

USING THE <CFGRIDUPDATE> TAG

As the user edits the values in the grid, she is changing the values only on her local machine (that is, the Java-based grid applet generated by <CFGRID> is not connected in real time to the database on the ColdFusion server). After a user has edited the grid to her satisfaction, she should have a way to commit her edits to the underlying database table. ColdFusion makes this easy to accomplish by providing the <CFGRIDUPDATE> tag, which takes care of updating the database accordingly when your users submit forms that contain editable grids.

The <CFGRIDUPDATE> tag is conceptually similar to the <CFUPDATE> tag you learned about in Chapter 14. In general, you need only provide the tag with the GRID, DATASOURCE, and TABLENAME attributes; the tag will take care of the rest. Any rows the user has added to the grid will be inserted into the specified database table, any rows the user has removed from the grid will be deleted from the table, and any existing cells the user has edited will be updated accordingly.

Table 25.6 is an abbreviated list of the attributes supported by <CFGRIDUPDATE>.; We've shortened the list here to make it easier for you to concentrate on the most important attributes. The other attributes (see the following note) are explained in Appendix A.

Table 25.6 An Abbreviated List of <CFGRIDUPDATE> Attributes

Name	Status	Description
GRID	Required	The NAME of the <CFGRID> form element being submitted.
DATASOURCE	Required	The name of the data source for the update action. Presumably the same DATASOURCE name you provided to the <CFGRID> tag.
TABLENAME	Required	The name of the table you want to update. Presumably the same table from which you selected records to populate the <CFGRID>.
KEYONLY	Optional	Yes or No. Yes specifies that in the update action, the WHERE criteria is confined to the key values. No specifies that in addition to the key values, the original values of any changed fields are included in the WHERE criteria. Default is Yes. In other words, if this attribute is set to No, records that have been changed by some other user since the page was loaded will not be changed again when the grid is submitted. Only those database rows that are unchanged since the grid was originally displayed will be affected by the <CFGRIDUPDATE> action. This is a simple but very effective way of ensuring that several users who are editing the same table at the same time do not overwrite each other's changes.

Note

The <CFGRIDUPDATE> tag also supports the DATASOURCE, DBTYPE, DBSERVER, DBNAME, CONNECTSTRING, USERNAME, PASSWORD, TABLEOWNER, TABLEQUALIFIER, PROVIDER, and PROVIDERDSN attributes, which work the same way as the corresponding attributes for the <CFUPDATE> tag discussed in Chapter 14. See Appendix A for details about these attributes.

Committing the User's Edits to the Database

Listing 25.7 takes the previous version of the template (refer to Listing 25.6) and makes it editable. After the user makes whatever edits she desires and submits the form, the `<CFIF>` test at the top of the template evaluates to `True`, which causes the `<CFGRIDUPDATE>` tag to execute.

So, the user can now edit the data in the grid, add new records, delete existing records, and submit the changes to the server. Figure 25.6 shows how the grid looks when this example is visited with a browser.

Tip

Always consider setting the `KEYONLY` attribute to `No` (see Table 25.6) to prevent multiple users from accidentally overwriting each other's edits to the database.

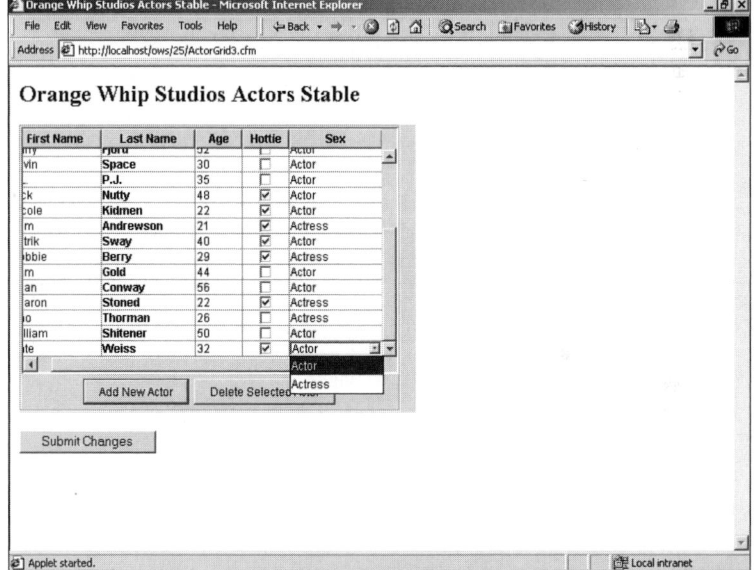

Figure 25.6
Editable grids provide an easy way to enable users to edit multiple rows of data.

Listing 25.7 ActorGrid3.cfm—An Editable Grid

```
<!--- If form is being submitted, commit changes to the database --->
<CFIF CGI.REQUEST_METHOD is "Post">
  <CFGRIDUPDATE
    DATASOURCE="ows"
    TABLENAME="Actors"
    GRID="ActorGrid"
    KEYONLY="No">
</CFIF>

<!--- Get list of Actors from database --->
<CFQUERY NAME="GetActors" DATASOURCE="ows">
  SELECT * FROM Actors
```

LISTING 25.7 CONTINUED

```
  ORDER BY NameFirst, NameLast
</CFQUERY>


<HTML>
<HEAD><TITLE>Orange Whip Studios Actors Stable</TITLE></HEAD>
<BODY>
<H2>Orange Whip Studios Actors Stable</H2>


<!--- Data entry form --->
<CFFORM ACTION="#CGI.SCRIPT_NAME#" METHOD="Post">

  <!--- Grid control for expenses --->
  <CFGRID
    NAME="ActorGrid"
    QUERY="GetActors"
    WIDTH="425"
    HEIGHT="300"
    ROWHEADERS="No"
    COLHEADERBOLD="Yes"
    COLHEADERALIGN="CENTER"
    SELECTMODE="EDIT"
    INSERT="Yes"
    DELETE="Yes"
    INSERTBUTTON="Add New Actor"
    DELETEBUTTON="Delete Selected Actor">
    <!--- Hidden column for ActorID - does not actually get displayed --->
    <CFGRIDCOLUMN
      NAME="ActorID"
      DISPLAY="No">
    <!--- Column for actor's first name --->
    <CFGRIDCOLUMN
      NAME="NameFirst"
      HEADER="First Name"
      WIDTH="100">
    <!--- Column for actor's last name --->
    <CFGRIDCOLUMN
      NAME="NameLast"
      HEADER="Last Name"
      WIDTH="100"
      BOLD="Yes">
    <!--- Column for actor's age--->
    <CFGRIDCOLUMN
      NAME="Age"
      HEADER="Age"
      WIDTH="50"
      NUMBERFORMAT="999.">
    <!--- Column for babe factor --->
    <CFGRIDCOLUMN
      NAME="IsTotalBabe"
      HEADER="Hottie"
      WIDTH="50"
      TYPE="boolean">
    <!--- Column for gender --->
    <CFGRIDCOLUMN
```

```
      NAME="Gender"
      HEADER="Sex"
      WIDTH="100"
      VALUES="M,F"
      VALUESDISPLAY="Actor,Actress">
  </CFGRID>

  <P><INPUT TYPE="Submit" VALUE="Submit Changes">
</CFFORM>

</BODY>
</HTML>
```

Note

This template uses the automatic `CGI.REQUEST_METHOD` variable to determine whether the form is currently being submitted. If the `REQUEST_METHOD` is `Post`, that is an indication that the form (which has a `METHOD` attribute of `Post`) is being submitted. If the page is simply being viewed normally (not as part of a form submission), the REQUEST_METHOD is `Get` instead. See Appendix C for details.

PROCESSING GRID EDITS WITHOUT <CFGRIDUPDATE>

As Listing 25.7 shows, the <CFGRIDUPDATE> tag makes updating a database table after a user makes changes to an editable grid easy. It handles all the appropriate inserts, updates, and deletes for you, all with just one line of code. In most cases, the <CFGRIDUPDATE> tag provides everything you need.

In some cases, however, you might want to handle each edit operation on your own. For instance, perhaps you want the user to be able to delete records from the Actors table, but only those actors who have not actually appeared in any films. ColdFusion enables you to handle this type of integrity check or other special processing by exposing a number of special arrays you can inspect to find out which edits the user made to the grid. Using the arrays, you can handle each edit operation separately, even ignoring some of the edits when appropriate.

Table 25.7 shows the special arrays ColdFusion makes available when a <CFGRID> is submitted. Normally, these array variables are used internally by the <CFGRIDUPDATE> tag to update the database automatically, but you can use them to create customized update handling behavior.

Each of the variables listed in Table 25.7 is a one-dimensional array. Each of the arrays always has the same number of elements in it, one for each grid row that was changed (edited, inserted, or deleted). Therefore, you can use the ArrayLen() function to find out how many edits were made to the grid.

TABLE 25.7 SPECIAL ARRAYS AVAILABLE AFTER A <CFGRID> SUBMISSION

Form Attribute	Description
`gridname.RowStatus.Action[index]`	The type of edit made to the row. Will be `U`, `I`, or `D` to indicate that the row was updated, inserted, or deleted, respectively.
`gridname.colname[index]`	The new value of the column indicated by `colname`.
`gridname.original.colname[index]`	The original value of the column indicated by `colname`.

Note

> It is important to understand that these arrays will *not* contain an entry for each row in the grid; they will contain only entries for each row in the grid that has been changed (edited, inserted, or deleted).

Listing 25.8 demonstrates how to use these special arrays. As you can see, using these arrays instead of <CFGRIDUPDATE> generally requires a lot of additional code. Of course, much of this code could be eliminated if your grid did not allow inserts or deletes (see Table 25.4).

LISTING 25.8 ActorGrid3b.cfm—HANDLING EACH UPDATE ON YOUR OWN

```
<HTML>
<HEAD><TITLE>Orange Whip Studios Actors Stable</TITLE></HEAD>
<BODY>
<H2>Orange Whip Studios Actors Stable</H2>

<!--- If form is being submitted, commit changes to the database --->
<CFIF CGI.REQUEST_METHOD is "Post">
  <!--- The RowStatus.Action array contains a value for each change --->
  <CFSET NumChanges = ArrayLen(FORM.ActorGrid.RowStatus.Action)>

  <!--- For each change made to the grid... --->
  <CFLOOP FROM="1" TO="#NumChanges#" INDEX="i">
    <!--- What type of change was made? --->
    <CFSET ThisAction = FORM.ActorGrid.RowStatus.Action[i]>

    <!--- Depending on the type of change (update, insert, or delete) --->
    <CFSWITCH EXPRESSION="#ThisAction#">
      <!--- Handle updates (if existing values were edited in grid) --->
      <CFCASE VALUE="U">
        <CFQUERY DATASOURCE="ows">
          UPDATE Actors SET
            NameFirst = '#FORM.ActorGrid.NameFirst[i]#',
            NameLast = '#FORM.ActorGrid.NameLast[i]#',
            Age = #FORM.ActorGrid.Age[i]#,
            IsTotalBabe = #FORM.ActorGrid.IsTotalBabe[i]#,
            Gender = '#FORM.ActorGrid.Gender[i]#'
          WHERE
            ActorID = #FORM.ActorGrid.original.ActorID[i]#
        </CFQUERY>
      </CFCASE>
```

```
      <!--- Handle inserts (if record was added to the grid) --->
      <CFCASE VALUE="I">
        <!--- The boss says we're only hiring beautiful people from now on --->
        <CFIF FORM.ActorGrid.IsTotalBabe[i] EQ 1>
          <CFQUERY DATASOURCE="ows">
            INSERT INTO Actors (
              NameFirst,
              NameLast,
              NameFirstReal,
              NameLastReal,
              Age,
              IsTotalBabe,
              Gender
            ) VALUES (
              '#FORM.ActorGrid.NameFirst[i]#',
              '#FORM.ActorGrid.NameLast[i]#',
              '#FORM.ActorGrid.NameFirst[i]#',
              '#FORM.ActorGrid.NameLast[i]#',
              #FORM.ActorGrid.Age[i]#,
              #FORM.ActorGrid.IsTotalBabe[i]#,
              '#FORM.ActorGrid.Gender[i]#'
            )
          </CFQUERY>
        <CFELSE>
          <CFOUTPUT>
            <P>Sorry, #FORM.ActorGrid.NameFirst[i]# #FORM.ActorGrid.NameLast[i]#
            cannot be added because it's company policy to only hire Hotties.<BR>
          </CFOUTPUT>
        </CFIF>
      </CFCASE>
      <!--- Handle deletes (if existing row was deleted from grid) --->
      <CFCASE VALUE="D">
        <!--- Find out if this actor is in any films --->
        <CFQUERY DATASOURCE="ows" NAME="GetActorFilms">
          SELECT FilmID FROM FilmsActors
          WHERE ActorID = #FORM.ActorGrid.original.ActorID[i]#
        </CFQUERY>
        <!--- Only allow a delete if the actor is not in any films --->
        <CFIF GetActorFilms.RecordCount EQ 0>
          <CFQUERY DATASOURCE="ows">
            DELETE FROM Actors
            WHERE ActorID = #FORM.ActorGrid.original.ActorID[i]#
          </CFQUERY>
        <CFELSE>
          <CFOUTPUT>
            <P>Sorry, #FORM.ActorGrid.original.NameFirst[i]#
            #FORM.ActorGrid.original.NameLast[i]#
            cannot be deleted because that actor has been in
            #GetActorFilms.RecordCount# of our films already.<BR>
          </CFOUTPUT>
        </CFIF>
      </CFCASE>
    </CFSWITCH>
  </CFLOOP>
</CFIF>

<!--- Get list of Actors from database --->
<CFQUERY NAME="GetActors" DATASOURCE="ows">
```

LISTING 25.8 CONTINUED

```
  SELECT * FROM Actors
  ORDER BY NameFirst, NameLast
</CFQUERY>


<!--- Data entry form --->
<CFFORM ACTION="#CGI.SCRIPT_NAME#" METHOD="Post">

  <!--- Grid control for expenses --->
  <CFGRID
    NAME="ActorGrid"
    QUERY="GetActors"
    WIDTH="425"
    HEIGHT="300"
    ROWHEADERS="No"
    COLHEADERBOLD="Yes"
    COLHEADERALIGN="CENTER"
    SELECTMODE="EDIT"
    INSERT="Yes"
    DELETE="Yes"
    INSERTBUTTON="Add New Actor"
    DELETEBUTTON="Delete Selected Actor">
    <!--- Hidden column for ActorID - does not actually get displayed --->
    <CFGRIDCOLUMN
      NAME="ActorID"
      DISPLAY="No">
    <!--- Column for actor's first name --->
    <CFGRIDCOLUMN
      NAME="NameFirst"
      HEADER="First Name"
      WIDTH="100">
    <!--- Column for actor's last name --->
    <CFGRIDCOLUMN
      NAME="NameLast"
      HEADER="Last Name"
      WIDTH="100"
      BOLD="Yes">
    <!--- Column for actor's age--->
    <CFGRIDCOLUMN
      NAME="Age"
      HEADER="Age"
      WIDTH="50"
      NUMBERFORMAT="999.">
    <!--- Column for babe factor --->
    <CFGRIDCOLUMN
      NAME="IsTotalBabe"
      HEADER="Hottie"
      WIDTH="50"
      TYPE="boolean">
    <!--- Column for gender --->
    <CFGRIDCOLUMN
      NAME="Gender"
      HEADER="Sex"
      WIDTH="100"
      VALUES="M,F"
```

```
        VALUESDISPLAY="Actor,Actress">
  </CFGRID>

  <P><INPUT TYPE="Submit" VALUE="Submit Changes">
</CFFORM>

</BODY>
</HTML>
```

First, the NumChanges variable is set to the length of the FORM.ActorGrid.RowStatus.Action array. This is the number of edits (inserts, updates, or deletes) the user made to the grid. If the user submitted the form without making any changes, the value of NumChanges is 0.

Next, a <CFLOOP> tag is used to loop over each of the elements in the special arrays. For instance, for each iteration of the loop, the value of RowStatus.Action[i] is U, D, or I to indicate an update, delete, or insert. This value is stored in the ThisAction variable. A <CFSWITCH> block is then used to execute a different <CFCASE> block for each of the possible values of ThisAction (U, D, or I).

Within each of the <CFCASE> tags, the original and updated values for each column of the grid are available for use in queries or other CFML code. For instance, within the <CFCASE> for deletes, the value of FORM.ActorGrid.original.ActorID[i] is used to determine which actor's record was deleted from the grid. A quick query named GetActorFilms is used to determine whether the actor is already in any films. If the actor is not in any films, the record is deleted. If the actor is in at least one film, the deletion is skipped, as shown in Figure 25.7.

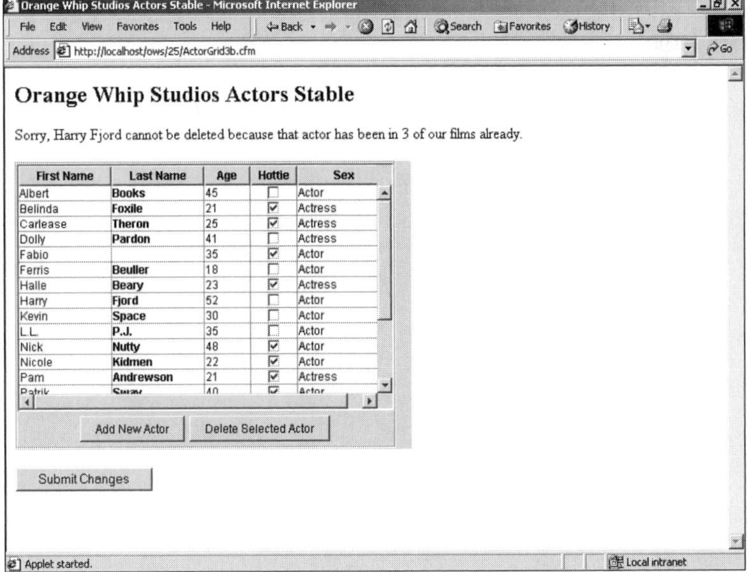

Figure 25.7 If the user attempts to delete an actor whose ID number is already used in some other table, the deletion is cancelled.

Conditional Color-Coding

A new feature in ColdFusion 5 is the capability to display grid cells in various colors based on the current grid values. Similar conceptually to the Conditional Formatting feature in Microsoft Excel, this gives you a way to visually highlight values that are particularly low, high, or otherwise unusual or noteworthy. The color-coding is applied in real time, so if the grid is updatable, cell colors can change while the user is editing.

To use the conditional color-coding feature, you use a special formula syntax in the `TEXTCOLOR` or `BGCOLOR` attribute of the `<CFGRIDCOLUMN>` tag (refer to Table 25.5). This formula looks similar to CFML and JavaScript and always must appear within parentheses, as shown in the following. The formula syntax is simple and is really much easier to show than to describe. Consider the following:

```
TEXTCOLOR="(CX GT 25 ? black : red)"
```

This would cause each cell in the column to appear in black when the current value of the cell was more than `25` and in red when less than or equal to `25`. The `CX` stands for the value of the current cell. The GT means *greater than*, just like in CFML. The `?` and `:` characters are used to specify the colors that should be used if the condition is met or not met, respectively. The color can be specified as a named color or as a hexadecimal RGB color value, like so:

```
TEXTCOLOR="(CX GT 25 ? 000000 : FF0000)"
```

You can use a numbered column number in place of the `CX`. The first column is `C0`, the second is `C1`, and so on. This enables you to set a cell's text color based on the values in other cells in the same row of the grid. So, this expression would set the cell's color based on the current value of the third column in the grid:

```
TEXTCOLOR="(C2 GT 25 ? black : red)"
```

You can also use `LT` (less than) or `EQ` (equal to) in place of the `GT` in the previous snippet.

Listing 25.9 shows how to use the conditional formatting feature in your code. This example displays actors who are `25` or older in black and younger actors in red. If the user changes the age column for an actor, the cells in that row will be colored accordingly. The results are shown in Figure 25.8.

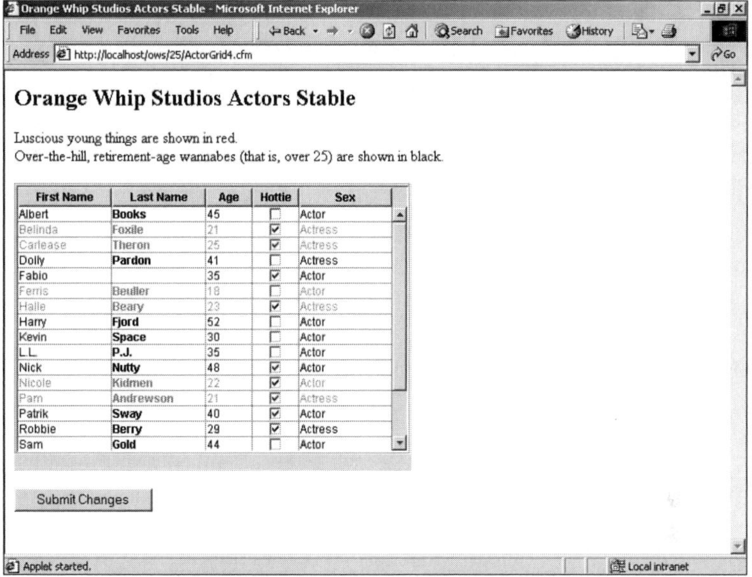

Figure 25.8
Conditional formatting can be used to color-code cells in real time as the user edits the grid.

Tip

When using conditional formatting, be sure to give your users some type of legend or explanation to help them understand what each color means. This listing provides such an explanation at the top of the page (see Figure 25.8).

Note

You might not be able to see the difference between the red and black type in Figure 25.8 as printed in this book, but you will see the difference if you visit this listing with your browser.

LISTING 25.9 ActorGrid4.cfm—HIGHLIGHTING CERTAIN VALUES WITH CONDITIONAL FORMATTING

```
<!--- If form is being submitted, commit changes to the database --->
<CFIF CGI.REQUEST_METHOD is "Post">
  <CFGRIDUPDATE
    DATASOURCE="ows"
    TABLENAME="Actors"
    GRID="ActorGrid"
    KEYONLY="No">
</CFIF>

<!--- Get list of Actors from database --->
<CFQUERY NAME="GetActors" DATASOURCE="ows">
  SELECT * FROM Actors
  ORDER BY NameFirst, NameLast
</CFQUERY>
```

Listing 25.9 Continued

```
<HTML>
<HEAD><TITLE>Orange Whip Studios Actors Stable</TITLE></HEAD>
<BODY>
<H2>Orange Whip Studios Actors Stable</H2>

Luscious young things are shown in red.<BR>
Over-the-hill, retirement-age wannabes (that is, over 25) are shown in black.<BR>

<!--- Data entry form --->
<CFFORM ACTION="#CGI.SCRIPT_NAME#" METHOD="Post">

  <!--- Grid control for expenses --->
  <CFGRID
    NAME="ActorGrid"
    QUERY="GetActors"
    WIDTH="425"
    HEIGHT="300"
    ROWHEADERS="No"
    COLHEADERBOLD="Yes"
    COLHEADERALIGN="CENTER"
    SELECTMODE="EDIT">
    <!--- Hidden column for ActorID - does not actually get displayed --->
    <CFGRIDCOLUMN
      NAME="ActorID"
      DISPLAY="No">
    <!--- Column for actor's first name --->
    <CFGRIDCOLUMN
      NAME="NameFirst"
      HEADER="First Name"
      WIDTH="100"
      TEXTCOLOR="(C2 GT 25 ? black : red )">
    <!--- Column for actor's last name --->
    <CFGRIDCOLUMN
      NAME="NameLast"
      HEADER="Last Name"
      WIDTH="100"
      BOLD="Yes"
      TEXTCOLOR="(C2 GT 25 ? black : red )">
    <!--- Column for actor's age--->
    <CFGRIDCOLUMN
      NAME="Age"
      HEADER="Age"
      WIDTH="50"
      NUMBERFORMAT="999."
      TEXTCOLOR="(CX GT 25 ? black : red )">
    <!--- Column for babe factor --->
    <CFGRIDCOLUMN
      NAME="IsTotalBabe"
      HEADER="Hottie"
      WIDTH="50"
      TYPE="boolean">
    <!--- Column for gender --->
    <CFGRIDCOLUMN
      NAME="Gender"
      HEADER="Sex"
```

```
        WIDTH="100"
        VALUES="M,F"
        VALUESDISPLAY="Actor,Actress"
        TEXTCOLOR="(C2 GT 25 ? black : red )">
  </CFGRID>

  <P><INPUT TYPE="Submit" VALUE="Submit Changes">
</CFFORM>

</BODY>
</HTML>
```

Tip

This example uses conditional formatting for the TEXTCOLOR attribute only, but you can also use it with the BGCOLOR attribute (using the same formula syntax).

DISPLAYING IMAGES IN GRIDS

The <CFGRID> tag is capable of displaying images in individual cells. To display images in a grid column, set the TYPE attribute of the <CFGRIDCOLUMN> to Image; then make sure that the values in the corresponding column of your query contain URLs for the appropriate images to display in each cell. If the grid is editable, the user will be able to double-click the image to edit the path and submit the changes to the server.

Listing 25.10 demonstrates how to use TYPE="Image" to display images in a grid. Each film record is shown with the appropriate image, if one is currently available for the film. If no image exists for the film, the Image column appears as empty. The results are shown in Figure 25.9.

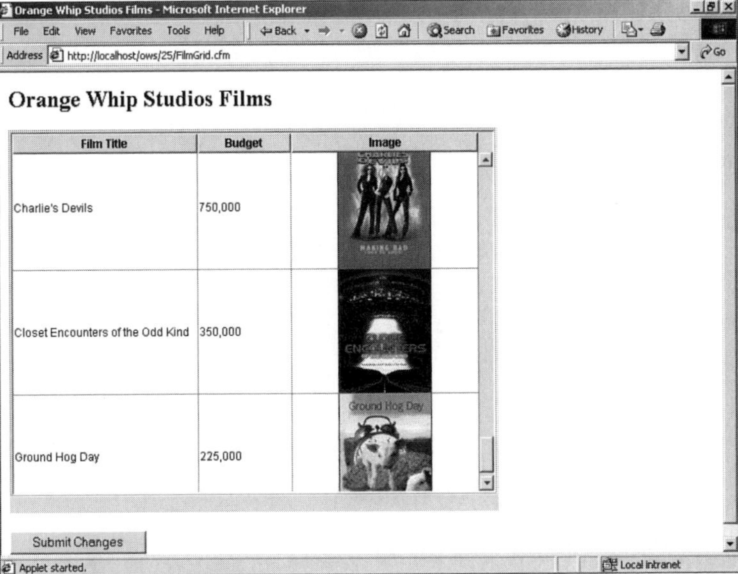

Figure 25.9
GIF and JPEG images can be displayed in grids, along with other types of information.

LISTING 25.10 `FilmGrid.cfm`—**DISPLAYING IMAGES IN AN EDITABLE GRID**

```
<!--- If form is being submitted, commit changes to the database --->
<CFIF CGI.REQUEST_METHOD is "Post">
  <CFGRIDUPDATE
    DATASOURCE="ows"
    TABLENAME="Actors"
    GRID="ActorGrid"
    KEYONLY="No">
</CFIF>

<!--- Get list of films from database --->
<!--- Include a column of blank values called ImagePath --->
<CFQUERY NAME="GetFilms" DATASOURCE="ows">
  SELECT FilmID, MovieTitle, AmountBudgeted, '' AS ImagePath
  FROM Films
  ORDER BY MovieTitle
</CFQUERY>

<!--- For each film, check to see if we have an image for it --->
<CFLOOP QUERY="GetFilms">
  <!--- This is the relative URL path for the image --->
  <CFSET TestImagePath = "../images/f#GetFilms.FilmID#.gif">
  <!--- If the image file actually exists on this server's drive --->
  <CFIF FileExists(ExpandPath(TestImagePath))>
    <!--- Set the ImagePath column of the current row --->
    <CFSET GetFilms.ImagePath[CurrentRow] = TestImagePath>
  </CFIF>
</CFLOOP>

<HTML>
<HEAD><TITLE>Orange Whip Studios Films</TITLE></HEAD>
<BODY>
<H2>Orange Whip Studios Films</H2>

<!--- Data entry form --->
<CFFORM ACTION="#CGI.SCRIPT_NAME#" METHOD="Post">

  <!--- Grid control for expenses --->
  <CFGRID
    NAME="ActorGrid"
    QUERY="GetFilms"
    WIDTH="525"
    HEIGHT="400"
    ROWHEADERS="No"
    ROWHEIGHT="130"
    COLHEADERBOLD="Yes"
    COLHEADERALIGN="Center"
    SELECTMODE="EDIT">
    <!--- Hidden column for FilmID - does not actually get displayed --->
    <CFGRIDCOLUMN
      NAME="FilmID"
      DISPLAY="No">
    <!--- Column for film's title --->> tag;subtags;<CFGRID>> tag>
    <CFGRIDCOLUMN
      NAME="MovieTitle"
      HEADER="Film Title"
      WIDTH="200">
```

```
    <!--- Column for film's budget --->
    <CFGRIDCOLUMN
      NAME="AmountBudgeted"
      HEADER="Budget"
      WIDTH="100"
      NUMBERFORMAT="999,999,999,999.">
    <!--- Column for film's publicity image, if any --->
    <CFGRIDCOLUMN
      TYPE="Image"
      NAME="ImagePath"
      HEADER="Image"
      WIDTH="200">

  </CFGRID>

  <P><INPUT TYPE="Submit" VALUE="Submit Changes">
</CFFORM>

</BODY>
</HTML>
```

First, a query called `GetFilms` is executed. Simple `AS` syntax is used to add another column called `ImagePath` to the query as it is being returned to ColdFusion. This column will be filled with the relative URL to each film's image, if an image is currently available for the film.

Next, a `<CFLOOP>` block is used to iterate over each row of the `GetFilms` query. Within the loop, the `TestImagePath` variable is set to what the relative path for the film's image should be, which is based on the film's ID number. The `ExpandPath()` and `FileExists()` functions are then used to determine whether an image file actually exists for the film; if so, the URL path for the image is placed in the `ImagePath` column of the query. When the loop has finished its work, each film that has an image will have the relative path to the image (starting with `../images`) as the `ImagePath` column; other films will still have an empty string in that column.

Finally, the `ImagePath` column name is passed as the `NAME` attribute of a `<CFGRIDCOLUMN>` tag of `TYPE="Image"`, which causes the images to be displayed in the grid (as shown in Figure 25.9).

About the <CFGRIDROW> Tag

Up to this point, you've been dealing with grids that get their data from a query. You also can add rows to a grid without using a query by omitting the `QUERY` attribute from the `<CFGRID>` tag and then adding a `<CFGRIDROW>` tag between the `<CFGRID>` tag pair.

However, the `<CFGRIDROW>` tag is not particularly well-designed, and we don't recommend that you use it. The main problem is that it requires you to supply all data for the row as a comma-separated list, in which the commas indicate where the data should be split into separate columns. However, in contrast to most uses of lists within ColdFusion, you have no opportunity to supply an alternative delimiter character, which leads to problems if any of the row's values are empty strings or contain commas. It's too bad that `<CFGRIDROW>` doesn't take a `COLUMN` attribute; that would solve the problem and turn it into a useful tag.

The good news is that there is really no need for <CFGRIDROW> in the first place. If you need to supply nondatabase data to a query, simply create a query object yourself, using the `QueryNew()`, `QueryAddRow()`, and `QuerySetCell()` functions. You can read more about these functions in Appendix B; there is also an example in Chapter 29, "Online Commerce."

If you want find out more about the <CFGRIDROW> tag, consult the CFML Reference section of the ColdFusion documentation.

USING <CFSLIDER>

The <CFSLIDER> tag places a sliding bar control on a page that enables you to select a numeric value by moving a knob from side to side (or up and down). This type of control is ideal for situations in which you need to collect some kind of rating or ranking from your users. The slider control can be defined with a number of settings for its range, alignment, default value, and other features.

Table 25.8 is an abbreviated list of the attributes supported by by the <CFSLIDER> tag. We've shortened the list here to make it easier for you to concentrate on the most important attributes. The complete list is provided in Appendix A.

TABLE 25.8 ABBREVIATED LIST OF <CFSLIDER> ATTRIBUTES

Name	Status	Description
NAME	Required	A name for the slider, which must be a unique name within the form. When the form is submitted, the slider's value will be available as the `FORM` variable indicated by this name.
VALUE	Optional	The value that should be preselected in the slider when the page first appears. If omitted, defaults to the minimum `RANGE` value (see the following).
RANGE	Optional	Determines the minimum and maximum values selectable with the slider. Separate values by a comma. For example `RANGE="0,500"` Default is `0,100`. Valid only for numeric data.
SCALE	Optional	A number that indicates which values the slider should be capable of being set to within the `RANGE`. So, if the `RANGE` is `0,500` and the `SCALE` is 50, the user would be able to use the slider to choose only `0`, `50`, `100`, `150`, and so on. If omitted, the user can select any value within the `RANGE`.
LABEL	Optional	A label that appears on the slider control so the user can easily see the numeric value he has selected by sliding the control's knob. Use the word `%value%` (surrounded by percent signs, as shown) to represent the current value of the slider, like so: `LABEL="Volume: %value%"` Remember to set the `REFRESHLABEL` attribute to `Yes` whenever you provide a `LABEL` attribute.

Name	Status	Description
REFRESHLABEL	Optional	Yes or No. If Yes, the label is not refreshed when the slider is moved. Default is Yes.
VERTICAL	Optional	Yes or No. If No, the slider knob can be moved from side to side. If Yes, the knob moves up and down. Default is No.
TICKMARKMAJOR	Optional	Yes or No. If Yes, large tick marks appear along the slider control to help the user see where particular values will fall. Default is No. There is also a TICKMARKMAJOR attribute (see Appendix A).
TICKMARKLABELS	Optional	If No (the default), no labels are shown along the slider control to mark where particular values fall. If Yes or Numeric, labels are automatically displayed based on the RANGE and SCALE attributes. If any other value is supplied, it is assumed to be a comma-separated list of tick labels to display (see Listing 25.11 for an example).

Note

The <CFSLIDER> tag also supports most of the look-and-feel attributes listed in Table 25.3, earlier in this chapter.

To use the slider control, just add the <CFSLIDER> tag to your <CFFORM> code. Most of the time, you will want to specify values for (at least) the NAME, WIDTH, HEIGHT, and RANGE attributes (see Table 25.8). Listing 25.11 shows how to use the slider control in your ColdFusion templates. This example takes advantage of the VERTICAL, TICKMARKMAJOR, and TICKMARKLABELS attributes introduced in ColdFusion 5.0. The results are shown in Figure 25.10.

LISTING 25.11 FilmEntry.cfm—ADDING A SLIDER CONTROL TO A DATA-ENTRY FORM

```
<!--- Insert film into database when form is submitted --->
<CFIF IsDefined("FORM.RatingID")>
  <CFQUERY DATASOURCE="ows">
    INSERT INTO Films(MovieTitle, RatingID, AmountBudgeted)
    VALUES ('#FORM.MovieTitle#', #FORM.RatingID#, #FORM.AmountBudgeted#)
  </CFQUERY>
</CFIF>

<!--- Get list of ratings from database --->
<CFQUERY NAME="GetRatings" DATASOURCE="ows">
  SELECT RatingID, Rating
  FROM FilmsRatings
  ORDER BY RatingID
</CFQUERY>

<!--- Use query of queries feature to get highest and lowest rating ID --->
<CFQUERY NAME="GetMinMax" DBTYPE="query">
  SELECT MIN(RatingID) AS MinRating, MAX(RatingID) As MaxRating
  FROM GetRatings
```

LISTING 25.11 CONTINUED

```
</CFQUERY>

<HTML>
<HEAD><TITLE>Film Entry Form</TITLE></HEAD>
<BODY>
<H2>Film Entry Form</H2>

<!--- Data entry form --->
<CFFORM ACTION="#CGI.SCRIPT_NAME#" METHOD="POST">

  <!--- Slider control for selecting the film's rating --->
  <CFSLIDER
    NAME="RatingID"
    VALUE="2"
    LABEL="Rating: %value%"
    RANGE="#GetMinMax.MinRating#,#GetMinMax.MaxRating#"
    TICKMARKMAJOR="Yes"
    TICKMARKLABELS="#ValueList(GetRatings.Rating)#"
    VERTICAL="Yes"
    WIDTH="160"
    HEIGHT="200"
    LOOKANDFEEL="Metal"
    ALIGN="LEFT"
    HSPACE="5">

  <!--- Text entry field for expense description --->
  <P><B>New Film Title:</B><BR>
  <CFINPUT NAME="MovieTitle" SIZE="50" MAXLENGTH="50"
    REQUIRED="Yes" MESSAGE="Please don't leave the film title blank."><BR>

  <!--- Text entry field for expense description --->
  <P><B>Short Description / One-Liner:</B><BR>
  <CFINPUT NAME="PitchText" SIZE="50" MAXLENGTH="50"
    REQUIRED="Yes" MESSAGE="Please don't leave the one-liner blank."><BR>

  <!--- Text entry field for expense description --->
  <P><B>New Film Budget:</B><BR>
  <CFINPUT NAME="AmountBudgeted" SIZE="15"
    REQUIRED="Yes" MESSAGE="Please don't leave the film title blank."
    VALIDATE="float"><BR>



  <!--- Submit button for form --->
  <P><INPUT TYPE="Submit" VALUE="Submit New Film">
</CFFORM>

</BODY>
</HTML>
```

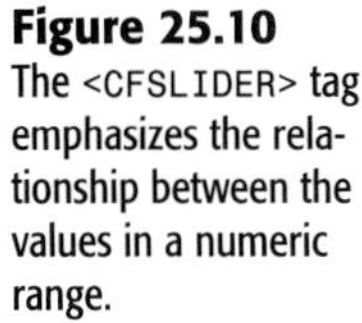

Figure 25.10
The <CFSLIDER> tag emphasizes the relationship between the values in a numeric range.

About <CFTEXTINPUT> and <CFAPPLET>

This section describes two <CFFORM> tags that were not covered in detail in this chapter: <CFTEXTINPUT> and <CFAPPLET>. Because these tags aren't generally used in the majority of ColdFusion applications, we aren't providing specific examples for them here. You can find out more about them in the ColdFusion documentation.

About <CFTEXTINPUT>

In this chapter, you have learned about the sophisticated Java-based controls provided by ColdFusion for use in your forms (the tree control, grid control, and slider control). ColdFusion also provides a Java-based alternative to HTML text form fields, called <CFTEXTINPUT>. It provides all the validation options provided by the <CFINPUT> tag you learned about in Chapter 13, plus a number of additional attributes to control font color, size, and so on.

In general, we don't recommend that you use this tag, so we aren't providing a specific code example for it in this chapter. You can get all the same validation functionality from <CFINPUT> without the added overhead of Java, and recent versions of the major browsers allow you to specify font size and color for text form fields via CSS formatting.

To learn more about <CFTEXTINPUT>, consult Appendix A or the CFML Language Reference section of the ColdFusion documentation.

ABOUT <CFAPPLET>

One of the least used or understood ColdFusion form features is the `<CFAPPLET>` tag. This tag enables you to extend the power of `<CFFORM>` by adding new Java elements that you create (or acquire or buy from other companies or developers). You can have the results of the Java applet submitted with the form, as if it were an ordinary form element. In addition, much of the code you normally would write for a Java applet is handled by ColdFusion using default values you set during registration.

Because the writing of Java applets is a topic well beyond the scope of this book, and because free, prebuilt Java controls that can effectively be used as form controls are in short supply, we aren't providing any specific `<CFAPPLET>` examples in this chapter. In general, you will be provided with prebuilt syntax for using a particular applet in your code, so the services provided by the `<CFAPPLET>` tag are not generally of much real-world benefit.

To use `<CFAPPLET>`, you first add an entry in the Java Applets page of the ColdFusion Administrator, and then use the `<CFAPPLET>` tag in your form templates. For more information, consult Appendix A or the ColdFusion documentation.

CHAPTER 26

INTEGRATING WITH MACROMEDIA FLASH

In this chapter

USING THE FLASH COMPONENT KIT

Macromedia provides a set of prebuilt user interface components that make including certain types of visual widgets in your ColdFusion pages remarkably easy. These stylish, highly interactive components are implemented as Macromedia Flash movies. The Macromedia Flash 5 Player—which must be present on the user's machine—takes care of presenting the components to the user.

The components are available as a part of the Macromedia Flash Component Kit for ColdFusion, which Macromedia makes available to developers free of charge. The latest available version of the kit has been included on this book's CD-ROM for your convenience. Updates will be made available from the ColdFusion Developers Exchange site at `http://devex.allaire.com/developer/gallery` (search for Flash Component Kit).

INTRODUCING THE FLASH COMPONENT KIT

The Macromedia Flash Component Kit for ColdFusion serves two purposes:

- **It provides a set of prebuilt, visual components, which you can use in your pages**—Each component is encapsulated within a custom tag, which makes them very easy to use. Sample templates that use each of the components are provided in this chapter.
- **It also provides tips, technical resources, and best practices information about creating additional components of your own**—This topic is beyond the scope of this chapter, but you are encouraged to look through the PDF documents provided with the Component Kit to learn more about creating your own user-interface widgets with Macromedia Flash.

Currently, four prebuilt components are included in the Flash Component Kit:

- **The Calendar component**—Used for letting your users pick dates visually
- **The Calculator component**—Embeds a calculator on your Web pages
- **The Navigation Bar component**—Used for placing an interactive toolbar at the top of your application pages
- **The IE Cascading Menu component**—A more advanced type of navigation bar

All the components provide slick-looking, interactive widgets, which can be used to give a more exciting, dynamic feel to your application. Because they rely on the Macromedia Flash Player to provide the interactivity, they work exactly the same way in nearly all browsers that support the Flash Player (except for the Cascading Menu component, which works with Internet Explorer on Windows only).

Note

In general, you could build similar components using Dynamic HTML, but developing Dynamic HTML that works properly in all the major browsers is usually quite difficult. That said, a great place to look for cross-browser Dynamic HTML solutions is `http://www.webreference.com`.

Installing the Component Kit

To install the Component Kit, follow these steps:

1. The Component Kit is provided in the form of a Zip archive named `componentkit.zip` (for use on Windows servers) or a TAR archive named `componentkit.tar` (for Linux/Unix users). Extract the appropriate archive to a temporary directory, making sure that the archive's directory structure is maintained during the extraction process.
2. Copy the entire `componentkittags` folder from the extracted archive to the `CustomTags` folder, which is located within the `CFUSION` folder. There should now be a `CFUSION\CustomTags\componentkittags` folder, with a number of ColdFusion templates in it.
3. Create a new folder called `componentkit` in your Web server's root directory.
4. Copy the `support` and `samples` folders from the extracted archive to the `componentkit` folder you just created.

Note

You are free to use a different folder name instead of `componentkit`. Actually, you can use any folder location you want, as long as it is accessible via your Web server. If you use a different folder location, just be sure to provide the relative path to that location in the `uiToolkitCFPath` and `uiToolkitSupportPath` variables later (see Listing 26.1).

To test the installation, visit the following URL with your Web browser (if you installed the Component Kit onto a ColdFusion server other than your local machine, use that server's name or IP address instead of `localhost`):

```
http://localhost/componentkit/samples/index.htm
```

An introductory page should appear, with links to live examples of the four prebuilt components included with the kit. At this point, you should be able to interact with the examples and see components in action. If not, make sure the Flash Player 5 (or later) is installed on your browser machine; then try going through the installation process on the server machine again.

Using the Calendar Component

The Calendar component is a handy date-picking widget you can use to collect dates from your users. Rather than typing a date into a plain text box, your users can interact with a visual calendar. This makes it a lot easier for them to understand which day of the week they are committing to, and to generally get a better sense of how far away from the present the dates might actually be.

From your perspective as a developer, the Calendar component behaves similarly to the form fields you have seen throughout this book. Used in a form page, it collects date information from the user and makes the date value available to the receiving template when the form is submitted. The Calendar component will usually be used within a `<CFFORM>` tag.

To include the Calendar in one of your pages, use the `<CF_uicalendar>` tag. Table 26.1 lists the attributes this tag supports.

TABLE 26.1 `<CF_uicalendar>` TAG ATTRIBUTES

Attribute	Description
FORMFIELD	A name for the component's value, which will be available to the form's ACTION page when the form is submitted. This attribute is equivalent to the NAME attribute of an ordinary form control, such as <INPUT>, <TEXTAREA>, or <CFINPUT>.
POPUP	Yes or No. If Yes, which is the default, the user has an ordinary text field for entering the date. The text field has a small calendar icon next to it, which the user can use to invoke the calendar. If No, the calendar appears right away, without any separate text entry field next to it.
MONTH	The month that should be shown by default when the calendar first appears. If this attribute is not provided, the current month is used.
DAY	The day that should appear selected when the calendar first appears. If it's not provided, the current day is used.
YEAR	The year that should be shown when the calendar first appears. If it's not provided, the current year is used.
DATEFORMAT	The format used to display (and submit) the date the user selects with the calendar control. Unfortunately, you cannot specify a date mask here, as with the DateFormat() function. Instead, the only choices are date and eurodate, which correspond to the date and eurodate values for the VALIDATE attribute of the <CFINPUT> tag.
WIDTH	The width of the calculator, in pixels.
HEIGHT	The height of the calculator, in pixels.
stFORMATTING	A ColdFusion structure containing the generic formatting properties supported by the Flash Component Kit. See Listing 26.3, later in this chapter, for details.
SELBDRCOLOR	A color for the border that indicates the currently selected date. Provide the value in RGB hexadecimal format, preceded by two # signs, such as ##FFFFFF for white or ##0000FF for blue. You can't use named colors, such as red or blue.
ZINDEX	A zindex value for the calculator component, which can be used to control whether the calculator appears in front of or behind other dynamic elements on the page. If it's not provided, a default value of 100 is used; use a higher number if the calendar appears behind other absolutely positioned elements on the page. Currently relevant only when the Calendar is viewed with Internet Explorer. For more information about zindex and absolutely positioned elements, refer to a DHTML reference book or the DHTML References section of http://msdn.microsoft.com/.

Attribute	Description
REQUIRED	Undocumented. Yes or No. If Yes, the user must provide a date before the form can be submitted. Corresponds to the REQUIRED attribute of the <CFINPUT> tag. This attribute is relevant only when POPUP="Yes". It has no effect if POPUP="No".
MESSAGE	Undocumented. The message to be shown if REQUIRED="Yes" and the user leaves the value blank. Corresponds to the MESSAGE attribute of the <CFINPUT> tag. If it's omitted, a default message (Invalid Date Format) is used. This attribute is relevant only when POPUP and REQUIRED are both Yes.

Note

The attributes marked as Undocumented are implemented in the custom tags provided in the Component Kit but are not documented for some reason. They work in the version of the Component Kit that was available when this book was written. There is no explicit guarantee that they will continue to work in future versions of the kit.

GETTING READY TO USE THE CALENDAR

As you are about to see, including the Calendar component in your application pages is very easy.

Before you can do so, you must set a few special variables in your Application.cfm file. All the components in the Flash Component Kit rely on these variables to locate the various images, Flash movie (.swf) files, and other elements used to display the components to your users.

The required variables are

- REQUEST.uiToolkitCFPath—This should always be set to /componentkit/support/, as long as you used the suggested folder names while installing the Component Kit. If you used a different folder location when installing, provide the relative path to the Component Kit's support folder. The <CF_uicalendar> and other custom tags provided by the Component Kit tags will use this value internally in <CFINCLUDE> tags, which means that any mappings established in the ColdFusion Administrator will be respected.
- REQUEST.uiToolkitSupportPath—This should also always be set to /componentkit/support/ as long as you used the suggested folder names while installing the Component Kit. If you used a different folder location when installing, provide the relative URL path to the Component Kit's support folder. The <CF_uicalendar> and other custom tags provided by the Component Kit tags will use this value internally in the SRC for images and script files, and in the MOVIE path for the Flash Player. Therefore, any folder or virtual Web server mappings established at the Web server level will be respected.

Note

To learn how the `REQUEST` scope might be helpful to use in your own custom tags, see Chapter 22, "Building Reusable Components."

Note

In most situations, the values for `REQUEST.uiToolkitCFPath` and `REQUEST.uiToolkitSupportPath` are the same.

Listing 26.1 is a typical `Application.cfm` template, with the two required variables added. The variables have each been set to `/componentkit/support/` under the assumption that you installed the Component Kit using the suggested folder locations.

Save this file as `Application.cfm`, not `Application1.cfm`.

LISTING 26.1 `Application1.cfm`**—ADDING THE COMPONENT KIT'S REQUIRED VARIABLES TO THE REQUEST SCOPE**

```
<!---
  Filename:     Application.cfm
  Created by:   Nate Weiss (NMW)
  Date Created: 2/18/2001
  Please Note:  Executes for each page request
--->

<!--- Any variables set here can be used by all our pages --->
<CFSET REQUEST.DataSource  = "ows">
<CFSET REQUEST.CompanyName = "Orange Whip Studios">

<!--- These variables required by the Flash Component Kit --->
<CFSET REQUEST.uiToolkitCFPath = "/componentkit/support/">
<CFSET REQUEST.uiToolkitSupportPath = "/componentkit/support/">
```

Note

The Component Kit does not specifically require that you define these variables in `Application.cfm`, but it does require that the variables be set in the `REQUEST` scope before you use any of the components in a ColdFusion template. The easiest way to do this is to set them in `Application.cfm`, but you could just set them at the top of each page that uses a Component Kit component instead.

Note

Like all file paths, the values of the `uiToolkitCFPath` and `uiToolkitSupportPath` variables are case sensitive on Unix/Linux servers. They are not case sensitive on Windows servers.

USING THE POP-UP CALENDAR FOR DATA ENTRY

Now that the required variables have been added to the REQUEST scope, you are free to use the Calendar component in your application pages. Simply create a form page using <CFFORM>, and then place the <CF_uicalendar> tag between the <CFFORM> tags.

Listing 26.2 shows how to use the Calendar component in a basic data-entry form. This example creates a simple form for inserting new records in the Films table. The user uses conventional text entry fields to provide the new film's MovieTitle, PitchText, and AmountBudgeted values. The Calendar component assists the user in providing the DateInTheaters value, as shown in Figure 26.1.

LISTING 26.2 FilmEntry1.cfm—USING THE CALENDAR COMPONENT

```
<HTML>
<HEAD><TITLE>New Film</TITLE></HEAD>
<BODY>
<H2>Adding New Film</H2>

<!--- If User is Submitting the Form --->
<CFIF IsDefined("FORM.MovieTitle")>
  <!--- Insert new record into Films table in database --->
  <CFINSERT
    DATASOURCE="#REQUEST.DataSource#"
    TABLENAME="Films">

  <!--- Display success message --->
  <CFOUTPUT>
    <B>#FORM.MovieTitle#</B> was added.<BR>
  </CFOUTPUT>
</CFIF>

<!--- Self-submitting data-entry form --->
<CFFORM ACTION="#CGI.SCRIPT_NAME#" METHOD="POST">
  <TABLE>
    <!--- Text entry field for: MovieTitle --->
    <TR>
      <TH>Film Title:</TH>
      <TD>
        <CFINPUT
          NAME="MovieTitle"
          SIZE="30"
          MAXLENGTH="50"
          REQUIRED="Yes"
          MESSAGE="You may not leave the title blank.">
      </TD>
    </TR>

    <!--- Text entry field for: MovieTitle --->
    <TR>
      <TH>One-Liner:</TH>
      <TD>
        <CFINPUT
          NAME="PitchText"
          SIZE="60"
```

LISTING 26.2 CONTINUED

```
        MAXLENGTH="200"
        REQUIRED="Yes"
        MESSAGE="You may not leave the One-Liner blank.">
    </TD>
  </TR>

  <!--- Text entry field for: AmountBudgeted --->
  <TR>
    <TH>Film Budget:</TH>
    <TD>
      <CFINPUT
        NAME="AmountBudgeted"
        SIZE="10"
        MAXLENGTH="200"
        VALIDATE="float"
        REQUIRED="Yes"
        MESSAGE="You may not leave the Film Budget blank.">
    </TD>
  </TR>

  <!--- Text entry field for: DateInTheaters --->
  <!--- Augmented with Flash Calendar component from FCK --->
  <TR>
    <TH>Release Date:</TH>
    <TD>
      <CF_uicalendar
        FORMFIELD="DateInTheaters"
        WIDTH="200"
        HEIGHT="200"
        POPUP="Yes"
        SELBDRCOLOR="##FFFF00"
        REQUIRED="Yes"
        MESSAGE="You must provide a release date.">
    </TD>
  </TR>

</TABLE>

<!--- Submit Button to create new film record --->
<P><INPUT TYPE="Submit" VALUE="Insert New Film Record Now">
</CFFORM>

</BODY>
</HTML>
```

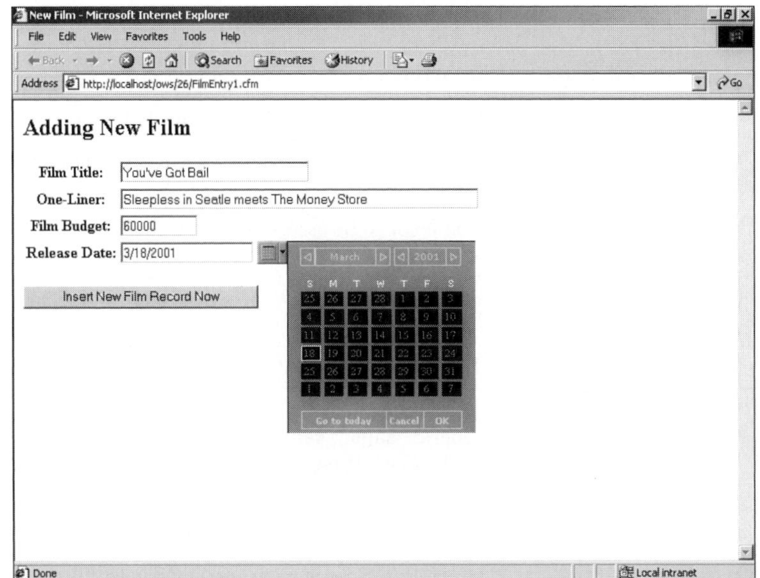

Figure 26.1
The Calendar Component provides a convenient way for your users to enter dates.

Note

To use the Calendar with POPUP="Yes", you must place the <CF_uicalendar> tag between opening and closing <CFFORM> tags. For more information about <CFFORM>, see Chapter 13, "Form Data Validation," and Chapter 25, "Enhancing Forms with Client-Side Java."

CONTROLLING THE LOOK AND FEEL

The Flash Component Kit gives you a lot of flexibility when it comes to customizing the look of the individual controls. To adjust properties such as the color and fonts used in a control, create a ColdFusion structure that contains the properties you want to adjust. The structure can contain any or all of the properties shown in Table 26.2. Then provide the structure to the optional `stFORMATTING` attribute of the `<CF_uicalendar>` or other Component Kit controls.

TABLE 26.2 FORMATTING ATTRIBUTES

Structure Attribute	Description
`bgcolor`	Component background color, as an RGB hexadecimal value.
`bgtrans`	Whether to set background transparency as a Boolean value. Currently, it works only with Internet Explorer and not on all platforms.
`bdrstate`	Whether to display a border as a Boolean value.
`bdrcolor`	The border color, as an RGB hexadecimal value.
`btncolor`	Background color for buttons, as an RGB hexadecimal value.
`btntxtcolor`	Text color for buttons, as an RGB hexadecimal value.

TABLE 26.2 CONTINUED

Structure Attribute	Description
`btnbdrcolor`	Border color for buttons, as an RGB hexadecimal value.
`btnhicolor`	Background color to be used when a button is clicked, as an RGB hexadecimal value.
`btntxthicolor`	Text color to be used when a button is clicked, as an RGB hexadecimal value.
`btnbdrhicolor`	Border color to be used when a button is clicked, as an RGB hexadecimal value.
`txtcolor`	Text color, as an RGB hexadecimal value.
`txtfont`	Text font name, such as `Arial` or `Helvetica`. You can also use the generic `_sans`, `_serif`, or `_typewriter` font names, which are defined by the Flash Player and should look the same on all machines, regardless of which fonts are actually installed on the user's machine.
`rdonly`	Whether component should be considered read-only, as a Boolean value.
`submitcontrols`	Whether the component should include OK and Cancel buttons.

You can create the formatting structure right before using each component, in your `Application.cfm` file, or in a separate file that you include via `<CFINCLUDE>` before using a component. (For more information about `<CFINCLUDE>`, see Chapter 10, "CFML Basics.")

Listing 26.3 is a revised version of `Application.cfm`. It creates a formatting structure called `REQUEST.uiToolkitFormatting` to create an attractive look for the Calendar component, using shades of blue. Save this listing as `Application.cfm`, not `Application2.cfm`.

LISTING 26.3 `Application2.cfm`—**DEFINING A LOOK AND FEEL FOR COMPONENT KIT WIDGETS**

```
<!---
  Filename:     Application.cfm
  Created by:   Nate Weiss (NMW)
  Date Created: 2/18/2001
  Please Note:  Executes for each page request
--->

<!--- Any variables set here can be used by all our pages --->
<CFSET REQUEST.DataSource  = "ows">
<CFSET REQUEST.CompanyName = "Orange Whip Studios">

<!--- These variables required by the Flash Component Kit --->
<CFSET REQUEST.uiToolkitCFPath = "/componentkit/support/">
<CFSET REQUEST.uiToolkitSupportPath = "/componentkit/support/">

<!--- Formatting Structure for Flash Component Kit components --->
<CFSET REQUEST.uiToolkitFormatting = StructNew()>
<CFSET REQUEST.uiToolkitFormatting.txtfont = "_sans">
<CFSET REQUEST.uiToolkitFormatting.bgcolor = "##0000CD">
<CFSET REQUEST.uiToolkitFormatting.btncolor = "##FFFFFF">
```

```
<CFSET REQUEST.uiToolkitFormatting.btntxtcolor = "##000080">
<CFSET REQUEST.uiToolkitFormatting.btnbdrcolor = "##0000FF">
<CFSET REQUEST.uiToolkitFormatting.bdrcolor = "##0000FF">
```

Now that the formatting structure has been set up, you just need to go back to Listing 26.2 and add `stFORMATTING="#REQUEST.uiToolkitFormatting#"` to the `<CF_uicalendar>` tag. When you reload Listing 26.2 in your browser, you will see that your formatting instructions have been applied.

USING THE INLINE CALENDAR

You can also use the Calendar in an inline mode, using `POPUP="No"` in the `<CF_uicalendar>` tag. The Calendar will appear on the page right away, with the `WIDTH` and `HEIGHT` that you indicate.

Unlike ordinary images, the Calendar will appear on top of (obscuring) the other elements on the page (like text). Therefore, you need to be sure to leave space for the Calendar to appear. An easy way to do this is to place the Calendar in its own table cell that has the same `WIDTH` and `HEIGHT` as the component itself. This will reserve the correct amount of space in the page layout for the Calculator to appear in.

Unfortunately, the undocumented `REQUIRED` and `MESSAGE` attributes of the Calendar have no effect when `POPUP="No"` (which might be part of why they are undocumented at this time). You must add a bit of JavaScript to require that the user pick a date (by double-clicking the date) before submitting the form. Using JavaScript for ad-hoc form validation is beyond the scope of this chapter, but it is easy to do. With the help of a JavaScript reference, you will be able to easily adapt the JavaScript code shown in Listing 26.4.

Listing 26.4 demonstrates how to use the inline version of the Calendar. The results are shown in Figure 26.2.

LISTING 26.4 `FilmEntry2.cfm`—**USING THE CALENDAR COMPONENT IN INLINE MODE**

```
<HTML>
<HEAD>
  <TITLE>New Film</TITLE>
  <!--- Validation script for when the form is submitted --->
  <SCRIPT LANGUAGE="JavaScript">
    function checkForm() {
      var result;
      with (document.forms[0]) {
        // Make DateInTheaters be a required field
        if (DateInTheaters.value == '') {
          alert('You must provide a release date.');
          result = false;
        };
      };
      return result;
    };
  </SCRIPT>
</HEAD>
<BODY>
<H2>Adding New Film</H2>
```

LISTING 26.4 CONTINUED

```
<!--- If User is Submitting the Form --->
<CFIF IsDefined("FORM.MovieTitle")>
  <!--- Insert new record into Films table in database --->
  <CFINSERT
    DATASOURCE="#REQUEST.DataSource#"
    TABLENAME="Films">

  <!--- Display success message --->
  <CFOUTPUT>
    <B>#FORM.MovieTitle#</B> was added.<BR>
  </CFOUTPUT>
</CFIF>

<!--- Self-submitting data-entry form --->
<CFFORM ACTION="#CGI.SCRIPT_NAME#" METHOD="POST" ONSUBMIT="return checkForm()">
  <TABLE>
    <!--- Text entry field for: MovieTitle --->
    <TR>
      <TH>Film Title:</TH>
      <TD>
        <CFINPUT
          NAME="MovieTitle"
          SIZE="30"
          MAXLENGTH="50"
          REQUIRED="Yes"
          MESSAGE="You may not leave the title blank.">
      </TD>
    </TR>

    <!--- Text entry field for: MovieTitle --->
    <TR>
      <TH>One-Liner:</TH>
      <TD>
        <CFINPUT
          NAME="PitchText"
          SIZE="60"
          MAXLENGTH="200"
          REQUIRED="Yes"
          VALUE=""
          MESSAGE="You may not leave the One-Liner blank.">
      </TD>
    </TR>

    <!--- Text entry field for: DateInTheaters --->
    <!--- Augmented with Flash Calculator component from FCK --->
    <TR>
      <TH>Film Budget:</TH>
      <TD>
        <CFINPUT
          NAME="AmountBudgeted"
          SIZE="10"
          MAXLENGTH="200"
          VALIDATE="float"
          REQUIRED="Yes"
          MESSAGE="You may not leave the Film Budget blank.">
      </TD>
```

```
    </TR>

    <!--- Text entry field for: DateInTheaters --->
    <!--- Augmented with Flash Calendar component from FCK --->
    <TR>
      <TH VALIGN="top">Release Date:</TH>
      <TD VALIGN="top" WIDTH="200" HEIGHT="200">
        <CF_uiCALENDAR
          FORMFIELD="DateInTheaters"
          WIDTH="200"
          HEIGHT="200"
          POPUP="No"
          SELBDRCOLOR="##FFFFFF"
          stFORMATTING="#REQUEST.uiToolkitFormatting#"
          REQUIRED="Yes"
          MESSAGE="You must provide a release date.">
      </TD>
    </TR>


  </TABLE>

  <!--- Submit Button to create new film record --->
  <P><INPUT TYPE="Submit" VALUE="Insert New Film Record Now">
</CFFORM>

</BODY>
</HTML>
```

Figure 26.2
The Calendar component can also be used in an inline mode.

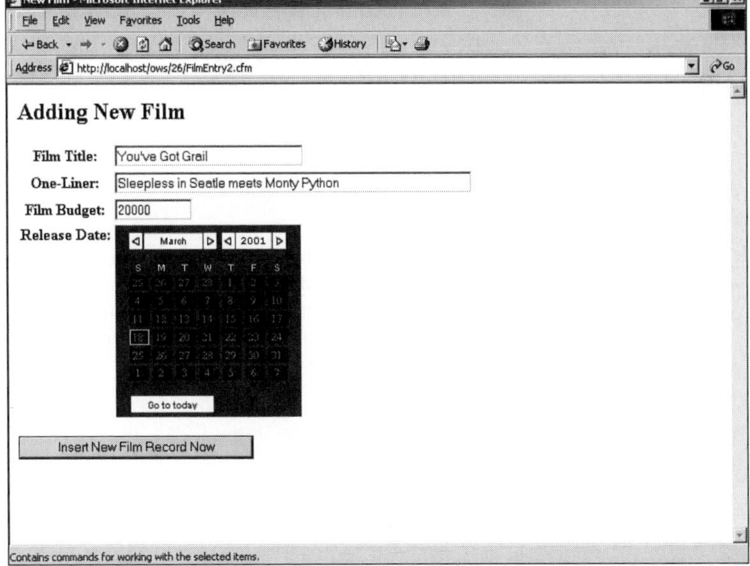

The ONSUBMIT attribute of the <CFFORM> tag causes the JavaScript checkForm() function to be called whenever the user attempts to submit the form. If a date value has not been selected yet, the function will display a "required" type of message to the user and return a value of `false`, which is what causes the form submission to be blocked. If the date value has been provided, the function returns `true`, which enables the form to be submitted.

USING THE CALCULATOR COMPONENT

The Calculator component is similar conceptually to the Calendar. It behaves in either a pop-up or an inline mode (controlled by the `POPUP` attribute) and is well suited for augmenting a normal data-entry form.

To include the Calculator in one of your pages, use the `<CF_uicalculator>` tag. Table 26.3 lists the attributes this tag supports.

TABLE 26.3 `<CF_uicalculator>` TAG ATTRIBUTES

Attribute	Description
FORMFIELD	A name for the component's value, which will be available to the form's ACTION page when the form is submitted. This attribute is equivalent to the NAME attribute of an ordinary form control, such as <INPUT>, <TEXTAREA>, or <CFINPUT>.
POPUP	Yes or No. If Yes, which is the default, the user has an ordinary text field for entering the date. The text field has a small calculator icon next to it, which the user can use to invoke the calculator. If No, the calculator appears right away, without any separate text entry field next to it.
WIDTH	The width of the calculator, in pixels.
HEIGHT	The height of the calculator, in pixels.
stFORMATTING	A ColdFusion structure containing the generic formatting properties supported by the Flash Component Kit. Refer to Listing 26.3 for details.
ZINDEX	A zindex value for the Calculator component, which can be used to control whether the calculator appears in front of or behind other dynamic elements on the page. If not provided, a default value of 100 is used; use a higher number if the calculator appears behind other absolutely positioned elements on the page. Currently relevant only when the Calculator is viewed with Internet Explorer. For more information about zindex and absolutely positioned elements, refer to a DHTML reference book or the DHTML References section of http://msdn.microsoft.com/.
REQUIRED	Undocumented. Yes or No. If Yes, the user must provide a value before the form can be submitted. Corresponds to the REQUIRED attribute of the <CFINPUT> tag. This attribute is relevant only when POPUP="Yes". It has no effect if POPUP="No".
MESSAGE	Undocumented. The message to be shown if REQUIRED="Yes" and the user leaves the value blank. Corresponds to the MESSAGE attribute of the <CFINPUT> tag. If omitted, a default message (Error in numeric data entry field) is used. This attribute is relevant only when POPUP and REQUIRED are both Yes.

Listing 26.5 is a revised version of the `FilmEntry.cfm` template from Listing 26.2. Now, in addition to being able to use the calendar icon to provide a date, the user can use the calculator icon to provide the film's budget. The user can use the Calculator component to perform any estimations or calculations to help come up with an accurate estimate of the film's final cost. Most functions available in a traditional handheld calculator are available here, including square roots, memory recall, and so on. When finished calculating, the user just clicks the OK button on the Calculator, which places the final calculated value onto the form, as shown in Figure 26.3.

Listing 26.5 `FilmEntry3.cfm`—Adding the Calculator Component to a Form

```
<HTML>
<HEAD><TITLE>New Film</TITLE></HEAD>
<BODY>
<H2>Adding New Film</H2>

<!--- If User is Submitting the Form --->
<CFIF IsDefined("FORM.MovieTitle")>
  <!--- Insert new record into Films table in database --->
  <CFINSERT
    DATASOURCE="#REQUEST.DataSource#"
    TABLENAME="Films">

  <!--- Display success message --->
  <CFOUTPUT>
    <B>#FORM.MovieTitle#</B> was added.<BR>
  </CFOUTPUT>
</CFIF>

<!--- Self-submitting data-entry form --->
<CFFORM ACTION="#CGI.SCRIPT_NAME#" METHOD="POST">
  <TABLE>
    <!--- Text entry field for: MovieTitle --->
    <TR>
      <TH>Film Title:</TH>
      <TD>
        <CFINPUT
          NAME="MovieTitle"
          SIZE="30"
          MAXLENGTH="50"
          REQUIRED="Yes"
          MESSAGE="You may not leave the title blank.">
      </TD>
    </TR>

    <!--- Text entry field for: MovieTitle --->
    <TR>
      <TH>One-Liner:</TH>
      <TD>
        <CFINPUT
          NAME="PitchText"
          SIZE="60"
          MAXLENGTH="200"
          REQUIRED="Yes"
          MESSAGE="You may not leave the One-Liner blank.">
```

LISTING 26.5 CONTINUED

```
      </TD>
    </TR>

    <!--- Text entry field for: AmountBudgeted --->
    <!--- Augmented with Flash Calendar component from FCK --->
    <TR>
      <TH>Film Budget:</TH>
      <TD>
        <CF_uiCALCULATOR
          FORMFIELD="AmountBudgeted"
          WIDTH="200"
          HEIGHT="200"
          POPUP="Yes"
          stFORMATTING="#REQUEST.uiToolkitFormatting#"
          REQUIRED="Yes"
          MESSAGE="You must provide the budget for the film.">
      </TD>
    </TR>

    <!--- Text entry field for: DateInTheaters --->
    <!--- Augmented with Flash Calendar component from FCK --->
    <TR>
      <TH>Release Date:</TH>
      <TD>
        <CF_uicalendar
          FORMFIELD="DateInTheaters"
          WIDTH="200"
          HEIGHT="200"
          POPUP="Yes"
          SELBDRCOLOR="##FFFF00"
          stFORMATTING="#REQUEST.uiToolkitFormatting#"
          REQUIRED="Yes"
          MESSAGE="You must provide a release date.">
      </TD>
    </TR>

  </TABLE>

  <!--- Submit Button to create new film record --->
  <P><INPUT TYPE="Submit" VALUE="Insert New Film Record Now">
</CFFORM>

</BODY>
</HTML>
```

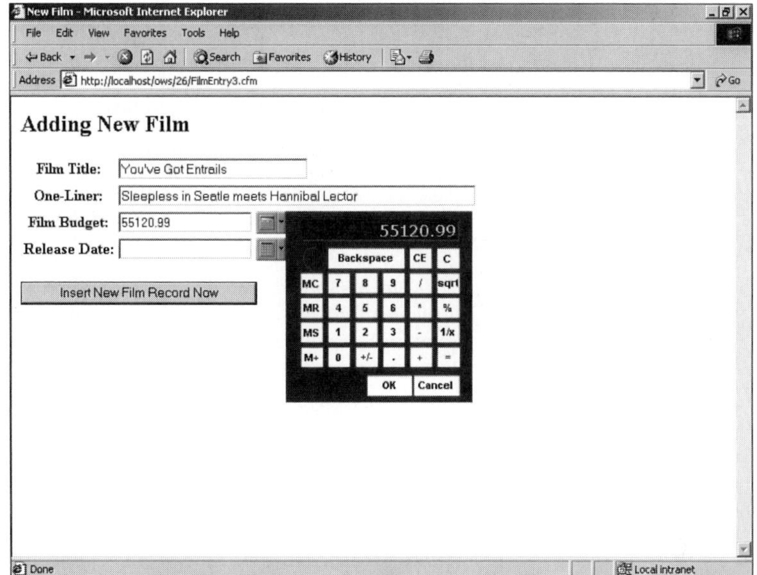

Figure 26.3
The Calculator provides a terrific way for users to make quick computations while filling out a form.

USING THE NAVIGATION BAR COMPONENT

The Navigation Bar component is used to provide an interactive navigation bar for your application pages. The Navigation Bar supports two levels of navigation choices. The top-level choices are always visible. The second-level choices become visible when the user selects the corresponding top-level choice, creating a pull-down-menu effect.

Because of the way most browsers work with plug-ins such as the Macromedia Flash Player, the Navigation Bar must always take up the same amount of space onscreen, regardless of whether any of the top-level choices are currently selected. If the second-level choices are too numerous to display at once within the space you specify with the `WIDTH` and `HEIGHT` attributes, arrow elements will be provided to enable the user to scroll through the second-level choices.

INTRODUCING THE NAVIGATION BAR TAGS

To include the Navigation Bar component in your pages, use the `<CF_uihnavbar>` tag. Then, within the `<CF_uihnavbar>` tag, add a `<CF_uihnavbaroption>` tag for each top-level navigation choice. Finally, within each `<CF_uihnavbaroption>` tag, add a `<CF_uihnavbaroptionitem>` tag for each second-level choice.

Tables 26.4, 26.5, and 26.6 list the attributes supported by each of the Navigation Bar tags.

TABLE 26.4 <CF_uihnavbar> TAG ATTRIBUTES

Attribute	Description
WIDTH	The width of the navigation bar, in pixels.
HEIGHT	The height of the navigation bar, in pixels.
stFORMATTING	A ColdFusion structure containing the generic formatting properties supported by the Flash Component Kit. Refer to Listing 26.3 for details.
DROPSPEED	A number between 0 and 100 that indicates how quickly the second-level elements should drop down. The higher the number, the faster the elements appear. The default value of 0 is far too slow for most situations; we recommend experimenting with an initial value of 99. Use 100 for an instant drop-down effect.
SUBSTEP	A number between 0 and 100 that indicates how quickly the user will scroll through the second-level elements, if there are too many elements to show in the navigation bar at once. We recommend experimenting with an initial value of 25.
TOPHEIGHT	The height, in pixels, of the top portion of the navigation bar (where the top-level choices appear). For best results, the TOPHEIGHT and BOTTOMHEIGHT should add up to the overall HEIGHT.
BOTTOMHEIGHT	The height, in pixels, of the bottom portion of the navigation bar (where the second-level choices appear). For best results, the TOPHEIGHT and BOTTOMHEIGHT should add up to the overall HEIGHT.
MIDLINECOLOR	The color of the line that separates the top and bottom portions of the navigation bar, as an RGB hexadecimal value.
ARROWCOLOR	The color of the arrow icon that appears when the user needs to scroll through the second-level choices, as an RGB hexadecimal value.
ARROWBGCOLOR	The background color that surrounds the arrow icon that appears when the user needs to scroll through the second-level choices, as an RGB hexadecimal value.

TABLE 26.5 <CF_uihnavbaroption> TAG ATTRIBUTES

Attribute	Description
NAME	The text that should appear for the top-level navigation choice.
WIDTH	The width of the top-level item, in pixels. If it's not provided, a default width of 50 pixels is used.

TABLE 26.6 <CF_uihnavbaroptionitem> TAG ATTRIBUTES

Attribute	Description
NAME	Required. The text that should appear for the top-level navigation choice.
URL	Required. The URL the user should be sent to if he clicks the item.
WIDTH	The width of the second-level navigation item, in pixels. If it's not provided, a default width of 50 pixels is used.

USING THE NAVIGATION BAR IN A PAGE HEADER

Listing 26.6 demonstrates one way the Horizontal Navigation Bar component can be used. It creates an interactive pull-down header that can be placed at the top of any page via a `<CFINCLUDE>` tag.

Using the navigation bar, the user can navigate to the Orange Whip Studios home page or to the online store. Users also can scroll through lists of current films, actors, and actresses; when they click one of these menu items, they are sent to the appropriate page, with the appropriate `FilmID` or `ActorID` passed as a URL parameter.

LISTING 26.6 `NavBarHeader.cfm`—**USING THE HORIZONTAL NAVIGATION BAR COMPONENT**

```
<!--- Fetch a listing of current films from the database --->
<CFQUERY NAME="GetFilms" DATASOURCE="#REQUEST.DataSource#"
  CACHEDWITHIN="#CreateTimeSpan(0,0,10,0)#">
  SELECT FilmID, MovieTitle
  FROM Films
  ORDER BY MovieTitle
</CFQUERY>

<!--- Fetch a listing of current actors from the database --->
<CFQUERY NAME="GetActors" DATASOURCE="#REQUEST.DataSource#"
  CACHEDWITHIN="#CreateTimeSpan(0,0,10,0)#">
  SELECT ActorID, NameFirst, NameLast, Gender
  FROM Actors
  WHERE IsTotalBabe = 1
</CFQUERY>

<!--- Use Query-of-queries to extract just the female actors --->
<CFQUERY NAME="GetFemaleActors" DBTYPE="Query">
  SELECT ActorID, NameFirst, NameLast
  FROM GetActors
  WHERE Gender = 'F'
  ORDER BY NameLast, NameFirst
</CFQUERY>

<!--- Use Query-of-queries to extract just the male actors --->
<CFQUERY NAME="GetMaleActors" DBTYPE="Query">
  SELECT ActorID, NameFirst, NameLast
  FROM GetActors
  WHERE Gender = 'M'
  ORDER BY NameLast, NameFirst
</CFQUERY>

<!--- Create formatting structure --->
<CFSET Formatting = StructNew()>
<CFSET Formatting.bgcolor = "##F5DEB3">
<CFSET Formatting.btncolor = "##FF8C00">
<CFSET Formatting.btnhicolor = "##FFA500">

<TABLE>
<TR>
  <TD>
    <IMG SRC="../images/logo_c.gif" WIDTH="101" HEIGHT="101" ALT="" BORDER="0">
  </TD>
```

LISTING 26.6 CONTINUED

```
<TD>
  <!--- Include Navigation Bar component, from Flash Component Kit --->
  <CF_uihnavbar
    WIDTH="500"
    HEIGHT="70"
    DROPSPEED="99"
    SUBSTEP="25"
    ARROWCOLOR="##FFFF00"
    ARROWBGCOLOR="##FF0000"
    BGCOLOR="##FF0000"
    TOPHEIGHT="25"
    BOTTOMHEIGHT="45"
    stFORMATTING="#Formatting#">

    <!--- Include Top-Level navigation choice --->
    <CF_uihnavbaroption NAME="Orange Whip Studios" WIDTH="200">
      <!--- Include Second-Level navigation choice --->
      <CF_uihnavbaroptionitem
        NAME="Home"
        URL="../"
        WIDTH="100">
      <!--- Include Second-Level navigation choice --->
      <CF_uihnavbaroptionitem
        NAME="Store"
        URL="../29/Store.cfm"
        WIDTH="100">
    </CF_uihnavbaroption>


    <!--- Include Top-Level navigation choice for Films --->
    <CF_uihnavbaroption NAME="Films" WIDTH="100">
      <!--- For each Film --->
      <CFLOOP QUERY="GetFilms">
        <!--- URL to send user to if they click on this film --->
        <CFSET LinkURL = "ShowFilm.cfm?FilmID=#GetFilms.FilmID#">
        <!--- Calculate appropriate width, based on length of film title --->
        <CFSET LinkWidth = 30 + (Len(GetFilms.MovieTitle) * 6)>
        <!--- Include Second-Level navigation choice for this film --->
        <CF_uihnavbaroptionitem
          NAME="#GetFilms.MovieTitle#"
          URL="#LinkURL#"
          WIDTH="#LinkWidth#">
      </CFLOOP>
    </CF_uihnavbaroption>

    <!--- Include Top-Level navigation choice for Actors (Female) --->
    <CF_uihnavbaroption NAME="Hot Actresses" WIDTH="100">
      <!--- For each Film --->
      <CFLOOP QUERY="GetFemaleActors">
        <CFSET FullName = NameFirst & " " & NameLast>
        <!--- URL to send user to if they click on this film --->
        <CFSET LinkURL = "ShowActor.cfm?ActorID=#GetFemaleActors.ActorID#">
        <!--- Calculate appropriate width, based on length of FullName --->
        <CFSET LinkWidth = 30 + (Len(FullName) * 6)>
        <!--- Include Second-Level navigation choice for this Actor --->
```

```
        <CF_uihnavbaroptionitem
          NAME="#FullName#"
          URL="#LinkURL#"
          WIDTH="#LinkWidth#">
      </CFLOOP>
    </CF_uihnavbaroption>

    <!--- Include Top-Level navigation choice for Actors (Male) --->
    <CF_uihnavbaroption NAME="Hot Actors" WIDTH="100">
      <!--- For each Film --->
      <CFLOOP QUERY="GetMaleActors">
        <CFSET FullName = NameFirst & " " & NameLast>
        <!--- URL to send user to if they click on this film --->
        <CFSET LinkURL = "ShowActor.cfm?ActorID=#GetMaleActors.ActorID#">
        <!--- Calculate appropriate width, based on length of FullName --->
        <CFSET LinkWidth = 30 + (Len(FullName) * 6)>
        <!--- Include Second-Level navigation choice for this Actor --->
        <CF_uihnavbaroptionitem
          NAME="#FullName#"
          URL="#LinkURL#"
          TXTCOLOR="##FF0000"
          WIDTH="#LinkWidth#">
      </CFLOOP>
    </CF_uihnavbaroption>

  </CF_uihnavbar>

</TD>
</TR>
</TABLE>
```

This template uses four `<CFQUERY>` tags. The first query gets a listing of all films currently in the `Films` table. The second query gets a listing of all `Actors` in the Actors table. Per a new company-wide mandate from the marketing department, only the really attractive actors are retrieved. (It seems that next month's ad campaign goes something like "Only Hotties On This Web Site!") Then, two query-of-queries are run, which split the records for attractive men and attractive women into two separate queries called `GetFemaleActors` and `GetMaleActors`.

Next, the `<CF_uihnavbar>` tag is used to create the navigation bar. Within the navigation bar, `<CF_uihnavbaroption>` is used to create a top-level navigation choice titled Orange Whip Studios. Within this top-level choice, two `<CF_uihnavbaroptionitem>` tags are used to provide links to the company's home page and the online store template from Chapter 29, "Online Commerce."

Another `<CF_uihnavbaroption>` is then used to create another top-level navigation choice, called Films. Within this top-level choice, a `<CF_uihnavbaroptionitem>` is generated for each film in the `GetFilms` query. Because the movie titles are of differing lengths, a simple calculation is performed to come up with an appropriate width for each film's menu item: All menu items start at a base width of 30 pixels, plus an additional 8 pixels for each letter in the movie title. Because the font being used is not monospaced, this is just an approximate value, but it works quite well for the film titles in the database.

A similar loop is used to create top-level options named Actresses and Actors, including a menu item for each record returned by the `GetFemaleActors` and `GetMaleActors` queries. The result is an attractive menu that includes four top-level choices and however many second-level choices are appropriate, based on the number of film and actor records currently in the database.

Listing 26.7 places the pull-down header at the top of a hypothetical home page with a `<CFINCLUDE>` tag. Figure 26.4 shows the results when this template is viewed in a Web browser. You could add this `<CFINCLUDE>` tag to any template on which you want the navigation header to appear.

Tip

If you want the navigation header to appear at the top of each of your application's pages, you could simply add the `<CFINCLUDE>` tag to your `Application.cfm` file.

LISTING 26.7 `HomePage1.cfm`—**INCLUDING THE NAVIGATION BAR HEADER AT THE TOP OF A PAGE**

```
<HTML>
<HEAD><TITLE>Hypothetical Home Page</TITLE></HEAD>
<BODY>

<!--- Flash-Based Navigation Bar --->
<CFINCLUDE TEMPLATE="NavBarHeader.cfm">

<P>This is the home page of Orange Whip Studios.
We hope you enjoy your visit to our web site.<BR>

<P>You can be assured that we at Orange Whip Studios have exacting standards
for our films.  We bring you only the best in entertainment.
For instance, all of our actors and actresses are especially attractive.
Also, we mix the soundtracks and voice-overs especially loud in our historical
dramas and WWII films, like Girl Harbor (coming soon).

</BODY>
</HTML>
```

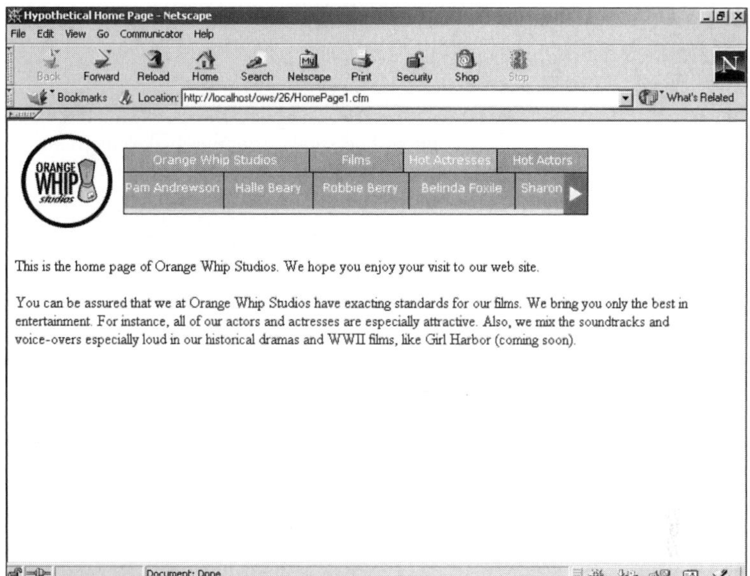

Figure 26.4
The Horizontal Navigation Bar component provides a slick, interactive way for users to navigate your site.

USING THE IE CASCADING MENU COMPONENT

In addition to the Horizontal Navigation Bar component, the Component Kit also provides an interactive, expanding Cascading Menu component. This component is similar to the Horizontal Navigation Bar, but it can expand over the Web page as necessary (somewhat similar to the Windows Start menu), creating a more pleasant experience for your users.

To add the IE Cascading Menu component to one of your application pages, use the `<CF_uicascadingmenu>` and `<CF_uicascadingmenuitem>` tags. The attributes supported by these tags are listed in Tables 26.7 and 26.8.

Note

The Cascading Menu component works only with Internet Explorer and doesn't work on the Macintosh. See Listing 26.9 for an example of how to show the appropriate component according to each user's browser and platform.

TABLE 26.7 `<CF_uicascadingmenu>` **TAG ATTRIBUTES**

Attribute	Description
`WIDTH`	The width, in pixels, of the Cascading Menu component.
`HEIGHT`	The height, in pixels, of the Cascading Menu component. This does not affect how tall the menu is when it first appears. It just puts a boundary on how large the menu can get as it expands to display the items the user pulls down from the initial menu items.
`stFORMATTING`	A ColdFusion structure containing the generic formatting properties supported by the Flash Component Kit. Refer to Listing 26.3 for details.

TABLE 26.7 CONTINUED

Attribute	Description
SCALE	A relative measure that affects the size of the individual items in the menu. The default is 1. A smaller number makes the items smaller, and a larger number makes them larger. The maximum number is 10. You can specify nonintegers, such as 1.3 or 0.9.
ELASTICITY	A number from 1 to 100 that governs how much the top-level items expand when selected. The lower the number, the more they will expand. We recommend experimenting with an initial value of 30.
BOOST	A number that indicates how fast the top-level items expand when selected. A 1 indicates an almost nonanimated expansion, and 100 indicates a very animated expansion. We recommend experimenting with an initial value of 20.
DAMPING	A number that affects the bouncing effect when top-level items are selected. 100 indicates no bouncing, and 1 causes the bouncing to go on for a long time. We recommend experimenting with an initial value of 50.
TRANSPARENCY	A transparency measure for the menu, between 0 and 100.

TABLE 26.8 <CF_uicascadingmenuitem> TAG ATTRIBUTES

Attribute	Description
ID	A numeric identifier for this menu item. This should be unique within the cascading menu.
PARENTID	The parent item of this menu item. If it's provided, this menu item becomes a child of (appears beneath or beside) the parent. If it's not provided, the menu item becomes a top-level item that is visible when the menu first appears on the page.
NAME	The text to display in the menu item.
HREF	The URL the user should be brought to if she clicks the menu item.
TARGET	The target frame, if any, that should be used when the user clicks the menu item. Corresponds to the TARGET attribute of the A tag. For details about frames and targets, see Chapter 11, "Creating Data-Driven Pages."
BGCOLOR	The background color for the menu item, as a hexadecimal RGB color. If not provided, the color is inherited from the parent item or from the value specified by the formatting structure provided to the stFORMATTING attribute for the Cascading Menu as a whole.
BGHICOLOR	The background color to use when the item is moused over. If not provided, it is inherited (see BGCOLOR).
TXTCOLOR	The text color for the menu item. If not provided, it is inherited (see BGCOLOR).
TXTHICOLOR	The text color to use when the item is moused over. If not provided, it is inherited (see BGCOLOR).
SUBBGCOLOR	The background color for this item's children, if any.

Attribute	Description
SUBBGHICOLOR	The mouse-over color for this item's children, if any.
SUBTXTCOLOR	The text color for this item's children, if any.
SUBTXTHICOLOR	The mouse-over text color for this item's children, if any.

USING THE CASCADING MENU IN A PAGE HEADER

Listing 26.8 shows how the Cascading Menu component can be put to work in your application pages. Here, it is used to provide the same set of menu choices that was presented with the Navigation Bar component (refer to Listing 26.6). Instead of having to scroll through the second-level options, the user can see all the items at once, in a somewhat more intuitive pull-down format. The results are shown in Figure 26.5.

LISTING 26.8 `CascadingHeader.cfm`—**USING THE CASCADING MENU COMPONENT**

```
<!--- Fetch a listing of current films from the database --->
<CFQUERY NAME="GetFilms" DATASOURCE="#REQUEST.DataSource#"
  CACHEDWITHIN="#CreateTimeSpan(0,0,10,0)#">
  SELECT FilmID, MovieTitle
  FROM Films
  ORDER BY MovieTitle
</CFQUERY>

<!--- Fetch a listing of current actors from the database --->
<CFQUERY NAME="GetActors" DATASOURCE="#REQUEST.DataSource#"
  CACHEDWITHIN="#CreateTimeSpan(0,0,10,0)#">
  SELECT ActorID, NameFirst, NameLast, Gender
  FROM Actors
  WHERE IsTotalBabe = 1
</CFQUERY>

<!--- Use Query-of-queries to extract just the female actors --->
<CFQUERY NAME="GetFemaleActors" DBTYPE="Query">
  SELECT ActorID, NameFirst, NameLast
  FROM GetActors
  WHERE Gender = 'F'
  ORDER BY NameLast, NameFirst
</CFQUERY>

<!--- Use Query-of-queries to extract just the male actors --->
<CFQUERY NAME="GetMaleActors" DBTYPE="Query">
  SELECT ActorID, NameFirst, NameLast
  FROM GetActors
  WHERE Gender = 'M'
  ORDER BY NameLast, NameFirst
</CFQUERY>

<!--- Create formatting structure --->
<CFSET Formatting = StructNew()>
<CFSET Formatting.bgcolor = "##F5DEB3">
<CFSET Formatting.btncolor = "##FF8C00">
<CFSET Formatting.btnhicolor = "##FFA500">
```

LISTING 26.8 CONTINUED

```
<TABLE>
<TR VALIGN="top">
  <TD>
    <IMG SRC="../images/logo_c.gif" WIDTH="101" HEIGHT="101" ALT="" BORDER="0">
  </TD>
  <TD>
    <!--- Include Navigation Bar component, from Flash Component Kit --->
    <CF_uicascadingmenu
      WIDTH="500"
      HEIGHT="300"
      ELASTICITY="30"
      BOOST="20"
      SCALE="1"
      DAMPING="50"
      stFORMATTING="#Formatting#">

      <!--- Include Top-Level navigation choice --->
      <CF_uicascadingmenuitem
        ID="1"
        NAME="Orange Whip Studios">
      <!--- Include Second-Level navigation choice --->
      <CF_uicascadingmenuitem
        NAME="Home"
        ID="2"
        PARENTID="1"
        HREF="../">
      <!--- Include Second-Level navigation choice --->
      <CF_uicascadingmenuitem
        NAME="Store"
        ID="3"
        PARENTID="1"
        HREF="../29/Store.cfm">


      <!--- Include Top-Level navigation choice for Films --->
      <CF_uicascadingmenuitem
        ID="4"
        BGCOLOR="##FF0000"
        NAME="Films">
      <!--- Include sub-navigation choice for A-M films --->
      <CF_uicascadingmenuitem
        ID="1000"
        PARENTID="4"
        NAME="A-L">
      <!--- Include sub-navigation choice for N-Z films --->
      <CF_uicascadingmenuitem
        ID="1500"
        PARENTID="4"
        NAME="M-Z">

      <!--- For each Film --->
      <CFLOOP QUERY="GetFilms">
        <!--- URL to send user to if they click on this film --->
        <CFSET LinkURL = "ShowFilm.cfm?FilmID=#GetFilms.FilmID#">
        <!--- ID number for this menu item (1000 plus current row) --->
```

```
      <CFSET ParentID = IIF(Left(MovieTitle, 1) LTE "M", 1000, 1500)>
      <CFSET LinkID = ParentID + GetFilms.CurrentRow>

      <!--- Include Second-Level navigation choice for this film --->
      <CF_uicascadingmenuitem
        ID="#LinkID#"
        PARENTID="#ParentID#"
        NAME="#GetFilms.MovieTitle#"
        HREF="#LinkURL#">
    </CFLOOP>


    <!--- Include Top-Level navigation choice for Actors (Female) --->
    <CF_uicascadingmenuitem
      ID="2000"
      NAME="Hot Actresses" WIDTH="100">
    <!--- For each Film --->
    <CFLOOP QUERY="GetFemaleActors">
      <CFSET FullName = NameFirst & " " & NameLast>
      <!--- URL to send user to if they click on this actor --->
      <CFSET LinkURL = "ShowActor.cfm?ActorID=#GetFemaleActors.ActorID#">
      <!--- ID number for this menu item (1000 plus current row) --->
      <CFSET LinkID = 1000 + GetFilms.CurrentRow>
      <!--- Include Second-Level navigation choice for this Actor --->
      <CF_uicascadingmenuitem
        ID="#LinkID#"
        PARENTID="2000"
        NAME="#FullName#"
        HREF="#LinkURL#">
    </CFLOOP>

    <!--- Include Top-Level navigation choice for Actors (Female) --->
    <CF_uicascadingmenuitem
      ID="3000"
      NAME="Hot Actors" WIDTH="100">
    <!--- For each Film --->
    <CFLOOP QUERY="GetMaleActors">
      <CFSET FullName = NameFirst & " " & NameLast>
      <!--- URL to send user to if they click on this actor --->
      <CFSET LinkURL = "ShowActor.cfm?ActorID=#GetMaleActors.ActorID#">
      <!--- ID number for this menu item (1000 plus current row) --->
      <CFSET LinkID = 3000 + GetFilms.CurrentRow>
      <!--- Include Second-Level navigation choice for this Actor --->
      <CF_uicascadingmenuitem
        ID="#LinkID#"
        PARENTID="3000"
        NAME="#FullName#"
        HREF="#LinkURL#">
    </CFLOOP>

  </CF_uicascadingmenu>

 </TD>
</TR>
</TABLE>
```

This listing uses the same queries and basic looping strategy that was used in the Navigation Bar header (refer to Listing 26.6). The main difference between the two versions is the need to have unique numbers to provide to the `ID` attribute for each `<CF_uicascadingmenuitem>` tag.

The simple technique used in this template is to give each of the static menu items (the ones marked Films, Hot Actors, and so on) a hard-coded ID number. For each of the dynamically generated menu items, an ID number is created by adding the current query row number to the parent item's ID number. For instance, the ID number for the Hot Actresses menu item is `2000`. So, within the `<CFLOOP>` for the `GetFemaleActors` query, a `LinkID` is created for each actress's menu item by adding the value of `GetFemaleActors.CurrentRow` to `2000`. The first actress's menu item will have an ID of `2001`, the next will have an ID of `2002`, and so on.

As long as there aren't more than 1,000 actresses, this technique will work fine (and if there were more than 1,000, it probably wouldn't make sense to display them in a cascading menu like this).

Displaying the Cascading Menu Only for IE

Because the Cascading Menu component works only if Internet Explorer is being used (and not on the Macintosh platform), it makes sense to add a bit of code that detects which browser the user is using to visit the page.

Listing 26.9 adds a simple `<CFIF>` test to the `HomePage.cfm` file, which displays the new Cascading Menu version of the page header if the user is visiting the page with IE on a Windows machine, as shown in Figure 26.5. If not, the Navigation Bar version of the page header from Listing 26.6 is displayed (refer to Figure 26.4).

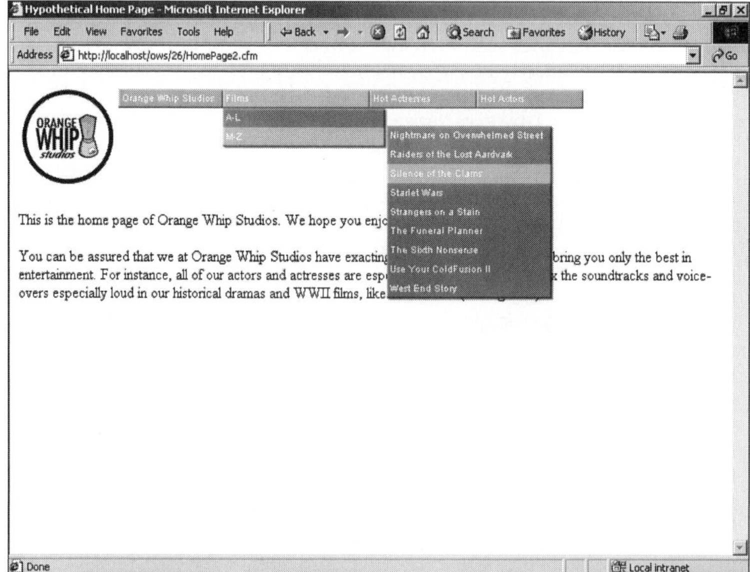

Figure 26.5 The Cascading Menu component provides an interactive menu that expands as the user drills down into it.

Listing 26.9 `HomePage2.cfm`—**Using the Cascading or Horizontal Version of the Page Header, Depending on the Browser**

```
<HTML>
<HEAD><TITLE>Hypothetical Home Page</TITLE></HEAD>
<BODY>

<!--- Flash-Based Navigation Bar --->
<CFIF (CGI.HTTP_USER_AGENT contains "MSIE")
  AND (CGI.HTTP_USER_AGENT contains "Windows")>
  <CFINCLUDE TEMPLATE="CascadingHeader.cfm">
<CFELSE>
  <CFINCLUDE TEMPLATE="NavBarHeader.cfm">
</CFIF>

<P>This is the home page of Orange Whip Studios.
We hope you enjoy your visit to our web site.<BR>

<P>You can be assured that we at Orange Whip Studios have exacting standards
for our films.  We bring you only the best in entertainment.
For instance, all of our actors and actresses are especially attractive.
Also, we mix the soundtracks and voice-overs especially loud in our historical
dramas and WWII films, like Girl Harbor (coming soon).

</BODY>
</HTML>
```

Note

For more information about the `CGI.HTTP_USER_AGENT` variable used here to do the browser detection, see Appendix C, "Special ColdFusion Variables and Result Codes."

Using Your Own Flash Movies in ColdFusion Pages

So far, this chapter has focused on how to use the prebuilt interactive widgets Macromedia has made available in the Flash Component Kit. Of course, you are also free to create your own Flash movies for inclusion in your pages. These movies might be navigational elements, data-collection widgets, or just pretty animations that contribute to the overall look and feel of your application.

To create Flash movies, you use the program called Macromedia Flash, which is sold separately from ColdFusion. A free 30-day trial version of Macromedia Flash 5 has been provided on the CD-ROM for this book and is also available from the Downloads section at `http://www.macromedia.com`.

Unfortunately, it just isn't possible for us to teach you how to create Flash movies in this chapter. If you would like to learn how to create your own Flash movies, please consult a book about Flash 5 or take a look at the tutorial provided in Flash 5 itself. The movies for the examples in this chapter have been provided on the CD-ROM for this chapter.

Note

Don't confuse Macromedia Flash with the Macromedia Flash *Player*. Macromedia Flash is what you use to create Flash movies and must be purchased separately. The Flash Player is what's used to view Flash movies in a browser and is available for free download. The Player is also automatically installed with most recent Web browsers, so most users already have the Player installed on their machines.

Note

You can find out the percentage of users who currently have the Flash Player installed on their machines by visiting `www.macromedia.com/software/player_census`.

Flash Movie Concepts

Macromedia Flash movies provide a method to supply compact, vector-based animations and other interactive elements for your Web pages. Macromedia Flash movies generally work identically across browsers and platforms and can even be displayed on devices such as WebTV, PocketPC handhelds, and soon on the Sony PlayStation 2.

Flash movies can collect information from users via form-like interfaces, be printed, be zoomed in on, and generally provide an exciting experience for your users. Best of all, you can create Flash movies that do a great deal but that are extremely small in terms of file size, so your users will not have to wait for a long time to view them. For instance, all the sample movies used in this chapter are less than 10KB. The Flash Player can even begin displaying a movie before the entire file has been downloaded.

In other words, Flash is a terrific way to present interactive elements to your users, without the programming hassles associated with Dynamic HTML or client-side Java.

Flash File Types

The three types of Flash-related files that you are likely to encounter are as follows:

- **`.fla` files**—While you are creating a movie in the Macromedia Flash authoring environment, your work is saved as an `.fla` file. This file can't be displayed on a Web page by the Flash Player. The Flash environment refers to these `.fla` files as *Flash Movie* files, which is somewhat confusing. Just think of `.fla` files as the author-able version of the final Flash presentation. You would share this file with others only if you wanted them to be able to edit the movie.
- **`.swf` files**—These are the files the Flash Player can display on a Web page. An `.swf` file is the unchangeable, compiled, compressed output generated by the corresponding `.fla` file. For instance, if you were creating an animation for Orange Whip Studios, you might be working with a file called `owsAnimation.fla`. When finished, you would tell Flash to publish the `owsAnimation.swf` file, which you could then display on your application's pages. The Flash IDE refers to these `.swf` files as *Flash Player* files.
- **`.swt` files**—These are *Generator templates*, which are used by the Macromedia Generator product (sold separately) to produce customized versions of movies on the

server. Conceptually, a Generator template is similar to a ColdFusion template, except that the output is a Flash Player file (`.swf`) instead of HTML. If you are curious about Generator templates, you are encouraged to download a trial version of Macromedia Generator from `http://www.macromedia.com`.

Note

If you are familiar with Java, think of `.fla` files as being conceptually equivalent to `.java` files (they are both source material that has not yet been compiled for delivery), and `.swf` files as being similar to the resulting `.class` files (they are both pseudocompiled files that need to be interpreted at runtime). Continuing the analogy, you can thus think of the Macromedia Flash Player as the rough equivalent to the Java Virtual Machine (both provide platform-specific host environments for miniature, platform-agnostic programs), and the Macromedia Flash IDE as being equivalent to your Java IDE or compiler.

Including Flash Movies in Your Pages

For the purposes of this chapter, pretend that you already have a Flash Player (`.swf`) file you want to incorporate into your ColdFusion application. Perhaps you created the movie yourself with the Flash IDE, or perhaps a graphic artist supplied it to you. In any case, to include the movie in a page, you must use `<OBJECT>`, `<PARAM>`, and `<EMBED>` tags.

Note

The `<OBJECT>` and `<PARAM>` tags are understood by Internet Explorer, and `<EMBED>` is used to specify the same properties for Netscape browsers. For the movie to be displayed correctly in all browsers, you must use the tags together as shown in this section.

Table 26.9 explains the special properties you can use to control how the Flash movie is displayed. Most of these properties are supplied twice—once to the `<EMBED>` tag and once for the `<OBJECT>` and `<PARAM>` tags. You see how to use these properties in Listing 26.10, later in this chapter.

Table 26.9 Important Properties to Use When Displaying a Flash Movie with `<OBJECT>` and `<EMBED>`

Property	Description
`SRC` and `MOVIE`	The relative URL path to the Flash Player (`.swf`) file you want to display. Similar conceptually to the `SRC` attribute of the `<IMG>` tag you are already familiar with. In your code, you should provide `SRC` for the `<EMBED>` tag and `MOVIE` for the `<OBJECT>` tag, using the same path value for both.
`WIDTH`	The width at which you want to show the movie, in pixels (such as `WIDTH="50"`) or as a percentage (such as `WIDTH="100%"`). Flash movies are scalable, so you typically can display a movie at whatever width you choose, regardless of how big it was when it was created.

TABLE 26.9 CONTINUED

Property	Description
HEIGHT	The height at which you want to show the movie, in pixels or as a percentage.
PLAY	Whether the movie should be playing when the page first appears. If `true` (the default), the movie starts playing on its own. If `false`, the movie appears stopped at the first frame until the user starts it via the right-click menu (or it is started programmatically via some type of script).
LOOP	Whether the movie repeats indefinitely or stops when it reaches the last frame. If `true` (the default), the movie repeats indefinitely. If `false`, it stops at the last frame. Note that the movie's author is free to override this behavior by adding ActionScript to the movie during its creation.
MENU	Whether a pop-up menu displays when the user right-clicks the movie area. If `true` (the default), the default menu appears, which provides the user with options to print the movie, zoom in or out, start and stop the movie, and so on. If `false`, the pop-up menu contains only an About Macromedia Flash Player option.
QUALITY	Can be set to `low`, `high`, `autolow`, `autohigh`, or `best`. The default value of `high` is usually the most appropriate. See the Flash documentation for details.
BGCOLOR	Specifies an optional background color for the movie, which overrides the background color applied when the movie was created.
WMODE	Whether the movies displays transparently or as a background layer. If set to `Window` (the default), the movie displays normally. `Opaque` makes the movie hide everything behind it on the page. `Transparent` makes the HTML page show through the unfilled portions of the movie and can slow movie performance. Works only in Internet Explorer and only for Windows users.
BASE	Optional. Specifies the base directory or URL used to resolve all relative path statements in the Flash Player movie. This attribute is helpful when your Flash movies are kept in a different directory from your other files.
DEVICEFONT	Optional. If set to `true`, antialiased (smooth-edged) system fonts are substituted for device fonts—such as `_sans` and `_serif`—not installed on the user's system. If `false` (the default), device fonts are not antialiased. Currently, this setting has an effect only when displayed on Windows machines.
SWLIVECONNECT	Optional. Values are `true` and `false`. Whether Java should be started when the page first appears; you should set this to `true` if you will use scripting to control the movie. See the Flash documentation for details.

Note

A few additional properties are available, including `SCALE`, `ALIGN`, and `SALIGN`, which have to do with how the movie is scaled in certain–generally unusual–situations. See the Flash documentation for details.

Listing 26.10 shows how to use the <OBJECT>, <PARAM>, and <EMBED> tags to include a Flash movie file called owsAnimation.swf. The results are shown in Figure 26.6. For your convenience, the owsAnimation.swf file has been included on this book's CD-ROM to enable you to easily test this template.

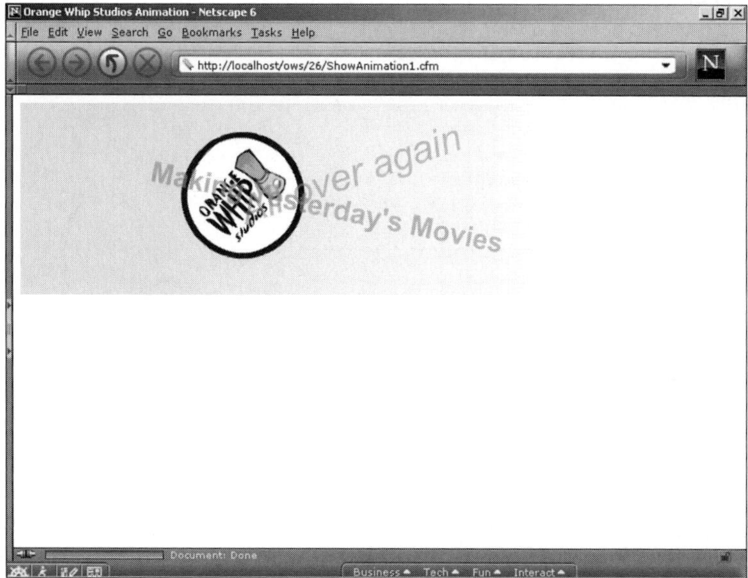

Figure 26.6
Including a Flash movie in your application pages is easy.

LISTING 26.10 ShowAnimation1.cfm—INCLUDING A FLASH MOVIE IN A COLDFUSION TEMPLATE

```
<HTML>
<HEAD>
<TITLE>Orange Whip Studios Animation</TITLE>
</HEAD>
<BODY>

<!--- Include Flash movie --->
<!--- The <OBJECT> and <PARAM> tags are for Internet Explorer --->
<OBJECT
  CLASSID="clsid:D27CDB6E-AE6D-11cf-96B8-444553540000"
  CODEBASE="http://download.macromedia.com/pub/shockwave/cabs/flash/swflash.cab
➥#version=5,0,0,0"
  WIDTH="550"
  HEIGHT="200">
  <PARAM NAME="movie" VALUE="owsAnimation.swf">
  <PARAM NAME="loop" VALUE="false">
  <PARAM NAME="quality" VALUE="high">
  <PARAM NAME="bgcolor" VALUE="#FFFFFF">
  <PARAM NAME="wmode" VALUE="opaque">

  <!--- The <EMBED> tag is for Netscape browsers --->
  <EMBED
```

LISTING 26.10 CONTINUED

```
    SRC="owsAnimation.swf"
    LOOP="false"
    QUALITY="high"
    BGCOLOR="#FFFFFF"
    WIDTH="550"
    HEIGHT="200"
    TYPE="application/x-shockwave-flash"
    PLUGINSPAGE="http://www.macromedia.com/shockwave/download/index.cgi?
➥P1_Prod_Version=ShockwaveFlash"></EMBED>

</OBJECT>

</BODY>
</HTML>
```

Tip

If you have Macromedia Flash, you can use its Publish command to produce this code automatically. See the Flash documentation for details.

As you can see, the values for the `WIDTH`, `HEIGHT`, `LOOP`, `QUALITY`, and other properties from Table 26.9 are supplied twice. First, the property is provided as an attribute of the `<OBJECT>` tag (for `WIDTH` and `HEIGHT`) or as a `<PARAM>` tag (for the other properties). Then, the property is provided again as an attribute of the `<EMBED>` tag.

Note

You always should provide `CLASSID` and `CODEBASE` attributes for the `<OBJECT>` tag and `TYPE` and `PLUGINSPAGE` attributes for the `<EMBED>` tag, as shown in this section. The values of these attributes always are the same, regardless of the Flash movie you are displaying.

INCLUDING FLASH MOVIES USING A CUSTOM TAG

A custom tag called `<CF_EmbedFlashMovie>` has been included on the CD-ROM for this chapter. The custom tag makes including a Flash movie in one of your ColdFusion templates much easier, outputting all the necessary `<OBJECT>`, `<PARAM>`, and `<EMBED>` code for you.

The attributes supported by the custom tag are shown in Table 26.10. Don't worry about the large number of attributes in this table. In many cases, you will need to use only the `MovieFile`, `Width`, and `Height` attributes.

Note

Because the job of the `<CF_EmbedFlashMovie>` custom tag is to output the appropriate `<OBJECT>`, `<PARAM>`, and `<EMBED>` code for you, most of these attributes correspond closely to the properties listed in Table 26.9.

TABLE 26.10 ATTRIBUTES SUPPORTED BY THE <CF_EmbedFlashMovie> CUSTOM TAG

Attribute	Description
MovieFile	The relative URL path to the Flash Player (.swf) file you want to display.
Width	The width at which you want to show the movie, in pixels (such as WIDTH="50") or as a percentage (such as WIDTH="100%").
Height	The height at which you want to show the movie, in pixels or as a percentage.
Play	Optional. Yes or No. Whether the movie starts automatically when the page appears. Default is Yes.
Loop	Optional. Yes or No. Whether the movie loops repeatedly or just plays once. Default is Yes.
Menu	Optional. Yes or No. Whether the default pop-up menu is available if the user right-clicks the movie. Default is No.
DeviceFont	Optional. Yes or No. Whether device fonts are shown using anti-aliased type on Windows systems. Default is No.
Quality	Can be set to low, high, autolow, autohigh, or best. The default value of high is usually the most appropriate. See the Flash documentation for details.
BGColor	Specifies an optional background color for the movie, which overrides the background color applied when the movie was created.
MovieName	Optional. A name for the movie, if you want to be able to control the movie via script. The value you provide is set as the ID attribute of the generated <OBJECT> tag and the NAME attribute of the generated <EMBED> tag.
Style	Optional CSS-style information.
IndentCode	Optional. Yes or No. Whether the <OBJECT> and <EMBED> code generated by the custom tag should be indented nicely. Default is No.
IncludeObject	Optional. Yes or No. Whether the custom tag should generate <OBJECT> and <PARAM> tags, which enables the movie to be seen by Internet Explorer users. Default is Yes.
IncludeEmbed	Optional. Yes or No. Whether the custom tag should generate <EMBED> code, which enables the movie to be seen by Netscape users. Default is Yes.
EnableFSCommand	Optional. Yes or No. Whether the custom tag should generate the <SCRIPT> blocks necessary for the Flash movie to be capable of carrying out fscommand operations via ActionScript in the movie file itself. If Yes, you can include actual fscommand code between opening and closing <CF_EmbedFlashMovie> tags. This attribute gets set to Yes automatically if you use opening and closing <CF_EmbedFlashMovie> tags. See the section "Interacting with the Underlying Web Page via fscommand," later in this chapter.
swLiveConnect	Optional. Yes or No. Whether Java should be started when the page first appears. Defaults to the value of EnableFSCommand. See the Flash documentation for details.
MovieVar	Relevant only if EnableFSCommand="Yes". Optional string that can be used to refer to the player object from script in an fscommand operation. Default is player.

Note

The custom tag also supports the same `Quality`, `BGColor`, `Scale`, `Align`, `SAlign`, `Base`, and `WMode` attributes that are supported by the Flash player. Refer to Table 26.9 for details.

Listing 26.11 shows how to use the `<CF_EmbedFlashMovie>` custom tag. As you can see, this code is much more straightforward than the previous version of this template (refer to Listing 26.9).

Note

For this example to work, the `EmbedFlashMovie.cfm` file (on the CD-ROM for this chapter) must be placed in the special `CustomTags` folder or in the same folder as Listing 26.11 itself. See Chapter 22 for more information about the special `CustomTags` folder and CFML custom tags in general.

LISTING 26.11 `ShowAnimation2.cfm`—USING THE `<CF_EmbedFlashMovie>` CUSTOM TAG

```
<HTML>
<HEAD>
<TITLE>Orange Whip Studios Animation</TITLE>
</HEAD>
<BODY>

<!--- Include Flash movie, via Custom Tag --->
<!--- Automatically generates all needed <OBJECT>, <PARAM> and <EMBED> tags --->
<CF_EmbedFlashMovie
  MovieFile="owsAnimation.swf"
  Width="550"
  Height="200">

</BODY>
</HTML>
```

If you visit this template with your browser, you will find that the results are the same as those shown previously in Figure 26.6. However, if you use your browser's View Source command, you will find that the HTML code that was actually sent to the browser is similar to the code shown in Listing 26.9. This is yet another example of how ColdFusion's excellent custom tag feature can simplify your life as a coder.

Tip

`<CF_EmbedFlashMovie>` is written in CFML, so you can feel free to adapt it to suit your own needs. See Chapter 22 for details about how to write CFML custom tags.

LOADING VARIABLES FROM COLDFUSION INTO A FLASH MOVIE

Note

This section assumes that you know a bit about ActionScript, which is Flash's internal scripting language for creating interactive movies. In particular, you should be familiar with the `loadVariables` action and with the Flash concepts of timelines and events. You might need to consult the Flash ActionScript Reference (part of the online Help in the Macromedia Flash IDE) to follow along.

If you are familiar with JavaScript, you will find ActionScript's semantics refreshingly similar.

You can integrate a Flash Movie with ColdFusion in a number of ways. Perhaps the easiest way is with the `loadVariables` action provided by ActionScript, which enables a Flash movie to grab values from a URL. Rather than being a conventional Web page, the URL should return just a single line of code, which specifies the names and values of variables that should be set in the Flash movie (see the Flash ActionScript Reference for details).

Therefore, if you create a ColdFusion template called `ExposeFilmInfo.cfm`, and the template returns a single line of code in the proper format, the Flash movie will be capable of grabbing values from ColdFusion in real time just by calling `loadVariables`. The `loadVariables` calls might be in response to user actions, such as mouse clicks, or attached to particular frames in the movie's timelines.

The format required by `loadVariables` is a simple one. It's the same format you use to pass URL parameters to your ColdFusion templates. Each variable is passed with an = sign between the variable's name and its value. If a variable's value contains spaces or other funny characters, they must be encoded using the same encoding scheme normally used in URLs.

So, if your `ExposeFilmInfo.cfm` template returns output that looks like this (without any HTML tags, whitespace, or other characters)

```
NAME=Nate%20Weiss&AGE=32
```

then a Flash movie can use a command like this, which sets variables named `NAME` and `AGE` in the current movie clip:

```
// Load variables from ColdFusion
loadVariables ("ExposeFilmInfo.cfm", this);
```

The Flash movie could then refer to `NAME` and `AGE` as normal `ActionScript` variables. The value of `NAME` will be `Nate Weiss`, and the value of `AGE` will be `32`.

EXPOSING COLDFUSION VARIABLES TO FLASH

Listing 26.12 creates a convenient CFML custom tag called *<CF_ExposeDataToFlash>*, which converts the contents of a ColdFusion structure or query to the URL-encoded format needed by Flash's `loadVariables` action. The tag takes one attribute, `Data`, which should be a structure or a query object.

Note

Don't worry too much about understanding the code in this listing right now. You will be able to use this custom tag without knowing exactly what it is doing internally. You can always study it more closely later.

LISTING 26.12 ExposeDataToFlash.cfm—**CREATING THE** <CF_ExposeDataToFlash> **CUSTOM TAG**

```
<!--- Tag attributes --->
<CFPARAM NAME="ATTRIBUTES.Data" TYPE="any">

<!--- If the passed-in value is a structure --->
<CFIF IsStruct(ATTRIBUTES.Data)>
  <!--- Start with an empty string --->
  <CFSET FinalString = "">

  <!--- For each value in the Data, add key/value pair to FinalString --->
  <CFLOOP COLLECTION="#ATTRIBUTES.Data#" ITEM="ThisKey">
    <!--- Get the value of this key/value pair --->
    <CFSET ThisValue = ATTRIBUTES.Data[ThisKey]>
    <!--- Make sure it's possible to express this value as a string --->
    <CFIF IsSimpleValue(ThisValue)>
      <!--- Add key/value pair to FinalString, with the value encoded --->
      <CFSET ThisPair = "#ThisKey#=#URLEncodedFormat(ThisValue)#">
      <CFSET FinalString = ListAppend(FinalString, ThisPair, "&")>
    </CFIF>
  </CFLOOP>


<!--- If the passed-in value is a query --->
<CFELSEIF IsQuery(ATTRIBUTES.Data)>
  <!--- Start by providing the record count --->
  <CFSET FinalString = "RecordCount=#ATTRIBUTES.Data.RecordCount#">

  <!--- For each row in the query --->
  <CFLOOP QUERY="ATTRIBUTES.Data">
    <!--- Loop through the column names --->
    <CFLOOP LIST="#ATTRIBUTES.Data.ColumnList#" INDEX="ThisCol">
      <!--- Add key/value pair to FinalString, with the value encoded --->
      <!--- Resulting variable names will be in the form COLUMNNAME_ROW --->
      <CFSET ThisValue = Attributes.Data[ThisCol][CurrentRow]>
      <CFSET ThisPair = "#ThisCol#_#CurrentRow#=#URLEncodedFormat(ThisValue)#">
      <CFSET FinalString = ListAppend(FinalString, ThisPair, "&")>
    </CFLOOP>
  </CFLOOP>

<!--- Show an error message if value was not a structure or a query --->
<CFELSE>
  <CFTHROW
    MESSAGE="Error Encountered by &lt;CF_ExposeDataToFlash&gt;"
    DETAIL="The value of the Data attribute must be a structure or a query.
            Don't forget to use pound signs around the query or structure name.">
</CFIF>

<!--- Output final string, using <CFCONTENT> to discard any prior output --->
<CFCONTENT TYPE="text/html" RESET="Yes"><CFOUTPUT>&#FinalString#</CFOUTPUT>
```

If the passed-in Data attribute is a structure, the tag creates a variable called FinalString and then loops through the key in the structure, adding the names and values for each key in the proper format. The URLEncodedFormat() function is used to encode any special characters in the values. At the bottom of the template, the FinalString variable is output, preceded with a <CFCONTENT> tag with RESET="Yes" to discard any prior output. This ensures that the value of FinalString appears on the very first line of the generated page. (For more information about <CFCONTENT>, see Chapter 34.)

If Data is a query object, the tag populates the FinalString variable a bit differently. It includes a name/value pair for a variable called RecordCount, the value of which is the number of rows in the query. Then, a separate name/value pair is included for each column and row in the query results, using the column name and row number as the name of the pair. Because of the way ColdFusion's automatic ColumnList property works, the column names always are represented in uppercase. For instance, if the query contains two columns named FilmID and MovieTitle, and the query returns three rows, FinalString includes pairs for RecordCount, FILMID_1, FILMID_2, FILMID_3, MOVIETITLE_1, MOVIETITLE_2, and MOVIETITLE_3.

This custom tag can be tested with the code in Listing 26.13. It creates a structure called s with two values, Name and Age. The structure is then passed to the <CF_ExposeDataToFlash> custom tag.

LISTING 26.13 ExposeDataTest.cfm—**TESTING THE** <CF_ExposeDataToFlash> **CUSTOM TAG**

```
<!--- Create structure --->
<CFSET s = StructNew()>
<CFSET s.Age = 32>
<CFSET s.Name = "NateWeiss">

<!--- Output data in URL-like format expected by Flash Player --->
<CF_ExposeDataToFlash
  Data="#s#">
```

If you visit this template with your browser, it outputs a single line, which looks like this:

```
AGE=32&NAME=Nate%20Weiss
```

Note

Because of the way ColdFusion stores structures internally, the name part of each name/value pair is uppercase.

Now all you need is a Flash movie that uses the loadVariables action to fetch the values from the ExposeDataTest.cfm template shown in Listing 26.13.

Note

You need Macromedia Flash 5 to follow along. A trial version is available at http://www.macromedia.com.

To create a Flash movie that fetches data from `ExposeDataTest.cfm`, follow these steps:

1. In Macromedia Flash, create a new movie and save it as `LoadVariablesTest.fla` in the same folder you're using for this chapter's ColdFusion templates.
2. In the Timeline, select the first frame of the movie; then open the Frame Actions panel by selecting Window, Actions from the main menu.
3. Add a `loadVariables` action. For the URL, provide `ExposeDataTest.cfm`. Leave the Location at Level 0 and the Variables field at Don't Send.
4. Place a text object on the stage. Using the Text Options panel (which you can reveal using Window, Panels if it is not showing already), change the type from Static Text to Dynamic Text. For the Variable field, type **`Name`**.
5. Repeat step 4, this time providing `Age` for the variable field.
6. If you want, add labels for the two text fields you just added, or whatever formatting you feel is appropriate, as shown in Figure 26.7.
7. Save the movie, and then publish it by pressing Shift+F12. Verify that a file called `LoadVariablesTest.swf` was created in the folder you are using for this chapter's listings.

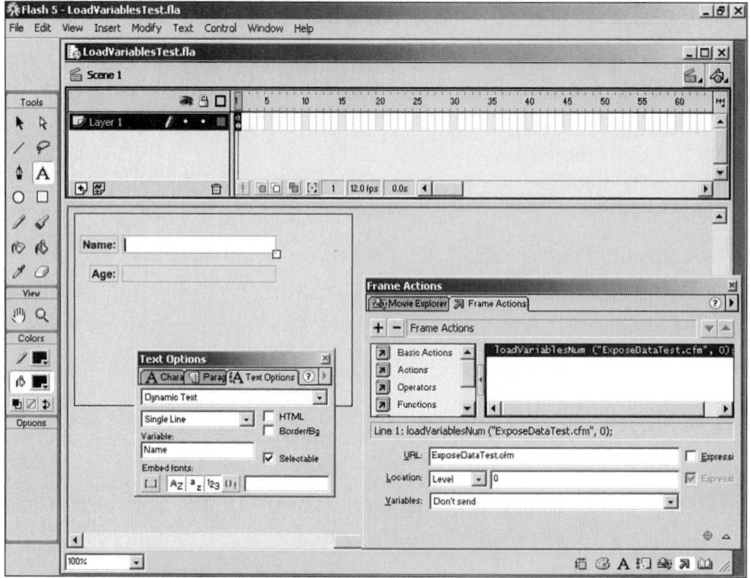

Figure 26.7
Text fields can be used to reflect the values of variables retrieved with the `loadVariables` action.

Now you can test the movie with the code shown in Listing 26.14. Note that this is essentially the same code used in Listing 26.11.

Listing 26.14 `LoadVariablesTest.cfm`—**Displaying the** `LoadVariablesTest.swf` **Flash Movie**

```
<HTML>
<HEAD>
<TITLE>loadVariables Test</TITLE>
</HEAD>
<BODY>

<!--- Include Flash movie, via Custom Tag --->
<!--- Automatically generates all needed <OBJECT>, <PARAM> and <EMBED> tags --->
<CF_EmbedFlashMovie
  MovieFile="LoadVariablesTest.swf"
  Width="300"
  Height="200">

</BODY>
</HTML>
```

When you visit this template with your browser, the Flash movie you created (`LoadVariablesTest.swf`) should display with the appropriate name and age values, as shown in Figure 26.8. If you go back and edit Listing 26.13 (so that the name and age values are different) and then reload this template, you should see the values change in the Flash movie.

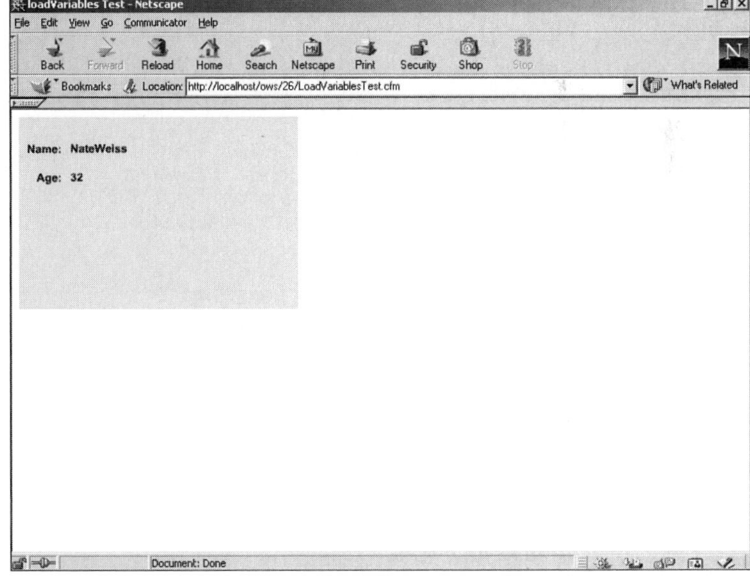

Figure 26.8
Flash movies can fetch variables from ColdFusion templates.

Note

The Flash movie you created in this section is very simple and just fetches the values once when the movie first appears. Of course, you could choose to use the `loadVariables` action at any point in your movie or in response to some type of user interaction, such as a button press.

WORKING WITH A QUERY OBJECT

The `FilmChooser.fla` file included on the CD-ROM for this chapter creates a Flash Player file called `FilmChooser.swf` that fetches query data from a ColdFusion template. The basic technique is the same as demonstrated in the previous section, except this time Flash's `loadVariables` action is used to fetch data from a template that supplies a query object to the `<CF_ExposeDataToFlash>` custom tag (instead of a structure).

Listing 26.15 provides the code for a ColdFusion template called `ExposeFilmInfo.cfm`, which is used by the `FilmChooser.swf` movie via the `loadVariables` action. It simply runs a query named `GetFilms` and then passes the query object to the `<CF_ExposeDataToFlash>` custom tag. If you visit this template with your browser, you will find that a long string of data is returned, including the `FilmID` and `MovieTitle` for each film in the `Films` table.

LISTING 26.15 `ExposeFilmInfo.cfm`—**SUPPLYING QUERY INFORMATION FOR THE FLASH** `loadVariables` **ACTION**

```
<!--- Select film titles from database --->
<CFQUERY NAME="GetFilms" DATASOURCE="ows"
  CACHEDWITHIN="#CreateTimeSpan(0,0,5,0)#">
  SELECT FilmID, MovieTitle
  FROM Films
  ORDER BY MovieTitle DESC
</CFQUERY>

<!--- Output query data in URL-like format expected by Flash Player --->
<CF_ExposeDataToFlash
  Data="#GetFilms#">
```

Unfortunately, it isn't possible for us to explain all the ActionScript code used in the `FilmChooser.swf` Flash movie (ActionScript is well beyond the scope of this book). That said, you should be able to understand most of what is going on just by exploring the `FilmChooser.fla` file (perhaps consulting the Flash documentation as you go). The most important code, as far as integration with ColdFusion is concerned, is attached to the first two frames of the movie's main timeline.

In the first frame of the timeline, the `loadVariables` action is used to fetch the variables from the `ExposeFilmInfo.cfm` template (Listing 26.15), like so:

```
// Load variables from ColdFusion
loadVariables ("ExposeFilmInfo.cfm", this);
```

The second frame of the timeline uses the ActionScript code shown in Listing 26.16 to loop through the variables produced by Listing 26.15. Because it is in the second frame of the timeline, this code executes after the `loadVariables` action.

LISTING 26.16 ACTIONSCRIPT CODE USED IN THE SECOND FRAME OF `FilmChooser.swf`

```
// If loadVariables call in previous frame fetched a RecordCount
if (RecordCount > 0) {

  // Loop through records
  for (i=1; i<RecordCount; i++) {
    // Get this FilmID and MovieTitle
    ThisFilmID = eval("FILMID_" add i);
    ThisMovieTitle = eval("MOVIETITLE_" add i);

    // Create new copy of FilmDisplay movie clip
    ClipName = "Film" add ThisFilmID;
    duplicateMovieClip ("FilmDisplay", ClipName, i);

    // Set the title in the new movie clip
    set (ClipName add ":FilmID", ThisFilmID);
    set (ClipName add ":MovieTitle", ThisMovieTitle);
  }

  // Make original FilmDisplay movie clip invisible
  setProperty ("FilmDisplay", _visible, 0);

  // Stop animation in main timeline
  // (the FilmDisplay clips will move around on their own)
  stop ();
}
```


The basic idea in this template is to use the `RecordCount` variable (which is one of the variables automatically exposed by the `ExposeFilmInfo.cfm` template from Listing 26.15) to loop through the query data fetched by the first frame's `loadVariables` action. A simple `for` loop is used to do the looping; for each iteration through the loop, the value of the `i` variable holds the current row number.

As explained just before Listing 26.13, the values from the first row of the query are available as `FILMID_1` and `MOVIETITLE_1`. The first two lines inside the `for` loop use the ActionScript `eval` function (which is comparable to the `Evaluate()` function in CFML) to get the value of those two variables and set them as new variables named `ThisFilmID` and `ThisMovieTitle`.

Next, a new movie clip is created using the `duplicateMovieClip` action. The new clip is a copy of the clip named `FilmDisplay` (which is located just off the stage). The `set` statement is then used to set local variables called `FilmID` and `MovieTitle` in the new clip's timeline. Because the clip contains a text field that displays the value of the `MovieTitle` variable, the film's title is now visible to the user. The loop then repeats for all the remaining film records (that is, until `i` reaches the value of `RecordCount`).

After the loop is finished, the `FilmDisplay` movie clip (which has just been copied once for each film) is made invisible, and then the movie's main timeline is halted with the `stop` action. The end result is that now a separate movie clip is on the stage for each film. Each of the clips—because of code in the clip symbol itself, which we don't have space to explain here—floats around on the stage on its own and responds to the user's mouse movements and clicks.

Note

The `FilmDisplay` movie clip has a bit of ActionScript in its own timeline, which causes it to move around on the stage. Although the code is certainly not sophisticated as far as the larger world of Flash programming is concerned, you are encouraged to take a glance at it if you are at all unfamiliar with how to make things move around in a Flash movie.

All that is left to do now is to display the movie on a Web page, which can be done with the `<CF_EmbedFlashMovie>` custom tag as shown in Listing 26.17. When this template is visited in a Web browser, the Flash movie begins playing automatically.

LISTING 26.17 `ShowFilmChooser1.cfm`**—DISPLAYING THE** `FilmChooser.swf` **MOVIE**

```
<HTML>
<HEAD><TITLE>Film Animation</TITLE></HEAD>
<BODY>

  <!--- Show Flash movie --->
  <CF_EmbedFlashMovie
    MovieFile="FilmChooser.swf"
    Width="100%"
    Height="100%">

</BODY>
</HTML>
```

Assuming that Listing 26.15 has been saved in the same folder as this listing, the titles of each movie will creep onto the page, each floating at its own speed. The titles will continue to move around, bouncing from side to side and top to bottom. If you hover your mouse over one of the titles, it moves forward and stops, as shown in Figure 26.9. When you move your mouse away from the title, it begins moving again. This provides the user with a fun, unconventional way to browse through the list of films.

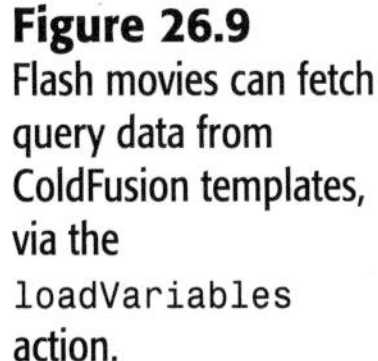

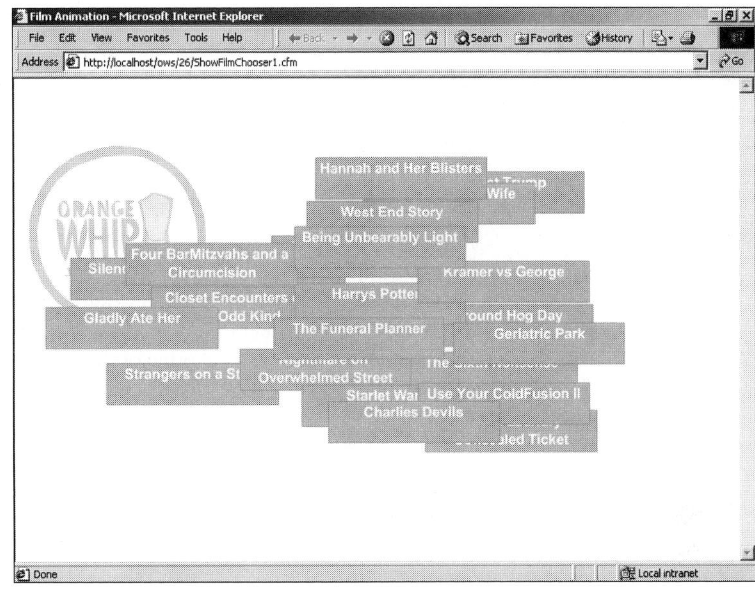

Figure 26.9
Flash movies can fetch query data from ColdFusion templates, via the `loadVariables` action.

Interacting with the Underlying Web Page via `fscommand`

Another way to get a Flash movie to interact with ColdFusion is via the `fscommand` action provided by ActionScript. The `fscommand` action is a simple mechanism that enables a Flash movie to execute JavaScript code on the Web page on which the movie is being displayed.

If you open the `FilmChooser.fla` file and look at the Invisible Button layer of the `FilmRecord` symbol's timeline, you will see that it includes an invisible button symbol that includes the following lines of ActionScript code:

```
on (release) {
    // Show detail when user clicks on symbol
    fscommand ( "showFilmDetail", FilmID );
}
```

What this means is that the `fscommand` action executes when the user clicks a film's title (refer to Figure 26.9). This causes the Flash movie to attempt to call a special script function on the Web page. The function is passed two parameters, `command` and `args`. In this example, the `command` is `showFilmDetail` and `args` is the `FilmID` of the film the user clicks.

Tip

For more information about `fscommand`, see the Flash documentation.

Normally, you would need to insert a number of special `<SCRIPT>` blocks and other code before you could respond to an `fscommand` action. If you use the `<CF_EmbedFlashMovie>` custom tag to display the movie, however, this is all taken care of for you.

Simply add a closing `</CF_EmbedFlashMovie>` tag to the template. Now add one or more `<CF_EmbedFlashMovieCommand>` tags between the opening and closing `<CF_EmbedFlashMovie>` tags. The `<CF_EmbedFlashMovieCommand>` takes two arguments, as shown in Table 26.11.

Table 26.11 Attributes Supported by the `<CF_EmbedFlashMovieCommand>` Custom Tag

Attribute	Description
`Command`	The first argument of the `fscommand` action to which you want to respond. If the movie executes the command, the JavaScript code between the opening and closing `<CF_EmbedFlashMovieCommand>` tags is executed. Please note that the value of this attribute is case sensitive.
`ArgsVariable`	A variable name you want to be able to use to refer to the second argument of the `fscommand` action. You can then use the variable in the JavaScript code between the `<CF_EmbedFlashMovieCommand>` tags, effectively enabling you to pass values from the Flash movie to your JavaScript code.

Listing 26.18 shows how easy responding to `fscommand` actions is with the `<CF_EmbedFlashMovieCommand>` custom tag. Note that the value of the `Command` attribute matches the first argument of the `fscommand` action call (refer to the code snippet before Table 26.11).

Note

For this example to work, the `EmbedFlashMovieCommand.cfm` file (on the CD-ROM for this chapter) must be placed in the special `CustomTags` folder or in the same folder as Listing 26.11 itself. See Chapter 22 for more information about the special `CustomTags` folder and CFML custom tags in general.

Listing 26.18 `ShowFilmChooser2.cfm`—Responding to `fscommand` Actions

```
<HTML>
<HEAD><TITLE>Film Animation</TITLE></HEAD>
<BODY>

  <!--- Show Flash movie --->
  <CF_EmbedFlashMovie
    MovieFile="FilmChooser.swf"
    Width="100%"
    Height="100%"
    IndentCode="Yes">

    <!--- If the movie executes an FSCommand of command "showFilmDetail" --->
    <CF_EmbedFlashMovieCommand
      Command="showFilmDetail"
      ArgsVariable="FilmID">
      var url = "http://"+location.host+"/ows/26/ShowFilm.cfm?FilmID=" + FilmID;
      window.open(url, "wFilm", "width=250,height=200,scrollbars=yes");
    </CF_EmbedFlashMovieCommand>
```

```
    </CF_EmbedFlashMovie>

  </BODY>
  </HTML>
```

Tip

For more information about the `window.open` and `location.host` code used in this listing, consult a JavaScript reference text or visit the online JavaScript documentation at `http://developer.netscape.com`.

When the user clicks a film title, the `fscommand` action shown previously is executed. This causes the JavaScript code between the `<CF_EmbedFlashMovieCommand>` to execute. The JavaScript code itself is quite simple. It opens a ColdFusion template called `ShowFilm.cfm` in a small pop-up window, passing the `FilmID` of the selected movie as a URL parameter.

The `ShowFilm.cfm` template displays the details for the film the user selected. In other words, the user is able to click the floating film titles to see more information about each film, as shown in Figure 26.10.

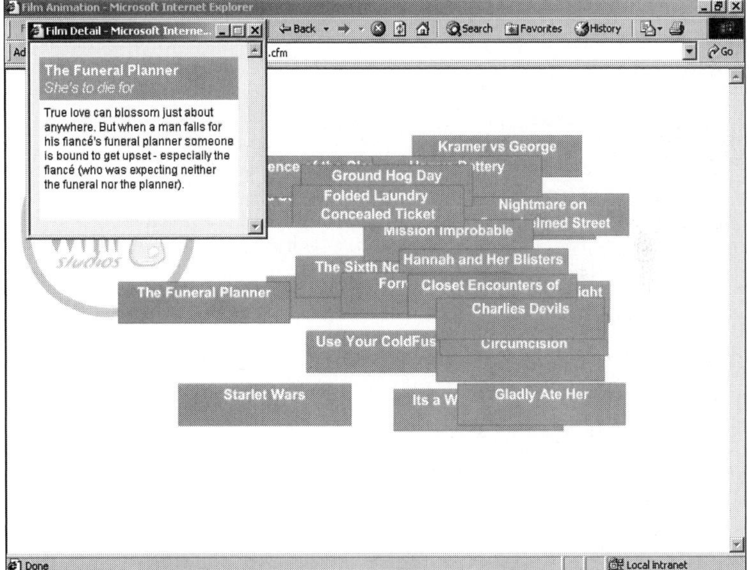

Figure 26.10
The `fscommand` action can be used to pop up browser windows or other JavaScript interactions.

Listing 26.19 provides the code for the `ShowFilm.cfm` template displayed in the pop-up window for each film (refer to Figure 26.10). There is nothing particularly special about this template. It simply queries the database for the details about the specified film and then displays the information in a simple HTML table.

Note

The code in this template uses the Query-of-Queries feature to requery the cached `GetFilms` query for each request, rather than recontacting the database separately for each film. See Chapter 31, "More About SQL and Queries," for more information.

LISTING 26.19 ShowFilm.cfm—DISPLAYING FILM INFORMATION IN A POP-UP WINDOW

```
<!--- FilmID must be passed in URL --->
<CFPARAM NAME="URL.FilmID" TYPE="numeric">

<!--- Retrieve information about films from database --->
<CFQUERY NAME="GetFilms" DATASOURCE="ows"
  CACHEDWITHIN="#CreateTimeSpan(0,0,15,0)#">
  SELECT FilmID, MovieTitle, PitchText, Summary
  FROM Films
</CFQUERY>

<!--- Use Query-of-Queries to grab this film's information --->
<CFQUERY DBTYPE="query" NAME="GetFilm">
  SELECT * FROM GetFilms
  WHERE FilmID = #URL.FilmID#
</CFQUERY>


<HTML>
<HEAD>
  <TITLE>Film Detail</TITLE>

  <!--- Some CSS-based classes for formatting --->
  <STYLE TYPE="text/css">
    .Title {font-family:sans-serif;font-size:15px;background:orange;color:white;}
    .Summary {font-family:sans-serif;font-size:12px;background:white;color:black;
      height:110px}
  </STYLE>
</HEAD>

<BODY
  BGCOLOR="yellow"
  onLoad="focus()">

<!--- Display film information --->
<CFOUTPUT>
  <TABLE WIDTH="100%" HEIGHT="100%" BORDER="0" CELLPADDING="5" CELLSPACING="0">
    <TR HEIGHT="20%">
      <TD CLASS="Title">
        <B>#GetFilm.MovieTitle#</B><BR>
        <I>#GetFilm.PitchText#</I>
      </TD>
    </TR>
    <TR HEIGHT="80%">
      <TD CLASS="Summary" VALIGN="top">
        #GetFilm.Summary#
      </TD>
    </TR>
  </TABLE>
```

```
</CFOUTPUT>

</BODY>
</HTML>
```

Tip

The call to `focus()` in the `onLoad` attribute of the `<BODY>` tag ensures that the pop-up window appears in front of the main browser window. It's a handy line of code to add to any template that will be displayed in a pop-up.

Note

The `fscommand` action does not work with all browsers, especially Netscape 6 and Internet Explorer on the Macintosh. For details and alternatives, see TechNote Article 14159 at `http://www.macromedia.com/support/flash/`.

OTHER TOPICS

Although you have learned a lot in the second half of this chapter, these examples have really only scratched the surface. You can get Flash and ColdFusion to work together in many ways. If this topic interests you, you are encouraged to investigate the following:

- **XML support in Flash 5**—The Flash 5 Player enables you to fetch XML content from URLs, somewhat like the `loadVariables` function. The difference, of course, is that XML content can be far more structured, validated, and so on. For details, see the ActionScript Reference portion of the Flash 5 documentation.
- **WDDX support provided by the Component Kit**—One of the files included in the Macromedia Flash Component Kit for ColdFusion is an ActionScript file called `wddx.as`, which sits on top of the Flash Player's native XML support. You can use this script file to fetch data from a ColdFusion template that uses the `<CFWDDX>` tag to expose structured information. Documentation for the `wddx.as` file is somewhat scant as of this writing, but it is conceptually similar to the `wddx.js` file that ships with ColdFusion, which is documented in the WDDX SDK from `http://www.openwddx.org`.
- **Scripting methods supported by the Flash Player**—You can control Flash movie playback, zooming, panning, and so on with the scripting methods described in Article 04160 at `http://www.macromedia.com/support/flash/`.
- **ColdFusion templates as Macromedia Generator data sources**—ColdFusion template URLs easily can be used as data sources for Macromedia Generator templates. For details, download an evaluation copy of Macromedia Generator from `http://www.macromedia.com`.

CHAPTER 27

GRAPHING

In this chapter

ENHANCING YOUR APPLICATIONS WITH GRAPHS

In the last chapter, "Integrating with Macromedia Flash," you learned how to integrate ColdFusion with Flash dynamically using the Harpoon kit. You enhanced the user interface with Flash-based menus, navigation bars, and so on.

Flash also plays a part in one of ColdFusion 5's most anticipated features, built-in graphing. For years, when confronted with the need to visualize data, ColdFusion developers had to buy and integrate separate third-party graphing solutions into their applications. With the introduction of ColdFusion 5, you can include a simple tag in your applications to create powerful, dynamic graphs.

In this chapter, you learn about the new graphing tags, `<CFGRAPH>` and `<CFGRAPHDATA>`, and the available graph types. In addition, you will build a simple report application in which the user can choose what data to graph, what graph type to use, and how the graph will look.

Before we begin, it is helpful to gain a basic understanding of how ColdFusion graphing works. An OEM version of Macromedia Generator, a server that produces Flash output, powers ColdFusion's graphing engine. Basically, here's what happens when you use a graphing tag:

1. ColdFusion passes data to Generator using the graphing tag attributes.
2. Generator translates that data into a graph and returns a graph image to ColdFusion.
3. ColdFusion relays that image to the user's Web browser.

Of course, this requires Macromedia Generator to reside on your server, which the ColdFusion installation installs automatically. Generator is a Java-based application. In fact, it uses JRun, another popular Macromedia server, as its Java runtime.

Let's start graphing.

Note

Save all the files created in this chapter in a directory named `27` under the `ows` directory in the Web root.

INTRODUCING <CFGRAPH>

The Orange Whip Studio board of directors is concerned about the lack of movies geared toward younger audiences. You are instructed to build a page that shows all the movies currently available and their ratings. Pressed for time, Listing 27.1 shows your initial attempt.

LISTING 27.1 RATING LIST

```
<!---
Name:         ratings.cfm
Author:       David Golden (d_golden73@hotmail.com)
```

```
Description: Ratings Chart
Created:     4/15/01
--->

<!--- Get ratings list from database --->
<CFQUERY NAME="GetRatings" DATASOURCE="ows">
  SELECT Rating, Count(*) AS FilmCount
  FROM FilmsRatings, Films
  WHERE FilmsRatings.RatingID = Films.RatingID
  GROUP BY Rating
  ORDER BY Rating
</CFQUERY>


<!--- Create HTML page --->
<!DOCTYPE HTML PUBLIC "-//W3C//DTD HTML 4.0 Transitional//EN">
<HTML>
<HEAD>
    <TITLE>Orange Whip Studios - Ratings List</TITLE>
</HEAD>

<BODY>

<H1>Ratings List</H1>

<!--- Display ratings --->
<TABLE BORDER="1">
<TR>
 <TH>Rating Category</TH>
 <TH>Movies</TH>
</TR>
<CFOUTPUT QUERY="GetRatings">
<TR>
 <TD>#GetRatings.Rating#</TD>
 <TD>#GetRatings.FilmCount#</TD>
</TR>
</CFOUTPUT>
</TABLE>

</BODY>
</HTML>
```


The results are shown in Figure 27.1.

Even though the simple query output satisfies the requirements, your boss is not impressed. She wants a graphical representation of the same data. Thankfully, you just upgraded to ColdFusion 5.

Aptly named, `<CFGRAPH>` represents your primary interface with the ColdFusion graphing engine. Enter the code as it appears in Listing 27.2, and save it in the `27` directory as `ratings_graph1.cfm`.

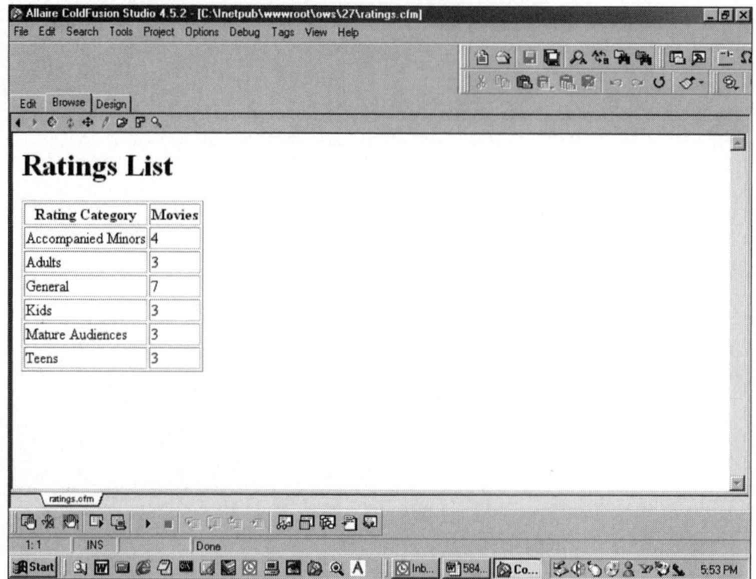

Figure 27.1 A simple table displays the query results.

LISTING 27.2 `ratings_graph1.cfm`—**RATINGS GRAPH**

```
<!---
Name:        ratings_graph1.cfm
Author:      David Golden (d_golden73@hotmail.com)
Description: ratings graph
Created:     4/15/01
--->

<!--- Get rating list from database --->
<CFQUERY NAME="GetRatings" DATASOURCE="ows">
  SELECT Rating, Count(*) AS FilmCount
  FROM FilmsRatings, Films
  WHERE FilmsRatings.RatingID = Films.RatingID
  GROUP BY Rating
  ORDER BY Rating
</CFQUERY>

<!--- Create HTML page --->
<!DOCTYPE HTML PUBLIC "-//W3C//DTD HTML 4.0 Transitional//EN">
<HTML>
<HEAD>
    <TITLE>Orange Whip Studios - Movie Ratings</TITLE>
</HEAD>

<BODY>

<!--- Displays graph--->
<CFGRAPH
  TYPE="Pie"
  QUERY="GetRatings"
  VALUECOLUMN="FilmCount"
```

```
  ITEMCOLUMN="Rating"
  FILEFORMAT="Flash">
</CFGRAPH>

</BODY>
</HTML>
```

Now execute this page in your browser as

`http://localhost/ows/27/ratings_graph1.cfm`

The results are shown in Figure 27.2.

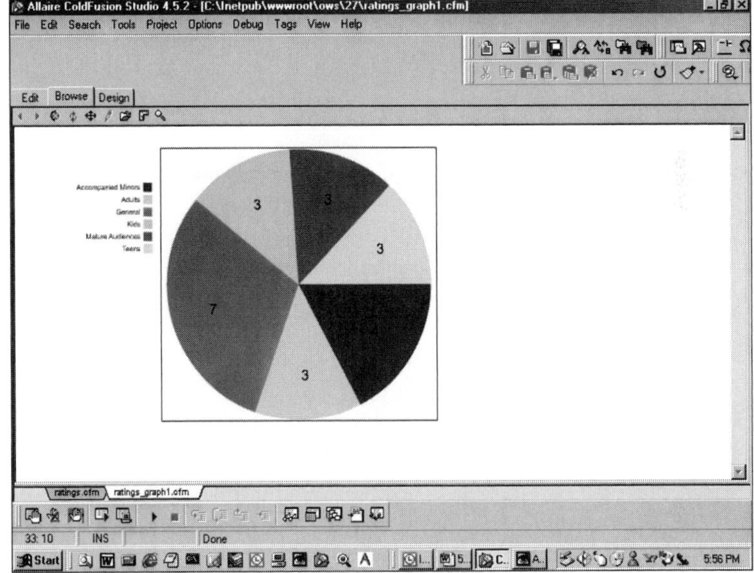

Figure 27.2
A pie graph shows the OWS movies by rating.

Listing 27.2 begins with the obligatory comment block. Next, the `<CFQUERY>` tag performs a `SELECT` operation on the OWS database on the `Ratings` column, as well as `GROUP` and `ORDER` operations to organize the query results by rating.

After the HTML comes the `<CFGRAPH>` tag. As you can see, the `<CFGRAPH>` attributes define which query data is graphed and the appearance of the graph. Table 27.1 provides a breakdown of the `<CFGRAPH>` tag in Listing 27.2.

Table 27.1 `<CFGRAPH>` Attributes

Attribute	Value	Description
`TYPE`	`Pie`	Type of graph
`QUERY`	`GetRatings`	Query to use
`VALUECOLUMN`	`FilmCount`	Query column that contains the data to graph

Table 27.1 Continued

Attribute	Value	Description
ITEMCOLUMN	Rating	Query column that contains labels for the items
FILEFORMAT	Flash	Graph file format

As you can see, you can build a pie graph with `<CFGRAPH>` with only five attributes without changing the SQL or `<CFQUERY>` tag. A legend is even produced automatically.

Your boss is impressed with your speed but not with how the graph looks. Fortunately, the `<CFGRAPH>` tag provides a variety of attributes that enable you to adjust the appearance of the graph.

In a new file, enter the code shown in Listing 27.3, and save the new file as `ratings_graph2.cfm` in the Web root. Notice the four new attributes in bold.

Listing 27.3 `ratings_graph2.cfm`**—Changing Graph Appearance**

```
<!---
Name:        ratings_graph2.cfm
Author:      David Golden (d_golden73@hotmail.com)
Description: Changing graph appearance
Created:     4/15/01
--->

<!--- Get rating list from database --->
<CFQUERY NAME="GetRatings" DATASOURCE="ows">
  SELECT Rating, Count(*) AS FilmCount
  FROM FilmsRatings, Films
  WHERE FilmsRatings.RatingID = Films.RatingID
  GROUP BY Rating
  ORDER BY Rating
</CFQUERY>

<!--- Create HTML page --->
<!DOCTYPE HTML PUBLIC "-//W3C//DTD HTML 4.0 Transitional//EN">
<HTML>
<HEAD>
    <TITLE>Orange Whip Studios - Movie Rating Analysis</TITLE>
</HEAD>

<BODY>

<!--- Displays graph from query data --->
<CFGRAPH
  TYPE="Pie"
  QUERY="GetRatings"
  VALUECOLUMN="FilmCount"
  ITEMCOLUMN="Rating"
  FILEFORMAT="Flash"
  TITLE="Movie Ratings"
  BORDERWIDTH="1"
  BORDERCOLOR="Black"
```

```
  Depth="20">
</CFGRAPH>


</BODY>
</HTML>
```

Now execute this page in your browser as

`http://localhost/ows/27/ratings_graph2.cfm`

The results are shown in Figure 27.3.

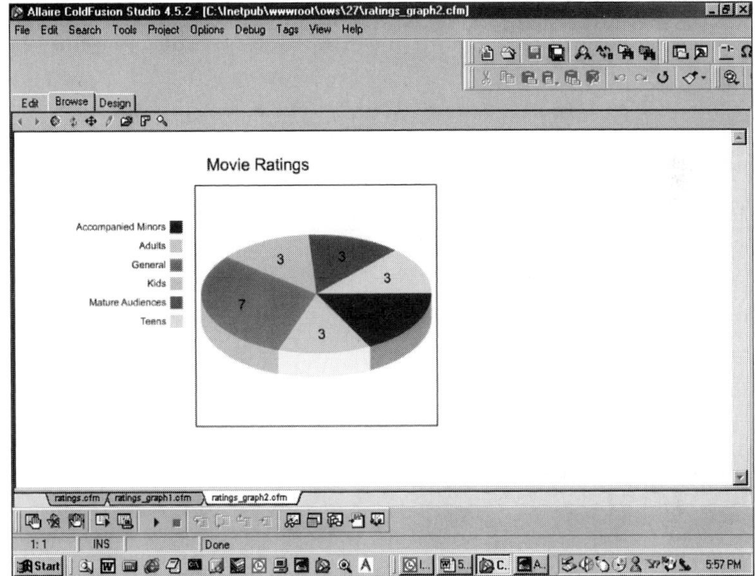

Figure 27.3
The pie graph now appears three dimensional with a border and title.

These attributes give ColdFusion instructions regarding how the graph should be presented in a browser. Table 27.2 describes the new attributes in Listing 27.3.

Table 27.2 <CFGRAPH> Attributes

Attribute	Value	Description
`TITLE`	`Movie Ratings`	Title for graph
`BORDERCOLOR`	`BLACK`	Border color
`BORDERWIDTH`	`1`	Border size in pixels
`DEPTH`	`20`	3D chart depth in pixels

Your boss thinks you're amazing but now thinks that a bar graph would work better. On second thought, your boss wants a bar graph and a pie graph on the same page. Before you build two graphs, you should learn more about the available graph types.

GRAPH TYPES

Currently, ColdFusion produces five types of graphs:

- Pie
- Bar
- Horizontal bar
- Line
- Area

Which type of graph you choose to use depends on what type of data you want to graph. ColdFusion graphs share the same strengths and weaknesses as any other visual representation of data. Table 27.3 describes each graph, including available file formats and an example of its use.

TABLE 27.3 COLDFUSION GRAPHS

Graph Type	Available Formats	Description	Example Use
Pie	Flash (SWF), JPG	Best used to show percentage of a whole	Percentage of total revenue by product
Bar and Horizontal Bar	Flash (SWF), JPG	Best used to compare different values	Compare actual revenue numbers by product
Line and Area	Flash (SWF), JPG	Best used to track change in values over time	Compare monthly sales numbers over the course of a year

Of course, with the flexibility of ColdFusion, these graphs can be used for a vast number of purposes. Your imagination is the only limit. Now, let's return to your assignment.

You need two graphs of the same data—one pie and one graph. Create a new file, and enter the code as it appears in Listing 27.4; then save it as `ratings_graph3.cfm`.

LISTING 27.4 `ratings_graph3.cfm`—TWO GRAPHS OF THE SAME DATA

```
<!---
Name:        ratings_graph3.cfm
Author:      David Golden (d_golden73@hotmail.com)
Description: Two graphs of the same data
Created:     4/15/01
--->

<!--- Get rating list from database --->
<CFQUERY NAME="GetRatings" DATASOURCE="ows">
```

```
  SELECT Rating, Count(*) AS FilmCount
  FROM FilmsRatings, Films
  WHERE FilmsRatings.RatingID = Films.RatingID
  GROUP BY Rating
  ORDER BY Rating
</CFQUERY>

<!--- Create HTML page --->
<!DOCTYPE HTML PUBLIC "-//W3C//DTD HTML 4.0 Transitional//EN">
<HTML>
<HEAD>
    <TITLE>Orange Whip Studios - Movie Rating Analysis</TITLE>
</HEAD>

<BODY>
<!--- Displays graph from query data --->

<CFGRAPH
    TYPE="Pie"
    QUERY="GetRatings"
    VALUECOLUMN="FilmCount"
    ITEMCOLUMN="Rating"
    FILEFORMAT="Flash"
      TITLE="Movie Ratings"
      BORDERWIDTH="1"
      BORDERCOLOR="Black"
      Depth="20">
 </CFGRAPH>

<!--- Displays second graph from query data --->

<CFGRAPH
    TYPE="Bar"
    QUERY="GetRatings"
      VALUECOLUMN="FilmCount"
      ITEMCOLUMN="Rating"
      FILEFORMAT="Flash"
    SCALETO="10"
      BORDERWIDTH="1"
      BORDERCOLOR="Black"
      Depth="20">
</CFGRAPH>

</BODY>
</HTML>
```

Now execute this page in your browser as

`http://localhost/ows/27/ratings_graph3.cfm`

The results are shown in Figure 27.4.

As you can see, a second `<CFGRAPH>` tag was inserted. For this tag, you changed only the attribute `TYPE="BAR"` and inserted a new attribute `SCALETO="10"`. For bar, horizontal bar, area, and line graphs, you can specify a maximum value for the value axis. In addition, `SCALEFROM` lets you dictate the starting value for the value axis.

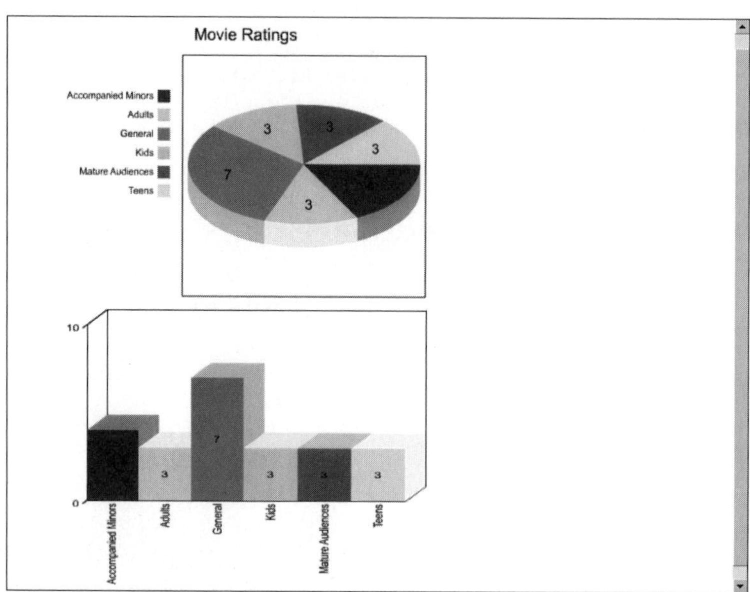

Figure 27.4
A pie graph and a bar graph are generated from the same data.

Note

The SCALETO and SCALEFROM attributes can contain only numbers.

INTRODUCING <CFGRAPHDATA>

Impressed by your speed and skill at producing graphs with ColdFusion, your boss makes one last tweak to the ratings graphs. One of the board members wants the graphs to show the average number of movies geared toward children produced by other studios. He even provided a number, 7.

Although this is a simple request, `<CFGRAPH>` poses a problem because it can graph only data supplied by a query. On top of everything else, your boss stands behind you tapping her foot while you make the change. To make matters worse, your boss doesn't want you to create a new entry in the database.

Luckily, you have the `<CFGRAPHDATA>` tag. `<CFGRAPHDATA>` lets you specify any number of specific data points within your graphs that don't depend on database information.

Create a new file, and enter the code as it appears in Listing 27.5; then save it as `ratings_graph4.cfm`.

LISTING 27.5 `ratings_graph4.cfm—<CFGRAPHDATA>`

```
<!---
Name:        ratings_graph4.cfm
Author:      David Golden (d_golden73@hotmail.com)
Description: CFGRAPHDATA
```

```
Created:     4/15/01
--->

<!--- Get rating list from database --->
<CFQUERY NAME="GetRatings" DATASOURCE="ows">
  SELECT Rating, Count(*) AS FilmCount
  FROM FilmsRatings, Films
  WHERE FilmsRatings.RatingID = Films.RatingID
  GROUP BY Rating
  ORDER BY Rating
</CFQUERY>

<!--- Create HTML page --->
<!DOCTYPE HTML PUBLIC "-//W3C//DTD HTML 4.0 Transitional//EN">
<HTML>
<HEAD>
    <TITLE>Orange Whip Studios - Movie Rating Analysis</TITLE>
</HEAD>

<BODY>
<!--- Displays graph from query data --->

<CFGRAPH
    TYPE="Pie"
    QUERY="GetRatings"
    VALUECOLUMN="FilmCount"
    ITEMCOLUMN="Rating"
    FILEFORMAT="Flash"
      TITLE="Movie Ratings"
      BORDERWIDTH="1"
      BORDERCOLOR="Black"
      Depth="20">

<!--- Displays graph from item value --->

<CFGRAPHDATA
    value="7"
    item="Industry Average for Kids">
</CFGRAPHDATA>

</CFGRAPH>

<!--- Displays second graph from query data --->

<CFGRAPH
    TYPE="Bar"
    QUERY="GetRatings"
      VALUECOLUMN="FilmCount"
      ITEMCOLUMN="Rating"
      FILEFORMAT="Flash"
    SCALETO="10"
      BORDERWIDTH="1"
      BORDERCOLOR="Black"
      Depth="20">

<!--- Displays graph from item value --->
```

LISTING 27.5 CONTINUED

```
<CFGRAPHDATA
    value="7"
    item="Industry Average for Kids">
</CFGRAPHDATA>

</CFGRAPH>

</BODY>
</HTML>
```

Now execute this page in your browser as

```
http://localhost/ows/27/ratings_graph4.cfm
```

The results are shown in Figure 27.5.

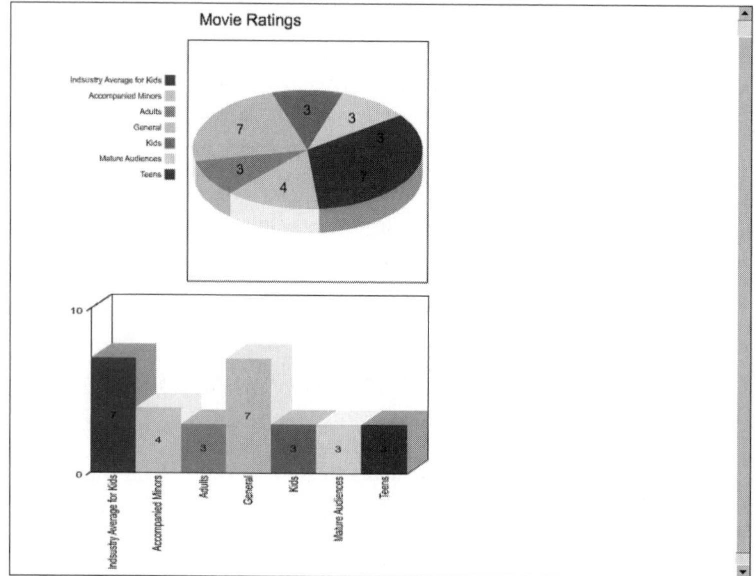

Figure 27.5
<CFGRAPHDATA> supplies nonquery data to the graphs.

Notice the code in bold. The `VALUE` attribute supplies the graph value, and the `ITEM` attribute supplies the label.

Note

A <CFGRAPHDATA> tag must reside inside the opening and closing tags of <CFGRAPH>.

FILE FORMATS

ColdFusion's graphing engine produces graphs in three file formats:

- Flash (SWF)
- JPG

The JPG file format looks exactly like the Flash version. JPG is a good choice if you're not sure whether users have the Flash player installed on their systems.

The Flash format provides a level of interactivity not found in other image formats. In addition, `<CFGRAPH>` lets you capitalize on the power of Flash to build graphs with which the user can interact.

You must put that additional interactivity into use because your boss just sent you a high-priority e-mail.

INTERACTIVE GRAPHS

You boss is now sitting in the board meeting. Apparently, the directors found your graphs useful and want to redirect funds to more children's movies. They now want a bar graph showing the current budgets of all OWS movies greater than $750,000. That will be a snap with `<CFGRAPH>`, you think. However, your boss adds another requirement. She wants the directors to be able to click a bar and see a details page of the expenses according to the movie.

This application will require two pages. The first page will contain the graph, and the second page—the details page—will contain the information.

Let's start with the details page first. Create a new file, and enter the code as it appears in Listing 27.6; then save it as `budget_details.cfm`.

LISTING 27.6 `ratings_graph5.cfm`**—BUDGET DETAILS PAGE**

```
<!---
Name:        budget_details.cfm
Author:      David Golden (d_golden73@hotmail.com)
Description: Budget details page
Created:     4/15/01
--->

<!--- Get title and budget information from database --->

<CFQUERY NAME="GetBudgets" DATASOURCE="ows">
  SELECT FilmID, MovieTitle, AmountBudgeted
  FROM Films
  WHERE AmountBudgeted > 0
  AND GetBudgets.FilmID = '#URL.FilmID#'
</CFQUERY>

<!--- Creates HTML page --->
```

LISTING 27.6 CONTINUED

```
<!DOCTYPE HTML PUBLIC "-//W3C//DTD HTML 4.0 Transitional//EN">

<html>
<head>
    <title>Budget Details - Orange Whip Studios</title>
</head>

<body>

<!--- Displays movie title and budget in table --->

<H1><CFOUTPUT>#GetBudgets.FilmID# Budget Details</CFOUTPUT></H1>

<TABLE BORDER="1">
<TR>
 <TH>Movie Title</TH>
 <TH>Amount Budgeted</TH>
</TR>
<CFOUTPUT QUERY="GetBudgets">
<TR>
 <TD>#GetBudgets.MovieTitle#</TD>
 <TD>#GetBudgets.AmountBudgeted#</TD>
</TR>
</CFOUTPUT>
</TABLE>
</cfoutput>

</body>
</html>
```

Listing 27.6 creates a simple details page. The first block of code performs the query. Notice the line `AND GetBudgets.FilmID = '#URL.FilmID#'`. The graph page passes the URL variable when the user clicks one of the bars, thereby telling the details page which `FilmID` to display.

Now, let's build the graph page.

Create a new file, and enter the code as it appears in Listing 27.7; then save it as `budget_graph.cfm` in the Web root.

LISTING 27.7 budget_graph.cfm—INTERACTIVE BUDGET GRAPH

```
<!---
Name:        budget_graph.cfm
Author:      David Golden (d_golden73@hotmail.com)
Description: Interactive Budget Graph
Created:     4/15/01
--->

<!--- Get title and budget information from database --->

<CFQUERY NAME="GetBudgets" DATASOURCE="ows">
  SELECT FilmID, MovieTitle, AmountBudgeted
```

```
  FROM Films
  WHERE AmountBudgeted > 750000
</CFQUERY>

<!--- Create HTML page --->

<!DOCTYPE HTML PUBLIC "-//W3C//DTD HTML 4.0 Transitional//EN">

<html>
<head>
    <title>Interactive Budget Graph - Orange Whip Studios</title>
</head>

<body>

<!--- Displays graph from query data --->

<CFGRAPH
    TYPE="bar"
    QUERY="GetBudgets"
      VALUECOLUMN="AmountBudgeted"
      ITEMCOLUMN="MovieTitle"
    TITLE="Current Production Budgets"
      FILEFORMAT="FLASH"
    Depth="10"
    SCALETO="10000000"
    SCALEFROM="0"
    GRAPHWIDTH="700"
    GRAPHHEIGHT="600"
    BARSPACING="15"
      URL="budget_details.cfm?FilmID="
    URCOLUMN="FilmID"
      SHOWITEMLABELS="Yes"
    SHOWVALUELABEL="Rollover"
    GRIDLINES="3"
    VALUELOCATION="over bar">
</CFGRAPH>

</body>
</html>
```

The budget graph page begins with the same `<CFQUERY>` as the budget details page, minus the `AND GetBudgets.FilmID='#URL.FilmID#'` line. However, the number of attributes specified in the `<CFGRAPH>` tag has more than doubled. The new attributes are bolded.

Pay close attention to the `URL` and `URLCOLUMN` attributes. The `URL` attribute sets the location of the details template and the `URL` variable to pass. The `URL` column supplies the value for the variable to pass. In this case, the `URL` attribute points to the `budget_details.cfm` page you just created. It also includes which variable to pass. The `URLCOLUMN` attribute supplies the value—in this case, the `FILMID` of the bar clicked, which is appended to the `URL` attribute value.

For an explanation of the other new attributes, see Table 27.4.

TABLE 27.4 <CFGRAPH> ATTRIBUTES

Attribute	Value	Description
`SCALEFROM`	`0`	Sets the number to start on the value axis
`GRAPHWIDTH`	`700`	Sets the graph's size in pixels
`GRAPHHEIGHT`	`600`	Sets the graph's size in pixels
`BARSPACING`	`10`	Sets the spacing between the bars in pixels
`SHOWITEMLABELS`	`Yes`	Sets the graph to display the bar labels (`AmountBudgeted`)
`SHOWVALUELABEL`	`Rollover`	Sets the graph to display the item labels on mouse rollover
`GRIDLINES`	`3`	Sets the graph to display grid lines along the value axis
`VALUELOCATION`	`over bar`	Sets the graph to display the value labels on top of the bar

Now execute this page in your browser as

```
http://localhost/ows/27/budget_graph.cfm
```

The results are shown in Figure 27.6.

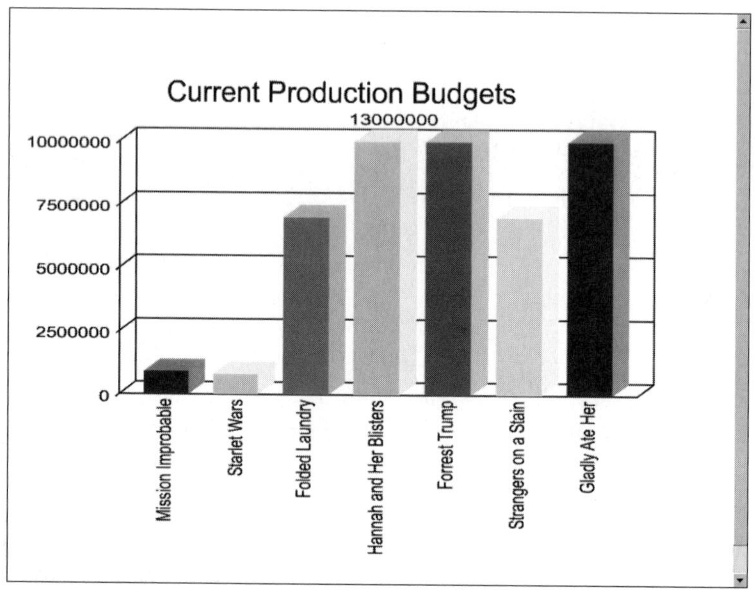

Figure 27.6 The movie budget graph is displayed.

Now click the bar labeled Hannah and Her Blisters. The Hannah and Her Blisters Budget details page appears, as shown in Figure 27.7.

Figure 27.7 After you click the Hannah and Her Blisters bar, the details page appears.

Look at the URL for this page:

```
http://localhost/ows/27/budget_details.cfm?FilmID=20
```

The `FilmID` for *Hannah and Her Blisters* is appended to the URL specified in the URL attribute of `<CFGRAPH>`.

> **Note**
>
> The `<CFGRAPH>` tag supplies many more attributes to manipulate the appearance of the graph. For more information, see the *CFML Reference Guide*.

> **Note**
>
> When setting the value for the `GRIDLINES` attribute, be sure to take the `SCALETO` and `SCALEFROM` attributes into account. For example, the budget graph's `SCALETO` attribute is set to `10000000`, and the `SCALEFROM` attribute is set to `0`. Therefore, you need to specify only `3` in the `GRIDLINES` attribute to produce the proper number of gridlines.

Building a Graphing Application

The board of directors loves your graphing application. In fact, your e-mail inbox is filled with messages requesting various budget graphs, usually either bar or pie, for a variety of movie budgets. You are now spending your days building budget graphs, and your project list is starting to languish.

So, you decide to build a simple graphing application so the board of directors can build their own budget graphs. You decide that users of this application will need the following options:

- Type of graph
- The minimum budget needed for a file to be included in the graph
- Background color

For this project, you will need three pages:

- A form page for users to make their choices
- An action page that creates and displays the graph
- A details page to show movie budget details

Let's build the form page first.

Create a new file, and enter the code as it appears in Listing 27.8; then save it as `budget_graph_form.cfm` in the Web root.

LISTING 27.8 budget_graph_form.cfm—BUDGET GRAPH FORM PAGE

```
<!---
Name:        budget_graph_form.cfm
Author:      David Golden (d_golden73@hotmail.com)
Description: Budget Graph Form Page
Created:     4/15/01
--->


<!--- Create HTML page --->

<!DOCTYPE HTML PUBLIC "-//W3C//DTD HTML 4.0 Transitional//EN">

<html>
<head>
    <title>Build Your Own Budget Graph</title>
</head>

<body>

<H1>Build Your Own Budget Graph</H1>

<p><i>All options are required.</i></p>


<!--- Create Form page --->

<FORM ACTION="generate_budget_graph.cfm"
      METHOD="post">


<table cellspacing="2" cellpadding="2" border="0" align="left">
<tr>
```

```
    <th>Graph Name</th>
    <td><input type="text"
               name="GraphName"></td>
</tr>
<tr>
    <th>Select Graph Type</th>
    <td><select name="GraphType">
    <option value="Pie" SELECTED>Pie</option>
    <option value="Bar">Bar</option>
        </select></td>
</tr>
<tr>
    <th>Enter Minimum Movie Budget (numbers only)</th>
    <td><input type="text"
               name="MinBudget"></td>
</tr>
<tr>
    <th>Background Color (select one)</th>
    <td><select name="BGColor">
    <option value="White" SELECTED>White</option>
    <option value="Yellow">Yellow</option>
    <option value="Blue">Blue</option>
    </select></td>
</tr>
<tr>
    <td>When finished, click Submit.</td>
</tr>
<tr>
    <td><input type="submit"
            value="Generate Graph"></td>
    <td><input type="Reset"></td>
</tr>
</table>



</FORM>

</body>
</html>
```


This page contains simple `FORM` controls that enable the user to enter a title for the graph, select either a pie or bar graph, enter the minimum budget for the movies to be graphed, and select a background color for the graph.

Now execute this page in your browser as

```
http://localhost/ows/27/budget_graph_form.cfm
```

The results are shown in Figure 27.8.

Next, you need to build the action page that will generate the graph according to the values passed by `budget_graph_form.cfm`.

Create a new file, and enter the code as it appears in Listing 27.9; then save it as `generate_budget_graph.cfm` in the Web root.

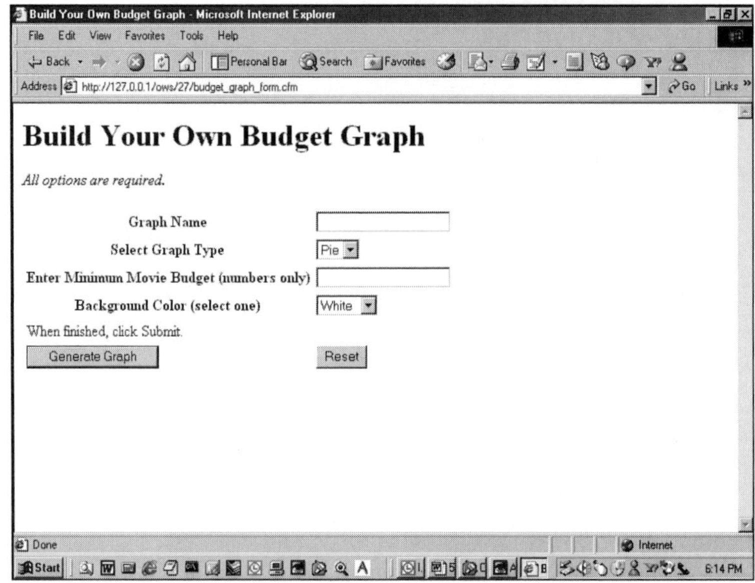

Figure 27.8
The form page displays the available controls to the user.

LISTING 27.9 generate_budget_graph.cfm—BUDGET GRAPH ACTION PAGE

```
<!---
Name:        generate_budget_graph.cfm
Author:      David Golden (d_golden73@hotmail.com)
Description: Budget Graph Action Page
Created:     4/15/01
--->

<CFOUTPUT>

<!--- Get title and budget information from database --->

<CFQUERY NAME="GetBudgets" DATASOURCE="ows">
  SELECT FilmID, MovieTitle, AmountBudgeted
  FROM Films
  WHERE AmountBudgeted > #Form.MinBudget#
</CFQUERY>

<!--- Set variables to URL variables --->


<!--- Create HTML page --->

<!DOCTYPE HTML PUBLIC "-//W3C//DTD HTML 4.0 Transitional//EN">

<html>
<head>
    <title>Interactive Budget Graph - Orange Whip Studios</title>
</head>
```

```
<body>

<!--- Displays graph from query data --->

<CFGRAPH
    TYPE="#Form.GraphType#"
    BACKGROUNDCOLOR="#Form.BGColor#"
    QUERY="GetBudgets"
      VALUECOLUMN="AmountBudgeted"
      ITEMCOLUMN="MovieTitle"
      FILEFORMAT="FLASH"
    TITLE="#Form.GraphName#"
    Depth="10"
    URL="budget_details.cfm?FilmID="
    URLCOLUMN="FilmID"
    SHOWVALUELABEL="Rollover">
</CFGRAPH>

</CFOUTPUT>

</body>
</html>
```

Notice the lines of bolded code. For this action page, the values were simply replaced with form variables passed by `budget_graph_form.cfm`.

Note

As always, be sure to enclose your variables with the `<CFOUTPUT>` tag.

Let's try it out. Go back to `budget_graph_form.cfm` in your browser. Enter **`New`** for the graph name, select Pie, enter **`10000000`** for the minimum budget, and select yellow for the background color. Click the Submit button.

The results are shown in Figure 27.9.

For the details page, you can just use the page you made in Listing 27.6. You don't even need to rename the file because the `<CFGRAPH> URL` attribute in the action page, `generate_budget_graph.cfm`, points to `budget_details.cfm`.

Congratulations, you have just built a graphing application.

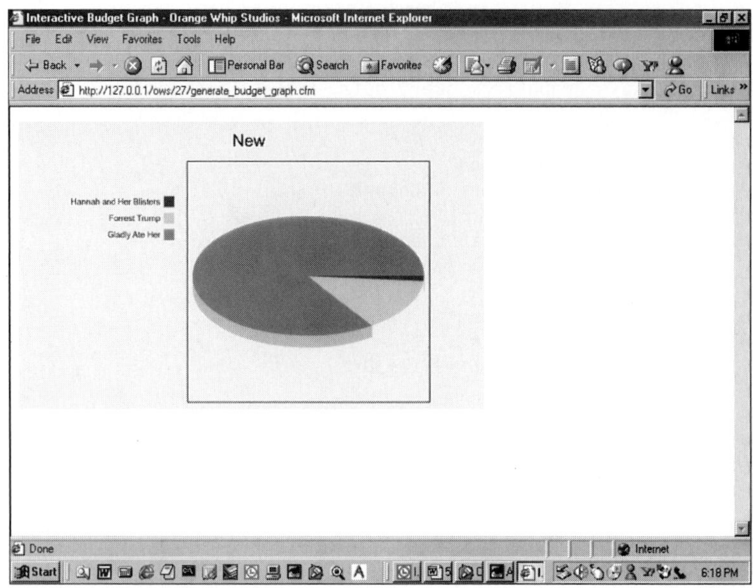

Figure 27.9
According to your selections in the form page, the graph titled New appears with only movies with budgets greater than $500,000 and with a yellow background.

CHAPTER 28

Interacting with E-mail

In this chapter

SENDING E-MAIL FROM COLDFUSION

Clearly, ColdFusion's main purpose is to create dynamic, data-driven Web pages. However, ColdFusion also provides a set of e-mail–related tags that enable you to send e-mail messages that are just as dynamic and data-driven as your Web pages. You can also write ColdFusion templates that check and retrieve e-mail messages, and even respond to them automatically.

Note

<CFMAIL> sends standard, Internet-style e-mail messages using the Simple Mail Transport Protocol (SMTP). SMTP is not explained in detail in this book; for now, all you need to know about SMTP is that it is the standard for sending e-mail on the Internet. Virtually all e-mail programs, such as Netscape, Outlook Express, Eudora, and so on send standard SMTP mail. The exceptions are proprietary messaging systems, such as Lotus Notes or older Microsoft Mail (MAPI-style) clients.

Tip

If you want to learn more about the underpinnings of the SMTP protocol, visit the World Wide Web Consortium's Web site at `http://www.wc3.org`.

INTRODUCING THE <CFMAIL> TAG

You can use the <CFMAIL> tag to send e-mail messages from your ColdFusion templates. After the server is set up correctly, you can use <CFMAIL> to send e-mail messages to anyone with a standard Internet-style e-mail address. As far as the receiver is concerned, the e-mail messages you send with <CFMAIL> are just like messages sent via a normal e-mail sending program, such as Netscape, Outlook Express, Eudora, or the like.

Table 28.1 shows the key attributes for the <CFMAIL> tag. These are the attributes you will use most often, and they are presented in a separate table here for clarity. Assuming that you have sent e-mail messages before, you will understand what almost all of these attributes do right away.

Note

Some additional <CFMAIL> attributes are introduced later in this chapter (see Table 28.2 in the "Sending Data-Driven Mail" section and Table 28.4 in the "Overriding the Default Mail Server Settings" section).

TABLE 28.1 KEY <CFMAIL> ATTRIBUTES FOR SENDING E-MAIL MESSAGES

Attribute	Purpose
SUBJECT	Required. The subject of the e-mail message.
FROM	Required. The e-mail address that that should be used to send the message. This is the address the message will be from when it is received. The address must be a standard Internet-style e-mail address (see the section "Using Friendly E-mail Addresses").

Attribute	Purpose
TO	Required. The address or addresses to send the message to. To specify multiple addresses, simply separate them with commas. Each must be a standard Internet-style e-mail address (see the section "Using Friendly E-mail Addresses," later in this chapter).
CC	Optional. Address or addresses to send a carbon copy of the message to. This is the equivalent to using the CC feature when sending mail with a normal e-mail program. To specify multiple addresses, simply separate them with commas. Each must be a standard Internet-style e-mail address (see the section "Using Friendly E-mail Addresses,").
BCC	Optional. Address or addresses to send a blind carbon copy of the message to. Equivalent to using the BCC feature when sending mail with a normal e-mail program. To specify multiple addresses, simply separate them with commas. Each must be a standard Internet-style e-mail address (see the section "Using Friendly E-mail Addresses,"later in this chapter).
TYPE	Optional. `Text` or `HTML`. `Text` is the default, which means that the message will be sent as a normal, plain text message. `HTML` means that HTML tags within the message will be interpreted as HTML, so you can specify fonts and include images in the e-mail message. See "Sending HTML-Formatted Mail," later in this chapter.
MAILERID	Optional. Can be used to specify the *X-Mailer header* that is sent with the e-mail message. The X-Mailer header is meant to identify which software program was used to send the message. This header is generally never seen by the recipient of the message but can be important to systems in between, such as firewalls. Using the `MAILERID`, you can make it appear as if your message is being sent by a different piece of software. If you find that your outgoing messages are being filtered out when sent to certain users, try using a `MAILERID` that matches some other mail client (such as Outlook Express or some other popular, end-user mail client).
MIMEATTACH	Optional. A document on the server's drive that should be included in the mail message as an attachment. This is an older way to specify attachments, maintained for backward compatibility. It is now recommended that you use the `<CFMAILPARAM>` tag to specify attachments. See "Adding Attachments," later in this chapter, for details.

SPECIFYING A MAIL SERVER IN THE ADMINISTRATOR

Before you can actually use the `<CFMAIL>` tag to send e-mail messages, you need to specify a mail server in the ColdFusion Administrator. This is the mail server with which ColdFusion will interact to actually send the messages that get generated by your templates.

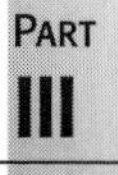

To set up ColdFusion to send e-mail, follow these steps:

1. If you don't know it already, find out the hostname or IP address for the SMTP mail server ColdFusion should use to send messages. Usually, this is the same server your normal e-mail client program (Outlook Express, Eudora, and so on) uses to send your own mail, so you typically can find the hostname or IP address somewhere in your mail

client's Settings or Preferences. Often, the hostname starts with something such as `mail`, `smtp`, or `sendmail`, as in `mail.orangewhipstudios.com`.

2. Open the ColdFusion Administrator, and navigate to the Mail/Mail Logging page, as shown in Figure 28.1.
3. Provide the mail server's hostname or IP address in the Mail Server field.
4. Check the Verify Mail Server Connection option.
5. If your mail server operates on a port other than the usual port number 25, provide the port number in the Server Port field. This is usually unnecessary.
6. Save your changes by clicking the Submit Changes button.

Note

These settings can be overridden in individual ColdFusion templates by the `<CFMAIL>` tag. See the "Overriding the Default Mail Server Settings" section, later in this chapter.

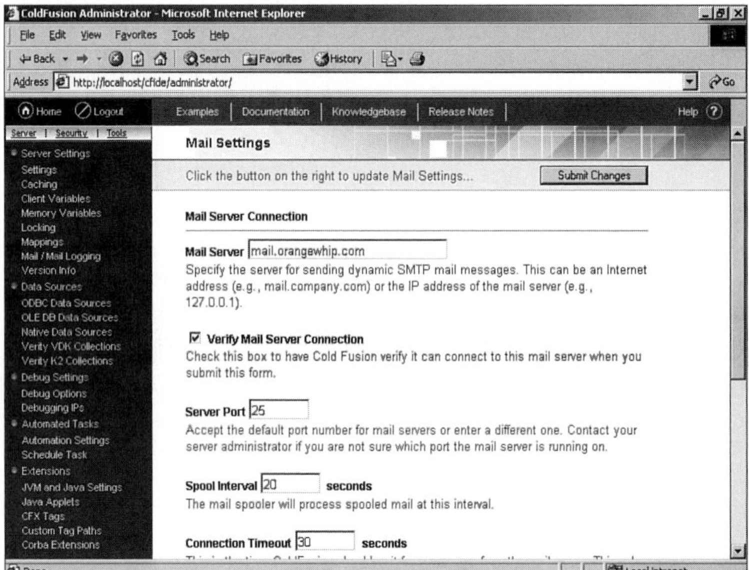

Figure 28.1
Before messages can be sent, ColdFusion needs to know which mail server to use.

SENDING E-MAIL MESSAGES

Sending an e-mail message via a ColdFusion template is easy. Simply code a pair of opening and closing `<CFMAIL>` tags, and provide the `TO`, `FROM`, and `SUBJECT` attributes as appropriate. Between the tags, type the actual message that should be sent to the recipient.

Of course, you can use ColdFusion variables and functions between the `<CFMAIL>` tags to build the message dynamically, using the `#` sign syntax you're used to. You don't need to place `<CFOUTPUT>` tags within (or outside) the `<CFMAIL>` tags; your `#` variables and expressions will be evaluated as if there were a `<CFOUTPUT>` tag in effect.

Note

In fact, as you look through the examples in this chapter, you will find that the <CFMAIL> tag is basically a specially modified <CFOUTPUT> tag. It has similar behavior (variables and expressions are evaluated) and attributes (GROUP, MAXROWS, and so on, as listed in Table 28.4).

SENDING A SIMPLE MESSAGE

Listing 28.1 shows how easy it is to use the <CFMAIL> tag to send a message. The idea behind this template is to provide a simple form for people working in Orange Whip Studio's Personnel Department. Rather than having to open their normal e-mail client programs, they can just use this Web page. It displays a simple form for the user to type a message and specify a recipient, as shown previously in Figure 28.1. When the form is submitted, the message is sent.

LISTING 28.1 PersonnelMail1.cfm—SENDING E-MAIL WITH COLDFUSION

```
<HTML>
<HEAD>
  <TITLE>Personnel Office Mailer</TITLE>
  <!--- Apply simple CSS formatting to <TH> cells --->
  <STYLE>
    TH {background:blue;color:white;text-align:right}
  </STYLE>
</HEAD>
<BODY>

<H2>Personnel Office Mailer</H2>

<!--- If the user is submitting the Form... --->
<CFIF IsDefined("FORM.Subject")>

<!--- We do not want ColdFusion to suppress whitespace here --->
<CFPROCESSINGDIRECTIVE SUPPRESSWHITESPACE="No">

<!--- Send the mail message, based on form input --->
<CFMAIL
  SUBJECT="#FORM.Subject#"
  FROM="personnel@orangewhipstudios.com"
  TO="#FORM.ToAddress#"
  BCC="personneldirector@orangewhipstudios.com"
>This is a message from the Personnel Office:
#FORM.MessageBody#

If you have any questions about this message, please
write back or call us at extension 352.  Thanks!</CFMAIL>

</CFPROCESSINGDIRECTIVE>

  <!--- Display "success" message to user --->
  <P>The email message was sent.<BR>
  By the way, you look fabulous today.
  You should be in pictures!<BR>
```

LISTING 28.1 CONTINUED

```
<!--- Otherwise, display the form to user... --->
<CFELSE>
  <!--- Provide simple form for recipient and message --->
  <CFFORM ACTION="#CGI.SCRIPT_NAME#" METHOD="POST">

    <TABLE CELLPADDING="2" CELLSPACING="2">
      <!--- Table row: Input for Email Address --->
      <TR>
        <TH>E-Mail Address:</TH>
        <TD>
          <CFINPUT
            TYPE="Text"
            NAME="ToAddress"
            REQUIRED="Yes"
            SIZE="40"
            MESSAGE="You must provide an e-mail address.">
        </TD>
      </TR>

      <!--- Table row: Input for E-mail Subject --->
      <TR>
        <TH>Subject:</TH>
        <TD>
          <CFINPUT
            TYPE="Text"
            NAME="Subject"
            REQUIRED="Yes"
            SIZE="40"
            MESSAGE="You must provide a subject for the e-mail.">
        </TD>
      </TR>

      <!--- Table row: Input for actual Message Text --->
      <TR>
        <TH>Your Message:</TH>
        <TD>
          <TEXTAREA
            NAME="MessageBody"
            COLS="30"
            ROWS="5"
            WRAP="Hard"></TEXTAREA>

        </TD>
      </TR>

      <!--- Table row: Submit button to send message --->
      <TR>
        <TD></TD>
        <TD>
          <INPUT
            TYPE="Submit"
            VALUE="Send Message Now">
        </TD>
      </TR>
    </TABLE>
```

```
  </CFFORM>
</CFIF>

</BODY>
</HTML>
```

There are two parts to this listing, divided by the large <CFIF>/<CFELSE> block. When the page is first visited, the second part of the template executes, which displays the form shown in Figure 28.2.

When the form is submitted, the first part of the template kicks in, which actually sends the e-mail message with the <CFMAIL> tag. The message's subject line and "to" address are specified by the appropriate form values, and the content of the message itself is constructed by combining the #FORM.MessageBody# variable with some static text. Additionally, each message sent by this template is also sent to the personnel director as a blind carbon copy, via the BCC attribute.

Around the <CFMAIL> tag, the <CFPROCESSINGDIRECTIVE> tag is used to turn off ColdFusion's default whitespace-suppression behavior. This is needed in this template because the <CFMAIL> tag that follows is written to output the exact text of the e-mail message, which includes "newlines" and other whitespace characters that should be included literally in the actual e-mail message. Without the <CFPROCESSINGDIRECTIVE> tag, ColdFusion would see the newlines within the <CFOUTPUT> tags as evil whitespace, deserving to be ruthlessly suppressed.

Note

For more information about whitespace suppression and the <CFPROCESSINGDIRECTIVE> tag, see the "Controlling Whitespace" section in Chapter 24, "Improving Performance."

Note

The opening and closing <CFMAIL> tags are not indented in this listing for a reason. If they were, the spaces or tabs used to do the indenting would show up in the actual e-mail message. You will generally need to make exceptions to your usual indenting practices when using <CFMAIL>. The exception would be when using TYPE="HTML", as discussed in the "Sending HTML-Formatted Mail" section, because whitespace is not significant in HTML.

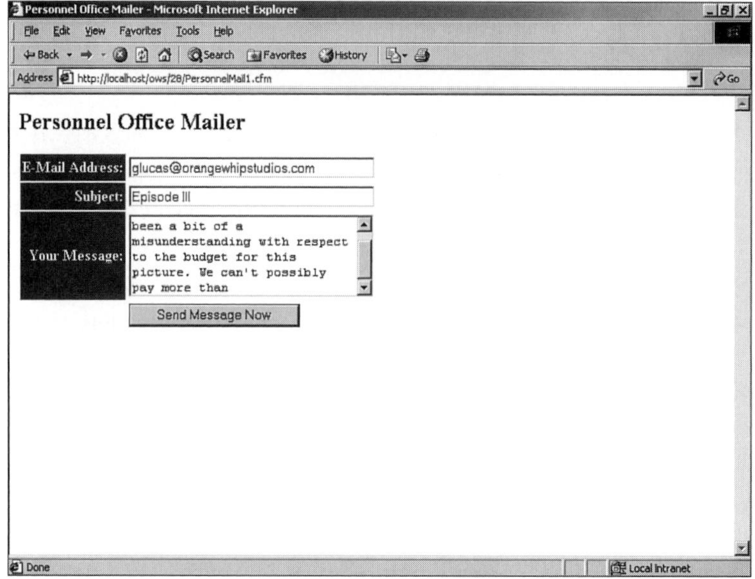

Figure 28.2
Creating a Web-based mail-sending mechanism for your users is easy.

Using Friendly E-mail Addresses

The e-mail addresses provided to the `TO`, `FROM`, `CC`, and `BCC` attributes can all be specified as just the e-mail address itself (such as `bforta@orangewhipstudios.com`), or as a combination of the address and the address's friendly name. The *friendly name* is usually the person's real-life first and last names.

To specify a friendly name along with an e-mail address, place the friendly name between double quotation marks, followed by the actual e-mail address between angle brackets. So, instead of

```
bforta@orangewhipstudios.com
```

you would provide

```
"Ben Forta" <bforta@orangewhipstudios.com>
```

To provide such an address to the `FROM`, `TO`, `CC`, or `BCC` attribute of the `<CFMAIL>` tag, you must double up each double quotation mark shown above, assuming that you are already using double quotation marks around the whole attribute value. So, you might end up with something such as the following:

```
<CFMAIL
  SUBJECT="Dinner Plans"
  FROM="""Nate Weiss"" <nweiss@orangewhipstudios.com>"
  TO="""Belinda Foxile"" <bfoxile@orangewhipstudios.com>">
```

Or, if you find the use of the doubled-up double quotation marks confusing, you could surround the `FROM` and `TO` attributes with single quotation marks instead of double quotation marks, which would allow you to provide the double-quotation characters around the friendly name normally, like so:

```
<CFMAIL
  SUBJECT="Dinner Plans"
  FROM='"Nate Weiss" <nweiss@orangewhipstudios.com>'
  TO='"Belinda Foxile" <bfoxile@orangewhipstudios.com>'>
```

Now, when the message is sent, the "to" and "from" addresses shown in the recipient's e-mail program can be shown with each person's real-life name along with his e-mail address. How the friendly name and e-mail address are actually presented to the user is up to the e-mail client software.

The version of the `PersonnelMail.cfm` template shown in Listing 28.2 is nearly the same as the one from Listing 28.1, except that this version collects the recipient's friendly name in addition to his e-mail address. Additionally, this version uses a bit of JavaScript to attempt to prefill the e-mail address field based on the friendly name. When the user changes the value in the `FirstName` or `LastName` field, the `ToAddress` field is filled in with the first letter of the first name, plus the whole last name.

Note

There isn't space to go through the JavaScript code used in this template in detail. It is provided to give you an idea of one place where JavaScript can be useful. Consult a JavaScript reference or online tutorial for details.

Limiting Input

This version of the form makes it impossible to send messages to anyone outside of Orange Whip Studios, by simply hard-coding the `@orangewhipstudios.com` part of the e-mail address into the `<CFMAIL>` tag itself. Also, it forces the user to select from a short list of Subject lines, rather than being able to type his own Subject, as shown in Figure 28.3.

In a real-world application, you probably would make different choices about what exactly to allow the user to do. The point is that by limiting the amount of input required, you can make it simpler for users to send consistent e-mail messages, thus increasing the value of your application. This can be a lot of what differentiates Web pages that send mail from ordinary e-mail programs, which can be more complex for users to learn.

Listing 28.2 `PersonnelMail2.cfm`—**Providing Friendly Names Along with E-mail Addresses**

```
<HTML>
<HEAD>
  <TITLE>Personnel Office Mailer</TITLE>
  <!--- Apply simple CSS formatting to <TH> cells --->
  <STYLE>
    TH {background:blue;color:white;
        font-family:sans-serif;font-size:12px;
        text-align:right;padding:5px;}
  </STYLE>

  <!--- Function to guess email based on first/last name --->
  <SCRIPT LANGUAGE="JavaScript">
```

Listing 28.2 Continued

```
    function guessEmail() {
      var guess;

      with (document.mailForm) {
        guess = FirstName.value.substr(0,1) + LastName.value;
        ToAddress.value = guess.toLowerCase();
      };
    };
  </SCRIPT>
</HEAD>

<!--- Put cursor in FirstName field when page loads --->
<BODY <CFIF NOT IsDefined("FORM.Subject")>
        onLoad="document.mailForm.FirstName.focus()"
      </CFIF>>

<!--- If the user is submitting the form... --->
<CFIF IsDefined("FORM.Subject")>
  <CFSET RecipEmail = ListFirst(FORM.ToAddress, "@") & "@orangewhipstudios.com">

  <!--- We do not want ColdFusion to suppress whitespace here --->
  <CFPROCESSINGDIRECTIVE SUPPRESSWHITESPACE="No">

  <!--- Send the mail message, based on form input --->
  <CFMAIL
    SUBJECT="#Form.Subject#"
    FROM="""Personnel Office"" <personnel@orangewhipstudios.com>"
    TO="""#FORM.FirstName# #FORM.LastName#"" <#RecipEmail#>"
    BCC="personneldirector@orangewhipstudios.com"
>This is a message from the Personnel Office:

#UCase(FORM.Subject)#

#FORM.MessageBody#

If you have any questions about this message, please
write back or call us at extension 352.  Thanks!</CFMAIL>

  </CFPROCESSINGDIRECTIVE>

  <!--- Display "success" message to user --->
  <P>The email message was sent.<BR>
  By the way, you look fabulous today.
  You should be in pictures!<BR>

<!--- Otherwise, display the form to user... --->
<CFELSE>
  <!--- Provide simple form for recipient and message --->
  <CFFORM ACTION="#CGI.SCRIPT_NAME#" NAME="mailForm" METHOD="POST">

    <TABLE CELLPADDING="2" CELLSPACING="2">
      <!--- Table row: Input for Recipient's Name --->
      <TR>
        <TH>Recipient's Name:</TH>
        <TD>
```

```
    <CFINPUT
      TYPE="Text"
      NAME="FirstName"
      REQUIRED="Yes"
      SIZE="15"
      MESSAGE="You must provide a first name."
      onChange="guessEmail()">

    <CFINPUT
      TYPE="Text"
      NAME="LastName"
      REQUIRED="Yes"
      SIZE="20"
      MESSAGE="You must provide a first name."
      onChange="guessEmail()">
  </TD>
</TR>

<!--- Table row: Input for Email Address --->
<TR>
  <TH>E-Mail Address:</TH>
  <TD>
    <CFINPUT
      TYPE="Text"
      NAME="ToAddress"
      REQUIRED="Yes"
      SIZE="20"
      MESSAGE="You must provide the recipient's e-mail."
    >@orangewhipstudios.com
  </TD>
</TR>

<!--- Table row: Input for E-mail Subject --->
<TR>
  <TH>Subject:</TH>
  <TD>
    <CFSELECT
      NAME="Subject">
      <OPTION>Sorry, but you have been fired.
      <OPTION>Congratulations! You got a raise!
      <OPTION>Just FYI, you have hit the glass ceiling.
    </CFSELECT>
  </TD>
</TR>

<!--- Table row: Input for actual Message Text --->
<TR>
  <TH>Your Message:</TH>
  <TD>
    <TEXTAREA
      NAME="MessageBody"
      COLS="50"
      ROWS="5"
      WRAP="Hard"></TEXTAREA>

  </TD>
</TR>
```

LISTING 28.2 CONTINUED

```
      <!--- Table row: Submit button to send message --->
      <TR>
        <TD></TD>
        <TD>
          <INPUT
            TYPE="Submit"
            VALUE="Send Message Now">
        </TD>
      </TR>
    </TABLE>
  </CFFORM>
</CFIF>

</BODY>
</HTML>
```

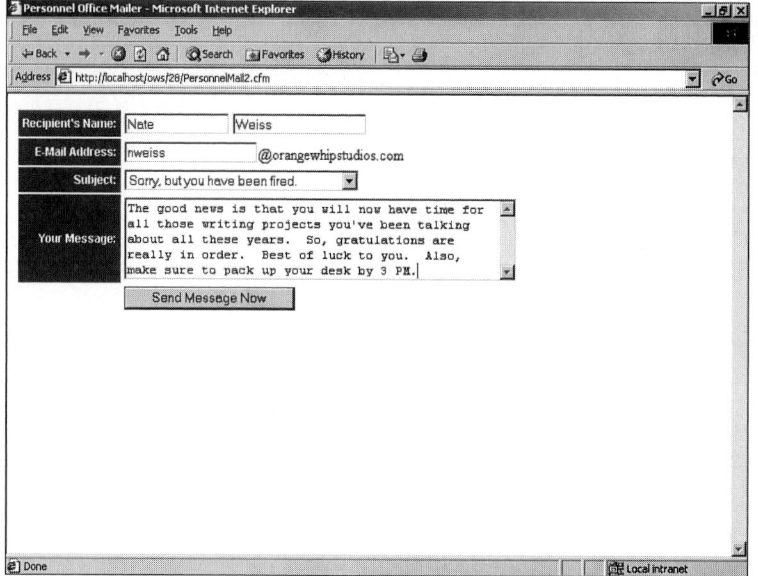

Figure 28.3
Web-based forms can make sending e-mail almost foolproof.

Figure 28.4 shows what an e-mail message generated by Listing 28.2 might look like when received and viewed in a typical e-mail client (here, Microsoft Outlook Express 5).

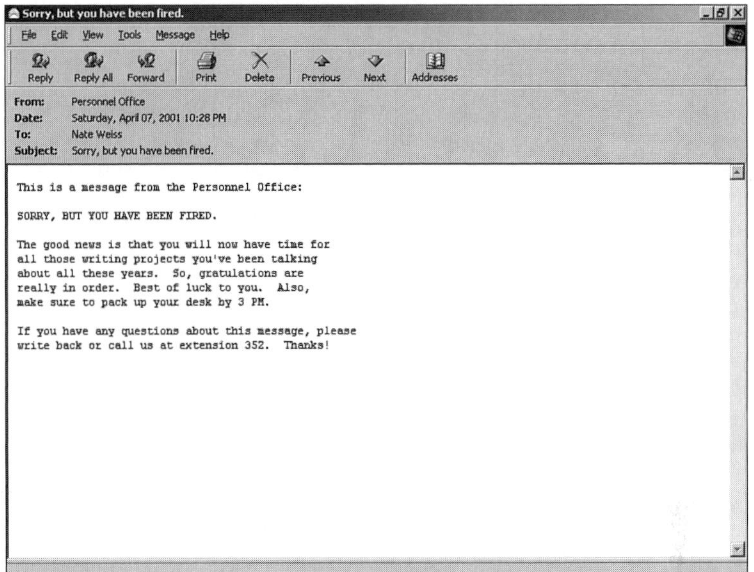

Figure 28.4
Providing a friendly name along with an e-mail address makes for a more personal-feeling e-mail message.

SENDING DATA-DRIVEN MAIL

In the last section, you learned that <CFMAIL> can be thought of as an extended version of the <CFOUTPUT> tag because ColdFusion variables and expressions are evaluated without the need for an explicit <CFOUTPUT> within the <CFMAIL>. The similarity between the two tags doesn't end there. They also share attributes specific to the notion of looping over query records. This capability enables you to send data-driven e-mail messages using nearly the same syntax and techniques that you use to output data-driven HTML code.

Table 28.2 shows the <CFMAIL> attributes relevant to sending data-driven mail. Each of these attributes behaves the same way as the corresponding attributes for <CFOUTPUT>. Instead of causing HTML output to be repeated for each row in a query, these attributes have to do with repeating e-mail message content for each row in a query.

TABLE 28.2 ADDITIONAL <CFMAIL> ATTRIBUTES FOR SENDING DATA-DRIVEN E-MAIL MESSAGES

Attribute	Purpose
`QUERY`	Optional. A query to use for sending data-driven e-mail. Very similar to the `QUERY` attribute of the `<CFOUTPUT>` tag.
`STARTROW`	Optional. A number that indicates which row of the query to consider when sending data-driven e-mail. The default is to start at the first row. Equivalent to the `STARTROW` attribute of the `<CFOUTPUT>` tag.
`MAXROWS`	Optional. A maximum number of query rows to consider when sending data-driven e-mail. Equivalent to the `MAXROWS` attribute of the `<CFOUTPUT>` tag.

Table 28.2 Continued

Attribute	Purpose
GROUP	Optional. A column name from the query that indicates groups of records. Additional output or processing can occur when each new group is encountered. You can indicate nested groups by providing a comma-separated list of column names. Equivalent to the GROUP attribute of the <CFOUTPUT> tag.
GROUPCASESENSITIVE	Optional. Whether to consider text case when determining when a new group of records has been encountered in the column(s) indicated by GROUP. Equivalent to the GROUPCASESENSITIVE attribute of the <CFOUTPUT> tag.

Note

Some ColdFusion developers will note that these additional attributes aren't really necessary. In today's ColdFusion, you usually can achieve the same results using a <CFLOOP> tag around a <CFMAIL> tag to send out multiple messages or using <CFLOOP> within <CFMAIL> to include queried information in the message itself. However, the <CFMAIL> tag appeared in CFML before the <CFLOOP> tag existed, which is one reason why these attributes exist today.

Including Query Data in Messages

By adding a QUERY attribute to the <CFMAIL> tag, you easily can include query data in the e-mail messages your application sends. Adding the QUERY attribute to <CFMAIL> is similar to adding QUERY to a <CFOUTPUT> tag—the content inside the tags will repeat for each row of the query.

Additionally, if you add a GROUP attribute, you can nest a pair of <CFOUTPUT> tags within the <CFMAIL> tag. If you do, the inner <CFOUTPUT> block is repeated for every record from the query, and everything outside the <CFOUTPUT> block is output only when the value in the GROUP column changes. This is just like the GROUP behavior of the <CFOUTPUT> tag itself; see Chapter 11, "Creating Data-Driven Pages," for more information about grouping query results.

Listing 28.3 shows how the <CFMAIL> tag can be used with the QUERY and GROUP attributes to send data-driven e-mail messages. This example creates a CFML custom tag called <CF_SendOrderConfirmation>, which takes one attribute called OrderID, like this:

```
<!--- Send Confirmation E-Mail, via Custom Tag --->
<CF_SendOrderConfirmation
  OrderID="3">
```

The idea is for the tag to compose an order confirmation type of e-mail message for the person who placed the order, detailing the items she purchased and when. If you have ever purchased something online, you likely received such a confirmation e-mail immediately after placing your order. This custom tag is used in Chapter 29, "Online Commerce," after a user makes an actual purchase.

Note

You should save this listing as a file called `SendOrderConfirmation.cfm`, either in the special `CustomTags` folder or just in the same folder as the other examples from this chapter. See Chapter 22, "Building Reusable Components," for information about the `CustomTags` folder and CFML custom tags in general.

Listing 28.3 `SendOrderConfirmation1.cfm`—**Sending a Data-Driven E-mail Message**

```
<!--- Tag attributes --->
<CFPARAM NAME="ATTRIBUTES.OrderID" TYPE="numeric">

<!--- Retrieve order information from database --->
<CFQUERY DATASOURCE="#REQUEST.Datasource#" NAME="GetOrder">
  SELECT
    c.ContactID, c.FirstName, c.LastName, c.Email,
    o.OrderDate, o.ShipAddress, o.ShipCity,
    o.ShipState, o.ShipZip, o.ShipCountry,
    oi.OrderQty, oi.ItemPrice,
    m.MerchName,
    f.MovieTitle
  FROM
    Contacts c,
    MerchandiseOrders o,
    MerchandiseOrdersItems oi,
    Merchandise m,
    Films f
  WHERE
    o.OrderID = #ATTRIBUTES.OrderID#
    AND c.ContactID = o.ContactID
    AND m.MerchID   = oi.ItemID
    AND o.OrderID   = oi.OrderID
    AND f.FilmID    = m.FilmID
  ORDER BY
    m.MerchName
</CFQUERY>

<!--- Re-Query the GetOrders query to find total $ spent --->
<!--- The DBTYPE="Query" invokes CF's "Query Of Queries" --->
<CFQUERY DBTYPE="Query" NAME="GetTotal">
  SELECT SUM(ItemPrice * OrderQty) AS OrderTotal
  FROM GetOrder
</CFQUERY>

<!--- We do not want ColdFusion to suppress whitespace here --->
<CFPROCESSINGDIRECTIVE SUPPRESSWHITESPACE="No">

<!--- Send E-mail to the user --->
<!--- Because of the GROUP attribute, the inner <CFOUTPUT> --->
<!--- block will be repeated for each item in the order --->
<CFMAIL
  QUERY="GetOrder"
  GROUP="ContactID"
  GROUPCASESENSITIVE="No"
  STARTROW="1"
  SUBJECT="Thanks for your order (Order number #ATTRIBUTES.OrderID#)"
  TO="""#FirstName# #LastName#"" <#Email#>"
```

Listing 28.3 Continued

```
  FROM="""Orange Whip Online Store"" <orders@orangewhipstudios.com>"
>Thank you for ordering from Orange Whip Studios.
Here are the details of your order, which will ship shortly.
Please save or print this E-mail for your records.

Order Number:  #ATTRIBUTES.OrderID#
Items Ordered: #RecordCount#
Date of Order: #DateFormat(OrderDate, "dddd, mmmm d, yyyy")#
               #TimeFormat(OrderDate)#

------------------------------------------------------
<CFOUTPUT>
#CurrentRow#. #MerchName#
   (in commemoration of the film "#MovieTitle#")
   Price: #LSCurrencyFormat(ItemPrice)#
   Qty:   #OrderQty#
</CFOUTPUT>
------------------------------------------------------
Order Total: #LSCurrencyFormat(GetTotal.OrderTotal)#

This order will be shipped to:;;
#FirstName# #LastName#
#ShipAddress#
#ShipCity#
#ShipState# #ShipZip# #ShipCountry#

If you have any questions, please write back to us at
orders@orangewhipstudios.com, or just reply to this email.
</CFMAIL>

</CFPROCESSINGDIRECTIVE>
```

The first thing this listing needs to do is to retrieve all the relevant information about the order from the database, including the orderer's name and shipping address; the name, price, and quantity of each item ordered; and the title of the movie that goes along with each item. This is all obtained using a single query called `GetOrder`, which is somewhat long but is fairly straightforward.

The `GetOrders` query returns one row for each item that was ordered in the specified `OrderID`. Because there is, by definition, only one row for each `OrderID` and only one `ContactID` for each order, the columns from the `MerchandiseOrders` and `Contacts` tables (marked with the `o` and `c` aliases in the query) will have the same values for each row. Therefore, the query can be thought of as being grouped by the `ContactID` column (or any of the other columns from the `MerchandiseOrders` or `Contacts` tables).

Next, ColdFusion's Query Of Queries feature is used to get the grand total of the order, which is simply the sum of each price times the quantity ordered. This query returns just one row (because there is no `GROUP BY` clause) and just one column (called `OrderTotal`), which means that the total can be output at any time by referring to `GetTotal.OrderTotal`. For more information about `DBTYPE="Query"`, the Query of Queries feature, and the `SUM` function used in this query, see Chapter 31, "More About SQL and Queries."

Tip

You could forgo the GetTotal query and just add the prices by looping over the GetOrders query, as in the OrderHistory2.cfm template from Chapter 21. However, getting the total via the Query Of Queries feature is a quick and convenient way to obtain the total, using familiar SQL-style syntax.

Tip

In general, you should use the <CFPROCESSINGDIRECTIVE> tag with SUPPRESSWHITESPACE="No" whenever you send data-driven e-mail. The exception would be if you were using TYPE="HTML" in the <CFMAIL> tag, in which case you should leave the whitespace-suppression options alone. See the section "Sending HTML-Formatted Mail," later in the chapter, for details.

Now the <CFMAIL> tag is used to actually send the confirmation message. Because the QUERY attribute is set to the GetOrder query, the columns in that query can be freely referred to in the TO attribute and the body of the e-mail message itself. Columns specific to each item ordered are referred to within the <CFOUTPUT> block. Columns specific to just the order in general are referred to outside the <CFOUTPUT> block, which will be repeated only once because there is only one group of records as defined by the GROUP attribute (that is, all the query records have the same ContactID value).

The custom tag you just created is used in Chapter 29, "Online Commerce," after a user makes an actual purchase.

SENDING BULK MESSAGES

You easily can use ColdFusion to send messages to an entire mailing list. Simply execute a query that returns the e-mail addresses of all the people the message should be sent to, and then refer to the e-mail column of the query in the <CFMAIL> tag's TO attribute.

Listing 28.4 shows how easy sending a message to a mailing list is. This listing is similar to the Personnel Office Mailer templates from earlier (refer to Listings 28.1 and 28.2). It enables the user (presumably someone within Orange Whip Studio's Public Relations Department) to type a message, which will be sent to everyone on the studio's mailing list.

LISTING 28.4 SendBulkMail.cfm—SENDING A MESSAGE TO EVERYONE ON A MAILING LIST

```
<HTML>
<HEAD>
  <TITLE>Mailing List</TITLE>
  <!--- Apply simple CSS formatting to <TH> cells --->
  <STYLE>
    TH {background:blue;color:white;
        font-family:sans-serif;font-size:12px;
        text-align:right;padding:5px;}
  </STYLE>
</HEAD>

<!--- Put cursor in FirstName field when page loads --->
<BODY>
```

LISTING 28.4 CONTINUED

```
<!--- Page Title --->
<H2>Send Message To Mailing List</H2>

<!--- If the user is submitting the form... --->
<CFIF IsDefined("FORM.Subject")>
  <!--- Retrieve "mailing list" records from database --->
  <CFQUERY DATASOURCE="#REQUEST.DataSource#" NAME="GetList">
    SELECT FirstName, LastName, EMail
    FROM Contacts
    WHERE MailingList = 1
  </CFQUERY>

  <!--- Send the mail message, based on form input --->
  <CFMAIL
    QUERY="GetList"
    SUBJECT="#Form.Subject#"
    FROM="""Orange Whip Studios"" <mailings@orangewhipstudios.com>"
    TO="""#FirstName# #LastName#"" <#EMail#>"
    BCC="personneldirector@orangewhipstudios.com"
>#FORM.MessageBody#

-----------------------------------------------------
We respect your privacy here at Orange Whip Studios.
To be removed from this mailing list, reply to this
message with the word "Remove" in the subject line.
-----------------------------------------------------
</CFMAIL>

  <!--- Display "success" message to user --->
  <P>The email message was sent.<BR>
  By the way, you look fabulous today.
  You should be in pictures!<BR>

<!--- Otherwise, display the form to user... --->
<CFELSE>
  <!--- Provide simple form for recipient and message --->
  <CFFORM ACTION="#CGI.SCRIPT_NAME#" NAME="mailForm" METHOD="POST"
    onSubmit="return confirm('Are you sure? This message will be sent to everyone
➥ on the mailing list.
➥  This is your last chance to cancel the bulk mailing.')">

    <TABLE CELLPADDING="2" CELLSPACING="2">
      <!--- Table row: Input for E-mail Subject --->
      <TR>
        <TH>Subject:</TH>
        <TD>
          <CFINPUT
            TYPE="Text"
            NAME="Subject"
            REQUIRED="Yes"
            SIZE="40"
            MESSAGE="You must provide a subject for the e-mail.">
        </TD>
      </TR>
```

```
      <!--- Table row: Input for actual Message Text --->
      <TR>
        <TH>Your Message:</TH>
        <TD>
          <TEXTAREA
            NAME="MessageBody"
            COLS="30"
            ROWS="5"></TEXTAREA>

        </TD>
      </TR>

      <!--- Table row: Submit button to send message --->
      <TR>
        <TD></TD>
        <TD>
          <INPUT
            TYPE="Submit"
            VALUE="Send Message Now">
        </TD>
      </TR>
    </TABLE>
  </CFFORM>
</CFIF>

</BODY>
</HTML>
```

Like Listings 28.1 and 28.2, this listing presents a simple form to the user, in which a subject and message can be typed. When the form is submitted, the <CFIF> block at the top of the template is executed.

The GetList query retrieves the name and e-mail address for each person in the Contacts table who has consented to be on the mailing list (that is, where the Boolean MailingList column is set to 1, which represents true or yes). Then, the <CFMAIL> tag is used to send the message to each user. Because of the QUERY="GetList" attribute, <CFMAIL> executes once for each row in the query.

A few lines of text at the bottom of the message let each recipient know that he can remove himself from the mailing list by replying to the e-mail message with the word "Remove" in the subject line. Listing 28.12—in the "Creating Automated POP Agents" section of this chapter—demonstrates how ColdFusion can respond to these remove requests.

SENDING HTML-FORMATTED MAIL

As noted in Table 28.1, you can set the optional TYPE attribute of the <CFMAIL> tag to HTML, which enables you to use ordinary HTML tags to add formatting, images, and other media elements to your mail messages.

The following rules apply:

- **The recipient's e-mail client program must be HTML enabled**—Most modern e-mail clients (for instance, version 4 or later of Outlook Express or Netscape

Communicator) know how to display the contents of e-mail messages as HTML. However, if the message is read in a program that is not HTML enabled, the user will see the message literally, including the actual HTML tags.

- **The mail message should be a well-formed HTML document**—This includes opening and closing `<HTML>`, `<HEAD>`, and `<BODY>` tags.
- **All references to external URLs must be fully qualified, absolute URLs, including the `http://` or `https://`**—In particular, this includes the `HREF` attribute for links and the `SRC` attribute for images.

The version of the `<CF_SendOrderConfirmation>` tag in Listing 28.5 expands on the previous version (refer to Listing 28.3) by adding a `UseHTML` attribute. If the tag is called with `UseHTML="Yes"`, an HTML-formatted version of the confirmation e-mail is sent, including small pictures of each item that was ordered (see Figure 28.5). If `UseHTML` is `No` or is omitted, the e-mail is sent as plain text (as in the previous version).

Note

Although it is not something that is supported by ColdFusion directly, you can use <CFMAIL> to send *multipart mail messages*, which include both a plain-text and HTML-formatted version of the same message. This would enable you to send the same message to all users, without needing to know whether their mail clients can render HTML-formatted mail messages. The downside is that the doubling-up makes each mail message that much larger. Search the ColdFusion Developers Exchange for CFML custom tags that provide multipart mail functionality.

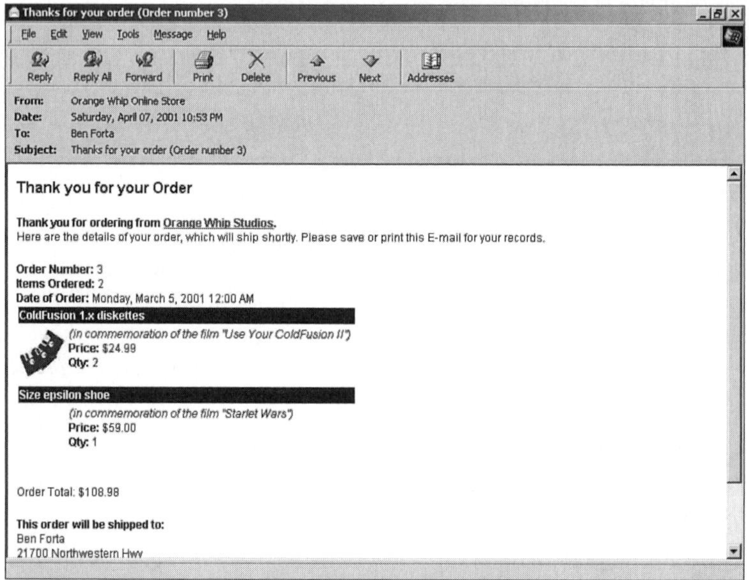

Figure 28.5 As long as the recipient's e-mail program supports HTML, your messages can include formatting, images, and so on.

LISTING 28.5 SendOrderConfirmation2.cfm—USING HTML TAGS TO FORMAT A MAIL MESSAGE

```
<!--- Tag attributes --->
<CFPARAM NAME="ATTRIBUTES.OrderID" TYPE="numeric">
<CFPARAM NAME="ATTRIBUTES.UseHTML" TYPE="boolean" DEFAULT="Yes">

<!--- Local variables --->
<CFSET ImgSrcPath  = "http://#CGI.HTTP_HOST#/ows/images">

<!--- Retrieve order information from database --->
<CFQUERY DATASOURCE="#REQUEST.Datasource#" NAME="GetOrder">
  SELECT
    c.ContactID, c.FirstName, c.LastName, c.Email,
    o.OrderDate, o.ShipAddress, o.ShipCity,
    o.ShipState, o.ShipZip, o.ShipCountry,
    oi.OrderQty, oi.ItemPrice,
    m.MerchName, m.ImageNameSmall,
    f.MovieTitle
  FROM
    Contacts c,
    MerchandiseOrders o,
    MerchandiseOrdersItems oi,
    Merchandise m,
    Films f
  WHERE
    o.OrderID = #ATTRIBUTES.OrderID#
    AND c.ContactID = o.ContactID
    AND m.MerchID   = oi.ItemID
    AND o.OrderID   = oi.OrderID
    AND f.FilmID    = m.FilmID
  ORDER BY
    m.MerchName
</CFQUERY>

<!--- Display an error message if query returned no records --->
<CFIF GetOrder.RecordCount EQ 0>
  <CFTHROW
    MESSAGE="Failed to obtain order information."
    DETAIL="Either the Order ID was incorrect, or order has no detail records.">
<!--- Display an error message if email blank or not valid --->
<CFELSEIF (GetOrder.Email does not contain "@")
  OR (GetOrder.Email does not contain ".")>
  <CFTHROW
    MESSAGE="Failed to obtain order information."
    DETAIL="E-Mail addresses need to have an @ sign and at least one 'dot'.">
</CFIF>

<!--- Query the GetOrders query to find total $$ --->
<CFQUERY DBTYPE="Query" NAME="GetTotal">
  SELECT SUM(ItemPrice * OrderQty) AS OrderTotal
  FROM GetOrder
</CFQUERY>


<!--- *** If we are sending HTML-Formatted Email *** --->
<CFIF ATTRIBUTES.UseHTML>
```

LISTING 28.5 CONTINUED

```
<!--- Send E-mail to the user --->
<!--- Because of the GROUP attribute, the inner <CFOUTPUT> --->
<!--- block will be repeated for each item in the order --->
<CFMAIL
  QUERY="GetOrder"
  GROUP="ContactID"
  GROUPCASESENSITIVE="No"
  STARTROW="1"
  SUBJECT="Thanks for your order (Order number #ATTRIBUTES.OrderID#)"
  TO="""#FirstName# #LastName#"" <#Email#>"
  FROM="""Orange Whip Online Store"" <orders@orangewhipstudios.com>"
  TYPE="HTML">

  <HTML>
  <HEAD>
    <STYLE TYPE="text/css">
      BODY {font-family:sans-serif;font-size:12px;color:navy}
      TD   {font-size:12px}
      TH   {font-size:12px;color:white;
            background:navy;text-align:left}
    </STYLE>
  </HEAD>
  <BODY>

  <H2>Thank you for your Order</H2>

  <P><B>Thank you for ordering from
  <A HREF="http://www.orangewhipstudios.com">Orange Whip Studios</A>.</B><BR>
  Here are the details of your order, which will ship shortly.
  Please save or print this E-mail for your records.<BR>

  <P>
  <STRONG>Order Number:</STRONG> #ATTRIBUTES.OrderID#<BR>
  <STRONG>Items Ordered:</STRONG> #RecordCount#<BR>
  <STRONG>Date of Order:</STRONG>
  #DateFormat(OrderDate, "dddd, mmmm d, yyyy")#
  #TimeFormat(OrderDate)#<BR>

  <TABLE>
    <CFOUTPUT>
      <TR VALIGN="top">
        <TH COLSPAN="2">
          #MerchName#
        </TH>
      </TR>
      <TR>
        <TD>
          <!--- If there is an image available... --->
          <CFIF ImageNameSmall NEQ "">
            <IMG SRC="#ImgSrcPath#/#ImageNameSmall#"
              ALT="#MerchName#"
              WIDTH="50" HEIGHT="50" BORDER="0">
          </CFIF>
        </TD>
        <TD>
```

```
            <EM>(in commemoration of the film "#MovieTitle#")</EM><BR>
            <STRONG>Price:</STRONG> #LSCurrencyFormat(ItemPrice)#<BR>
            <STRONG>Qty:</STRONG>   #OrderQty#<BR> <BR>
          </TD>
        </TR>
      </CFOUTPUT>
    </TABLE>

    <P>Order Total: #LSCurrencyFormat(GetTotal.OrderTotal)#<BR>

    <P><STRONG>This order will be shipped to:</STRONG><BR>
    #FirstName# #LastName#<BR>
    #ShipAddress#<BR>
    #ShipCity#<BR>
    #ShipState# #ShipZip# #ShipCountry#<BR>

    <P>If you have any questions, please write back to us at
    <a href="orders@orangewhipstudios.com">orders@orangewhipstudios.com</a>,
    or just reply to this email.<BR>
    </BODY>
    </HTML>
  </CFMAIL>


<!--- *** If we are NOT sending HTML-Formatted Email *** --->
<CFELSE>

<!--- We do not want ColdFusion to suppress whitespace here --->
<CFPROCESSINGDIRECTIVE SUPPRESSWHITESPACE="No">

<!--- Send E-mail to the user --->
<!--- Because of the GROUP attribute, the inner <CFOUTPUT> --->
<!--- block will be repeated for each item in the order --->
<CFMAIL
  QUERY="GetOrder"
  GROUP="ContactID"
  GROUPCASESENSITIVE="No"
  STARTROW="1"
  SUBJECT="Thanks for your order (Order number #ATTRIBUTES.OrderID#)"
  TO="""#FirstName# #LastName#"" <#Email#>"
  FROM="""Orange Whip Online Store"" <orders@orangewhipstudios.com>"
>Thank you for ordering from Orange Whip Studios.
Here are the details of your order, which will ship shortly.
Please save or print this E-mail for your records.

Order Number:  #ATTRIBUTES.OrderID#
Items Ordered: #RecordCount#
Date of Order: #DateFormat(OrderDate, "dddd, mmmm d, yyyy")#
               #TimeFormat(OrderDate)#

-------------------------------------------------------
<CFOUTPUT>
#CurrentRow#. #MerchName#
   (in commemoration of the film "#MovieTitle#")
   Price: #LSCurrencyFormat(ItemPrice)#
   Qty:   #OrderQty#
</CFOUTPUT>
-------------------------------------------------------
```

LISTING 28.5 CONTINUED

```
Order Total: #LSCurrencyFormat(GetTotal.OrderTotal)#

This order will be shipped to:
#FirstName# #LastName#
#ShipAddress#
#ShipCity#
#ShipState# #ShipZip# #ShipCountry#

If you have any questions, please write back to us at
orders@orangewhipstudios.com, or just reply to this email.
</CFMAIL>

</CFPROCESSINGDIRECTIVE>

</CFIF>
```

In most respects, Listing 28.5 is nearly identical to the prior version (refer to Listing 28.3). A simple `<CFIF>` determines whether the tag is being called with `UseHTML="Yes"`. If so, `<CFMAIL>` is used with `TYPE="HTML"` to send an HTML-formatted message. If not, a separate `<CFMAIL>` tag is used to send a plain-text message. Note that the `<CFPROCESSINGDIRECTIVE>` tag is needed only around the plain-text version of the message because HTML is not sensitive to whitespace.

As already noted, a fully qualified URL must be provided for images to be correctly displayed in e-mail messages. To make this easier, a variable called `ImgSrcPath` is defined at the top of the template, which will always hold the fully qualified URL path to the `ows/images` folder. This variable can then be used in the `SRC` attribute of any `<IMG>` tags within the message. For instance, assuming that you are visiting a copy of ColdFusion server on your local machine, this variable will evaluate to something such as `http://localhost/ows/images/`.

Note

The `CGI.HTTP_HOST` variable can be used to refer to the hostname of the ColdFusion server. The `CGI.SERVER_NAME` also could be used to get the same value. For details, see Appendix C, "Special ColdFusion Variables and Result Codes."

In addition, Listing 28.5 does two quick checks after the `GetOrder` query to ensure that it makes sense for the rest of the template to continue. If the query fails to return any records, the `OrderID` passed to the tag is assumed to be invalid, and an appropriate error message is displayed. An error message is also displayed if the `E-mail` column returned by the query is blank or appears not to be a valid e-mail address (specifically, if it doesn't contain both an `@` sign and at least one dot (.) character).

Note

The error messages created by the `<CFTHROW>` tags in this example can be caught with the `<CFCATCH>` tag, as discussed in Chapter 33, "Error Handling."

Caution

If the recipient doesn't use an HTML-enabled mail client to read the message, the message will be shown literally, including the actual HTML tags. Therefore, you should send messages of TYPE="HTML" only if you know the recipient is using an HTML-enabled e-mail client program.

ADDING CUSTOM MAIL HEADERS

All SMTP e-mail messages contain a number of *mail headers*, which give Internet mail servers the information necessary to route the message to its destination. Mail headers also provide information used by the e-mail client program to show the message to the user, such as the message date and the sender's e-mail address.

ColdFusion allows you to add your own mail headers to mail messages, using the <CFMAILPARAM> tag.

Tip

You can see what these mail headers look like by using an ordinary e-mail client program. For instance, in Outlook Express, highlight a message in your Inbox, select Properties from the File menu, and then click the Details tab.

INTRODUCING THE <CFMAILPARAM> TAG

ColdFusion provides a tag called <CFMAILPARAM> that can be used to add custom headers to your mail messages. It also can be used to add attachments to your messages, which is discussed in the next section. The <CFMAILPARAM> tag is allowed only between opening and closing <CFMAIL> tags. Table 28.3 shows which attributes can be provided to <CFMAILPARAM>.

Note

Because <CFMAILPARAM> serves two distinct purposes, it might have made more sense if there were two separate tags—one called <CFMAILHEADER> and the other called <CFMAILATTACHMENT>. For whatever reason, CFML uses just the one tag (<CFMAILPARAM>) to represent both ideas (headers and attachments).

TABLE 28.3 <CFMAILPARAM> TAG ATTRIBUTES

Attribute	Purpose
NAME	The name of the custom mail header you want to add to the message. You can provide any mail header name you want; a common one is Reply-To, as discussed in this section. (You must provide a NAME or FILE attribute, but not both in the same <CFMAILPARAM> tag.)
VALUE	The actual value for the mail header specified by NAME. The type of string you provide for VALUE will depend on which mail header you are adding to the message. For instance, if NAME="Reply-To", the VALUE should be the e-mail address that should be used when people reply to the message. Required if the NAME attribute is provided.

TABLE 28.3 CONTINUED

Attribute	Purpose
FILE	The filename of document or other file that should be sent as an attachment to the mail message. The filename must include a fully qualified, filesystem-style path—for instance a drive letter if ColdFusion is running on a Windows machine. (You must provide a NAME or FILE attribute, but not both in the same <CFMAILPARAM> tag.)

SPECIFYING THE REPLY-TO ADDRESS

Before you use <CFMAILPARAM> to add a custom header to a mail message, you first need to know the name of the mail header you want to add and what its value should be. This book doesn't discuss all possible mail headers. You will need to refer to the SMTP specification or reference for a list of mail header names.

That said, probably the most common use of the <CFMAILPARAM> tag is to provide a *Reply-To* address for a mail message. As the name implies, the Reply-To address is the address that is used when a user uses the Reply feature in her e-mail client program. If a Reply-To address is present in the mail message, the reply will be sent to that address. If not, the reply is sent to the From address. In other words, the Reply-To address is a way to override the From address for the purpose of sending reply messages.

To include a Reply-To address for a message, simply add a <CFMAILPARAM> tag between the opening and closing <CFMAIL> tags, supplying a NAME of Reply-To and the desired e-mail address as the VALUE. This would look something like the following:

```
<!--- Include "Reply-To" address --->
<CFMAILPARAM
  NAME="Reply-To"
  VALUE="help@orangewhipstudios.com">
```

Or, to include a friendly name (as discussed in the "Using Friendly E-mail Addresses" section, earlier in this chapter), you would use something such as this:

```
<!--- Include "Reply-To" address --->
<CFMAILPARAM
  NAME="Reply-To"
  VALUE="""Customer Service"" <help@orangewhipstudios.com>">
```

ADDING ATTACHMENTS

As noted in Table 28.3, you can also use the <CFMAILPARAM> tag to add a file attachment to a mail message. Simply place a <CFMAILPARAM> tag between the opening and closing <CFMAIL> tags, specifying the attachment's filename with the FILE attribute. The filename must be provided as a fully qualified filesystem path, including the drive letter and/or volume name. It can't be expressed as a relative path or URL.

Note

The filename you provide for FILE must point to a location on the ColdFusion server's drives (or a location on the local network). It can't refer to a location on the browser machine. ColdFusion has no way to grab a document from the browser's drive. If you want a user to be able to attach a file to a <CFMAIL> e-mail, you first must have the user upload the file to the server. See Chapter 35, "Interacting with the Operating System," for details about file uploads.

Note

The attachment does not have to be within your Web server's document root. In fact, you might want to ensure that it is not, if you want people to be able to access it only via e-mail, rather than via the Web.

So, to add a Word document called BusinessPlan.doc as an attachment, you might include the following <CFMAILPARAM> tag between your opening and closing <CFMAIL> tags:

```
<!-- Attach business plan document to message --->
<CFMAILPARAM
  FILE="c:\OwsMailAttachments\BusinessPlan.doc">
```

Tip

To add multiple attachments to a message, simply provide multiple <CFMAILPARAM> tags, each specifying one FILE.

Note

As noted in Table 28.1, you also can use the older MIMEATTACH attribute of the <CFMAIL> tag to add an attachment, instead of coding a separate <CFMAILPARAM> tag. However, it is recommended that you use <CFMAILPARAM> instead because it is more flexible (it allows you to add more than one attachment to a single message).

OVERRIDING THE DEFAULT MAIL SERVER SETTINGS

Earlier in this chapter, you learned about the settings on the Mail/Mail Logging page of the ColdFusion Administrator (refer to Figure 28.1). These settings tell ColdFusion with which mail server to communicate to send the messages your templates generate. In most situations, you can simply provide these settings once, in the ColdFusion Administrator, and forget about them. ColdFusion will use the settings to send all messages.

However, you might encounter situations in which you want to specify the mail server settings within individual <CFMAIL> tags. For instance, your company might have two mail servers set up, one set aside for bulk messages and another for ordinary messages. Or, you might not have access to the ColdFusion Administrator for some reason, perhaps because your application is sitting on a shared ColdFusion server at an Internet service provider (ISP).

To specify the mail server for a particular <CFMAIL> tag, add the SERVER attribute, as explained in Table 28.4. You also can provide the PORT and TIMEOUT attributes to completely override all mail server settings from the ColdFusion Administrator.

Tip

If you need to provide these attributes for your `<CFMAIL>` tags, consider setting a variable called `REQUEST.MailServer` in your `Application.cfm` file and then specifying `SERVER="#REQUEST.MailServer#"` for each `<CFMAIL>` tag.

TABLE 28.4 ADDITIONAL <CFMAIL> ATTRIBUTES FOR OVERRIDING THE MAIL SERVER SETTINGS IN THE COLDFUSION ADMINISTRATOR

Attribute	Purpose
`SERVER`	Optional. The hostname or IP address of the mail server ColdFusion should use to actually send the message. If omitted, this defaults to the Mail Server setting on the Mail/Mail Logging page of the ColdFusion Administrator.
`PORT`	Optional. The port number on which the mail server is listening. If omitted, this defaults to the Server Port setting on the Mail/Mail Logging page of the ColdFusion Administrator. The standard port number is `25`. Unless your mail server has been set up in a nonstandard way, you should never need to specify the `PORT`.
`TIMEOUT`	Optional. The number of seconds ColdFusion should spend trying to connect to the mail server. If omitted, this defaults to the Connection Timeout setting on the Mail/Mail Logging page of the ColdFusion Administrator.

RETRIEVING E-MAIL WITH COLDFUSION

You already have learned how the `<CFMAIL>` tag can be used to send mail messages via your ColdFusion templates. You also can create ColdFusion templates that receive and process incoming mail messages. What your templates do with the messages is up to you. You might display each message to the user, or you might have ColdFusion periodically monitor the contents of a particular mailbox, responding to each incoming message in some way.

INTRODUCING THE <CFPOP> TAG

To check or receive e-mail messages with ColdFusion, you use the `<CFPOP>` tag, providing the username and password for the e-mail mailbox you want ColdFusion to look in. ColdFusion will connect to the appropriate mail server in the same way that your own e-mail client program connects to retrieve your mail for you.

Table 28.5 lists the attributes supported by the `<CFPOP>` tag.

Note

The `<CFPOP>` tag can only be used to check e-mail that is sitting on a mail server that uses the Post Office Protocol (POP, or POP3). POP servers are by far the most popular type of mailbox server, largely because the POP protocol is very simple. Some mail servers use the newer Internet Mail Access Protocol (IMAP, or IMAP4). The `<CFPOP>`

tag can't be used to retrieve messages from IMAP mailboxes. Perhaps a future version of ColdFusion will include a <CFIMAP> tag; until then, some third-party solutions are available at the Developers Exchange Web site (`http://www.allaire.com/developer/gallery/`).

TABLE 28.5 <CFPOP> TAG ATTRIBUTES

Attribute	Purpose
ACTION	`GetHeaderOnly`, `GetAll`, or `Delete`. Use `GetHeaderOnly` to quickly retrieve just the basic information (the subject, who it is from, and so on) about messages, without retrieving the messages themselves. Use `GetAll` to retrieve actual messages, including any attachments (which might take some time). Use `Delete` to delete a message from the mailbox.
SERVER	Required. The POP server to which ColdFusion should connect. You can provide either a hostname, such as `pop.orangewhipstudios.com`, or an IP address.
USERNAME	Required. The username for the POP mailbox ColdFusion should access. This is likely to be case sensitive, depending on the POP server.
PASSWORD	Required. The password for the POP mailbox ColdFusion should access. This is likely to be case sensitive, depending on the POP server.
NAME	ColdFusion places information about incoming messages into a query object. You will loop through the records in the query to perform whatever processing you need for each message. Provide a name (such as `GetMessages`) for the query object here. This attribute is required if the `ACTION` is `GetHeaderOnly` or `GetAll`.
MAXROWS	Optional. The maximum number of messages that should be retrieved. Because you don't know how many messages might be in the mailbox you are accessing, it is usually a good idea to provide `MAXROWS` unless you are providing `MESSAGENUMBER` (later in this table).
STARTROW	Optional. The first message that should be retrieved. If, for instance, you already have processed the first 10 messages currently in the mailbox, you could specify `STARTROW="11"` to start at the 11th message.
MESSAGENUMBER	Optional. If the `ACTION` is `GetHeaderOnly` or `GetAll`, you can use this attribute to specify messages to retrieve from the POP server. If the `ACTION` is `DELETE`, this is the message or messages you want to delete from the mailbox. In either case, you can provide either a single message number or a comma-separated list of message numbers.
ATTACHMENTPATH	Optional. If the `ACTION` is `GetAll`, you can specify a directory on the server's drive in which ColdFusion should save any attachments. If you don't provide this attribute, the attachments will not be saved.

TABLE 28.5 CONTINUED

Attribute	Purpose
GENERATEUNIQUEFILENAMES	Optional. This attribute should be provided only if you are using the ATTACHMENTPATH attribute. If Yes, ColdFusion will ensure that two attachments that happen to have the same filename will get unique filenames when they are saved on the server's drive. If No (the default), each attachment is saved with its original filename, regardless of whether a file with the same name already exists in the ATTACHMENTPATH directory.
PORT	Optional. If the POP server specified in SERVER is listening for requests on a nonstandard port, specify the port number here. The default value is 110, which is the standard port used by most POP servers.
TIMEOUT	Optional. This attribute indicates how many seconds ColdFusion should wait for each response from the POP server. The default value is 60.

When the `<CFPOP>` tag is used with `ACTION="GetHeaderOnly"`, it will return a query object that contains one row for each message in the specified mailbox. The columns of the query object are shown in Table 28.6.

TABLE 28.6 COLUMNS RETURNED BY <CFPOP> WHEN ACTION="GetHeaderOnly"

Column	Explanation
MESSAGENUMBER	A number that represents the slot the current message is occupying in the mailbox on the POP server. The first message that arrives in a user's mailbox is message number one. The next one to arrive is message number two. When a message is deleted, any message behind the deleted message moves into the deleted message's slot. That is, if the first message is deleted, the second message becomes message number one. In other words, the MESSAGENUMBER is not a unique identifier for the message. It is simply a way to refer to the messages currently in the mailbox.
DATE	The date the message was originally sent. Unfortunately, this date value is not returned as a native CFML Date object. You must use the ParseDateTime() function to turn the value into something with which you can use ColdFusion's date functions (see Listing 28.6, later in this chapter, for an example).
SUBJECT	The subject line of the message.
FROM	The e-mail address that the message is reported to be from. This address might or might not contain a friendly name for the sender, delimited by quotation marks and angle brackets (see the section "Using Friendly E-mail Addresses," earlier in this chapter). It is worth noting that the FROM address is not guaranteed to be a real e-mail address that can actually receive replies.

Column	Explanation
TO	The e-mail address to which the message was sent. This address might or might not contain a friendly name for the sender, delimited by quotation marks and angle brackets (see the section "Using Friendly E-mail Addresses," earlier in this chapter).
CC	The e-mail address or addresses to which the message was CC'd, if any. You can use ColdFusion's list functions to get the individual e-mail addresses. Each address might or might not contain a friendly name for the sender, delimited by quotation marks and angle brackets (see the section "Using Friendly E-mail Addresses," earlier in this chapter).
REPLYTO	The address to use when replying to the message, if provided. If the message's sender did not provide a Reply-To address, the column will contain an empty string, in which case it would be most appropriate for replies to go to the FROM address. This address might or might not contain a friendly name for the sender, delimited by quotation marks and angle brackets (see the section "Using Friendly E-mail Addresses," earlier in this chapter).

If the <CFPOP> tag is used with ACTION="GetAll", the returned query object will contain all the columns from Table 28.6, plus the columns listed in Table 28.7.

TABLE 28.7 ADDITIONAL COLUMNS RETURNED BY <CFPOP> WHEN ACTION="GetAll"

Column	Explanation
BODY	The actual body of the message, as a simple string. This string usually contains just plain text, but if the message was sent as an HTML-formatted message, it contains HTML tags. You can check for the presence of a Content-Type header value of text/html to determine whether the message is HTML formatted (see Listing 28.8, later in this chapter, for an example).
HEADER	The raw, unparsed header section of the message. This usually contains information about how the message was routed to the mail server, along with information about which program was used to send the message, the MIME content type of the message, and so on. You need to know about the header names defined by the SMTP protocol (see the section "Adding Custom Mail Headers," earlier in this chapter) to make use of the HEADER.
ATTACHMENTS	If you provided an ATTACHMENTPATH attribute to the <CFPOP> tag, this column contains a list of the attachment filenames as they were named when originally attached to the message. The list of attachments is separated by tab characters. You can use ColdFusion's list functions to process the list, but you must specify Chr(9) (which is the tab character) as the delimiter for each list function, as in ListLen(ATTACHMENTS, Chr(9)).

TABLE 28.7 CONTINUED

Column	Explanation
ATTACHMENTFILES	If you provided an ATTACHMENTPATH attribute to the <CFPOP> tag, this column contains a list of the attachment filenames as they were saved on the ColdFusion server (in the directory specified by ATTACHMENTPATH). You can use the values in this list to delete, show, or move the files after the message has been retrieved. Like the ATTACHMENTS column, this list is separated by tab characters.

RETRIEVING THE LIST OF MESSAGES

Most uses for <CFPOP> tag call for using all three of the ACTION values it supports. Whether you are using the tag to display messages to your users (such as a Web-based system for checking mail) or an automated agent that responds to incoming e-mail messages on its own, the sequence of events probably involves these steps:

1. Log in to the mail server with ACTION="GetHeaderOnly" to get the list of messages currently in the specified mailbox. At this point, you can display or make decisions based on who the message is from, the date, or the subject line.
2. Use ACTION="GetAll" to retrieve the full text of individual messages.
3. Use ACTION="Delete" to delete messages.

Listing 28.6 is the first of three templates that demonstrate how to use <CFPOP> by creating a Web-based system for users to check their mail. This template asks the user to log in by providing the information ColdFusion needs to access her e-mail mailbox (her username, password, and mail server). It then checks the user's mailbox for messages and displays the From address, date, and subject line for each. The user can click each message's subject to read the full message.

LISTING 28.6 CheckMail.cfm—THE BEGINNINGS OF A SIMPLE POP CLIENT

```
<HTML>
<HEAD><TITLE>Check Your Mail</TITLE></HEAD>
<BODY>

<!--- Simple CSS-based formatting styles --->
<STYLE>
  BODY {font-family:sans-serif;font-size:12px}
  TH   {font-size:12px;background:navy;color:white}
  TD   {font-size:12px;background:lightgrey;color:navy}
</STYLE>
<H2>Check Your Mail</H2>


<!--- If user is logging out --->
<CFIF IsDefined("URL.Logout")>
  <CFSET StructDelete(SESSION, "Mail")>
</CFIF>
```

```
<!--- If we don't have a username/password --->
<CFIF NOT IsDefined("SESSION.Mail")>
  <!--- Show "mail server login" form --->
  <CFINCLUDE TEMPLATE="CheckMailLogin.cfm">
</CFIF>


<!--- If we need to contact server for list of messages --->
<!--- (if just logged in, or if clicked "Refresh" link) --->
<CFIF NOT IsDefined("SESSION.Mail.GetMessages") OR IsDefined("URL.Refresh")>
  <!--- Flush page output buffer --->
  <CFFLUSH>

  <!--- Contact POP Server and retrieve messages --->
  <CFPOP
    ACTION="GetHeaderOnly"
    NAME="SESSION.Mail.GetMessages"
    SERVER="#SESSION.Mail.POPServer#"
    USERNAME="#SESSION.Mail.Username#"
    PASSWORD="#SESSION.Mail.Password#"
    MAXROWS="50">
</CFIF>


<!--- If no messages were retrieved... --->
<CFIF SESSION.Mail.GetMessages.RecordCount EQ 0>
  <P>You have no mail messages at this time.<BR>

<!--- If messages were retrieved... --->
<CFELSE>
  <!--- Display Messages in HTML Table Format --->
  <TABLE BORDER="0" CELLSPACING="2" CELLSPACING="2" COLS="3" WIDTH="550">
    <!--- Column Headings for Table --->
    <TR>
      <TH WIDTH="100">Date Sent</TH>
      <TH WIDTH="200">From</TH>
      <TH WIDTH="200">Subject</TH>
    </TR>
    <!--- Display info about each message in a table row --->
    <CFOUTPUT QUERY="SESSION.Mail.GetMessages">
      <!--- Parse Date from the "date" mail header --->
      <CFSET MsgDate = ParseDateTime(Date, "POP")>
      <!--- Let user click on Subject to read full message --->
      <CFSET LinkURL = "CheckMailMsg2.cfm?MsgNum=#MessageNumber#">

      <TR VALIGN="baseline">
        <!--- Show parsed Date and Time for message--->
        <TD>
          <STRONG>#DateFormat(MsgDate)#</STRONG><BR>
          #TimeFormat(MsgDate)# #ReplyTo#
        </TD>
        <!--- Show "From" address, escaping brackets --->
        <TD>#HTMLEditFormat(From)#</TD>
        <TD><STRONG><A HREF="#LinkURL#">#Subject#</A></STRONG></TD>
      </TR>
    </CFOUTPUT>
  </TABLE>
```

Listing 28.6 Continued

```
  <!--- "Refresh" link to get new list of messages  --->
  <B><A HREF="CheckMail.cfm?Refresh=Yes">Refresh Message List</A></B><BR>
  <!--- "Log Out" link to discard SESSION.Mail info --->
  <A HREF="CheckMail.cfm?Logout=Yes">Log Out</A><BR>
</CFIF>


</BODY>
</HTML>
```

This template maintains a structure in the SESSION scope called SESSION.Mail. The SESSION.Mail structure holds information about the current user's POP server, username, and password. It also holds a query object called GetMessages, which is returned by the <CFPOP> tag when the user's mailbox is first checked.

At the top of the template, a <CFIF> test checks to see whether a URL parameter named Logout has been provided. If so, the SESSION.Mail structure is deleted from the server's memory, which effectively logs the user out. You will see how this works later.

Next, a similar <CFIF> tests checks to see whether the SESSION.Mail structure exists. If not, the template concludes that the user has not logged in yet, so it displays a simple login form by including the CheckMailLogin.cfm template (see Listing 28.7). This is the same basic login-check technique explained in Chapter 21. In any case, all code after this <CFIF> test is guaranteed to execute only if the user has logged in. The SESSION.Mail structure will contain Username, Password, and POPServer values, which can later be passed to all <CFPOP> tags for the remainder of the session.

The next <CFIF> test checks to see whether ColdFusion needs to access the user's mailbox to get a list of current messages. ColdFusion should do this whenever SESSION.Mail.GetMessages does not exist yet (which means that the user has just logged in) or if the page has been passed a Refresh parameter in the URL (which means that the user has just clicked the Refresh Message List link, as shown in Figure 28.6). If so, the <CFPOP> tag is called with ACTION="GetHeaderOnly", which means that ColdFusion should just get a list of messages from the mail server (which is usually pretty fast), rather than getting the actual test of each message (which can be quite slow, especially if some of the messages have attachments). Note that the <CFPOP> tag is provided with the username, password, and POP server name that the user provided when she first logged in (now available in the SESSION.Mail structure).

Note

The SESSION.Mail.GetMessages object returned by the tag contains columns called Date, Subject, From, To, CC, ReplyTo, and MessageNumber, as listed previously in Table 28.6. Because it is a query object, it also contains the automatic CurrentRow and RecordCount attributes returned by ordinary <CFQUERY> tags.

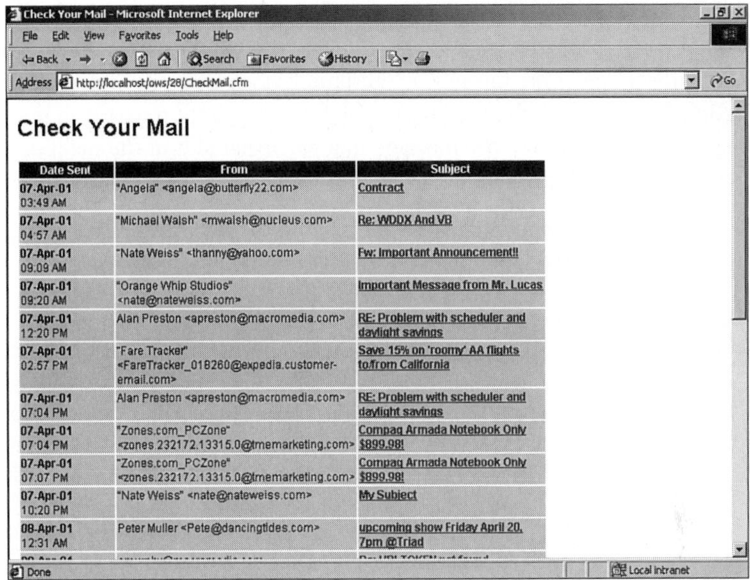

Figure 28.6
The <CFPOP> tag enables e-mail messages to be retrieved via ColdFusion templates.

At this point, the template has retrieved the list of current messages from the user's mailbox, so all that's left to do is to display them to the user. The remainder of Listing 28.6 simply outputs the list of messages in a simple HTML table format, using an ordinary `<CFOUTPUT>` block that loops over the `SESSION.Mail.GetMessages` query object. Within this loop, the code can refer to the `Date` column of the query object to access a message's date or to the `Subject` column to access the message's subject line. The first time through the loop, these variables refer to the first message retrieved from the user's mailbox. The second time, the variables refer to the second message, and so on.

Just inside the `<CFOUTPUT>` block, a ColdFusion date variable called `MsgDate` is created using the `ParseDateTime()` function with the optional `POP` attribute. This is necessary because the `Date` column returned by `<CFPOP>` does not contain native CFML date value as you might expect. Instead, it contains the date in the special date format required by the mail-sending protocol (SMTP). The `ParseDateTime()` function is needed to parse this special date string into a proper CFML `Date` value you can provide to ColdFusion's date functions (such as the `DateFormat()` and `DateAdd()` functions).

Note

Unfortunately, the format used for the date portion of mail messages varies somewhat. The `ParseDateTime()` function does not properly parse the date string that some incoming messages have. If the function encounters a date that it cannot parse correctly, an error message results. Some custom tag solutions to this problem are available at the ColdFusion Developers Exchange Web site (`http://www.allaire.com/developer/gallery`). Search for `POP and Date`.

Inside the <CFOUTPUT> block, the basic information about the message is output as a table row. The date of the message is shown using the DateFormat() and TimeFormat() functions. The Subject line of the message is presented as a link to the CheckMailMsg.cfm template (see Listing 28.8), passing the MessageNumber for the current message in the URL. Because the MessageNumber identifies the message in a particular slot in the mailbox, the user can click the subject to view the whole message.

At the bottom of the template, the user is provided with Refresh Message List and Log Out links, which simply reload the listing with either Refresh=Yes or Logout=Yes in the URL.

Note

Because e-mail addresses can contain angle brackets (see the section "Using Friendly E-mail Addresses," earlier in this chapter), you should always use the HTMLEditFormat() function when displaying an e-mail address returned by <CFPOP> in a Web page. Otherwise, the browser will think the angle brackets are meant to indicate an HTML tag, which means that the e-mail address will not show up visibly on the page (although it will be part of the page's HTML if you view source). Here, HTMLEditFormat() is used on the From column, but you should use it whenever you output the To, CC, or ReplyTo columns as well.

Listing 28.7 is a template that presents a login form to the user when he first visits CheckMail.cfm. It is included via the <CFINCLUDE> tag in Listing 28.6 whenever the SESSION.Mail structure does not exist (which means that the user has either logged out or has not logged in yet).

LISTING 28.7 CheckMailLogin.cfm—A SIMPLE LOGIN FORM, WHICH GETS INCLUDED BY CheckMail.cfm

```
<!--- If user is submitting username/password form --->
<CFIF IsDefined("FORM.POPServer")>
  <!--- Retain username, password, server in SESSION --->
  <CFSET SESSION.Mail = StructNew()>
  <CFSET SESSION.Mail.POPServer = FORM.POPServer>
  <CFSET SESSION.Mail.Username  = FORM.Username>
  <CFSET SESSION.Mail.Password  = FORM.Password>
  <!--- Remember server and username for next time --->
  <CFSET CLIENT.MailServer      = FORM.POPServer>
  <CFSET CLIENT.MailUsername    = FORM.Username>

<CFELSE>
  <!--- Use server/username from last time, if available --->
  <CFPARAM NAME="CLIENT.MailServer" TYPE="string" DEFAULT="">
  <CFPARAM NAME="CLIENT.MailUsername" TYPE="string" DEFAULT="">

  <!--- Simple form for user to provide mailbox info --->
  <CFFORM ACTION="#CGI.SCRIPT_NAME#" METHOD="POST">
    <P>To access your mail, please provide the
    server, username and password.<BR>

    <!--- FORM field: POPServer --->
    <P>Mail Server:<BR>
```

```
    <CFINPUT TYPE="Text" NAME="POPServer"
      VALUE="#CLIENT.MailServer#" REQUIRED="Yes"
      MESSAGE="Please provide your mail server.">
    (example: pop.yourcompany.com)<BR>

    <!--- FORM field: Username --->
    Mailbox Username:<BR>
    <CFINPUT TYPE="Text" NAME="Username"
      VALUE="#CLIENT.MailUsername#" REQUIRED="Yes"
      MESSAGE="Please provide your username.">
    (yourname@yourcompany.com)<BR>

    <!--- FORM field: Password --->
    Mailbox Password:<BR>
    <CFINPUT TYPE="Password" NAME="Password"
      REQUIRED="Yes"
      MESSAGE="Please provide your username."><BR>

    <INPUT TYPE="Submit" VALUE="Check Mail"><BR>
  </CFFORM>

  </BODY></HTML>
  <CFABORT>
</CFIF>
```

When the user first visits `CheckMail.cfm`, Listing 28.7 gets included. At first, the `FORM.POPServer` variable will not exist, so the `<CFELSE>` part of the code executes, which presents the login form to the user. When the form is submitted, it posts the user's entries to the `CheckMail.cfm` template, which in turn calls this template again. This time, `FORM.POPServer` exists, so the first part of the `<CFIF>` block executes. The `SESSION.Mail` structure is created, and the `POPServer`, `Username`, and `Password` values are copied from the user's form input into the structure so that they can be referred to during the rest of the session (or until the user logs out.

Note

If you accidentally enter an incorrect username or password while testing this listing, you will probably find that you have no way to reenter it (you must restart the ColdFusion server so the `SESSION.Mail` structure is discarded). This limitation is addressed in Chapter 33, "Error Handling."

Note

As a convenience to the user, Listing 28.7 stores the `POPServer` and `Username` values (which the user provides in the login form) as variables in the `CLIENT` scope. These values are passed to the `VALUE` attributes of the corresponding form fields the next time the user needs to log in. This way, the user must enter only his password on repeat visits.

RECEIVING AND DELETING MESSAGES

Listing 28.8 is the `CheckMailMsg.cfm` template the user will be directed to whenever she clicks the subject line in the list of messages (refer to Figure 28.6). This template requires that a URL parameter called `MsgNum` be passed to it, which indicates the `MESSAGENUMBER` of the message the user clicked. In addition, the template can be passed a `Delete` parameter, which indicates that the user wants to delete the specified message.

LISTING 28.8 `CheckMailMsg.cfm`—**RETRIEVING THE FULL TEXT OF AN INDIVIDUAL MESSAGE**

```
<HTML>
<HEAD><TITLE>Mail Message</TITLE></HEAD>
<BODY>

<!--- Simple CSS-based formatting styles --->
<STYLE>
  BODY {font-family:sans-serif;font-size:12px}
  TH   {font-size:12px;background:navy;color:white}
  TD   {font-size:12px;background:lightgrey;color:navy}
</STYLE>

<H2>Mail Message</H2>

<!--- A message number must be passed in the URL --->
<CFPARAM NAME="URL.MsgNum" TYPE="numeric">
<CFPARAM NAME="URL.Delete" TYPE="boolean" DEFAULT="No">

<!--- If we don't have a username/password --->
<!--- send user to main CheckMail.cfm page --->
<CFIF IsDefined("SESSION.Mail.GetMessages") EQ "No">
  <CFLOCATION URL="CheckMail.cfm">
</CFIF>

<!--- If the user is trying to delete the message --->
<CFIF URL.Delete>
  <!--- Contact POP Server and delete the message --->
  <CFPOP
    ACTION="Delete"
    MESSAGENUMBER="#URL.MsgNum#"
    SERVER="#SESSION.Mail.POPServer#"
    USERNAME="#SESSION.Mail.Username#"
    PASSWORD="#SESSION.Mail.Password#">

  <!--- Send user back to main "Check Mail" page --->
  <CFLOCATION URL="CheckMail.cfm?Refresh=Yes">


<!--- If not deleting, retrieve and show the message --->
<CFELSE>

  <!--- Contact POP Server and retrieve the message --->
  <CFPOP
    ACTION="GetAll"
    NAME="GetMsg"
    MESSAGENUMBER="#URL.MsgNum#"
    SERVER="#SESSION.Mail.POPServer#"
```

```
  USERNAME="#SESSION.Mail.Username#"
  PASSWORD="#SESSION.Mail.Password#">

<CFSET MsgDate = ParseDateTime(GetMsg.Date, "POP")>

<!--- If message was not retrieved from POP server --->
<CFIF GetMsg.RecordCount NEQ 1>
  <CFTHROW
    MESSAGE="Message could not be retrieved."
    DETAIL="Perhaps the message has already been deleted.">
</CFIF>

<!--- We will provide a link to Delete message --->
<CFSET DeleteURL = "#CGI.SCRIPT_NAME#?MsgNum=#MsgNum#&Delete=Yes">

<!--- Display message in a simple table format --->
<TABLE BORDER="0" CELLSPACING="0" CELLPADDING="3">
  <CFOUTPUT>
    <TR>
      <TH BGCOLOR="Wheat" ALIGN="left" NOWRAP>
        Message #URL.MsgNum# of #SESSION.Mail.GetMessages.RecordCount#
      </TH>
      <TD ALIGN="right" BGCOLOR="beige">
        <!--- Provide "Back" button, if appropriate --->
        <CFIF URL.MsgNum GT 1>
          <A HREF="CheckMailMsg.cfm?MsgNum=#Val(URL.MsgNum - 1)#">
            <IMG SRC="../images/BrowseBack.gif"
              WIDTH="40" HEIGHT="16" ALT="Back" BORDER="0"></A>
        </CFIF>
        <!--- Provide "Next" button, if appropriate --->
        <CFIF URL.MsgNum LT SESSION.Mail.GetMessages.RecordCount>
          <A HREF="CheckMailMsg.cfm?MsgNum=#Val(URL.MsgNum + 1)#">
            <IMG SRC="../images/BrowseNext.gif"
              WIDTH="40" HEIGHT="16" ALT="Next" BORDER="0"></A>
        </CFIF>
      </TD>
    </TR>
    <TR>
      <TH ALIGN="right">From:</TH>
      <TD>#HTMLEditFormat(GetMsg.From)#</TD>
    </TR>
    <CFIF GetMsg.CC NEQ "">
    <TR>
      <TH ALIGN="right">CC:</TH>
      <TD>#HTMLEditFormat(GetMsg.CC)#</TD>
    </TR>
    </CFIF>
    <TR>
      <TH ALIGN="right">Date:</TH>
      <TD>#DateFormat(MsgDate)# #TimeFormat(MsgDate)#</TD>
    </TR>
    <TR>
      <TH ALIGN="right">Subject:</TH>
      <TD>#GetMsg.Subject#</TD>
    </TR>
    <TR>
      <TD BGCOLOR="Beige" COLSPAN="2">
        <STRONG>Message:</STRONG><BR>
```

LISTING 28.8 CONTINUED

```
          <CFIF GetMsg.Header contains "Content-Type: text/html">
            #GetMsg.Body#
          <CFELSE>
            #HTMLCodeFormat(GetMsg.Body)#
          </CFIF>
        </TD>
      </TR>
    </CFOUTPUT>
  </TABLE>

  <CFOUTPUT>
    <!--- Provide link back to list of messages --->
    <STRONG><A HREF="CheckMail.cfm">Back To Message List</A></STRONG><BR>
    <!--- Provide link to Delete message --->
    <A HREF="#DeleteURL#">Delete Message</A><BR>
    <!--- "Log Out" link to discard SESSION.Mail info --->
    <A HREF="CheckMail.cfm?Logout=Yes">Log Out</A><BR>
  </CFOUTPUT>
</CFIF>

</BODY>
</HTML>
```

First, as a sanity check, the user is sent back to the `CheckMail.cfm` template (refer to Listing 28.6) if the `SESSION.Mail.GetMessages` query does not exist. This would happen if the user's session had timed out or if the user had somehow navigated to the page without logging in first. In any case, sending her back to `CheckMail.cfm` causes the login form to be displayed.

Next, a `<CFIF>` test is used to see whether `Delete=Yes` was passed in the URL. If so, the message is deleted using the `ACTION="Delete"` attribute of the `<CFPOP>` tag, specifying the passed `URL.MsgNum` as the `MESSAGENUMBER` to delete. The user is then sent back to `CheckMail.cfm` with `Refresh=Yes` in the URL, which causes `CheckMail.cfm` to recontact the mail server and repopulate the `SESSION.Mail.GetMessages` query with the revised list of messages (which should no longer include the deleted message).

If the user is not deleting the message, the template simply retrieves and displays it in a simple HTML table format. To do so, `<CFPOP>` is called again, this time with `ACTION="GetAll"` and the `MESSAGENUMBER` of the desired message. Then the columns returned by `<CFPOP>` can be displayed, much as they were in Listing 28.6. Because the `ACTION` was `GetAll`, this template could use the `BODY` and `HEADER` columns listed previously in Table 28.7. The end result is that the user has a convenient way to view, scroll through, and delete messages, as shown in Figure 28.7.

At the bottom of the template, the user is provided with the links to log out or return to the list of messages. She is also provided with a link to delete the current message, which simply reloads the current page with `Delete=Yes` in the URL, causing the Delete logic mentioned previously to execute.

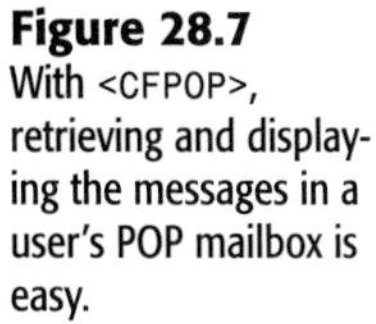

Figure 28.7
With <CFPOP>, retrieving and displaying the messages in a user's POP mailbox is easy.

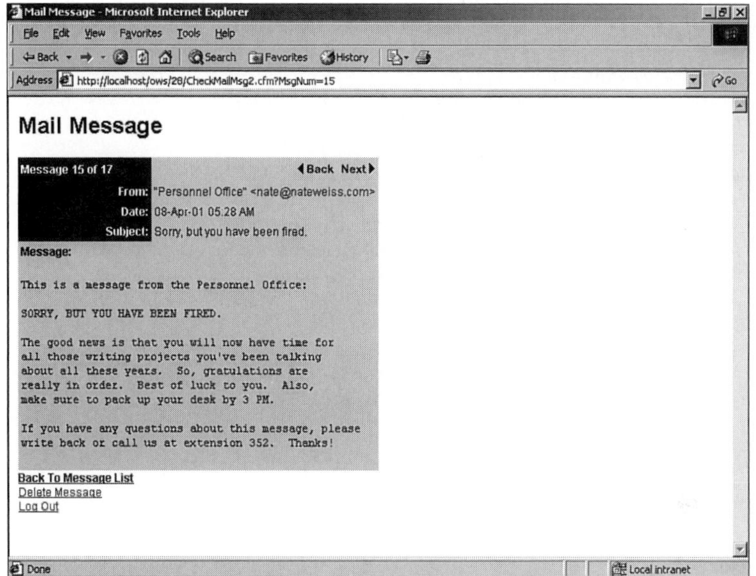

RECEIVING ATTACHMENTS

As noted previously in Table 28.5, the <CFPOP> tag includes an ATTACHMENTPATH attribute that, when provided, tells ColdFusion to save any attachments to a message to a folder on the server's drive. Your template can then process the attachments in whatever way is appropriate (move the files to a certain location, parse through them, display them to the user, or whatever your application needs).

RETRIEVING THE ATTACHMENTS

Listing 28.9 is a revised version of the CheckMailMsg.cfm template from Listing 28.8. This version enables the user to download and view any attachments that might be attached to each mail message. The most important change in this version is the addition of the ATTACHMENTPATH attribute, which specifies that any attachments should be placed in a subfolder named Attach (within the folder that the template itself is in).

LISTING 28.9 CheckMailMsg2.cfm—**ALLOWING THE USER TO ACCESS ATTACHMENTS**

```
<HTML>
<HEAD><TITLE>Mail Message</TITLE></HEAD>
<BODY>

<!--- Simple CSS-based formatting styles --->
<STYLE>
  BODY {font-family:sans-serif;font-size:12px}
  TH   {font-size:12px;background:navy;color:white}
  TD   {font-size:12px;background:lightgrey;color:navy}
</STYLE>
```

LISTING 28.9 CONTINUED

```
<H2>Mail Message</H2>

<!--- A message number must be passed in the URL --->
<CFPARAM NAME="URL.MsgNum" TYPE="numeric">
<CFPARAM NAME="URL.Delete" TYPE="boolean" DEFAULT="No">


<!--- Store attachments in "Attach" subfolder --->
<CFSET AttachDir = ExpandPath("Attach")>
<!--- Set a variable to hold the Tab character --->
<CFSET TAB = Chr(9)>

<!--- Create the folder if it doesn't already exist --->
<CFIF NOT DirectoryExists(AttachDir)>
  <CFDIRECTORY
    ACTION="Create"
    DIRECTORY="#AttachDir#">
</CFIF>

<!--- If we don't have a username/password --->
<!--- send user to main CheckMail.cfm page --->
<CFIF IsDefined("SESSION.Mail.GetMessages") EQ "No">
  <CFLOCATION URL="CheckMail.cfm">
</CFIF>

<!--- If the user is trying to delete the message --->
<CFIF URL.Delete>
  <!--- Contact POP Server and delete the message --->
  <CFPOP
    ACTION="Delete"
    MESSAGENUMBER="#URL.MsgNum#"
    SERVER="#SESSION.Mail.POPServer#"
    USERNAME="#SESSION.Mail.Username#"
    PASSWORD="#SESSION.Mail.Password#">

  <!--- Send user back to main "Check Mail" page --->
  <CFLOCATION URL="CheckMail.cfm?Refresh=Yes">


<!--- If not deleting, retrieve and show the message --->
<CFELSE>

  <!--- Contact POP Server and retrieve the message --->
  <CFPOP
    ACTION="GetAll"
    NAME="GetMsg"
    MESSAGENUMBER="#URL.MsgNum#"
    SERVER="#SESSION.Mail.POPServer#"
    USERNAME="#SESSION.Mail.Username#"
    PASSWORD="#SESSION.Mail.Password#"
    ATTACHMENTPATH="#AttachDir#"
    GENERATEUNIQUEFILENAMES="Yes">

  <!--- Parse message's date string to CF Date value --->
  <CFSET MsgDate = ParseDateTime(GetMsg.Date, "POP")>
```

```
<!--- If message was not retrieved from POP server --->
<CFIF GetMsg.RecordCount NEQ 1>
  <CFTHROW
    MESSAGE="Message could not be retrieved."
    DETAIL="Perhaps the message has already been deleted.">
</CFIF>

<!--- We will provide a link to Delete message --->
<CFSET DeleteURL = "#CGI.SCRIPT_NAME#?MsgNum=#MsgNum#&Delete=Yes">

<!--- Display message in a simple table format --->
<TABLE BORDER="0" CELLSPACING="0" CELLPADDING="3">
  <CFOUTPUT>
    <TR>
      <TH BGCOLOR="Wheat" ALIGN="left" NOWRAP>
        Message #URL.MsgNum# of #SESSION.Mail.GetMessages.RecordCount#
      </TH>
      <TD ALIGN="right" BGCOLOR="beige">
        <!--- Provide "Back" button, if appropriate --->
        <CFIF URL.MsgNum GT 1>
          <A HREF="CheckMailMsg.cfm?MsgNum=#Val(URL.MsgNum - 1)#">
            <IMG SRC="../images/BrowseBack.gif"
              WIDTH="40" HEIGHT="16" ALT="Back" BORDER="0"></A>
        </CFIF>
        <!--- Provide "Next" button, if appropriate --->
        <CFIF URL.MsgNum LT SESSION.Mail.GetMessages.RecordCount>
          <A HREF="CheckMailMsg.cfm?MsgNum=#Val(URL.MsgNum + 1)#">
            <IMG SRC="../images/BrowseNext.gif"
              WIDTH="40" HEIGHT="16" ALT="Next" BORDER="0"></A>
        </CFIF>
      </TD>
    </TR>
    <TR>
      <TH ALIGN="right">From:</TH>
      <TD>#HTMLEditFormat(GetMsg.From)#</TD>
    </TR>
    <CFIF GetMsg.CC NEQ "">
    <TR>
      <TH ALIGN="right">CC:</TH>
      <TD>#HTMLEditFormat(GetMsg.CC)#</TD>
    </TR>
    </CFIF>
    <TR>
      <TH ALIGN="right">Date:</TH>
      <TD>#DateFormat(MsgDate)# #TimeFormat(MsgDate)#</TD>
    </TR>
    <TR>
      <TH ALIGN="right">Subject:</TH>
      <TD>#GetMsg.Subject#</TD>
    </TR>
    <TR>
      <TD BGCOLOR="Beige" COLSPAN="2">
        <STRONG>Message:</STRONG><BR>

        <CFIF GetMsg.Header contains "Content-Type: text/html">
          #GetMsg.Body#
        <CFELSE>
          #HTMLCodeFormat(GetMsg.Body)#
```

LISTING 28.9 CONTINUED

```
          </CFIF>
        </TD>
      </TR>
      <!--- If this message has any attachments --->
      <CFSET NumAttachments = ListLen(GetMsg.Attachments, TAB)>
      <CFIF NumAttachments GT 1>
        <TR>
          <TH ALIGN="right">Attachments:</TH>
          <TD>
            <!--- For each attachment, provide a link  --->
            <CFLOOP FROM="1" TO="#NumAttachments#" INDEX="i">
              <!--- Original filename, as it was attached to message  --->
              <CFSET ThisFileOrig = ListGetAt(GetMsg.Attachments, i, TAB)>
              <!--- Full path to file, as it was saved on this server --->
              <CFSET ThisFilePath = ListGetAt(GetMsg.AttachmentFiles, i, TAB)>
              <!--- Relative URL to file, so user can click to get it --->
              <CFSET ThisFileURL  = "Attach/#GetFileFromPath(ThisFilePath)#">
              <!--- Actual link --->
              <A HREF="#ThisFileURL#">#ThisFileOrig#</A><BR>
            </CFLOOP>
          </TD>
        </TR>
      </CFIF>
    </CFOUTPUT>
  </TABLE>

  <CFOUTPUT>
    <!--- Provide link back to list of messages --->
    <STRONG><A HREF="CheckMail.cfm">Back To Message List</A></STRONG><BR>
    <!--- Provide link to Delete message --->
    <A HREF="#DeleteURL#">Delete Message</A><BR>
    <!--- "Log Out" link to discard SESSION.Mail info --->
    <A HREF="CheckMail.cfm?Logout=Yes">Log Out</A><BR>
  </CFOUTPUT>
</CFIF>

</BODY>
</HTML>
```

The first change is the addition of a variable called `AttachDir`, which is the complete path to the directory on the server that will hold attachment files. Additionally, a variable called `TAB` is created to hold a single Tab character (which is character number `9` in the standard character set). This way, the rest of the code can refer to `TAB` instead of `Chr(9)`, which improves code readability.

Tip

This code uses the variable name `TAB` in all caps instead of `Tab` to indicate the notion that the variable holds a *constant value*. A constant value is simply a value that will never change (that is, the Tab character will always be represented by ASCII code `9`). Developers often spell constants with capital letters to make them stand out. There is no need to do this, but you might find it helpful as you write your ColdFusion templates.

Note

This code uses the `ExpandPath()` function to set `AttachDir` to the subfolder named `Attach` within the folder that the template itself is in. See Appendix B, "ColdFusion Function Reference," for details about `ExpandPath()`.

Next, a `DirectoryExists()` test checks to see whether the `AttachDir` directory exists yet. If not, the directory is created via the `<CFDIRECTORY>` tag. See Chapter 35 for details about creating directories on the server. After the directory is known to exist, it is safe to provide the value of `AttachDir` to the `ATTACHMENTPATH` attribute of the `<CFPOP>` tag.

Note

This code also sets `GENERATEUNIQUEFILENAMES` to `Yes` so there is no danger of two attachment files with the same name (from different messages, say) being overwritten with one another. It is generally recommended that you do this to prevent the risk of two `<CFPOP>` requests interfering with one another.

Now, near the bottom of the template, the `ATTACHMENTS` and `ATTACHMENTFILES` columns of the `GetMsg` query object are examined to present any attachments to the user. As noted previously in Table 28.7, these two columns contain tab-separated lists of the message's file attachments (if any). Unlike most ColdFusion lists, these lists are separated with Tab characters, so any of ColdFusion's list functions must specify the Tab character as the delimiter.

For instance, the `NumAttachments` variable is set to the number of file attachments using a simple call to the `ListLen()` function. If at least one attachment exists, a simple `<CFLOOP>` block iterates through the list of attachments. Each time through the loop, the `ThisFileOrig` variable holds the original filename of the attachment (as the sender attached it), the `ThisFilePath` variable holds the unique filename used to save the file in `AttachDir`, and the `ThisFileURL` variable holds the appropriate relative URL for the file on the server. It is then quite easy to provide a simple link the user can click to view or save the file (as shown in Figure 28.8).

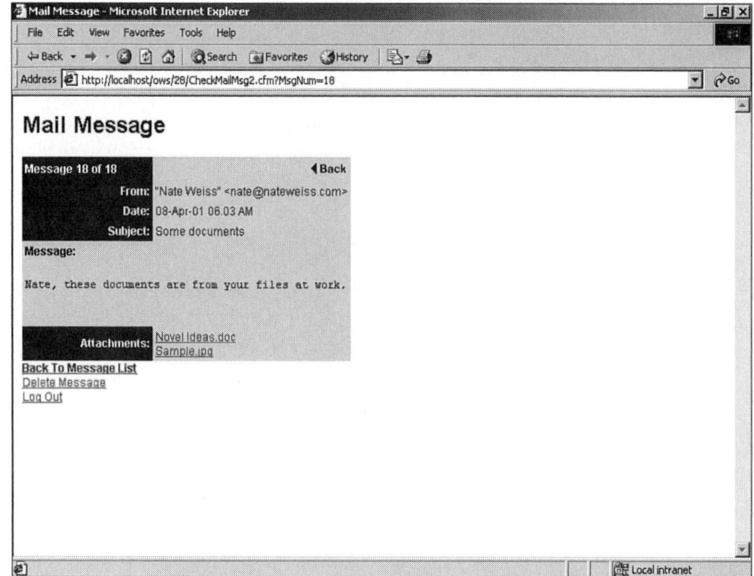

Figure 28.8
The <CFPOP> tag can retrieve files attached to messages in a mailbox.

DELETING ATTACHMENTS AFTER USE

One problem with Listing 28.9 is the fact that the attachment files that get placed into `AttachDir` are never deleted. Over time, the directory would fill up with every attachment for every message that was ever displayed by the template. It would be nice to delete the files when the user was finished looking at the message, but because of the stateless nature of the Web, you don' t really know when that is. You could delete each user's attachment files when he logs out, but the user could close his browser at any time, without logging out.

> **Note**
>
> Developers familiar with Active Server Pages (ASP) might point out that ASP provides a way to fire a template just before a session variable (similar to ColdFusion's `SESSION` scope) is discarded from the server's RAM. This template could take care of deleting the files in `AttachDir` that were created by each session. Unfortunately, there is no ColdFusion equivalent to ASP's `OnSessionEnd` event.

The most straightforward solution to this problem, strange at it might seem, is to simply create a ColdFusion template that deletes all files from the `AttachDir` folder that are older than, say, one hour. Then, use ColdFusion's template scheduler to execute the template once an hour, or whatever interval you feel is appropriate. This will keep the folder from filling up with old attachment files.

Listing 28.10 provides a template that deletes all files from `AttachDir` after they are more than one hour old. You could schedule this template to run periodically, using the ColdFusion Administrator. See Chapter 37, "Event Scheduling," for details.

LISTING 28.10 `DeleteAttachments.cfm`—**DELETING ATTACHMENT FILES PREVIOUSLY SAVED BY** `<CFPOP>`

```
<!--- Attachments are stored in "Attach" subfolder --->
<CFSET AttachDir = ExpandPath("Attach")>

<!--- Get a list of all files in the directory --->
<CFDIRECTORY
  DIRECTORY="#AttachDir#"
  NAME="GetFiles">

<!--- For each file in the directory --->
<CFLOOP QUERY="GetFiles">
  <!--- If it's a file (rather than a directory) --->
  <CFIF GetFiles.Type NEQ "Dir">
    <!--- If it's older than one hour --->
    <CFIF DateDiff("h", DateLastModified, Now()) GT 1>
      <!--- Get full filename of this file --->
      <CFSET ThisFile = ExpandPath("Attach\#GetFiles.Name#")>

      <!--- Go ahead and delete the file --->
      <CFFILE
        ACTION="DELETE"
        FILE="#ThisFile#">
    </CFIF>
  </CFIF>
</CFLOOP>
```

ANOTHER APPROACH

`CheckMailMsg3.cfm` (on this book's CD-ROM) is yet another version of `CheckMailMsg.cfm` that uses a different approach to provide the user with access to the attachments. When the user first views the message, the attachment filenames are displayed on the page, but the actual attachments are immediately deleted from disk. If the user clicks an attachment, the page is accessed again, this time passing the name of the desired attachment in the URL. The template code reexecutes, this time returning the requested file via the `<CFCONTENT>` tag. See Chapter 34, "Generating Non-HTML Content," for details about the `<CFCONTENT>` and `<CFHEADER>` tags used in this template.

The end result is that the user can access the files without the files ever needing to be stored on the server's drive. There is a significant downside, however, which is that the message is being re-retrieved from the server whenever the user clicks an attachment. If the attachments are many or large, this could mean quite a bit of extra processing time for ColdFusion. In general, the previous approach (Listing 28.9 coupled with Listing 28.10) is likely to serve you better in the long run.

Note

An interesting side effect of this approach is that the attachment files do not need to reside within the Web server's document root because they will be accessed only via `<CFCONTENT>`. Therefore, the `AttachDir` folder is set to the value returned by the `GetTempDirectory()` function, which is a reasonable place to store files that need to exist for only a short time. See Appendix B for information about `GetTempDirectory()`.

CREATING AUTOMATED POP AGENTS

You can create automated agents that watch for new messages in a particular mailbox and respond to the messages in some kind of intelligent way. First, you create an *agent template*, which is just an ordinary ColdFusion template that checks a mailbox and performs whatever type of automatic processing is necessary. This template should not contain any forms or links because it will not be viewed by any of your users. Then, using the ColdFusion scheduler, you schedule the template to be visited automatically every 10 minutes, or whatever interval you feel is appropriate.

CREATING THE AGENT TEMPLATE

Listing 28.11 creates a simple version of a typical agent template: an unsubscribe agent, which responds to user requests to be removed from mailing lists. If you look at the `SendBulkMail.cfm` template (refer to Listing 28.4), you will notice that all messages sent by the template include instructions for users who want to be removed from Orange Whip Studio's mailing list.

The instructions tell the user to send a reply to the e-mail with the word `Remove` in the subject line. Therefore, the main job of this template is to check the mailbox to which the replies will be sent (which is `mailings@orangewhipstudios.com` in this example). The template then checks each message's subject line. If it includes the word `Remove`, and the sender's e-mail address is found in the `Contacts` table, the user is removed from the mailing list by setting the user's `MailingList` field to `0` in the database. The next time the `SendBulkMail.cfm` is used to send a bulk message, the user will be excluded from the mailing.

LISTING 28.11 `ListUnsubscriber.cfm`—**AUTOMATICALLY UNSUBSCRIBING USERS FROM A MAILING LIST**

```
<!--- Mailbox info for "mailings@orangewhipstudios.com" --->
<CFSET POPServer = "pop.orangewhipstudios.com">
<CFSET Username  = "mailings">
<CFSET Password  = "ThreeOrangeWhips">

<!--- We will delete all messages in this list --->
<CFSET MsgDeleteList = "">

<HTML>
<HEAD><TITLE>List Unsubscriber Agent</TITLE></HEAD>
<BODY>
<H2>List Unsubscriber Agent</H2>
```

```
<P>Checking the mailings@orangewhipstudios.com mailbox for new messages...<BR>
This may take a minute, depending on traffic and the number of messages.<BR>

<!--- Flush output buffer so the above messages --->
<!--- are shown while <CFPOP> is doing its work --->
<CFFLUSH>

<!--- Contact POP Server and retrieve messages --->
<CFPOP
  ACTION="GetHeaderOnly"
  NAME="GetMessages"
  SERVER="#POPServer#"
  USERNAME="#Username#"
  PASSWORD="#Password#"
  MAXROWS="20">

<!--- Short status message --->
<CFOUTPUT>
  <P><STRONG>#GetMessages.RecordCount# messages to process.</STRONG><BR>
</CFOUTPUT>

<!--- For each message currently in the mailbox... --->
<CFLOOP QUERY="GetMessages">
  <!--- Short status message --->
  <CFOUTPUT>
    <P><STRONG>Message from:</STRONG> #HTMLEditFormat(GetMessages.From)#<BR>
  </CFOUTPUT>

  <!--- If the subject line contains the word "Remove" --->
  <CFIF GetMessages.Subject does not contain "Remove">
    <!--- Short status message --->
    Message does not contain "Remove".<BR>
  <CFELSE>
    <!--- Short status message --->
    Message contains "Remove".<BR>

    <!--- Which "word" in From address contains @ sign? --->
    <CFSET AddrPos = ListContains(GetMessages.From, "@", "<> ")>
    <!--- Assuming one of the "words" contains @ sign, --->
    <CFIF AddrPos EQ 0>
      <!--- Short status message --->
      Address not found in From line.<BR>
    <CFELSE>

      <!--- Email address is that word in From address --->
      <CFSET FromAddress = ListGetAt(GetMessages.From, AddrPos, "<> ")>

      <!--- Who in mailing list has this email address? --->
      <CFQUERY NAME="GetContact" DATASOURCE="#REQUEST.DataSource#" MAXROWS="1">
        SELECT ContactID, FirstName, LastName
        FROM Contacts
        WHERE Email = '#FromAddress#'
        AND MailingList = 1
      </CFQUERY>

      <!--- Assuming someone has this address... --->
      <CFIF GetContact.RecordCount EQ 0>
```

LISTING 28.11 CONTINUED

```
        <!--- Short status message --->
        <CFOUTPUT>Recipient #FromAddress# not on list.<BR></CFOUTPUT>
      <CFELSE>
        <!--- Short status message --->
        <CFOUTPUT>Removing #FromAddress# from list.<BR></CFOUTPUT>

        <!--- Update the database to take them off list --->
        <CFQUERY DATASOURCE="#REQUEST.DataSource#">
          UPDATE Contacts SET
            MailingList = 0
          WHERE ContactID = #GetContact.ContactID#
        </CFQUERY>

        <!--- Short status message --->
        Sending confirmation message via email.<BR>

        <!--- Mail user a confirmation note --->
        <CFMAIL
          TO="""#GetContact.FirstName# #GetContact.LastName#"" <#FromAddress#>"
          FROM="""Orange Whip Studios"" <mailings@orangewhipstudios.com>"
          SUBJECT="Mailing List Request"
        >You have been removed from our mailing list.</CFMAIL>

      </CFIF>
    </CFIF>
  </CFIF>

  <!--- Add this message to the list of ones to delete. --->
  <!--- If you wanted to only delete some messages, you --->
  <!--- would put some kind of <CFIF> test around this. --->
  <CFSET MsgDeleteList = ListAppend(MsgDeleteList, GetMessages.MessageNumber)>
</CFLOOP>


<!--- If there are messages to delete --->
<CFIF MsgDeleteList NEQ "">
  <!--- Short status message --->
  <P>Deleting messages...

  <!--- Flush output buffer so the above messages --->
  <!--- are shown while <CFPOP> is doing its work --->
  <CFFLUSH>

  <!--- Contact POP Server and delete messages --->
  <CFPOP
    ACTION="Delete"
    SERVER="#POPServer#"
    USERNAME="#Username#"
    PASSWORD="#Password#"
    MESSAGENUMBER="#MsgDeleteList#">

  Done.<BR>
</CFIF>

</BODY>
</HTML>
```

The code in Listing 28.11 is fairly simple. First, the `<CFPOP>` tag is used to retrieve the list of messages currently in the appropriate mailbox. Because the template needs to look only at the Subject line of each message, this template only ever needs to perform this `GetHeaderOnly` action (it never needs to retrieve the entirety of each message via `ACTION="GetAll"`).

Then, for each message, a series of tests are performed to determine whether the message is indeed a removal request from someone who is actually on the mailing list. First, it checks to see whether the Subject line contains the word `Remove`. If so, it now must extract the sender's e-mail address from the string in the message's `From` line (which might contain a friendly name or just an e-mail address). To do so, the template uses `ListContains()` to determine which word in the `From` line—if any—contains an `@` sign, where each word is separated by angle brackets or spaces. If such a word is found, that word is assumed to be the user's e-mail address and is stored in the `FromAddress` variable via the `ListGetAt()` function.

Next, the query named `GetContact` is run to determine whether a user with the e-mail address in question and who hasn't already been removed from the mailing list does indeed exist. If the query returns a row, the e-mail is coming from a legitimate e-mail address, and so represents a valid removal request.

Note

The `GetContact` query uses `MAXROWS="1"` just in case two users exist in the database with the e-mail address in question. If so, only one is removed from the mailing list.

The next `<CFQUERY>` updates the sender's record in the `Contacts` table, setting the `MailingList` column to `0`, effectively removing her from the mailing list. Finally, the sender is sent a confirmation note via a `<CFMAIL>` tag, so she knows her remove request has been received and processed.

The `<CFLOOP>` then moves on to the next message in the mailbox, until all messages have been processed. With each iteration, the current `MessageNumber` is appended to a simple ColdFusion list called `MsgDeleteList`. After all messages have been processed, they are deleted from the mailbox using the second `<CFPOP>` tag at the bottom of the template. As the template executes, messages are output for debugging purposes, so you can see what the template is doing if you visit using a browser (see Figure 28.9).

Tip

If you use the `<CFFLUSH>` tag before each `<CFPOP>` tag, as this template does, the messages output by the page is displayed in real time as the template executes. See Chapter 23, "Improving the User Experience," for details about `<CFFLUSH>`.

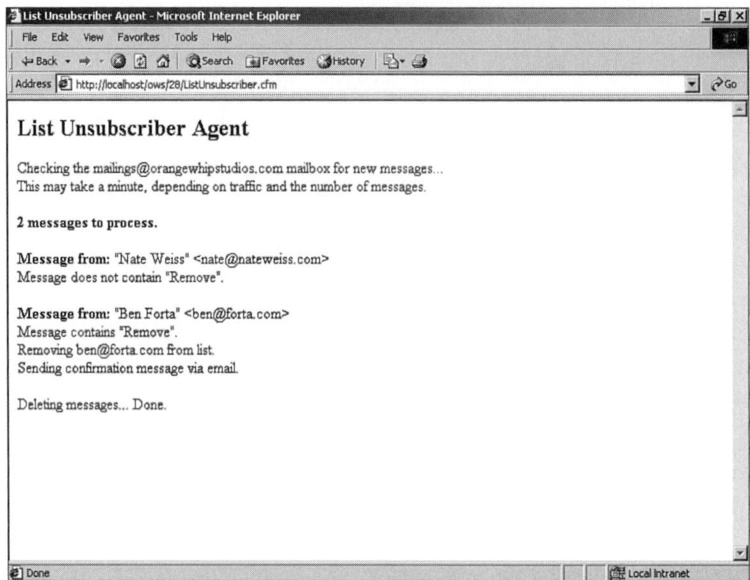

Figure 28.9
Automated POP agents can scan a mailbox for messages and act appropriately.

SCHEDULING THE AGENT TEMPLATE

After you have your agent template working properly, you should schedule for automatic, periodic execution using the ColdFusion Administrator or the `<CFSCHEDULE>` tag. See Chapter 37 for details.

OTHER USES FOR POP AGENTS

This example simply created a POP-based agent template that responds to unsubscribe requests. It could be expanded to serve as a full-fledged list server, responding to both subscribe and unsubscribe requests. It could even be in charge of forwarding incoming messages back out to members of the mailing list.

Note

That said, ColdFusion was not designed to be a round-the-clock, high-throughput, mail-generating engine. If you will be sending out tens of thousands of e-mail messages every hour, you should probably think about a different solution. You wouldn't want your ColdFusion server to be so busy tending to its mail delivery duties that it wasn't capable of responding to Web page requests in a timely fashion.

Other POP-based agents could be used to create auto-responder mailboxes that respond to incoming messages by sending back standard messages, perhaps with files attached. You could also create a different type of agent that examines incoming help messages for certain words and sends back messages that should solve the user's problem.

CHAPTER 29

Online Commerce

In this chapter

Building E-commerce Sites

For better or worse, more and more of today's World Wide Web is about selling goods and services, rather than providing freely available information for educational or other purposes. Once the realm of researchers, educators, and techies, the Net is now largely seen as a way to sell to a larger market with less overhead.

Whether this counts as progress is a debate that can be left for the history books. What it means for you as a Web developer is that sooner or later, you will probably need to build some type of e-commerce Web application, hopefully with ColdFusion.

Common Commerce Site Elements

No two commerce projects are exactly alike. Nearly every company will have its own idea about what its commerce application should look and feel like, complete with its own wish list and feature requirements.

That said, a number of common elements appear in one shape or another on most online commerce sites. If your project is about selling goods (or services) to the general public, it probably makes sense to implement something that users will be reasonably familiar with. This section discusses some of the elements that nearly all shopping sites have in common.

Storefront Area

Nearly any online shopping experience starts at some type of *storefront page*, where the user is presented with a top-level view of all the items or services for sale. Depending on the number of items, the items for sale are usually broken down by categories of some kind. From the main storefront page, users generally navigate to the item they want to purchase and then add the item to a shopping cart of some type.

Depending on the company, the storefront area might be the same thing as the company's home page and might occupy nearly all of its Web site. This is probably the case with an online bookstore or software reseller, for instance. In other situations, the storefront area is just a section of a larger site. For instance, Orange Whip Studio's online store is just a place to buy merchandise, such as posters and movie memorabilia. It's an important part of the site, but information about upcoming releases, lovely starlets, and investor relations will probably be the primary focus.

Note

The `Store.cfm` template presented in this chapter is Orange Whip Studio's storefront page.

Promotions and Featured Items

Most shopping sites also ensure that certain items really jump out at the user. Certain items are displayed prominently, labeled as a Sale Item, Featured Product, or other promotional term. These items are often sprinkled in callouts throughout the company's site, as a way of making users aware of items for sale without relying on them to find the product in the storefront.

Note

The <CF_MerchDisplay> custom tag provided in this chapter offers a simple way for featured merchandise to be displayed throughout Orange Whip Studio's Web site.

Shopping Cart

Of course, one of the most important aspects of most commerce sites is some notion of a shopping cart. Shopping carts are so ubiquitous on today's Web that users have come to expect them and navigate through them almost intuitively.

If you implement a shopping cart for your application, you should ensure that it looks and feels like carts on other sites, especially sites in similar industries. Typically, you will have some type of page where the user can see the contents of his cart. From there, the user should be able to remove items from his cart, change quantities, review the total price of the items in his cart, and enter some type of checkout process.

Note

The `StoreCart.cfm` template discussed in this chapter provides a simple shopping cart for the Orange Whip Studios online store.

Checkout Process

Again, most users coming to your site will already have a preconceived idea about what the checkout process will be like, so you should make it as straightforward and predictable as possible. This means forcing the user to fill out one or two pages of forms, on which he provides information such as shipping addresses and credit card information. Then, the user clicks some type of Purchase Now button, which generates some kind of Order Number and usually charges the user's credit card in real time.

Note

The `StoreCheckout.cfm` and `StoreCheckoutForm.cfm` templates in this chapter provide the checkout experience for Orange Whip Studio's virtual visitors.

Order Status and Package Tracking

If you are selling physical goods that need to be shipped after a purchase, users will expect there to be some way for them to check the status of their orders online. At a minimum, you should provide an e-mail address users can write to for finding the status of an order, but you should also consider building a page that allows the user to check the status of current and past orders in real time.

Many users also will expect to be able to track their packages online after they have been shipped. You usually can accomplish this via a simple link to the shipping carrier's Web site—such as `http://www.ups.com` or `http://www.fedex.com`—perhaps passing a tracking number in the URL). Visit the Web site of your shipping carrier for details (look for some type of developer's section).

Note

There isn't space in this chapter to explicitly discuss how to build such an order-tracking page, but the `OrderHistory.cfm` template discussed in Chapter 21, "Security with ColdFusion," is a solid start that gets you most of the way there.

Using a Secure Server

Before you deploy your commerce site onto a production server, you should consider investing in a Secure Sockets Layer (SSL) server certificate from a company such as VeriSign (`http://www.verisign.com`). You then can use the certificate to set up a secure Web server that uses encryption when communicating with Web browsers. This secured server might or might not reside on the same machines as the company's regular Web servers.

The secured Web server instance usually has its own document root (perhaps `c:\inetpub\secroot` instead of `c:\inetpub\wwwroot`), depending on your preferences and the Web server software you are using. Depending on your needs, some or all of your commerce application will be placed on the secure server. A typical scenario would put your checkout and order history pages on the secure server and leave the storefront and cart pages on the regular Web server. If so, the URL for the checkout page would likely be something such as `https://secure.orangewhipstudios.com/ows/Checkout.cfm` (instead of `http://www.orangewhipstudios.com/ows/Checkout.cfm`).

Note

SSL encryption is something you configure at the Web-server level and doesn't have anything to do with ColdFusion directly. Consult your Web server's documentation for details about how to enable SSL and HTTPS with the software you are using. See also Chapter 21.

Creating Storefronts

Before creating code for the shopping cart and checkout process, you should create a simple framework for displaying the products and services your company will be offering for purchase. Then, the items can be organized into an online storefront.

Displaying Individual Items

Listing 29.1 creates a CFML custom tag called `<CF_MerchDisplay>`. The tag displays a single piece of merchandise for sale, including a picture of the item and the appropriate Add to Cart link. This can be used to display a series of items in Orange Whip Studio's storefront page, as well as to feature individual items as callouts on the home page and throughout the site.

After this tag is in place, it can be used like this (where *`SomeMerchID`* is the name of a variable that identifies the desired item from the `Merchandise` table):

```
<!--- Show item for sale, via custom tag --->
<CF_MerchDisplay
```

```
MerchID="#SomeMerchID#"
ShowAddLink="Yes">
```


This custom tag is similar conceptually to the `<CF_ShowMovieCallout>` custom tag covered in Chapter 22, "Building Reusable Components." The two `<CFPARAM>` tags at the top force the tag to accept two attributes: the desired `MerchID` (which is required) and `ShowAddLink` (which is optional). If `ShowAddLink` is `Yes` or is not provided, the custom tag displays the merchandise item with a link for the user to add the item to her shopping cart. If `ShowAddLink` is `No`, the same content is displayed, but without the Add to Cart link.

Note

To make this custom tag available to ColdFusion, Listing 29.1 should be saved as a file called `MerchDisplay.cfm`, either within the special `CustomTags` folder or in the same folder as the templates that will call it. See Chapter 22 for more information about where to save custom tag templates and about CFML custom tags in general.

LISTING 29.1 `MerchDisplay.cfm`—**CREATING A CUSTOM TAG TO DISPLAY INDIVIDUAL ITEMS FOR SALE**

```
<CFSILENT>
  <!--- Tag Attributes --->
  <!--- MerchID to display (from Merchandise table) --->
  <CFPARAM NAME="ATTRIBUTES.MerchID" TYPE="numeric">
  <!--- Controls whether to show "Add To Cart" link --->
  <CFPARAM NAME="ATTRIBUTES.ShowAddLink" TYPE="boolean" DEFAULT="Yes">

  <!--- Get information about this part from database --->
  <!--- Query-Caching cuts down on database accesses. --->
  <CFQUERY NAME="GetMerch" DATASOURCE="#REQUEST.DataSource#"
    CACHEDWITHIN="#CreateTimeSpan(0,1,0,0)#">
    SELECT
      m.MerchName, m.MerchDescription, m.MerchPrice,
      m.ImageNameSmall, m.ImageNameLarge,
      f.FilmID, f.MovieTitle
    FROM
      Merchandise m INNER JOIN Films f
      ON m.FilmID = f.FilmID
    WHERE
      m.MerchID = #ATTRIBUTES.MerchID#
  </CFQUERY>

  <!--- Exit tag silently (no error) if item not found --->
  <CFIF GetMerch.RecordCount NEQ 1>
    <CFEXIT>
  </CFIF>

  <!--- URL for "Add To Cart" link/button --->
  <CFSET AddLinkURL = "StoreCart.cfm?AddMerchID=#ATTRIBUTES.MerchID#">
</CFSILENT>

<!--- Now display information about the merchandise --->
<CFOUTPUT>
  <TABLE WIDTH="300" CELLSPACING="0" BORDER="0">
    <TR>
```

Listing 29.1 Continued

```
      <!--- Pictures go on left --->
      <TD ALIGN="center">
        <!--- If there is an image available for item  --->
        <!--- (allow user to click for bigger picture) --->
        <CFIF GetMerch.ImageNameLarge NEQ "">
          <A HREF="../images/#GetMerch.ImageNameLarge#">
            <IMG SRC="../images/#GetMerch.ImageNameSmall#" BORDER="0"
            ALT="#GetMerch.MerchName# (click for larger picture)"></A>
        </CFIF>
      </TD>
      <!--- Item description, price, etc., go on right --->
      <TD STYLE="font-family:arial;font-size:12px">
        <!--- Name of item, associated movie title, etc --->
        <STRONG>#GetMerch.MerchName#</STRONG><BR>
        <FONT SIZE="1">From the film: #GetMerch.MovieTitle#</FONT><BR>
        #GetMerch.MerchDescription#<BR>
        <!--- Display Price --->
        <B>Price: #LSCurrencyFormat(GetMerch.MerchPrice)#</B>

        <!--- If we are supposed to show an "AddToCart" link --->
        <CFIF ATTRIBUTES.ShowAddLink>
          <A HREF="#AddLinkURL#">Add To Cart</A><BR>
        </CFIF>
      </TD>
    </TR>
  </TABLE>
</CFOUTPUT>
```

After the two `<CFPARAM>` tags, a simple query named `GetMerch` is used to get the relevant information about the piece of merchandise, based on the `MerchID` passed to the tag. If, for some reason, the `MerchID` no longer exists, the tag simply stops its processing via the `<CFEXIT>` tag (no error message is displayed and processing in the calling template continues normally). Next, a variable called `AddLinkURL` is constructed, which is the URL the user will be sent to if she decides to add the item to her shopping cart.

Tip

By using the `CACHEDWITHIN` attribute to cache the `GetMerch` query in ColdFusion's RAM, database interaction is kept to a minimum, which improves performance. See the section "Improving Query Performance with Caching" in Chapter 24, "Improving Performance," for details.

The rest of the template is straightforward. An HTML table is used to display a picture of the part (if available), based on the value of the `ImageNameSmall` column in the `Merchandise` table. The user can see a larger version of the image by clicking it.

This makes it easy to display various items for sale throughout a site, based on whatever logic your application calls for. For instance, assuming you already have run a query called `GetMerch` that includes a `MerchID` column, you could select a random `MerchID` from one of the query's rows, like so:

```
<!--- Pick an item at random to display as a "Feature" --->
<CFSET RandNum     = RandRange(1, GetMerch.RecordCount)>
<CFSET RandMerchID = GetMerch.MerchID[RandNum]>
```

The randomly selected merchandise could then be displayed with the following:

```
<!--- Display featured item --->
<CF_MerchDisplay
  MerchID="#RandMerchID#">
```


Collecting Items into a Store

Depending on the nature of the company, the actual store part of a Web site can be a sprawling, category-driven affair or something quite simple. Because Orange Whip Studios has a relatively low number of products for sale (less than 20 rows exist in the `Merchandise` table), the best thing might be to create a one-page store that just displays all items for sale.

Listing 29.2 outputs all the items currently available for sale in a two-column display, using ordinary HTML table tags. Because the job of actually displaying the product's name, image, and associated links is encapsulated within the `<CF_MerchDisplay>` custom tag, this simple storefront template turns out to be quite short.

Figure 29.1 shows what this storefront looks like in a user's browser.

Listing 29.2 `Store.cfm`—Displaying All Items for Sale

```
<!--- Get list of merchandise from database --->
<CFQUERY NAME="GetMerch" DATASOURCE="#REQUEST.DataSource#"
  CACHEDWITHIN="#CreateTimeSpan(0,1,0,0)#">
  SELECT MerchID, MerchPrice
  FROM Merchandise
  ORDER BY MerchName
</CFQUERY>

<!--- Show header images, etc., for Online Store --->
<CFINCLUDE TEMPLATE="StoreHeader.cfm">

<!--- Show merchandise in a HTML table --->
<P>
<TABLE>
  <TR>
    <!--- For each piece of merchandise --->
    <CFLOOP QUERY="GetMerch">
      <TD>
        <!--- Show this piece of merchandise --->
        <CF_MerchDisplay
          MerchID="#MerchID#">
      </TD>

      <!--- Alternate left and right columns --->
      <CFIF CurrentRow MOD 2 EQ 0></TR><TR></CFIF>
    </CFLOOP>
  </TR>
</TABLE>
```

Listing 29.2 Continued

```
</BODY>
</HTML>
```

Tip

By altering the `ORDER BY` part of the query, the items could be displayed in terms of popularity, price, or some other measure.

The `Store.cfm` template in Listing 29.2 displays a common storefront page header at the top of the page by including a file called `StoreHeader.cfm` via a `<CFINCLUDE>` tag. Listing 29.3 creates that header template, which displays Orange Whip Studio's logo, plus links marked Store Home, Shopping Cart, and Checkout. It also establishes a few default font settings via a `<STYLE>` block.

Listing 29.3 `StoreHeader.cfm`—Common Header for All Orange Whip's Shopping Pages

```
<!--- "Online Store" page title and header --->
<CFOUTPUT>
  <HTML>
  <HEAD><TITLE>#REQUEST.CompanyName# Online Store</TITLE></HEAD>
  <BODY>
  <STYLE TYPE="text/css">
    BODY {font-family:arial,helvetica,sans-serif;font-size:12px}
    TD   {font-size:12px}
    TH   {font-size:12px}
  </STYLE>

  <TABLE BORDER="0" WIDTH="100%">
    <TR>
      <TD WIDTH="101">
        <!--- Company logo, with link to company home page --->
        <A HREF="http://www.orangewhipstudios.com">
          <IMG SRC="../images/logo_c.gif"
            WIDTH="101" HEIGHT="101" ALT="" BORDER="0" ALIGN="left"></A>
      </TD>
      <TD>
        <HR>
        <STRONG>#REQUEST.CompanyName#</STRONG><BR>
        Online Store<BR CLEAR="all">
        <HR>
      </TD>
      <TD WIDTH="100" ALIGN="left">
        <!--- Link to "Shopping Cart" page --->
        <IMG SRC="../images/Arrow.gif" WIDTH="10" HEIGHT="9" ALT="" BORDER="0">
        <A HREF="Store.cfm">Store Home</A><BR>
        <!--- Link to "Shopping Cart" page --->
        <IMG SRC="../images/Arrow.gif" WIDTH="10" HEIGHT="9" ALT="" BORDER="0">
        <A HREF="StoreCart.cfm">Shopping Cart</A><BR>
        <!--- Link to "Checkout" page --->
        <IMG SRC="../images/Arrow.gif" WIDTH="10" HEIGHT="9" ALT="" BORDER="0">
        <A HREF="StoreCheckout.cfm">Checkout</A><BR>
```

```
        </TD>
      </TR>
    </TABLE>
     <BR>
</CFOUTPUT>
```

Figure 29.1
Orange Whip Studio's online store enables users to peruse the merchandise available for sale.

Note

This listing displays all the items for sale on the same page. If you will be selling many items, you might want to create a Next N interface for browsing through the merchandise in groups of 10 or 20 items per page. See Chapter 23, "Improving the User Experience," for information about how to build Next N interfaces.

Creating Shopping Carts

Not all shopping cart experiences are alike, but most are similar. After you have built one cart application, others will come naturally and quickly. This section presents one way of implementing a shopping cart, which you can adapt for your own applications. First, several approaches for remembering shopping cart contents are discussed. Then, a simple cart is assembled, using just a few ColdFusion templates.

Note

This section discusses a number of concepts that were introduced in Chapter 20, "Working with Sessions," including the definition of a Web-based session, as well as ColdFusion's special `CLIENT` and `SESSION` scopes. It is recommended that you read (or at least look through) Chapter 20 before you continue here.

STORING CART INFORMATION

One of the first things to consider when building a shopping cart is how the shopping cart information will be stored. Most users expect that they will be able to add items to a cart, go off somewhere else (perhaps back to your storefront page or to some other site to do comparison shopping), and then return sometime later to check out. This means you will need to maintain the contents of each user's cart somewhere.

No matter how you decide to store the information, you usually have at least two pieces of information to maintain:

- **The actual items the user has added to his cart**—In most situations, each item will have its own unique identifier (in the sample database, this is the `MerchID` column in the `Merchandise` table), so remembering which items the user has added to his cart is usually just a matter of remembering one or more ID numbers.
- **The desired quantity for each item**—Generally, when the item is first added to the cart, it is assumed that the user wants to purchase just one of that item. The user can usually increase the quantity for each item by adding the same item to his cart multiple times or by going to a View Cart page and entering the desired quantity directly into a text field.

As far as these examples are concerned, these two pieces of information—when considered together—comprise the user's shopping cart. In many situations, this is all you need to track. Sometimes, though, you will also need to track some kind of option for each item, such as a color or discounted price. You typically can deal with these extra modifiers in the same way that the quantity is dealt with in this chapter.

In any case, you can store this information in a number of ways. The most common approaches are summarized here.

`CLIENT`-SCOPED LISTS

Perhaps the simplest approach is to simply store the item IDs and quantities as variables in the `CLIENT` scope. As you learned in Chapter 20, the `CLIENT` scope can only be used to store simple values, rather than arrays, structures, and so on. So, the simplest option probably is to maintain two variables in the `CLIENT` scope, one being a ColdFusion-style list of `MerchIDs` and the other being a list of associated quantities.

Aside from its simplicity, one nice thing about this approach is that the user's cart will persist between visits, without you having to write any additional code (see Chapter 20 for details about how long `CLIENT` variables are maintained and how they can be stored in the server's registry, in a database, or as a cookie on the user's machine).

This is the principal approach taken by the examples in this chapter.

SESSION-SCOPED STRUCTURES AND ARRAYS

Another approach would be to maintain each user's shopping cart data in the `SESSION` scope. Unlike the `CLIENT` scope, the `SESSION` scope can contain structured data, such as structures and arrays. This means that your code can be a lot more elegant, especially if you have to track more information about each item than just the desired quantity.

For instance, you could have a structure called `SESSION.Cart`, which could hold an array of items called `SESSION.Cart.Items`. As the user adds items to the cart, you would add a corresponding structure to the `Items` array, where each structure contained `MerchID` and `Quant` values, plus whatever other modifiers you would need, such as color or size. So, you might refer to the ID of the first item in the user's cart as `SESSION.Cart.Items[1].MerchID` or the color of the second item as `SESSION.Cart.Items[2].Color`. The number of items in the cart would be available via `ArrayLen(SESSION.Cart.Items)`. To empty the cart, you would simply use `StructDelete(SESSION, "Cart")` or `ArrayClear(SESSION.Cart)`.

However, `SESSION` variables are RAM resident and not cluster aware, so you should stay away from this approach if you plan to run a number of ColdFusion servers together in a cluster. Another disadvantage is that shopping cart data would not persist between Web sessions, so users would not be able fill a cart on one day and then check out a couple of days later.

See Chapter 20 for more pros, cons, and techniques regarding session variables.

CART DATA IN A DATABASE

Another approach is to create additional tables in your database to hold cart information. If you were requiring your users to register before they could add items to their carts, you could use their `ContactID` (or whatever unique identifiers you were using for users) to associate cart contents with users. Therefore, you might have a table called `CartContents`, which would have columns such as `ContactID`, `MerchID`, `Quant`, `DateAdded`, plus whatever additional columns you might need, such as `Color` or `Size`. If you are not requiring users to register before using the cart, you could use the automatic `CLIENT.CFID` variable as a reasonably unique identifier for tracking cart contents.

This approach gives you more control than the others, in particular the capability to maintain easily queried historical information about which items have been added to carts most often and so on (as opposed to items that have actually been purchased). You would, however, probably need to come up with some type of mechanism for flushing very old cart records from the database because they would not automatically expire in the way that `SESSION` and `CLIENT` variables do.

Tip

This periodic table flushing could be done via a scheduled template, as explained in Chapter 37, "Event Scheduling."

Building a Shopping Cart

Now that a storefront has been constructed with Add To Cart links for each product, it is now time to build the actual shopping cart itself. This section creates two versions of a ColdFusion template called `StoreCart.cfm`.

If the `StoreCart.cfm` template is visited without any URL parameters, it displays the items in the user's cart and gives the user the opportunity to either change the quantity of each item or to check out, as shown in Figure 29.2. If a `MerchID` parameter is passed in the URL, that item is added to the user's cart before the cart is actually displayed. You will notice that the Add To Cart links generated by the `<CF_MerchDisplay>` custom tag (refer to Listing 29.1) do exactly that.

The Simplest Approach

The version of the `StoreCart.cfm` template in Listing 29.4 is probably one of the simplest shopping cart templates possible. As suggested in the "Storing Cart Information" section earlier in this chapter, each user's cart data is stored using two comma-separated lists in the `CLIENT` scope. The `CLIENT.CartMerchList` variable holds a comma-separated list of merchandise IDs, and `CLIENT.CartQuantList` holds a comma-separated list of corresponding quantities.

Tip

The next version of the template improves upon this one by removing all references to the way the user's cart data is actually being stored. It is recommended that you model your code after the next version of this template, rather than this one.

Note

For the links to the shopping cart page to work correctly, you should save Listing 29.4 as `StoreCart.cfm`, not `StoreCart1.cfm`.

Listing 29.4 `StoreCart1.cfm`—**A Simple Shopping Cart**

```
<!--- Show header images, etc., for Online Store --->
<CFINCLUDE TEMPLATE="StoreHeader.cfm">

<!--- URL parameter for MerchID --->
<CFPARAM NAME="URL.AddMerchID" TYPE="string" DEFAULT="">

<!--- These two variables track MerchIDs / Quantities  --->
<!--- for items in user's cart (start with empty cart) --->
<CFPARAM NAME="CLIENT.CartMerchList" TYPE="string" DEFAULT="">
<CFPARAM NAME="CLIENT.CartQuantList" TYPE="string" DEFAULT="">

<!--- If MerchID was passed in URL --->
<CFIF IsNumeric(URL.AddMerchID)>
  <!--- Get position, if any, of MerchID in cart list --->
  <CFSET CurrentListPos=ListFind(CartMerchList, URL.AddMerchID)>
  <!--- If this item *is not* already in cart, add it --->
  <CFIF CurrentListPos EQ 0>
    <CFSET CLIENT.CartMerchList=ListAppend(CLIENT.CartMerchList, URL.AddMerchID)>
```

```
    <CFSET CLIENT.CartQuantList=ListAppend(CLIENT.CartQuantList, 1)>
  <!--- If item *is* already in cart, change its qty --->
  <CFELSE>
    <CFSET CurrentQuant=ListGetAt(CLIENT.CartQuantList, CurrentListPos)>
    <CFSET UpdatedQuant=CurrentQuant + 1>
    <CFSET CLIENT.CartQuantList=ListSetAt(CLIENT.CartQuantList, CurrentListPos,
➥UpdatedQuant)>
  </CFIF>

<!--- If no MerchID passed in URL --->
<CFELSE>
  <!--- For each item currently in user's cart --->
  <CFLOOP FROM="1" TO="#ListLen(CLIENT.CartMerchList)#" INDEX="i">
    <CFSET ThisMerchID=ListGetAt(CLIENT.CartMerchList, i)>

    <!--- If FORM field exists for this item's Quant --->
    <CFIF IsDefined("FORM.Quant_#ThisMerchID#")>
      <!--- The FORM field value is the new quantity --->
      <CFSET NewQuant=FORM["Quant_#ThisMerchID#"]>
      <!--- If new quant is 0, remove item from cart --->
      <CFIF NewQuant EQ 0>
        <CFSET CLIENT.CartMerchList=ListDeleteAt(CLIENT.CartMerchList, i)>
        <CFSET CLIENT.CartQuantList=ListDeleteAt(CLIENT.CartQuantList, i)>
      <!--- Otherwise, Update cart with new quantity --->
      <CFELSE>
        <CFSET CLIENT.CartQuantList=ListSetAt(CLIENT.CartQuantList, i, NewQuant)>
      </CFIF>
    </CFIF>
  </CFLOOP>

  <!--- If user submitted form via "Checkout" button --->
  <CFIF IsDefined("FORM.IsCheckingOut")>
    <CFLOCATION URL="StoreCheckout.cfm">
  </CFIF>
</CFIF>

<!--- Stop here if user's cart is empty --->
<CFIF CLIENT.CartMerchList EQ "">
  There is nothing in your cart.
  <CFABORT>
</CFIF>

<!--- Create form that submits to this template --->
<CFFORM ACTION="#CGI.SCRIPT_NAME#">
  <TABLE>
    <TR>
      <TH COLSPAN="2" BGCOLOR="Silver">Your Shopping Cart</TH>
    </TR>
    <!--- For each piece of merchandise --->
    <CFLOOP FROM="1" TO="#ListLen(CLIENT.CartMerchList)#" INDEX="i">
      <CFSET ThisMerchID=ListGetAt(CLIENT.CartMerchList, i)>
      <CFSET ThisQuant=ListGetAt(CLIENT.CartQuantList, i)>
      <TR>
        <TD>
          <!--- Show this piece of merchandise --->
          <CF_MerchDisplay
            MerchID="#ThisMerchID#"
            ShowAddLink="No">
```

Listing 29.4 Continued

```
        </TD>
        <TD>
          <!--- Display Quantity in Text entry field --->
          <CFOUTPUT>
            Quantity:
            <INPUT TYPE="Text"
              NAME="Quant_#ThisMerchID#"
              SIZE="3"
              VALUE="#ThisQuant#">
          </CFOUTPUT>
        </TD>
      </TR>
    </CFLOOP>
  </TABLE>

  <!--- Submit button to update quantities --->
  <INPUT TYPE="Submit" VALUE="Update Quantities">

  <!--- Submit button to Check out --->
  <INPUT TYPE="Submit" VALUE="Checkout" NAME="IsCheckingOut">
</CFFORM>
```

The `<CFFORM>` section at the bottom of this template is what displays the contents of the user's cart, based on the contents of the `CLIENT.CartMerchList` and `CLIENT.CartQuantList` variables. Suppose for the moment that the current value of `CartMerchList` is `5,8` (meaning that the user has added items number 5 and 8 to his cart) and that `CartQuantList` is `1,2` (meaning that the user wants to buy one of item number 5 and two of item number 8). If so, the `<CFLOOP>` near the bottom of this template will execute twice. The first time through the loop, `ThisMerchID` will be `5` and `ThisQuant` will be `1`. Item number 5 is displayed with the `<CF_MerchDisplay>` tag, and then a text field called `Quant_5` is displayed, prefilled with a value of `1`. This text field enables the user to adjust the quantities for each item.

At the very bottom of the template, two submit buttons are provided, labeled Update Quantities and Checkout. Both submit the form, but the Checkout button sends the user on to the Checkout phase after the cart quantities have been updated.

Updating Cart Quantities

Three `<CFPARAM>` tags are at the top of Listing 29.4. The first makes it clear that the template can take an optional `AddMerchID` parameter. The next two ensure that the `CLIENT.CartMerchList` and `CLIENT.CartQuantList` variables are guaranteed to exist (if not, they are initialized to empty strings, which represent an empty shopping cart).

If a numeric `AddMerchID` is passed to the page, the first `<CFIF>` block executes. The job of this block of code is to add the item indicated by `URL.AddMerchID` to the user's cart. First, the `ListFind()` function is used to set the `CurrentListPos` variable. This variable is `0` if the `AddMerchID` value is not in `CLIENT.CartMerchList` (in other words, if the item is not in the user's cart). Therefore, the `AddMerchID` is placed in the user's cart by appending it to the current `CartMerchList` value, and by appending a quantity of `1` to the current `MerchQuantList` value.

If, on the other hand, the item is already in the user's cart, `CurrentListPos` is the position of the item in the comma-separated lists that represent the cart. Therefore, the current quantity for the passed `AddMerchID` value can be obtained with the `ListGetAt()` function and stored in `CurrentQuant`. The current quantity is incremented by one, and the updated quantity is placed in the appropriate spot in `CLIENT.CartQuantList`, via the `ListSetAt()` function.

The large `<CFELSE>` block executes when the user submits the form, using the Update Quantities or Checkout button (see Figure 29.2). The `<CFLOOP>` loops through the list of items in the user's cart. Again, supposing that `CLIENT.CartMerchList` is currently `5,8`, `ThisMerchID` is set to `5` the first time through the loop. If a form variable named `FORM.Quant_5` exists, that form value represents the user's updated quantity for the item. If the user has specified an updated quantity of `0`, it is assumed that the user wants to remove the item from the cart, so the appropriate values in `CartMerchList` and `CartQuantList` are removed using the `ListDeleteAt()` function. If the user has specified some other quantity, the quantity in `CartQuantList` is simply updated, using the `ListSetAt()` function.

Finally, if the user submitted the form using the Checkout button, the browser is directed to the `CartCheckout.cfm` template via the `<CFLOCATION>` tag.

At this point, the shopping cart is quite usable. The user can go to the `Store.cfm` template (refer to Figure 29.1) and add items to his shopping cart. Once at his shopping cart (see Figure 29.2), the user can update quantities or remove items by setting the quantity to `0`.

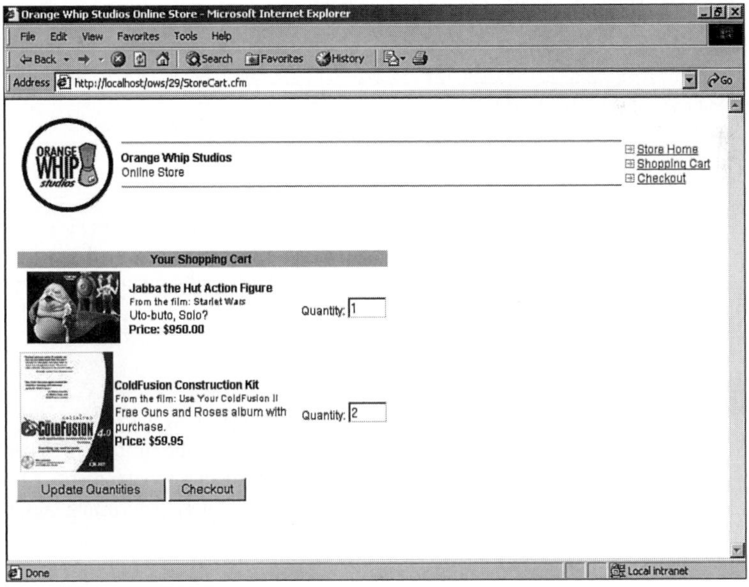

Figure 29.2 From the Shopping Cart page, users can update quantities or proceed to the Checkout phase.

Encapsulating the Shopping Cart in a Custom Tag

Although the version of `StoreCart.cfm` in Listing 29.4 works just fine, the code itself is a bit messy. It is forced to contain quite a few list functions, which don't necessarily have to do with the conceptual problem at hand (the user's cart). Worse, other templates that need to refer to the user's cart (such as the Checkout template) will need to use nearly all the same list functions over again, resulting in quite a bit of code for you to maintain.

Using the custom tag skills you learned in Chapter 22, you can create a custom tag that represents the abstract notion of the user's shopping cart. The code in Listing 29.5 creates a custom tag called `<CF_ShoppingCart>`, which encapsulates all the list-manipulation details necessary to maintain the user's shopping cart.

After Listing 29.5 is saved as `ShoppingCart.cfm` in the special `CustomTags` folder (or just in the same folder where it will be used), it will be capable of accomplishing any of the tasks shown in Table 19.1.

TABLE 19.1 SYNTAX SUPPORTED BY THE `<CF_ShoppingCart>` CUSTOM TAG EXAMPLE

Desired Action	Sample Code
Add an item to the user's cart	`<CF_ShoppingCart Action="Add" MerchID="5">`
Update the quantity of an item	`<CF_ShoppingCart Action="Update" MerchID="5" Quantity="10">`
Remove an item from the cart	`<CF_ShoppingCart Action="Remove" MerchID="5">`
Remove all items from cart	`<CF_ShoppingCart Action="Empty">`
Retrieve all items in cart	`<CF_ShoppingCart Action="List" ReturnVariable="GetCart">` (The cart contents are returned as aColdFusion query object; the query object will contain two columns, `MerchID` and `Quantity`.)

Note

Because the various `ACTION` tasks provided by this custom tag all relate to a single concept (a shopping cart), you can think of the custom tag as being an object-based representation of the cart. See the discussion about the `<CF_Film>` custom tag in Chapter 22 for further discussion about thinking of custom tags in this way.

Listing 29.5 ShoppingCart.cfm—Constructing the <CF_ShoppingCart> Custom Tag

```
<!--- Tag Parameters --->
<CFPARAM NAME="ATTRIBUTES.Action" TYPE="string">


<!--- These two variables track MerchIDs / Quantities  --->
<!--- for items in user's cart (start with empty cart) --->
<CFPARAM NAME="CLIENT.CartMerchList" TYPE="string" DEFAULT="">
<CFPARAM NAME="CLIENT.CartQuantList" TYPE="string" DEFAULT="">


<!--- This tag is being called with what ACTION? --->
<CFSWITCH EXPRESSION="#ATTRIBUTES.Action#">

  <!--- *** ACTION="Add" or ACTION="Update" *** --->
  <CFCASE VALUE="Add,Update">
    <!--- Tag attributes specific to this ACTION --->
    <CFPARAM NAME="ATTRIBUTES.MerchID" TYPE="numeric">
    <CFPARAM NAME="ATTRIBUTES.Quantity" TYPE="numeric" DEFAULT="1">

    <!--- Get position, if any, of MerchID in cart list --->
    <CFSET CurrentListPos = ListFind(CLIENT.CartMerchList, ATTRIBUTES.MerchID)>
    <!--- If this item *is not* already in cart, add it --->
    <CFIF CurrentListPos EQ 0>
      <CFSET CLIENT.CartMerchList =
        ListAppend(CLIENT.CartMerchList, ATTRIBUTES.MerchID)>
      <CFSET CLIENT.CartQuantList =
        ListAppend(CLIENT.CartQuantList, ATTRIBUTES.Quantity)>
    <!--- If item *is* already in cart, change its qty --->
    <CFELSE>
      <!--- If Action="Add", add new Qty to existing --->
      <CFIF ATTRIBUTES.Action EQ "Add">
        <CFSET ATTRIBUTES.Quantity =
          ATTRIBUTES.Quantity + ListGetAt(CLIENT.CartQuantList, CurrentListPos)>
      </CFIF> tag>>
      <!--- If new quantity is zero, remove item from cart --->
      <CFIF ATTRIBUTES.Quantity EQ 0>
        <CFSET CLIENT.CartMerchList =
          ListDeleteAt(CLIENT.CartMerchList, CurrentListPos)>
        <CFSET CLIENT.CartQuantList =
          ListDeleteAt(CLIENT.CartQuantList, CurrentListPos)>
      <!--- If new quantity not zero, update cart quantity --->
      <CFELSE>
        <CFSET CLIENT.CartQuantList =
          ListSetAt(CLIENT.CartQuantList, CurrentListPos, ATTRIBUTES.Quantity)>
      </CFIF>
    </CFIF>
  </CFCASE>


  <!--- *** ACTION="Remove" *** --->
  <CFCASE VALUE="Remove">
    <!--- Tag attributes specific to this ACTION --->
    <CFPARAM NAME="ATTRIBUTES.MerchID" TYPE="numeric">
    <!--- Treat "Remove" action same as "Update" with Quant=0 --->
    <CF_ShoppingCart
      ACTION="Update"
```

LISTING 29.5 CONTINUED

```
      MerchID="#ATTRIBUTES.MerchID#" tag>
      Quantity="0">
  </CFCASE>


  <!--- *** ACTION="Empty" *** --->
  <CFCASE VALUE="Empty">
    <CFSET CLIENT.CartMerchList = "">
    <CFSET CLIENT.CartQuantList = "">
  </CFCASE>


  <!--- *** ACTION="List" *** --->
  <CFCASE VALUE="List">
    <!--- Tag attributes specific to this ACTION --->
    <CFPARAM NAME="ATTRIBUTES.ReturnVariable" TYPE="variableName">

    <!--- Create a query, to return to calling template --->
    <CFSET q = QueryNew("MerchID,Quantity")>

    <!--- For each item in CLIENT lists, add row to query --->
    <CFLOOP FROM="1" TO="#ListLen(CLIENT.CartMerchList)#" INDEX="i">
      <CFSET QueryAddRow(q)>  tag>
      <CFSET QuerySetCell(q, "MerchID",  ListGetAt(CLIENT.CartMerchList, i))>
      <CFSET QuerySetCell(q, "Quantity", ListGetAt(CLIENT.CartQuantList, i))>
    </CFLOOP> tag>>

    <!--- Return query to calling template --->
    <CFSET "Caller.#ATTRIBUTES.ReturnVariable#" = q>
  </CFCASE>


  <!--- If an unknown ACTION was provided, display error --->
  <CFDEFAULTCASE>
     <CFTHROW
       MESSAGE="Unknown ACTION passed to &lt;CF_ShoppingCart&gt;"
       DETAIL="Recognized ACTION values are <B>List</B>, <B>Add</B>,
               <B>Update</B>, <B>Remove</B>, and <B>Empty</B>.">
  </CFDEFAULTCASE>
</CFSWITCH>
```

Note

Some of the `<CFSET>` tags in this template are broken somewhat unusually across two lines (the left side of the expression on one line and the right side on the next line) to make them easier to read in this book. In your actual code templates, you probably would have the whole `<CFSET>` statement on one line, but this listing does point out that ColdFusion can deal with expressions that span multiple lines without complaint.

Similar to the `<CF_Film>` custom tag in Chapter 22, this custom tag supports its various tasks by requiring an `ACTION` attribute (required by the `<CFPARAM>` tag at the top of Listing 29.5) and then handling each of the supported actions in separate `<CFCASE>` tags within a large <CFSWITCH> block. If the ACTION is Add or Update, the first <CFCASE> tag executes. If the ACTION is Remove, the second one executes, and so on.

If ACTION="Add" or ACTION="Update", the tag accepts two additional parameters—MerchID (required) and Quantity (optional, defaulting to 1). The <CFCASE> block for these actions is similar to the top portion of Listing 29.4, using ListFind() to determine whether the item is already in the user's cart and then adding it to the cart with ListAppend() or updating the quantity using ListSetAt(). Also, if ACTION="Update" and Quantity="0", the item is removed from the user's cart.

If the tag is called ACTION="Remove", the tag just calls itself again, using ACTION="Update" and Quantity="0" to remove the item from the user's cart. So, Remove is just a synonym for an Update that sets the quantity to 0.

If ACTION="Empty", the CLIENT.CartMerchList and CLIENT.CartQuantList are emptied by setting them both to empty strings. This has the effect of removing all items from the user's cart.

Finally, if ACTION="List", the tag creates a new ColdFusion query object using the QueryNew() function, which the calling template will be capable of using as if it were generated by an ordinary <CFQUERY> tag. The new query has two columns, MerchID and Quantity. For each item in the CartMerchList and CartQuantList lists, a row is added to the query using QueryAddRow(); then the MerchID and Quantity columns of the just-inserted row are set using the QuerySetCell() function. The end result is a simple two-column query that contains a row for each item in the user's cart. The query object is returned to the calling template with the name specified in the tag's ReturnVariable attribute.

Tip

It's worth learning more about returning nondatabase queries from custom tags. Check out QueryNew(), QueryAddRow(), and QuerySetCell() in Appendix B, "ColdFusion Function Reference."

Note

One of the goals for this custom tag is to ensure that the CLIENT.CartMerchList and CLIENT.CartQuantList variables will not need to be referred to in any other template. The custom tag will therefore be a clean abstraction of the concept of a user's cart, including the storage method (currently the two lists in the CLIENT scope). If you later decide to use SESSION variables or a database table to hold each user's cart data, you will have to change only the code in the custom tag template. See Chapter 22 for more discussion about getting to the holy grail of abstraction via custom tags.

PUTTING <CF_ShoppingCart> TO WORK

The version of StoreCart.cfm in Listing 29.6 is a revised version of the one from Listing 29.4. As far as the user is concerned, it behaves the same way. However, all references to the internal storage mechanisms (the CLIENT variables, list functions, and so on) have been removed. As a result, the code reads well, will be clearer to future coders, and will be easier for you to reuse and maintain.

Note

For the links to the shopping cart page to work correctly, you should save Listing 29.6 as `StoreCart.cfm`, not `StoreCart2.cfm`.

LISTING 29.6 `StoreCart2.cfm`—USING `<CF_ShoppingCart>` TO REBUILD THE `StoreCart.cfm` TEMPLATE

```
<!--- Show header images, etc., for Online Store --->
<CFINCLUDE TEMPLATE="StoreHeader.cfm">

<!--- If MerchID was passed in URL --->
<CFIF IsDefined("URL.AddMerchID")>
  <!--- Add item to user's cart data, via custom tag --->
  <CF_ShoppingCart
    Action="Add"
    MerchID="#URL.AddMerchID#">

<!--- If user is submitting cart form --->
<CFELSEIF IsDefined("FORM.MerchID")>
  <!--- For each MerchID on Form, Update Quantity --->
  <CFLOOP LIST="#Form.MerchID#" INDEX="ThisMerchID">
    <!--- Update Quantity, via Custom Tag --->
    <CF_ShoppingCart
      Action="Update"
      MerchID="#ThisMerchID#"
      Quantity="#FORM['Quant_#ThisMerchID#']#">
  </CFLOOP>

  <!--- If user submitted form via "Checkout" button, --->
  <!--- send on to Checkout page after updating cart. --->
  <CFIF IsDefined("FORM.IsCheckingOut")>
    <CFLOCATION URL="StoreCheckout.cfm">
  </CFIF>
</CFIF>

<!--- Get current cart contents, via Custom Tag --->
<CF_ShoppingCart
  Action="List"
  ReturnVariable="GetCart">

<!--- Stop here if user's cart is empty --->
<CFIF GetCart.RecordCount EQ 0>
  There is nothing in your cart.
  <CFABORT>
</CFIF>


<!--- Create form that submits to this template --->
<CFFORM ACTION="#CGI.SCRIPT_NAME#">
  <TABLE>
    <TR>
      <TH COLSPAN="2" BGCOLOR="Silver">Your Shopping Cart</TH>
    </TR>
    <!--- For each piece of merchandise --->
    <CFLOOP QUERY="GetCart">
      <TR>
```

```
        <TD>
          <!--- Show this piece of merchandise --->
          <CF_MerchDisplay
            MerchID="#GetCart.MerchID#"
            ShowAddLink="No">
        </TD>
        <TD>
          <!--- Display Quantity in Text entry field --->
          <CFOUTPUT>
            Quantity:
            <INPUT TYPE="Hidden"
              NAME="MerchID"
              VALUE="#GetCart.MerchID#">
            <INPUT TYPE="Text" SIZE="3"
              NAME="Quant_#GetCart.MerchID#"
              VALUE="#GetCart.Quantity#">
          </CFOUTPUT>
        </TD>
      </TR>
    </CFLOOP>
  </TABLE>

  <!--- Submit button to update quantities --->
  <INPUT TYPE="Submit" VALUE="Update Quantities">

  <!--- Submit button to Check out --->
  <INPUT TYPE="Submit" VALUE="Checkout" NAME="IsCheckingOut">
</CFFORM>
```

If the template receives an `AddMerchID` parameter in the URL, the `<CF_ShoppingCart>` tag is called with `ACTION="Add"` to add the item to the user's cart. If the user submits the shopping cart form with the Update Quantities or Checkout button, the template loops through the merchandise elements that were on the form, calling `<CF_ShoppingCart>` with `ACTION="Update"` for each one.

Then, to display the items in the user's cart, the `<CF_ShoppingCart>` tag is called again, this time with `Action="List"`. Because `GetCart` is specified for the `ReturnVariable` attribute, the display portion of the code just needs to use a `<CFLOOP>` over the `GetCart` query, calling `<CF_MerchDisplay>` for each row to get the merchandise displayed to the user.

PAYMENT PROCESSING

Now that Orange Whip Studio's storefront and shopping cart mechanisms are in place, it is time to tackle the checkout process. This part generally takes the most time to get into place because you must make some decisions about how the actual payments will be accepted from your users and how they will be processed.

Depending on the nature of your application, you might have no need for real-time payment processing. For instance, if your company operates by billing your customers at the end of each month, you probably just need to perform some type of query to determine the status of the user's account, rather than worrying about collecting a credit card number and charging the card right when the user checks out.

However, most online shopping applications call for getting a credit card number from a user at checkout time and charging the user's credit cart account in real time. That is the focus of this section.

PAYMENT PROCESSING SOLUTIONS

Assuming that you will be collecting credit card information from your users, the first thing you should decide is how you will process the credit card charges that come through your application. ColdFusion does not ship with any specific functionality for processing credit card transactions. However, a number of third-party packages are available that enable you to accept payments via credit cards and checks.

Because it is extremely popular, the examples in this chapter use the CashRegister payment-processing service from CyberCash (`www.cybercash.com`). CyberCash makes integrating their service into your ColdFusion applications particularly easy by providing a native ColdFusion extension tag called `<CFX_CyberCash>`.

That said, the CyberCash service is just one of several solutions available to you. You are encouraged to investigate other payment software packages to find the service or package that makes the most sense for your project.

To get you started, here are a few products you can take a look at:

- OpenMarket's Transact product (`www.openmarket.com`)
- The Payflow family of products and services from VeriSign (`www.verisign.com`)
- The ICVerify and `CashRegister` products from CyberCash (`www.cybercash.com`)

PROCESSING A PAYMENT

Of course, the exact ColdFusion code you use to process payments will vary according to the payment-processing package you decide to use. This section uses CyberCash, just as an example. Please understand, however, that other options are available and that CyberCash shouldn't necessarily be considered as superior or better-suited than other solutions just because it is discussed here.

GETTING STARTED WITH CYBERCASH

If you want to try the payment-processing code examples that follow in this section, you must download and install CyberCash's Merchant Connection Kit (MCK) and the `<CFX_CyberCash>` extension.

Note

At the time of this writing, the items discussed here were available for free download from CyberCash's Web site. Further, it was not necessary to establish a merchant account to be able to test the functionality.

These instructions (especially step 3) assume you are using the Windows version of ColdFusion Server for testing purposes. CyberCash also provides a Linux version of the `<CFX_CyberCash>` tag, so you should be able to use the code examples in this chapter under Linux, although the specific installation steps will differ somewhat. Consult the CyberCash documentation for details.

To get started, do the following:

1. Go to CyberCash's Web site and download the latest version of the Merchant Connection Kit (MCK) appropriate for your system. While you are there, also download the `<CFX_CyberCash>` extension for ColdFusion. At the time of this writing, the MCK was at version 3.3.1, and the CFX extension was at version 1.01.
2. Install the MCK on your ColdFusion server machine. During the install process, be sure to indicate that you want a test installation. If asked which development language you want to use (Perl, C, ASP, and so on), just pick whichever one you prefer. The specific ColdFusion support will be added when you install the CFX extension.
3. A test version of a file called `merchant_conf` should now be somewhere on the server's drive, probably within a folder called `test-mck`, within the folder that the MCK was installed in. For instance, when version 3.3.1 of the MCK is installed on a Windows machine, the `merchant_conf` file is stored in `C:\mck-3.3.1-NT\test-mck\conf`. In any case, make a note of the file's location. You will need it later for Listing 29.7.
4. Install the CFX extension on your ColdFusion server machine using the default options. When the installation is complete, navigate to the CFX Tags page of the ColdFusion Administrator and check to see whether the `<CFX_CyberCash>` tag has been registered by the installer. If not, look for a file called `cybercash.dll` on the ColdFusion server's drive (it will probably be in the `BIN` folder, within the `CFUSION` folder), and register it as `<CFX_CyberCash>` using the Administrator. The Procedure field should be left at `ProcessTagRequest`. See Chapter 30, "ColdFusion Server Configuration," for details.

Note

The CyberCash software on your server needs to communicate with CyberCash's network over the Internet, so your ColdFusion server must be capable of accessing the Internet before you can start testing. Depending on your situation, you might need to configure CyberCash to be capable of getting past your firewall or proxy software, or take other special steps. Most of these configuration tasks are accomplished by editing the `merchant_conf` file. See the CyberCash documentation for details. Please understand that successful installation of CyberCash's software is not the primary focus of this chapter.

Now that the appropriate software has been installed, you should be able to write code that uses `<CFX_CyberCash>` to process payments in real time.

WRITING A CUSTOM TAG WRAPPER TO ACCEPT PAYMENTS

To make the <CFX_CyberCash> tag easier to use in your own ColdFusion templates, and to make switching to some other payment-processing solution in the future easier, you might consider hiding all payment-package–specific code within a more abstract, general-purpose custom tag that encapsulates the notion of processing a payment.

Listing 29.7 creates a CFML custom tag called <CF_ProcessPayment>. It accepts a Processor attribute to indicate which payment-processing software should be used to process the payment. As you will see, this example supports only Processor="CyberCash". You would need to expand the tag by adding the package-specific code necessary for any additional software packages yourself.

The idea here is similar to the idea behind the <CF_ShoppingCart> tag created earlier in this chapter: Keep all the mechanics in the custom tag template, so each individual page can use simpler, more goal-oriented syntax. In addition to the Processor attribute mentioned previously, this sample version of the <CF_ProcessPayment> tag accepts the following attributes:

- OrderID—This is passed along to the credit card company as a reference number.
- OrderAmount, CreditCard, CreditExpM, CreditExpY, and CreditName—These describe the actual payment to be processed.
- ReturnVariable—This indicates a variable name the custom tag should use to report the status of the attempted payment transaction. The returned value is a ColdFusion structure that contains a number of status values.

LISTING 29.7 ProcessPayment.cfm—**CREATING THE** <CF_ProcessPayment> **CUSTOM TAG**

```
<!--- Tag Parameters --->
<CFPARAM NAME="ATTRIBUTES.Processor" TYPE="string">
<CFPARAM NAME="ATTRIBUTES.OrderID" TYPE="numeric">
<CFPARAM NAME="ATTRIBUTES.OrderAmount" TYPE="numeric">
<CFPARAM NAME="ATTRIBUTES.CreditCard" TYPE="string">
<CFPARAM NAME="ATTRIBUTES.CreditExpM" TYPE="string">
<CFPARAM NAME="ATTRIBUTES.CreditExpY" TYPE="string">
<CFPARAM NAME="ATTRIBUTES.CreditName" TYPE="string">
<CFPARAM NAME="ATTRIBUTES.ReturnVariable" TYPE="variableName">


<!--- Depending on the PROCESSOR attribute --->
<CFSWITCH EXPRESSION="#ATTRIBUTES.Processor#">
  <!--- If PROCESSOR="CyberCash" --->
  <CFCASE VALUE="CyberCash">
    <!--- Force expiration into MM and YY format --->
    <CFSET ExpM  = NumberFormat(ATTRIBUTES.CreditExpM, "00")>
    <CFSET ExpY  = NumberFormat(Right(ATTRIBUTES.CreditExpM, 2), "00")>

    <!--- Attempt to process the transaction --->
    <CFX_CYBERCASH
      VERSION="3.2"
      CONFIGFILE="C:\mck-3.3.1-NT\test-mck\conf\merchant_conf"
```

```
      MO_ORDER_ID="8767767#ATTRIBUTES.OrderID#"
      MO_VERSION="3.3.1"
      MO_PRICE="USD #NumberFormat(ATTRIBUTES.OrderAmount, '9.00')#"
      CPI_CARD_NUMBER="#ATTRIBUTES.CreditCard#"
      CPI_CARD_EXP="#ExpM#/#ExpY#"
      CPI_CARD_NAME="#ATTRIBUTES.CreditName#"
      OUTPUTPOPQUERY="Charge">

    <!--- Values to return to calling template --->
    <CFSET s = StructNew()>
    <!--- Always return IsSuccessful (Boolean) --->
    <CFSET s.IsSuccessful = Charge.STATUS EQ "success">
    <!--- Always return status of transaction --->
    <CFSET s.Status = Charge.STATUS>
    <!--- If Successful, return the Auth Code --->
    <CFIF s.IsSuccessful>
      <CFSET s.AuthCode     = Charge.AUTH_CODE>
      <CFSET s.OrderID      = ATTRIBUTES.ORDERID>
      <CFSET s.OrderAmount  = ATTRIBUTES.OrderAmount>
    <!--- If not successful, return the error --->
    <CFELSE>
      <CFSET s.ErrorCode    = Charge.ERROR_CODE>
      <CFSET s.ErrorMessage = Charge.ERROR_MESSAGE>
    </CFIF>
    <!--- Return values to calling template --->
    <CFSET "Caller.#ATTRIBUTES.ReturnVariable#" = s>
  </CFCASE>

  <!--- If the PROCESSOR attribute is unknown --->
  <CFDEFAULTCASE>
    <CFTHROW MESSAGE="Unknown PROCESSOR attribute.">
  </CFDEFAULTCASE>
</CFSWITCH>
```

Note

The CONFIGFILE attribute for the <CFX_CyberCash> tag needs to point to your own merchant_conf file, wherever it is located (see the previous section "Getting Started with CyberCash").

At the top of Listing 29.7, eight <CFPARAM> tags are used to establish the tag's various attributes, all of which are required. Then, a <CFSWITCH> tag is used to execute various payment-processing code, based on the Processor attribute passed to the custom tag. The syntax specific to <CFX_CyberCash> is the only code fleshed out in this template; you would add syntax for other packages in separate <CFCASE> blocks.

The actual code in the <CFCASE> block is quite simple. Most of the custom tag's attributes are fed directly to the <CFX_CyberCash> tag. Some of the values need to be tweaked just a bit to conform to what the CFX tag expects. For instance, the custom tag expects the expiration month and year to be provided as simple numeric values, but the CFX tag wants them provided as a single string in MM/YY format. Also, CyberCash expects the local currency to be specified using the appropriate three-character identifier, which is why USD appears in the MO_PRICE attribute.

After the `<CFX_CyberCash>` tag executes, a new structure named `s` is created using `StructNew()`. A Boolean value called `IsSuccessful` is added to the structure by examining the `STATUS` code returned by the CFX tag. The calling template will be able to look at `IsSuccessful` to tell whether the payment was completed successfully. Additionally, if the order was successful, `AuthCode`, `OrderID`, and `OrderAmount` values are added to the structure. If it was not successful, values called `ErrorCode` and `ErrorMessage` are added to the structure, so the calling template will be able to understand exactly what went wrong. Then the whole structure is passed back to the calling template using the quoted `<CFSET>` return variable syntax that was explained in Chapter 22.

Note

Consult the CyberCash documentation for details on the attributes provided to the `<CFX_CyberCash>` tag in this template. The tag is capable of a lot more than is demonstrated here.

If you adapt this custom tag to handle other payment processors, try to return a structure the same value names (`IsSuccessful`, `AuthCode`, and so on). In this way, you will be building a common API to deal with payment processing in an application-agnostic way.

Processing a Complete Order

In addition to explaining how to build commerce applications, this chapter is trying to emphasize the benefits of hiding the mechanics of complex operations within goal-oriented custom tag wrappers that know how to accomplish whole tasks on their own. Actual page templates that use these custom tags end up being very clean, dealing only with the larger concepts at hand—rather than including a lot of low-level code. That's the difference, for instance, between the two versions of the `StoreCart.cfm` template (Listings 29.4 and 29.6).

In keeping with that notion, Listing 29.8 creates another custom tag, called `<CF_PlaceOrder>`. This tag is in charge of handling all aspects of accepting a new order from a customer, including

- Inserting a new record into the `MerchandiseOrders` table
- Inserting one or more detail records into the `MerchandiseOrdersItems` table (one detail record for each item being ordered)
- Attempting to charge the user's credit card, using the `<CF_ProcessPayment>` custom tag created in the previous section (refer to Listing 29.7)
- If the charge is successful, sending an order confirmation message to the user via e-mail, using the `<CF_SendOrderConfirmation>` custom tag that was created in Chapter 28, "Interacting with E-mail"
- If the charge is not successful for whatever reason (because of an incorrect credit card number, expiration date, or the like), ensuring that the just-inserted records from `MerchandiseOrders` and `MerchandiseOrdersItems` are not actually permanently committed to the database

LISTING 29.8 PlaceOrder.cfm—CREATING THE <CF_PlaceOrder> CUSTOM TAG

```
<!--- Tag Parameters --->
<CFPARAM NAME="ATTRIBUTES.Processor" TYPE="string" DEFAULT="CyberCash">
<CFPARAM NAME="ATTRIBUTES.MerchList" TYPE="string">
<CFPARAM NAME="ATTRIBUTES.QuantList" TYPE="string">
<CFPARAM NAME="ATTRIBUTES.ContactID" TYPE="numeric">
<CFPARAM NAME="ATTRIBUTES.CreditCard" TYPE="string">
<CFPARAM NAME="ATTRIBUTES.CreditExpM" TYPE="string">
<CFPARAM NAME="ATTRIBUTES.CreditExpY" TYPE="string">
<CFPARAM NAME="ATTRIBUTES.CreditName" TYPE="string">
<CFPARAM NAME="ATTRIBUTES.ShipAddress" TYPE="string">
<CFPARAM NAME="ATTRIBUTES.ShipCity" TYPE="string">
<CFPARAM NAME="ATTRIBUTES.ShipCity" TYPE="string">
<CFPARAM NAME="ATTRIBUTES.ShipState" TYPE="string">
<CFPARAM NAME="ATTRIBUTES.ShipZIP" TYPE="string">
<CFPARAM NAME="ATTRIBUTES.ShipCountry" TYPE="string">
<CFPARAM NAME="ATTRIBUTES.HTMLMail" TYPE="boolean">
<CFPARAM NAME="ATTRIBUTES.ReturnVariable" TYPE="variableName">


<!--- Begin "order" database transaction here --->
<!--- Can be rolled back or committed later --->
<CFTRANSACTION ACTION="BEGIN">
  <!--- Insert new record into Orders table --->
  <CFQUERY DATASOURCE="#REQUEST.DataSource#">
    INSERT INTO MerchandiseOrders (
      ContactID,
      OrderDate,
      ShipAddress, ShipCity,
      ShipState, ShipZip,
      ShipCountry)
    VALUES (
      #ATTRIBUTES.ContactID#,
      <CFQUERYPARAM CFSQLTYPE="CF_SQL_TIMESTAMP"
        VALUE="#DateFormat(Now())# #TimeFormat(Now())#">,
      '#ATTRIBUTES.ShipAddress#', '#ATTRIBUTES.ShipCity#',
      '#ATTRIBUTES.ShipState#', '#ATTRIBUTES.ShipZip#',
      '#ATTRIBUTES.ShipCountry#'
    )
  </CFQUERY>

  <!--- Get just-inserted OrderID from database --->
  <CFQUERY DATASOURCE="#REQUEST.DataSource#" NAME="GetNew">
    SELECT MAX(OrderID) AS NewID
    FROM MerchandiseOrders
  </CFQUERY>

  <!--- For each item in user's shopping cart --->
  <CFLOOP FROM="1" TO="#ListLen(ATTRIBUTES.MerchList)#" INDEX="i">
    <CFSET ThisMerchID = ListGetAt(ATTRIBUTES.MerchList, i)>
    <CFSET ThisQuant   = ListGetAt(ATTRIBUTES.QuantList, i)>

    <!--- Add the item to "OrdersItems" table --->
    <CFQUERY DATASOURCE="#REQUEST.DataSource#">
      INSERT INTO MerchandiseOrdersItems
        (OrderID, ItemID, OrderQty, ItemPrice)
      SELECT
```

Listing 29.8 Continued

```
        #GetNew.NewID#, MerchID, #ThisQuant#, MerchPrice
      FROM Merchandise
      WHERE MerchID = #ThisMerchID#
    </CFQUERY>
  </CFLOOP>

  <!--- Get the total of all items in user's cart --->
  <CFQUERY DATASOURCE="#REQUEST.DataSource#" NAME="GetTotal">
    SELECT SUM(ItemPrice * OrderQty) AS OrderTotal
    FROM MerchandiseOrdersItems
    WHERE OrderID = #GetNew.NewID#
  </CFQUERY>

  <!--- Attempt to process the transaction  --->
  <CF_ProcessPayment
    Processor="CyberCash"
    OrderID="#GetNew.NewID#"
    OrderAmount="#GetTotal.OrderTotal#"
    CreditCard="#ATTRIBUTES.CreditCard#"
    CreditExpM="#ATTRIBUTES.CreditExpM#"
    CreditExpY="#ATTRIBUTES.CreditExpY#"
    CreditName="#ATTRIBUTES.CreditName#"
    ReturnVariable="ChargeInfo">

  <!--- If the order was processed successfully --->
  <CFIF ChargeInfo.IsSuccessful>
    <!--- Commit the transaction to database --->
    <CFTRANSACTION ACTION="Commit"/>
  <CFELSE>
    <!--- Rollback the Order from the Database --->
    <CFTRANSACTION ACTION="RollBack"/>
  </CFIF>
</CFTRANSACTION>


<!--- If the order was processed successfully --->
<CFIF ChargeInfo.IsSuccessful>
  <!--- Send Confirmation E-Mail, via Custom Tag --->
  <CF_SendOrderConfirmation
    OrderID="#GetNew.NewID#"
    UseHTML="#ATTRIBUTES.HTMLMail#">
</CFIF>

<!--- Return status values to callling template --->
<CFSET "Caller.#ATTRIBUTES.ReturnVariable#" = ChargeInfo>
```

At the top of the template is a rather large number of `<CFPARAM>` tags that define the various attributes for the `<CF_PlaceOrder>` custom tag. The `Processor`, `ReturnVariable`, and four `Credit` attributes are passed directly to `<CF_ProcessPayment>`. The `MerchList` and `QuantList` attributes specify which item is actually being ordered, in the same comma-separated format that the `CLIENT` variables use in Listing 29.4. The `ContactID` and the six `Ship` attributes are needed for the `MerchandiseOrders` table. The `HTMLMail` attribute is used to send an e-mail confirmation to the user if the payment is successful.

After the tag attributes have been defined, a large <CFTRANSACTION> block is started. The <CFTRANSACTION> tag is ColdFusion's representation of the idea of a database transaction. You saw it in action in Chapter 14, "Using Forms to Add or Change Data," and you will learn about it more formally in Chapter 31, "More About SQL and Queries," and Chapter 33, "Error Handling." The <CFTRANSACTION> tag tells the database that all queries and other database operations within the block are to be considered as a single transaction, which cannot be interrupted by other operations.

The use of <CFTRANSACTION> in this template accomplishes two things. First, it makes sure that no other records are inserted between the first `INSERT` query and the `GetNew` query that comes right after it. This in turn ensures that the ID number retrieved by the `GetNew` query is indeed the correct one, rather than a record that was inserted by some other process. Second, the <CFTRANSACTION> tag allows any database changes (inserts, deletes, or updates) to be rolled back if some kind of problem occurs. A *rollback* is basically the database equivalent of the Undo function in a word processor—all changes are undone, leaving the database in the state that it was in at the start of the transaction. Here, the transaction is rolled back if the credit card transaction fails (perhaps because of an incorrect credit card number), which means that all traces of the new order will be removed from the database.

After the opening <CFTRANSACTION> tag, the following actions are taken:

1. A new order record is inserted into the `MerchandiseOrders` table.
2. The `GetNew` query obtains the `OrderID` number for the just-inserted order record.
3. A simple <CFLOOP> tag inserts one record into the `MerchandiseOrdersItems` table for each item supplied to the `MerchList` attribute. Each record includes the new `OrderID`, the appropriate quantity from the `QuantList` attribute, and the current price for the item (as listed in the `Merchandise` table). (The `INSERT/SELECT` syntax used here is explained in Chapter 31.)
4. The `GetTotal` query obtains the total price of the items being purchased, by adding up the price of each item times its quantity.
5. The <CF_ProcessPayment> tag (refer to Listing 29.7) is used to attempt to process the credit card transaction. The structure of payment-status information is returned as a structure named `ChargeInfo`.
6. If the charge was successful, the database transaction is committed by using the <CFTRANSACTION> tag with `ACTION="Commit"`. This permanently saves the inserted records in the database and ends the transaction.
7. If the charge was not successful, the database transaction is rolled back with a <CFTRANSACTION> tag of `ACTION="RollBack"`. This permanently removes the inserted records from the database and ends the transaction.
8. If the charge was successful, a confirmation e-mail message is sent to the user, using the <CF_SendOrderConfirmation> custom tag from Chapter 28. Because this tag performs database interactions of its own, it should sit outside the <CFTRANSACTION> block.
9. Finally, the `ChargeInfo` structure returned by <CF_PlaceOrder> is passed back to the calling template, so the calling template can understand whether the order was placed successfully.

CHECKING OUT A SHOPPING CART

Now that the `<CF_PlaceOrder>` custom tag has been created, actually creating the Checkout page for Orange Whip Studio's visitors is a simple task. Listing 29.9 provides the code for the `StoreCheckout.cfm` page, which users can access via the Checkout link at the top of each page in the online store or by clicking the Checkout button on the `StoreCart.cfm` page (refer to Figure 29.2).

LISTING 29.9 StoreCheckout.cfm—ALLOWING THE USER TO COMPLETE HER ONLINE TRANSACTION

```
<!--- Show header images, etc., for Online Store --->
<CFINCLUDE TEMPLATE="StoreHeader.cfm">

<!--- Get current cart contents, via Custom Tag --->
<CF_ShoppingCart
  Action="List"
  ReturnVariable="GetCart">

<!--- Stop here if user's cart is empty --->
<CFIF GetCart.RecordCount EQ 0>
  There is nothing in your cart.
  <CFABORT>
</CFIF>

<!--- If user is not logged in, force them to now --->
<CFIF NOT IsDefined("SESSION.Auth.IsLoggedIn")>
  <CFINCLUDE TEMPLATE="LoginForm.cfm">
  <CFABORT>
</CFIF>

<!--- If user is attempting to place order --->
<CFIF IsDefined("FORM.IsPlacingOrder")>

  <!--- Attempt to process the transaction  --->
  <CF_PlaceOrder
    ContactID="#SESSION.Auth.ContactID#"
    MerchList="#ValueList(GetCart.MerchID)#"
    QuantList="#ValueList(GetCart.Quantity)#"
    CreditCard="#FORM.CreditCard#"
    CreditExpM="#FORM.CreditExpM#"
    CreditExpY="#FORM.CreditExpY#"
    CreditName="#FORM.CreditName#"
    ShipAddress="#FORM.ShipAddress#"
    ShipState="#FORM.ShipState#"
    ShipCity="#FORM.ShipCity#"
    ShipZIP="#FORM.ShipZIP#"
    ShipCountry="#FORM.ShipCountry#"
    HTMLMail="#FORM.HTMLMail#"
    ReturnVariable="OrderInfo">

  <!--- If the order was processed successfully --->
  <CFIF OrderInfo.IsSuccessful>
```

```
    <!--- Empty user's shopping cart, via custom tag --->
    <CF_ShoppingCart
      ACTION="Empty">

    <!--- Display Success Message --->
    <CFOUTPUT>
      <H2>Thanks For Your Order</H2>
      <P><B>Your Order Has Been Placed.</B><BR>
      Your order number is: #OrderInfo.OrderID#<BR>
      Your credit card has been charged:
      #LSCurrencyFormat(OrderInfo.OrderAmount)#<BR>
      <P>A confirmation is being E-mailed to you.<BR>
    </CFOUTPUT>

    <!--- Stop here. --->
    <CFABORT>
  <CFELSE>
    <!--- Display "Error" message --->
    <FONT COLOR="Red">
      <STRONG>Your credit card could not be processed.</STRONG><BR>
      Please verify the credit card number, expiration date, and
      name on the card.<BR>
    </FONT>

    <!--- Show debug info if viewing page on server --->
    <CFIF CGI.REMOTE_ADDR EQ "127.0.0.1">
      <CFOUTPUT>
        Status:  #OrderInfo.Status#<BR>
        Error:   #OrderInfo.ErrorCode#<BR>
        Message: #OrderInfo.ErrorMessage#<BR>
      </CFOUTPUT>
    </CFIF>
  </CFIF>
</CFIF>


<!--- Show Checkout Form (Ship Address/Credit Card) --->
<CFINCLUDE TEMPLATE="StoreCheckoutForm.cfm">
```

First, the standard online store page header is displayed with the `<CFINCLUDE>` tag at the top of Listing 29.9. Next, the `<CF_ShoppingCart>` tag is used with `ACTION="List"`. If `GetCart.RecordCount` is `0`, the user's cart must be empty, so the template displays a short your-cart-is-empty message and stops further processing. Next, the template ensures that the user has logged in, using the same `<CFINCLUDE>` file developed in Chapter 21.

At the bottom of the template, a `<CFINCLUDE>` tag is used to include the form shown in Figure 29.3, which asks the user for her shipping and credit card information. The form is self-submitting, so when the user clicks the Place Order Now button, the code in Listing 29.9 is executed again. This is when the large `<CFIF>` block kicks in.

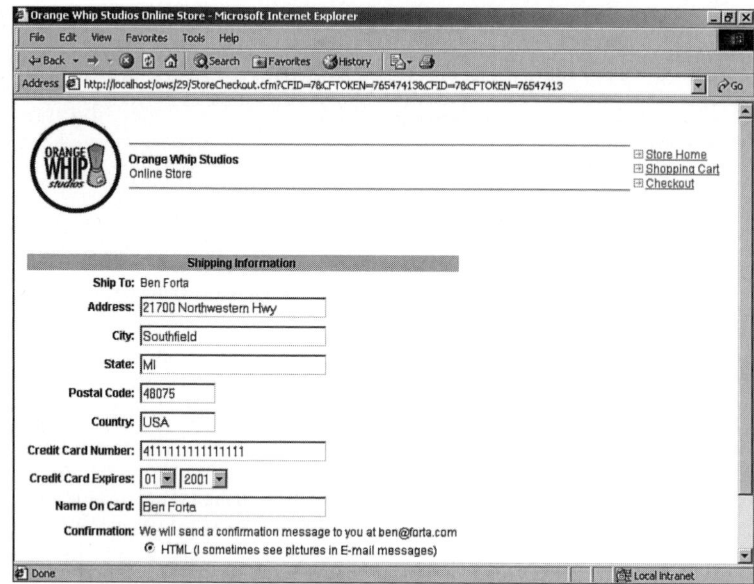

Figure 29.3
Users provide credit card information on the Checkout page.

Within the <CFIF> block, the <CF_PlaceOrder> tag attempts to complete the user's order. If all goes well, the order will be committed to the database, the confirmation e-mail message will be sent, the `OrderInfo.IsSuccessful` value will be `True`, and the new order's ID number will be returned as `OrderInfo.OrderID`.

If the order is actually successful, the user's cart is emptied using a final call to <CF_ShoppingCart>, and a thanks-for-your-order message is displayed, as shown in Figure 29.4. If not, an error message is displayed (along with helpful diagnostic informa–tion if the page is being visited from `127.0.0.1`), and the checkout form (see Listing 29.10) is redisplayed.

Listing 29.10 is the `StoreCheckoutForm.cfm` template that is included via the <CFINCLUDE> tag at the bottom of Listing 29.9. It is a simple template that uses <CFFORM> and <CFINPUT> to display a Web-based form with some simple data validation (such as the `VALIDATE="creditcard"` attribute for the `CreditCard` field). As a convenience to the user, the shipping address fields are prefilled based on the address information currently in the `Contacts` table. The resulting form was shown in Figure 29.3.

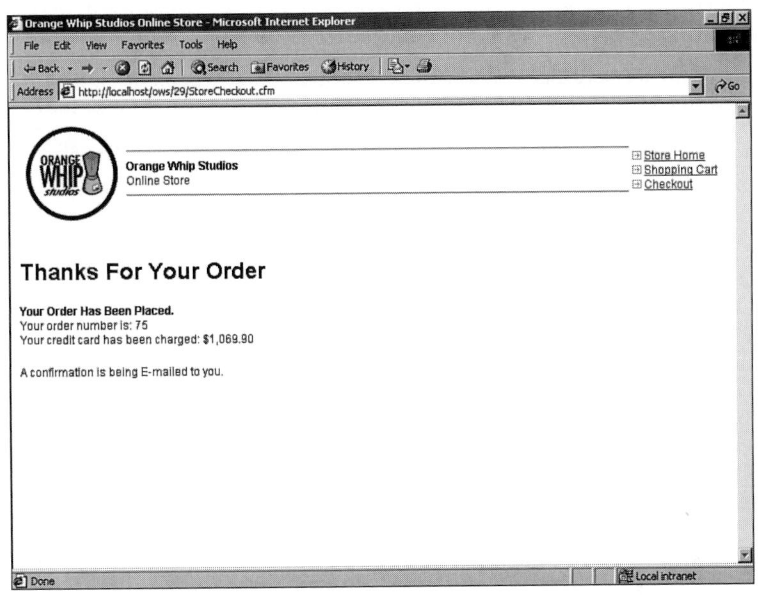

Figure 29.4 Credit card numbers can be verified and charged in real time to facilitate immediate confirmation of orders.

LISTING 29.10 `StoreCheckoutForm.cfm`—**COLLECTING SHIPPING AND CREDIT CARD INFORMATION FROM THE USER**

```
<!--- Get the user's contact info from database --->
<CFQUERY NAME="GetContact" DATASOURCE="#REQUEST.DataSource#">
  SELECT
    FirstName, LastName, Address,
    City, State, Zip, Country, Email
  FROM Contacts
  WHERE ContactID = #SESSION.Auth.ContactID#
</CFQUERY>

<CFOUTPUT>
  <CFFORM ACTION="#CGI.SCRIPT_NAME#" METHOD="POST" PRESERVEDATA="Yes">
    <INPUT TYPE="Hidden" NAME="IsPlacingOrder" VALUE="Yes">

    <TABLE BORDER="0" CELLSPACING="4">
      <TR>
        <TH COLSPAN="2" BGCOLOR="Silver">Shipping Information</TH>
      </TR>

      <TR>
        <TH ALIGN="right">Ship To:</TH>
        <TD>
          #GetContact.FirstName# #GetContact.LastName#
        </TD>
      </TR>
      <TR>
        <TH ALIGN="right">Address:</TH>
        <TD>
          <CFINPUT
            NAME="ShipAddress" SIZE="30"
```

LISTING 29.10 CONTINUED

```
          REQUIRED="Yes" VALUE="#GetContact.Address#"
          MESSAGE="Please don't leave the Address blank!">
      </TD>
    </TR>
    <TR>
      <TH ALIGN="right">City:</TH>
      <TD>
        <CFINPUT
          NAME="ShipCity" SIZE="30"
          REQUIRED="Yes" VALUE="#GetContact.City#"
          MESSAGE="Please don't leave the City blank!">
      </TD>
    </TR>
    <TR>
      <TH ALIGN="right">State:</TH>
      <TD>
        <CFINPUT
          NAME="ShipState" SIZE="30"
          REQUIRED="Yes" VALUE="#GetContact.State#"
          MESSAGE="Please don't leave the State blank!">
      </TD>
    </TR>
    <TR>
      <TH ALIGN="right">Postal Code:</TH>
      <TD>
        <CFINPUT
          NAME="ShipZIP" SIZE="10"
          REQUIRED="Yes" VALUE="#GetContact.ZIP#"
          MESSAGE="Please don't leave the ZIP blank!">
      </TD>
    </TR>
    <TR>
      <TH ALIGN="right">Country:</TH>
      <TD>
        <CFINPUT
          NAME="ShipCountry" SIZE="10"
          REQUIRED="Yes" VALUE="#GetContact.Country#"
          MESSAGE="Please don't leave the Country blank!">
      </TD>
    </TR>
    <TR>
      <TH ALIGN="right">Credit Card Number:</TH>
      <TD>
        <CFINPUT
          NAME="CreditCard" SIZE="30"
          REQUIRED="Yes" VALIDATE="creditcard"
          MESSAGE="You must provide a credit card number.">
      </TD>
    </TR>
    <TR>
      <TH ALIGN="right">Credit Card Expires:</TH>
      <TD>
        <SELECT NAME="CreditExpM">
          <CFLOOP FROM="1" TO="12" INDEX="i">
            <OPTION VALUE="#i#">#NumberFormat(i, "00")#
```

```
          </CFLOOP>
        </SELECT>
        <SELECT NAME="CreditExpY">
          <CFLOOP FROM="#Year(Now())#" TO="#Val(Year(Now())+5)#" INDEX="i">
            <OPTION VALUE="#i#">#i#
          </CFLOOP>
        </SELECT>
      </TD>
    </TR>
    <TR>
      <TH ALIGN="right">Name On Card:</TH>
      <TD>
        <CFINPUT
          NAME="CreditName" SIZE="30" REQUIRED="Yes"
          VALUE="#GetContact.FirstName# #GetContact.LastName#"
          MESSAGE="You must provide the Name on the Credit Card.">
      </TD>
    </TR>
    <TR VALIGN="baseline">
      <TH ALIGN="right">Confirmation:</TH>
      <TD>
        We will send a confirmation message to you at
        #GetContact.EMail#<BR>
        <CFINPUT TYPE="Radio" NAME="HTMLMail" VALUE="Yes" CHECKED="Yes">
        HTML (I sometimes see pictures in E-mail messages)<BR>
        <CFINPUT TYPE="Radio" NAME="HTMLMail" VALUE="No">
        Non-HTML (I never see any pictures in my messages)<BR>
      </TD>
    </TR>
    <TR>
      <TD></TD>
      <TD>
        <INPUT TYPE="Submit" VALUE="Place Order Now">
      </TD>
    </TR>
  </TABLE>

  </CFFORM>
</CFOUTPUT>
```

The online store for Orange Whip Studios is now complete. Users can add items to their shopping carts, adjust quantities, remove items, and check out. And all the code has been abstracted in a reasonable and maintainable fashion, thanks to ColdFusion's wonderful custom tag feature.

OTHER COMMERCE-RELATED TASKS

For a real-world online commerce site, there are some other tasks that your application pages will need to take care of. These tasks are not covered explicitly in this book, but they should be well within reach now that you've been introduced to the basic concepts and have walked through the construction of the main shopping experience for your users.

ORDER TRACKING

Most users who place orders online will expect some mechanism to be available to them to check the status of their orders, and they generally expect that mechanism to be online. Depending on what is being sold, simply making an e-mail address available for status inquiries might be enough. However, some type of secured order-tracking page will usually satisfy more people and cut down on support costs.

The `OrderHistory.cfm` templates from Chapter 21 are a great start. You would just need to ensure that the user has a way to see the `ShipDate` as well as the `OrderDate`, and you might even add a button the user could use to cancel her order.

ORDER FULFILLMENT

This chapter hasn't even touched upon the notion of actually fulfilling an order after it has been placed. How this works will depend entirely on the company for which you are building your commerce application. For instance, you might provide an Order Queue page for employees in Orange Whip Studio's shipping department. This Order Queue page could be similar to the `OrderHistory.cfm` templates (see the previous section, "Order Tracking"), except they would show all pending orders, not just the ones for a particular user.

Or, you might decide that an e-mail message should be sent to the shipping department using the `<CFMAIL>` tag. If your company's needs are simple, it might be sufficient to simply `BCC` the shipping department on the e-mail message sent by the `<CF_SendOrderConfirmation>` custom tag from Chapter 28.

CANCELLATIONS, RETURNS, AND REFUNDS

If you are taking money from your visitors, there is always the possibility that you will need to give some of it back at some point. You must ensure that your company has some means for dealing with returns and refunds, including the ability to recredit any charges that have been made to the user's credit card.

You might build your own Web-based interface for refunds and cancellations, using the `<CFX_CyberCash>` tag (which does support things such as refunds), if that is the payment-processing mechanism you are using. Many of the payment-processing services provide their own Web-based systems that your company's accounting or customer service employees can use to handle such special cases.

INVENTORY TRACKING

The examples in this chapter assume that all items in the `Merchandise` table are always available for sale. Orange Whip Studios might not need to be concerned about its merchandise ever selling out, but your company probably does. At a minimum, you probably should add an `InStock` Boolean field to the `Merchandise` table and ensure that users can't add items to their carts unless the `InStock` field is `1`. More sophisticated applications might call for maintaining a `NumberOnHand` field for each item, which gets decremented each time an item is ordered and incremented each time new shipments come in from the supplier.

Reporting

Of course, after a company is doing business online, it will need to know how much business its online store is generating. You should supply your company's executives with some type of reporting functionality that shows purchase trends over time, which products are profitable, and so on. To build such reports, you could use Crystal Reports with the `<CFREPORT>` tag (see Appendix A, "ColdFusion Tag Reference") or build your own reporting templates, perhaps illustrating the data visually using ColdFusion's dynamic graphing and charting capabilities (see Chapter 27, "Graphing").

PART IV

Advanced ColdFusion

CHAPTER 30

ColdFusion Server Configuration

In this chapter

THE COLDFUSION ADMINISTRATOR

The ColdFusion Administrator serves as a Web-based console to manage and configure your ColdFusion server. Because the ColdFusion Administrator works through a Web browser, you can use a Windows-based system to manage a Linux-, Solaris-, or HP-UX–based ColdFusion server or vice versa.

The Administrator provides a spectrum of controls and services for you to control. For example, you can

- Improve server performance in the Caching page
- Connect to a data source in the ODBC Data Sources page
- Configure debugging settings in the Debugging Options page
- Register CFX tags in the CFX Tags page
- Change the Administrator password in the CF Admin Password page
- Analyze application performance in the Server Reports page

In short, you can change almost any facet of your ColdFusion Server using the Adminstrator. Let's begin.

STARTING THE COLDFUSION ADMINISTRATOR

To start the Administrator in Windows, select Start, Programs, ColdFusion Server 5, ColdFusion Administrator. In other operating systems, enter the following URL in a Web browser:

```
http://hostname/CFIDE/Administrator/index.cfm
```

Note

Because Linux, Solaris, and HP-UX filenames are case sensitive, be sure you enter the URL exactly as it appears here.

A login screen will appear, as shown in Figure 30.1. Enter the password you specified during the installation.

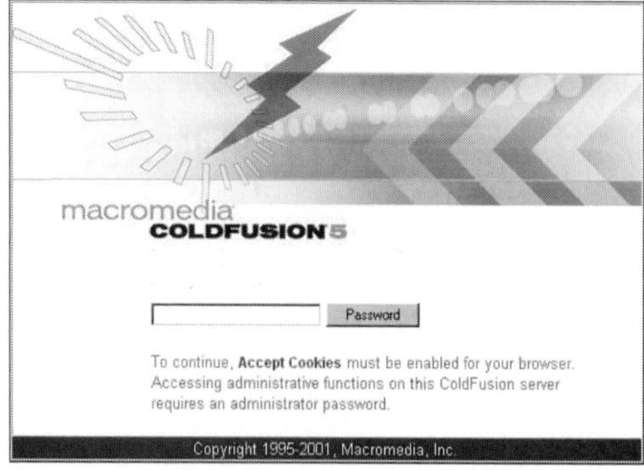

Figure 30.1
Enter the ColdFusion Administrator password you specified in the installation process.

After you have entered your password, the ColdFusion Administrator Welcome Page appears (see Figure 30.2). From this page, you can access almost any administration page in less than two clicks of the mouse.

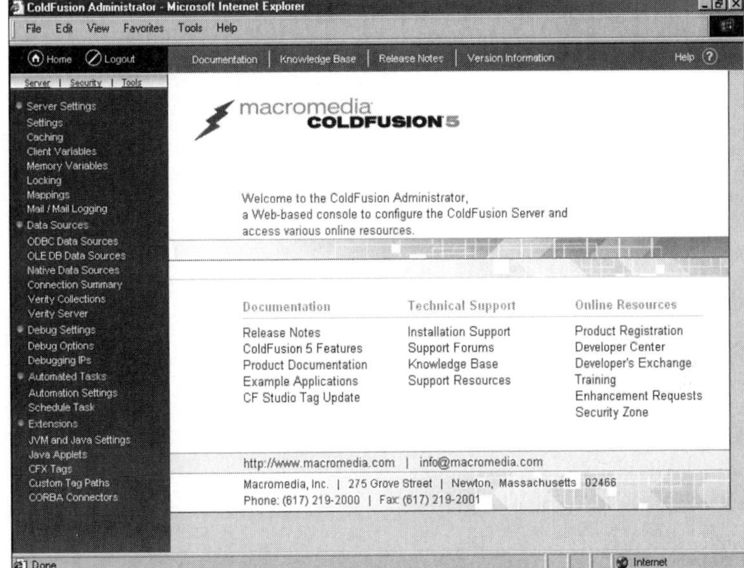

Figure 30.2 The ColdFusion Welcome Page greets you upon login.

The Administrator home page consists of a left navigation bar that contains all the available administration options. You also can access sample applications, documentation, online developer resources, and release notes.

In the left navigation bar, you will notice three links at the top: Server, Security, and Tools. These links, referred to as *tabs*, represent the major functional divisions of the Administrator:

- **The Server tab**—Lets you configure the majority of ColdFusion settings, such as data sources, debugging, variables, and so on.
- **The Security tab**—Lets you set passwords, restrict certain tags, and so on.
- **The Tools tab**—Provides a variety of features to analyze site performance.

The following sections describe how to use the features contained in these tabs.

THE SERVER TAB

Whether you're developing an enterprise-level e-commerce Web site that will handle hundreds of thousands of hits per day or a simple company intranet, you will need to spend a few minutes configuring ColdFusion's basic settings.

Here are the options available in the Server tab:

- Server Settings
- Data Sources
- Debug Settings
- Automated Settings
- Extensions

SERVER SETTINGS

The Server Settings section of the Server tab contains a great number of useful and powerful server configuration settings. The majority of these settings directly affect ColdFusion performance. Here are the available pages:

- Settings
- Caching
- Client Variables
- Memory Variables
- Locking
- Mapping
- Mail/Mail Logging

SETTINGS

In the Settings page, you can configure a variety of server options for ColdFusion (see Figure 30.3). You can manipulate many of these settings, such as Simultaneous Requests and Suppress Whitespace, for optimal performance. The following sections describe the available options.

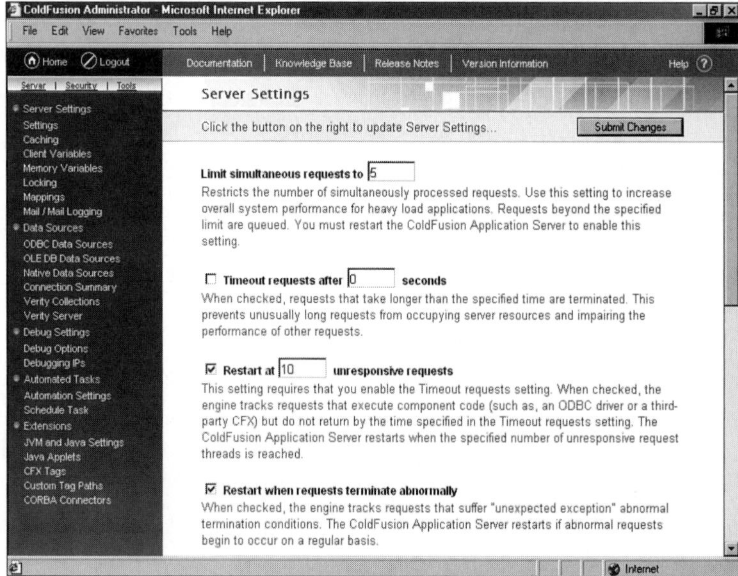

Figure 30.3
In the Server Settings page, you can configure general settings for your ColdFusion server.

LIMIT SIMULTANEOUS REQUESTS TO X

ColdFusion's processing resources are not unlimited. Thus, you must enter the number of simultaneous request that ColdFusion will process at a time.

To understand this setting, let's use a metaphor. Let's say your ColdFusion Server is a short-order cook in a busy downtown diner. This cook, who goes by the name of Gus, is new to the job and can handle five orders (page requests) at a time efficiently. However, at lunch hour, when office workers crowd the diner, Gus is suddenly flooded with twenty orders at a time. Bewildered by the avalanche of orders, Gus tries to fill all the orders at once. Unfortunately, because of his lack of experience, Gus's efficiency plunges, all the orders take longer, and the diner patrons become impatient.

If Gus had more experience, he could handle more orders at one time, or in other words, simultaneous requests. Gus's level of experience directly translates into your server's hardware specifications. The more powerful your hardware, such as a greater amount of RAM, faster processor, quicker hard drive, and SCSI connections, the more requests it can handle at one time.

Note

Application design also plays a prominent role in application performance. See Chapter 17, "Planning an Application," for an introduction to application design.

Let's go back to the lunch-hour pandemonium at the diner. Although inexperienced, Gus can think on his feet. He instructs the waitresses to herd the hungry patrons into one line and take five orders at a time. That way, Gus stays at peak efficiency and can cook the maximum number of orders.

Therefore, depending on your hardware specifications, limiting the number of requests forces ColdFusion to devote its resources to a small number of tasks, thus executing all tasks more quickly. The default value is `5`. If you think your server can handle more requests, try your ColdFusion applications with the increased setting under load in a staging environment.

Caution

If no value is specified, ColdFusion processes all requests that come to it. This can lead to instability and potential crashes.

Note

ColdFusion must be restarted for this change to take effect.

TIMEOUT REQUESTS AFTER X SECONDS

With his simultaneous request line working, Gus is working efficiently and customers are satisfied. Suddenly, Gus receives an order for a lobster roll. He realizes that the seafood distributor didn't make the delivery this morning, and there's no lobster meat with which to make lobster roll. Gus sends a dishwasher out to the nearest seafood market to procure some lobster fast. Unfortunately, this one order, or request, will take too long.

As Gus continues to fill other orders, he keeps an eye on the clock, counting the minutes until the dishwasher returns. More lobster roll orders are coming in and starting to pile up. Therefore, even though Gus has limited the simultaneous requests, the lobster roll requests are taking too long and diverting his attention from the matter at hand. Gus makes a decision and throws the orders in the trash can. The customers will just have to submit their requests again, he thinks.

The Timeout Requests After X Seconds setting works the same way. For requests that take a long time to process, whether the latency is due to a slow legacy database or a credit card verification service, ColdFusion must devote resources to maintaining that request. This setting enables you to apply a time limit to requests. If the request takes longer than the timeout setting, ColdFusion drops the request and processes other requests in the queue.

RESTART AT X UNRESPONSIVE REQUESTS

The dishwasher has yet to return with the lobster, and the customers are getting tired of resubmitting their orders (that is, page requests). With no other option available to him, Gus announces to everyone that all lobster roll orders cannot be filled. At the same time, Gus sends another dishwasher to the seafood market for lobster.

The Restart at X Unresponsive Requests setting instructs ColdFusion to restart services that do no respond after a specified number of requests. Restarting a service might resolve the problem, but it can also prove costly for site users if e-commerce transactions are involved. If a pattern of problems develops, you should investigate the problem. The default value is `10`.

RESTART WHEN REQUESTS TERMINATE ABNORMALLY

Selecting this check box instructs ColdFusion to restart services that terminate page requests abnormally. If a pattern of problems develops, you should investigate the problem.

Enabling this option is a double-edged sword. If the problem lies with ColdFusion, restarting the server could remedy the situation. However, if the problem lies with a service that is out of your control and rebooting seems to be the only way to remedy the situation, you've got a small dilemma on your hands.

In a development environment, you should disable this setting so that you can examine the error before ColdFusion reboots. In a production environment, the situation is more complicated. Because you want maximum uptime for ColdFusion applications, enabling this option might come at the cost of declining reliability. Then again, you do not want an application to malfunction. The best solution can be to enable the option and, if users begin to complain about downtime, consider disabling the option and finding another workaround.

Suppress Whitespace by Default

Despite the proliferation of broadband access, the Internet's bandwidth limitations continue to be a performance-sapping factor in Web site performance. Therefore, smaller files, even HTML files, are always desirable.

Select this check box to compress extraneous spaces, tabs, carriage returns, and linefeeds into a single space. This can significantly reduce the HTML file size that is sent to the user's Web browser. ColdFusion must be restarted for this change to take effect.

Note

The `SUPPRESSWHITESPACE` attribute of the `<CFPROCESSINGDIRECTIVE>` tag takes precedent over the Administrator's whitespace suppression.

Enforce Strict Attribute Validation

Irrelevant CFML tag attributes require ColdFusion to expend server resources evaluating unnecessary attributes. Although potentially annoying during development, selecting this check box instructs ColdFusion to not process any tags with superfluous attributes. ColdFusion's template processing speed will increase, while coding errors will decrease.

Note

See Appendix A, "ColdFusion Tag Reference," for a comprehensive CFML tag reference.

Note

If you currently run ColdFusion applications that are more than two years old, ColdFusion 5 might not recognize some older tag attributes. Try these older applications in a staging environment with this setting enabled to ensure that they work.

Missing Template Handler

You can create a custom page to display when ColdFusion can't find a template. Enter the absolute file path to the page in the Missing Template Handler text box. If no file path is specified, ColdFusion uses the standard missing template message.

Site-Wide Error Handler

You can create a custom page to display when ColdFusion throws an error when processing a page request. Enter the absolute file path to the page in the Site-Wide Error Handler text box. If no file path is specified, ColdFusion uses the standard error message.

Note

Remember to click the Submit Changes button to save your changes.

CACHING

Rather than storing all data in a database, ColdFusion can hold some data in server memory. This eliminates costly database reads and speeds up page processing. Finding the optimal caching settings depends on your hardware and application needs. In addition, many Web servers provide their own caching settings that can increase performance. For more information, consult the documentation included with your Web server.

Note

See Chapter 24, "Improving Performance," for a detailed explanation of caching.

Like the Simultaneous Requests setting, you must test your cache settings in a staging environment under load to target the appropriate settings properly. Never implement untested settings on your production servers before testing.

The Administrator's Caching page provides the general configuration settings for ColdFusion caching (see Figure 30.4). Read the following sections to learn more.

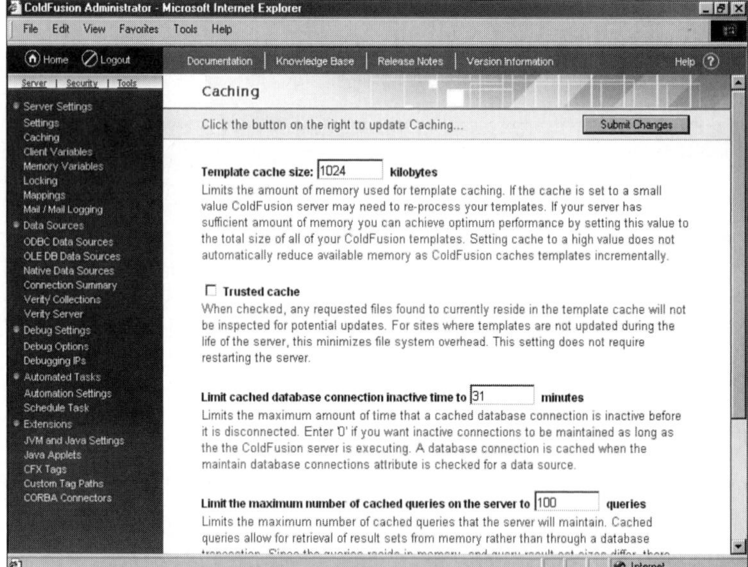

Figure 30.4
In the Caching page, you can set general caching preference for ColdFusion, such as cache sizes.

Note

For information on programmatic caching, see Chapter 24.

Template Cache Size

Select this check box and specify the amount (in kilobytes) of server memory to allocate for template caching. If the value is set too small, ColdFusion must continually reprocess templates, thus consuming server resources. If your memory size allows, set the template cache to four or five times the size of all your templates. This value will account for the additional data added by the database queries. The default is 1024KB.

One method to derive the appropriate template cache size is to add all the templates together associated with your ColdFusion applications. Next, take that sum and double it. This number represents the total template size of your ColdFusion applications plus some room for expansion. If your server has sufficient memory resources available, enter the value in the Template Cache Size setting and click the Submit Changes button. Keep in mind that you should always do testing in a staging environment. Never experiment with server settings on your production servers.

Caution

Be careful when calculating the size of your template cache. If you do not leave a sufficient amount of server memory available for other ColdFusion processes, the server can become unstable and crash.

Trusted Cache

To further decrease database calls, select this check box to stop ColdFusion from checking whether the template cache is up-to-date. The Trusted Cache setting should be used only when you are certain that the data will not change. Some examples of data that changes very infrequently are the number of U.S. states, income tax rates, annual rainfall averages, and so on.

Limit Cached Database Connection Inactive Time to X Minutes

Most databases can handle only a certain number of database connections. To keep close database connections and make those connections available for other applications, enter the number of minutes for ColdFusion to wait before terminating an inactive cached database connection. Enter `0` if you want ColdFusion to maintain inactive database connections indefinitely.

Obviously, if your ColdFusion applications make many database calls at the same time, you should set this value to a lower number to free up connections for other applications. At the same time, you also must take into account the nature of the database calls. Opening database connections take time. If your applications require the fastest possible access to data, such as an application that must provide a constant stream of mission-critical data, enter `0` to keep database connections open indefinitely.

Note

Entering 0 is not advisable unless you're certain that ColdFusion will not require additional database connections at some point. Therefore, this setting should be specified only for ColdFusion Servers dedicated to one application.

LIMITING THE MAXIMUM NUMBER OF CACHED QUERIES ON THE SERVER TO X QUERIES

Cached database queries enable ColdFusion to retrieve information from memory rather than querying the database itself. To conserve server memory, enter the number of cached queries that ColdFusion will store in server memory. When this value is exceeded, the oldest query is dropped from the cache and is replaced with the specified query. The default value is `100`.

Note

Because database query size can vary greatly, average your database queries and multiply the result by the number of cached queries you want to specify. If the number exceeds the available memory, reduce the number of cached queries.

Note

Remember to click the Submit Changes button to save your changes.

CLIENT VARIABLES

The Client Variables page enables you to store client variables via four mechanisms: the default store, the system Registry, cookies on the client, or in a database. The storage mechanism specified in this page is used system-wide in your ColdFusion server when an alternative variable storage location is not specified in the `<CFAPPLICATION>` tag.

→ **See** Chapter 9, "Using ColdFusion," for an introduction to ColdFusion variables.

Keep the following points in mind:

- **Registry**—Unix-based operating systems store Registry information in a flat text file. Therefore, performance and scalability might not be adequate for your ColdFusion applications' demands. On Windows, carefully monitor the amount of virtual memory allocated to the Registry. If your ColdFusion applications consume more memory than specified, Windows might become unstable and crash.
- **Cookies**—In the past, cookies have come under scrutiny for privacy reasons. Although some of these concerns have subsided, keep the users' concerns in mind. To that end, a note that your site uses cookies might be in order. In addition, some users might have disabled the storage of cookies in their Web browsers, or their browsers might not support cookies.
- **Database**—Storing client variables in a database can provide a scalable and secure storage mechanism. However, it can also pose a potential reliability and performance problem. Be sure your database server is hosted on a dependable, high-performance server.

If your database is unavailable or performs poorly, your users will probably not appreciate the loss of functionality or long wait times.

To set the client variable storage mechanism, select the radio button next to the desired mechanism and click the Apply button (see Figure 30.5).

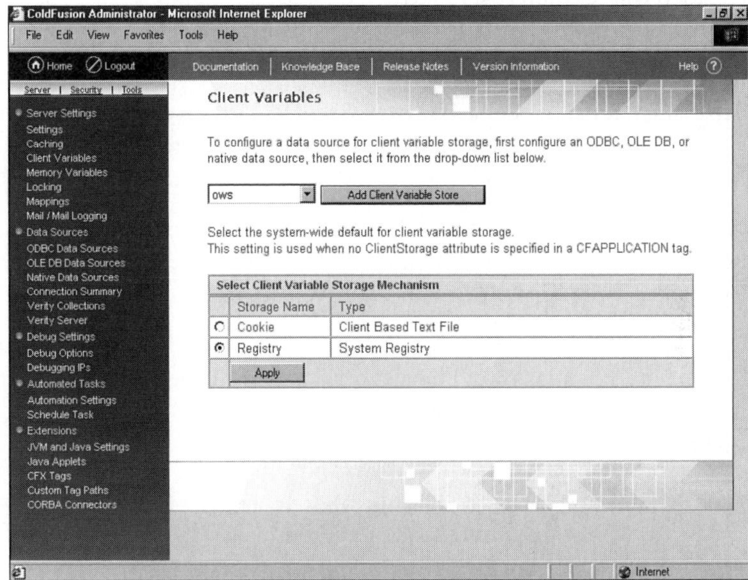

Figure 30.5
In the Client Variables page, you can choose which client variable storage mechanism for ColdFusion to use, modify existing storage mechanisms, or add more storage mechanisms.

Note

See Chapter 9 for more information on variables.

ESTABLISHING A DATABASE FOR CLIENT VARIABLE STORAGE

To establish a database as a client variable storage mechanism, do the following:

1. In the Client Variables page, select the DSN data source ows from the drop-down menu, and click the Add Client Variable Store button.
2. In the Add/Edit Store page, change any settings you want. See the next section, "Modifying a Client Variable Storage Mechanism," for further instructions.

Note

If you have configured this data source for client variable storage before, be sure to clear the Create Client Database Tables check box. Otherwise, multiple database tables will be created.

3. Click the Submit Changes button.

MODIFYING A CLIENT VARIABLE STORAGE MECHANISM

To modify an existing mechanism, click the name in the Storage Name column of the Select Client Variable Storage Mechanism table. Depending on the storage mechanism being modified, you will be presented with an Add/Edit Client Store page with various options.

The following sections describe your client variable options.

PURGE DATA FOR CLIENTS THAT REMAIN UNVISITED FOR X DAYS

Depending on the level of activity for your ColdFusion application, the number of stored client variables can quickly balloon to enormous proportions, which can cause problems if the system Registry is used as the storage mechanism.

To solve this problem, you can set ColdFusion to delete variables automatically that are not used (that is, unvisited) for X number of days. The default value for system storage is 30 days. The default value for Registry storage is 10 days, and the default value for database storage is 90 days.

To enable this option, select the check box and enter the desired number of days. Click the Submit Changes button to apply the setting.

Note

If you cluster your servers, be sure only one server in the cluster is set to purge variables. Multiple servers purging client variable can cause problems with application processing.

DISABLE GLOBAL CLIENT VARIABLE UPDATES

Use this option to control how global client variables are updated. When global client variable updates are enabled, ColdFusion updates global client variables when a page is requested. When disabled, global client variables are updated only when set or explicitly changed.

To disable global client variable updates, select the check box and click the Submit Changes button.

DELETE

Click the Delete button to remove the client variable storage mechanism.

MEMORY VARIABLES

The Memory Variables page lets you enable and specify the timeout interval for application and session variables (see Figure 30.6).

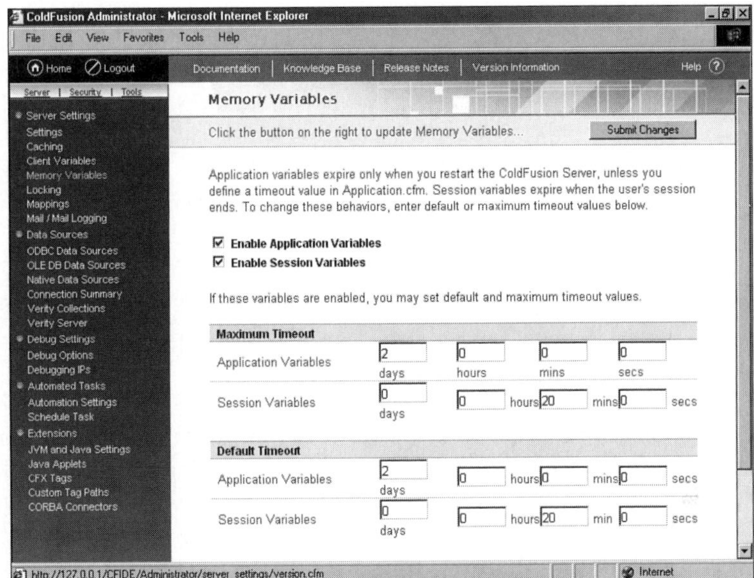

Figure 30.6
In the Memory Variables page, you can enable application and server variables, as well as specify timeout intervals.

Note

See Chapter 9 for more information on variables.

ENABLE APPLICATION VARIABLES

Application variables are stored in ColdFusion's memory. If your ColdFusion applications do not use application variables, deselect the check box to free up valuable server memory for other processing tasks, and then click the Submit Changes button.

ENABLE SESSION VARIABLES

Session variables are stored in ColdFusion's memory. If your ColdFusion applications do not use session variables, deselect the check box to conserve server memory.

APPLICATION AND SESSION VARIABLE TIMEOUTS

Application and session variables reside in ColdFusion's memory until they are released from memory, or time out. If support for these variables is enabled, you can specify the timeout interval. The default timeout for application variables is 2 days, whereas the default timeout for session variables is 20 minutes.

PART IV

CH 30

Note

Because the timeout settings in the Memory Variables page affect all application and session variables on your ColdFusion server, you must take care that the default and maximum timeouts specified at the application level in the `<CFAPPLICATION>` tag parallel those set in the Administrator. For more information, see Chapter 19, "Introducing the Web Application Framework," for more information on using the `<CFAPPLICATION>` tag.

Note

Remember to click the Submit Changes button to save your changes.

LOCKING

ColdFusion applications read and write numerous variables during the processing of a page request. Further, multiple application processes accessing variables simultaneously in the shared data scopes, including server, application, and session scopes, can corrupt data.

Note

See Chapter 19 for an introduction to locking.

Because some data referenced in variables cannot become corrupted, such as payment information in an e-commerce application, ColdFusion provides a locking method to restrict access to designated variables. Enclosing variables in the `<CFLOCK>` tag accomplishes this.

You also can use the Locking page in the Administrator to lock variables in shared data scopes (see Figure 30.7). You can enable single threaded sessions, configure whether ColdFusion should check that all variables are locked within each scope, and automatically lock variables for read access only.

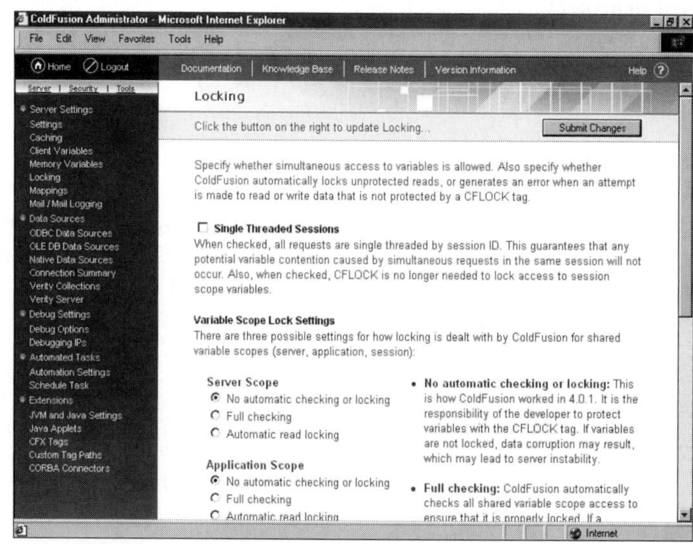

Figure 30.7 In the Locking page, you can configure locking settings for server, application, and session scopes.

ENABLE SINGLE THREADED SESSIONS

Select this check box to instruct ColdFusion to queue access to session scope variables. When enabled, reading and writing session variables occurs one at a time, with each waiting for all other requests to finish.

Let's return to the diner metaphor, but this time, let's make a change. Instead of a mob of customers submitting orders all at once or a few simultaneous requests at a time, Gus will take only one order at a time, cook the meal, and serve it to the customer before taking the next order. Gus can take extra care with every order to ensure everything is perfect, but his overall efficiency decreases.

Single-threaded sessions provide the highest level of protection against sessions accessing variables at the same time and potentially corrupting data. If you enable Single Threaded Sessions, you do not need to use the `<CFLOCK>` tag to protect session variables. However, single-threaded sessions can retard application performance. For example, because each session request occurs sequentially, applications that use Web browser frames will load each frame consecutively.

In addition, enabling single-threaded sessions can prove a useful debugging tool. If you are experiencing an unidentifiable page error, enable single-threaded sessions. If the error disappears, the problem is likely an unlocked session variable.

VARIABLE SCOPE LOCK SETTINGS

For server, application, and session scopes, the Administrator supplies three options for automatic locking: No Automatic Checking or Locking, Full Checking, and Automatic Read Locking. When any of these options is selected, ColdFusion scans variables for the `<CFLOCK>` tag. Table 30.1 describes the locking options.

TABLE 30.1 LOCKING OPTIONS FOR SERVER, APPLICATION, AND SESSION SCOPES

Option	Description
No Automatic Checking or Locking	Variables will not be scanned for the `<CFLOCK>` tag. As a result, data corruption can occur.
Full Checking	Variables are scanned for the `<CFLOCK>` tag. If it's not locked, an error page is thrown.
Automatic Read Locking	Variable reads automatically are locked. If a write is attempted on an unlocked variable, an error is thrown.

Click the Submit Changes button when finished. For more information on locking, see Chapter 19.

Note

The Full Checking option must be used only with the `SCOPE` attribute of the `<CFLOCK>` tag. If the `NAME` attribute is used, an error is thrown.

Note

Remember to click the Submit Changes button to save your changes.

MAPPINGS

ColdFusion mappings allow you to specify directories to use in your CFML code file paths. Specifically, the `<CFINCLUDE>` and `<CFMODULE>` tags use the server mappings. By default, the only mapping specified is the Web server root. You can add more mappings to direct ColdFusion to look in other directories on your server, or to another mapped drive in your network, for certain files.

Mappings are useful for separating files in different directories. For example, the Webmaster of the Orange Whip Studio site wants to store all the site images in the directory `C:\IMAGES`. In the Mappings page (see Figure 30.8), follow these steps:

1. Enter **`/images`** in the Logical Path text box. This is the file path you will use in your tags.
2. In the Directory Path text box, enter **`C:\IMAGES`**. This is the directory on your server to which ColdFusion will direct requests from `/images`.
3. Click the Apply Mapping button.

The mapping should now appear in the list of mappings.

Note

Mappings apply only to CFML tags. You must still specify the absolute file path for all HTML paths.

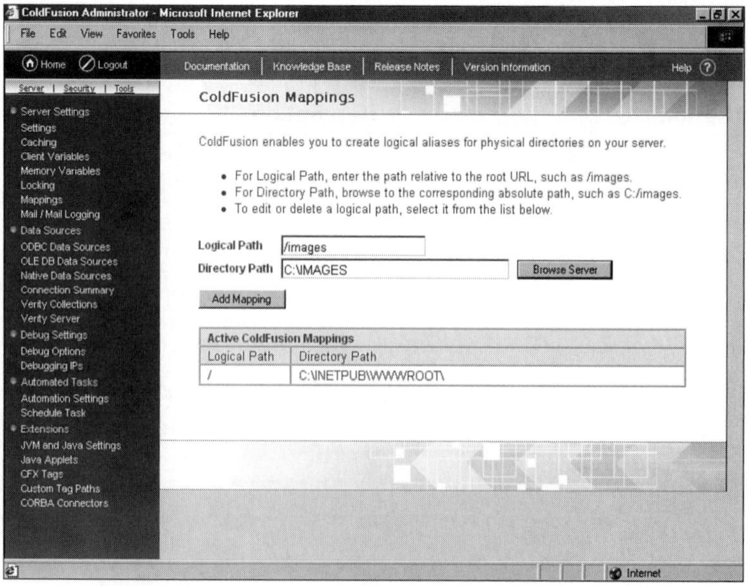

Figure 30.8
Enter your mapping information in the Mappings page.

To update or delete the mapping, click the entry in either the Logical Path or Directory Path column. Make your changes, and then click the Update Mapping button. To delete the mapping, simply click the Delete Mapping button.

Mail/Mail Logging

Use the Mail/Mail Logging page to establish an SMTP e-mail server connection for ColdFusion to use (see Figure 30.9). ColdFusion can use e-mail in a variety of ways, including the `<CFMAIL>` tag and automatically generated reports to server administrators in case of problems.

> **Note**
>
> See Chapter 28, "Interacting with E-mail," to learn more about generating e-mail with ColdFusion.

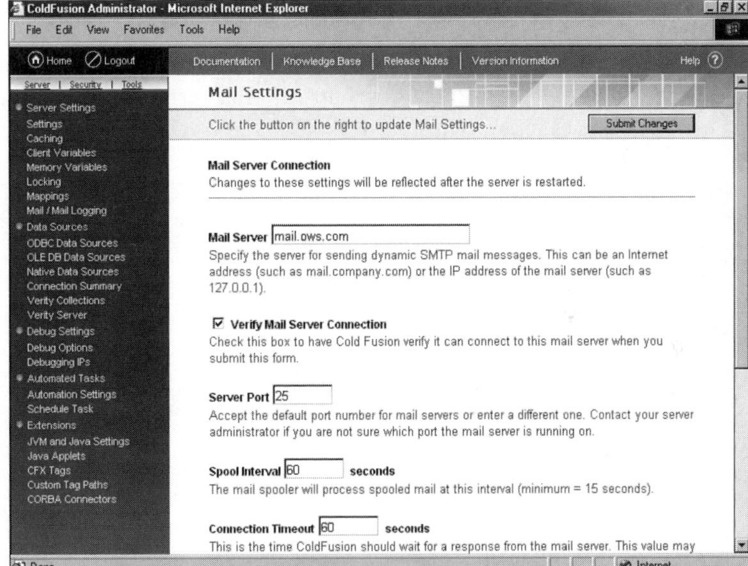

Figure 30.9
Use the Mail/Mail Logging page to specify server settings, set logging options, and verify e-mail servers.

To set up a mail server, do the following:

1. Enter either the Internet domain name or the IP address for the SMTP server in the Mail Server Connection text box. For the Orange Whip Studio site, enter **`MAIL.OWS.COM`**.
2. Click the Verify Mail Server check box for ColdFusion to validate the e-mail server when the Submit Changes button is clicked. This isn't required, but it is recommended.
3. Enter your e-mail server's port number. If you don't know the port number for your e-mail server, check with your network administrator.

4. The Spool Interval setting enables you to specify the number of seconds ColdFusion waits before sending e-mail.

Tip

> When scheduling the spool interval, keep in mind that any scheduled tasks might need to generate an important e-mail. For example, if a scheduled task runs every 30 seconds, set the Spool Interval to 35 for the scheduled task to complete and generate all pertinent e-mails.

5. The Connection Timeout setting enables you to set the number of seconds ColdFusion should wait for a response from the e-mail server. An interval in excess of 60 seconds is unusual and might point to problems with the e-mail server.

The Mail Logging settings give you the ability to either log the e-mail messages generated by ColdFusion by severity (including Information, Warning, and Error) or just log all ColdFusion-generated e-mails.

The logs are saved in `\CFUSION\LOG` in Windows and `\OPT\COLDFUSION\LOG` in Unix-based operating systems. The `MAIL.LOG` file contains e-mail error messages, and the `MAILSENT.LOG` file contains entries for all e-mails sent by ColdFusion.

Note

> Remember to click the Submit Changes button to save your changes.

DATA SOURCES

The Data Sources section of the Administrator lets you establish data source connections to databases for your ColdFusion applications and create, index, and maintain Verity collections to build search interfaces for your Web site.

The Data Sources section contains the following pages:

- ODBC Data Sources
- OLE DB Data Sources
- Native Data Sources
- Connection Summary
- Verity Collections
- Verity Server

The following sections describe the available pages.

ODBC, OLE DB, AND NATIVE DATA SOURCES

ColdFusion includes drivers for ODBC, OLE DB, and Native database drivers.

Note

See Chapter 1, "Introducing ColdFusion," and Chapter 3, "Building the Databases," for more information on DNS and an introduction to databases.

Determining which kind of database driver to use depends on the data source to which you want to connect and your server operating system. Consider the following:

- **Open DataBase Connectivity (ODBC) connections**—Can be established in any operating system after you have registered them in your operating system.
- **OLE DB connections**—Can be made only in Windows NT and Windows 2000. They enable you to connect to alternative data sources, such as LDAP servers, Microsoft Exchange and Lotus Notes servers, legacy mainframes, and so on.
- **Native database drivers**—Available only in ColdFusion Enterprise, these are drivers specifically designed for certain database systems. These drivers offer arguably better performance than their ODBC counterparts as well as enhanced functionality, such as robust support for stored procedures.

The following ODBC drivers are available in ColdFusion 5 Enterprise Edition for Windows:

- Microsoft Access (MDB)
- Microsoft SQL Server
- Microsoft dBase
- Microsoft FoxPro
- Microsoft Visual FoxPro
- Microsoft Excel
- Microsoft Text
- Merant dBase/FoxPro
- Merant Paradox
- Merant Text
- Merant Excel Workbook
- Merant IBM DB2/UDB
- Merant Informix 7.x/9.x
- Merant Informix Dynamic Server
- Merant Progress
- Merant SQLBase 7/9
- Merant Sybase ASE
- Merant Oracle 8

The following OLE DB drivers are available in ColdFusion 5 Enterprise Edition for Windows:

- SQLOLEDB
- Microsoft Jet OLEDB 3.51

The following native database drivers are available in ColdFusion 5 Enterprise Edition for Windows:

- Sybase 11
- Oracle 7.3
- Oracle 8
- Informix 7.3
- DB2

Note

Consult the Data Sources chapters in the ColdFusion documentation for a complete listing of the available database drivers for all operating systems and editions of ColdFusion.

CONNECTING TO A DATA SOURCE

The process for creating a data source in the Administrator is similar for ODBC, OLE DB, and native database drivers. An ODBC database is used for the example.

To create an ODBC connection, do the following:

1. Under the Data Sources heading, click the ODBC Connection link. The ODBC Data Sources page appears (see Figure 30.10).

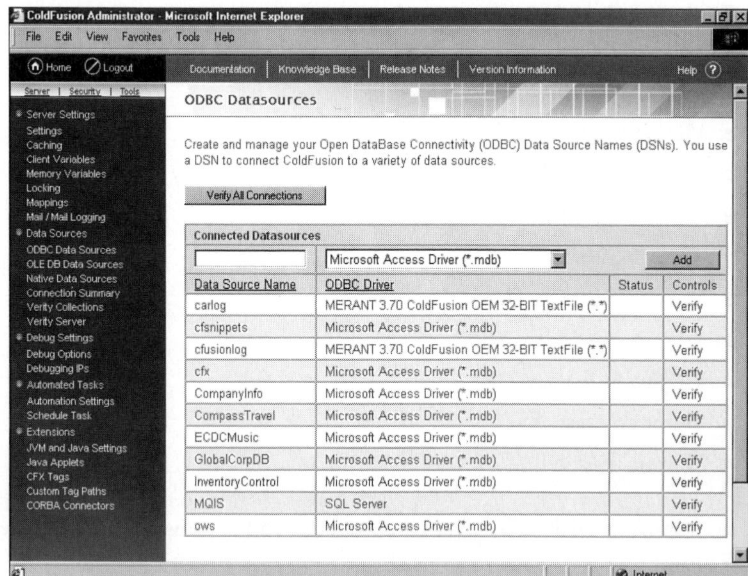

Figure 30.10 The ODBC Data Sources page displays all active ODBC connections.

2. Enter **ows** (Orange Whip Studios) in the text box above the Data Source Name column. Select Microsoft Access Driver (*.mdb) in the drop-down menu above the ODBC Driver column.
3. Click the Add button. The Create ODBC Data Source page appears (see Figure 30.11).

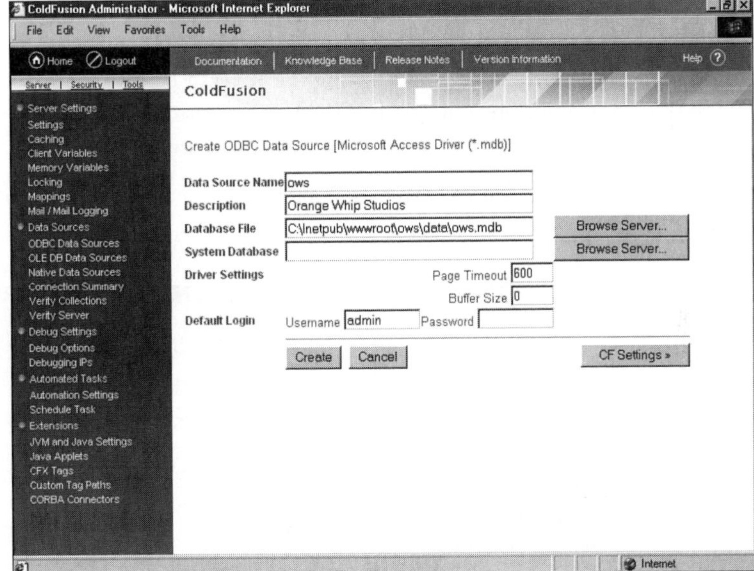

Figure 30.11 Enter your ODBC data source connection information in the Create ODBC Data Source page.

4. In the Description text box, enter **Orange Whip Studios** to identify the connection.
5. Click the Browse Server button next to the Database File text box. In the Browse Server page, navigate to the directory in which you saved the `ows.mdb` file and click the Apply button.
6. Click the Create button.

Tip

To further customize your ODBC connection, click the CF Settings button in the Create ODBC Data Source page. The list of available settings expands to include connection limits and timeout, settings to restrict SQL statements, the text buffer size, and other options.

In the ODBC Data Source page, ows should now appear in the Data Source Name column. To verify the connection, click the Verify link in the Controls column.

Tip

To validate all ODBC data sources, click the Verify All Data Sources button.

After a data source is created, you can edit and update settings by clicking the data source's name in the Data Source Name column. When you have finished making the changes, click the Update button to apply the settings.

CONNECTION SUMMARY

The Connection Summary page provides a consolidated management console to all ODBC, OLE DB, and native data sources for ColdFusion (see Figure 30.12). You can release all cached data source connections by clicking the Release All button, and you can verify all data source connections by clicking the Verify All button. You can also verify individual data source connections by clicking the data source's name in the Connected DataSources table.

The results of the data source verification appear in the Status column of the Connected DataSources table.

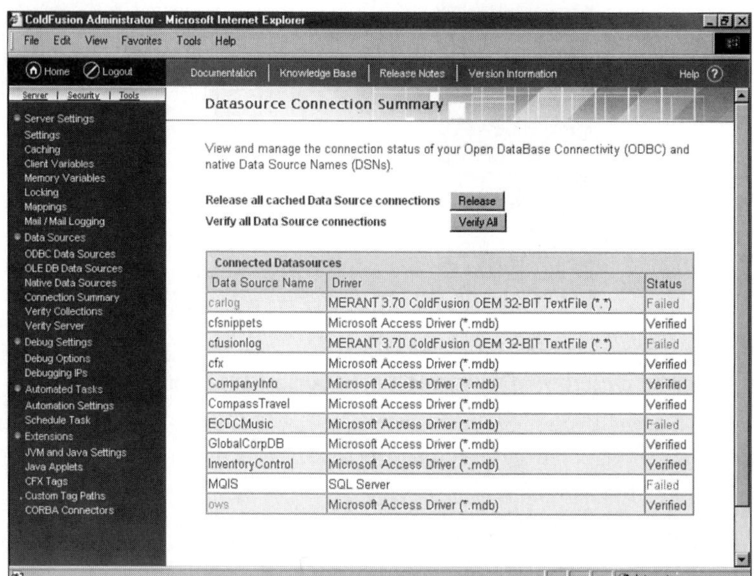

Figure 30.12
In the Connection Summary page, you can verify and release all cached data sources with one click.

VERITY COLLECTIONS

ColdFusion bundles the Verity Development Kit (VDK) 2.6.1 search engine for indexing your site's content for efficient site searches. ColdFusion also includes an OEM version of Verity's K2 Server for high-performance searching.

Note

See Chapter 36, "Full-Text Searching with Verity," to learn how to build search interfaces into your ColdFusion applications.

Verity creates *collections*, Verity's proprietary databases that enable full-text searches of site files, such as HTML and HTML files, database queries, word-processing documents, and so on. You also can use the `<CFCOLLECTION>` and `<CFINDEX>` tags to create and index collections programmatically. For more information on Verity indexing and searching and building search functionality into your ColdFusion applications, see Chapter 36.

The Administrator provides two pages to create, modify, and configure Verity collections—Verity VDK Collections and Verity K2 Collections.

VERITY VDK COLLECTIONS

In the Verity Collections page, you can create, modify, and delete Verity collections (see Figure 30.13). Before you can actually index a collection, however, you must create it.

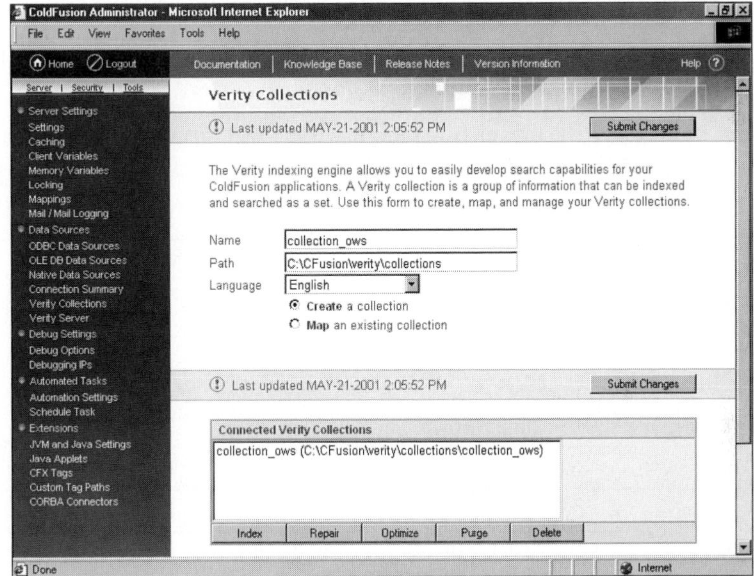

Figure 30.13
In the Verity Collections page, you can create, modify, and delete Verity collections.

To create a collection, perform the following steps:

1. Enter **`collection_ows`** in the Name text box.
2. If you want to store the collection files in a directory other than the default, enter the file path in the Path text box.
3. Select the language of your site in the Language drop-down menu.
4. Select the Create a Collection radio button.
5. Click the Submit Changes button.

The collection `ows` should now appear in the Connected Verity Collections window.

Note

You can also map an existing collection using the previously described procedure by selecting the Map an Existing Collection radio button. Mapping a collection creates an alias for you to use as a reference to that collection in the `<CFCOLLECTION>` tag. This is useful if you reinstalled ColdFusion but want to use an existing collection.

After a collection is created, you must populate it with the index of your site's contents. To index your site, select the collection in the Connected Verity Collections window and click the Index button.

In the next page that appears, do the following:

1. Enter the file extensions for the file types you want the VDK engine to index.
2. Click the Browse Server button, and navigate to the directory you want the VDK engine to index.
3. Select the Recursively Index Sub Directories check box to instruct the VDK engine to index all subdirectories automatically.
4. Enter the URL to which the VDK engine will return the indexed documents. For example, if you were indexing a hypothetical In Production directory in the Orange Whip Studios site, the return URL would be `http://www.ows.com/inproduction`.
5. Click the Submit Changes button to begin indexing.

Table 30.2 describes the other four buttons you can use to manage collections.

TABLE 30.2 COLLECTION MANAGEMENT BUTTONS

Button	Description
Repair	Repairs corrupted collections
Optimize	Compacts collections for faster searching
Purge	Deletes all data from a collection
Delete	Deletes the collection completely from ColdFusion

VERITY SERVER

Although you can specify the IP address and connection port in the Administrator, you must manually edit the Verity K2 Server's `SERVER.INI` file to register the collections for the K2 Server to search.

After you have registered the collections in the `SERVER.INI` file, the registered collections appear in the Server Managed Online Collection window.

Enter the IP address for the server on which the K2 Server will reside in the K2 Server IP Address text box. In the K2 Server Connection Port text box, enter the connection port ColdFusion will use to connect to the K2 Server.

You will still use the Verity Collections page to create, manage, and delete collections. For more information on configuring the K2 Server and the number of documents your edition of ColdFusion supports, consult the ColdFusion documentation.

Note

Remember to click the Submit Changes button to save your changes.

DEBUG SETTINGS

Debugging applications is a critical part of all software development, including ColdFusion development. ColdFusion provides a copious amount of processing information that lets you locate the problems in your applications with minimal effort.

The Administrator provides the following pages for debugging configurations:

- Debugging Options
- Debugging IPs

DEBUGGING OPTIONS

In the Debugging Settings page, the Administrator enables you to customize the debugging information that is appended to the bottom of the page returned to the browser (see Figure 30.14).

Note

See Chapter 15, "Debugging and Troubleshooting," for more information on debugging.

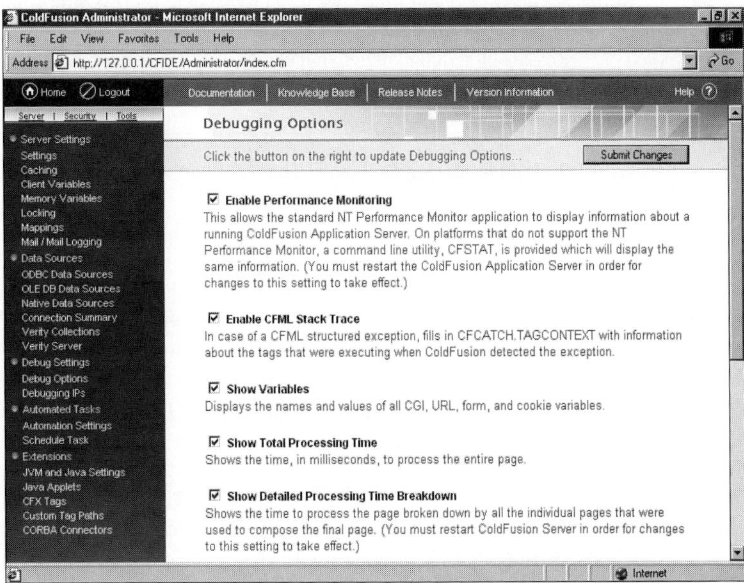

Figure 30.14
In the Debugging Settings page, you can configure the debugging information that ColdFusion returns to your Web browser.

Table 30.3 describes the available debugging options.

TABLE 30.3 DEBUGGING OPTIONS

Option	Description
Enable Performance Monitoring	Configures the Microsoft Management Console's Performance Monitor to display ColdFusion performance information
Enable CFML Stack Trace	Displays the list of tags that executed until the error occurred in `CFCATCH.TAGCONTEXT`
Show Variables	Displays all variable names and values for all variables
Show Total Processing Time	Displays the time in milliseconds the page request takes to process
Show Detailed Processing Time Breakdown	Displays the time in milliseconds each page involved in the page request takes to process
Show SQL and Data Source Name	Displays the data source name and the SQL statement in database query error messages
Show Query Information	Displays the record count, processing time, and SQL statement for each query executed
Display the Template Path in Error Messages	Displays the file path for the template producing the error

Tip

To determine how long ColdFusion is taking to process your code itself without query processing, subtract the total amount of time spent processing all queries from the processing time option mentioned earlier.

Note

Remember to click the Submit Changes button to save your changes.

DEBUGGING IPS

If you do not specify an IP address(es) to restrict debugging reporting in the Debugging IPs page, debugging information is sent to all users, including customers. If you have installed ColdFusion on your personal system and it will not be serving pages to anyone other than yourself, there is little reason to restrict IP addresses. However, you always should restrict IP addresses in debugging environments.

To add an IP address, enter the desired IP address into the IP Address text box and click the Add button (see Figure 30.15). The IP address should appear in the window below. You also can click the Add Current button to add the IP address of the system you are using to access the Administrator.

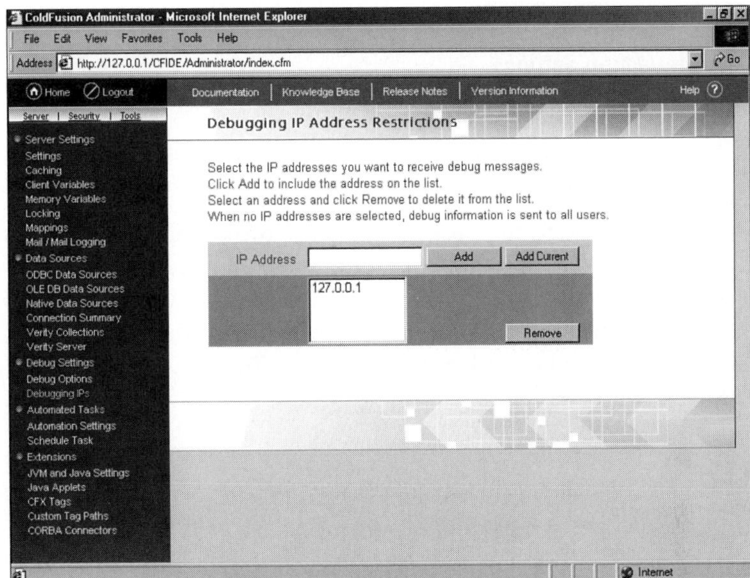

Figure 30.15
In the Debugging IP Address Restrictions page, you can restrict the debugging information to certain IP addresses.

Tip

The I.P. address for your local system, usually 127.0.0.1, should always be present. This restricts the debugging information from being displayed to all users. Click the Use Current button to add the IP address of the system accessing the ColdFusion Administrator.

Automated Tasks

Querying databases remains one of the most resource-intensive, yet critical, operations in database-driven Web site performance. To improve the efficiency of Web page delivery, the Administrator provides a scheduling tool that enables you to schedule the execution of CFML templates at specified intervals and store the resulting HTML for quick delivery to users' Web browsers.

Note

See Chapter 37, "Event Scheduling," for more information on automating tasks programmatically in your ColdFusion applications.

Automating page generation works best for CFML templates in which the data rarely changes, such as home pages, company directories, and so on. In addition, scheduling pages enables you to update pages on a regular basis to show progress, such as sales reports, development updates, and so on. In other words, a page that rarely changes is a prime candidate for automation.

The Administrator provides the following pages for automating tasks:

- Automation Settings
- Schedule Tasks

AUTOMATION SETTINGS

In the Automation Settings page, you will see two configuration options: Scheduler Refresh Interval and Enable Logging. Enter the number of minutes for ColdFusion to wait before it checks for new scheduled tasks. If your development environment does not require constant changing of scheduled tasks or all your schedule tasks run infrequently—such as daily—enter a higher number, such as 660. Select the Enable Logging check box to log scheduled task actions.

Note

Remember to click the Submit Changes button to save your changes.

SCHEDULE TASKS

The Schedule Tasks page enables you to create new scheduled tasks and modify and delete existing scheduled tasks. Any changes applied to the home page are installed once a day at 7:15 a.m. Let's create a scheduled task that executes the home page template every day at 7:30 a.m. and saves the resulting HTML file.

To schedule a new task, follow these steps:

1. In the Schedule Tasks page, click the Schedule New Task button.
2. In the Add/Edit Scheduled Task page (see Figure 30.16), enter **`OWS Homepage Cache`** in the Task Name text box.
3. Because you want this task to run daily, select the radio button next to Recurring. Because you want this task to run at 7:30 a.m., enter **`07:30:00`** in the text box to the right.
4. This will be an HTTP request operation. Besides, it's the only available operation.
5. Enter **`http://www.ows.com/`** for the home page.
6. Accessing the home page doesn't require a username, password, or proxy server settings. So, leave those text fields blank.
7. In the Path text box, enter the absolute file path to which ColdFusion should save the resulting HTML file. For this example, you want this file easily available, so enter **`C:\INETPUB\WWWROOT\OWS`**.
8. In the File text box, you supply the name for the HTML file. Enter **`OWS_HOMEPAGE_CACHE`**.
9. Because the HTML will be presented to site visitors, check the Resolve URLs check box.
10. Click the Submit Changes button.

Your scheduled task will now appear on the Scheduled Task page in the Schedule Tasks table. Now, all you have to do is reference the page in your existing home page template using <CFINCLUDE>.

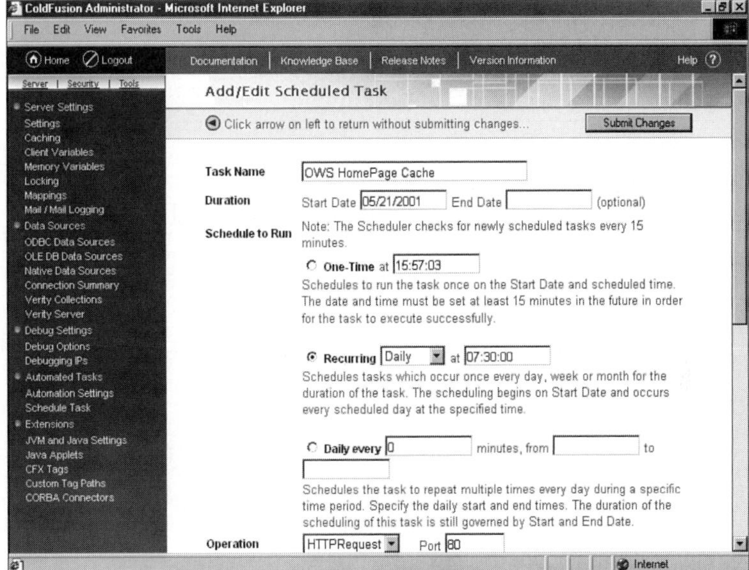

Figure 30.16
In the Add/Edit Scheduled Task page, you create and modify scheduled tasks.

To modify an existing scheduled task, click its name in the Name column or click the Edit Scheduled Task icon in the Actions column. To delete a scheduled task, click the Delete Scheduled Task icon.

EXTENSIONS

Use the Extensions section to integrate various Web technologies into ColdFusion. The Administrator provides pages for the following technologies:

- JVM and Java settings
- Java applets
- CFX tags
- Custom tag paths
- CORBA extensions

Note

See *Advanced ColdFusion 5 Application Development* (Que, ISBN: 0-7897-2585-1) for an in-depth examination of extending ColdFusion with other technologies.

JVM AND JAVA SETTINGS

Java functionality requires a Java Virtual Machine (JVM). The JVM and Java Settings page enables you to specify the file paths and configuration options for your JVM (see Figure 30.17). The available configuration options are described in Table 30.4.

TABLE 30.4 JVM AND JAVA SETTINGS

Setting	Description
Java Virtual Machine Path	Enter the file path to your desired JVM.
Initial Heap and Max Heap Size	Enter the initial and maximum amount of memory your JVM uses.
Load JVM When Starting ColdFusion	Select this check box if your ColdFusion application needs instant access to the JVM. To conserve server resources, deselect the check box to instruct ColdFusion to load the JVM only when needed.
Class Path	Enter the file path to the Java classes for your JVM.
System Options	Enter any initialization options needed by your JVM as name/value pairs. Be sure to insert a space between pairs.
Implementation Options	Enter any implementation options needed by your JVM. Be sure to insert a space between options.
CFX Jar Paths	Enter the file path for the interface needed by any `CFX.JAR` files.

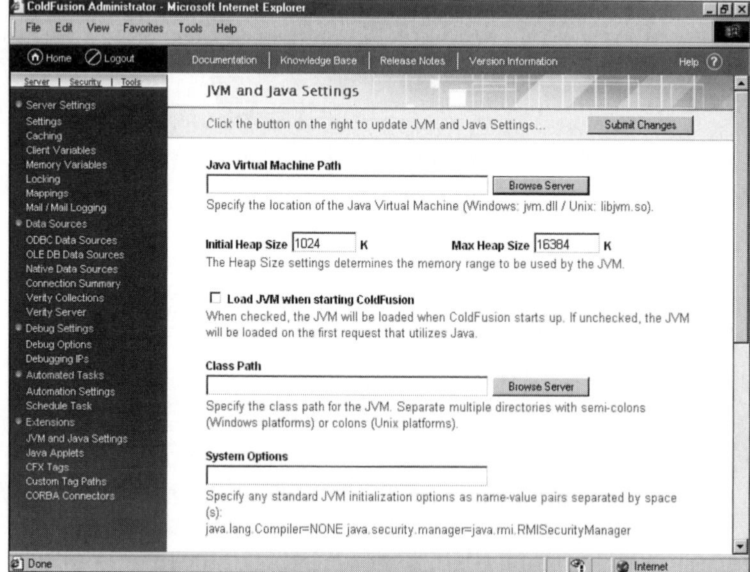

Figure 30.17 In the JVM and Java Settings page, you can configure the JVM for your ColdFusion applications.

JAVA APPLETS

Using the <CFAPPLET> tag, Java applets provide a rich, dynamic user interface environment for a variety of tasks, such as complex client-side validation. The Java Applets page lets you register Java applets for use in your ColdFusion applications (see Figure 30.18). In addition, you can modify and delete existing applet registrations.

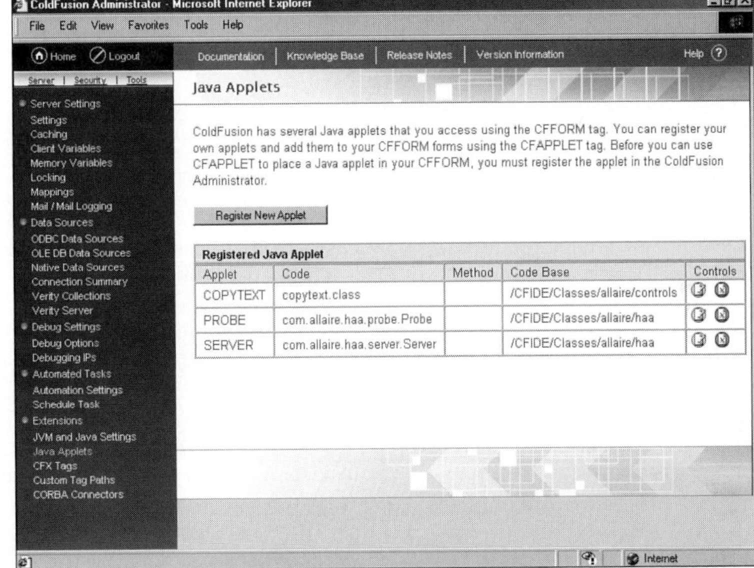

Figure 30.18
In the Java Applets page, you can register, modify, and delete Java applets for use in your ColdFusion application.

To register a Java applet, follow these steps:

1. Click the Register New applet button.
2. In the Add/Register Applets page, enter the applicable information described in Table 30.5.

TABLE 30.5 SETTINGS FOR ADDING JAVA APPLETS

Setting	Description
Name (Required)	Enter the name for your applet.
Code (Required)	Enter the filename of the code for your applet.
Code Base (Required)	Enter the relative file path for the location of your applet's code.
Archive	Enter the name(s) of the JAR file(s) of your applet. Separate multiple JAR filenames by a comma.
Method	Enter the method(s) for your applet. Separate multiple methods by a comma.
Height	Enter the height for your applet window in pixels.

TABLE 30.5 CONTINUED

Setting	Description
Width	Enter the width for your applet window in pixels.
Vspace	Enter the vertical position for your applet window in pixels.
Hspace	Enter the horizontal position for your applet window in pixels.
Align	Select the alignment for your applet window.
Not Supported Message	Enter the message to display if the user's Web browser does not support Java applets.
Parameter Name	Enter the name for a parameter for your applet.
Value	Enter the value for a parameter.

When finished, click the Submit Changes button. Your applet should now appear in the Registered Java Applets table in the Java Applet page.

To modify an existing applet registration, click the applet name or the Edit Applet icon. To delete an applet, click the Delete Applet icon.

CFX TAGS

CFX tags enable you to efficiently encapsulate C++ and Java code in your CFML for the intricate processing of tasks. The CFX Tags page enables you to register C++ and Java CFX tags for use in your ColdFusion applications (see Figure 30.19). You also can modify and delete existing registrations.

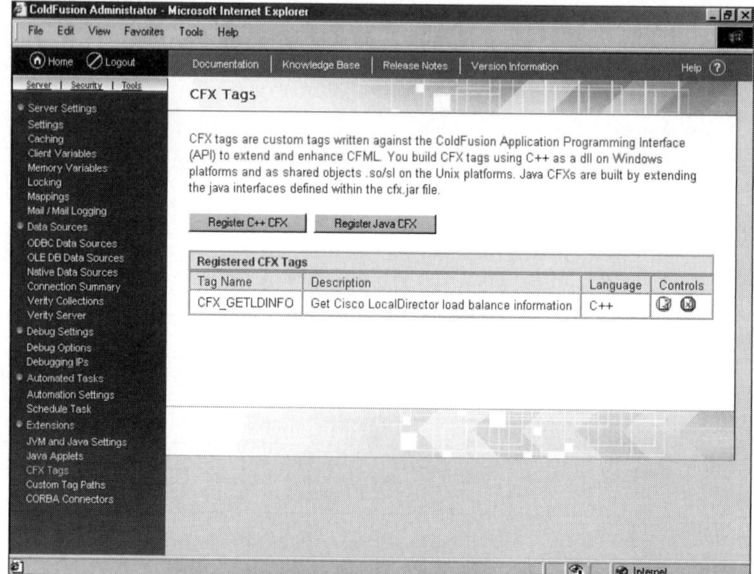

Figure 30.19
In the CFX Tags page, you can register, modify, and delete C++ and Java CFX tags for use in your ColdFusion application.

To register a CFX tag, do the following:

1. Click either the Register C++ CFX button or the Register Java CFX button.
2. In the Add/Edit Java/CFX page, enter the applicable information described in Table 30.6.

TABLE 30.6 JAVA AND C++ CFX TAG SETTINGS

Setting	Description
Tag Name	Enter the tag name for both C++ and Java CFX tags, which must be in the form `CFX_name`.
Server Library (DLL)/Class Name	Enter the location of the DLL for C++ CFX tags or the class name for Java CFX tags.
Procedure	Enter the name of the procedure to use with a C++ CFX tag.
Keep Library Loaded	Select this check box to keep the DLL in ColdFusion's memory. If the CFX tag will be called infrequently, deselect the check box to preserve server resources.
Description	Enter a description for the C++ or Java CFX tag.

Click the Submit Changes button. The CFX tag should now appear in the Register CFX tags on the CFX Tags page.

To modify an existing CFX tag registration, click the tag name or the Edit Tag icon. To delete an applet, click the Delete Tag icon.

CUSTOM TAG PATHS

If you use a directory for custom tags other than the default (`C:/CFUSION/CustomTags`), you must register the directory in the Custom Tag Paths page.

Note

See Chapter 22, "Building Reusable Components," for more information on custom tags.

To register a custom tag file path, follow these steps:

1. Click the Browse Server button, and navigate to the desired directory in the Browse Server page. Click the Apply button.
2. In the Custom Tag Paths page, click the Add button.

The directory should now appear in the Custom Tag Paths window (see Figure 30.20).

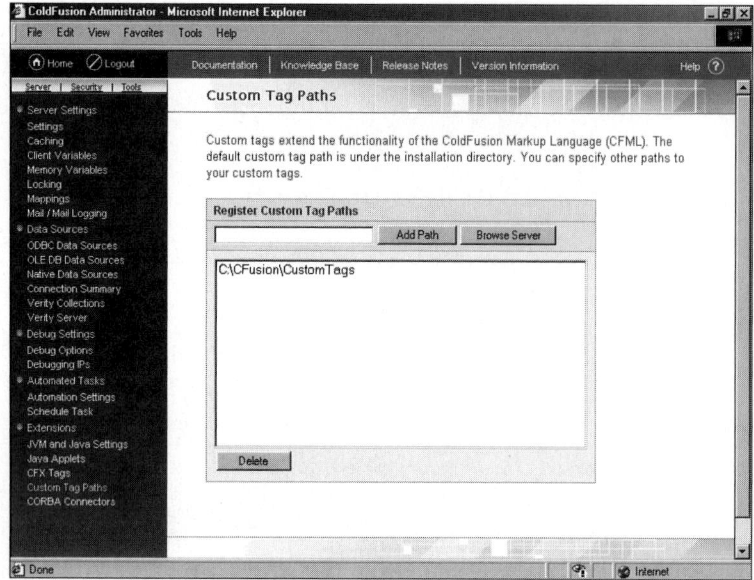

Figure 30.20
In the Custom Tag Paths page, you can register additional directories for custom tags.

CORBA Extensions

To use CORBA with ColdFusion, you must register the ORB in the CORBA Extensions page. You can also modify and delete an ORB registration.

To register an ORB, do the following:

1. Click the Register CORBA Extension button.
2. In the Add/Registered CORBA page, enter the applicable information described in Table 30.7 (see Figure 30.21).

Table 30.7 CORBA Settings

Setting	Description
ORB Vendor	Enter the name of the ORB vendor.
Location of ORB Connector DLL	Click the Browse Server button to navigate to the ORB DLL.
ORB Init Options	Enter any `init` options the ORB requires.

Click the Submit Changes button. The ORB Vendor name should now appear in the Registered CORBA table in the CORBA Extensions page.

To modify an existing CORBA registration, click the extension name or the Edit Extension icon. To delete an extension, click the Delete Extension icon.

To instruct ColdFusion to load the ORB whenever ColdFusion starts, select the Load ORB on Startup box.

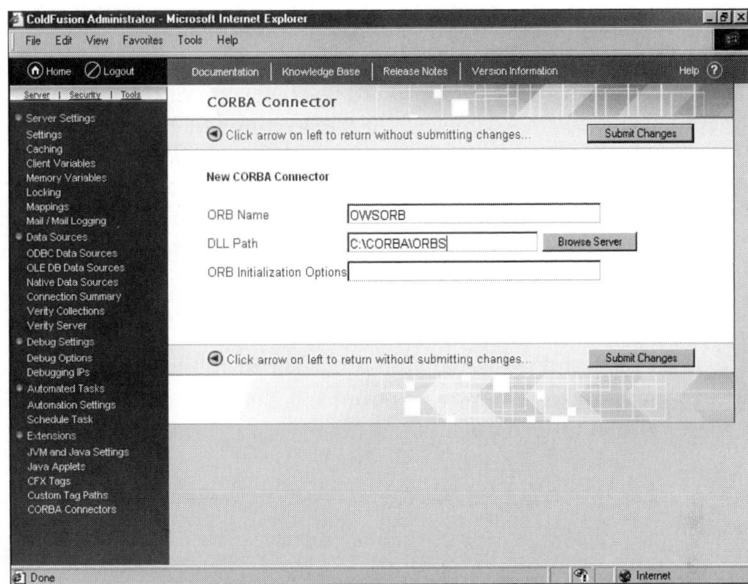

Figure 30.21
In the Add/Registered CORBA page, you can register additional ORBs.

THE SECURITY TAB

Clicking the Security tab at the top of the Administrator's left navigation bar reveals the pages that enable you to configure ColdFusion's security measures. ColdFusion's security features are divided into two groups, Basic and Advanced:

- **Basic security**—Lets you assign and change passwords for the Administrator and ColdFusion Studio and restrict certain tags.
- **Advanced security**—Lets you integrate ColdFusion security with other security servers in your network, your operating system (Windows NT 4.0 and Windows 2000 only), and so on.

Note

See Chapter 21, "Security with ColdFusion," for an introduction to ColdFusion security.

BASIC SECURITY

ColdFusion basic security essentially consists of assigning and changing passwords and restricting CFML tag use. The following pages are available to configure basic security:

- CF Admin Password
- Tag Restrictions
- CF Studio Password

CF ADMIN PASSWORD

The ColdFusion Administrator password provides a simple yet effective level of security to your ColdFusion server. If no password is set, anyone with the proper URL and network access could alter and possibly disrupt the operation of your ColdFusion applications.

Caution

The Administrator is a powerful management console to your ColdFusion server. To protect administrative settings from unauthorized tampering, always set a secure password for the ColdFusion Administrator.

To change the ColdFusion Administrator password in the CF Admin page (see Figure 30.22), type your password in the New Password and Confirmation text boxes. Click the Submit Changes button to set the new password.

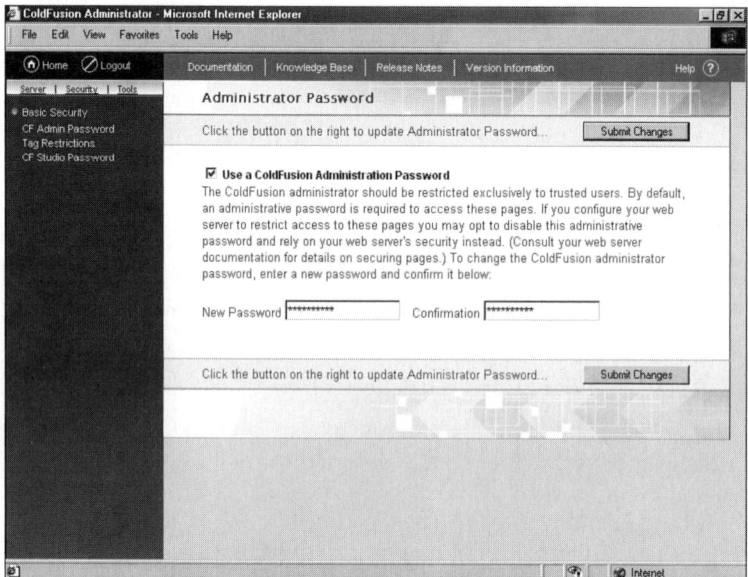

Figure 30.22
The CF Admin Password page enables you to change your Administrator password.

Although it's not advisable to do so, you can also disable the ColdFusion Administrator password by deselecting the Use a ColdFusion Administrator Password box. You might want to disable the ColdFusion Administrator password if you have other security measures in place, such as Web server security or network security provisions.

TAG RESTRICTIONS

If your ColdFusion server will be used by a number of developers, such as a co-location hosting provider, you might need to restrict the use of some tags to ensure that files are not accidentally or intentionally deleted, directories changed, security settings altered, or private files downloaded.

The Tag Restrictions page enables you to disable the following tags and tag attributes (see Figure 30.23):

- <CFCONTENT>
- <CFDIRECTORY>
- <CFFILE>
- <CFOBJECT>
- <CFREGISTRY>
- <CFADMINSECURITY>
- <CFEXECUTE>
- <CFFTP>
- <CFLOG>
- <CFMAIL>
- DBTYPE=DYNAMIC
- CONNECTSTRING

To disable a tag(s) or attribute(s), deselect the check box next to the desired tag(s) and click the Submit Changes button.

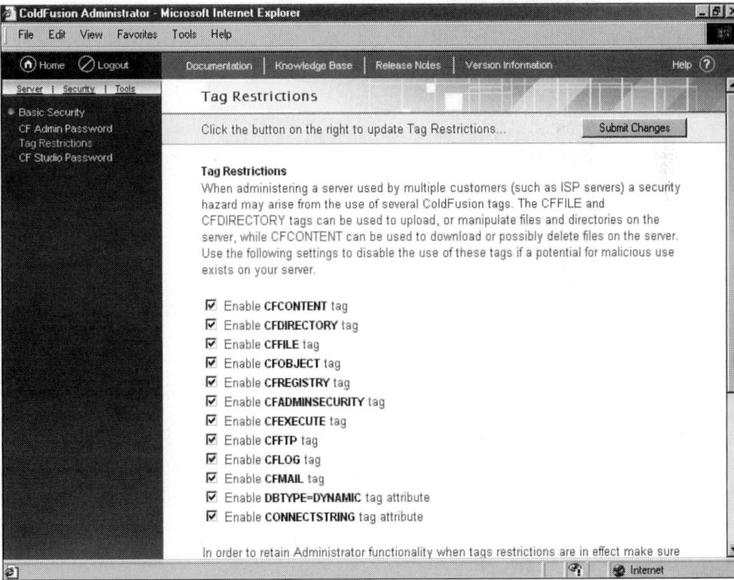

Figure 30.23
The Tag Restrictions page displays a list of tags and tag attributes to disable to provide enhanced security for ColdFusion servers used by multiple developers.

Note

In the Unsecured Tags Directory text box, you can specify a directory in which the tag restrictions do not apply. This directory could be used as your personal development directory or a restricted-use directory for other developers.

CF Studio Password

ColdFusion Studio RDS gives users access to server directories and databases over a network or the Internet. Although this is convenient for remote development, this level of access also poses serious security problems.

To change the ColdFusion Studio password in the CF Studio Password page, type your password in the New Password and Confirmation text boxes (see Figure 30.24). Click the Submit Changes button to set the new password.

Caution

To protect the files in your Web development projects, always set a password for ColdFusion Studio.

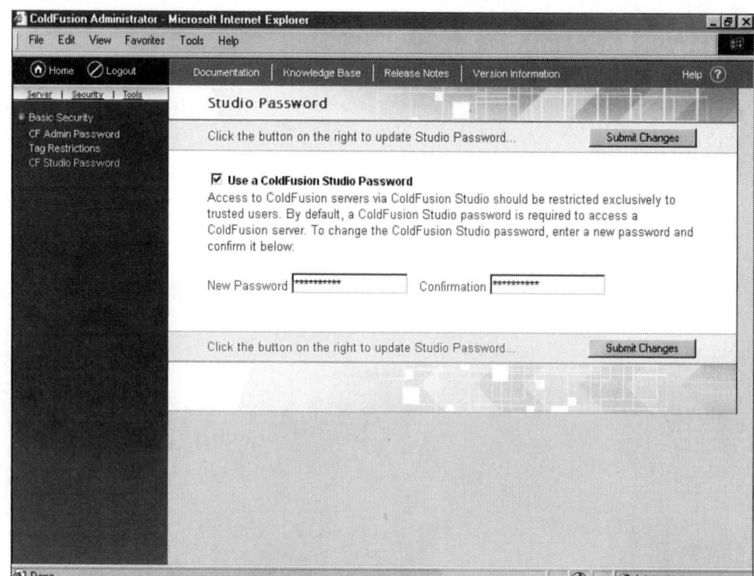

Figure 30.24 The CF Studio Password page enables you to change your Studio password.

Advanced Security

ColdFusion's Advanced Security functionality provides granular control over server resources during development, application components in a production environment, and access to the Administrator.

Security Configuration

The Security Configuration page provides a variety of configuration options, including security server settings; buttons for accessing user directories, security contexts, resources, and security sandboxes; and check boxes to enable advanced security (see Figure 30.25).

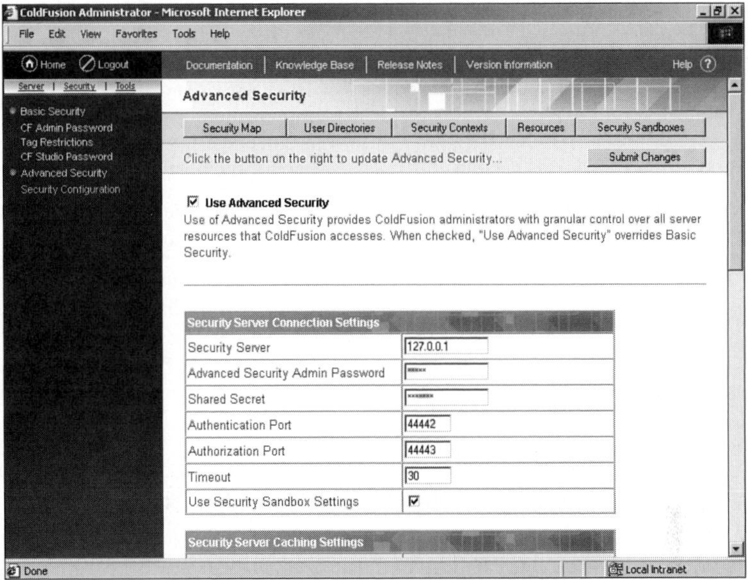

Figure 30.25
The Security Configuration page gives you centralized access to all advanced security features.

Note

See *Advanced ColdFusion 5 Application Development* (Que, ISBN: 0-7897-2585-1) for an in-depth examination of security implementations for your ColdFusion applications.

USE ADVANCED SECURITY

Select the Use Advanced Security check box to enable Advanced Security on your ColdFusion server. This will supplant any basic security settings.

SECURITY SERVER CONNECTION SETTINGS

Use the settings in Table 30.7 to configure the settings for your security server.

TABLE 30.7 SECURITY SERVER CONNECTION SETTINGS

Setting	Description
Security Server	Enter the IP address of your security server. If the security server is the ColdFusion server on your own system, use 127.0.0.1. You also can use a logical name.
Shared Secret	A shared secret represents a portion of the encryption key that validates the security server's transactions. You should change the shared secret at least once.
Authentication Port	Enter the port number for ColdFusion to communicate with the security server. Do not change from the default unless you're certain the port number is not used by other resources.

TABLE 30.7 CONTINUED

Setting	Description
Authorization Port	Enter the port number for ColdFusion to communicate with the security server. Do not change from the default unless you're certain the port number is not used by other resources.
Timeout	Enter the time in minutes you want ColdFusion to wait when connecting to the security server. The default is 20 minutes.
Use Security Sandbox Settings	Select this check box to enable Security Sandbox settings. See the section "Security Sandboxes," later in this chapter, for more information.

SECURITY SERVER CACHING SETTINGS

As with any server caching, security caching can enhance the performance of your security server. The security server cache settings are listed in Table 30.8.

TABLE 30.8 SECURITY SERVER CACHING SETTINGS

Setting	Description
Use Security Cache	Select this check box to enable security caching.
Load Policy Store at Startup	Select this check box to instruct the security server to load policy store information into server memory at startup.
Refresh Interval	Enter the number of minutes to elapse before the security server refreshes the security cache. If security settings rarely change, increase the interval to conserve server resources.
Use Authorization Cache	Select this check box to enable authorization caching. Because every authentication call will be cached, a popular Web application with thousands of users will quickly expand the cache to the point that the security server can become unstable. Use this cache only for ColdFusion applications that will experience relatively light usage.
Refresh Interval	Enter the number of minutes to elapse before the security server refreshes the security cache. If security settings rarely change, increase the interval to conserve server resources.

COLDFUSION SECURITY CACHE SETTINGS

ColdFusion provides user authentication natively. ColdFusion cache settings provide general configuration settings (see Table 30.9).

TABLE 30.9 SECURITY CACHE SETTINGS

Setting	Description
Use ColdFusion Authorization Cache	Select this check box to enable ColdFusion authorization caching.

Setting	Description
Refresh Interval	Select this checkbox to instruct ColdFusion to load policy store information into server memory at startup.
Refresh Interval	Enter the number of minutes to elapse before the security server refreshes the security cache. If security settings rarely change, increase the interval to conserve server resources.
Use Authorization Cache	Select this check box to enable authorization caching. Because every authentication call will be cached, a popular Web application with thousands of users will quickly expand the cache to the point that ColdFusion can become unstable. Use this cache only for ColdFusion application that will experience relatively light usage.
Refresh Interval	Enter the number of minutes to elapse before ColdFusion refreshes the security cache. If security settings rarely change, increase the interval to conserve server resources.

Flush ColdFusion and Security Server Caches

You can flush authentication and authorization caches immediately by clicking one of the three buttons in the Flush ColdFusion and Security Server Caches.

Use ColdFusion Administrator Authentication

Select the Use ColdFusion Administrator Authentication check box to enable ColdFusion Administrator to use a user directory for user access. This supplants the ColdFusion Administrator password set in basic security.

Enter the name of the administrator in the Administrator text field, and select the user directory to use in the User Directory drop-down menu.

Use ColdFusion Studio Authentication

Select the Use ColdFusion Authentication check box to enable ColdFusion Studio to use a security context to restrict access to server resources by user. Select the security context to use in the Security Context drop-down menu.

Tip

To secure the Administrator, you should secure the `CFIDE` directory at the operating-system or Web-server level. To do this in Windows 2000 with IIS 5.0, open the Microsoft Management Console. Under the Internet Information Services tree in the Services and Applications directory, right-click Default Web Site (for example) and select Permissions Wizard. Select the options you want in the wizard to secure the directory. For other operating systems and Web servers, consult the appropriate documentation.

CONFIGURING ADVANCED SECURITY

Although the Administrator provides a centralized repository for all security-related features in ColdFusion, setting up a robust and scalable security framework is no small task. Depending on your security needs, some or all of the following components must be configured to implement Advanced Security:

- User directories
- Security contexts
- Resources
- Security sandboxes

USER DIRECTORIES

Any level of advanced security requires the registration of user directories for use with ColdFusion. You can think of user directories as essentially a secure contact list of network users. However, instead of containing addresses, phone numbers, and e-mail addresses, a user directory contains login names, passwords, and affiliations to other groups of users.

ColdFusion can integrate with three types of user directories: Windows NT/2000 domains, LDAP directories, and ODBC data sources. Because of this integration, you do not have to maintain multiple user directories.

Let's say you want to connect to a user directory for the OWS ColdFusion development staff. To establish a connection to a user directory, do the following:

1. In the Security Configuration page (see Figure 30.26), click the User Directories button.
2. In the next page that appears, enter the directory to which you want to connect, and click the Add button.
3. In the next page, you configure your connection. You will notice that the setting you must configure depends on the type of user directory to which you're connecting: LDAP, Windows NT/2000 domain, or ODBC.

   For this example, connect to a Windows NT user directory. In the Namespace drop-down menu, select Windows NT. In the location text box, enter the directory for OWS development on `\OWS\dev`. Enter the administrator username, such as **`bforta`**, and the password.
4. When finished, click the Add button.

Note

Consult the ColdFusion documentation and the documentation for your user directory for detailed explanations of these settings.

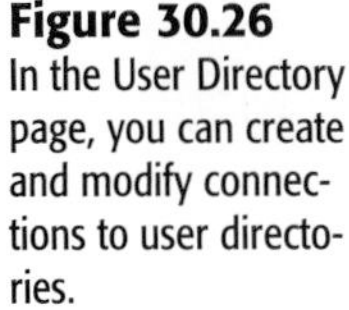

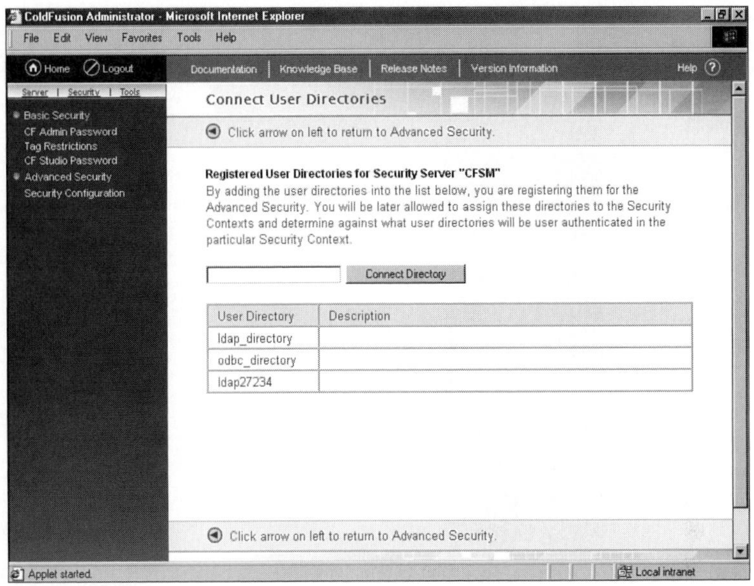

Figure 30.26
In the User Directory page, you can create and modify connections to user directories.

The user directory should now appear in the user directory list.

To modify or delete a user directory connection, click the name of the connection. Its detail page will appear, in which you can change settings or delete the connection altogether.

User directories can authenticate users, but security contexts provide the basis for controlling access to server, network, and application resources.

SECURITY CONTEXTS

As the name implies, security contexts represent a virtual container, or context, in which policies and rules reside. You refer to security contexts in the `SECURITYCONTEXT` attribute of the `<CFAUTHENTICATE>` tag and the `<CFIMPERSONATE>` tag.

To define a security context, do the following:

1. In the Security Configurations page, click the Security Contexts button (see Figure 30.27).
2. In the next page that appears, enter **`OWS_DEV`** for the context that you're about to create, and click the Add button.
3. In the next page, you assign resources, user directories, rules, and policies to the security context. Consult the ColdFusion documentation more details about creating rules and policies and assigning resources.
4. When finished, click the Submit Changes button.

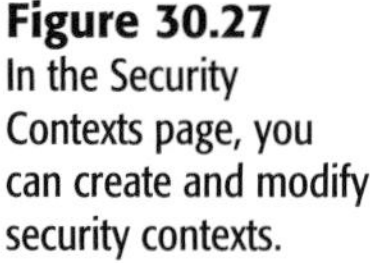

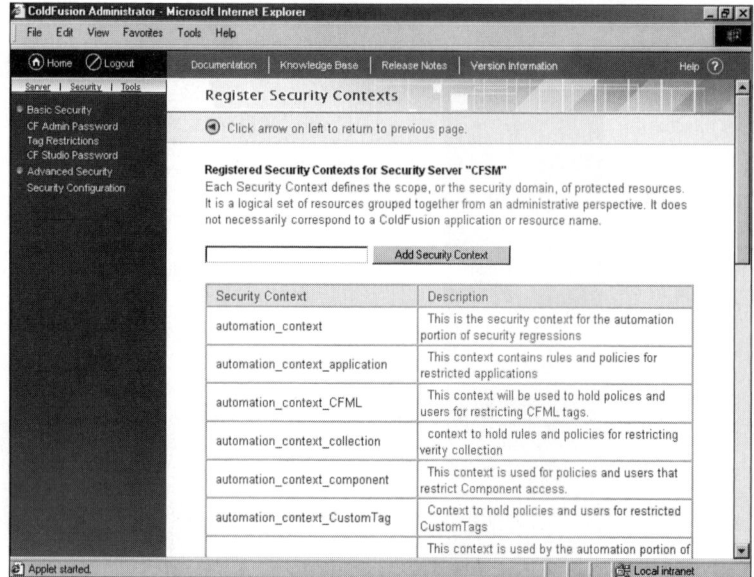

Figure 30.27
In the Security Contexts page, you can create and modify security contexts.

You can also modify and delete security contexts by clicking the name in the Security Context page.

Note

To conserve server resources, do not assign resources to a context if they do not need protection.

RESOURCES

ColdFusion Advanced Security enables you to protect virtually all server resources, including data sources, file directories, CFML tags, and so on.

To add a resource, follow these steps:

1. In the Security Configurations page, click the Resources button.
2. In the next page that appears, select the security context to which you want to assign resources from the Current Security Context drop-down menu.
3. According to the resources you added in the Security Contexts page to the selected context, you will see a list of resources displayed in the Resource Browser. Select the resource you want to add, and click the Add Resource button. The Add Resource page displays a detailed listing of the resource according to the resource selected. Select the specific resource and click the OK button.
4. The Policy Editor now appears. Click the Add Policy button.
5. Enter a name and description for the policy, and click OK. The Resources page appears, and the Resource Browser now includes your policy.

6. Select the policy, and click the check boxes for the actions you want to protect.
7. Add user groups to the policy or enter user logins to add individual users.
8. Click the Submit Changes button when finished.

You can also modify and delete security contexts by clicking the name in the Security Context page.

SECURITY SANDBOXES

To restrict ColdFusion to a specific area of Windows NT/2000—especially useful for hosting providers—you can use the Security Sandboxes page (see Figure 30.28).

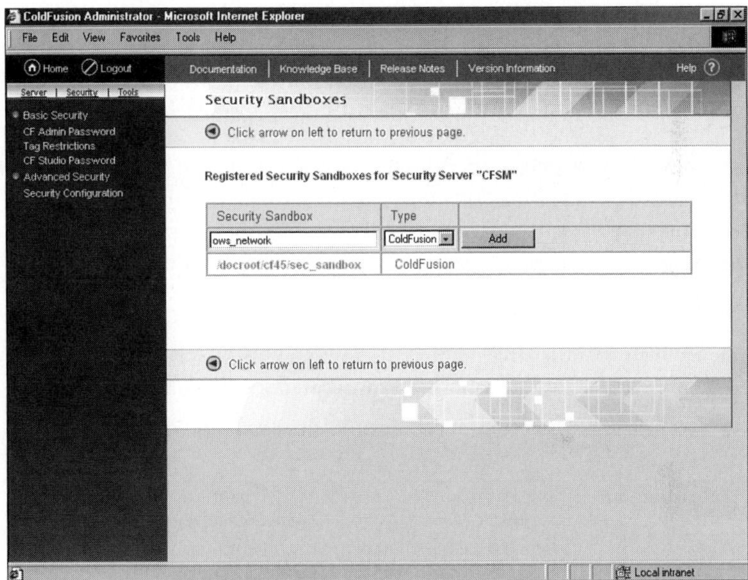

Figure 30.28 In the Security Sandboxes page, you can create and modify sandboxes inside Windows NT/2000 and inside ColdFusion itself.

To create a security sandbox, follow these steps:

1. In the Security Configuration page, click the Security Sandboxes button.
2. In the next page that appears, enter the name for the sandbox, such as **`OWS_DEV`**, and select either Operating System or ColdFusion in the Type drop-down menu. Click the Add button.
3. In the next page, enter the file path in the Location text box, such as **`\OWS\Dev`**, for the directory you want to protect.
4. If you selected Operating System in the Type menu in the previous page, select the NT domain to use in the NT Domain text box. If you selected ColdFusion in the Type menu in the previous page, select the security context to use in the Security Context drop-down menu.

5. Enter a username, such as **`bforta`**, and password in the Username and Password text boxes for the NT domain.
6. When finished, click the Apply button.

Tip

Click the Security Map button in the Security Configuration page to display an outline of your security framework.

THE TOOLS TAB

Speedy Web site performance is no longer a wish-list item. With the explosion of Web alternatives, users who become frustrated with tardy performance are just one click away from leaving your site for another. Information on the performance of your ColdFusion server and your ColdFusion applications allows you to tweak server settings and modify your ColdFusion applications to increase performance.

To accomplish this task, the Administrator's Tool tab provides a plethora of tools for tuning your ColdFusion applications for peak performance. Clicking the Tools tab at the top of the Administrator's left navigation bar reveals a number of pages. The pages are categorized into Logs and Statistics, System Monitoring, and Archive and Deploy:

- **Logs and Statistics**—Provides tools for examining site and application performance.
- **System Monitoring**—Provides tools to cluster servers, configure automatic e-mail alerts, and integrate with hardware-based load balancers.
- **Archive and Deploy**—Provides tools to back up your site and restore archives.

Note

See *Advanced ColdFusion 5 Application Development* (Que, ISBN: 0-7897-2585-1) for a detailed examination of improving Web site scalability.

LOGS AND STATISTICS

Information on the performance of your ColdFusion server and ColdFusion applications enables you to tweak server settings and modify your ColdFusion applications to increase performance. To accomplish this task, the Administrator provides detailed server reports and a browser-based log viewer for performance analysis.

The following pages are available in the Logs and Statistics section:

- Logging Settings
- Log Files
- Server Reports

LOGGING SETTINGS

The Logging Settings page lets you to configure, view, and manage how ColdFusion logs warnings and errors (see Figure 30.29). Analyzing log files and statistics provides valuable insight into the operation of your ColdFusion server for debugging and troubleshooting.

Table 30.10 describes the available configuration options.

TABLE 30.10 LOGGING OPTIONS

Option	Description
Administrator E-mail	If an error occurs, ColdFusion displays a message describing the error condition. If you enter an e-mail address here, ColdFusion also displays it and instructs the visitor to notify that address of the error condition. You can override this address for a specific application by specifying an address in the `<CFAPPLICATION>` tag in the `APPLICATION.CFM` file. To learn more, see Chapter 19.
Log Directory	By default, ColdFusion log files are stored in a directory called `LOG` beneath the ColdFusion root directory (usually `C:\CFUSION`). If desired, you can specify an alternative directory.
Log Slow Pages Taking Longer Than X	Select this check box to log files that take longer than the value you enter in the text box (in seconds).
Use Operating System Logging Facilities	Select this check box to instruct ColdFusion to write error logs to your operating system's log files in addition to ColdFusion's logs.
Disable Version 5 Logging Format	Select this check box to use ColdFusion 4.5's logging format. Keep in mind that ColdFusion 5's enhanced Log Viewer requires version 5's log format.

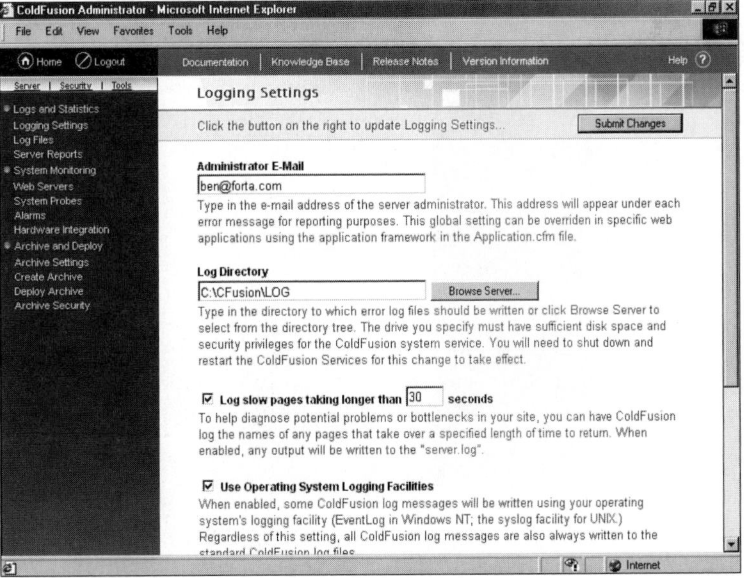

Figure 30.29
In the Logging Settings page, you can configure how ColdFusion generates error logs, where it stores them, and which logging options to use.

Tip

ColdFusion enables you to specify only a single e-mail address for the mail administrator. To have messages sent to multiple recipients, create a mail group on your mail server and specify that group address in the Administrator E-mail text box.

Log Files

Log files can be thought of as your server's personal diary. The Log Files page lets you view and manage three ColdFusion log files, `APPLICATION.LOG`, `CFADMIN.LOG`, and `SERVER.LOG`. These files are listed in the Available Log Files table (see Figure 30.30).

The APPLICATION log records error messages by application, such as failed page requests. The CFADMIN log records configuration setting changes in the ColdFusion Administrator, such as changing the ColdFusion Studio password or enabling single threaded sessions. The SERVER log records server events for ColdFusion, such as server startup and shutdown.

Note

Any files that end in the .log suffix, are present in the directory specified in the Log Directory text box on the Log Settings page, and are written in the ColdFusion 5 log format are available for viewing in the Log Files page.

Viewing a log is as simple as selecting the check box next to the log file you want to view and clicking the View Log File button. the log files will display in the administrator.

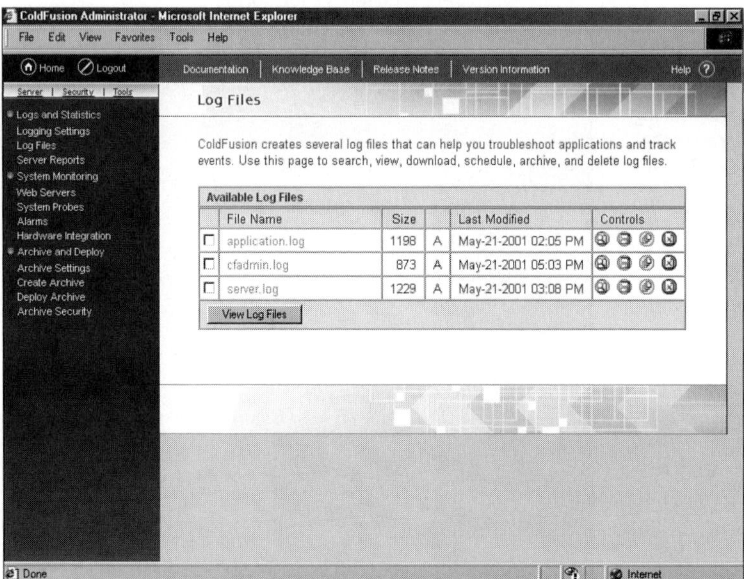

Figure 30.30
In the Log Files page, you can view and manage the ColdFusion log files.

The icons at the far right of the Available Log Files table do the following:

- Search and View
- Download
- Archive
- Delete

Tip

> To conserve server resources during times of heavy server load, schedule log archiving actions for late at night or early in the morning.

When you view a log page, you can filter the log file results by keywords, application name, date, and so on (see Figure 30.31). Consult the online help in the Log Files page for a complete list of options.

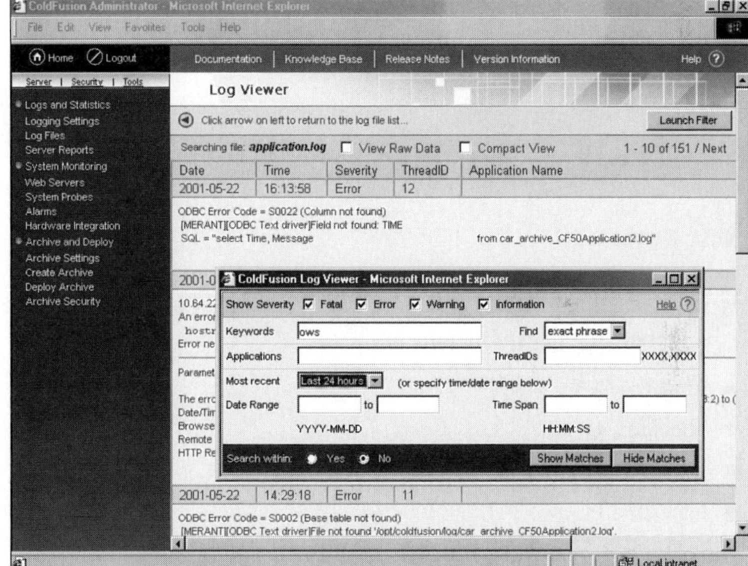

Figure 30.31 When viewing a log file, you can filter log file results using a variety of criteria.

SERVER REPORTS

The Server Reports page enables you to see server performance statistics over time. This tool provides valuable data analysis for tracking your application performance under load and showing the effects of any configuration changes.

As shown in Figure 30.32, the Server Reports page is divided into left and right frames. In the left frame, you set the reports options. The right pane displays the reports you select in the left pane.

The Administrator's server report options are divided into two sections: Select Timeframe and Available Reports.

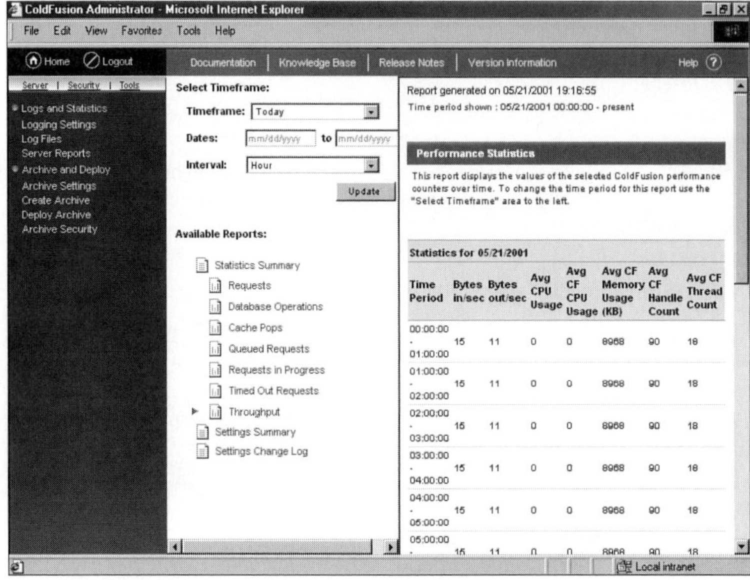

Figure 30.32
In the Server Reports page, you can view server statistics, configuration changes, and setting summaries.

SELECTING A TIMEFRAME

You must select a timeframe to view server statistics. The following timeframes are available in the Timeframe drop-down menu:

- Anytime
- Specified Time
- Today
- Last Two Days
- Last Three Days
- One Week
- Two Weeks
- One Month
- Two Months
- Six Months

Select the timeframe that fits your review criteria. If you select Specified Time in the Timeframe drop-down menu, enter the dates you want to review in the Dates text boxes. In the Interval drop-down menu, select the interval for ColdFusion to check to record server statistics.

Tip

If you're using the Server Statistics page to examine server performance under load over a period of several months, select Day as the interval. Otherwise, you could be presented with thousands of report entries.

AVAILABLE REPORTS

The Server Reports page provides reports for numerous server statistics. The types of reports are described in Table 30.11.

TABLE 30.11 SERVER REPORT TYPES

Type	Description
Statistics Summary	Displays summary of ColdFusion server stats
Requests	Displays record page request stats to ColdFusion
Database Operations	Displays ColdFusion database call stats
Cache Pops	Displays ColdFusion cache population stats
Queued Requests	Displays ColdFusion queued page request stats
Request in Progress	Displays ColdFusion page request processing stats
Timed Out Request	Displays ColdFusion page request timeout stats
Throughput	Displays ColdFusion throughput of data

Tip

The Server Reports page reflects changes in the Available Reports section dynamically. So, you don't need to click any buttons to apply the changes.

You can also click Settings Summary to see the current configuration settings. In addition, you can view configuration changes over time by clicking Settings Change Log.

Tip

You can go directly to the corresponding Administrator page in either Settings Summary or Settings Change Log by clicking individual report entries.

SYSTEM MONITORING

The Administrator provides dynamic monitoring tools in the form of System Monitoring. These tools enable you to communicate with hardware load-balancing solutions, monitor system resources dynamically, and configure alarms to alert you when there is a problem.

To access these tools, click the Tools link at the top of the Administrator's left navigation bar. Under the System Monitoring section are four pages to configure ColdFusion dynamic monitoring:

- Web Servers
- System Probes
- Alarms
- Hardware Integration

Tip

My *Advanced ColdFusion Application Development* book (Que, ISBN: 0-7897-2585-1) goes into great detail about ColdFusion's scalability and availability features.

WEB SERVERS

In the Web Servers page, you will see an Excel-like window listing all the servers clustered by your hardware load balancer, such as Cisco LocalDirector (see Figure 30.33). This window displays a variety of information, such as availability, probes, current load, load-balancer availability, and so on.

In this page, you can specify to restrict this server to a certain threshold of traffic load, set the threshold that triggers a restriction, and enable the server for control through this window.

Note

Refer to the ColdFusion documentation for detailed instructions on load-balancing options.

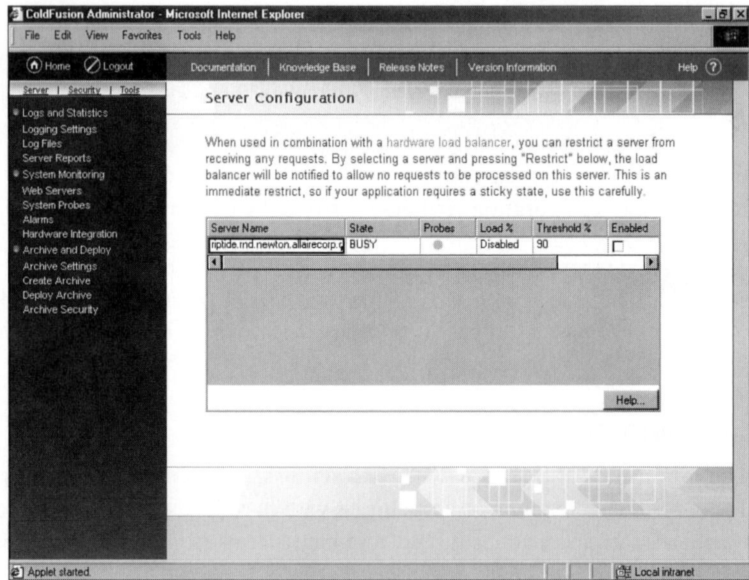

Figure 30.33
In the Web Servers page, you can select servers for hardware-based clustering and designate server cluster load thresholds.

SYSTEM PROBES

As the name implies, system probes automatically monitor system resources. Usually, a system probe takes the form of an HTTP request to verify that a resource is available. However, a probe can be customize to perform a variety of actions, such as a database query, and calculate the availability of the resource on the results.

In the Server Probes page, you can create, modify, and delete system probes (see Figure 30.34). Similar to the Web Servers page, you will see an Excel-like window listing all the probes. To create a new probe, click the New button and configure the probe settings in the page that appears next.

When finished, the probe will appear in the window. You will be able to see the status of the probe, edit the probe by clicking the Edit button, and delete the probe by clicking the Delete button.

Note

Refer to the ColdFusion documentation for detailed instructions on creating and managing system probes.

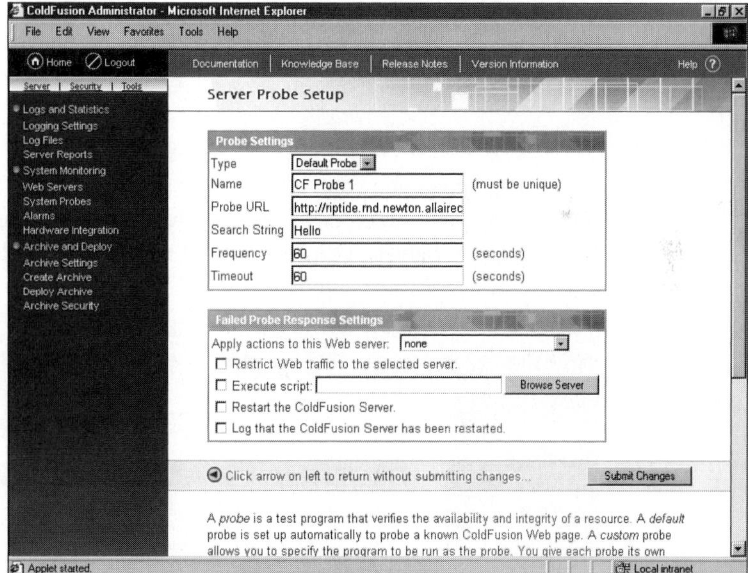

Figure 30.34
In the Server Probe Setup page, you can create server probes.

ALARMS

In the Alarms page, you can specify e-mail addresses that will be notified in the event of a Web server failure, when a Web server reaches its load threshold, when the load balancer becomes unavailable, and when a probe fails. To use this feature, you must specify an SMTP server to send the alarm e-mails.

HARDWARE INTEGRATION

In the Hardware Integration page, you can configure ColdFusion to integrate with your hardware load-balancing solution.

Note

ColdFusion requires Cisco Local Director 3.1.4 or later for its load-balancing integration features.

ARCHIVE AND DEPLOY

The Administrator now supports building and deploying archives of your ColdFusion applications. Archiving applications is useful as a secondary backup measure, comparing changes in different versions of applications and porting applications to other servers.

Access the Archive and Deploy section by clicking the Tools link at the top of the left navigation bar. Four pages make up the Archive and Deploy section:

- Archive Settings
- Create Archive
- Deploy Archive
- Archive Security

ARCHIVE SETTINGS

The Archive Settings page gives you control over basic archive settings (see Figure 30.35). Specifically, you can change the directory to which archives will be stored, define log files settings, and create archive variables. The archives will be stored as CAR files.

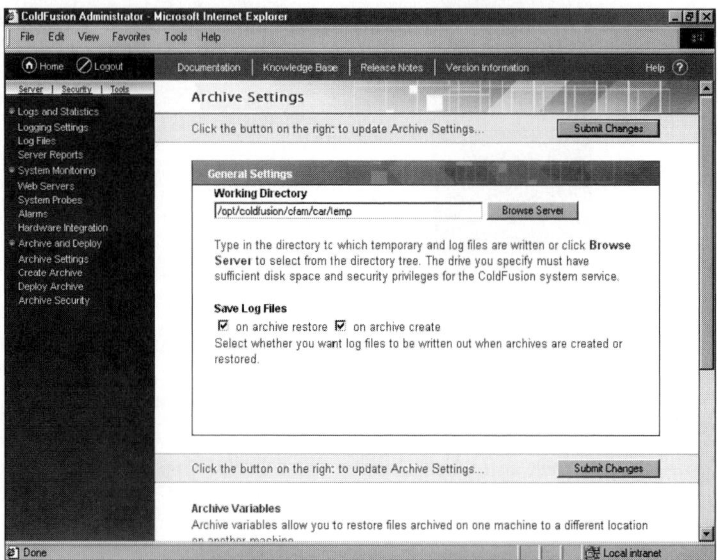

Figure 30.35
In the Archive Settings page, you can define general archive settings applicable to all archive creation and management.

General Settings

You can change the directory to which archives are stored by entering the file path in the Working Directory text box or clicking the Browse Server button. Under the Save Logs heading, you can also specify whether to create log files when creating or deploying archives by selecting or deselecting the On Archive Create and On Archive Deploy check boxes.

Note

Ensure that the directory in which you intend to store the archive has sufficient space.

Archive Variables

Archive variables enable you to define a directory or file that is archived on one machine in a certain location and deploy it at a different location in another machine.

For example, in preparation to migrate your ColdFusion application to a new system, you have just archived a ColdFusion application that requires a customized Java class. You're ready to deploy that ColdFusion application to the new system, but the new system's JDK resides in a different directory.

Rather than going through the trouble of copying and pasting the require Java class manually, you can specify an archive variable. When deployed, the archive variable will instruct ColdFusion to write the Java class to the new directory.

To create an archive variable, do the following:

1. On the Archive Settings page, click the Add Variable button.
2. Enter a name for the variable in the Name text box.
3. In the Value text box, enter the relative file path for the existing system, an equal sign (=), and the absolute file path on the new system.
4. Enter a description of the variable's action.
5. Click the Save button.

The variable name should now appear in the Archive Settings page in the Variable name table. You can also modify or delete existing variables by clicking a variable name in the table.

Create Archive

The Create Archive page allows you to create an archive (see Figure 30.36).

To create an archive, follow these steps:

1. Enter a name for the archive, such as **OWS_CURRENT**, and enter a description of the archive. To select every file, setting, and object associated with your application, click the Global Select All button.

2. The archive name will appear in the Create ColdFusion Archive. Click Build Archive.
3. A list of site components that will be archived is presented for your review. Click Next.
4. Enter a filename for the archive, and click Generate Archive.

   The archive is created.

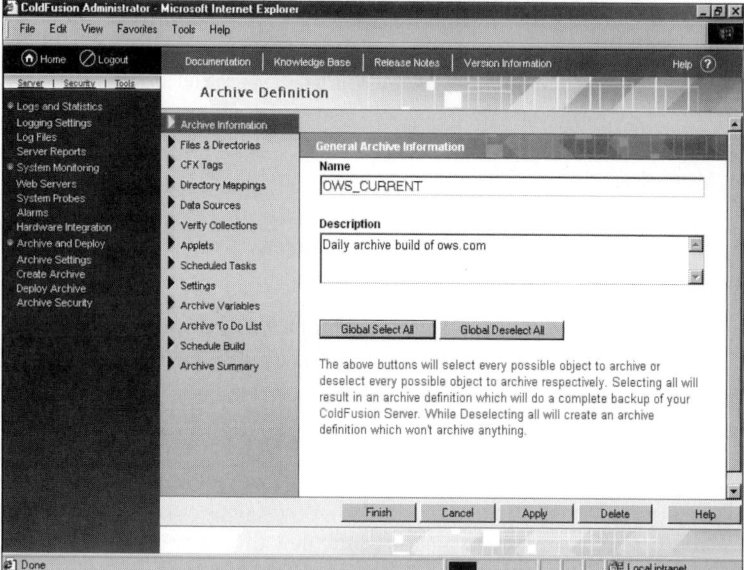

Figure 30.36
In the Create Archive page, you can create an archive by entering a name and description for the archive.

5. Select the Files & Directories tab and enter the directory of the ColdFusion application to archive, such as **`C:Inetpub\wwwroot\ows`**, in the Web Application Directory text box. You can also click the Browse Server button and navigate to the directory.

   Select the Archive Web Application Directory check box to archive all files in the selected directory.

   In the File List window, you can select additional files to include in the archive. Separated by a semicolon, you can enter the file paths for the files in window. You can also click the Add button to navigate to the file you want to archive.

   In the Files to Exclude window, you can select which files to be excluded from archiving. Separated by a semicolon, you can enter the file paths for the files in window. You can also click the Add button to navigate to the file you want to archive.
6. If you don't select the Global Select All option, you can specify individual objects for archiving. The following objects are available for archiving:

   - CFX Tags
   - Directory Mappings
   - Data Sources

- Verity Collections
- Applets
- Scheduled Tasks
- Settings
- Archive Variables

Also available are Archive To Do Lists for instructions, Schedule Build to set up autmomatic archiving, and Archive Summary.

DEPLOY ARCHIVE

In the Deploy Archive page, specify the directory from which to retrieve the archive and the retrieval method (FTP, HTTP, or local network). Next, you choose the destination file for archive, whether to back up the archive, and configuration settings before deployment.

Note

Ensure that the directory to which you intend to deploy the archive has sufficient space.

ARCHIVE SECURITY

In the Archive Security page, you import certificate, PKCS12, and Sun Store files to encrypt your archives for secure delivery and receipt of sensitive data.

The following archive procedures can also be performed in the Archive Security page:

- Sign Certificate
- Verify Signature
- Encrypt Archive
- Decrypt Archive

Tip

To get an RSA DESX certificate, visit RSA Security's Web site (`http://www.rsasecurity.com`).

CHAPTER 31

More About SQL and Queries

In this chapter

ADVANCED SQL TOPICS

You have already learned quite a bit about SQL in this book. In Chapter 6, "Introduction to SQL," you learned how to retrieve records using SELECT, WHERE, and ORDER BY. In Chapter 7, "SQL Data Manipulation," you learned how to change the data in your database with INSERT, UPDATE, and DELETE and how to use the AS keyword to create aliases. You have also seen how ColdFusion's <CFQUERY> tag lets you create SQL statements dynamically, based on form parameters and other variables.

This chapter introduces you to some additional topics related to querying your databases with ColdFusion. This section explains certain aspects of SQL that haven't been discussed yet, and which will be particularly relevant when putting together report style pages. The section "Additional <CFQUERY> Topics" explains how to use several advanced features of the <CFQUERY> tag, several of which are new for ColdFusion 5.

Note

The discussion in this section assumes that you have already read Chapters 6 and 7 or that you have used SQL on your own in the past. If not, it's recommended that you take a few minutes to look through Chapters 6 and 7 (especially Chapter 6) before reading on here.

GETTING UNIQUE RECORDS WITH DISTINCT

In Chapter 6, you learned how to use the SELECT statement to retrieve records from your database tables, with or without WHERE or ORDER BY clauses. You can add DISTINCT to these SELECT statements in situations in which you don't want to retrieve duplicate rows from your tables.

In general, all you have to do is to add the DISTINCT keyword directly after the SELECT keyword. As an example, Listing 31.1 shows the results of two queries, side by side. The first query retrieves the descriptions for all expenses logged in the Expenses table. The second query is exactly the same as the first, except it uses the DISTINCT keyword to ensure that any repeats in the resultset are eliminated before the query results are returned to ColdFusion. As you can see from Figure 31.1, the first query returns multiple entries for Costumes and Extras, whereas the second query does not.

Tip

It's often appropriate to remove duplicated values when creating report-style pages. Even if duplicated entries don't exist in your database yet, keep DISTINCT in the back of your mind when putting together such pages.

LISTING 31.1 Distinct.cfm—USING DISTINCT TO ELIMINATE DUPLICATES

```
<!--- Retrieve Expense Descriptions from Expense table; --->
<!--- This query may include any repeated descriptions  --->
<CFQUERY NAME="GetExp" DATASOURCE="#REQUEST.DataSource#">
```

```
  SELECT Description
  FROM Expenses
  ORDER BY Description
</CFQUERY>

<!--- Retrieve Expense Descriptions from Expense table; --->
<!--- The DISTINCT means we won't get any repeated rows --->
<CFQUERY NAME="GetUniqueExp" DATASOURCE="#REQUEST.DataSource#">
  SELECT DISTINCT Description
  FROM Expenses
  ORDER BY Description
</CFQUERY>

<HTML>
<HEAD><TITLE>Film Expenses</TITLE></HEAD>
<BODY>
<H2>What Are We Spending Money On?</H2>

<TABLE BORDER="1">
  <TR VALIGN="Top">
    <!--- First, ordinary SELECT records --->
    <TD>Ordinary SELECT statement:
      <OL>
      <CFOUTPUT QUERY="GetExp">
        <LI>#GetExp.Description#</LI>
      </CFOUTPUT>
      </OL>
    </TD>
    <!--- Now the SELECT DISTINCT records --->
    <TD>SELECT DISTINCT statement:
      <OL>
      <CFOUTPUT QUERY="GetUniqueExp">
        <LI>#GetUniqueExp.Description#</LI>
      </CFOUTPUT>
      </OL>
    </TD>
  </TR>
</TABLE>

</BODY>
</HTML>
```


Note

There are other ways you could get the same unique effect. For instance, you could just run the first query and then add a `GROUP="Description"` attribute to the `<CFOUTPUT>` tag, causing ColdFusion to display a record only if its `Description` value were different from the previous row's (see Chapter 11, "Creating Data-Driven Pages," for more information about `GROUP`). However, the `DISTINCT` approach would be more efficient because the duplicate records never leave the database in the first place.

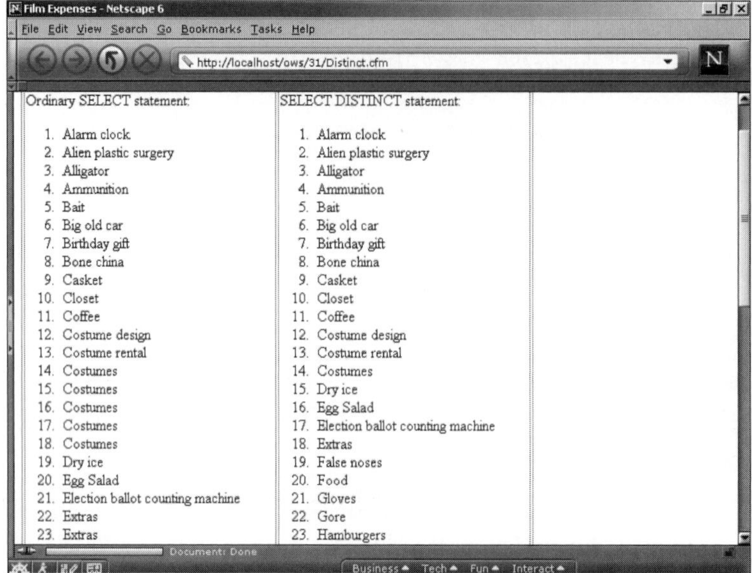

Figure 31.1
The value `Costumes`, which appears several times in the `Expenses` table, appears only once when `DISTINCT` is used.

Note

It is important to understand that the `DISTINCT` keyword applies to all columns in each row being returned by the query, not just the first column. So, if the `SELECT` statements in Listing 31.1 were selecting the `ExpenseAmount` column as well as the `Description` column, rows would be eliminated only in the unlikely event that the descriptions *and* expense amounts were exactly the same.

SUMMARIZING DATA WITH AGGREGATE FUNCTIONS

SQL provides a number of *aggregate functions* for your use. Aggregate functions are used to crunch information from any number of rows into a summarized overview of your data. Again, you will find yourself using these functions most often when trying to present some type of big picture to your users, such as with report-style summaries or overviews in your ColdFusion applications.

Tip

Aggregate functions are sometimes called *set functions*, or *set-based functions*.

STANDARD AGGREGATE FUNCTIONS

There are five standard aggregate functions, which any SQL-compliant database system should support: `COUNT`, `SUM`, `AVG`, `MIN`, and `MAX`. Table 31.1 explains what each of these functions does and the types of columns they can generally be used with (although certain database systems might make exceptions).

Table 31.1 Standard SQL Aggregate Functions

Function	On Numeric Columns	On Date Columns	On Character Columns
`COUNT(*)`	Counts the number of rows in a table	*(same)*	*(same)*
`COUNT(column)`	Counts the number of values found in a column	*(same)*	*(same)*
`SUM(column)`	Adds the total of the values found in a column	*(not allowed)*	*(not allowed)*
`AVG(column)`	Computes the average of values found in a column	*(not allowed)*	*(not allowed)*
`MIN(column)`	Finds the smallest value in a column	Finds the earliest date	Finds the first value (alphabetically)
`MAX(column)`	Finds the largest value in a column	Finds the latest date	Finds the last value (alphabetically)

Note

Some database systems might support additional aggregate or aggregate-like functions, such as `FIRST` and `LAST`, and related keywords, such as `PIVOT`, `CUBE`, and `ROLLUP`. Consult your database documentation for details.

Listing 31.2 shows how aggregate functions can be used in a ColdFusion template. This example uses `COUNT`, `SUM`, `AVG`, `MIN`, and `MAX` on numeric and date values in Orange Whip Studio's `Expenses` table. The results are shown in Figure 31.2.

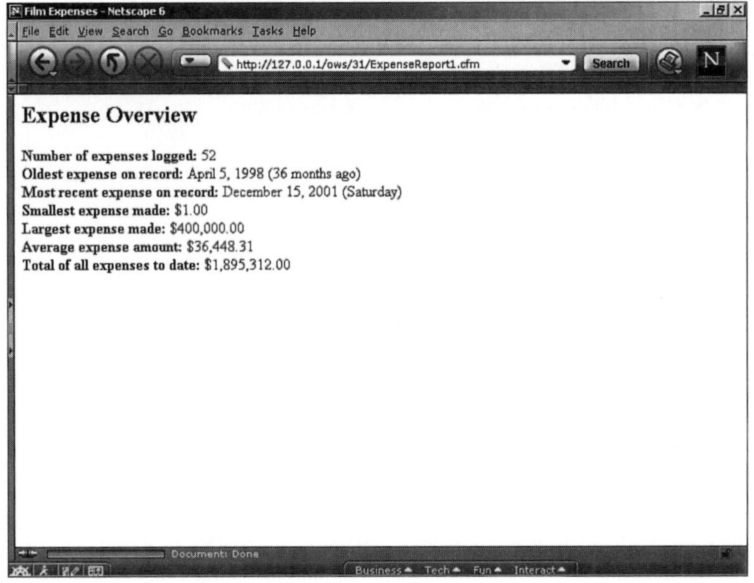

Figure 31.2 Aggregate functions can be used to report on trends in your data.

LISTING 31.2 `ExpenseReport1.cfm`—**USING AGGREGATE FUNCTIONS ON ALL RECORDS OF A TABLE**

```
<!--- Retrieve summarized expense data from database --->
<CFQUERY NAME="GetExp" DATASOURCE="#REQUEST.DataSource#">
  SELECT
    COUNT(*) AS ExpenseCount,
    MIN(ExpenseDate)   AS DateMin,
    MAX(ExpenseDate)   AS DateMax,
    MIN(ExpenseAmount) AS ExpenseMin,
    MAX(ExpenseAmount) AS ExpenseMax,
    SUM(ExpenseAmount) AS ExpenseSum,
    AVG(ExpenseAmount) AS ExpenseAvg
  FROM Expenses
</CFQUERY>


<HTML>
<HEAD><TITLE>Film Expenses</TITLE></HEAD>
<BODY>
<H2>Expense Overview</H2>

<!--- Output high-level expense summary --->
<CFOUTPUT>
  <B>Number of expenses logged:</B>
    #GetExp.ExpenseCount#<BR>

  <B>Oldest expense on record:</B>
    #LSDateFormat(GetExp.DateMin, "mmmm d, yyyy")#
    (#DateDiff("m", GetExp.DateMin, Now())# months ago)<BR>

  <B>Most recent expense on record:</B>
    #LSDateFormat(GetExp.DateMax, "mmmm d, yyyy (dddd)")#<BR>

  <B>Smallest expense made:</B>
    #LSCurrencyFormat(GetExp.ExpenseMin)#<BR>

  <B>Largest expense made:</B>
    #LSCurrencyFormat(GetExp.ExpenseMax)#<BR>

  <B>Average expense amount:</B>
    #LSCurrencyFormat(GetExp.ExpenseAvg)#<BR>

  <B>Total of all expenses to date:</B>
    #LSCurrencyFormat(GetExp.ExpenseSum)#<BR>
</CFOUTPUT>

</BODY>
</HTML>
```

Note

Queries that use only aggregate functions in their `SELECT` lists, such as the query in Listing 31.2, will never return more than one row.

It's important to note that no columns are being selected on their own by the query in this listing (the only columns are those used by the aggregate functions). To mix ordinary column references and aggregate columns together in the same SELECT list, you also must add a GROUP BY clause (discussed in the next section). Otherwise, you will get an error message from the database driver.

GETTING MORE SELECTIVE WITH WHERE

You can use WHERE and aggregates together in the same query to get summarized records about only certain rows in your database tables. For instance, if a parameter named FilmID might be passed to the page in the URL, you could show the summarized expense information for just that film by adding the following to the <CFQUERY> tag in Listing 31.2 (right after the FROM line of the query):


```
<!--- Limit expense summary to single film, if provided --->
<CFIF IsDefined("URL.FilmID")>
  WHERE FilmID = #URL.FilmID#
</CFIF>
```

The results would look the same when viewed in a browser, except that the various totals and dates would apply only to the FilmID specified in the URL (if any). When no FilmID parameter is provided, the data for all expenses would continue to be shown (as shown previously in Figure 31.2).

Tip

Be careful not to confuse WHERE with HAVING (discussed later in this section). As a rule, you almost always should use WHERE when specifying criteria. HAVING is generally used for special cases only.

ColdFusion Studio's Query Builder can be handy when putting together queries that use aggregate functions. Just right-click the ows database's Expenses table from the Resource tab's Database pane and then select New Query from the pop-up menu. At the top of the Query Builder, double-click each of the columns you are interested in. Next, select the aggregate functions you want from the drop-down list provided in the Group By column, as shown in Figure 31.3. With just a few clicks, you can build the same type of query as shown in Listing 31.2, without having to concentrate as hard on the actual SQL syntax involved.

Note

See Chapter 8, "Introduction to ColdFusion Studio," for more information about using the Query Builder.

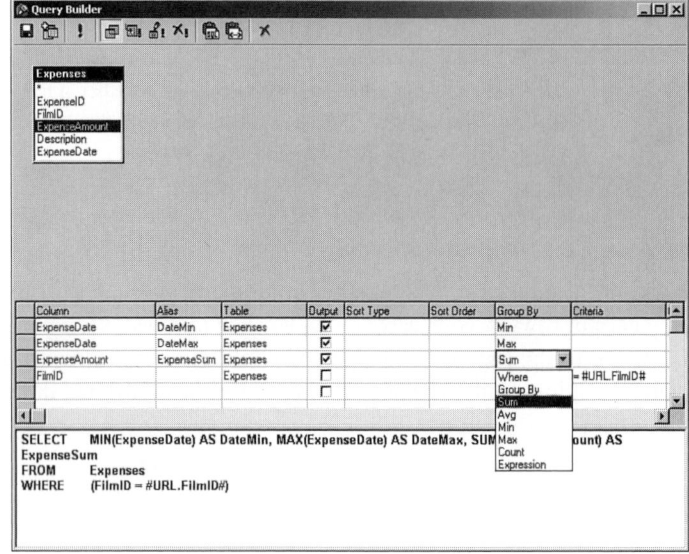

Figure 31.3 ColdFusion Studio's Query Builder supports aggregate functions.

BREAKING IT DOWN WITH GROUP BY

So far, you have seen how aggregate functions can be used to run simple computations that return only one row of data, which reports the computed sums (or averages, or counts) of all matching records at once. You'll often want to break the computations down further, returning a separate set of summary data results for each value in a particular column. You can get this effect by adding a `GROUP BY` clause to your query.

To use `GROUP BY`, you add the column(s) you want to get summarized data for in two places: the query's `SELECT` list and the new `GROUP BY` clause, which should come right after the `FROM` part of your query (but before any `ORDER BY` clause).

Behind the scenes, your database breaks down your data into groups, one group for each value found in your `GROUP BY` columns. Each of your aggregate functions is computed separately for each group. When the results are returned to ColdFusion, one row will exist for each unique value in your `GROUP BY` column(s). That is, there will be one row for each group.

Listing 31.3 shows how `GROUP BY` can be used to apply aggregate functions, such as `SUM`, to each group in the `Expenses` table. Here, the results are broken down (or *grouped*) by `FilmID`. The results are shown in Figure 31.4.

LISTING 31.3 `ExpenseReport2.cfm`—**USING** `GROUP BY` **WITH AGGREGATE FUNCTIONS TO BREAK DOWN YOUR DATA**

```
<!--- Retrieve summarized expense data from database --->
<CFQUERY NAME="GetExp" DATASOURCE="#REQUEST.DataSource#">
  SELECT
    f.FilmID, f.MovieTitle,
    SUM(ExpenseAmount) AS ExpenseSum
```

```
  FROM Expenses e, Films f
  WHERE e.FilmID = f.FilmID
  GROUP BY f.FilmID, f.MovieTitle
  ORDER BY f.MovieTitle
</CFQUERY>


<HTML>
<HEAD><TITLE>Film Expenses</TITLE></HEAD>
<BODY>
<H2>Expense Overview</H2>

<!--- Output film-level expense summary --->
<CFTABLE
  QUERY="GetExp"
  HTMLTABLE="Yes"
  BORDER="Yes"
  COLHEADERS="Yes">

  <CFCOL
    HEADER="Film Title"
    TEXT="#MovieTitle#">
  <CFCOL
    HEADER="Amount"
    TEXT="#LSCurrencyFormat(ExpenseSum)#"
    ALIGN="RIGHT">

</CFTABLE>

</BODY>
</HTML>
```

Film Title	Amount
Being Unbearably Light	$25,800.00
Charlie's Devils	$221,000.00
Charlie's Devils 3	$143,000.00
Closet Encounters of the Odd Kind	$80.00
Folded Laundry, Concealed Ticket	$28,500.00
Forrest Trump	$101,245.50
Four Bar-Mitzvah's and a Circumcision	$10,250.00
Geriatric Park	$10,451.00
Gladly Ate Her	$600,000.00
Ground Hog Day	$2,000.00
Hannah and Her Blisters	$39,900.00
Harry's Pottery	$20,500.00
It's a Wonderful Wife	$55,500.00
Kramer vs. George	$75,000.00
Mission Improbable	$609.00
Nightmare on Overwhelmed Street	$255,000.00

Figure 31.4 Aggregate functions become more powerful when combined with GROUP BY to break the results down.

Note

If you specify more than one column in the GROUP BY part of your query, the results will include one record for each unique permutation of values amongst the specified columns. That is, each unique permutation of values in the GROUP BY columns is what defines a new group.

FILTERING SUMMARIZED RECORDS WITH HAVING

You've seen how you can use WHERE to cause only certain rows to be considered by aggregate functions such as SUM and MAX. That's fine for filtering totals based on something fixed, such as an ID number. But what if you wanted to apply a different type of filtering criteria, based not on what the values were *before* the aggregate functions do their work, but *after*?

The HAVING keyword enables you to do just that. You get to provide criteria using the same syntax you use in a WHERE clause, using the =, <, and > operators. The difference is that HAVING criteria is applied to the final grouped rows just before they are returned to ColdFusion, whereas WHERE criteria is applied before any of the values are considered for grouping in the first place.

To use HAVING, place it directly after the GROUP BY part of your query (but before the ORDER BY part, if any). For instance, if you wanted to keep films with a small amount of expenses from being shown in the report from Listing 31.3, you could change the query code from this

```
WHERE e.FilmID = f.FilmID
GROUP BY f.FilmID, f.MovieTitle
```

to this

```
WHERE e.FilmID = f.FilmID
GROUP BY f.FilmID, f.MovieTitle
HAVING SUM(ExpenseAmount) > 1000
```

Now only those groups that have a total expense of more than 1000 will be returned to ColdFusion. Note that this is *very, very different* from the following:

```
WHERE e.FilmID = f.FilmID
AND ExpenseAmount > 1000
GROUP BY f.FilmID, f.MovieTitle
```

The previous snippet simply means that no individual expenses that are less than 1000 will be considered, but the total amount for any group (film) could exceed 1000. The HAVING snippet, by contrast, considers only the total for each film, with no regard to how big the individual payments are.

Of course, you can combine both concepts, like so:

```
WHERE e.FilmID = f.FilmID
AND ExpenseAmount < 50000
GROUP BY f.FilmID, f.MovieTitle
HAVING SUM(ExpenseAmount) > 1000
```

The previous snippet shows total spending only for films that have 1000 in expenses or more. However, in coming up with these totals, it ignores any individual expenses that are very large (more than 50000). This might be useful to an executive at Orange Whip Studios who probably doesn't care about movies that are spending very small amounts of money (less than 1000 total) and who also probably already knows about the really big expenditures (more than 50000 each). This report lets the executive focus on the middle ground, where movie executives seem to feel most at home.

Listing 31.4 is a simple revision of the template from Listing 31.3, which presents the data returned from this last version of the query. Figure 31.5 shows the results.

Note

Compared to everything else you're learning in this chapter, HAVING is relatively obscure, and you may not find yourself using it much. Having said that, it's still good to know everything that's available to you.

LISTING 31.4 ExpenseReport3.cfm—USING GROUP BY, HAVING, WHERE, AND AGGREGATE FUNCTIONS TOGETHER

```
<!--- These values will control the filtering --->
<CFSET FilterMinTotal = 1000>
<CFSET FilterMaxIndiv = 50000>

<!--- Retrieve summarized expense data from database --->
<CFQUERY NAME="GetExp" DATASOURCE="#REQUEST.DataSource#">
  SELECT
    f.FilmID, f.MovieTitle,
    SUM(ExpenseAmount) AS ExpenseSum
  FROM Expenses e, Films f
  WHERE e.FilmID = f.FilmID
  AND ExpenseAmount < #FilterMaxIndiv#
  GROUP BY f.FilmID, f.MovieTitle
  HAVING SUM(ExpenseAmount) > #FilterMinTotal#
  ORDER BY f.MovieTitle
</CFQUERY>


<HTML>
<HEAD><TITLE>Film Expenses</TITLE></HEAD>
<BODY>
<H2>Expense Overview</H2>
<CFOUTPUT>
  <!--- Note that we are filtering out small numbers --->
  For clarity, films that haven't reported more than <BR>
  #LSCurrencyFormat(FilterMinTotal, "international")#
  have been ommitted from this list.<BR>
  In addition, large payments
  (over #LSCurrencyFormat(FilterMaxIndiv, "international")#) <BR>
  have not been considered in the totals.<BR>
</CFOUTPUT>

<!--- Output film-level expense summary --->
<CFTABLE
  QUERY="GetExp"
```

Listing 31.4 Continued

```
  HTMLTABLE="Yes"
  BORDER="Yes"
  COLHEADERS="Yes">

  <CFCOL
    HEADER="Film Title"
    TEXT="#MovieTitle#">
  <CFCOL
    HEADER="Amount"
    TEXT="#LSCurrencyFormat(ExpenseSum)#"
    ALIGN="RIGHT">

</CFTABLE>

</BODY>
</HTML>
```

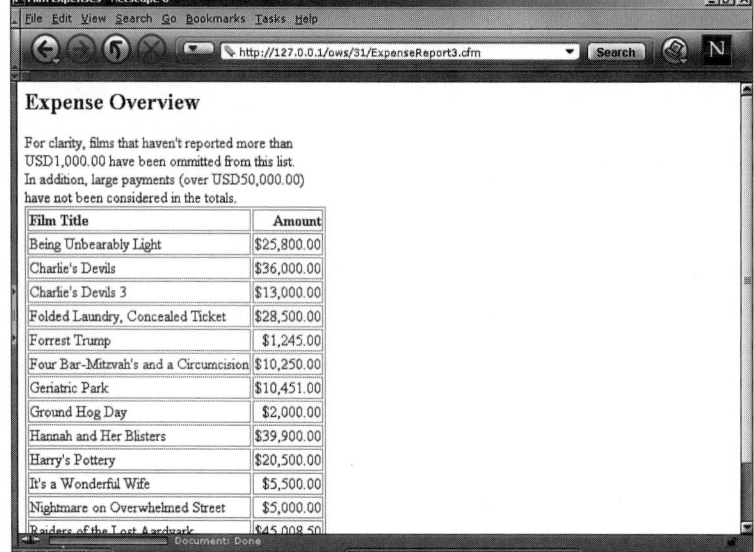

Figure 31.5
The `HAVING` keyword enables you to filter records based on the results of your aggregate functions

Selecting Related Data with Joins

The design of the tables in Orange Whip Studio's database calls for a number of relationships between the various tables. This section focuses on the relationships between the `Films`, `Actors`, and `FilmsActors` tables.

You will recall that the `Films` and `Actors` tables contain relatively straightforward information about the studio's films and actors (the title of each movie, the name of each actor, and so on). That is, the principal purpose of these two tables is to remember the attributes of each film and actor. In contrast, the principal purpose of the `FilmsActors` table is to connect each film with its actors (and vice versa). Yes, there are a couple of extra columns in

FilmsActors (the Salary and IsStarringRole columns), but the really important columns are the FilmID and ActorID columns. Because of these two columns, the database knows what the relationship is between the other two tables (Films and Actors).

Because tables such as FilmsActors define the relationship, or connection, between other tables, they can be thought of as *connector* tables. Much of the SQL language's power comes from its capability to return records from several tables at once, using something called a *join*. A join is simply a way to describe the relationship between tables, right in a SQL query statement. This means you can use join syntax in a SELECT query, for example, to easily retrieve information about the actors who have appeared in each film.

Note

For clarity, this section refers to tables such as Films and Actors as *data tables* and tables such as FilmsActors as *connector tables*. These aren't official SQL terms. They are just used here to keep the discussion as clear as possible.

Joining Two Tables

When you need to join two tables in a query, you actually have your choice of several syntax forms. The simplest and most common method is to add a piece of criteria in the query's WHERE clause, using this basic form:

```
SELECT Columns
FROM TableA, TableB
WHERE TableA.SomeID = TableB.SomeID
```

Applying this basic form to the Films and FilmsActors tables, say, might translate to

```
SELECT Films.FilmID, Films.MovieTitle, FilmsActors.ActorID
FROM Films, FilmsActors
WHERE Films.FilmID = FilmsActors.FilmID
```

The WHERE keyword is clearly being used in a new way here. Rather than merely specifying selection criteria, it is used here to bind the Films and FilmsActors tables together. Translated into plain English, this statement might read, "Using the FilmID as a guide, show me the FilmID and MovieTitle for each row in the Films table, along with the corresponding ActorID numbers from the FilmsActors table."

Listing 31.5 shows how the previous join query can be used in a ColdFusion template. For each film, the query results include one record for each actor in that film, as shown in Figure 31.6.

Listing 31.5 FilmCast1.cfm—Retrieving Data from Two Tables at Once, Using a Join

```
<!--- Retrieve Films and Related Actors from database --->
<CFQUERY NAME="GetFilmInfo" DATASOURCE="#REQUEST.DataSource#">
  SELECT
    Films.FilmID, Films.MovieTitle,
    FilmsActors.ActorID
```

LISTING 31.5 CONTINUED

```
  FROM Films, FilmsActors
  WHERE Films.FilmID = FilmsActors.FilmID
  ORDER BY Films.MovieTitle
</CFQUERY>

<HTML>
<HEAD><TITLE>Films and Actors</TITLE></HEAD>
<BODY>
<H2>Films And Actors</H2>

<!--- Display retrieved information in HTML table --->
<CFTABLE QUERY="GetFilmInfo" HTMLTABLE BORDER COLHEADERS>
  <CFCOL HEADER="Film ID" TEXT="#FilmID#">
  <CFCOL HEADER="Film Title" TEXT="#MovieTitle#">
  <CFCOL HEADER="Actor ID" TEXT="#ActorID#">
</CFTABLE>

</BODY>
</HTML>
```

Note

If a film has no associated actors (that is, if there are no rows in the `FilmsActors` table with the same `FilmID`), no records are returned for that film. Therefore, the query results return records only for each combination of film and actor that can actually be found in both tables. If you wanted to get information about all films, even ones with no corresponding actors, you would need to use an outer join (see the section "Using Outer Joins," later in this chapter).

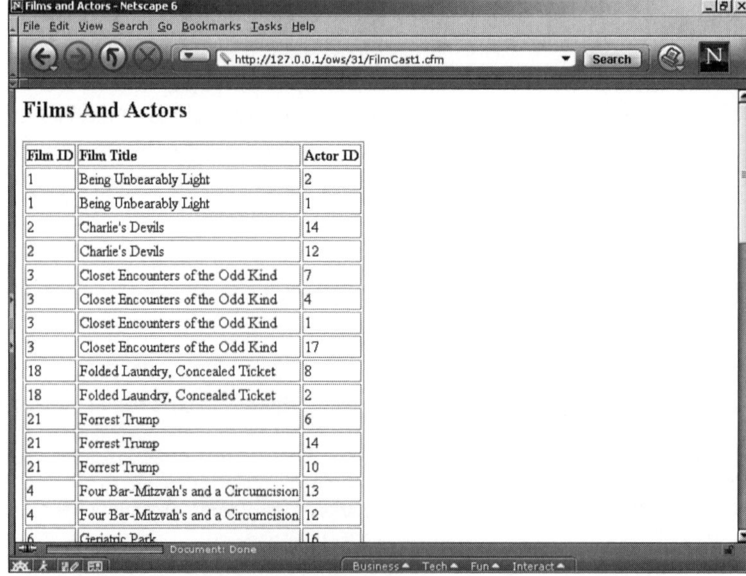

Film ID	Film Title	Actor ID
1	Being Unbearably Light	2
1	Being Unbearably Light	1
2	Charlie's Devils	14
2	Charlie's Devils	12
3	Closet Encounters of the Odd Kind	7
3	Closet Encounters of the Odd Kind	4
3	Closet Encounters of the Odd Kind	1
3	Closet Encounters of the Odd Kind	17
18	Folded Laundry, Concealed Ticket	8
18	Folded Laundry, Concealed Ticket	2
21	Forrest Trump	6
21	Forrest Trump	14
21	Forrest Trump	10
4	Four Bar-Mitzvah's and a Circumcision	13
4	Four Bar-Mitzvah's and a Circumcision	12
6	Geriatric Park	16

Figure 31.6
Two tables can be queried together, using simple join syntax.

The WHERE clause in this listing is absolutely critical to understand. As a human, you know that the conceptual relationship between the two tables hinges on the fact that the rows of the Films table in which the FilmID is 1 correspond to the rows in the FilmsActors table in which the FilmID is 1, and so on. The WHERE clause explains this fact to your database system.

Note

Notice the simple dot notation used to specify which columns are in which tables. Now that two tables are participating in the SELECT, this dot notation is necessary. Otherwise, your database system wouldn't know which table to retrieve the FilmID from (because a column called FilmID exists in each one).

You actually have to use the dot notation only for columns that exist in both tables (that is, where the column name alone would be ambiguous). However, it is recommended that you use the dot notation for all columns in any query that involves more than one table, simply to make your code clearer and remove any possibility of (gasp!) human error.

Joining Three Tables

Joining three tables is not much different from joining two tables, and it is what's needed to turn the results shown in Figure 31.6 into something more intuitive for your users. You simply specify two join conditions in your WHERE clause using AND between them.

So, to retrieve each actor's last name instead of just retrieving the actors' ID numbers, you would join the Films table to the FilmsActors table (as you have already seen) and then join the FilmsActors table to the Actors table (to pick up the last name associated with each actor's ID number). The resulting query would look like this:

```
SELECT Films.FilmID, Films.MovieTitle, Actors.NameLast
FROM Films, FilmsActors, Actors
WHERE Films.FilmID = FilmsActors.FilmID
  AND FilmsActors.ActorID = Actors.ActorID
```

Listing 31.6 shows how this three-table join can be used to revise the previous example (refer to Listing 31.5) to create a much friendlier display for your users. Now, instead of just seeing each actor's ID number, your users can see each actor's first and last names, as shown in Figure 31.7. If you wanted to display other information from the Actors table, you could just add them to the query's SELECT list.

Listing 31.6 FilmCast2.cfm—**Joining Three Tables at Once**

```
<!--- Retrieve Films and Related Actors from database --->
<CFQUERY NAME="GetFilmInfo" DATASOURCE="#REQUEST.DataSource#">
  SELECT
    Films.FilmID, Films.MovieTitle,
    Actors.NameFirst, Actors.NameLast
  FROM Films, FilmsActors, Actors
  WHERE Films.FilmID        = FilmsActors.FilmID
    AND FilmsActors.ActorID = Actors.ActorID
  ORDER BY Films.MovieTitle, Actors.NameLast
</CFQUERY>
```

LISTING 31.6 CONTINUED

```
<HTML>
<HEAD><TITLE>Films and Actors</TITLE></HEAD>
<BODY>
<H2>Films And Actors</H2>

<!--- Display retrieved information in HTML table --->
<CFTABLE QUERY="GetFilmInfo" HTMLTABLE BORDER COLHEADERS>
  <CFCOL HEADER="Film ID" TEXT="#FilmID#">
  <CFCOL HEADER="Film Title" TEXT="#MovieTitle#">
  <CFCOL HEADER="Actor (First Name)" TEXT="#NameFirst#">
  <CFCOL HEADER="Actor (Last Name)" TEXT="#NameLast#">
</CFTABLE>

</BODY>
</HTML>
```

Note

To create queries that join four or more tables together, just continue to add additional lines of criteria in your `WHERE` clause, using the `AND` keyword between each one.

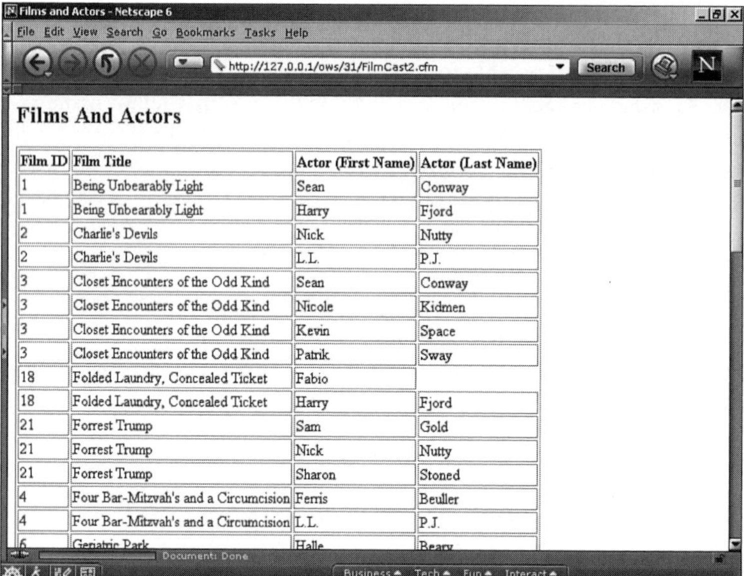

Figure 31.7
Three-table joins are common when you need to display names, labels, or titles from related data tables.

IMPROVING READABILITY WITH TABLE ALIASES

When you start using table joins more and more frequently, you will probably find it helpful to use *table aliases* to make the queries easier to read (and easier to type!). A table alias is just a temporary nickname for a table, good only within the context of the current query.

You can define a very short table alias that is only one or two letters long, allowing you to remove clutter from the remainder of the query statement.

To define a table alias, just provide a short nickname right after the table's real name in the `FROM` part of your query. Now you can use the short alias in the other parts of the query, in place of the actual table name. Many developers choose to use just the first letter or two of the table name (in lowercase) for an alias. For instance, this query

```
SELECT Films.FilmID, Films.MovieTitle, Actors.NameLast
FROM Films, FilmsActors, Actors
WHERE Films.FilmID = FilmsActors.FilmID
  AND FilmsActors.ActorID = Actors.ActorID
```

could become this, which is relatively easy on the eyes (like the actors themselves):

```
SELECT f.FilmID, f.MovieTitle, a.NameLast
FROM Films f, FilmsActors fa, Actors a
WHERE f.FilmID   = fa.FilmID
  AND fa.ActorID = a.ActorID
```


If you prefer, you can use the `AS` keyword between the table's real name and the alias, like so:

```
SELECT f.FilmID, f.MovieTitle, a.NameLast
FROM Films AS f, FilmsActors AS fa, Actors AS a
WHERE f.FilmID   = fa.FilmID
  AND fa.ActorID = a.ActorID
```

THE TWO TYPES OF JOIN SYNTAX

So far, you have seen how tables can be joined using the `WHERE` part of a query. This is the simplest and most common method, but there is another. The two types of join syntax generate the same results (except in very rare circumstances that are well beyond the scope of this book, and which you are unlikely to encounter). You can use whichever syntax you like better.

The two forms of join syntax are

- **`WHERE` join syntax**—You have already learned about this simple syntax.
- **`INNER JOIN` syntax**—This is somewhat more complex-looking but is formally preferred by some SQL scholars, mainly because it keeps your table relationships separate from any filter criteria (that is, it gets the join description out of the `WHERE` clause).

The first join syntax describes the join as part of the query's `WHERE` criteria, as you have already seen:

```
SELECT f.FilmID, f.MovieTitle, fa.ActorID
FROM Films f,
     FilmsActors fa
WHERE f.FilmID   = fa.FilmID
```

The `INNER JOIN` syntax describes the join in the `FROM` part of the query, instead of the `WHERE` part. Instead of separating the table names with commas, you separate them with the words `INNER JOIN`. Each pair of table names is followed by the word `ON`, followed by the equality condition that describes the join. For instance, the `WHERE`-style join shown above would translate into the following:

```
SELECT Films.FilmID, Films.MovieTitle, FilmsActors.ActorID
FROM Films INNER JOIN
     FilmsActors ON Films.FilmID = FilmsActors.FilmID
```

Or, adding table aliases to improve readability somewhat, it would look like this:

```
SELECT f.FilmID, f.MovieTitle, fa.ActorID
FROM Films f INNER JOIN
     FilmsActors fa ON f.FilmID = fa.FilmID
```

To join three or more tables using `INNER JOIN` syntax, use parentheses to isolate the individual `INNER JOIN` pieces from one another, like so:

```
SELECT f.FilmID, f.MovieTitle, a.NameFirst, a.NameLast
FROM (Films f INNER JOIN
     FilmsActors fa ON f.FilmID = fa.FilmID) INNER JOIN
     Actors a ON fa.ActorID =  a.ActorID
```

Listings 31.7 and 31.8 are revisions of Listings 31.5 and 31.6, respectively, using `INNER JOIN` syntax instead of the `WHERE`-style of join syntax. Use whichever syntax you find more straightforward.

Listing 31.7 `FilmCast1a.cfm`—**Using `INNER JOIN` Syntax to Join Two Tables**

```
<!--- Retrieve Films and Related Actors from database --->
<CFQUERY NAME="GetFilmInfo" DATASOURCE="#REQUEST.DataSource#">
  SELECT f.FilmID, f.MovieTitle, fa.ActorID
  FROM Films f INNER JOIN
       FilmsActors fa ON f.FilmID = fa.FilmID
  ORDER BY f.MovieTitle
</CFQUERY>

<HTML>
<HEAD><TITLE>Films and Actors</TITLE></HEAD>
<BODY>
<H2>Films And Actors</H2>

<!--- Display retrieved information in HTML table --->
<CFTABLE QUERY="GetFilmInfo" HTMLTABLE BORDER COLHEADERS>
  <CFCOL HEADER="Film ID" TEXT="#FilmID#">
  <CFCOL HEADER="Film Title" TEXT="#MovieTitle#">
  <CFCOL HEADER="Actor ID" TEXT="#ActorID#">
</CFTABLE>

</BODY>
</HTML>
```

Listing 31.8 `FilmCast2a.cfm`—**Using `INNER JOIN` Syntax to Join Three Tables**

```
<!--- Retrieve Films and Related Actors from database --->
<CFQUERY NAME="GetFilmInfo" DATASOURCE="#REQUEST.DataSource#">
  SELECT
    f.FilmID, f.MovieTitle,
    a.NameFirst, a.NameLast
  FROM (Films f INNER JOIN
       FilmsActors fa ON f.FilmID = fa.FilmID) INNER JOIN
```

```
        Actors a ON fa.ActorID =  a.ActorID
  ORDER BY f.MovieTitle, a.NameLast
</CFQUERY>

<HTML>
<HEAD><TITLE>Films and Actors</TITLE></HEAD>
<BODY>
<H2>Films And Actors</H2>

<!--- Display retrieved information in HTML table --->
<CFTABLE QUERY="GetFilmInfo" HTMLTABLE BORDER COLHEADERS>
  <CFCOL HEADER="Film ID" TEXT="#FilmID#">
  <CFCOL HEADER="Film Title" TEXT="#MovieTitle#">
  <CFCOL HEADER="Actor (First Name)" TEXT="#NameFirst#">
  <CFCOL HEADER="Actor (Last Name)" TEXT="#NameLast#">
</CFTABLE>

</BODY>
</HTML>
```


USING OUTER JOINS

So far, all the joins in this chapter have been *inner joins*, which just means only those records that match up in both tables are included in the results. From time to time, you will run into situations in which you need to use an *outer join*, which means that all records in one of the tables are returned, regardless of whether any matching records exist in the other.

For instance, say you need to create a simple report page—similar to Listing 31.5 or 31.6—but that shows each film and the rating it has been given. You decide to join the `Films` table to the `Ratings` table, using the `RatingID` column as the join criteria. Putting your new join skills to work, you come up with something such as this:

```
SELECT f.FilmID, f.MovieTitle, r.Rating
FROM Films f INNER JOIN
     FilmsRatings r ON f.RatingID = r.RatingID
ORDER BY f.MovieTitle
```

The query seems to work fine, and no one notices any kind of problem for the first few weeks that your application is up and running. But after a while, people start complaining that some movies never show up on the list. After a bit of trial and error, you realize that whenever a movie doesn't have a rating (when the `RatingID` column is null), it gets excluded from the query results. This is because inner joins return records only when matching rows exist in both tables.

To solve the problem, you need to change the query to use an outer join instead of an inner join. To do so, you simply change the words `INNER JOIN` to `OUTER JOIN`, preceded by either `LEFT` or `RIGHT`, depending on whether the outer table (the table that should always get included in the query results) is on the left or the right side of the `OUTER JOIN` statement.

So, the query statement shown previously could become this:

```
SELECT f.FilmID, f.MovieTitle, r.Rating
FROM Films f LEFT OUTER JOIN
     FilmsRatings r ON f.RatingID = r.RatingID
```

or this:

```
SELECT f.FilmID, f.MovieTitle, r.Rating
FROM FilmsRatings r RIGHT OUTER JOIN
     Films f ON f.RatingID = r.RatingID
```

These two queries will behave in exactly the same way. They will always return all records from the `Films` table, regardless of whether any corresponding rows exist in the `Ratings` table. When matching records exist in `Ratings`, a row gets added to the query results for each combination of film and rating, just like a normal inner join.

But, because these are outer joins, when no matching rating exists for a film (because the film's `RatingID` is null or is set to some number that doesn't exist in the `Ratings` table), the film is still included in the results. Any columns from the `Ratings` table—in this case, just the `Rating` column—are left blank (the `Rating` column will be an empty string).

Note

Technically, the `Rating` column isn't returned to ColdFusion as an empty string; it's returned as a null value. However, ColdFusion converts null values to empty strings as it receives them, so as far as your CFML code is concerned, the column is an empty string. You would need to test for it as such in any `<CFIF>` statements. See "Working with NULL Values," later in this chapter, for details.

Listing 31.9 shows how this outer join query can be used in an actual template. To test this template, add a few new films to the `Films` table, being sure to leave the `RatingID` to null, `0`, or some other unknown rating ID number. Then, visit Listing 31.9 with your browser. The new films will appear, but their ratings will be blank, as shown in Figure 31.8. If you then change Listing 31.9 so that it uses ordinary inner join syntax, you will see that the new films disappear altogether when you revisit the page.

LISTING 31.9 `FilmRatings.cfm`—USING AN OUTER JOIN TO SHOW ALL FILMS, EVEN ONES WITH NO CORRESPONDING RATING

```
<!--- Retrieve Films and Related Actors from database --->
<CFQUERY NAME="GetFilmInfo" DATASOURCE="#REQUEST.DataSource#">
  SELECT
    f.FilmID, f.MovieTitle,
    r.Rating
  FROM Films f LEFT OUTER JOIN
       FilmsRatings r ON f.RatingID = r.RatingID
  ORDER BY f.MovieTitle
</CFQUERY>

<HTML>
<HEAD><TITLE>Film Ratings</TITLE></HEAD>
<BODY>
<H2>Film Ratings</H2>

<!--- Display retrieved information in HTML table --->
<CFTABLE QUERY="GetFilmInfo" HTMLTABLE BORDER COLHEADERS>
  <CFCOL HEADER="Film ID" TEXT="#FilmID#">
```

```
  <CFCOL HEADER="Film Title" TEXT="#MovieTitle#">
  <CFCOL HEADER="Rating" TEXT="#Rating#">
</CFTABLE>

</BODY>
</HTML>
```

Note

If you want, you can leave the word `OUTER` out of your outer join queries. That is, `LEFT JOIN` and `LEFT OUTER JOIN` are synonyms; so are `RIGHT JOIN` and `RIGHT OUTER JOIN`. However, most people find it clearer to leave the word `OUTER` in there, to emphasize what is going on.

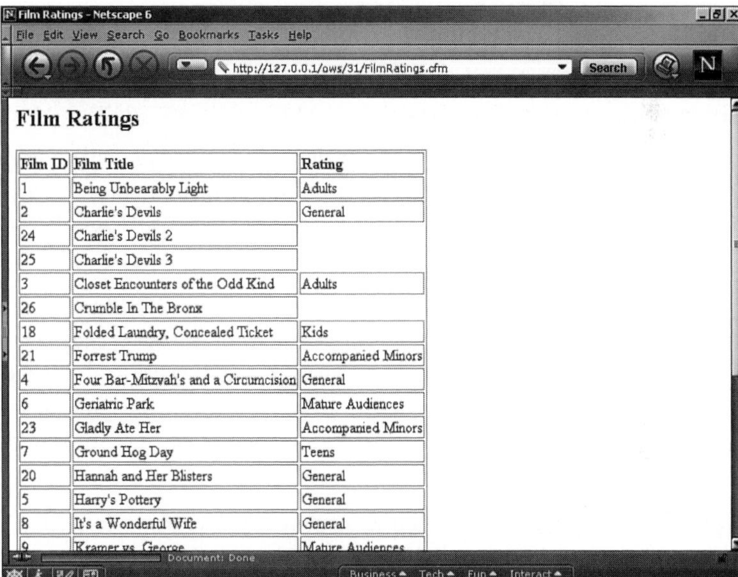

Film ID	Film Title	Rating
1	Being Unbearably Light	Adults
2	Charlie's Devils	General
24	Charlie's Devils 2	
25	Charlie's Devils 3	
3	Closet Encounters of the Odd Kind	Adults
26	Crumble In The Bronx	
18	Folded Laundry, Concealed Ticket	Kids
21	Forrest Trump	Accompanied Minors
4	Four Bar-Mitzvah's and a Circumcision	General
6	Geriatric Park	Mature Audiences
23	Gladly Ate Her	Accompanied Minors
7	Ground Hog Day	Teens
20	Hannah and Her Blisters	General
5	Harry's Pottery	General
8	It's a Wonderful Wife	General
9	Kramer vs. George	Mature Audiences

Figure 31.8 Because an outer join is used, unrated movies simply show up with a blank rating, instead of being eliminated from the list altogether.

Note

Many database systems place restrictions on whether you can use inner and outer joins together in the same `SELECT` statement. See your database documentation for details.

SUBQUERIES

SQL enables you to nest complete `SELECT` statements within other statements for various purposes. These nested queries are known as *subqueries*. Subqueries provide great flexibility and really allow your queries to get into those hard-to-reach places.

Subqueries can be included in your queries in a number of ways. The most common are

- In the WHERE part of a SQL statement to correlate data in various tables.
- In the SELECT part of a SQL statement to return an additional column.

Either way, the subquery itself is put inside parentheses and can contain just about any valid SELECT statement. The subquery can use dot notation to refer to tables outside the parentheses, but not vice versa (the main statement can't reach in and refer to tables inside the parentheses, but the subquery can reach out and refer to tables in the main statement).

Note

Most database systems support subqueries, but some place certain restrictions on their use. If you run into problems, consult your database system's documentation for details.

Subqueries in WHERE Criteria

The simplest way to include a subquery in your SQL statements is as part of your WHERE criteria, using the = operator. In general, this type of subquery statement is best for quickly and easily looking up information based on some type of ID number.

Say you were constructing a set of pages that will enable the folks in Orange Whip Studio's accounting department to view a list of merchandise orders. On the first page, the user sees a list of all orders, retrieved straightforwardly from the MerchandiseOrders table. Each order can be clicked to view the name and other information about the person who placed the order. This link (for each order's contact information) passes the OrderID in the URL. Therefore, the code in the contact details page must retrieve information from the Contacts table, based on the given OrderID.

The following statement, which uses a subquery, does this job nicely:

```
<CFQUERY NAME="GetContact" DATASOURCE="ows">
  SELECT * FROM Contacts
  WHERE ContactID =
    (SELECT ContactID FROM MerchandiseOrders
     WHERE OrderID = #URL.OrderID#)
</CFQUERY>
```

Tip

This example uses the = operator to include the subquery in the larger query statement, but you also could use <>, >, <, >=, or <= in place of the = sign.

When this query is executed, your database system works on it from the inside out, starting with the subquery. Say the URL.OrderID value is passed as 2. The subquery looks in the MerchandiseOrders table and finds that the corresponding ContactID number is 4. Now the outer query statement is run, using the value of 4 in place of the subquery, almost as if the outer query had used WHERE ContactID = 4.

The result is that all contact information from the `Contacts` table is returned to ColdFusion, based only on the `OrderID`. This type of subquery technique is great for situations such as this, in which there is a conceptual step-by-step process to go through (first, get the `ContactID` from the `MerchandiseOrders` table; then use that to retrieve the correct record from the `Contacts` table).

Caution

When you include a subquery in a SQL statement with the = operator, be sure that only one record will ever be found by the subquery. If the subquery part of the statement shown previously were to return more than one record, a database error message would be displayed. If the subquery might return more than one record, you should use the `IN` operator (discussed shortly) instead of the = operator.

Subqueries Are Often Just Alternatives

Take another look at the previous subquery code snippet. There are other ways that the same information could be retrieved from the database. For instance, you could simply use two separate `<CFQUERY>` tags, which represent the two steps mentioned previously. First, you could get the correct `ContactID`, like so:

```
<CFQUERY NAME="GetID" DATASOURCE="ows">
  SELECT ContactID FROM MerchandiseOrders
  WHERE OrderID = #URL.OrderID#
</CFQUERY>
```

Then, you would pass the retrieved `ContactID` to a second query, like so:

```
<CFQUERY NAME="GetContact" DATASOURCE="ows">
  SELECT * FROM Contacts
  WHERE ContactID = #GetID.ContactID#
</CFQUERY>
```

This method returns the same information to ColdFusion; you are free to use either method. However, you can expect slightly better performance from the subquery approach because only one database operation is necessary. Also, if you conceptually ask your questions all at once, your database system often can make optimizations based on indexes and other tuning algorithms, which usually are bypassed if you run two separate queries. As a general rule of thumb, the fewer times ColdFusion must interact with the database, the better.

You also could get the same information using a join, as you learned about in the last section. The following query (which uses a join) returns the same results as the subquery statement shown earlier or the two `<CFQUERY>` tags shown most recently:

```
<CFQUERY NAME="GetContact" DATASOURCE="ows">
  SELECT c.*
  FROM Contacts c INNER JOIN MerchandiseOrders o
    ON c.ContactID = o.ContactID
  WHERE o.OrderID = #URL.OrderID#
</CFQUERY>
```

Again, you are free to use the join syntax instead of the subquery syntax. They will both return the same data to ColdFusion. In this case, you could theoretically expect slightly better performance from the subquery because it implies that there is only one relevant `ContactID` and only one matching `OrderID` (whereas the database system would potentially need to scan all rows of the tables to see how many matching records might exist). Whether any real-world performance difference really exists between the two, however, depends on the database system being used, how the columns are indexed, and other factors too numerous to discuss here. In fact, many database systems will decide to treat a subquery and a join in exactly the same manner internally. In general, deciding whether to use a subquery or a join in any given situation is often a matter of personal choice. Joins are frequently more powerful, mainly because they can return multiple columns from all tables at once. Subqueries are often easier to write and understand and can sometimes be more efficient. The best rule of thumb is to simply use the method that springs to mind first as you are thinking about the query you need to write. You can always make changes later.

Note

As a general rule, joins are more likely to run more quickly than subqueries, so use a join when in doubt. That said, you should feel free to experiment and use whichever seems more straightforward for a given situation.

USING SUBQUERIES WITH IN

You just saw how a subquery can be introduced into a larger query statement by including it on the right side of the `=` operator in the `WHERE` clause. That type of subquery is useful when you know the subquery will never return more than one record. If the subquery can return any number of records, you must introduce the subquery using the `IN` keyword. Conceptually, the values found by the subquery will be turned into a comma-separated list. Then, the comma-separated list is used to complete the outer query statement.

For instance, to get information from the `Merchandise` table about the items included in a particular order, you could do the following:

```
SELECT * FROM Merchandise
WHERE MerchID IN
 (SELECT ItemID FROM MerchandiseOrdersItems
  WHERE OrderID = #URL.OrderID# )
```

You also can nest subqueries within other subqueries. For instance, this statement first retrieves all the `OrderID` numbers from the `MerchandiseOrders` table that a particular contact has made. The list of order numbers is passed to the middle subquery, which retrieves a list of corresponding `ItemID` numbers from the `MerchandiseOrdersItems` table. Finally, the list of item numbers is passed to the outermost query, which retrieves the list of merchandise. The result is a set of records that provide information about all merchandise items a particular customer has ordered:

```
SELECT * FROM Merchandise WHERE MerchID IN
  (SELECT ItemID FROM MerchandiseOrdersItems
   WHERE OrderID IN
```

```
    (SELECT OrderID FROM MerchandiseOrders
     WHERE ContactID = #URL.ContactID#))
```

Again, you could get this same information using join syntax. The following join returns the same information as the nested subquery syntax used in the previous snippet:

```
SELECT m.*
FROM Merchandise m, MerchandiseOrders o, MerchandiseOrdersItems oi
WHERE m.MerchID = oi.ItemID AND o.OrderID = oi.OrderID
AND o.ContactID = #URL.ContactID#
```

The different syntaxes will feel more natural to different developers. The thought process to get to the first query is more step by step, whereas the second requires a more relational mindset. In general, you can just use the approach that seems more intuitive to you.

Note

The `IN` keyword isn't just for subqueries. It's for any situation in which you need to provide a comma-separated list of values as criteria. For instance, you could use `WHERE OrderID IN (4,7,9)` to get information about order numbers 4, 7, and 9. Or, if you have several check boxes named `OrderID` on a form, you could use `WHERE OrderID IN (#FORM.OrderID#)` to retrieve information about the orders the user checked.

USING SUBQUERIES WITH `NOT IN`

One interesting way to use subqueries is with the `NOT IN` operator. You can use `NOT IN` just like `IN`, as discussed previously. The difference is that the outer query will retrieve records that *do not* correspond to the values found by the subquery. In other words, the query as a whole will return the opposite set of records.

So, to select the merchandise items a user has *not* ordered in the past, you could do the following. This is exactly the same as the first example in the previous section, "Using Subqueries with `IN`," except that it adds the word `NOT` to invert the results:

```
SELECT * FROM Merchandise
WHERE MerchID NOT IN
 (SELECT ItemID FROM MerchandiseOrdersItems
  WHERE OrderID = #URL.OrderID# )
```

Listing 31.10 shows how to use several nested `IN` and `NOT IN` subqueries together to create a lightweight collaborative filtering effect. The term *collaborative filtering* is sometimes used to describe the online merchandising technique of presenting a list of suggested items to a user, based on what similar people have ordered in the past. The technique can be seen most visibly at Amazon.com ("People who bought *Raiders of the Lost Aardvark* also bought *The Mommy Returns*"). The listing that follows is relatively simple and might not count as true collaborative filtering. However, it does show how subqueries can be used to create something fairly similar.

The idea behind this listing is simple: It updates the `StoreCart.cfm` template from Chapter 29, "Online Commerce." When the user goes to check out by visiting the version of `StoreCart.cfm` shown in Listing 31.10, the query called `GetSimilar` is run. `GetSimilar` looks at the items in the user's cart and finds the completed orders in which the items have appeared. In addition, if the user has logged in, the query uses a `NOT IN` subquery to ensure that the user's own orders are not included in the list of completed orders being considered.

Then, for each of the other completed orders, the query retrieves all items that were included in those orders (not counting the items in the current user's cart). These items are then shown to the user with the message, *people who have purchased items in your cart have also bought the following*, as shown in Figure 31.9.

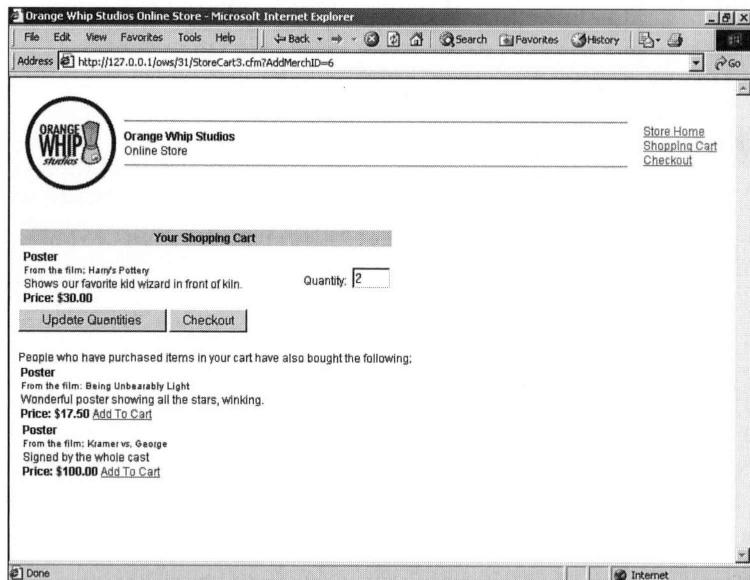

Figure 31.9 You can use `IN` *and* `NOT IN` subqueries to build interesting takes on your data, such as this lightweight collaborative filtering example.

Note

To test this listing, save it as `StoreCart.cfm` in the same folder with Chapter 29's listings. Now visit the `Store.cfm` template in that folder, and add a few items to your cart. Be sure to add items that already are in the `MerchandiseOrdersItems` table. Now visit this listing.

LISTING 31.10 `StoreCart3.cfm`**—USING SUBQUERIES TO MIMIC A COLLABORATIVE FILTERING FEATURE**

```
<!--- Show header images, etc., for Online Store --->
<CFINCLUDE TEMPLATE="StoreHeader.cfm">

<!--- If MerchID was passed in URL --->
<CFIF IsDefined("URL.AddMerchID")>
  <!--- Add item to user's cart data, via custom tag --->
  <CF_ShoppingCart
    Action="Add"
    MerchID="#URL.AddMerchID#">
```

```
<!--- If user is submitting cart form --->
<CFELSEIF IsDefined("FORM.MerchID")>
  <!--- For each MerchID on Form, Update Quantity --->
  <CFLOOP LIST="#Form.MerchID#" INDEX="ThisMerchID">
    <!--- Update Quantity, via Custom Tag --->
    <CF_ShoppingCart
      Action="Update"
      MerchID="#ThisMerchID#"
      Quantity="#FORM['Quant_#ThisMerchID#']#">
  </CFLOOP>

  <!--- If user submitted form via "Checkout" button, --->
  <!--- send on to Checkout page after updating cart. --->
  <CFIF IsDefined("FORM.IsCheckingOut")>
    <CFLOCATION URL="StoreCheckout.cfm">
  </CFIF>
</CFIF>

<!--- Get current cart contents, via Custom Tag --->
<CF_ShoppingCart
  Action="List"
  ReturnVariable="GetCart">


<!--- Stop here if user's cart is empty --->
<CFIF GetCart.RecordCount EQ 0>
  There is nothing in your cart.
  <CFABORT>
</CFIF>



<!--- Create form that submits to this template --->
<CFFORM ACTION="#CGI.SCRIPT_NAME#">
  <TABLE>
    <TR>
      <TH COLSPAN="2" BGCOLOR="Silver">Your Shopping Cart</TH>
    </TR>
    <!--- For each piece of merchandise --->
    <CFLOOP QUERY="GetCart">
      <TR>
        <TD>
          <!--- Show this piece of merchandise --->
          <CF_MerchDisplay
            MerchID="#GetCart.MerchID#"
            ShowAddLink="No">
        </TD>
        <TD>
          <!--- Display Quantity in Text entry field --->
          <CFOUTPUT>
            Quantity:
            <INPUT TYPE="Hidden"
              NAME="MerchID"
              VALUE="#GetCart.MerchID#">
            <INPUT TYPE="Text" SIZE="3"
              NAME="Quant_#GetCart.MerchID#"
              VALUE="#GetCart.Quantity#"><BR>
          </CFOUTPUT>
```

LISTING 31.10 CONTINUED

```
        </TD>
      </TR>
    </CFLOOP>

  </TABLE>

  <!--- Submit button to update quantities --->
  <INPUT TYPE="Submit" VALUE="Update Quantities">

  <!--- Submit button to Check out --->
  <INPUT TYPE="Submit" VALUE="Checkout" NAME="IsCheckingOut">
</CFFORM>



<!--- Convert current cart contents to comma-sep list --->
<CFSET CurrentMerchList = ValueList(GetCart.MerchID)>

<!--- Run query to suggest other items for user to buy --->
<CFQUERY NAME="GetSimilar" DATASOURCE="#REQUEST.DataSource#"
  CACHEDWITHIN="#CreateTimeSpan(0,0,5,0)#" MAXROWS="3">
  <!--- We want all items NOT in user's cart... --->
  SELECT ItemID
  FROM MerchandiseOrdersItems
  WHERE ItemID NOT IN (#CurrentMerchList#)
  <!--- ...but that *were* included in other orders --->
  <!--- along with items now in the user's cart... --->
  AND OrderID IN
    (SELECT OrderID FROM MerchandiseOrdersItems
     WHERE ItemID IN (#CurrentMerchList#)
     <!--- ...not including this user's past orders! --->
     <CFIF IsDefined("SESSION.Auth.ContactID")>
     AND OrderID NOT IN
       (SELECT OrderID FROM MerchandiseOrders
        WHERE ContactID = #SESSION.Auth.ContactID#)
     </CFIF> )
</CFQUERY>

<!--- If at least one "similar" item was found --->
<CFIF GetSimilar.RecordCount GT 0>
  <P>People who have purchased items in your cart
  have also bought the following:<BR>

   <!--- For each similar item, display it, via Custom Tag --->
   <!--- (show five suggestions at most) --->
   <CFLOOP QUERY="GetSimilar">
     <CF_MerchDisplay
       MerchID="#GetSimilar.ItemID#">
   </CFLOOP>
</CFIF>
```

Note

This `StoreCart.cfm` listing is meant to work with the other listings from Chapter 29. For all the links to work properly, you should save Listing 31.10 as `StoreCart.cfm` in the same folder with Chapter 29's listings.

CALCULATING NEW COLUMNS WITH SUBQUERIES

Another convenient place to use subqueries is in the `SELECT` part of an ordinary query statement. Simply include the subquery in the `SELECT` list, as if it were a column. Within the subquery, add criteria to its `WHERE` clause using dot notation, similar to a join. The idea is to connect the subquery somehow to the outer query, usually based on a common ID number of some type.

For instance, to get a list of all contacts in the `Contacts` table, along with a simple count of the number of orders that each contact has made, you could use the following query:

```
SELECT ContactID, FirstName, LastName,
  (SELECT COUNT(*) FROM MerchandiseOrders o
   WHERE c.ContactID = o.ContactID) AS OrderCount
FROM Contacts c
```

You could get this same information using an outer join, as discussed earlier in this chapter, but it would be a bit more tedious to write and may not feel as straightforward:

```
SELECT c.ContactID, c.FirstName, c.LastName,
  COUNT(o.OrderID) AS OrderCount
FROM Contacts c LEFT OUTER JOIN MerchandiseOrders o
ON c.ContactID = o.ContactID
GROUP BY c.ContactID, c.FirstName, c.LastName
```

Note

Because an aggregate function is in this join query's `SELECT` list, all other columns must be repeated in the `GROUP BY` list. Depending on the situation and the database system being used, queries that have a long `GROUP BY` list can start to perform somewhat poorly when the number of rows in the tables gets to be large.

COMBINING RECORDSETS WITH UNION

You can use SQL's `UNION` operator to combine the results from two different queries. Compared to joins, subqueries, aggregates, and the like, `UNION` is pretty simple. `UNION` is simply about combining the results of two different `SELECT` statements. Each `SELECT` can be based on the same table or on different tables.

Say someone at Orange Whip Studios has asked you to come up with a little report page that shows which actors and directors are involved with each of the studio's films. For each film, the people should be sorted by last name.

Listing 31.11 shows how the `UNION` operator makes this task easy. The `<CFQUERY>` in this template contains two `SELECT` statements. The first retrieves information about the actors in each film. If it were run on its own, it would return four columns: `MovieTitle`, `NameFirst`, `NameLast`, and `Credit`. The second `SELECT` retrieves information about the directors of each film. Run on its own, it would also return four columns, with slightly different names (`MovieTitle`, `FirstName`, `LastName`, and `Credit`). The `UNION` statement causes the records from both statements to be returned together, in the order specified by the `ORDER BY` at the end of the query (first by `MovieTitle` and then by the last names of each actor or director involved with that movie).

The results are shown in Figure 31.10.

Tip

ColdFusion 5.0's new query-of-query feature enables you to perform `UNION`s between queries that come from different data sources or database systems. See the section "Queries of Queries," later in this chapter.

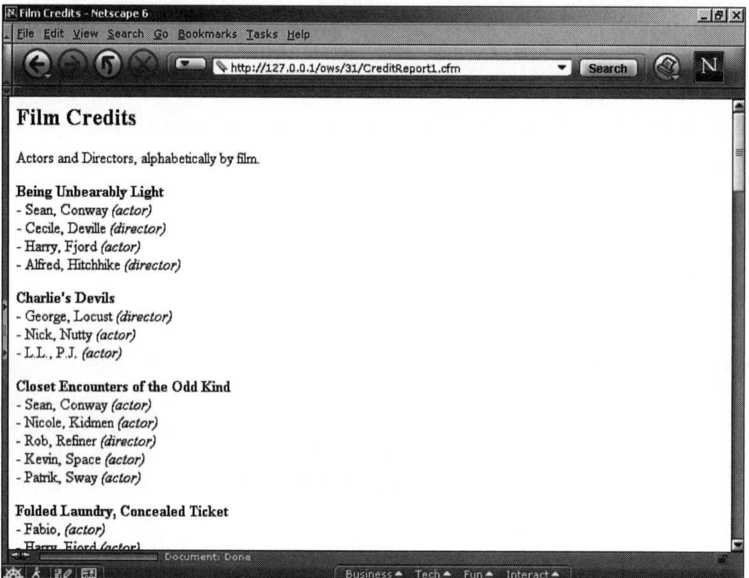

Figure 31.10 `UNION` statements enable you combine the results of several `SELECT` statements.

Note

Even though the column names are not exactly the same, the query is still valid (see the following list of rules and considerations). Use the column names in the first `SELECT` statement in your ColdFusion code.

LISTING 31.11 `CreditReport1.cfm`—**USING `UNION` TO COMBINE TWO RESULTSETS**

```
<HTML>
<HEAD><TITLE>Film Credits</TITLE></HEAD>
<BODY>
```

```
<H2>Film Credits</H2>
Actors and Directors, alphabetically by film.

<!--- Retrieve Films and Actors, then --->
<!--- Retrieve Films and Directors, then order everyone --->
<!--- by related Film Title and the person's last name. --->
<CFQUERY NAME="GetExp" DATASOURCE="#REQUEST.DataSource#">
    SELECT
      f.FilmID, f.MovieTitle,
      a.NameFirst, a.NameLast, 'actor' AS Credit
    FROM
      Films f, Actors a, FilmsActors fa
    WHERE
      f.FilmID  = fa.FilmID AND
      a.ActorID = fa.ActorID
  UNION
    SELECT
      f.FilmID, f.MovieTitle,
      d.FirstName, d.LastName, 'director' AS Credit
    FROM
      Films f, Directors d, FilmsDirectors fd
    WHERE
      f.FilmID     = fd.FilmID AND
      d.DirectorID = fd.DirectorID
  ORDER BY
    f.MovieTitle, NameLast
</CFQUERY>

<!--- For each film, show the title --->
<CFOUTPUT QUERY="GetExp" GROUP="FilmID">
  <P><B>#MovieTitle#</B><BR>

  <!--- Within each film, show each person involved --->
  <CFOUTPUT>
    - #NameFirst#, #NameLast# <I>(#Credit#)</I><BR>
  </CFOUTPUT>
</CFOUTPUT>

</BODY>
</HTML>
```


Note

The `Credit` column for the first `SELECT` statement has a constant value of `actor`. Every row returned by that statement will hold the actual word `actor` in the `Credit` column. The same column for the second `SELECT` has a constant value of `director`. This enables the user to see whether each person is an actor or a director (otherwise, there would be no way to tell because they are all mixed together in alphabetical order). This is not something that is done very often, but you can actually return constant values from any query. Just provide the constant value (a string in single quotes or a number without any quotes) where you would normally provide the column name; then give the new psdeuocolumn an alias using the AS keyword.

Tip

You can use more than one `UNION` in a SQL statement–which means that you can combine records from more than two `SELECT` statements.

When you are using `UNION` in your queries, the following rules and considerations apply:

- **All the `SELECT` statements must specify the same number of columns.**
- **The columns' data types, `Text`, `Numeric`, `Date`, and so on, must match**—However, the text width or numeric precision of the columns might not need to match, depending on the type of database you are using. See your database documentation for details.
- **The column names in the `SELECT` statements *don't* have to match**—In fact, the column names from the first `SELECT` are the only ones that matter and are the only ones that will be returned to ColdFusion.
- **Duplicate rows (rows that are the same from more than one of the `SELECT` statements) are automatically eliminated**—This is true unless you use `UNION ALL` instead of `UNION`.
- **There might be only one `ORDER BY` statement, at the very end, and it must only refer to column names from the first `SELECT` statement**—It orders all the rows from all the queries involved in the `UNION`, intermingling the rows with one another.
- **With most database systems, you may not use `DISTINCT` and `UNION` in the same query.**
- **In general, so-called BLOb (Binary Large Object) columns that allow unlimited amounts of data to be stored (such as `Memo` columns in Access or `Image` columns in SQLServer) cannot be used in `UNION` statements**—Some database systems might make an exception to this rule if you are using `UNION ALL` instead of `UNION`.

WORKING WITH NULL VALUES

One of the most confusing concepts when starting out with databases is the idea of a *null value*. A null value indicates that there is literally nothing recorded in the table for that row and column (in layman's terms, the value was left blank). For instance, consider the `MerchandiseOrders` table's `ShipDate` column. When the order is indeed shipped, the date is recorded here. Until that point, there is nothing in the column; its value is `NULL`.

SETTING VALUES TO NULL

To indicate that you want to set a column to a null value, use the keyword `NULL` where you would normally provide the value. It is important to understand that you should not surround the `NULL` keyword with quotation marks; that would set the column to the four-character string "NULL", rather than the single, special value of `NULL`.

If you need to record a null value when a form field has been left blank, ColdFusion's `<CFIF>` and `<CFELSE>` tags come in handy. For instance, imagine a form with `OrderID` and `ShipDate` fields on it. The following code snippet would set the `ShipDate` column to whatever the user provides, as long as it is a valid date. If the form field has been left blank, or if ColdFusion doesn't recognize it as a date value, it will be set to NULL to indicate that no date is known:

```
UPDATE MerchandiseOrders
SET ShipDate = <CFIF IsDate(FORM.ShipDate)>
                '#DateFormat(FORM.ShipDate, "m/d/yyyy")#'
               <CFELSE> NULL </CFIF>
WHERE OrderID = #FORM.OrderID#
```

TESTING FOR NULL VALUES IN SQL CODE

SQL statements that deal with null values can produce unexpected results if you don't know what to watch out for. There isn't time to get into the formal theory behind null values here, but the basic idea is that a null value, by its very definition, is not equal *or unequal* to anything—not even another null value. Therefore, the following statement should not return any records, even if null values exist for ShipDate in the table:


```
SELECT * FROM MerchandiseOrders
WHERE ShipDate = NULL
```

Instead, to retrieve the orders that have not shipped yet, you must use the special IS operator, which is used only for testing for NULL values. In addition, a special IS NOT operator is available, which can be used to return values that do not have NULL values.

So, the following could be used to find orders that have not shipped yet:

```
SELECT * FROM MerchandiseOrders
WHERE ShipDate IS NULL
```

Conversely, to find records that have already been shipped, you would use this:

```
SELECT * FROM MerchandiseOrders
WHERE ShipDate IS NOT NULL
```

Note

Some database systems, especially older versions, don't make a distinction between = NULL and IS NULL.

It is also important to note that *any* comparison (not just equality comparisons done with the = operator) against a null value must, by definition, return false. Therefore, inequality tests (with the <> operator) and other comparisons (such as < or >=) often produce what end users might consider to be counterintuitive results. You need to take a bit of extra time to think about how any null values might affect your application's queries. For instance, at first glance, you would probably expect the following snippet to return all films except for one (*The Lice Storm*):

```
SELECT * FROM MerchandiseOrders
WHERE MovieTitle <> 'The Lice Storm'
```

Strange as it might seem, if any of the films have a null value in the MovieTitle column (perhaps the studio's focus groups haven't determined a title yet), those films will *not* be returned by the previous snippet. To get all rows except *The Lice Storm*, including ones that have NULL titles, you would need to use the following:

```
SELECT * FROM MerchandiseOrders
WHERE (MovieTitle <> 'The Lice Storm' OR MovieTitle IS NULL)
```

TESTING FOR NULL VALUES IN CFML CODE

The situation is further complicated by the fact that CFML doesn't include the concept of a null value (which is somewhat surprising, given the database-centric nature of the product). When ColdFusion receives a NULL value from a database query, it converts the value into an empty string.

Note

SQL purists generally wince when they hear this because it means that there is no way to tell the difference between a NULL value and a value that has actually been set to an empty string. In practice, though, this isn't usually too much of a problem because such a distinction rarely is significant in a real-world application. Would there ever be a need, for instance, to distinguish between a film title that hasn't been named yet (a null value) and a film that has actually been named "" (an empty string)? Probably not.

So, if you want to display a date only when it is has not been set to a null value in the database, you can test for an empty string in your CFML code, like so:

```
<CFIF GetOrders.ShipDate EQ "">
  (this order has not shipped yet)
<CFELSE>
  Shipped on: #LSDateFormat(GetOrders.ShipDate)#
</CFIF>
```

WORKING WITH DATE VALUES

Working with date values in databases and ColdFusion can be confusing. The confusion often stems from the fact that a date value in a database is recorded conceptually as a *moment in history*, rather than a simple string (such as 4/15/01). How exactly the date is stored internally is up to the database system (often it's stored as a very long number that represents the number of milliseconds before or after some fixed reference date). Only when the date is returned to ColdFusion and then output using a CFML function such as DateFormat() or LSDateFormat() does it look like a date to us humans.

Note

This discussion assumes that you are storing your dates in actual date-type columns in your database tables. Depending on the database system you're using, these columns can be called *Date* columns, *Date/Time* columns, or something similar.

SPECIFYING DATES IN <CFQUERY> TAGS

First, the bad news: Not all database systems agree on the syntax that should be used to specify a date in a query. Some are willing to parse the date based on a number of formats; others have a strict format that must be used at all times. The good news is that the ODBC specification defines a common format that can be used for any ODBC data source. Also, ColdFusion provides a `CreateODBCDate()` function that can be used to automatically get dates into this format in your <CFQUERY> tags.

So, as long as you are using an ODBC (or OLE-DB) data source, you can use `CreateODBCDate()` to correctly format the date in your `INSERT` and `UPDATE` queries. Here's a sample snippet that updates a column based on a form field called `DateInTheaters`:

```
<CFQUERY DATASOURCE="ows">
  UPDATE Films
  SET DateInTheaters = #CreateODBCDate(FORM.DateInTheaters)#
  WHERE FilmID = #FORM.FilmID#
</CFQUERY>
```


Tip

If your situation is such that you can use <CFUPDATE> or <CFINSERT> to update your database, you don't even have to worry about this part. ColdFusion takes care of writing the correct query syntax for you.

If you are using a native database driver, however, the date format generated by `CreateODBCDate()` generally results in an error message from your database server. You then must become familiar with the method preferred by the database system itself for providing dates. For instance, to supply a date and time to a database with the Oracle native driver, you must use the `TO_DATE()` function provided by Oracle itself.

To enable your query to work with any database system, you can substitute the `CreateODBCDate()` function with a <CFQUERYPARAM> tag that uses a `CFSQLTYPE` attribute of `CF_SQL_TIMESTAMP`. ColdFusion will take care of adapting your SQL statement so the date is sent to the database in a format it will understand.

You will learn more about <CFQUERYPARAM> later in this chapter. For now, just think of it as a way to tell ColdFusion to convert the `VALUE` you supply into whatever format is appropriate for the type of database you are using (ODBC or otherwise). The query shown previously, then, would become this:

```
<CFQUERY DATASOURCE="ows">
  UPDATE Films
  SET DateInTheaters =
    <CFQUERYPARAM CFSQLTYPE="CF_SQL_DATE" VALUE="#FORM.DateInTheaters#">
  WHERE FilmID = #FORM.FilmID#
</CFQUERY>
```

For more about <CFQUERYPARAM>, see the section "Parameterized Queries," later in this chapter.

DATES IN QUERY CRITERIA

For instance, consider the `ShipDate` column of the `MerchandiseOrders` table in the Orange Whip Studios database. This column contains the date and time the order was shipped. The date and time are not stored separately. They are stored as one value, which you can think of as a moment in history.

If, when a date is being recorded in a database, a time is not supplied, the database assumes that you mean midnight at the beginning of that day and will store it as such. If, later, you retrieve that date value with a `SELECT` statement and output the time portion of it with CFML's `TimeFormat()` function, the time will display as `12:00 AM`.

All of this makes perfect sense. But you will often need to query the database based on a date value, where the time portions of the date values can feel like they are working against you. For instance, say you are allowing the user to see all orders made on a particular day. You decide to allow the user to specify the date in a form field called `SearchDate`, using a `<CFINPUT>` tag, like this:

```
<CFINPUT
  NAME="SearchDate"
  VALIDATE="date"
  REQUIRED="Yes" MESSAGE="You must provide a date first!">
```

The user expects to be able to type a simple date into this field (perhaps `3/18/2001`) to see all orders placed on that date. You decide, quite sensibly, to write a query such as the following, which executes when the form is submitted:

```
<CFQUERY NAME="GetOrders" DATABASE="ows">
  SELECT * FROM MerchandiseOrders
  WHERE OrderDate = #CreateODBCDate(FORM.SearchDate)#
</CFQUERY>
```

When you test the template, though, you find that it doesn't work as planned. Users are expecting to see all orders placed on the date they specify, no matter what time during that day the order was placed. However, your code never seems to find any records. This is because no time is specified in the query criteria, so the database assumes a time of midnight. If the user types `3/18/2001` in the search field, your query is sent as something such as the following to your database system (conceptually):

```
  SELECT * FROM MerchandiseOrders
  WHERE OrderDate = '3/18/2001 12:00 AM'
```

After you see it this way, it becomes clear what's going on. Your query will return only records that were shipped at exactly midnight on whatever day the user specifies. You need to translate the user-specified date into a range between two moments in time (the beginning of that day and the end). The following will work as expected, returning all orders placed on or after midnight at the beginning of the specified day, all the way up to (but not including) midnight at the end of that same day:

```
<CFQUERY NAME="GetOrders" DATABASE="ows">
  SELECT * FROM MerchandiseOrders
  WHERE OrderDate >= #CreateODBCDate(FORM.SearchDate)#
    AND OrderDate <  #CreateOBDCDate(DateAdd("d", Form.SearchDate, 1))#
</CFQUERY>
```

The following query will also work as expected and can be used interchangeably with the one shown previously. It uses a special keyword provided by SQL, called BETWEEN:

```
<CFQUERY NAME="GetOrders" DATABASE="ows">
  SELECT * FROM MerchandiseOrders
  WHERE OrderDate BETWEEN
    #CreateODBCDate(FORM.SearchDate)# AND
    #CreateOBDCDate(DateAdd("d", Form.SearchDate, 1))#
</CFQUERY>
```

Note

If you are not using an ODBC database, you should substitute all the CreateODBCDate() functions shown in this section with a <CFQUERYPARAM> tag, as explained in the previous section "Specifying Dates in <CFQUERY> Tags."

MILLISECOND-LEVEL PRECISION

Date-type columns in many database systems are accurate to the millisecond, but Date objects in ColdFusion are accurate only to the second. When you query a table with <CFQUERY>, the millisecond information is lost as it is being returned to ColdFusion.

If you need to display dates with millisecond-level precision in your templates, you must convert the value to a string as part of your SQL statement, using whatever syntax is appropriate for your database system (often a function called Convert or CAST). The CONVERT scalar function provided by ODBC also can be used for this conversion (see the section "Manipulating Data with Scalar Functions," later in this chapter).

Note

After you return a date as a string that includes millisecond information, however, it will no longer be recognized by ColdFusion as a date value. Therefore, CFML's date functions, such as DateAdd() and DatePart(), will no longer work. In situations in which you need to display millisecond precision *and* use CFML date functions, consider selecting the column from the database in both forms (the actual date and its CONVERTed string representation).

UNDERSTANDING VIEWS

Many database systems support something called a *view*. The idea behind a view is to be able to save the SQL code for a particular SELECT query as a permanent part of the database. From that point on, the name of the view can be used like a table name in other queries.

Note

The exact definition of what a view is called, how you create it, and what it can do varies a bit depending on the database system you use. For instance, if you use CREATE VIEW with an Access database, Access will create what it normally calls a query.

CREATING A VIEW

Again, the exact syntax needed to create a view might vary depending on your database system, but you usually can create one by typing the words CREATE VIEW, then a name for the view, then the word AS, and then the actual SELECT statement you want to use to create the view, like so:

```
CREATE VIEW OrdersPending AS
SELECT * FROM MerchandiseOrders
WHERE ShipDate IS NULL
```

After you execute this SQL statement once (either via a <CFQUERY> tag; by executing it with ColdFusion Studio's Query Builder; or via whatever command-line, graphical, or other query tools your database system provides), it becomes a part of your database. You can now refer to the OrdersPending view in your queries as if it were a table. It's as if you have created a virtual or shadow table that always contains the exact same data as the MerchandiseOrders table, except that all the orders that have already shipped (where the ShipDate is not a null value) are excluded.

For instance, the following would return all pending orders:

```
SELECT * FROM OrdersPending
ORDER BY OrderDate
```

ADVANTAGES OF USING VIEWS

You almost never would *need* to create a view when building a ColdFusion application, but they can be helpful. Here, the OrdersPending view makes separating the abstract idea of a pending order with its implementation in the database (the NULL value) easier. If you are working on a part of the application that deals only with pending orders (a section of the company intranet for the shipping department, say), you can use the OrdersPending view in each of your queries, instead of having to remember to use ShipDate IS NULL each time.

Also, if, in the future, you decide to keep pending orders in a different table, you would need to change only the definition of the view, rather than having to alter each individual query. In this respect, views become, somewhat like CFML custom tags, a method of abstraction—a way to separate your application's logic from the physical details of how the data is stored behind the scenes.

In fact, if your database is being designed by a different person in your team, or if you are connecting ColdFusion to some type of legacy database that is already in place, your database administrator might decide to give you access to only the OrdersPending view, rather than the underlying MerchandiseOrders table. You might not even know the difference. This way, the administrator knows that your ColdFusion application will not be capable of displaying inappropriate records (in this case, orders that have already shipped).

You can also create views that involve more than one table by using ordinary join syntax in the SELECT statement that follows CREATE VIEW. For instance, you could create a view called ActorsInFilms, which uses a join to select the FilmID and MovieTitle of each film, plus the ActorID and name of each actor in that film. The CREATE VIEW statement would look like this:

```
CREATE VIEW ActorsInFilms AS
SELECT f.FilmID, f.MovieTitle, a.ActorID, a.NameFirst, a.NameLast
FROM Actors a, Films f, FilmsActors fa
WHERE a.ActorID = fa.ActorID AND f.FilmID = fa.FilmID
```

After the previous snippet is executed once, you can retrieve the title and actors for any film without having to use any joins at all. For instance

```
SELECT * FROM ActorsInFilms
WHERE FilmID = #URL.FilmID#
```

Note

Views that involve more than one table are considered read-only by most database systems. You can `SELECT` from them but not make changes via `INSERT`, `UPDATE`, or `DELETE`.

Manipulating Data with Scalar Functions

Caution

This discussion is relevant only for ODBC data sources. If you are using a native database driver, these scalar functions are not available to you. You must use whatever database-specific syntax (usually proprietary functions) is appropriate for your system. Consult the SQL reference section of your database documentation for details.

You might want to create queries that do things such as manipulate dates or perform arithmetic on your data. The ODBC standard defines a number of scalar functions for performing date, time, numeric, and string operations on your data. Basically, ODBC says that if the database supports a function natively, it should be mapped to the appropriate scalar function to provide some common ground between systems. However, nothing is required here. Most databases support only a subset of the complete list.

Tip

A complete reference and discussion of scalar functions is provided in the Microsoft Data Access Components SDK, which is currently available at `http://www.microsoft.com/data`.

Using Scalar Functions in Queries

You can use scalar functions to create computed columns on-the-fly for each row your query returns. Use the following syntax to use scalar functions in your queries:

```
{ fn function_name(parameter, parameter ... )}
```

The curly braces indicate that this is an ODBC command (as opposed to ordinary SQL). The `fn` indicates that a scalar function is to follow. A list of parameters follows, in parentheses (the appropriate parameters for the most common functions are listed in Table 31.2).

For instance, the following query uses the scalar function called `MONTH()` to return all orders made during the month of December (of any year):

```
<CFQUERY NAME="GetHolidayOrders" DATASOURCE="ows">
  SELECT * FROM MerchandiseOrders
  WHERE { fn MONTH(OrderDate) } = 12
</CFQUERY>
```

The following example returns two columns, one called `DayNum` (an integer representing the day of the week, from 1 to 7) and a `TotalAmount` column (the total of all expenses that have ever been made on that day of the week, for all months and years). This would be a useful query for creating some type of expense breakdown report page:

```
<CFQUERY NAME="GetExpenseBreakdown" DATASOURCE="ows">
  SELECT
    { fn DAYOFWEEK(ExpenseDate) } AS DayNum,
    SUM(ExpenseAmount) AS TotalAmount
  FROM Expenses
  GROUP BY { fn DAYOFWEEK(ExpenseDate) }
</CFQUERY>
```

Tip

You could use the CFML `DayOfWeekAsString()` function to display the value of `GetExpenseBreakdown.DayNum` in your `<CFOUTPUT>` code. See Appendix B for details.

A SHORT LIST OF SCALAR FUNCTIONS

Table 31.2 summarizes the scalar functions supported by the Microsoft desktop family of ODBC drivers. These are not the only scalar functions defined by ODBC, but it is the list that is most commonly supported in real-world driver implementations. You will need to experiment a bit or consult your driver's documentation (if any) to determine which functions are supported by your driver.

TABLE 31.2 SCALAR FUNCTION QUICK REFERENCE

Scalar Function	What It Returns	Similar to CFML Expression
`CONVERT (value, datatype)`	`value` converted to data type*	n/a
`CONCAT (string1, string)`	*`string1`* concatenated with *`string2`*	*`string1`* and *`string2`*
`LCASE(string)`	*`string`* converted to lowercase	`LCase(string)`
`LEFT(string, count)`	First *`count`* characters of *`string`*	`Left(string, count)`
`LENGTH(string)`	Number of characters in *`string`*	`Len(string)`
`LOCATE(substring, string [, start])`	Position of *`substring`* in string after *`start`*	`Find (substring, string [, start])`

Scalar Function	What It Returns	Similar to CFML Expression
`LTRIM(string)`	*string* without leading spaces	`LTrim(string)`
`RIGHT(string, count)`	Last *count* characters of string	`Right(string, count)`
`RTRIM(string)`	*string* without trailing spaces	`RTrim(string)`
`SUBSTRING(string, start, count)`	*count* characters of *string* after *start*	`Mid(string, start, count)`
`UCASE(string)`	*string* converted to uppercase	`UCase(string)`
`CURDATE()`	The current date	`DateFormat(Now())`
`CURTIME()`	The current time	`TimeFormat(Now())`
`DAYOFMONTH(date)`	The day (between 1 and 31)	`Day(date)`
`DAYOFWEEK(date)`	The day (between 1 and 7)	`DayOfWeek(date)`
`MONTH(date)`	The month (between 1 and 12)	`Month(date)`
`YEAR(date)`	The year	`Year(date)`
`MOD(integer1, integer2)`	Remainder of *integer1* divided by *integer2*	`integer1 MOD integer2`

**The following are the keywords for use as the data type for the* CONVERT *function listed earlier:* SQL_BIGINT, SQL_INTERVAL_HOUR_TO_MINUTE, SQL_BINARY, SQL_INTERVAL_HOUR_TO_SECOND, SQL_BIT, SQL_INTERVAL_MINUTE_TO_SECOND, SQL_CHAR, SQL_LONGVARBINARY, SQL_DECIMAL, SQL_LONGVARCHAR, SQL_DOUBLE, SQL_NUMERIC, SQL_FLOAT, SQL_REAL, SQL_INTEGER, SQL_SMALLINT, SQL_INTERVAL_MONTH, SQL_TYPE_DATE, SQL_INTERVAL_YEAR, SQL_TYPE_TIME, SQL_INTERVAL_YEAR_TO_MONTH, SQL_TYPE_TIMESTAMP, SQL_INTERVAL_DAY, SQL_TINYINT, SQL_INTERVAL_HOUR, SQL_VARBINARY, SQL_INTERVAL_MINUTE, SQL_VARCHAR, SQL_INTERVAL_SECOND, SQL_WCHAR, SQL_INTERVAL_DAY_TO_HOUR, SQL_WLONGVARCHAR, SQL_INTERVAL_DAY_TO_MINUTE, SQL_WVARCHAR, *and* SQL_INTERVAL_DAY_TO_SECOND. *Do not use quotation marks around these keywords. You will probably need to experiment a little to figure out which of these corresponds to the desired data type your database system supports natively.*

ADDITIONAL <CFQUERY> TOPICS

The remainder of this chapter discusses several advanced features provided by the <CFQUERY> tag. Each of these features provides you with finer-grained control over how ColdFusion interacts with your database or database server.

Queries of Queries

One of the most interesting and unique new features in ColdFusion 5.0 is its new query of queries capability. As the name implies, this feature enables you to retrieve information from queries that have already been run, using standard SQL syntax. The feature is simple but has many uses. This section introduces you to the query of queries feature and suggests several ways to put it to use in your ColdFusion applications.

> **Note**
>
> For brevity, this chapter uses the abbreviation *QofQ* to refer to the query of queries feature.

The Basics

Considering all the problems it can solve, the actual process of using the query of queries feature is surprisingly straightforward. Perhaps the nicest thing about it is that it enables you to get new benefits from the SQL skills you already have.

To use the QofQ feature, follow these steps:

1. Run one or more ordinary queries using the `<CFQUERY>` tag in the way that you are already familiar with. These are the queries you will be able to query further in a moment. You can think of these as *source queries*.
2. Create a new `<CFQUERY>` tag, this time with `DBTYPE="query"`. This tells ColdFusion you don't intend to contact a traditional database (via ODBC, OLE-DB, or a native database driver). Instead, you will query the results returned by the queries from step 1.
3. Within this new `<CFQUERY>` tag, write SQL code that retrieves the records you want, using the names of the source queries as if they were table names. You can't do everything you would be able to within a traditional database query, but the most important SQL concepts and keywords are supported.
4. Now you can use the results of the query normally, just as you would any other query. You can output its records in a `<CFOUTPUT>` block, loop through them using `<CFLOOP>`, and so on. You can even query the records again, using yet another query of queries.

Using QofQ for Heterogeneous Data Analysis

Say Orange Whip Studios has some type of legacy database in place, which predates your ColdFusion application. Perhaps the studio is experimenting with direct phone sales, trying to get people to buy collector's editions of coins (complete with certificates of authenticity) that commemorate the studio's classic films.

This database has just one table, called `Calls`, which contains the `ContactID` of each person called and columns named `CallID`, `CallDate`, `Status`, and `Comments`. Using the ColdFusion Administrator, you set up a new ODBC data source called `DirectSales` and then write a query that retrieves all the records from the `Calls` table, like so:

```
<CFQUERY DATASOURCE="DirectSales" NAME="GetCalls">
  SELECT ContactID, CallID, CallDate, Status, Comments
  FROM Calls
</CFQUERY>
```

Next, you run a second query against the `Contacts` table, using the usual ows data source:

```
<CFQUERY DATASOURCE="ows" NAME="GetContacts">
  SELECT ContactID, FirstName, LastName
  FROM Contacts
</CFQUERY>
```

Now you can use the QofQ feature to join the results of the `GetCalls` and `GetContacts` queries, like so:

```
<CFQUERY DBTYPE="query" NAME="GetJoined">
  SELECT *
  FROM GetCalls, GetContacts
  WHERE GetCalls.ContactID = GetContacts.ContactID
</CFQUERY>
```


That's it. Now you can use the `GetJoined` query just like the results of any other `<CFQUERY>` tag. Its results will contain one row for each row of the `GetCalls` and `GetContacts` queries that contain the same `ContactID`. All columns from the original query will be included.

Note

What makes this really interesting is the fact that the records from the two source queries do not have to have come from the same database or even the same type of database system. In fact, as you will see shortly, the source queries don't even have to come from databases at all. Any ColdFusion tag or function that returns a query object, such as the `<CFDIRECTORY>`, `<CFPOP>`, or `<CFSEARCH>` tags, can be requeried using the query of queries feature.

USING QOFQ TO REDUCE DATABASE INTERACTION

In Chapter 24, "Improving Performance," you learned about ColdFusion's query caching mechanism, which enables you to transparently share query results between page requests, thereby cutting down on the interaction with the database system. You can use the QofQ feature in combination with query caching to reduce the actual communication with the database system even further.

You can use QofQ and query caching together in many ways; most are variations on the following basic idea. First, you write a source query using a normal `<CFQUERY>` tag that queries your database in the usual way and that uses the `CACHEDWITHIN` attribute to cache the query's results. For instance, you might retrieve all records from the `Films` table and cache them for 30 minutes at a time, like so:

```
<CFQUERY DATASOURCE="ows" NAME="GetFilms"
  CACHEDWITHIN="#CreateTimeSpan(0,0,30,0)#">
  SELECT * FROM Films
  ORDER BY MovieTitle
</CFQUERY>
```

Now, you can get information about individual film records by querying the `GetFilms` query, instead of running a separate query. For instance, if you wanted to retrieve a film record based on a URL parameter called `FilmID`, you could use code such as the following, which uses the query of queries feature to fetch a single row from the `GetFilms` query:

```
<CFQUERY DBTYPE="query" NAME="GetThisFilm">
  SELECT * FROM GetFilms
  WHERE FilmID = #URL.FilmID#
</CFQUERY>
```

The `GetThisFilm` query can now be used to output the film record. The net effect is that you have access to all the data you need, even though the database is hit only once every 30 minutes (at most). If you accept the notion that cutting down on database communication typically has a positive impact on overall system performance, then using QofQ in this way makes a lot of sense.

But why is this necessarily better than simply letting ColdFusion run separate cached queries for each individual record? That is, why not just use this version of `GetThisFilm` (rather than the combination of the `GetFilms` and `GetThisFilm` shown previously):

```
<CFQUERY DATASOURCE="ows" NAME="GetThisFilm "
  CACHEDWITHIN="#CreateTimeSpan(0,0,30,0)#">
  SELECT * FROM Films
  WHERE FilmID = #URL.FilmID#
</CFQUERY>
```

The answer is that neither approach is necessarily better than the other; it depends on the situation. For the moment, let's suppose that 100 films exist in the `Films` table and that the individual film records are all being accessed about five times in any 30-minute period. The first approach retrieves all 100 records at the beginning of the 30 minutes and serves the individual queries from the cached source query; however, all 100 records must be remembered in ColdFusion's RAM. The second approach contacts the database more often (up to 100 times during a 30-minute period, one for each film), but each query is very small and takes up only a small amount of memory in ColdFusion's RAM.

So, all other things being equal, the first approach probably makes the most sense when a significant number of the individual records will actually be accessed during the 30-minute period. If it turns out that only 3 out of the 100 records get accessed during the 30 minutes, the memory that was being used by the other 97 was essentially wasted; therefore, the second approach is probably a bit more efficient. On the other hand, if almost all of the individual records were actually accessed during the 30 minutes, the first approach is likely to be more efficient.

Note

Also, depending on the situation, the cached `GetFilms` query might be capable of being used by a large number of other QofQ queries in the application. Some pages might retrieve individual records from it using `WHERE`, as shown previously. Other pages might need to obtain counts or summaries from the data using aggregate functions and `GROUP BY` statements in QofQ queries. Still other pages might simply need to display the records as is, using the cached query results directly. Using the query of queries feature, you could have all these pages using the same cached version of the `GetFilms` query, so there is still only one access to the database every 30 minutes, even though the query is being massaged and reinterpreted by the various pages in various ways.

But ColdFusion Is Not a Database Server

It is also critical to understand that ColdFusion's query of query feature, while certainly very useful, is unlikely to be better at searching through large sets of records than a dedicated database system. Whereas database systems can rely on indexes, active query optimizers, and other tools to find the correct record in a large database table, ColdFusion's query of query feature just iterates through the rows, looking for the correct values. This is what database server products call an *iterative table scan*, which is unlikely to scale well in extreme conditions.

So, if the number of records in the cached `GetFilms` query becomes very large over time (say, 100 million records instead of 100), the performance of the first approach will start to degrade because ColdFusion will have to look through all those records each time it needs to find an individual record. In contrast, a decent database system should be capable of returning the correct record very quickly, regardless of the size of the table (especially if a well-tuned index exists on the `FilmID` column), making the second approach more efficient.

To put it another way, the introduction of the query of queries feature in ColdFusion 5.0 does not mean that ColdFusion should now be considered a database server, competing directly with high-performance database products such as Oracle 8i and Microsoft SQLServer. The fact that query records are maintained in ColdFusion's RAM *does not* automatically mean ColdFusion will be capable of requerying the records more efficiently than your database server would. Today's database servers are very sophisticated animals indeed and are difficult for ColdFusion to outsmart.

As a general rule of thumb, a practice of caching queries of 1,000 records or less (and then requerying those records using QofQ) is likely to serve you very well. When the record count starts to climb toward five digits, the benefit of having the records already in RAM will eventually be overcome by the sheer weight of the large recordset and will probably be further hampered by ColdFusion's iterative approach to requerying the data.

A Real-World Example

In Chapter 23, "Improving the User Experience," several versions of a Next N interface were created, allowing the user to click through records in pages of 10 rows at a time. Then, in Chapter 24, the Next N interface was revised to use ColdFusion's query-caching feature via the `CACHEDWITHIN` attribute to improve perfomance.

The code in Listing 31.12 revises the Next N interface again, this time using ColdFusion's query of queries feature to allow the user to re-sort the records by clicking the column names. When the user first visits the page, the records are sorted by date (most recent expense first), just as in the previous versions of the template. Then, if the user clicks the `Film` column, the page reloads with the records sorted alphabetically by film title. If the user clicks the `Film` column again, the sort order is reversed. A small triangle image indicates which column the records are sorted by, and in what order.

Note

This listing uses `<CFINCLUDE>` tags to include the `NextNIncludePageLinks.cfm` and `NextNIncludeBackNext.cfm` templates from Chapter 23. Either save this template in the same directory as Chapter 23's listings or copy the included templates into the folder you are using for this chapter.

Listing 31.12 `NextN6.cfm`—**Allowing Users to Re-sort Cached Query Results**

```
<!--- Remember sort order for user, using SESSION scope --->
<CFPARAM NAME="SESSION.NextNSortCol" TYPE="string" DEFAULT="d">
<CFPARAM NAME="SESSION.NextNSortAsc" TYPE="boolean" DEFAULT="No">

<!--- If user is asking to change sort order --->
<CFIF IsDefined("URL.SortCol") AND IsDefined("URL.SortDir")>
  <!--- Save new order column/order in SESSION scope --->
  <CFSET SESSION.NextNSortCol = URL.SortCol>
  <CFSET SESSION.NextNSortAsc = URL.SortDir>
  <!--- Send user back to first row of query results --->
  <CFSET URL.StartRow = 1>
</CFIF>

<!--- Retrieve Expense Records from Database --->
<!--- Will be sorted by default order (expense date) --->
<CFQUERY NAME="GetExp" DATASOURCE="#REQUEST.DataSource#"
  CACHEDWITHIN="#CreateTimeSpan(0,0,30,0)#">
  SELECT
    f.FilmID, f.MovieTitle,
    e.Description, e.ExpenseAmount, e.ExpenseDate
  FROM
    Expenses e INNER JOIN Films f
    ON e.FilmID = f.FilmID
  ORDER BY
    ExpenseDate DESC
</CFQUERY>

<!--- If user's current sort order differs from the --->
<!--- default, use Q-of-Q to re-sort original query --->
<CFIF NOT (SESSION.NextNSortCol EQ "d" AND SESSION.NextNSortAsc EQ "No")>
  <!--- Re-query "GetExp" with appropriate ORDER BY --->
  <CFQUERY NAME="GetExp" DBTYPE="query">
    SELECT * FROM GetExp
    ORDER BY
    <!--- Use appropriate sort column --->
    <CFSWITCH EXPRESSION="#SESSION.NextNSortCol#">
      <CFCASE VALUE="f">MovieTitle</CFCASE>
      <CFCASE VALUE="e">Description</CFCASE>
      <CFCASE VALUE="a">ExpenseAmount</CFCASE>
      <CFDEFAULTCASE>   ExpenseDate</CFDEFAULTCASE>
    </CFSWITCH>
```

```
    <!--- Appropriate sort direction --->
    <CFIF SESSION.NextNSortAsc>ASC<CFELSE>DESC</CFIF>
  </CFQUERY>
</CFIF>



<!--- Number of Rows to display per Next/Back page  --->
<CFSET RowsPerPage = 10>
<!--- What row to start at? Assume first by default --->
<CFPARAM NAME="URL.StartRow" DEFAULT="1" TYPE="numeric">
<!--- Allow for "Show All" parameter in the URL --->
<CFPARAM NAME="URL.ShowAll" TYPE="boolean" DEFAULT="No">

<!--- We know the total number of rows from query   --->
<CFSET TotalRows    = GetExp.RecordCount>
<!--- Show all on page if "ShowAll" passed in URL   --->
<CFIF URL.ShowAll>
  <CFSET RowsPerPage = TotalRows>
</CFIF>
<!--- Last row is 10 rows past the starting row, or --->
<!--- total number of query rows, whichever is less --->
<CFSET EndRow       = Min(URL.StartRow + RowsPerPage - 1, TotalRows)>
<!--- "Next" button goes to 1 past current end row  --->
<CFSET StartRowNext = EndRow + 1>
<!--- "Back" button goes back N rows from start row --->
<CFSET StartRowBack = URL.StartRow - RowsPerPage>


<!--- Page Title --->
<HTML>
<HEAD><TITLE>Expense Browser</TITLE></HEAD>
<BODY>
<CFOUTPUT><H2>#REQUEST.CompanyName# Expense Report</H2></CFOUTPUT>

<!--- Simple Style Sheet for formatting --->
<STYLE>
  TH        {font-family:sans-serif;font-size:smaller;
             background:navy;color:white}
  TD        {font-family:sans-serif;font-size:smaller}
  TD.DataA  {background:silver;color:black}
  TD.DataB  {background:lightgrey;color:black}
  A.Head    {color:white}
  A.Head:visited {color:white}
</STYLE>

<TABLE WIDTH="600" BORDER="0" CELLSPACING="0" CELLPADDING="1">
  <!--- Row at top of table, above column headers --->
  <TR>
    <TD WIDTH="500" COLSPAN="3">
      <!--- Message about which rows are being displayed --->
      <CFOUTPUT>
        Displaying <B>#URL.StartRow#</B> to <B>#EndRow#</B>
        of <B>#TotalRows#</B> Records<BR>
      </CFOUTPUT>
    </TD>
    <TD WIDTH="100" ALIGN="right">
      <CFIF NOT URL.ShowAll>
```

LISTING 31.12 CONTINUED

```
      <!--- Provide Next/Back links --->
      <CFINCLUDE TEMPLATE="../23/NextNIncludeBackNext.cfm">
    </CFIF>
  </TD>
</TR>

<!--- Row for Column Headers --->
<TR>
  <CFOUTPUT>
    <!--- For each of the four columns... --->
    <CFLOOP LIST="Date,Film,Expense,Amount" INDEX="Col">
      <!--- Use 1st letter of column as "Alias" to pass in URL --->
      <CFSET Letter    = LCase(Left(Col, 1))>
      <!--- If user already viewing by this col, link should   --->
      <!--- reverse order; otherwise, order should be ASC for  --->
      <!--- all columns except Date, when order should be DESC --->
      <CFIF SESSION.NextNSortCol EQ Alias>
        <CFSET SortDir = NOT SESSION.NextNSortAsc>
      <CFELSE>
        <CFSET SortDir = Col NEQ "Date">
      </CFIF>
      <!--- URL for when user clicks on column name --->
      <CFSET SortLink = "#CGI.SCRIPT_NAME#?SortCol=#Alias#&SortDir=#SortDir#">
      <TH>
        <!--- Show column heading as link that changes order --->
        <A HREF="#SortLink#" CLASS="Head">#Col#</A>
        <!--- If this is current column, show icon to indicate sort order --->
        <CFIF SESSION.NextNSortCol EQ Alias>
          <CFSET SortImgSrc = IIF(SESSION.NextNSortAsc, "'SortA.gif'",
➥"'SortD.gif'")>
          <IMG SRC="../images/#SortImgSrc#" WIDTH="12" HEIGHT="12" ALT="">
        </CFIF>
      </TH>
    </CFLOOP>
  </CFOUTPUT>
</TR>

<!--- For each query row that should be shown now --->
<CFLOOP QUERY="GetExp" StartRow="#URL.StartRow#" ENDROW="#EndRow#">
  <!--- Use class "DataA" or "DataB" for alternate rows --->
  <CFSET Class = IIF(GetExp.CurrentRow MOD 2 EQ 0, "'DataA'", "'DataB'")>

  <CFOUTPUT>
    <TR VALIGN="baseline">
      <TD CLASS="#Class#" WIDTH="100">#LSDateFormat(ExpenseDate)#</TD>
      <TD CLASS="#Class#" WIDTH="250">#MovieTitle#</TD>
      <TD CLASS="#Class#" WIDTH="150"><I>#Description#</I></TD>
      <TD CLASS="#Class#" WIDTH="100">#LSCurrencyFormat(ExpenseAmount)#</TD>
    </TR>
  </CFOUTPUT>
</CFLOOP>

<!--- Row at bottom of table, after rows of data --->
<TR>
  <TD WIDTH="500" COLSPAN="3">
```

```
      <CFIF NOT URL.ShowAll>
        <!--- Shortcut links for "Pages" of search results --->
        Page <CFINCLUDE TEMPLATE="../23/NextNIncludePageLinks.cfm">
        <!--- "Show All" Link --->
        <CFOUTPUT>
          <A HREF="#CGI.SCRIPT_NAME#?ShowAll=Yes">Show All</A>
        </CFOUTPUT>
      </CFIF>
    </TD>
    <TD WIDTH="100" ALIGN="right">
      <CFIF NOT URL.ShowAll>
        <!--- Provide Next/Back links --->
        <CFINCLUDE TEMPLATE="../23/NextNIncludeBackNext.cfm">
      </CFIF>
    </TD>
  </TR>
</TABLE>

</BODY>
</HTML>
```


Most of the code in this template is identical to the versions presented in Chapters 23 and 24. The most important additions are discussed here.

First, two `<CFPARAM>` tags have been added, which define `SESSION.NextNSortCol` and `SESSION.NextNSortAsc` variables to track the user's current sort column and sort direction. The `NextNSortCol` value will be `d`, `f`, `e`, or `a` to signify the `ExpenseDate`, `MovieTitle`, expense `Description`, and `ExpenseAmount` columns, respectively. The Boolean `NextNSortAsc` value will be `True` if the sort column is being sorted in ascending order, and will be `False` if it is being sorted in descending order.

A `<CFIF>` block at the top of the template changes the sort order and sort direction for the user's session if URL parameters called `SortCol` and `SortDir` are provided. If provided, the values provided in the URL are copied to the two `SESSION` variables mentioned previously, which causes the template to show the records in the new sort order for the rest of the session. In addition, the `StartRow` variable is set to `1`, so the user is always shown the first page of records whenever the sort is changed.

After the cached `GetExp` query, a second `<CFQUERY>` tag that uses the query of queries feature is used to re-sort the cached query results, depending on the current values of the two `SESSION` variables. For instance, if `SESSION.NextNSortCol` is `f` and `SESSION.NextNSortAsc` is `True`, the resulting `ORDER BY` statement would be `MovieTitle ASC`, thereby providing the user with the desired sorting effect. Simple `<CFIF>` logic skips this requerying step if the user is viewing the template with the default sort options.

The rest of the code is largely unchanged from prior versions. The only other major change is in the middle of the template, where the column headings are displayed.

A `<CFLOOP>` is used to output the four columns. For each column, the `Alias` variable is set to the first letter of the column name; this is passed in the URL when the user clicks a column heading. Then, a `SortDir` variable is set to `True` or `False`, depending on whether the results are already being sorted by that column. The `SortDir` determines which in direction the records should be sorted if the user clicks the column heading. For instance, for the `Date` column, if the user is already viewing the records by date, the `SortDir` is the opposite of the current `SESSION.NextNSortAsc` value. If the user is currently viewing records by some other column, the `SortDir` is `NO`, meaning the sort direction is changed to a descending sort if the user clicks the `Date` column.

The column name is then displayed as a link, passing the appropriate values as URL parameters called `SortCol` and `SortDir`. Plus, if the column heading being output corresponds with the current sort order, a small triangle icon is displayed (`SortA.gif` or `SortD.gif`), depending on whether the column is currently sorted in ascending or descending order, respectively. The results are shown in Figure 31.11.

Note

In this example, the query of queries feature is used to reorder the original, cached resultset. The same basic technique could be used for other types of requerying needs. For instance, the second QofQ query might retrieve a subset of the original records, using some type of `WHERE` filter criteria.

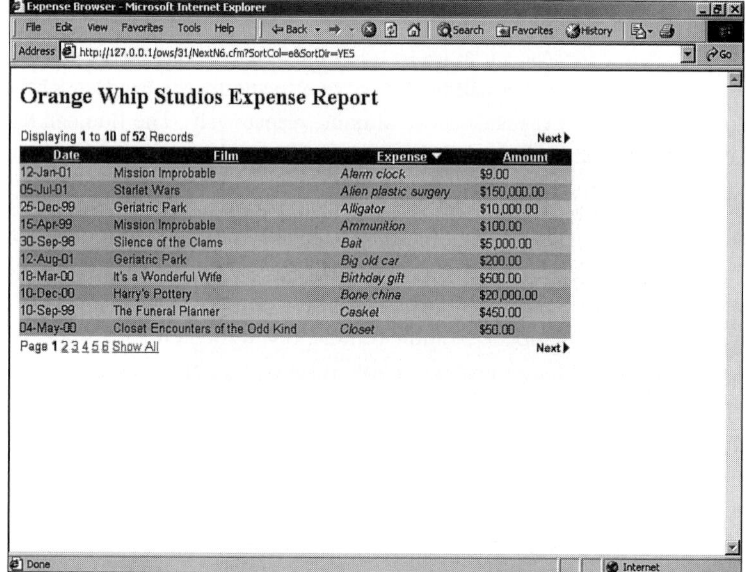

Figure 31.11
When users click a column header, the results are re-sorted using a QofQ query.

USING QOFQ WITH NONDATABASE QUERIES

The query of queries feature can be used on any ColdFusion query object. Most commonly, this is the result of a `<CFQUERY>` tag that retrieves records from a database. However, a number of other CFML tags return information as ColdFusion query objects, which means they can be requeried using QofQ.

Table 31.3 provides a short list of tags that return query objects. More information about each of these tags is available in Appendix A, "ColdFusion Tag Reference."

TABLE 31.3 CFML TAGS THAT RETURN QUERY OBJECTS, WHICH CAN BE REQUERIED USING QOFQ

CFML Tag	Returns Query Object That Contains
`<CFDIRECTORY>`	A listing of files in a particular directory (when used with `ACTION="List"`). See Chapter 35, "Interacting with the Operating System."
`<CFFTP>`	A listing of files on a remote FTP server (when used with `ACTION="ListDir"`).
`<CFLDAP>`	Directory listings retrieved from a remote LDAP server (when used with `ACTION="Query"`).
`<CFPOP>`	Incoming mail messages, as retrieved from a remote e-mail mailbox (when used with `ACTION="GetHeaderOnly"` or `ACTION="GetAll"`). See Chapter 28, "Interacting with E-mail."
`<CFREGISTRY>`	Information from the Windows Registry (when used with `ACTION="GetAll"`). See Chapter 35.
`<CFSEARCH>`	Search results found by a Verity full-text search operation. See Chapter 36, "Full-Text Searching with Verity."
`<CFPROCRESULT>`	A result set returned by a stored procedure in a database. See Chapter 32, "Working with Stored Procedures."
Custom Tags	CFML custom tags can use the `QueryNew()` function to create and return query objects, filled with rows and columns of whatever data is appropriate. The `<CF_ShoppingCart>` custom tag from Chapter 29 is an example of such a tag. For more about CFML custom tags, see Chapter 22, "Building Reusable Components."
CFX Tags	Many CFX tags return query objects, filled with whatever specialized data is appropriate. The `<CFX_CyberCash>` tag used in Chapter 29 is one example. For information about writing your own CFX tags (using Java or C++), see our companion volume, *Advanced ColdFusion 5 Application Development* (Que, ISBN: 0-7897-2585-1).

For instance, Listing 31.13 shows how ColdFusion's query of queries feature can be used to combine resultsets from two different query objects. Here, QofQ is used to get around a limitation of the `<CFDIRECTORY>` tag. It is a good example of how QofQ can add flexibility and power to CFML tags that return query objects (refer to Table 31.3).

The purpose of this listing is to display all the GIF and JPEG images in a particular directory. As explained in Chapter 35, the `<CFDIRECTORY>` tag can be used to easily obtain a list of files, and it even provides a `FILTER` attribute that enables you to filter the files based on DOS-style wildcards. For instance, a `FILTER` of `*.jpg` returns all JPEG files in a directory, and a `FILTER` of `*.gif` lists all the GIF files. Unfortunately, `<CFDIRECTORY>` doesn't allow you to provide a single filter that returns all GIF and JPEG files together as a single, sorted query object.

Listing 31.13 overcomes this limitation by using separate `<CFDIRECTORY>` tags to retrieve the GIF and JPEG directory listings. Then, the query of queries feature is used to combine the two resultsets as a single query object, sorted by filename.

LISTING 31.13 `MultiDirectory1.cfm`—COMBINING THE RESULTS OF TWO `<CFDIRECTORY>` TAGS WITH `UNION`

```
<!--- Directory to scan for images --->
<CFSET Dir = ExpandPath("../images")>

<!--- First, get query object of JPEG files --->
<CFDIRECTORY
  ACTION="LIST"
  DIRECTORY="#Dir#"
  FILTER="*.jpg"
  NAME="GetJPG">

<!--- Next, get query object of GIF files --->
<CFDIRECTORY
  ACTION="LIST"
  DIRECTORY="#Dir#"
  FILTER="*.gif"
  NAME="GetGIF">

<!--- Use CF's Query-of-Queries feature to --->
<!--- combine the queries with a SQL UNION --->
<!--- Sort the resulting query by filename --->
<CFQUERY DBTYPE="query" NAME="GetAll">
  SELECT * FROM GetJPG
  UNION
  SELECT * FROM GetGIF
  ORDER BY Name
</CFQUERY>


<HTML>
<HEAD><TITLE>Images Folder</TITLE></HEAD>
<BODY>
<H2>Images Folder</H2>

<!--- Display all files together as a list --->
<CFOUTPUT>
  <P>There are #GetAll.RecordCount# images in #Dir#:<BR>
  <OL>
    <CFLOOP QUERY="GetAll">
      <LI><A HREF="../images/#Name#">#GetAll.Name#</A><BR>
    </CFLOOP>
  </OL>
</CFOUTPUT>

</BODY>
</HTML>
```

First, the `ExpandPath()` function is used to get the absolute filesystem path of Orange Whip Studio's `images` folder. It is assumed that the `images` folder and the current folder are both contained within the same parent folder.

Next, two `<CFDIRECTORY>` tags are used to retrieve listings of all JPEG and GIF files in the `images` folder. The query objects returned by the two tags are named `GetJPG` and `GetGIF`, respectively.

Now the two query objects can be combined in the QofQ query named `GetAll`. The SQL syntax used here is extremely simple. All that's needed is a standard `UNION` statement that retrieves all records from both source queries and sorts the combined resultset by filename (see the section "Combining Recordsets with `UNION`," earlier in this chapter). The result is a single ColdFusion query object that can be used just like any other. It contains a row for each GIF and JPEG file. The filenames can be displayed using a standard `<CFLOOP>` block that loops over the `GetAll` query, as shown in Figure 31.12.

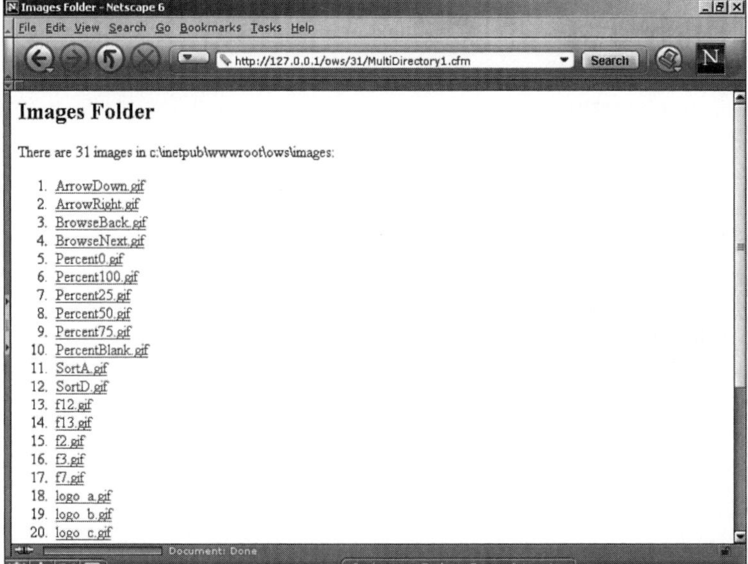

Figure 31.12
The query of query feature makes obtaining flexible directory listings easier.

You can wrap such QofQ operations in CFML custom tags. Listing 31.14 takes the code from Listing 31.13 and turns it into a custom tag called `<CF_GetDirectoryContents>`. The custom tag takes `Directory`, `Filter`, `Sort`, and `Name` attributes, which correspond to the same attributes of ColdFusion's native `<CFDIRECTORY>` tag. The advantage of this custom tag is that its `Filter` attribute accepts multiple wildcard filters. The individual filters are separated with semicolons, like so:

```
<CF_GetDirectoryContents
  Directory="c:\inetpub\wwwroot\ows\images\"
  Filter="*.gif;*.jpg"
  Name="GetAll">
```

Note

Because this is a custom tag template, it should be saved in the special `CustomTags` folder. As an alternative, you can just save a copy of it in the folder where you intend to use it (the same folder you are using for the other code listings in this chapter).

LISTING 31.14 `GetDirectoryContents.cfm`—**CREATING THE** `<CF_GetDirectoryContents>` **CUSTOM TAG**

```
<!--- Tag Parameters ---> tag>
<CFPARAM NAME="ATTRIBUTES.Directory">
<CFPARAM NAME="ATTRIBUTES.Filter" TYPE="string" DEFAULT="*.*">
<CFPARAM NAME="ATTRIBUTES.Sort" TYPE="string" DEFAULT="Name">
<CFPARAM NAME="ATTRIBUTES.Name" TYPE="variableName">

<!--- For each filter (filters separated by semicolons) --->
<CFLOOP LIST="#ATTRIBUTES.Filter#" INDEX="ThisFilter" DELIMITERS=";">

  <!--- Get query object of matching files --->
  <CFDIRECTORY
    ACTION="LIST"
    DIRECTORY="#ATTRIBUTES.Directory#"
    FILTER="#ThisFilter#"
    NAME="GetFiles">

  <!--- If this is first time through loop, --->
  <!--- Save GetFiles as our "ResultQuery". --->
  <CFIF NOT IsDefined("ResultQuery")>
    <CFSET ResultQuery = GetFiles>
  <!--- If ResultQuery already exists, add --->
  <!--- GetFiles's records to it via UNION --->
  <CFELSE>
    <CFQUERY DBTYPE="query" NAME="ResultQuery">
      SELECT * FROM ResultQuery
      UNION
      SELECT * FROM GetFiles
      ORDER BY #ATTRIBUTES.Sort#
    </CFQUERY>
  </CFIF>

</CFLOOP>

<!--- Return completed resultset to calling template ---> tag>
<CFSET "Caller.#ATTRIBUTES.Name#" = ResultQuery>
```

First, four `<CFPARAM>` tags are used to establish the tag's parameters. Then, a `<CFLOOP>` tag is used to loop through the semicolon-delimited list provided to the tag's `Filter` attribute. If the `Filter` is provided as `*.gif;*.jpg`, the loop runs twice. The first time through the loop, `ThisFilter` is `*.gif`, and so on.

Within the loop, the `<CFDIRECTORY>` tag called `GetFiles` is used to retrieve the files in the directory that correspond to the current `ThisFilter` value. Then, if this is the first time through the loop, the `GetFiles` object is set to a new variable named `ResultQuery`, which is what gets passed back to the calling template when the tag is finished with its work. The next time through the loop, the results of the GetFiles query are added to the ResultsQuery, using the UNION technique from Listing 31.13.

When the loop is finished, the ResultsQuery variable contains the complete file listing. It is returned to the calling template using quoted <CFSET> syntax. See Chapter 22 for details.

Listing 31.15 shows how this custom tag can be used in a normal ColdFusion template. It is the same as Listing 31.13, except that the <CFDIRECTORY> and <CFQUERY> tags have been replaced with the <CF_GetDirectoryContents> custom tag. Refer to Figure 31.12 to see what the results will look like.

Listing 31.15 MultiDirectory2.cfm—Executing a QofQ Operation Via the <CF_GetDirectoryContents> Custom Tag

```
<!--- Directory to scan for images --->
<CFSET Dir = ExpandPath("../images")>

<!--- Get GIF and JPG file listing, via custom tag --->
<CF_GetDirectoryContents
  Directory="#Dir#"
  Filter="*.gif;*.jpg"
  Name="GetAll">

<HTML>
<HEAD><TITLE>Images Folder</TITLE></HEAD>
<BODY>
<H2>Images Folder</H2>

<!--- Display all files together as a list --->
<CFOUTPUT>
  <P>There are #GetAll.RecordCount# images in #Dir#:<BR>
  <OL>
    <CFLOOP QUERY="GetAll">
      <LI><A HREF="../images/#Name#">#GetAll.Name#</A>
    </CFLOOP>
  </OL>
</CFOUTPUT>

</BODY>
</HTML>
```

Part IV Ch 31

Joining Database and Nondatabase Queries

You have seen how ColdFusion's QofQ feature can be used to join or combine query objects returned by database queries or nondatabase tags, such as <CFDIRECTORY>. You also can use QofQ to merge the results of database queries with nondatabase query objects, using UNION or join syntax.

Listing 31.16 is another revision of the StoreCart.cfm templates created in Chapter 29. Similar to the version in Listing 31.10, this template displays suggestions to the user using a pseudocollaborative filtering technique. In addition, this version displays a subtotal for each item in the user's cart, along with a grand total of all the items. Versions provided up to this point did not display totals.

Note

Because this listing relies on other templates from Chapter 29, you should save this template in the same folder as Chapter 29's listings.

LISTING 31.16 `StoreCart4.cfm`**—USING SEVERAL QOFQ QUERIES TOGETHER, WITH DATABASE AND NONDATABASE SOURCE QUERIES**

```
<!--- Show header images, etc., for Online Store --->
<CFINCLUDE TEMPLATE="StoreHeader.cfm">

<!--- If MerchID was passed in URL --->
<CFIF IsDefined("URL.AddMerchID")>
  <!--- Add item to user's cart data, via custom tag --->
  <CF_ShoppingCart
    Action="Add"
    MerchID="#URL.AddMerchID#">

<!--- If user is submitting cart form --->
<CFELSEIF IsDefined("FORM.MerchID")>
  <!--- For each MerchID on Form, Update Quantity --->
  <CFLOOP LIST="#Form.MerchID#" INDEX="ThisMerchID">
    <!--- Update Quantity, via Custom Tag --->
    <CF_ShoppingCart
      Action="Update"
      MerchID="#ThisMerchID#"
      Quantity="#FORM['Quant_#ThisMerchID#']#">
  </CFLOOP>

  <!--- If user submitted form via "Checkout" button, --->
  <!--- send on to Checkout page after updating cart. --->
  <CFIF IsDefined("FORM.IsCheckingOut")>
    <CFLOCATION URL="StoreCheckout.cfm">
  </CFIF>
</CFIF>

<!--- Get current cart contents, via Custom Tag --->
<CF_ShoppingCart
  Action="List"
  ReturnVariable="GetCart">


<!--- Stop here if user's cart is empty --->
<CFIF GetCart.RecordCount EQ 0>
  There is nothing in your cart.
  <CFABORT>
</CFIF>


<!--- Retrieve items in user's cart from database --->
<CFQUERY NAME="GetMerch" DATASOURCE="ows">
  SELECT MerchID, MerchPrice
  FROM Merchandise
  WHERE MerchID IN (#ValueList(GetCart.MerchID)#)
</CFQUERY>
```

```
<!--- Use QofQ to join queried records against cart data --->
<!--- The SubTotal column is Quantity times MerchPrice --->
<CFQUERY NAME="GetPrices" DBTYPE="query">
  SELECT
    GetMerch.MerchID AS MerchID,
    GetCart.Quantity AS Quantity,
    GetCart.Quantity * GetMerch.MerchPrice AS SubTotal
  FROM GetMerch, GetCart
  WHERE GetMerch.MerchID = GetCart.MerchID
</CFQUERY>

<!--- Use QofQ again to get a grand total of all items --->
<CFQUERY NAME="GetTotal" DBTYPE="query">
  SELECT SUM(SubTotal) AS GrandTotal
  FROM GetPrices
</CFQUERY>

<!--- Create form that submits to this template --->
<CFFORM ACTION="#CGI.SCRIPT_NAME#">
  <TABLE>
    <TR>
      <TH COLSPAN="2" BGCOLOR="Silver">Your Shopping Cart</TH>
    </TR>
    <!--- For each piece of merchandise --->
    <CFLOOP QUERY="GetPrices">
      <TR>
        <TD>
          <!--- Show this piece of merchandise --->
          <CF_MerchDisplay
            MerchID="#GetPrices.MerchID#"
            ShowAddLink="No">
        </TD>
        <TD>
          <!--- Display Quantity in Text entry field --->
          <CFOUTPUT>
            Quantity:
            <INPUT TYPE="Hidden"
              NAME="MerchID"
              VALUE="#GetPrices.MerchID#">
            <INPUT TYPE="Text" SIZE="3"
              NAME="Quant_#GetCart.MerchID#"
              VALUE="#GetPrices.Quantity#"><BR>
            Subtotal: #LSCurrencyFormat(SubTotal)#
          </CFOUTPUT>
        </TD>
      </TR>
    </CFLOOP>

    <TR>
      <TD></TD>
      <TD>
        <!--- Display Grand Total for all items in cart --->
        <CFOUTPUT>
          <B>Total: #LSCurrencyFormat(GetTotal.GrandTotal)#</B>
        </CFOUTPUT>
      </TD>
    </TR>
  </TABLE>
```

LISTING 31.16 CONTINUED

```
  <!--- Submit button to update quantities --->
  <INPUT TYPE="Submit" VALUE="Update Quantities">

  <!--- Submit button to Check out --->
  <INPUT TYPE="Submit" VALUE="Checkout" NAME="IsCheckingOut">
</CFFORM>



<!--- Convert current cart contents to comma-sep list --->
<CFSET CurrentMerchList = ValueList(GetCart.MerchID)>

<!--- Run query to suggest other items for user to buy --->
<CFQUERY NAME="GetSimilar" DATASOURCE="#REQUEST.DataSource#"
  CACHEDWITHIN="#CreateTimeSpan(0,0,5,0)#" MAXROWS="3">
  <!--- We want all items NOT in user's cart... --->
  SELECT ItemID
  FROM MerchandiseOrdersItems
  WHERE ItemID NOT IN (#CurrentMerchList#)
  <!--- ...but that *were* included in other orders --->
  <!--- along with items now in the user's cart... --->
  AND OrderID IN
    (SELECT OrderID FROM MerchandiseOrdersItems
     WHERE ItemID IN (#CurrentMerchList#)
     <!--- ...not including this user's past orders! --->
     <CFIF IsDefined("SESSION.Auth.ContactID")>
     AND OrderID NOT IN
       (SELECT OrderID FROM MerchandiseOrders
        WHERE ContactID = #SESSION.Auth.ContactID#)
     </CFIF> )
</CFQUERY>

<!--- If at least one "similar" item was found --->
<CFIF GetSimilar.RecordCount GT 0>
  <P>People who have purchased items in your cart
  have also bought the following:<BR>

   <!--- For each similar item, display it, via Custom Tag --->
   <!--- (show five suggestions at most) --->
   <CFLOOP QUERY="GetSimilar">
     <CF_MerchDisplay
       MerchID="#GetSimilar.ItemID#">
   </CFLOOP>
</CFIF>
```

Listing 31.16 is identical to Listing 31.10 in most respects. The important additions are the GetMerch, GetPrices, and GetTotal prices near the middle of the template.

First, the GetMerch query retrieves the MerchID and MerchPrice for each item in the user's cart (from the database). This works because the ValueList function returns a comma-separated list of the values in the MerchID column of the GetCart query object that was returned by the <CF_ShoppingCart> custom tag. Therefore, the IN criteria causes the database to return just the records that are actually in the user's cart at the moment.

Next, a QofQ query named `GetPrices` is used to calculate the subtotals for each item in the user's cart by joining the `MerchID` columns from the `GetMerch` query (which came from a database) and the `GetCart` query (which did not). The resulting query contains three columns for each item in the cart: `MerchID`, `Quantity`, and `SubTotal`.

Finally, a second QofQ query called `GetTotal` is used to calculate the grand total of all items in the user's cart by applying the aggregate `SUM()` function against the `SubTotal` column from the `GetPrices` query. The result is a query with one value, `GrandTotal`, which represents the total value of all cart items. This proves that you can use QofQ to retrieve information from query objects that were *themselves* created with QofQ.

Now outputting the rest of the page, including the subtotals and totals, is a simple matter. Note that the `<CFLOOP>` that displays each item now iterates over the `GetPrices` query created by the first QofQ. The results are shown in Figure 31.13.

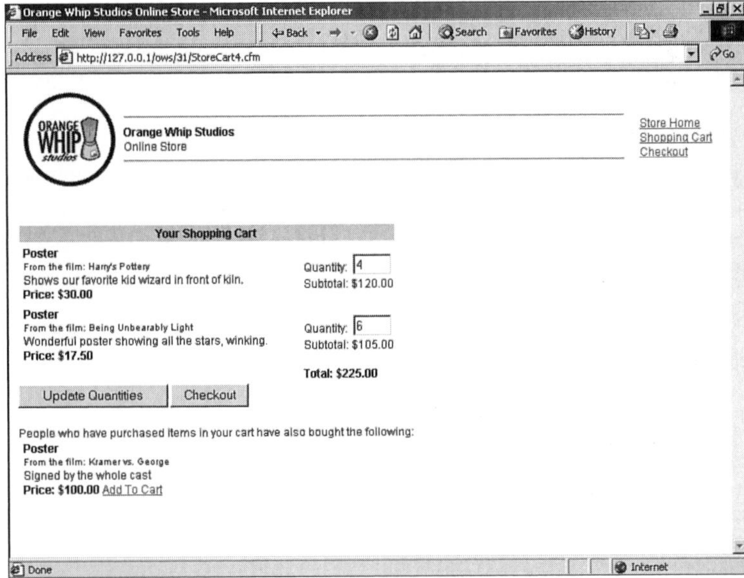

Figure 31.13 Using ColdFusion's query of queries feature to `SUM` data that lives both inside and outside a database.

PARAMETERIZED QUERIES

ColdFusion enables you to create parameterized queries by placing `<CFQUERYPARAM>` tags within the SQL code you supply to `<CFQUERY>`. The value of each `<CFQUERYPARAM>` tag is sent to the database.

Behind the scenes, as ColdFusion sends your query to the database, it substitutes a SQL bind parameter for each `<CFQUERYPARAM>` tag you supply. Unfortunately, a proper discussion of what a SQL bind parameter is would be beyond the scope of this book. In a nutshell, *bind parameters* enable a database client (here, ColdFusion) to send a SQL statement to the database with placeholders in it, followed by the actual values for each placeholder. This method is a bit more formalized than the usual method of sending completed, ad-hoc query statements to the database.

Note

Bind parameters are supported by most database systems. If the database you are using does not support them, ColdFusion simply inserts the correct value into your query for you.

Theoretically, depending on the database system, this could result in slightly faster performance because the database system might be capable of compiling a parameterized query for later reuse. If your knowledge of your database system is such that you believe a performance boost would result from the use of SQL bind parameters, `<CFQUERYPARAM>` is the way to implement the bind parameters in your ColdFusion applications. In practice, however, real-world testing suggests that you will not see an actual performance boost of any noticeable margin.

There are other reasons to use parameterized queries in your templates, however. In some cases, the tag can prevent a certain type of hack and can make your query code more database independent. This section introduces the `<CFQUERYPARAM>` tag and explains how to use it in your code and why.

INTRODUCING `<CFQUERYPARAM>`

At its simplest, you can parameterize a query by adding a `<CFQUERYPARAM>` tag to a query wherever you would normally provide a variable name. For instance, suppose you want to run a query called `GetFilm`, which retrieves a record from the `Films` table, based on a `FilmID` value passed in the URL.

Normally, you would do this:

```
<CFQUERY NAME="GetFilm" DATASOURCE="ows">
  SELECT * FROM Films
  WHERE FilmID = #URL.FilmID#
</CFQUERY>
```

Instead, you could do the following, which supplies the dynamic part of the query (the value of `URL.FilmID`) as a SQL bind parameter:

```
<CFQUERY NAME="GetFilm" DATASOURCE="ows">
  SELECT * FROM Films
  WHERE FilmID = <CFQUERYPARAM VALUE="#URL.FilmID#">
</CFQUERY>
```

In general, you should provide ColdFusion with the data type of the corresponding column in your database via the `CFSQLTYPE` attribute. This enables ColdFusion to send the data to the database system correctly (rather than relying on the database to convert the parameter on-the-fly), which reduces overhead. Because the `FilmID` column contains integers, you would specify a `CFSQLTYPE` of `CF_SQL_INTEGER`:

```
<CFQUERY NAME="GetFilm" DATASOURCE="ows">
  SELECT * FROM Films
  WHERE FilmID = <CFQUERYPARAM VALUE="#URL.FilmID#" CFSQLTYPE="CF_SQL_INTEGER">
</CFQUERY>
```

In most situations, you can use <CFQUERYPARAM> with just the VALUE and SQLTYPE attributes, as shown previously. A number of other attributes can be used to deal with special situations, as listed in Table 31.4. Table 31.5 shows the values you can supply to the CFSQLTYPE attribute and helps you understand which CFSQLTYPE to use for corresponding column data types in Access, SQLServer, and Oracle databases.

TABLE 31.4 ATTRIBUTES FOR THE <CFQUERYPARAM> TAG

Attribute	Purpose
VALUE	Required. The value you want ColdFusion to send to your database system in place of the <CFQUERYPARAM> tag.
CFSQLTYPE	Optional. One of the CFSQLTYPE values listed in Table 31.5. If you do not provide this attribute, the parameter is treated as a CFSQLCHAR.
MAXLENGTH	Optional. The maximum number of characters to allow for the VALUE. If you provide this attribute, it should reflect the maximum number of characters (width) allowed by the corresponding column in your database.
SCALE	Optional. The number of decimal places to allow. If you provide this attribute, it should reflect the numeric scale defined for the corresponding column in your database (see your database documentation about the concepts of scale and precision for numeric columns). Applicable only if the CFSQLTYPE is CF_SQL_NUMERIC or CF_SQL_DECIMAL.
LIST	Optional. If set to Yes, indicates that the value you are supplying to VALUE should be treated as a comma-separated list of values. Typically, you use this if the <CFQUERYPARAM> tag is being placed between the parentheses of SQL's IN keyword. ColdFusion takes care of quoting each element in the list for you, if appropriate for the data type of the column. If you want to use a different delimiter for the list (instead of a comma), provide the delimiter as the SEPARATOR attribute (see the following).
SEPARATOR	The delimiter character to use to separate the VALUE into separate values. Relevant only if LIST="Yes". The default is a comma.
NULL	Optional. Set this attribute to Yes to send a null value to the database, instead of the VALUE. The default, of course, is No.

TABLE 31.5 WHICH CFSQLTYPE TO USE WITH WHICH NATIVE DATA TYPE

CFSQLTYPE	Use with (Access)	Use with (SQLServer)	Use with (ORACLE)
CF_SQL_BIGINT		bigint	
CF_SQL_BIT	Yes/No	bit	
CF_SQL_CHAR		char, nchar	CHAR, NCHAR
CF_SQL_DATE			
CF_SQL_DECIMAL		numeric, decimal	
CF_SQL_DOUBLE		double, float	
CF_SQL_FLOAT		double, float	

TABLE 31.5 CONTINUED

CFSQLTYPE	Use with (Access)	Use with (SQLServer)	Use with (ORACLE)
CF_SQL_IDSTAMP		timestamp	
CF_SQL_INTEGER	AutoNumber	int	
CF_SQL_LONGVARCHAR	Memo	text	LONG, CLOB, NCLOB
CF_SQL_MONEY	Currency	money	
CF_SQL_MONEY4		smallmoney	
CF_SQL_NUMERIC	Number	numeric, decimal	NUMBER
CF_SQL_REAL		real	
CF_SQL_REFCURSOR		cursor	
CF_SQL_SMALLINT		smallint	
CF_SQL_TIME			
CF_SQL_TIMESTAMP	Date/Time	datetime, smalldatetime	DATE
CF_SQL_TINYINT		tinyint	
CF_SQL_VARCHAR	Text	varchar, nvarchar, uniqueidentifier	VARCHAR2, NVAR CHAR2, VARCHAR

USING PARAMETERIZED QUERIES FOR DATABASE INDEPENDENCE

In the section "Specifying Dates in <CFQUERY> Tags," earlier in this chapter, you learned how the <CFQUERYPARAM> tag can be used to avoid having to provide dates in the format required for the particular database system you are using. Instead of having to use the `CreateODBCDate()` function for ODBC data sources and other code for native data sources, you can just write the query using <CFQUERYPARAM>, which makes that part of the query database independent.

Note

This can be especially helpful if you are creating custom tags or complete ColdFusion applications that need to interact with different types of databases. As long as your queries use standard SQL statements, and as long as tricky data types such as dates are handled with <CFQUERYPARAM>, you can feel reasonably confident that the queries will work on just about any database ColdFusion encounters.

USING PARAMETERIZED QUERIES FOR SECURITY

Parameterized queries can also help you prevent a certain type of database hack. The hack depends on the fact that many database systems enable you to execute multiple SQL statements in the same <CFQUERY> tag. If your queries are being built dynamically, using information being passed via URL or form parameters, your database could be subject to this form of attack.

For instance, take another look at this unparameterized query:

```
<CFQUERY NAME="GetFilm" DATASOURCE="ows">
  SELECT * FROM Films
  WHERE FilmID = #URL.FilmID#
</CFQUERY>
```

Normally, you would expect that the value of `URL.FilmID` to be a number. But what if it's not? What if the user changes the URL parameter from `2`, say, to a value that includes actual SQL code? For instance, consider what would happen if some pesky user changed a template's URL from this:

```
ShowFilm.cfm?FilmID=2
```

to this:

```
ShowFilm.cfm?FilmID=2%3BDELETE%20FROM%20Films
```

You guessed it. The actual SQL sent to the database would be:

```
SELECT * FROM Films
WHERE FilmID = 2;DELETE FROM Expenses
```

Most database systems would consider the semicolon to indicate the start of a new SQL statement, and would thus dutifully carry out the `DELETE` statement, removing all records from your `Expenses` table. Try explaining this one to your colleagues in the Accounting Department!

Note

Of course, this isn't a bug or security hole in ColdFusion itself, or in your database or database driver. Both ColdFusion and your database are only doing what they are being told to do.

If you use the `<CFQUERYPARAM>` tag in your query, specifying the appropriate data type with `CFSQLTYPE`, it becomes impossible for users to violate your database in this way because the `<CFQUERYPARAM>` tag displays an error message if the URL parameter doesn't contain the expected type of information.

So, the unsafe, unparameterized query shown previously would become the following, which should defeat the type of attack described in this section:

```
<CFQUERY NAME="GetFilm" DATASOURCE="ows">
  SELECT * FROM Films
  WHERE FilmID = <CFQUERYPARAM VALUE="#URL.FilmID#" CFSQLTYPE="CF_SQL_INTEGER">
</CFQUERY>
```

Note

There are other ways to deal with this problem. For instance, you could put a `<CFPARAM>` tag at the top of the template, with `NAME="URL.FilmID"` and `TYPE="numeric"`. This would prevent users from being able to cause damage because an error message would be generated by the `<CFPARAM>` tag if the value is not a simple number, stopping all further template execution. Another option is to use `#Val(URL.FilmID)#` instead of just `#URL.FilmID#` in the original `<CFQUERY>` tag.

Or you could just use a simple <CFIF> test at the top of the template that uses the IsNumeric() function to ensure that URL.FilmID is valid; if not, you could skip the query or abort all processing with <CFABORT>.

PARAMETERIZED QUERIES AND QUERY CACHING

Unfortunately, parameterized queries cannot be used with ColdFusion's query-caching feature. If you attempt to use <CFQUERYPARAM> in a query that also uses the CACHEDWITHIN or CACHEDAFTER attribute, ColdFusion displays an error message.

Note

See Chapter 24 for more information about CACHEDWITHIN and CACHEDAFTER.

CONNECTION STRINGS

The ODBC framework includes the concept of *connection strings*, which can be used when an ODBC client (such as ColdFusion) makes a connection to a database. As of version 5 of the server, ColdFusion enables you to specify ODBC connection strings via the new CONNECTIONSTRING attribute.

Connection strings allow you to do the following:

- **Provide additional options and parameters ColdFusion should use when connecting to a database via an ODBC data source**—You can provide these options at the data-source level in the ColdFusion Administrator (see Figure 31.14, later in this chapter) or in the CONNECTSTRING attribute for each <CFQUERY> (or other database-related tag). The actual options and parameters that can be specified in the connection string vary, depending on the database system and ODBC driver you are using.
- **Connect to a database without creating an ODBC data source first in the ColdFusion Administrator**—This requires providing a CONNECTSTRING that includes all information ColdFusion will need to connect to the database, including the name of the ODBC driver to use, the name or location of the database, the username and password, and any other relevant information.
- **Use a single database connection to connect with a number of similar databases, such as a number of different databases on a particular SQLServer machine**—You would create the data source as usual in the ColdFusion Administrator and then override the database name specified in the data source in the CONNECTSTRING.

Note

The CONNECTIONSTRING attribute is applicable to the <CFQUERY>, <CFINSERT>, <CFUPDATE>, <CFSTOREDPROC>, and <CFGRIDUPDATE> tags.

CONNECTION STRING FORMAT KEYWORDS

Connections strings are specified using a simple name-value pair format, much like the format used for passing URL parameters. The name of each option or parameter in the connection string is called a *keyword*. Each keyword is followed by an = sign and then the keyword's value. Semicolons are used to separate each keyword-value pair.

For instance, two common keywords found in many connection strings are `UID` and `PWD`, which are used to specify a username and password for the database. A connection string that uses these two keywords would look similar to this:

```
UID=MyUsername;PWD=MyPassword
```

Note

Be careful about whitespace (spaces, tabs, newlines, and so on) in connection strings. No whitespace should be on either side of each = sign, and no whitespace should be before each semicolon. In addition, no whitespace should appear at the very beginning of the connection string. If you want, you can include whitespace after each semicolon or at the very end of the connection string.

The actual keywords you will use in a connection string depend on the type of database to which you are connecting and the version of the ODBC driver you are using. In general, you should consult your database or driver documentation to find a complete list of keywords supported. To help you get started, the most commonly used connection string keywords for Access, SQLServer, and Oracle databases are listed in Tables 31.6, 31.7, and 31.8, respectively. In addition, the keywords supported by the Merant Text driver that ships with ColdFusion are listed in Table 31.9.

TABLE 31.6 BASIC CONNECTION STRING KEYWORDS FOR THE MICROSOFT ACCESS ODBC DRIVER

Keyword	Description
`DRIVER`	To connect to an Access database, the `DRIVER` keyword should be set to `{Microsoft Access Driver (*.mdb)}`.
`DBQ`	The name of the database filename, including the `.mdb` extension, but without directory path information.
`DefaultDir`	The directory in which the database file is sitting.
`UID`	The username to use when connecting to the database. Many Access databases can be connected to with a username of `Admin`, so you would provide `UID=Admin;` in the connection string.
`PWD`	The password to use when connecting to the database. If you are using `Admin` for the username, the password is often blank by default, unless you have changed it using Access itself. Therefore, you would provide `PWD=;` in the connection string.

TABLE 31.7 BASIC CONNECTION STRING KEYWORDS FOR THE MICROSOFT SQLSERVER ODBC DRIVER

Keyword	Description
`DRIVER`	To connect to a SQLServer database, the `DRIVER` keyword should be set to `{SQL SERVER}`.
`SERVER`	The name of the SQLServer machine to connect to. To connect to a SQLServer running on the same machine as ColdFusion, use `SERVER=(local)`. Depending on how the SQLServer is configured, you usually can specify the `SERVER` using a Windows-style machine name; an Internet-style hostname; or an IP address, such as `SERVER=MySQLServer`, `SERVER=127.0.0.1`, or `SERVER=mysqlserver.mycompany.com`.
`DATABASE`	The name of the database on the SQLServer to which you want to connect, as shown in the SQL Enterprise Manager. If not provided, ColdFusion will be connected to the default database for the user you specify in `UID`.
`APP`	An optional application name, which you can specify as anything you want. This application name will be visible in SQL Profiler and other tools supplied with SQLServer, so it might be useful for logging or debugging purposes.
`WSID`	An optional workstation identifier, which you can specify as anything you want. This workstation ID will be visible in the SQL Profiler and other tools supplied with SQLServer, so it might be useful for logging or debugging purposes.
`UID`	The username to use when connecting to the database.
`PWD`	The password to use when connecting to the database.

Tip

For information about additional keywords you can provide in the connect string with SQLServer, look up `SQLDriverConnect` in your SQLServer documentation (or the SQLServer Books Online).

TABLE 31.8 BASIC CONNECTION STRING KEYWORDS FOR THE ORACLE ODBC DRIVER

Keyword	Description
`DRIVER`	To connect to an Oracle database, the `DRIVER` keyword should be set to `{Oracle ODBC Driver}`.
`DBQ`	The Oracle service name to which you want to connect.
`DBA`	Type of access needed; `W`=write access; `R`=read-only access.
`UID`	The username to use when connecting to the database.
`PWD`	The password to use when connecting to the database.

Tip

For information about additional keywords you can provide in the connect string with Oracle, select an existing Oracle data source in the Windows ODBC Administrator, select Configure, select Help, and then look in the For Programmers section of the Help Contents.

Note

Table 31.8 pertains to the OBDC driver installed by Oracle as part of the Oracle installation process, which is listed as Oracle ODBC Driver in the Windows ODBC Administrator. The Microsoft ODBC for Oracle driver, which is supplied by Microsoft as part of the standard Windows ODBC distribution, takes slightly different parameters.

Table 31.9 Connection String Keywords for the Merant Text Driver That Ships with ColdFusion 5

Keyword	Description
DRIVER	To connect to an Oracle database, the DRIVER keyword should be set to {MERANT 3.70 ColdFusion OEM 32-BIT TextFile (*.*)}.
AUD	To use UPDATE and DELETE statements on a text file with this driver, you must set this keyword to 1. The default value of 0 allows SELECT and INSERT statements—but not UPDATE and DELETE—for performance reasons.
DB	The directory in which the text file(s) are stored.
DC	The character to use as a field delimiter within each row of data. The default delimiter is a comma.
FLN	Determines whether the driver looks for column names in the first line of the file. Set this keyword to 1 if your text file has the column names as its first line. If it's set to 0 (the default), the first line is assumed to hold actual data.
UT	If set to GUESS (the default), the driver attempts to guess the file's structure if necessary. The driver also supports a value of PROMPT for this keyword, but you should not use PROMPT with ColdFusion.

Tip

For information about additional keywords you can provide in the connect string with the Merant Text driver, select an existing text data source in the Windows ODBC Administrator, select Configure, Help, and then look at the Connecting Using a Connection String page in the Connecting to a Data Source section of the Help Contents.

Note

Chapter 25, "Enhancing Forms with Client-Side Java," and Chapter 33, "Error Handling," include examples that illustrate how the Merant Text driver can be used in your ColdFusion templates.

Note

The information in Table 31.9 was correct when this book went to press. The correct value for the `DRIVER` keyword might be slightly different in the final version of ColdFusion 5.

USING CONNECTION STRINGS WITH <CFQUERY>

To use a connection string to query a database with `<CFQUERY>`, do the following:

1. Provide a `DBTYPE` attribute of `dynamic`.
2. Provide the actual connection string using the `CONNECTSTRING` attribute.

Listing 31.17 is a revised version of the `FilmCast2.cfm` template from Listing 31.6. This version uses a connection string to connect to the `ows.mdb` database, instead of using the `ows` data source from the ColdFusion Administrator.

LISTING 31.17 `FilmCast3.cfm`—USING A CONNECTION STRING TO PERFORM A DATASOURCELESS QUERY

```
<!--- Our Access database is in "data" folder --->
<CFSET DBPath=ExpandPath("../data")>
<CFSET DBFile="ows.mdb">
<!--- Build ODBC Connection String --->
<CFSET Driver="{Microsoft Access Driver (*.mdb)}">
<CFSET ConStr="DRIVER=#Driver#;DBQ=#DBFile#;DefaultDir=#DBPath#;UID=Admin;PWD=;">

<!--- Retrieve Films and Related Actors from database --->
<CFQUERY NAME="GetFilmInfo" DBTYPE="dynamic" CONNECTSTRING="#ConStr#">
  SELECT
    Films.FilmID, Films.MovieTitle,
    Actors.NameFirst, Actors.NameLast
  FROM Films, FilmsActors, Actors
  WHERE Films.FilmID        = FilmsActors.FilmID
    AND FilmsActors.ActorID = Actors.ActorID
  ORDER BY Films.MovieTitle, Actors.NameLast
</CFQUERY>

<HTML>
<HEAD><TITLE>Films and Actors</TITLE></HEAD>
<BODY>
<H2>Films And Actors</H2>

<!--- Display retrieved information in HTML table --->
<CFTABLE QUERY="GetFilmInfo" HTMLTABLE BORDER COLHEADERS>
  <CFCOL HEADER="Film ID" TEXT="#FilmID#">
  <CFCOL HEADER="Film Title" TEXT="#MovieTitle#">
```

```
  <CFCOL HEADER="Actor (First Name)" TEXT="#NameFirst#">
  <CFCOL HEADER="Actor (Last Name)" TEXT="#NameLast#">
</CFTABLE>

</BODY>
</HTML>
```

At the top of the template, four `<CFSET>` tags are used to assemble an appropriate connection string. First, the `ExpandPath()` function is used to obtain the complete directory path to the `data` folder (where the database file should be sitting), which is assumed to be a subfolder of the current folder's parent. The actual filename of the database file is assumed to be `ows.mdb`, and the `Driver` variable is set to the appropriate `DRIVER` string, as noted previously in Table 31.6.

The complete connection string is then assembled and stored in the `ConStr` variable. The `<CFQUERY>` tag is adjusted to provide a `DBTYPE` of `dynamic`, and the newly assembled connection string is provided to the `CONNECTSTRING` attribute. When the template is visited, it looks exactly the same as the previous version (refer to Figure 31.7). There is no difference as far as your users are concerned.

Note

Of course, you could use a single `<CFSET>` tag to set the `REQUEST.ConStr` variable all at once. The four tags are used here for clarity.

If you are going to use connection strings in the queries throughout your application, you might consider setting the connection string to a variable in the `REQUEST` scope in your `Application.cfm` file, so that it is available to the rest of your ColdFusion templates. Listing 31.18 shows what this might look like.

LISTING 31.18 `Application.cfm`—**SETTING THE CONNECTION STRING IN THE** `REQUEST` **SCOPE**

```
<!---
  Filename:     Application.cfm
  Created by:   Nate Weiss (NMW)
  Date Created: 2/18/2001
  Please Note:  Executes for each page request
--->

<!--- Any variables set here can be used by all our pages --->
<CFSET REQUEST.DataSource  = "ows">
<CFSET REQUEST.CompanyName = "Orange Whip Studios">

<!--- Name our app, and enable Application vars --->
<CFAPPLICATION
  NAME="OrangeWhipSite"
  CLIENTMANAGEMENT="Yes"
  SESSIONMANAGEMENT="Yes">
```

Listing 31.18 Continued

```
<!--- Our Access database is in "data" folder --->
<CFSET DBPath=ExpandPath("../data")>
<CFSET DBFile="ows.mdb">
<!--- Build ODBC Connection String --->
<CFSET Driver="{Microsoft Access Driver (*.mdb)}">
<CFSET REQUEST.ConStr="DRIVER=#Driver#;DBQ=#DBFile#;"
                    & "DefaultDir=#DBPath#;UID=Admin;PWD=;">
```

After the connection string is set in `Application.cfm`, you can just refer to the `REQUEST` variable in each of your `<CFQUERY>` tags, as shown in Listing 31.19.

Listing 31.19 `FilmCast4.cfm`—Using a Connection String Set in `Application.cfm`

```
<!--- Retrieve Films and Related Actors from database --->
<CFQUERY NAME="GetFilmInfo" DBTYPE="dynamic" CONNECTSTRING="#REQUEST.ConStr#">
  SELECT
    Films.FilmID, Films.MovieTitle,
    Actors.NameFirst, Actors.NameLast
  FROM Films, FilmsActors, Actors
  WHERE Films.FilmID        = FilmsActors.FilmID
    AND FilmsActors.ActorID = Actors.ActorID
  ORDER BY Films.MovieTitle, Actors.NameLast
</CFQUERY>

<HTML>
<HEAD><TITLE>Films and Actors</TITLE></HEAD>
<BODY>
<H2>Films And Actors</H2>

<!--- Display retrieved information in HTML table --->
<CFTABLE QUERY="GetFilmInfo" HTMLTABLE BORDER COLHEADERS>
  <CFCOL HEADER="Film ID" TEXT="#FilmID#">
  <CFCOL HEADER="Film Title" TEXT="#MovieTitle#">
  <CFCOL HEADER="Actor (First Name)" TEXT="#NameFirst#">
  <CFCOL HEADER="Actor (Last Name)" TEXT="#NameLast#">
</CFTABLE>

</BODY>
</HTML>
```

When to Use Connection Strings

As you can see in Listings 31.17 and 31.19, ColdFusion's `CONNECTSTRING` attribute is easy to use. However, whether there is actually any advantage to using connection strings instead of named data sources is another matter. In general, just setting up a named data source in the ColdFusion Administrator, ignoring all this connection string business, is more convenient.

That said, there are certain situations in which the ability to connect to databases without defining a data source is useful, such as the following:

- **If you are creating a custom tag that needs to connect to a database internally**—Or, if you are creating a complete ColdFusion application for sale, your code can interact with your database without anyone needing to do anything special in the ColdFusion Administrator first.
- **If you don't have access to the ColdFusion Administrator for whatever reason**—For instance, if you are using a ColdFusion server hosted at an Internet service provider (ISP). Note, however, that it is anticipated that many ISPs will disable the connection string feature for the entire server (see Chapter 30 for details) for security reasons.
- **If, for whatever reason, you have many file-based databases with which you need to interact**—It might not be practical to create a named data source for each one. For instance, you might build an intranet application in which your users can upload small Access databases to the server. Using a connection string, you could connect to the just-uploaded database by setting the `DBQ` keyword (refer to Table 31.6) to the value of `File.ServerFile`. You could run any needed queries and then delete the uploaded database from the server when you're finished with it. For information about file uploading, see Chapter 35.

OVERRIDING DATA SOURCE OPTIONS WITH CONNECTION STRINGS

You also can use the `CONNECTSTRING` attribute, along with `DATASOURCE`, to change or override the data source's connection options for a specific `<CFQUERY>` tag. For instance, suppose a SQLServer data source called `MySQLServer` exists in the ColdFusion Administrator, which points to a SQLServer machine that has several separate databases on it. If, for whatever reason, you wanted to be able to query the various databases on that server without having to create a separate data source for each one, you could just override the database name using the `DATABASE` connection string keyword (refer to Table 31.7)

```
<CFQUERY NAME="GetFilm" DATASOURCE="MySQLServer"
  CONNECTSTRING="DATABASE=OrangeWhipStudios">
  SELECT * FROM Films
</CFQUERY>
```

ABOUT THE SPECIAL __DYNAMIC__ DATA SOURCE NAME

ColdFusion reserves a special data source name called `__DYNAMIC__` to enable you to control ColdFusion-specific options for your queries that don't use an ordinary data source name (such as Listings 31.17 and 31.19). Whenever you use `DBTYPE="dynamic"`, the `DATASOURCE` attribute is set to a default of `__DYNAMIC__` for you (that's the word `DYNAMIC` with two underscore characters at the beginning and end).

If you want to change the ColdFusion-specific settings used by dynamic queries (such as turning off the Maintain Database Connections setting, which is on by default), create a dummy data source (using any driver) called `__DYNAMIC__` in the OBDC Data Sources page of the ColdFusion Administrator. You could then tell ColdFusion to allow only `SELECT` statements in dynamic queries by checking the Restrict SQL Operations to SELECT option (see Figure 31.14).

You could also create another fake data source name in the ColdFusion Administrator and specify that data source in the `DATASOURCE` for a `DBTYPE="dynamic"` query. You can provide a different set of ColdFusion-specific options for each dummy data source you create.

In addition, ColdFusion will consider each `DATASOUCE` name to represent a separate connection pool. Assuming that the Maintain Database Connections setting is enabled for each dummy data source, ColdFusion will maintain and reuse connections on a per-dummy-data-source basis, up to the limit (if any) specified in the Enable the Limit of Simultaneous Connections setting for the dummy data sources. See Figure 31.14 and Chapter 30, "ColdFusion Server Configuration," for details.

SPECIFYING CONNECTION STRINGS IN THE COLDFUSION ADMINISTRATOR

As of ColdFusion 5, the ColdFusion Administrator provides a Connection String field for each ODBC data source. You can use this field to specify additional connection options for which the ColdFusion Administrator doesn't provide specific form fields. For instance, for a SQLServer data source, you might use this field to provide the optional `APP` and `WSID` keywords, to enable your database administrator (dba) to more easily understand which queries are being made by which of your ColdFusion applications.

To specify additional options using connection string keywords, follow these steps:

1. Navigate to the ODBC Data Sources page of the ColdFusion Administrator, and select the desired data source.
2. Provide the additional connection string information in the Connection String field, as shown in Figure 31.14.
3. Click Update to save your changes.

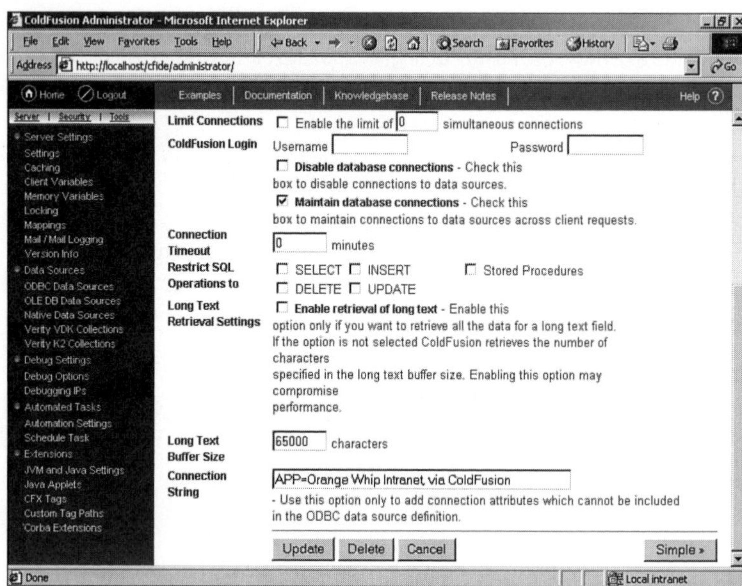

Figure 31.14
You can add to the connection string normally used for a data source by using the ColdFusion Administrator.

Note

You should not use the ColdFusion Administrator option to provide connection string keywords you can set using the Administrator page normally. For instance, do not provide `UID` or `PWD` keywords because those can be provided in the Username and Password fields (shown in Figure 31.14).

Note

In this release of ColdFusion (5), connection strings are relevant only for OBDC data sources. They are not relevant for OLE-DB data sources or native data sources.

BUILDING QUERY RESULTS PROGRAMMATICALLY

ColdFusion provides functions that enable you to create new query objects programmatically. These functions are called `QueryNew()`, `QueryAddRow()`, and `QuerySetCell()`. For instance, the `<CF_ShoppingCart>` custom tag created in Chapter 29 uses these functions to return a query object that represents the items currently in a user's shopping cart.

Furthermore, Listing 29.5 showed you how query results that are built using these functions can be requeried further, using ColdFusion's query of queries feature. You can find out more about `QueryNew()`, `QueryAddRow()`, and `QuerySetCell()`in Chapter 29 or Appendix B.

USING DATABASE TRANSACTIONS

ColdFusion provides a tag called `<CFTRANSACTION>`, which can be used to explicitly specify the beginning and end of a *database transaction*. A database transaction is a way of telling your database system that several SQL statements should be thought of as representing a single unit of work.

For instance, for the Orange Whip Studios project, the series of related inserts that need to occur to record a merchandise order should be thought of as a single transaction. An order really hasn't been properly recorded unless the appropriate records have been added to both the `MerchandiseOrders` and `MerchandiseOrdersItems` tables. During the moments between those inserts, the database is in what's called an *inconsistent state*, meaning that the data doesn't properly represent the real-world facts yet. Database transactions ensure that your database doesn't expose this inconsistent state to other connections.

Using `<CFTRANSACTION>` is simple:

- **Whenever you need to make several related changes to your database, you should use a `<CFTRANSACTION>` tag around the `<CFQUERY>` tags that perform all the various steps**—This tells your database system that the changes made by the queries should not be considered a permanent part of the database until the transaction has completed all its work.

- **Until the transaction has finished its work, any changes made to the database during the transaction will not be visible to any other connections that might be querying the database at the same time**—This means that queries made by other ColdFusion page requests will be incapable of interrupting your database transaction or catching the database in an inconsistent state (for instance, between the moments during which two related changes are made).
- **Because changes made to the database during the transaction are not considered a permanent part of the database until the transaction is finished, you are actually free to undo all the changes at any time during the transaction**—This is called *rolling back* the transaction and is supported by ColdFusion via `ACTION="Rollback"` (see Table 31.10). Or, you can permanently commit the transaction using `ACTION="Commit"`. After a transaction is committed, it can't be rolled back.

Table 31.10 shows the attributes supported by `<CFTRANSACTION>` in ColdFusion 5.0.

Table 31.10 `<CFTRANSACTION>` Tag Attributes

Attribute	Description
`ACTION`	Can be set to `BEGIN`, `COMMIT`, or `ROLLBACK`. If you do not provide an `ACTION`, it defaults to `BEGIN`.
`ISOLATION`	Can be set to `Read_Uncommitted`, `Read_Committed`, `Repeatable_Read`, or `Serializable`. These values enable you to control the appropriate balance between concurrency and consistency. Consult your database documentation to find out which isolation levels are actually supported by your database system and how your database vendor has chosen to implement the various isolation levels.

Tip

Database scholars generally define the concept of a database transaction as having a number of properties, often referred to as the so-called *ACID Properties* (atomicity, consistency, isolation, and durability). If you are interested in the theory behind database transactions, you are encouraged to consult your database's documentation (or a dedicated SQL text) to learn about them formally.

Note

A complete discussion about database transactions is, unfortunately, beyond the scope of this book. Again, you are encouraged to consult your database system's documentation to find out more about how transactions are implemented in the database software you are using.

Using the `<CFTRANSACTION>` Tag

You have already seen `<CFTRANSACTION>` used in several of this book's listings. In general, this book's examples use `<CFTRANSACTION>` to explicitly mark the beginning and end of database transactions to accomplish one of two things:

- To correctly retrieve an automatically generated ID number after a new record is inserted into the database
- To be able to commit or roll back changes within the transaction, based on the success or failure of some type of external processing

USING TRANSACTIONS FOR ID NUMBER SAFETY

In Chapter 14, "Using Forms to Add or Change Data," you learned how the `<CFTRANSACTION>` tag should be used around the two-step process that's often necessary when inserting a new record into a database. First, the actual insert is performed (via `<CFINSERT>` or a SQL `INSERT` statement), and then the SQL `MAX()` function is used to retrieve the ID number of the just-inserted record.

The examples in this book always use `<CFTRANSACTION>` around such a multistep process. Without `<CFTRANSACTION>`, the wrong ID number could occasionally be retrieved if the ColdFusion template was being visited by several users at the same time. With `<CFTRANSACTION>`, you are assured that you will get back the correct number because no other database operations are allowed to affect the state of each transaction until it is finished. Conceptually, you are asking your database to freeze the database just before the changes are made and unfreeze it only after the changes are complete.

You generally end up with code that follows this basic pattern:

```
<CFTRANSACTION>
  <!--- 1) insert record, via <CFINSERT> or SQL INSERT --->
  <!--- 2) get new id number, via a SELECT MAX() query --->
</CFTRANSACTION>
```

See Chapter 14 for a complete example that uses `<CFTRANSACTION>` in this manner.

Note

The mechanics of how the database actually preserves the integrity of the transaction varies somewhat from database to database. Some implement transactions by simply blocking all other accesses to the relevant database (or table or portions of the table) until your transaction is finished. Others use a more sophisticated approach, in which simultaneous transactions each affect their own version of the data. Consult your database documentation for details.

USING TRANSACTIONS FOR THE ABILITY TO UNDO

In Chapter 29, a CFML custom tag called `<CF_PlaceOrder>` was created, which takes care of all the various steps that must be completed each time a user decides to buy merchandise from Orange Whip Studios. The custom tag inserts a new record into the `MerchandiseOrders` table and inserts several new records into the `MerchandiseOrdersItems` table. It also attempts to charge the user's credit card and is smart enough to undo all the changes to the database if, for whatever reason, the user's credit card can't be successfully charged at the time. The `<CFTRANSACTION>` tag makes this possible.

When using <CFTRANSACTION> to enable rollback processing, you usually end up with code that follows this basic pattern:

```
<CFTRANSACTION ACTION="Begin">
  ... database changes here ...
  <CFIF Everything Goes Well>
    <CFTRANSACTION ACTION="Commit"/>
  <CFELSE>
    <CFTRANSACTION ACTION="Rollback"/>
  </CFIF>
</CFIF>
```

Note

The trailing forward slashes at the end of the previous `ACTION="Commit"` and the `ACTION="Rollback"` are important. Be sure to include the slashes when performing a `Commit` or `Rollback` in your own code.

If you take a look at Listing 29.8 in Chapter 29, you will see that it follows this pattern. First, the transaction is begun, using the opening <CFTRANSACTION> tag. Within the transaction, the various INSERT queries needed to record the order are executed. Because the queries are being executed within the safe space of the transaction, you do not need to worry about what might happen if only part of the database changes were able to take place.

Then, after the records have been inserted and after the attempt to charge the user's credit card, a <CFIF> statement is used to determine whether the credit cart charge was successful. If so, the transaction is committed via an `ACTION="Commit"`. If not, the transaction is rolled back via an `ACTION="Rollback"`.

Note

With two important exceptions, you can't use more than one data source within a single <CFTRANSACTION> block. The first exception is when you're using ColdFusion's query of queries feature; queries of `DBTYPE="query"` are always allowed, even in transactions that involve other data sources. The second exception is after an explicit `COMMIT`; you can run queries that refer to other data sources after a transaction has been committed. Otherwise, any queries that need to use other data sources must be placed outside the <CFTRANSACTION> block.

TRANSACTIONS AND CFML ERROR HANDLING

Database transactions commonly are committed or rolled back based on the results of ColdFusion's structured exception-handling mechanisms. In general, this means using <CFTRANSACTION> inside a <CFTRY> block. Within the <CFTRY> block, any database errors are caught using the <CFCATCH> tag, which causes the transaction to be rolled back with an `ACTION="Rollback"`.

Note

For details, see Chapter 33.

Transactions and Stored Procedures

In general, it often makes the most sense to create stored procedures that encapsulate an entire database transaction. Rather than creating several <CFQUERY> tags and wrapping <CFTRANSACTION> around them, you would just make a single stored procedure that takes care of performing all the steps. Within the stored procedure, you would use whatever syntax your database requires to ensure the database server considers the whole process to be a single database transaction.

This way, everything about the transaction is owned conceptually by the database server and occurs entirely under its watch. Also, the stored procedure can then be used by other systems within your company (not just ColdFusion).

You will learn all about stored procedures in the next chapter.

Note

With Oracle systems, you use the SET TRANSACTION, COMMIT, and ROLLBACK statements to declare the beginning and end of a transaction within a stored procedure. With SQLServer, you use BEGIN TRANSACTION, COMMIT TRANSACTION, and COMMIT TRANSACTION.

CHAPTER 32

Working with Stored Procedures

In this chapter

Most server-based database systems—SQL Server, Oracle, and Sybase—support stored procedures. A *stored procedure* is a chunk of SQL code that's given a name and stored as a part of your database, along with your actual data tables. After the stored procedure has been created, you can invoke it in your ColdFusion templates using the `<CFSTOREDPROC>` tag.

Tip

The use of stored procedures in database applications is a relatively advanced topic. As the saying goes, it's not exactly rocket science, but it probably makes sense to start working with stored procedures only after you have become pretty familiar with the SQL concepts introduced in the previous chapter or have a specific reason for using stored procedures in a particular ColdFusion application.

Note

At the time of this writing, stored procedures are supported by most server-based database systems (such as SQL Server, Oracle, and Sybase) but are not generally supported by file-based databases (such as Access, FoxPro, Paradox, dBASE, and so on). If you don't plan on using a server-based database system, you can skip this chapter without missing out on anything essential.

WHY USE STORED PROCEDURES?

Stored procedures provide a way to consolidate any number of SQL statements—such as `SELECT`, `INSERT`, `UPDATE`, and so on—into a little package that encapsulates a complete operation to be carried out in your application.

For instance, consider Orange Whip Studio's online store. When a customer places an order, the application needs to verify that the customer's account is in good standing and then carry out `INSERT` statements to the `MerchandiseOrders` and `MerchandiseOrdersItems` tables to record the actual order. In the future, the application might be expanded to first ensure that the selected merchandise is in stock; if not, the application needs to display some type of "sorry, out of stock" message for the user, and it might need to update another table somewhere else to indicate that the merchandise needs to be reordered from the supplier.

This type of complex, causally related set of checks and record-keeping is often referred to generally as a *business rule* or *business process.* Using the techniques you've learned so far in this book, you already know that you could accomplish the steps with several `<CFQUERY>` tags and some conditional processing using `<CFIF>` and `<CFELSE>` tags. In fact, in Chapter 29, "Online Commerce," you learned how all the relevant processing can be bundled up into a CFML custom tag called `<CF_PlaceOrder>`.

In this chapter, you see that you could wrap up all the database-related actions required to place an order into a single stored procedure called, say, `PlaceOrder`, thus encapsulating the entire business process into one smart routine your ColdFusion templates need only refer to.

This shifts the responsibility for ensuring that the steps are followed properly away from your ColdFusion code and places that responsibility in the hands of the database server itself. This shift generally requires a little bit of extra work on your part up front but offers some real advantages later.

Advantages of Using Stored Procedures

Depending on the situation, a number of possible advantages exist to using a stored procedure in your application (rather than a series of `<CFQUERY>` and `<CFIF>` tags). Some of the most important advantages are outlined in this chapter. You might want to consult your database server documentation for further details and remarks on the advantages of using stored procedures.

Modularity Is a Good Thing

When developing any type of application, it generally pays to keep pieces of code—whether it be CFML code, SQL statements, or some other type of code—broken into small, self-explanatory modules that know how to perform a specific task on their own. This type of practice keeps your code readable, easier to maintain, and easier to reuse in other applications you might need to write later.

It can also enable several people to more easily work on the same project at the same time without stepping on each other's toes. Developer A might say to Developer B, "Make me a stored procedure that does such-and-such. Meanwhile, I'll be putting together the ColdFusion templates that use the procedure." Because the procedure runs independently of the templates and vice versa, neither developer needs to wait for the other to get started. The result can be an application that gets up and running more quickly.

Sharing Code Between Applications

After a stored procedure has been created, it enables you to share code between different types of applications, even applications written with different development tools. For instance, a ColdFusion template, a Visual Basic program, and a Java application might all refer to the same stored procedure on your server. Clearly, this cuts down on development time and ensures that all three applications enforce the various business rules in exactly the same way.

This type of consistent enforcement of business rules can be particularly important if the three applications are being developed by different teams or developers. In addition, if the business rules change for order-taking in the future, it's likely that only the stored procedure would need to be adapted, rather than the code in all three applications needing to be revised.

Increasing Performance

Depending on the situation, using stored procedures can often cause an application to perform better. For two basic reasons, the use of stored procedures will speed your application. First, most database systems do some type of precompilation of the stored procedure so that it runs more quickly when it is actually used. For instance, Microsoft SQL Server makes all its performance-optimizing decisions (such as which indexes and which join algorithms to use) the first time a stored procedure is run. Subsequent executions of the stored procedure do not need to be parsed and analyzed, which causes the procedure to run somewhat more quickly than if you executed its SQL statements in an ad hoc fashion every time. Generally, the more steps the procedure represents, the more of a difference this precompilation makes. Oracle servers do something very similar.

Second, if you compare the idea of having one stored procedure versus several `<CFQUERY>` and `<CFIF>` tags in a template, the stored procedure approach is often more efficient because much less communication is necessary between ColdFusion and the database server. Instead of sending the information about the number of books in stock and customer account status back and forth between the ColdFusion server and the database server, all the querying and decision-making steps are kept in one place. Because less data needs to move between the two systems, and because the database drivers aren't really involved at all until the very end, you are likely to have a slightly faster process in the end if you use the stored-procedure approach. Generally, the more data that needs to be examined to enforce the various business rules, the more of a difference the use of stored procedures is likely to have on overall application performance.

Note

In general, the performance increases mentioned here will be relatively modest. Of course, your mileage will vary from application to application and from database to database, but you should expect speed increases of 10% or so as a ballpark figure in your mind. In other words, don't expect your application to work 20 times faster just because you put all your SQL code into stored procedures.

MAKING TABLE SCHEMAS IRRELEVANT

Because a stored procedure is invoked simply by referring to it by name, a database administrator can shield whoever is actually using a stored procedure from having to be familiar with the database tables' underlying structure. In fact, in a team environment, it's easy to imagine a situation in which you are developing a ColdFusion application but don't even know the names of the tables in which the various data is being stored.

You can get your work done more quickly if whoever designed the database provides you with a number of stored procedures you can use to get your job done without having to learn the various table and column names involved. In return, the database designer can be comforted by the knowledge that if the relationships between the tables change at some point in the future, only the stored procedure will need to be changed, rather than the ColdFusion code you're working on.

ADDRESSING SECURITY CONCERNS

Depending on the type of database server you're using, stored procedures can provide advantages in terms of security. For instance, you might have some confidential data in some of your database tables, so the database administrator might not have granted `SELECT` or `INSERT` privileges to whatever database username ColdFusion uses to interact with the database server. By creating a few stored procedures, your administrator could provide the needed information to ColdFusion without granting more general privileges than are necessary.

By only granting privileges to the stored procedures rather than enabling the actual tables to be queried or updated, the database administrator can be confident that the data in the tables does not become compromised or lose its real-world meaning. Because all database servers enable the administrator to grant `SELECT`, `UPDATE`, `DELETE`, and `INSERT` privileges separately, the administrator could enable your ColdFusion application to retrieve data but make changes only via stored procedures. That gives the administrator a lot of control and keeps you from worrying about harming the organization's data because of some mistake in your code.

Such a policy would enable the ColdFusion developer, the database administrator, and the company in general to feel very confident about the development of a ColdFusion application. Everyone involved can see that nothing crazy is going to happen as the company shifts toward Web-based applications.

COMPARING STORED PROCEDURES TO CFML CUSTOM TAGS

It's worth noting that stored procedures are similar in many conceptual ways to CFML custom tags (also known as *modules*), which you learned about in Chapter 22, "Building Reusable Components." You can think about a stored procedure as the database server equivalent of a custom tag, which might help you get a handle on when you should consider writing a stored procedure.

Here are some of the ways stored procedures are similar to custom tags:

- Both stored procedures and custom tags enable you to take a bunch of code, wrap it up, slap a name on it, and use it as you develop your applications almost as if it were part of the language all along.
- Both encourage code reuse, cutting development times and costs in the long run.
- Both can accept parameters as input.
- Both can set ColdFusion variables in the calling template that can be used in subsequent CFML code.
- Both can generate one or more query resultsets for the calling template.
- Both make integrating other people's work into your own easier.

CALLING STORED PROCEDURES FROM COLDFUSION TEMPLATES

Now that you have an idea about what kinds of things stored procedures can be used for, this is a good time to see how to integrate them into your ColdFusion templates. For the moment, assume that several stored procedures have already been created and are ready for use within your ColdFusion application. Perhaps you put the stored procedures together yourself, or maybe they were created by another developer or by the database administrator (DBA). At this point, all you care about is what the name of the stored procedure is and what it does. You learn how to actually create the stored procedures later in this chapter.

The two ways to execute a stored procedure from your ColdFusion templates are

- **With the `<CFSTOREDPROC>` tag**—The `<CFSTOREDPROC>` tag is the formal, recommended way to call stored procedures. You can pass input parameters to the stored procedure, collect return codes and output parameters passed back by the procedure, and use any recordsets (queries) the procedure returns. In theory, `<CFSTOREDPROC>` should also result in the fastest performance.

  However, using `<CFSTOREDPROC>` has two disadvantages. First, you can't use ColdFusion's query-caching feature with the recordsets the procedure returns.

  Second, for ODBC and OLE-DB data sources, the parameters you pass to the stored procedure via `<CFSTOREDPROC>` are referenced by ordinal position, rather than by name. This means your ColdFusion code can break if parameters are added to the procedure in the future. This is a particularly unfortunate limitation and can be enough to keep you from using the tag altogether, especially if you are using Microsoft SQLServer. For details, see the section "Ordinal Versus Named Parameter Positioning," later in this chapter.

- **With the `<CFQUERY>` tag**—As an alternative to `<CFSTOREDPROC>`, you can execute stored procedures via ordinary `<CFQUERY>` tags. Recordsets returned by stored procedures called in this way can be cached via ColdFusion's `CACHEDWITHIN` attribute (see Chapter 24, "Improving Performance"). Also, this method allows you to refer to the procedure's parameter by name instead of by ordinal position.

  Unfortunately, this method has two big disadvantages as well. First, you can't capture any output parameters or result codes returned by the procedure (only query-style output).

  Second, if the procedure returns multiple recordsets, you can capture only one of them for use in your ColdFusion code. See the section, "Calling Procedures with `<CFQUERY>` Instead of `<CFSTOREDPROC>`," later in this chapter.

Using the <CFSTOREDPROC> Tag

To call an existing stored procedure from a ColdFusion template, you refer to the procedure by name using the `<CFSTOREDPROC>` tag. The `<CFSTOREDPROC>` tag is similar to the `<CFQUERY>` tag in that it knows how to interact with data sources you've defined in the ColdFusion Administrator. However, rather than accepting ad hoc SQL query statements (such as `SELECT` and `DELETE`), `<CFSTOREDPROC>` is very structured, optimized specifically for dealing with stored procedures.

The `<CFSTOREDPROC>` tag takes a number of relatively simple parameters, as listed in Table 32.1.

TABLE 32.1 IMPORTANT <CFSTOREDPROC> ATTRIBUTES

Attribute	Purpose
PROCEDURE	The name of the stored procedure you want to execute. You usually can just provide the procedure name directly, as in PROCEDURE="MyProcedure". Depending on the database system you are using, however, you might need to qualify the procedure name further using dot notation.
DATASOURCE	The appropriate data source name. Just like the DATASOURCE attribute for <CFQUERY>, this could be the name of an ODBC, an OLE-DB, or a native data source as configured in the ColdFusion Administrator.
RETURNCODE	Optional. Yes or No. This attribute determines whether ColdFusion should capture the status code (sometimes called the *return code* or *return value*) reported by the stored procedure after it executes. If you set this attribute to Yes, the status code will be available to you in a special variable called CFSTOREDPROC.StatusCode. See the section "Stored Procedures That Take Parameters and Return Status Codes," later in this chapter.

Note

The <CFSTOREDPROC> tag also supports CONNECTSTRING, USERNAME, PASSWORD, DBSERVER, DBNAME, BLOCKFACTOR, PROVIDER, PROVIDERDSN, and DEBUG attributes. All these attributes work similarly to the corresponding attributes of the <CFQUERY> tag. See Appendix A, "ColdFusion Tag Reference," for details.

For simple stored procedures, you can just use its PROCEDURE and DATASOURCE attributes. When the template is executed in a Web browser, the stored procedure executes on the database server, accomplishing whatever it was designed to accomplish as it goes.

For instance, suppose you have access to an imaginary stored procedure called PerformInventoryMaintenance. It has been explained to you that this stored procedure performs some type of internal maintenance on the data in the Merchandise table, and that people need some way to execute the procedure via the company intranet. Listing 32.1 shows a ColdFusion template called InventoryMaintenanceRun.cfm, which does exactly that.

Note

The code listings in this chapter refer to a data source called owsServer to indicate a copy of the ows sample database sitting on a Microsoft SQLServer or Sybase server, and a data source called owsOra to indicate a version of the database sitting on an Oracle server. You can't work through the examples in this chapter using the Access version of the ows database used elsewhere in this book. Microsoft and Oracle each provide migration tools that can import the Access version of the ows database into the database server. See the section titled "Creating Stored Procedures," later in this chapter.

Listing 32.1 InventoryMaintenanceRun.cfm—**Calling a Stored Procedure with** <CFSTOREDPROC>

```
<HTML>
<HEAD><TITLE>Inventory Maintenance</TITLE></HEAD>
<BODY>
<H2>Inventory Maintenance</H2>

<!--- If the submit button was not just pressed, display form --->
<CFIF NOT ParameterExists(Form.ExecuteNow)>
  <!--- Provide button to start stored procedure --->
  <CFFORM ACTION="#CGI.SCRIPT_NAME#" METHOD="POST">
     <INPUT TYPE="SUBMIT" NAME="ExecuteNow" VALUE="Perform Inventory
➥Maintenance">
  </CFFORM>

<!--- If the user just clicked the submit button --->
<CFELSE>
   <P>Executing stored procedure...</P>

   <!--- Go ahead and execute the stored procedure --->
   <CFSTOREDPROC
     PROCEDURE="PerformInventoryMaintenance"
     DATASOURCE="owsServer">

   <P>Done executing stored procedure!</P>

</CFIF>

</BODY>
</HTML>
```

As you can see, the code to execute the stored procedure is extremely simple. You see in a moment how to use stored procedures that receive input and respond by providing output back to you. This particular stored procedure doesn't require any information to be provided to it, so the only things you must specify are the `PROCEDURE` and `DATASOURCE` parameters.

The `PROCEDURE` parameter tells ColdFusion what the name of the stored procedure is. The `DATASOURCE` parameter works just like it does for the `<CFQUERY>` tag; it must be the name of the appropriate ODBC, OLE-DB, or native-driver data source as defined in the ColdFusion Administrator.

Note

Listing 32.1 uses a simple piece of `<CFIF>` logic that tests to see whether a form parameter called `ExecuteNow` exists. Assuming that it does not exist, the template puts a simple form—with a single submit button—on the page. Because the submit button is named `ExecuteNow`, the `<CFIF>` logic executes the second part of the template when the form is submitted; the second part contains the `<CFSTOREDPROC>` tag that executes the stored procedure. The template is put together this way so you can see the form code and the form-processing code in one listing. See the section titled "Understanding Conditional Forms" in Chapter 14, "Using Forms to Add or Change Data," for further discussion of this type of single-template technique.

When the `InventoryMaintenanceRun.cfm` template from Listing 32.1 is first brought up in a Web browser, it displays the simple form shown in Figure 32.1. When the Perform Inventory Maintenance button is clicked, the procedure is executed and a simple message is displayed to the user to indicate that the work has been done. Figure 32.2 shows what the user sees after the procedure runs.

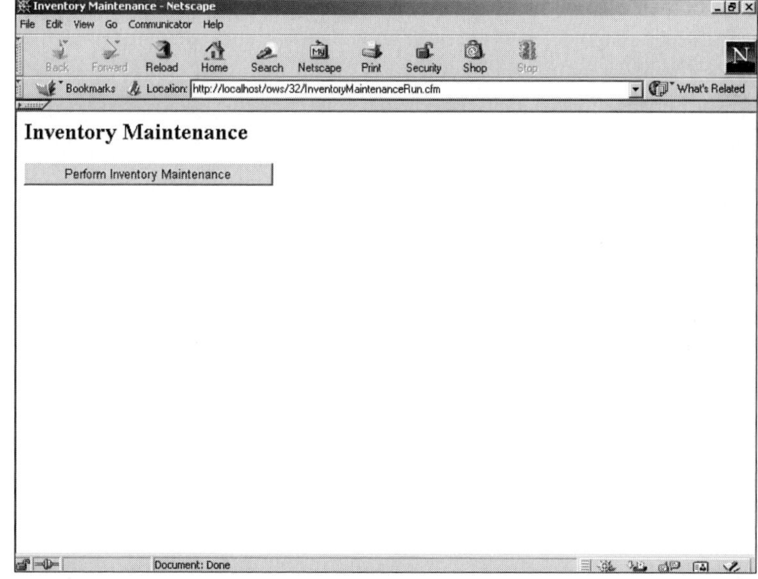

Figure 32.1
The `InventoryMaintenanceRun.cfm` template first displays a simple form.

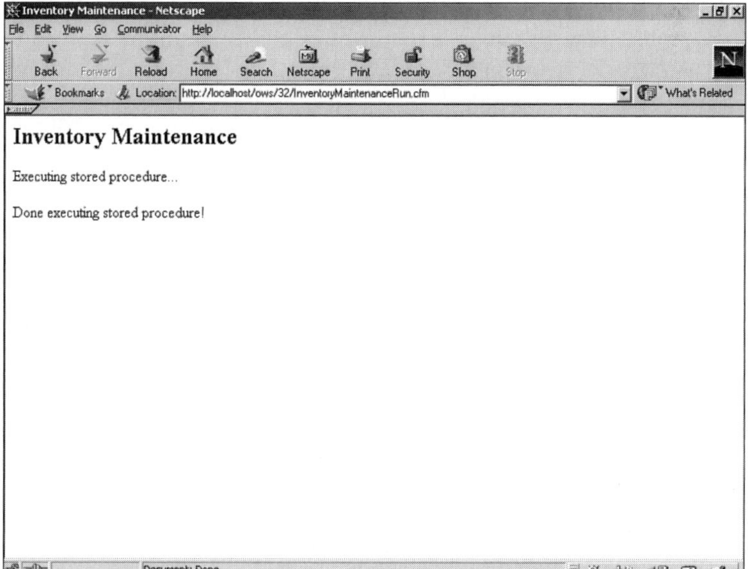

Figure 32.2
The stored procedure executes when the form is submitted.

STORED PROCEDURES THAT RETURN RECORDSETS

Stored procedures also can return recordsets to your ColdFusion templates. As far as your ColdFusion code is concerned, recordsets are just like query results. They contain columns and rows of data—usually from one or more of the database's tables—that you can then use the way you'd use rows of data fetched by a `<CFQUERY>` tag.

For instance, consider a stored procedure called `FetchRatingsList` that returns rating information straight from the `FilmsRatings` table in the `owsServer` database. This stored procedure sends back its information as a recordset, just as if you had performed a simple `SELECT` type of query with a `<CFQUERY>` tag.

It has been explained to you by whomever created the stored procedure that the recordset will contain two columns: `RatingID` and `Rating`, which correspond to the columns of the `FilmsRatings` table. In other words, executing this particular stored procedure is similar to running an ordinary `SELECT * FROM FilmsRating` query (you will see more complex examples shortly).

THE <CFPROCRESULT> TAG

To use a recordset returned by a stored procedure, you must use the `<CFPROCRESULT>` tag, which tells ColdFusion to capture the recordset as the stored procedure is executed. The `<CFPROCRESULT>` tag takes just a few attributes and is easy to use.

Table 32.2 lists the attributes supported by `<CFPROCRESULT>`. Most of the time, you will need to use only the `NAME` attribute.

TABLE 32.2 <CFPROCRESULT> TAG ATTRIBUTES

Attribute	Purpose
NAME	A name for the recordset. The recordset will become available as a query object with whatever name you specify; the query object can be used just like any other (like the results of a `<CFQUERY>` or `<CFPOP>` tag).
RESULTSET	An optional number that indicates which recordset you are referring to. This attribute is important only for stored procedures that return several recordsets. See the section, "Multiple Recordsets Are Fully Supported," later in this chapter. Defaults to 1.
MAXROWS	Optional; similar to the `MAXROWS` attribute of the `<CFQUERY>` tag. The maximum number of rows ColdFusion should retrieve from the database server as the stored procedure executes. If not provided, ColdFusion simply retrieves all the rows.

Tip

Because a recordset captured from a stored procedure is made available to your ColdFusion templates as an ordinary CFML query object, the query object has the `RecordCount`, `ColumnList`, and `CurrentRow` properties. You can use these to find out how much data the recordset contains. See Appendix C, "Special ColdFusion Variables and Result Codes," for details about these properties.

Note

The <CFPROCRESULT> tag must be used between opening and closing <CFSTOREDPROC> tags, as shown in Listing 32.3.

USING <CFPROCRESULT>

The FilmEntry1.cfm template in Listing 32.2 shows how to retrieve and use a recordset returned from a stored procedure. As you can see, a <CFSTOREDPROC> tag is used to refer to the stored procedure itself. Then the <CFPROCRESULT> tag is used to capture the recordset returned by the procedure.

Note

Remember, it is assumed that you have created a version of the Orange Whip Studios sample database for SQLServer (or whatever database server you are using), and that the database is accessible via the data source name owsServer.

In addition, for this template to work, you must have created the FetchRatingsList stored procedure. See the "Creating Stored Procedures" section in this chapter for details.

LISTING 32.2 FilmEntry1.cfm—RETRIEVING A RECORDSET FROM A STORED PROCEDURE

```
<!--- Get list of ratings from database --->
<CFSTOREDPROC PROCEDURE="FetchRatingsList" DATASOURCE="owsServer">
  <CFPROCRESULT NAME="GetRatings">
</CFSTOREDPROC>

<HTML>
<HEAD><TITLE>Film Entry Form</TITLE></HEAD>
<BODY>
<H2>Film Entry Form</H2>

<!--- Data entry form --->
<CFFORM ACTION="#CGI.SCRIPT_NAME#" METHOD="POST" PRESERVEDATA="Yes">

  <!--- Text entry field for film title --->
  <P><B>Title for New Film:</B><BR>
  <CFINPUT NAME="MovieTitle" SIZE="50" MAXLENGTH="50"
    REQUIRED="Yes" MESSAGE="Please don't leave the film's title blank."><BR>

  <!--- Text entry field for pitch text --->
  <P><B>Short Description / One-Liner:</B><BR>
  <CFINPUT NAME="PitchText" SIZE="50" MAXLENGTH="100"
    REQUIRED="Yes" MESSAGE="Please don't leave the one-liner blank."><BR>

  <!--- Text entry field for expense description --->
  <P><B>New Film Budget:</B><BR>
  <CFINPUT NAME="AmountBudgeted" SIZE="15"
    REQUIRED="Yes" MESSAGE="Please enter a valid number for the film's budget."
    VALIDATE="float"><BR>
```

LISTING 32.2 CONTINUED

```
  <!--- Drop-down list of ratings --->
  <P><B>Rating:</B><BR>
  <CFSELECT
    NAME="RatingID"
    QUERY="GetRatings"
    VALUE="RatingID"
    DISPLAY="Rating"/>

  <!--- Text areas for summary --->
  <P><B>Summary:</B><BR>
  <TEXTAREA NAME="Summary" COLS="40" ROWS="3" WRAP="soft"></TEXTAREA>

  <!--- Submit button for form --->
  <P><INPUT TYPE="Submit" VALUE="Submit New Film">
</CFFORM>

</BODY>
</HTML>
```

Note

The syntax shown in Listing 33.2 should work with most database server systems, including Microsoft SQLServer and Sybase. If you are using Oracle, you will need to make a minor change, as discussed in the next section.

Because this listing specifies `NAME="GetRatings"` in the `<CFPROCRESULT>` tag, the rest of the template is free to refer to `GetRatings` just like the results of a `<CFQUERY>`. Here, the `GetRatings` query object is provided to a `<CFSELECT>` tag to populate a drop-down list. Figure 32.3 shows the results.

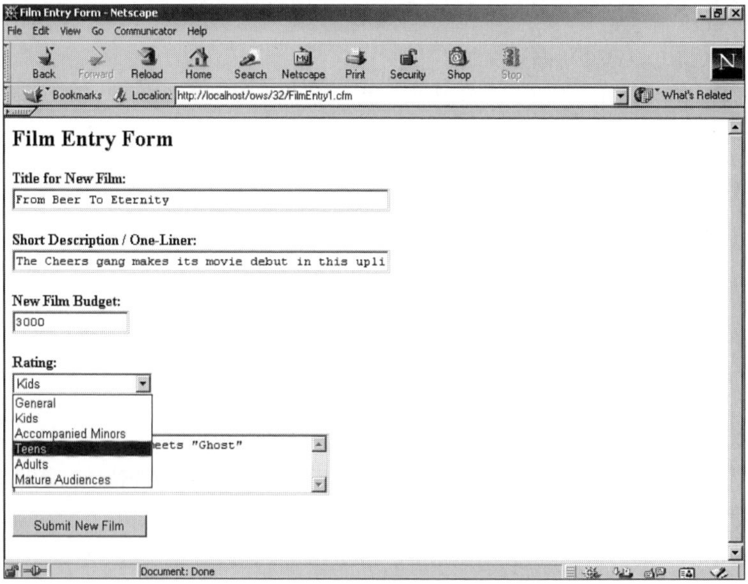

Figure 32.3
The `<CFPROCRESULT>` tag captures a record-set returned by a stored procedure.

Tip

If you are using ColdFusion Studio to edit your templates, you can use the Tag Inspector or the `<CFPROCRESULT>` Tag Editor to help you add the `<CFPROCRESULT>` tag to your code (see Figure 32.4).

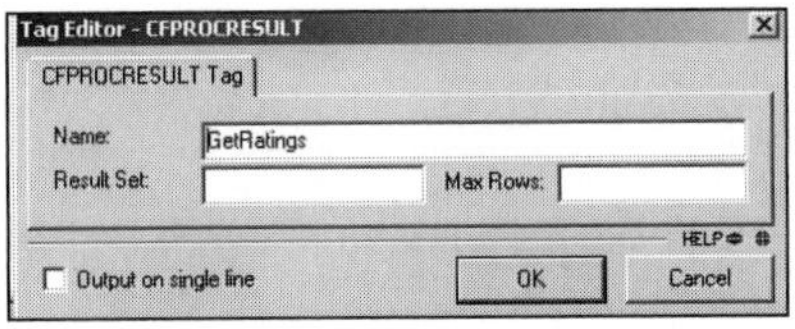

Figure 32.4 ColdFusion Studio makes adding `<CFPROCRESULT>` tags to your code even easier.

Tip

If you don't know the column names the procedure outputs, you could run the procedure and output the value of the automatic `#GetRatings.ColumnList#` variable, just as you could do for any normal query resultset.

USING `<CFPROCRESULT>` WITH ORACLE

With Oracle databases, stored procedures can't return recordsets in the traditional sense. They can return recordset-like data, but only via something called a *reference cursor*. You will need to consult your Oracle documentation if you want to learn all about reference cursors and the various ways in which they can be used.

That said, ColdFusion makes using the data returned by reference cursors in Oracle stored procedures easy. The steps are slightly different from those for SQLServer, Sybase, or other database systems, but the end result is the same: ColdFusion provides you with a CFML query object that you can use just like the results of a `<CFQUERY>` tag.

To capture the data from a reference cursor, do the following:

1. Add a `<CFPROCPARAM>` tag between the opening and closing `<CFSTOREDPROC>` tags, with `CFSQLTYPE="REFCURSOR"`, `TYPE="OUT"`, and `MAXROWS="-1"` attributes. These attributes tell ColdFusion that it will be receiving a pointer to a reference cursor on the server. ColdFusion takes care of communicating with the Oracle client software to iterate through and fetches the rows of data from the cursor. The `TYPE` attribute should be set to `Out`.

   You are also required to provide a `VARIABLE` attribute for the `<CFPROCPARAM>` tag, but it is not used for anything. Just set it to some value that makes it clear that it should be ignored, such as `VARIABLE="IgnoreThis"`.

   You will learn more about `<CFPROCPARAM>` later in this chapter.

2. Now add a `<CFPROCRESULT>` tag, using the `NAME` attribute to supply a name for the query object. This special data type string tells ColdFusion that it will be receiving a pointer to a reference cursor on the server. ColdFusion takes care of communicating with the Oracle client software to iterate through and fetch the rows of data from the cursor.

3. If the stored procedure exposes more than one reference cursor, just add another <CFPROCPARAM> and <CFPROCRESULT> tag for each reference cursor. For details, see the section "Multiple Recordsets Are Fully Supported," later in this chapter.

Note

The need to add a MAXROWS="-1" attribute to the <CFPROCPARAM> tag that corresponds to the reference cursor is a new requirement in ColdFusion 5. If you do not add this attribute, only one row of data will be fetched from the stored procedure. This behavior is undocumented and counterintuitive, and it is hoped that Macromedia will remove this requirement in a service release or some future version of the server.

Listing 32.3 is almost the same as the previous version of this template (refer toListing 32.2), except that the extra <CFPROCPARAM> tag has been added to give ColdFusion the information it needs to fetch the data properly. Assuming that a procedure called owsWeb.FetchRatingsList exists on your Oracle server, and assuming that it exposes information from the FilmsRatings table as a reference cursor, this template will behave just like the previous listing (refer to Figure 32.3).

Note

Remember, it is assumed that you have created a version of the Orange Whip Studios sample database for Oracle, and that the database is accessible via a native Oracle data source named owsOra.

In addition, for this template to work, you must have created the owsWeb.FetchRatingsList stored procedure. See the "Creating Stored Procedures with Oracle" section in this chapter for details.

LISTING 32.3 FilmEntry1Oracle.cfm—RETRIEVING DATA FROM A REFERENCE CURSOR IN AN ORACLE STORED PROCEDURE

```
<!--- Get list of ratings from database --->
<CFSTOREDPROC PROCEDURE="owsWeb.FetchRatingsList" DATASOURCE="owsOra">
  <!--- This output parameter gives ColdFusion a pointer to reference cursor --->
  <CFPROCPARAM
    TYPE="Out"
    CFSQLTYPE="CF_SQL_REFCURSOR"
    VARIABLE="IgnoreThis"
    MAXROWS="-1">
  <!--- Make the data from reference cursor available as CFML query object --->
  <CFPROCRESULT NAME="GetRatings">
</CFSTOREDPROC>

<HTML>
<HEAD><TITLE>Film Entry Form</TITLE></HEAD>
<BODY>
<H2>Film Entry Form</H2>

<!--- Data entry form --->
<CFFORM ACTION="#CGI.SCRIPT_NAME#" METHOD="POST" PRESERVEDATA="Yes">
```

```
<!--- Text entry field for film title --->
<P><B>Title for New Film:</B><BR>
<CFINPUT NAME="MovieTitle" SIZE="50" MAXLENGTH="50"
  REQUIRED="Yes" MESSAGE="Please don't leave the film's title blank."><BR>

<!--- Text entry field for pitch text --->
<P><B>Short Description / One-Liner:</B><BR>
<CFINPUT NAME="PitchText" SIZE="50" MAXLENGTH="100"
  REQUIRED="Yes" MESSAGE="Please don't leave the one-liner blank."><BR>

<!--- Text entry field for expense description --->
<P><B>New Film Budget:</B><BR>
<CFINPUT NAME="AmountBudgeted" SIZE="15"
  REQUIRED="Yes" MESSAGE="Please enter a valid number for the film's budget."
  VALIDATE="float"><BR>

<!--- Drop-down list of ratings --->
<P><B>Rating:</B><BR>
<CFSELECT
  NAME="RatingID"
  QUERY="GetRatings"
  VALUE="RatingID"
  DISPLAY="Rating"/>

<!--- Text areas for summary --->
<P><B>Summary:</B><BR>
<TEXTAREA NAME="Summary" COLS="40" ROWS="3" WRAP="soft"></TEXTAREA>

<!--- Submit button for form --->
<P><INPUT TYPE="Submit" VALUE="Submit New Film">
</CFFORM>


</BODY>
</HTML>
```


Note

In the stored procedure name `owsWeb.FetchRatingsList`, the `owsWeb` part refers to the name of the package that the stored procedure is in, and `FetchRatingsList` is the name of the procedure itself. For more information about packages, see your Oracle documentation.

Note

To see the Oracle code required to create the `owsWeb.FetchRatingsList` Procedures referred to in this template, see the section, "Creating Stored Procedures with Oracle," later in this chapter.

Stored Procedures That Take Parameters and Return Status Codes

So far you've been working with stored procedures that always work the same exact way each time they are called. The `PerformInventoryMaintenance` and `FetchRatingsList` procedures used in the first two examples doesn't accept any input from the calling application (in this case, a ColdFusion template) to do their work.

Most stored procedures, however, take *input parameters* or *output parameters* and also can return *status codes*. Here's what each of these terms means:

- **Input parameters**—Values you supply by name when you execute a stored procedure, similar to providing parameters to a ColdFusion tag. The stored procedure can then use the values of the input parameters internally, similar to variables. The stored procedure can take as many input parameters as needed for the task at hand. Similar to attributes for a ColdFusion tag, some input parameters are required, and others are optional.

  To supply an input parameter to a stored procedure, you use the `<CFPROCPARAM>` tag (see Table 32.3 in the next section).
- **Output parameters**—Values the procedure can pass back to ColdFusion, or whatever other program might call the stored procedure. Each output parameter has a name, and the stored procedure can return as many output parameters as necessary.

  To capture the value of an output parameter from a stored procedure, use the `<CFPROCPARAM>` tag with `TYPE="OUT"` (see Table 32.3).
- **Status codes**—Values returned by a stored procedure after it executes. Each stored procedure can return only one status code; the code is usually used to indicate whether the stored procedure was capable of successfully carrying out its work. With most database systems, the status code must be numeric, and defaults to `0`.

  To capture a procedure's status code, use `RETURNCODE="Yes"` in the `<CFSTOREDPROC>` tag (refer to Table 32.1, earlier in this chapter).

For instance, consider a new stored procedure called `InsertFilm` that enables the user to add a new film to Orange Whip Studio's `Films` table. Whoever created the stored procedure set it up to require five input parameters called `@MovieTitle`, `@PitchText`, `@AmountBudgeted`, `@RatingID`, and `@Summary`, which supply information about the new film. The procedure uses these values to insert a new record into the `Films` table.

The procedure also has one output parameter called `@NewFilmID`, which passes the ID number of the newly inserted film record back to ColdFusion (or whatever program is executing the stored procedure).

Note

Stored procedure parameter names start with an `@` sign with Microsoft SQLServer and Sybase databases. Other databases systems, such as Oracle, do not require the `@` sign.

In addition, the stored procedure has been designed to perform a few sanity checks before blindly recording the new film:

- **First, it ensures that the film doesn't already exist in the `Films` table**—If a film with the same title is already in the table, the procedure stops with a return value of `-1`.
- **It ensures that the rating specified by the `@RatingID` parameter is valid**—If the rating number does not exist in the `Ratings` table, the procedure stops with a return value of `-2`.

Provided that both of the tests are okay, the procedure inserts a new row in the Inventory table using the values of the supplied parameters. Finally, it sends a return value of 1 to indicate success.

Providing Parameters with <CFPROCPARAM>

ColdFusion makes supplying input and output parameters to a stored procedure easy, via the <CFPROCPARAM> tag. Table 32.3 shows the attributes supported by the <CFPROCPARAM> tag.

Table 32.3 <CFPROCPARAM> Tag Attributes

Attribute	Purpose
TYPE	In, Out, or InOut. Use TYPE="In" (the default) to supply an input parameter to the stored procedure. Use TYPE="Out" to capture the value of an output parameter. Use TYPE="InOut" if the parameter behaves as both an input and output parameter (such parameters are rather rare). This attribute is meant to be optional, but in the initial release version of ColdFusion 5, you always must provide it. If you do not, an error message appears. It is hoped that Macromedia will fix have fixed this behavior in a service release by the time you read this book.
VALUE	*For input parameters only.* The actual value you want to provide to the procedure.
NULL	*For input parameters only.* Yes or No. If NULL="Yes", the VALUE attribute is ignored; instead, a null value is supplied as the parameter's value. For more information about null values, see the section, "Working with NULL Values" in Chapter 31, "More About SQL and Queries."
DBVARNAME	*For input parameters only.* The name given to the parameter by the person who created the stored procedure. Unfortunately, this attribute is completely ignored unless you are using a native database driver. See "Ordinal Versus Named Parameter Positioning," later in this chapter.
VARIABLE	*For output parameters only.* A variable name you want ColdFusion to place the value of the output parameter into. For instance, if you provide VARIABLE="InsertedFilmID", you can output the value using #InsertedFilmID# after the <CFSTOREDPROC> tag executes.
CFSQLTYPE	Required. The parameter's data type. Unlike ColdFusion variables, stored procedure parameters are strongly typed, so you have to specify whether the parameter expects a numeric, string, date, or other type of value. The list of data types that you can supply to this attribute is the same as for the <CFQUERYPARAM> tag; see Table 31.5 in Chapter 31 for the list of data types. In addition, you can use CF_SQL_REFCURSOR for Oracle, in which case you must add a MAXROWS="-1" attribute to the <CFPROCPARAM> tag as well. See the "Using <CFPROCRESULT> with Oracle" section earlier in this chapter for details.
MAXLENGTH	Optional. The maximum length of the parameter's value.
SCALE	Optional. The number of significant decimal places for the parameter. Relevant only for numeric parameters.

`FilmEntry2.cfm`, shown in Listing 32.4, builds on the previous version of the data entry template from Listing 32.3. It creates a simple form a user can use to fill in the title, description, budget, rating, and summary for a new book. The form collects the information from the user and posts it back to the same template, which executes the stored procedure, feeding the user's entries to the procedure's input parameters.

Listing 32.4 `FilmEntry2.cfm`**—A Simple Form for Collecting Input Parameters**

```
<!--- Is the form being submitted? --->
<CFSET WasFormSubmitted = IsDefined("FORM.RatingID")>

<!--- Insert film into database when form is submitted --->
<CFIF WasFormSubmitted>
  <CFSTOREDPROC
    PROCEDURE="InsertFilm"
    DATASOURCE="owsServer"
    RETURNCODE="Yes">

    <!--- Provide form values to the procedure's input parameters --->
    <CFPROCPARAM
      TYPE="In"
      DBVARNAME="@MovieTitle"
      MAXLENGTH="50"
      CFSQLTYPE="CF_SQL_VARCHAR"
      VALUE="#Form.MovieTitle#">
    <CFPROCPARAM
      TYPE="In"
      DBVARNAME="@PitchText"
      MAXLENGTH="100"
      CFSQLTYPE="CF_SQL_VARCHAR"
      VALUE="#Form.PitchText#">
    <CFPROCPARAM
      TYPE="In"
      DBVARNAME="@AmountBudgeted"
      MAXLENGTH="100"
      CFSQLTYPE="CF_SQL_MONEY"
      VALUE="#Form.AmountBudgeted#"
      NULL="#YesNoFormat(FORM.AmountBudgeted EQ '')#">
    <CFPROCPARAM
      TYPE="In"
      DBVARNAME="@RatingID"
      MAXLENGTH="100"
      CFSQLTYPE="CF_SQL_INTEGER"
      VALUE="#Form.RatingID#">
    <CFPROCPARAM
      TYPE="In"
      DBVARNAME="@Summary"
      CFSQLTYPE="CF_SQL_LONGVARCHAR"
      VALUE="#Form.Summary#">

    <!--- Capture @NewFilmID output parameter --->
    <!--- Value will be available in CFML variable named #InsertedFilmID# --->
    <CFPROCPARAM
      TYPE="Out"
      DBVARNAME="@NewFilmID"
```

```
      CFSQLTYPE="CF_SQL_INTEGER"
      VARIABLE="InsertedFilmID">

  </CFSTOREDPROC>

  <!--- Remember the status code returned by the stored procedure --->
  <CFSET InsertStatus = CFSTOREDPROC.StatusCode>
</CFIF>

<!--- Get list of ratings from database --->
<CFSTOREDPROC PROCEDURE="FetchRatingsList" DATASOURCE="owsServer">
  <CFPROCRESULT NAME="GetRatings">
</CFSTOREDPROC>


<HTML>
<HEAD><TITLE>Film Entry Form</TITLE></HEAD>
<BODY>
<H2>Film Entry Form</H2>

<!--- Data entry form --->
<CFFORM ACTION="#CGI.SCRIPT_NAME#" METHOD="POST" PRESERVEDATA="Yes">

  <!--- Text entry field for film title --->
  <P><B>Title for New Film:</B><BR>
  <CFINPUT NAME="MovieTitle" SIZE="50" MAXLENGTH="50"
    REQUIRED="Yes" MESSAGE="Please don't leave the film's title blank."><BR>

  <!--- Text entry field for pitch text --->
  <P><B>Short Description / One-Liner:</B><BR>
  <CFINPUT NAME="PitchText" SIZE="50" MAXLENGTH="100"
    REQUIRED="Yes" MESSAGE="Please don't leave the one-liner blank."><BR>

  <!--- Text entry field for expense description --->
  <P><B>New Film Budget:</B><BR>
  <CFINPUT NAME="AmountBudgeted" SIZE="15"
    REQUIRED="No" MESSAGE="Only numbers may be provided for the film's budget."
    VALIDATE="float"> (leave blank if unknown)<BR>

  <!--- Drop-down list of ratings --->
  <P><B>Rating:</B><BR>
  <CFSELECT
    NAME="RatingID"
    QUERY="GetRatings"
    VALUE="RatingID"
    DISPLAY="Rating"/>

  <!--- Text areas for summary --->
  <P><B>Summary:</B><BR>
  <TEXTAREA NAME="Summary" COLS="40" ROWS="3" WRAP="soft"></TEXTAREA>

  <!--- Submit button for form --->
  <P><INPUT TYPE="Submit" VALUE="Submit New Film">
</CFFORM>


<!--- If we executed the stored procedure --->
<CFIF WasFormSubmitted>
```

Listing 32.4 Continued

```
  <!--- Display message based on status code reported by stored procedure --->
  <CFSWITCH EXPRESSION="#InsertStatus#">
    <!--- If the stored procedure returned a "success" status --->
    <CFCASE VALUE="1">
      <CFOUTPUT>
        <P>Film "#Form.MovieTitle#" was inserted as Film ID #InsertedFilmID#.<BR>
      </CFOUTPUT>
    </CFCASE>
    <!--- If the status code was -1 --->
    <CFCASE VALUE="-1">
      <CFOUTPUT>
        <P>Film "#Form.MovieTitle#" already exists in the database.<BR>
      </CFOUTPUT>
    </CFCASE>
    <!--- If the status code was -2 --->
    <CFCASE VALUE="-2">
      <P>An invalid rating was provided.<BR>
    </CFCASE>
    <!--- If any other status code was returned --->
    <CFDEFAULTCASE>
      <P>The procedure returned an unknown status code.<BR>
    </CFDEFAULTCASE>
  </CFSWITCH>
</CFIF>

</BODY>
</HTML>
```

When the form is submitted, the `<CFIF>` block at the top of the template is executed, which executes the `InsertFilm` stored procedure via the `<CFSTOREDPROC>` tag. Within the `<CFSTOREDPROC>` tag, six `<CFPROCPARAM>` tags are used. The first five provide values for the `@MovieTitle`, `@PitchText`, and other input parameters. The last `<CFPROCPARAM>` captures the value of the output parameter called `@NewFilmID`.

Note that the `CFSQLTYPE` for each of the parameters has been set to the correct value for the type of information being passed. Also, the `NULL` attribute is used for the fifth `<CFPROCPARAM>`, so that the film's budget will be recorded as a null value if the user leaves the budget blank on the form. After the procedure executes, the status code reported by the procedure is placed into the `InsertStatus` variable.

At the bottom of the template, a `<CFSWITCH>` block is used to output a message to the user depending on the status code reported by the stored procedure. If the procedure returns a value of `1`, a success message is displayed, along with the new film's `FilmID` number (which was captured by the first `<CFPROCPARAM>` tag at the top of the template), as shown in Figure 32.5. If the procedure returns some other status code, it is assumed that something went wrong, so the status code is shown to the user.

Note

In an actual application, you would probably do more than just display the new FilmID. For instance, you might provide some type of Click Here link to a screen on which the user could do further data entry about the film. The point is that a stored procedure can give back whatever information its creator desires as output parameters, and you can use that information in just about any way you please.

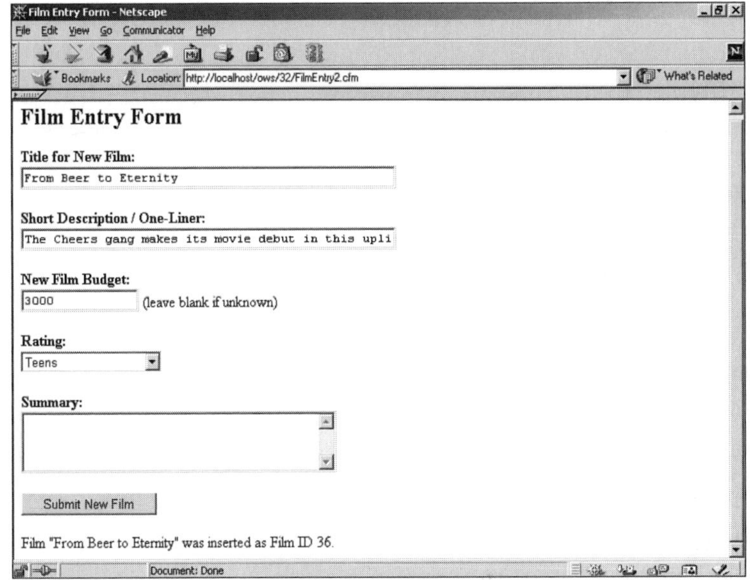

Figure 32.5 Parameters can be passed in and out of stored procedures.

Note

The template in Listing 32.4 uses ColdFusion's <CFSWITCH>, <CFCASE>, and <CFDEFAULTCASE> tags to analyze the return code from the stored procedure. Making decisions based on return codes is a perfect situation to use these case-switching tags because a single expression (the return code) exists that will have one of several predetermined values. See Appendix A for more information about <CFSWITCH> and related tags.

Tip

If you are using ColdFusion Studio to edit your templates, you can use the Tag Inspector or the <CFPROCPARAM> Tag Editor to help you add <CFPROCPARAM> tags to your code (see Figure 32.6).

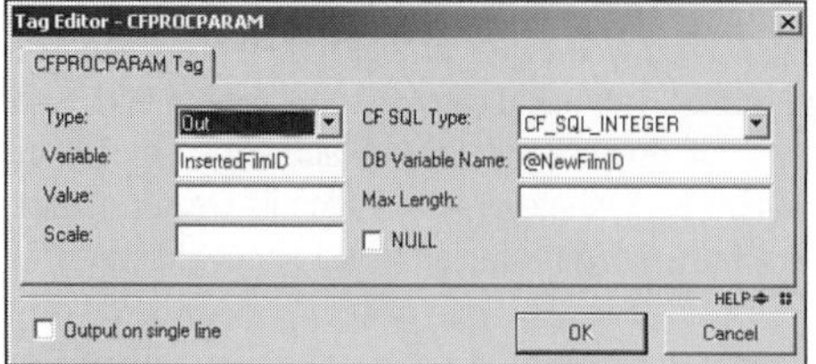

Figure 32.6
Using ColdFusion Studio as your editor makes coding <CFPROCPARAM> tags easy.

ORDINAL VERSUS NAMED PARAMETER POSITIONING

As you saw in Table 32.3 and Listing 32.4, the <CFPROCPARAM> tag accepts an attribute called DBVARNAME, which allows you to specify the name of each parameter you pass to a stored procedure. Atlhough we recommend that you always include this attribute for clarity, you can choose to omit the DBVARNAME as long as you provide the parameters in the same order in which they appear in the actual stored procedure code. In fact, some stored procedures are created without giving the parameters names; if so, any DBVARNAME attributes that you provide will be ignored, and the order of the <CFPROCPARAM> tags will be significant.

Also, ColdFusion does not pass <CFSTOREDPROC> parameters by name for ODBC or OLE-DB data sources, so the DBVARNAME you provide will always be ignored, and the order of the <CFPROCPARAM> tags will always be significant. Unfortunately, this means that if the order of the parameters changes on the database server, your ColdFusion templates will likely need to be edited to match. It is hoped that a future version of ColdFusion will eliminate this limitation. Until then, you might want to consider using <CFQUERY> instead of <CFSTOREDPROC> whenever possible (see the section, "Calling Procedures with <CFQUERY> Instead of <CFSTOREDPROC>," later in this chapter).

Note that because Microsoft SQLServer is always accessed via a ODBC or OLE-DB connection, the inferior ordinal positioning method is always used.

PARAMETER DATA TYPES

As you saw in Listing 32.4, when you provide parameters to a stored procedure with the <CFPROCPARAM> tag, you must specify the data type of the parameter, as defined by whomever created the procedure. ColdFusion requires that you provide the data type for each parameter you refer to in your templates, so that it does not have to determine the data type itself on-the-fly each time the template runs. That would require a number of extra steps for ColdFusion, which in turn would slow your application.

It's important to specify the correct data type for each parameter. If you use the wrong data type, you might run into problems. The data type you provide for CFSQLTYPE in a <CFPROCPARAM> tag must be one of ColdFusion's SQL data types, as listed in Table 31.5 in Chapter 31. These data types are based on the data types defined by the ODBC standard—one of them will map to each of the database-specific data types used when your stored procedure was created.

For instance, if you have a stored procedure sitting on a Microsoft SQL Server that takes a parameter of SQL Server data type `int`, you should specify the `CF_SQL_INTEGER` data type in the corresponding `<CFPROCPARAM>` tag.

WRAPPING A STORED PROCEDURE CALL IN A CUSTOM TAG

If you have a stored procedure that you plan to use often in your ColdFusion applications, you may want to consider creating a CFML Custom Tag that wraps all the needed `<CFSTOREDPROC>` and related code into an easier-to-use module. For instance, you might create a custom tag called `<CF_spInsertFilm>` that calls the `InsertFilm` stored procedure.

The `spInsertFilm.cfm` template included on the CD-ROM for this chapter creates such a custom tag, which could be used like this:

```
<!--- Insert film via Stored Procedure (via custom tag) --->
<CF_spInsertFilm
  MovieTitle="#FORM.MovieTitle#"
  PitchText="#FORM.PitchText#"
  RatingID="#FORM.RatingID#"
  AmountBudgeted="#FORM.AmountBudgeted#"
  Summary="#FORM.Summary#"
  ReturnFilmID="InsertedFilmID"
  ReturnStatusCode="InsertStatus">
```


The FilmEntry3.cfm template (also on the CD-ROM) is a revision of Listing 32.4. Instead of calling the `<CFSTOREDPROC>` tag directly, the template simply calls the custom tag when the form is submitted. For more information about how to create and use CFML custom tags, see Chapter 22.

MULTIPLE RECORDSETS ARE FULLY SUPPORTED

Some stored procedures return more than one recordset. For instance, consider a stored procedure called `FetchFilmInfo`. You are told that the procedure accepts one input parameter called `@FilmID`, and the procedure responds by returning five recordsets of information related to the specified film. The first recordset contains information about the film record itself; the second returns related records from the `Expenses` table; the third returns related records from the `Actors` table; the fourth returns related records from `Directors`; and the fifth returns information from the `Merchandise` table.

As you can see in Listing 32.5, the key to receiving more than one recordset from a stored procedure is to include one `<CFPROCRESULT>` tag for each recordset, specifying `RESULTSET="1"` for the first recordset, `RESULTSET="2"` for the second, and so on.

LISTING 32.5 `ShowFilmExpenses.cfm`—DEALING WITH MULTIPLE RECORDSETS FROM A SINGLE STORED PROCEDURE

```
<!--- Execute stored procedure to fetch film information --->
<CFSTOREDPROC PROCEDURE="FetchFilmInfo" DATASOURCE="owsServer">
  <!--- Provide the FilmID parameter --->
  <CFPROCPARAM
    TYPE="In"
    DBVARNAME="@FilmID"
```

LISTING 32.5 CONTINUED

```
    CFSQLTYPE="CF_SQL_INTEGER"
    VALUE="#URL.FilmID#">

  <!--- Film information --->
  <CFPROCRESULT NAME="GetFilm" RESULTSET="1">
  <!--- Expense information --->
  <CFPROCRESULT NAME="GetExpenses" RESULTSET="2">
  <!--- Actor information --->
  <CFPROCRESULT NAME="GetActors" RESULTSET="3">
  <!--- Director information --->
  <CFPROCRESULT NAME="GetDirectors" RESULTSET="4">
  <!--- Merchandise information --->
  <CFPROCRESULT NAME="GetMerch" RESULTSET="5">
</CFSTOREDPROC>

<!--- Get subtotals from the recordsets returned by stored procedure --->
<CFSET ExpenseSum  = ArraySum(ListToArray(ValueList(GetExpenses.ExpenseAmount)))>
<CFSET ActorSum    = ArraySum(ListToArray(ValueList(GetActors.Salary)))>
<CFSET DirectorSum = ArraySum(ListToArray(ValueList(GetDirectors.Salary)))>
<CFSET MerchSum    = ArraySum(ListToArray(ValueList(GetMerch.TotalSales)))>

<!--- Add up all expenses --->
<CFSET TotalExpenses = ExpenseSum + ActorSum + DirectorSum - MerchSum>
<!--- Determine how much money is left in the budget --->
<CFSET LeftInBudget = GetFilm.AmountBudgeted - TotalExpenses>

<HTML>
<HEAD><TITLE>Film Expenses</TITLE></HEAD>
<BODY>

<!--- Company logo and page title --->
<IMG SRC="../images/logo_b.gif" WIDTH="73" HEIGHT="73" ALIGN="absmiddle">
<FONT SIZE="+2"><B>Film Expenses</B></FONT><BR CLEAR="all">

<CFOUTPUT>
  <!--- Show film title--->
  <P><B>Film:</B> #GetFilm.MovieTitle#<BR>

  <!--- Film budget, expense total, and amount left in budget --->
  <P><B>Budget:</B> #LSCurrencyFormat(GetFilm.AmountBudgeted)#<BR>
  <B>Expenses:</B> #LSCurrencyFormat(TotalExpenses)#<BR>
  <B>Currently:</B> #LSCurrencyFormat(LeftInBudget)#
  <!--- Are we currently over or under budget? --->
  #IIF(LeftInBudget LT 0, "'over budget'", "'under budget'")#<BR>

  <!--- Output information about actors --->
  <P><B>Actors:</B>
  <CFLOOP QUERY="GetActors">
    <LI>#NameFirst# #NameLast# (Salary: #LSCurrencyFormat(Salary)#)
  </CFLOOP>

  <!--- Output information about directors --->
  <P><B>Directors:</B>
  <CFLOOP QUERY="GetDirectors">
    <LI>#FirstName# #LastName# (Salary: #LSCurrencyFormat(Salary)#)
  </CFLOOP>
```

```
  <!--- Output information about expenses --->
  <P><B>Other Expenses:</B>
  <CFLOOP QUERY="GetExpenses">
    <LI>#Description# (#LSCurrencyFormat(ExpenseAmount)#)
  </CFLOOP>

  <!--- Output information about merchandise --->
  <P><B>Income from merchandise:</B>
  <CFLOOP QUERY="GetMerch">
    <LI>#MerchName# (Sales: #LSCurrencyFormat(TotalSales)#)
  </CFLOOP>
</CFOUTPUT>

</BODY>
</HTML>
```

After the `<CFSTOREDPROC>` tag, the ColdFusion template is free to refer to the five recordsets named in the `<CFPROCRESULT>` tags just as if they were the results of five separate `<CFQUERY>`-type queries. Because only one database transaction needed to take place, though, you can expect performance to be faster using the single stored procedure. Figure 32.7 shows the results if you visit this listing with `FilmID=1` passed in the URL.

Figure 32.7 ColdFusion makes capturing multiple recordsets from a single stored procedure easy.

Tip

Your template doesn't have to handle or receive all the recordsets a stored procedure spits out. For instance, if you weren't interested in the second recordset from the `FetchFilmInfo` procedure, you could simply leave out the second `<CFPROCRESULT>` tag. Neither ColdFusion nor your database server will mind.

If you are using Oracle, just be sure to add a <CFPROCPARAM> tag of TYPE="REFCURSOR" before adding each <CFPROCRESULT> tag. As long as you are providing the names of each parameter via <CFPROCPARAM>'s DBVARNAME attribute, you can provide the <CFPROCPARAM> tags in whatever order you want. However, the <CFPROCPARAM> tags must appear in the same order as the <CFPROCRESULT> tags.

So, if you had a procedure called owsWeb.FetchFilmInfo on your Oracle server that exposed five reference cursors (such as the five recordsets returned by the SQLServer used in the previous listing), you could simply add a few <CFPROCPARAM> lines to Listing 32.5, as shown in Listing 32.6.

Listing 32.6 ShowFilmExpensesOracle.cfm—**Dealing with Multiple Reference Cursors from an Oracle Stored Procedure**

```
<!--- Execute stored procedure to fetch film information --->
<CFSTOREDPROC PROCEDURE="owsWeb.FetchFilmInfo" DATASOURCE="owsOra">
  <!--- Provide the FilmID parameter --->
  <CFPROCPARAM
    TYPE="In"
    DBVARNAME="pFilmID"
    CFSQLTYPE="CF_SQL_INTEGER"
    VALUE="#URL.FilmID#">

  <!--- Output parameters return reference cursor pointers --->
  <CFPROCPARAM TYPE="OUT" CFSQLTYPE="CF_SQL_REFCURSOR"
    DBVARNAME="pFilmsCur" VARIABLE="IgnoreThis" MAXROWS="-1">
  <CFPROCPARAM TYPE="OUT" CFSQLTYPE="CF_SQL_REFCURSOR"
    DBVARNAME="pExpesnesCur" VARIABLE="IgnoreThis" MAXROWS="-1">
  <CFPROCPARAM TYPE="OUT" CFSQLTYPE="CF_SQL_REFCURSOR"
    DBVARNAME="pActorsCur" VARIABLE="IgnoreThis" MAXROWS="-1">
  <CFPROCPARAM TYPE="OUT" CFSQLTYPE="CF_SQL_REFCURSOR"
    DBVARNAME="pDirectorsCur" VARIABLE="IgnoreThis" MAXROWS="-1">
  <CFPROCPARAM TYPE="OUT" CFSQLTYPE="CF_SQL_REFCURSOR"
    DBVARNAME="pMerchCur" VARIABLE="IgnoreThis" MAXROWS="-1">

  <!--- Film information --->
  <CFPROCRESULT NAME="GetFilm" RESULTSET="1">
  <!--- Expense information --->
  <CFPROCRESULT NAME="GetExpenses" RESULTSET="2">
  <!--- Actor information --->
  <CFPROCRESULT NAME="GetActors" RESULTSET="3">
  <!--- Director information --->
  <CFPROCRESULT NAME="GetDirectors" RESULTSET="4">
  <!--- Director information --->
  <CFPROCRESULT NAME="GetMerch" RESULTSET="5">
</CFSTOREDPROC>

<!--- Get subtotals from the recordsets returned by stored procedure --->
<CFSET ExpenseSum  = ArraySum(ListToArray(ValueList(GetExpenses.ExpenseAmount)))>
<CFSET ActorSum    = ArraySum(ListToArray(ValueList(GetActors.Salary)))>
<CFSET DirectorSum = ArraySum(ListToArray(ValueList(GetDirectors.Salary)))>
<CFSET MerchSum    = ArraySum(ListToArray(ValueList(GetMerch.TotalSales)))>

<!--- Add up all expenses --->
<CFSET TotalExpenses = ExpenseSum + ActorSum + DirectorSum - MerchSum>
```

```
<!--- Determine how much money is left in the budget --->
<CFSET LeftInBudget = GetFilm.AmountBudgeted - TotalExpenses>

<HTML>
<HEAD><TITLE>Film Expenses</TITLE></HEAD>
<BODY>

<!--- Company logo and page title --->
<IMG SRC="../images/logo_b.gif" WIDTH="73" HEIGHT="73" ALIGN="absmiddle">
<FONT SIZE="+2"><B>Film Expenses</B></FONT><BR CLEAR="all">

<CFOUTPUT>
  <!--- Show film title--->
  <P><B>Film:</B> #GetFilm.MovieTitle#<BR>

  <!--- Film budget, expense total, and amount left in budget --->
  <P><B>Budget:</B> #LSCurrencyFormat(GetFilm.AmountBudgeted)#<BR>
  <B>Expenses:</B> #LSCurrencyFormat(TotalExpenses)#<BR>
  <B>Currently:</B> #LSCurrencyFormat(LeftInBudget)#
  <!--- Are we currently over or under budget? --->
  #IIF(LeftInBudget LT 0, "'over budget'", "'under budget'")#<BR>

  <!--- Output information about actors --->
  <P><B>Actors:</B>
  <CFLOOP QUERY="GetActors">
    <LI>#NameFirst# #NameLast# (Salary: #LSCurrencyFormat(Salary)#)
  </CFLOOP>

  <!--- Output information about directors --->
  <P><B>Directors:</B>
  <CFLOOP QUERY="GetDirectors">
    <LI>#FirstName# #LastName# (Salary: #LSCurrencyFormat(Salary)#)
  </CFLOOP>

  <!--- Output information about expenses --->
  <P><B>Other Expenses:</B>
  <CFLOOP QUERY="GetExpenses">
    <LI>#Description# (#LSCurrencyFormat(ExpenseAmount)#)
  </CFLOOP>

  <!--- Output information about merchandise --->
  <P><B>Income from merchandise:</B>
  <CFLOOP QUERY="GetMerch">
    <LI>#MerchName# (Sales: #LSCurrencyFormat(TotalSales)#)
  </CFLOOP>
</CFOUTPUT>

</BODY>
</HTML>
```


Note

This code assumes that the procedure parameter named `pFilmsCur` is a reference cursor that exposes records from the `Films` table, `pExpensesCur` exposes data from the `Expenses` table, and so on.

CALLING PROCEDURES WITH <CFQUERY> INSTEAD OF <CFSTOREDPROC>

The <CFSTOREDPROC> and related tags were added back in ColdFusion 4. Before that, the only way to call a stored procedure from a ColdFusion template was to use special procedure-calling syntax in a normal CFQUERY tag, where you would normally provide a SQL statement. You can still call stored procedures this way, and you actually mightprefer to do so in some situations.

When you execute a stored procedure with <CFQUERY>, ColdFusion treats the response from the database server similar to how it would treat the response from an ordinary SELECT query. In fact, ColdFusion doesn't even realize that it's executing a stored procedure exactly; it's just passing on what it assumes to be a valid SQL statement and hopes to get some rows of table-style data in return.

The fact that ColdFusion is treating the stored procedure in the same way it treats a <SELECT> statement brings with it several important limitations:

- ColdFusion cannot directly access the return code generated by the stored procedure.
- ColdFusion cannot directly access any output parameters generated by the stored procedure.
- If the stored procedure returns more than one recordset, only one of the recordsets will be captured by ColdFusion and available for your use in your templates. Details about this limitation might vary between types of database servers. With some database servers, only the first recordset will be available for your use; with others, only the last will be available. The point is that stored procedures that return multiple recordsets are not fully supported when using CFQUERY.

However, using <CFQUERY> has some important advantages over <CFSTOREDPROC>, as well:

- **A recordset returned by a stored procedure via <CFQUERY> can be cached using the CACHEDWITHIN attribute**—Recordsets captured via <CFSTOREDPROC> and <CFPROCRESULT> can't be cached in ColdFusion 5.
- **With <CFQUERY>, if you refer to a stored procedure's parameters by name, they will be passed to the server properly when using an ODBC connection**—With <CFSTOREDPROC>, parameters are passed by position rather than by name, even if you supply a DBVARNAME attribute to the <CFPROCPARAM> tag.

USING ODBC'S CALL COMMAND

If you are using an ODBC or OLE-DB data source to connect to your database server, you can use the CALL command defined by the ODBC standard to execute a stored procedure. Listing 32.7 demonstrates how the FetchRatingsList stored procedure can be called using this method.

Note

This method of calling stored procedures can be used only with ODBC and OLE-DB data sources. It can't be used with ColdFusion's native driver support.

Note that this template is almost exactly the same as the `FilmEntry1.cfm` template shown in Listing 32.2. The only change is that `<CFQUERY>` is being used instead of `<CFSTOREDPROC>`. When this template is brought up in a browser, it should display its results exactly the same way.

Listing 32.7 `FilmEntry1a.cfm`—**Calling a Stored Procedure Using** `CALL` **in a** `<CFQUERY>`

```
<!--- Get list of ratings from database --->
<CFQUERY NAME="GetRatings" DATASOURCE="owsServer">
  { CALL FetchRatingsList }
</CFQUERY>

<HTML>
<HEAD><TITLE>Film Entry Form</TITLE></HEAD>
<BODY>
<H2>Film Entry Form</H2>

<!--- Data entry form --->
<CFFORM ACTION="#CGI.SCRIPT_NAME#" METHOD="POST" PRESERVEDATA="Yes">

  <!--- Text entry field for film title --->
  <P><B>Title for New Film:</B><BR>
  <CFINPUT NAME="MovieTitle" SIZE="50" MAXLENGTH="50"
    REQUIRED="Yes" MESSAGE="Please don't leave the film's title blank."><BR>

  <!--- Text entry field for pitch text --->
  <P><B>Short Description / One-Liner:</B><BR>
  <CFINPUT NAME="PitchText" SIZE="50" MAXLENGTH="100"
    REQUIRED="Yes" MESSAGE="Please don't leave the one-liner blank."><BR>

  <!--- Text entry field for expense description --->
  <P><B>New Film Budget:</B><BR>
  <CFINPUT NAME="AmountBudgeted" SIZE="15"
    REQUIRED="Yes" MESSAGE="Please enter a valid number for the film's budget."
    VALIDATE="float"><BR>

  <!--- Drop-down list of ratings --->
  <P><B>Rating:</B><BR>
  <CFSELECT
    NAME="RatingID"
    QUERY="GetRatings"
    VALUE="RatingID"
    DISPLAY="Rating"/>

  <!--- Text areas for summary --->
  <P><B>Summary:</B><BR>
  <TEXTAREA NAME="Summary" COLS="40" ROWS="3" WRAP="soft"></TEXTAREA>

  <!--- Submit button for form --->
  <P><INPUT TYPE="Submit" VALUE="Submit New Film">
```

Listing 32.7 Continued

```
</CFFORM>


</BODY>
</HTML>
```

As you can see in Listing 32.7, the syntax for using the `CALL` command is simply the word `CALL` and then the procedure name. The entire command is surrounded by a set of curly braces, which indicate that the command must be interpreted by ODBC before it gets sent on to the database server.

Input parameters can be supplied in parentheses after the procedure name, separated by commas. If no input parameters exist for the procedure, leave out the parentheses. Because you are not referring to them by name, input parameters must be supplied in the proper order (as defined by whomever wrote the stored procedure). If an input parameter is of a character type (such as `char`, `varchar`, or `text`), enclose the parameter's value in single quotation marks. For instance, to call the `InsertFilm` stored procedure from Listing 32.4, you could replace the `<CFSTOREDPROC>` block in that template with the following snippet (see `FilmEntry2a.cfm` on the CD-ROM to see this snippet in a complete template):

```
<CFQUERY DATASOURCE="owsServer">
  { CALL InsertFilm (
    '#Form.MovieTitle#',
    '#Form.PitchText#',
     #Form.AmountBudgeted#,
     #Form.RatingID#,
    '#Form.Summary#') }
</CFQUERY>
```

Remember, however, that ColdFusion is not aware of the return code or output parameters returned by the procedure, so the code in the rest of the listing would fail. You would need to have the stored procedure rewritten so that the information provided by the return code or output parameters instead get returned as a recordset.

Using Your Database's Native Syntax

In addition to using the `CALL` command, most database drivers also enable you to use whatever native syntax you would use normally with that database system. All the same limitations (regarding return codes, output parameters, and so on) listed at the beginning of this section apply.

The native syntax to use varies according to the database server you're using. You need to consult your database server documentation for the details. Just as an example, if you were using Microsoft SQL Server, you could replace the `<CFQUERY>` shown in Listing 32.7 with the following code; the results would be the same:

```
<CFQUERY NAME="GetRatings" DATASOURCE="owsServer">
   EXEC FetchRatingsList
</CFQUERY>
```

One advantage of using the native syntax over the CALL syntax is that you may be able to refer to the input parameters by name, which leads to cleaner and more readable code. So, if you were using Microsoft SQL Server, the InsertFilm procedure could be called with the following. Consult your database server documentation for specific details:

```
<CFQUERY DATASOURCE="owsServer">
  EXEC InsertFilm
    @MovieTitle = '#Form.MovieTitle#',
    @PitchText = '#Form.PitchText#',
    @AmountBudgeted = #Form.AmountBudgeted#,
    @RatingID = #Form.RatingID#,
    @Summary = '#Form.Summary#'
</CFQUERY>
```

Depending on your database server, you might be able to add more code to the <CFQUERY> tag to be able to capture the status code and output parameters from the stored procedure. Again, just as an example, if you were using Microsoft SQL Server, you would be able to use something similar to the following:

```
<CFQUERY DATASOURCE="owsServer" NAME="ExecProc">
  -- Declare T-SQL variables to hold values returned by stored procedure
  DECLARE @StatusCode INT, @NewFilmID INT
  -- Execute the stored procedure, assigning values to T-SQL variables
  EXEC @StatusCode = InsertFilm
    @MovieTitle = '#Form.MovieTitle#',
    @PitchText = '#Form.PitchText#',
    @AmountBudgeted = #Form.AmountBudgeted#,
    @RatingID = #Form.RatingID#,
    @Summary = '#Form.Summary#',
    @NewFilmID = @NewFilmID OUTPUT
  -- Select the T-SQL variables as a one-row recordset
  SELECT @StatusCode AS StatusCode, @NewFilmID AS NewFilmID
</CFQUERY>
```

You then could refer to ExecProc.StatusCode and ExecProc.NewFilmID in your CFML template code. The FilmEntry2b.cfm template on the CD-ROM for this chapter is a revised version of Listing 32.4 that uses this <CFQUERY> snippet instead of <CFSTOREDPROC> to execute the InsertFilm stored procedure.

Note

You will need to consult your database documentation for more information about how to use this type of syntax. In general, it is really best to use <CFSTOREDPROC> instead of <CFQUERY> if the stored procedure you want to use generates important status codes or output parameters.

CREATING STORED PROCEDURES

Now that you've seen how to use stored procedures in your ColdFusion templates, you are probably curious about how you can create some stored procedures of your own. We can't cover everything about creating stored procedures in this book, but you learn enough here to hit the ground running.

Before you begin, a short note: The examples you see in this section—and the procedure-creating code you're likely to use as you write your own stored procedures—are not standard SQL. Stored procedures are implemented slightly differently by different database servers, and you often will want to use code within the stored procedures that take advantage of various extensions proprietary to the database system you are using. In other words, when you get to the point of writing your own stored procedures, you likely will be tying yourself to the database system you're using to some extent. The procedures probably will not be portable to other database systems (like ordinary SQL generally is) without reworking the procedures to some extent.

CREATING STORED PROCEDURES WITH MICROSOFT SQL SERVER

To create a stored procedure with Microsoft SQL Server, you use the SQL Server Enterprise Manager tool, which helps you submit a `CREATE PROCEDURE` statement to the SQL Server itself. After it's created, the procedure is available to whoever has appropriate permissions.

Note

This chapter assumes that you are using SQLServer 7.0. If you are using a different version (such as SQLServer 6.5 or SQLServer 2000), the specific steps might be slightly different, but the basic concepts will be the same.

Note

To follow along with this chapter, you need to have a database on your SQL Server machine that has the same tables and columns as the A2Z sample database. With SQL Server 7.0, select Tools, Wizards from the Enterprise Manager's menu to start the DTS Import Wizard. In just a few steps, the wizard can import the Access version of the database (the `a2z.mdb` file), with all tables, columns, and data intact.

CREATING YOUR FIRST STORED PROCEDURE

As a simple example, you can create the `FetchRatingsList` stored procedure that was used in Listing 32.2. This procedure is a good one to start with because it's very simple and does not use any input or output parameters.

To create the stored procedure, follow these simple steps:

1. Start the SQL Server Enterprise Manager. Click your server, expand the databases tree, and click your database.
2. Click the Stored Procedures folder; right-click to select New Stored Procedure from the pop-up menu, as shown in Figure 32.8.

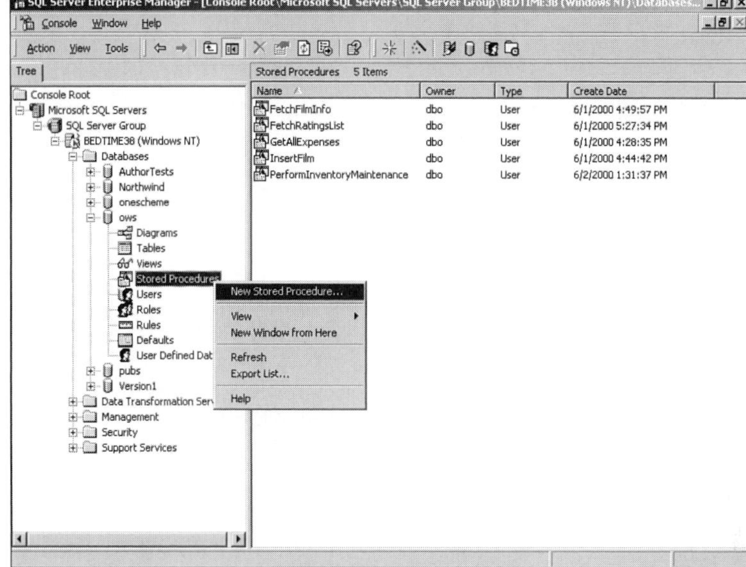

Figure 32.8
Use the Enterprise Manager to create a new stored procedure.

3. Type the actual code for the procedure—provided in Listing 32.8—in the window that appears, as shown in Figure 32.9.

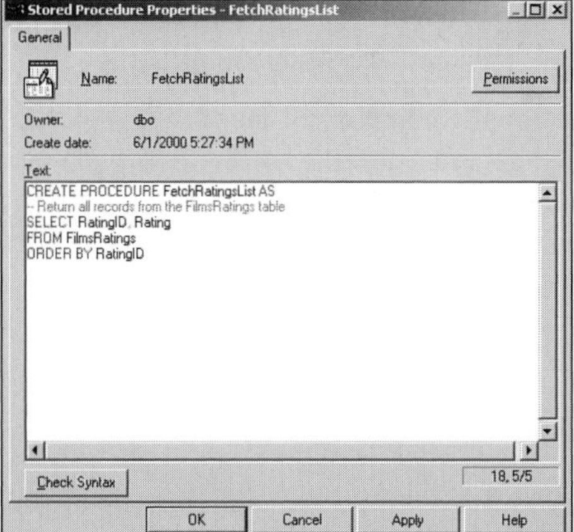

Figure 32.9
Enter the procedure's code in the New Stored Procedure window.

4. Click the OK button to create the stored procedure.

Listing 32.8 shows the actual code for the `FetchRatingsList` stored procedure. This is the code you should enter after selecting New Procedure from the pop-up menu (refer to Figure 32.12). As you can see, it's fairly simple. First, a `CREATE PROCEDURE` statement is used to provide a name for the new stored procedure, followed by the `AS` keyword. Everything after AS is the code for the stored procedure itself—the actual SQL statements you want to execute each time the procedure is called.

LISTING 32.8 THE FetchRatingsList STORED PROCEDURE

```
CREATE PROCEDURE FetchRatingsList AS
-- Return all records from the FilmsRatings table
SELECT RatingID, Rating
FROM FilmsRatings
ORDER BY RatingID
```

Note

You also can execute the CREATE PROCEDURE statements shown in this section with the Query Analyzer (called iSQL/w in SQL Server 6.5 and earlier) or the isql.exe command-line utility that ships with SQL Server. You could even execute these CREATE PROCEDURE statements in a tag within a ColdFusion template.

This procedure's actual body is simple. It just uses a simple SELECT statement to return all the records from the FilmsRatings table. The records can be captured and accessed in your ColdFusion code via the <CFSTOREDPROC> tag (refer to Listing 32.2) or <CFQUERY> tag (refer to Listing 32.7).

DEFINING STATUS CODES, INPUT PARAMETERS, AND OUTPUT PARAMETERS

As demonstrated in Listing 32.4, stored procedures can accept input parameters, return values via output parameters, and return a status code.

With SQL Server, you define input parameters in the CREATE PROCEDURE part of the procedure code, between the procedure name and the AS keyword. Each input parameter is given a name, which must begin with the @ symbol and can't contain any spaces or other unusual characters. The SQL Server data type for each parameter is provided after the parameter's name. If more than one parameter exists, separate them with commas.

If you want the parameter to be optional, type an = sign after the data type and then type the default value. To create an output parameter, provide an initial value for the parameter (usually NULL is most appropriate) using the = sign and then type the word **OUTPUT**.

For instance, Listing 32.9 shows the code to create the InsertFilm stored procedure used in Listing 32.4. As you can see, each of the parameters provided in <CFPROCPARAM> tags in that template matches the corresponding parameters in the CREATE PROCEDURE statement here. Then, in the SQL statements that follow, the procedure is free to refer to the parameters by name—similar to how you refer to ColdFusion variables in your CFML templates. The values of the parameters are automatically plugged in with the appropriate values each time the procedure is actually used.

Listing 32.9 The `InsertFilm` Procedure Accepts Input Parameters

```
CREATE PROCEDURE InsertFilm
  @MovieTitle varchar(100),
  @PitchText varchar(100),
  @AmountBudgeted money,
  @RatingID int,
  @Summary text,
  @NewFilmID int = null OUTPUT
AS

-- Make sure there isn't a film by this name in the database already
IF EXISTS (SELECT * FROM Films WHERE MovieTitle = @MovieTitle)
  -- If film exists already, return status of -1 to ColdFusion (or other program)
  RETURN -1

-- Make sure the specified rating is valid
ELSE IF NOT EXISTS (SELECT * FROM FilmsRatings WHERE RatingID = @RatingID)
  -- If specified rating code does not exist, return status of -2
  RETURN -2

-- Assuming that the film is not i nthe database already
ELSE
  BEGIN
    -- Insert the new film into the Films table
    INSERT INTO Films (MovieTitle, PitchText, AmountBudgeted, RatingID, Summary)
    VALUES (@MovieTitle, @PitchText, @AmountBudgeted, @RatingID, @Summary)

    -- Set output parameter called @NewFilmID to the ID of the just-inserted film
    SET @NewFilmID = @@IDENTITY

    -- Return a status of 1 to ColdFusion (or other program) to indicate success
    RETURN 1
  END
```


Note that the `InsertFilm` procedure uses SQL Server's `IF` keyword to do some conditional processing as the template executes. Similar conceptually to the `CFIF` tag in CFML, the `IF` keyword as used here enables you to execute certain chunks of SQL code depending on conditions you define. You'll find `IF` extremely helpful when you need to write a stored procedure that must perform some kind of sanity check before committing changes to the database. For instance, the first `IF` line in Listing 32.11 halts processing and sends a return code of `-1` to the calling application if the `SELECT` subquery inside the parentheses returns any rows.

Note also that the `@NewFilmID` output parameter is set to the value of SQL Server's built-in `@@IDENTITY` variable, which always contains the newly generated identity value for the last `INSERT` to a table that contained an identity-type column. (Identity columns are similar to AutoNumber columns in Access tables.) Thus, the parameter gets set to the `FilmID` that was just assigned to the row just inserted into the `Films` table.

Note

IF is not part of SQL as most people would define it, but rather it is part of SQL Server's extensions to SQL, which Microsoft calls Transact-SQL. Transact-SQL provides many other control-of-flow keywords you might want to become familiar with, such as BEGIN, END, ELSE, DECLARE, and WHILE. Sybase also supports most of the same Transact-SQL extensions to standard SQL. Consult your database documentation about these keywords.

RETURNING MULTIPLE RECORDSETS TO COLDFUSION

As you saw in Listing 32.5, stored procedures can return multiple recordsets to ColdFusion (or whatever program is calling the procedures). Again, think of a *recordset* as a set of rows and columns generated by a SELECT statement that outputs data from a database table.

To return recordsets, simply use the appropriate SELECT statements as you would normally. Whatever would be returned by the SELECT statement outside a stored procedure is what will be returned to the calling application (in this case, your ColdFusion template) as a recordset each time the procedure executes.

Your stored procedure can output as many recordsets as it pleases. The calling ColdFusion template need only provide a <CFPROCRESULT> tag for each recordset that it wants to be aware of after the procedure runs. The second SELECT statement in the procedure that outputs rows can be captured by using RECORDSET="2" in the <CFPROCRESULT> tag, and so on.

For instance, Listing 32.10 provides the code to create the FetchFilmInfo procedure that is used by the ShowFilmExpenses.cfm template from Listing 32.5. As you can see, each <CFPROCRESULT> tag used in that template matches with a corresponding SELECT statement in the procedure code itself.

LISTING 32.10 RETURNING MULTIPLE RECORDSETS FROM A STORED PROCEDURE

```
CREATE PROCEDURE FetchFilmInfo
  @FilmID int
AS

-- Recommended setting; see SET in your SQLServer documentation
SET NOCOUNT ON

-- Return information about the film itself
SELECT * FROM Films
WHERE FilmID = @FilmID

-- Return all expense records related to the film
SELECT * FROM Expenses
WHERE FilmID = @FilmID
ORDER BY ExpenseDate DESC

-- Return all actor records related to the film
SELECT a.ActorID, a.NameFirst, a.NameLast, fa.Salary
FROM Actors a, FilmsActors fa
WHERE a.ActorID = fa.ActorID
```

```
AND fa.FilmID = @FilmID
ORDER BY NameFirst, NameLast

-- Return all director records related to the film
SELECT d.DirectorID, d.FirstName, d.LastName, fd.Salary
FROM Directors d, FilmsDirectors fd
WHERE d.DirectorID = fd.DirectorID
AND fd.FilmID = @FilmID
ORDER BY LastName, FirstName

-- Return all merchandise records related to the film
SELECT m.MerchID, m.MerchName, SUM(ItemPrice) AS TotalSales
FROM Merchandise m, MerchandiseOrdersItems oi
WHERE m.MerchID = oi.ItemID
AND m.FilmID = @FilmID
GROUP BY m.MerchID, m.MerchName
ORDER BY m.MerchName
```

CREATING STORED PROCEDURES WITH ORACLE

Stored procedures work somewhat differently with Oracle than they do with SQL Server and Sybase. The basic concepts are the same, and many of the stored procedure examples in this chapter can be implemented on an Oracle server quite easily.

Note

This section assumes you are using Oracle8i for Windows NT or 2000. If you're using a different version of Oracle (such as Oracle 7.3, 8, or 9i), some of the figures shown in this chapter may look a little different from what you see on your screen.

Note

With Oracle, procedures that send back a return value are actually called *stored functions*, rather than stored procedures. Stored functions are not supported by the `<CFSTOREDPROC>` tag (even if you set `RETURNCODE="Yes"`). Therefore, you need to write your procedures so they send back any status information as an output parameter instead of a return value.

Note

To follow along with this section, you must have the tables from the A2Z sample database available on your Oracle server. You can do this relatively easily by using the Oracle Migration Workbench with the Microsoft Access Plug-In, which is a simple wizard you can use to automatically migrate the Access version of the Orange Whip Studios database (the `a2z.mdb` file from this book's CD) to your Oracle server. At the time of this writing, the Migration Workbench was available as a free 55MB download from `http://www.oracle.com`.

CREATING THE `ImportCustomers` STORED PROCEDURE

The easiest way to create a stored procedure is to use the Oracle DBA Studio, which is installed as part of the standard Oracle 8i installation. For instance, follow these steps to create the `InsertFilm` stored procedure:

1. Using the Windows Start menu, start the Oracle DBA Studio application and enter a valid username and password when prompted.
2. Navigate to the Schema item within your database, right-click the Procedure folder, and then select Create from the pop-up menu, as shown in Figure 32.10. The Create Procedure dialog box appears.
3. For the procedure's Name, type `INSERTFILM`; then select the correct Schema from the drop-down list.
4. Type the code shown in Listing 32.11 into the Source box, as shown in Figure 32.11. Do not include the first line of the listing (the `CREATE OR REPLACE PROCEDURE` line). The dialog box includes this line for you.

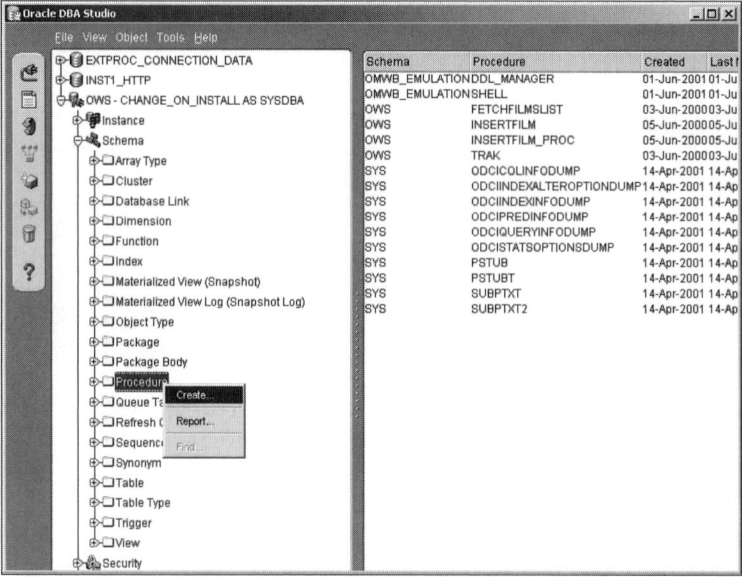

Figure 32.10
Creating a stored procedure is simple with the Oracle DBA Studio.

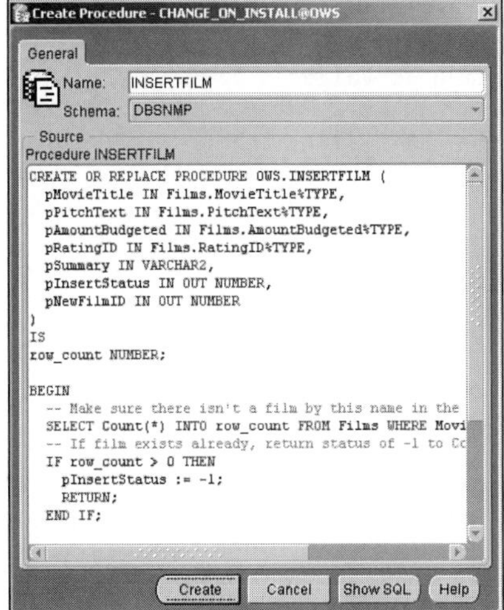

Figure 32.11 Enter the actual SQL code for the procedure into the Create Procedure dialog box.

5. Click the Create button. Your new procedure is created and the dialog box disappears. You can now expand the Procedures folder along the left side of the screen and click the new procedure to confirm that it was created correctly.

Tip

Instead of following the steps, you can just execute the code in Listing 32.11 directly into the Oracle SQL*Plus Worksheet utility. See your Oracle documentation for details.

LISTING 32.11 CREATING THE `InsertFilm` STORED PROCEDURE FOR ORACLE

```
CREATE OR REPLACE PROCEDURE OWS.INSERTFILM (
  pMovieTitle IN Films.MovieTitle%TYPE,
  pPitchText IN Films.PitchText%TYPE,
  pAmountBudgeted IN Films.AmountBudgeted%TYPE,
  pRatingID IN Films.RatingID%TYPE,
  pSummary IN VARCHAR2,
  pInsertStatus IN OUT NUMBER,
  pNewFilmID IN OUT NUMBER
)
IS
row_count NUMBER;

BEGIN
  -- Make sure there isn't a film by this name in the database already
  SELECT Count(*) INTO row_count FROM Films WHERE MovieTitle = pMovieTitle;
  -- If film exists already, return status of -1 to ColdFusion (or other program)
  IF row_count > 0 THEN
    pInsertStatus := -1;
    RETURN;
  END IF;
```

LISTING 32.11 CONTINUED

```
  -- Make sure the specified rating is valid
  SELECT Count(*) INTO row_count FROM FilmsRatings WHERE RatingID = pRatingID;
  -- If specified rating code does not exist, return status of -2
  IF row_count = 0 THEN
    pInsertStatus := -2;
    RETURN;
  END IF;

  -- Insert the new film into the Films table
  INSERT INTO Films (
    FilmID, MovieTitle, PitchText,
    AmountBudgeted, RatingID, Summary)
  VALUES (
    FilmsSeq.NEXTVAL, pMovieTitle, pPitchText,
    pAmountBudgeted, pRatingID, pSummary);

  -- Set output parameter called NewFilmID to the ID of the just-inserted film
  SELECT FilmsSeq.CURRVAL INTO pNewFilmID FROM DUAL;
  -- Return a status of 1 to ColdFusion (or other program) to indicate success
  pInsertStatus := 1;
END;
```

Note

Listing 32.11 assumes that an Oracle sequence called `FilmsSeq` is being used to auto-generate `FilmID` values. See your Oracle documentation for details about sequences.

Note that the SQL syntax for creating the stored procedure is slightly different from what it is for SQL Server, but the basic idea is the same. There's nothing here that's conceptually different from the SQL Server version of the procedure (refer to Listing 32.9).

The procedure name is provided first and follows the words `CREATE OR REPLACE PROCEDURE`. Then the procedure's parameters, if any, are provided within a pair of parentheses. The parentheses are followed by the `IS` keyword, and then the procedure's actual SQL code is provided between `BEGIN` and `END` keywords. Within the code, the actual value for the output parameter is set using Oracle's assignment operator, which is a colon followed by an equal sign (`:=`).

Tip

Oracle requires that you place a semicolon after each statement in your SQL code. If you've done any work with C or C++ in the past, that semicolon is a familiar friend. See your Oracle documentation for details.

Because the Oracle version of the `InsertFilm` stored procedure created in Listing 32.11 returns the insert status as an output parameter rather than as the status code, the ColdFusion code that uses the stored procedure must be changed slightly. Listing 32.12 is a revised version of Listing 32.4, which adds a `<CFPROCPARAM>` tag to capture the value of `pNewFilmID`. It also eliminates the `RETURNCODE="Yes"` attribute from the first `<CFSTOREDPROC>` tag.

LISTING 32.12 `FilmEntry2Oracle.cfm`**—USING THE ORACLE VERSION OF THE** `InsertFilm` **STORED PROCEDURE**

```
<!--- Is the form being submitted? --->
<CFSET WasFormSubmitted = IsDefined("FORM.RatingID")>

<!--- Insert film into database when form is submitted --->
<CFIF WasFormSubmitted>
  <CFSTOREDPROC
    PROCEDURE="InsertFilm"
    DATASOURCE="owsOra"
    RETURNCODE="No">

    <!--- Provide form values to the procedure's input parameters --->
    <CFPROCPARAM
      TYPE="In"
      DBVARNAME="pMovieTitle"
      MAXLENGTH="50"
      CFSQLTYPE="CF_SQL_VARCHAR"
      VALUE="#Form.MovieTitle#">
    <CFPROCPARAM
      TYPE="In"
      DBVARNAME="pPitchText"
      MAXLENGTH="100"
      CFSQLTYPE="CF_SQL_VARCHAR"
      VALUE="#Form.PitchText#">
    <CFPROCPARAM
      TYPE="In"
      DBVARNAME="pAmountBudgeted"
      MAXLENGTH="100"
      CFSQLTYPE="CF_SQL_MONEY"
      VALUE="#Form.AmountBudgeted#"
      NULL="#YesNoFormat(FORM.AmountBudgeted EQ '')#">
    <CFPROCPARAM
      TYPE="In"
      DBVARNAME="pRatingID"
      MAXLENGTH="100"
      CFSQLTYPE="CF_SQL_INTEGER"
      VALUE="#Form.RatingID#">
    <CFPROCPARAM
      TYPE="In"
      DBVARNAME="pSummary"
      CFSQLTYPE="CF_SQL_LONGVARCHAR"
      VALUE="#Form.Summary#">

    <!--- Capture @NewFilmID output parameter --->
    <!--- Value will be available in CFML variable named #InsertedFilmID# --->
    <CFPROCPARAM
      TYPE="Out"
      DBVARNAME="pInsertStatus"
      CFSQLTYPE="CF_SQL_INTEGER"
      VARIABLE="InsertStatus">

    <CFPROCPARAM
      TYPE="Out"
      DBVARNAME="pNewFilmID"
      CFSQLTYPE="CF_SQL_INTEGER"
      VARIABLE="InsertedFilmID">
```

LISTING 32.12 CONTINUED

```
  </CFSTOREDPROC>

</CFIF>

<!--- Get list of ratings from database --->
<CFSTOREDPROC PROCEDURE="owsWeb.FetchRatingsList" DATASOURCE="owsOra">
  <!--- This output parameter gives ColdFusion a pointer to reference cursor --->
  <CFPROCPARAM
    TYPE="Out"
    CFSQLTYPE="CF_SQL_REFCURSOR"
    VARIABLE="IgnoreThis"
    MAXROWS="-1">
  <!--- Make the data from reference cursor available as CFML query object --->
  <CFPROCRESULT NAME="GetRatings">
</CFSTOREDPROC>


<HTML>
<HEAD><TITLE>Film Entry Form</TITLE></HEAD>
<BODY>
<H2>Film Entry Form</H2>

<!--- Data entry form --->
<CFFORM ACTION="#CGI.SCRIPT_NAME#" METHOD="POST" PRESERVEDATA="Yes">

  <!--- Text entry field for film title --->
  <P><B>Title for New Film:</B><BR>
  <CFINPUT NAME="MovieTitle" SIZE="50" MAXLENGTH="50"
    REQUIRED="Yes" MESSAGE="Please don't leave the film's title blank."><BR>

  <!--- Text entry field for pitch text --->
  <P><B>Short Description / One-Liner:</B><BR>
  <CFINPUT NAME="PitchText" SIZE="50" MAXLENGTH="100"
    REQUIRED="Yes" MESSAGE="Please don't leave the one-liner blank."><BR>

  <!--- Text entry field for expense description --->
  <P><B>New Film Budget:</B><BR>
  <CFINPUT NAME="AmountBudgeted" SIZE="15"
    REQUIRED="No" MESSAGE="Only numbers may be provided for the film's budget."
    VALIDATE="float"> (leave blank if unknown)<BR>

  <!--- Drop-down list of ratings --->
  <P><B>Rating:</B><BR>
  <CFSELECT
    NAME="RatingID"
    QUERY="GetRatings"
    VALUE="RatingID"
    DISPLAY="Rating"/>

  <!--- Text areas for summary --->
  <P><B>Summary:</B><BR>
  <TEXTAREA NAME="Summary" COLS="40" ROWS="3" WRAP="soft"></TEXTAREA>

  <!--- Submit button for form --->
  <P><INPUT TYPE="Submit" VALUE="Submit New Film">
</CFFORM>
```

```
<!--- If we executed the stored procedure --->
<CFIF WasFormSubmitted>
  <!--- Display message based on status code reported by stored procedure --->
  <CFSWITCH EXPRESSION="#InsertStatus#">
    <!--- If the stored procedure returned a "success" status --->
    <CFCASE VALUE="1">
      <CFOUTPUT>
        <P>Film "#Form.MovieTitle#" was inserted as Film ID #InsertedFilmID#.<BR>
      </CFOUTPUT>
    </CFCASE>
    <!--- If the status code was -1 --->
    <CFCASE VALUE="-1">
      <CFOUTPUT>
        <P>Film "#Form.MovieTitle#" already exists in the database.<BR>
      </CFOUTPUT>
    </CFCASE>
    <!--- If the status code was -2 --->
    <CFCASE VALUE="-2">
      <P>An invalid rating was provided.<BR>
    </CFCASE>
    <!--- If any other status code was returned --->
    <CFDEFAULTCASE>
      <P>The procedure returned an unknown status code.<CFOUTPUT>#InsertStatus#
➥</CFOUTPUT><BR>
    </CFDEFAULTCASE>
  </CFSWITCH>
</CFIF>

</BODY>
</HTML>
```


Creating the FetchRatingsList Stored Procedure

As you learned in Listing 32.3, Oracle stored procedures can't return recordsets per se; instead, they can expose reference cursors as output parameters. Although this is an important distinction within the Oracle universe, you can treat reference cursors just like traditional recordsets in your ColdFusion template code, just by adding an additional `<CFPROCPARAM>` tag with `TYPE="REFCURSOR"`.

Creating a stored procedure that exposes a reference cursor requires a bit more code than the equivalent SQLServer procedure; however, the concepts are very similar. You should consult your Oracle documentation for all the details. That said, we can provide you with enough information here to help get you started.

The first step is to create a package to hold the cursor definition and your procedure. Within the package, define a cursor type that contains the columns you want to send back to ColdFusion (if you are going to select all columns from a single table, consider using the special `%ROWTYPE` attribute, as shown in the next listing). Also within the package, provide a declaration for the stored procedure itself, which is basically the first line of the procedure without the words `CREATE OR REPLACE`.

Within the package body, create the stored procedure itself, using the OPEN, FOR, and SELECT keywords to open the cursor and fill it with the appropriate data.

Listing 32.13 shows how the FetchRatingsList stored procedure can be created on an Oracle server. You could issue this code from the Oracle SQL*Plus Worksheet application. Or, you could provide the first part of the code (starting with the first AS) to the Oracle DBA Studio application in the Create Package dialog box, and the second part (starting with the second AS) to the Create Procedure dialog box.

LISTING 32.13 EXPOSING REFERENCE CURSORS FROM ORACLE STORED PROCEDURES

```
CREATE OR REPLACE PACKAGE OWS.OWSWEB AS
  TYPE RatingsCurType IS REF CURSOR RETURN FilmsRatings%ROWTYPE;
  PROCEDURE FetchRatingsList(RatingsCur OUT RatingsCurType);
END owsWeb;
/

CREATE OR REPLACE PACKAGE BODY OWS.OWSWEB AS
  PROCEDURE FetchRatingsList(RatingsCur OUT RatingsCurType) IS
  BEGIN
    OPEN RatingsCur FOR
    SELECT * FROM FilmsRatings ORDER BY RatingID;
  END FetchRatingsList;
END owsWeb;
/
```

Note

An Oracle stored procedure that returns multiple resultsets would simply include additional IS REF CURSOR lines in the package declaration and then include output parameters for each cursor type between the parentheses that follow the procedure name.

CREATING STORED PROCEDURES WITH SYBASE

Creating stored procedures with Sybase is extremely similar to creating them with Microsoft SQL Server. This has a lot to do with the fact that SQL Server originally was developed as a joint effort between Microsoft and Sybase. Both products supported almost the same functionality until relatively recently. See your Sybase documentation for details.

CHAPTER 33

Error Handling

In this chapter

CATCHING ERRORS AS THEY OCCUR

Unless you are a really, really amazing developer—and an incredibly fast learner—you have seen quite a few error messages from ColdFusion, both during development and after your applications have been deployed. ColdFusion is generally very good about providing diagnostic messages that help you understand what the problem is. So, as a developer, error messages are your friends. They're these clever little helpers, selflessly providing you with hints and observations about the state of your code, so you can get it fixed as soon as possible. It's almost romantic.

Unfortunately, your users aren't likely to see error messages through the rose-colored glasses that we coders tend to wear. They are likely to call you or page you or flood your mailbox with unfriendly e-mail messages until you get the error message (which is perceived as some kind of ugly monster) under control.

Wouldn't it be great if you could have your code watch for certain types of errors and respond to them on-the-fly, before the error even gets shown to the user? After all, as a developer, you often know the types of problems that might occur while a particular chunk of code does its work. If you could teach your code to recover from predictable problems on its own, you could lead a less stressful, healthier (albeit somewhat lonely) coding lifestyle.

This, and more, is what this chapter is all about. ColdFusion provides a small but powerful set of *structured exception handling* tags, which enable you to respond to problems as they occur.

Note

Many ColdFusion developers do not use the structured exception tags discussed in this chapter, perhaps because they sound too complicated (or out of an optimistic feeling that nothing will ever go wrong). The truth is, the structured exception framework is really easy to use and is likely to save you time in the long run.

Give this chapter a shot. This is ColdFusion, after all. How hard can it be, really?

WHAT IS AN EXCEPTION?

When ColdFusion displays an error message, it is responding to something called an *exception*. Whenever a CFML tag or function is incapable of doing whatever your code has asked it to do—such as connect to a database or process a variable—it lets ColdFusion know what exactly went wrong and provides information about why. This process of reporting the fact that something has gone wrong is called *raising an exception*. After an exception is raised, ColdFusion's job is to respond to the exception somehow. Out of the box, ColdFusion responds to nearly all exceptions in the same way: by displaying an error message that describes the exception. The fact that the exception occurred is also noted in ColdFusion's logs. If you want, you can use ColdFusion's exception-handling tags to respond to an exception in some different, customized way. When you do this, you are telling ColdFusion to run special code of your own devising, instead of displaying an error message as it would normally. This process—of responding to an exception with your own code—is called *catching* the exception.

Note

After an exception has been caught by your code, ColdFusion no longer considers itself responsible for displaying any type of error message. That is, the error message is suppressed.

Note

Although subtle distinctions exist between the exact meanings of each term, for now you can just consider *exception*, *exception condition*, *error*, and *error condition* to all mean the same thing: the state that occurs whenever an operation can't be completed. Also, for purposes of this discussion, consider *raising* and *throwing* to be synonyms as well. So, *raising an exception*, *throwing an error*, and *throwing an exception* all mean pretty much the same thing.

Note

As you learned in Chapter 19, "Introducing the Web Application Framework," the look and feel of ColdFusion's error messages can be customized. If all you want is to change the way error messages look, you can skip this chapter and just use what you learned in Chapter 19. If, however, you want to be able to take active recovery steps when an error occurs, read on.

Introducing <CFTRY> and <CFCATCH>

ColdFusion provides two basic CFML tags for handling exception conditions:

- **The `<CFTRY>` tag**—A paired tag you place around the portions of your templates that you think might fail under certain conditions.

  The <CFTRY> tag does not take any attributes. You simply place opening and closing <CFTRY> tags around the block of code you want ColdFusion to attempt to execute.
- **The `<CFCATCH>` tag**—Used to catch exceptions that occur within a <CFTRY> block.

  <CFCATCH> takes only one attribute, TYPE, as shown in Table 33.1. If that type of problem occurs, ColdFusion executes the code between the <CFCATCH> tags.

Part IV Ch 33

Table 33.1 <CFCATCH> Tag Attributes

Attribute	Description
TYPE	The type of exceptions to catch or respond to. It can be any of the types shown in Table 33.2. For instance, if you are interested in trying to recover from errors that occur while executing a <CFQUERY> or other database-related operation, you would use a <CFCATCH> of TYPE="Database".

TABLE 33.2 PREDEFINED EXCEPTION TYPES

Exception Type	Description
`Any`	Catches any exception, even exceptions you might not have any way of dealing with (such as an "out of memory" type of exception message). Use this exception value if you need to catch errors that do not fall into one of the other exception types in this table. It is recommended that you consider using one of the more specific exception types listed in this table, if at all possible.
`APPLICATION`	Catches application-level exception conditions. These exceptions are reported by your own CFML code, using the `<CFTHROW>` tag. In other words, catch errors of `TYPE="APPLICATION"` if you want to catch your own, custom errors.
`Database`	Catches database errors, which could include errors such as not being able to connect to a database, an incorrect column or table name, a locked database record, and so on.
`Expression`	Catches errors that occur while attempting to evaluate a CFML expression. For instance, if you refer to an unknown variable name or provide a function parameter that doesn't turn out to make sense when your template is actually executed, an exception of type `Expression` is thrown.
`Lock`	Catches errors that occur while attempting to process a `<CFLOCK>` tag. Most frequently, this type of error is thrown when a lock cannot be obtained within the `TIMEOUT` period specified by the `<CFLOCK>` tag, which usually means that some other page request (which also uses a similar lock) is taking a long time to complete its work.
`MissingInclude`	Catches errors that arise when you use a `<CFINCLUDE>` tag but the CFML template that you specify for the `TEMPLATE` attribute cannot be found.
Object	Catches errors that occur while attempting to process a `<CFOBJECT>` tag or `CreateObject()` function—or while attempting to access a property or method of an object that was returned by `<CFOBJECT>` or `CreateObject()`.
Security	Catches errors that occur while using one of ColdFusion's built-in security-related tags, such as `<CFAUTHENTICATE>` (see Appendix A, "ColdFusion Tag Reference").
`Template`	Catches general application page errors that occur while processing a `<CFINCLUDE>`, `<CFMODULE>`, or `<CFERROR>` tag.

Note

You can also provide an *advanced exception type* for `<CFCATCH>`'s `TYPE` attribute. The advanced exception types typically are used for catching specific errors generated while processing a `<CFPOP>` or `<CFHTTP>` tag. See Table 33.4 for more information.

Basic Exception Handling

The easiest way to understand exception handling is to actually go through the process of adding `<CFTRY>` and `<CFCATCH>` to an existing template. The next two listings (Listings 33.1 and 33.2) show the effects of ColdFusion's exception-handling tags, using a before-and-after scenario.

A Typical Scenario

Say you have been asked to create a page that enables users to select from two drop-down lists. The first drop-down provides a list of films; the second drop-down shows a list of film ratings. Each drop-down list has a Go button next to it, which presumably takes the user to some type of detail page when clicked.

Here's the catch: For whatever reason, you know ahead of time that the database tables that populate these drop-down lists (the `Films` and `FilmsRatings` tables) will not always be available. There might be any number of reasons for this. Perhaps you are connecting to a database server that is known to crash often, is down during certain times of the day for maintenance, or is accessed via an unreliable network connection.

Your job is to make your new drop-down list page operate as gracefully as possible, even when the database connections fail. At the very least, users should not see some type of ugly database error message. If you can pull off something more elegant, such as querying some kind of backup database in the event that the normal database tables are not available, that's even better. It seems that your yearly review is coming up, and it has been hinted that you might get a hefty raise if you can pull this project off with aplomb. Let's see whether ColdFusion can help you get that raise.

A Basic Template, Without Exception Handling

Listing 33.1 is the basic template, before any error handling is added. This template works just fine as long as no problems occur while connecting to the database. Two queries are run, and two drop-down lists are displayed, as shown in Figure 33.1. If an error occurs, though, an ugly error message is displayed to the user, which keeps the user from getting any further information.

Note

The examples in this chapter assume that an `Application.cfm` file has been created that sets the `REQUEST.DataSource` variable and also turns on Session and Client management via the `<CFAPPLICATION>` tag (as discussed in Chapter 19). For your convenience, the appropriate `Application.cfm` file has been included on the CD-ROM for this chapter.

Listing 33.1 `ChoicePage1.cfm`—**A Basic Display Template, Without any Error Handling**

```
<HTML>
<HEAD><TITLE>Film Information</TITLE></HEAD>
<BODY>
<H2>Film Information</H2>

<!--- Retrieve Ratings from database --->
<CFQUERY NAME="GetRatings" DATASOURCE="#REQUEST.DataSource#">
  SELECT RatingID, Rating
  FROM FilmsRatings
  ORDER BY Rating
</CFQUERY>

<!--- Retrieve Films from database --->
<CFQUERY NAME="GetFilms" DATASOURCE="#REQUEST.DataSource#">
  SELECT FilmID, MovieTitle
  FROM Films
  ORDER BY Films.MovieTitle
</CFQUERY>


<!--- Create self-submitting form --->
<CFFORM ACTION="#CGI.SCRIPT_NAME#" METHOD="Post">
  <!--- Display Film names in a drop-down list --->
  <P>Films:
  <CFSELECT
    QUERY="GetFilms" NAME="FilmID"
    VALUE="FilmID" DISPLAY="MovieTitle"/>

  <!--- Display Rating names in a drop-down list --->
  <P>Ratings:
  <CFSELECT
    QUERY="GetRatings" NAME="RatingID"
    VALUE="RatingID" DISPLAY="Rating"/>

</CFFORM>

</BODY>
</HTML>
```

There is nothing new in this template yet. Two `<CFQUERY>` tags named `GetRatings` and `GetFilms` are run, and the results from each query are displayed in a drop-down list that enables the user to select a film or rating. If any of this looks unfamiliar, take a look back at Chapter 14, "Using Forms to Add or Change Data."

If, for whatever reason, `GetRatings` and `GetFilms` are not capable of executing normally, an error message is displayed, leaving the user with nothing useful (other than a general impression that your site isn't maintained very carefully). For instance, if you go into the ColdFusion Administrator and sabotage the connection by providing an invalid filename in the Database File field for the `ows` data source, the error shown in Figure 33.2 is displayed.

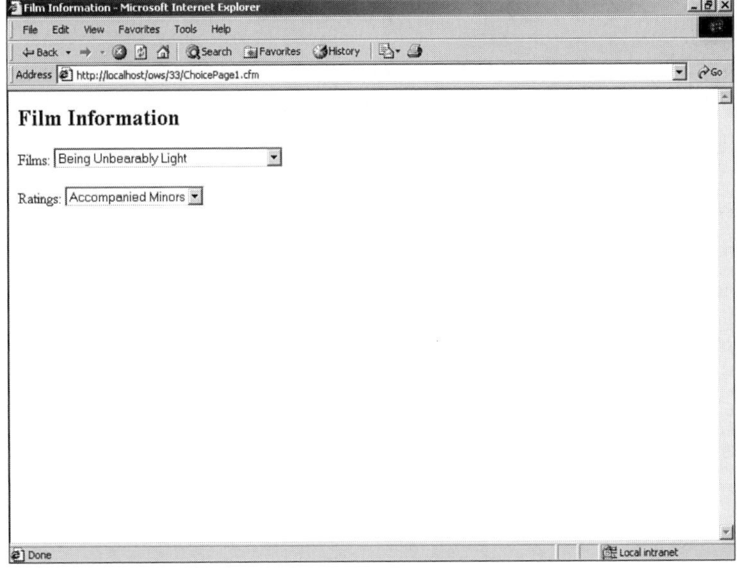

Figure 33.1
This is what the drop-down page looks like, as long as no errors occur.

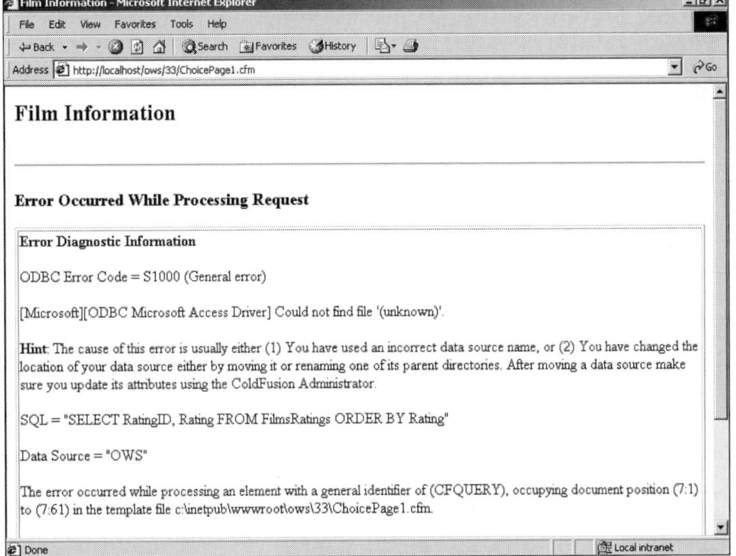

Figure 33.2
If an error occurs while connecting to the database, the default error message is displayed.

Adding <CFTRY> and <CFCATCH>

To add ColdFusion's structured exception handling to Listing 33.1, simply wrap a pair of opening and closing `<CFTRY>` tags around the two `<CFQUERY>` tags. Then, add a `<CFCATCH>` block that specifies an exception `TYPE` of `Database`, just before the closing `</CFTRY>` tag. The code inside the `<CFCATCH>` tag will be executed whenever a database exception is raised by either of the `<CFQUERY>` tags.

Listing 33.2 is a revised version of Listing 33.1. The code is almost exactly the same, except for the addition of the <CFTRY> and <CFCATCH> blocks, which display a basic "Sorry, we are not able to connect" type of error message. Now, if any problems occur when connecting to the database, the error message is displayed, as shown in Figure 33.3. This really isn't that much better than what the user saw in Figure 33.2, but it's a start.

LISTING 33.2 ChoicePage2.cfm—**ADDING A SIMPLE <CFTRY> BLOCK TO CATCH DATABASE ERRORS**

```
<HTML>
<HEAD><TITLE>Film Information</TITLE></HEAD>
<BODY>
<H2>Film Information</H2>

<CFTRY>
  <!--- Retrieve Ratings from database --->
  <CFQUERY NAME="GetRatings" DATASOURCE="#REQUEST.DataSource#">
    SELECT RatingID, Rating
    FROM FilmsRatings
    ORDER BY Rating
  </CFQUERY>

  <!--- Retrieve Films from database --->
  <CFQUERY NAME="GetFilms" DATASOURCE="#REQUEST.DataSource#">
    SELECT FilmID, MovieTitle
    FROM Films
    ORDER BY Films.MovieTitle
  </CFQUERY>

  <!--- If any database errors occur during above query, --->
  <CFCATCH TYPE="Database">
    <!--- Let user know that the Films data can't be shown right now --->
    <I>Sorry, we are not able to connect to our real-time database at the moment,
    due to carefully scheduled database maintenance.<BR></I>
    <CFABORT>
  </CFCATCH>
</CFTRY>


<!--- Create self-submitting form --->
<CFFORM ACTION="#CGI.SCRIPT_NAME#" METHOD="Post">
  <!--- Display Film names in a drop-down list --->
  <P>Films:
  <CFSELECT QUERY="GetFilms" NAME="FilmID"
    VALUE="FilmID" DISPLAY="MovieTitle"/>

  <!--- Display Rating names in a drop-down list --->
  <P>Ratings:
  <CFSELECT QUERY="GetRatings" NAME="RatingID"
    VALUE="RatingID" DISPLAY="Rating"/>

</CFFORM>

</BODY>
</HTML>
```

Even though it's rather simplistic, take a close look at Listing 33.2. First, the <CFTRY> block is used to tell ColdFusion you are interested in trapping exceptions. Within the <CFTRY> block, all of the queries needed by the page are executed. If any type of problem occurs—which could be anything from a crashed database server to a mere typo in your SQL code—the code inside the <CFCATCH> block executes, which displays the static message shown in Figure 33.3. Otherwise, the <CFCATCH> block is skipped entirely.

Note

It's important to note that the <CFCATCH> block in Listing 33.2 includes a <CFABORT> tag to halt all further processing. If it were not for the <CFABORT> tag, ColdFusion would continue processing the template, including the code that follows the <CFTRY> block altogether. This would just result in a different error message being shown because the <CFSELECT> tags would be referring to queries that never ended up being run.

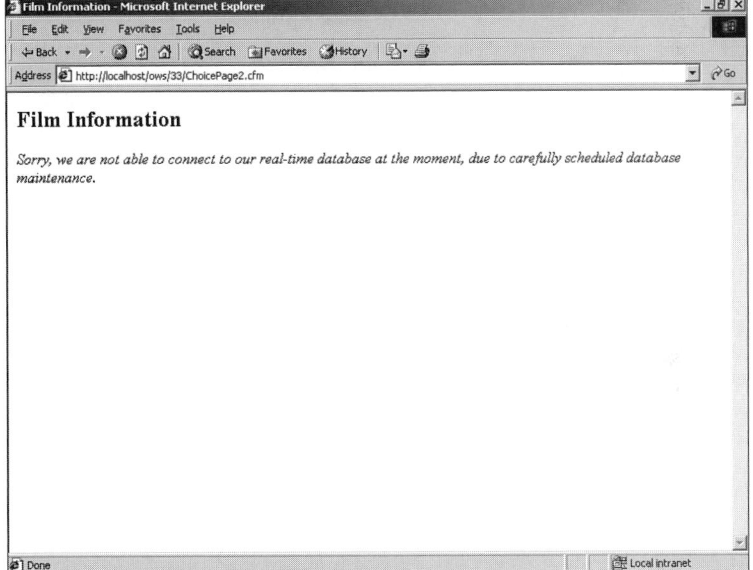

Figure 33.3
In its simplest form, a <CFCATCH> block can be used to display context-specific error messages.

Note

Because all this code is doing so far is displaying a custom error message, without taking any specific action to help the user, there really isn't anything about Listing 33.2 that's any better than the templates in Chapter 19 that used the <CFERROR> tag to customize the display of error messages. The advantages of using <CFTRY> and <CFCATCH> will become apparent shortly. In practice, you often will use <CFTRY> and <CFCATCH> along with <CFERROR>.

UNDERSTANDING WHAT CAUSED THE ERROR

When an exception is caught, ColdFusion populates a number of special variables that contain information about the problem that actually occurred. These variables are available to you via the special `CFCATCH` scope. Your code can examine these `CFCATCH` variables to get a better understanding of what exactly went wrong, or you can just display the `CFCATCH` values to the user in a customized error message.

Table 33.3 lists the variables available to you within a `<CFCATCH>` block.

TABLE 33.3 CFCATCH VARIABLES AVAILABLE AFTER AN EXCEPTION IS CAUGHT

`CFCATCH` **Variable**	**Available for These Exception Types**	**Description**
`CFCATCH.Type`	All types	The type of exception that was caught. This will be one of the exception types listed in Table 33.2.
`CFCATCH.Message`	All types	The text error message that goes along with the exception that was caught. Nearly all ColdFusion errors include a reasonably helpful `Message` value; this is the message that shows up at the top of normal error messages. For instance, the value of `CFCATCH.Message` for the exception shown in Figure 33.2 is `ODBC Error Code = S1000 (General error).`
`CFCATCH.Detail`	All types	Detail information that goes along with the exception that was caught. Most ColdFusion errors include a helpful `Detail` value. For the error shown in Figure 33.2, the value of `CFCATCH.Detail` begins with `[Microsoft]` and ends with `Data Source = "OWS".`
`CFCATCH.SqlState`	`Database`	A standardized error code that should be reasonably consistent for the same type of error, even between different database systems.

CFCATCH **Variable**	**Available for These Exception Types**	**Description**
`CFCATCH.NativeErrorCode`	`Database`	The native error code reported by the database system when the problem occurred. These error codes usually are not consistent between database systems.
`CFCATCH.ErrNumber`	`Expression`	Available only if the type of exception is `Expression`. A code that identifies the type of error that threw the exception.
`CFCATCH.MissingFileName`	`MissingInclude`	Available only if the type of exception is `MissingInclude`. The name of the ColdFusion template that could not be found.
`CFCATCH.LockName`	`Lock`	Available only if the type of exception is `Lock`. The name of the lock, if any, that was provided to the `<CFLOCK>` tag that failed.
`CFCATCH.LockOperation`	`Lock`	Available only if the type of exception is `Lock`. At this time, this value will always be `Timeout`, `Create Mutex`, or `Unknown`.
`CFCATCH.ErrorCode`	Exceptions thrown with `<CFTHROW>`	Available only for custom exceptions that are thrown by your code, using the `<CFTHROW>` tag. The value, if any, that was supplied to the `ERRORCODE` attribute of the `<CFTHROW>` tag that threw the exception.
`CFCATCH.ExtendedInfo`	Exceptions thrown with `<CFTHROW>`	The value, if any, that was supplied to the `EXTENDEDINFO` attribute of the `<CFTHROW>` tag.
`CFCATCH.TagContext`	Any	An array of structures that contains information about the ColdFusion templates involved in the page request when the exception occurred.

Listing 33.3 is a slightly revised version of Listing 33.2. This time, the message shown to the user includes information about the exception, by outputting the value of `CFCATCH.SqlState`. The results are shown in Figure 33.4.

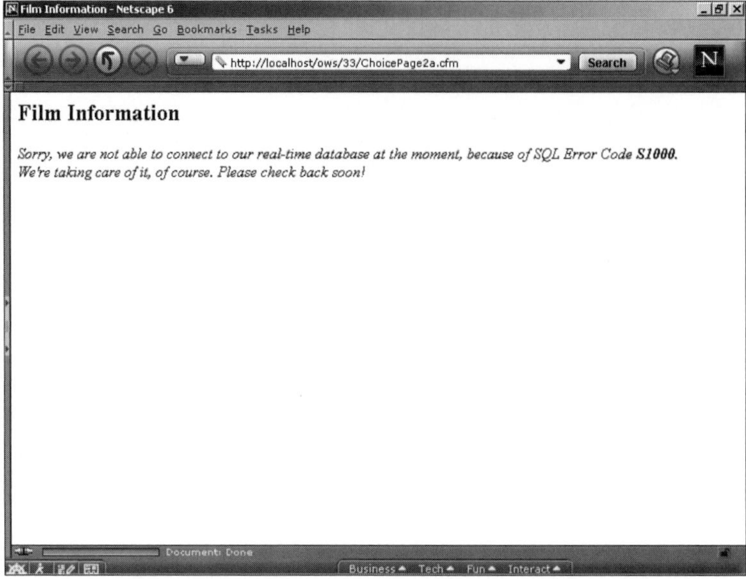

Figure 33.4
You can use the `CFCATCH` variables to examine or display diagnostic information.

LISTING 33.3 `ChoicePage2a.cfm`—DISPLAYING THE SQL ERROR CODE FOR A DATABASE ERROR

```
<HTML>
<HEAD><TITLE>Film Information</TITLE></HEAD>
<BODY>
<H2>Film Information</H2>

<CFTRY>
  <!--- Retrieve Ratings from database --->
  <CFQUERY NAME="GetRatings" DATASOURCE="#REQUEST.DataSource#">
    SELECT RatingID, Rating
    FROM FilmsRatings
    ORDER BY Rating
  </CFQUERY>

  <!--- Retrieve Films from database --->
  <CFQUERY NAME="GetFilms" DATASOURCE="#REQUEST.DataSource#">
    SELECT FilmID, MovieTitle
    FROM Films
    ORDER BY Films.MovieTitles
  </CFQUERY>

  <!--- If any database errors occur during above query, --->
  <CFCATCH TYPE="Database">
    <!--- Let user know that the Films data can't be shown right now --->
    <CFOUTPUT>
```

```
      <I>Sorry, we are not able to connect to our real-time database right now,
      because of SQL Error Code <B>#CFCATCH.SqlState#</B>.<BR>
      We're taking care of it, of course. Please check back soon!</I><BR>
    </CFOUTPUT>
    <CFABORT>
  </CFCATCH>
</CFTRY>

<!--- Create self-submitting form --->
<CFFORM ACTION="#CGI.SCRIPT_NAME#" METHOD="Post">
  <!--- If, after all is said and done, we were able to get Film data --->
  <CFIF IsDefined("GetFilms")>
    <!--- Display Film names in a drop-down list --->
    <P>Films:
    <CFSELECT QUERY="GetFilms" NAME="FilmID"
      VALUE="FilmID" DISPLAY="MovieTitle"/>
  </CFIF>

  <!--- If, after all is said and done, we were able to get Ratings data --->
  <CFIF IsDefined("GetRatings")>
    <!--- Display Rating names in a drop-down list --->
    <P>Ratings:
    <CFSELECT QUERY="GetRatings" NAME="RatingID"
      VALUE="RatingID" DISPLAY="Rating"/>
  </CFIF>

</CFFORM>

</BODY>
</HTML>
```

Note

This template only outputs the value of `CFCATCH.SqlState`. Of course, if you want to give the user more information, you are free to use the other `CFCATCH` variables from Table 33.3 that are relevant to the type of exception that was thrown.

WRITING TEMPLATES THAT WORK AROUND ERRORS

As shown in Figure 33.4, you can use `<CFTRY>` and `<CFCATCH>` to respond to errors by displaying a customized error message. But that's really not so different from the way you learned to use `<CFERROR>` in Chapter 19. The real value of `<CFTRY>` and `<CFCATCH>` is the fact that they enable you to create templates that actively respond to or work around exception conditions. In other words, they let you write Web pages that continue to be at least somewhat helpful to your users, even after an error has occurred.

WORKING AROUND A FAILED QUERY

Take a look at Listing 33.4, which is similar to the other listings you have looked at so far in this chapter. This version isolates each `<CFQUERY>` within its own `<CFTRY>` block. Within each `<CFTRY>` block, if any database errors occur, a static message is displayed to the user, but the template execution is not stopped.

Note

No errors are thrown when you first visit this message with your browser. To see the results shown in Figure 33.5, sabotage one of the queries in some way and then visit the template again. For instance, change one of the columns in the SQL statement to an invalid column name—or go into the `Application.cfm` file and the `Request.DataSource` variable to a data source name that doesn't exist.

LISTING 33.4 ChoicePage3a.cfm—USING <CFTRY> AND <CFCATCH> TO DISPLAY INFORMATION ONLY WHEN IT IS ACTUALLY AVAILABLE

```
<HTML>
<HEAD><TITLE>Film Information</TITLE></HEAD>
<BODY>
<H2>Film Information</H2>

<!--- Create self-submitting form --->
<CFFORM ACTION="#CGI.SCRIPT_NAME#" METHOD="Post">

  <!--- Attempt database operation --->
  <CFTRY>
    <!--- Retrieve Films from database --->
    <CFQUERY NAME="GetFilms" DATASOURCE="#REQUEST.DataSource#">
      SELECT FilmID, MovieTitle
      FROM Films
      ORDER BY Films.MovieTitle
    </CFQUERY>

    <!--- If any database errors occur during above query, --->
    <CFCATCH TYPE="Database">
      <!--- Let user know that the Films data can't be shown right now --->
      <P><I>Sorry, we can't show a real-time list of Films right now.<BR></I>
    </CFCATCH>
  </CFTRY>


  <!--- Attempt database operation --->
  <CFTRY>
    <!--- Retrieve Ratings from database --->
    <CFQUERY NAME="GetRatings" DATASOURCE="#REQUEST.DataSource#">
      SELECT RatingID, Rating
      FROM FilmsRatings
      ORDER BY Rating
    </CFQUERY>

    <!--- If any database errors occur during above query, --->
    <CFCATCH TYPE="Database">
      <!--- Let user know that the Ratings data can't be shown right now --->
      <P><I>Sorry, we can't show a real-time list of Ratings right now.<BR></I>
    </CFCATCH>
  </CFTRY>


  <!--- If, after all is said and done, we were able to get Film data --->
  <CFIF IsDefined("GetFilms")>
    <!--- Display Film names in a drop-down list --->
```

```
    <P>Films:
    <CFSELECT
      QUERY="GetFilms" NAME="FilmID"
      VALUE="FilmID" DISPLAY="MovieTitle"/>
    <INPUT TYPE="Submit" VALUE="Go">
  </CFIF>

  <!--- If, after all is said and done, we were able to get Ratings data --->
  <CFIF IsDefined("GetRatings")>
    <!--- Display Ratings in a drop-down list --->
    <P>Ratings:
    <CFSELECT
      QUERY="GetRatings" NAME="RatingID"
      VALUE="RatingID" DISPLAY="Rating"/>
    <INPUT TYPE="Submit" VALUE="Go">
  </CFIF>

</CFFORM>

</BODY>
</HTML>
```

For instance, if for some reason the `GetFilms` query fails to run properly, a *not able to get a real-time list of Films* message is displayed. Template execution then continues on normally, right after the first `<CFTRY>` block. Because the `<CFQUERY>` was incapable of completing its work, the `GetFilms` variable does not exist; otherwise, everything is fine.

At the bottom of the template, the display of each drop-down list is protected by an `IsDefined()` check to see whether the corresponding query actually exists. If the `GetFilms` query was completed without error, the first `<CFIF>` test passes and the Films drop-down list is displayed. If not, the code inside the `<CFIF>` block is skipped.

So, if the first query causes an error, the user simply sees a friendly little status message instead of the Films drop-down list, as shown in Figure 33.5. Assuming that the second query is capable of executing successfully, however, the Ratings drop-down list still is displayed normally.

The result is a page that is still useful when it is partially disabled because of a problem with the database. It is, in a small but very helpful way, self-healing.

Note

To see the results shown in Listing 33.5, sabotage the `GetFilms` query in some way, such as changing the value supplied to the `DATASOURCE` attribute to a data source name that doesn't exist.

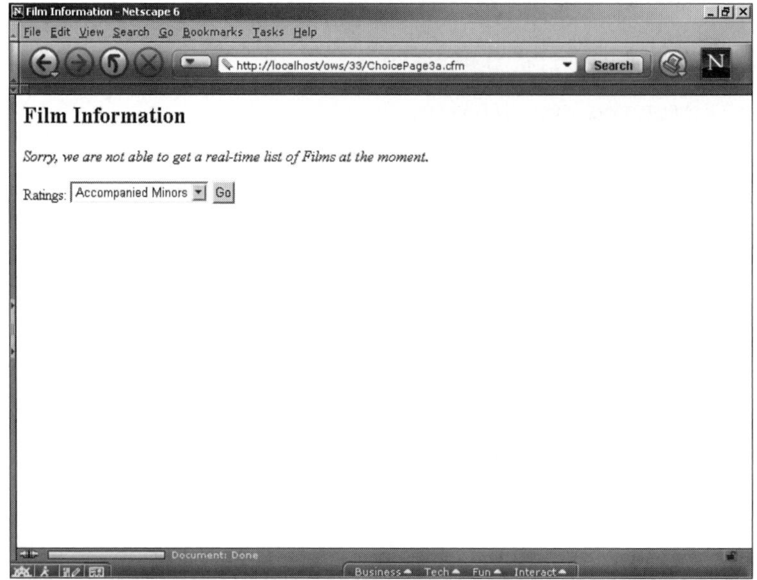

Figure 33.5 ColdFusion's exception-handling capabilities enable your templates to recover gracefully from error conditions.

Listing 33.5 shows a slightly different way to structure the code from Listing 33.4. Almost all the code lines are the same between the two versions; they are just placed in a different order. Instead of placing both `<CFSELECT>` tags together, at the end of the template, each `<CFSELECT>` is output in the corresponding `<CFTRY>` block, right after the query that populates it. If one of the queries fails, the `<CFSWITCH>` block immediately takes over, thus skipping over the `<CFSELECT>` for the failed query.

The result is a template that behaves in exactly the same way as Listing 33.4. Depending on your preference and on the situation, placing code in self-contained `<CFTRY>` blocks as shown in Listing 33.5 can make your templates easier to understand and maintain. On the other hand, in many situations, the approach taken in Listing 33.4 is more sensible because it keeps the database access code separate from the HTML generation code.

Tip

Use whichever approach results in the simplest-looking, most straightforward code.

LISTING 33.5 ChoicePage3b.cfm—AN ALTERNATIVE WAY OF STRUCTURING THE CODE IN LISTING 33.4

```
<HTML>
<HEAD><TITLE>Film Information</TITLE></HEAD>
<BODY>
<H2>Film Information</H2>

<!--- Create self-submitting form --->
<CFFORM ACTION="#CGI.SCRIPT_NAME#" METHOD="Post">
```

```
<!--- Attempt database operation --->
<CFTRY>
  <!--- Retrieve Films from database --->
  <CFQUERY NAME="GetFilms" DATASOURCE="#REQUEST.DataSource#">
    SELECT FilmID, MovieTitle
    FROM Films
    ORDER BY Films.MovieTitle
  </CFQUERY>

  <!--- Display Film names in a drop-down list --->
  <P>Films:
  <CFSELECT
    QUERY="GetFilms" NAME="FilmID"
    VALUE="FilmID" DISPLAY="MovieTitle"/>
  <INPUT TYPE="Submit" VALUE="Go">

  <!--- If any database errors occur during above query, --->
  <CFCATCH TYPE="Database">
    <!--- Let user know that the Films data can't be shown right now --->
    <P><I>Sorry, we can't show a real-time list of Films right now.<BR></I>
  </CFCATCH>
</CFTRY>


<!--- Attempt database operation --->
<CFTRY>
  <!--- Retrieve Ratings from database --->
  <CFQUERY NAME="GetRatings" DATASOURCE="#REQUEST.DataSource#">
    SELECT RatingID, Rating
    FROM FilmsRatings
    ORDER BY Rating
  </CFQUERY>

  <!--- Display Ratings in a drop-down list --->
  <P>Ratings:
  <CFSELECT
    QUERY="GetRatings" NAME="RatingID"
    VALUE="RatingID" DISPLAY="Rating"/>
  <INPUT TYPE="Submit" VALUE="Go">

  <!--- If any database errors occur during above query, --->
  <CFCATCH TYPE="Database">
    <!--- Let user know that the Ratings data can't be shown right now --->
    <P><I>Sorry, we can't show a real-time list of Ratings right now.<BR></I>
  </CFCATCH>
</CFTRY>

</CFFORM>

</BODY>
</HTML>
```


WORKING AROUND ERRORS SILENTLY

Listing 33.6 is another version of Listing 33.4. This time, no action of any type is taken in the <CFCATCH> block (not even the display of an error message). Because nothing needs to be placed between the <CFCATCH> and </CFCATCH> tags, they can be coded using the shorthand notation of <CFCATCH/> alone. The trailing slash is just an abbreviated way of providing an empty tag pair.

Tip

You can use this trailing-slash notation whenever you need to use a CFML tag that requires a closing tag, but where you don't actually need to place anything between the tags. Most of the templates in this chapter use this shorthand in their <CFSELECT> tags.

The result is a template that recovers silently from database errors, without even acknowledging that anything has gone wrong. If the GetFilms query can't execute, the Films drop-down list just doesn't get displayed. As far as the user is concerned, there never was an error of any type. The template simply displays what it can and gracefully omits what it cannot.

LISTING 33.6 ChoicePage3c.cfm—HANDLING ERRORS SILENTLY, WITHOUT LETTING THE USER KNOW THAT ANYTHING WENT WRONG

```
<HTML>
<HEAD><TITLE>Film Information</TITLE></HEAD>
<BODY>
<H2>Film Information</H2>

<!--- Create self-submitting form --->
<CFFORM ACTION="#CGI.SCRIPT_NAME#" METHOD="Post">

  <!--- Attempt database operation --->
  <CFTRY>
    <!--- Retrieve Films from database --->
    <CFQUERY NAME="GetFilms" DATASOURCE="#REQUEST.DataSource#">
      SELECT FilmID, MovieTitle
      FROM Films
      ORDER BY Films.MovieTitle
    </CFQUERY>

    <!--- Display Film names in a drop-down list --->
    <P>Films:
    <CFSELECT
      QUERY="GetFilms" NAME="FilmID"
      VALUE="FilmID" DISPLAY="MovieTitle"/>
    <INPUT TYPE="Submit" VALUE="Go">

    <!--- Silently catch any database errors from above query --->
    <CFCATCH TYPE="Database"/>
  </CFTRY>


  <!--- Attempt database operation --->
  <CFTRY>
    <!--- Retrieve Ratings from database --->
    <CFQUERY NAME="GetRatings" DATASOURCE="#REQUEST.DataSource#">
      SELECT RatingID, Rating
      FROM FilmsRatings
```

```
      ORDER BY Rating
    </CFQUERY>

    <!--- Display Ratings in a drop-down list --->
    <P>Ratings:
    <CFSELECT
      QUERY="GetRatings" NAME="RatingID"
      VALUE="RatingID" DISPLAY="Rating"/>
    <INPUT TYPE="Submit" VALUE="Go">

    <!--- Silently catch any database errors from above query --->
    <CFCATCH TYPE="Database"/>
  </CFTRY>

</CFFORM>

</BODY>
</HTML>
```

WRITING TEMPLATES THAT RECOVER FROM ERRORS

Listings 33.4–33.6 created templates that continue to be useful for your users by skipping the blocks of code that rely on failed queries. Depending on the situation, you often can go a step further, creating templates that continue to provide the basic functionality they are supposed to (albeit in some type of scaled-back manner), even when a problem occurs.

For instance, Listing 33.7 creates yet another version of the drop-down page example. It looks similar to Listing 33.4, except for first `<CFCATCH>` block, which has been expanded. The idea here is to use a backup copy of the `Films` database table, which exists for the sole purpose of providing a fallback when the primary database system can't be reached.

LISTING 33.7 `ChoicePage4.cfm`—QUERYING A BACKUP TEXT FILE WHEN THE PRIMARY DATABASE IS UNAVAILABLE

```
<HTML>
<HEAD><TITLE>Films</TITLE></HEAD>
<BODY>
<H2>Film Information</H2>

<CFTRY>
  <!--- Retrieve Films from live database --->
  <CFQUERY NAME="GetFilms" DATASOURCE="#REQUEST.DataSource#">
    SELECT FilmID, MovieTitle
    FROM Films
    ORDER BY Films.MovieTitle
  </CFQUERY>

  <!--- If any database errors occur during above query, --->
  <CFCATCH TYPE="Database">
    <!--- Construct connection string so we can query Films.txt file --->
    <CFSET Driver = "{MERANT 3.70 ColdFusion OEM 32-BIT TextFile (*.*)}">
    <CFSET DBDir  = GetDirectoryFromPath(GetCurrentTemplatePath())>
    <CFSET ConStr = "DRIVER=#Driver#;DB=#DBDir#;FLN=1;tT=COMMA;UT=GUESS">
```

LISTING 33.7 CONTINUED

```
    <!--- Retrieve Films from Text file --->
    <CFQUERY NAME="GetFilms" DBTYPE="dynamic" CONNECTSTRING="#ConStr#">
      SELECT FilmID, MovieTitle
      FROM Films.txt
      ORDER BY Films.MovieTitle
    </CFQUERY>

    <!--- Let user know that text file is being used --->
    <I><P>NOTE:
    We are not able to connect to our real-time Films database at the moment.<BR>
    Instead, we are using data from our archives to display the Films list.<BR>
    Please try again later today for an up to date listing.<BR></I>
  </CFCATCH>
</CFTRY>

<!--- Attempt database operation --->
<CFTRY>
  <!--- Retrieve Ratings from database --->
  <CFQUERY NAME="GetRatings" DATASOURCE="#REQUEST.DataSource#">
    SELECT RatingID, Rating
    FROM FilmsRatings
    ORDER BY Rating
  </CFQUERY>

  <!--- Silently catch any database errors from above query --->
  <CFCATCH TYPE="Database"/>
</CFTRY>


<!--- Create self-submitting form --->
<CFFORM ACTION="#CGI.SCRIPT_NAME#" METHOD="Post">

  <!--- If, after all is said and done, we were able to get Film data --->
  <CFIF IsDefined("GetFilms")>
    <!--- Display Film names in a drop-down list --->
    <P>Films:
    <CFSELECT
      QUERY="GetFilms" NAME="FilmID"
      VALUE="FilmID" DISPLAY="MovieTitle"/>
    <INPUT TYPE="Submit" VALUE="Go">
  </CFIF>

  <!--- If, after all is said and done, we were able to get Ratings data --->
  <CFIF IsDefined("GetRatings")>
    <!--- Display Ratings in a drop-down list --->
    <P>Ratings:
    <CFSELECT
      QUERY="GetRatings" NAME="RatingID"
      VALUE="RatingID" DISPLAY="Rating"/>
    <INPUT TYPE="Submit" VALUE="Go">
  </CFIF>

</CFFORM>

</BODY>
</HTML>
```

You will notice that there are two queries named `GetFilms` in this template. The first one queries the `ows` data source normally. If that query fails, the first `<CFCATCH>` block kicks in, which runs the second version of the query.

Note that the second `GetFilms` query, instead of querying against the `ows` data source, queries against a standalone comma-separated text file called `Films.txt`. The Merant ODBC driver for text files, which ships with ColdFusion 5, is used to do the actual querying. This query doesn't need a data source name; it uses `DBTYPE="Dynamic"` and `CONNECTSTRING` to connect to the `Films.txt` file on its own. The `Films.txt` file is expected to be in the same folder as Listing 33.7 itself.

Note

The Merant Text File driver that ships with ColdFusion 5 is used here just as an example. In a real-world scenario, your backup database would probably be something more sophisticated than a text file.

The result is a version of the template that still provides the basic functionality it is supposed to, even when the first `GetFilms` query fails. Assuming that the second query succeeds, the user is presented with the drop-down list of films she is expecting. She also sees a message that alerts her to the fact that the list is not being populated from the live database, but rather an archived backup copy, as shown in Figure 33.6.

Tip

To find out more about using `DBTYPE="Dynamic"` and `CONNECTSTRING` to query a table without a normal data source, see Chapter 31, "More About SQL and Queries."

Note

The `Films.txt` file was created by exporting the `Films` table from the `ows.mdb` database and is provided on this book's CD-ROM so you easily can test Listing 33.7. To create the text file yourself, open the database in Microsoft Access. Select the `Films` table, and select Export from the File menu. Next, type **`Films.txt`** for the filename, select Text Files as the file type, and then click Save, which should launch the Export Text Wizard. On the first wizard step, select Delimited. On the second step, select Comma for the delimiter, check the Include Field Names on First Row option, and then click Finish. (Some of these steps might be slightly different if you are using a version of Access other than Access 2000.)

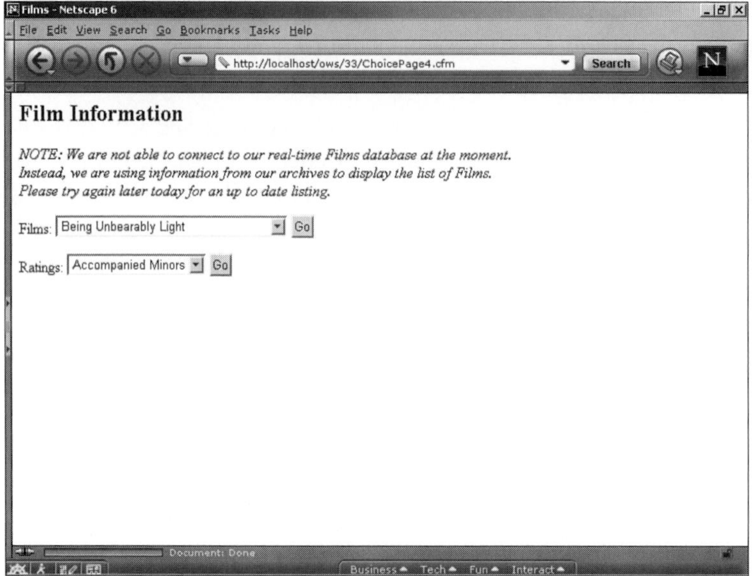

Figure 33.6
This version of the template connects to a backup text file if the usual database is not accessible.

Nesting <CFTRY> Blocks

You can nest <CFTRY> blocks within one another. There are generally two ways you can nest the blocks, depending on the behavior you want.

If you nest a <CFTRY> within another <CFTRY> block (but not within a <CFCATCH>), the code inside the inner <CFTRY> is doubly protected. This first type of nesting typically follows this basic form:

```
<CFTRY>
  <CFTRY>
    ...important code...
    <CFCATCH></CFCATCH>
  </CFTRY>
  <CFCATCH></CFCATCH>
</CFTRY>
```

If something goes wrong, ColdFusion will see whether any of the <CFCATCH> tags within the inner <CFTRY> are appropriate (that is, whether a <CFCATCH> of the same TYPE as the exception itself exists). If so, the code in that block is executed. If not, it looks to see whether the <CFCATCH> tags within the *outer* <CFTRY> block are appropriate. If no appropriate <CFCATCH> blocks are found there either, the exception is considered *uncaught*, so the default error message is displayed.

Alternatively, if you nest a <CFTRY> within a <CFCATCH> that belongs to another <CFTRY>, you are essentially creating a two-step process. This second type of nesting is typically structured like this:

```
<CFTRY>
  ...important code...
```

```
  <CFCATCH>
    <CFTRY>
      ...fallback code...
      <CFCATCH></CFCATCH>
    </CFTRY>
  </CFCATCH>
</CFTRY>
```

If the code in the outer `<CFTRY>` fails, the inner `<CFTRY>` attempts to deal with the situation in some other way. If the code in the inner `<CFTRY>` also fails, its `<CFCATCH>` tags can catch the error and perform some type of last-ditch processing (such as displaying an error message).

Listing 33.8 is an example of this second form of `<CFTRY>` nesting. It revises Listing 33.7 by surrounding the backup version of the `GetFilms` query within its own `<CFTRY>` block. This enables the page to still display something coherent to the user, even if both `GetFilms` queries fail.

LISTING 33.8 ChoicePage5.cfm—NESTING <CFTRY> BLOCKS WITHIN EACH OTHER

```
<HTML>
<HEAD><TITLE>Films</TITLE></HEAD>
<BODY>
<H2>Film Information</H2>

<CFTRY>
  <!--- Retrieve Films from live database --->
  <CFQUERY NAME="GetFilms" DATASOURCE="#REQUEST.DataSource#">
    SELECT FilmID, MovieTitle
    FROM Films
    ORDER BY Films.MovieTitle
  </CFQUERY>

  <!--- If any database errors occur during above query, --->
  <CFCATCH TYPE="Database">

    <!--- Attempt to get information from txt file instead --->
    <CFTRY>
      <!--- Construct connection string so we can query Films.txt file --->
      <CFSET Driver = "{MERANT 3.70 ColdFusion OEM 32-BIT TextFile (*.*)}">
      <CFSET DBDir  = GetDirectoryFromPath(GetCurrentTemplatePath())>
      <CFSET ConStr = "DRIVER=#Driver#;DB=#DBDir#;FLN=1;tT=COMMA;UT=GUESS">

      <!--- Retrieve Films from Text file --->
      <CFQUERY NAME="GetFilms" DBTYPE="dynamic" CONNECTSTRING="#ConStr#">
        SELECT FilmID, MovieTitle
        FROM Films.txt
        ORDER BY Films.MovieTitle
      </CFQUERY>

      <!--- Let user know that text file is being used --->
      <I><P>NOTE:
      We are not able to connect to our real-time database at the moment.<BR>
      Instead, we are using information from our most recent archives.<BR>
      Please try again later today for an up to date listing.<BR></I>
```

LISTING 33.8 CONTINUED

```
      <!--- If any database occurs *during this second query* --->
      <CFCATCH TYPE="Database">
        <!--- Let user know that the Films data can't be shown right now --->
        <I>Sorry, we are not able to provide you with a list of films.<BR></I>
      </CFCATCH>
    </CFTRY>
  </CFCATCH>
</CFTRY>

<!--- Attempt database operation --->
<CFTRY>
  <!--- Retrieve Ratings from database --->
  <CFQUERY NAME="GetRatings" DATASOURCE="#REQUEST.DataSource#">
    SELECT RatingID, Rating
    FROM FilmsRatings
    ORDER BY Rating
  </CFQUERY>

  <!--- Silently catch any database errors from above query --->
  <CFCATCH TYPE="Database"/>
</CFTRY>

<!--- Create self-submitting form --->
<CFFORM ACTION="#CGI.SCRIPT_NAME#" METHOD="Post">

  <!--- If, after all is said and done, we were able to get Film data --->
  <CFIF IsDefined("GetFilms")>
    <!--- Display Film names in a drop-down list --->
    <P>Films:
    <CFSELECT
      QUERY="GetFilms" NAME="FilmID"
      VALUE="FilmID" DISPLAY="MovieTitle"/>
    <INPUT TYPE="Submit" VALUE="Go">
  </CFIF>

  <!--- If, after all is said and done, we were able to get Ratings data --->
  <CFIF IsDefined("GetRatings")>
    <!--- Display Ratings in a drop-down list --->
    <P>Ratings:
    <CFSELECT
      QUERY="GetRatings" NAME="RatingID"
      VALUE="RatingID" DISPLAY="Rating"/>
    <INPUT TYPE="Submit" VALUE="Go">
  </CFIF>

</CFFORM>

</BODY>
</HTML>
```

If the first `<CFQUERY>` raises an error, the error causes the first `<CFCATCH>` block to execute. That `<CFCATCH>` contains a nested `<CFTRY>` tag, which attempts to query the `Films.txt` file using the Merant ODBC driver, as explained during the discussion for Listing 33.7. If this second query fails—perhaps because the `Films.txt` file is missing or is invalid or the Merant driver is not present for some reason—the inner <CFCATCH> block executes. The inner <CFCATCH> block displays a short error message—which could be repressed altogether (as shown previously in Listing 33.6—but does not abort further processing. Template execution thus picks up again right after the outer <CFTRY> block. The rest of the template is unchanged from the previous version.

The result is a version of the template that normally looks like Figure 33.1. If the usual `Films` table is not available, it uses the backup version of the table, as shown in Figure 33.6. If the backup version is also unavailable, it simply skips over the parts of the template that rely on the query, as shown in Figure 33.5. This is quite an improvement over the original version of the template (refer to Listing 33.1), which could do no better than display a user-unfriendly error message when something went wrong (refer to Figure 33.2).

DECIDING NOT TO HANDLE AN EXCEPTION

When your code catches an exception with <CFCATCH>, it assumes all responsibility for dealing with the exception in an appropriate way. After the exception is caught by your code, ColdFusion is no longer responsible for logging an error message or halting further page processing.

For instance, take a look back at Listing 33.8 (`ChoicePage5.cfm`). The <CFCATCH> tags in this template declare themselves fit to handle any and all database-related errors by specifying a `TYPE="Database"` attribute in the <CFCATCH> tag. No matter what type of database-related exception gets raised, those <CFCATCH> tags will catch the error.

The purpose of the first <CFCATCH> block in Listing 33.8 is to attempt to connect with the backup version of the database when the first <CFQUERY> fails. This backup plan is activated no matter what the actual problem is. Even a simple syntax error or misspelled column name in the SQL statement will cause the `Films.txt` table to be queried.

It would be a better policy for the backup version of the database to be used only when the original query failed due to a connection problem. Other types of errors, such as syntax errors and so on, should probably not be caught and dealt with in this same way.

ColdFusion provides the <CFRETHROW> tag for exactly this type of situation. This section explains how to use <CFRETHROW> and when to use it.

EXCEPTIONS AND THE NOTION OF BUBBLING UP

Similar to the error or exception constructs in many other programming languages, ColdFusion's exceptions can do something called *bubbling up*. Say you have some code that includes several layers of nested <CFTRY> blocks and that an exception has taken place in the innermost block.

If the exception is not caught the innermost <CFTRY> block, ColdFusion looks in the containing <CFTRY> block, if any, to see whether it contains any appropriate <CFCATCH> tags. If not, the exception continues to *bubble up* through the layers of <CFTRY> blocks until the exception is caught. If the error bubbles up through all the layers of the <CFTRY> blocks (that is, if none of the <CFCATCH> tags in the <CFTRY> blocks choose to catch the exception), that is when ColdFusion displays its default error message.

USING <CFRETHROW>

The <CFRETHROW> tag is basically the opposite of <CFCATCH>. After an error has been caught with <CFCATCH>, it can be uncaught using <CFRETHROW>. The error is then free to bubble up to the next containing <CFTRY> block, if any.

The <CFRETHROW> tag takes no attributes and can be used only inside a <CFCATCH> tag. Typically, you will decide to use it by testing the value of one of the special `CFCATCH` variables shown previously in Table 33.3.

For instance, earlier in this chapter, you learned that the Access driver reports a `CFCATCH.SQLState` value of `S1000` when the database file—in this case, `ows.mdb`—cannot be found (refer to Figure 33.4). If you wanted your code to handle only errors of this specific type, letting all other errors bubble up normally, you would use code similar to the following within a <CFCATCH> block:

```
<CFIF CFCATCH.SQLState NEQ "S1000">
  <CFRETHROW>
</CFIF>
```

Listing 33.9 is a revision of Listing 33.8, which uses the basic <CFIF> test shown in the previous snippet to ensure that the backup data file (`Films.txt`) is queried only if the database exception has a `SQLState` value of `S1000`.

> **Note**
>
> To test the exception-handling behavior of this template, try crippling it by changing the filename for the `ows` data source in the ColdFusion Administrator. That should cause error `S1000`, so the backup version of the `Films` table will be used (refer to Figure 33.6).
>
> Now correct the filename in the ColdFusion Administrator, and try sabotaging the first <CFQUERY> in some other way–for instance by changing one of the column names to something invalid. That should cause the <CFRETHROW> tag at line 18 to fire, which in turn causes the error to be raised again. Because there are no other <CFCATCH> tags to handle the reraised exception, ColdFusion displays its usual error message (which you would customized with <CFERROR>, as discussed in Chapter 19).

LISTING 33.9 `ChoicePage6.cfm`—USING <CFRETHROW> TO PROCESS ONLY DATABASE ERRORS OF CODE `S1000`

```
<HTML>
<HEAD><TITLE>Films</TITLE></HEAD>
<BODY>
<H2>Film Information</H2>

<CFTRY>
  <!--- Retrieve Films from live database --->
  <CFQUERY NAME="GetFilms" DATASOURCE="#REQUEST.DataSource#">
```

```
    SELECT FilmID, MovieTitle
    FROM Films
    ORDER BY Films.MovieTitle
  </CFQUERY>

  <!--- If any database errors occur during above query, --->
  <CFCATCH TYPE="Database">
    <!--- Unless this is SQL Error S0001, un-catch the exception --->
    <CFIF CFCATCH.SQLState NEQ "S1000">
      <CFRETHROW>

    <!--- If it is SQL Error, S0001, attempt to get data from txt file --->
    <CFELSE>
      <CFTRY>
        <!--- Construct connection string so we can query Films.txt file --->
        <CFSET Driver = "{MERANT 3.70 ColdFusion OEM 32-BIT TextFile (*.*)}">
        <CFSET DBDir  = GetDirectoryFromPath(GetCurrentTemplatePath())>
        <CFSET ConStr = "DRIVER=#Driver#;DB=#DBDir#;FLN=1;tT=COMMA;UT=GUESS">

        <!--- Retrieve Films from Text file --->
        <CFQUERY NAME="GetFilms" DBTYPE="dynamic" CONNECTSTRING="#ConStr#">
          SELECT FilmID, MovieTitle
          FROM Films.txt
          ORDER BY Films.MovieTitle
        </CFQUERY>

        <!--- Let user know that text file is being used --->
        <I><P>NOTE:
        We are not able to connect to our real-time database at the moment.<BR>
        Instead, we are using information from our most recent archives.<BR>
        Please try again later today for an up to date listing.<BR></I>

        <!--- If any database error occurs *during this second query* --->
        <CFCATCH TYPE="Database">
          <!--- Let user know that the Films data can't be shown right now --->
          <I>Sorry, we can't display a list of current films right now.<BR></I>
        </CFCATCH>
      </CFTRY>
    </CFIF>
  </CFCATCH>
</CFTRY>

<!--- Attempt database operation --->
<CFTRY>
  <!--- Retrieve Ratings from database --->
  <CFQUERY NAME="GetRatings" DATASOURCE="#REQUEST.DataSource#">
    SELECT RatingID, Rating
    FROM FilmsRatings
    ORDER BY Rating
  </CFQUERY>

  <!--- Silently catch any database errors from above query --->
  <CFCATCH TYPE="Database"/>
</CFTRY>

<!--- Create self-submitting form --->
<CFFORM ACTION="#CGI.SCRIPT_NAME#" METHOD="Post">
```

Listing 33.9 Continued

```
  <!--- If, after all is said and done, we were able to get Film data --->
  <CFIF IsDefined("GetFilms")>
    <!--- Display Film names in a drop-down list --->
    <P>Films:
    <CFSELECT QUERY="GetFilms" NAME="FilmID"
      VALUE="FilmID" DISPLAY="MovieTitle"/>
    <INPUT TYPE="Submit" VALUE="Go">
  </CFIF>

  <!--- If, after all is said and done, we were able to get Ratings data --->
  <CFIF IsDefined("GetRatings")>
    <!--- Display Ratings in a drop-down list --->
    <P>Ratings:
    <CFSELECT QUERY="GetRatings" NAME="RatingID"
      VALUE="RatingID" DISPLAY="Rating"/>
    <INPUT TYPE="Submit" VALUE="Go">
  </CFIF>

</CFFORM>

</BODY>
</HTML>
```

Of course, you are free to have as many `<CFIF>` tests as you need to make the decision whether to rethrow the error. For instance, if you wanted your `<CFCATCH>` code to handle only errors of types `S1000`, `S1005`, and `S1010` instead of only `S1000`, you could replace the `<CFIF>` test in Listing 33.19 with something such as the following:

```
<CFIF ListFindNoCase("S1000,S1005,S1010", CFCATCH.SQLState) EQ 0>
  <CFRETHROW>
</CFIF>
```

Catching Advanced Exception Types

ColdFusion defines a large number of what Macromedia calls *advanced exception types*, which can help you catch very specific error conditions that might occur while processing certain CFML tags. At the moment, most of the advanced exception types are thrown only by the `<CFPOP>` and `<CFHTTP>` tags.

Table 33.4 is an abbreviated list of the advanced exception types that have been documented for ColdFusion 5, along with a short description of what each exception type means. Only those types that you would most likely want to catch in a real-world application are listed here. The complete list is available in the ColdFusion documentation.

Note

This is not meant to be an exhaustive list. For the complete list of advanced exception types, see the documentation for the `<CFTRY>` tag in the CFML Language Reference section of the ColdFusion documentation.

Table 33.4 A Short List of Advanced Exception Types

Exception Type	Description
COM.Allaire.ColdFusion.HTTPAuthFailure	Thrown by <CFHTTP> when the Web page specified in the URL attribute requires different USERNAME and PASSWORD attributes to be provided.
COM.Allaire.ColdFusion.HTTPFailure	Thrown by <CFHTTP> when the Web server specified in the URL attribute cannot be reached, often because of a misspelled server name.
COM.Allaire.ColdFusion.HTTPMovedTemporarily	Thrown by <CFHTTP> when the Web server specified in the URL attribute is reporting the requested page as having been moved. Generally, this means that a <CFLOCATION> (or equivalent function, if ColdFusion is not being used for the remote page) is being used to do a page redirect.
COM.Allaire.ColdFusion.HTTPNotFound	Thrown by <CFHTTP> if the Web page specified in the URL attribute cannot be found.
COM.Allaire.ColdFusion.POPAuthFailure	This error is thrown if an invalid username or password is provided to the <CFPOP> tag.
COM.Allaire.ColdFusion.POPConnectionFailure	Thrown by <CFPOP> if the mail server cannot be reached, usually because of an invalid SERVER attribute.
COM.Allaire.ColdFusion.POPDeleteError	Thrown by <CFPOP> when an e-mail message cannot be deleted.

Listing 33.10 is a revised version of the `CheckMail.cfm` template that was created and explained in detail in Chapter 28, “Interacting with E-mail.” This version uses <CFTRY> and <CFCATCH> in two places. The first <CFTRY> block surrounds the <CFPOP> tag and catches the special exceptions that occur if the user’s mail server can’t be connected to or if the username and password the user provides are not accepted by the mail server.

The second <CFTRY> block is used to catch the `Expression` exceptions that can occur when the `ParseDateTime()` function is incapable of parsing the date string provided by the application that originally sent the incoming mail message. Unfortunately, the `ParseDateTime()` function is not capable of parsing many of the date formats in common use on the Net. This template demonstrates how <CFTRY> can be used to trap the error that gets raised when `ParseDateTime()` can’t do its work properly.

Note

This template relies on the `CheckMailLogin.cfm` and `CheckMailMsg2.cfm` templates that were created in Chapter 28. It also requires client and session variables to be turned on in the `Application.cfm` file. For your convenience, these files are included in this chapter's folder on the CD-ROM for this book.

Listing 33.10 `CheckMail2.cfm`—**Catching Advanced Exceptions Raised During a** `<CFPOP>` **Operation**

```
<HTML>
<HEAD><TITLE>Check Your Mail</TITLE></HEAD>
<BODY>

<!--- Simple CSS-based formatting styles --->
<STYLE>
  BODY {font-family:sans-serif;font-size:12px}
  TH   {font-size:12px;background:navy;color:white}
  TD   {font-size:12px;background:lightgrey;color:navy}
</STYLE>
<H2>Check Your Mail</H2>


<!--- If user is logging out --->
<CFIF IsDefined("URL.Logout")>
  <CFSET StructDelete(SESSION, "Mail")>
</CFIF>

<!--- If we don't have a username/password --->
<CFIF NOT IsDefined("SESSION.Mail")>
  <!--- Show "mail server login" form --->
  <CFINCLUDE TEMPLATE="CheckMailLogin.cfm">
</CFIF>


<!--- If we need to contact server for list of messages --->
<!--- (if just logged in, or if clicked "Refresh" link) --->
<CFIF NOT IsDefined("SESSION.Mail.GetMessages") OR IsDefined("URL.Refresh")>
  <!--- Flush page output buffer --->
  <CFFLUSH>

  <CFTRY>
    <!--- Contact POP Server and retrieve messages --->
    <CFPOP
      ACTION="GetHeaderOnly"
      NAME="SESSION.Mail.GetMessages"
      SERVER="#SESSION.Mail.POPServer#"
      USERNAME="#SESSION.Mail.Username#"
      PASSWORD="#SESSION.Mail.Password#"
      MAXROWS="50">


    <!--- If the username/password were rejected by mail server --->
    <CFCATCH TYPE="COM.Allaire.ColdFusion.POPAuthFailure">
      <!--- Discard login information from SESSION scope --->
      <!--- This will force user to re-provide credentials --->
```

```
      <CFSET StructDelete(SESSION, "Mail")>
      <!--- Explain what happened, with link to try again --->
      <CFOUTPUT>
        <P>The username and password you provided were not accepted.<BR>
        <P><A HREF="#CGI.SCRIPT_NAME#">Click Here To Try Again</A><BR>
        <CFABORT>
      </CFOUTPUT>
    </CFCATCH>

    <!--- If the connection to the mail server failed --->
    <CFCATCH TYPE="COM.Allaire.ColdFusion.POPConnectionFailure">
      <!--- Discard login information from SESSION scope --->
      <!--- This will force user to re-provide credentials --->
      <CFSET StructDelete(SESSION, "Mail")>
      <!--- Explain what happened, with link to try again --->
      <CFOUTPUT>
        <P>The mail server you specified could not be reached.<BR>
        <P><A HREF="#CGI.SCRIPT_NAME#">Click Here To Try Again</A><BR>
        <CFABORT>
      </CFOUTPUT>
    </CFCATCH>

  </CFTRY>
</CFIF>


<!--- If no messages were retrieved... --->
<CFIF SESSION.Mail.GetMessages.RecordCount EQ 0>
  <P>You have no mail messages at this time.<BR>

<!--- If messages were retrieved... --->
<CFELSE>
  <!--- Display Messages in HTML Table Format --->
  <TABLE BORDER="0" CELLSPACING="2" CELLSPACING="2" COLS="3" WIDTH="550">
    <!--- Column Headings for Table --->
    <TR>
      <TH WIDTH="100">Date Sent</TH>
      <TH WIDTH="200">From</TH>
      <TH WIDTH="200">Subject</TH>
    </TR>
    <!--- Display info about each message in a table row --->
    <CFOUTPUT QUERY="SESSION.Mail.GetMessages">
      <CFTRY>
        <!--- Parse Date from the "date" mail header --->
        <CFSET d = ParseDateTime(Date, "POP")>
        <CFSET MsgDate = "<B>#DateFormat(d)#</B><BR>#TimeFormat(d)#">
        <!--- If the date can't be parsed, just use raw date header --->
        <CFCATCH TYPE="Expression">
          <CFIF CFCATCH.ErrNumber EQ 16394>
            <CFSET MsgDate = Date>
          <CFELSE>
            <CFRETHROW>
          </CFIF>
        </CFCATCH>
      </CFTRY>
      <!--- Let user click on Subject to read full message --->
      <CFSET LinkURL = "CheckMailMsg2.cfm?MsgNum=#MessageNumber#">
```

Listing 33.10 Continued

```
      <TR VALIGN="baseline">
        <!--- Show parsed Date and Time for message--->
        <TD>
          #MsgDate#
        </TD>
        <!--- Show "From" address, escaping brackets --->
        <TD>#HTMLEditFormat(From)#</TD>
        <TD><STRONG><A HREF="#LinkURL#">#Subject#</A></STRONG></TD>
      </TR>
    </CFOUTPUT>
  </TABLE>

  <!--- "Refresh" link to get new list of messages  --->
  <B><A HREF="CheckMail.cfm?Refresh=Yes">Refresh Message List</A></B><BR>
  <!--- "Log Out" link to discard SESSION.Mail info --->
  <A HREF="CheckMail.cfm?Logout=Yes">Log Out</A><BR>
</CFIF>

</BODY>
</HTML>
```

Note

This template uses two `<CFCATCH>` tags within the same `<CFTRY>` block to catch two different types of specific exception types. You can use as many `<CFCATCH>` tags as you need within a single `<CFTRY>`. Just be sure that each one specifies a different `TYPE` attribute.

Most of the code in Listing 33.10 is unchanged from the version in Chapter 28, so only the two `<CFTRY>` blocks are discussed here. The first `<CFTRY>` block displays a simple login-failed type of error message if the `<CFPOP>` tag raises an exception of type `COM.Allaire.ColdFusion.POPAuthFailure` while it tries to check the user's mailbox for messages. It also deletes the `Mail` structure from the `SESSION` scope, which effectively logs the user out of the page. When the user clicks the Click Here To Try Again link, he gets the login screen again, where he can specify a different username and password. A similar response is generated if the `<CFPOP>` tag raises an exception of `COM.Allaire.ColdFusion.POPConnectionFailure`, as shown in Figure 33.7.

The job of the second `<CFTRY>` block is to catch the error thrown by `ParseDateTime()` when it is incapable of parsing a message's date value correctly. First, the `<CFCATCH>` block catches all errors of type `Expression`. Then, a simple `<CFIF>` test is used to determine whether the error is expression error number `16394` (which means that `ParseDateTime()` doesn't consider the `Date` value for the message to be valid). If the exception is error number `16394`, the `MsgDate` variable is just set to the raw `Date` value for the message, so the date won't be formatted nicely). If the exception has some other error number, the exception is re-released via the `<CFRETHROW>` tag.

The result is a template that simply asks the user to verify his login credentials if his messages can't be retrieved and that can deal reasonably with date values that normally would cause an error message to be displayed.

Note

No published list of all the possible `ErrNumber` values that might be returned along with a particular `Expression` exception was available at the time of this writing. The number `16394` was found by first coding the `<CFCATCH>` block to display the value of `CFCATCH.ErrNumber` when the exception occurred. That value proved to be `16394`.

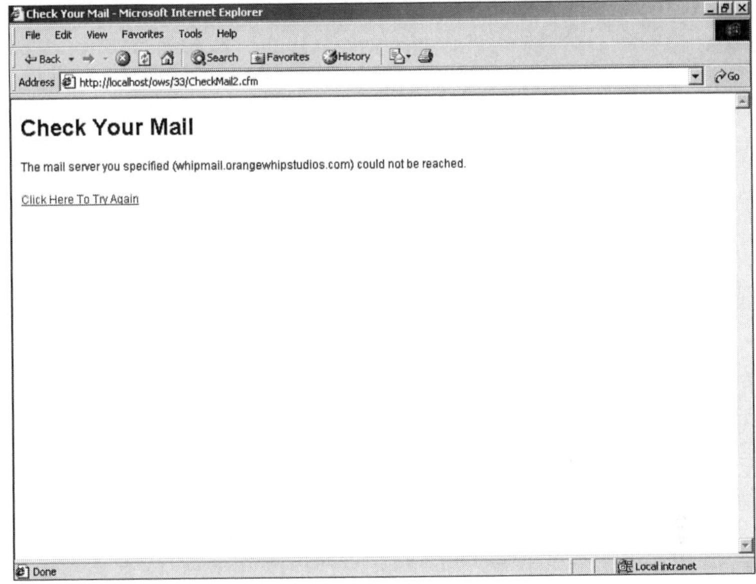

Figure 33.7 If a POP server can't be reached, the exception can be caught so a sensible message can be shown to the user.

Throwing and Catching Your Own Errors

You can throw custom exceptions whenever your code encounters a situation that should be considered an error within the context of your application, perhaps because it violates some type of business rule. Therefore, custom exceptions give you a way to teach your ColdFusion code to treat certain conditions—which ColdFusion wouldn't be capable of identifying as problematic on its own—as exceptions, just like the built-in exceptions thrown by ColdFusion itself.

Introducing <CFTHROW>

To throw your own custom exceptions, you use the `<CFTHROW>` tag. The exceptions you raise with `<CFTHROW>` can be caught with a `<CFTRY>`/`<CFCATCH>` block, just like the exceptions thrown by ColdFusion internally. If your custom exception is not caught (or is caught and then rethrown via the `<CFRETHROW>` tag), ColdFusion simply displays the text you provide for the `MESSAGE` and `DETAIL` attributes in a standard error message.

Table 33.5 lists the attributes that can be provided to the <CFTHROW> tag. All of them are optional, but it is strongly recommended that you at least provide the MESSAGE attribute whenever you use <CFTHROW>.

TABLE 33.5 <CFTHROW> TAG ATTRIBUTES

Attribute	Description
TYPE	A string which classifies your exception into a category. You can provide either TYPE="APPLICATION", which is the default, or a TYPE of your own choosing. You cannot provide any of the predefined exception types listed in Table 33.1. You can specify custom exception types that include dots, which enables you to create hierarchical families of custom exceptions. See the next section, "Creating Custom Exception Families."
MESSAGE	A text message that describes the error you are raising. This message should briefly describe the error that has occurred. If the exception is caught in a <CFCATCH> block, the value you provide here is available as CFCATCH.Message. If the exception is not caught, ColdFusion displays this value in an error message to the user. This value is optional, but it is strongly recommended that you provide it.
DETAIL	A second text message that describes the error in more detail, or any background information or hints that will help other people understand the cause of the error. If the exception is caught in a <CFCATCH> block, the value you provide here is available as CFCATCH.Detail. If the exception is not caught, ColdFusion displays this value in an error message to the user.
ERRORCODE	An optional error code, of your own devising. If the exception is caught in a <CFCATCH> block, the value you provide here is available as CFCATCH.ErrorCode.
EXTENDEDINFO	A second optional error code of your own devising. If the exception is caught in a in a <CFCATCH> block, the value you provide here will be available as CFCATCH.ExtendedInfo.

THROWING CUSTOM EXCEPTIONS

Say you are working on a piece of code that performs some type of operation (such as placing an order) based on a ContactID value. As a kind of sanity check, you should verify that the ContactID is actually valid before going further.

If you find that the ContactID is not valid, you can throw a custom error using the <CFTHROW> tag, like so:

```
<CFTHROW
  MESSAGE="Invalid Contact ID"
  DETAIL="No record exists for that Contact ID.">
```

This exception can be caught using a <CFCATCH> tag, as shown in the following. Within this <CFIF> block, you could take whatever action is appropriate in the face of an invalid contact ID (perhaps you insert a new record into the Contacts table or use <CFMAIL> to send a message to your customer service manager):

```
<CFCATCH TYPE="APPLICATION">
  <CFIF Message EQ "Invalid Contact ID">
    ...recovery code here...
  </CFIF>
</CFIF>
```

This <CFCATCH>code catches the *Invalid Contact ID* exception because the exception's type is APPLICATION, which is the default exception type used when no TYPE attribute is provided to <CFTHROW>. If you want, you can specify your own exception type, like so:

```
<CFTHROW
  TYPE="InvalidContactID"
  MESSAGE="Invalid Contact ID"
  DETAIL="No record exists for that Contact ID.">
```

This exception will be caught by any <CFCATCH> tag that has a matching TYPE, like this one:

```
<CFCATCH TYPE="InvalidContactID">
   ...recovery code here...
</CFCATCH>
```

Note

You can also use the <CFABORT> tag with the SHOWERROR attribute to throw a custom exception. If the exception is caught, the text you provide for SHOWERROR becomes the CFCATCH.Message value. However, the use of <CFTHROW> is preferred because you can provide more complete information about the error you are raising, via the TYPE, DETAIL, and other attributes shown in Listing 33.5.

Creating Custom Exception Families

You can create hierarchical families of exceptions by including dots in the TYPE attribute you provide to the <CFTHROW> tag. If you do so, you can catch whole groups of exceptions using a single <CFCATCH> tag.

For instance, you could throw an error such as the following:

```
<CFTHROW
  TYPE="OrangeWhipStudios.InternalData.InvalidContactID"
  MESSAGE="Invalid Contact ID"
  DETAIL="No record exists for that Contact ID.">
```

The previous exception could be caught with a matching <CFCATCH> tag, like this one:

```
<CFCATCH TYPE="OrangeWhipStudios.InternalData.InvalidContactID">
```

If no <CFCATCH> matches the TYPE exactly, ColdFusion looks for a <CFCATCH> tag that matches the next most specific type of exception, using the dots to denote levels of specificity. So, the error thrown by the previous <CFTHROW> would be caught with this <CFCATCH> tag:

```
<CFCATCH TYPE="OrangeWhipStudios.InternalData">
```

If no `<CFCATCH>` such as the previous one was present, this `<CFCATCH>` would catch the error, which would also catch other errors in the `OrangeWhipStudios` hierarchy, such as `OrangeWhipStudios.InternalData.InvalidMerchID` and `OrangeWhipStudios.DatabaseNotAvailable`:

```
<CFCATCH TYPE="OrangeWhipStudios">
```

Custom Exceptions and Custom Tags

Listing 33.11 is an example of a ColdFusion template that includes several `<CFTHROW>` tags that know how to report helpful, diagnostic information when problems arise. It is a revision of the `<CF_PlaceOrder>` custom tag from Chapter 29, "Online Commerce." This version performs all the same operations as the original version; the main difference is the addition of several sanity checks at the top of the template, which ensure that the various ID numbers passed to the tag make sense. If not, custom exceptions are thrown, which the calling template can catch with `<CFCATCH>` if it wants. If the calling template does not catch the exceptions thrown by the tag, ColdFusion displays the exception to the user in the form of an error message.

Note

This template relies on many of the templates from Chapter 29. To test this template, save it as `PlaceOrder.cfm` in the same folder as the examples from Chapter 29.

Listing 33.11 `PlaceOrder.cfm`—**Throwing Your Own Exceptions with `<CFTHROW>`**

```
<!--- Tag Parameters --->
<CFPARAM NAME="ATTRIBUTES.Processor" TYPE="string" DEFAULT="CyberCash">
<CFPARAM NAME="ATTRIBUTES.MerchList" TYPE="string">
<CFPARAM NAME="ATTRIBUTES.QuantList" TYPE="string">
<CFPARAM NAME="ATTRIBUTES.ContactID" TYPE="numeric">
<CFPARAM NAME="ATTRIBUTES.CreditCard" TYPE="string">
<CFPARAM NAME="ATTRIBUTES.CreditExpM" TYPE="string">
<CFPARAM NAME="ATTRIBUTES.CreditExpY" TYPE="string">
<CFPARAM NAME="ATTRIBUTES.CreditName" TYPE="string">
<CFPARAM NAME="ATTRIBUTES.ShipAddress" TYPE="string">
<CFPARAM NAME="ATTRIBUTES.ShipCity" TYPE="string">
<CFPARAM NAME="ATTRIBUTES.ShipCity" TYPE="string">
<CFPARAM NAME="ATTRIBUTES.ShipState" TYPE="string">
<CFPARAM NAME="ATTRIBUTES.ShipZIP" TYPE="string">
<CFPARAM NAME="ATTRIBUTES.ShipCountry" TYPE="string">
<CFPARAM NAME="ATTRIBUTES.HTMLMail" TYPE="boolean">
<CFPARAM NAME="ATTRIBUTES.ReturnVariable" TYPE="variableName">

<CFTRY>
  <!--- Make sure the MerchList and QuantList Attributes make sense --->
  <CFIF (ListLen(ATTRIBUTES.MerchList) EQ 0)
    OR ListLen(ATTRIBUTES.MerchList) NEQ ListLen(ATTRIBUTES.QuantList)>
    <!--- If not, throw an error --->
    <CFTHROW
      MESSAGE="Invalid MerchList or QuantList attribute"
      DETAIL="Both must have same number of list elements, and cannot be empty.">
  </CFIF>
```

```
  <!--- Quick query to verify the ContactID is valid --->
  <CFQUERY NAME="GetCount" DATASOURCE="#REQUEST.DataSource#">
    SELECT Count(*) AS ContactCount
    FROM Contacts
    WHERE ContactID = #ATTRIBUTES.ContactID#
  </CFQUERY>

  <!--- If any of the MerchIDs are not valid, throw custom error --->
  <CFIF GetCount.ContactCount NEQ 1>
    <CFTHROW
      TYPE="ows.MerchOrder.InvalidContactID"
      MESSAGE="Invalid Contact ID"
      DETAIL="The ContactID you provided (#ATTRIBUTES.ContactID#) is not valid."
      ERRORCODE="1">
  </CFIF>

  <!--- Quick query to verify that all MerchIDs are valid --->
  <CFQUERY NAME="GetCount" DATASOURCE="#REQUEST.DataSource#">
    SELECT Count(*) AS ItemCount
    FROM Merchandise
    WHERE MerchID IN (#ATTRIBUTES.MerchList#)
  </CFQUERY>

  <!--- If any of the MerchIDs are not valid, throw custom error --->
  <CFIF GetCount.ItemCount NEQ ListLen(ATTRIBUTES.MerchList)>
    <CFTHROW
      TYPE="ows.MerchOrder.InvalidMerchID"
      MESSAGE="Invalid Merchandise ID"
      DETAIL="At least one of the MerchID values you supplied is not valid."
      ERRORCODE="2">
  </CFIF>

  <!--- If any database problems came up during above validation steps --->
  <CFCATCH TYPE="Database">
    <CFTHROW
      TYPE="ows.MerchOrder.ValidationFailed"
      MESSAGE="Order Validation Failed"
      DETAIL="A database problem occurred while validating the order.">
  </CFCATCH>
</CFTRY>

<!--- Begin "order" database transaction here --->
<!--- Can be rolled back or committed later --->
<CFTRANSACTION ACTION="BEGIN">
  <CFTRY>
    <!--- Insert new record into Orders table --->
    <CFQUERY DATASOURCE="#REQUEST.DataSource#">
      INSERT INTO MerchandiseOrders (
        ContactID,
        OrderDate,
        ShipAddress, ShipCity,
        ShipState, ShipZip,
        ShipCountry)
      VALUES (
        #ATTRIBUTES.ContactID#,
        <CFQUERYPARAM CFSQLTYPE="CF_SQL_TIMESTAMP"
          VALUE="#DateFormat(Now())# #TimeFormat(Now())#">,
```

LISTING 33.11 CONTINUED

```
      '#ATTRIBUTES.ShipAddress#', '#ATTRIBUTES.ShipCity#',
      '#ATTRIBUTES.ShipState#', '#ATTRIBUTES.ShipZip#',
      '#ATTRIBUTES.ShipCountry#'
    )
  </CFQUERY>

  <!--- Get just-inserted OrderID from database --->
  <CFQUERY DATASOURCE="#REQUEST.DataSource#" NAME="GetNew">
    SELECT MAX(OrderID) AS NewID
    FROM MerchandiseOrders
  </CFQUERY>

  <!--- For each item in user's shopping cart --->
  <CFLOOP FROM="1" TO="#ListLen(ATTRIBUTES.MerchList)#" INDEX="i">
    <CFSET ThisMerchID = ListGetAt(ATTRIBUTES.MerchList, i)>
    <CFSET ThisQuant   = ListGetAt(ATTRIBUTES.QuantList, i)>

    <!--- Add the item to "OrdersItems" table --->
    <CFQUERY DATASOURCE="#REQUEST.DataSource#">
      INSERT INTO MerchandiseOrdersItems
        (OrderID, ItemID, OrderQty, ItemPrice)
      SELECT
        #GetNew.NewID#, MerchID, #ThisQuant#, MerchPrice
      FROM Merchandise
      WHERE MerchID = #ThisMerchID#
    </CFQUERY>
  </CFLOOP>

  <!--- Get the total of all items in user's cart --->
  <CFQUERY DATASOURCE="#REQUEST.DataSource#" NAME="GetTotal">
    SELECT SUM(ItemPrice * OrderQty) AS OrderTotal
    FROM MerchandiseOrdersItems
    WHERE OrderID = #GetNew.NewID#
  </CFQUERY>

  <!--- Attempt to process the transaction  --->
  <CF_ProcessPayment
    Processor="CyberCash"
    OrderID="#GetNew.NewID#"
    OrderAmount="#GetTotal.OrderTotal#"
    CreditCard="#ATTRIBUTES.CreditCard#"
    CreditExpM="#ATTRIBUTES.CreditExpM#"
    CreditExpY="#ATTRIBUTES.CreditExpY#"
    CreditName="#ATTRIBUTES.CreditName#"
    ReturnVariable="ChargeInfo">

  <!--- If the order was processed successfully --->
  <CFIF ChargeInfo.IsSuccessful>
    <!--- Commit the transaction to database --->
    <CFTRANSACTION ACTION="Commit"/>
  <CFELSE>
    <!--- Rollback the Order from the Database --->
    <CFTRANSACTION ACTION="RollBack"/>
  </CFIF>
```

```
    <!--- If any errors occur while processing the order --->
    <CFCATCH TYPE="Any">
      <!--- Rollback the Order from the Database --->
      <CFTRANSACTION ACTION="RollBack"/>
      <!--- Throw a custom exception --->
      <CFTHROW
        TYPE="ows.MerchOrder.OrderFailed"
        MESSAGE="Order Could Not Be Completed"
        DETAIL="The order (ID #GetNew.NewID#) was rolled back from the database."
        ERRORCODE="3">
    </CFCATCH>
  </CFTRY>
</CFTRANSACTION>

<!--- If the order was processed successfully --->
<CFIF ChargeInfo.IsSuccessful>
  <!--- Send Confirmation E-Mail, via Custom Tag --->
  <CF_SendOrderConfirmation
    OrderID="#GetNew.NewID#"
    UseHTML="#ATTRIBUTES.HTMLMail#">
</CFIF>

<!--- Return status values to calling template --->
<CFSET "Caller.#ATTRIBUTES.ReturnVariable#" = ChargeInfo>
```

The first use of `<CFTHROW>` just performs a bit of simple data validation on the `MerchList` and `QuantList` attributes. The custom tag needs these two lists to have the same number of elements; additionally, neither list should be allowed to be empty. So, if the `ListLen()` function reports that the lists contain different numbers of elements, or if the lists are empty, an exception is raised with a `MESSAGE` that reads `Invalid MerchList or QuantList attribute`.

Next, the `<CFTHROW>` tag is used again to raise an exception of type `ows.MerchOrder.InvalidContactID` if the `ContactID` attribute passed to the custom tag is not a valid contact ID number. First, the `GetCount` query counts the number of records in the `Contacts` table with the given `ContactID`. If the ID number is legitimate, the query returns a `ContactCount` of `1`. If not, the custom exception is thrown.

Similar logic is used to ensure that all the merchandise IDs in the `MerchList` attribute are legitimate. If the `ItemCount` value returned by the second `GetCount` query is the same as the number of items in the list, all the merchandise IDs must be legitimate (and do not contain any duplicate values). If not, a custom exception of type `ows.MerchOrder.InvalidMerchID` is thrown.

The whole top portion of the template (the portion that performs the sanity checks) is also wrapped in its own `<CFTRY>` block, so a custom exception of type `ows.MerchOrder.ValidationFailed` is thrown if any database errors occur while performing either of the `GetCount` queries.

Listing 33.12 is a revised version of the `StoreCheckout.cfm` template, also from Chapter 29. It calls the `<CF_PlaceOrder>` custom tag from Listing 33.11, catching any of the custom exceptions the custom tag might throw. Because the exceptions the tag throws all start with `ows.MerchOrder`, they are all capable of being caught with a single `<CFCATCH>` of `TYPE="owsMerchOrder"`.

Note

This template relies on many of the templates from Chapter 29. To test this template, save it as `StoreCheckout.cfm` in the same folder as the examples from Chapter 29. Be sure that Listing 33.11 also has been saved as `PlaceOrder.cfm` in the same folder.

LISTING 33.12 `StoreCheckout.cfm`—CATCHING CUSTOM EXCEPTIONS THROWN BY A CUSTOM TAG

```
<!--- Show header images, etc., for Online Store --->
<CFINCLUDE TEMPLATE="StoreHeader.cfm">

<!--- Get current cart contents, via Custom Tag --->
<CF_ShoppingCart
  Action="List"
  ReturnVariable="GetCart">

<!--- Stop here if user's cart is empty --->
<CFIF GetCart.RecordCount EQ 0>
  There is nothing in your cart.
  <CFABORT>
</CFIF>

<!--- If user is not logged in, force them to now --->
<CFIF NOT IsDefined("SESSION.Auth.IsLoggedIn")>
  <CFINCLUDE TEMPLATE="LoginForm.cfm">
  <CFABORT>
</CFIF>

<!--- If user is attempting to place order --->
<CFIF IsDefined("FORM.IsPlacingOrder")>

  <CFTRY>
    <!--- Attempt to process the transaction  --->
    <CF_PlaceOrder
      ContactID="#SESSION.Auth.ContactID#"
      MerchList="#ValueList(GetCart.MerchID)#"
      QuantList="#ValueList(GetCart.Quantity)#"
      CreditCard="#FORM.CreditCard#"
      CreditExpM="#FORM.CreditExpM#"
      CreditExpY="#FORM.CreditExpY#"
      CreditName="#FORM.CreditName#"
      ShipAddress="#FORM.ShipAddress#"
      ShipState="#FORM.ShipState#"
      ShipCity="#FORM.ShipCity#"
      ShipZIP="#FORM.ShipZIP#"
      ShipCountry="#FORM.ShipCountry#"
      HTMLMail="#FORM.HTMLMail#"
      ReturnVariable="OrderInfo">

    <!--- If any exceptions in the "ows.MerchOrder" family are thrown... --->
    <CFCATCH TYPE="ows.MerchOrder">
      <P>Unfortunately, we are not able to process your order at the moment.<BR>
      Please try again later.  We apologize for the inconvenience.<BR>
      <CFABORT>
```

```
    </CFCATCH>
  </CFTRY>


  <!--- If the order was processed successfully --->
  <CFIF OrderInfo.IsSuccessful>

    <!--- Empty user's shopping cart, via custom tag --->
    <CF_ShoppingCart
      ACTION="Empty">

    <!--- Display Success Message --->
    <CFOUTPUT>
      <H2>Thanks For Your Order</H2>
      <P><B>Your Order Has Been Placed.</B><BR>
      Your order number is: #OrderInfo.OrderID#<BR>
      Your credit card has been charged:
      #LSCurrencyFormat(OrderInfo.OrderAmount)#<BR>
      <P>A confirmation is being E-mailed to you.<BR>
    </CFOUTPUT>

    <!--- Stop here. --->
    <CFABORT>
  <CFELSE>
    <!--- Display "Error" message --->
    <FONT COLOR="Red">
      <STRONG>Your credit card could not be processed.</STRONG><BR>
      Please verify the credit card number, expiration date, and
      name on the card.<BR>
    </FONT>

    <!--- Show debug info if viewing page on server --->
    <CFIF CGI.REMOTE_ADDR EQ "127.0.0.1">
      <CFOUTPUT>
        Status:  #OrderInfo.Status#<BR>
        Error:   #OrderInfo.ErrorCode#<BR>
        Message: #OrderInfo.ErrorMessage#<BR>
      </CFOUTPUT>
    </CFIF>
  </CFIF>
</CFIF>


<!--- Show Checkout Form (Ship Address/Credit Card) --->
<CFINCLUDE TEMPLATE="StoreCheckoutForm.cfm">
```

This listing is exactly the same as the original version from Chapter 29, except for the addition of the `<CFTRY>` and `<CFCATCH>` tags. Please see Chapter 29 for a complete discussion.

Note

Listing 33.11 has also added a `<CFTRY>` block around the main portion of the template, where the order is actually processed. See the next section, "Exceptions and Database Transactions," for an explanation.

EXCEPTIONS AND DATABASE TRANSACTIONS

Listing 33.11 uses `<CFTRY>` and `<CFCATCH>` together with the `<CFTRANSACTION>` tag, so that the database transaction can be rolled back if any errors occur. The `<CFTRY>` block is wrapped around all the database interactions, as well as the call to the `<CF_ProcessPayment>` custom tag.

If any database errors or syntax errors occur while the order is being processed (even inside `<CF_ProcessPayment>`), they are caught by the `<CFCATCH>` tag near the end of Listing 33.11. The `<CFCATCH>` tag uses `<CFTRANSACTION>` with `ACTION="Rollback"`, which has the effect of undoing all the database changes that were made since the beginning of the first `<CFTRANSACTION>` tag. This greatly minimizes the risk that any type of erroneous or inconsistent order information will ever get recorded in the `MerchandiseOrders` or `MerchandiseOrdersItems` table.

In many respects, `<CFTRANSACTION>` can be thought of as the database equivalent of `<CFTRY>` because they both are about being able to recover gracefully when problems arise. Used together, they become even more powerful.

Note

As noted in Chapter 31, it is generally preferable to keep transactions contained within stored procedures whenever possible. However, when that isn't possible, you can use `<CFTRY>` and `<CFTRANSACTION>` together as shown here. For more information, see Chapter 31, "More About SQL and Queries" and Chapter 32, "Working with Stored Procedures."

CHAPTER 34

Generating Non-HTML Content

In this chapter

ABOUT COLDFUSION AND NON-HTML CONTENT

Normally, ColdFusion is used to generate Web pages and Web pages only. Its main purpose in life is to wait for requests from Web browsers and send back chunks of HTML in response. The Web browsers then render the HTML visually for your users. In one form or another, that's what every code example in this book has been about.

However, there's no law that says your ColdFusion templates have to send HTML back to the Web browser. If you think about it, the only reason HTML tags such as `<body>` and `<title>` are in the pages ColdFusion serves up is because *you* put them there. Take away the HTML tags, and your ColdFusion templates are really just sending back plain old text files, such as you would create in Notepad.

Okay, so if you remove the HTML tags from a page, could you format or mark up the text in some other way? Sure you could. If the user's browser knows how to display text formatted in that particular way, it will do so. If not, it will try to invoke some other application to display the content to the user.

In this chapter, you learn about doing just that: getting ColdFusion to create other types of content on-the-fly.

ABOUT MIME CONTENT TYPES

If you've been working with Web pages for long, you might have heard of strange things called *MIME types* or *content types*. But you may not have heard much of an explanation regarding what exactly they are or what they are good for.

Basically, a MIME type is a short label that determines what type of content a particular document or URL contains. The idea is that every file format—word processing files, spreadsheets, HTML files, image files, multimedia files, and so on—has (or could have) its own MIME type. Any Web browser, e-mail client, or other device can use the MIME type to determine what do to with a file (or stream of content from a server), such as showing it as a picture, interpreting it as a document, or opening up the file in some other program (such as the appropriate word processing or spreadsheet application).

Note

In a way, the concept of a MIME type is similar to the notion of a file extension in Windows; the file extension tells Windows which icon to display in the Windows Explorer and which program should be launched when a user double-clicks a file. MIME types are more flexible and appropriate for the Internet because they are not a Windows-specific concept. But both are simple schemes for describing what exactly a computer should expect to find in a particular file or chunk of data.

Note

Although purists might disagree, the terms *MIME type*, *MIME content type*, and *content type* are often used interchangeably. For purposes of this discussion, please consider them to be synonyms.

A MIME content type is always made up of two parts, separated by a forward slash:

- **The first part describes the broad category that the content can be thought to belong to**—The common ones are text (generally something that could sensibly be opened in Notepad or some other text editor), image, audio, video, and application. The application type is somewhat of a catchall, generally meaning that the content is meant for a specific application, such as Word, Photoshop, or something of that nature.
- **The second part, or *subtype*, is a more specific description of what exactly the content's format is**—For instance, JPEG images, GIF images, and TIFF images been given MIME types of `image/jpeg`, `image/gif`, and `image/tiff`, respectively.

Some common content types are listed in Table 34.1.

Table 34.1 Common MIME Content Types

MIME Type	Description
`text/html`	Content that should be interpreted as HTML markup and thus rendered by a Web browser natively. By far the most common in use on the Web. Anything you would normally call a Web page has this content type.
`text/plain`	Just normal text content, such as you would create if you were just typing a note for yourself in Notepad or some other text editor.
`text/vnd.wap.wml` `text/vnd.wap.wmlscript`	Markup and script content intended for WAP-enabled wireless devices, such as cell phones. This subject is discussed in the section "Getting Started with Wireless Applications," later in this chapter.

`image/gif`
`image/jpeg`
`image/jpg`
	Common types of image content. Unlike the various text types listed above, images are binary files that mostly contain information about individual pixels and can't be opened in a text editor, such as Notepad.

`application/msword` `application/msexcel`	Content tailored specifically for, and probably generated or saved by, a specific application (in these cases, Microsoft Word and Excel).

`application/x-shockwave-flash`
`video/x-msvideo`
`video/vnd.rn-realvideo`
	Multimedia presentations or movies to be displayed by the Macromedia Flash Player, Windows Media Player, or Real Player, respectively.

`application/unknown` `application/octet-stream`	In general, a file or content that isn't really meant to be opened or viewed in any particular way. When you download an executable program (an .exe file, perhaps) from a Web site, the content type typically is set to this value. Web browsers usually respond to this content type by prompting the user for a download location by displaying a Save As prompt.

How Your Browser Handles MIME Types

A good way to get a list of MIME content types—and which program your particular browser will launch if it can't display the content itself—is to examine how the browser has been configured.

If you are using a Netscape browser, select Preferences from the Edit menu, and then select the Applications or Helper Applications option (depending on the version). You will be able to scroll through the list of applications and see the types of content the browser has been configured to launch for each application. For instance, Figure 34.1 shows that URLs that return a content type of `application/msexcel` are passed off to Microsoft Excel for processing and viewing. This is how the dialog box looks with Netscape 4.7; other versions will look different but provide the same basic information.

If you are using Internet Explorer on a Windows machine, the equivalent place to look is in the File Types tab of the Folder Options dialog box, which you can get to by selecting Folder Options from the Tools menu in the Windows Explorer (not Internet Explorer).

Note

If no content type is provided by the Web server for a given file or steam of content, the browser will not know what to do with the content. It usually will ask you what you want to do with the file, often by presenting a dialog box in which you select the appropriate viewer or helper application. The exact behavior varies from browser to browser; it is generally the same behavior as when a content type of `application/unknown` or `application/octet-stream` is specified (refer to Table 34.1).

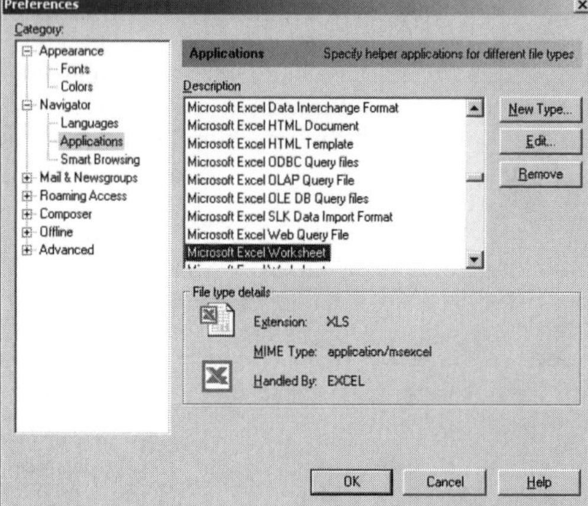

Figure 34.1
You can see how Netscape associates content types with applications in its Preferences dialog box.

Note

Although it's not exactly bedtime reading, you can read the formal specification for the MIME type scheme by visiting the WC3's Web site at `http://www.w3.org`.

Introducing the <CFCONTENT> Tag

The HTTP specification requires that every response from a Web server include the appropriate content type information. By default, ColdFusion always sends back a MIME type of `text/html`, which is why Web browsers assume that the text returned by your templates should be rendered as Web pages.

The `<CFCONTENT>` tag is provided for situations in which you want to send a different content type back to the browser along with the content your template generates. Table 34.2 lists the various attributes the `<CFCONTENT>` tag can take. The most important of these, as you might guess, is the `TYPE` attribute.

Table 34.2 <CFCONTENT> Tag Syntax

Attribute	Purpose
`TYPE`	Required. The `MIME` content type you want to send back to the browser along with the content your template is generating. This could be one of the types listed in Table 34.1 or some other type. For instance, if your template is written to generate plain text (rather than HTML), you would set this value to `text/plain`.
`FILE`	Optional. The complete path of a file on the server that you want to send back to the browser. The actual content of the file should match up with the content type you specified with the `TYPE` attribute. You can use this to respond to a page request with an image or some other type of file that you want the user to download (perhaps a .zip or an .exe file).
`DELETEFILE`	Optional. You can set this attribute to `Yes`, which causes a file to be deleted from the server's drive after it has been sent to the browser. The default is `No`. Relevant only if the `FILE` attribute is provided.
`RESET`	Optional. Defaults to `Yes`, which means that any text that might have been output before the `<CFCONTENT>` tag should be discarded (not sent to the browser). This is handy if your code needs to make some decisions before deciding which content type to specify. If it's set to `No`, all content, even spaces and other whitespace, that precedes the `<CFCONTENT>` tag will be sent back to the browser. This attribute is discussed later in this chapter, in the section "Generating Comma-Separated Text."

Experimenting with Plain Text

As mentioned previously, ColdFusion always sends back a content type of `text/html` unless you specify a different one using the `<CFCONTENT>` tag. As an experiment, you can try setting the content type to `text/plain`, which means the browser is not obligated to parse the content as HTML. Instead, the browser can display the content literally, just as you would expect to see the content in a simple text editor such as Notepad.

Here's a simple exercise to illustrate this point. Visit Listings 34.1 and 34.2 with your Web browser, and compare the results. You can probably guess what Listing 34.1 will look like: The words `The time is now` will be in italics, and then the current time will appear in bold on the next line. Listing 34.2, on the other hand, tells the browser that the content type is plain text rather than HTML, so it shows the text quite literally, without attempting to apply any tag-based formatting (see Figure 34.2).

LISTING 34.1 `TestMessage1.cfm`**—A SIMPLE MESSAGE, WITHOUT SPECIFYING A CONTENT TYPE**

```
<P><I>The time is now:</I><BR>
<CFOUTPUT><B>#TimeFormat(Now())#</B></CFOUTPUT>
```

LISTING 34.2 `TestMessage2.cfm`**—THE SAME SIMPLE MESSAGE, SPECIFYING** `text/plain` **AS THE CONTENT TYPE**

```
<CFCONTENT TYPE="text/plain"><P><I>The time is now:</I><BR>
<CFOUTPUT><B>#TimeFormat(Now())#</B></CFOUTPUT>
```

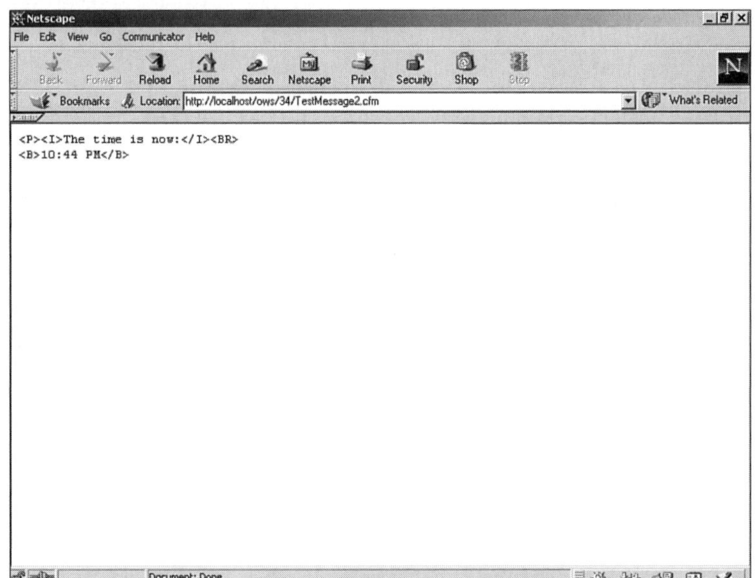

Figure 34.2
If the MIME type is set to `text/plain`, the browser won't know to interpret any HTML tags in your documents.

Note

Unlike the other listings in this book, Listings 34.1 and 34.2 were purposefully written to not be well-formed HTML (no `<html>` or `<body>` tags and so on). This is because Internet Explorer browsers try to second-guess the situation by assuming that any document that contains well-formed HTML should be displayed as HTML, regardless of the content type specified by the Web server. Whether that's a bug or a feature depends on who you ask (see "Adding a `Content-Disposition` Header for Internet Explorer," later in this chapter). We just chose these short listings to avoid any confusion. You'll find that Netscape browsers will correctly display even a well-formed HTML document as plain text if you specify a content type of `text/plain`.

Tip

The `TimeFormat()` and `Now()` functions are both explained in Appendix B, "ColdFusion Function Reference."

Comma-Separated Text

Now that you know how to use ColdFusion to serve plain text rather than HTML, let's try to put that knowledge to good use. One thing people do with plain-text files is to use them to hold *comma-separated* text. Comma-separated text is a simple data format that gets used for many purposes. Because it's simple and easy to parse through, it's often used for various types of logging and simple integration projects. In fact, ColdFusion's own log files are kept in a comma-separated format (take a look at the files in the `LOG` folder, within ColdFusion's program directory). Many types of Web server software packages keep their logs in comma-separated format as well.

There are slightly different flavors of comma-separated text in common use, but they usually follow these rules:

- Each row of information usually sits in its own line in the text.
- Within each line, each column or field of information has a comma separating it from the next column or field.
- If the data in a particular column can contain commas, it's traditional to put double-quote characters around the data so the "real" commas can be distinguished from the commas that separate the fields.
- It's common to put the names of each column on the first line, with each name surrounded by quotation marks and separated from one another with commas.

Generating Comma-Separated Text

To generate comma-separated text with a ColdFusion template, you are generally going to create a .cfm file that does the following:

1. Retrieves the information that should be presented in column-separated format, using a database query or some other means.
2. Sets the content type for the request to `text/plain` using the `<CFCONTENT>` tag, so the generated content is not mistaken for HTML.
3. Outputs the names of the columns as the first line of the generated content.
4. Outputs the actual rows of data, each on its own line.

The code in Listing 34.3 retrieves some data from a database table and sends the data back to the browser in a comma-separated text format. If you were to visit this page in your browser, it would look similar to Figure 34.3, if viewed with a Netscape browser.

Listing 34.3 `FilmsCommaSep.cfm`—**Presenting Queried Data As Comma-Separated Text**

```
Retrieving information about films...
<CFQUERY DATASOURCE="ows" NAME="GetFilms">
  SELECT FilmID, MovieTitle
  FROM Films
  ORDER BY MovieTitle
</CFQUERY>

<!--- Now output as simple comma-separated text --->
<!--- Put the column names on first line, then  --->
<!--- the actual data rows on their own lines   --->
<CFCONTENT TYPE="text/plain">"FilmID","MovieTitle"
<CFOUTPUT QUERY="GetFilms">#FilmID#,"#MovieTitle#"
</CFOUTPUT>
```

Note

In HTML, whitespace (such as multiple spaces together or new lines) is ignored—not so with comma-separated text. That's why there is a new line after the list of column names but not before; it is important that the names show up as the first line of text. That's also why there is a new line before the closing `</CFOUTPUT>` tag but not after the opening `<CFOUTPUT>` tag. You want ColdFusion to output a new line only after each row of data, so you can't freely indent and skip lines the way you can when you are outputting normal HTML content.

You'll notice that the `Retrieving information about films` message is not displayed by the browser. Because you have not explicitly set the `RESET` attribute of the `<CFCONTENT>` tag to `No`, it defaults to its `Yes` behavior, which is for all content that was generated before the tag to be discarded. If you were to remove the `<CFCONTENT>` tag, not only would the data no longer be displayed as plain text by the browser, but the retrieving message would be displayed, as you would expect it to normally. Figure 34.4 shows the results if you were to remove the `<CFCONTENT>` tag from Listing 34.3. The same results would appear if you added `RESET="No"` to the `<CFCONTENT>` tag.

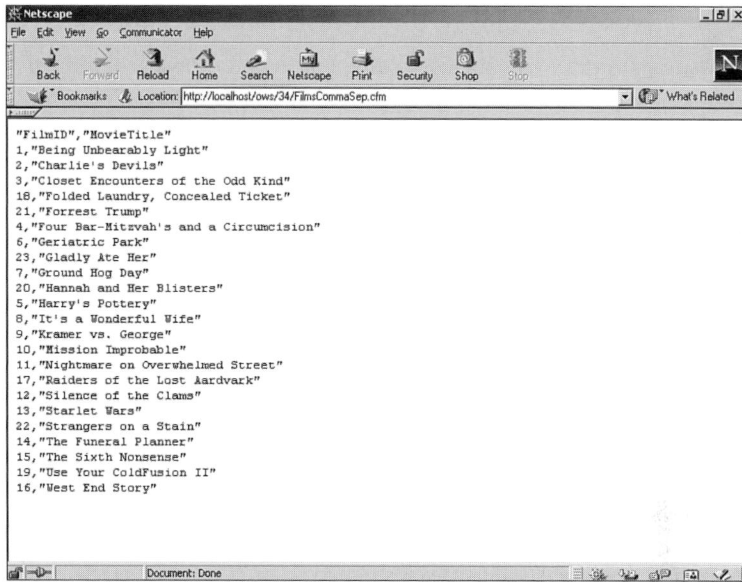

Figure 34.3
The <CFCONTENT> tag makes generating comma-separated text on-the-fly easy.

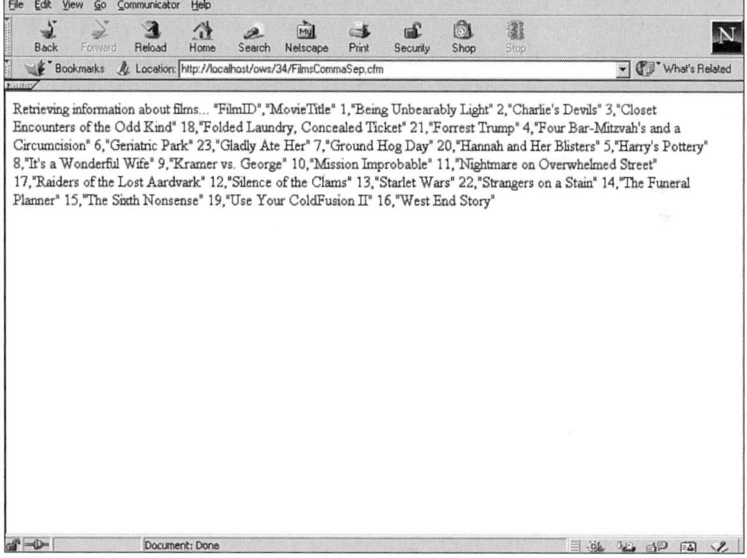

Figure 34.4
Without <CFCONTENT>, the new lines in the text are no longer displayed. Also, the message from earlier in the template is included in the output.

Adding a Content-Disposition Header for Internet Explorer

If you test Listing 34.3 with a Netscape browser, it should look similar to Figure 34.3. If you visit the listing with Internet Explorer, you might see much different behavior. For instance, you might find that the comma-separated text opens in ColdFusion Studio as a file named `FilmsCommaSep[1].cfm` or similar. Internet Explorer takes the `.cfm` extension in the URL as an indication that the returned content is a ColdFusion template, which it clearly is not.

This illustrates one of Internet Explorer's policies, which, contrary to most other browsers, is to think of the file extension—and the format of the actual content itself—as being more important than the specified content type. Only if the file extension does not have an associated program—or when there is no file extension—is the content type considered.

To get consistent behavior with IE, add a `content-disposition` header to the page request, using a `<CFHEADER>` tag, such as the following. The `<CFHEADER>` tag is the method ColdFusion provides to enable you to send custom HTTP headers back to the browser, along with the content your template generates. You would add this line right before the `<CFCONTENT>` line in Listing 34.3:

```
<CFHEADER NAME="Content-Disposition" VALUE="filename=films">
```

We don't have space here to discuss the `content-disposition` header in detail. The short explanation is that the `content-disposition` header suggests a filename for the file, if the user were to save it. After Internet Explorer sees this header, it will think of the content as having an implied filename of `films`, rather than of `FilmsCommaSep.cfm`. Because `films` has no extension, Internet Explorer will then use the content type to decide how to display the content. The content therefore will be shown as plain text, similar to Figure 34.3.

You could also provide a filename with an extension, like so:

```
<CFHEADER NAME="Content-Disposition" VALUE="filename=films.txt">
```

Now, if you visit the listing with Internet Explorer and then select Save As from the File menu, the Save Web Page dialog box will appear with `films.txt` prefilled as the filename. You can also add the word `Attachment` to the header, as shown here:

```
<CFHEADER NAME="Content-Disposition" VALUE="Attachment; filename=films.txt">
```

This will cause Internet Explorer to prompt the user to save the content as an attachment right away when Listing 34.3 is visited, rather than displaying the content in the browser window. Netscape browsers do not do anything special with the `Attachment` keyword, so the added line of code should not cause any harm. The `FilmsCommaSepIE.cfm` template (on this book's CD-ROM) includes this `content-disposition` line.

Note

To read more about the `content-disposition` header and the `Attachment` and `filename` keywords (there is an `Inline` keyword, too), see RFC 1806 at `http://www.ietf.org`.

Note

If you want to know more about the way IE decides how to display incoming content, please refer to Article number Q293336 in the Microsoft Knowledge Base at `http://support.microsoft.com`.

Retrieving the Comma-Separated Text with <CFHTTP>

Listing 34.4 is a bit of a digression, but it demonstrates a way you actually can use comma-separated text in your applications. You can use ColdFusion's `<CFHTTP>` tag to visit the URL for Listing 34.3, as if ColdFusion itself were a Web browser. The `<CFHTTP>` tag grabs the comma-separated text generated by `FilmsCommaSep.cfm` and parses through it, effectively re-creating the query result set. You can then use the resultset just as if it were returned by the original `<CFQUERY>` tag. This enables you to share data between two different ColdFusion servers over the Internet.

Note

We're using the `<CFHTTP>` tag a bit ahead of ourselves here. It's discussed in full in the "Creating Intelligent Agents" chapter in our companion volume, *Advanced ColdFusion 5 Application Development* (ISBN: 0-7897-2585-1). You can find the syntax for the `<CFHTTP>` tag in Appendix A, "ColdFusion Tag Reference" on the accompanying CD-ROM.

Tip

ColdFusion's `<CFWDDX>` tag gives you an even easier and more powerful way to share content between servers over the Internet, using a clever XML format instead of comma-separated text. Unfortunately, that discussion is beyond the scope of this book. To learn more about WDDX, please refer to the "Using WDDX" chapter in *Advanced ColdFusion 5 Application Development* (ISBN: 0-7897-2585-1), or visit `http://www.openwddx.org`.

Listing 34.4 `FetchCommaSep.cfm`—The `<CFHTTP>` Tag Knows How to Grab Comma-Separated Text Over the Internet and Return It to You As a Query Object

```
<!--- Visit our new "comma-separated" page, --->
<!--- and parse content into a query object --->
<CFHTTP
  METHOD="Get"
  URL="http://localhost/ows/34/FilmsCommaSep.cfm"
  NAME="GetFilmsViaHTTP">

<HTML>
<HEAD><TITLE>Fetching Comma-Separated Content</TITLE></HEAD>
<BODY>

<H3>Comma-separated text has been fetched via CFHTTP</H3>

<!--- Now the "fetched" query may be used normally --->
<CFOUTPUT QUERY="GetFilmsViaHTTP">
  Film <B>#FilmID#</B> is: <I>#MovieTitle#</I><BR>
```

Listing 34.4 Continued

```
</CFOUTPUT>

</BODY>
</HTML>
```

Generating Excel Files

You might have seen Web sites that enable users to access or view some type of information in spreadsheet or Excel format. For instance, the check stock quotes area at Yahoo! enables users to download stock quotes in spreadsheet format. Because Microsoft Excel has become the de facto standard for spreadsheet applications, and because so many PCs come with it preinstalled, this type of feature can be very useful for people.

In this section, you learn how you can add this type of functionality to your own ColdFusion applications. This will enable you to provide your users with a way to open customized data in Excel (such as kind of personalized purchase history or a list of other employees if you're building an intranet application).

Creating Spreadsheets with Tab-Separated Text

One of the file formats Excel knows how to import is *tab-separated* text. Tab-separated text is basically the same as comma-separated text, except it uses tab characters instead of commas to separate the columns on each line.

If you create a ColdFusion template that generates tab-separated text and specify a content type of `application/msexcel`, the user's browser will display the content to the user by launching Excel. Excel should then seamlessly import the tab-separated text and display it in the same way it would display a native Excel worksheet (.xls) file. As far as the end user is concerned, your Web site presented him with a personalized spreadsheet file. Only you know that it was simply some tab-separated text.

Listing 34.5 shows how easy getting this effect is. Note that this code is essentially the same as the code from Listing 34.3, with just a few minor changes. Most importantly, the `TYPE` attribute of the `<CFCONTENT>` tag has been changed to `application/msexcel`.

Listing 34.5 `FilmsToExcel.cfm`—Generating Tab-Separated Text for Use with Excel on the Client

```
<!--- Don't output anything *not* in CFOUTPUT tags --->
<!--- This makes it easier to deal with whitespace --->
<CFSETTING ENABLECFOUTPUTONLY="Yes">

<!--- Retrieve information about films --->
<CFQUERY DATASOURCE="ows" NAME="GetFilms">
  SELECT MovieTitle, AmountBudgeted
  FROM Films
  ORDER BY MovieTitle
</CFQUERY>
```

```
<!--- Set variables for special characters --->
<CFSET TabChar = Chr(9)>
<CFSET NewLine = Chr(13) & Chr(10)>

<!--- Set the content-type so Excel is invoked --->
<CFCONTENT TYPE="application/msexcel">

<!--- Suggest default filename for spreadsheet --->
<CFHEADER NAME="Content-Disposition" VALUE="filename=FilmBudgets.xls">

<!--- Output the header row, with column names --->
<!--- Put tab between columns, and newline at end --->
<CFOUTPUT>MOVIE TITLE#TabChar#BUDGET#NewLine#</CFOUTPUT>

<!--- Output actual data rows, each on own line --->
<!--- Put tab between columns, and newline at end  --->
<CFLOOP QUERY="GetFilms">
  <CFOUTPUT>#MovieTitle##TabChar##AmountBudgeted##NewLine#</CFOUTPUT>
</CFLOOP>
```

Note

When the spreadsheet is displayed in Excel, you might see hash marks (a series of # signs) where the budget numbers belong. Just make the budget column a bit wider (by dragging in Excel) to see the full numbers. This is normal Excel behavior and does not represent a problem or bug.

Another difference is that this code uses the `<CFHEADER>` tag mentioned earlier to send a custom `Content-Disposition` header to the browser, along with the content type. The `Content-Disposition` header is used to suggest a default filename for the content going back to the browser (see the following notes and the section, "Adding a `Content-Disposition` Header for Internet Explorer," earlier in this chapter).

Note

A complete discussion of all HTTP headers and the various things they are used for is beyond the scope of this book (and is something you generally don't need to know about because ColdFusion takes care of this kind of thing for you). In short, custom headers can be used to provide the browser with various pieces of information, or *metadata*, about the server's response.

Note

The `Content-Disposition` header really should be optional, but because of the way Internet Explorer determines how to handle incoming content, this particular `<CFHEADER>` tag is required for the code to work properly with IE. To make the decision about which application to launch, IE doesn't look only at the MIME content type the code provides; it also relies on other factors, such as the suggested filename. Additionally, the extension of the suggested filename must be associated with Excel (that is, .xls), but the first part of the filename is up to you. If you want to know more about the way IE decides how to display incoming content, please refer to Article number Q293336 in the Microsoft Knowledge Base at `http://support.microsoft.com`.

Listing 34.5 also sets a couple of variables for the two special characters needed to produce the correct text, by using the `Chr()` function. This can be a more manageable way to get special characters into your page output. Instead of actually pressing the Tab key to insert a Tab character into your code (which would work but might be hard to notice or understand when you edit the code later), you can use the `Chr()` function, which returns the character specified by the ASCII code you supply.

Tip

`Chr(9)` always returns a Tab character, and a `Chr(13)` followed by a `Chr(10)` always returns a linefeed character followed by a carriage return. A linefeed followed by a carriage return is known as a *newline*, which is the standard way to indicate the end of a line in a text file.

Another difference is that this listing turns on the `ENABLECFOUTPUTONLY` mode of the `<CFSETTING>` tag, which causes ColdFusion not to output anything that is not between `CFOUTPUT` tags. Together with the `TabChar` and `NewLine` variables, this enables the code to explicitly tell ColdFusion about every single character that needs to be output to the browser, rather than having to be overly careful about positioning the tags within the code (refer to Listing 34.3). See Appendix A for more information about the `<CFSETTING>` tag.

In any case, if you visit the URL for Listing 34.5 with your browser, it should launch Excel with the film data loaded as a spreadsheet. Depending on the browser and platform being used, Excel might be launched as a separate application, or it might appear within the browser window, as shown in Figure 34.5.

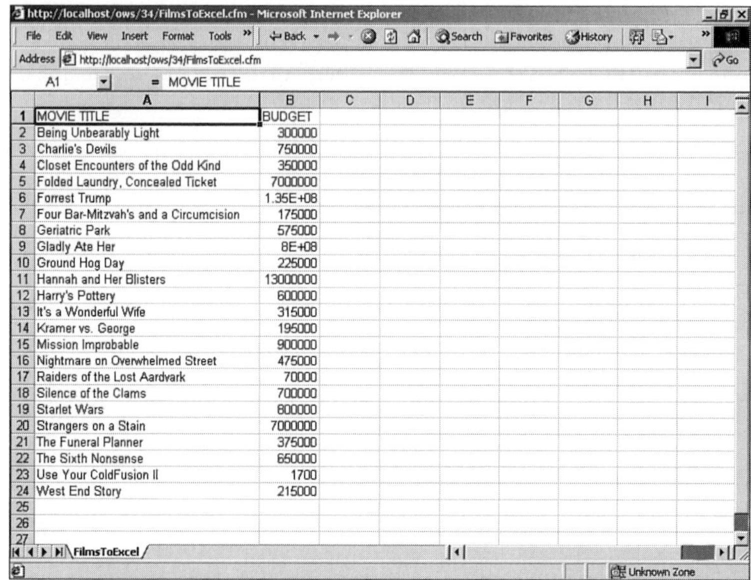

	A	B
1	MOVIE TITLE	BUDGET
2	Being Unbearably Light	300000
3	Charlie's Devils	750000
4	Closet Encounters of the Odd Kind	350000
5	Folded Laundry, Concealed Ticket	7000000
6	Forrest Trump	1.35E+08
7	Four Bar-Mitzvah's and a Circumcision	175000
8	Geriatric Park	575000
9	Gladly Ate Her	8E+08
10	Ground Hog Day	225000
11	Hannah and Her Blisters	13000000
12	Harry's Pottery	600000
13	It's a Wonderful Wife	315000
14	Kramer vs. George	195000
15	Mission Improbable	900000
16	Nightmare on Overwhelmed Street	475000
17	Raiders of the Lost Aardvark	70000
18	Silence of the Clams	700000
19	Starlet Wars	800000
20	Strangers on a Stain	7000000
21	The Funeral Planner	375000
22	The Sixth Nonsense	650000
23	Use Your ColdFusion II	1700
24	West End Story	215000
25		
26		
27		

Figure 34.5
If you send tab-separated text back to the browser with the correct content type, it should be opened in Excel.

Tip

Of course, you could create a template based on Listing 34.5 that uses a URL parameter to dynamically return spreadsheet data based on some type of Film ID, actor, and so on.

CREATING SPREADSHEETS WITH HTML

For Excel 2000, Microsoft created a special flavor of HTML, which Excel can import as if it were a normal .xls file. If you have Excel 2000 or later, try creating a quick spreadsheet with a few columns and rows. Select Save As from the File menu, and save the spreadsheet as an HTML file. Now open that HTML file in ColdFusion Studio. You will find a decent amount of what seems like extraneous code in there, but after a moment you'll realize that the spreadsheet has basically just been converted into an ordinary HTML table, using the `<table>`, `<tr>`, and `<td>` tags you are already familiar with.

If you were to create a ColdFusion template that created a similar HTML file, Excel could render it as a spreadsheet, just as it could render the tab-separated text from Listing 34.5 as a spreadsheet. The advantage to using the special HTML format over the tab-separated format is that Microsoft designed the special HTML format to be more than just a data-export format; it actually holds all the Excel-specific information about the spreadsheet, as well. This means you can dynamically specify formatting options such as font, color, and alignment, and even provide autocalculating formulas for specific cells. So, you easily can create a fully functioning Excel spreadsheet on-the-fly, using relatively familiar HTML-looking syntax.

Listing 34.6 and Listing 34.7 are two examples that demonstrate how you can create formatted spreadsheets for Excel by using HTML table syntax. Listing 34.6 again creates a spreadsheet that lists the title and budget for each film. Note that you can provide width and alignment for the columns and specify formatting using ordinary `<font>` and `<b>` tags.

LISTING 34.6 `FilmsToExcelPretty.cfm`—**OUTPUTTING AN HTML TABLE FOR DISPLAY IN EXCEL**

```
<!--- Retrieve information about films --->
<CFQUERY DATASOURCE="ows" NAME="GetFilms">
  SELECT MovieTitle, AmountBudgeted
  FROM Films
  ORDER BY MovieTitle
</CFQUERY>

<!--- Set the content-type so Excel is invoked --->
<CFCONTENT TYPE="application/msexcel">

<!--- Suggest default filename for spreadsheet --->
<CFHEADER NAME="Content-Disposition" VALUE="filename=FilmBudgets.xls">

<html>
<head><title>Film Budgets</title></head>
<body>
```

LISTING 34.6 CONTINUED

```
<!--- Output ordinary HTML table, which will --->
<!--- be displayed by Excel as a spreadsheet --->
<table>
  <tr><th>Film</th><th>Budget</th></tr>
  <CFOUTPUT QUERY="GetFilms">
    <tr>
      <td width="400">
        <font face="verdana">#MovieTitle#</font>
      </td>
      <td align="center">
        <font color="red"><b>#AmountBudgeted#</b></font>
      </td>
    </tr>
  </CFOUTPUT>
</table>

</body>
</html>
```

Listing 34.7 is similar to Listing 34.6, except that it includes some additional color and formatting instructions, so the resulting spreadsheet looks quite nice. It also adds another row of cells to the bottom of the spreadsheet, which shows the total of the second column (the budgets of all films combined), as shown in Figure 34.6. This is a live, formula-based total; if the user changes any of the prices, Excel updates the total accordingly.

LISTING 34.7 `FilmsToExcelPrettier.cfm`—ADDING CSS FORMATTING AND CELL FORMULAS TO GENERATED SPREADSHEET

```
<!--- Retrieve information about films --->
<CFQUERY DATASOURCE="ows" NAME="GetFilms">
  SELECT MovieTitle, AmountBudgeted
  FROM Films
  ORDER BY MovieTitle
</CFQUERY>

<!--- Set the content-type so Excel is invoked --->
<CFCONTENT TYPE="application/msexcel">

<!--- Suggest default filename for spreadsheet --->
<CFHEADER NAME="Content-Disposition" VALUE="filename=FilmBudgets.xls">

<!--- Include "XML Namespace" information to --->
<!--- allow using Excel "extensions" to HTML --->
<html
  xmlns:o="urn:schemas-microsoft-com:office:office"
  xmlns:x="urn:schemas-microsoft-com:office:excel"
  xmlns="http://www.w3.org/TR/REC-html40">
<head><title>Film Budgets</title></head>


<body>

<style TYPE="text/css">
```

```
  .rowHeads {
    color:white;
    background:blue;
  }
  .titleCol {
    width:400px;
    font-style:italic;
    font-family:verdana;
  }
  .priceCol {
    width:150px;
    font-family:verdana;
    color:red;
    mso-number-format:"\0022$\0022\#\,\#\#0\.00"
  };
</style>


<!--- Output ordinary HTML table, which will --->
<!--- be displayed by Excel as a spreadsheet --->
<table>
  <!--- Top row --->
  <tr>
    <th class="rowHeads">Movie Title</th>
    <th class="rowHeads">Amount Budgeted</th>
  </tr>

  <!--- Data rows --->
  <CFOUTPUT QUERY="GetFilms">
    <tr>
      <td class="titleCol">#MovieTitle#</td>
      <td class="priceCol">#AmountBudgeted#</td>
    </tr>
  </CFOUTPUT>

  <!--- Last row, with "total" formula --->
  <CFSET FirstPriceCell = "B2">
  <CFSET LastPriceCell  = "B" & GetFilms.RecordCount + 1>
  <CFSET TotalFormula   = "SUM(#FirstPriceCell#:#LastPriceCell#)">
  <CFOUTPUT>
    <tr>
      <td
        class="titleCol"
        style="font-weight:bold;background:yellow">Total:</td>
      <td
        class="priceCol"
        style="font-weight:bold;background:yellow"
        x:fmla="=#TotalFormula#"></td>
    </tr>
  </CFOUTPUT>
</table>

</body>
</html>
```

Near the end of Listing 34.7, a ColdFusion variable called `TotalFormula` is created, which will end up having a value of `SUM(B2:B24)` if 23 rows of film information exist. That formula is then supplied to the special `x:fla` attribute of the `<td>` tag, which is one of the Microsoft extensions to HTML geared especially for use with Excel. To use these extensions, the three `xmlns` attributes must be included for the `<html>` tag at the top of the template.

Tip

We couldn't possibly explain everything about these special extensions to HTML (and how they are implemented using XML standards) in the space we have in this book. For purposes of putting together nice-looking and functional spreadsheets for Excel, you will need to experiment a bit to figure out how to express the specific formatting or features you want using HTML. A good way to do this is to simply create a similar spreadsheet using Excel normally; then save the spreadsheet as HTML, as explained earlier in this section. By examining the HTML file in ColdFusion Studio, you will be able to figure out how to get the results you want on-the-fly.

Note

Remember that the HTML approach used in Listing 34.7 is a solution only for Excel 2000 (sometimes called Excel 9) and later. This technique will not work for earlier versions of the product.

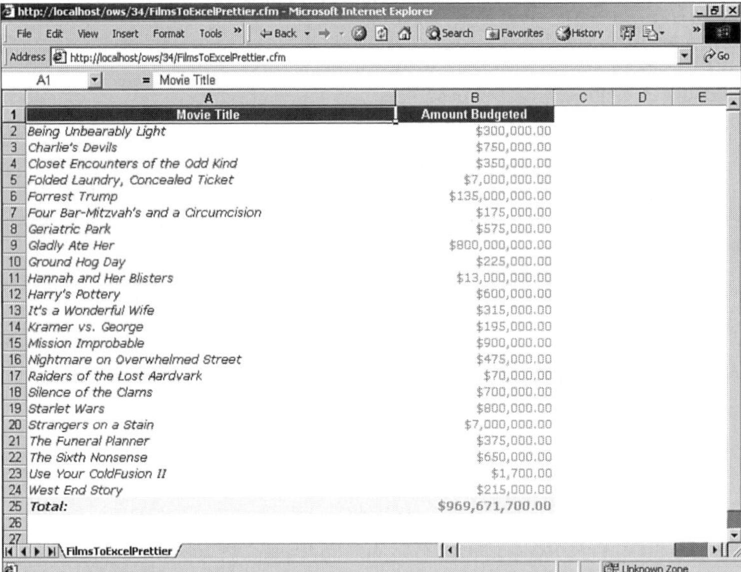

Figure 34.6
You can create dynamic spreadsheets that include live cell formulas.

Other Options for Creating Excel Files

A few other options are available with regard to generating Excel spreadsheets dynamically with ColdFusion. Unfortunately, there isn't space to go into a specific discussion about each of these options here.

Creating Files Server-Side

Instead of generating a new Excel spreadsheet on-the-fly for every request, you could write the necessary tab-delimited or HTML content to a file on the server, using the `<CFFILE>` tag. Then, you could send that file to the browser in response to successive page requests, using the `FILE` attribute of the `<CFCONTENT>` tag. You still would need the `<CFHEADER>` tag, as shown in Listing 34.7. The file could be updated on a periodic basis (perhaps once a day) using the `<CFSCHEDULE>` tag.

For more information about `<CFFILE>`, see Chapter 35, "Interacting with the Operating System." For more information about `<CFSCHEDULE>`, see Chapter 37, "Event Scheduling."

Talking to Excel via <CFOBJECT>

ColdFusion can also communicate directly with a copy of Excel installed on the server by using COM automation. You use the `<CFOBJECT>` tag with the `TYPE` attribute set to `COM` and the `CLASS` attribute set to `Excel.Application`. You then use the objects, methods, and properties provided by Excel (the same ones people normally use to create Excel macros, generally using the Visual Basic for Applications (VBA) language) to create whatever spreadsheet you want, and save it to the server's drive as a temporary file. You then can use the `FILE` attribute of the `<CFCONTENT>` tag to send the file back to the browser, perhaps also specifying a `DELETEFILE` attribute of `Yes` so the temporary file is deleted from the server after it is delivered to the browser.

Tip

Two Web sites that might help you to find additional information about creating Excel content via COM/ActiveX are `http://www.cfcomet.com` and `http://www.softartisans.com`.

For more information about `<CFOBJECT>`, see the *Advanced ColdFusion 5 Application Development* (ISBN: 0-7897-2585-1) book or Appendix A in this book. For the Excel-specific objects, methods, and properties mentioned previously, see your Excel documentation, the Microsoft Web site, or a third-party book about writing Excel macros using VBA.

Generating Word Files

You can also use ColdFusion to create Microsoft Word files on-the-fly, using techniques similar to the ones for creating Excel files (see the previous section). This opens up the possibility of creating personalized or customized sales documents, pricing sheets, product documentation, and other documents you might want to deliver in the common Microsoft Word file format.

Although the idea of using a proprietary document format to deliver such documents—rather than something more open, such as HTML—might rub some people the wrong way, there are some clear benefits. Most obviously, you can produce documents that the end user can edit further, using her own, familiar copy of Word. Also, in a Word document you generally have much greater control over the way the document will look when printed (margins, headers, footers, leading, kerning, widow and orphan paragraphs, and so on) than you do with HTML.

CREATING DOCUMENTS WITH RTF

If you have needed to exchange documents between word-processing programs, you might have run into a file format called the Rich Text Format (RTF). RTF is a somewhat older file format, designed to be a reasonably generic way to store formatted information, especially documents such as those you create with a word processor. Word lets you work with RTF (.rtf) files in almost all the same ways you can work with real Word (.doc) files.

Most importantly to you, RTF is a plain-text format, so it is made up of normal ASCII characters, which ColdFusion is good at generating. So, just as you were able to create a tab-separated text to be sent to Excel via `<CFCONTENT>`, you can create RTF files to be sent to Word.

CREATING A TEMPLATE DOCUMENT

There are several approaches you could take to creating RTF files with ColdFusion. This section discusses a relatively simple one, which is similar to performing a mail merge operation within a word processor. First, you will create a template document and save it as an RTF file on your ColdFusion server. Then, you will customize the document using simple string-manipulation functions and send the customized version of the document back to the browser using the `<CFCONTENT>` tag.

Note

The following instructions assume you are using a recent version of Word, such as Word 2000. Earlier versions will also work just fine, although the specific steps you take to save a document as RTF might be slightly different.

To create your template document, do the following:

1. Open Word. Create some type of document, such as a form letter.
2. In the document, insert six placeholders by including the following terms somewhere in the text, including the percent signs: `%CurrentDate%`, `%NameFirst%`, `%NameLast%`, `%NameFirstReal%`, `%NameLastReal%`, and `%FreePrize%`.
3. Feel free to add some formatting to the document, using whatever features you want (styles, margins, font colors, tables, and so on). Just try to stay away from including large pictures in the document for the moment.
4. Select Save As from Word's File menu, select Rich Text Format from the drop-down list of file types, and save the document as `DocTemplate.rtf` in the same folder you're using to save code for this chapter.
5. Be sure you close the document in Word (otherwise, Word might keep it locked).

Note

If you prefer, you can just use the `DocTemplate.rtf` file included on this book's CD-ROM.

Now you can create a ColdFusion template that creates a personalized copy of the template, based on information you retrieve with a database query. Listing 34.8 shows one way to get this done. As you can see, this template has two sections. When you visit the template normally (with no URL parameters), the top portion of the code executes and displays a list of actors. The user can then click an actor's name to cause the template to be executed again, this time with the appropriate ActorID passed as a URL parameter.

LISTING 34.8 `RetireActor.cfm`—**PRODUCING A PERSONALIZED WORD DOCUMENT FROM AN RTF TEMPLATE**

```
<!--- If no Actor ID passed, diplay list of links --->
<CFIF IsDefined("URL.ActorID") EQ False>
  <!--- Get a list of actors from database --->
  <CFQUERY NAME="GetActors" DATASOURCE="ows">
    SELECT ActorID, NameFirst, NameLast
    FROM Actors
    ORDER BY NameLast, NameFirst
  </CFQUERY>

  <!--- Page Title, etc --->
  <html>
  <head><title>Actor Retirement System</title></head>
  <body>
  <h3>Which Actor Would You Like To Retire?</h3>

  <!--- For each Actor, include simple link to --->
  <!--- this page, passing the Actor ID in URL --->
  <CFOUTPUT QUERY="GetActors">
    <CFSET LinkURL = "#CGI.SCRIPT_NAME#?ActorID=#ActorID#">
    <a href="#LinkURL#">#NameFirst# <B>#NameLast#</B></a><br>
  </CFOUTPUT>

  </body>
  </html>


<!--- If Actor ID passed, generate Word document --->
<CFELSE>
  <!--- Make sure Actor ID in URL is a number --->
  <CFPARAM NAME="URL.ActorID" TYPE="numeric">

  <!--- Get this Actor's name from database --->
  <CFQUERY NAME="GetActor" DATASOURCE="ows">
    SELECT NameFirst, NameLast,
      NameFirstReal, NameLastReal,
      (SELECT Min(DateInTheaters)
       FROM Films f, FilmsActors fa
       WHERE fa.FilmID = f.FilmID
       AND fa.ActorID = a.ActorID) AS DateFirstFilm
```

Listing 34.8 Continued

```
    FROM Actors a
    WHERE ActorID = #URL.ActorID#
  </CFQUERY>

  <!--- How long has Actor been with company? --->
  <CFSET MonthsEmployed = DateDiff("m", GetActor.DateFirstFilm, Now())>

  <!--- Determine severance package --->
  <CFIF MonthsEmployed GTE 12>
    <CFSET SevPackage = "Gold Watch (Digital)">
  <CFELSEIF MonthsEmployed GTE 6>
    <CFSET SevPackage = "$100 Starbucks Gift Certificate">
  <CFELSE>
    <CFSET SevPackage = "ColdFusion Web Application Construction Kit">
  </CFIF>


  <!--- Location of our RTF "template" document --->
  <CFSET ThisFolder   = GetDirectoryFromPath(GetCurrentTemplatePath())>
  <CFSET TemplatePath = ThisFolder & "DocTemplate.rtf">

  <!--- Read RTF template into variable called "RTF" --->
  <CFFILE
    ACTION="Read"
    FILE="#TemplatePath#"
    VARIABLE="RTF">

  <!--- Replace "placeholders" with specific information --->
  <CFSET TodaysDate = DateFormat(Now(), "dddd, mmmm d, yyyy")>
  <CFSET RTF = Replace(RTF, "%CurrentDate%", TodaysDate)>
  <CFSET RTF = Replace(RTF, "%FreePrize%", SevPackage)>
  <CFSET RTF = Replace(RTF, "%NameFirst%", GetActor.NameFirst)>
  <CFSET RTF = Replace(RTF, "%NameLast%",  GetActor.NameLast )>
  <CFSET RTF = Replace(RTF, "%NameFirstReal%", GetActor.NameFirstReal)>
  <CFSET RTF = Replace(RTF, "%NameLastReal%", GetActor.NameLastReal )>

  <!--- Suggest default filename for document --->
  <CFHEADER NAME="Content-Disposition" VALUE="filename=RetireMemo.doc">

  <!--- Set the content-type so Word is invoked --->
  <CFCONTENT TYPE="application/msword"><CFOUTPUT>#RTF#</CFOUTPUT>

</CFIF>
```

When an actor ID is provided, the second part of the template executes, which is where the dynamic Word generation occurs. First, some basic information about the employee is retrieved from the database, using an ordinary `<CFQUERY>` tag. Then, a severance package is determined, depending on how long ago the actor's first film was released (if he was hired more than 12 months ago, he gets a gold watch).

Next, the `<CFFILE>` tag is used to read the `DocTemplate.rtf` file (which is just a text file) into an ordinary ColdFusion string variable called `RTF`. Now, you can use ColdFusion's `Replace()` function to replace the simple placeholders in the RTF file with the actor's actual first and last names and replace the `%FreePrize%` placeholder with the value of the `SevPackage` variable (which contains the determined severance package).

Tip

See Chapter 35 for more information about using `<CFFILE>` to read in the contents of text files.

Note

In this example, ColdFusion looks for the `DocTemplate.rtf` file in the same folder the `RetireActor.cfm` file is in. The `GetCurrentTemplatePath()` function makes this possible. In practice, you might want to keep the RTF template somewhere else, outside the Web server's document root, so it can't be downloaded directly.

Now the customized RTF text is sitting in the `RTF` variable. All that's left is to stream the RTF text to the browser. As with the Excel examples earlier in this chapter, this is done by including a `<CFCONTENT>` tag—this time with the `TYPE` attribute set to `application/msword`. This causes the browser to launch the user's copy of Microsoft Word on the local machine. Note that you also must include the `<CFHEADER>` tag, which suggests a sensible default filename for the document (see the discussion of Listing 34.5).

If you use the `DocTemplate.rtf` file that was included on this book's CD-ROM, the resulting Word document would look similar to Figure 34.7.

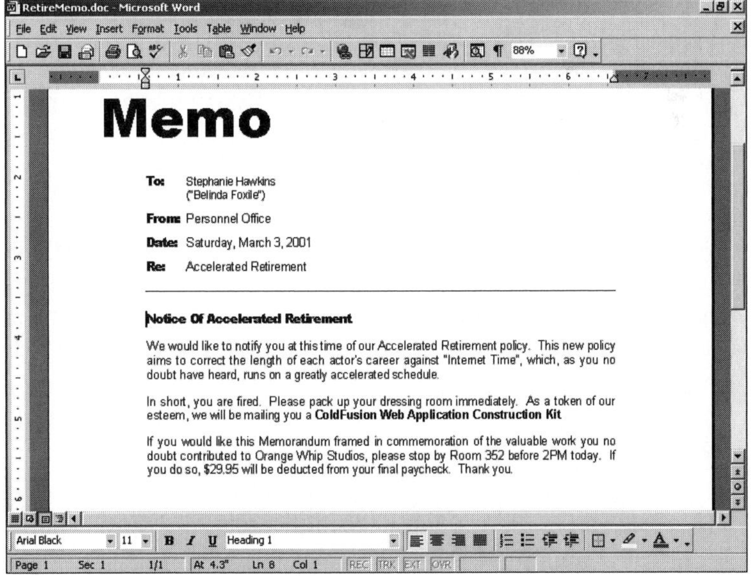

Figure 34.7
You can create Word files on-the-fly that the user can print or modify.

OTHER OPTIONS FOR CREATING WORD FILES

A few other options are available if you want to learn more about creating Word documents with ColdFusion:

- Similar to Excel 2000, Word 2000 understands an extended version of HTML that can include extra code to deal with all the Word-specific features not normally found in HTML documents. You could adapt the basic technique described in the "Creating Spreadsheets with HTML" section of this chapter to generate the Word version of HTML.
- It should also be possible to communicate with a copy of Word installed on the ColdFusion server via the `<CFOBJECT>` tag. See "Other Options for Creating Excel Files," earlier in this chapter, for a few pointers.

SERVING MEDIA FILES

You have seen how you can create various types of document-type files with a little help from the `<CFCONTENT>` tag. You also can use `<CFCONTENT>` to serve up images or other types of multimedia files, such as audio or video.

TURNING COLDFUSION INTO AN IMAGE SERVER

For instance, say you have been asked to create a banner ad server application with ColdFusion. One of the requirements is that your ad server must be capable of working for sites built with static HTML files. You need to be able to provide a simple `<IMG>` tag people can cut and paste into their pages. But, if the `SRC` of the `<IMG>` tag doesn't change each time a user views a page, how will the banner ad rotate? Similar to the other solutions discussed in this chapter, the answer to this head-scratcher involves the `<CFCONTENT>` tag.

Although it's certainly the norm, there is no law that says the `SRC` for an image has to have a `.gif` or `.jpg` extension. The `SRC` can be the URL for a ColdFusion template, perhaps called `AdServer.cfm`. Rather than returning some type of text, such as HTML code, the template should return an image. In addition, it should specify a MIME content type of `image/gif` instead of the usual `text/html` content type. Because of the content type, the browser will understand that it is receiving what it expects to receive (an image) and should have no problems displaying it.

SERVING UP IMAGES

Listing 34.9 shows what this ad server template might look like. It assumes that a number of banner images are located in a subfolder called `Ads`. It selects one of the ads at random and then uses `<CFCONTENT>` to send the image back to the browser with the appropriate content type.

Before this example will work, however, you must do the following:

1. Save the code shown in Listing 34.9 to a ColdFusion template named `AdServer.cfm`.
2. Create a subdirectory called `Ads`, within the same folder you just saved `AdServer.cfm` in.

3. Place several banner ads or other GIF files in the `Ads` subfolder. If you want, you can simply copy the images from the `Ads` subfolder from this chapter's folder on the CD-ROM that accompanies this book.

Listing 34.9 AdServer1.cfm—Using <CFCONTENT> to Respond with an Image Instead of HTML Content

```
<!---
  Filename:     AdServer.cfm
  Created by:   Nate Weiss (NMW)
  Date Created: 2/18/2001
--->

<!--- Ad Images are in "Ads" subfolder, within current folder --->
<CFSET AdDir = GetDirectoryFromPath(GetCurrentTemplatePath()) & "Ads\">

<!--- Get a listing of GIF image files in the Ads folder --->
<!--- Result is a query object with a row for each image --->
<CFDIRECTORY
  DIRECTORY="#AdDir#"
  ACTION="LIST"
  FILTER="*.gif"
  NAME="GetAds">

<!--- Pick random number between one and number of images --->
<CFSET AdNum  = RandRange(1, GetAds.RecordCount)>
<!--- Grab the filename in chosen row of the GetAds query --->
<CFSET AdFileName = GetAds.Name[AdNum]>
<!--- Prepend directory to get full filesystem path to ad image --->
<CFSET AdFilePath = AdDir & AdFileName>

<!--- Send the chosen image back to the client --->
<CFCONTENT TYPE="image/gif" FILE="#AdFilePath#">
```

Note

Because it is not returning HTML content, Listing 34.9 doesn't contain the `<HTML>`, `<BODY>`, and other standard tags you're used to seeing.

As you can see, you don't need a lot of code to serve up an image with ColdFusion. You simply select the file you want to serve and supply its complete filename to the `FILE` attribute of the `<CFCONTENT>` tag, which is being used for the first time in this chapter (see Table 34.2). Any streaming and network communication issues are handled for you.

First, the `AdDir` variable is set to the full filesystem path of the `Ads` folder. This is a nice use for the `GetDirectoryFromPath()` and `GetCurrentTemplatePath()` functions. When you use the two together as shown in Listing 34.9, they always return the full path to the folder in which the currently executing template is located.

Next, the `<CFDIRECTORY>` tag is used to get a listing of all GIF files within the `Ads` folder. You can find out more about `<CFDIRECTORY>` in Chapter 35. Here, it is used in a very basic way. It returns a query object, such as the results of a `<CFQUERY>`, where each row of the query represents a file that matches the `FILTER` attribute. The query object contains a column called `NAME`, which contains the filename (with extension, but not the path) of each file.

Now, the `RandRange()` function is used to pick a number between 1 and the number of rows in the query, which in turn is the number of GIF files in the `Ads` folder. So, if eight images are in the folder, the `AdNum` variable will be set to a random number between 1 and 8. Next, the `AdFileName` variable is set to the value of the `NAME` column of the appropriate row of the `GetAds` query object. If `AdNum` turns out to be `5`, `AdFileName` is set to the filename in the fifth row of the query.

Tip

> You can gain more control over how random numbers are generated by using the `Rand()` and `Randomize()` functions together. See Appendix B for details.

Finally, another variable called `AdFilePath` is created, which just concatenates the `AdDir` and `AdFileName` variables together, resulting in the complete filesystem path to the randomly selected image file. All that's left is to feed the path to the `FILE` attribute of the `<CFCONTENT>` tag.

You should be able to test the template at this point by visiting the `AdServer.cfm` template with your browser. All you should see is the randomly selected banner ad. If you reload the template's URL a few times, you should see that the ads rotate on a fairly even, random basis.

Note

> If you visit the `AdServer.cfm` template and then try to View Source with your browser, you will find that your browser either prevents it or shows garbage characters. This is because there is no HTML source to show. The template is returning the binary image information itself, not an `<IMG>` tag, which is a pointer to an image on the Net.

Displaying the Images in Other Web Pages

The goal of this exercise was to use a simple `<IMG>` tag to create a rotating banner ad system that could be used by static HTML files—and that's exactly what you have. You can include the following line of code in a static HTML file:

```
<IMG SRC="http://localhost/ows/34/AdServer.cfm">
```

When the browser encounters the `<IMG>` tag, it communicates with the `AdServer.cfm` template and displays whatever image content is returned. As long as you use a fully qualified URL (including the `http://`), you are free to save the HTML file on any server in the world. It doesn't have to be on the same machine as the ad server.

Handling Click-Throughs

Listing 34.9 now correctly serves up banner ads, but it can't be really considered a fully featured ad-management system at this point. For instance, what about tracking the number of ads served? What happens when the user clicks an ad?

Unfortunately, there isn't space to develop and discuss a world-class ad server here that would meet everyone's needs. That said, a few lines of code can be added to the `AdServer.cfm` template to make the example a bit more complete.

Note

The main purpose of these examples is to demonstrate how `<CFCONTENT>` can be combined with client or session variables to build a useful application based on serving media files, such as images. If you were building a real-world ad-server utility, you would probably do some things differently (for instance, use a database).

Listing 34.10 shows an `Application.cfm` file that turns on ColdFusion's Session Management feature and then creates a structure called `SESSION.AdsOnPages` if it doesn't exist already. Because the structure is kept in the `SESSION` scope, it is maintained separately for each user who is shown an ad. You'll see how this structure is used in a moment.

Caution

The following examples use variables in the `SESSION` scope without locking the accesses with the `<CFLOCK>` tag. This is an acceptable practice if the Single Threaded Sessions option is checked in the Locking page of the ColdFusion Administrator. Otherwise, you must add `<CFLOCK>` tags around all accesses to the `SESSION` scope. See the section "Locking Revisited" in Chapter 20, "Working with Sessions."

Listing 34.10 `Application.cfm`—**Getting Ready to Track Ad Views Per Page and Per User**

```
<!---
  Filename:     Application.cfm
  Created by:   Nate Weiss (NMW)
  Date Created: 2/18/2001
  Please Note:  Executes for every page request!
--->

<!--- Give application a name, and enable Session variables --->
<CFAPPLICATION
  NAME="AdServer"
  SESSIONMANAGEMENT="Yes">

<!--- Make sure AdsOnPage structure exists for this session --->
<!--- Each time we serve an ad, we'll record page/ad in this. --->
<CFIF NOT IsDefined("Session.AdsOnPages")>
  <CFSET SESSION.AdsOnPages = StructNew()>
</CFIF>
```

The version of AdServer.cfm in Listing 34.11 is almost the same as Listing 34.9. Only one line of code has been added, before the <CFCONTENT> tag at the end:

```
<!--- Record fact that this ad is now placed on this page --->
<!--- You could record the ad-showing in database instead --->
<CFSET SESSION.AdsOnPages[CGI.HTTP_REFERER] = AdFileName>
```

LISTING 34.11 AdServer2.cfm—RECORDING EACH AD HIT IN A SESSION VARIABLE

```
<!---
  Filename:     AdServer.cfm
  Created by:   Nate Weiss (NMW)
  Date Created: 2/18/2001
--->

<!--- Ad Images are in "Ads" subfolder, within current folder --->
<CFSET AdDir = GetDirectoryFromPath(GetCurrentTemplatePath()) & "Ads\">

<!--- Get a listing of GIF image files in the Ads folder --->
<!--- Result is a query object with a row for each image --->
<CFDIRECTORY
  DIRECTORY="#AdDir#"
  ACTION="LIST"
  FILTER="*.gif"
  NAME="GetAds">

<!--- Pick random number between one and number of images --->
<CFSET AdNum  = RandRange(1, GetAds.RecordCount)>
<!--- Grab the filename in chosen row of the GetAds query --->
<CFSET AdFileName = GetAds.Name[AdNum]>
<!--- Prepend dir to get full filesystem path to ad image --->
<CFSET AdFilePath = AdDir & AdFileName>

<!--- Record fact that this ad is now placed on this page --->
<!--- You could record the ad-showing in database instead --->
<CFSET SESSION.AdsOnPages[CGI.HTTP_REFERER] = AdFileName>

<!--- Send the chosen image back to the client --->
<CFCONTENT TYPE="image/gif" FILE="#AdFilePath#">
```

The idea here is to exploit the fact that the browser will provide the referring page when it requests the image from the AdServer.cfm page. That is, the URL of the page in which the image is to appear will be available in the CGI.HTTP_REFERER variable. Therefore, the <CFSET> line shown previously places a new name/value pair in the AdsOnPages structure, where the referring URL is used as the name portion of the structure entry, and the filename of the ad being shown is the value portion.

Later, you easily can look up the ad's filename using the page's URL as the structure's key. In other words, the template is now tracking which users have seen which ads, on which pages. (See Chapter 9, "Using ColdFusion," for a discussion about ColdFusion structures.)

Tip

For more information about HTTP_REFERER and the other variables in the CGI scope, see Appendix C, "Special ColdFusion Variables and Result Codes."

Tip

In addition to (or instead of) maintaining the AdsOnPages structure, you could record each banner ad view in a database table—for example, called AdViews. The table might have columns such as AdID, PageURL, and ViewDate. This would enable you to easily create reports based on usage.

Now that each ad view is being recorded in the AdsOnPages structure, you can create a template to respond when an ad is clicked. You can use the code in Listing 34.12, assuming that this is template that will be called when a user clicks an ad. It again uses the CGI.HTTP_REFERER variable to determine the URL of the referring document, which should be the URL that the ad is on. The idea is to use the referrer URL to look up the last ad shown to this user on that page.

Listing 34.12 AdClick.cfm—**Responding to a Banner Ad Click**

```
<!---
  Filename:     AdClick.cfm
  Created by:   Nate Weiss (NMW)
  Date Created: 2/18/2001
--->

<!--- Assuming we have shown an ad on the referring page --->
<CFIF StructKeyExists(SESSION.AdsOnPages, CGI.HTTP_REFERER)>
  <!--- What ad was last shown to this user on referring page? --->
  <CFSET AdFileName = SESSION.AdsOnPages[CGI.HTTP_REFERER]>

  <!---
    At this point, you might record the "click" in database
    and then redirect the user to the appropriate site via
    the <CFLOCATION> tag.  Here, we will simply output the
    ad that the user clicked on, just to prove the concept.
  --->
  <CFOUTPUT>
    You just came from: #CGI.HTTP_REFERER#<BR>
    You got here by clicking the <B>#AdFileName#</B> ad.
  </CFOUTPUT>

<!--- If "KeyExists" fails, we don't know what ad was shown --->
<CFELSE>
  We don't have any ad on record for you.  Perhaps you didn't
  come here after seeing an ad, or your session timed out.
</CFIF>
```

First, the StructKeyExists() function is used to see whether a record exists for the URL. If so, the <CFSET> line retrieves the value from the structure, assigning the ad's filename to the AdFileName variable. This code then outputs the original filename of the ad, without redirecting the user somewhere else. As an exercise, you could take things further by using the filename to determine where to send the user in response to the ad click, log the click-through in a database, and then use <CFLOCATION> to redirect the user to the advertiser's Web site.

The code in Listing 34.13 can be used to test the new ad server templates. The <IMG> tag displays the banner ad served up by AdServer.cfm, and the <A> tag causes the AdClick.cfm page to be called when the ad is clicked. This is an ordinary, static HTML file that doesn't need to be processed by ColdFusion. The results are shown in Figure 34.8.

LISTING 34.13 AdServerTest.htm—DISPLAYING AN IMAGE SERVED BY A COLDFUSION TEMPLATE

```
<!---
  Filename:      AdServerTest.htm
  Created by:    Nate Weiss (NMW)
  Date Created: 2/18/2001
  Please Note:   This is a static HTML file, not a CF template
--->

<HTML>
<HEAD><TITLE>Ad Server Test</TITLE></HEAD>
<BODY>

<H2>Ad Server Test</H2>

The randomly chosen ad should appear below:<BR>

<!--- Include banner ad supplied by "Ad Server" --->
<A HREF="http://localhost/ows/34/AdClick.cfm">
  <IMG SRC="http://localhost/ows/34/AdServer.cfm"
    WIDTH="468" HEIGHT="60" ALT="" BORDER="0"></A>

</BODY>
</HTML>
```

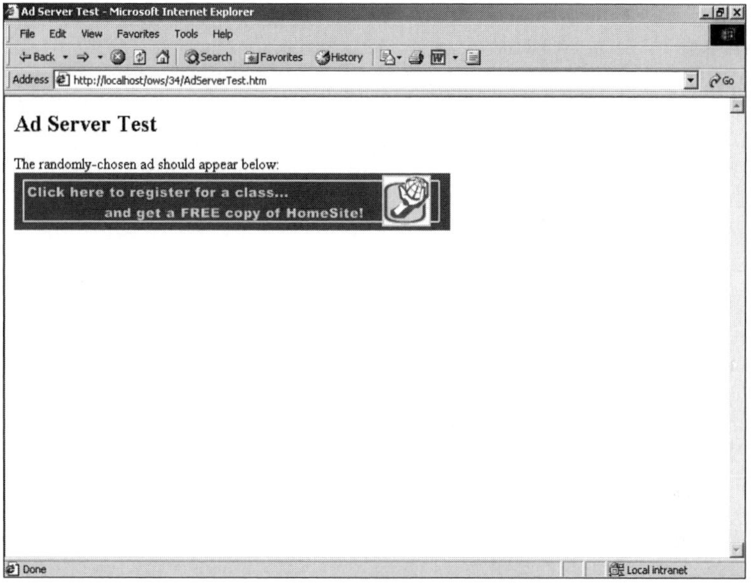

Figure 34.8
ColdFusion templates can serve images, such as this banner ad, instead of documents.

OTHER USES

You could apply this same idea—using ColdFusion to serve up media files—to many other situations. Here are just a few ideas.

CREATING OR CHANGING THE ADS ON-THE-FLY

Using third-party extensions to ColdFusion, you can create or manipulate images on-the-fly. This means you could adapt the ad server idea to create personalized images of some kind (such as greeting cards). Take a look in the ColdFusion Developers Exchange at `http://www.allaire.com/developer/gallery` to find out which CFX and other tags are available for creating dynamic images with ColdFusion.

Tip

If you did start to create images on-the-fly for each user, you could use the `DELETEFILE="Yes"` attribute for the `<CFCONTENT>` tag. This would cause each dynamically created image to be deleted from disk after it was delivered to the browser.

OTHER TYPES OF MEDIA CONTENT

You also could adapt this ad server idea to serve up other types of multimedia content, such as Macromedia Flash movies, or audio or video files. As long as you provide the correct MIME content type to the `TYPE` attribute of the `<CFCONTENT>` tag, you can serve up just about any type of content with ColdFusion.

Secure Downloads

If you look back at Listing 34.9, you will notice that `<CFCONTENT>`'s `FILE` attribute requires a full filesystem path (including the `c:\`, for instance, if you're using ColdFusion on a Windows machine). This means the banner images could be stored anywhere on the server's drives or local network. That is, you are free to store the images in a folder that is not within the Web server's document root, and thus not accessible via the Internet using an ordinary URL (a URL ending with `.gif`). The only way to get to the files would be via the `AdServer.cfm` template. In fact, if you think about it, there isn't even any way for the outside world to know what the name of each image file is.

This means you easily can set up a secure download system for documents or other important files your company wants to be accessible to only certain people. Or, you could set up a software download page that requires people to register (or pay) before they can obtain your software. Because ColdFusion is in charge, you can use whatever queries or other special processing you need to determine whether the user has the right to get a particular image or file.

Tip

If you want to give the downloaded file a name, or if you find that you don't get the Save As behavior you want, try using a `Content-Disposition` header, such as the Word and Excel examples earlier in this chapter.

Getting Started with Wireless Applications

Just as you can use ColdFusion to create interactive applications for Web browsers, you can use ColdFusion to create interactive applications for cell phones and other wireless devices. This opens up exciting ways to provide information and services to your users while they are on the move.

This section explains what's needed to create wireless applications with ColdFusion, using the WAP standard. You also can adapt these basic concepts to produce wireless applications for PalmOS handhelds, I-Mode–compliant devices, or any other wireless standard that uses text-based markup.

Basic Concepts

Before you get started, you need to understand the ways in which wireless development is different from normal Web application development. You will see that the framework for building wireless applications borrows very heavily from the Web development world. That's good for you because you will be able to apply your knowledge of ColdFusion to the wireless universe very quickly.

Here are some important terms to keep in mind as you follow along:

- **WAP**—*WAP* stands for Wireless Application Protocol. It defines the way wireless devices talk to Web servers. Although the analogy is not perfect, you can think of WAP as the wireless equivalent to HTTP. It grew out of efforts led by a company called

Phone.com (now Openwave.com) to create a standard for wireless application development. WAP's home on the Web is the WAP Forum site, at `http://www.wapforum.com`.

- **WML**—*WML* stands for Wireless Markup Language. WML is the wireless equivalent to HTML and is similar to HTML in many respects. WML grew out of an earlier specification called HDML (Handheld Device Markup Language).
- **WAP Device**—Any cell phone or other device that understands WAP and WML. If you don't have such a phone yourself, you can use a phone simulator on your computer while you develop your application; it looks and behaves similarly to a real cell phone.
- **WAP Gateway**—A server that sits between a wireless device and the Web. When a user uses her cell phone to connect to your ColdFusion application, the communication passes through a gateway computer, which is generally supplied by the user's cell phone company.

Installing the UP.SDK

The first thing to do is to install the UP.SDK on your workstation. The UP.SDK is a set of tools for wireless application developers. Installing it gives you access to an onscreen simulation of a cell phone, which you can use to develop and test your applications.

A copy of the UP.SDK setup program has been included on the CD-ROM for this book. You can also download the most recent version of the UP.SDK from `http://developer.openwave.com`.

To install the UP.SDK, follow these steps:

1. Locate the setup program on this book's CD-ROM, or download it from the URL shown previously. Depending on the version, the filename will be similar to `upsdkW41e.exe`.
2. Double-click the setup program to start the installation process.
3. Follow the simple instructions to install the UP.SDK.

A Crash Course in WML

Instead of writing your ColdFusion templates to generate HTML as you would normally, you write them to generate WML.

You'll find that many tags from HTML have been adopted by WML with hardly any changes. In general, most of the differences between the languages have to do with preserving bandwidth because cell phones and other devices have relatively slow connections. Also, cell phones obviously don't have all the processing power that an average computer does, so the language has been kept very simple.

WML has a number of rules, which must be followed exactly:

- **WML is case sensitive**—In WML, tag names and attributes are case sensitive; therefore, you can't type WML tags using your choice of uppercase or lowercase as you can with HTML. You must type them as shown.

- **All tags must be nested properly**—In WML, all tags must have opening and closing tags. In HTML, you can use a `<p>` tag without ever providing the matching `</p>` tag—not so in WML.
- **Unpaired tags must use slash notation**—You are familiar with the `<br>` tag in HTML. The equivalent in WML is the `<br/>` tag. The slash indicates that no matching `</br>` tag exists, so the device's parser needn't waste time looking for it. Actually, this slash notation is a shortcut for writing `<br></br>`, which is also valid WML (but more tedious to type). The same rule applies to other unpaired tags, so you will see the slash used at the end of `<img>` and `<a>` tags in WML code.

Note

Most of these rules are the result of the fact that the WML language is actually a subset of XML. HTML is not directly related to XML and doesn't adhere to many of XML's rules regarding syntax.

Explaining the entire WML language in one chapter isn't possible. You will learn enough to get you started, though. Table 34.3 shows the WML tags are used in this chapter's code samples. The table also attempts to explain what each tag's equivalent is in HTML. Although the comparisons are not always perfect, they should help you feel comfortable as you start looking at the examples.

Tip

Studio's Help tab contains a WML Reference section, which explains each tag's syntax in detail.

TABLE 34.3 COMMON WML TAGS AND THEIR ROUGH EQUIVALENTS IN HTML

WML Tag	Compares to HTML	Purpose
`<wml>`	`<html>`	Marks beginning and end of a WML document, more commonly called a *deck*
`<card>`	`<body>`	Marks beginning and end of a card
`<p>`	`<p>`	Marks beginning and end of a paragraph
`<a>`	`<a>`	Defines a hyperlink to another card
` `	` `	Starts a new line
`<do>`	`<button>`	Assigns actions to buttons on the WAP device
`<go>`	`<form>`	Performs an action, such as submitting data or linking to another page
`<input>`	`<input>`	Collects input from user
`<postfield>`	hidden `<input>`	Submits form-style input to the server

Tip

ColdFusion Studio can provide context-sensitive help about any of the WML tags listed in Table 34.3. Just select the tag in your code and press F1.

YOUR FIRST WML CARD

In WML, you deal with *cards* instead of pages. Just as a Web browser always shows one page at a time (ignoring frames for the moment), a WAP device always shows one card at a time. The first card to write is a home card for your wireless application. This gives the user some basic links to the information you are going to provide.

WRITING THE CODE

Listing 34.14 shows a ColdFusion template that displays a simple welcome message to the user. It also presents the user with two links that he can use to navigate to get information about Orange Whip Studio's movies.

This chapter includes several version of this template. Save the code in this listing as a file called `WapIndex.cfm`, not `WapIndex1.cfm`.

Tip

The first few lines of code can be a bit tricky to type correctly. To have ColdFusion Studio start a new document with these lines already typed for you, select New from the File menu, and then select Dynamic (using CF) on the WML tab of the New Document dialog box.

LISTING 34.14 `WapIndex1.cfm`—**PRESENTING SIMPLE TEXT AND LINKS TO THE USER**

```
<!---
  Filename:      WapIndex.cfm
  Created by:    Nate Weiss (NMW)
  Date Created: 2/18/2001
--->

<!--- Send back the proper WAP content type --->
<CFCONTENT TYPE="text/vnd.wap.wml">

<!--- Send back the proper WAP "prologue" --->
<?xml version="1.0"?>
<!DOCTYPE wml PUBLIC "-//PHONE.COM//DTD WML 1.1//EN"
  "http://www.phone.com/dtd/wml11.dtd" >


<wml>
  <card>
    <p>
      <!--- Welcome message --->
      <b>OrangeWAP Studios</b><br/>
      <i>Celluloid by Cell</i><br/>
```

Listing 34.14 Continued

```
      <!--- Links to other pages --->
      <a href="#movies">Browse Movies</a><br/>
      <a href="#search">Search Movies</a><br/>
    </p>
  </card>
</wml>
```

Note

Because the WML language is case sensitive, it is important that you use lowercase letters as shown for `<wml>`, `<card>`, and other tags in this example.

The first line uses the `<CFCONTENT>` tag to specify that ColdFusion should respond with a content type of `text/vnd.wap.xml` when it sends back the code your template generates. Otherwise, the user's WAP device would receive the default content type of `text/html`, which it wouldn't know what to do with.

The next two lines (the `?xml` line and the `!DOCTYPE` line) include the *WML document prologue*, which must always appear before any actual WML content. It is very important that these lines appear exactly as shown here.

Next, the opening and closing `<wml>` tags indicate the beginning and end of the WML content itself. This is equivalent to the opening and closing `<html>` tags you are used to. Within the opening and closing `<card>` tags, a WML card is defined; it is conceptually similar to the `<body>` section of an HTML page.

Within the card, things start to look pretty familiar. The `<p>`, `<b>`, `<i>`, and `<a>` tags all do the same things they do in HTML. Just be careful to open and close them correctly, and use the slash notation for any unpaired tags, such as `<br/>`.

Tip

You can use Studio's Tag Chooser to insert the various WML tags (`<wml>`, `<card>`, and so on). Select Tag Chooser from the Tools menu, and then expand the WML Tags folder.

Trying It Out with UP.Simulator

When you installed the UP.SDK, you also installed the UP.Simulator, which enables you to visit your WAP templates to see how they will look and behave with a cell phone. You can use the simulator to view the `WapIndex.cfm` page you just created.

To view your new page with the simulator, follow these steps:

1. Start the UP.Simulator by clicking its icon in the Start menu, which is in a program folder labeled `UP.SDK 4.1` or something similar—depending on the version of the UP.SDK you installed.

2. Select UP.Link Settings from the Settings menu.
3. Type the URL for the `WapIndex.cfm` template in the Home Url field, as shown in Figure 34.9. This is the same localhost URL you would use to access the template if it were a normal Web page. Leave the other settings as shown.
4. Click OK. The simulator should now connect to your Web server and display your welcome card, as shown in Figure 34.10.

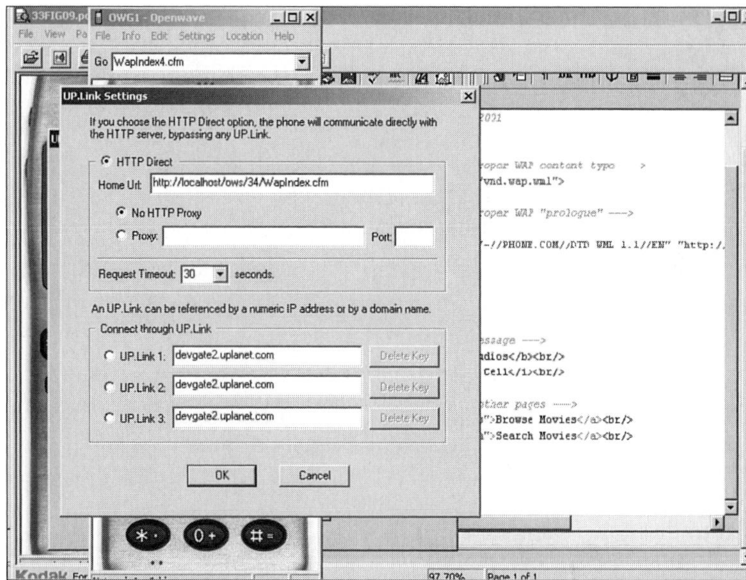

Figure 34.9
Set your simulator's Home URL to your `WapIndex` template to make testing easier.

Figure 34.10
Your WML is interpreted by the simulated phone and displayed on its small LCD screen.

When you have a chance, you should explore the various menu options for the UP.Simulator to become familiar with what it can do for you. In particular, note the following:

- **Open Configuration**—You can select this from the File menu to simulate various makes and models of real-world WAP phones.
- **Reload**—You can select this from the Edit menu to reload the current card. This is similar to using the Reload button on a Web browser.
- **Source**—You can select this from the Info menu to view the source code for the current deck. This is similar to Viewing Source in a Web browser.
- **Clear Cache**—You can select this from the Edit menu to clear the simulator's cache. It also returns you to the Home URL you entered previously. It's a good way to start over after you change some code.

USING <CFINCLUDE> FOR THE PROLOGUE

As explained previously, it is very important to get the `<CFCONTENT>` and prologue parts of Listing 34.14 exactly right in every WML template you build. For that reason, it would probably be helpful to put those lines in a separate template, so you can just use `<CFINCLUDE>` to include the proper prologue each time.

Listing 34.15 shows a template called `WapIncludePrologue.cfm`. Listing 34.16 is the `WapIndex.cfm` file again, this time using `<CFINCLUDE>` to include the content type and prologue—much easier.

LISTING 34.15 `WapIncludePrologue.cfm`—SENDING THE WAP PROLOGUE IN AN INCLUDED TEMPLATE

```
<!---
  Filename:      WAPIncludePrologue.cfm
  Created by:    Nate Weiss (NMW)
  Date Created: 2/18/2001
  Please Note:   Can be used via <CFINCLUDE>, or as a CFML
                 Custom Tag (<CF_WapIncludePrologue>)
--->

<!--- Send back the proper WAP content type --->
<CFCONTENT TYPE="text/vnd.wap.wml">

<!--- Send back the proper WAP "prologue" --->
<?xml version="1.0"?>
<!DOCTYPE wml PUBLIC "-//PHONE.COM//DTD WML 1.1//EN"
  "http://www.phone.com/dtd/wml11.dtd" >
```

LISTING 34.16 `WapIndex2.cfm`—USING `<CFINCLUDE>` TO INCLUDE WAP CONTENT TYPE AND PROLOGUE

```
<!---
  Filename:      WapIndex.cfm
  Created by:    Nate Weiss (NMW)
```

```
  Date Created: 2/18/2001
--->

<!--- Include WAP Content-Type and Prologue --->
<CFINCLUDE TEMPLATE="WapIncludePrologue.cfm">

<wml>

  <card>
    <p>
      <!--- Welcome message --->
      <b>OrangeWAP Studios</b><br/>
      <i>Celluloid by Cell</i><br/>

      <!--- Links to other pages --->
      <a href="#movies">Browse Movies</a><br/>
      <a href="#search">Search Movies</a><br/>
    </p>
  </card>

</wml>
```

Tip

Listing 34.15 can also be used as a CFML Custom tag. Just save `WapIncludePrologue.cfm` in ColdFusion's `CustomTags` folder. You can then replace the `<CFINCLUDE>` line in Listing 34.16 with `<CF_WapIncludePrologue>`. See Chapter 22, "Building Reusable Components," for details.

Multiple Cards in One Deck

One interesting feature of WML is that you can include more than one card within each document. That is, each `<wml>` tag can include more than one `<card>` tag. The WML document, or collection of cards, is therefore called a *Deck*. You can include links from one card to another, and the user can move from card to card within the deck without recontacting the server.

Note

You certainly don't have to include multiple cards in each of your WML templates, but it is definitely encouraged. Because WAP devices generally have slow connections, you should keep the number of requests to your server to a minimum. By including multiple cards with each request, you potentially save a lot of time for your users.

The version of `WapIndex.cfm` in Listing 34.17 creates a simple deck of three cards. From the first card, the user can navigate to the other two cards. Note that each card has been given an `id` attribute. Links to other cards in the same deck are made by referring to the target card's `id`, using the `#` notation shown in the two `href` attributes.

Listing 34.17 `WapIndex3.cfm`—**Including Multiple Cards in the Same Deck**

```
<!---
  Filename:     WapIndex.cfm
  Created by:   Nate Weiss (NMW)
  Date Created: 2/18/2001
--->

<!--- Include WAP Content-Type and Prologue --->
<CFINCLUDE TEMPLATE="WapIncludePrologue.cfm">


<wml>
  <card id="home">
    <p>
      <!--- Welcome message --->
      <b>OrangeWAP Studios</b><br/>
      <i>Celluloid by Cell</i><br/>

      <!--- Links to other pages --->
      <a href="#movies">Browse Movies</a><br/>
      <a href="#search">Search Movies</a><br/>
    </p>
  </card>

  <card id="movies">
    <p>
      <b>Movie List</b>
    </p>
  </card>

  <card id="search">
    <p>
      <b>Movie Search</b>
    </p>
  </card>
</wml>
```

Tip

Much of the finesse of WAP development is sending a sensible set of cards in each request. Even if you don't know that the user will want to look at all the cards in a deck, you still should include them if you can. Of course, you don't want to include cards that no one ever seems to use, either.

Note

As long as there is a reasonable chance the user will navigate to each card, it's worth putting the card in there. The additional cost (in time) of including each additional card is generally much lower than the cost of additional connections back to your server.

CREATING DATA-DRIVEN CARDS

So far, you have created static cards that always look the same. What about creating cards dynamically—for instance to display information from a database? It's really quite simple. Just use <CFQUERY> and <CFOUTPUT> tags as you would normally, ensuring that the content your template generates is valid WML.

Listing 34.18 demonstrates how easy generating data-driven WML is. This is essentially the same as the last listing, except for the addition of a query to retrieve a list of current movies. Then, within the movies card, a link in the form of the <a> tag is generated for each film. The results are shown in Figure 34.11.

LISTING 34.18 `WapIndex4.cfm`—**GENERATING WML DYNAMICALLY FROM QUERY RESULTS**

```
<!---
  Filename:      WapIndex.cfm
  Created by:    Nate Weiss (NMW)
  Date Created: 2/18/2001
  Please Note:
--->

<!--- Include WAP Content-Type and Prologue --->
<CFINCLUDE TEMPLATE="WapIncludePrologue.cfm">

<!--- Get movies from database --->
<CFQUERY
  DATASOURCE="OrangeWhipStudios"
  NAME="GetMovies"
  CACHEDWITHIN="#CreateTimeSpan(0,0,15,0)#">
  SELECT FilmID, MovieTitle, Summary
  FROM Films
  ORDER BY MovieTitle
</CFQUERY>


<wml>

  <card id="home">
    <p>
      <!--- Welcome message --->
      <b>OrangeWAP Studios</b><br/>
      <i>Celluloid by Cell</i><br/>

      <!--- Links to other pages --->
      <a href="#movies">Browse Movies</a><br/>
      <a href="#search">Search Movies</a><br/>
    </p>
  </card>

  <card id="movies">
    <!--- Present a link for each movie --->
    <p>
      <b>Orange Whip Movies</b>
      <CFOUTPUT QUERY="GetMovies">
        <CFSET MovieCardURL = "WapMov.cfm?FilmID=#FilmID#">
```

LISTING 34.18 CONTINUED

```
        <a href="#MovieCardURL#">#MovieTitle#</a><br/>
      </CFOUTPUT>
    </p>
  </card>


  <card id="search">
    <p>
      <b>Movie Search</b>
    </p>
  </card>
</wml>
```

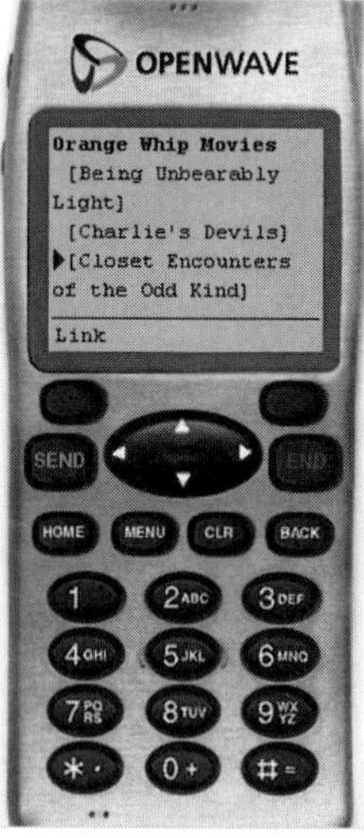

Figure 34.11
Creating data-driven wireless applications is easy with ColdFusion and WML.

BROWSING THROUGH RECORDS

When the user clicks any of the links in Listing 34.18, she will be linked to `WapMov.cfm`, with the selected film's ID passed as a URL parameter. Listing 34.19 shows one way that template can be written.

Rather than responding with a single card, this code sends back a card for the requested movie, plus one card each for the next four movies. Each card enables the user to click the Next button to navigate to the next card in the deck. When the user clicks the Next button on the fifth card, the template is revisited: As the user scrolls through the list of films, the server is contacted only for every fifth film.

Note

Most WAP devices display an error message if your code contains more than 2,000 characters or so. You can adjust the number of cards sent back per deck by adjusting the `MaxRowsPerDeck` variable. In general, the number should be as high as possible without the whole deck exceeding the 2,000-character limit. See the UP.SDK documentation for more details regarding code-size limits.

Listing 34.19 `WapMov.cfm`—**Enabling the User to Browse Through the List of Movies**

```
<!---
  Filename:     WapMov.cfm
  Created by:   Nate Weiss (NMW)
  Date Created: 2/18/2001
--->

<!--- Include WAP Content-Type and Prologue --->
<CFINCLUDE TEMPLATE="WapIncludePrologue.cfm">

<!--- We need to limit how many cards we send --->
<CFSET MaxCardsPerDeck = 5>

<!--- Get movies from database --->
<CFQUERY
  DATASOURCE="ows"
  NAME="GetMovies"
  CACHEDWITHIN="#CreateTimeSpan(0,0,15,0)#">
  SELECT FilmID, MovieTitle, Summary, DateInTheaters
  FROM Films
  ORDER BY MovieTitle
</CFQUERY>

<!--- A FilmID must be passed in the URL --->
<CFPARAM NAME="URL.FilmID" TYPE="numeric">
<!--- Find the passed FilmID's row in query --->
<CFSET StartRow = ListFind(ValueList(GetMovies.FilmID), URL.FilmID)>
<!--- We'll start at that row, and end 5 rows later --->
<CFSET EndRow   = StartRow + MaxCardsPerDeck - 1>


<wml>
  <!--- All cards need a way back to movie list --->
  <template>
    <do type="accept" label="List">
      <go href="WapIndex.cfm#movies"/>
    </do>
  </template>

  <!--- Create a card for each movie --->
  <CFOUTPUT QUERY="GetMovies"
    STARTROW="#StartRow#"
    MAXROWS="#MaxCardsPerDeck#">

    <card id="Film#FilmID#">
```

LISTING 34.19 CONTINUED

```
      <!--- Show "Next" navigation, unless at end --->
      <CFIF CurrentRow LT RecordCount>
        <!--- What is the next film? --->
        <CFSET NextID = FilmID[CurrentRow + 1]>

        <do type="options" label="Next">
          <!--- If next film is in this deck --->
          <CFIF CurrentRow NEQ EndRow>
            <go href="##Film#NextID#"/>
          <!--- If next film not in this deck --->
          <CFELSE>
            <go href="?FilmID=#NextID#"/>
          </CFIF>
        </do>
      </CFIF>

      <!--- Display information about this movie--->
      <p>
        <b>#MovieTitle#</b><br/>
        <i>Opens #DateFormat(DateInTheaters, "mmm d")#.</i><br/>
        #Summary#<br/>
      </p>
    </card>
  </CFOUTPUT>
</wml>
```

RESPONDING TO FORM INPUT

Just like normal Web applications, your WAP applications can include forms for the user to fill in and submit. For instance, you might want the user to be able to search for a movie by typing in a word or two.

The last version of `WapIndex.cfm` included a movie search card, but it didn't actually work. To enable the user to specify his search criteria, the `search` card from Listing 34.18 needs to be completed, as shown in Listing 34.20.

LISTING 34.20 `WapIndex5.cfm`—ALLOWING THE USER TO RUN SEARCHES

```
<!---
  Filename:     WapIndex.cfm
  Created by:   Nate Weiss (NMW)
  Date Created: 2/18/2001
  Please Note:
--->

<!--- Include WAP Content-Type and Prologue --->
<CFINCLUDE TEMPLATE="WapIncludePrologue.cfm">

<!--- Get movies from database --->
<CFQUERY
  DATASOURCE="ows"
  NAME="GetMovies"
```

```
  CACHEDWITHIN="#CreateTimeSpan(0,0,15,0)#">
  SELECT FilmID, MovieTitle, Summary
  FROM Films
  ORDER BY MovieTitle
</CFQUERY>


<wml>

  <card id="home">
    <p>
      <!--- Welcome message --->
      <b>OrangeWAP Studios</b><br/>
      <i>Celluloid by Cell</i><br/>

      <!--- Links to other pages --->
      <a href="#movies">Browse Movies</a><br/>
      <a href="#search">Search Movies</a><br/>
    </p>
  </card>

  <card id="movies">
    <!--- Give user a way to get back home --->
    <do type="options" label="Home">
      <go href="#home"/>
    </do>

    <!--- Present a link for each movie --->
    <p>
      <b>Orange Whip Movies</b>
      <CFOUTPUT QUERY="GetMovies">
        <a href="WapMov.cfm?FilmID=#FilmID#">#MovieTitle#</a><br/>
      </CFOUTPUT>
    </p>
  </card>


  <card id="search">
    <!--- Run search when "Accept" button pressed --->
    <do type="accept" label="Submit">
      <go method="post" href="WapSearch.cfm?">
        <postfield name="criteria" value="$criteria"/>
      </go>
    </do>

    <!--- Allow user to type search criteria --->
    <p>
      <b>Movie Search</b><br/>
      Keywords: <input name="criteria"/>
    </p>
  </card>
</wml>
```

This is roughly equivalent to a simple search form on an HTML page. The `<input>` field gives the user a place to enter his search criteria, and the `<do>` tag gives the user a way to submit the search by clicking the Accept button on the phone.

When the user clicks the Accept button, the `<go>` action fires, essentially acting like a `<form>` tag in HTML. The `method` attribute can be set to `get` or `post`; the `href` attribute, on the other hand, indicates the page to submit to, such as a Web form's `action` attribute. And just as with Web forms, you should use `method="post"`. The `<postfield>` tag causes the value of the `<input>` to be submitted as a form-like value.

Note

The value of `<input>` automatically becomes known to the phone as a variable called `$criteria`, which can be used in various ways. Here, the variable is just passed to the `<postfield>` tag so its value gets submitted to ColdFusion. But you can do a lot more with these variables. Refer to the documentation that was installed with the UP.SDK to see what else you can do with WAP variables and the $ notation used here.

Now you can write a ColdFusion template called `WapSearch.cfm`. Listing 34.21 shows one way to respond to the user's search request. Note that you can refer to the user's search criteria as `#Form.Criteria#`, just as if the search request were coming from a normal Web form.

Listing 34.21 `WapSearch.cfm`**—Responding to Form Input**

```
<!---
  Filename:     WapSearch.cfm
  Created by:   Nate Weiss (NMW)
  Date Created: 2/18/2001
--->

<!--- Include WAP Content-Type and Prologue --->
<CFINCLUDE TEMPLATE="WapIncludePrologue.cfm">

<!--- We must have search criteria --->
<CFPARAM NAME="Form.Criteria" TYPE="string">

<!--- Get movies from database --->
<CFQUERY
  DATASOURCE="ows"
  NAME="GetMovies"
  CACHEDWITHIN="#CreateTimeSpan(0,0,15,0)#">
  SELECT FilmID, MovieTitle, Summary
  FROM Films
  WHERE MovieTitle LIKE '%#Form.Criteria#%'
     OR PitchText  LIKE '%#Form.Criteria#%'
     OR Summary    LIKE '%#Form.Criteria#%'
  ORDER BY MovieTitle
</CFQUERY>


<wml>
  <card id="search">
    <!--- Give user a way back to "Search" card --->
    <do type="options" label="Again">
      <go href="WapIndex.cfm#search"/>
    </do>
```

```
    <p>
      <!--- Show "Results" message, with criteria --->
      <b>Search Results For</b><br/>
      <CFOUTPUT>&quot;<b>#Form.Criteria#</b>&quot;<br/></CFOUTPUT>

      <!--- For each matching movie, provide link --->
      <CFOUTPUT QUERY="GetMovies">
        <a href="WapMov.cfm?FilmID=#FilmID#">#MovieTitle#</a><br/>
      </CFOUTPUT>
    </p>
  </card>
</wml>
```

Tip

It's not easy for users to type on the tiny keypads cell phones come with. Try to keep the amount of typing down to a bare minimum. Elaborate data-entry screens with many fields probably will be too time-consuming for your users to actually use.

LEARNING MORE

Even though these examples should give you enough to hit the ground running, this section has really only scratched the surface with regard to what you can do with WML. You probably need to learn more about the WML language before you can build the wireless application of your dreams. All the following are great resources:

- The WML Reference section of the Help Tab in ColdFusion Studio
- The WAP, WML, and WMLScript documentation that was installed when you installed the UP.SDK
- The WAP Forum Web site, at `http://www.wapforum.com`
- The Openwave Web site, at `http://www.openwave.com`
- *WAP Development with WML and WMLScript*, by Ben Forta
- *Learning WML & WMLScript*, by Martin Frost (O'Reilly)

CHAPTER 35

INTERACTING WITH THE OPERATING SYSTEM

In this chapter

WORKING WITH THE OPERATING SYSTEM

ColdFusion provides the developer with many tools with which to interact with the operating system. These tools include functions and tags to manipulate files and directories using <CFFILE> and <CFDIRECTORY>, execute applications on the server using the <CFEXECUTE> tag, and manipulate the system Registry using the <CFREGISTRY> tag. This chapter shows how these tags can be used to interact with the file system and operating system.

LOCAL FILE MANIPULATION

<CFFILE> permits local file access through CFML templates. Files can be moved, copied, renamed, or deleted by using various action attributes for the <CFFILE> tag. Additionally, <CFFILE> provides mechanisms for reading and writing ASCII files with ColdFusion. Taking advantage of the <CFFILE> tag provides you with the ability to produce complex applications with file manipulation using a single interface, without having to deal with the additional complexities of protocols such as File Transport Protocol (FTP) and Networked File System (NFS). The templates in which the <CFFILE> tag is used can be protected using native server security when the templates are stored in directories below the document root defined for the HTTP server. In addition to the ability to access the local file system, <CFFILE> provides the ability to upload files using the HTTP protocol.

The general structure of the <CFFILE> tag and its attributes are shown in Listing 35.1.

LISTING 35.1 <CFFILE> TAG SYNTAX

```
<CFFILE ACTION="action" ATTRIBUTE="attribute"
➥ATTRIBUTE="attribute" ATTRIBUTE="attribute">
```

Note

Local file manipulation in this case means accessing the filesystem on the server where ColdFusion is installed. <CFFILE> provides no capabilities to manipulate the client filesystem. Because ColdFusion operates on the server, it has no access to the client file system. Keep this in mind when developing your applications.

The <CFFILE> tag's attributes can be set to multiple values, which enables the behavior of the tag to be modified to fit your needs. Each of the attributes can be set dynamically using variables created via the <CFSET> tag or with the values of query or form fields. When using form fields, extreme care should be taken to ensure that security restrictions are in place to prevent malicious action as a result of dynamic file action. Table 35.1 indicates the attributes and the valid values permitted for specific values of the ACTION attribute. Table 35.2 shows the possible values for the NAMECONFLICT attribute and the corresponding ColdFusion actions that will occur based on those values.

Caution

When using FORM fields, URL variables, or other user-entered data to set the attributes for the <CFFILE> tag, extreme caution should be used to ensure only valid entries are processed.

Table 35.1 <CFFILE> Tag ACTION Attributes

Action	Attributes	Comments
APPEND	OUTPUT FILE ADDNEWLINE MODE ATTRIBUTES	Writes the contents of the string specified in OUTPUT to the end of the file specified in FILE.
COPY	SOURCE DESTINATION	Copies file from location specified in SOURCE to location specified in DESTINATION.
DELETE	FILE	Deletes file specified in FILE attribute.
MOVE	SOURCE DESTINATION	Moves file from location specified in SOURCE to location specified in DESTINATION.
READ	FILE VARIABLE	Reads the contents of the file specified in FILE into the variable specified in VARIABLE. The VARIABLE is created if it does not exist.
READBINARY	FILE VARIABLE	Reads the contents of the binary file specified in FILE into the variable specified in VARIABLE. The VARIABLE is created if it does not exist.
RENAME	SOURCE DESTINATION ATTRIBUTES MODE	Renames file specified in SOURCE to the filename specified in DESTINATION.
UPLOAD	ACCEPT DESTINATION FILEFIELD NAMECONFLICT ATTRIBUTES MODE	Used to upload files to the server using the filename found in FILEFIELD from the form and resolves filename conflicts using the value of the NAMECONFLICT attribute.
WRITE	OUTPUT FILE ADDNEWLINE	Writes the contents of the string specified as OUTPUT to the file specified in FILE. The file is overwritten if it exists.

TABLE 35.2 EXPLANATION OF NAMECONFLICT ATTRIBUTE

Value	Meaning
`ERROR`	Generates an error if the file specified already exists.
`SKIP`	Enables the problem file to be skipped. The file cannot be saved.
`OVERWRITE`	The file is overwritten with a new file.
`MAKEUNIQUE`	Automatically generates a unique filename for the uploaded file.

After a `<CFFILE>` operation is completed, information about the file is available in reference keys of the `FILE` structure. Similar to the `URL`, `FORM`, and `CGI` structures, the `FILE` structure maintains status information about the most recent file operation completed or attempted. Keys in the `FILE` structure are referenced in the same manner as other ColdFusion variables (for example, `#FILE.ContentType#`). Table 35.3 identifies the attributes maintained and their meanings.

TABLE 35.3 FILE STRUCTURE KEYS

Key	Explanation
`AttemptedServerFile`	Did ColdFusion attempt to save the file? (Yes/No)
`ClientDirectory`	Client-side directory in which the file was located.
`ClientFile`	Client-side filename (with extension).
`ClientFileExt`	Client-side filename extension without the period.
`ClientFileName`	Client-side filename (without extension).
`ContentSubType`	MIME content subtype of file.
`ContentType`	MIME content type of file.
`DateLastAccessed`	Returns the date and time the uploaded file was last accessed.
`FileExisted`	Did a file with the same name exist in the specified destination prior to upload, copy, or move? (Yes/No)
`FileSize`	Size of the uploaded file.
`FileWasAppended`	Was the file appended to an existing file by ColdFusion? (Yes/No)
`FileWasOverwritten`	Was an existing file overwritten by ColdFusion? (Yes/No)
`FileWasRenamed`	Was the uploaded file renamed to avoid a conflict? (Yes/No)
`FileWasSaved`	Was the file saved by ColdFusion? (Yes/No)
`OldFileSize`	Size of the file that was overwritten during an upload operation.
`ServerDirectory`	Directory on server where file was saved.
`ServerFile`	Filename of the saved file.
`ServerFileExt`	Extension of the uploaded file without the period.

Key	Explanation
ServerFileName	Filename without extension of the uploaded file.
TimeCreated	Returns the time the uploaded file was created.
TimeLastModified	Returns the date and time of the last modification to the uploaded file.

The previous ariables are used in several of the examples that follow, specifically in Listing 35.8 and the examples that follow it.

ACCESSING THE LOCAL FILESYSTEM

During application development you might need to perform local filesystem operations (local here refers to the Web server's file system). This need might manifest itself in the requirement to read or write ASCII files or to copy, move, rename, or delete various application files.

READING AND WRITING FILES

Using <CFFILE> to read and write ASCII files is fairly straightforward. For example, to read the contents of AUTOEXEC.BAT into a ColdFusion variable for processing, the code would be similar to Listing 35.2.

LISTING 35.2 <CFFILE> CALL TO READ CFDIST.INI INTO A VARIABLE

```
<!--- Read the contents of C:\CFUSION\CFDIST.INI into a
➥variable (cfdist) for processing --->

<CFFILE ACTION="READ" FILE="C:\CFUSION\CFDIST.INI"
➥VARIABLE="cfdist">
```

Note

<CFFILE> can read both ASCII and binary files. To read a binary file, the ACTION attribute must be set to ReadBinary.

This is a simple yet powerful feature. The example in Listing 35.2 is trivial, but it serves as the basis for the power of reading files using <CFFILE>. After the <CFFILE> operation is completed, the contents of the file are available in the variable specified during the call. If this file contained delimited data, it could be parsed using <CFLOOP> and various string functions.

Writing a file using <CFFILE> is just as easy. Listing 35.3 shows an example of writing a modified version of the CFDIST.INI file back out to disk.

Listing 35.3 <CFFILE> Call to Read CFDIST.INI and Write CFDIST.INI to Disk

```
<!--- Read the contents of C:\CFUSION\CFDIST.INI into a variable
 (cfdist) for processing -CFDIST.INI is a configuration file that
is optionally used to allow the ColdFusion server to operate on a machine
that does not have a web server installed, using a listener module
[--->

<CFFILE ACTION="READ" FILE="C:\CFUSION\CFDIST.INI " VARIABLE="cfdist">
<!--- modify the contents of the variable --->
<CFSET header="; File Modified using ColdFusion 5.0 on: ">
<CFSET header=header & DateFormat(Now(),"MM/DD/YYYY") & "at ">
<CFSET header=header & TimeFormat(Now(),"HH:MM:SS") & CHR(13) & CHR(10)>
<CFSET cfdist=header & cfdist>
<!--- Write the contents of the variable back out to disk --->
<CFFILE ACTION="WRITE" FILE="C:\CFUSION\CFDIST.INI" OUTPUT="#cfdist#"
➥ ADDNEWLINE="NO">
<HTML>
<HEAD>
<TITLE>Listing 35.2 - CFFILE READ/WRITE Example</TITLE>
</HEAD>
<BODY>
C:\CFUSION\CFDIST.INI has been modified, as shown below:
<PRE>
<CFOUTPUT>#cfdist#</CFOUTPUT>
</PRE>
</BODY>
</HTML>
```

The code in Listing 35.3 builds on the example in Listing 35.2. First, it uses `<CFFILE>` to read the contents of `CFDIST.INI` into a variable. Next, a new line is added to the beginning of the variable by concatenating a remark statement coupled with a date/time stamp to the contents of the variable. Lastly, `<CFFILE>` is called again to write the contents of the variable back out to disk. The resulting file output is displayed as it would be seen on disk.

Caution

`<CFFILE>` with the `ACTION` attribute set to `Write` creates the file if it does not exist and overwrites the file if it exists. Care should be taken to ensure that existing content is not deleted inadvertently. If the contents of an existing ASCII file are to be kept, `<CFFILE>` should be used with the `ACTION` set to `Append`, which will concatenate the contents of the variable specified in the `OUTPUT` attribute to the end of the disk file. The `FileExists()` function can be used to determine whether a `Write` or `Append` operation should take place.

At this time, `<CFFILE>` can only be used to write ASCII files.

Copying, Moving, Renaming, and Deleting Files

The `<CFFILE>` tag provides the capability to perform local file operations, such as `COPY`, `MOVE`, `RENAME`, and `DELETE`. *Local* in this example means local to the HTTP server—not local to the client. These actions have the potential for causing severe damage to the filesystem.

Security considerations should therefore be evaluated carefully before developing ColdFusion templates that provide the ability to copy, rename, move, or delete files.

Note

Security measures can vary by operating system and from one Web server to another. Consult documentation specific to the configuration of your Web server for detailed information about security issues.

To provide local file access, the `<CFFILE>` tag is used with the `ACTION` attribute set to `COPY`, `MOVE`, `RENAME`, or `DELETE`. The `DESTINATION` attribute is not required in the case of the `DELETE` action value; it is required in all other cases.

Listing 35.3 shows ColdFusion's capability to copy files on the local filesystem. The `ACTION` attribute is set to `COPY`; the `SOURCE` attribute is set to the name of the file that is to be copied. The `DESTINATION` attribute is set to the directory into which the file will be copied. The `DESTINATION` attribute also can specify a filename in addition to the directory name, which enables you to copy one file to another while changing the name in the process.

LISTING 35.4 <CFFILE> TAG WITH ACTION ATTRIBUTE SET TO COPY

```
<!--- Copy a file from one location to another --->
<CFFILE ACTION="COPY" SOURCE="C:\INETPUB\WWWROOT\OWS\FILE1.TXT"
➥ DESTINATION="C:\INETPUB\WWWROOT\OWS\PROCESS\">
```

Listing 35.4 shows ColdFusion's capability to move files on the local filesystem. The `ACTION` attribute is set to `MOVE`; the `SOURCE` attribute is set to the name of the file that is to be moved. The `DESTINATION` attribute is set to the directory into which the file will be moved. Listing 35.4 shows the use of the `DELETE` value of the `ACTION` attribute.

LISTING 35.5 <CFFILE> TAG WITH ACTION ATTRIBUTE SET TO MOVE

```
<!--- Move an existing file from one location to another --->
<CFFILE ACTION="MOVE" SOURCE="C:\INETPUB\WWWROOT\OWS\FILE2.TXT"
➥DESTINATION="C:\INETPUB\WWWROOT\OWS\PROCESS\">
```

The `ACTION` attribute in Listing 35.6 is set to `DELETE`, and the `FILE` attribute is set to the name of the file you will delete. The `DESTINATION` attribute is not used when the `ACTION` attribute is set to `DELETE`.

LISTING 35.6 <CFFILE> TAG WITH ACTION ATTRIBUTE SET TO DELETE

```
<!--- Delete an existing file --->
<CFFILE ACTION="DELETE" FILE="C:\INETPUB\WWWROOT\OWS\FILE3.TXT">
```

Caution

Use the `DELETE` action carefully. Access to templates that delete files should be carefully restricted.

Listing 35.7 shows `<CFFILE>` being used to `RENAME` an existing file.

LISTING 35.7 `<CFFILE>` TAG WITH `ACTION` ATTRIBUTE SET TO `RENAME`

```
<!--- Rename an existing file --->
<CFFILE ACTION="RENAME" SOURCE="C:\INETPUB\WWWROOT\OWS\FILE3.TXT"
➥DESTINATION="C:\INETPUB\WWWROOT\OWS\FILE4.TXT">
```

UPLOADING FILES USING THE <CFFILE> TAG

Browser-based file uploads in ColdFusion are provided through the `<CFFILE>` tag. This tag takes advantage of features introduced in Web browsers that support file uploads using the HTTP protocol. The method by which files are uploaded to the server using HTTP is documented in the Internet Request for Comment (RFC) 1867, which can be found at `http://www.faqs.org/rfcs/rfc1867.html`. These features are browser specific; you should therefore use them carefully to provide the maximum capability to your users, while also providing the maximum level of flexibility.

Note

RFC 1867 is the formal documentation of the HTTP file upload process. It specifies the concepts related to file uploads using MIME file extensions.

Caution

The file upload mechanism is browser specific. Netscape Navigator 2.0 and later support this feature. Microsoft Internet Explorer 4.0 and higher supports this feature natively, whereas Internet Explorer 3.02 provides file upload support through the addition of an ActiveX control. Other browsers, such as Lynx and Mosaic, might not support this feature. Use of the file upload mechanism should be implemented with this in mind.

The syntax of the `<CFFILE>` tag can be used with selected attributes to facilitate the uploading of files to the server. You must carefully examine a number of issues prior to writing the HTML/CFML necessary to process a file upload. First and foremost is security. The directory to which the files will be uploaded must be secure from outside view, and the templates used to perform the file operations must be protected from unauthorized access. Because the threat of computer viruses is increasing, you must take precautions to protect your system from malicious users. The second issue to examine is the reason you are providing file operations to the users. Is it necessary? Can it be accomplished using other means?

After you have decided to use `<CFFILE>` to upload a file, you can move on to the next step of the process, which is preparing the user interface. This requires the development of an HTML form, either through writing static HTML or by creating an HTML form using dynamic code generated via CFML. In either case, the form's structure is basically the same.

The next series of listings is used to create an add-on to the actor listings that will allow a photo to be linked to an actor record. First, the general syntax is shown, and then specific modifications to the actor templates are made.

Listing 35.8 shows the HTML code necessary to create a form that prompts the user for a file to be uploaded to the server. The result of Listing 35.8 is shown in Figure 35.1. Figure 35.2 shows the file selection dialog box produced by the `INPUT TYPE="File"` tag, and Figure 35.3 shows the form after a file has been selected for uploading.

Listing 35.8 UPLOADFORM.HTML—HTML Form for File Upload Using the <CFFILE> Tag

```
<!--- Create HTML form to upload a file --->


<HTML>
<HEAD>
<TITLE>&lt;CFFILE&gt; Upload Demonstration - Example 1</TITLE>
</HEAD>
<BODY>
<CENTER>&lt;CFFILE&gt; Upload Demonstration - Example 1</CENTER>
<HR>
<FORM ACTION="uploadfile.cfm" ENCTYPE="multipart/form-data" METHOD="POST">
File to upload: <INPUT NAME="FileName" SIZE="50" TYPE="FILE"><BR>
<INPUT TYPE="SUBMIT" VALUE="Upload the File">
</FORM>
</BODY>
</HTML>
```

Figure 35.1
Example HTML form for file upload.

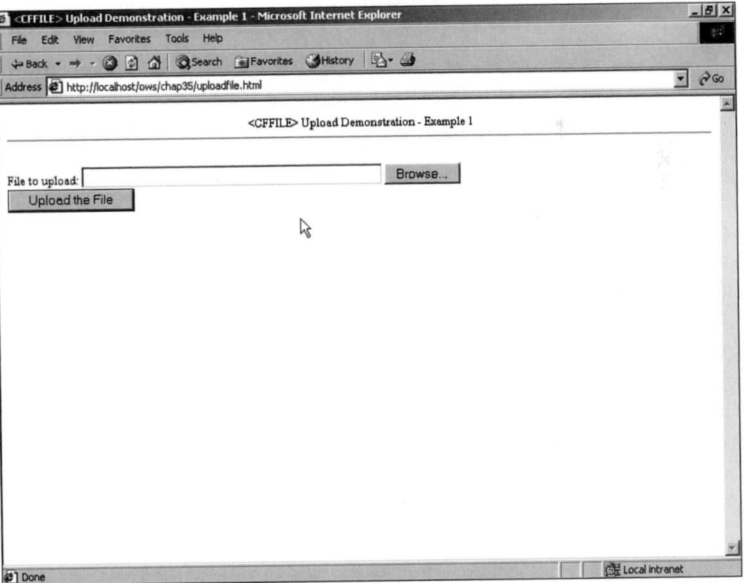

The primary difference between this form and a standard HTML form is the specification of the `ENCTYPE` value `"multipart/form-data"`, which is necessary to process the uploaded file. A second difference is the addition of an `INPUT` type called `FILE`, which tells the browser to process file selection using the standard user-interface functionality of the underlying operating system. The `FORM` tag's `ACTION` attribute identifies which ColdFusion template will be used to process the file. The `METHOD` attribute is set to `POST`, which is required by ColdFusion. Figure 35.2 shows the operating system's file selection dialog box.

The dialog box shown in Figure 35.2 is specific to the operating system on which a browser is running and changes from one operating system to another. Figure 35.3 shows the HTML form with the text box filled with the selected filename.

Figure 35.2
Example file selection dialog box.

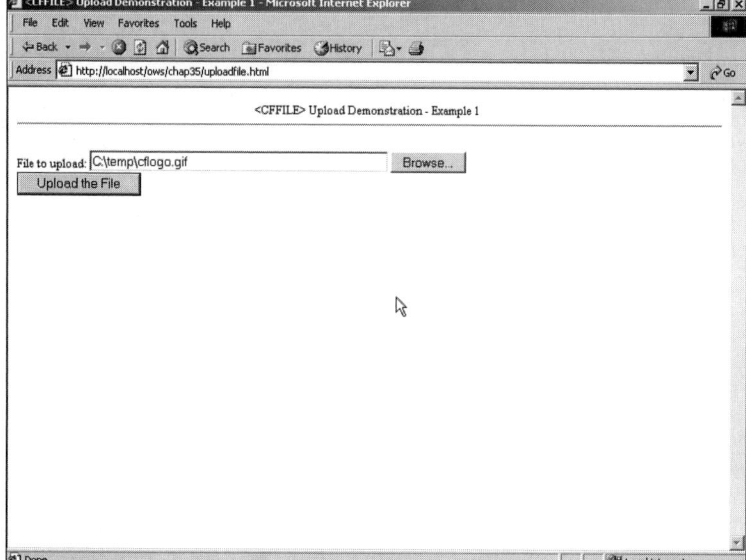

Figure 35.3
Example HTML form for file upload with selected filename.

When this form is submitted, the FORM tag's ACTION attribute causes the selected file to be uploaded. Listing 35.9 shows the CFML code required to process the uploaded file. This example enumerates the values of the keys in the FILE structure after the file has been written to the file server. Details of the keys in the FILE structure can be seen in Table 35.3.

LISTING 35.9 UPLOADFILE.CFM—CFML CODE REQUIRED TO PROCESS AN UPLOADED FILE

```
<!--- Template to process uploaded files from user --->
<HTML>
<HEAD>
<TITLE>CFFILE Tag File Upload Demonstration
➥Results - Example 1</TITLE>
</HEAD>
<BODY>
<CFFILE
DESTINATION="C:\INETPUB\WWWROOT\OWS\CHAP35\FILES\"
ACTION="UPLOAD"
NAMECONFLICT="OVERWRITE"
FILEFIELD="FileName">
<CFOUTPUT>
<CENTER>
&lt;CFFILE&gt; Tag File Upload Demonstration Results - Example 1<P>
File Upload was Successful! Information about the file is detailed below
</CENTER>
<HR>
<TABLE>
<CAPTION><B>File Information</B></CAPTION>
<TR>
<TH VALIGN="TOP" ALIGN="LEFT">File Name:</TH>
➥<TD>#File.ServerDirectory#\#FILE.ServerFile#</TD>
<TH VALIGN="TOP" ALIGN="LEFT">Content Type:</TH><TD>#File.ContentType#</TD>
</TR>
<TR>
<TH VALIGN="TOP" ALIGN="LEFT">Content SubType:</TH>
➥<TD>#File.ContentSubType#</TD>
<TH VALIGN="TOP" ALIGN="LEFT">Client Path:</TH>
➥<TD>#File.ClientDirectory#</TD>
</TR>
<TR>
<TH VALIGN="TOP" ALIGN="LEFT">Client File:</TH><TD>#File.ClientFile#</TD>
<TH VALIGN="TOP" ALIGN="LEFT">Client FileName:</TH>
➥<TD>#File.ClientFileName#</TD>
</TR>
<TR>
<TH VALIGN="TOP" ALIGN="LEFT">Client FileExt:</TH>
➥<TD>#File.ClientFileExt#</TD>
<TH VALIGN="TOP" ALIGN="LEFT">Server Path:</TH><TD>#File.ServerDirectory#</TD>
</TR>
<TR>
<TH VALIGN="TOP" ALIGN="LEFT">Server File:</TH><TD>#File.ServerFile#</TD>
<TH VALIGN="TOP" ALIGN="LEFT">Server FileName:</TH>
➥<TD>#File.ServerFileName#</TD>
</TR>
<TR>
<TH VALIGN="TOP" ALIGN="LEFT">Server FileExt:</TH>
➥<TD>#File.ServerFileExt#</TD>
```

LISTING 35.9 CONTINUED

```
<TH VALIGN="TOP" ALIGN="LEFT">Attempted ServerFile:</TH>
➥<TD>#File.AttemptedServerFile#</TD>
</TR>
<TR>
<TH VALIGN="TOP" ALIGN="LEFT">File Existed?</TH><TD>#File.FileExisted#</TD>
<TH VALIGN="TOP" ALIGN="LEFT">File Was Saved?</TH><TD>#File.FileWasSaved#</TD>
</TR>
<TR>
<TH VALIGN="TOP" ALIGN="LEFT">File Was Overwritten?</TH>
➥<TD>#File.FileWasOverWritten#</TD>
<TH VALIGN="TOP" ALIGN="LEFT">File Was Appended?</TH>
➥<TD>#File.FileWasAppended#</TD>
</TR>
<TR>
<TH VALIGN="TOP" ALIGN="LEFT">File Was Renamed?</TH>
➥<TD>#File.FileWasRenamed#</TD>
<TH VALIGN="TOP" ALIGN="LEFT">File Size:</TH><TD>#File.Filesize#</TD></TH>
</TR>
<TR>
<TH VALIGN="TOP" ALIGN="LEFT">Old File Size:</TH><TD>#File.OldFileSize#</TD>
<TH VALIGN="TOP" ALIGN="LEFT">Date Last Accessed:</TH>
➥<TD>#DateFormat(File.DateLastAccessed,'DD MMM YYYY')#</TD>
</TR>
<TR>
<TH VALIGN="TOP" ALIGN="LEFT">Date/Time Created:</TH>
➥<TD>#DateFormat(File.TimeCreated,'DD MMM YYYY')# #Timeformat(File.
➥TimeCreated,'HH:MM:SS')#</TD>
<TH VALIGN="TOP" ALIGN="LEFT">Date/Time Modified:</TH>
➥<TD>#DateFormat(File.TimeLastModified,'DD MMM YYYY')
➥# #Timeformat(File.TimeLastModified,'HH:MM:SS')#</TD>
</TR>
</TABLE>
</CFOUTPUT>
</BODY>
</HTML>
```

The CFML template shown in Listing 35.9 processes the uploaded file, stores it in the directory indicated in the `<CFFILE>` tag's `DESTINATION` attribute, and then prints out the contents of the keys in the `FILE` structure. Some of the `FILE` keys might not have values, depending on the attributes passed to the `<CFFILE>` tag. Figure 35.4 shows the output resulting from the file upload.

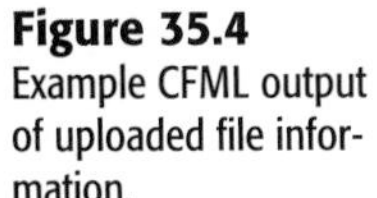

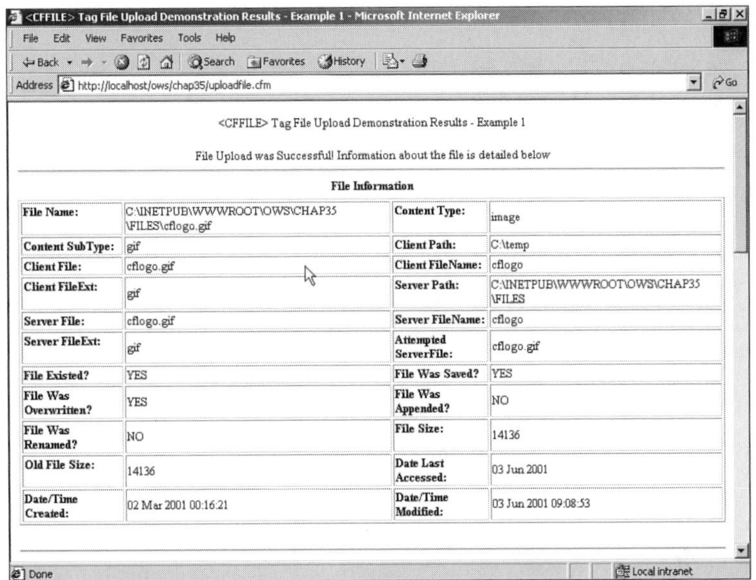

Figure 35.4 Example CFML output of uploaded file information.

Now take a look at the use of the `<CFFILE>` tag in Listing 35.9. Four of the attributes for the `<CFFILE>` tag were used:

```
<CFFILE
ACTION="UPLOAD"
DESTINATION="C:\INETPUB\WWWROOT\OWS\CHAP35\FILES\"
NAMECONFLICT="OVERWRITE"
FILEFIELD="FileName">
```

The `ACTION` attribute is set to `"UPLOAD"`. The `DESTINATION` attribute was set to the value `"C:\INETPUB\WWWROOT\OWS\CHAP35\FILES\"`, which is a directory created on a server specifically for storing uploaded files. The directory you choose can be anywhere on the server, provided the appropriate file access privileges (read, write, delete, and so on) are set. The `NAMECONFLICT` attribute is set to `"OVERWRITE"`, indicating that ColdFusion should overwrite the file if it finds a file with the same name in the destination directory. The last attribute set is the `FILEFIELD` attribute. Its value is `"FileName"`, indicating the name of the field on the form from which the `multipart/form-data` containing the file data will be passed. The remaining code in the example uses attributes from the `FILE` structure to show details about the selected file.

Caution

The trailing slash (\) in the destination directory name is required.

Listing 35.10 shows an example that builds on the HTML/CFML code you just wrote; it demonstrates the use of variables to set the various attributes of the `<CFFILE>` tag. The HTML form is modified by adding a radio button group that sets the `NAMECONFLICT` attribute in the `<CFFILE>` tag.

LISTING 35.10 UPLOADFORM2.HTML—MODIFICATION OF HTML TO DEMONSTRATE DATA-DRIVEN ATTRIBUTE SETTING

```
<!--- Modified Form to Dynamically Change Attributes  --->
<HTML>
<HEAD>
<TITLE>&lt;CFFILE&gt; Upload Demonstration - Example 2</TITLE>
</HEAD>
<BODY>
<CENTER>&lt;CFFILE&gt; Upload Demonstration - Example 2</CENTER>
<HR>
<FORM ACTION="uploadfile2.cfm" ENCTYPE="multipart/form-data" METHOD="POST">
File to upload: <INPUT NAME="FileName" SIZE="50" TYPE="FILE"><BR>
Action if File Exists:
<INPUT TYPE=RADIO NAME="FileAction" VALUE="OVERWRITE" CHECKED>Overwrite
<INPUT TYPE=RADIO NAME="FileAction" VALUE="MAKEUNIQUE">Make Unique
<INPUT TYPE=RADIO NAME="FileAction" VALUE="SKIP">Skip
<INPUT TYPE=SUBMIT VALUE="Upload the File">
</FORM>
</BODY>
</HTML>
```

The radio button group was added with the name of `FileAction`, which is used in the template to identify the appropriate action to take if a duplicate file is detected. Figure 35.5 shows what the modified form looks like in the browser.

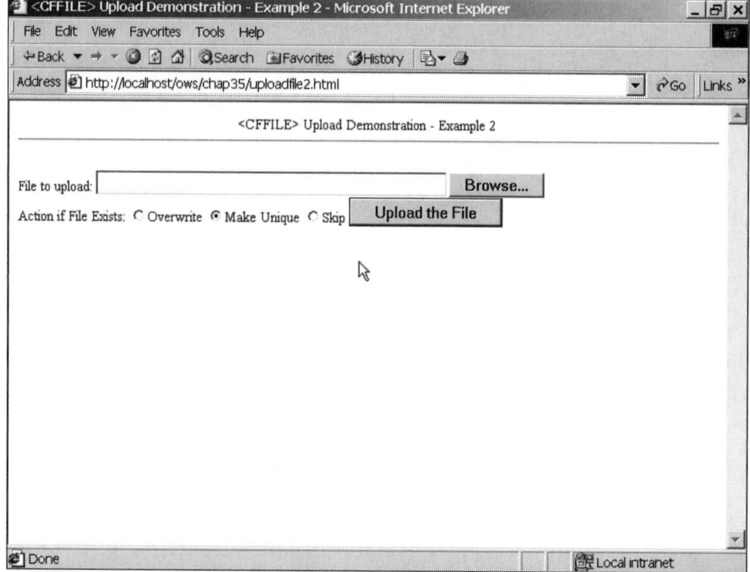

Figure 35.5 Modified file upload form with radio buttons.

The CFML from Listing 35.9 has to be modified to specify the action to take when data is being passed to the template and a duplicate file exists. Listing 35.11 shows the modifications required.

Listing 35.11 UPLOADFILE2.CFM—Modified CFML Code with Data-Driven Attribute Setting

```
<!--- Modified Template that will dynamically set the
➥NAMECONFLICT attribute based on form input --->
<HTML>
<HEAD>
<TITLE>&lt;CFFILE&gt; Tag File Upload Demonstration Results - Example 2</TITLE>
</HEAD>
<BODY>
<CFFILE
DESTINATION="C:\INETPUB\WWWROOT\OWS\CHAP35\FILES\"
ACTION="UPLOAD"
NAMECONFLICT="#FORM.FILEACTION#"
FILEFIELD="FileName">
<CFOUTPUT>
<CENTER>
&lt;CFFILE&gt; Tag File Upload Demonstration Results - Example 2<P>
File Upload was Successful! Information about the file is detailed below.
</CENTER>
<HR>
<TABLE BORDER WIDTH="100%">
<CAPTION><B>File Information</B></CAPTION>
<TR>
<TH VALIGN="TOP" ALIGN="LEFT">File
Name:</TH><TD>#File.ServerDirectory#\#FILE.ServerFile#</TD>
<TH VALIGN="TOP" ALIGN="LEFT">Content Type:</TH><TD>#File.ContentType#</TD>
</TR>
<TR>
<TH VALIGN="TOP" ALIGN="LEFT">Content SubType:</TH>
<TD>#File.ContentSubType#</TD>
<TH VALIGN="TOP" ALIGN="LEFT">Client Path:</TH>
<TD>#File.ClientDirectory#</TD>
</TR>
<TR>
<TH VALIGN="TOP" ALIGN="LEFT">Client File:</TH><TD>#File.ClientFile#</TD>
<TH VALIGN="TOP" ALIGN="LEFT">Client
FileName:</TH><TD>#File.ClientFileName#</TD>
</TR>
<TR>
<TH VALIGN="TOP" ALIGN="LEFT">Client
FileExt:</TH><TD>#File.ClientFileExt#</TD>
<TH VALIGN="TOP" ALIGN="LEFT">Server Path:</TH><TD>#File.ServerDirectory#</TD>
</TR>
<TR>
<TH VALIGN="TOP" ALIGN="LEFT">Server File:</TH><TD>#File.ServerFile#</TD>
<TH VALIGN="TOP" ALIGN="LEFT">Server
FileName:</TH><TD>#File.ServerFileName#</TD>
</TR>
<TR>
<TH VALIGN="TOP" ALIGN="LEFT">Server
FileExt:</TH><TD>#File.ServerFileExt#</TD>
```

LISTING 35.11 CONTINUED

```
<TH VALIGN="TOP" ALIGN="LEFT">Attempted
ServerFile:</TH><TD>#File.AttemptedServerFile#</TD>
</TR>
<TR>
<TH VALIGN="TOP" ALIGN="LEFT">File Existed?</TH><TD>#File.FileExisted#</TD>
<TH VALIGN="TOP" ALIGN="LEFT">File Was Saved?</TH><TD>#File.FileWasSaved#</TD>
</TR>
<TR>
<TH VALIGN="TOP" ALIGN="LEFT">File Was
Overwritten?</TH><TD>#File.FileWasOverWritten#</TD>
<TH VALIGN="TOP" ALIGN="LEFT">File Was
Appended?</TH><TD>#File.FileWasAppended#</TD>
</TR>
<TR>
<TH VALIGN="TOP" ALIGN="LEFT">File Was
Renamed?</TH><TD>#File.FileWasRenamed#</TD>
<TH VALIGN="TOP" ALIGN="LEFT">File Size:</TH><TD>#File.Filesize#</TD></TH>
</TR>
<TR>
<TH VALIGN="TOP" ALIGN="LEFT">Old File Size:</TH><TD>#File.OldFileSize#</TD>
<TH VALIGN="TOP" ALIGN="LEFT">Date Last
Accessed:</TH><TD>#DateFormat(File.DateLastAccessed,'DD MMM YYYY')#</TD>
</TR>
<TR>
<TH VALIGN="TOP" ALIGN="LEFT">Date/Time
Created:</TH><TD>#DateFormat(File.TimeCreated,'DD MMM YYYY')#
#Timeformat(File.TimeCreated,'HH:MM:SS')#</TD>
<TH VALIGN="TOP" ALIGN="LEFT">Date/Time
Modified:</TH><TD>#DateFormat(File.TimeLastModified,'DD MMM YYYY')#
#Timeformat(File.TimeLastModified,'HH:MM:SS')#</TD>
</TR>
</TABLE>
</CFOUTPUT>
</BODY>
</HTML>


All the following is deleted and replaced with above code to match the file on
➥disk.
```

Note that in the example in Figure 35.5, the radio button marked Make Unique was checked. This caused the CFML to dynamically change its behavior. Because in the first example you uploaded `cflogo.gif` to the server, the result of submitting the same file (with the make unique parameter) is that the server is forced to create a unique name for the file when it is uploaded the second time. Figure 35.6 shows the results, with the new filename `ACF3EB.GIF` and the fact that the `FILE.FileWasRenamed` variable was set to `Yes`.

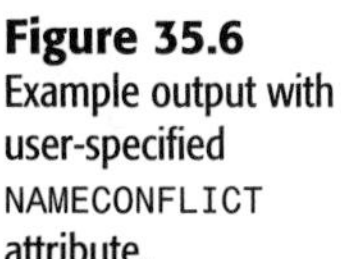

Figure 35.6
Example output with user-specified NAMECONFLICT attribute.

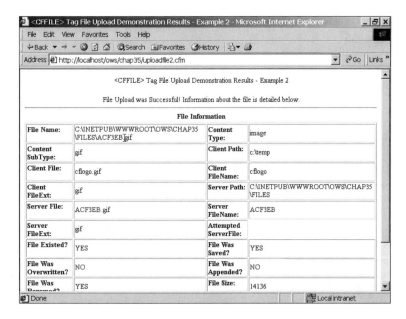

The <CFFILE> tag in this example uses data passed from the form in the FileAction field to set the value of the NAMECONFLICT attribute. The field was referenced in the <CFFILE> tag as follows:

```
NAMECONFLICT="#FORM.FILEACTION#"
```

Any of the other attributes can also be set using CFSET variables, FORM attributes, or URL attributes. Note, however, that setting the SOURCE or DESTINATION attribute based on user input can have far-reaching consequences. For security reasons, users should not be permitted to specify SOURCE or DESTINATION attributes using TEXT input fields. The SOURCE and DESTINATION attributes should be set using only template-based code, which is conditionally executed, to provide maximum security.

Now that you have seen the <CFFILE> tag used in simple examples, you can modify the sample application to add file upload capabilities. You accomplish this by creating three CFML templates for the purposes of uploading an actor's photo to the server. The first template provides a list of actors from which to choose. The second template prompts you for the name of the file containing the photo. The third template actually accepts the file and saves it to the server. You start by creating the template to provide the actor list, which is shown in Listing 35.12.

Listing 35.12 ACTORPHOTO1.CFM—Actor Listing Template

```
<!--- Query the database to get a listing of actors to choose from --->
<CFQUERY DATASOURCE="OWS" NAME="Actors">
SELECT NameFirst, NameLast, ActorId FROM Actors
      ORDER BY NameLast, NameFirst
</CFQUERY>
```

LISTING 35.12 CONTINUED

```
<HTML>

<HEAD>
<TITLE>Maintain Actor Photos</TITLE>
</HEAD>

<BODY BGCOLOR="#FFFFFF">

<H1>Maintain Actor Photos</H1>
<HR>
<H3>Click on Actor Name to Add Photo</H3>
<TABLE BORDER>
<TR>
<TH>Name</TH>
<TH>ID</TH>
</TR>
<CFOUTPUT QUERY="Actors">
<TR>
<TD><A HREF="actorphoto2.cfm?ActorID=#ActorID#">
➥#NameLast#, #NameFirst#</A></TD>
<TD>#NumberFormat(ActorId,'0000')#</TD>
</TR>
</CFOUTPUT>
</TABLE>
</BODY>
</HTML>
```

Figure 35.7 shows what the screen looks like using the template created in Listing 35.11. This template selects a list of actors from the `actors` table and presents a table to select an actor for photo processing.

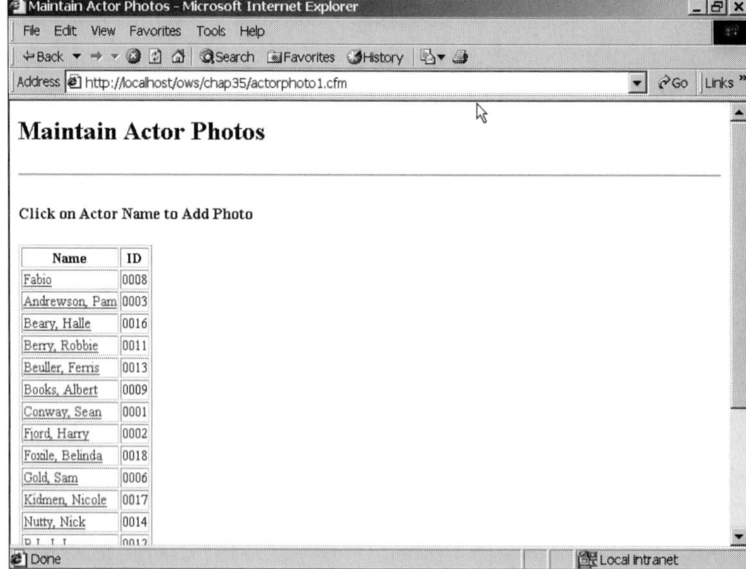

Figure 35.7 Actor photo maintenance list.

A link is created for each actor in the Actors table; the link takes you to another template, where the photo information can be added or updated. Listing 35.13 shows the CFML code used to create the form necessary to upload the file to the server.

Listing 35.13 actorphoto2.cfm—Actor Photo Maintenance Form

```
<!--- Query the database and then present a form for uploading the photo --->
<CFQUERY NAME="Actor" DATASOURCE="OWS">
SELECT NameLast,NameFirst,ActorID from Actors where
ActorID=#Val(URL.ActorID)#
</CFQUERY>

<HTML>
<TITLE>Actor Photo Maintenance Form</TITLE>
<BODY BGCOLOR="#FFFFFF">
<CENTER>Actor Photo Maintenance Form</CENTER>
<HR>
<FORM ACTION="actorphoto3.cfm"
ENCTYPE="multipart/form-data"
METHOD=POST>
<CFOUTPUT>
<INPUT TYPE="hidden" NAME="ActorID" VALUE=#Actor.ActorId#>
<B>
Actor ID: #NumberFormat(Actor.ActorId,'0000')#<BR>
Name: <CFIF Len(Trim(Actor.NameLast))>#Actor.NameLast#, </CFIF>
#Actor.NameFirst#<BR>
</B>
</CFOUTPUT>
<BR>
Photo File to upload: <INPUT NAME="PhotoFile" SIZE="50" TYPE="FILE"><BR>
<INPUT TYPE=SUBMIT VALUE="Upload the Photo">
</FORM>
</BODY>
</HTML>
```

This template is a simple modification of the first file upload template you wrote. Figure 35.8 shows what this template would look like. The value of the actor ID is retrieved from the URL.ActorId variable and used to retrieve the actor's name from the Actors table.

The actor name and actor ID are displayed with leading 0s using the NumberFormat() function. A file selection box is also displayed. The button labeled Upload the Photo causes the browser to upload the file to the server, where it will be processed by the template in Listing 35.14.

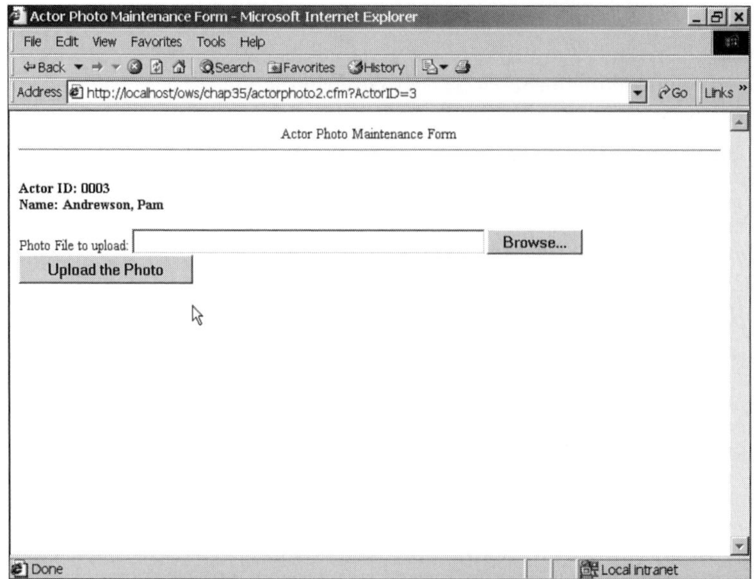

Figure 35.8
Actor photo upload form.

LISTING 35.14 ACTORPHOTO3.CFM—ACTOR PHOTO UPLOAD PROCESS TEMPLATE

```
<CFQUERY NAME="Actor" DATASOURCE="OWS">
SELECT NameLast,NameFirst,ActorId from Actors
➥ where ActorID=# Form.actorid#
</CFQUERY>

<HTML>
<TITLE>OWS Actor Photo Upload Results</TITLE>
<BODY>
<CFFILE
DESTINATION="C:\INETPUB\WWWROOT\OWS\CHAP35\FILES\"
ACTION="UPLOAD"
NAMECONFLICT="OVERWRITE"
FILEFIELD="PhotoFile"
ACCEPT="image/gif,image/jpeg">

<CFOUTPUT>
Actor Photo Upload was Successful!
Information about the file is detailed below.
<HR>
<TABLE BORDER WIDTH="100%">
<CAPTION><B>Photo Information</B></CAPTION>
<TR>
<TH VALIGN="TOP" ALIGN="LEFT">Actor
Id:</TH><TD>#NumberFormat(Actor.ActorId,'0000')#</TD>
<TH VALIGN="TOP" ALIGN="LEFT">Actor Name:</TH>
<TD>#Actor.NameLast#, #Actor.NameFirst#</TD>
</TR>
<TR>
<TH VALIGN="TOP" ALIGN="LEFT">Photo File Name:</TH>
<TD>#File.ServerDirectory#\#FILE.ServerFile#</TD>
```

```
<TH VALIGN="TOP" ALIGN="LEFT">Content Type:</TH><TD>#File.ContentType#</TD>
</TR>
<TR>
<TH VALIGN="TOP" ALIGN="LEFT">Content SubType:</TH>
<TD>#File.ContentSubType#</TD>
<TH VALIGN="TOP" ALIGN="LEFT">Client Path:</TH>
<TD>#File.ClientDirectory#</TD>
</TR>
</CFOUTPUT>
<!--- rename the file to point to the actor based on actor ID --->
<CFSET NewFile="ACTOR_#ACTOR.ACTORID#.#File.ServerFileExt#">
<CFFILE ACTION="RENAME" SOURCE="#File.ServerDirectory#\#FILE.ServerFile#"
➥DESTINATION="#File.ServerDirectory#\#NewFile#">
<TR>
<TD COLSPAN="4" ALIGN="CENTER"><CFOUTPUT><IMG SRC="FILES/#NewFile#"></CFOUTPUT>
➥</TD>
</TR>
</TABLE>
</BODY>
</HTML>
```

Figure 35.9 shows the screen results. The template you just completed processes the uploaded file and stores it in the specified directory. The <CFFILE> tag's ACCEPT attribute is set to allow only GIF and JPEG (including Progressive JPEG) images to be uploaded to the server.

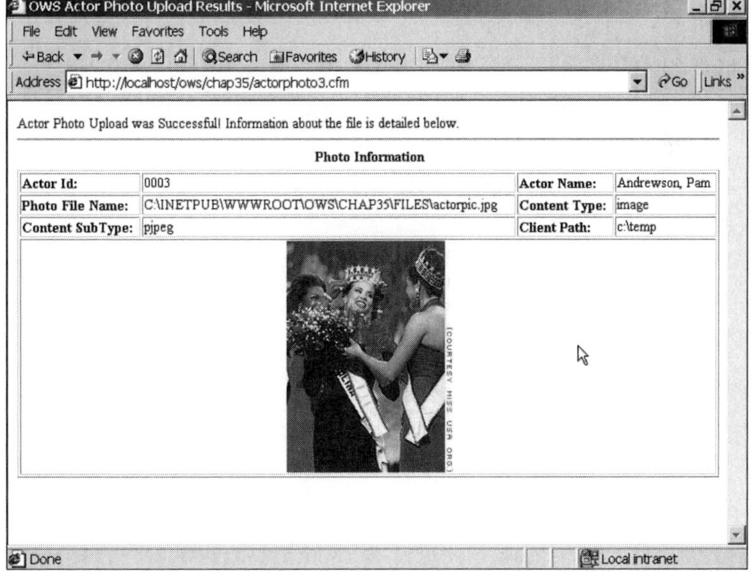

Figure 35.9
Actor photo upload results.

Combining <CFFILE> Actions

You have seen the capabilities of <CFFILE> to manipulate files on the local filesystem by moving, copying, deleting, or renaming them. The previous sets of examples demonstrated the ability to upload files to the server from the browser using <CFFILE>. Earlier in the chapter, you looked at the capability of ColdFusion to read and write files with <CFFILE>. The last piece of the puzzle is to combine some of these capabilities. <CFFILE> combined with other constructs available in ColdFusion—looping over the results of a query and evaluating expressions—provides a powerful tool to developers. The next example highlights the capability to read and write files and utilizes several functions to assist in the process.

To see this capability in action, you write a template that queries the `Actors` table and writes out an ASCII file containing the following items:

- The name of the actor
- The actor ID
- If present, the name of the file in which the actor's photo is maintained

The template then reads the file into a variable and displays it in the browser window. Listing 35.15 shows the code necessary to accomplish these tasks.

Listing 35.15 READWRITE.CFM—Read and Write an ASCII File Using <CFFILE>

```
<!-- Template queries the database to get list of actors and checks for photos -->
<CFQUERY NAME="ACTORS" DATASOURCE="OWS">
select NameLast,NameFirst,ActorID from Actors
</CFQUERY>
<!--- Setup variables to be used in writing the file --->
<!--- Variable to hold output string, with column names in first line,
 terminated by CRLF --->
<CFSET TXTOUTPUT = '"NAMELAST","NAMEFIRST","ACTORID","PHOTOEXISTS","PHOTOFILE"'>
<!--- Set File Name to write string into, getting a temporary file name
 using the GetTempFile() Function--->
<CFSET OUTFILE = GetTempFile("C:\INETPUB\WWWROOT\OWS\CHAP35\FILES\","CHAP35")>

<!--- Check for the existence of the file.  If it exists, delete it --->
<CFIF FileExists(OUTFILE) is "Yes">
   <CFFILE ACTION="DELETE" FILE="#OUTFILE#">
</CFIF>

<!--- Write out the Header Line --->
<CFFILE ACTION="WRITE" FILE="#OUTFILE#" OUTPUT="#TXTOUTPUT#" ADDNEWLINE="YES">



<CFLOOP QUERY="ACTORS">
<!--- use the GetDirectoryFromPath() and GetBaseTemplatePath() functions to build
 part of the variable  based on currently executing template path --->
<CFSET PhotoFile_GIF=GetDirectoryFromPath(GetBaseTemplatePath()) &
➥"FILES\ACTOR_#ACTORS.ACTORID#.GIF">
<CFSET PhotoFile_JPG=GetDirectoryFromPath(GetBaseTemplatePath()) &
➥"FILES\ACTOR_#ACTORS.ACTORID#.JPG">
```

```
    <!--- Check for a GIF image --->
    <CFIF FileExists(PhotoFile_GIF)>
        <CFSET PhotoExists="YES">

        <CFSET PhotoFile=PhotoFile_GIF>
    <!--- Check for a JPG image --->
    <CFELSEIF FileExists(PhotoFile_JPG)>
        <CFSET PhotoExists="YES">
        <CFSET PhotoFile=PhotoFile_JPG>
    <!--- Otherwise --->
    <CFELSE>
        <CFSET PhotoExists="NO">
        <CFSET PhotoFile="">
    </CFIF>
    <CFSET TXTOUTPUT = '"#NAMELAST#","#NAMEFIRST#","#NumberFormat
➥(ACTORID,'0000')#","#PHOTOEXISTS#","#PHOTOFILE#"'>
    <!--- Determine if file is to be written or appended to --->
    <CFIF NOT FileExists(OUTFILE)>
        <CFFILE ACTION="WRITE" FILE="#OUTFILE#" OUTPUT="#TXTOUTPUT#"
➥ADDNEWLINE="YES">
    <CFELSE>
        <CFFILE ACTION="APPEND" FILE="#OUTFILE#" OUTPUT="#TXTOUTPUT#"
➥ADDNEWLINE="YES">
    </CFIF>
</CFLOOP>

<!--- Read the file back in for display --->
<CFFILE ACTION="READ" FILE="#OUTFILE#" VARIABLE="TXTINPUT">

<HTML>
<HEAD>
    <TITLE>&lt;CFFILE&gt; Read/Write Demonstration</TITLE>
</HEAD>

<BODY bgcolor="white">
&lt;CFFILE&gt; Read/Write Demonstration<P>
<CFOUTPUT>
Information from the Actors table was written into the file located at
➥#OUTFILE#.<P>
The contents of the file are shown below:
<HR>
<PRE>
#TXTINPUT#
</PRE>
</CFOUTPUT>
</BODY>
</HTML>
```

Figure 35.10 shows the output from the template you just created. The code in the template creates a comma-delimited ASCII file containing the `NameLast`, `NameFirst`, `ActorID`, and `Photo` information from the `Actors` table.

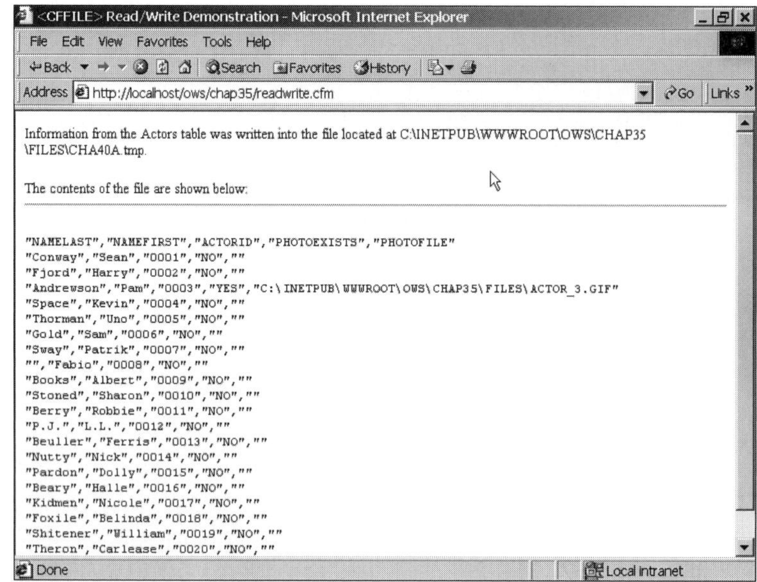

Figure 35.10
Output from the read/write demonstration template.

Let's take a closer look at this template to see what makes it tick. The first part of the template runs a simple query, which selects a number of fields from the `Actors` table. The following lines are responsible for the query:

```
<CFQUERY NAME="Actors" DATASOURCE="OWS">
SELECT NameLast, NameFirst, ActorID FROM Actors
</CFQUERY>
```

The next few lines of code set up a number of variables that are used to pass values to the `<CFFILE>` tag. The comments in the following code indicate what the variables are to be used for:

```
<!--- Set up variables to be used in writing the file --->
<!--- Variable to hold output string, with column names
 in first line, terminated by CRLF --->
<CFSET TXTOUTPUT = '"NAMELAST","NAMEFIRST","ACTORID","PHOTOEXISTS","PHOTOFILE"'>
<!--- Set file name to write string into, getting a
temporary file name using the GetTempFile() function--->
<CFSET OUTFILE = GetTempFile("C:\INETPUB\WWWROOT\OWS\CHAP35\FILES\","CHAP35")>
```

After setting up the variables, you use the `FileExists` function to determine whether the output file you want to create is on the disk. If it does exist there, you use the `<CFFILE>` tag with the `DELETE` action to remove it before proceeding:

```
<CFIF FileExists(OUTFILE) >
    <CFFILE ACTION="DELETE" FILE="#OUTFILE#">
</CFIF>
```

The next few lines of code perform the meat of the work in this template. The `CFLOOP` tag processes each record in the resultset from your query; a text variable is set with the values of the fields, separated by commas and enclosed in quotation marks. The following code results in a comma-delimited file when you are finished:

```
<!--- Loop over the query building a string to
 be written to the file.  Since the photos --->
<!--- are not directly referenced in the database,
➥the FileExists() function will be used to --->
<!--- read the directory to check for it --->
<CFLOOP QUERY="ACTORS">
    <!--- use the GetBaseTemplatePath()
➥function to build part of the variable  _--->
    <CFSET PhotoFile_GIF=GetBaseTemplatePath() & "\FILES\ACTOR_#ACTORID#.GIF">
    <CFSET PhotoFile_JPG=GetBaseTemplatePath() & "\FILES\ACTOR_#ACTORID#.JPG">
    <!--- Check for a GIF image --->
    <CFIF FileExists(PhotoFile_GIF)>
        <CFSET PhotoExists="YES">

        <CFSET PhotoFile=PhotoFile_GIF>
    <!--- Check for a JPG image --->
    <CFELSEIF FileExists(PhotoFile_JPG)>
    <!--- Otherwise --->
    <CFELSE>
        <CFSET PhotoExists="NO">
        <CFSET PhotoFile="">
    </CFIF>
    <CFSET TXTOUTPUT = '"#NAMELAST#","#NAMEFIRST#","#NumberFormat
➥(ACTORID,'0000')#","#PHOTOEXISTS#","#PHOTOFILE#"'>
    <!--- Determine if file is to be written or appended to --->
    <CFIF NOT FileExists(OUTFILE)>
        <CFFILE ACTION="WRITE" FILE="#OUTFILE#" OUTPUT="#TXTOUTPUT#"
➥ADDNEWLINE="YES">
    <CFELSE>
        <CFFILE ACTION="APPEND" FILE="#OUTFILE#" OUTPUT="#TXTOUTPUT#"
➥ADDNEWLINE="YES">
    </CFIF>
</CFLOOP>
```

The `<CFFILE>` tag is executed within the loop, and its behavior is changed depending on the existence of the output file specified in the variable `OUTFILE`. If it does not exist (which is true for the first iteration of the loop), the `<CFFILE>` tag's `ACTION` attribute is set to `"WRITE"`, which creates the file and writes the contents of the `TXTOUTPUT` variable into the file. Because the file exists, the `ACTION` attribute is set to `"APPEND"` on the remaining iterations through the loop; this results in the value of the `#TXTOUTPUT#` variable being written to the end of the file.

The last few lines of the template are used to read the contents of the file you created into a variable and then display the contents in the browser window. This is accomplished by setting the `<CFFILE>` tag's `ACTION` attribute to `"READ"` and specifying the name of the variable where the file contents will be stored:

```
<!--- Read the file back in for display --->
<CFFILE ACTION="READ" FILE="#OUTFILE#" VARIABLE="TXTINPUT">

<HTML>
<HEAD>
    <TITLE>&lt;CFFILE&gt; Read/Write Demonstration</TITLE>
</HEAD>

<BODY bgcolor="white">
&lt;CFFILE&gt; Read/Write Demonstration<P>
```

```
<CFOUTPUT>
Information from the Actors table was written into the file
➥located at #OUTFILE#.<P>
The contents of the file are shown below:
<HR>
<PRE>
#TXTINPUT#
</PRE>
</CFOUTPUT>
</BODY>
</HTML>
```

This example builds on the foundation of the code shown earlier in the chapter. It exercises several ColdFusion functions—for example, `GetTempFile()`, which returns a unique name that can be used for building dynamic files, and `FileExists()`, which checks for the existence of a file on disk, and `GetBaseTemplatePath()`, which returns the physical directory where the currently executing template is located. Finally, it uses the `<CFLOOP>` tag to loop over a query, combining text and data and then writing it out to disk again using the `<CFFILE>` tag. This puts all the pieces of `<CFFILE>` in one place.

USING <CFEXECUTE>

ColdFusion provides a powerful tool for interacting with the operating system in the `<CFEXECUTE>` tag. It enables the execution of server processes at the command-line level. It is powerful yet simple.

Caution

Executing processes on the server can have disastrous consequences, so extreme care should be taken to control access to templates that use the `<CFEXECUTE>` tag. Arbitrary user input of arguments to the tag should be prohibited.

Listing 35.16 shows the basic arguments for the `<CFEXECUTE>` tag.

LISTING 35.16 <CFEXECUTE> ARGUMENTS

```
<CFEXECUTE
    NAME=" ApplicationName "
    ARGUMENTS="CommandLine Arguments"
    OUTPUTFILE="Output file name"
    TIMEOUT="Timeout interval in seconds" >
```

Table 35.4 shows the definitions of the arguments and attributes for the `<CFEXECUTE>` tag.

TABLE 35.4 <CFEXECUTE> AND ITS ATTRIBUTES

Attribute	Description
NAME	Required. The fully qualified name of the application to execute.
ARGUMENTS	Optional. Command-line arguments to be passed to the program.

Attribute	Description
OUTPUTFILE	Optional. File in which output of program will be written.
TIMEOUT	Optional. Indicates how long in seconds ColdFusion will wait for the process to complete. Values must be integers greater than or equal to 0.

Note

On Windows systems, the NAME argument must contain the fully qualified path to the program to be executed, including the extension (e.g.: C:\WINNT\SYSTEM32\IPCONFIG.EXE).

Several things are worth noting about the attributes of the <CFEXECUTE> tag.

If ARGUMENTS is passed as a string, it is processed in the following ways:

- On Windows systems, the entire string is passed to the Windows process for parsing.
- On Unix, the string is tokenized into an array of arguments. The default token separator is a space; arguments with embedded spaces can be delimited by double quotes.

If ARGUMENTS is passed as an array, it is processed as follows:

- On Windows systems, the array elements is concatenated into a string of tokens, separated by spaces. This string is then passed to the Windows process.
- On Unix, the elements of the ARGUMENTS array is copied into a corresponding array of exec() arguments.

If TIMEOUT and OUTPUTFILE are not provided as attributes to the tag, the resulting output from the executed process is ignored.

The TIMEOUT attribute is used to determine whether ColdFusion should execute the called process asynchronously (that is, spawn process and continue) or synchronously (spawn process and wait). A value of 0 spawns the process asynchronously, with the ColdFusion execution picking up at the next line of CFML code immediately. Any positive integer value causes the process to be spawned synchronously, with ColdFusion waiting for TIMEOUT seconds before proceeding.

If errors occur during the process, exceptions are thrown that can be handled with <CFTRY>/<CFCATCH>. These exceptions are

- If the application name is not found, an Application File Not Found exception is thrown.
- If the output file cannot be opened, an Output File Cannot Be Opened exception is thrown.
- If ColdFusion does not have permissions to execute the process, a security exception is thrown.

Listing 35.17 shows an example of using the <CFEXECUTE> tag to determine IP configuration information about the server using the IPCONFIG utility. The results are shown in Figure 35.11.

Listing 35.17 <CFEXECUTE> Example Showing Output from IPCONFIG

```
<HTML>
<HEAD>
    <TITLE>&lt;CFEXECUTE&gt; Demonstration</TITLE>
</HEAD>

<BODY>
&lt;CFEXECUTE&gt; Demonstration<P>

<!--- Set up output file --->
<CFSET OUTFILE=GETTEMPFILE("C:\INETPUB\WWWROOT\OWS\CHAP35\FILES\","CHAP35")>
<!--- Call the system utility, with output placed in the file --->
<CFEXECUTE NAME="C:\WINNT\SYSTEM32\IPCONFIG.EXE " ARGUMENTS="/ALL"
➥TIMEOUT="15" OUTPUTFILE="#OUTFILE#"/>
<!--- Read the file for display --->
<CFFILE ACTION="READ" VARIABLE="STDOUT" FILE="#OUTFILE#">

<!--- Display the contents of the file --->
<CFOUTPUT>
<PRE>#STDOUT#</PRE>
</CFOUTPUT>

</BODY>
</HTML>
```

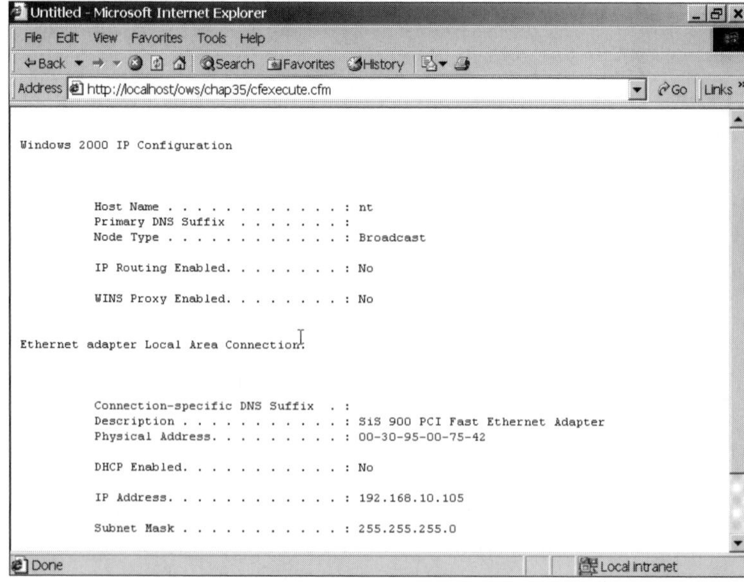

Figure 35.11 Output from the <CFEXECUTE> example.

The code in Listing 35.15 is fairly simple and straightforward. Using techniques learned earlier in the chapter, `GetTempFile()` is used to get a filename to be passed as the `OUTPUTFILE` argument to `<CFEXECUTE>`. The `NAME` attribute is set to the fully qualified pathname of the executable that is to be run, in this case the IPCONFIG utility, `C:\WINNT\SYSTEM32\IPCONFIG.EXE`. The `ARGUMENTS` attribute is set to `"/ALL"`, which tells the IPCONFIG utility to return information about all defined interfaces. Lastly, the `TIMEOUT` attribute is set to `15` seconds, indicating that the process should be spawned in a synchronous fashion. The output from the process is then read into a variable using `<CFFILE>`.

`<CFEXECUTE>` provides a powerful set of functionality, but its use should be carefully evaluated because any server process has the potential to affect the stability of the server. There are many potential uses for `CFEXECUTE`, including the capability to

- Submit batch processes to legacy command-line applications
- Use CF to communicate with external processes via the command line
- Execute CF templates asynchronously using batch files and the `CFML.exe` stub file

INTERACTING WITH THE SYSTEM REGISTRY USING <CFREGISTRY>

ColdFusion provides another powerful means of interacting with the operating system in the `<CFREGISTRY>` tag. However, that power comes at a price: `<CFREGISTRY>` is potentially the most dangerous tag available to the developer.

Caution

`<CFREGISTRY>` has the potential for causing serious harm to the stability of a server, if improperly used. In fact, it can be disabled in the ColdFusion Administrator as a precaution. Bottom Line: Use extreme care when using the `<CFREGISTRY>` tag to modify the system Registry.

As its name implies, `<CFREGISTRY>` provides access to the system Registry.

WHAT IS THE REGISTRY?

The Registry is a system database that primarily holds information about where things are located in the operating system. Programs, paths, default values, and more are stored within it. Because it is a system database, it has very fast access to information. The only problem is that it is not designed for real database work. This is one of the reasons client variables can better be stored in a database rather than in the Registry, which is the default setting.

Note

Even though the Registry is a Windows-only construct, a simulation is provided on Unix platforms. This simulation has the same effect as the Windows Registry, and the tag reacts the same way to both.

Caution

If you are not familiar with the Windows Registry, you should not change any of the settings. This cannot be recommended strongly enough! If you decide to explore the Windows Registry, be sure to have a good Registry book on hand, such as *Troubleshooting and Configuring the Windows NT/95 Registry* (Sams Publishing, ISBN: 0-672-31066-X).

One important note is that the Registry is a system database for Windows machines. The structure and job of the Registry exist only for the Windows NT and Windows NT/95/98 versions of ColdFusion. This does not mean that these tags are of no use on the Unix platforms. The Unix versions of ColdFusion ship with a mock Registry that provides all the storage of ColdFusion information that the Windows NT/95/98 Registry does. Therefore, all the code that relates to ColdFusion and the Registry works on all platforms. In addition, other information—Web server data, program mappings, and other things that are in the Windows Registry—are inaccessible in Unix.

Certain terms are used in conjunction with the Windows Registry that you need to become familiar with to use the `<CFREGISTRY>` tag:

- **Key**—This is the same as a directory in a filesystem. It holds subkeys (subdirectories) and entries (files).
- **Entry**—A variable within a key that holds a data value. Entries do not change unless they are deleted and re-created. Only their content can be altered.
- **Value**—The data contained within an entry. ColdFusion does not allow binary data to be set or retrieved from values.
- **Branch**—A specific path mapping from the root of a Registry tree to a specific subkey.

Certain Registry paths are used more than others in ColdFusion. These include the following:

Standard ColdFusion path:

```
HKEY_LOCAL_MACHINE\SOFTWARE\Allaire\ColdFusion\CurrentVersion\
```

Caution

The Registry key values for ColdFusion information might change over time as the merger with Macromedia takes shape. For CF5, the Allaire key is still used; however, some information for CFGRAPH and the ColdFusion Application Manager are found in the `HKEY_LOCAL_MACHINE\SOFTWARE\Macromedia` path.

ODBC information:

```
HKEY_LOCAL_MACHINE\SOFTWARE\ODBC\ODBC.INI\
```

The `<CFREGISTRY>` tag has only two attributes. These are shown in Table 35.5.

TABLE 35.5 <CFREGISTRY> TAG ATTRIBUTES

Attribute	Required	Description
ACTION	Required	The type of Registry action you want to perform
BRANCH	Required	The name of the Registry branch containing the keys or values you want to access

Four values exist for the ACTION attribute of the <CFREGISTRY> tag to manipulate the Registry:

- Get
- GetAll
- Set
- Delete

Each of the actions of the <CFREGISTRY> tag is examined in the following sections.

Get ACTION

The Get action of <CFREGISTRY> is similar to the <CFSET> tag. It sets a variable with a value, derived from the Registry. Table 35.6 shows the attributes for the <CFREGISTRY> tag when the action is set to GET.

TABLE 35.6 <CFREGISTRY> TAG ATTRIBUTES WITH GET ACTION

Attribute	Required?	Description
ENTRY	Required	The Registry value to be accessed
TYPE	Optional	The type of data you want to access: ■ String—Returns a string value (default) ■ DWord—Returns a DWord value ■ Key—Returns a key's default value
VARIABLE	Required	Variable into which <CFREGISTRY> places the value

One important note is that this tag tries to set the variable with the entry value no matter what. So, if the entry value does not exist, it fails. However, the GetAll section of this chapter shows a way around this. Listing 35.18 uses <CFREGISTRY> with the Get action to retrieve the company name to whom the ColdFusion server is registered. Figure 35.12 shows the results.

LISTING 35.18 RegistryGet.CFM—<CFREGISTRY> WITH THE Get ATTRIBUTE

```
<html>
<head>
    <title>&lt;CFREGISTRY&gt; Action=Get Example</title>
</head>
```

Listing 35.18 Continued

```
<body>

<!---
This example uses CFREGISTRY with the Get Action to retrieve the default
directory for File ODBC Datasources
 --->
<cfregistry action="GET"
    branch="HKEY_LOCAL_MACHINE\SOFTWARE\ODBC\ODBC.INI\ODBC File DSN"
    entry="DefaultDSNDir"
    type="String"
    variable="ODBC_Information">

The value returned by the <CFREGISTRY> call is:
<p>
<cfoutput>
Directory = #ODBC_Information#<br><br>
</cfoutput>

</body>
</html>
```

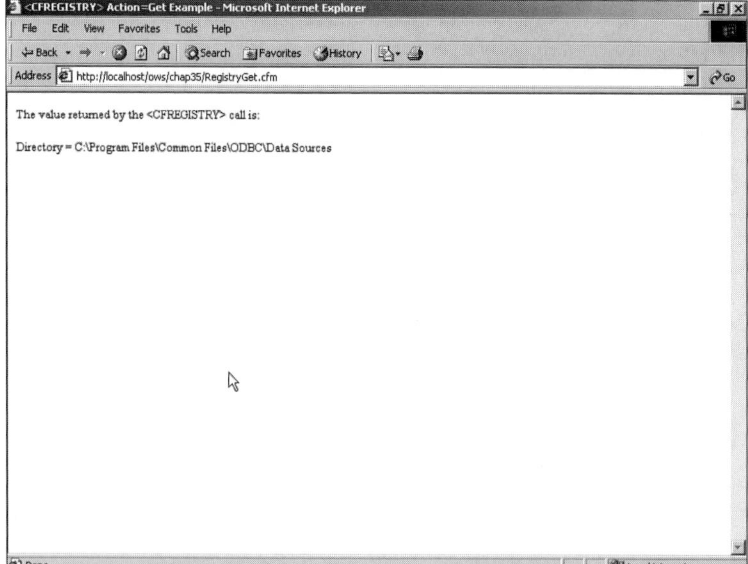

Figure 35.12 Output from the `<CFREGISTRY>` `ACTION=Get` example.

`GetAll` Action

The `GetAll` action is the broadest of the `<CFREGISTRY>` actions. It searches and returns all values within a key. This capability covers both `Key` and `Entry` values. The result of this action is a standard ColdFusion query with a name equal to the `NAME` attribute. Table 35.7 shows the attributes as used with the `GetAll` action.

TABLE 35.7 ATTRIBUTES FOR THE GetAll ACTION OF THE <CFREGISTRY> TAG

Attribute	Required?	Description
TYPE	Optional	The type of data you want to access: ■ String—Returns string values (default) ■ DWord—Returns DWord values ■ Key—Returns keys ■ Any—Returns keys and values
NAME	Required	The name of the resultset to contain returned keys and values.
SORT	Optional	Used to sort query column data returned with ACTION="GETALL". Ignored for all other actions. Sorts on Entry, Type, and Value fields as text. Any combination of columns from a query output can be specified in a comma-separated list. ASC (ascending) or DESC(descending) can be specified as qualifiers for column names. ASC is the default.

When run, this version of the <CFREGISTRY> tag returns a query with three columns:

- Entry—The name of the key or entry.
- Type—The data type (refer to Table 35.7).
- Value—If the type is not a key, this holds the value of the entry.

Listing 35.19 shows an example of using the GetAll action to read the registration information from the Registry and display it. Figure 35.13 shows the results.

LISTING 35.19 RegistryGetAll.CFM—<CFREGISTRY> Action=GetAll EXAMPLE

```
<html>
<head>
    <title>CFREGISTRY GETALL Example</title>
</head>

<body>

<cfregistry action="GETALL"
    branch="HKEY_LOCAL_MACHINE\SOFTWARE\ODBC\ODBC.INI\ODBC Data Sources"
    type="Any"
    name="ODBC_Information"
    sort="entry ASC, value DESC">

The GETALL action returns a CF query object containing the following columns:<BR>
<cfoutput>#ODBC_Information.columnlist#</cfoutput>
<p>
The results of reading the ODBC\ODBC.INI\ODBC Data Sources entry are shown below:
<table border>
<tr>
<th valign="left">Entry</th><th valign="left">Type</th><th valign="left">Value
➥</th>
```

LISTING 35.19 CONTINUED

```
</tr>
<cfoutput query="ODBC_Information">
<tr><td valign="left">#entry#</td><td valign="left">#type#</td>
➥<td valign="left">#value#</td></tr>
</cfoutput>
</table>
</body>
</html>
```

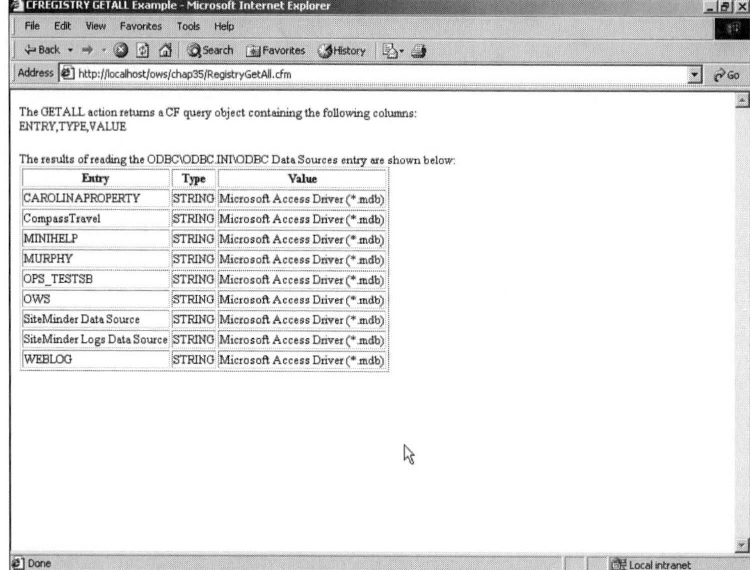

Figure 35.13
Output from the `<CFREGISTRY>` `ACTION=GetAll` example.

DIRECTORY MANIPULATION WITH <CFDIRECTORY>

Just as `<CFFILE>` can be used to read, write, and manipulate local files, `<CFDIRECTORY>` can be used to manage directories. Similar to `<CFFILE>`, `<CFDIRECTORY>` takes an `ACTION` attribute, which specifies the action to be performed. Listing 35.20 shows the basic format of the `<CFDIRECTORY>` tag. The supported actions are shown in Table 35.7, and attributes are listed in Table 35.8.

LISTING 35.20 `<CFDIRECTORY>` SYNTAX

```
<CFDIRECTORY ACTION="directory action"
    DIRECTORY="directory name"
    NAME="query name"
    FILTER="list filter"
    MODE="permission"
    SORT="sort specification"
    NEWDIRECTORY="new directory name">
```

Table 35.7 <CFDIRECTORY> Actions

Action	Description
CREATE	Creates the directory specified in the DIRECTORY attribute.
DELETE	Deletes the directory specified in the DIRECTORY attribute.
LIST	Returns the contents of the directory specified in the DIRECTORY attribute into a query named in the NAME attribute. An optional FILTER can be specified as well, as can a SORT order.
RENAME	Renames the directory specified in the DIRECTORY attribute to the name specified in the NEWDIRECTORY attribute.

Table 35.8 <CFDIRECTORY> Attributes

Attribute	Description
DIRECTORY	Directory on which action will be taken. Required with all ACTION values.
FILTER	Optional. Used with ACTION="List" to filter the files returned in the query. An example is *.txt. Only one filter can be applied at a time. It's ignored for all other actions.
MODE	Optional. Used on Unix versions of ColdFusion to set directory permissions when ACTION="Create". Ignored on Windows. Standard Unix style modes are accepted.
NAME	Required for ACTION="List". Ignored for other actions. Specifies name of output query created by the action.
NEWDIRECTORY	Required for ACTION="Rename". Ignored for all other actions. Specifies new name of directory.
SORT	Optional for ACTION="List". Ignored for other actions. Lists the columns in the query to sort the results with. Specified in a comma-delimited list. Ascending order is the default (ASC). Descending order is specified by the use of DESC. An example is "dirname ASC, name DESC, size".

The ACTION="LIST" call to <CFDIRECTORY> returns a query as specified in the NAME attribute. This query contains five or six columns: Name (filename), Size (file size), Type (file type, such as file or dir), DateLastModified (Date file was last modified), Attributes (file attributes), Mode (Unix file settings; Unix versions only). The query can be used like any other ColdFusion query for processing.

Essentially, the <CFDIRECTORY> tag provides the fundamental pieces to build a File Manager–type application. The CREATE, DELETE, and RENAME actions are potentially dangerous, and access to templates that use them should be carefully controlled.

Listing 35.21 shows an example of a directory drill-down application that lists the files in a specified directory, with the ability to click the name of a file to execute it, view it, download it, or (in the case of a directory) drill down. It also steps back up the directory tree. Figure 35.14 shows a sample of the output.

Caution

The CREATE, DELETE, and RENAME actions of the <CFDIRECTORY> tag can be dangerous. Care should be taken to restrict access to templates that use these actions.

Listing 35.20 uses <CFDIRECTORY> to enhance and modify the template used to maintain actor photos. <CFDIRECTORY> is used to determine whether a actor photo exists for a particular actor. If one does, the option to replace, view, or delete the photo is presented to the user. If no photo is found, an option to add a photo is presented. Figure 35.14 shows the output from Listing 35.21.

Listing 35.21 ACTORPHOTO4.CFM—<CFDIRECTORY> Example

```
<!---
 use CFDIRECTORY to get a list of photo files in the files subdirectory
--->
<cfdirectory action="LIST"
             directory="#GetDirectoryFromPath(GetbaseTemplatePath())#FILES\"
             name="PHOTOS"
             filter="actor_*.*"
             sort="name asc">

<!--- Query the database to get a listing of actors to chose from --->
<CFQUERY DATASOURCE="OWS" NAME="Actors">
SELECT NameFirst, NameLast, ActorId FROM Actors
      ORDER BY NameLast, NameFirst
</CFQUERY>

<HTML>

<HEAD>
<TITLE>Maintain Actor Photos</TITLE>
</HEAD>

<BODY BGCOLOR="#FFFFFF">

<H1>Maintain Actor Photos</H1>
<HR>
<H3></H3>
<TABLE BORDER>
<TR>
<TH>Name</TH>
<TH>ID</TH>
<TH>Action</th>
</TR>
<CFOUTPUT QUERY="Actors">
<TR>
<TD><CFIF Len(Trim(NameLast))>#NameLast#, </CFIF>#NameFirst#</A></TD>
<TD>#NumberFormat(ActorId,'0000')#</TD>
<TD>
<CFIF findnocase("actor_#actorid#",valuelist(photos.name))>
<a href="actorphoto2.cfm?actorid=#actorid#">Replace Photo</a> |
<a href="actorphoto5.cfm?actorid=#actorid#">View Photo</a> |
<a href="actorphoto6.cfm?actorid=#actorid#"
```

```
onClick="return confirm('Are you sure you want to delete this photo?');">Delete
➥Photo</a>
<CFELSE>
<a href="actorphoto3.cfm?actorid=#actorid#">Add Photo</a>
</CFIF>
</td>
</TR>
</CFOUTPUT>
</TABLE>
</BODY>
</HTML>
```

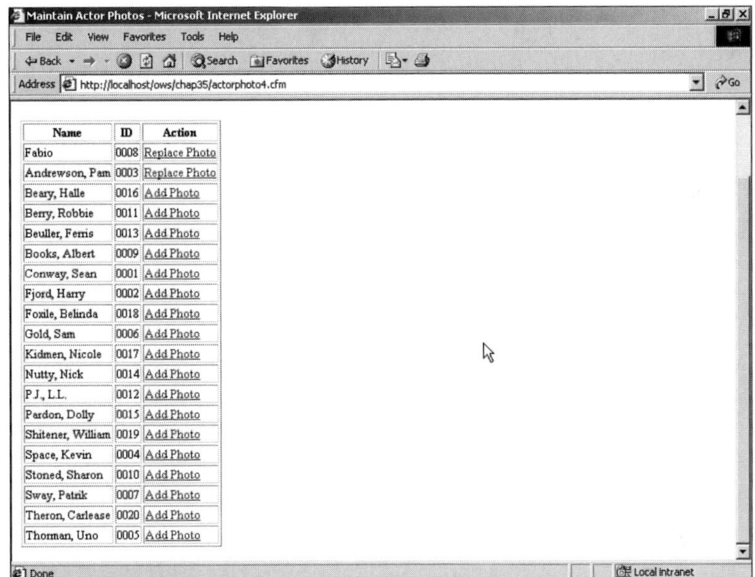

Figure 35.14 Output from the example in Listing 35.18 (actorphoto4.cfm).

A new template was created to view the actor's photo. The code is shown in Listing 35.22, and the output is shown in Figure 35.15. <CFDIRECTORY> is used here to find the photo in the appropriate directory with the resulting query object used to populate the source of the image on the screen.

Listing 35.22 ACTORPHOTO5.CFM—<CFDIRECTORY> Example (Continued)

```
<!--- Get the actor information from the database --->
<CFQUERY NAME="Actor" DATASOURCE="OWS">
SELECT NameLast,NameFirst,ActorId from Actors
 where ActorID=#URL.ActorId#
</CFQUERY>
<cfdirectory action="LIST"
             directory="#GetDirectoryFromPath(GetbaseTemplatePath())#FILES\"
             name="PHOTOS"
             filter="actor_#url.actorid#.*"
             sort="name asc">
```

Listing 35.22 (Continued)

```
<HTML>
<TITLE>OWS Actor Photo Scren</TITLE>
<BODY>
<HR>
<CFOUTPUT>
<TABLE BORDER WIDTH="100%">
<CAPTION><B>Photo Information</B></CAPTION>
<TR>
<TH VALIGN="TOP" ALIGN="LEFT">Actor
Id:</TH><TD>#NumberFormat(Actor.ActorId,'0000')#</TD>
</TR>
<TR>
<TH VALIGN="TOP" ALIGN="LEFT">Actor Name:</TH>
<TD><CFIF Len(Trim(Actor.NameLast))>#Actor.NameLast#,
➥</CFIF>#Actor.NameFirst#</TD>
</TR>
<TR>
<TD COLSPAN="2"><DIV ALIGN="CENTER"><IMG SRC="files/#photos.name#"><DIV></TD>
</TR>
</TABLE>
</CFOUTPUT>
</BODY>
</HTML>
```

Rounding out the modifications to the templates to manage the actor's photos, Listing 35.23 and Figure 35.16 show the code and output of the template that deletes the photo. As in Listing 35.22, `<CFDIRECTORY>` is used to get a list of photos to be processed. Combining the results of the `<CFDIRECTORY>` call with a loop and `<CFFILE>`, the photos are then deleted.

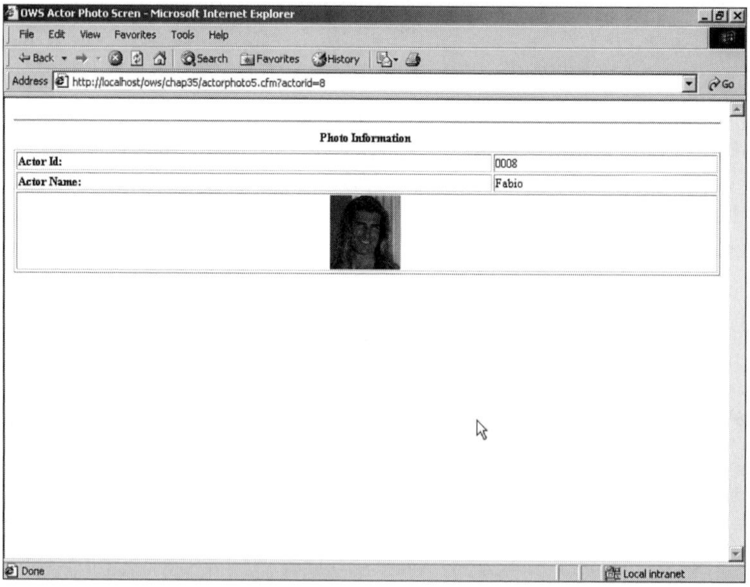

Figure 35.15 Output from the example in Listing 35.19 (`actorphoto5.cfm`).

LISTING 35.23 ACTORPHOTO6.CFM—<CFDIRECTORY> EXAMPLE (CONTINUED)

```
<HTML>
<HEAD>
    <TITLE>Actor Photo Delete - Example</TITLE>
</HEAD>

<BODY>
Actor Photo Delete Screen<P>
<!--- Get a list of files to be deleted --->
<CFDIRECTORY ACTION="LIST"
  DIRECTORY="#GetDirectoryFromPath(GetbaseTemplatePath())#FILES\"
  NAME="PHOTOS"
  FILTER="actor_#url.actorid#.*"
  SORT="name asc">

<!--- if photos exist --->
<CFIF PHOTOS.RECORDCOUNT>
    <CFLOOP QUERY="PHOTOS">
        <cffile action="DELETE"
         file="#GetDirectoryFromPath(GetBaseTemplatePath())#FILES\#PHOTOS.NAME#">
         <CFOUTPUT>Deleted: #PHOTOS.NAME#<BR></CFOUTPUT>
    </CFLOOP>
</CFIF>
</BODY>
</HTML>
```

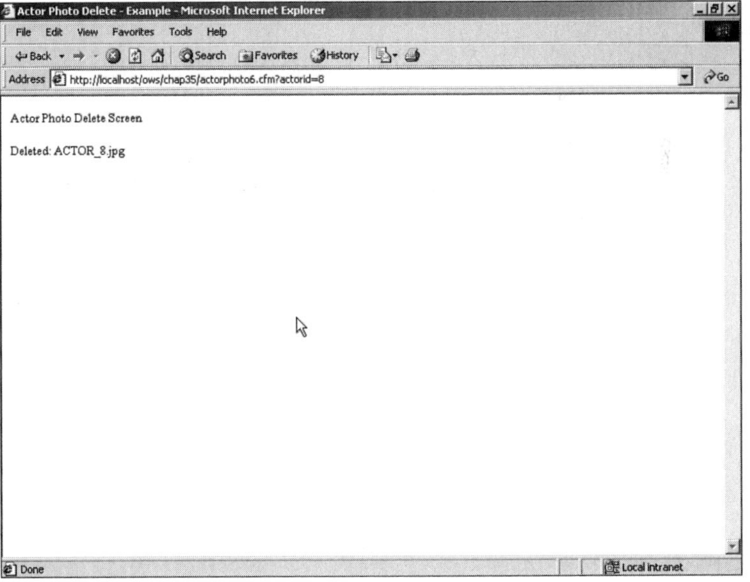

Figure 35.16 Output from the example in Listing 35.22 (actorphoto6.cfm).

With a bit of creativity, `<CFDIRECTORY>` can be used to create powerful file-management applications. Examples are content management systems and document libraries.

Caution

The example shown for `<CFDIRECTORY>` was designed for instructional purposes and should not be used in production. This is primarily due to the means in which the drill-down functionality is provided using URL parameters. This not secure.

SUMMARY

ColdFusion provides several powerful tools to interact with the operating system, including the `<CFFILE>`, `<CFDIRECTORY>`, `<CFEXECUTE>`, and `<CFREGISTRY>` tags. With this power comes potential for harm to the system, so extreme caution needs to be exercised when using these tags in applications, especially if user input is used to drive the tags.

CHAPTER 36

Full-Text Searching with Verity

In this chapter

GETTING TO KNOW VERITY

By now you're convinced that ColdFusion is the greatest package on the planet for publishing database data to the Web—but you have not yet learned how to create that most popular of Web-based applications: the search engine. The success of Yahoo!, Excite, and so on has made the concept of a Web-based search tool nearly as ubiquitous on the Internet as the word *ubiquitous* itself. An intelligent search tool is a must-have for an increasing number of sites. This chapter shows how to integrate the Verity search engine into your ColdFusion applications.

Verity's search technology—which is included and can be integrated with ColdFusion—is a high-performance search engine built specifically for searching text. It excels at finding words in large chunks of unstructured text, such as the documents human beings tend to write. As a developer, you tell it what to search—and what to search for—and it faithfully tries to find it.

Verity can search a variety of files in a variety of languages, and it does all the fancy stuff you'd expect from a sophisticated search engine, such as handling `AND`s, `OR`s, wildcards, and so on. If you've ever used the search interface provided by LEXIS/NEXIS, you can expect the same type of functionality from your own applications that use Verity.

Support for Verity's powerful K2 search technology is new in ColdFusion 5. Verity's K2 server is faster, supports simultaneous indexing, and enables you to index more than 100,000 documents.

Conceptually, the Verity layer you learn about in this chapter is similar to the ODBC/SQL layer you learned so much about earlier in this book. The main difference is that whereas ODBC and SQL excel at accessing neat rows and columns of information in structured database tables, Verity excels at accessing messy chunks of text, strewn about in various folders on your hard drives.

Most of the inner workings of the Verity engine are thoughtfully hidden from ColdFusion developers. All you are primarily concerned with is creating collections of documents with the ColdFusion Administrator and including the `<CFINDEX>` and `<CFSEARCH>` tags in your ColdFusion templates.

Note

The word *Verity* in this chapter really refers to ColdFusion's integration with search technology from a company called Verity. Just as people tend to say Netscape when they are really referring to the program called Navigator (which is made by Netscape Communications), ColdFusion developers tend to just say Verity when they are talking about putting together full-text search applications.

You might not have realized it yet, but you probably already have a Verity-based application running on your server. Unless you chose not to install the documentation files when you installed ColdFusion, full online documentation was installed for you in the `CFDOCS` folder, directly off your Web server's root directory. As you can see in Figure 36.1, the documentation has a handy search tool. The search tool uses the same Verity functionality you'll learn about in this chapter.

Note

Note that starting with version 5.0, this documentation is accessible from within the ColdFusion Administrator. Just click the DOCUMENTATION link in the top frame of the Administrator, as seen in Figure 36.2.

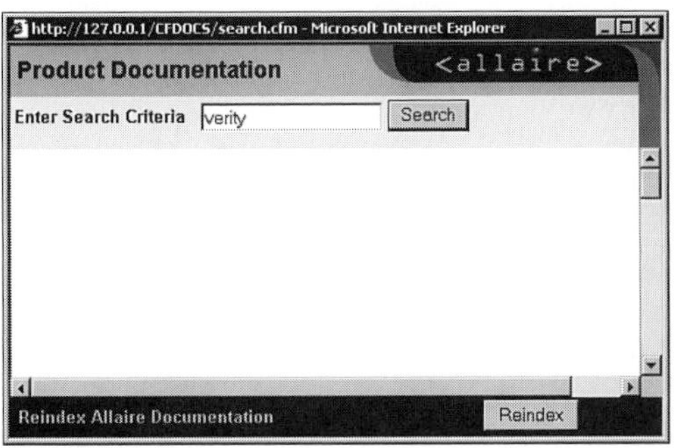

Figure 36.1 The search tool for the ColdFusion online documentation uses Verity to carry out its searches.

Tip

Check out your ColdFusion documentation's search tool anytime by opening this URL in your browser and then clicking Search: `http://`*`localhost`*`/CFDOCS/dochome.htm`. (*`localhost`* is your computer's name or IP address.)

Note

The first time you try to run a search in the ColdFusion documentation (after installing or upgrading), you'll be prompted to index the documentation.

Searching for Different Types of Files with Verity

ColdFusion's Verity functionality supports more than 200 file types, including native files, such as documents produced with many of the Microsoft Office applications. This provides great flexibility when it comes to making files searchable via a Web browser.

For instance, in an intranet situation, employees can continue to use the word-processing and spreadsheet applications they use every day. All they have to do is save the documents in a folder tree that is indexed in a Verity collection. With literally a few lines of code, you can turn those documents into a fully searchable company library. And with K2 server support in ColdFusion 5, these libraries can include *enterprise-level* volumes of information. Table 36.1 shows the various types of files Verity can index and search.

Note

Support for searching binary file formats (word processor, spreadsheet, and other native types of files) was introduced in ColdFusion 3.1; version 3.0 supported only plain-text files (which included HTML files).

Table 36.1 File Types Verity Can Index and Search

Category	File Type	Limited to Versions
Word Processing	Acrobat PDF files	All
	Adobe Frame-maker	All
	Aplix Words	4.2
	Lotus AMI Pro	2.*x*, 3.0, 3.1
	WordPerfect	DOS: 5.0, 5.1, 6.0*x*, 6.1, 7.0 Windows: 5.1, 5.2, 6.0*x*, 6.1, 7.0, 8.0 Macintosh: 2.0, 2.1, 3.0-3.5
	Microsoft Word	Windows: 2.0, 6.0, 95 (7.0), 97 (8.0), 2000 DOS: 4.*x*, 5.*x*, 6.*x* Macintosh: 4.0, 5.0, 6.0
	Microsoft Wordpad	All
	Microsoft Write	All
	XY Write	4.12
Spreadsheets	1-2-3	DOS, Windows: 2.0, 3.0, 4.0, 5.0, 96, 97 OS/2: Release 2
	Microsoft Excel	Windows: 3.0, 4.0, 5.0, 95 (7.0), 97 (8.0), 2000 Macintosh: 3.0, 4.0
	Corel Quattro Pro	7, 8
	Microsoft Works	All
Text-Based Files	HTML Plain Text Rich Text Format (RTF) ASCII and ANSI Text	1.*x*, 2.0
Other	Corel Presentations	7, 8
	Lotus Freelance	96, 97
	Microsoft PowerPoint	Windows: 95 (7.0), 97 (8.0)

Note

The term *document files* is used in reference to files that are being indexed with Verity. As you can see, Verity can handle 1-2-3 spreadsheets, PowerPoint presentations, and so on. Document files means any word processor, spreadsheet, or other file type listed in Table 36.1.

Tip

Different file types can be freely mixed and matched in a Verity collection. Don't worry about keeping the HTML and Word files in separate folders or collections. Store them wherever you want.

Integrating ColdFusion with Other Search Engines

Including Verity functionality is a terrific way to add search capability to your application, making it behave somewhat like a mini-AltaVista. However, it has nothing to do with actually integrating with AltaVista, Google, Yahoo!, or any other commercial search engines. If you want to integrate with one of these search engines, you certainly can include standard `HREF` links from your application to a commercial search engine—but doing so really has nothing to do with the Verity functionality explained in this chapter.

You also could place a search form on one of your pages that has an appropriate URL (within the commercial search engine's domain) as the form's `ACTION` parameter. Many of the commercial search engines have instructions about how to set this up—such as what to name the form `<INPUT>` tags, for instance. See their sites for details.

Finally, you could use the `<CFHTTP>` tag to place a search request to a commercial search engine and display the results on your page with the `#CFHTTP.FileContent#` variable. See Appendix A, "ColdFusion Tag Reference," for information about this extremely flexible tag. You can also refer to the chapter on building intelligent agents in our companion book, *Advanced ColdFusion 5 Application Development* (Que, ISBN: 0-7897-2585-1).

Creating a Search Tool for Your Documents

Say that Orange Whip Studio's Human Resources Department wants to make the company's personnel policies available online so that employees can see what they are allowed to do (and not do) at any time.

The documents are saved as various Word, plain-text, and Excel files. Collect all the documents into one folder on your Web server's local drive; explore what is necessary to make these documents searchable and retrievable from a Web browser using ColdFusion's Verity functionality as the back end. It's really pretty simple.

Note

If you want to follow along with the examples in this section exactly, make a copy of the folder named HR from this chapter's directory on the CD-ROM. You can either place the folder directly off your Web server's document root or use any random folder of your own documents that you like. Just be sure that the folder is accessible to your Web server.

Creating a New Collection for the Documents

Verity's search functionality centers around a concept of a collection. A Verity *collection* is a mass of documents you want Verity to keep track of and make searchable. (Note that a collection also can consist of a query resultset, which is explored later in this chapter.)

After Verity has been told which documents belong to a collection, it can index the documents and compile metadata about them for its own use. This enables it to search through your documents quickly, without actually parsing through them line by line at runtime. Conceptually, the key to Verity's strength is its capability to invest a certain amount of time up front in indexing and compiling information about your documents. You get the payoff on that investment when your users run their searches; Verity has already studied the documents and can therefore return information about them very quickly.

Again, you might find it useful to think of Verity collections as being the full-text search equivalent of ODBC data sources. Just as you need to set up an ODBC data source before you can use `<CFQUERY>` to retrieve data with SQL, you need to set up a collection before you can get started with Verity. Just as with setting up a new ODBC data source, you go to the ColdFusion Administrator to set up a new collection.

Creating a New Verity Collection

To set up a new collection, go to the ColdFusion Administrator and click the Verity VDK Collections link, as shown in Figure 36.2.

You'll probably notice right away that a document collection named `cfdocumentation` is already created and visible (assuming you have indexed the documentation from the search tool, as described at the beginning of the chapter). This collection represents the ColdFusion documentation, which uses the Verity engine for its search interface.

Here is how to create the Verity collection to which your human resources documents will belong. Enter **`HRDocs`** as the name of the new collection, in the top portion of the page.

You can change the path if you want the collection to be stored in a location other than the default, but you might as well use the default unless you have a specific reason not to (such as drive space or file-permissions issues).

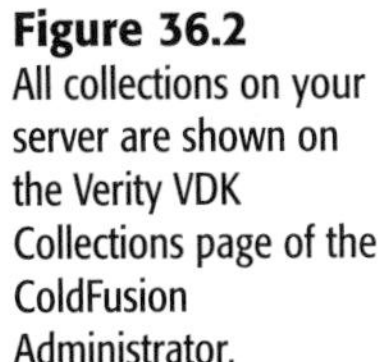

Figure 36.2
All collections on your server are shown on the Verity VDK Collections page of the ColdFusion Administrator.

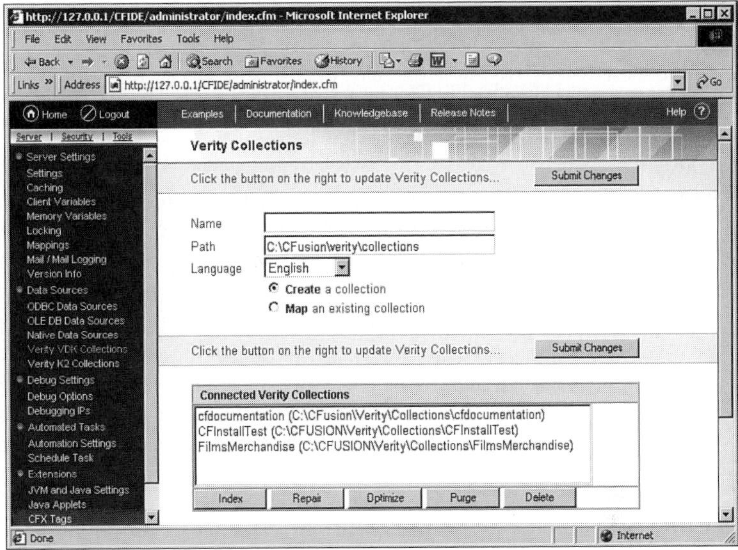

Click the Submit Changes button (see Figure 36.3). After a moment, your new collection will appear in the list at the top of the page, right along with the predefined `cfdocumentation` collection.

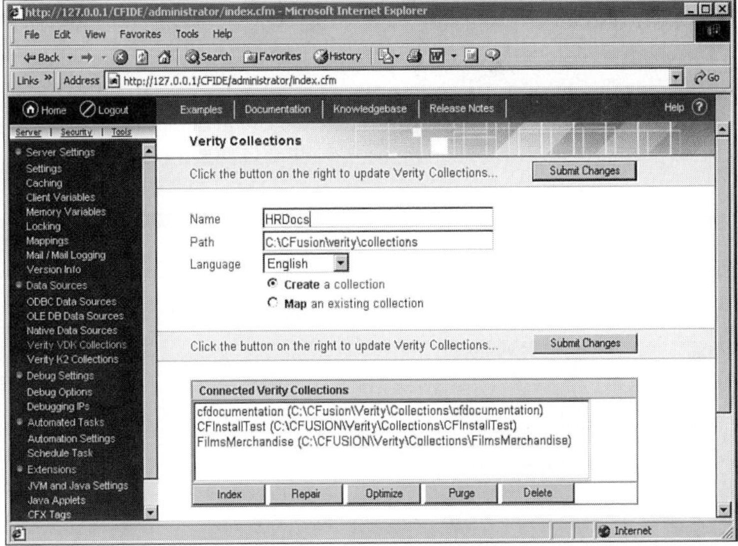

Figure 36.3
Simply type the name for the new collection and then click Submit Changes at the top of the page.

Note

The path you fill in when creating a new collection is simply where Verity's internal data about your documents will be kept. You don't have to point to the path to where the actual documents are at this point.

Note

If you already had created this collection on another ColdFusion server on your local network, you could check the Map an Existing Collection radio button and enter a complete UNC path to the collection's folder on the other server.

This feature can be used in situations in which you have several ColdFusion servers—perhaps operating in a cluster—that all need to be capable of searching the same information. By creating this mapped collection, the Verity engine uses the index files maintained by the other ColdFusion server. When the collection is reindexed on the other server, all collections that are mapped to it reflect the new data in search results. This keeps you from having to maintain separate collections on each ColdFusion server.

SPECIFYING A LANGUAGE

If you have the optional ColdFusion International Search Pack, you can specify a language other than English when creating a new collection. The language should match the language the documents were written in. Verity can pull off a few neat tricks when it knows which language the documents are written in, such as understanding the role of accented characters. It also uses knowledge of the language to pull off variations on the same word stem, or root.

You must choose the language when you are creating the collection. Simply select the language from the drop-down list in the Administrator before you click the Submit Changes button (see Figure 36.4). The International Search Pack supports the following languages: Danish, Dutch, English, Finnish, French, German, Italian, Norwegian, Portuguese, Spanish, and Swedish. Support for the language pack was added to ColdFusion in version 3.1.

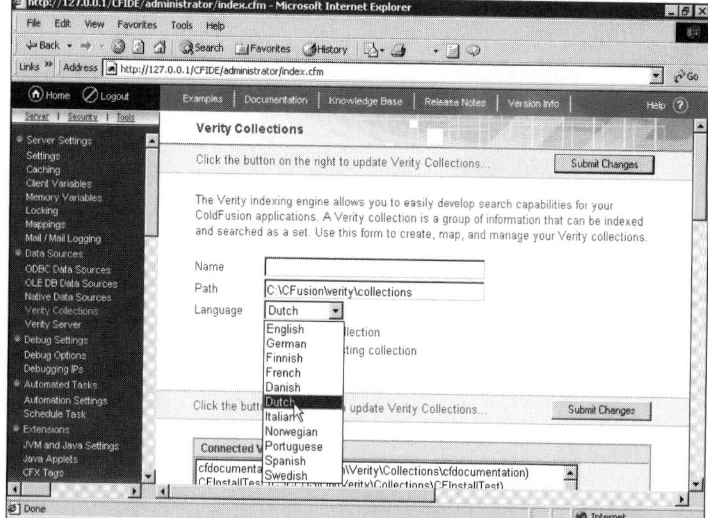

Figure 36.4
When the International Search Pack is installed, you can select from 11 languages when creating a collection.

Note

You must have purchased the ColdFusion International Search Pack from Macromedia to use languages other than English. If you attempt to do so without the Search Pack installed, you get an error message when you click Create.

Try not to mix documents written in different languages in the same collection. If you have documents in several languages, make separate collections for them.

CREATING A WORKING SEARCH INTERFACE

Now that you've created the `HRDocs` collection, you can start putting together the ColdFusion templates to make your documents searchable. You'll see that the code you use to do this is similar in concept to the examples presented in Chapter 12, "ColdFusion Forms."

A terrific way to get started is to use the Verity Wizard included in ColdFusion Studio. The wizard helps you create a search tool page, search results page, and detail page. After letting the wizard create these basic templates for you, you can examine each of the templates to see how they work and what you can add to them.

Note

If you're not using ColdFusion Studio, don't worry. All the code the wizard generates is included here as you work through the steps, and it is on the CD-ROM that comes with this book for your convenience. The wizard makes setting up basic Verity templates quick and easy, but it is by no means required.

In ColdFusion Studio, follow these steps to bring the Verity Wizard up on your screen:

1. Select New from the File menu. The New Document window appears.
2. Click the CFML tab in the New Document window.
3. Double-click the Verity Wizard from the list of wizards.

Tip

You can also start the Verity Wizard—or any other wizard—by right-clicking anywhere in the editor and selecting File, New from the pop-up menu.

As you can see in Figure 36.5, the first step of the Verity Wizard wants you to select a title for the application and where the ColdFusion templates should be stored. To complete the first step, do the following:

1. Type **`Personnel Policy Documents`** for the title. The wizard puts this title at the top of each of the ColdFusion (.cfm) templates it generates.
2. Select the directory in which the ColdFusion (.cfm) templates should be generated. The folder must already exist and should be located somewhere within your Web server's document root (so people will be able to access the .cfm files with their Web

browsers). My Web server's document root is `C:\Inetpub\wwwroot`, so I've created a folder named `C:\Inetpub\wwwroot\HRSearch` and selected the path on the server to that folder.

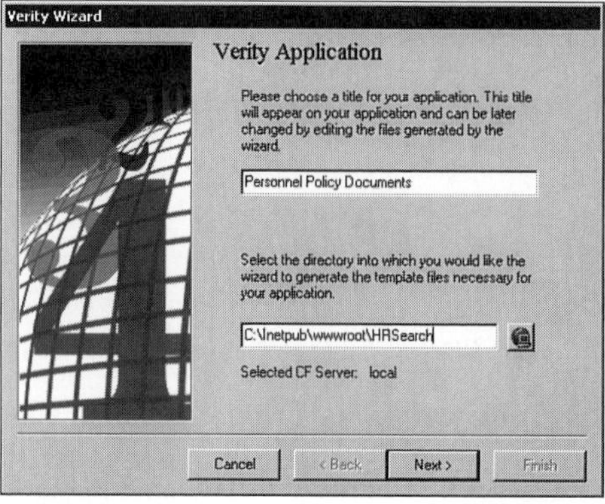

Figure 36.5
The first step of the Verity Wizard wants an application title and location for the generated .cfm files.

When you're finished with the first step, click the Next button to get to step 2. As you can see in Figure 36.6, this second step asks you about the Verity collection to which the generated ColdFusion templates should refer. Do the following to complete this second step:

1. For the collection name, enter **`HRDocs`**, which is the name of the collection you created in the ColdFusion Administrator.
2. Leave the language selection at English, unless you chose a different language when creating the `HRDocs` collection. The language you select here should always match the language with which you created the collection in the ColdFusion Administrator.

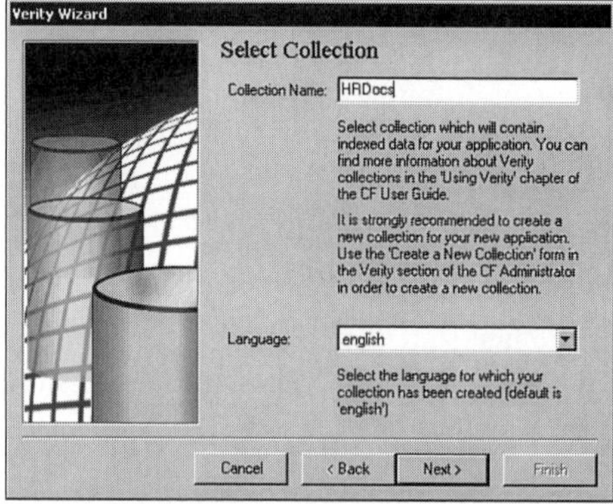

Figure 36.6
The second step of the wizard asks you about the Verity collection to be used by the generated .cfm files.

When you're finished with the second step, click the Next button to get to the third step. As you can see in Figure 36.7, you're asked about the document files you actually want Verity to index and make searchable. Do the following to complete this third step:

1. For Directory Path, select the folder that contains the actual documents you want to make searchable. The documents on my server are in a folder called `Docs`, which is in a folder called `HR`, directly off my Web server's root directory. I've entered `C:\Inetpub\wwwroot\HR\Docs\` here.
2. The Recursively Index Subdirectories check box indicates whether Verity is to look inside any subdirectories of the directory path you just entered. My `C:\Inetpub\wwwroot\HR\Docs` folder includes a `Days Off` subfolder that has documents in it that I want searched, so I've left this check box selected.
3. For File Extensions, type a list of file extensions that Verity should index. Separate the extensions with commas. I want Verity to make all the HTML, Word, Excel, and plain-text files available for searching, so I've entered `.HTM, .HTML, .TXT, .DOC, .XLS` in this field. I do not, however, want any files with the `.CFM` extension to be indexed, so I've excluded `.CFM` from the list.
4. For Return URL, type the URL version of the document path you entered earlier. In other words, what would a user need to type before a filename to pull up a file from the folder in his Web browser? I have entered `http://127.0.0.1/HR/Docs` here because that is what I would need to enter to get to my Web server's `C:\Inetpub\wwwroot\HR\Docs\` folder with my browser.

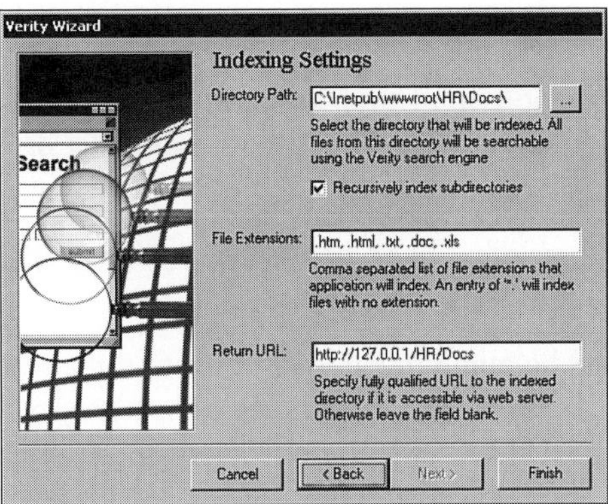

Figure 36.7
The third step of the Verity Wizard asks about the actual document files.

Click the Finish button when you are done with the third step. The wizard generates and saves four files to the `C:\Inetpub\wwwroot\HRSearch` folder (or whatever directory you specified in the first step of the wizard). As you can see in Figure 36.8, the wizard then displays the four files that it generated in the Wizard Output Summary.

Figure 36.8
The Verity Wizard generates four .CFM files in all.

Finally, click the Close button to exit the wizard. ColdFusion Studio automatically brings up the four files in the editor for your convenience.

Take a look at the search interface the Verity Wizard put together. Bring up the search form in your Web browser. The URL depends on what you entered in step 1 of the wizard—on my system, it's called `PERSONNELPOLICYDOCUMENTS_VSEARCHFORM.CFM`. (The `PERSONNELPOLICYDOCUMENTS` part came from the application title I supplied in step 1 of the wizard.) Because `HRSEARCH` was specified as the directory in the example, the complete URL from this example is `HTTP://127.0.0.1/HRSEARCH/PERSONNELPOLICYDOCUMENTS_VSEARCHFORM.CFM`. Be sure to bring it up in your browser with an HTTP URL (starting with `http://`), rather than as a local file (starting with `c:/` or some other drive letter). Figure 36.9 shows what the search form looks like.

It looks the way you'd expect a search tool to look—there's a text INPUT field to type keywords into and a Submit button to start the search.

However, no documents would be found if you were to try to run a search right now, regardless of what you were searching for. That's because the Verity collection you created in the ColdFusion Administrator has not been indexed yet—the collection has been set up, but it's still empty.

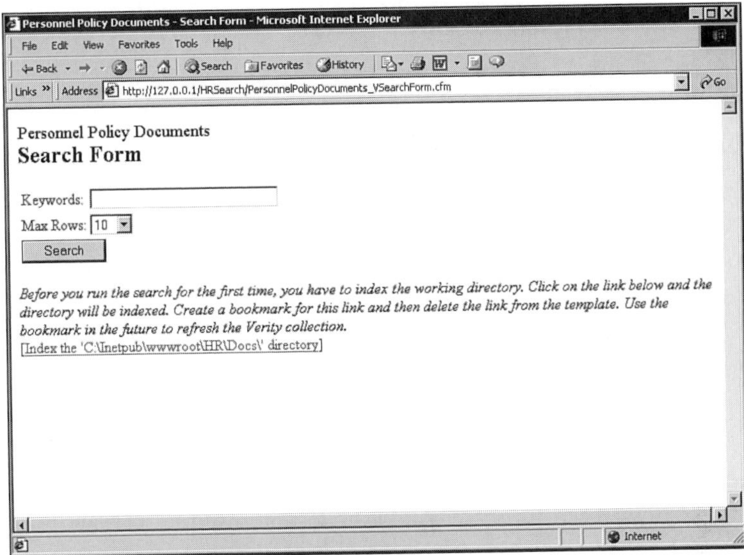

Figure 36.9
The search form includes a link that indexes the actual documents.

At the bottom of the search page (shown in Figure 36.9), the Verity Wizard has provided a link that indexes the collection. Go ahead and click that link now. Your server's hard drive will whir around for a bit as Verity examines the actual documents and saves its internal data about the documents to disk. When the indexing is complete, an Indexing Finished message appears, as shown in Figure 36.10.

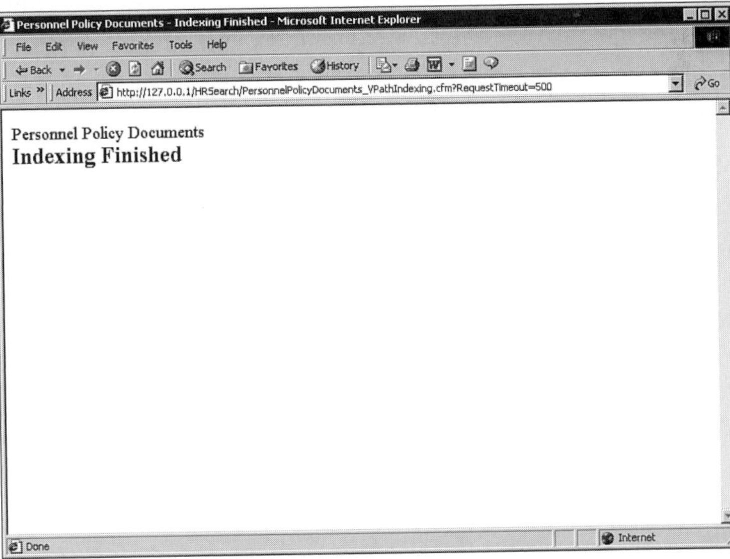

Figure 36.10
The `PERSONNELPOLICY DOCUMENTS_ VPATHINDEXING.CFM` file indexes the collection, populating it with your actual documents.

If you run a search with the search form shown in Figure 36.9, it should work. The documents have successfully been indexed by Verity and are searchable.

INDEXING YOUR FILES WITH THE <CFINDEX> TAG

You've seen that clicking that link on the search page causes Verity to index the collection, populating it with the contents of your actual documents. Take a look at what that link is actually doing.

The link is bringing up a separate ColdFusion template that was generated by the Verity Wizard. On my machine, this template is named PERSONNELPOLICYDOCUMENTS_VPATHINDEXING.CFM. It's shown in Listing 36.1 and is actually a simple template, with only one ColdFusion tag you haven't seen before: <CFINDEX>.

The <CFINDEX> tag is what cues Verity to wake up and index (or reindex) the files in the folder you specify. This is the second step in the overall process of making a Verity application come alive. (The first step is creating the collection in the ColdFusion Administrator, and the third is actually searching the collection with the <CFSEARCH> tag, which is covered shortly.)

Tip

Remember, there's nothing special about the code the Verity Wizard generates. You can use this code–or any code that uses <CFINDEX> in a similar way–to get the job done, whether you use ColdFusion Studio and its Verity Wizard.

LISTING 36.1 PERSONNELPOLICYDOCUMENTS_VPATHINDEXING.CFM—INDEXING A COLLECTION

```
<CFSET IndexCollection = "HRDocs">
<CFSET IndexDirectory = "C:\INETPUB\WWWROOT\HR\Docs">
<CFSET IndexRecurse = "YES">
<CFSET IndexExtensions = ".htm, .html, .txt, .doc, .xls">
<CFSET IndexLanguage = "english">

<CFINDEX
  collection="#IndexCollection#"
  action="REFRESH"
  type="PATH"
  key="#IndexDirectory#\"
  extensions="#IndexExtensions#"
  recurse="#IndexRecurse#"
  language="#IndexLanguage#"
  urlPath="http://127.0.0.1/HR/Docs"
>

<HTML><HEAD>
    <TITLE>Personnel Policy Documents - Indexing Finished</TITLE>
</HEAD><BODY bgcolor="ffffff">

<FONT size="+1">Personnel Policy Documents</FONT> <BR>
<FONT size="+2"><B>Indexing Finished</B></FONT>
```

This template simply sets a few constants at the top of the template with some <CFSET> tags. It then plugs the values of those constants into the <CFINDEX> tag. The Verity Wizard has used the <CFSET> tags at the top—rather than hard coding the values in the parameters of the <CFINDEX> tag itself—so changing the values later is easy.

Because the <CFINDEX> tag is what tells Verity to index your actual documents, the <CFINDEX> tag's various parameters simply give Verity the particulars about what you want it to do. Take a look at each of the parameters:

- COLLECTION—Simply tells Verity which collection to use. In Listing 36.11, later in this chapter, the value passed to the COLLECTION parameter is HRDocs, which is the value I supplied to the wizard.
- ACTION—Tells Verity that you're interested in refreshing any data currently in the collection with new information. Other values are possible for ACTION other than REFRESH, which are discussed in the section "Maintaining Collections" at the end of this chapter.
- TYPE—Tells Verity you're interested in adding documents from a directory path on your Web server. You learn about another possible value for TYPE later, when using Verity to index database data rather than document files is covered. Refer to the section "Indexing Your Table Data: Verity to the Rescue," later in this chapter.
- KEY—Tells Verity from which directory path to add documents. This must evaluate to a complete physical file system path to the actual documents you want to index.
- EXTENSIONS—Tells Verity which documents in the specified folder should be indexed. This is useful if you want only certain types of documents to become searchable.
- RECURSE—Tells Verity whether you want it to index files that are sitting in subfolders of the folder you specified with the KEY parameter. Possible values are YES and NO—usually, you specify YES for this parameter.
- LANGUAGE—Tells Verity in which language the documents are written. For the possible values, see the section "Specifying a Language," earlier in this chapter.
- URLPATH—Tells Verity to maintain URLs for each document, as it does its indexing, by appending the filename to the value you supply with this parameter. If RECURSE="YES" and the file is in a subfolder, the folder name is appended as well. So, as long as the value you supply here is the URL version of the value you supplied for KEY, Verity automatically records the correct URL for each file as it does its indexing. You see this in action later, when you use the #URL# column returned by the <CFSEARCH> tag. This is discussed later in the section "The Search Results Page."

That's about all there is to indexing document files. Now all you have to do is ensure that the code in Listing 36.1 runs whenever somebody saves new documents to the C:\Inetpub\wwwroot\HR\Docs folder.

You can now delete the link to the PERSONNELPOLICYDOCUMENTS_VSEARCHFORM.CFM template as the message at the bottom of the search page suggests (refer to Figure 36.9 and Listing 36.2), or you can leave it there so that your users can reindex the documents on their own whenever they want.

The Search Form Page

Take a look at the search form the Verity Wizard created for you. The name of the file depends on what application title you supplied in the first step of the wizard; on my machine, the file is called PERSONNELPOLICYDOCUMENTS_VSEARCHFORM.CFM (refer to Listing 36.2).

This search form is similar to the search forms you worked through in Chapter 12. Refer to that chapter if you need to refresh your memory about the <INPUT> and <SELECT> tags that appear in Listing 36.2.

Listing 36.2 PERSONNELPOLICYDOCUMENTS_VSEARCHFORM.CFM—The Search Form Page the Wizard Created

```
<!--- template settings --->
<CFSET SearchDirectory = "C:\INETPUB\WWWROOT\HR\Docs">

<HTML><HEAD>
    <TITLE>Personnel Policy Documents - Search Form</TITLE>
</HEAD><BODY bgcolor="ffffff">

<FONT size="+1">Personnel Policy Documents</FONT> <BR>
<FONT size="+2"><B>Search Form</B></FONT>


<!--- search form definition --->
<FORM action="PersonnelPolicyDocuments_VSearchResult.cfm" method="post">
  <INPUT type="hidden" name="StartRow" value="1">

  <TABLE>

    <TR>
      <TD>Keywords:</TD>
      <TD><INPUT type="text" name="Criteria" size="30"></TD>
    </TR>

    <TR>
      <TD>Max Rows:</TD>
      <TD>
➥<SELECT name="MaxRows"> <OPTION> 10 <OPTION> 25 <OPTION> 100 </SELECT></TD>
    </TR>

    <TR>
      <TD colspan=2><INPUT type="submit" value="   Search   "></TD>
    </TR>

  </TABLE>

</FORM>

<P>
<I>
Before you run the search for the first time, you have to index the working
directory. The directory is indexed when you click the link. Create a
bookmark for it and then delete the link from the template. Use the bookmark
in the future to refresh the Verity collection.
```

```
</I>
<BR>
[<A href="PersonnelPolicyDocuments_VPathIndexing.cfm?RequestTimeout=500">
➥Index the 'C:\INETPUB\WWWROOT\HR\Docs' directory</A>]

</BODY></HTML>
```


If you refer to Figure 36.9, you can see that your search form template contains a form that collects two pieces of information from the user. Most importantly, it collects the keywords the user wants to search for (the INPUT named Criteria). It also collects the maximum number of hits to display per page of search results (the <SELECT> named MaxRows).

The Search Results Page

The Verity Wizard's search form submits these two pieces of information to the PERSONNELPOLICYDOCUMENTS_VSEARCHRESULT.CFM template, which contains the code that actually runs the Verity search and displays the results of the search to the user.

Take a look at that template now. As you can see in Listing 36.3, it contains only one ColdFusion tag that you're not familiar yet—the <CFSEARCH> tag.

Listing 36.3 PERSONNELPOLICYDOCUMENTS_VSEARCHRESULT.CFM—The Search Results Page the Wizard Created

```
<!--- template settings --->
<CFSET SearchDirectory = "C:\Inetpub\wwwroot\HR\Docs\">
<CFSET SearchCollection = "HRDocs">
<CFSET UseURLPath = "YES">



<!--- retrieve requested files --->
<CFSEARCH
   name = "GetResults"
   collection = "#SearchCollection#"
   criteria = "#Form.Criteria#"
   maxRows = "#Evaluate(Form.MaxRows + 1)#"
   startRow = "#Form.StartRow#"
>



<HTML><HEAD>
    <TITLE>Personnel Policy Documents - Search Results</TITLE>
</HEAD><BODY bgcolor="ffffff">

<FONT size="+1">Personnel Policy Documents</FONT> <BR>
<FONT size="+2"><B>Search Results</B></FONT>

<P>

<!--- no files found for specified criteria? --->
<CFIF GetResults.RecordCount is 0>
   <B>No files found for specified criteria</B>
```

Listing 36.3 PersonnelPolicyDocuments_VSearchResult.cfm—The Search Results

```
<!--- ... else at least one file found --->
<CFELSE>

   <TABLE cellspacing=0 cellpadding=2>

   <!--- table header --->
   <TR bgcolor="cccccc">
      <TD><B>No</B></TD>
      <TD><B>Score</B></TD>
      <TD><B>File</B></TD>
      <TD><B>Title</B></TD>
   </TR>

   <CFOUTPUT query="GetResults" maxRows="#Form.MaxRows#">
   <TR bgcolor="#IIf(CurrentRow Mod 2, DE('ffffff'), DE('ffffcf'))#">

      <!--- current row information --->
      <TD>#Evaluate(Form.StartRow + CurrentRow - 1)#</TD>

      <!--- score --->
      <TD>#Score# </TD>

      <!--- file name with the link returning the file --->
      <TD>
         <CFIF UseURLPath>   <!--- URL parameter from cfsearch contains URL
         path info --->
            <CFSET href = Replace(URL, " ", "%20", "ALL")>
         <CFELSE>          <!--- ... else use OpenFile to return the file --->
            <CFSET href = "MyApplication_VOpenFile.cfm?serverFilePath
            =#URLEncodedFormat(Key)#">
         </CFIF>
         <A href="#href#">#GetFileFromPath(Key)#</A>
      </TD>

      <!--- title for HTML files --->
      <TD>#Title# </TD>

   </TR>
   </CFOUTPUT>

   </TABLE>


  <!--- CFSEARCH tried to retrieve one more file than the number specified in the
     Form.MaxRows parameter. If number of retrieved files is greater than MaxRows
     we know that there is at least one file left. The following form contains
     only one button which reloads this template with the new StartRow parameter.
  --->
   <CFIF GetResults.RecordCount gt Form.MaxRows>
      <FORM action="PersonnelPolicyDocuments_VSearchResult.cfm" method="post">
      <CFOUTPUT>
         <INPUT type="hidden" name="Criteria" value="#Replace(Form.Criteria,
          """", "'", "ALL")#">
         <INPUT type="hidden" name="MaxRows" value="#Form.MaxRows#">
```

```
        <INPUT type="hidden" name="StartRow" value="#Evaluate(Form.StartRow +
         Form.MaxRows)#">
        <INPUT type="submit" value="    More ...    ">
     </CFOUTPUT>
     </FORM>
  </CFIF>

</CFIF>

</BODY></HTML>
```


Note

Some earlier versions of ColdFusion Studio do not produce this code correctly as in Listing 36.3. Just below the <CFOUTPUT>, look for this code:

```
<TR bgcolor="#IIf(CurrentRow Mod 2, DE('#FFFFFF'),
DE('#FFFFCF'))#">
```

If you find that the wizard has written this code, you must remove the pound signs in the two DE() functions. When you're finished, the code should look as it does in Listing 36.3.

The problem is that the pound signs should not be used in this context within the <CFOUTPUT> body.

Clearly, the focus of this template is the <CFSEARCH> tag near the top. The <CFSEARCH> tag tells Verity to actually run a search—take the search criteria the user supplies and try to find documents that match.

Do you remember that Verity searches are similar to ODBC/SQL queries? With that similarity in mind, it's worth noting that the <CFSEARCH> tag acts a lot like the <CFQUERY> tag when you're dealing with database tables.

Take a look at the specific parameters you're supplying to the <CFSEARCH> tag in Listing 36.3. As you do so, keep in mind that most of these parameters look similar to the type of parameters you'd supply to a <CFQUERY> tag.

Note

The MAXROWS and STARTROW parameters listed here are used in the templates the wizard generated to create a Next 10 Records feature–where the user can move through pages of search results–just like you see on commercial search engines. The Next 10 Records functionality isn't explained in this chapter because it's not directly related to Verity. See Chapter 11, "Creating Data-Driven Pages," for an explanation of how to use MAXROWS and STARTROW to put together Next 10 Records types of solutions.

The following are the parameters for <CFSEARCH>, as used in Listing 36.3:

- NAME —Gives the search a name. Whatever results are found by Verity are available (for your use as a developer) as a query that has the name you supply here. You can use the search results in <CFOUTPUT> tags and in any of the other ways you normally use query results.

- COLLECTION—Tells Verity in which collection to search for documents. In this case, I'm directing it to the HRDocs collection I created and indexed in this chapter.
- CRITERIA—Is probably the most important parameter here. This is what you're actually asking Verity to look for. Here, you're simply passing whatever the user types in the search form to this parameter.
- MAXROWS—Tells Verity to return only a certain number of rows. This is similar to using the MAXROWS parameter with the <CFQUERY> tag. Here, you're taking whatever the user indicated in the MaxRows SELECT on the search form and adding one to it.
- STARTROW—Tells Verity to return only the search results from a certain row in the search results on down. Here, you're taking the value specified by the hidden field named StartRow on the search form, so this value is always 1 for now. In other words, you're telling Verity to start returning the search results starting with the very first row.

Note

<CFSEARCH> also takes another parameter, TYPE. You can use TYPE="SIMPLE" or TYPE="EXPLICIT" in your search templates. TYPE="SIMPLE" places the STEM and MANY operators into effect automatically (see Appendix D, "Verity Search Language Reference," for information on the STEM and MANY operators). Unless you specify EXPLICIT, SIMPLE is used by default. I recommend that you do not use EXPLICIT unless you have a specific reason to do so.

After the <CFSEARCH> is executed, the rest of Listing 36.3 displays the results to the user; it's fairly straightforward. The main thing to keep in mind is that now that the <CFSEARCH> has found its results, you will treat it just as if it were a <CFQUERY> named GetResults.

First, a <CFIF> tag performs the now-familiar check to ensure that the built-in RecordCount variable is not 0 (which would mean Verity didn't find any results). See Chapter 11 for more information on the RecordCount variable.

Provided there are results to display, your code moves into the large <CFELSE> block that encompasses the remainder of the template. <TABLE>, <TR>, and <TD> tags are used to establish an HTML table in which to display the results, with headers. Look back at Chapter 11 for more examples of building tables row by row with query results.

Most of the important stuff happens in the large <CFOUTPUT> block that follows. The QUERY="GetResults" parameter in the <CFOUTPUT> tag causes this code to be executed once for each row in the search results, where each row represents a document found. Unlike a resultset returned by a <CFQUERY>—where you've specified which columns your resultset will contain by including them in the SELECT part of your SQL statement—resultsets returned by Verity searches always contain the same, predefined column names, which are shown in Table 36.2.

Table 36.2 Columns Returned by Verity Searches

Column	Contains
Key	The document's filename.
TITLE	The title of the document, if Verity is capable of determining what the title is. For example, if the file is an HTML document, Verity obtains the title from the <TITLE> tags in the document's <HEAD> section. Verity might not provide a title for other types of documents.
SCORE	The *relevancy score* for the document, which indicates how closely the document matched the search criteria. The score is always a value between 0 and 1, where a score of 1 indicates a perfect match.
URL	The URL that can be used to obtain the file from your Web server. This is based on the information you supplied to the <CFINDEX> tag with its URLPATH parameter. If you did not specify a URLPATH parameter when indexing the collection, this column is blank.
CUSTOM1	This is the value of a custom field you specify when you populate the collection with <CFINDEX>. This will become useful later in the chapter when you build searches against collections consisting of database query results. See the section "Indexing Additional Columns with Custom Fields."
CUSTOM2	This is the value of a second custom field you specify when you populate the collection with <CFINDEX>. Again, this is used in the same way as CUSTOM1.
RECORDSSEARCHED	The number of records Verity searched. In other words, the number of records in the collection(s).

As you can see, the code in Listing 36.3 uses these columns to display the score, title, and filename for each document. It also uses the URL column in an HTML anchor tag's HREF attribute to provide a link to the document.

In addition, two predefined variables are available to you after a search runs. Table 36.3 explains these variables.

Table 36.3 Properties Available After a <CFSEARCH> Tag Executes

Property	Indicates
ColumnList	Comma-separated list of the columns in this query result.
CurrentRow	This works just like the CurrentRow column returned by a <CFQUERY>. In a <CFOUTPUT> block that uses the search results in its QUERY parameter, CurrentRow is 1 for the first document returned by the <CFSEARCH>, 2 for the second document, and so on. See Chapter 11 for more discussion on CurrentRow.
RecordCount	Just as with <CFQUERY>, this is the number of matches Verity found. In this example, you access this variable using #GetResults.RecordCount# in your code.

You saw `RecordCount` in action in Listing 36.3. `RecordsSearched` can be used in much the same way, if you want to let the user know how many documents were searched to find his hits. For example, a code similar to the following would display something such as `10 out of 4363 documents found`:

```
<CFOUTPUT>
#GetResults.RecordCount#
out of
#GetResults.RecordsSearched#
documents found.
</CFOUTPUT>
```

RUNNING A SEARCH

Your search tool should already be operational. Pull the search form up in your browser and type **`employee`** in the blank. When you click Search, you should get a list of relevant documents from your Human Resources Department, as shown in Figure 36.11.

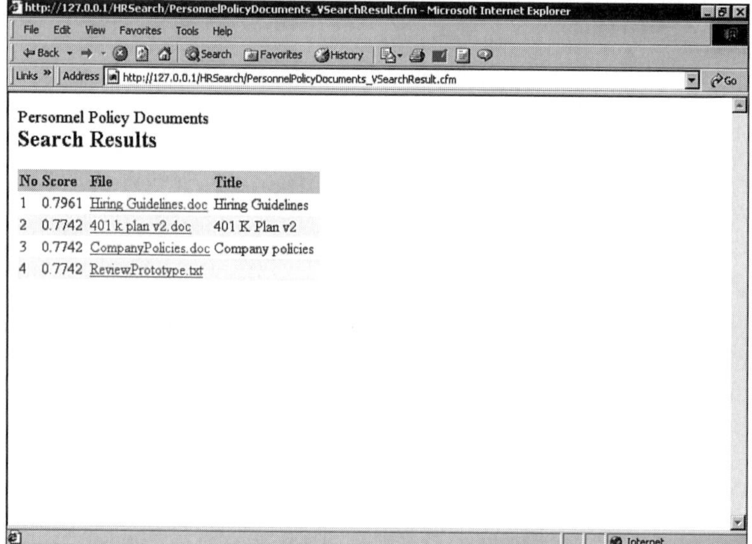

Figure 36.11
Your search results page shows a relevancy score, filename, and title (when available) for each document found.

Note

If you look at Listing 36.3, you'll see a reference to a file called `MYAPPLICATOIN_VOPENFILE.CFM`. That code is in the template to provide access to documents that do not reside in the Web server's document root, and it goes into effect only if the URL path is left blank when the collection is indexed. This `OPENFILE` template uses the `<CFCONTENT>` tag to get its job done. See Appendix A for more information on using the `<CFCONTENT>` tag.

REFINING YOUR SEARCH

Often, just typing a few keywords isn't enough to find the documents you want. Verity provides a wealth of search operators to help you get the job done. By including special words such as AND, OR, and NOT in your search criteria, or by using various wildcards, your users can tweak their searches so they find exactly what they're looking for.

As you're reading through this section, note how Verity search criteria end up looking similar to SQL statements. It's nice that some common ground exists between the two, but it's also important to keep in mind that Verity's search language is not the same thing as SQL.

USING AND, OR, AND NOT

If you want to refine your search a little, you can use special search operators in your search criteria to get more specific. Only the most common search operators are discussed at this point. Many others are available for your use. See Appendix C, "Special ColdFusion Variables and Result Codes," for all the details on each of the search operators in Verity's search language.

Table 36.4 briefly describes the effect of using AND, OR, and NOT in your search criteria. These operators are very similar to the AND, OR, and NOT Boolean operators discussed in Chapter 6, "Introduction to SQL."

TABLE 36.4 BASIC SEARCH OPERATORS

Operator	Effect	Example
AND	Searches for documents that have both words in it	`Verity AND Macromedia`
OR	Searches for documents that have either word in it	`Verity OR Macromedia`
NOT	Eliminates documents in which the word is found	`Verity NOT Macromedia`

Tip

A comma can be used instead of `OR` in search criteria. A search for `Verity, Macromedia` is therefore the same as a search for `Verity OR Macromedia`.

USING PARENTHESES AND QUOTATION MARKS

Search criteria can look ambiguous after more than two search words are present. For instance, if you typed in `Verity AND Macromedia OR ColdFusion`, what would that mean exactly? Documents that definitely contain Verity but that only need to contain Verity or ColdFusion? Documents that contain ColdFusion in addition to documents that contain both Verity and Macromedia?

Use parentheses and quotation marks to indicate this type of criteria, in which the order of evaluation needs to be specified. They make your intentions clear to Verity and are fairly easy to explain to users. Table 36.5 summarizes the use of parentheses and quotation marks.

TABLE 36.5 EXAMPLES: QUOTATION MARKS AND PARENTHESES

Character	Purpose	Examples
(Parentheses)	Determines how ANDs and ORs are treated. Words within parentheses are considered a unit and are considered first.	`Macromedia OR (Cold AND Fusion)` `Fusion AND (Cold NOT Hot)`
"Quotation Marks"	Quoted words or phrases are searched for literally. Useful when you want to search for the actual words *and* or *or*.	`"Simple AND Explicit"` `Macromedia AND "not installed"`

USING WILDCARDS

Verity provides a few wildcards you can use in your searches, so you can find documents based on incomplete search words or phrases. The wildcards should look pretty familiar to you if you've used the `LIKE` operator with SQL queries, as discussed in Chapter 6. Table 36.6 summarizes the use of wildcard operators.

TABLE 36.6 THE TWO MOST COMMON WILDCARDS

Wildcard	Purpose
*	Similar to the `%` wildcard in SQL, `*` stands in for any number of characters (including 0). A search for `Fu*` would find `Fusion`, `Fugazi`, and `Fuchsia`.
?	Just as in SQL, `?` stands in for any single character. More precise—and thus generally less helpful—than the `*` wildcard. A search for `?ar?et` would find both `carpet` and `target`, but not `Learjet`.

Note

These aren't the only wildcards available for your use. See the `WILDCARD` operator in "Evidence Operators," in Appendix D.

TAKING CASE SENSITIVITY INTO ACCOUNT

By default, a Verity search automatically becomes case sensitive whenever the characters provided as the `CRITERIA` parameter are of mixed case. A search for `employee`—or for `EMPLOYEE`—finds `employee`, `Employee`, or `EMPLOYEE`, but a search for `Employee` finds only `Employee`, not `employee` or `EMPLOYEE`. You might want to make this fact clear to your users by providing a message on your search forms, such as `Type in all uppercase or all lowercase unless you want the search to be case sensitive.`

To have your application always ignore case regardless of what the user types, use ColdFusion's `LCase` function to convert the user's search words to lowercase when you supply them to `<CFSEARCH>`. For instance, by replacing the `<CFSEARCH>` in Listing 36.3 with the code in Listing 36.4, you guarantee that the search criteria passed to Verity is not of mixed case—you know the search will not be case sensitive.

LISTING 36.4 USING `LCase` TO DEFEAT CASE-SENSITIVITY EVEN IF USER'S KEYWORDS ARE OF MIXED CASE

```
<!--- retrieve requested files --->
<CFSEARCH
    name = "GetResults"
    collection = "#SearchCollection#"
    criteria = "#LCase(Form.Criteria)#"
    maxRows = "#Evaluate(Form.MaxRows + 1)#"
    startRow = "#Form.StartRow#"
>
```

INDEXING YOUR FILES INTERACTIVELY

You've explored how to use the `<CFINDEX>` tag to index your collections. ColdFusion provides two ways to index a Verity collection:

- Programmatically, with the `<CFINDEX>` tag (see Listing 36.11)
- Interactively, with the ColdFusion Administrator

The programmatic method you've explored is best suited for the following situations:

- When the documents are always changing
- When it's critical that new documents become searchable right away
- When it's important that your application is as self-tuning as possible; if you are working as an outside consultant, for instance
- More complicated applications

However, you also have the option of indexing your documents interactively, using the Index button in the ColdFusion Administrator. This method is handy for the following situations:

- When the documents change infrequently, or not on a fixed or predictable schedule
- When the documents live outside your ColdFusion application, such as a folder full of Word files that employees might save and edit without your application knowing about it
- Testing and development
- Less complicated, in-house applications

Take a look at the interactive approach. To do this, go to the ColdFusion Administrator's Verity VDK Collections page, highlight your collection, and click the Index button. As you can see, all you have to do is fill in a few form fields and click the Submit Changes button (see Figure 36.12). After a few seconds—or minutes, depending on the number of files you're indexing—you see a message in the Administrator that the operation is complete.

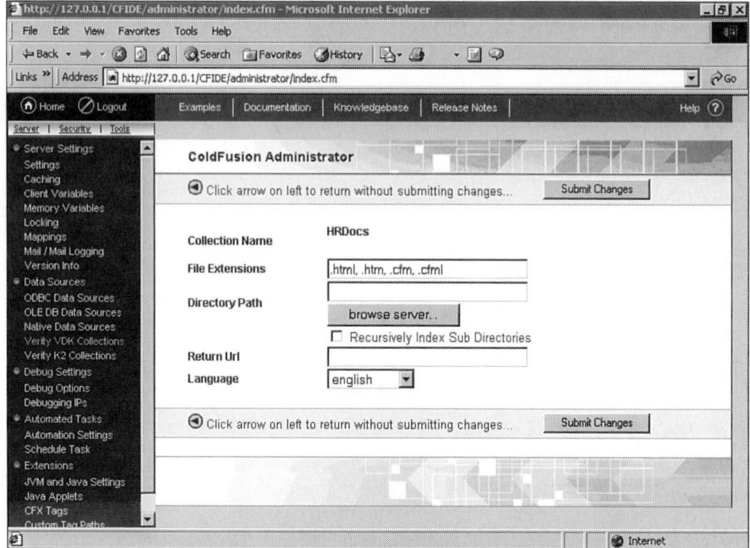

Figure 36.12
Indexing your files interactively is as simple as filling in a few blanks.

To index files, you must supply four pieces of information:

- File extensions
- Directory path
- Recursively index subdirectories
- Return URL

The File Extensions field corresponds to the `<CFINDEX>` tag's `EXTENSIONS` parameter. Just provide a simple list of file extensions—including the periods—that indicate which documents you want to index. I used `.HTM`, `.HTML`, `.TXT`, `.DOC`, `.XLS` in the previous example.

The Directory Path field corresponds to the `KEY` parameter of the `<CFINDEX>` tag. Just indicate which directory on your Web server—or local network—Verity should index. This value must be given as an absolute filesystem path, not a URL, so it cannot start with `http://`. In the previous example, I used `C:\Inetpub\wwwroot\HR\Docs`.

The Recursively Index Subdirectories check box corresponds to the `RECURSE` parameter of the `<CFINDEX>` tag. Check this box if you want Verity to search all folders within the directory you specify.

The Return URL field corresponds to the URLPATH parameter of the <CFINDEX> tag. Enter the URL equivalent of the directory path you entered. In other words, what would you put before the filename if you wanted to open a file in this directory in a Web browser? This value should start with http:// or https://. In the previous example, this was http://127.0.0.1/HR/Docs. (Note that your URL might be different. This URL assumes you're working on the ColdFusion server machine.)

A collection indexed using this method will work the same way as a collection indexed using the <CFINDEX> tag in a ColdFusion template. It's really just a matter of whether you want to create a template that uses the <CFINDEX> tag.

Indexing SQL Data

You've seen how easy using ColdFusion's Verity functionality to index all sorts of files on your system is. What if you want to index and search information in your database files? ColdFusion enables you to build a Verity index from data in your database as if the data were a bunch of document files.

In this section you see how Verity enables you to very neatly get around the limitations that make SQL less than perfect for true text-based searching. By the time you're finished, you'll have a good understanding of when you should unleash Verity's rich search capabilities on your database data and when you're better off leaving things to SQL instead.

Note

The examples in this section use the code listings directory located on the CD-ROM. The tables are populated with some actual book and order data with which to work.

Doing It Without Verity

You don't need to use Verity to make your database searchable, but it can make implementing a search interface much easier and enable your users to more easily find what they want. Take a look at what you'd need to do to search your data using the tools you already know: <CFQUERY> and SQL.

Say you want to set up a little search tool to enable your users to search the OWS database's Merchandise table. You just want the user to be able to type a word or two into a form field and click Search to get the matching item.

The code in Listing 36.5 is a simple search form. This will remind you a lot of the search forms explained in Chapter 12. The form is displayed in a browser, as shown in Figure 36.13.

Listing 36.5 MerchandiseSearch_Form.cfm—A Simple Merchandise Search Form

```
<HTML>
<HEAD>
<TITLE>Merchandise Search</TITLE>
```

LISTING 36.5 CONTINUED

```
</HEAD>

<BODY>

<H2>Please enter keywords to search for.</H2>

<FORM ACTION="MerchandiseSearch_Action.cfm" METHOD="POST">
Keywords: <INPUT TYPE="text" NAME="Criteria"><BR>
<P><INPUT TYPE="submit" VALUE="Search">
</FORM>

</BODY>
</HTML>
```

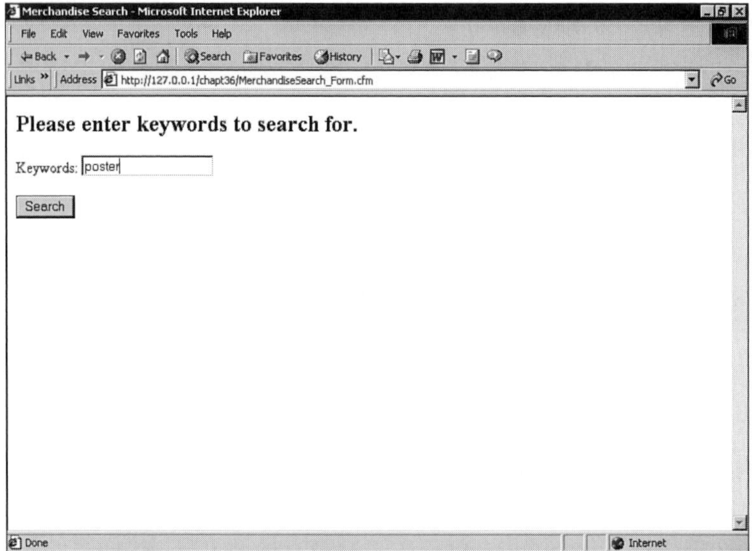

Figure 36.13 The Inventory Search tool collects one or more keywords from the user.

Again borrowing heavily from Chapter 11, you could come up with the code in Listing 36.6 for searching and displaying the results from the `Merchandise` table. Note that the `LIKE` keyword is used along with the `%` wildcard to search any part of the description. See Chapter 11 if you need to jog your memory on the use of the `LIKE` keyword.

LISTING 36.6 `MerchandiseSearch_Action.cfm`—CODE FOR SEARCHING THE INVENTORY TABLE

```
<CFQUERY NAME="GetResults" DATASOURCE="ows">
  SELECT MerchID, MerchDescription
  FROM Merchandise
  WHERE (MerchDescription LIKE '%#Form.Criteria#%')
</CFQUERY>
```

```
<HTML>
<HEAD>
<TITLE>Search Results</TITLE>
</HEAD>

<BODY>

<H2><CFOUTPUT>
#GetResults.RecordCount# Merchandise record(s) found for "#Form.Criteria#".
</CFOUTPUT>
</H2>

<UL>
<CFOUTPUT QUERY="GetResults">
  <LI>#MerchDescription#
</CFOUTPUT>
</UL>

</BODY>
</HTML>
```

This would work fine, as long as your application required only simple searching. If the user entered *poster* for the search criteria, SQL's `LIKE` operator would faithfully find all the merchandise that had the word *poster* somewhere in the description, as shown in Figure 36.14.

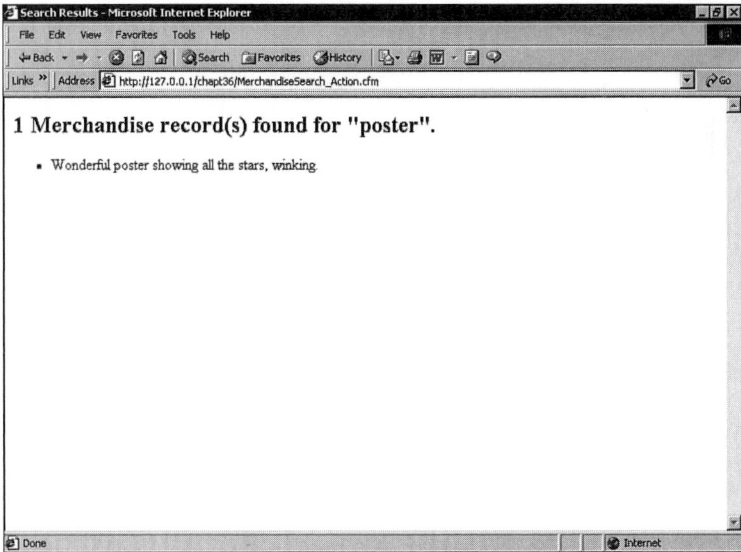

Figure 36.14
Your Verity-free code works fine for simple, one-word searches.

What if the user entered something such as *West End Tee*? No records would be found because no records have those exact words in them (although one merchandise item does have the phrase "...West End Story Tee"). That's a limitation your users probably won't find acceptable.

Maybe you need to modify your <CFQUERY> a little, to account for multiple-word searches. Listing 36.7 contains a revised query that should take multiple words into account. Each word is treated separately because the <CFLOOP> adds an additional AND condition to the query for each word in the user's input. Only books that contain all the words entered in the blank will be found. See Chapter 10, "CFML Basics," for a detailed discussion of the <CFLOOP> tag.

LISTING 36.7 MerchandiseSearch_Action2.cfm—GETTING SQL TO ACCOUNT FOR MULTIPLE WORDS

```
<CFQUERY NAME="GetResults" DATASOURCE="ows">
  SELECT MerchID, MerchDescription
  FROM Merchandise
  WHERE (0=0
  <CFLOOP LIST="#Form.Criteria#" INDEX="ThisWord" DELIMITERS=" ">
    AND (MerchDescription LIKE '%#ThisWord#%')
  </CFLOOP>)
</CFQUERY>


<HTML>

<HEAD>
<TITLE>Search Results</TITLE>
</HEAD>

<BODY>

<H2><CFOUTPUT>
#GetResults.RecordCount# Merchandise record(s) found for "#Form.Criteria#".
</CFOUTPUT>
</H2>

<UL>
<CFOUTPUT QUERY="GetResults">
  <LI>#MerchDescription#
</CFOUTPUT>
</UL>

</BODY>
</HTML>
```

Now the appropriate merchandise item will be found if the user enters *West End Tee*. What if your user wants to search for *Tee, West End*? There are other reasons SQL searches just won't cut it when a real search engine is needed. For example, if the search phrase includes some symbols, such as apostrophes or hyphens, SQL won't find matches unless the user's criteria is an exact match.

This is the kind of intelligence users have come to expect from a real search engine. Theoretically, you could come up with various CFLOOPs and CFIFs that build SQL code to cover all those scenarios, but that many WHEREs, LIKEs, ANDs, and ORs would be a real pain to code, debug, and maintain. In addition, performance degrades as the number of books grows. Indexing the text columns won't improve performance because the `LIKE` operator can't take advantage of indexes when a wildcard operator precedes the search string. There has to be a better way.

INDEXING YOUR TABLE DATA: VERITY TO THE RESCUE

ColdFusion's Verity functionality provides a well-performing, easy-to-implement solution that addresses all these concerns. You create a *custom* Verity collection filled with documents that aren't really documents at all. Each *document* is actually just a record from your database tables.

It works like this: You write a `<CFQUERY>` that retrieves the data you want to make searchable. You pass this data to a `<CFINDEX>` tag, which indexes the data as if it were documents. Additionally, you tell Verity which column from the query should be considered a document "filename," which column should be considered a document "title," and which column(s) should be considered a document's "body." Figure 36.15 illustrates the idea.

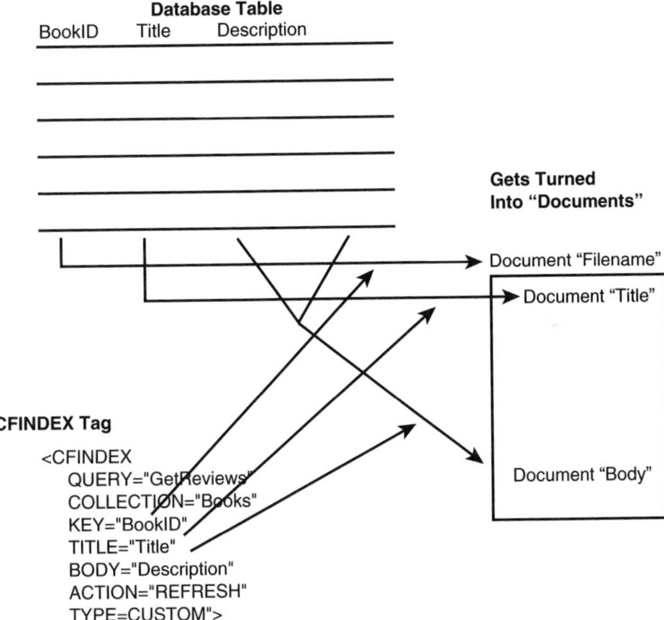

Figure 36.15
Database data becomes searchable, just like regular documents.

Assume you've just used the ColdFusion Administrator to create a new Verity collection called `Merchandise`, as discussed earlier in this chapter. You'll populate this new collection with data from the `Merchandise` database table.

Take a look at the code in Listing 36.8. Notice that the `<CFINDEX>` tag looks similar to Listing 36.1, in which you indexed your document files. The central differences here are the fact that you're setting `TYPE` to `CUSTOM` instead of `PATH` and that you're referring to column names from a `<CFQUERY>`.

LISTING 36.8 IndexData.cfm—CODE TO INDEX A COLLECTION WITH DATABASE DATA

```
<CFQUERY NAME="GetResults" DATASOURCE="OWS">
  SELECT MerchID, MerchName, MerchDescription
  FROM Merchandise
</CFQUERY>

<CFINDEX
   ACTION="REFRESH"
   COLLECTION="Merchandise"
   KEY="MerchID"
   TYPE="CUSTOM"
   TITLE="MerchName"
   QUERY="GetResults"
   BODY="MerchDescription"
>

<HTML>
<HEAD>
<TITLE>Indexing Complete</TITLE>
</HEAD>
<BODY>

<H2>Indexing Complete</H2>

</BODY>

</HTML>
```

The `<CFQUERY>` part is very simple—just get the basic information about the books. (Obviously, if you only want certain books to be indexed, a `WHERE` clause could be added to the `<CFQUERY>`'s SQL statement.) Next comes a `<CFINDEX>` tag, which looks a lot like the `<CFINDEX>` tag you used earlier to index your normal document files.

This time around, though, you specify a few new parameters that are necessary when indexing a database table instead of normal documents:

`ACTION="REFRESH"`	As before, this tells Verity that you're supplying new data.
`TYPE="CUSTOM"`	Says that you're dealing with table data, rather than document files.
`QUERY="GetResults"`	Specifies from which `<CFQUERY>` to get the data.
`KEY, TITLE, BODY`	Specifies which query columns should be treated like which parts of a document.

That's really about all there is to it! After the `INDEXDATA.CFM` template is executed, you should be able to search the `Merchandise` collection in much the same way as you searched the `HRDocs` collection back in Listing 36.3.

The code in Listing 36.9 searches through the newly indexed `Merchandise` collection, based on whatever criteria the user types in the search form. Except for the introduction of the `<CFSEARCH>` tag, this code is virtually unchanged from Listing 36.6; the results are displayed to the user as shown in Figure 36.14.

Note

You're still using Listing 36.5's Merchandise Search form—just be sure to change the `ACTION` parameter of the `FORM` tag to `"MerchandiseSearch_Action3.cfm"`.

LISTING 36.9 `MerchandiseSearch_Action3.cfm`**—SEARCHING AND DISPLAYING RECORDS THAT CAME FROM A DATABASE**

```
<CFSEARCH COLLECTION="Merchandise"
          NAME="GetResults"
          CRITERIA="#Form.Criteria#">

<HTML>

<HEAD>
<TITLE>Search Results</TITLE>
</HEAD>

<BODY>

<H2><CFOUTPUT>
#GetResults.RecordCount# merchandise item(s) found for "#Form.Criteria#".
</CFOUTPUT></H2>

<UL>
<CFOUTPUT QUERY="GetResults">
  <LI>#MerchDescription#
</CFOUTPUT>
</UL>

</BODY>

</HTML>
```

As you can see, exposing your database data to Verity was easy. You really didn't have to do much work at all. Of course, the user will notice a tremendous difference: All Verity's `AND`, `OR`, `NOT`, wildcarding, and other searching niceties are all of a sudden very much available.

DISPLAYING A SUMMARY FOR EACH RECORD

In addition to the score and title, Verity also provides a summary for each record in the search results. The summary is the first three sentences—or the first 500 characters—of the information you specified for the `BODY` back when you indexed the collection with the `<CFINDEX>` tag. The summary helps the user to eyeball which documents he is interested in.

To display the summary to the user, simply refer to it in your ColdFusion templates in the same way you refer to the `KEY`, `SCORE`, or `TITLE`. Listing 36.10 adds the summary to your Search Results page. Figure 36.16 shows what the search results will look like to the user.

Listing 36.10 `MerchandiseSearch_Action4.cfm`—**Code to Include a Summary for Each Document**

```
<CFSEARCH
   COLLECTION="Merchandise"
   NAME="GetResults"
   CRITERIA="#Form.Criteria#"
>

<HTML>
<HEAD>
<TITLE>Search Results</TITLE>
</HEAD>

<BODY>

<H2><CFOUTPUT>
#GetResults.RecordCount# books found for "#Form.Criteria#".
</CFOUTPUT></H2>

<DL>
<CFOUTPUT QUERY="GetResults">
  <DT><I>#NumberFormat(Round(Score * 100))#%</I>
      <B>#Title#</B>
  <DD><FONT SIZE="-1">#Summary#</FONT>
</CFOUTPUT>
</DL>

</BODY>

</HTML>
```

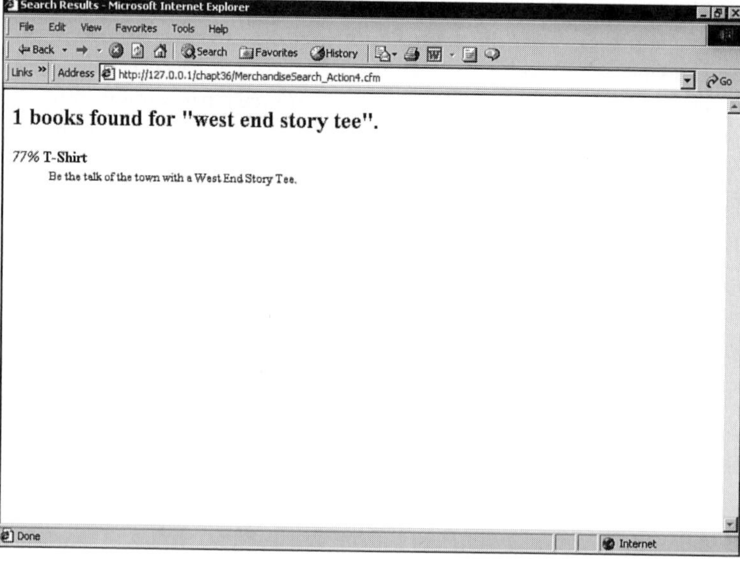

Figure 36.16 Displaying the document summary is a slick, professional-looking touch.

Don't expect Verity summaries to always show the parts of the document that contain the search keywords; that's not how Verity summarization works. Verity selects each record's summary at the time the collection is indexed, and it is always the same for any given record, regardless of whatever the search criteria were that found it. The summary does not necessarily contain the keywords that were used as the search criteria.

Indexing Multiple Query Columns as the BODY

In Listing 36.8 you indexed the `Merchandise` collection with the results from a query. In that listing, you declared that the `MerchDescription` column from the `Merchandise` table should be considered the body of each book record (by setting the `BODY` parameter of the `<CFINDEX>` tag to `"MerchDescription"`).

By default, when your application runs a Verity search, only the `BODY` part of each record is actually searched for matching words. The information in the `TITLE` part of the record is not searched.

There are two ways to make the title searchable. One is to specify the title in the `CRITERIA` parameter, using relational operators and the `SUBSTRING` operator.

Note

See the section "Indexing Additional Columns with Custom Fields."

An easier way is to go back to your `<CFINDEX>` tag and simply supply the information you're giving to the `TITLE` parameter to the `BODY` parameter as well. The `BODY` parameter can take a comma-separated list of column names (`"MerchName,MerchDescription"`), rather than only one column name (`"MerchDescription"`). The searchable part of each record in your database is comprised of the `MerchName` of the item, followed by the `MerchDescription` of the item.

There's no need to stop there. You can put a bunch of column names in the `BODY` parameter, as shown in Listing 36.11. For each row returned by the query, ColdFusion concatenates the `MerchDescription` and `MerchName` columns and presents them to Verity as the `BODY` of each document. The result is that all textual information about the merchandise description and name is now part of your collection and instantly searchable. You don't have to change a thing about the code in any of your search templates.

Listing 36.11 IndexData2.cfm—Supplying More Than One Column to the BODY Parameter

```
<CFQUERY NAME="GetResults" DATASOURCE="OWS">
  SELECT MerchID, MerchName, MerchDescription
  FROM Merchandise
</CFQUERY>

<CFINDEX
   ACTION="REFRESH"
   COLLECTION="Merchandise"
```

Listing 36.11 Continued

```
   TYPE="CUSTOM"
   KEY="MerchID"
   TITLE="MerchName"
   QUERY="GetResults"
   BODY="MerchName,MerchDescription"
>

<HTML>
<HEAD>
<TITLE>Indexing Complete</TITLE>
</HEAD>
<BODY>

<H2>Indexing Complete</H2>

</BODY>

</HTML>
```

It's important to note that when you supply several columns to the `BODY` like this, Verity does not maintain the information in separate columns, fields, or anything else. The underlying table's structure is not preserved; all the information is pressed together into one big, searchable mass. Don't expect to be able to refer to a `#MerchName#` variable, for instance, in the same way you can refer to the `#Title#` and `#Score#` variables after a `<CFSEARCH>` is executed.

That might or might not feel like a limitation, depending on the nature of the applications you're building. In a way, it's just the flip side of Verity's concentrating on text in a natural-language kind of way, rather than being obsessed with columns the way SQL is.

However, ColdFusion and Verity do enable you to store a limited amount of information in a more database-type of way, using something called *custom fields*.

Indexing Additional Columns with Custom Fields

ColdFusion enables you to index up to two additional Verity fields when you're indexing database data. The fields—`CUSTOM1` and `CUSTOM2`—are treated similarly to the `Title` field you've already worked with. These custom fields come in handy when you have precise, code-style data you want to keep associated with each record.

In Listing 36.12, you adjust the code from Listing 36.8 to fill the `CUSTOM1` field with your `FilmID`. Conceptually, it's as if Verity were making a little note on each document that it makes from the rows of your query. The `CUSTOM1` note is the `FilmID`. This example doesn't use the `CUSTOM2` attribute, but it is used exactly the same way as `CUSTOM1`.

Listing 36.12 `IndexData3.cfm`**—Adding Custom Fields to a Collection**

```
<CFQUERY NAME="GetResults" DATASOURCE="OWS">
  SELECT MerchID, MerchName, MerchDescription, FilmID
  FROM Merchandise
</CFQUERY>
```

```
<CFINDEX
   ACTION="REFRESH"
   COLLECTION="Merchandise"
   TYPE="CUSTOM"
   KEY="MerchID"
   TITLE="MerchName"
   QUERY="GetResults"
   BODY="MerchName,MerchDescription"
   CUSTOM1="FilmID"
>

<HTML>
<HEAD>
<TITLE>Indexing Complete</TITLE>
</HEAD>
<BODY>

<H2>Indexing Complete</H2>

</BODY>

</HTML>
```

Now that Verity knows the `FilmID` for each record in the collection, you easily can create a more sophisticated search tool that enables the user to select films along with her search words, similar to Listing 36.13. Figure 36.17 shows what the search form looks like.

LISTING 36.13 `MerchandiseSearch_Form2.cfm`**—SEARCH FORM WITH USER INTERFACE FOR CUSTOM SEARCH CRITERIA**

```
<CFQUERY NAME="GetFilms" DATASOURCE="ows">
   SELECT FilmID, MovieTitle
   FROM Films
</CFQUERY>

<HTML>
<HEAD>
<TITLE>Merchandise Search</TITLE>
</HEAD>

<BODY>

<H2>Please enter keywords to search for.</H2>

<FORM ACTION="MerchandiseSearch_Action5.cfm" METHOD="POST">
Keywords: <INPUT TYPE="text" NAME="Criteria"><BR>
<P>Film:<BR>
<SELECT SIZE="4" NAME="FilmID">
<CFOUTPUT QUERY="GetFilms"><OPTION VALUE="#FilmID#">#MovieTitle#
</CFOUTPUT>
</SELECT>
<P><INPUT TYPE="submit" VALUE="Search">
</FORM>

</BODY>
</HTML>
```

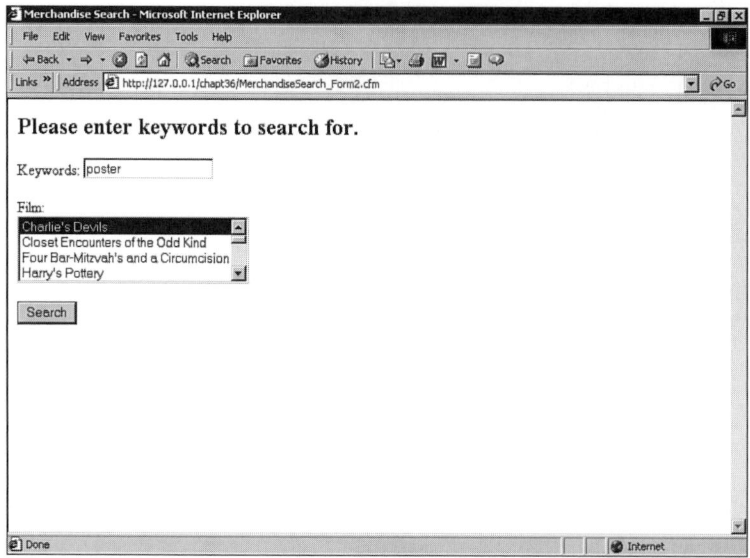

Figure 36.17
Custom fields provide a simple way to handle search forms such as this one.

Now you just need to teach the receiving template how to deal with the user's entries for the FilmID field. To specify the additional criteria, use Verity's MATCHES operator, which you use here for the first time.

The MATCHES operator searches specific document fields—rather than the body—and finds only exact matches. Document fields you can use MATCHES with include CF_CUSTOM1, CF_CUSTOM2, CF_TITLE, and CF_KEY, all of which correspond to the values you supply to the <CFINDEX> tag when you index the data.

Note

Depending on the situation, you could use the Verity operators CONTAINS, STARTS, ENDS, and SUBSTRING in place of MATCHES in the this code. You also could use numeric operators, such as =, <, and >, with the CF_CUSTOM2 field. See the section "Relational Operators" in Appendix D for more information.

Listing 36.14 demonstrates the use of the MATCHES search operator. At the top of the template, you use some <CFIF>, <CFELSE>, and <CFELSEIF> tags to decide what you're going to ask Verity to look for. If the user specifies a specific film (using the <SELECT> list, FilmID), you will ignore the keywords. If the FilmID is blank, search for the keywords the user enters—but, be sure he specified either keywords or a film.

Depending on which field the user might have left blank, the TheCriteria variable will have slightly different values. The TheCriteria variable is then supplied to the <CFSEARCH> tag in its CRITERIA parameter.

LISTING 36.14 MerchandiseSearch_Action5.cfm—USING THE MATCHES OPERATOR TO SEARCH A CUSTOM FIELD

```
<CFIF IsDefined("Form.FilmID")>
   <!--- FilmID is specified --->
   <CFSET TheCriteria = "CF_CUSTOM1 <MATCHES> #Form.FilmID#">
<CFELSEIF (Form.Criteria NEQ "")>
   <!--- Film and keywords were specified --->
   <CFSET TheCriteria = "#Form.Criteria#">
<CFELSE>
   <!--- Neither keywords nor FilmID were specified --->
   <CFABORT SHOWERROR="Please enter your criteria">
</CFIF>

<CFSEARCH
   COLLECTION="Merchandise"
   NAME="GetResults"
   CRITERIA="#TheCriteria#"
>
<HTML>

<HEAD>
<TITLE>Search Results</TITLE>
</HEAD>

<BODY>

<H2><CFOUTPUT>#GetResults.RecordCount# merchandise item(s) found.</CFOUTPUT></H2>

<P ALIGN="RIGHT">
<CFOUTPUT>Actual Criteria Used:#HTMLEditFormat(TheCriteria)#
</CFOUTPUT>
</P>

<DL>
<CFOUTPUT QUERY="GetResults">
  <DT><I>#NumberFormat(Round(Score * 100))#%</I>
      <B>#Title#</B>
  <DD><FONT SIZE="-1"><I>FilmID #Custom1#.</I> #Summary#</FONT>
</CFOUTPUT>
</DL>

</BODY>

</HTML>
```

As you can see in Figure 36.18, this code presents the FilmID to the user by using the #Custom1# variable in the <CFOUTPUT> block, along with the summary, score, and other information. Also note that this code displays the criteria that is actually being passed to Verity at the top of the page, so you can fool around with the template a bit if you want and see the effect your <CFIF> logic is having.

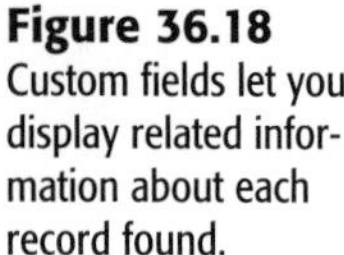

Figure 36.18
Custom fields let you display related information about each record found.

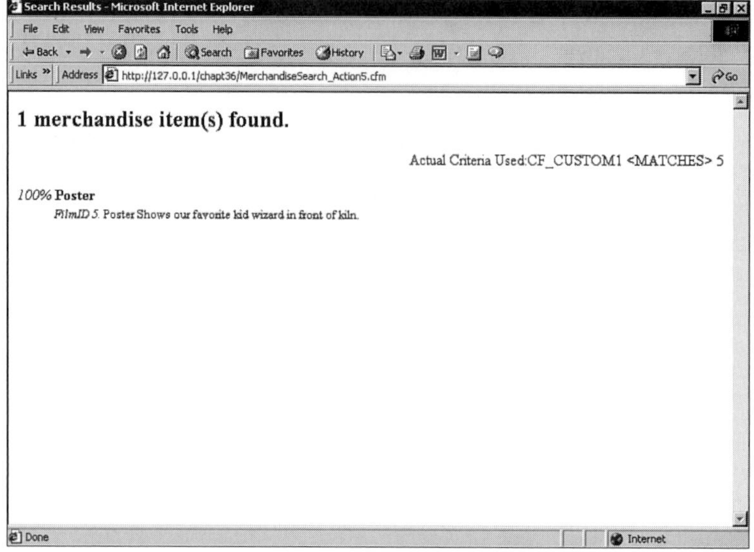

Combining Verity Searches with SQL Queries On-the-Fly

The custom fields you just learned about give you a lot of flexibility. In most cases, you'll be able to search and display records straight from your Verity collection(s), without bothering the underlying database tables.

You might encounter situations in which you want to get information from Verity and from your database tables, presenting the information together to the user. This is quite easy to pull off: Use ColdFusion's `ValueList` function along with SQL's `IN` operator.

Say you want to run a Verity search on the `Merchandise` collection, but you want to be able to show the current, up-to-the minute price on each item. You consider the idea of feeding the `MerchPrice` column to `CUSTOM1` or `CUSTOM2`, but you know that Orange Whip Studios changes the prices, well, hourly! So you decide you must get the live value directly from the database table.

You run a `<CFSEARCH>` just as you already have, but you won't display anything from it. Instead, you just use Verity's results as criteria for a normal SQL query. Verity supplies you with the key value for each document it finds, which you know happens to be the `MerchID` from your `Merchandise` table. You'll supply those `MerchIDs` to a normal `<CFQUERY>`.

Listing 36.15 shows how to use `<CFSEARCH>` results to drive a `<CFQUERY>` in this manner. Figure 36.19 shows the results.

Listing 36.15 InvSrch6.cfm—Using Verity Results as Criteria for a Normal SQL Query

```
<CFIF IsDefined("Form.FilmID")>
   <!--- FilmID is specified --->
   <CFSET TheCriteria = "CF_CUSTOM1 <MATCHES> #Form.FilmID#">
<CFELSEIF (Form.Criteria NEQ "")>
   <!--- Film and keywords were specified --->
   <CFSET TheCriteria = "#Form.Criteria#">
<CFELSE>
   <!--- Neither keywords nor FilmID were specified --->
   <CFABORT SHOWERROR="Please enter your criteria">
</CFIF>

<CFSEARCH
   COLLECTION="Merchandise"
   NAME="GetResults"
   CRITERIA="#TheCriteria#"
>

<CFQUERY NAME="GetPrices" DATASOURCE="ows">
   SELECT MerchID, MerchDescription, MerchPrice
   FROM Merchandise
   WHERE MerchID IN (#ValueList(GetResults.Key)#)
</CFQUERY>

<HTML>

<HEAD>
<TITLE>Search Results</TITLE>
</HEAD>

<BODY>

<H2><CFOUTPUT>#GetPrices.RecordCount# merchandise item(s) found.</CFOUTPUT></H2>

<P ALIGN="RIGHT">
<CFOUTPUT>Actual Criteria Used:#HTMLEditFormat(Variables.TheCriteria)#
</CFOUTPUT>
</P>

<CFTABLE QUERY="GetPrices" COLHEADERS HTMLTABLE BORDER>
  <CFCOL HEADER="ID" TEXT="#MerchID#">
  <CFCOL HEADER="Description" TEXT="#MerchDescription#">
  <CFCOL HEADER="Price" TEXT="#MerchPrice#">
</CFTABLE>

</BODY>

</HTML>
```

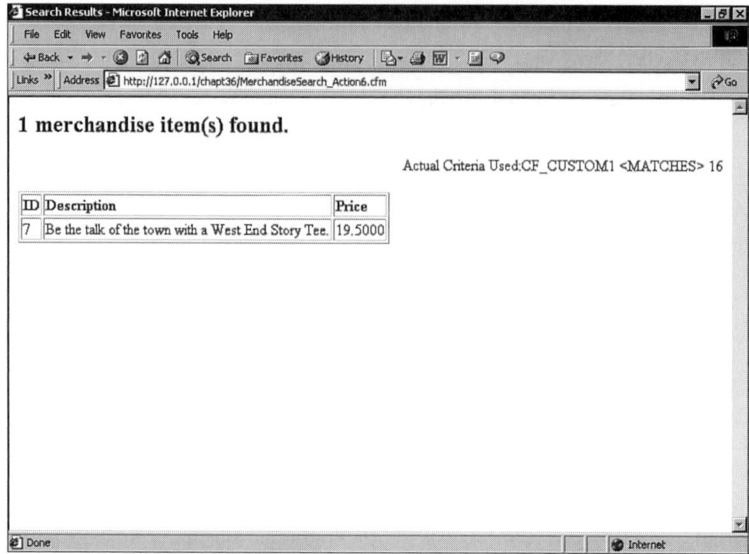

Figure 36.19 <CFSEARCH> and <CFQUERY> can work well together, through SQL's `IN` keyword and ColdFusion's `ValueList` function.

Tip

When you use this strategy, the search results no longer are sorted by relevance. Instead, they are sorted according to the `ORDER BY` part of your SQL statement. This can be a good or a bad thing, depending on your situation. Keep it in mind.

Understanding Verity and Your Table's Key Values

When you're indexing table data, it's important to understand that Verity doesn't think of the concept of a key in the same way that your database tables do. Specifically, Verity does not assume or enforce any rules about uniqueness of values you feed it with `<CFINDEX>`'s `KEY` parameter. This means Verity can and will index two separate documents that have the same key value. This can lead to problems, especially if the data you're indexing is derived from two tables that have a master-detail relationship to one another.

For instance, say you want to include the names of the people who placed orders for each of the merchandise items into the Verity collection. As you learned in Chapter 31, "More About SQL and Queries," creating a join query that retrieves this information from your database tables is fairly simple.

The problem is that any number of orders can be placed for each piece of merchandise. Therefore, if an item has been ordered by seven customers, seven rows will exist for that item in the resultset. This poses a problem. Verity will dutifully index each of these rows as a separate document, without understanding that the seven rows all represent the same item. So, a search that matches with the description of the item finds all seven records and displays them to the user. This can make your application look buggy.

ColdFusion provides no built-in way out of this. `<CFINDEX>` doesn't have a `GROUP` parameter like `CFOUTPUT` does; you can't use `GROUP` when you're displaying the records because the seven rows aren't guaranteed to be in consecutive rows when Verity finds them. You need to either avoid this kind of situation altogether or figure out some way of processing the data between `<CFQUERY>` and `<CFINDEX>`.

Here's one approach. The code in Listing 36.16 takes the query results and manually creates a second query, line by line. The new query has the same structure as the original, except that it is guaranteed to have only one row for each `MerchID`. If the original query had more than one row for a particular `MerchID` (because of multiple orders), the customer names from all the rows would be turned into a comma-separated list when they were put into the new query. The result is a query that can be used to index a Verity collection without problems.

Listing 36.16 `IndexData4.cfm`—Solving the Problem by Creating a New, Unique Query

```
<CFQUERY NAME="GetResults" DATASOURCE="OWS">
SELECT
   M.MerchID, M.MerchName, M.MerchDescription,
   C.LastName
FROM
   Contacts C, Merchandise M, MerchandiseOrders O, MerchandiseOrdersItems OI
WHERE
       M.MerchID = OI.ItemID AND
       OI.OrderID = O.OrderID AND
       O.ContactID = C.ContactID
ORDER BY
       M.MerchID
</CFQUERY>

<!--- Create new query with same column names --->
<CFSET MerchCustomers = QueryNew(GetResults.ColumnList)>
<CFOUTPUT QUERY="GetResults" GROUP="MerchID">
  <!--- Make a comma-separated list of all papers for this MerchID --->
  <CFSET LastNameList = "">
  <CFOUTPUT><CFSET LastNameList = ListAppend(LastNameList,
  ➥GetResults.LastName)>
  </CFOUTPUT>
  <!--- Make new row in MerchCustomers, with other data just copied from
  ➥GetResults --->
  <CFSET Temp = QueryAddRow(MerchCustomers)>
  <CFSET Temp = QuerySetCell(MerchCustomers,"MerchID",GetResults.MerchID)>
  <CFSET Temp = QuerySetCell(MerchCustomers,"MerchName",GetResults.MerchName)>
  <CFSET Temp = QuerySetCell(MerchCustomers,"MerchDescription",
  ➥GetResults.MerchDescription)>
  <CFSET Temp = QuerySetCell(MerchCustomers,"LastName",LastNameList)>
</CFOUTPUT>

<CFINDEX
   ACTION="UPDATE"
   COLLECTION="Merchandise"
   KEY="MerchID"
   TYPE="CUSTOM"
   TITLE="MerchDescription"
```

Listing 36.16 Continued

```
    QUERY="MerchCustomers"
    BODY="MerchDescription, LastName"
>

<HTML>

<HEAD>
<TITLE>Indexing Complete</TITLE>
</HEAD>

<BODY>

<H2>Indexing Complete</H2>

</BODY>

</HTML>
```

After this code is run, if the user types a company name in a search form, the `<CFSEARCH>` finds books the specified company has actually ordered.

Searching on More Than One Collection

To specify more than one Verity collection in a `<CFSEARCH>` tag, just specify all the collection names for the `COLLECTION` parameter and separate them with commas. All the collections are searched for matching documents.

If you want to allow your users to choose from several collections, you could add the code from Listing 36.17 to your search form.

Listing 36.17 `MerchandiseSearch_Form3.cfm`—Adding Check Boxes for Multiple Collections

```
<HTML>

<HEAD>
<TITLE>Collection Search</TITLE>
</HEAD>

<BODY>

<H2>Please enter keywords to search for.</H2>

<FORM ACTION="search_action.cfm" METHOD="POST">
<INPUT TYPE="Hidden" NAME="Collections_required"
       VALUE="You must choose at least one collection.">

Keywords: <INPUT TYPE="text" NAME="Criteria"><BR>

<INPUT TYPE="Checkbox" NAME="Collections" VALUE="Merchandise">Merchandise
<INPUT TYPE="Checkbox" NAME="Collections" VALUE="HRDocs">Personnel Policies
```

```
<P>
<INPUT TYPE="submit" VALUE="Search">

</FORM>

</BODY>

</HTML>
```

Because of the convenient way check boxes are handled by ColdFusion, the value of the `Form.Collections` variable is set to `"Merchandise,HRDocs"` if the user checks both boxes. You would pass the variable directly to the `COLLECTION` parameter of the receiving template's `<CFSEARCH>` tag.

Tip

> **Note that you can freely mix normal document collections with database-table collections within a single `<CFSEARCH>` operation.**

DISPLAYING RECORDS IN A DIFFERENT ORDER

The search results returned by a `<CFSEARCH>` tag are ranked in *order of relevance*. The closest matches—the ones with the highest score—are first, and the weakest matches are last.

Verity provides a few ways to tweak the way the score is computed (see the section "Score Operators" in Appendix D), which gives you a little bit of control over how the documents are ordered. What if you wanted to display the search results in, say, alphabetical order by title?

No built-in function is available to handle this in ColdFusion. A few custom tags in the custom tag library on Macromedia's site could be used to sort the results, though. Listing 36.18 provides a CFML custom tag developed by Nate Weiss that you can use to order your Verity results. Actually, you can use it to sort the output of any ColdFusion tag that presents its data as a query, such as `<CFPOP>`, `<CFLDAP>`, and so on.

LISTING 36.18 `QuerySort.cfm`—A CUSTOM TAG THAT SORTS QUERY (AND VERITY) RESULTS

```
<!---  Example of use

<CF_QuerySort
  QUERY="MyQuery"
  SORTCOLUMN="MyColumn"
  SORTORDER="Desc"              <- optional, defaults to Asc
  SORTTYPE="Numeric"            <- optional, defaults to Textnocase
  SORTEDQUERY="MySortedQuery">  <- optional, defaults to "Sorted"

 --->

<!--- COLD FUSION 3.1 OR HIGHER NEEDED --->
<CFIF Val(ListGetAt(Server.ColdFusion.ProductVersion, 1)) &"."&
```

Listing 36.18 Continued

```
  Val(ListGetAt(Server.ColdFusion.ProductVersion, 2)) less than
  "3.1">This tag only works in Cold Fusion 3.1 and higher.
  <CFABORT>
</CFIF>

<!--- SUSPEND OUTPUT --->
<CFSETTING ENABLECFOUTPUTONLY="YES">

<!--- REQUIRED PARAMETERS --->
<CFPARAM NAME="Attributes.QUERY">
<CFPARAM NAME="Attributes.SortColumn">
<!--- OPTIONAL PARAMETERS --->
<CFPARAM NAME="Attributes.SortType" DEFAULT="Textnocase">
<CFPARAM NAME="Attributes.SortOrder" DEFAULT="Asc">
<CFPARAM NAME="Attributes.SortedQuery" DEFAULT="Sorted">

<!--- ESTABLISH LOCAL VERSIONS OF QUERIES --->
<CFSET MyArray = ArrayNew(1)>
<CFSET MyQuery = Evaluate("Caller.#Attributes.Query#")>
<CFSET NewQuery = QueryNew(MyQuery.ColumnList)>
<CFIF MyQuery.RecordCount greater than 999999>
   <CFABORT SHOWERROR="Only Queries  with less than one million rows can
    be sorted.  Your Query has #MyQuery.RecordCount# rows.">
</CFIF>

<!--- ADD ROWNUMBER TO END OF EACH ROW'S VALUE --->
<CFOUTPUT QUERY="MyQuery">
  <CFSET MyArray[CurrentRow] = Evaluate("MyQuery.#Attributes.SortColumn#") &
         NumberFormat(CurrentRow, "000009")>
  <CFSET Temp = QueryAddRow(NewQuery)>
</CFOUTPUT>

<!--- SORT ARRAY --->
<CFSET Temp = ArraySort(MyArray, Attributes.SortType, Attributes.SortOrder)>

<!--- POPULATE NEW QUERY, ROW BY ROW, WITH APPROPRIATE ROW OF OLD QUERY --->
<CFLOOP FROM=1 TO=#MyQuery.RecordCount# INDEX="This">
  <CFSET Row = Val(Right(MyArray[This], 6))>
  <CFLOOP LIST="#MyQuery.ColumnList#" INDEX="Col">
    <CFSET Temp = QuerySetCell(NewQuery, Col, Evaluate("MyQuery.#Col#[Row]"),
     This)>
  </CFLOOP>
</CFLOOP>

<!--- PASS SORTED QUERY BACK TO CALLING TEMPLATE --->
<CFSET "Caller.#Attributes.SortedQuery#" = NewQuery>

<!--- RESTORE OUTPUT --->
<CFSETTING ENABLECFOUTPUTONLY="NO">
```

If you save the `QUERYSORT.CFM` file to your server's `CustomTags` directory, sorting your Verity results should be easy, as shown in Listing 36.19.

LISTING 36.19 `Sorted.cfm`—**SORTING VERITY RESULTS BY TITLE**

```
<CFSEARCH
   COLLECTION="Merchandise"
   NAME="GetResults"
   CRITERIA="#Form.Criteria#"
>

<CF_QUERYSORT
   QUERY="GetResults"
   SORTEDQUERY="GetResults"
   SORTCOLUMN="Title"
>

<HTML>

<HEAD>
<TITLE>Search Results</TITLE>
</HEAD>

<BODY>

<H2><CFOUTPUT>#GetResults.RecordCount# merchandise item(s) found for
➥"#Form.Criteria#".
</CFOUTPUT>
</H2>

<UL>
<CFOUTPUT QUERY="GetResults">
  <LI>#Title#
</CFOUTPUT>
</UL>

</BODY>

</HTML>
```

MAINTAINING COLLECTIONS

In some situations, you might be able to simply create a Verity collection, index it, and forget about it. If the documents or data that make up the collection never change, you're in luck—you get to skip this whole section of the chapter.

It's likely, though, that you'll have to refresh that data at some point. Even when you don't have to refresh it, you might want to get it to run more quickly.

REPOPULATING YOUR VERITY COLLECTION

Whenever the original documents change from what they were when you indexed them, your collection will be a little bit out of sync with reality. The search results will be based on Verity's knowledge of the documents back when you did your indexing. If a document or database record has since been edited so that it no longer has certain words in it, it might be found in error if someone types in a search for those words. If the document is deleted altogether, Verity will still find it in its own records, which means your application might show a bad link that leads nowhere.

In a perfect world, Verity would dynamically watch your document folders and data tables and immediately reflect any changes, additions, or deletions in your collections. Unfortunately, the world isn't perfect, and this stuff doesn't happen automatically for you. The good news is that it's no major chore.

IF YOU INDEX YOUR COLLECTIONS INTERACTIVELY

If you recall, there are two ways of indexing a Verity collection: interactively with the ColdFusion Administrator or programmatically with the `<CFINDEX>` tag. If you did it interactively, there's not much I need to tell you; just go back to the Verity page in the Administrator and click the Purge button for your collection. Click the Index button, and do the same thing you did the first time. This should bring your collection up to date.

Tip

You'd do the same basic thing if the location of the documents had changed.

IF YOU INDEX YOUR COLLECTIONS PROGRAMMATICALLY

If you indexed the collection using `<CFINDEX>`—and you used `ACTION="REFRESH"` in the `<CFINDEX>` tag, as shown in Listing 36.1 and Listing 36.8—you should be able to bring your collection up to date simply by running it again.

Tip

You might consider scheduling this refresh template to be executed automatically at the end of each week, during off-peak hours. The indexing process can be resource intensive. It is therefore best to schedule this type of activity during off-peak hours. For more information on ColdFusion's built-in template scheduler, see Chapter 37, "Event Scheduling."

Instead of `ACTION="REFRESH"`, you can use `ACTION="UPDATE"` in your `<CFINDEX>` tag. This updates information on documents already indexed but without deleting information on documents that no longer exist. You also can use `ACTION="PURGE"` to completely remove all data from the collection. The `ACTION="REFRESH"` previously recommended is really the same thing as a `PURGE` followed by an `UPDATE`.

DELETING/REPOPULATING SPECIFIC RECORDS

If your application is aware of the moment that a document or table record is deleted or edited, you might want to update the Verity collection right then, so your collection stays in sync with the actual information. Clearly, you don't have to repopulate the entire collection just because one record has changed. ColdFusion and Verity address this by enabling you to delete items from a collection via the key value.

For instance, after an edit has been made to the `Merchandise` database table, you could use the code shown in Listing 36.20 to remove the record from the `Merchandise` collection and put the new data in its place. This should run much more quickly than a complete repopulation. This listing assumes that a form that passes the `MerchID` as a hidden field has just been submitted and contains some other fields that are meant to allow them to update certain columns in the `Merchandise` table (the description, perhaps) for a particular item.

LISTING 36.20 `DelAdd.cfm`**—DELETING AND RE-ADDING A SPECIFIC RECORD TO A COLLECTION**

```
<!--- Perform the update to the database table --->
<CFUPDATE DATASOURCE="OWS" TABLENAME="Merchandise">

<!--- Retrieve updated data back from the database --->
<CFQUERY NAME="GetMerchandise" DATASOURCE="OWS">
  SELECT MerchID, MerchName, MerchDescription
  FROM Merchandise
  WHERE MerchID = #Form.MerchID#
</CFQUERY>

<!--- Delete the old record from the Verity collection --->
<CFINDEX ACTION="DELETE"
  COLLECTION="Merchandise"
  KEY="#Form.MerchID#">

<!--- Get updated version back into the Verity collection --->
<CFINDEX
  ACTION="UPDATE"
  COLLECTION="Merchandise"
  TYPE="CUSTOM"
  QUERY="GetMerchandise"
  KEY="MerchID"
  TITLE="MerchName"
  BODY="MerchDescription"
>

<HTML>

<HEAD>
<TITLE>Update Complete</TITLE>
</HEAD>

<BODY>

<H2>Update Complete</H2>

</BODY>

</HTML>
```

Administrating Collections with <CFCOLLECTION>

The <CFCOLLECTION> tag enables you to administer collections programmatically in your own templates, as an alternative to using the ColdFusion Administrator. If you want your application to be capable of creating, deleting, and maintaining a collection on its own, the <CFCOLLECTION> tag is here to help.

This section might be especially interesting if you are developing prebuilt applications that other people will deploy on their servers without your help, or if you are presented with a project in which you want to completely remove any need for anyone to interact with the ColdFusion Administrator interface. For example, you could use <CFCOLLECTION> in a template that acted as a setup script, creating the various files, Registry entries, database tables, and Verity collections your application needs to operate.

Optimizing a Verity Collection

After a Verity collection gets hit many times, performance can start to degrade. Depending on your application, this might never become a problem. If you notice your Verity searches becoming slower over time, you might want to try optimizing your collection. Optimizing your collection is similar conceptually to running Disk Defragmenter on a Windows 2000 machine.

Two ways to optimize a collection are available: You can use the ColdFusion Administrator or create a ColdFusion template that uses the <CFCOLLECTION> tag to optimize the collection programmatically.

To optimize a collection with the ColdFusion Administrator, highlight the collection in the ColdFusion Administrator and click Optimize (refer to Figure 36.2). Verity whirs around for a minute or two as the collection is optimized. Because optimization can take some time—especially with large collections—you should optimize a collection during off-peak hours if possible.

To optimize a collection with the <CFCOLLECTION> tag, just include the tag in a simple ColdFusion template. The tag must include an ACTION="OPTIMIZE" parameter, and the collection name must be provided in the COLLECTION parameter. For instance, the code in Listing 36.21 can be used to optimize the HRDocs collection created earlier in this chapter.

Tip

You might find that you want to optimize your collections on a regular basis. You could schedule the template shown in Listing 36.21 to be automatically run once a week, for example, by using the ColdFusion scheduler. See Chapter 32.

Listing 36.21 Optimize.cfm—**Optimizing a Collection with the <CFCOLLECTION> Tag**

```
<!--- Optimize the Verity collection --->
<CFCOLLECTION
```

```
  ACTION="OPTIMIZE"
  COLLECTION="HRDocs">

<HTML>

<HEAD>
<TITLE>Optimizing Verity Collection</TITLE>
</HEAD>

<BODY>

<H2>Optimizing Complete</H2>
The HRDocs collection has been optimized successfully.

</BODY>

</HTML>
```


Note

Use ACTION="OPTIMIZE" in a <CFCOLLECTION> tag when coding for ColdFusion 4.0 and later. In previous versions of ColdFusion, the way to optimize a collection programmatically was to use ACTION="OPTIMIZE" in a <CFINDEX> tag. This use of <CFINDEX> is now deprecated.

REPAIRING OR DELETING A COLLECTION

If, for some reason, Verity's internal index files for a collection become damaged, ColdFusion provides repairing functionality that enables you to get the collection back up and running quickly in most cases. Most likely, you will never need to repair a Verity collection. However, if you do need to, use the <CFCOLLECTION> tag with ACTION="REPAIR". For instance, you could use the code shown in Listing 36.21—just change the ACTION parameter to REPAIR.

Tip

You also can use the Repair button on the Verity VDK Collections page in the ColdFusion Administrator (refer to Figure 36.2) to repair a collection. Simply highlight the collection to be repaired, and then click the Repair button.

Note

While a collection is being repaired, searches against the collection can't take place.

To delete a collection altogether, use the <CFCOLLECTION> tag with ACTION="DELETE". Again, you could use the basic code shown in Listing 36.21 by simply changing the ACTION to DELETE. After the collection has been deleted, ColdFusion displays an error message if a <CFSEARCH> tag that uses that collection name is encountered. The collection name will no longer appear in the ColdFusion Administrator, and Verity's index files will be removed from your server's hard drive. Note that only Verity's internal index files will be deleted, not the actual documents that had been made searchable by the collection.

Tip

Alternatively, you could use the Delete button on the Verity page of the ColdFusion Administrator (refer to Figure 36.2) to delete the collection.

CREATING A COLLECTION PROGRAMMATICALLY

The `<CFCOLLECTION>` tag also can be used to create a collection from scratch. Basically, you supply the same information to the tag as you would normally supply to the ColdFusion Administrator when creating a new collection there. Provide a name for the new collection in the tag's `NAME` parameter, and provide the path for the new collection's internal index files with the `PATH` parameter.

Under most circumstances, you would supply the same path that appears by default in the ColdFusion Administrator, which typically would be `c:\CFUSION\Verity\Collections\` on Windows platforms, as shown previously in Figure 36.3. Verity will create a new subfolder within the directory that you specify as the `PATH`.

Listing 36.22 demonstrates how to use `<CFCOLLECTION>` to create a new collection called `MoreHRDocs`.

Note

If you have the ColdFusion International Search Pack installed on your ColdFusion server, you also can provide a `LANGUAGE` attribute to specify a language other than English. The languages you can supply with the `LANGUAGE` attribute include Danish, Dutch, English, Finnish, French, German, Italian, Norwegian, Portuguese, Spanish, and Swedish.

LISTING 36.22 `Create.cfm`—**CREATING A COLLECTION WITH THE `<CFCOLLECTION>` TAG**

```
<!--- Create the Verity collection --->
<CFCOLLECTION
  ACTION="CREATE"
  COLLECTION="MoreHRDocs"
  PATH="c:\CFUSION\Verity\Collections\">

<HTML>

<HEAD>
<TITLE>Creating Verity Collection</TITLE>
</HEAD>

<BODY>

<H2>Collection Created</H2>
The MoreHRDocs collection has been created successfully.

</BODY>

</HTML>
```

Note

Remember that the newly created collection cannot be searched yet because no information has been indexed. You still need to use the <CFINDEX> tag–after the <CFCOLLECTION> tag–to index documents or data from your database tables, as discussed earlier in this chapter.

If the collection already exists on another server in your local network, you can create a mapping to the existing collection, rather than creating a new one. This is useful when you are using several ColdFusion servers in a cluster because only one copy of Verity's internal index files will need to be maintained.

Tip

You also can use these techniques to map to an existing collection that was produced by Verity outside of ColdFusion.

To create the mapping, change the `ACTION` parameter in Listing 36.22 to `MAP` and provide a complete UNC-style path to the collection's folder on the other ColdFusion server. For instance, Listing 36.23 shows the code you could use to create a mapping to the collection named `HRDocs`, which is on another machine named `MAINSERVER` (it's assumed that the `Collections` folder on the other server is available as a share called `Collections`). Note that you can't use a URL in the `PATH` parameter—`PATH` can't start with `http://` to point to another server over the Internet.

Tip

You also can create a mapping with the ColdFusion Administrator by using the Map an Existing Collection option when filling out the onscreen form for a new collection (refer to Figure 36.3).

After the mapping has been created, you can use the `HRDocs` collection name normally in <CFSEARCH> and <CFINDEX> tags. The Verity engine installed on the local ColdFusion server does the indexing and searching work, but it accesses the index files that are located on the other ColdFusion server.

Listing 36.23 `Map.cfm`—**Creating a Mapping to an Existing Collection on Another Server**

```
<!--- Create the Verity collection --->
<CFCOLLECTION
  ACTION="MAP"
  COLLECTION="HRDocs"
  PATH="\\otherserver\drive\cfusion\verity\collections\HRDocs"
>

<HTML>

<HEAD>
```

LISTING 36.23 CONTINUED

```
<TITLE>Creating Verity Collection</TITLE>
</HEAD>

<BODY>

<H2>Collection Created</H2>
The HRDocs collection has been mapped successfully.

</BODY>

</HTML>
```

Note

If you create a collection by using `ACTION="MAP"` to point to an existing collection on another machine, you do not need to index it, assuming it has already been populated. You only need to use `<CFSEARCH>`.

Tip

Depending on how your local network is configured, you might have permissions issues to deal with before ColdFusion can access the files on the other server. On Windows NT, you might need to go to the Services applet in the Control Panel; there you adjust the Windows NT username that the Macromedia ColdFusion service logs in as.

Note

If you delete a collection that was created with `ACTION="MAP"`, Verity's internal index files on the other ColdFusion server do not get deleted–only the mapping itself does. The same goes for collections created using the Map an Existing Collection option in the ColdFusion Administrator, as shown previously in Figure 36.3.

EXPANDING VERITY'S POWER

ColdFusion version 5 introduces a new, more powerful way of using the Verity search engine. When you install ColdFusion (Professional and Enterprise editions), a somewhat limited version of Verity's new K2 server technology is installed as well.

The new K2 server is significantly faster than the VDK version. It also supports simultaneous indexing (which VDK does not). When using ColdFusion Professional Edition, you can index 150,000 documents, and when using ColdFusion Enterprise, you can index 250,000 documents!

Using this powerful new Verity technology is quite simple. Before you can use the K2 server, you must create *aliases* to the collections you want the K2 server to search. You then use `<CFSEARCH>` as you normally would, but you refer to the K2 server alias name for the collection (in the `COLLECTION` attribute) rather than the collection name itself. ColdFusion will then recognize that you are not searching one of the Verity VDK Collections and will direct your search to the Verity K2 server. The section "Starting the Verity K2 Server," later in this chapter describes how you configure the K2 server and create these aliases.

K2 SERVER SETTINGS IN THE COLDFUSION ADMINISTRATOR

You must enter your server's IP address and port (the default is 9900) in the Verity K2 Collection page in the ColdFusion Administrator (see Figure 36.20).

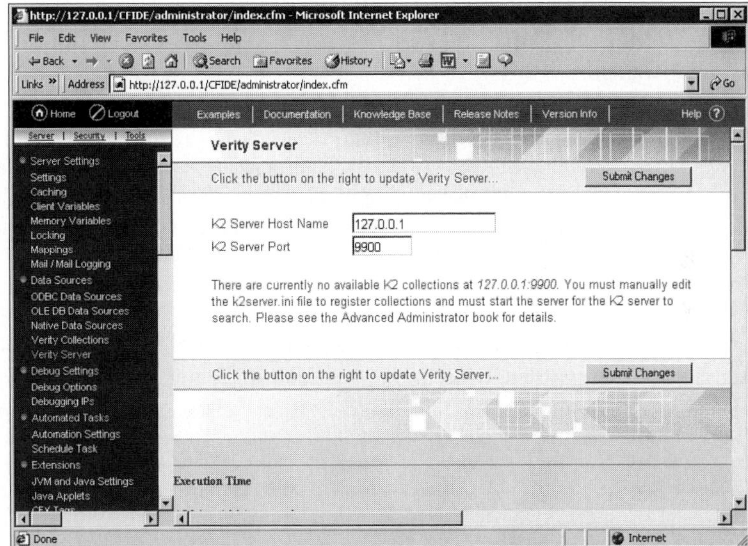

Figure 36.20
The IP address and port for the K2 server default to 127.0.0.1 and 9900, respectively.

STARTING THE VERITY K2 SERVER

You must ensure that your the K2 server is up and running on your machine before your searches can employ it. To verify that it's running under Windows NT or 2000, check the Windows Task Manager. Under the Processes tab, look for k2server.exe, as in Figure 36.21.

The K2 server uses an initialization file that contains a lot of its basic configuration settings. A sample, named `server.ini`, ships with ColdFusion server and is located in the ColdFusion installation directory under `BIN\` (typically, `c:\cfusion\bin`).

Two basic sections must be edited in the `server.ini` file. You must enter a valid server alias with the `serverAlias=` setting, and you must create an entry for each VDK collection you want to search with the K2 server. Listing 36.24 shows the changes you must make to the Server section of the .INI file. You need to specify the full path to where your Verity resources are installed in the `vdkHome` parameter. The default is `c:\cfusion\verity`. You also must specify a name of your K2 server in the `serverAlias` parameter.

Listing 36.24 The Server Section of Your server.ini

```
vdkHome=c:\cfusion\verity
serverAlias=myK2Server
```

Listing 36.25 shows the entries you must make in the section for each collection you want to be searched by the K2 server. You must specify the path to the existing Verity VDK collection. Note that if the collection was built by indexing a group of files, you should point to the `file` subdirectory. If it was built by indexing a query or some other custom data, you should point to the `custom` subdirectory instead. You also must specify the value of the `onLine` parameter.

> **Note**
>
> The value you use in the `vdkHome` setting in your `server.ini` file will be different from the value in Listing 36.24. If you didn't install ColdFusion in the default directory (`c:\cfusion`), that part of the value will be different. The second subdirectory, `verity`, is correct.

With the online parameter set to `0`, the server starts with the collection offline. A value of `1` starts the server with the collection in a hidden state, and a value of `2` starts the server with the collection online. When hidden, a collection can't be searched, but it is primed and tested.

Listing 36.25 The COLL-N Section of Your server.ini

```
[Coll-1]
collPath=c:\cfusion\verity\collections\cfdocumentation\file
collAlias=docs
topicSet=
knowledgeBase=
onLine=2
```

> **Note**
>
> Note again that the path to the collection you want to include will be somewhat different from the example in Listing 36.25. It will be in the `verity\collections` subdirectory below the directory in which you installed ColdFusion. As mentioned earlier in the chapter, the final subdirectory you point to will be either `\file` (as in listing 36.25) or `\custom`. If the collection consists of a ColdFusion query result, use `\custom`; if it consists of a group of files, use `\file`.

Note that you must add new `COLL-N` sections for each VDK collection you want the K2 server to search. Be sure to increment *n* in each new `COLL-N` section you add.

If the K2 server isn't running, you must start it. Assuming you used the default directory when you installed ColdFusion, you can do this from the Windows command line with the following code:

```
C:\cfusion\bin\k2server -inifile c:\cfusion\bin\server.ini
```

Check the Windows Task Manager to verify that the K2 server is running. This is displayed in Figure 36.21.

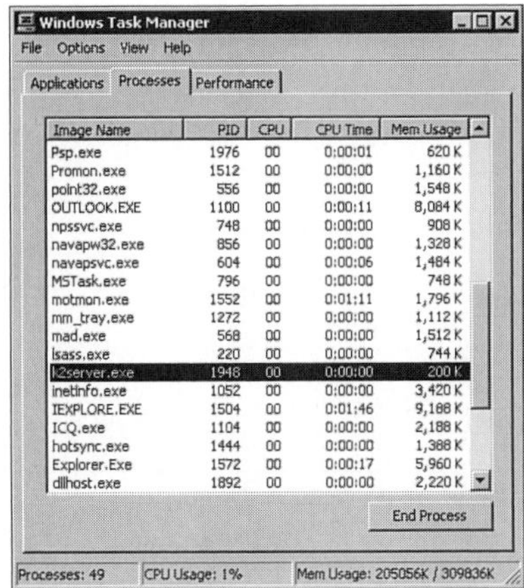

Figure 36.21
You can tell whether the K2 Server is running by checking the Windows Task Manager.

SEARCHING WITH THE VERITY K2 SERVER

As mentioned earlier, to use the Verity K2 Server in your searches, you use `<CFSEARCH>` as you have learned earlier in this chapter. The only change is that instead of referring to one of the VDK collections in the `COLLECTION` parameter, you refer to the alias name specified in the `collAlias` setting in one of the `COLL-N` sections in your `server.ini` file.

In Listing 36.25, the `cfdocumentation` collection was given the alias `docs`. To search this collection with the K2 Server, you'd use `<CFSEARCH>` as demonstrated here:

```
<CFSEARCH COLLECTION="docs" NAME="GetResults" CRITERIA="#Form.Criteria#">
```

UNDERSTANDING VERITY'S SEARCH SYNTAX

You've explored a number of ways to index information and make it searchable on the Web. You've also discovered using AND, OR, and wildcards, which make your search criteria work more easily for you.

It doesn't stop at AND and OR. Verity provides a fairly rich set of operators you can use in your search criteria. Your users probably won't use these operators along with their keywords when they are running a search—most people won't go beyond ANDs and ORs. However, you might, in certain circumstances, want to use some of these operators behind the scenes. Table 36.7 lists all the operators available by category. See Appendix D for explanations of each of the operators listed in Table 36.7.

TABLE 36.7 VERITY OPERATOR QUICK REFERENCE

Category	Operator	Purpose	Description
Concept Operators	`AND`	To find *documents* where:	all words/conditions are found
	`OR`		any one word/condition is found
Evidence Operators	`STEM`	To find *words* that:	are derived from the search words;
	`WORD`		match the search words
	`WILDCARD`		match search words with `*`, `?`, and so on
Proximity Operators	`NEAR`	To find *words* that are:	close together
	`NEAR/N`		within N words of each other
	`PARAGRAPH`		in same paragraph
	`PHRASE`		in same phrase
	`SENTENCE`		in same sentence
Relational Operators	`CONTAINS`	To find *words* that are:	within a specific field (see following)
	`MATCHES`		the text of an entire field
	`STARTS`		at the start of a specific field
	`ENDS`		at the end of a specific field
	`SUBSTRING`		within a specific field as fragments
	`=, <, >, <=, >=`		(for numeric and date values only)
Search Modifiers	`CASE`	To change Verity's behavior so that:	the search is case-sensitive
	`MANY`		documents are ranked by relevance
	`NOT`		matching documents should not be found
	`ORDER`		words must appear in documents in order

Category	Operator	Purpose	Description
Score Operators	YESNO	To *rank* documents found:	equally (no ranking)
	COMPLEMENT		in reverse order
	PRODUCT		by pushing multiple hits up faster
	SUM		by pushing multiple hits up much faster

The document fields you can specify with relational operators, such as CONTAINS, STARTS, ENDS, and so on, are as follows:

- CF_TITLE
- CF_KEY
- CF_URL
- CF_CUSTOM1
- CF_CUSTOM2

These fields correspond to the values (TITLE, KEY, URL, and so on) you specify in the <CFINDEX> tag used to index a collection.

Finally, it's worth noting that ColdFusion employs a limited version of the Verity engine and K2 Server. For example, you can't index more than 250,000 documents with the ColdFusion Enterprise version of the Verity K2 Server. You can overcome these limitations by upgrading to the commercial versions of the Verity products from Verity.

CHAPTER 37

Event Scheduling

In this chapter

Understanding Event Scheduling

Automation has become a normal part of modern life. We set VCRs to record our favorite sitcoms, schedule monthly mortgage payments to be deducted automatically from our checking accounts, and water our lawns with timed sprinkler systems. In short, automation makes our lives easier and increases our efficiency by letting us focus on other, more important tasks.

ColdFusion development is no different. Using event scheduling, you can specify the execution of a CFML template at some point in the future. The event can be scheduled to execute only one time or at a recurring interval. Depending on the template being executed, ColdFusion's event scheduling can become a powerful tool.

Here are some possible uses for event scheduling:

- **Increase site performance**—By scheduling the generation of a static HTML file from a CFML template
- **Perform site maintenance**—By scheduling the update and optimization of a Verity collection
- **Generate e-mails automatically**—By scheduling the creation of a promotional e-mail and sending it automatically

You can schedule events, also called *tasks*, in ColdFusion using two methods:

- The ColdFusion Administrator's Schedule Task page
- The `<CFSCHEDULE>` tag

The Schedule Task page and the `<CFSCHEDULE>` tag contain essentially the same functionality. In fact, the Administrator page is just form-based front-end for the tag. However, there are a few minor differences between the two:

- The Schedule Task page lets you see the entire list of scheduled events in one location.
- Using the Schedule Task page, you don't need to worry about making mistakes in your code.
- If you use the `<CFSCHEDULE>` tag, you don't need access to the Administrator, and you don't need to give others access to the Administrator—an important security consideration for hosting providers.

ColdFusion Event Scheduling Versus Operating System/Database Event Scheduling

Because CFML templates require only an HTTP request (Web browser request) to execute, operating system scheduling facilities can be used to automate tasks as well. Windows NT and Windows 2000 include the Scheduled Tasks feature; Unix-based operating systems, such as Solaris, Linux, and HP-UX, include the cron utility. In addition, many database systems let you create scheduled tasks, such as caching common database queries.

Deciding whether to use your operating system's scheduling facilities or ColdFusion's event scheduling depends more on your circumstances than differences in functionality between the two methods. Here are a few points to consider:

- If you already have a number of tasks scheduled in your operating system, using ColdFusion's event scheduling would separate ColdFusion-centric tasks from other tasks, thereby providing a level of abstraction.
- If you use a hosting provider for your ColdFusion applications, you might not have another choice than to use ColdFusion's event scheduling.
- If you want ColdFusion to manipulate the results of database queries, database event scheduling will not provide enough functionality.
- If you want to build a "trigger" mechanism using ColdFusion to create a scheduled task, such as X number of content additions made in X timeframe causes a scheduled task to increase the frequency of Verity collection updates, ColdFusion's event scheduling is your best choice.
- If you use other Web application platforms in addition to ColdFusion, such as Active Server Pages (ASP) or Perl, that integrate into the operating system itself, you might want to use your operating system's event scheduling facilities.

CREATING, MODIFYING, AND DELETING SCHEDULED TASKS WITH THE COLDFUSION ADMINISTRATOR

The Automated Tasks section of the ColdFusion Administrator lets you create, run, and delete scheduled tasks. It also provides a centralized interface to see all tasks scheduled in your ColdFusion application. However, this also means that developers must have access to the ColdFusion Administrator. Some administrators might not want to give all users access to the Administrator, such as ColdFusion hosting providers.

Note

See Chapter 30, "ColdFusion Server Configuration," for an introduction to the ColdFusion Administration.

When you create a new scheduled task, ColdFusion does not recognize it until the scheduling service searches for new or updated scheduled tasks. You can set the interval for the scheduled service to check for new or updated entries in the Automation Settings page of the Automated Tasks section of the left navigation bar (see Figure 37.1). Once added, the new entry appears in the queue of to-do tasks. ColdFusion checks the scheduled event list every 60 seconds to find out whether any events should be executed at that time.

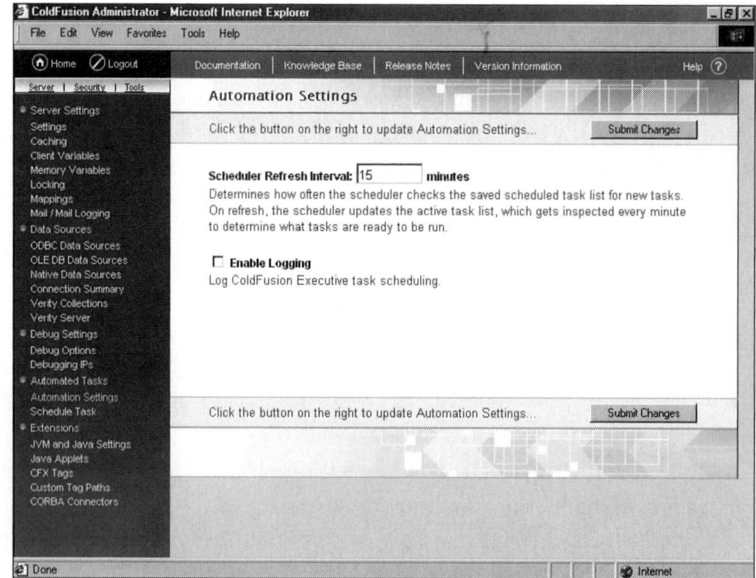

Figure 37.1 The Automation Settings page shows the Scheduler Refresh Interval and Enable Logging options.

You can alter this interval to any number. For example, you could set the refresh interval to `60` (one minute), wait for the scheduling service to run, and then reset it to `900` (15 minutes). This causes the ColdFusion scheduling service to read all new or updated tasks immediately. Even though the scheduling service consumes very little server memory, to preserve server resources, you should keep the refresh interval to at least the default value (`900`) and lower it only when new events are added.

> **Note**
>
> You can also reset the refresh interval by stopping and restarting the ColdFusion service in Windows. However, that is not recommended because it interrupts ColdFusion.

If you want to log scheduled task activity, select the Enable Logging checkbox. The execution of all scheduled files is recorded in the `SCHEDULE.LOG` file, which is located in the `\cfusion\log\` directory. The log is a comma-delimited list of information, each surrounded by quotation marks (see Listing 37.1).

LISTING 37.1 `SCHEDULE.LOG` SAMPLE LINE FROM SCHEDULE LOG

```
"Information","TID=378","07/01/01","20:01:00","Scheduled action FOO, template
http://127.0.0.1/Inetpub/wwwroot/ows/37/OPTIMIZE_COLLECTION.cfm completed
successfully."
```

Table 37.1 Log File Values

Value	Description
`"Information"`	Displays the information
`"TID=378"`	Displays the process's thread ID
`"07/01/01"`	Displays the process's date of execution
`"20:01:00"`	Displays the process's time of execution
`"Scheduled action, Get_Industry_Headlines2, template http://127.0.0.1/Inetpub/wwwroot/ows/37/GetIndustryHeadlines3.cfm completed successfully."`	Displays the template run by a scheduled event

Using the Scheduled Tasks Page to Create Tasks

Open the Schedule Tasks page by clicking the Schedule Task link (located on the left navigation bar). From this page, you can perform all maintenance related to scheduled tasks, including creation, execution, modification, and deletion.

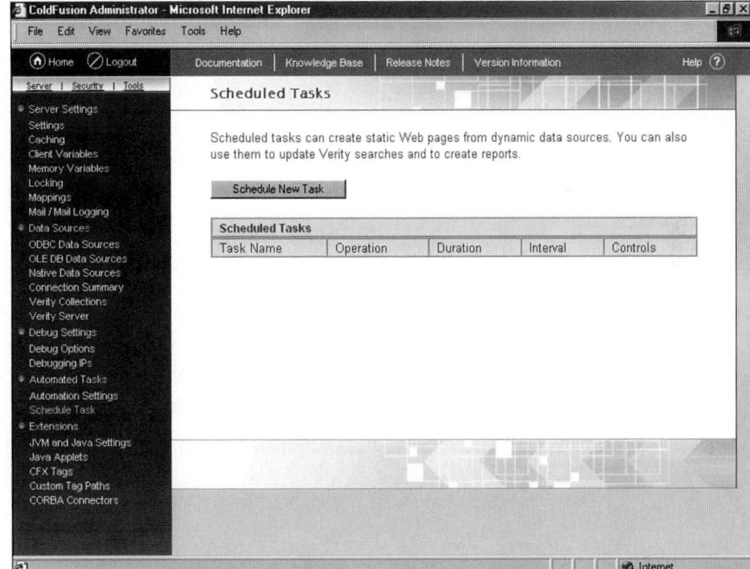

Figure 37.2 The Scheduled Tasks page displays all currently scheduled tasks.

To create a new scheduled task, simply click the Schedule New Task button. As shown in Figure 37.3, this causes the Add/Edit Scheduled Task page to appear.

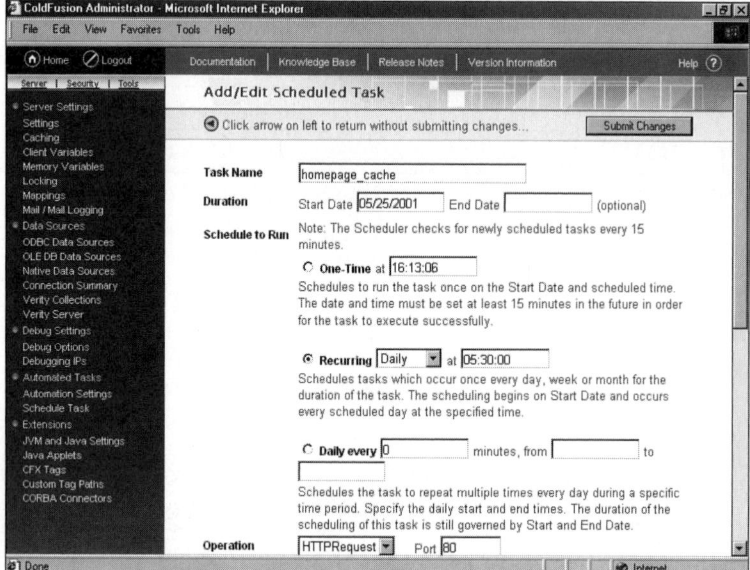

Figure 37.3
Create or modify a scheduled task in the Add/Edit Scheduled Tasks page.

In the Add/Edit Scheduled Task page, you are presented with a variety of options. These options fall into four general categories:

- Name
- Timeframe Options
- Operation
- Publish to a File

Name

Enter a name in the Task Name text box. For this example, the scheduled task executes the OWS home page template and saves the resulting HTML to a static page on the server. Therefore, rather than generating HTML from the OWS home page every time a user requests the file and thereby taxing server resources unnecessarily, this file is sent to users who visit the OWS home page. Name this task `homepage_cache`.

Timeframe Options

In the Duration section, the start date setting defaults to the current date. You should change this value only if you want the scheduled task to execute at some time in the future. Use the end date value to specify the number of days that the task will run. For `homepage_cache`, you want this task to run indefinitely.

In the Schedule to Run section, you can schedule tasks to execute once at a specific time; a recurring time every day, week, or month; or a recurring time every day.

If you click the One-Time radio button to execute a task once. Even though the task will continue to appear in the Scheduled Task page, it will not execute again unless the time and date values are reset.

Note

If no end date is set in the Duration section for a One-Time task, the task will execute once a year.

Click the Recurring radio button and select Daily in the drop-down menu. (Weekly and Monthly are the other options.) In the text box to the right of the drop-down menu, enter **05:30:00** to run the scheduled task at 5:30 a.m. This collects all the new content from the previous day's content changes that appear on the home page.

If you click the radio button for the Daily Every section and you do not need to specify an end date in the Duration section, the scheduled task will run every x number of minutes that you specify. In addition, you must supply times between which the task will execute.

Tip

Remember that every scheduled task that executes a page on your site is the same as any other HTTP request. Thus, it contributes to the overall traffic load, which adds up quickly. As always, you should make every effort to create compact and efficient code, especially for large, highly trafficked sites.

Operation

In the Operation drop-down menu, only one available option appears, HTTPRequest. If necessary, enter the port to use with your Web server. In the URL text box, enter the URL to execute. For the homepage example, use **`http://www.ows.com`**.

Note

Be sure to add a forward slash (/) after the URL if it is an external site, such as `http://www.forta.com/`.

Table 37.2 describes the additional settings in the Add/Edit Scheduled Task page.

Table 37.2 Additional Options in the Add/Edit Scheduled Task Page

Option	Description
Username	Enter a value in the Username text box only if the server your scheduled task will be using requires such authentication.
Password	Enter a value in the Password text box only if the server your scheduled task will be using requires such authentication.
Request Timeout	You should set a timeout value (in seconds) for each scheduled task. This eliminates the chance of the scheduled task request hanging if the server is unavailable.

TABLE 37.2 CONTINUED

Proxy Server	Enter a value in the Proxy Server text box only if your network requires a proxy server to access the Web.
Proxy Port	Enter a value in the Proxy Port text box only if your network requires a proxy server to access the Web.

PUBLISH TO A FILE

Because you want to use the static HTML file for the OWS home page, select the Publish check box to instruct the ColdFusion scheduling service to save the data returned by the `homepage_cache` scheduled task to a file on a local server.

For the example, you want to publish this to a file, so select the Publish check box. For the file path, use `C:\Inetpub\wwwroot\ows\37`, and name the file `homepage_cache`. Because the URLs returned will come from outside servers, you definitely want ColdFusion to resolve all URLs automatically.

The `<CFCACHE>` tag can also be used to cache files. In addition to enabling browser-side caching, the `<CFCACHE>` tag constantly checks to see whether the original template has changed. When it detects a change, it executes the template, saves the resulting HTML to a temporary file, and serves that file to Web browsers.

Although it provides similar functionality, the `<CFCACHE>` tag can't be set to run at a specified time. This does not matter to many developers, but if you have instituted a standard time that all updates go live on the site, such as 7 p.m. every day, scheduled tasks are your best alternative.

Click the Submit Changes button. As shown in Figure 37.4, the scheduled task `homepage_cache` should now appear in the Scheduled Tasks table on the Scheduled Tasks page.

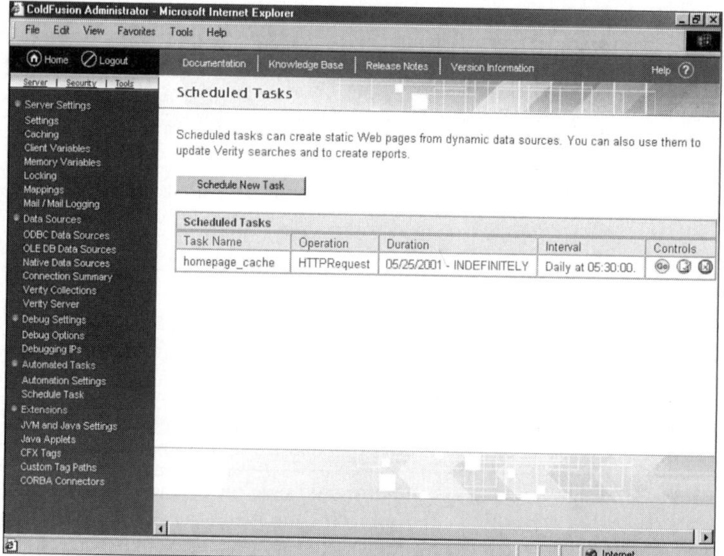

Figure 37.4
The `homepage_cache` scheduled task is now available.

MODIFYING AND DELETING SCHEDULED TASKS IN THE SCHEDULED TASKS PAGE

The Scheduled Task page displays a list of all the scheduled tasks that exist, which operations they are performing (currently limited to HTTP requests), the duration of the tasks, the interval between each execution, and the available controls (see Figure 37.4).

The Scheduled Tasks page also enables you to modify a scheduled task by clicking its name or clicking the corresponding Edit icon. The Add/Edit Scheduled Task page appears in which you can change any setting. When finished making changes, remember to click the Submit Changes button.

To delete a task, simply follow these steps:

1. Click the corresponding Delete icon. A confirmation page will appear.
2. Click the Yes button to delete the task.

Tip

You can also run a scheduled task immediately by clicking the Run Scheduled Task button in the Controls column of the Scheduled Tasks table.

CREATING, MODIFYING, AND DELETING SCHEDULED TASKS WITH THE <CFSCHEDULE> TAG

As described previously in the "Understanding Event Scheduling" section, the ColdFusion Administrator's Automated Tasks section essentially provides a form-based GUI interface for the `<CFSCHEDULE>` tag. In this section, you will use the tag itself to update and optimize Verity collections automatically.

Tip

Even if you want to restrict users' access to the Administrator, you can still let them use the Automated Tasks pages. Copy the appropriate form templates from the Administrator, and use that as a front end when dealing with users who want to add tasks. This is helpful to them, maintains the security of your Administration pages, and ensures that the `<CFSCHEDULE>` tag is always formatted properly. Keep in mind that this means you must write a page to test the data before running the `<CFSCHEDULE>` tag. See Chapter 13, "Form Data Validation," to learn more about data validation.

For the example, let's assume that the summer movie season is about to begin, and the Orange Whip Studios marketing staff is busily updating the site with promotional material for the new releases. The site's contents are changing rapidly and frequently. To keep the site search facilities fresh, update and optimize the Verity collections twice per day.

Let's start by building the template that will update and optimize the Verity collection. For this example, the Verity collection is called `ows`.

UPDATING THE VERITY COLLECTION

The template that actually optimizes the Verity collection is very simple. Look at Listing 37.2.

LISTING 37.2 THE COLLECTION UPDATE AND OPTIMIZATION TEMPLATE

```
<!---
Name:        OPTIMIZE_COLLECTION.cfm
Author:      David Golden (d_golden73@hotmail.com)
Description: ColdFusion Event Scheduling Collection Optimization Template
Created:     4/15/01
--->

<CFINDEX
    ACTION="UPDATE"
    COLLECTION="OWS"
    KEY="OWS"
    TYPE="FILE"
    URLPATH="http://www.ows.com"
    LANGUAGE="English">
</CFINDEX>

<CFCOLLECTION
    ACTION="OPTIMIZE"
    COLLECTION="OWS"
    PATH="C:\CFusion\verity\collections">
</CFCOLLECTION>
```

As you can see in Listing 27.2, you must insert the `<CFINDEX>` tag to update the collection, which reindexes the site files. In addition, you must also insert the `<CFCOLLECTION>` tag to optimize the collection, which consolidates directories within the collection.

Note

See Chapter 36, "Full-Text Searching with Verity," for an introduction to ColdFusion's search functionality.

Save this file as `Optimize_Collection.cfm` in the `37` folder under the `OWS` directory.

Now let's build the scheduling template itself.

USING THE <CFSCHEDULE> TAG

Table 37.3 lists all the `<CFSCHEDULE>` tag attributes and provides a brief description for each attribute. Status items with an asterisk (*) are optional in some cases and required in others. The specific cases in which the attribute is required are always noted.

TABLE 37.3 <CFSCHEDULE> TAG ATTRIBUTES

Attribute	Required	Description
ACTION	Required	Enter DELETE, UPDATE, or RUN to specify which action the schedule task is to perform. UPDATE creates a new task if one does not exist. If a task already exists, UPDATE overwrites the current task of the same name. RUN executes a task now. DELETE removes the task from the list of current tasks.
TASK	Required	Enter the name of the task to update, run, or delete.
OPERATION	Required*	This attribute is required when the ACTION attribute is set to UPDATE. ColdFusion 5 supports only OPERATION="HTTPRequest". It can be used for calling remote and local pages for execution.
STARTDATE	Required*	This attribute is required when the ACTION attribute is set to UPDATE. Enter the date you want the scheduled task to start (in XX/XX/XX format).
STARTTIME	Required*	This attribute is required when the ACTION attribute is set to UPDATE. Enter the time you want the scheduled task to start. This should be a complete time value either in military standard format (13:00:00=1:00:00pm) or with the a.m./p.m. appended to it.
URL	Required*	This attribute is required when the ACTION attribute is set to UPDATE. Enter the URL for the scheduled task to use.
INTERVAL	Required*	This attribute is required when the ACTION attribute is set to UPDATE. Enter the interval for the scheduled task to run. You can use DAILY, WEEKLY, MONTHLY, and EXECUTE (immediately). In addition, you can specify a number of seconds for the scheduled task to execute throughout the day. The INTERVAL attribute defaults to one hour with the minimum interval being one minute
PUBLISH	Optional	Enter either YES or NO to specify whether the results of the scheduled task will be saved to a file.
FILE	Optional*	This attribute is required when the PUBLISH attribute is set to YES. Enter a filename for the results of the scheduled task.
PATH	Optional*	This attribute is required when the PUBLISH attribute is set to YES. Enter the file path for the results of the scheduled task.
ENDDATE	Optional	Specify the date when the scheduled task should end.
ENDTIME	Optional	Specify the time when the scheduled task should end. This value should be in a valid time format.
REQUESTTIMEOUT	Optional	Enter a timeout value for operations that require more time.

Table 37.3 Continued

Attribute	Required	Description
USERNAME	Optional	Specify a username if the URL is protected.
PASSWORD	Optional	Specify a password if the URL is protected.
PROXYSERVER	Optional	Specify a hostname or an IP address of a proxy server.
RESOLVEURL	Optional	Enter either YES or NO. If you are retrieving data from a remote server or an external server instance, this guarantees that links to other pages and graphics still work by changing relative links to fully qualified URLs.
PORT	Optional	If you need to specify a Web server port for the HTTP request, enter a value here. Default is 80. If used in tandem with the RESOLVEURL attribute, the URLs of scheduled task are resolved to preserve links.
PROXYPORT	Optional	If you need to specify a port for the proxy server, enter a value here. Default is 80. If used in tandem with the RESOLVEURL attribute, the URLs of scheduled task are resolved to preserve links.

For this example, you won't use all these attributes (see Listing 37.3).

Listing 37.3 The Collection Optimization and Update Template

```
<!---
Name:        opt_coll_scheduler.cfm
Author:      David Golden (d_golden73@hotmail.com)
Description: Scheduling Template for Optimizing Collections
Created:     4/15/01
--->

<CFSCHEDULE
    ACTION="UPDATE"
    TASK="optimize_collection"
    OPERATION="HTTPRequest"
    URL="/ows/37/optimize_collection.cfm"
    STARTDATE="06/01/01"
    STARTTIME="07:00:00"
    ENDDATE="09/01/01"
    INTERVAL="43200"
    RESOLVEURL="No"
    PUBLISH="No">
</CFSCHEDULE>
```

As Listing 37.3 shows, 10 attributes are used. Here is a listing of the attributes used and what they do:

- `ACTION="UPDATE"`—Creates the scheduled task.
- `TASK="optimize_collection"`—Names the task to be scheduled.

- OPERATION="HTTPRequest"—Specifies the nature of the action.
- STARTDATE="06/01/01"—Creates the date for the scheduled task to begin. This translates to June 1, 2001, the unofficial start of the summer movie season.
- STARTTIME="07:00:00"—Creates the time for the scheduled task to begin. This translates to 1 a.m.
- ENDDATE="09/01/01"—Creates the time for the scheduled task to begin. This translates to September 1, 2001, the unofficial end of the summer movie season.
- INTERVAL="43200"—Creates the interval for ColdFusion to wait before running the scheduled task again. This value translates to the number of seconds in 12 hours. Because you specified 7 a.m. to begin the scheduled task, it will run again at 7 p.m.

Save this file as opt_coll_scheduler.cfm in the 37 folder in the OWS directory, and you're done. You now have a ColdFusion scheduled event that runs twice a day for the rest of the summer and automatically updates and optimizes the Verity collections.

Modifying and Deleting Scheduled Tasks with the <CFSCHEDULE> Tag

To modify a scheduled task, simply open the template file, change any attributes you want, and save the file. The ColdFusion scheduler service will pick up the changes in about a minute.

To delete a schedule task, create a file and insert the <CFSCHEDULE> tag in it. Set the ACTION attribute to "DELETE" and the TASK attribute to the task name you specified when you created the scheduled task; then save the file. For example, the following code would delete the OWS scheduled task:

```
<cfschedule action="DELETE"
    task="OWS">
```

Tip

To execute a scheduled task immediately, simply substitute RUN with DELETE in the previous example.

The <CFSCHEDULE> Button in ColdFusion Studio

One fast and easy way to create the <CFSCHEDULE> code is to use the <CFSCHEDULE> button in ColdFusion Studio (see Figure 37.5). The <CFSCHEDULE> button does not appear on a toolbar by default. Therefore, you must add it to a toolbar. For more information on customizing Studio, see Chapter 8, "Introduction to ColdFusion Studio."

The <CFSCHEDULE> tag editor gives you full access to all attributes. This tag generator does almost everything necessary to write the tag (see Figure 37.6).

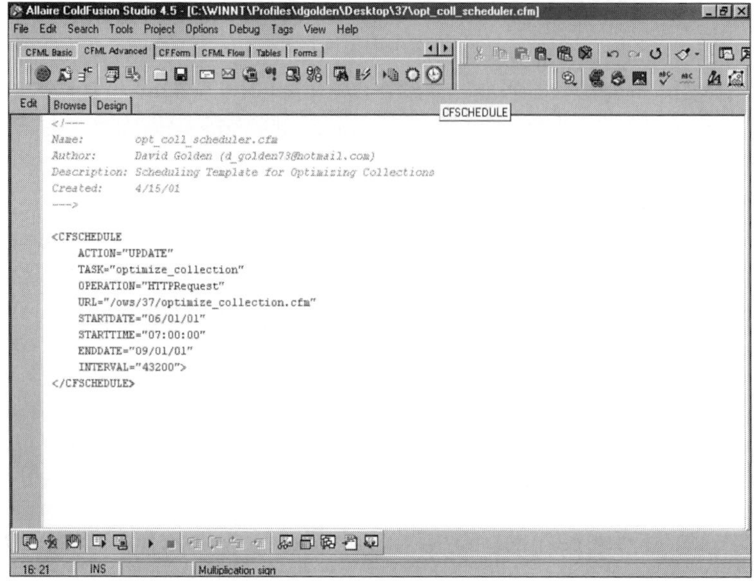

Figure 37.5
The <CFSCHEDULE> button gives you access to the <CFSCHEDULE> tag editor.

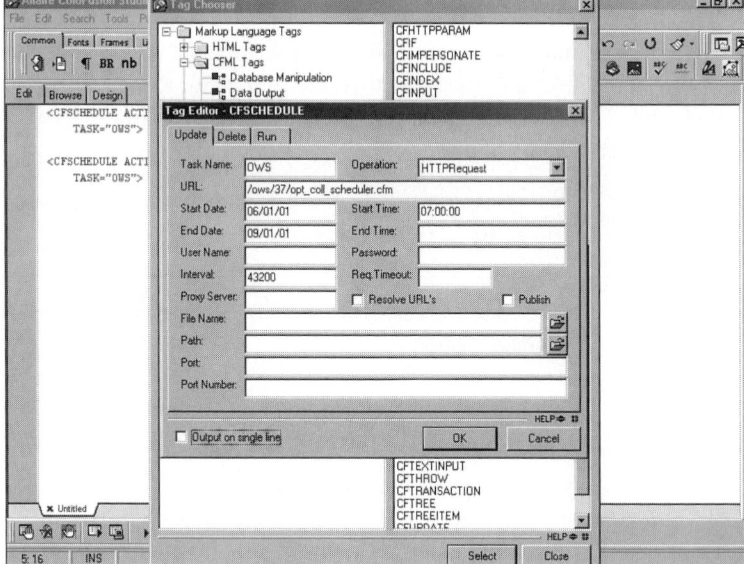

Figure 37.6
The <CFSCHEDULE> tag editor lets you access to all attributes in <CFSCHEDULE>.

BUILDING AN AUTOMATIC PROMOTIONAL E-MAIL APPLICATION

Until now, the sample applications have not employed any database operations. That's about to change.

Let's assume that the OWS marketing department wants to capitalize on the large media blitz underway to support the new releases. It wants you to send out promotional e-mails to local memorabilia dealers once a week that list the current merchandise available at the online store. To make matters tougher, the marketing department wants the e-mail to be waiting in the dealers' inboxes when they first check their e-mail each Monday morning.

Therefore, you must build a ColdFusion application that contains two parts:

- A page that queries the database for the current merchandise available, displays the results in an HTML table, and sends the e-mail page to the group e-mail alias
- A scheduled event page that sends the promotional e-mail once a week on Monday morning

Let's start with the e-mail application.

Building the E-mail Application

The e-mail application consists of two parts: the <CFMAIL> tag that actually sends the e-mail and the <CFQUERY> and <CFOUTPUT> tags that generate the merchandise list (see Listing 37.4).

Listing 37.4 The E-mail Application

```
<!---
Name:        promo_email.cfm
Author:      David Golden (d_golden73@hotmail.com)
Description: Promotional E-Mail Generator
Created:     4/15/01
--->

<!--- Get Merchandise Info from database --->
<CFQUERY NAME="GetMerchInfo" DATASOURCE="ows">
  SELECT *
  FROM Merchandise
  ORDER BY FilmID
</CFQUERY>


<!--- Create HTML E-Mail --->
<cfmail to="dealers@ows.com"
        from="store@ows.com"
        subject="Merchandise Currently Available"
        server="mail.ows.com"
        port=25
        type="HTML"
        groupcasesensitive="Yes">

<!DOCTYPE HTML PUBLIC "-//W3C//DTD HTML 4.0 Transitional//EN">
<HTML>
<HEAD>
    <TITLE>Available Merchandise from OWS Online Store</TITLE>
</HEAD>

<BODY>
```

Listing 37.4 Continued

```
Greetings from Orange Whip Studios!

Here is a list of the merchandise currently
available from the online store at Orange Whip
Studios. To order any of these items, go to
<a href="http://www.ows.com/store">http://www.ows.com/store</a>.

<!--- Display merchandise info --->
<TABLE BORDER="1">
<TR>
 <TH>Item Name</TH>
 <TH>Description</TH>
 <TH>Price</TH>
</TR>
<CFOUTPUT QUERY="GetMerchInfo">
<TR>
 <TD>#GetMerchInfo.MerchName#</TD>
 <TD>#GetMerchInfo.MerchDescription#</TD>
 <TD># DollarFormat (GetMerchInfo.MerchPrice) #</td>
</TR>
</CFOUTPUT>
</TABLE>

</BODY>
</HTML>

</cfmail>
```

The `<CFQUERY>` tag sets the query parameters. The `<CFMAIL>` tag actually sends the e-mail to the recipients. Notice that most of the attributes reflect that of a normal e-mail, such as `TO`, `FROM`, and `SUBJECT`. The HTML page itself is a simple HTML table with a `<CFOUTPUT>` tag wrapping the table rows in which the query variables reside.

Note

See Chapter 28, "Interacting with E-mail," for more information on using ColdFusion to generate e-mails.

Save this file as `promo_email.cfm`. Let's move on to the actual scheduled task.

Building the Scheduled Event

The second part of this application requires building the page that will schedule sending the e-mail. Much like the previous `<CFSCHEDULE>` example, this will be a simple tag. (see Listing 37.5).

Listing 37.5 Sending the E-mail Each Monday

```
<!---
Name:         email_scheduler.cfm
Author:       David Golden (d_golden73@hotmail.com)
```

```
Description: Scheduling Template for Sending Promotional E-Mail
Created:     4/15/01
--->

<CFSCHEDULE
    ACTION="UPDATE"
    TASK="send_email"
    OPERATION="HTTPRequest"
    URL="/ows/37/promo_email.cfm"
    STARTDATE="06/04/01"
    STARTTIME="07:00:00"
    ENDDATE="09/01/01"
    INTERVAL="Weekly">
</CFSCHEDULE>
```


Using the `<CFSCHEDULE>` tag, you set the `promo_email.cfm` to execute every Monday at 7 a.m. (The first Monday in June 2001 is June 4.) Notice the bolded code. Rather than entering the number of seconds in a week, which would amount to a very large number, `"Weekly"` instructs the ColdFusion scheduling service to run the task every seven days.

Note

As an alternative, you could separate the merchandise listing to a separate file and create a scheduled event that would execute the template and save the resulting HTML to a static HTML file. Using the `<CFMAILPARAM>` tag in combination with the `<CFMAIL>` tag, the static HTML file containing the merchandise listing would be attached to the e-mail sent by ColdFusion.

Save this file as `email_scheduler.cfm` in the `37` folder in the `OWS` directory, and you're finished. You now have an application that sends an e-mail automatically containing the current list of available merchandise.

CHAPTER 38

Managing Your Code

In this chapter

CODING STANDARDS

When developing an application with ColdFusion, remember that how you code can sometimes have as much of an effect on your application's performance as what you code. There are some disparate opinions within the community as to which coding methodology is the best choice and how certain CFML operations can and should be performed. In truth, the best methodology is to have a methodology. In Chapter 39, "Development Methodologies," some of the more prevalent ColdFusion development methodologies are discussed in greater detail.

What you need to understand prior to thinking about implementing a specific methodology is that you can do certain things as a developer that can cause degradation in your application's performance. Even though you can code the exact same functionality a hundred different ways, there are some general guidelines you should consider when writing your code. These will help keep your application performing at the best level possible.

Note

The coding standards in this chapter outline some things you should be cautious of as you develop any application with ColdFusion. Some of the most common things you can do as a developer to improve performance are covered in this chapter. As you gain more experience and confidence, you might find that you can add several of your own suggestions to this list.

The guidelines are as follows:

- Avoid overuse of subqueries in a select statement
- Remember to lock all shared scope variables
- Don't reassign variable values with each request
- Don't use if statements to test for existence of variables
- Use `<CFSWITCH/CFCASE>` in place of `<CFIF>`
- Don't overuse the `#` sign
- Avoid overusing the `<CFOUTPUT>` tag
- Comment, comment, comment

AVOID OVERUSE OF SUBQUERIES IN A SELECT STATEMENT

Using subqueries within a select statement can, in some cases, cause a database to create an inefficient execution plan for the overall query. The database has no way to know what the results of the subquery contained in your SQL statement will be, so it is forced to examine the table as many times as there are possible results for the subquery.

In other words, if you can break a large query that contains another query nested inside it into two or three smaller queries, you will generally see page execution time improve.

Remember to Lock All Shared Scope Variables

One of the most powerful features of the ColdFusion Application Server is the capability to create session, server, and application variables. Anything you store in these variables is written directly to the physical memory of the server and can be retrieved for later use in the application.

Although having the ability to store things in server memory is a powerful development tool, it requires you to take some responsibility for application stability if you choose to use any of these three scopes.

One of the things that you must do as a developer to ensure that your code is stable and does not misuse system resources is to consistently use the `<CFLOCK>` tag anytime you are making a read to or a write from the shared scope. Failure to consistently lock these reads and writes can cause memory corruption on the server on which your code is being executed. Memory corruption will in turn cause application instability, and you will begin to see all kinds of strange things appear in your logs as corruption errors are encountered.

Most of the time, this type of corruption becomes evident only when your application starts to see a lot of use. You can avoid any surprises by using `<CFLOCK>` from the very beginning and consistently implementing it through all your code.

When you are going to perform a write to a shared scope variable, use `<CFLOCK>` with the `TYPE="EXCLUSIVE"` attribute, as shown in the following example:

```
<cflock scope="Application" type="exclusive" timeout="10">
    <cfset Application.FirstName = "Laura">
</cflock>
```

When reading from a shared scope variable, use `<CFLOCK>` with the `TYPE="READONLY"` attribute, as shown in the following example:

```
<cflock scope="Application" type="readonly" timeout="10">
    <cfset myNewVar = Application.FirstName >
</cflock>
```

Tip

If you need to perform multiple reads or writes to or from the shared scope, you can put them all in a single `<CFLOCK>` block, provided that everything inside the block is either being read or written to.

You can't mix reads and writes from the shared scope inside a single `<CFLOCK>` tag because the `TYPE` for the lock is defined only once for each `<CFLOCK>` statement.

Don't Reassign Variable Values with Each Request

Developers commonly define certain variables—a data source, for example—inside the `application.cfm` file. There is nothing wrong with doing this, but keep in mind when working with your `application.cfm` file that this file is loaded with each and every page request. Because of this, you should avoid forcing ColdFusion to reassign values to all of the variables inside of your `application.cfm` if they are already present.

One way to avoid this unnecessary processing is to encapsulate variable assignments within a <CFIF> statement. In this way, you can check whether a variable value already has been assigned, instead of asking ColdFusion to perform this work again.

The following example assumes that you are assigning a value to the variable application.datasource within your application.cfm page. This example demonstrates the concept of testing for the existence of this variable and writing a value for the variable only if one is not already present:

```
<cflock scope="Application" type="exclusive" timeout="10">
<cfif NOT IsDefined("Application.DataSource">
    <cfset application.datasource = "MyDSN">
</cfif>
</cflock>
```

Don't Use If Statements to Test for Existence of Variables

If you know that you need to evaluate a specific variable inside a ColdFusion template, you likely will need to check to see whether that variable is already present. Then, if it's not, you should create it and assign a default value to it. You can do this with the <CFIF> statement, as shown in the following code:

```
<cfif NOT IsDefined("myCat")>
    <cfset myCat = "Carbon">
</cfif>
```

This method of testing for the existence of a variable will work, but it is not the most efficient way to perform this task. As a matter of fact, the ColdFusion Markup Language provides an even easier method of testing for the existence of variables and assigning default values. The following example accomplishes the same thing that the previous <CFIF> evaluation accomplished, but in a much more efficient manner:

```
<cfparam name="myCat" default="Carbon">
```

Use <CFSWITCH/CFCASE> in Place of <CFIF>

If you know you will want to have several pieces of code run depending on the value of a single parameter, you might assume that you should just create multiple <CFIF> statements to check for the value of the desired parameter and run the code inside your <CFIF> if that value is met. To demonstrate what I mean, let's think about a task that many developers replicate when first working with ColdFusion. Suppose you are returning a list of users from a database. You want to be able to list these users in alphabetical order by either first name or last name, depending on how the user of your application decides that he best likes these results displayed. To accomplish this, you must allow the user of your application to pass in a simple parameter, perhaps on the URL, telling your application to order the results by either the last names or first names of the users. You could accomplish this as shown in the following example:

```
<cfquery name="ListTheUsers" datasource="MyDSN">
SELECT User.FirstName, User.LastName
FROM   tbl_Users
<CFIF URL.OrderBy EQ "LastName">
```

```
ORDERBY LastName DESC
</CFIF>
<CFIF URL.OrderBy EQ "FirstName">
ORDERBY FirstName DESC
</CFIF>
</CFQUERY>
```

Now, even though the preceding code will work to accomplish your goal, ColdFusion provides you with a more efficient way to complete this type of evaluation—using the `<CFSWITCH/CFCASE>` tags, as shown in the following example:

```
<cfquery name="ListTheUsers" datasource="MyDSN">
SELECT User.FirstName, User.LastName
FROM   tbl_Users
<CFSWITCH EXPRESSION="URL.OrderBy">
<CFCASE VALUE="LastName">
ORDERBY LastName DESC
</CFCASE>
<CFCASE VALUE="FirstName">
ORDERBY FirstName DESC
</CFCASE>
<CFDEFAULTCASE>
ORDERBY LastName DESC
</CFDEFAULTCASE>
</CFSWITCH>
</CFQUERY>
```


Both of these examples produce the same results, but using the `<CFSWITCH/CFCASE>` tags doesn't force evaluation of logic unless the specific conditions being watched for are met, making it more efficient than a long list of `<CFIF>` statements.

Don't Overuse the # Sign

As you get started with ColdFusion, one of the characters you will become most familiar with typing is the # sign. Surrounding a variable, function call, or variable-function combination with the # sign flags that bit of code to let ColdFusion know that it is a variable you want ColdFusion to evaluate. Otherwise, the ColdFusion engine would have no way of distinguishing what you wanted evaluated from other text within your CFML templates.

Any time a variable is used as a parameter for a standard CFML tag, the pound signs are not necessary, as shown in the following example:

```
<cif #MyName# = "John">
    <!--- Some conditional ColdFusion code --->
</cfif>
```

This is the same thing as

```
<cif MyName = "John">
    <!--- Some conditional ColdFusion code --->
</cfif>
```

Notice how having the # sign around the `"MyName"` variable makes no difference in how the code is processed.

Now, let's assume that you wanted to run a special bit of code if, in fact, my name is John. The following example demonstrates this:

```
<cfif myName = "John">
    <cfset formAction = "updateData.cfm?MyName=#MyName#">
</cfif>
```

Notice how, in the preceding code, when you want to use the "MyName" variable as part of a URL, pound signs are required to let ColdFusion know you want this variable to be evaluated so that the string "John" will be passed to the page you're calling. Without the pound signs here, the string "MyName" is passed to the next page.

AVOID OVERUSING THE <CFOUTPUT> TAG

In general, you should try to use as few <CFOUTPUT> tags per page as possible. Overusing the <CFOUTPUT> tag can put undue strain on the ColdFusion parser, and under heavy load conditions this potentially can slow down your application. Because of this, you should try to combine as much of your code as possible that requires <CFOUTPUT> statements in to a single <CFOUTPUT> block. The following example demonstrates <CFOUTPUT> being overused in a CFML template and subsequently shows how to correct that problem:

```
<input type="text" value="<cfoutput>#Variable1#</cfoutput>"
<input type="text" value="<cfoutput>#Variable2#</cfoutput>"
<input type="text" value="<cfoutput>#Variable3#</cfoutput>"
```

The preceding code will work as you would expect it to, but using multiple output statements in this way creates a lot of extra work for ColdFusion's parser. A much better way to code this and achieve the same result is demonstrated in the following example:

```
<cfoutput>
    <input type="text" value="#Variable1#">
    <input type="text" value="#Variable2#">
    <input type="text" value="#Variable3#">
</cfoutput>
```

COMMENT, COMMENT, COMMENT

Nothing is more frustrating than having to dig into another developer's code attempting to resolve a problem or add functionality, only to discover that none of the code you have to work with has been commented.

Trying to follow the flow of uncommented code is not unlike trying to find your way around an unfamiliar city without a map. You have no idea what the person before you was doing or what her thought process was in developing her code. This can make your job extremely difficult if you are tasked with doing something with another developer's uncommented code base.

Be conscious of these truths when developing your own application, and be sure that you effectively comment your own CFML code. Place comments in your code that will make it easier for someone else to come in behind you and pick up work right where you left off. Ensure that comments are clear, concise, easy to understand, and relevant to the code. You might find that in six months or so you won't even be able to remember how you accomplished a specific task within your code. Having comments there to guide you will help get you thinking the way you were thinking when the code was written.

DOCUMENTATION

By nature, the first thing any ColdFusion developer wants to do when presented with a project is open ColdFusion Studio and start coding away. That's understandable because writing the code is the fun part and the part that most of us became ColdFusion developers to actually do.

Still, you must consider a few other things if you really want your development project to be successful. One of the most important of these is ensuring that you have every step of the project documented as clearly and completely as possible.

Finding out exactly what works for you in the way of project documentation is a deeply personal process. Keep in mind that there really is no right or wrong in this regard. So long as you are aware that your project, from start to finish, needs to be documented completely, how you choose to do it is not that important.

Table 38.1 outlines some key steps you should take along the path to complete documentation of a project of any size to ensure that you have a complete record.

TABLE 38.1 STEPS TO COMPLETE DOCUMENTATION OF A PROJECT

Item	Description
Key Players	Be sure you have a record of all the people who are involved in the project, along with a description of what their specific roles and responsibilities are relevant to this project.
Application Diagram	One of the first steps to building a successful ColdFusion application is laying out that application on paper before you begin to code. This way, by the time you start development, you already will have solved many problems.
Problem/Solution Guides	As you begin to actually work through the development of your application, you will undoubtedly encounter some unexpected—and perhaps complex—problems. Be sure you keep a good record of what these problems were and how they were solved. Not only do these documents add to your understanding of the current application, but they also provide a valuable reference should you run into a similar problem in the future.
Lists of Resources	Be sure to keep a good record of all resources involved in the development of a specific application. In this instance, the term *resources* refers to all CFML templates, their functions in the application, and their archived locations, as well as references to any data sources or third-party software used in conjunction with the application.

Part of having complete documentation of any project is making sure that all the CFML templates used in any application are commented completely and clearly. Remember to comment your code along the way so you or anyone else can come back to any file and easily determine its function and logic flow.

VERSION CONTROL

In the development of any ColdFusion application, the ability to control access to the templates being developed, track changes, and roll back to earlier versions if necessary is an important part of ensuring that the application is completed on time and the entire project is successful.

Often, developers today work within teams made up of other developers, sometimes dispersed over large geographic distances. In these cases, it is also important to know that what you are working on isn't affecting what someone else has already done, or will be doing in the near future.

Oftentimes, a developer will experiment with his code, only to find that a change that was made has just created a template that no longer functions. Worse still, a template can be changed by someone else and no longer function, in which case it is extremely helpful to have the ability to roll back to a known stable version of the code.

Implementing some form of version control speaks to all these issues. Having version control in place enables you to know which developer, regardless of where he or she is located, made changes to any given template. You have the ability to roll back to previous versions of code if an unexpected error is encountered, and you can allow large groups of people to work on the same project without having to worry about them stepping on each other's work.

PLANNING FOR VERSION CONTROLLING

Before you jump into implementing a version-controlling solution, you need to ask yourself some questions about how your project will be designed, implemented, and managed. You should look at all the people who will be involved in working on the project, as well as how the project itself will be organized.

You can save yourself some time by answering the following questions before you attempt to implement a specific version-controlling solution:

- **Should I define this as a single project?**—Chances are, if the application you are developing is of any size, you should consider dividing the development into multiple "subprojects" beneath the banner of a larger, all encompassing project. A good example of this is if you will be developing an administrative section of the site, as most developers do. This type of functionality would be a good candidate for a subproject that could reside in a layer below the larger application project.

- **What does the development team look like?**—Who are you working with on this project? Chances are, if you're implementing source control, you aren't the sole developer. You must clearly define the role and responsibilities of each person involved with the development process so that you can determine which members of the team need access to which resources. Try to avoid giving team members unnecessary access to resources for which they are not directly responsible or on which they shouldn't be working.
- **Where will the source files reside?**—Determine where you want to store the project database and source files. The location you choose should be convenient to all those involved with the project.

After you've answered all these questions, you can begin to think about the version-controlling system you want to implement.

VERSION-CONTROLLING SYSTEMS

Several good third-party tools provide version controlling for ColdFusion code. Most of these tools share some common key functionality:

- The capability to control access to source files
- The capability to log changes to files as they occur
- Maintenance of old source files providing rollback capabilities
- An easy way to compare an older version of the source to the current version

Having a version-controlling system in place is particularly important when your development team is large or members of the team are far away from one another. It is also very important to have version controlling in place if your project is likely to have a long life span, in which case there might be several builds of the application in existence at any given time.

After you understand why it's important to consider putting a version-controlling system in place, you can begin to examine which version-controlling software is right for you. As mentioned earlier, most of these systems have similar core functionality, but the degree to which they allow you to manipulate the source, track changes, and roll back coding errors fluctuates with quality and price. The various products available run the gamut from freeware tools to solutions that can be extremely pricey.

For the purposes of this book, we'll look at two of the most popular and widely used version-controlling products on the market today: Microsoft's Visual SourceSafe (VSS) and Merant's PVCS product.

MICROSOFT VISUAL SOURCESAFE

VSS enables you to create and manage projects that consist of many types of files, from CFML code and images to sound and video files.

When working with a project that is managed in Visual SourceSafe, a project database is set up that enables you to store recent and past versions of source files (including code and supporting documentation), track access to those files, and re-create previous versions of any file.

When any user working with you on a project wants to make changes to a file, the file must be *checked out*, which effectively locks any other users from being able to make modifications to the same file while it is in the checked out state.

If all your developers are not in the same location as your source file database, third-party plug-ins for VSS exist that enable those offsite developers to gain access to the VSS database using a standard TCP/IP connection and Web browser. This enables developers working in separate physical locations to safely contribute to the same project without having to worry about gaining access to specific network resources.

If you are using Macromedia's ColdFusion Studio to develop your CFML code, you can use the Projects tool within ColdFusion Studio to integrate directly with VSS. In this instance, the machine on which you are running your copy of ColdFusion Studio will act as a VSS client, connecting to a predefined VSS server to work on a project.

Caution

When talking about integrating a version-controlling product with ColdFusion Studio, the language can get confusing, primarily because you have the ability to create "projects" inside ColdFusion Studio. Be aware that, although you must create a ColdFusion Studio project to integrate with a Visual SourceSafe project, the two are not the same and can exist independently of one another.

Integrating VSS with ColdFusion Studio

To integrate a Visual SourceSafe project with ColdFusion Studio, you first must have created the VSS project by following the instructions included with the VSS software.

After this project is set up, you can take on the task of setting up your copy of ColdFusion Studio to work with this project. This is a relatively simple thing to do.

The first step is to create a project from within ColdFusion Studio. Open your copy of ColdFusion Studio and from the toolbar, select Project, New Project, as shown in Figure 38.1.

Tip

Before you create your new ColdFusion Studio project, copy the directory structure from your VSS project over to your local machine, and then point your new Studio project to this directory with the Include Subfolders flag checked. This will make it much easier for you when you get ready to integrate your Studio project with your VSS project.

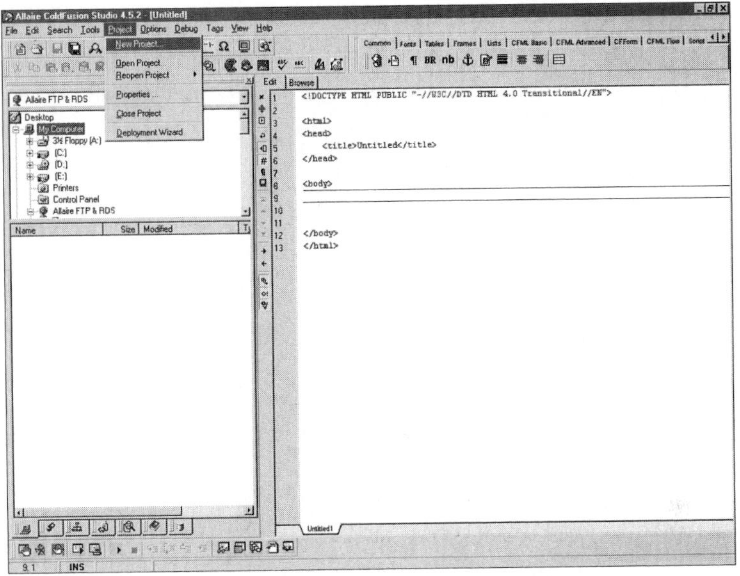

Figure 38.1
Step 1: Create a new project in ColdFusion Studio.

You will see a context dialog box similar to the one shown in Figure 38.2. Enter the name for your new project in the Project Name box. Next, enter the directory in which you want the `.apf` file (the file that holds the definitions for your Studio project) saved, or click the folder icon to browse to a directory for saving this file. If the directory you are browsing to contains any subfolders, check the Add All Subfolders check box if you want to have these included. After you click OK, the project will show up under the projects tab in ColdFusion Studio, as shown in Figure 38.3.

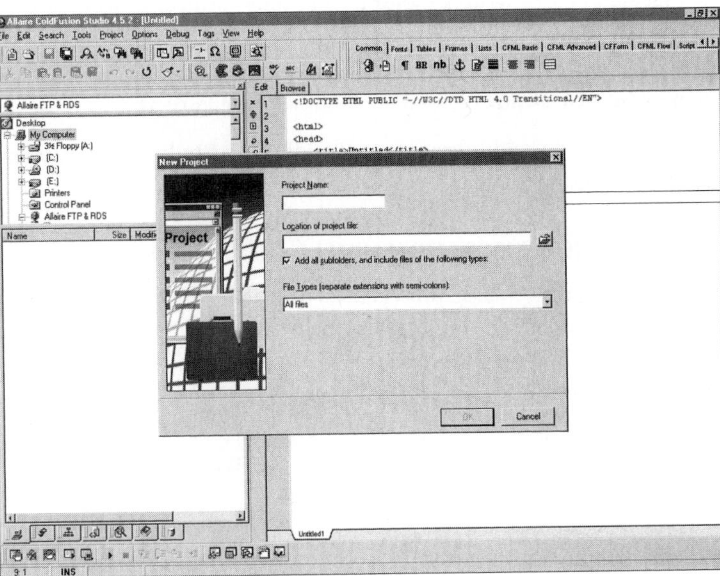

Figure 38.2
Step 2: Define the project name and locations of the files.

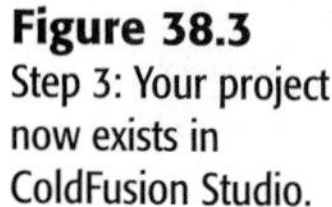

Figure 38.3
Step 3: Your project now exists in ColdFusion Studio.

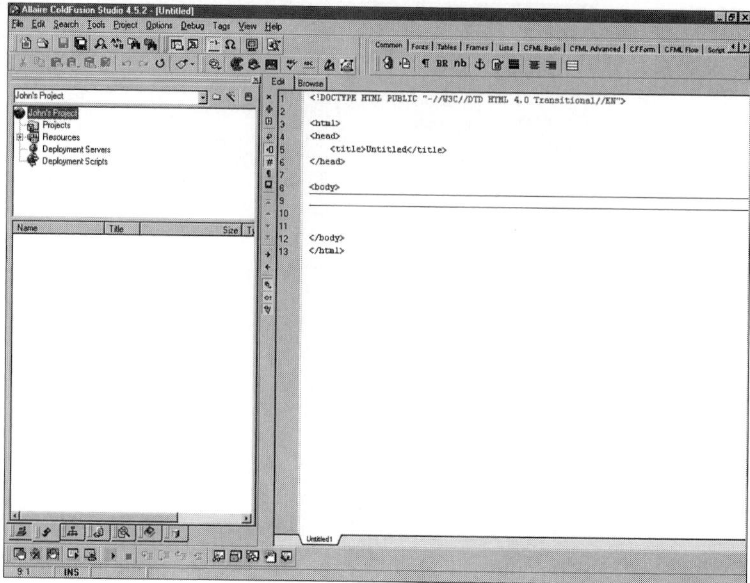

Now you are ready to integrate the project you just created inside ColdFusion Studio with your Microsoft Visual SourceSafe project.

If you look at Figure 38.3, you'll see that a project is now displayed under the projects tab in ColdFusion Studio, called John's Project. If I right mouse-click the project name (the main project name will always have the globe icon next to it), a list of various actions that can be performed on this project is displayed.

The first step in setting up a ColdFusion Studio project to work with a Visual SourceSafe project is to point the Studio project to a source control provider. You can do this by right-clicking the project name, and then selecting from the pop-up menu Source Control, Choose a Source Control Provider, as shown in Figure 38.4.

Now all you need to do is point your ColdFusion Studio project to your Visual SourceSafe project to integrate the two.

Merant PVCS and Integration with ColdFusion Studio

Similar to Microsoft Visual SourceSafe, Merant PVCS provides the same basic source control functionality. Integrating Microsoft Visual SourceSafe projects with ColdFusion Studio is a relatively simple operation, as is ColdFusion Studio's integration with Merant PVCS. You go through the same steps to integrate PVCS with Studio as you would to integrate VSS with Studio—the only difference being that you choose a different source control provider when you come to that step. Also, this time you point ColdFusion Studio to your PVCS project root.

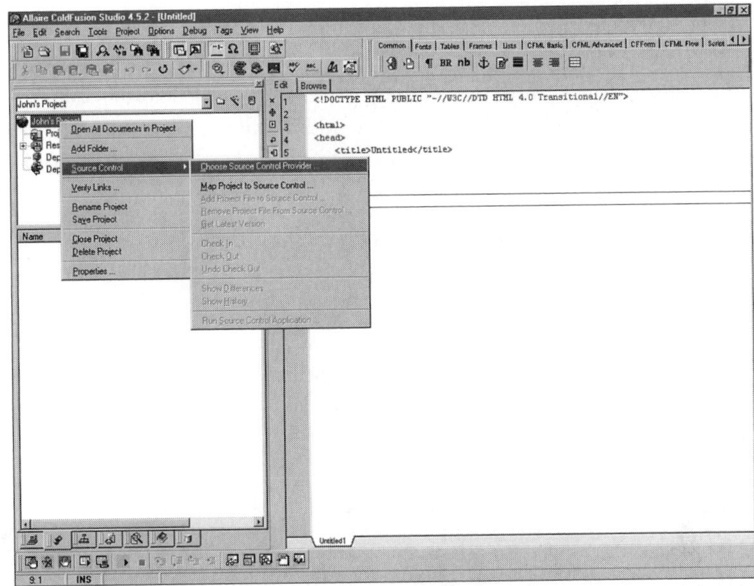

Figure 38.4
Choosing a source control provider for your project.

MULTIPLE USERS AND INTEGRATION WITH COLDFUSION STUDIO

When you are dealing with multiple developers, all of whom will be accessing your VSS or PVCS source database through a Studio project, you must perform a few special steps to ensure that all your developers can share access to the version-controlling software through the ColdFusion Studio project.

In this case, each of the developers accessing the source database through ColdFusion Studio will act as a client of the version-controlling software, as demonstrated in Figure 38.5.

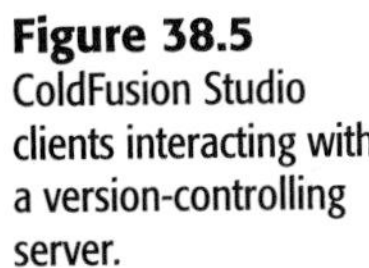

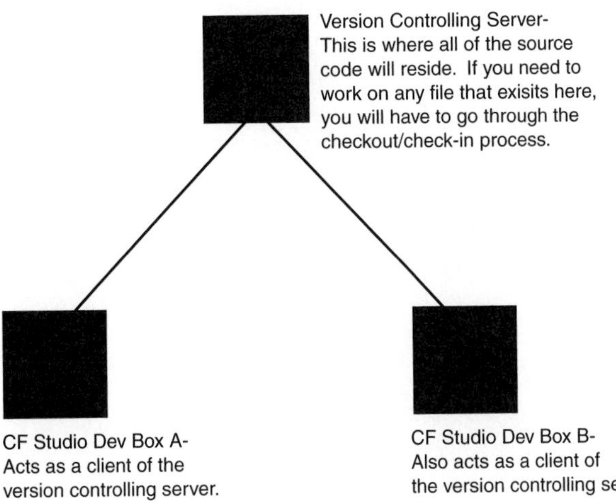

Figure 38.5
ColdFusion Studio clients interacting with a version-controlling server.

Because your copy of ColdFusion Studio is now essentially a client of the version-controlling server, and you are now working within a ColdFusion Studio project as well, each time you add a file or folder anywhere under the root directory of your ColdFusion Studio project, you will be asked whether you want to add the file to your Studio project and whether you want to add it to your source control project. In most cases, you should answer yes to both of these questions.

Each time you open ColdFusion Studio while working as a client of a version-controlling system, you should ensure that you have the latest copy of the source files and tree displayed locally on your machine. To do this, each time you open Studio, go to the Projects tab, right-click your ColdFusion Studio project name, and select Run Source Control Application. After your source control application is running, right-click the project name again and select Get Latest Version. After you've done this, you'll see the dialog box shown in Figure 38.6.

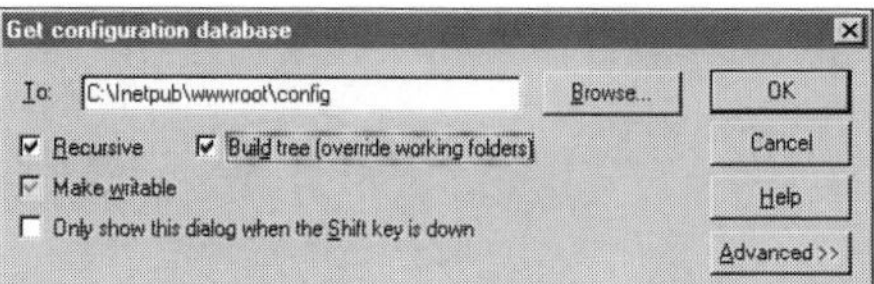

Figure 38.6
Be sure ColdFusion Studio is set up to run against the latest version of your code.

Check both the Recursive and Build Tree options. You must do this each time you open ColdFusion Studio to work as a client of your version-controlling system. You also must do this on each developer's machine that is running Studio as a client of your version-controlling system.

CHAPTER 39

Development Methodologies

In this chapter

WHY USE A DEVELOPMENT METHODOLOGY?

If you've been building Web applications for a while, you've probably run into this situation: You're asked to work on something that you originally wrote many months ago. Perhaps you're asked to change the way a complex set of forms works. As you pour over your old code, you're bewildered and having a bit of difficulty figuring out which pages call which and why you did certain things the way you did. Sound familiar?

Of course, this can happen to the most experienced developer. You should recognize that when you spend *n* hours developing an application, you will probably spend 2*n* or 3*n* hours maintaining the application over time. The predicament described in the previous paragraph can be largely avoided—or at least significantly mitigated—by employing a well-defined and thought-out development methodology.

A good development methodology defines file—and perhaps other—naming conventions. It provides an organizational structure for your application directories and source files (Web pages, ColdFusion templates, graphical images, and other content). It also probably provides directives on how to structure your program code as well.

Employing these types of conventions enables you to more easily maintain your code. It also enables a team of developers—all employing the same methodology—to debug and support each other's code. Take it one step further, and it's easy to imagine how a methodology employed by unrelated individuals can produce code that can be understood and maintained by anyone who uses the methodology.

A robust methodology also enables you to build large applications with many, many sections and pages. The methodology provides a meaningful way of organizing all the content and program logic so as to make maintaining it easier.

So, development methodologies are useful to individuals because we can't remember how we programmed something a long time ago (or sometimes, just last week!). Development methodologies are useful to teams and remote programmers because they make the team members more interchangeable and better able to support each other's efforts. And development methodologies are useful when organizing large applications with many components and pages.

This chapter looks at two methodologies—Fusebox and cfObjects—in detail and provides an overview of several others. Let's say you need to build a simple contact manager for Orange Whip Studios. In this chapter, you construct a simple contact manager in both Fusebox and cfObjects so you can better understand how these frameworks address a common application.

Note

For more information on cfObjects, see `http://www.cfobjects.com`.

FUSEBOX

First developed in 1998, Fusebox is the granddaddy of all ColdFusion development methodologies. Steve Nelson and Gabe Roffman are responsible for creating the original Fusebox specification, and Joshua Cyr was perhaps the first person to employ the methodology on a real application. Many ColdFusion developers have subsequently contributed to and popularized the Fusebox methodology.

Partly because of its longevity, but mostly because of its practicality, Fusebox is perhaps the most widely used ColdFusion development methodology. (It's worth noting that it isn't really specific to ColdFusion per se. It can be applied—and is being developed—for other development environments.)

Fusebox enables you to write applications so they are easily ported and reused. It provides a set of directory and filenaming conventions that enable anyone familiar with the methodology to easily understand someone else's code. It also defines a number of special templates that are used for controlling program flow and managing global variables.

The basic idea behind Fusebox is that you develop applications that resemble the fuse box in your house (see Figure 39.1, later in this chapter). All the circuits (business functions) come from the fuse box (the main template that controls program flow to the sections). The concept extends beyond the fuse box/circuitry metaphor to make it possible to develop application components as standalone, miniapplications that are relatively portable and interchangeable.

HOW FUSEBOX WORKS

To build an application, you create a directory for the application and place a file named `index.cfm` in the home directory. The `index.cfm` file is essentially just a `switch/case` statement. In the metaphor, it is the fuse box. The fuse box (`index.cfm`) gets requests through the URL variable, form variable, or attribute named `fuseaction`. The box directs all user requests for various application functions to the appropriate part of your application in a `switch/case` statement. Each `fuseaction` corresponds to a business function and leads to either a fuse or a circuit. A *fuse* is a template that executes a function. A *circuit* is a subapplication within your application. You can see a sample box in Listing 39.1.

LISTING 39.1 AN `index.cfm` TEMPLATE IN A FUSEBOX APPLICATION

```
<CFSWITCH EXPRESSION="#Attributes.Fuseaction#">
<CFCASE VALUE="MainApp">
  <CFINCLUDE TEMPLATE="dsp_main.cfm">
</CFCASE>
<CFCASE VALUE="Search">
  <CFINCLUDE TEMPLATE="dsp_searchform.cfm">
</CFCASE>
<CFCASE VALUE="MaintainProfile">
  <CFINCLUDE TEMPLATE="dsp_profile.cfm">
```

Listing 39.1 Continued

```
</CFCASE>
<CFCASE VALUE="Forum">
  <CFINCLUDE TEMPLATE="dsp_forum.cfm">
</CFCASE>
</CFSWITCH>
```

When an application is large enough to be broken down into smaller component applications, each application is put in a subdirectory with its own `index.cfm`. These are referred to as *circuits*.

Five types of fuses exist, as presented in Table 39.1.

Table 39.1 Fuse Template Types

Fuse	Description
Application	`app_Locals.cfm` is used to define variables that are local to the circuit. `app_Globals.cfm` is used to define variables that are global to the entire application and all circuits. These files are included in other files.
Display	You create display files to display content to the user, which are named like `dsp_MyFile.cfm`. These files don't modify anything on the server or perform any actions.
Action	You create action files to perform actions on the server, which are named like `act_MyAction.cfm`. Action templates do tasks such as updating data and sending e-mail.
Query	Named `qry_MyQuery.cfm`, query files execute queries and stored procedures, usually one per file.
Custom tags	These are ColdFusion custom tags. These can be written in ColdFusion or—when using the CFAPI—in C++, Delphi, or Java.

Note that when following the Fusebox methodology, you do not use the ColdFusion `Application.cfm` file. One of the early goals of Fusebox was to provide a mechanism for running an entire application as a custom tag. Because `Application.cfm` is not automatically invoked inside custom tags, it isn't considered useful. So, you use the application fuses—`app_Globals.cfm` and `app_Locals.cfm`—instead.

Note also that you are not supposed to invoke fuses directly. You always invoke fuses through the box (`index.cfm`) by passing it the appropriate `fuseaction` param, for example

```
<A HREF="index.cfm?fuseaction=Search">Search the site</A>
```

If your application is programmed this way, anyone should be able to look at the `index.cfm` and determine which template performs a particular action.

An `index.cfm` template in a Fusebox application normally contains the following tags at the top:

```
<CFINCLUDE TEMPLATE="app_Locals.cfm">
```

The `app_Locals.cfm` template is included so that variables local to this box are defined before any fuse template is included. It also includes the `app_Globals.cfm` file to ensure that all variables global to the entire application are defined. Here's what an `app_Locals.cfm` template might look like:

```
<!--- in app_Locals.cfm --->
<CFINCLUDE TEMPLATE="../app_Globals.cfm">
<CFPARAM NAME="MyLocalVar" DEFAULT="value">
```

The `app_Globals.cfm` template serves several purposes. First, it defines variables global to the application and all its component applications. Second, it executes the `Formurl2attributes.cfm` custom tag, which converts all form and URL variables to the `ATTRIBUTES` scope. The intent is to enable the application to function as a standalone application or custom tag. Finally, it is used to execute the `<CFAPPLICATION>` tag. A sample `app_Globals.cfm` template is presented later in this chapter, in Listing 39.2.

When you're producing a larger application, you'll probably want to break it up into smaller functional chunks. Each of these chunks is referred to as a *circuit application*. Each has its own directory, `index.cfm`, `app_Locals.cfm`, and associated template files. Its `app_Locals.cfm` file will include the `app_Globals.cfm` for the entire application.

Figure 39.1 depicts how a typical Fusebox application might look. The figure presents a box (an `index.cfm`) and its branching logic. It is invoked through a URL and is passed a `fuseaction` that tells it which function a user is requesting. The box's branching logic tells it which fuses or circuit applications to run.

Figure 39.1
Fusebox works like the fuse box in your house.

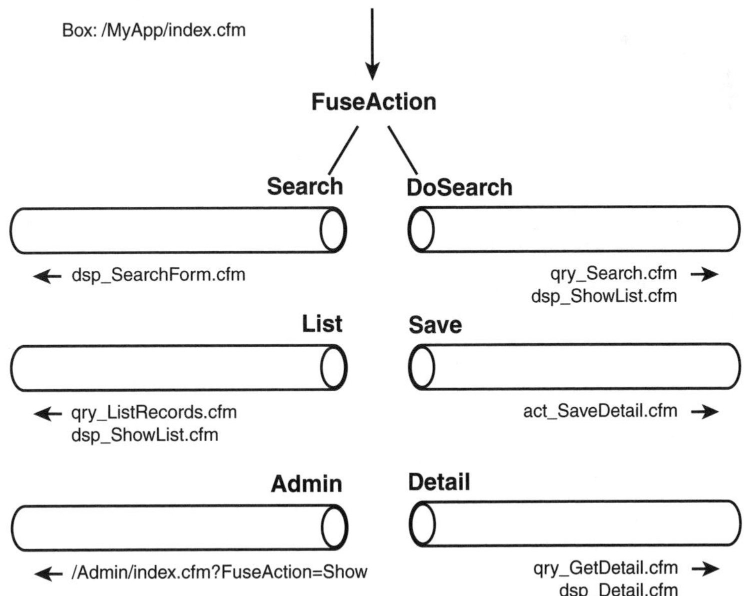

BUILDING A SIMPLE CONTACT MANAGER WITH FUSEBOX

Now that you understand a bit of the mechanics behind Fusebox, let's review an example of how the Fusebox methodology could be used by Orange Whip Studios to build a simple contact manager. The main templates used in this application are described in Table 39.2.

The contact manager enables Orange Whip Studios to list, view, create, update, and delete contact records.

TABLE 39.2 FUSEBOX CONTACT MANAGER TEMPLATES

Template	Description
`app_Globals.cfm`	Defines data source name and executes the `FormURL2Attributes.cfm` custom tag.
`app_Locals.cfm`	Creates a few local variables.
`index.cfm`	The `index.cfm` file is passed the `fuseaction` URL variable to indicate which action the user has requested. It then includes the appropriate templates.
`qry_GetAllContacts.cfm`	Runs a query to get the list of contacts.
`qry_GetContactRecord.cfm`	Selects a specified contact or returns an empty recordset.
`FormURL2Attributes.cfm`	This custom tag converts all `FORM` and URL variables to `ATTRIBUTES` scope.
`dsp_ContactList.cfm`	Displays a list of contacts, grouped by last name.
`dsp_ContactForm.cfm`	Template with a form for creating and modifying contact records.
`Dsp_Menu.cfm`	Creates a simple drop-down list that acts as a menu.
`dsp_ContactDetail.cfm`	Form for viewing a contact record.
`act_ContactUpdate.cfm`	Queries for either inserting, updating, or deleting contact records.

DEFINING GLOBAL VARIABLES

This is a very simplistic application, but it effectively demonstrates the basic Fusebox constructs we've been talking about. Let's first look at the `app_Globals.cfm` file for this application, seen in Listing 39.2.

LISTING 39.2 `app_Globals.cfm` CALLS THE `FormURL2Attributes` CUSTOM TAG

```
<CFSETTING ENABLECFOUTPUTONLY="Yes">

<!--- define an application --->
<CFAPPLICATION NAME="FuseActionContact">

<CFPARAM NAME="DSN" default="OWS">
```

```
<CFIF NOT ISDEFINED("attributes.fuseaction")>
   <CFMODULE TEMPLATE="formURL2attributes.CFM">
</CFIF>

<CFSETTING ENABLECFOUTPUTONLY="No">
```

Note that `app_Globals.cfm` defines variables global to an entire application or set of related applications. It is included in `app_Locals.cfm`. `app_Locals.cfm` is included in your `index.cfm`, so it's executed for every page included in `index.cfm`. `app_Locals.cfm` is used to define variables local to just this application (your contact manager). It is presented in Listing 39.3, and `index.cfm` is presented in Listing 39.4.

LISTING 39.3 `app_Locals.cfm` DEFINES THE DEFAULT `fuseaction`

```
<CFINCLUDE TEMPLATE="app_globals.cfm">
<CFPARAM NAME="Attributes.fuseaction" DEFAULT="contactlist">
```

YOUR CONTACT MANAGER'S FUSE BOX

LISTING 39.4 AN `index.cfm` TEMPLATE IN A FUSEBOX APPLICATION

```
<CFINCLUDE TEMPLATE="app_locals.cfm">

<HTML>
<HEAD>
   <TITLE>Simple Contact Management</TITLE>
   <LINK REL="STYLESHEET" TYPE="text/css" HREF="default.css">
</HEAD>
<BODY>
<CFINCLUDE TEMPLATE="dsp_menu.cfm">

<CFSWITCH EXPRESSION="#Attributes.fuseaction#">
   <CFCASE VALUE="contactlist">
      <CFINCLUDE TEMPLATE="qry_getallcontacts.cfm">
      <CFINCLUDE TEMPLATE="dsp_contactlist.cfm">
   </CFCASE>
   <CFCASE VALUE="contactdetail">
      <CFINCLUDE TEMPLATE="qry_getcontactrecord.cfm">
      <CFINCLUDE TEMPLATE="dsp_contactdetail.cfm">
   </CFCASE>
   <CFCASE VALUE="contactform">
      <CFINCLUDE TEMPLATE="qry_getcontactrecord.cfm">
      <CFINCLUDE TEMPLATE="dsp_contactform.cfm">
   </CFCASE>
   <CFCASE VALUE="updatecontact">
      <CFINCLUDE TEMPLATE="act_contactupdate.cfm">
   </CFCASE>
   <CFCASE VALUE="addcontact">
      <CFINCLUDE TEMPLATE="act_contactupdate.cfm">
   </CFCASE>
   <CFCASE VALUE="deletecontact">
      <CFINCLUDE TEMPLATE="act_contactupdate.cfm">
```

Listing 39.4 Continued

```
   </CFCASE>
</CFSWITCH>
</BODY>
</HTML>
```

You can see that by looking at this one file, you get a darn good idea what all the templates in this application do and know how they're invoked.

If no `fuseaction` is passed, the contact list is displayed because it is the default `fuseaction` defined in `app_Locals.cfm` (refer to Listing 39.3).

Adding a New Contact

To add a new contact, you select Add a New Contact from the drop-down menu. You could use any other mechanism you chose to implement a navigational menu—there's nothing special about it. When you make a selection from the list, it executes a Java script that redirects the user to the URL provided in the `<OPTION> VALUE` attribute, as shown in Listing 39.5.

Listing 39.5 Menu Choices Are Executed from an Option List in `dsp_Menu.cfm`

```
<OPTION VALUE="index.cfm?fuseaction=contactform&event=add">
➥Add a New Contact</option>
```

So, adding a new contact invokes `index.cfm` with a `fuseaction` of `contactform` and sets an additional parameter, `event`, to `add`. Looking at Listing 39.4, you can see that this `fuseaction` runs the `qry_GetContactRecord.cfm` and then the template `dsp_ContactForm.cfm`.

Tip

If you've been working with ColdFusion for a while, you might recognize that it's often convenient to use the same HTML form for adding and modifying simple data. When you're editing, you use a query to retrieve a specific record to work on; then you populate all the form fields with the values from your query. But when you're adding, you must do something to populate the fields with null values. How can you do this with one form?

If you look at `qry_GetContactRecord.cfm`, in Listing 39.6, you'll see it uses the same query to retrieve a recordset. This way, you have all the same field values you need to populate the form.

Listing 39.6 The Query in `qry_GetContactRecord.cfm` Is Run Prior to Adding or Modifying a Contact

```
<CFPARAM NAME="Attributes.Con_ID" DEFAULT="0">
<CFQUERY NAME="GetContactDetail" DATASOURCE="#DSN#">
   SELECT ContactID, FirstName, LastName, Phone, Address, City, State, Zip,
➥      Country,
```

```
      Email, UserLogin, UserPassword, MailingList
   FROM Contacts
   <CFIF attributes.Con_ID NEQ 0>
      WHERE ContactID = #Attributes.Con_ID#
   <CFELSE>
      <!--- When adding, will return empty resultset --->
      WHERE 0 = 1
   </CFIF>
</CFQUERY>
```

After `index.cfm` includes `qry_GetContactRecord.cfm` (seen in Listing 39.6), it includes `dsp_ContactForm.cfm`, which is displayed in Listing 39.7.

LISTING 39.7 FORM FOR ADDING AND MODIFYING CONTACTS

```
<CFOUTPUT>
<TABLE BORDER="0">
<CFFORM ACTION="index.cfm?fuseaction=#Attributes.event#Contact" METHOD="post">
<INPUT TYPE="Hidden" NAME="con_id" VALUE="#GetContactDetail.ContactID#">
<!--- Hidden field to store the event type ( update or add ) --->
<INPUT TYPE="Hidden" NAME="event" VALUE="#attributes.event#">
<TR VALIGN="top">
    <TD COLSPAN="2">* indicates required field</TD>
</TR>
<TR VALIGN="top">
   <TD>Name:</TD>
   <TD><CFINPUT TYPE="Text" NAME="FirstName"
➥       VALUE="#GetContactDetail.FirstName#" SIZE="25" REQUIRED="Yes"
➥       MESSAGE="First Name is required">
      <CFINPUT TYPE="Text" NAME="LastName" VALUE="#GetContactDetail.LastName#"
➥        SIZE="25" REQUIRED="Yes" MESSAGE="Last Name is required">*</TD>
</TR>
<TR VALIGN="top">
   <TD>Address:</TD>
   <TD>
      <INPUT TYPE="Text" NAME="Address" VALUE="#GetContactDetail.Address#"
➥        SIZE="50">
   </TD>
</TR>
<TR VALIGN="top">
   <TD>City/State/Zip</TD>
   <TD>
      <INPUT TYPE="Text" NAME="City" VALUE="#GetContactDetail.City#" SIZE="25">
      <INPUT TYPE="Text" NAME="State" VALUE="#GetContactDetail.State#" SIZE="3">
      <INPUT TYPE="Text" NAME="Zip" VALUE="#GetContactDetail.Zip#" SIZE="10">
   </TD>
</TR>
<TR VALIGN="top">
   <TD>Country:</TD>
   <TD>
      <INPUT TYPE="Text" NAME="Country" VALUE="#GetContactDetail.Country#">
   </TD>
</TR>
<TR VALIGN="top">
   <TD>Phone:</TD>
   <TD><INPUT TYPE="Text" NAME="phone" VALUE="#GetContactDetail.phone#"></TD>
```

LISTING 39.7 CONTINUED

```
</TR>
<TR VALIGN="top">
   <TD>E-Mail:</TD>
   <TD><INPUT TYPE="Text" NAME="email" VALUE="#GetContactDetail.email#"
➥        SIZE="50"></TD>
</TR>
<TR VALIGN="top">
   <TD>Login Name:</TD>
   <TD><CFINPUT TYPE="Text" NAME="UserLogin" VALUE="#GetContactDetail.userlogin#"
➥        REQUIRED="Yes" MESSAGE="Login name is required">*</TD>
</TR>
<TR VALIGN="top">
   <TD>Password:</TD>
   <TD><CFINPUT TYPE="password" NAME="UserPassword"
➥        VALUE="#GetContactDetail.userpassword#" REQUIRED="Yes"
➥        MESSAGE="Password is required">*</TD>
</TR>
<TR VALIGN="top">
   <TD>Mailing List?:</TD>
   <TD><INPUT TYPE="Checkbox" NAME="MailingList" #IIF
➥        (GetContactDetail.mailinglist EQ 0, DE(""), DE("CHECKED"))#></TD>
</TR>
<TR VALIGN="top">
   <TD> </TD>
   <TD>
       <BR>
      <CFIF attributes.event EQ "update">
         <INPUT TYPE="submit" VALUE="Save Changes">
      <CFELSE>
         <INPUT TYPE="submit" VALUE="Add Contacts">
      </CFIF>
      <INPUT TYPE="button" VALUE="Cancel" onClick="history.back();">
   </TD>
</TR>
</CFFORM>
</TABLE>
</CFOUTPUT>
```

Note that the URL associated with the Add a Contact menu item includes a parameter named `event`, which is set to `add` (refer to Listing 39.5). This parameter will be created in the `ATTRIBUTES` scope by the `FormURL2Attribute.cfm` custom tag (which executes in `app_Globals.cfm`). Now look at the `<CFFORM>` tag at the top of Listing 39.7. Note that this `ATTRIBUTES.event` is used in the form's action to dynamically generate the name of the `fuseaction`. In this case, the `fuseaction` will be set to `addcontact`.

When `index.cfm` (refer to Listing 39.4) executes with a `fuseaction` of `'addcontact'`, it executes the template, `act_ContactUpdate.cfm`. This template then looks at the value of the event parameter and then runs either an insert, an update, or a delete query.

The other templates in this example work in a similar fashion: Everything executes via the `index.cfm`.

BENEFITS

The example demonstrates how you can tell a lot about how a Fusebox application works by looking at the `index.cfm` file. In a properly constructed Fusebox application, everything traces back to `fuseaction`. This makes understanding and maintaining a Fusebox application much easier: You just follow the `fuseactions`.

Many ColdFusion developers use Fusebox. If you learn to use this methodology, you'll certainly be in a great position to work and share code with other developers.

More to the point, Fusebox will make you more productive. You'll derive all the general benefits associated with employing a development methodology that were outlined earlier in the chapter. Maintaining old Fusebox code or code that someone else wrote will be much easier. Understanding an application's structure is really just a question of following the `fuseactions`. You'll also be able to tell what a file does by where it's located and what it is named.

Also, note that because Fusebox applications are quite modular—they originally were intended to be written as custom tags—they can be swapped in and out of larger applications relatively easily.

As you can see from the example, using this methodology, you also can separate much of the application logic from the presentation. This makes for applications that will scale better and be easier to maintain.

DRAWBACKS

Ironically, some people argue that Fusebox applications can be harder to debug than non-Fusebox applications. All templates are included in the `index.cfm` template and refer back to it. So when something isn't working, it can be harder to tell from which template the offending code came.

This also makes it quite difficult for your Web log reporting software to get an accurate hit count on individual pages because every page in the application appears to be `index.cfm`.

Fusebox's filenaming convention is based on files' technical roles in the application, rather than on their functional roles. You should be careful to use filenames that also describe the business function being performed.

Note For more information on Fusebox, see `http://www.fusebox.org`.

CFOBJECTS

This fascinating methodology was architected by Ralph Fiol of ActiveTier Technologies in late 1999 and introduced to the ColdFusion developer community in early 2000. This methodology brings the basic principles of object-oriented programming to the ColdFusion development environment—a markedly non–object-oriented platform. cfObjects brings the promise of being able to separate presentation from application logic, originally described in SmallTalk's Model-View-Controller architecture.

Employing this methodology enables you to write ColdFusion applications that use classes, encapsulation, polymorphism, and inheritance! Confused? Well, object-oriented programming can indeed be confusing for the uninitiated. If you need a brief review of these concepts, please read the sidebar titled "A Review of Object-Oriented Programming Concepts."

A Review of Object-Oriented Programming Concepts

The basic idea is that you design your code based around logical *objects* or *classes*. A class represents a prototype of an object and defines the object's attributes and behaviors. For example, in a contact management application, you might have classes for contacts and phone calls. These objects have attributes (*properties*) and behaviors (*methods*). A contact will have properties such as first name, last name, company name, address, phone number, and so on.

When you actually create a contact, it is referred to as an *instance* of the contact class.

The contact class will probably employ methods such as Fetch, Remove, and List. Methods are similar to procedures–they're the code that does most of the work.

If you think about it, you could create the same methods for most of the other objects in the contact management system. For example, the phone call object probably needs Fetch and List capabilities, too. This demonstrates the concept of *polymorphism*–the notion that functions with the same names can be used to do different things in the same application. In this example, both the contact object and phone call object will have Fetch, Remove, and List methods.

In a contact management system, you'll want to track phone calls you make. A follow-up is a certain type of phone call related to an earlier phone call. In the object-oriented contact management application, you might want to create a special class of phone call called a follow-up. You could create it as a subclass of your phone call class. This would save time because your subclass would *inherit* the property methods of its parent class, so you would only have to produce those that are new or modified.

The cfObjects methodology dictates the use of a directory structure, some filenaming conventions, and some tag-naming conventions, and requires the use of some specific tags. Moreover, you also must use a set of framework tags that are available from the `www.cfObjects.com` Web site. The framework tags provide low-level services that you'll use throughout your applications, such as initializing your application, creating objects, and declaring methods. The Web site contains an excellent tutorial on the methodology. It's strongly recommended that you go through the tutorial before sitting down to code anything. Note that the tutorial provides instructions on downloading and installing a custom toolbar and set of wizards in CF Studio, which are also highly recommended but not required.

USING CFOBJECTS

First, you must create a CF mapping to the cfObjects framework. This is a one-time task that is part of the installation process.

Now, in each cfObjects application, you first must initialize the framework. This is done by including one of the framework's custom tags—<CF_CFOINIT>—in your Application.cfm file (which you might recall is executed before every CF template in your application). So, your Application.cfm might look like this:

```
<!--- define your application --->
<CFAPPLICATION NAME="MyNewCfoApp">

<!--- initialize cfObjects framework --->
<CF_CFOINIT LIBPATH="cfo20lib">
```

Here, cfo20lib is the name of the CF mapping you created during installation. When you begin building your own object class libraries, you'll wind up including mappings to them in the <CF_CFOINIT> LIBPATH attribute.

To instantiate an object, you could use the framework tag, <CF_CFOCREATEOBJECT>, like this:

```
<CF_CFOCREATEOBJECT
   CLASS="Object"
   OBJECT="aContact"
   FIRSTNAME="Jenny"
   LASTNAME="Jenny"
   PHONENBR="333-867-5309"
>
```


This code creates three instance variables along with the object: FirstName, LastName, and PhoneNbr. These variables are similar to properties of this instance of the class.

Creating Your Own Classes

In reality, you won't create instances of objects this way. You create your own objects by creating a set of files that define the class. These are stored in a subdirectory named after the class. Your applications probably will include several classes (at least), and these will be stored in class libraries. A class library is simply a directory named classes that contains one or more subdirectories, named for the various classes they represent.

When creating classes that you're likely to use in many applications, you should create a class library under the shared custom tags folder (normally located in c:\cfusion\custom tags\). This is where the cfObjects framework class library is located.

You normally will create classes that are specific to your current application. You put their class subdirectories in a /class directory, located under your application's root directory. See Figure 39.2 for an example of what your application directory structure might look like.

Figure 39.2 shows subdirectories for the Contact and PhoneCall classes under the Classes directory. The public directory is where you would put other files used by your application, such as Application.cfm.

Before you can use them, you must first create ColdFusion mappings (in the CF Administrator) for each of your class library locations. Figure 39.3 depicts how you use the CF Administrator to do this. In this chapter's example, you would create a mapping to the /classes directory in the Contact Manager application's directory.

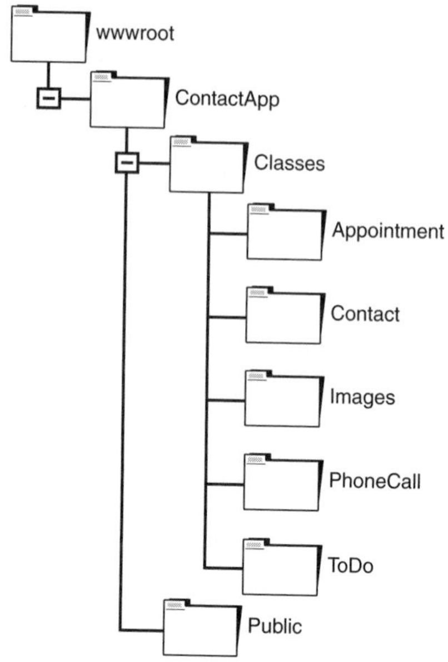

Figure 39.2 The directory structure associated with a cfObjects application.

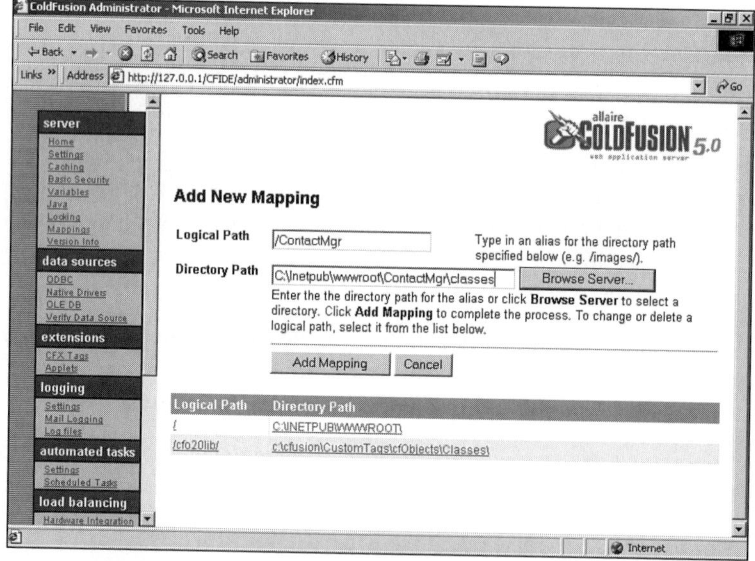

Figure 39.3 Adding mappings in the ColdFusion Administrator.

You must then include the name of the mapping in your application's call to the `<CF_CFOINIT>` custom tag. Your application's `Application.cfm` might contain this code:

```
<!--- define our application --->
<CFAPPLICATION NAME="ContactManager">

<!--- initialize our classes --->
<CF_CFOINIT LIBPATH="ContactMgr, cf20lib">
```

ContactMgr, in the LIBPATH attribute of the <CF_CFOINIT> tag, is the CF mapping that was defined to map to your application's classes.

So what goes in a class's folder? Typically, at least two files: class.cfm and constructor.cfm. The class.cfm file is a simple CF template that defines several specific variables that are part of the framework, like this:

```
<!--- class.cfm for the Contact class --->
<CFSCRIPT>
   stClassDef = structNew();
   stClassDef.className = "Contact";
   stClassDef.superClass = "Object";
   // define optional class variables below here.
</CFSCRIPT>
```

A constructor.cfm template for your contact is presented in Listing 39.8.

Listing 39.8 The Constructor.cfm Template (Constructor Method)

```
<CF_CFODECLAREMETHOD TYPE="public">
<!---///
   This file is automatically invoked by CreateObject.
   Use CFPARAM to define instance variables.
///--->
<CFPARAM NAME="self.con_id" DEFAULT="0">
<CFPARAM NAME="self.con_fname" DEFAULT="">
<CFPARAM NAME="self.con_lname" DEFAULT="">
<CFPARAM NAME="self.con_company" DEFAULT="">
<CFPARAM NAME="self.con_street1" DEFAULT="">
<CFPARAM NAME="self.con_street2" DEFAULT="">
<CFPARAM NAME="self.con_city" DEFAULT="">
<CFPARAM NAME="self.con_state" DEFAULT="">
<CFPARAM NAME="self.con_zip" DEFAULT="">
<CFPARAM NAME="self.con_phone" DEFAULT="">
<CFPARAM NAME="self.con_fax" DEFAULT="">
<CFPARAM NAME="self.con_email" DEFAULT="">
```


The constructor.cfm template is used to initialize the object's properties (also known as instance variables). The two templates, class.cfm and constructor.cfm, are executed by the framework when you use the <CF_CFOCREATEOBJECT> custom tag to create an instance (an object) of the contact class.

Creating a Class's Methods

As you might recall, objects have methods, and methods are similar to an object's behaviors. So, when you want an object to do something, or when you want something done to it, you use the object's methods. For example, you might want to display an individual contact, display a list of contacts, edit a contact, save a contact, delete a contact, and so on.

In the cfObjects framework, methods are simply templates stored in an object's class directory. The filenames correspond to the method names. So the contact object's save method is stored in the file save.cfm in the /contact directory within the /classes directory of your contact manager application. This makes finding the code that performs a particular function for a particular object very easy!

In the context of a database application—where your contacts are stored in a database—the save method is simply the code that writes a contact record to the database.

Most methods operate on an instance object of a class. For example, the save method saves the data in a specific object to the database. Static methods, on the other hand, do not operate on a specific instance and do not require that you instantiate the object before the method can be used. The `displayList` method, for example, presents a list of contacts, rather than an individual contact.

At the top of each method, you must declare it as either static or public using the framework tag, `<CF_CFODECLAREMETHOD>`, like this:

```
<CF_CFODECLAREMETHOD TYPE="public">
```

EXAMPLE

Well, this has been an interesting discussion on a conceptual level. Now, let's flesh it out with an example. This example—Simple Contact Manager 2.0—was developed by Ralph Fiol and is available on the cfObjects.com Web site. (Note, however, that I've modified the original to work with the Orange Whip Studios database.) The Contact Manager lets you review, create, and modify contacts and basic contact information. You can also remove contacts from the list.

Only one application-specific object exists in this example: a contact. The contact object methods are described in Table 39.3.

TABLE 39.3 CONTACT OBJECT METHODS

Method	Description
`load`	Loads a contact record from the database into the current contact object.
`save`	This method saves the contact information to a database. If the `con_id` is `0`, a new contact is inserted. If the `con_id` is greater than `0`, the record is updated.
`edit`	Presents a form for editing a contact.
`delete`	Deletes a contact record from the database and empties the instance variables of the current contact object.
`display`	Presents an individual contact in a noneditable format.
`getAll`	This static method is simply a query to retrieve all contact records from the database.
`displayList`	Invoked after `getAll`, this static method displays a list of contacts retrieved from the database.

The contact object properties (and instance variables) are easily understood. The `con_id` is a unique identifier used in the database. It defaults to `0` when a contact object is instantiated.

As you can guess, con_fname is the contact's first name. There are fields for company, address, phone number, and so on.

Figure 39.4 presents the directory structure for the Simple Contact Manager when installed. The database subdirectory contains a simple Microsoft Access database used in this application.

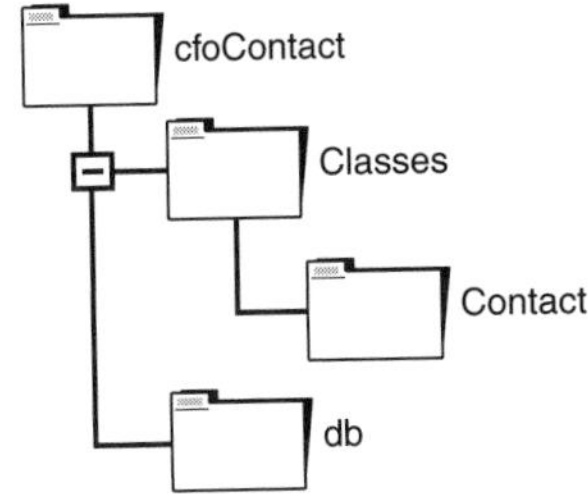

Figure 39.4
The directory structure used in the cfObjects Contact Manager application.

Note

Normally, you wouldn't keep the database in a directory under the Web root because it would represent a security risk. If a user could guess the name of your database, he might be able to download it directly! You should normally keep your file-oriented databases in a directory outside the realm of your Web server.

The root application directory, cfoContact, contains files not part of a class. The Application.cfm invokes the <CF_CFOINIT> custom tag to preserve the use of the framework on each page in the application and to identify the class libraries used in this application. The index.cfm page is where a user's interaction with the application begins. Listing 39.9 displays the index.cfm page.

Figure 39.5 diagrams the flow of the application. As you can see, the application can be conceptually divided into application templates and object-related templates. The application templates pretty much all wind up calling Handler.cfm to process some sort of function or event, and Handler.cfm in turn includes object templates, which implement the contact object's methods.

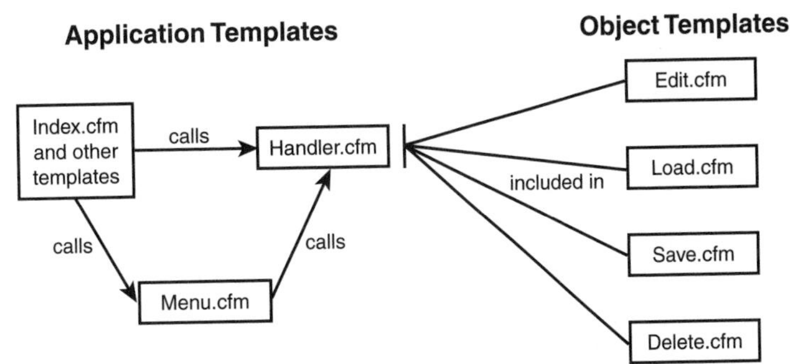

Figure 39.5
The flow of the cfObjects Contact Manager application.

Listing 39.9 The `index.cfm` Page

```
<HTML>
<HEAD>
      <TITLE>Simple Contact Manager</TITLE>
    <LINK REL="STYLESHEET" TYPE="text/css" HREF="default.css">
</HEAD>

<BODY>

<CF_MENU>
<H1>My Contacts</H1>

<!---/// First, we begin by getting a list of all contacts.  The getAll
   method will return a query with all contacts.  Note that we are calling
   this method on the class (not an instance of the class).  The getAll
   method is known as a "static method" -- it does not require that you
   first call CreateObject.  After getAll executes, there will be a local
   variable named getAll.contacts that contains the contacts as a query.
///--->
<CF_CFOINVOKEMETHOD CLASS="Contact" METHOD="getAll">

<!---/// Next, call another class method to display the query
   in a nice tabular format organized by last name.  If a contact
   is selected, it triggers the "contactSelected" event.
///--->
<CF_CFOINVOKEMETHOD CLASS="Contact" METHOD="displayList"
➥   QUERY="#getAll.contacts#" EVENT="contactSelected">

</BODY>
</HTML>
```

This very simple page displays all the contacts in the database by calling the static methods, `getAll` and `displayList`. Figure 39.6 presents the output from this template.

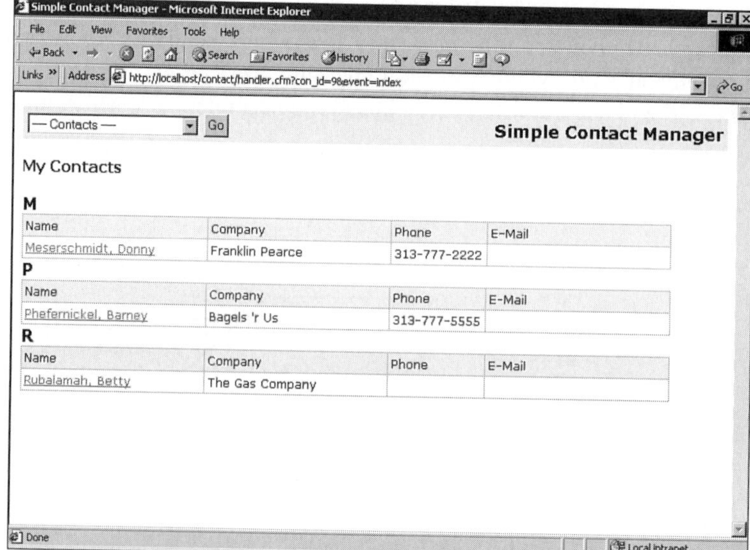

Figure 39.6
The Contact Manager List.

Note how effectively this template separates the business logic from the presentation of the data.

Listing 39.10 The <CF_MENU> Custom Tag

```
<CFPARAM NAME="attributes.con_id" DEFAULT="0">

<FORM NAME="menu_form" ACTION="handler.cfm" METHOD="get">
<CFOUTPUT>
    <INPUT TYPE="hidden" NAME="con_id" VALUE="#attributes.con_id#">
</CFOUTPUT>
<TABLE CELLPADDING="5" WIDTH="100%" CELLSPACING="0">
<TR BGCOLOR="#efefef">
   <TD>
      <!---/// Events ///--->
      <SELECT NAME="event" SIZE="1" onchange="menu_form.submit();">
         <OPTION VALUE="index">---- Contacts ----</OPTION>
         <OPTION VALUE="add">Add a New Contact</OPTION>
      <CFIF VAL(ATTRIBUTES.CON_ID) GT 0>
         <OPTION VALUE="edit">Edit Contact</OPTION>
         <OPTION VALUE="delete">Delete</OPTION>
      </CFIF>
         <OPTION VALUE="index">-------------------------------------</OPTION>
         <OPTION VALUE="index">Display All</OPTION>
      </SELECT>
      <!---/// End of Events ///--->
      <INPUT TYPE="submit" VALUE="Go">
   </TD>
   <TD ALIGN="right">
      <FONT SIZE="+1"><B>Simple Contact Manager</B></FONT>
   </TD>
</TR>
</TABLE>
</FORM>
```

The <CF_MENU> custom tag (refer to Listing 39.10) at the top of the index.cfm page produces the drop-down list. The output is presented in Figure 39.6. When working on a specific contact, the form containing the menu also contains a hidden field with the contact ID in it. Under those circumstances, it also provides menu choices that you'd expect when working on a single contact, such as Edit and Delete. It also always contains choices to add a new contact and view all the contacts.

Note that the menu introduces the concept of events and calls Handler.cfm (see Listing 39.15, later in this chapter) to process the events. Events include index, add, edit, delete, contactSelected, and several others used elsewhere in the application. These event names translate into templates names that Handler.cfm includes.

Let's look at how creating a new contact works. First, you select Add a New Contact from the drop-down menu. The Handler.cfm page is called. Handler.cfm interprets the selected menu option as the event. When selecting Add a New Contact, Handler.cfm includes the template named Add.cfm. Note that this template is not a method on the contact object; it's just a template stored in the root directory.

Add.cfm is presented in Listing 39.11. This template creates a new contact object with the <CF_CFOCREATEOBJECT> tag. Note that the contact object will be instantiated with a contact ID of 0 and other instance variables set to null strings (refer to Listing 39.1 for the contact object's Constructor.cfm). The Add.cfm template then invokes the edit method on the new contact object. The Edit.cfm template output is displayed in Figure 39.7.

LISTING 39.11 THE Add.cfm TEMPLATE

```
<HTML>
<HEAD>
   <TITLE>Simple Contact Manager</TITLE>
   <LINK REL="STYLESHEET" TYPE="text/css" HREF="default.css">
</HEAD>

<BODY>

<CF_MENU>
<H1>Add a New Contact</H1>

<CF_CFOCREATEOBJECT CLASS="Contact" OBJECT="aContact">
<CF_CFOINVOKEMETHOD OBJECT="#aContact#" METHOD="edit"
   EVENT="contactChanged">

</BODY>
</HTML>
```

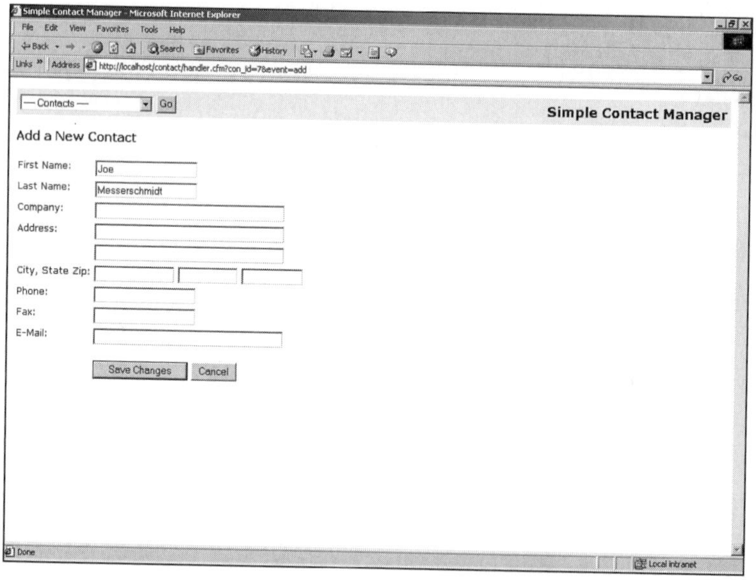

Figure 39.7
This form is used for adding new contacts.

The Edit.cfm template is a public method of the contact class. It presents a form that is used to edit the contact, as seen in Figure 39.7. The top portion of this form is presented in Listing 39.12.

LISTING 39.12 THE Edit.cfm TEMPLATE (THE edit METHOD)

```
<CF_CFODECLAREMETHOD TYPE="public">
<CFPARAM NAME="attributes.event" DEFAULT="contactChanged">
<!---/// Display the contact in a simple HTML table ///--->
<CFFORM ACTION="handler.cfm" METHOD="post">
<CFOUTPUT>
   <INPUT TYPE="hidden" NAME="event" VALUE="#attributes.event#">
   <INPUT TYPE="hidden" NAME="con_id" VALUE="#self.con_id#">
</CFOUTPUT>
<CFOUTPUT>
<TABLE BORDER="0">
<TR VALIGN="top">
   <TD COLSPAN="2">* indicates required field</TD>
</TR>
<TR VALIGN="top">
   <TD>Name:</TD>
   <TD><CFINPUT TYPE="Text" NAME="firstName" VALUE="#self.FirstName#" SIZE="25"
➥         REQUIRED="Yes" MESSAGE="First name is required">
   <CFINPUT TYPE="Text" NAME="lastName" VALUE="#self.LastName#" SIZE="25"
➥    REQUIRED="Yes" MESSAGE="Last name is required">*</TD>
</TR>
<TR VALIGN="top">
   <TD>Address:</TD>
   <TD><INPUT TYPE="Text" NAME="Address" VALUE="#self.Address#" SIZE="50"></TD>
</TR>
<TR VALIGN="top">
   <TD>City/State/Zip</TD>
   <TD>
      <INPUT TYPE="Text" NAME="City" VALUE="#self.City#" SIZE="25">
      <INPUT TYPE="Text" NAME="State" VALUE="#self.State#" SIZE="3">
      <INPUT TYPE="Text" NAME="Zip" VALUE="#self.Zip#" SIZE="10">
   </TD>
</TR>
<TR VALIGN="top">
   <TD>Country:</TD>
   <TD><INPUT TYPE="Text" NAME="Country" VALUE="#self.Country#"></TD>
</TR>
<TR VALIGN="top">
   <TD>Main Phone:</TD>
   <TD><INPUT TYPE="Text" NAME="phone" VALUE="#self.phone#"></TD>
</TR>
<TR VALIGN="top">
   <TD>E-Mail:</TD>
   <TD><INPUT TYPE="Text" NAME="email" VALUE="#self.email#" SIZE="50"></TD>
</TR>
<TR VALIGN="top">
   <TD>Login name:</TD>
   <TD><CFINPUT TYPE="Text" NAME="UserLogin" VALUE="#self.userlogin#"
➥         REQUIRED="Yes" MESSAGE="Login name is required.">*</TD>
</TR>
<TR VALIGN="top">
   <TD>Password:</TD>
   <TD><CFINPUT TYPE="password" NAME="UserPassword" VALUE="#self.UserPassword#"
➥         REQUIRED="Yes" MESSAGE="Password is required.">*</TD>
</TR>
<TR VALIGN="top">
```

LISTING 39.12 CONTINUED

```
    <TD>Mailing List?:</TD>
    <TD><INPUT TYPE="Checkbox" NAME="MailingList" #IIF((SELF.MAILINGLIST EQ "" OR
➥        SELF.MAILINGLIST EQ 0), DE(""), DE("CHECKED"))#></TD>
</TR>
<TR VALIGN="top">
    <TD> </TD>
    <TD>
        <BR>
       <INPUT TYPE="submit" VALUE="Save Changes">
       <INPUT TYPE="button" VALUE="Cancel" onClick="history.back();">
    </TD>
</TR>
</TABLE>
</CFOUTPUT>
</CFFORM>
```

Note the use of the pronoun `self`. In object-oriented programming, `self` refers to the current object. So, `self.con_fname` refers to the value of the contact's first name in the current contact object. In some languages, the pronoun `this` is used instead of `self`.

> **Note**
>
> The `Edit.cfm` method is used for both new contacts (being added) and existing contacts (being modified). When creating a new contact, the `con_fname` and other instance variables are initialized to null strings. When editing, these variables are populated with values from the query invoked in the `load` method. See the Load.cfm template. The load method is invoked in the `Edit.cfm` file located in the root application directory.

The user clicks the Save button in the edit form (in `Edit.cfm`) to save the new contact object to the database. This calls `Handler.cfm`, passing it the event—`contactChanged`. `Handler.cfm` then includes the `ContactChanged.cfm` template. `ContactChanged.cfm`, displayed in Listing 39.13, creates a new object. You might wonder why it needs to create a new object. It must create another object because the object instantiated in the `Edit.cfm` template does not persist into this template.

So, after the new contact object is created, you use a method of the object class (that is, part of the cfObjects framework)—`collectFields`—to collect all current field values and calls the contact class method, `save`. `collectFields` works when the values you want to populate an object's instance variables are in Form or URL variables. In this case, these values come from the Form variables created in `Edit.cfm`.

After the object is saved, the `ContactSelected.cfm` template is used to display the new record.

LISTING 39.13 THE `ContactChanged.cfm` TEMPLATE

```
<CF_CFOCREATEOBJECT CLASS="Contact" OBJECT="aContact">
<CF_CFOINVOKEMETHOD OBJECT="#aContact#" METHOD="collectFields">
```

```
<CF_CFOINVOKEMETHOD OBJECT="#aContact#" METHOD="save">

<!---/// Display new contact screen ///--->
<CFLOCATION URL="contactSelected.cfm?con_id=#aContact.con_id#">
```

The save method, presented in Listing 39.14, executes either an insert query or an update on the contact table. The value of the contact ID (con_id) in the contact object acts as a semaphore for which query to run. If the contact ID is 0—to which it is initialized when adding a new contact—the insert query is executed. Otherwise, the update query is executed. Note that the database is set up to generate a new contact ID when inserting a record. The save method then updates the current contact object with the newly created contact ID.

LISTING 39.14 THE Save.cfm TEMPLATE (save METHOD)

```
<CF_cfoDeclareMethod type="public">

<!---///
   This method will save the contact information to a database.
   If the con_id is 0 then a new contact is inserted.  If the
   con_id is greater than 0 then an update is performed.
///--->

<CFIF VAL(self.con_id) EQ 0>
   <!------------------------------------------------------------------
      Add a New Contact
     ------------------------------------------------------------------>
   <CFTRANSACTION>

      <CFIF self.mailinglist NEQ "">
         <CFSET VARIABLES.mailinglist = 1>
      <CFELSE>
         <CFSET VARIABLES.mailinglist = 0>
      </CFIF>
      <CFQUERY NAME="InsertContact" DATASOURCE="#request.dsn#">
         INSERT INTO Contacts (FirstName, LastName, Address, City, State, Zip,
➥             Country,
            Email, Phone, UserLogin, UserPassword,  MailingList)
         VALUES (
            '#self.firstname#',
            '#self.lastname#',
            <CFIF self.Address NEQ "">'#self.Address#' <CFELSE> Null </CFIF>,
            <CFIF self.city NEQ "">'#self.city#' <CFELSE> Null </CFIF>,
            <CFIF self.state NEQ "">'#self.state#' <CFELSE> Null </CFIF>,
            <CFIF self.zip NEQ "">'#self.zip#' <CFELSE> Null </CFIF>,
            <CFIF self.country NEQ "">'#self.country#' <CFELSE> Null </CFIF>,
            <CFIF self.email NEQ "">'#self.email#' <CFELSE> Null </CFIF>,
            <CFIF self.phone NEQ "">'#self.phone#' <CFELSE> Null </CFIF>,
           '#self.userlogin#', '#self.userpassword#',
            #Variables.MailingList# )
      </CFQUERY>
      <CFQUERY NAME="q_contact" DATASOURCE="#request.dsn#">
         SELECT max(contactid) as new_id
         FROM   contacts
      </CFQUERY>
```

Listing 39.14 Continued

```
   </CFTRANSACTION>

   <!---/// Save New ID ///--->
   <CFSET self.con_id = q_contact.new_id>

<CFELSE>
   <!------------------------------------------------------------------
      Update Existing Contact
     ----------------------------------------------------------------->
   <CFIF self.mailinglist NEQ "">
      <CFSET VARIABLES.mailinglist = 1>
   <CFELSE>
      <CFSET VARIABLES.mailinglist = 0>
   </CFIF>
   <CFQUERY NAME="UpdateContact" DATASOURCE="#request.dsn#">
      UPDATE Contacts SET
         FirstName = '#self.firstName#',
         LastName = '#self.lastName#',
         Address = <CFIF self.Address NEQ "">'#self.Address#' <CFELSE> Null
➥                   </CFIF>,
         City = <CFIF self.city NEQ "">'#self.city#' <CFELSE> Null </CFIF>,
         State = <CFIF self.state NEQ "">'#self.state#' <CFELSE> Null </CFIF>,
         Zip = <CFIF self.zip NEQ "">'#self.zip#' <CFELSE> Null </CFIF>,
         Country = <CFIF self.country NEQ "">'#self.country#' <CFELSE> Null
➥                   </CFIF>,
         Email = <CFIF self.email NEQ "">'#self.email#' <CFELSE> Null </CFIF>,
         Phone = <CFIF self.phone NEQ "">'#self.phone#' <CFELSE> Null </CFIF>,
         UserLogin = '#self.userlogin#',
         UserPassword = '#self.userpassword#',
         MailingList = #Variables.MailingList#
       WHERE ContactID = #self.con_id#
   </CFQUERY>
</CFIF>
```

The approach to editing is quite similar. The user selects a contact record by clicking the record in the `Index.cfm` display. This invokes `Handler.cfm`, seen in Listing 39.15, passing it the selected contact ID and the event flag `contactSelected`, indicating that the user has selected this contact.

Listing 39.15 The `Handler.cfm` Template

```
<CFPARAM NAME="FORM.event" DEFAULT="index">
<CFPARAM NAME="URL.event" DEFAULT="#FORM.event#">

<CFTRY>
   <CFINCLUDE TEMPLATE="#URL.event#.cfm">

   <CFCATCH TYPE="MissingInclude">
      <CFTHROW MESSAGE="<b>cfObjects</B>: There is no handler for event
➥         '<B>#URL.event#</B>'.">
   </CFCATCH>
</CFTRY>
```

Passing `Handler.cfm` the `contactSelected` event again causes it to include the `ContactSelected.cfm` template. This creates a contact object and uses the `collectFields` framework method to get the contact ID (passed through the URL) into the current contact record. `ContactSelected.cfm` then loads the contact record from the database into the object (using the contact object `load` method). It then invokes the contact object `display` method, which simply presents the contact data from the database in a read-only form.

This presentation form includes a button to edit the selected contact. As you might guess, this action invokes `Handler.cfm`, passing it the `edit` event, which executes the contact edit method and passes it the contact ID.

Now the process becomes almost the same as adding: The `edit` method presents the current contact object (this time, as loaded from the database) in an editable form (refer to Figure 39.7). When the user is done, she clicks the Save Changes button.

Please refer again to Listing 39.14. The process of saving a modified contact is similar to the process of saving a new contact. However, because the contact ID is not `0`, the update query is executed, rather than the insert query.

BENEFITS

If you look at the code in the example, you'll see that cfObjects enables you to do an extremely good job of separating presentation code from application logic. This is a powerful benefit because it enables you to build scalable applications that are easier to maintain. This is quite helpful if you need to change aspects of the presentation (the language, for example).

Organizational benefits exist as well. By organizing your application into objects, you organize your logically related files into directories, and this makes locating code easier when maintenance is required. cfObjects also provides some naming conventions that will help make your code more consistent and therefore easier to maintain.

cfObjects also delivers on the promise of object orientation—the ability to work more productively by building reusable objects. If you are an experienced object-oriented programmer, you'll be able to do a good job of identifying and creating generic, reusable objects.

DRAWBACKS

As you might have guessed, producing object-oriented programs is more difficult. At first, the code appears somewhat more complex or confusing.

Because CF isn't a truly object-oriented development environment, implementing certain concepts is somewhat clumsy—for example, the manner in which you invoke a method with the `cfoInvokeMethod` custom tag.

Finally, it can be argued that if you really seek the benefits of an object-oriented development environment, perhaps you'll be better off simply using a real object-oriented development tool, such as Java.

BLACKBOX, SMART-OBJECTS, AND SWITCH_BOX

The next three methodologies to be investigated are somewhat less well known than Fusebox and cfObjects. Blackbox was developed by Dan Chick (with assistance from Joel Mueller and Mike Imhoff) in 1999. As you might expect from the name, it has some similarities to Fusebox. Similarly, some analogies exist between Smart-Objects and cfObjects. Smart-Objects was developed by Benjamin Pate in the summer of 2000. Like cfObjects, Smart-Objects enables you to write object-oriented ColdFusion applications. Switch_Box was developed by Joseph Flanigan. It is an interesting cross between some elements of Fusebox and some object-oriented concepts.

BLACKBOX

The Blackbox framework intends to provide many of the benefits of using Fusebox, but in a somewhat less restrictive manner. The notion is that other developers might prefer their own filenaming conventions, for example. Blackbox also enables you to structure your applications so that all the URLs don't all point back to `index.cfm`.

How does it do this? It does this with a special custom tag called `Blackbox.cfm` and a simple directory structure that you employ. It does not provide a real filenaming convention or tell you how to structure your application.

The `Blackbox.cfm` template somewhat takes the place of `index.cfm` in Fusebox. But instead of it being a long `switch/case` statement that you code, it is a custom tag that navigates your application directory tree looking for a directory and template you specify in two attributes you pass it.

You create your application directory and put the `Blackbox.cfm` custom tag in it, along with templates you'll use to invoke the major sections of your application. You then create a directory named `Blackbox` in your application's root. Now, think of the logical sections of your application: You'll create a subdirectory of `/Blackbox` for each logical section.

In a robust contact management system, the sections might be contacts, phone calls, appointments, and to-do lists. Each of these sections would become a directory in your `/Blackbox` directory, as shown in Figure 39.8. Within each directory, you might have templates for listing, creating, modifying, and deleting.

Invoking your contact listing from your application's home page might look something like this:

```
<A HREF="Contacts.cfm">List of Contacts</A>
```

Assume you've created templates named `PageHeader.cfm` and `PageFooter.cfm` (in your application root directory) that provide common page header and footer code, respectively. Then, the `Contacts.cfm` page, also located in your application root directory, might look like the code in Listing 39.16.

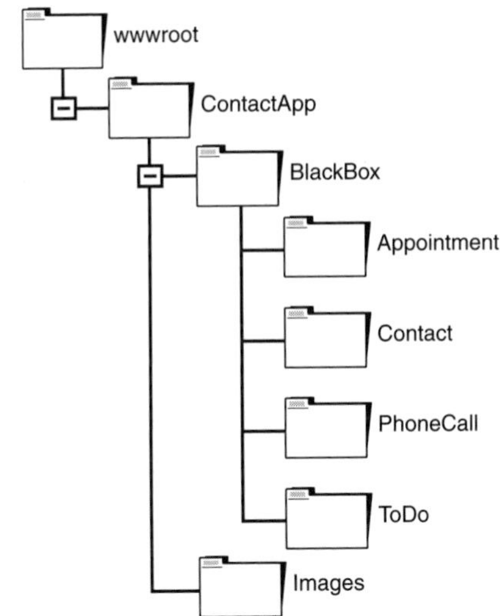

Figure 39.8
The directory structure that might be used in a Blackbox implementation of a ContactMgr.

LISTING 39.16 INVOKING A CONTACT LISTING THROUGH THE BLACKBOX CUSTOM TAG

```
<CFINCLUDE TEMPLATE="PageHeader.cfm">
<CF_BLACKBOX TOOL="Contact" ACTION="ContactList">
<CFINCLUDE TEMPLATE="PageFooter.cfm">
```

The `Blackbox.cfm` custom tag recursively searches `/Blackbox` for a directory named `Contact` containing a template named `ContactList.cfm`. The `ContactList.cfm` template contains functionality for listing contacts. You can alternatively specify the `TOOL` attribute like this:

```
"Contact.ContactList"
```

`Blackbox.cfm` will treat this just like the call in Listing 39.16.

The `Blackbox.cfm` template is a custom tag. It finds your template and `<CFINCLUDE>`s it. This means that your template is now part of a custom tag and can be written like one—meaning it can read attributes and read and write to the `CALLER` scope.

Now, suppose a template in one of your functional subdirectories needs to run another template in the same directory. A common way of doing this is to include another copy of `Blackbox.cfm` in the functional subdirectory and execute the template through it.

So, most of the functionality in your application is written through related sets of custom tags that are `<CFINCLUDE>`d in the `Blackbox.cfm` custom tag. The `Blackbox.cfm` tag itself is executed inside your application templates. This means your URLs will look like this:

```
http://localhost/MyApp/Contacts.cfm
http://localhost/MyApp/PhoneCalls.cfm
```

Whereas in Fusebox, your URLs might look like this:

```
http://localhost/MyApp/index.cfm?FuseAction=Contacts
http://localhost/MyApp/index.cfm?FuseAction=PhoneCalls
```

Note

For more information on SmartObjects, see `http://www.cfblackbox.com`.

SmartObjects

SmartObjects is intended to be easier to learn and use than cfObjects, while providing a similar set of benefits (that is, the benefits of object-oriented programming). It also supports multiple inheritance—the capability to encapsulate functions from more than one base class.

Similar to cfObjects, the methodology consists of a set of framework templates and a set of special directories and templates you create.

You create classes in their own directories. In each class directory, you create a file named `Public.cfm`. This defines the class and registers it using the framework's custom tag, `Class.cfm`. You specify the class name, its base classes (from which it inherits properties and methods), and its methods.

You use the custom tag `Object.cfm` to create instances of objects. As with cfObjects, instances of objects are implemented as structures.

Each of an object's methods is a template in the object's directory. For example, if a contact object is to have add, update, and delete methods, you'd create templates named `Add.cfm`, `Update.cfm`, and `Delete.cfm` and store them in the contact object directory. You invoke methods using the framework custom tag, `Call.cfm`. `Call.cfm` simply includes your method template, so it, too, is essentially a custom tag.

Similar to cfObjects, the directories for your objects must either be in the Web root directory or referenced by a ColdFusion virtual directory mapping (which you create in the administrator). So, your application structure might wind up looking like the structure depicted in Figure 39.9.

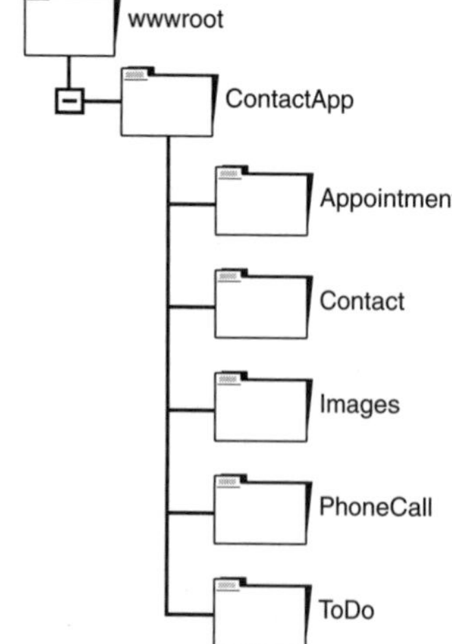

Figure 39.9 The directory structure for a SmartObjects version of the Contact Manager application.

As you can see, SmartObjects is quite similar to cfObjects. Where it really differs is that it registers objects in an application structure (an Application variable). They are retrieved quickly, and there's no equivalent call to an initialization routine in your `Application.cfm`.

Note

For more information on SmartObjects, see `http://www.smart-objects.com`.

SWITCH_BOX

You might assume from its name that Switch_Box is another derivative of the Fusebox framework. But this wouldn't really be accurate. It incorporates some object-oriented terminology and concepts, as well as bringing some its own unique concepts to the table.

Like Fusebox and Blackbox, this intriguing framework is built around the notion that you use one template to handle the logic associated with executing all application functions. This template is referred to as the *box*, as in Fusebox. However, this one template is the only template your application *ever* points to! There might be many boxes providing other functions in your application, but the main box hides them from the user. You include special URL parameters (such as fuseactions) that provide instructions on what the application is to do. (You'll look at these in more detail in a minute.)

In fact, the notion of using this one, reentrant template is one of the key benefits of Switch_Box. Whenever a regular CF application employs its filename and directory name in the URL (address field in the browser), it reveals some of its internal structure. And this can be considered, to some degree, a security issue.

You divide your Switch_Box application files into subdirectories, as in cfObjects and SmartObjects. Each subdirectory has its own box template, which represents a different type of object.

But the real power of Switch_Box is the notion that messages you pass to the box on the URL can include *message vectors*.

So, what the heck is a message vector? A message vector is Switch_Box parlance for a specially designed URL parameter used to direct program flow. It is a multivalued variable consisting of an object tree (for example, a directory) and a method tree to execute within the object. Similar to Blackbox, a special custom tag is required to interpret the message vector. The custom tag, `Switch_Box.cfm`, parses the message vectors and makes the switch to another object (`box`), if necessary.

A simple message vector has two parts and might look like this:

```
member.contact.address:display.home
```

The first part, `member.contact.address`, is referred to as the *object tree*. It points to the address object. This is just a directory structure containing box templates. The second part of the vector, `display.home`, is a `method tree`. This implements the object-oriented notion of polymorphism. This code identifies the home method within the display method. (There might be several display methods in your application, but we're referring to the particular method used to display home.)

Figure 39.10
This table illustrates the various parts of the box message.

Message Vector	
Composite Message	
member.contact.address:display.home	
compound object tree	compound method tree
member.contact.address	display.home
top box object or root	boxaction method
member	display
stem object	method template task
member.contact	home
target box object	
address	

So what do message vectors get you? Because Switch_Box applications use one reentrant box template, message vectors—in conjunction with the <SWITCH_BOX> tag that parses them and does the switching—identify objects and methods to which the program flow is directed, without revealing the internal structure of your application. The Switch_Box Web site describes how (and provides code examples) to make message vectors even more secure. The basic idea behind symbolic message vectors is to replace entire trees in regular message vectors with tokens, and then construct a sort of hash table that reassembles the vectors in one of your global application templates (for example, Application.cfm).

Switch_Box also recommends (but doesn't mandate) a set of filenaming conventions. Part of the filename identifies the technical role of the file in the application (qry for query, dsp for display, and so on) and the other part identifies the functional role (for example, ContactMaintenance). But here, the convention is to use a suffix rather than a prefix (such as ContactMaintenance_dsp.cfm). This way, when you look at a directory structure, files are sorted together based on their functional roles, rather than their technical roles.

The Switch-box.org site also provides a wizard for creating simple application shells, which can be very handy. This fascinating methodology provides some unique benefits and improves on the Fusebox naming convention.

Note

For more information on Switch_Box, see http://www.switch-box.org.

Issues to Consider with All Development Methodologies

Recognize that adopting a methodology is not a decision to take lightly. It can be a significant commitment. Varying learning curves are associated with the methodologies you've looked at in this chapter. Some require that you structure your applications a certain way, which might be contrary to what you or others you work with are accustomed to.

For example, a commitment to an object-oriented methodology by a team of less-experienced programmers can prove to be challenging.

Another important point is that different methodologies exploit different features of the CFML language, and this language is not static. It has evolved quite significantly over the years. Moreover, Macromedia has indicated that ColdFusion will soon be completely rewritten in Java (although you'll still be able to write applications in CFML). The point is you should be concerned with the effect that future changes might have on the approach taken by the methodology.

A final note: Most application-development tools provide some degree of a programming framework themselves. They often include features that support certain types of coding. There is some inherent danger in coding approaches that attempt to circumvent the way the developer (Macromedia in this case) intended for the product to be used.

Conclusions

ColdFusion provides a rich development environment in which the developer has a great deal of freedom. If you're in the business of developing ColdFusion (or any other) applications, however, it might make sense to adopt a methodology when developing applications. The most significant benefit from taking this approach is that you and others you work with will be able to more easily maintain applications you create. Other benefits will vary a bit from one methodology to the next. However, all the methodologies discussed in this chapter are intended to help you build more modular reusable code. Along with generally good coding practices, all these methodologies also help you write code more efficiently.

It's important to note that you do not need to use any of these methodologies to produce good ColdFusion applications. You should, however, adopt some sort of methodical approach to developing applications—perhaps something you and your associates develop on your own—so that you can still attain the benefits associated with using a methodology.

PART V

Appendixes

APPENDIX 

ColdFusion Tag Reference

ColdFusion tags are the instructions to ColdFusion to perform database queries, process results, generate output, control program flow, handle errors, send and receive e-mail, and much more.

The following is a complete alphabetical list of CFML tags with a description of each.

The accompanying CD-ROM contains a complete reference of all these tags in PDF format so as to facilitate electronic searching and printing.

Tag	Description
<CFABORT>	Immediately halt processing of a ColdFusion template.
<CFAPPLET>	Embed user-supplied Java applets in <CFFORM> forms.
<CFAPPLICATION>	Define the scope of an application and to specify several aspects of the application's configuration.
<CFASSOCIATE>	Associate subtags, or child tags, with base tags.
<CFAUTHENTICATE>	Authenticates a user against a security context, defining a security context for the application.
<CFBREAK>	Break out of a looping process, unlike <CFABORT> does not stop ColdFusion processing.
<CFCACHE>	Improve the performance on pages in which content doesn't need to be dynamically created each time the page is requested, ColdFusion instead returns static HTML output created during prior processing.
<CFCASE>	Specify a case statement within a <CFSWITCH> block.
<CFCATCH>	Create catch blocks to catch errors in a <CFTRY> block.
<CFCOL>	Specify columns in a <CFTABLE> HTML table.
<CFCOLLECTION>	Programmatically create and administer Verity collections.
<CFCONTENT>	Set the MIM type so as to be able to send non-HTML documents to a client's browser.
<CFCOOKIE>	Set cookies, persistent client-side variables, on the client browser.
<CFDEFAULTCASE>	Specify a default case statement within a <CFSWITCH> block.
<CFDIRECTORY>	Obtain directory lists, manipulate directories.
<CFDUMP>	Output the contents of simple variables, queries, structures, arrays, and serialized WDDX packets for debugging.
<CFELSE>	The else portion of a <CFIF> statement.

Tag	Description
<CFELSEIF>	The else if portion of a <CFIF> statement.
<CFERROR>	Override the standard ColdFusion error messages and replace them with special error-handling templates that you specify.
<CFEXECUTE>	Execute processes on the ColdFusion server machine.
<CFEXIT>	Aborts the processing of a custom tag without aborting processing of the calling template.
<CFFILE>	Perform file-management operations, including uploading files from a browser; moving, renaming, copying, and deleting files; and reading and writing files.
<CFFLUSH>	Flushes ColdFusion's output buffer, sending the contents back to the Web browser.
<CFFORM>	Enables the use of other tags (<CFGRID>, <CFINPUT>, <CFSELECT>, <CFTEXTINPUT>, <CFSLIDER>, <CFTREE>, or any Java applets using <CFAPPLET>).
<CFFTP>	Interface to FTP—the Internet standard file transfer protocol.
<CFGRAPH>	Dynamically create Web-based data driven graphs.
<CFGRAPHDATA>	Provide data points for a <CFGRAPH>.
<CFGRID>	Create a Java applet data grid.
<CFGRIDCOLUMN>	Specify a <CFGRID> column explicitly.
<CFGRIDROW>	Specify a <CFGRID> data row.
<CFGRIDUPDATE>	Backend support for <CFGRID> in edit mode.
<CFHEADER>	Control the contents of specific HTTP headers.
<CFHTMLHEAD>	Write text into the header section of your Web page.
<CFHTTP>	Interface to HTTP—the Internet standard hypertext transfer protocol.
<CFHTTPPARAM>	Pass parameters to a <CFHTTP> request.
<CFIF>	Perform conditional processing.
<CFIMPERSONATE>	Impersonate another user defined in a security context.
<CFINCLUDE>	Include the contents of another template in the one being processed.
<CFINDEX>	Populate Verity collections with index data.
<CFINPUT>	Embed JavaScript client-side validation code in your HTML forms.
<CFINSERT>	Add a single row to a database table.
<CFLDAP>	Interact with LDAP servers.
<CFLOCATION>	Redirect a browser to a different URL.
<CFLOCK>	Place exclusive or read-only locks around a block of code.
<CFLOG>	Produce user-defined log files.

Tag	Description
<CFLOOP>	Implement programmatic looping.
<CFMAIL>	Generate SMTP mail from within ColdFusion templates.
<CFMAILPARAM>	Specify <CFMAIL> headers or provide file attachments.
<CFMODULE>	Execute a custom tag explicitly stating its full or relative path.
<CFOBJECT>	Use COM, Java, and CORBA objects within your ColdFusion applications.
<CFOUTPUT>	Output the results of a <CFQUERY> or any time text includes variables that are to be expanded.
<CFPARAM>	Specify default values for parameters and flag parameters that are required.
<CFPOP>	Retrieve and manipulate mail in a POP3 mailbox.
<CFPROCESSINGDIRECTIVE>	Suppress whitespace between the start and end tags.
<CFPROCPARAM>	Pass and retrieve parameters to and from <CFSTOREDPROC> invoked stored procedures.
<CFPROCRESULT>	Specify the result sets to be retrieved with <CFSTOREDPROC> invoked stored procedures.
<CFQUERY>	Submit SQL statements to a data source that is either previously configured or dynamically generated, or to another query.
<CFQUERYPARAM>	Define <CFQUERY> query parameters and their data types.
<CFREGISTRY>	Directly manipulate the system Registry.
<CFREPORT>	Interface to reports created with the Crystal Reports Professional report writer.
<CFRETHROW>	Force the current error to be invoked again within a <CFCATCH> block.
<CFSAVECONTENT>	Save the output of a page or portion of a page in a variable.
<CFSCHEDULE>	Programmatically create, update, delete, and execute tasks in the ColdFusion Administrator's scheduler.
<CFSCRIPT>	Mark blocks of ColdFusion script.
<CFSEARCH>	Performs searches against Verity collections (in much the same way <CFQUERY> performs searches against ODBC data sources).
<CFSELECT>	Simplify the process of creating data-driven <SELECT> form controls.
<CFSERVLET>	Execute Java Servlets running on a JRun server.
<CFSERVLETPARAM>	Pass parameters by value or by reference to a <CFSERVLET> invoked Java Servlet running on a JRun server.
<CFSET>	Assign a value to a variable.
<CFSETTING>	Control various aspects of page processing, such as controlling the output of HTML code in your pages or enabling and disabling debug output.

Tag	Description
<CFSILENT>	Suppress generated output.
<CFSLIDER>	Create a Java applet slider control.
<CFSTOREDPROC>	Invoke a SQL stored procedure.
<CFSWITCH>	Create a ColdFusion switch statement.
<CFTABLE>	Create a complete data-driven HTML <TABLE> automatically.
<CFTEXTINPUT>	Create a Java applet text input control.
<CFTHROW>	Force an error condition in a <CFTRY> block.
<CFTRANSACTION>	Group multiple <CFQUERY> uses into a single transaction.
<CFTREE>	Create a Java applet tree control.
<CFTREEITEM>	Specify tree elements for a <CFTREE> tree control.
<CFTRY>	Catch exceptions thrown by ColdFusion or explicitly with <CFTHROW> or <CFRETHROW>.
<CFUPDATE>	Update a single row in a database table.
<CFWDDX>	Serialize and deserialize ColdFusion data structures to the XML-based WDDX format.

APPENDIX B

ColdFusion Function Reference

Using ColdFusion Functions

ColdFusion provides a complete set of data manipulation and formatting functions. Here are some things to remember when using functions:

- Function names are not case sensitive, so `NOW()` is the same as `now()`, which is the same as `Now()`.
- When functions are used in body text rather than within a ColdFusion tag, they must be enclosed within `<CFOUTPUT>` tags.
- Functions can be nested.

The following is a complete list of CFML functions with a description of each. For added convenience, the functions have been grouped into logical sets.

The accompanying CD-ROM contains a complete reference of all these functions in PDF format so as to facilitate electronic searching and printing.

- **String manipulation functions**—A complete set of text parsing, comparison, and conversion functions
- **Date and time functions**—Can be used to create, parse, compare, and manipulate date and time values
- **Data formatting functions**—Enable you to display data in a variety of formats
- **Mathematical functions**—Can be used to perform calculations, perform conversions, and generate random numbers
- **International functions**—Provide localization support for dates, times, and other data types
- **List manipulation functions**—Used to control lists of values
- **Array manipulation functions**—Used to create and manage two- and three-dimensional arrays
- **Structure manipulation functions**—Used to create and manage ColdFusion structures
- **Query manipulation functions**—Used to create and manage ColdFusion queries
- **Security functions**—Give you access to security information returned by a `<CFAUTHENTICATE>` call

- **System functions**—Give you access to system directories, temporary files, and path manipulation functions
- **Client variable manipulation functions**—Enable you to control client variables
- **Expression evaluation functions**—Enable you to create and evaluate expressions on-the-fly
- **Bit and set manipulation functions**—Can be used to perform bit-level operations
- **Conversion functions**—Used to convert data from one form to another
- **Miscellaneous functions**—An assortment of functions that you can use to check for the existence of parameters, format URLs, and manipulate lists to be passed to SQL statements

STRING MANIPULATION FUNCTIONS

The ColdFusion string manipulation functions can be used to perform operations on character data. Strings can be hard-coded constants, table column values, or ColdFusion fields. As with all ColdFusion functions, these string manipulation functions can be nested.

Function	Description
`Asc()`	Returns the ASCII value of the leftmost character of a string, `0` if the string is empty.
`Chr()`	Converts an ASCII value into a printable character.
`CJustify()`	Centers a string within a field of a specified length.
`Compare()`	Perform a case-sensitive comparison on two strings.
`CompareNoCase()`	Perform a case-insensitive comparison on two strings.
`Decrypt()`	Decrypt a string encrypted with `Encrypt()`.
`Encrypt()`	Encrypt a string using a user specified key.
`Find()`	Performs a case-sensitive sub-string search.
`FindNoCase()`	Performs a case-insensitive sub-string search.
`FindOneOf()`	Returns the position of the first target string character that matches any of the characters in a specified set.
`GetToken()`	Extract specific sets of data within a string by specifying its index.
`Hash()`	Converts a string into a 32-byte hexadecimal string using the one-way MD5 algorithm.
`InputBaseN()`	Converts a string into a number using the base specified by radix.
`Insert()`	Insert text into a string.
`LCase()`	Converts a string to lowercase.
`Left()`	Returns the specified leftmost characters from the beginning of a string.
`Len()`	Returns the length of a specified string.

Function	Description
`LJustify()`	Left-aligns a string within a field of a specified length.
`LTrim()`	Trims whitespace from the beginning of a string.
`Mid()`	Returns a string of characters from any location in a string.
`REFind()`	Performs a case-sensitive search using regular expressions.
`REFindNoCase()`	Performs a case-insensitive search using regular expressions.
`RemoveChars()`	Returns a string with specified characters removed from it.
`RepeatString()`	Returns a string made up of a specified string repeated multiple times.
`Replace()`	Replace text within strings with alternative text.
`ReplaceList()`	Replaces all occurrences of elements in one string with corresponding elements in another.
`REReplace()`	Performs a case-sensitive search and replace using regular expressions.
`REReplaceNoCase()`	Performs a case-insensitive search and replace using regular expressions.
`Reverse()`	Reverses the characters in a string.
`Right()`	Returns the specified rightmost characters from the end of a string.
`RJustify()`	Right-aligns a string within a field of a specified length.
`RTrim()`	Trims whitespace from the end of a string.
`SpanExcluding()`	Extracts characters from the beginning of a string until a character that is part of a specified set is reached.
`SpanIncluding()`	Extracts characters from the beginning of a string only as long as they match characters in a specified set.
`StripCR()`	Removes all carriage return characters from a string.
`ToBase64()`	Returns the Base64 representation of a specified string or binary object.
`ToBinary()`	Converts a Base64 encoded string to a binary object.
`Trim()`	Trims whitespace from the beginning and end of a string.
`UCase()`	Converts a string to uppercase.
`Val()`	Converts the beginning of a string to a number.

DATE AND TIME FUNCTIONS

The ColdFusion Date and Time functions enable you to perform date and time manipulation on table columns and user-supplied fields.

Many of these functions work with date/time objects. A *date/time object* is a ColdFusion internal representation of a complete date and time with accuracy to the second. These objects are designed to facilitate the passing of date/time information between various ColdFusion functions and are not designed to be displayed as is. If you need to display a date/time object, you must use one of the date/time formatting functions.

Function	Description
`CreateDate()`	Returns a ColdFusion date/time object that can be used with other date-manipulation or formatting functions.
`CreateDateTime()`	Returns a ColdFusion date/time object that can be used with other date and time manipulation or formatting functions.
`CreateODBCDate()`	Returns a date in an ODBC date/time field that can safely be used in SQL statements.
`CreateODBCDateTime()`	Returns an ODBC date/time field that safely can be used in SQL statements.
`CreateODBCTime()`	Returns a time in an ODBC date/time field that can safely be used in SQL statements.
`CreateTime()`	Returns time in a ColdFusion date/time object that can be used with other time-manipulation or formatting functions.
`CreateTimeSpan()`	Creates a date/time object that can be used to rapidly perform date and time-based calculations.
`DateAdd()`	Add or subtract values to a date/time object.
`DateCompare()`	Compare two dates to determine whether they are the same or whether one is greater than the other.
`DateConvert()`	Converts local machine time to UTC (Universal Coordinated Time) time or vice versa.
`DateDiff()`	Returns the difference between two dates.
`DatePart()`	Returns the specified part of a passed date.
`Day()`	Returns a date/time object's day of month as a numeric value.
`DayOfWeek()`	Returns a date/time object's day of week as a numeric value.
`DayOfWeekAsString()`	Returns the English weekday name for a passed day of week number.
`DayOfYear()`	Returns a date/time object's day of year as a numeric value.
`DaysInMonth()`	Returns the number of days in a specified month.
`DaysInYear()`	Returns the number of days in a specified year.
`FirstDayOfMonth()`	Returns the day of the year on which the specified month starts.
`GetHTTPTimeString()`	Formats a ColdFusion date/time object according to the HTTP standard outlined in RFC 1123.
`GetTimeZoneInfo()`	Returns a structure containing relevant server time zone information.
`Hour()`	Returns a date/time object's hour as a numeric value.
`IsDate()`	Checks whether a string contains a valid date.
`IsLeapYear()`	Checks whether a specified year is a leap year.
`IsNumericDate()`	Checks whether a value passed as a date in the ColdFusion internal date format is in fact a legitimate date.
`Minute()`	Returns a date/time object's minute as a numeric value.
`Month()`	Returns a date/time object's month as a numeric value.

Function	Description
`MonthAsString()`	Returns the English month name for a passed month number.
`Now()`	Returns a date/time object containing the current date and time.
`ParseDateTime()`	Converts a date in string form into a ColdFusion date/time object.
`Quarter()`	Returns a date/time object's quarter as a numeric value.
`Second()`	Returns a date/time object's second as a numeric value.
`Week()`	Returns a date/time object's week in year as a numeric value.
`Year()`	Returns a date/time object's year as a numeric value.

DATA FORMATTING FUNCTIONS

Powerful data-manipulation functions and database-interaction capabilities are pretty useless unless you have ways to display data in a clean, readable format. ColdFusion data addresses this need by providing an array of highly capable formatting functions.

Many of these functions take optional format masks as parameters, thereby giving you an even greater level of control over the final output.

Function	Description
`DateFormat()`	Displays the date portion of a date/time object in a readable format.
`DecimalFormat()`	Outputs numbers with two decimal places, commas to separate the thousands, and a minus sign for negative values.
`DollarFormat()`	Outputs numbers with a dollar sign at the front, two decimal places, commas to separate the thousands, and a minus sign for negative values.
`FormatBaseN()`	Converts a number to a string using the base specified.
`HTMLCodeFormat()`	Displays text with HTML codes with a preformatted HTML block.
`HTMLEditFormat()`	Converts supplied text into a safe format, with any HTML control characters converted to their appropriate entity codes.
`NumberFormat()`	Displays numeric values in a readable format.
`TimeFormat()`	Displays the time portion of a date/time object in a readable format.
`ParagraphFormat()`	Converts text with embedded carriage returns for correct HTML display.
`YesNoFormat()`	Converts `TRUE` and `FALSE` values to `Yes` and `No`.

APP B

MATHEMATICAL FUNCTIONS

To assist you in performing calculations, ColdFusion comes with a complete suite of mathematical functions, random-number–generation functions, and arithmetic expressions. As with all ColdFusion functions, these mathematical functions can be nested.

Some of the mathematical functions take one or more numeric values as parameters. You may pass real values, integer values, and ColdFusion fields to these functions.

Function	Description
`Abs()`	Absolute value of passed number.
`Acos()`	The arc cosine of a passed number.
`Asin()`	The arc sine of a passed number in radians.
`Atn()`	Arc tangent of passed number.
`Ceiling()`	The closest integer greater than passed number.
`Cos()`	Cosine of passed number.
`DecrementValue()`	Number decremented by 1.
`Exp()`	E to the power of passed number.
`Fix()`	If passed number is greater than or equal to `0`, it returns the closest integer smaller than the passed number. If not, it returns the closest integer greater than the passed number.
`IncrementValue()`	Number incremented by 1.
`Int()`	The closest integer smaller than passed number.
`Log()`	Natural logarithm of passed number.
`Log10()`	Base 10 log of passed number.
`Max()`	The greater of the two passed numbers.
`Min()`	The smaller of the two passed numbers.
`Pi()`	Value of pi as 3.14159265359.
`Rand()`	A random number between 0 and 1.
`Randomize()`	Seeds the random number generator with the passed number.
`RandRange()`	A random integer value between the two passed numbers.
`Round()`	The integer closest (either greater or smaller) to the passed number.
`Sgn()`	Sign—either –1, 0, or 1, depending on whether the passed number is negative, 0, or positive.
`Sin()`	Sine of passed number.
`Sqr()`	Square root of passed number.
`Tan()`	Tangent of passed number.

INTERNATIONAL FUNCTIONS

ColdFusion fully supports the display, formatting, and manipulation of international dates, times, numbers, and currencies. To use ColdFusion's international support, you must specify the locale. A *locale* is an encapsulation of the set of attributes that govern the display and formatting of international date, time, number, and currency values. All locale functions (those beginning with LS use the current locale value which must be set using SetLocale().

Function	Description
GetLocale()	Returns the name of the locale currently in use.
LSCurrencyFormat()	Displays currency information formatted for the current locale.
LSDateFormat()	Displays the date portion of a date/time object in a readable format.
LSEuroCurrencyFormat()	Displays Euro currency formatted correctly.
LSIsCurrency()	Checks whether a string contains a valid currency for the current locale.
LSIsDate	Checks whether a string contains a valid date for the current locale.
LSIsNumeric	Checks whether a specified value is numeric taking into account the current locale.
LSNumberFormat()	Displays numeric values in a locale-specific readable format.
LSParseCurrency()	Converts a locale-specific number in string form into a valid number.
LSParseDateTime()	Converts a locale-specific date in string form into a ColdFusion date/time object.
LSParseEuroCurrency()	Converts a currency string that contains the Euro symbol or sign to a number.
LSParseNumber()	Converts a locale-specific number in string form into a valid number.
LSTimeFormat()	Displays the time portion of a date/time object in a locale-specific readable format.
SetLocale()	Sets the name of the locale to be used by any subsequent calls to the LS functions.

LIST MANIPULATION FUNCTIONS

ColdFusion lists are an efficient way to manage groups of information. Lists are made up of elements, which are values separated by delimiting characters. The default delimiter is a comma, but you can change it to any character or string if required. Lists are actually simple two-dimensional arrays. For more complex or multidimensional lists, you should use arrays instead.

This list format is well suited for ColdFusion applications; it is both the format that HTML forms use to submit fields with multiple values and the format used by SQL to specify lists in SQL statements.

Function	Description
ListAppend()	Adds an element to the end of a list.
ListChangeDelims()	Changes a lists delimiters.
ListContains()	Case-sensitive list search for an element containing specified text.

Function	Description
`ListContainsNoCase()`	Case-insensitive list search for an element containing specified text.
`ListDeleteAt()`	Deletes an element from a list.
`ListFind()`	Case-sensitive list search for a specific element.
`ListFindNoCase()`	Case-insensitive list search for a specific element.
`ListFirst()`	Returns the first element in a list.
`ListGetAt()`	Gets a specific list element by index.
`ListInsertAt()`	Inserts an element into a list.
`ListLast()`	Returns the last element in a list.
`ListLen()`	Returns the number of elements in a list.
`ListPrepend()`	Inserts an element at the beginning of a list.
`ListSort()`	Sorts a list.
`ListQualify()`	Returns the contents of a specified list with qualifying characters around each list element.
`ListRest()`	Returns a list containing all the elements after the first element.
`ListSetAt()`	Sets a specific list element by index.
`ListValueCount()`	Performs a case-sensitive search and returns the number of matching elements in a list.
`ListValueCountNoCase()`	Performs a case-insensitive search and returns the number of matching elements in a list.

ARRAY MANIPULATION FUNCTIONS

Arrays are special variables made up of collections of data. Array elements are accessed via their indexes into the array; to access the third element of a simple array, you would refer to `array[3]`, for example.

ColdFusion supports arrays with one to three dimensions. A one-dimensional array is similar to a list, whereas a two-dimensional array is similar to a grid. (In fact, under the hood, ColdFusion queries are essentially two-dimensional arrays.) Three-dimensional arrays are more like cubes.

Arrays are created using the `ArrayNew()` function. To create an array, you must specify the number of dimensions needed, between one and three. You don't need to specify how many elements will be stored in the array; ColdFusion automatically expands the array as necessary.

Function	Description
`ArrayAppend()`	Appends an element to an array.
`ArrayAvg()`	Returns the average numeric value in an array.
`ArrayClear()`	Deletes all data from an array.

Function	Description
`ArrayDeleteAt()`	Deletes a specific array element.
`ArrayInsertAt()`	Inserts an element into an array.
`ArrayIsEmpty()`	Checks whether an array has any data.
`ArrayLen()`	Returns the length of an array.
`ArrayMax()`	Returns the greatest numeric value in an array.
`ArrayMin()`	Returns the lowest numeric value in an array.
`ArrayNew()`	Creates a new array.
`ArrayPrepend()`	Inserts an element at the beginning of an array.
`ArrayResize()`	Resizes an array.
`ArraySet()`	Sets a specific array element.
`ArraySort()`	Sorts an array.
`ArraySum()`	Returns the sum of numeric values in an array.
`ArraySwap()`	Swaps the values in two array elements.
`ArrayToList()`	Converts a one-dimensional array to a list.
`IsArray()`	Checks whether a variable is a valid ColdFusion array.
`ListToArray()`	Converts a list to one-dimensional array.

STRUCTURE MANIPULATION FUNCTIONS

ColdFusion *structures* are special data types that contain one or more other variables. Structures are a way to group related variables together.

To create a structure you must use the `StructNew()` function. Unlike arrays, structures have no dimensions and grow dynamically as needed.

Function	Description
`Duplicate()`	Returns a deep copy of a structure.
`IsStruct()`	Checks whether a variable is a valid ColdFusion structure.
`StructClear()`	Deletes all data from a structure.
`StructCopy()`	Returns a clone of the specified structure, with all the keys and values of the specified structure intact.
`StructCount()`	Returns the number of items in a specified structure.
`StructDelete()`	Deletes an item from a structure.
`StructFind()`	Searches through a structure to find the key that matches the specified search text.
`StructInsert()`	Inserts an item into a structure.
`StructIsEmpty()`	Checks whether a structure has data.

Function	Description
StructKeyArray()	Returns the keys of a specified structure in an array.
StructKeyExists()	Checks whether a structure contains a specific key.
StructKeyList()	Returns a list of keys in the specified ColdFusion structure.
StructNew()	Creates a new structure.
StructUpdate()	Updates the specified key in a given structure with a specified value.

QUERY MANIPULATION FUNCTIONS

ColdFusion uses queries to return sets of data. Most queries are created with the `<CFQUERY>` tag, but other tags (`<CFPOP>` and `<CFLDAP>`) also return data in queries. ColdFusion also enables you to programmatically create your own queries using the `QueryNew()` function and set query values using `QuerySetCell()`.

Function	Description
IsQuery()	Checks whether a variable is a valid ColdFusion query.
QueryAddColumn()	Adds a new column to a specified query.
QueryAddRow()	Adds a row to an existing ColdFusion query.
QueryNew()	Returns a new query object, optionally with specified columns.
QuerySetCell()	Sets the values of specific cells in a query.

SECURITY FUNCTIONS

ColdFusion supports advanced security contexts that let you create complete security systems to secure your applications. Security is managed and maintained using the ColdFusion Administrator. After security is established, you can make a call to the `<CFAUTHENTICATE>` tag to return security information. Use these security functions to interact with that security information.

Function	Description
AuthenticatedContext()	Returns the name of the currently valid security context.
AuthenticatedUser()	Returns the name of the currently authenticated user.
IsAuthenticated()	Checks whether a user has been authenticated with the `<CFAUTHENTICATE>` tag.
IsAuthorized()	Checks whether a user is authorized to perform specific actions.
IsProtected()	Checks whether the resource that is being accessed is protected in the security context of the authenticated user.

SYSTEM FUNCTIONS

The ColdFusion system functions enable you to perform manipulation of file paths, create temporary files, and verify file existence.

Function	Description
`DirectoryExists()`	Checks for the existence of a specified directory.
`ExpandPath()`	Converts a relative path into a fully qualified path.
`FileExists()`	Checks for the existence of a specified file.
`GetCurrentTemlatePath()`	Returns the complete path of the template calling this function.
`GetDirectoryFromPath()`	Extracts the drive and directory (with a trailing backslash) from a fully specified path.
`GetFileFromPath()`	Extracts the filename from a fully specified path.
`GetMetricData()`	Returns a structure containing system and application metrics based on the mode specified.
`GetProfileString()`	Gets the value of a profile entry in an INI format initialization file.
`GetTempDirectory()`	Returns the full path of the operating system temporary directory.
`GetTempFile()`	Creates and returns the full path to a temporary file for use by your application.
`GetTemplatePath()`	Returns the fully qualified path of the base template being processed.
`SetProfileString()`	Sets the value of a profile entry in an INI format initialization file.

CLIENT VARIABLE MANIPULATION FUNCTIONS

Client variables enable you to store client information so it is available between sessions. Client variables can be accessed just like any other ColdFusion variables; standard variable access tools, such as `<CFSET>`, can therefore be used to set variables. In addition, these functions provide special variable manipulation capabilities.

Function	Description
`DeleteClientVariable()`	Deletes specified client variables.
`GetClientVariableList()`	Returns a comma-delimited list of the read/write client variables available for use.

APP B

EXPRESSION EVALUATION FUNCTIONS

ColdFusion enables you to perform *dynamic expression evaluation*. This is an advanced technique that allows you to build and evaluate expressions on-the-fly.

Dynamic expression evaluations are performed on string expressions. A string expression is just that—a string that contains an expression. The string `"1+2"` contains an expression that, when evaluated, returns `3`. String expressions can be as simple or as complex as necessary.

Function	Description
`DE()`	Flags an expression for delayed evaluation.
`Evaluate()`	Evaluates string expressions.
`IIf()`	Performs an inline if statement.
`SetVariable()`	Sets a specified variable to a passed value.

BIT AND SET MANIPULATION FUNCTIONS

ColdFusion provides a complete set of bit manipulation functions for use by advanced developers only. These functions enable you to manipulate the individual bits within a 32-bit integer.

Function	Description
`BitAnd(x, y)`	Return `x` and `y`.
`BitMaskClear(x, start, length)`	Return `x` with length bits starting from start cleared.
`BitMaskRead(x, start, length)`	The value of length bits starting from start.
`BitMaskSet(x, mask, start, length)`	Return `x` with mask occupying the length bits starting from start.
`BitNot(x)`	Return not `x`.
`BitOr(x, y)`	Return `x	y`.
`BitSHLN(x, n)`	Return `x << n`.
`BitSHRN(x, n)`	Return `x >> n`.
`BitXor(x, y)`	Return `x^y`.

CONVERSION FUNCTIONS

These functions are provided to enable you to easily convert data from one type to another.

Function	Description
`JavaCast()`	Cast a variable for use within a Java object.
`JSStringFormat()`	Formats a specified string so that it is safe to use with JavaScript.
`ToString()`	Convert any value, including binary values, into a string.
`XMLFormat()`	Formats a specified string so that it is safe to use with XML.

MISCELLANEOUS FUNCTIONS

The following functions are listed here to give you access to some of the lesser-known, yet nonetheless important, functions available to you in ColdFusion 5.

Function	Description
`CreateObject()`	Invoke COM, CORBA, or Java objects (equivalent to the `<CFOBJECT>` tag).
`CreateUUID()`	Returns a 35-character string representation of a unique 128-bit number.
`GetBaseTagData()`	Returns an object containing data from a specified ancestor tag.
`GetBaseTagList()`	Returns a comma-delimited list of base tag names.
`GetBaseTemplatePath()`	Returns the full path of the base template.
`GetFunctionList()`	Returns a structure containing all built-in functions available in ColdFusion.
`GetHTTPRequestData()`	Retrieves the HTTP request headers and body and makes them available for use.
`GetTickCount()`	Returns a tick count used to perform timing tests with millisecond accuracy.
`IsBinary()`	Tests whether a specified value is binary.
`IsBoolean()`	Determines whether a value can be converted to a Boolean value.
`IsCustomFunction()`	Checks whether or not a specified function is a user-defined function.
`IsDebugMode()`	Checks whether a page is being sent back to the user in debug mode.
`IsDefined()`	Determines whether a specified variable exists.
`IsNumeric()`	Checks whether a specified value is numeric.
`IsSimpleValue()`	Checks whether a value is a string, number, `TRUE/FALSE` value, or a date/time object.
`ParameterExists()`	Checks to see whether a specified variable exists (deprecated, use `IsDefined()` instead).
`PreserveSingleQuotes()`	Instructs ColdFusion to not escape single quotation marks contained in values derived from dynamic parameters.
`QuotedValueList()`	Returns a list of values in a specified query column, all values enclosed within quotes.
`URLDecode()`	Decodes a URL encoded string.
`URLEncodedFormat()`	Encodes a string in a format that safely can be used within URLs.
`ValueList()`	Returns a list of values in a specified query column.
`WriteOutput()`	Appends text to the page output stream.

MISCELLANEOUS FUNCTIONS

APPENDIX C

Special ColdFusion Variables and Result Codes

In this appendix

Special ColdFusion Variables and Result Codes

ColdFusion provides access to many special variables that can be used within your applications. These variables generally fall into one of several categories:

- System variables
- Scope-related variables
- Tag-specific variables
- Query-related variables

All these variables can be used like any variables, by simply referencing them. Some have specific prefixes; others use specified names (for example, a query name) as their prefixes.

The following is a complete list of all special ColdFusion variables. Descriptions are provided for those that are not tag related (tag-related variables are described along with the appropriate tags in Appendix A, "ColdFusion Tag Reference"). For your convenience, cross references to appropriate chapters in this book are provided as well.

APPLICATION Variables

APPLICATION is a special scope whose contents are available to all requests within an application. APPLICATION primarily is used for storage of custom information, but one predefined variable exists within it, as listed in Table C.1.

Table C.1 APPLICATION Variables

Variable	Description
APPLICATION.ApplicationName	Application name, as specified in the <CFAPPLICATION> tag

Caution

APPLICATION variables must be locked (using <CFLOCK>) before they are accessed.

Note

APPLICATION variables and the <CFAPPLICATION> tag are covered in detail in Chapter 19,"Introducing the Web Application Framework."

ATTRIBUTE Variables

ATTRIBUTE is a special scope within ColdFusion, but it does not contain any predefined variables.

CALLER Variables

CALLER is a special scope that contains no predefined variables. Only valid for use within custom tags, CALLER provides access to the caller page's scope.

Note The CALLER scope is explained in Chapter 22, "Building Reusable Components."

CGI VARIABLES

CGI variables are read-only variables that are prepopulated by ColdFusion for your use. They contain information about the server, request, and client. Some of the more common CGI variables are listed in Table C.2.

Caution Not all servers and clients set all these variables; check for their existence before use.

TABLE C.2 CGI VARIABLES

Variable	Description
CGI.ALL_HTTP	All HTTP headers in header:value sets
CGI.ALL_RAW	All HTTP headers in raw form (as submitted by the client)
CGI.APPL_MD_PATH	Metabase path for the application when using ISAPI
CGI.APPL_PHYSICAL_PATH	Physical metabase path for the application when using ISAPI
CGI.AUTH_GROUP	Authentication group
CGI.AUTH_PASSWORD	Authentication password as specified by the client (if AUTH_TYPE is Basic)
CGI.AUTH_REALM	Authentication realm
CGI.AUTH_REALM_DESCRIPTION	Authentication realm browser string
CGI.AUTH_TYPE	Authentication method if authentication is supported and used, usually null or Basic
CGI.AUTH_USER	Authenticated username if authenticated by the operating system
CGI.CERT_COOKIE	Unique ID of client certificate
CGI.CERT_FLAGS	Certification flags; first bit will be on if client certificate is present; second bit will be on if the client certificate certifying authority (CA) is unknown
CGI.CERT_ISSUER	Client certificate issuer
CGI.CERT_KEYSIZE	Number of bits in SSL connection key size
CGI.CERT_SECRETKEYSIZE	Number of bits in server certificate private key
CGI.CERT_SERIALNUMBER	Client certificate serial number
CGI.CERT_SERVER_ISSUER	Server certificate issuer field
CGI.CERT_SERVER_SUBJECT	Server certificate subject field
CGI.CERT_SUBJECT	Server certificate subject field
CGI.CF_TEMPLATE_PATH	Path of ColdFusion file being executed

Table C.2 Continued

Variable	Description
`CGI.CONTENT_LENGTH`	Length of submitted content (as reported by the client)
`CGI.CONTENT_TYPE`	Content type of submitted data
`CGI.DATE_GMT`	Current GMT date and time
`CGI.DATE_LOCAL`	Current local date and time
`CGI.DOCUMENT_NAME`	The complete local directory path of the current document
`CGI.DOCUMENT_URI`	The local path of the current document relative to the Web site base directory
`CGI.GATEWAY_INTERFACE`	CGI interface revision number (if CGI interface is used)
`CGI.HTTP_ACCEPT`	List of content types that will be accepted by the client browser
`CGI.HTTP_ACCEPT_CHARSET`	ID of client browser ISO character set in use
`CGI.HTTP_ACCEPT_ENCODING`	List of types of encoded data that will be accepted by the browser
`CGI.HTTP_ACCEPT_LANGUAGE`	The human languages that can be accepted by the client
`CGI.HTTP_AUTHORIZATION`	Authorization string within the Web server (used by IIS)
`CGI.HTTP_CONNECTION`	HTTP connection type; usually `Keep-Alive`
`CGI.HTTP_COOKIE`	The cookie sent by the client
`CGI.HTTP_FORWARDED`	Any proxies or gateways that forwarded the request
`CGI.HTTP_HOST`	HTTP hostname, as sent by client
`CGI.HTTP_IF_MODIFIED_SINCE`	Cache request value as submitted by the client
`CGI.HTTP_PRAGMA`	Any pragma directives
`CGI.HTTP_REFERER`	The URL of the referring document (if referred)
`CGI.HTTP_UA_CPU`	Client computer CPU (processor) identifier (as provided by the client browser)
`CGI.HTTP_UA_COLOR`	Client computer color capabilities (as provided by the client browser)
`CGI.HTTP_UA_OS`	Client computer operating system (as provided by the client browser)
`CGI.HTTP_UA_PIXELS`	Client computer display resolution
`CGI.HTTP_USER_AGENT`	Client browser identifier (as provided by the client itself)
`CGI.HTTPS`	Flag indicating if the request was via a secure HTTPS connection
`CGI.HTTPS_KEYSIZE`	Number of bits in SSL connection key size
`CGI.HTTPS_SECRETKEYSIZE`	Number of bits in server certificate private key
`CGI.HTTPS_SERIALNUMBER`	Server certificate serial number

Variable	Description
CGI.HTTPS_SERVER_ISSUER	Server certificate issuer field
CGI.HTTPS_SERVER_SUBJECT	Server certificate subject field
CGI.INSTANCE_ID	ID of IIS instance
CGI.INSTANCE_META_PATH	Metabase path for the instance of IIS responding to a request
CGI.LAST_MODIFIED	Date and time of last modification of document
CGI.LOCAL_ADDRESS	IP address of server on which request came in (used primarily in multihomed hosts)
CGI.LOGON_USER	Windows account the user is logged in to
CGI.PATH_INFO	Requested file path information (as provided by the client)
CGI.PATH_TRANSLATED	Server translation of `CGI.PATH_INFO` (can be set even if `CGI.PATH_INFO` is empty)
CGI.QUERY_STRING	Contents of the URL after the `?`
CGI.QUERY_STRING_UNESCAPED	Unescaped version of `CGI.QUERY_STRING`
CGI.REMOTE_ADDR	Client IP address
CGI.REMOTE_HOST	Client hostname (if available)
CGI.REMOTE_IDENT	Remote user identification (if server supports RFC 931)
CGI.REMOTE_USER	Authentication method if authentication is supported and used
CGI.REQUEST_BODY	Request body text (used by Apache)
CGI.REQUEST_METHOD	Request method (for example, `GET`, `HEAD`, or `POST`)
CGI.REQUEST_URI	Requested URL; useful when multiple hosts share a single IP address (used by Apache)
CGI.SCRIPT_FILENAME	Logical path of script being executed (used by Apache)
CGI.SCRIPT_NAME	Logical path of script being executed
CGI.SERVER_ADMIN	E-mail address of server administrator (used by Apache)
CGI.SERVER_CHARSET	Server default character set
CGI.SERVER_NAME	Server name
CGI.SERVER_PORT	Server port on which request was received
CGI.SERVER_PORT_SECURE	Server port on which secure request was received (usually `0` if not secure)
CGI.SERVER_PROTOCOL	Name and version of the server protocol with which request was received
CGI.SERVER_SIGNATURE	Server ID, host, and port (used by Apache)
CGI.SERVER_SOFTWARE	HTTP server software name and version
CGI.URL	URL base
CGI.WEB_SERVER_API	Web server API used (if not CGI)

Note

CGI variable support varies from server to server and from browser to browser. Not all the CGI variables listed in Table C.2 will always be available, so check for their existence before using them.

Tip

The ColdFusion function `GetHTTPRequestData()` returns a structure containing all browser-specified information, potentially including information not available via CGI variables.

<CFCATCH> Variables

<CFCATCH> is part of ColdFusion's error-handling system, and when errors occur, details are made available via these variables:

- `CFCATCH.Detail`
- `CFCATCH.ErrNumber`
- `CFCATCH.ErrorCode`
- `CFCATCH.ExtendedInfo`
- `CFCATCH.LockName`
- `CFCATCH.LockOperation`
- `CFCATCH.Message`
- `CFCATCH.MissingFileName`
- `CFCATCH.NativeErrorCode`
- `CFCATCH.SQLState`
- `CFCATCH.TagContext`
- `CFCATCH.Type`

These variables are described in Appendix A on the accompanying CD-ROM.

Note

CFCATCH variables and the <CFCATCH> tag are covered in detail in Chapter 33, "Error Handling."

<CFDIRECTORY ACTION="list"> Query Columns

<CFDIRECTORY> is used to perform operations on filesystem directories. When `ACTION="list"` is used to retrieve directory contents, a query is returned containing the following columns:

- `query.Attributes`
- `query.DateLastModified`

- `query.Mode`
- `query.Name`
- `query.Size`
- `query.Type`

These columns are described in Appendix A on the accompanying CD-ROM.

Note

As with all queries, the standard query variables can also be used with the resultset. The standard query variables are listed in the section "`Query` Variables," later in this appendix.

Note

The `<CFDIRECTORY>` tag is covered in detail in Chapter 35, "Interacting with the Operating System."

`<CFFILE ACTION="upload">` VARIABLES

`<CFFILE>` is used to perform filesystem operations. When `ACTION="upload"` is used to process uploaded files, process details are made available via the following variables:

- `CFFILE.AttemptedServerFile`
- `CFFILE.ClientDirectory`
- `CFFILE.ClientFile`
- `CFFILE.ClientFileExt`
- `CFFILE.ClientFileName`
- `CFFILE.ContentSubType`
- `CFFILE.ContentType`
- `CFFILE.DateLastAccessed`
- `CFFILE.FileExisted`
- `CFFILE.FileSize`
- `CFFILE.FileWasAppended`
- `CFFILE.FileWasOverwritten`
- `CFFILE.FileWasRenamed`
- `CFFILE.FileWasSaved`
- `CFFILE.OldFileSize`
- `CFFILE.ServerDirectory`
- `CFFILE.ServerFile`
- `CFFILE.ServerFileExt`
- `CFFILE.ServerFileName`

- `CFFILE.TimeCreated`
- `CFFILE.TimeLastModified`

These variables are described in Appendix A on the accompanying CD-ROM.

Note

CFFILE variables and the <CFFILE> tag are covered in detail in Chapter 35.

<CFFTP> VARIABLES

<CFFTP> is used to perform server-side FTP operations. Upon operation completion, the following variables will contain status information:

- `CFFTP.ErrorCode`
- `CFFTP.ErrorText`
- `CFFTP.ReturnValue`
- `CFFTP.Succeeded`

These variables are described in Appendix A.

Note

CFFTP variables and the <CFFTP> tag are covered in the sequel to this book, *Advanced ColdFusion 5 Development* (Que, ISBN: 0-7897-2585-1).

<CFFTP ACTION="ListDir"> QUERY COLUMNS

<CFFTP> is used to perform server-side FTP operations. When ACTION="listdir" is used to retrieve directory contents, a query is returned containing the following columns:

- `query.Attributes`
- `query.IsDirectory`
- `query.LastModified`
- `query.Length`
- `query.Mode`
- `query.Name`
- `query.Path`
- `query.URL`

These columns are described in Appendix A.

Note

As with all queries, the standard query variables can also be used with a resultset. The standard query variables are listed in the section "Query Variables," later in this appendix.

Note

<CFFTP> results and the <CFFTP> tag are covered in the sequel to this book, *Advanced ColdFusion 5 Development* (Que, ISBN: 0-7897-2585-1).

<CFHTTP> Variables

<CFHTTP> is used to perform server-side HTTP operations. Upon operation completion, the following variables will contain status information:

- `CFHTTP.FileContent`
- `CFHTTP.MimeType`
- `CFHTTP.Header`
- `CFHTTP.Response`
- `CFHTTP.ResponseHeader`
- `CFHTTP.StatusCode`

These variables are described in Appendix A on the accompanying CD-ROM.

Note

Not all available variables are returned when `METHOD="post"`.

Note

`CFHTTP` variables and the <CFHTTP> tag are covered in the sequel to this book, *Advanced ColdFusion 5 Development* (Que, ISBN: 0-7897-2585-1).

<CFLDAP ACTION="query"> Query Columns

<CFLDAP> is used to interact with LDAP servers. When `ACTION="query"` is used to retrieve directory information, a query is returned containing the requested data. There are no predefined query columns; the query will contain a column for each value specified in the `ATTRIBUTES` attribute.

Note

As with all queries, the standard query variables can also be used with a resultset. The standard query variables are listed in the section "`Query` Variables," later in this appendix.

Note

The <CFLDAP> tag is covered in the sequel to this book, *Advanced ColdFusion 5.0 Development* (ISBN: 0-7897-2585-1).

<CFPOP ACTION="GetHeaderOnly|GetAll> Query Columns

<CFPOP> is used to access POP3 mailboxes. When either ACTION="GetHeaderOnly" or ACTION="GetAll" is used to retrieve mailbox contents, a query is returned containing the following columns:

- query.AttachmentFiles
- query.Attachments
- query.Body
- query.CC
- query.Date
- query.From
- query.Header
- query.MessageNumber
- query.ReplyTo
- query.Subject
- query.To

These columns are described in Appendix A on the accompanying CD-ROM.

Note

As with all queries, the standard query variables can also be used with a resultset. The standard query variables are listed in the section "Query Variables," later in this appendix.

Note

Not all query columns are returned when ACTION="GetHeaderOnly".

Note

<CFPOP> results and the <CFPOP> tag are covered in detail in Chapter 28, "Interacting with E-mail."

<CFQUERY> Variables

<CFQUERY> is used to execute SQL statements. In addition to returning a query (named in the NAME attribute), one predefined variable exists, as listed in Table C.3.

Table C.3 <CFQUERY> Variables

Variable	Description
CFQUERY.ExecutionTime	Query execution time (in milliseconds)

Note

As with all queries, the standard query variables can also be used with a resultset. The standard query variables are listed in the section "Query Variables," later in this appendix.

Note

The <CFQUERY> is introduced in Chapter 11, "Creating Data-Driven Pages."

<CFREGISTRY> Query Variables

<CFREGISTRY> is used to access the Windows Registry. When ACTION="GetAll" is used to retrieve Registry data, a query is returned containing the following columns:

- query.Entry
- query.Type
- query.Value

These columns are described in Appendix A on the accompanying CD-ROM.

Note

As with all queries, the standard query variables can also be used with a resultset. The standard query variables are listed in the section "Query Variables," later in this appendix.

Note

The <CFREGISTRY> tag and returned query columns are covered in detail in Chapter 35.

<CFSEARCH> Results Variables

<CFSEARCH> is used to perform full-text searches using the integrated Verity search engine. When a search is performed, a query is returned containing the following columns:

- query.Custom1
- query.Custom2
- query.Key
- query.RecordsSearched
- query.Score
- query.Summary
- query.Title
- query.URL

These columns are described in Appendix A.

Note

As with all queries, the standard query variables can also be used with a resultset. The standard query variables are listed in the section "`Query` Variables," later in this appendix.

Note

The `<CFSEARCH>` tag and returned query columns are covered in detail in Chapter 36, "Full-Text Searching."

`<CFSERVLET>` VARIABLES

`<CFSERVLET>` is used to execute Java servlets within a Java Application Server. Upon operation completion, the following variable can contain results:

- CFSERVLET.Output
- `CFSERVLET.ServletResponseHeaderName`

This variable is described in Appendix A on the accompanying CD-ROM.

Note

`CFSERVLET` variables and the `<CFSERVLET>` tag are covered in the sequel to this book, *Advanced ColdFusion 5.0 Development* (ISBN: 0-7897-2585-1).

`<CFSTOREDPROC>` VARIABLES

`<CFSTOREDPROC>` is used to execute SQL stored procedures. In addition to returning one or more queries, two predefined variables exist, as listed in Table C.4.

TABLE C.4 `<CFSTOREDPROC>` VARIABLES

Variable	Description
`CFSTOREDPROC.ExecutionTime`	Stored procedure execution time (in milliseconds)
`CFSTOREDPROC.StatusCode`	Stored procedure returned status code

Note

Query-related tags are listed in the section "`Query` Variables," later in this appendix.

Note

The `<CFSTOREDPROC>` tag is covered in Chapter 32, "Working with Stored Procedures."

`CLIENT` VARIABLES

`CLIENT` is a special scope whose contents are client specific and persistent. `CLIENT` primarily is used for storage of custom information, but several predefined variables exist within it, as listed in Table C.5.

TABLE C.5 CLIENT VARIABLES

Variable	Description
CLIENT.CFID	Client ID, used as part of the client identification mechanism
CLIENT.CFToken	Client token, used as part of the client identification mechanism
CLIENT.HitCount	Request counter
CLIENT.LastVisit	Date and time of last client visit
CLIENT.TimeCreated	Date and time of first client visit
CLIENT.URLToken	String containing complete CFID and CFToken values (for URL embedding)

Note

CLIENT variables and the <CFAPPLICATION> tag are covered in detail in Chapter 20, "Working with Sessions."

COOKIE Variables

COOKIE is a special scope within ColdFusion, but it does not contain any predefined variables.

Note

The COOKIE scope is explained in Chapter 20.

ERROR Variables

<CFERROR> is used to create alternate error pages to be displayed when errors occur. Within those pages, the following ERROR variables are available for use:

- ERROR.Browser
- ERROR.DateTime
- ERROR.Detail
- ERROR.Diagnostics
- ERROR.ErrNumber
- ERROR.ErrorCode
- ERROR.ExtendedInfo
- ERROR.GeneratedContent
- ERROR.HTTPReferer
- ERROR.InvalidFields
- ERROR.LockName
- ERROR.LockOperation
- ERROR.MailTo
- ERROR.Message

- ERROR.MissingFileName
- ERROR.NativeErrorCode
- ERROR.QueryString
- ERROR.RemoteAddress
- ERROR.SQLState
- ERROR.TagContext
- ERROR.Template
- ERROR.Type
- ERROR.ValidationError
- ERROR.ValidationFooter

These variables are described in Appendix A on the accompanying CD-ROM.

Note Not all ERROR variables are always available; this varies based on the type of error and error page.

Note ERROR variables and the <CFERROR> tag are covered in detail in Chapter 19.

FORM VARIABLES

FORM is a special scope that contains form submissions. FORM also contains one predefined variable within it, as listed in Table C.6.

TABLE C.6 FORM VARIABLES

Variable	Description
FORM.FieldNames	Comma-delimited list of all submitted form field names

Note Form use within ColdFusion is introduced in Chapter 12, "ColdFusion Forms."

Query VARIABLES

Queries are resultsets returned by many ColdFusion tags (or created with the QueryNew() function). Queries primarily contain columns of data, but three predefined variables also exist, as listed in Table C.7.

Table C.7 Query Variables

Variable	Description
`ColumnList`	Comma-delimited list of query column names
`CurrentRow`	Current row (when being looped within `<CFOUTPUT>`)
`RecordCount`	Number of rows in query

Note

ColdFusion queries are introduced in Chapter 11.

REQUEST Variables

`REQUEST` is a special scope within ColdFusion, but it does not contain any predefined variables.

Note

The `CALLER` scope is explained in Chapter 22.

SERVER Variables

`SERVER` is a special scope whose contents are available to all requests within all applications. `SERVER` should generally not be used for storage of custom information, and several predefined variables exist within it, as listed in Table C.8.

Table C.8 SERVER Variables

Variable	Description
`SERVER.ColdFusion.ProductName`	ColdFusion product name
`SERVER.ColdFusion.ProductVersion`	ColdFusion product version
`SERVER.ColdFusion.ProductLevel`	ColdFusion product level
`SERVER.ColdFusion.SerialNumber`	ColdFusion serial number
`SERVER.ColdFusion.SupportedLocales`	List of supported ColdFusion locales
`SERVER.OS.Name`	Operating system name
`SERVER.OS.AdditionalInformation`	Operating system additional information
`SERVER.OS.Version`	Operating system version
`SERVER.OS.BuildNumber`	Operating system build number

Caution

`SERVER` variables must be locked (using `<CFLOCK>`) before they are accessed.

SESSION VARIABLES

SESSION is a special scope, the contents of which are client specific and persistent for a specified duration. SESSION primarily is used for the storage of custom information, but several predefined variables exist within it, as listed in Table C.9.

TABLE C.9 SESSION VARIABLES

Variable	Description
SESSION.CFID	Client ID, used as part of the client identification mechanism
SESSION.CFToken	Client token, used as part of the client identification mechanism
SESSION.URLToken	String containing complete CFID and CFToken values (for URL embedding)

Note

SESSION variables and the <CFAPPLICATION> tag are covered in detail in Chapter 20.

ThisTag VARIABLES

ThisTag is a special scope that exists only within ColdFusion custom tags. It can be used for storage of data and also includes several predefined variables within it, as listed in Table C.10.

TABLE C.10 ThisTag VARIABLES

Variable	Description
ThisTag.AssocAttribs	Associated attributes (if an associated tag is used)
ThisTag.ExecutionMode	Tag execution mode
ThisTag.GeneratedContent	Content between the tag pairs in the caller page
ThisTag.HasEndTag	Flag indicating calling convention (as a single tag, or as part of a tag pair)

Note

The ThisTag scope and custom tags in general are covered in detail in Chapter 22.

URL VARIABLES

URL is a special scope within ColdFusion, but it does not contain any predefined variables.

Note

URL use within ColdFusion is introduced in Chapter 11.

APPENDIX

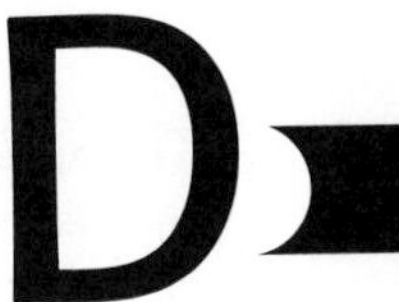

Verity Search Language Reference

In this appendix

This appendix describes each of the search operators that can be passed to Verity in the CRITERIA parameter of a <CFSEARCH> tag. See Chapter 36, "Full-Text Searching," for details on incorporating Verity into your ColdFusion applications.

This is not meant to be an exhaustive reference. You should consult your ColdFusion documentation for each operator's precise definition and syntax. Verity's Web site is also a good resource for information regarding the syntax and impact of the search operators discussed in this appendix. There are many FAQs (frequently asked questions) and examples of search syntax in action. Just keep in mind that Verity's search functionality is not a ColdFusion-only thing. You will find references to features that are not exposed to you as a ColdFusion developer. Verity's Web site can be found at http://www.verity.com/.

Using Angle Brackets Around Operators

With the exception of AND, OR, and NOT, you must use angle brackets around all Verity operators. This tells Verity that you're interested in actually using the NEAR operator, for example, rather than just trying to search for the word *near* in your document. The following line is not searching for the word *near*:

```
CRITERIA="Sick <NEAR> Days"
```

Again, AND, OR, and NOT do not need the angle brackets—the idea is they will be used very often, and people infrequently need to search for the actual words *and*, *or*, or *not* in their documents. The following two lines are equivalent:

```
CRITERIA="Sick AND Days"
CRITERIA="Sick <AND> Days"
```

Operators Are Not Case Sensitive

Verity search operators are not case sensitive, even when the search itself might be case sensitive. Therefore, these two statements are also equivalent:

```
CRITERIA="Sick <NEAR> Days"
CRITERIA="Sick <near> Days"
```

Using Prefix Instead of Infix Notation

All Verity operators except for the evidence operators (STEM, WILDCARD, and WORD) can be specified using something called *prefix notation*.

For instance, suppose you have several search words on which you want to use the NEAR operator. Instead of sticking <NEAR> between each word, you can just specify NEAR once and then put the list of words in parentheses. The following two lines are equivalent:

```
CRITERIA="sick <NEAR> days <NEAR> illness"
CRITERIA="<NEAR>(sick,days,illness)"
```

Searching for Special Characters as Literals

Special characters—most obviously, the < and > characters—have special meaning for Verity. If you want to actually search for these characters, you must use a backslash (\) to "escape" each special character. For example, if you want to search for documents that contain `<TABLE>`, you must do it like this:

```
CRITERIA="\<TABLE\>"
```

Understanding Concept Operators

Verity's *concept operators* are used when you specify more than one search word or search element. The concept operator tells Verity whether you mean that all the words/elements must be present in the document for it to count as a match, or if any one word/element makes the document count as a match. The concept operators include `AND` and `OR`.

The `AND` operator indicates that all the search words/elements must be present in a document for the document to count as a match. Here are some examples:

```
CRITERIA="sick AND days AND illness"
CRITERIA="sick <AND> days <AND> illness"
CRITERIA="AND (sick,days,illness)"
```


Tip

Remember that, unlike most other operators, `AND` does not need angle brackets around it.

The `OR` operator indicates that a document counts as a match as soon as any of the search words/elements are present in the document. The following are some examples:

```
CRITERIA="sick OR days OR illness"
CRITERIA="sick <OR> days <OR> illness"
CRITERIA="OR (sick,days,illness)"
```

Tip

Remember that, unlike the majority of operators, `OR` does not need angle brackets around it.

Understanding Evidence Operators

Verity's *evidence operators* control whether Verity steps in and searches for words that are slightly different from the search words you actually specify.

Remember that, unlike other operators, evidence operators cannot be used with prefix notation. Instead, they must be specified with *infix notation*—that is, they must be inserted between each word of a set. See the example for `STEM`, which follows.

Evidence operators include STEM, WILDCARD, and WORD.

The STEM operator tells Verity to expand the search to include grammatical variations of the search words you specify. In other words, Verity takes each word and finds its root and then searches for all the common variations of that root. If the search were for *permitting*, Verity would take it upon itself to also search for *permit* and *permitted*. Here are some examples:

```
CRITERIA="<STEM> permitting"
CRITERIA="AND (<STEM> permitting, <STEM> smoke)"
```

The WILDCARD operator tells Verity that the search words contain wildcards that should be considered while the search is occurring. Note that two of the wildcard characters—the question mark and asterisk—are automatically assumed to be wildcard characters, even if you don't specify the WILDCARD operator. The other wildcard characters will behave as such only if the WILDCARD operator is used. The following statements are examples:

```
CRITERIA="smok*"
CRITERIA="smok?"
CRITERIA="<WILDCARD>smok*"
CRITERIA="<WILDCARD>'smok{ed,ing}'"
```

Table D.1 summarizes the possible operators for a wildcard value.

TABLE D.1 VERITY WILDCARDS

Wildcard	Purpose
*	Like the % wildcard in SQL, * stands in for any number of characters (including 0).
	A search for Fu* would find *Fusion*, *Fugazi*, and *Fuchsia*.
?	Just as in SQL, ? stands in for any single character. More precise—and thus generally less helpful—than the * wildcard. A search for ?ar?et would find both *carpet* and *target*, but not *Learjet*.
{ }	Enable you to specify a number of possible word fragments, separated by commas. A search for {gr,frag,deodor}rant would find documents that contained *grant*, *fragrant*, or *deodorant*.
[ ]	Like { }, except brackets stand in for only one character at a time. A search for f[eao]ster would find documents that contained *fester*, *faster*, or *foster*.
-	Allows you to place a range of characters within square brackets. Searching for A[C-H]50993 is the same as searching for A[DEFGH]50993.

If you use any wildcard other than ? or *, you must use either single or double quotation marks around the actual wildcard pattern. I recommend that you use single quotation marks around the wildcard pattern because the criteria parameter as a whole should be within double quotation marks.

The WORD operator tells Verity to perform a simple word search, without any wildcarding or stemming. Including a WORD operator is a good way to suppress Verity's default use of the STEM operator; it is also effective if you don't want the ? in a search for Hello? to be treated as a wildcard character. Here are some examples:

```
CRITERIA="<WORD>smoke"
CRITERIA="<WORD>Hello?"
```

Understanding Proximity Operators

Verity's *proximity operators* are used to specify how close together search words must be to each other within a document for that document to count as a match. For example, if you were looking for rules about where smoking is permitted, you might want only documents that have the words *smoking* and *permitted* sitting pretty close to one another within the actual text. A document that has the word *smoking* at the beginning and the word *permitted* way at the end would probably not interest you. The proximity operators include NEAR, NEAR/N, PARAGRAPH, and SENTENCE.

The NEAR operator specifies that you are most interested in documents in which the search words are closest to one another. All documents in which the words are within 1,000 words of each other are considered "found," but the closer together the words, the higher the document's score, which means it will be up at the top of the list. The following is an example:


```
CRITERIA="smoking <NEAR> permitted"
```

The NEAR/N operator is just like NEAR, except that you get to specify how close together the words have to be to qualify as a match. Documents are still ranked based on the closeness of the words. In reality, NEAR is just shorthand for NEAR/1000. Some examples of the NEAR/N operator are as follows:

```
CRITERIA="smoking <NEAR/3> permitted"
CRITERIA="<NEAR/3>(smoking,permitted)"
```

The PARAGRAPH and SENTENCE operators specify that the words need to be in the same paragraph or sentence, respectively. Sometimes using these is better than NEAR or NEAR/N because you know that the words are related in some way having to do with their actual linguistic contexts, rather than their physical proximity to one another. Some examples are as follows:

```
CRITERIA="smoking <PARAGRAPH> permitted"
CRITERIA="<SENTENCE> (smoking,permitted)"
```

Understanding Relational Operators

Verity's *relational operators* enable you to search for words within specific document fields, such as the title of the document or a custom field. Searches that use these operators are not ranked by relevance. The relational operators include the following:

- CONTAINS
- MATCHES

- STARTS
- ENDS
- SUBSTRING
- =, <, >, <=, and >=

Table D.2 summarizes the document fields available for use with relational operators.

TABLE D.2 DOCUMENT FIELDS AVAILABLE FOR USE WITH RELATIONAL OPERATORS

Field	Explanation
CF_TITLE	The filename of the document if the collection is based on normal documents, or whatever table column you specified for TITLE if the collection is based on database data.
CF_CUSTOM1	Whatever table column you specified for CUSTOM1, if any, if your collection is based on database data.
CF_CUSTOM2	Whatever table column you specified for CUSTOM2, if any, if your collection is based on database data.
CF_KEY	The filename of the document if the collection is based on normal documents, or whatever table column you specified for KEY if the collection is based on database data. You use relational operators with this field if the user already knows the unique ID for the record you wanted, such as a knowledge base article number.
CF_URL	The URL path to the document, as defined when you indexed the collection.

The CONTAINS operator finds documents in which a specific field contains the exact word(s) you specify, similar to using the WORD operator on a specific field. If you specify more than one word, the words must appear in the correct order for the document to be considered a match. These are some examples:

```
CRITERIA="CF_TITLE <CONTAINS> smoking"
CRITERIA="CF_TITLE <CONTAINS>'smoking,policy'"
```

The MATCHES operator finds documents in which the entirety of a specific field is exactly what you specify. The field is looked at as a whole, not as individual words. A search for *Smoking Policy* in the CF_TITLE field would match only documents in which the title was literally *Smoking Policy*, verbatim. This feature is probably most useful with custom fields, if the custom field holds nothing more than some type of rating, category code, or the like. Here are some examples:

```
CRITERIA="CF_TITLE <MATCHES>'Smoking Policy'"
CRITERIA="CF_CUSTOM1 <MATCHES> Policies"
```

The `STARTS` operator finds documents in which a specific field starts with the characters you specify, such as this:

```
CRITERIA="CF_TITLE <STARTS> smok"
```

The `ENDS` operator finds documents in which a specific field ends with the characters you specify, such as the following:

```
CRITERIA="CF_TITLE <ENDS> olicy"
```

The `SUBSTRING` operator finds documents in which a specific field contains any portion of what you specify. Unlike `CONTAINS`, this matches incomplete words. Here is an example:

```
CRITERIA="CF_TITLE <SUBSTRING> smok"
```

The =, <, >, <=, and >= operators perform arithmetic comparisons on numeric and date values stored in specific fields. These are probably useful only with custom fields, if the table columns you specified for the custom fields held only numeric or date values. Note that these operators don't need angle brackets around them. The following are some examples:

```
CRITERIA="CF_CUSTOM1 = 5"
CRITERIA="CF_CUSTOM2 >= 1990"
CRITERIA="CF_CUSTOM2 < #DateFormat(Form.SearchDate, 'yyyy-mm-dd')
➥#"(c)Understanding Search Modifiers
```


Verity's search modifiers cause the search engine to behave slightly differently from how it would otherwise. The search modifiers include

- `CASE`
- `MANY`
- `NOT`
- `ORDER`

The `CASE` modifier forces Verity to perform a case-sensitive search, even if the search words are all lowercase or all uppercase. Here are some examples:

```
CRITERIA="<CASE>smoking"
CRITERIA="AND(<CASE>smoking,<CASE>policy)"
```

Verity often runs case-sensitive searches even if the `CASE` operator is not used.

The `MANY` operator ranks documents based on the density of search words or search elements found in a document. It is automatically in effect whenever the search type is `SIMPLE` and cannot be used with the concept operators `AND`, `OR`, and `ACCRUE`. Here are some examples:

```
CRITERIA="<MANY>(smoking,policy)"
CRITERIA="<MANY> smoking"
```

The `NOT` modifier causes Verity to eliminate documents that are found by the search word(s), such as

```
CRITERIA="NOT smoking"
CRITERIA="smoking NOT policy"
CRITERIA="NOT(smoking,days)"
CRITERIA="<NOT>(smoking,days)"
```

Note that if you want to find documents that contain *not smoking*, you must indicate this to Verity by using quotation marks:

```
CRITERIA="'not smoking'"
CRITERIA="AND('not',smoking)"
CRITERIA="AND(""not"",smoking)"
```

When used with a PARAGRAPH, SENTENCE, or NEAR/N operator, the ORDER modifier indicates that your search words must be found in the document—in the order that you specified them—for the document to be considered a match. The following is an example:

```
CRITERIA="<ORDER><PARAGRAPH>(smoking,policy)"
```

UNDERSTANDING SCORE OPERATORS

Every time Verity finds a document, it assigns the document a "score" that represents how closely the document matches the search criteria. The score is always somewhere from 0 to 1, where 1 is a perfect match and 0 is a perfectly miserable match. In most cases, Verity orders the search results in score order, with the highest scores at the top.

Score operators tell Verity to compute this score differently from what it would normally. To a certain extent, this allows you to control the order of the documents in the resultset. The score operators include the following:

- YESNO
- COMPLEMENT
- PRODUCT
- SUM

The YESNO operator forces the score for any match to be 1, no matter what. In other words, all documents that are relevant at all are equally relevant. The records will not appear in any particular order—even though Verity is trying to rank the search results by relevance—because sorting by a bunch of 1s doesn't really do anything. Here is an example:

```
CRITERIA="YESNO(policy)"
```

The COMPLEMENT operator is kind of strange. With this operator, the score is subtracted from 1 before it's returned to you. A closely matching document that ordinarily would get a score of .97 would now get a score of only .03. If Verity is ranking records by relevance, using COMPLEMENT makes the search results appear in reverse order (best matches last instead of first). Unfortunately, this also means that a score of 0 now has a score of 1, which means that all documents that didn't match at all will be returned—and returned first.

If for some bizarre reason you wanted only documents that were completely unrelated to smoking—ranked by irrelevance—you could use this:

```
CRITERIA="<COMPLEMENT>smoking"
```

The PRODUCT operator causes Verity to calculate the score for the document by multiplying the scores for each search word found. The net effect is that relevant documents appear to be even more relevant, and less relevant documents are even less relevant. This operator can cause fewer documents to be found. The following is an example:

```
CRITERIA="<PRODUCT>smoking"
```

The SUM operator causes Verity to calculate the score for the document by adding the scores for each search word found, up to a maximum document score of 1. The net effect is that more documents appear to get perfect scores. Here is an example:

```
CRITERIA="<SUM>smoking"
```

APPENDIX

Sample Application Data Files

In this appendix

Sample Application Data Files

"Orange Whip Studios" is a fictitious company used in the examples throughout this book. The various examples and applications use a total of 11 database tables, as described in the following sections.

The `Actors` Table

The `Actors` table contains a list of all the actors along with name, address, and other personal information. `Actors` contains the columns listed in Table E.1.

Table E.1 The `Actors` Table

Column	Datatype	Description
`ActorID`	Numeric (Auto Numer)	Unique actor ID
`NameFirst`	Text (50 chars)	Actor's (stage) first name
`NameLast`	Text (50 chars)	Actor's (stage) last name
`Age`	Numeric	Actor's (stage) age
`NameFirstReal`	Text (50 chars)	Actor's real first name
`NameLastReal`	Text (50 chars)	Actor's real last name
`AgeReal`	Numeric	Actor's real age
`IsEgomaniac`	Bit (Yes/No)	Egomaniac flag
`IsTotalBabe`	Bit (Yes/No)	Total babe flag
`Gender`	Text (1 char)	Gender (`M` or `F`)

Primary Key

- `ActorID`

Foreign Keys

- None

The `Contacts` Table

The `Contacts` table stores all contacts, including mailing list members and online store customers. `Contacts` contains the columns listed in Table E.2.

Table E.2 The `Contacts` Table

Column	Datatype	Description
`ContactID`	Numeric (Auto Number)	Unique contact ID
`FirstName`	Text (50 chars)	Contact first name

Column	Datatype	Description
`LastName`	Text (50 chars)	Contact last name
`Address`	Text (100 chars)	Contact address
`City`	Text (50 chars)	Contact city
`State`	Text (5 chars)	Contact state
`Zip`	Text (10 chars)	Contact ZIP
`Country`	Text (50 chars)	Contact country
`Email`	Text (100 chars)	Contact e-mail address
`Phone`	Text (50 chars)	Contact phone number
`UserLogin`	Text (50 chars)	Contact user login
`UserPassword`	Text (50 chars)	Contact login password
`MailingList`	Bit (Yes/No)	Mailing list flag

PRIMARY KEY

- `ContactID`

FOREIGN KEYS

- None

THE `Directors` TABLE

The `Directors` table stores all movie directors. `Directors` contains the columns listed in Table E.3.

TABLE E.3 THE `Directors` TABLE

Column	Datatype	Description
`DirectorID`	Numeric (Auto Number)	Unique director ID
`FirstName`	Text (50 chars)	Director first name
`LastName`	Text (50 chars)	Director last name

PRIMARY KEY

- `DirectorID`

FOREIGN KEYS

- None

THE Expenses TABLE

The Expenses table lists the expenses associated with listed movies. Expenses contains the columns in Table E.4.

TABLE E.4 THE Expenses TABLE

Column	Datatype	Description
ExpenseID	Numeric (Auto Number)	Unique expense ID
FilmID	Numeric	Movie ID
ExpenseAmount	Currency (or numeric)	Expense amount
Description	Text (100 chars)	Expense description
Expense Date	Date Time	Expense date

PRIMARY KEY

- ExpenseID

FOREIGN KEYS

- FilmID related to primary key in Films table

THE Films TABLE

The Films table lists all movies and related information. Films contains the columns in Table E.5.

TABLE E.5 THE Films TABLE

Column	Datatype	Description
FilmID	Numeric (Auto Number)	Unique movie ID
MovieTitle	Text (255 chars)	Movie title
PitchText	Text (100 chars)	Movie one-liner
AmountBudgeted	Currency (or numeric)	Movie budget (planned)
RatingID	Numeric	Movie rating ID
Summary	Memo (or text)	Movie plot summary
ImageName	Text (50 chars)	Movie poster image filename
DateInTheaters	Date Time	Date movie is in theaters

PRIMARY KEY

- FilmID

Foreign Keys

- `RatingID` related to primary key in `FilmsRatings` table

The `FilmsActors` Table

The `FilmsActors` table associates actors with the movies they are in. `FilmsActors` contains the columns in Table E.6. Retrieving actors with their movies requires a three-way join (`Films`, `Actors`, and `FilmsActors`).

Table E.6 The `FilmsActors` Table

Column	Datatype	Description
`FARecID`	Numeric (Auto Number)	Unique film actor ID
`FilmID`	Numeric	Movie ID
`ActorID`	Numeric	Actor ID
`IsStarringRole`	Bit (Yes/No)	Is star flag
`Salary`	Currency (or numeric)	Actor salary

Primary Key

- `FARecID`

Foreign Keys

- `FilmID` related to primary key in `Films` table
- `ActorID` related to primary key in `Actors` table

The `FilmsDirectors` Table

The `FilmsDirectors` table associates directors with their movies. `FilmsDirectors` contains the columns in Table E.7. Retrieving actors with their movies requires a three-way join (`Films`, `Directors`, and `FilmsDirectors`).

Table E.7 The `FilmsDirectors` Table

Column	Datatype	Description
`FDRecID`	Numeric (Auto Number)	Unique films director ID
`FilmID`	Numeric	Movie ID
`DirectorID`	Numeric	Director ID
`Salary`	Currency (or numeric)	Director salary

PRIMARY KEY

- `FDRecID`

FOREIGN KEYS

- `FilmsID` related to primary key in `Films` table
- `DirectorID` related to primary key in `Directors` table

THE `FilmsRatings` TABLE

The `FilmsRatings` table lists all movie ratings. `FilmsRatings` contains the columns in Table E.8.

TABLE E.8 THE `FilmsRatings` TABLE

Column	Datatype	Description
`RatingID`	Numeric (Auto Number)	Unique rating ID
`Rating`	Text (50 chars)	Rating description

PRIMARY KEY

- `RatingID`

FOREIGN KEYS

- None

THE `Merchandise` TABLE

The `Merchandise` table lists the movie-related merchandise for sale in the online store. `Merchandise` contains the columns in Table E.9.

TABLE E.9 THE `Merchandise` TABLE

Column	Datatype	Description
`MerchID`	Numeric (Auto Number)	Unique merchandise ID
`FilmID`	Numeric	Movie ID
`MerchName`	Text (50 chars)	Merchandise name
`MerchDescription`	Text (100 chars)	Merchandise description
`MerchPrice`	Currency (or numeric)	Merchandise price
`ImageNameSmall`	Text (50 chars)	Item's small image filename
`ImageNameLarge`	Text (50 chars)	Item's large image filename

PRIMARY KEY

- `MerchID`

FOREIGN KEYS

- `FilmID` related to primary key in `Films` table

THE `MerchandiseOrders` TABLE

The `MerchandiseOrders` table stores online merchandise order information. `MerchandiseOrders` contains the columns in Table E.10.

TABLE E.10 THE `MerchandiseOrders` TABLE

Column	Datatype	Description
`OrderID`	Numeric (Auto Number)	Unique order ID
`ContactID`	Numeric	Buyer contact ID
`OrderDate`	Date Time	Order date
`ShipAddress`	Text (100 chars)	Ship to address
`ShipCity`	Text (50 chars)	Ship to city
`ShipState`	Text (5 chars)	Ship to state
`ShipZip`	Text (10 chars)	Ship to ZIP
`ShipCountry`	Text (50 chars)	Ship to country
`ShipDate`	Date Time	Ship date

PRIMARY KEY

- `OrderID`

FOREIGN KEYS

- `ContactID` related to primary key in `Contacts` table

THE `MerchandiseOrdersItems` TABLE

The `MerchandiseOrdersItems` table contains the items in each order. `MerchandiseOrdersItems` contains the columns in Table E.11.

TABLE E.11 THE `MerchandiseOrdersItems` TABLE

Column	Datatype	Description
`OrderItemID`	Numeric (Auto Number)	Unique order item ID
`OrderID`	Numeric	Order ID

TABLE E.11 CONTINUED

Column	Datatype	Description
`ItemID`	Numeric	Ordered item ID
`OrderQty`	Numeric	Number of items ordered
`ItemPrice`	Currency (or numeric)	Item sale price

PRIMARY KEY

- `OrderItemID`

FOREIGN KEYS

- `OrderID` related to primary key in `MerchandiseOrders` table
- `ItemID` related to primary key in `Merchandise` table

INDEX

Symbols & Numbers

A

B

C

D

E

G

H

I

J

M

N

O

P

Q

R

S

T

U

V

W

X-Z

CD-INDEX

A

B

C

D

E

F

G

H

I

J-K

L

M

Q

R

S

T

U

V

W

X-Z